Markets with cash and/or futures price histories

The following commodities are available on Knight-Ridder's DataPak. Please specify which market(s) you are interested in when you call.

Aluminum	Gold	Potatoes
Barley	Heating Oil	Rapeseed (Canola)
Broilers	Hides and Leather	Rice
Butter	Hogs	Rubber
Cattle and Calves	Knight-Ridder CRB Futures Index	Rye
Cheese	Interest Rates, U.S.	Silk
Cocoa	Interest Rates, Worldwide	Silver
Coconut Oil and Copra	Iron and Steel	Soybean Meal
Coffee	Lard	Soybean Oil
Copper	Lead	Soybeans
Corn	Lumber and Plywood	Stock Index Futures, U.S.
Corn Oil	Mercury	Stock Index Futures, Worldwide
Cotton	Milk	Sugar
Cottonseed and Products	Nickel	Tallow and Greases
Currencies	Oats	Tin
Eggs	Oranges and Orange Juice	Wheat and Flour
Fertilizers (Nitrogen, Phosphate and Potash)	Palm Oil	Wool
Flaxseed and Linseed Oil	Petroleum	Zinc
Gas	Platinum-Group Metals	
Gasoline	Pork Bellies	

THE CRB COMMODITY YEARBOOK 1996

Knight-Ridder Financial/
Commodity Research Bureau

John Wiley & Sons, Inc.
New York • Chichester • Brisbane • Toronto • Singapore

Published by John Wiley & Sons, Inc.

ISBN 0-471-15458-X

Printed in the United States of America
10 9 8 7 6 5 4 3 2 1

Knight-Ridder Financial Commodity Research Bureau
30 South Wacker Drive, Suite 1820
Chicago, IL 60606
(312) 454-1801/(800) 621-5271

TABLE OF CONTENTS

ACKNOWLEDGMENTS

The editors wish to thank the following for source material:

Aluminum Association
American Bureau of Metal Statistics
American Gas Association
American Iron and Steel Institute
American Metal Market
American Paper and Pulp Association
American Petroleum Institute
Atomic Industrial Forum Inc.
Chicago Board of Trade
Chicago Mercantile Exchange
Citrus Associates of the N.Y. Cotton Exchange
Coffee, Sugar & Cocoa Exchange
Commodity Exchange, N.Y.
Commodity Futures Trading Commission
Edison Electric Institute
F.W. Dodge Corp.
Federal Power Commission
Federal Reserve Board
Florida Department of Citrus
Futures Industry Association
General Services Administration
Gill & Duffus Ltd.
Gold Fields Mineral Services Ltd.
Handy & Harman
International Cotton Advisory Committee
International Monetary Market (Chicago)
International Rubber Study Group
International Tea Committee
Johnson Matthey Ltd.
The Journal of Commerce
Kansas City Board of Trade
Leather Industries of America Inc.
London Metal Exchange
MidAmerica Commodity Exchange
Minneapolis Grain Exchange
National Coffee Association of U.S.A., Inc.
New York Cotton Exchange
New York Futures Exchange
New York Mercantile Exchange
Newsprint Service Bureau
Nuclear Exchange Corp.
Nuclear Regulatory Commission
Oil World
Organization for Economic Co-operation and Development
Portland Cement Association
Random Lengths
Rubber Manufacturers Association
Shell Briefing Service
The Silver Institute
Society of the Plastics Industry Inc.
Tea Council Inc.
Textile Economics Bureau Inc.
Textile Organon
U.N. Conference on Trade and Development
U.N. Food and Agriculture Organization
U.S. Bureau of Mines
U.S. Department of Agriculture
U.S. Department of Commerce
U.S. Department of Energy
U.S. Department of the Interior
U.S. Department of Labor
U.S. Department of the Treasury
The Wall Street Journal
Winnipeg Commodity Exchange
Wool Services Co.
Zinc Institute

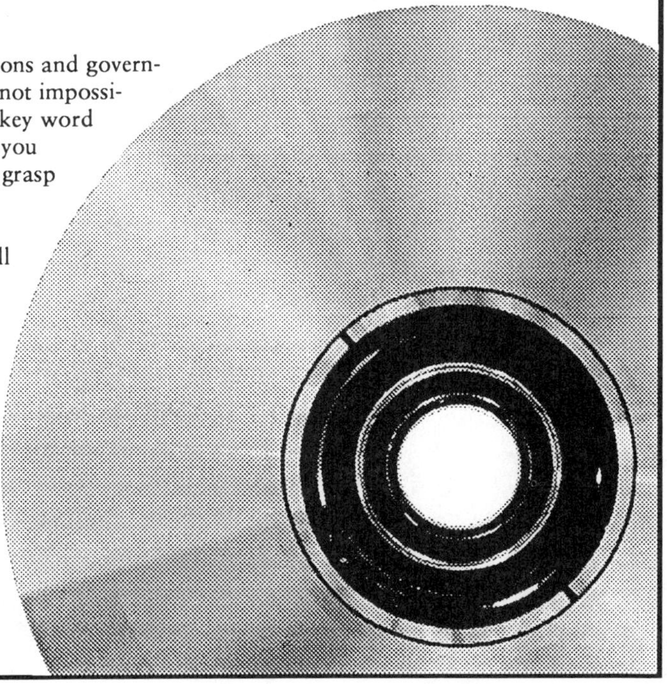

THE COMMODITY PRICE TREND

In 1995, the Knight-Ridder Commodity Research Bureau's Futures Price Index[1] rose for the third consecutive year. The December 29, 1995 closing value of 243.18 was 6.54 higher, or 2.76 percent above the December 30, 1994 level. Four of the six sub-index groups rose during the year led by a 47.71 percent increase in the grains index. The largest drop came in the imported group which declined 26.19 percent.

Grains and Oilseeds

The 47.71 percent rise in the grain index was largely due to the year-on-year reversal in corn prices. The 1995 closing corn price of $3.69, basis nearby futures, was nearly sixty percent higher than 1994's closing level of $2.31. A 54 million metric ton decline in world production, due largely to a very disappointing U.S. crop, coupled with a surge in Asian demand to cause the dramatic price rise.

Wheat prices followed 1994's six percent rise with a 27 percent increase in 1995 to a year-end value of $5.12. Concerns about declining world stocks were compounded by increased demand from importing countries.

The oilseed index rose 12.57 percent in 1995 led by a 33 percent increase in soybean prices. The year-end value of $7.35 nearly retraced all of the losses the market posted in 1994. Production declines in both the U.S. and Brazil accounted for the higher prices.

Imported

The imported index declined 26.19 percent in 1995, led by a 43 percent drop in coffee prices. The 1995 year-end coffee price of 94.9¢ per pound, basis nearby futures, was still 32 percent above the pre-freeze levels of 1993. The price drop was viewed as a return to normalcy after the wild gyrations caused by the Brazilian freeze of 1994.

Sugar prices also dropped considerably in 1995 ending the year at 11.6¢ per pound, 23 percent lower than 1994's closing value. A 1.2 million metric ton world production surplus helped build ending stock levels from 1994's five-year lows.

Cocoa prices registered a 1.7 percent decline in 1995, signaling an end to the uptrend which had begun in 1993. The 4 1/2 year planned liquidation of buffer cocoa stocks by the ICO seems to have put a cap on prices.

Energy

The energy sub-index registered a 3.53 percent increase in 1995. The gain would have been substantially higher if natural gas was a component of the sub-index.

Heating oil prices rose 14 percent due to very harsh winter weather in the the northeast U.S. The cold temperatures and heavy snowfall contributed to a significant drawdown on available stocks.

Crude oil prices rallied ten percent in 1995 to a year-end level of $19.55 compared to $17.76 the previous year, basis nearby futures. A rise in world demand of 500,000 barrels per day was blamed for the price increase.

Industrials

The industrial index declined 4.09 percent in 1995, breaking a string of three consecutive yearly advances. Copper prices declined 13 percent for the year but finished at 120.55¢ per pound in what was seen as a normal correction to 1994's dramatic advance.

Cotton prices had the wildest ride of any market in 1995 when they reached 117.20¢ per pound in May, the highest price for cotton since the Civil War. Dramatic increases in demand caught the market off guard and accounted for the startling price rise. In turn, the higher prices successfully "rationed" the available supply allowing prices to return to a more normal level of 81¢ per pound by year-end.

Livestock

The livestock index rose 14.22 percent in 1995 led by a 23 percent increase in hog prices. A three million head drop in the U.S. hog herd and the perception that rising feed costs could lead to further herd reductions fueled the price advance.

Precious Metals

The precious metal index rose a barely perceptible 0.22 percent in 1995 as all three markets ended 1995 very close to where they ended 1994. A mid-year rally in both silver and platinum fizzled as quickly as it began, while gold moved sideways in a very tight range for the second consecutive year.

[1] The Knight-Ridder Commodity Research Bureau Price Index was modified on December 6, 1995, to reflect changes in the marketplace. This was the ninth revision to the Index since its inception in 1957.

Monthly Knight-Ridder CRB Futures Price Index High,Low & Close 1967 = 100

Year		Jan.	Feb.	Mar.	Apr.	May	June	July	Aug.	Sept.	Oct.	Nov.	Dec.	Range
1986	High	231.1	216.6	216.5	213.5	216.1	205.7	203.7	207.1	212.3	213.4	213.3	212.0	231.1
	Low	219.9	209.9	209.4	203.0	205.5	201.6	196.9	201.0	208.2	209.7	208.4	207.5	196.9
	Close	219.9	209.9	209.6	213.5	205.5	201.6	200.1	207.1	210.9	211.3	210.7	209.1	----
1987	High	213.9	213.7	210.1	221.7	235.6	234.6	227.8	226.8	227.3	232.7	237.1	234.7	237.1
	Low	208.3	204.2	205.7	209.4	222.6	223.1	220.7	222.4	223.5	222.7	221.1	227.5	204.2
	Close	212.6	205.4	208.7	221.7	224.9	225.9	225.9	223.0	223.8	223.4	234.6	232.5	----
1988	High	239.3	232.9	233.5	236.0	248.4	270.5	265.8	251.0	248.6	246.5	247.0	252.8	270.5
	Low	230.4	224.3	224.5	232.7	232.5	249.8	242.0	243.7	237.1	237.6	236.0	244.1	224.3
	Close	230.4	225.7	233.0	234.4	248.4	265.1	246.2	246.2	238.8	243.9	244.9	251.8	----
1989	High	251.6	243.3	248.1	244.6	242.8	235.4	237.0	225.5	226.8	228.1	231.7	229.9	251.6
	Low	241.1	236.6	241.7	237.7	229.4	227.9	221.2	221.5	222.9	223.0	226.0	225.6	221.2
	Close	242.4	243.2	242.1	238.0	229.4	234.4	221.2	225.5	226.8	225.7	228.8	229.9	----
1990	High	235.1	236.3	239.0	245.8	247.8	241.2	240.0	244.7	239.8	242.0	231.1	223.8	247.8
	Low	228.8	229.9	234.2	238.4	241.5	233.8	230.3	233.1	234.9	228.6	223.2	220.1	220.1
	Close	229.9	234.6	238.2	245.8	241.5	236.9	235.0	233.7	239.2	229.8	223.3	222.6	----
1991	High	222.8	215.6	221.8	222.2	217.0	217.7	214.1	216.5	217.6	219.8	218.6	213.9	222.8
	Low	214.1	209.7	217.3	216.2	214.1	208.4	205.9	204.7	211.9	216.2	213.3	207.2	204.7
	Close	214.1	215.6	218.5	216.2	215.4	208.4	214.1	211.8	215.6	218.2	213.3	208.1	----
1992	High	212.2	215.3	212.9	210.3	211.7	212.9	209.1	204.9	203.5	202.9	203.6	204.3	215.3
	Low	206.9	207.2	208.6	204.5	204.9	208.0	203.0	198.2	199.3	199.1	199.2	201.2	198.2
	Close	211.2	209.6	209.8	204.8	208.0	209.3	203.1	201.0	200.4	199.9	203.1	202.8	----
1993	High	203.2	204.9	214.3	213.9	211.8	210.0	219.7	223.5	217.8	220.6	223.8	226.8	226.8
	Low	199.3	198.4	203.4	207.8	207.4	202.6	207.2	212.1	211.9	216.6	217.4	218.4	198.4
	Close	199.5	202.9	212.5	210.9	208.7	207.1	219.3	217.2	216.1	218.4	218.0	226.3	----
1994	High	229.8	229.2	231.0	227.8	239.2	239.7	234.7	235.4	234.4	235.2	234.7	237.2	239.7
	Low	226.2	225.7	227.4	227.8	225.2	235.9	230.4	228.0	228.6	227.0	228.8	227.0	225.2
	Close	225.6	227.6	227.7	225.0	235.5	230.4	233.7	231.9	229.9	233.3	229.2	236.6	----
1995	High	238.0	236.2	236.9	237.7	237.1	238.0	235.9	240.3	245.8	242.7	244.5	246.5	246.5
	Low	232.6	231.0	231.1	233.2	229.6	232.2	229.3	231.7	239.4	238.3	240.9	240.9	229.3
	Close	232.8	234.3	232.9	235.3	232.7	233.4	233.2	240.0	241.7	242.2	241.8	243.2	----

Source: Knight-Ridder Financial

MONTHLY CASH
AS OF:02/29/96
KR-CRB FUTURES PRICE INDEX
1967=100
KR-CRB Futures Price Index
17 Futures Markets
Cattle (Live)
Cocoa
Coffee
Copper
Corn
Cotton
Crude Oil
Gold (N.Y.)
Heating Oil #2
Hogs
Natural Gas
Orange Juice
Platinum
Silver (N.Y.)
Soybeans
Sugar #11 (World)
Wheat (CHI)
INDEX VALUE
320
300
280
260
240
220
200
180
160
140
120
100
72 73 74 75 76 77 78 79 80 81 82 83 84 85 86 87 88 89 90 91 92 93 94 95 96

MONTHLY CASH
AS OF:02/29/96
GOLDMAN SACHS COMMODITY INDEX
CASH
INDEX VALUE
320
300
280
260
240
220
200
180
160
140
120
100
72 73 74 75 76 77 78 79 80 81 82 83 84 85 86 87 88 89 90 91 92 93 94 95 96

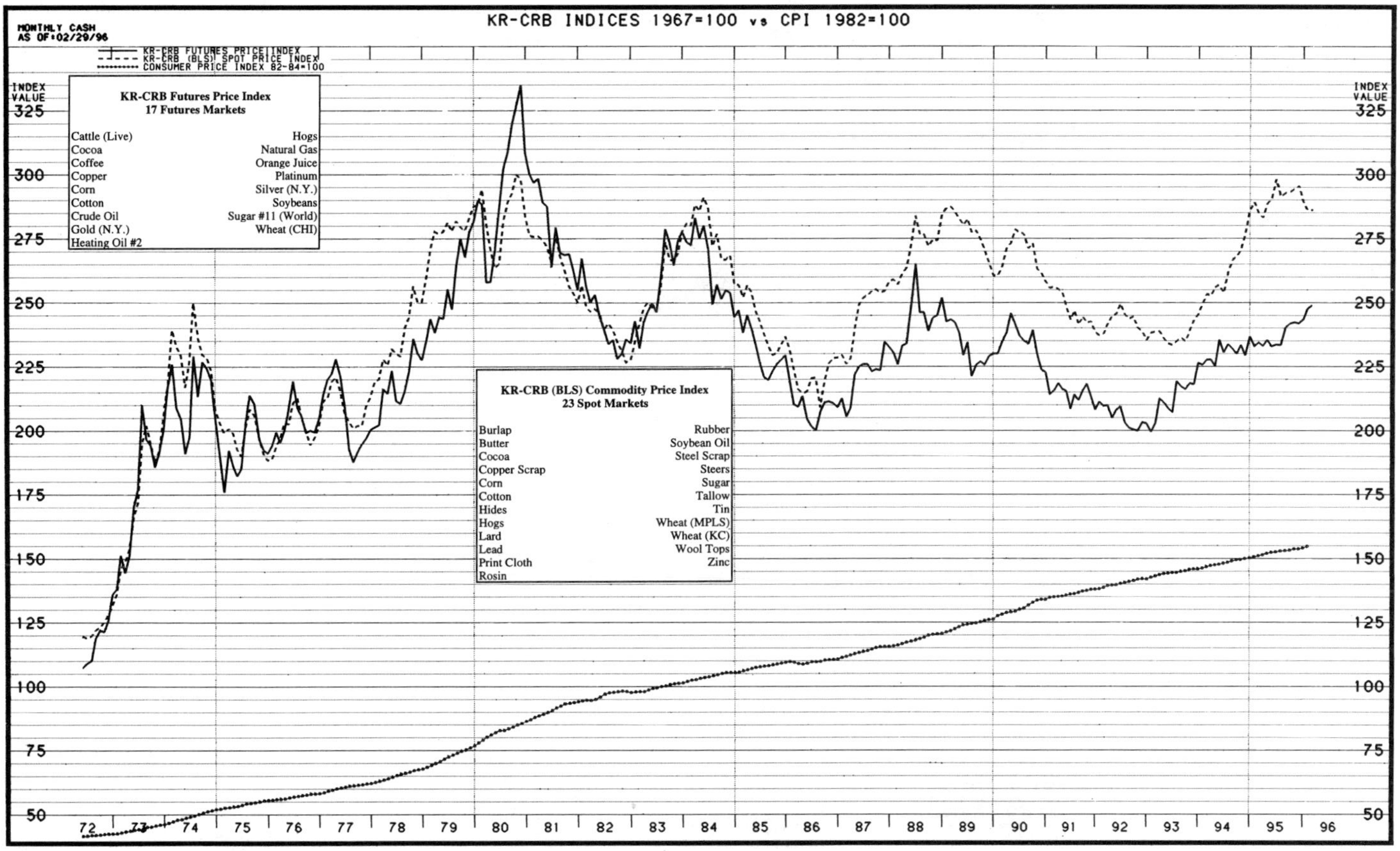
KR-CRB INDICES 1967=100 vs CPI 1982=100
MONTHLY CASH
AS OF:02/29/96
KR-CRB FUTURES PRICE INDEX
KR-CRB (BLS) SPOT PRICE INDEX
CONSUMER PRICE INDEX 82-84=100
INDEX VALUE
KR-CRB Futures Price Index
17 Futures Markets
Cattle (Live)
Cocoa
Coffee
Copper
Corn
Cotton
Crude Oil
Gold (N.Y.)
Heating Oil #2
Hogs
Natural Gas
Orange Juice
Platinum
Silver (N.Y.)
Soybeans
Sugar #11 (World)
Wheat (CHI)
KR-CRB (BLS) Commodity Price Index
23 Spot Markets
Burlap
Butter
Cocoa
Copper Scrap
Corn
Cotton
Hides
Hogs
Lard
Lead
Print Cloth
Rosin
Rubber
Soybean Oil
Steel Scrap
Steers
Sugar
Tallow
Tin
Wheat (MPLS)
Wheat (KC)
Wool Tops
Zinc
325
300
275
250
225
200
175
150
125
100
75
50
72 73 74 75 76 77 78 79 80 81 82 83 84 85 86 87 88 89 90 91 92 93 94 95 96

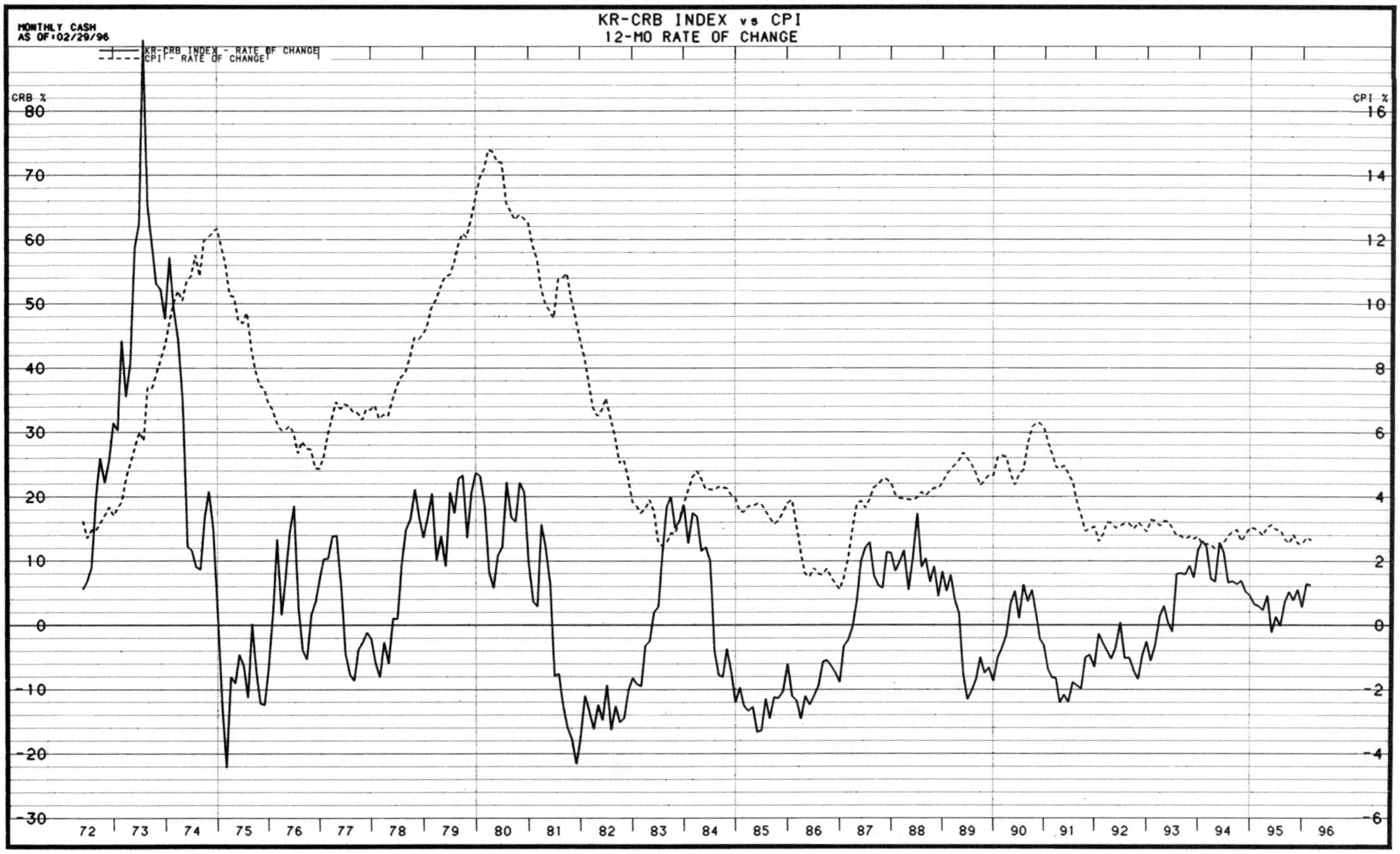
KR-CRB INDEX vs CPI
12-MO RATE OF CHANGE
MONTHLY CASH
AS OF:02/29/96
KR-CRB INDEX - RATE OF CHANGE
CPI - RATE OF CHANGE
CRB %
CPI %
80 70 60 50 40 30 20 10 0 -10 -20 -30
16 14 12 10 8 6 4 2 0 -2 -4 -6
72 73 74 75 76 77 78 79 80 81 82 83 84 85 86 87 88 89 90 91 92 93 94 95 96

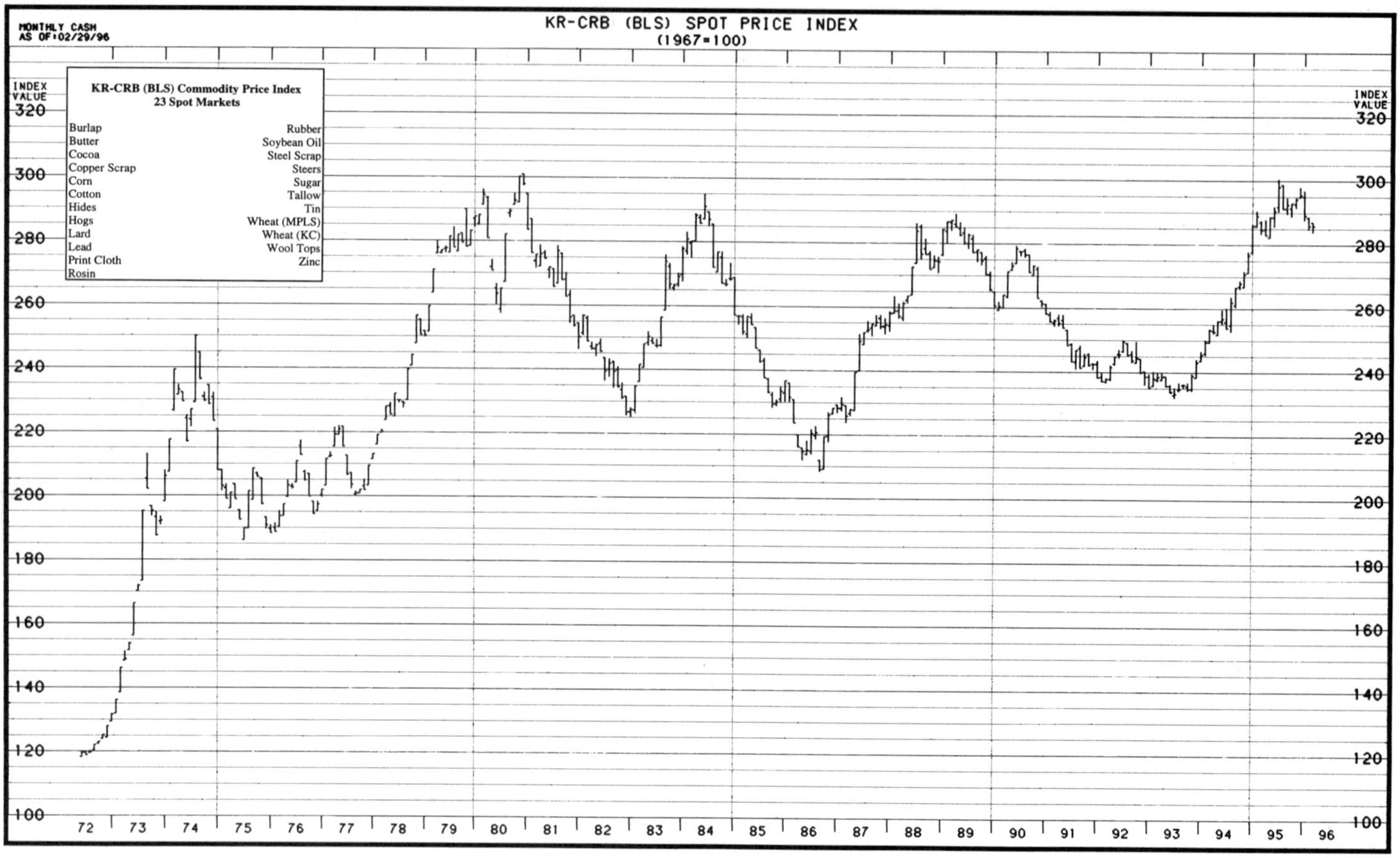
MONTHLY CASH
AS OF: 02/29/96
KR-CRB (BLS) SPOT PRICE INDEX
(1967=100)
INDEX VALUE
KR-CRB (BLS) Commodity Price Index
23 Spot Markets
Burlap
Butter
Cocoa
Copper Scrap
Corn
Cotton
Hides
Hogs
Lard
Lead
Print Cloth
Rosin
Rubber
Soybean Oil
Steel Scrap
Steers
Sugar
Tallow
Tin
Wheat (MPLS)
Wheat (KC)
Wool Tops
Zinc
320
300
280
260
240
220
200
180
160
140
120
100
72 73 74 75 76 77 78 79 80 81 82 83 84 85 86 87 88 89 90 91 92 93 94 95 96

WEEKLY CASH
AS OF: 03/15/96
KR-CRB (BLS) SPOT PRICE INDEX
(1967=100)
INDEX VALUE
KR-CRB (BLS) Commodity Price Index
23 Spot Markets
Burlap
Butter
Cocoa
Copper Scrap
Corn
Cotton
Hides
Hogs
Lard
Lead
Print Cloth
Rosin
Rubber
Soybean Oil
Steel Scrap
Steers
Sugar
Tallow
Tin
Wheat (MPLS)
Wheat (KC)
Wool Tops
Zinc
320
310
300
290
280
270
260
250
240
230
220
210
1990 1991 1992 1993 1994 1995

KR-CRB (BLS) FOODSTUFFS SUB-INDEX
WEEKLY CASH
AS OF:03/15/96
KR-CRB (BLS) FoodStuffs Sub-Index
10 Spot Markets
Hogs
Steers
Lard
Butter
Soybean Oil
Cocoa
Corn
Sugar
Wheat (KC)
Wheat (MPLS)
INDEX VALUE
245
240
235
230
225
220
215
210
205
200
195
190
1990
1991
1992
1993
1994
1995

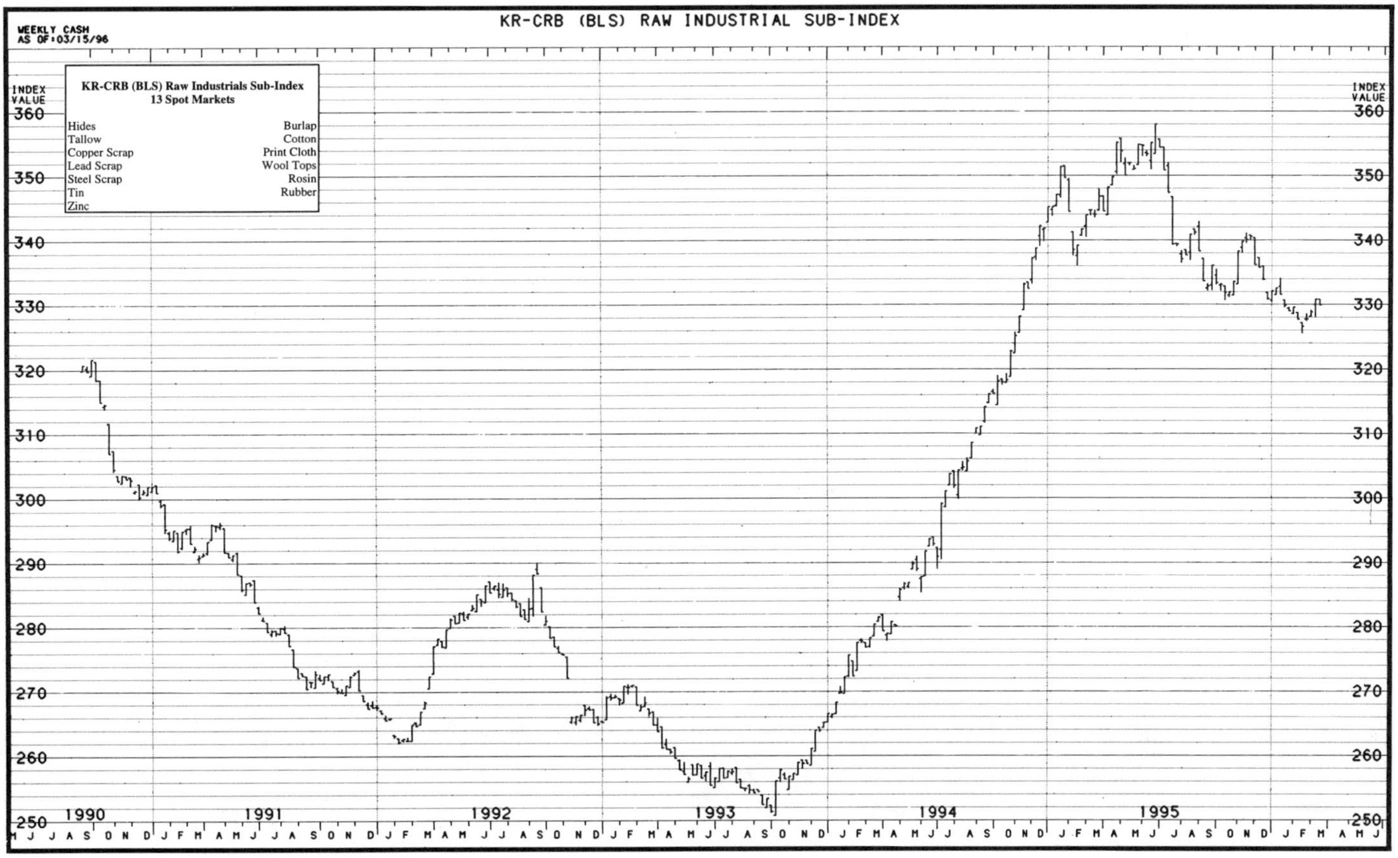
KR-CRB (BLS) RAW INDUSTRIAL SUB-INDEX
WEEKLY CASH
AS OF:03/15/96
KR-CRB (BLS) Raw Industrials Sub-Index
13 Spot Markets
Hides
Tallow
Copper Scrap
Lead Scrap
Steel Scrap
Tin
Zinc
Burlap
Cotton
Print Cloth
Wool Tops
Rosin
Rubber
INDEX VALUE
360
350
340
330
320
310
300
290
280
270
260
250
1990
1991
1992
1993
1994
1995

WEEKLY CASH
AS OF:03/15/96
KR-CRB IMPORTED INDEX
(1967=100)
KR-CRB Imported Index
4 Futures Markets
Cocoa
Coffee
Sugar
INDEX VALUE
1990
1991
1992
1993
1994
1995

WEEKLY CASH
AS OF:03/15/96
KR-CRB INDUSTRIAL INDEX
(1967=100)
KR-CRB Industrials Index
6 Futures Markets
Cotton
Copper
Crude Oil
Lumber
Platinum
Silver
INDEX VALUE
1990
1991
1992
1993
1994
1995

KR-CRB GRAINS INDEX
(1967=100)
WEEKLY CASH
AS OF:03/15/96
INDEX VALUE
KR-CRB Grains Index
4 Futures Markets
Corn
Oats
Soybean Meal
Wheat (CHI)
270
260
250
240
230
220
210
200
190
180
170
160
1990
1991
1992
1993
1994
1995
M J J A S O N D J F M A M J J A S O N D J F M A M J J A S O N D J F M A M J J A S O N D J F M A M J J A S O N D J F M A M J J A S O N D J F M A M J

KR-CRB OILSEEDS INDEX
(1967=100)
WEEKLY CASH
AS OF:03/15/96
INDEX VALUE
KR-CRB Oilseeds Index
3 Futures Markets
Flaxseed
Canola
Soybean Oil
360
340
320
300
280
260
240
220
200
180
160
140
1990
1991
1992
1993
1994
1995
M J J A S O N D J F M A M J J A S O N D J F M A M J J A S O N D J F M A M J J A S O N D J F M A M J J A S O N D J F M A M J J A S O N D J F M A M J

WEEKLY CASH
AS OF:03/15/96
KR-CRB LIVESTOCK INDEX
(1967=100)
KR-CRB Livestock & Meats Index
3 Futures Markets
Live Cattle
LIve Hogs
Pork Bellies
INDEX VALUE
260
250
240
230
220
210
200
190
180
170
160
150
1990
1991
1992
1993
1994
1995

WEEKLY CASH
AS OF:03/15/96
KR-CRB PRECIOUS METALS INDEX
(1967=100)
KR-CRB Precious Metals Index
3 Futures Markets
Gold (N.Y.)
Platinum
Silver (N.Y.)
INDEX VALUE
310
300
290
280
270
260
250
240
230
220
210
200
1990
1991
1992
1993
1994
1995

KR-CRB ENERGY INDEX
(1977=100)
WEEKLY CASH
AS OF:03/15/96
INDEX VALUE
KR-CRB Energy Index
3 Futures Markets
(1977=100)
Crude Oil
Unleaded Gas
Heating Oil #2
1990
1991
1992
1993
1994
1995

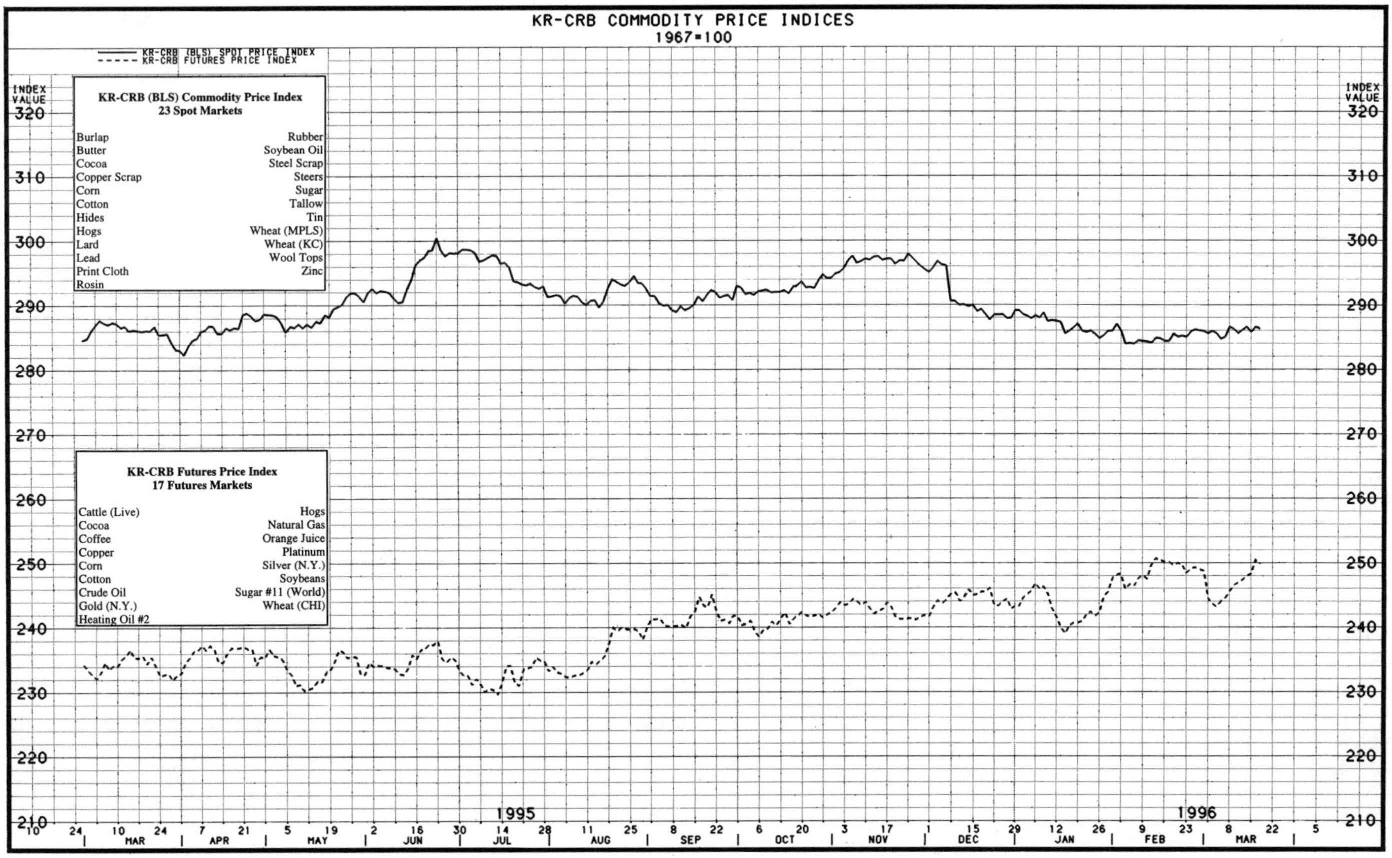
KR-CRB COMMODITY PRICE INDICES
1967=100
KR-CRB (BLS) SPOT PRICE INDEX
KR-CRB FUTURES PRICE INDEX
INDEX VALUE
KR-CRB (BLS) Commodity Price Index
23 Spot Markets
Burlap
Butter
Cocoa
Copper Scrap
Corn
Cotton
Hides
Hogs
Lard
Lead
Print Cloth
Rosin
Rubber
Soybean Oil
Steel Scrap
Steers
Sugar
Tallow
Tin
Wheat (MPLS)
Wheat (KC)
Wool Tops
Zinc
KR-CRB Futures Price Index
17 Futures Markets
Cattle (Live)
Cocoa
Coffee
Copper
Corn
Cotton
Crude Oil
Gold (N.Y.)
Heating Oil #2
Hogs
Natural Gas
Orange Juice
Platinum
Silver (N.Y.)
Soybeans
Sugar #11 (World)
Wheat (CHI)
1995
1996

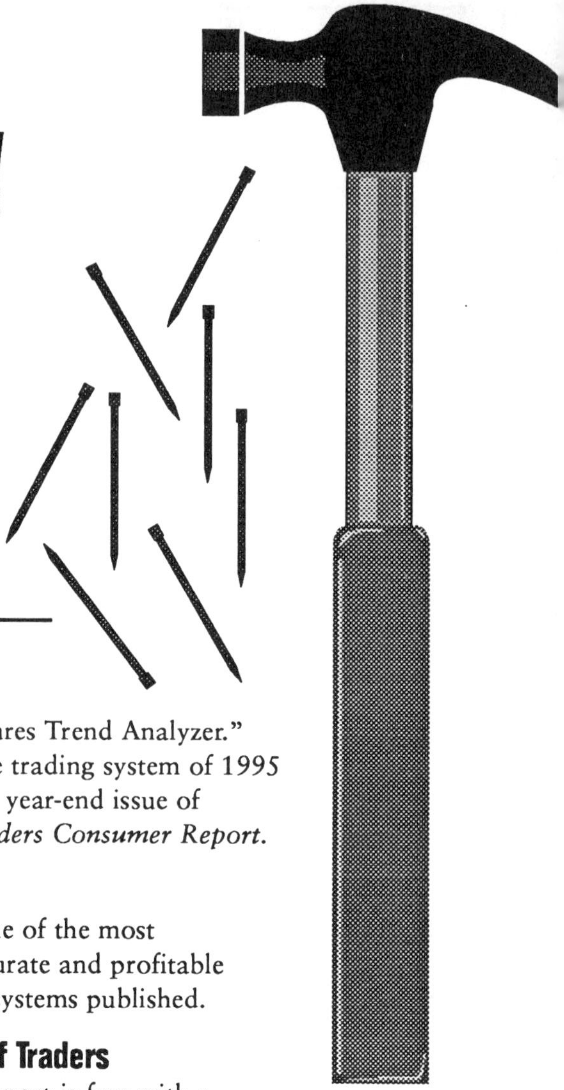

ANALYZING THE COMMITMENTS OF TRADERS REPORT

by Kenneth H. Shaleen

Every clearing member, futures clearing merchant, and foreign broker is required to report daily to the U.S. Commodity Futures Trading Commission (CFTC), the futures and futures options positions of any trader that exceeds a specified minimum reporting level. The reporting level on Treasury Bond Futures, for example, was 500 futures contracts at the beginning of 1996. The CFTC then classifies these reporting traders as either Commercial or Non-Commercial. The Commercial users are more commonly referred to as the Large Hedgers and the Non-Commercials as the Large Speculators. Since the total number of open futures contracts is known, a simple subtraction of these reportable positions yields the number (in contracts) of Non-Reportable futures positions. Analysts refer to this category as the Small Trader. Bi-weekly, the CFTC releases the Commitments of Traders Report which details the long and short positions of each of the three categories. This report has long been an important quasi-technical tool for futures traders and has been referred to as "an elaboration of open interest". Use of the Commitments Report in price forecasting has been chronicled in prior CRB Commodity Year Books, most recently in 1985 and 1990. Readers are encouraged to study the earlier practical examples.

A sample page of the Commitments Report for Crude Oil is shown in Figure 1. The pertinent facts from the reports are summarized in tabular format as a regular feature of Knight-Ridder Financial's *CRB FUTURES PERSPECTIVE* weekly chart ser-

Figure 1. Futures Only Report

CRUDE OIL, LIGHT 'SWEET' - NEW YORK MERCANTILE EXCHANGE

COMMITMENTS OF TRADERS IN ALL FUTURES COMBINED AND INDICATED FUTURES, JANUARY 2, 1996

	TOTAL	REPORTABLE POSITIONS								NONREPORTABLE POSITIONS	
		NON-COMMERCIAL				COMMERCIAL		TOTAL			
	OPEN INTEREST	LONG OR SHORT ONLY		LONG AND SHORT (SPREADING)							
		LONG	SHORT	LONG	SHORT	LONG	SHORT	LONG	SHORT	LONG	SHORT
		(CONTRACTS OF 1000 BARRELS)									
ALL	358,474	49,036	11,222	15,850	15,850	210,425	260,819	275,311	287,891	83,436	70,856
OLD	297,575	49,209	10,520	10,411	10,411	166,989	218,124	226,609	239,055	70,966	58,520
OTHER	61,172	37	912	5,229	5,229	43,436	42,695	48,702	48,836	12,470	12,336
		CHANGES IN COMMITMENTS FROM DECEMBER 26, 1995									
ALL	15,405	466	-700	1,200	1,200	11,087	11,937	12,753	12,437	2,652	2,968
		PERCENT OPEN INTEREST REPRESENTED BY EACH CATEGORY OF TRADERS									
ALL	100.00%	13.7	3.1	4.4	4.4	58.7	72.7	76.7	80.2	23.3	19.8
OLD	100.00%	16.5	3.5	3.5	3.5	56.1	73.3	76.2	80.3	23.8	19.7
OTHER	100.00%	0.1	1.5	8.5	8.5	71.0	69.8	79.6	79.8	20.4	20.2
	NUMBER OF TRADERS	NUMBER OF TRADERS IN EACH CATEGORY									
ALL	134	39	16	13	13	57	59	104	82		
OLD	133	39	16	12	12	55	58	102	80		
OTHER	26	2	2	4	4	16	16	20	20		

CONCENTRATION RATIOS

PERCENT OF OPEN INTEREST HELD BY THE INDICATED NUMBER OF LARGEST TRADERS

	BY GROSS POSITION				BY NET POSITION			
	4 OR LESS TRADERS		8 OR LESS TRADERS		4 OR LESS TRADERS		8 OR LESS TRADERS	
	LONG	SHORT	LONG	SHORT	LONG	SHORT	LONG	SHORT
ALL	22.4	25.6	34.0	36.7	11.9	14.0	18.9	21.4
OLD	20.8	25.2	30.9	37.0	12.1	16.2	19.9	23.7
OTHER	43.9	43.0	59.0	57.9	35.4	32.8	46.0	44.4

Figure 2. Futures and Options Report As Shown In CRB Futures Perspective

CFTC COMMITMENTS OF TRADERS - FINANCIAL FUTURES AND OPTIONS

Open Interest Positions shown in Percent (Rounded) as of 12 MARCH, 1996

	LARGE HEDGERS				LARGE SPECULATORS				SMALL TRADERS			
	LONG	*SHORT*	*NET*	*	*LONG*	*SHORT*	*NET*	*	*LONG*	*SHORT*	*NET*	*
BRITISH POUND	85	63	22	22	2	15	-13	-14	12	20	-8	-8
COPPER #1 (High Grade)	41	57	-16	-15	18	10	8	12	41	32	9	3
CANADIAN DOLLAR	39	72	-33	-31	13	5	8	16	48	23	25	14
CRUDE OIL(NY)	67	73	-6	0	6	1	5	0	18	17	1	-1
DEUTSCHE MARK	69	43	26	23	6	12	-6	-12	17	37	-20	-11
EURODOLLARS	69	67	2	0	2	1	1	0	19	22	-3	0
FED FUNDS (30-day)	72	78	-6	-5	2	2	0	0	21	16	5	4
GOLD (COMEX)	50	74	-24	4	12	4	8	-5	28	12	16	1
HEATING OIL #2	47	63	-16	2	6	1	5	-2	41	29	12	1
JAPANESE YEN	73	43	30	3	3	22	-19	-1	17	28	-11	-2
KR-CRB FUTURES +	0	0	0	0	27	56	-29	-10	46	17	29	9
LIBOR (1-mo.)	78	74	4	3	1	4	-3	2	19	20	-1	-5
MUNICIPAL BONDS	80	60	20	-6	2	12	-10	6	15	25	-10	0
NATURAL GAS	66	81	-15	1	8	0	8	-2	20	13	7	1
PLATINUM	41	81	-40	10	32	9	23	-8	26	8	18	-1
SILVER (COMEX)	25	70	-45	-3	22	2	20	0	41	16	25	4
SWISS FRANC	72	39	33	-6	3	16	-13	5	23	42	-19	2
S&P 500 INDEX	58	56	2	2	3	6	-3	-2	24	23	1	0
T-BILLS (90-Day)	56	56	0	16	3	12	-9	-12	38	28	10	-3
T-NOTES (2-yr.)	69	63	6	-1	3	7	-4	3	21	22	-1	0
T-NOTES (5-yr.)	75	71	4	-7	7	6	1	5	7	12	-5	1
T-NOTES (10-yr.)	74	65	9	-5	3	5	-2	3	13	20	-7	2
T-BONDS (30-yr.)	63	63	0	-1	6	5	1	0	20	21	-1	0
U.S. DOLLAR INDEX	0	29	-29	-6	57	54	3	-5	38	12	26	10
UNLEADED GAS	48	70	-22	2	10	1	9	-1	29	15	14	-1

The statistics in the Commitments of Traders Report are released by the Commodity Futures Trading Commission. The data will appear here in tabular form in the issue immediately following release of the report. It should be recognized that there are seasonal movements in the shifting interest between large and small trade interests. Release date: Every other Monday with data for the prior two Tuesdays.

Note: Positions may not equal 100% because intermarket statistics are not included.

NET Positive - increased long or decreased short.
NET Negative - increased short or decreased long.
* Change in % from previous report.
+ Futures only.

vice. A sample of this report can be seen in Figure 2. The CFTC makes the report available on it's INTERNET site at http://www.cftc.gov/cftc/.

Theory

The general theory behind the application of the Commitments Report report has not changed. The Large Hedgers are expected to possess the best fundamental long term market knowledge--and eventually be the best forecasters of future price movement. Years ago, the Large Speculator was also deemed to be the "smart money"--possessing insights not available to the Small Trader. But now this category is increasingly dominated by the trend following funds that control reportable positions. A simple method of investigating this new factor utilizes the mathematical trend direction as reported weekly as the Electronic Futures Trend Analyzer (EFTA) in *CRB FUTURES PERSPECTIVE.* This purely mechanical determination of price trend direction can be compared to the net long or short position of the Large Speculators (assumed now to be trend followers) in the Commitments Report. The Small Trader is still regarded as:

1) Lacking a trading plan
2) Undercapitalized
3) Tends to run "en-masse"

Thus, this class of trader remains the least desirable contingent to mimic.
Since the last look at this report in the 1990 yearbook, the CFTC has increased the frequency of the report from once a month to bi-weekly, and introduced a new report which adds options as futures-equivalent positions. This Futures + Options Commitments Report "delta adjusts" the options positions of the reportable traders. It should yield a more accurate overall picture of the market make up. Figure 1 is the January 2, 1996 Futures Only Report; figure 2 contains percentage data from a combined Futures + Options Report. This article will review the traditional method of analyzing the Commitments of Traders Report and suggest a slightly different approach.

The important key to successful analysis of the Commitments Report is the knowledge of the seasonally normal positions of each of the three categories. Knight-Ridder Financial has once again updated, in chart format, the historic normal positions (in futures only, not combined) for the ten year period ending in late 1995 (pages 23T-42T). Ken Shaleen has added a general observation of the most obvious idiosyncracy on each of the graphs.

Traditional Approach

The "traditional" method of analyzing the CFTC's Commitments of Traders Report is to:

1. Examine a futures price chart for:
   A. Any unusual changes in total open interest, especially upward.
   B. Ascertain the direction of the price trend using conventional trendline analysis.

2. Refer to the current Commitments Report to delineate the positions of the three categories of traders. This answers the question of who has been correct in their market judgement. It also reveals who has been wrong--a provided "fuel" for the price move.

3. Compare the current positions to the normal historic positions of each category at that date. Prior analytical work by the Commodity Research Bureau states:

A. If any of the current positions differ more than 5% from the historic norm--a definite directional bias exists.

B. Deviations of less than 5% should be disregarded.

C. Deviations of greater than 40% from normal indicate an unusual situation. This is a caution flag and traders should be "wary."

4. Make the assumptions that:

A. The Large Hedgers are the "smartest" money.

B. The Small Traders have the worst track record.

C. The Large Speculators used to be "smarter"; now this category is becoming dominated by trend following funds.

5. The most distinct conclusions:

A. Bullish: Large Hedgers are more heavily net long than usual, Large Speculators are clearly net long, and the Small Trader is net short more than normal.

B. Bearish: Large Hedgers are more heavily net short than usual, Large Speculators are clearly net short, and the Small Trader is net long more than normal.

A slightly different approach to analyzing the Commitments Report will be investigated. Instead of beginning with an actual futures price chart--each of the historic ten-year average commitments graphs is analyzed first. A determination is made of what constitutes the most obvious feature of the seasonally normal commitments chart at that specific date. Then the make-up of the three categories from the comparable current Commitments Report is noted. If the two are materially different it implies a strong directional belief on the part of the participants.

January 1996 Example

The first look at the strategic positions of the three categories in 1996 was available with the January 2, 1996, Commitments Report, released Monday January 8, 1996. The expected (normal) situation on 20 historic average charts at the beginning of each calendar year was compared to the actual make-up on January 2, 1996. Particular attention was focused on the current position of the Large Hedger versus their normal stance. Four of the 20 futures markets examined had pronounced differences with respect to both sign (long or short) and magnitude (greater than 5% deviation). These were T-Bonds, Crude Oil, Cotton, and Coffee. An example of the Commitments Report for Crude Oil is shown in Figure 1. The historic normal graph for Crude Oil is in Figure 3.

The situation of the four commodities under investigation:

1. <u>Treasury Bonds:</u>
Expectation = Large Hedgers net long 2.3%.
Actual situation= Large Hedgers net short 9.1%.
Forecast = Bearish

2. <u>Crude Oil:</u>
Expectation = Large Hedgers net long 3.3%
Actual situation = Large Hedgers net short 14.0%
Forecast = Bearish

3. <u>Cotton:</u>
Expectation = Large Hedgers net short 15.0%
Actual situation = Large Hedgers net long 14.1%
Forecast = Bullish

4. <u>Coffee:</u>
Expectation = Large Hedgers net short 20.3%
Actual situation = Large Hedgers net long 8.8%
Forecast = Bullish

Figure 4. Comparison of the two Commitments Reports for January 2, 1996.

U.S Treasury Bonds

Trader Category	Futures Only Report	Futures and Options Report	Conclusion
Large Hedger	-9.1%	-7.8%	Still Net Short
Large Speculator	+9.5%	+2.8%	Still Net Long
Small Trader	-0.5%	+5.0%	Now Net Long

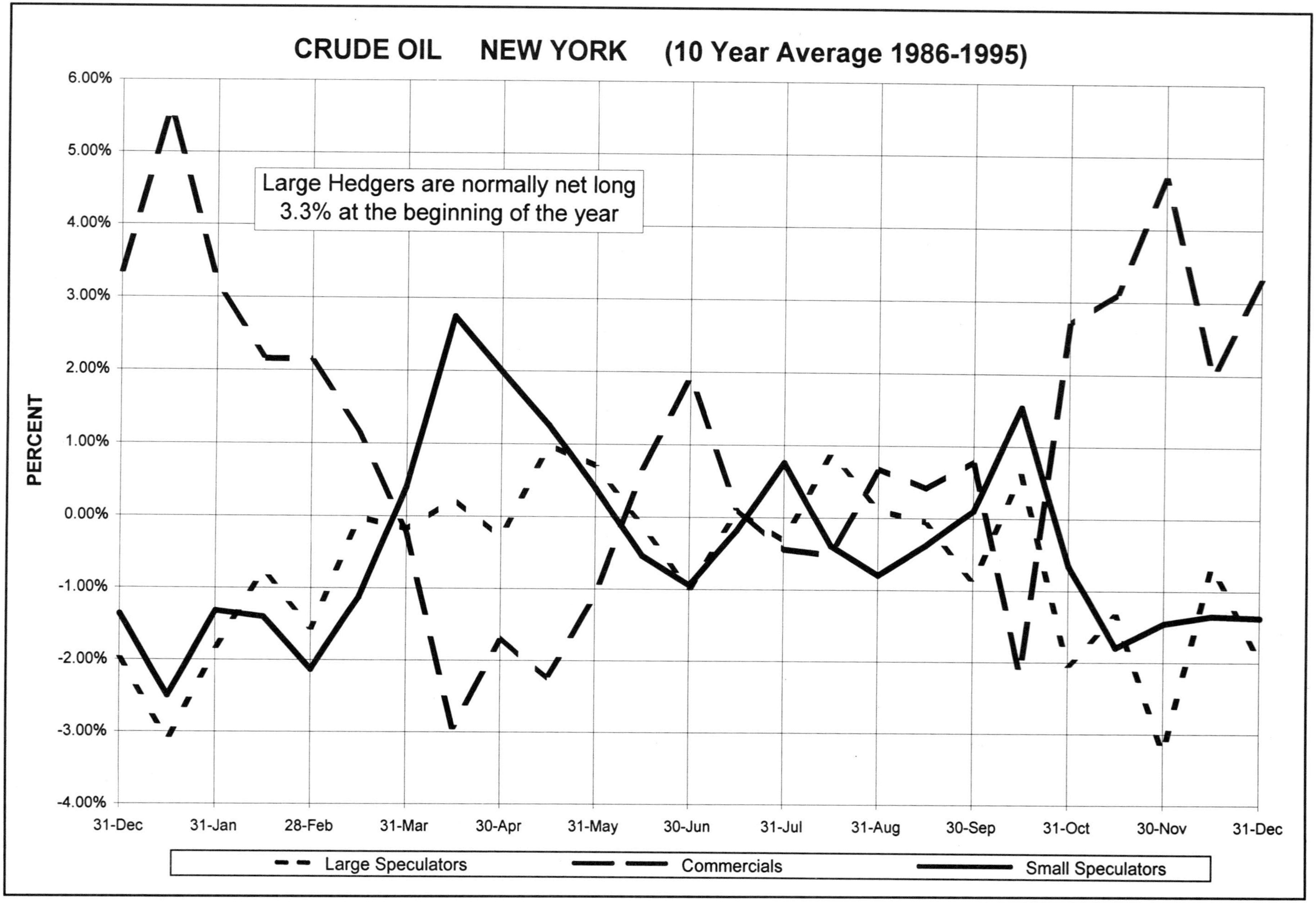

Figure 3. Seasonally Normal Graph

In the four situations isolated, the Large Hedgers in T-Bonds and Crude Oil were definitely inclined to hold net short futures positions on January 2, 1996. The Cotton and Coffee Large Hedgers were holding net long futures. *In the previous ten years, on average, these four Large Hedgers were facing exactly the opposite direction*--and by considerably more than a five percent swing--but less than 40 percent.

The remaining 16 historic normal charts vs. actual situations examined did not show a difference in sign from what was expected of the Large Hedgers. The grain and oilseed commitments did show a more bullish (than the normal bullish) bias on the part of both speculative categories.

The Large Hedgers are not always immediately correct in their market view. But if prices do start moving in their direction, the other side, the Small Trader, will begin to panic. The Large Speculator will receive a trend change signal and attempt to move to the sidelines. This environment creates the potential for an "air-pocket" in futures price movement against the positions of the Small Trader.

Adding Options

With the advent of the Combined Commitments of Traders Report in May of 1995, an analyst will want to make sure that the addition of futures equivalent options positions does not alter the bias of each category enough to negate the forecasting implications. This Combined Commitments Report is released the day after the Futures Only report. In the January 2, 1996 case study, the addition of options did not change the long/short classification of any category of any of the four situations under study, with one minor exception, T-Bonds. A detailed observation of the T-Bond Reports is shown in Figure 4. A positive sign equals net long, a negative sign equals net short.

The comparison of the futures only positions to futures + options shows that the Small Trader is now net long five percent. These traders are taking a bullish view via positive delta, options positions. These could be short T-Bond put options. But a much more likely scenario is that the small trader is long T-Bond calls. This bullish bias on the part of the Small Trader increases the bearish forecast of the Commitments Report.

Technical Analysis

Technically orientated traders might now want to apply their favorite technical tool to the price charts of the Bonds, Crude Oil, Cotton, and Coffee. The first step is to identify the direction of the current price trend and then look for any technical signs of a reversal. A classical bar chartist would see a very different "look" to the four price charts. A technical comment on each of the four charts could be summarized as follows:

T-Bonds: A price selloff in the last few trading sessions (early January) violated underlying support at the former price high of 121-12. This is the first major criteria necessary for a Head & Shoulders Top price pattern to form.

Crude Oil: A strong price uptrend is underway with no classical price signs of a top. This chart is shown in Figure 5.

Cotton: Prices have been moving net sideways within a large seven cent/lb. trading range between 80.00 and 87.00.

Coffee: A definite price downtrend is in progress, with prices below the 100.00 cent/lb. overhead resistance on the March 1996 future.

The Outcome

By the beginning of the next month, February 2, 1996, the following observations could be made:

T-Bonds: Still within a large trading range between 118 and 122.
Result of forecast: Result not in

Crude Oil: Refer to Figure 6 to see the sharp price break of more than 2.50 $/bbl.
Result of forecast: Large profit

Cotton: A rally of 3.45 cent/lb. occurred.
Result of forecast: Large profit

Coffee: A rally of $13.30 occurred.
Result of forecast: Large profit

Summary

The Crude Oil chart in Figure 6 is representative of the profitable outcomes in three of the four situations investigated. The directional forecasts based on the Commitments Report were impressive. Only the T-Bonds failed to produce a clear cut price move. However, any (small) trader with long T-Bond call options would have been holding wasting assets.

* * *

Figure 5. Chart When January 2 Commitments Report Data Was Available

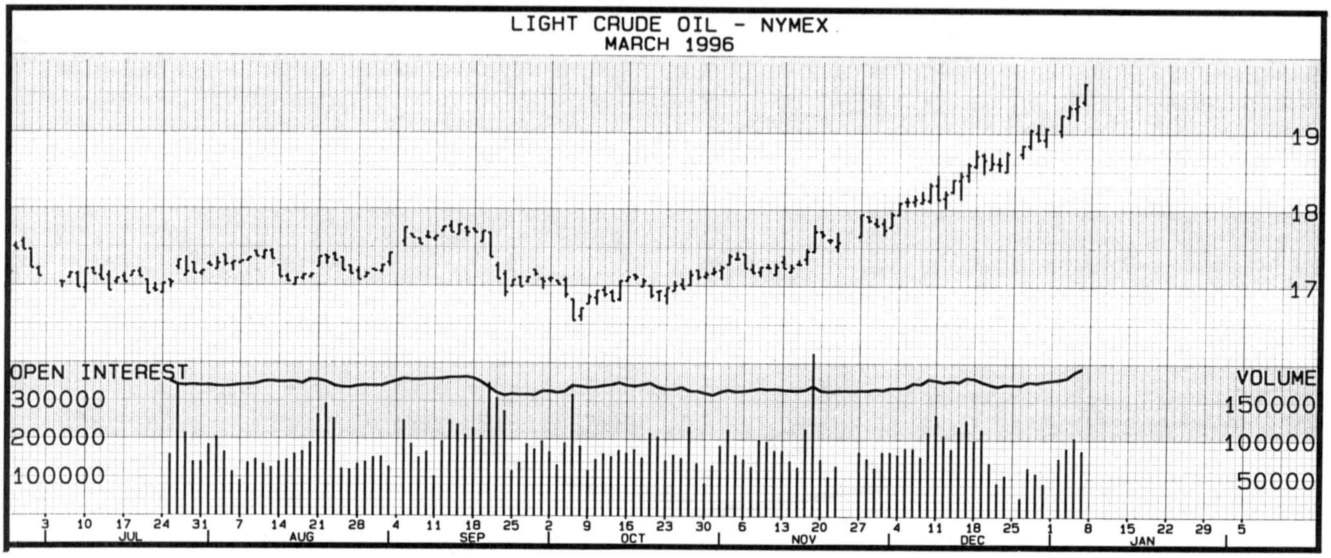

Figure 6. How It Came Out

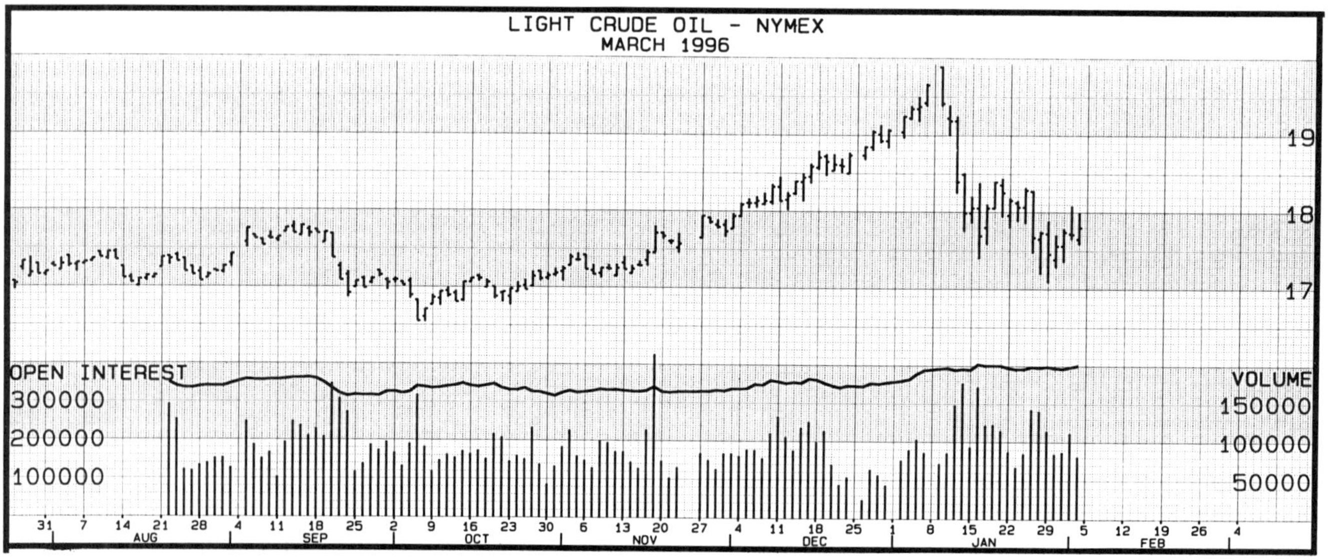

Author's Note: For further information on the use of open interest in technical analysis, refer to Mr. Shaleen's book *Volume and Open Interest: Cutting Edge Trading Strategies in the Futures Markets*, IRWIN Professional Publishing.

* * *

***Kenneth H. Shaleen** is President of CHARTWATCH, an international research firm to the futures industry. CHARTWATCH distributes a weekly technical publication and produces a daily telephone market update covering the financial instrument futures. Mr. Shaleen has instructed technical analysis courses for the Chicago Mercantile Exchange since 1978. These courses are also conducted in Singapore, Malaysia, Hong Kong, London ands numerous other locations throughout the world. Mr. Shaleen is the author of Volume and Open Interest: Cutting Edge Trading Strategies in the Futures Markets (Probus 1991), Technical Analysis & Option Strategies (Probus 1992), three Chicago Mercantile Exchange course books as well as numerous articles. Mr. Shaleen can be contacted at CHARTWATCH, Fulton House, 345 Canal Street, Chicago, IL 60606, 312-454-1130.*

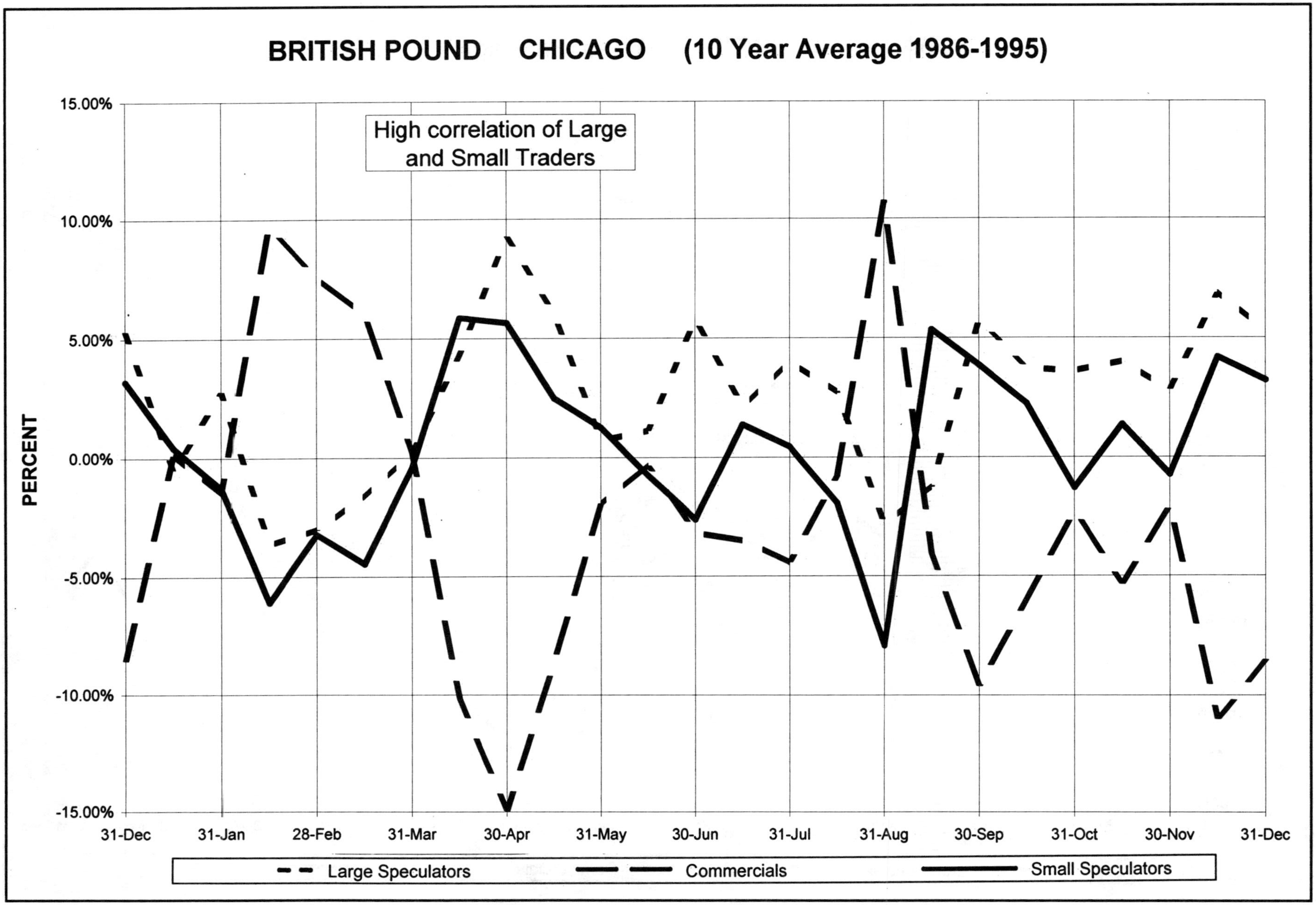
BRITISH POUND CHICAGO (10 Year Average 1986-1995)
High correlation of Large and Small Traders
PERCENT
15.00%
10.00%
5.00%
0.00%
-5.00%
-10.00%
-15.00%
31-Dec
31-Jan
28-Feb
31-Mar
30-Apr
31-May
30-Jun
31-Jul
31-Aug
30-Sep
31-Oct
30-Nov
31-Dec
Large Speculators
Commercials
Small Speculators

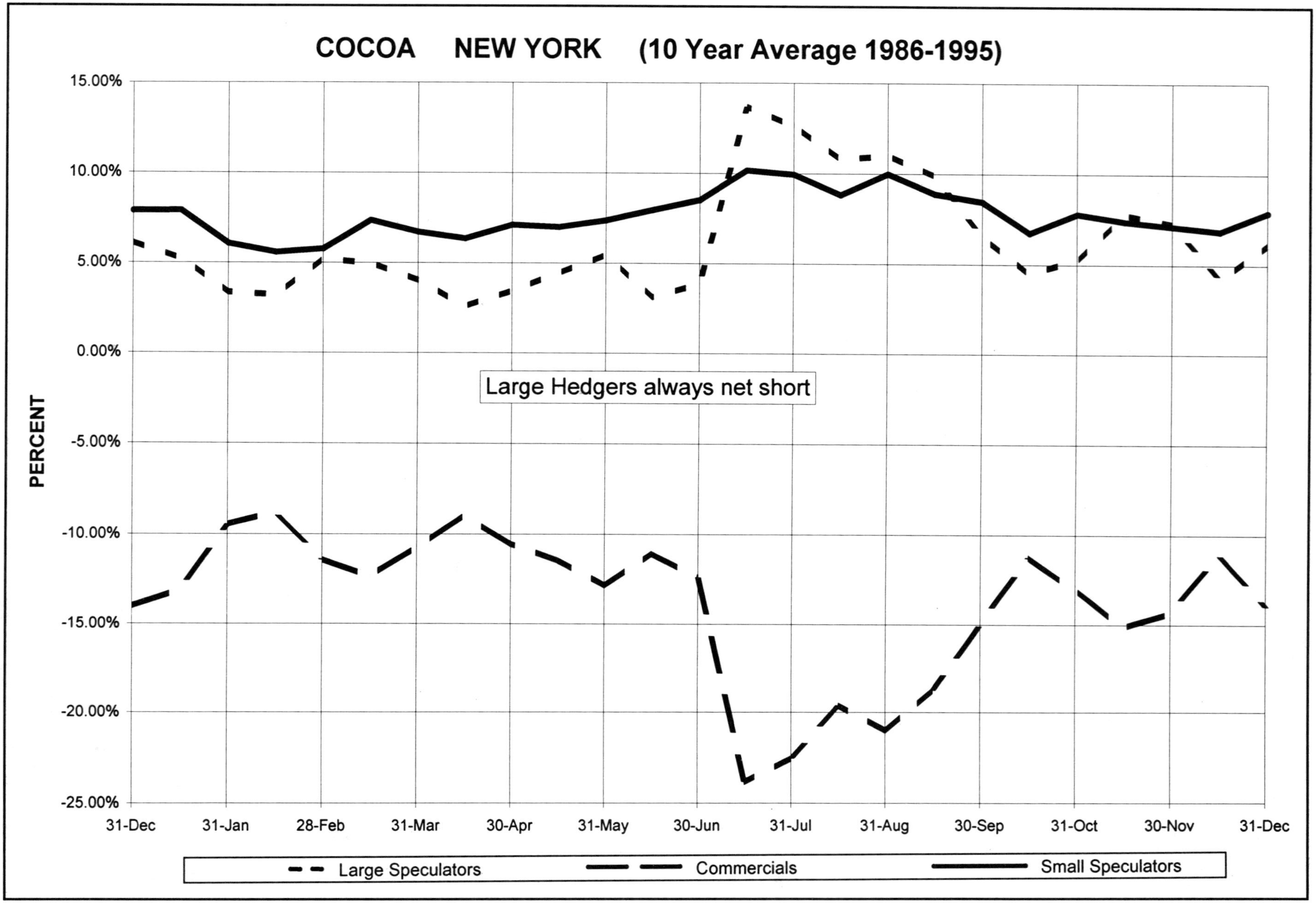
COCOA NEW YORK (10 Year Average 1986-1995)
PERCENT
15.00%
10.00%
5.00%
0.00%
-5.00%
-10.00%
-15.00%
-20.00%
-25.00%
31-Dec
31-Jan
28-Feb
31-Mar
30-Apr
31-May
30-Jun
31-Jul
31-Aug
30-Sep
31-Oct
30-Nov
31-Dec
Large Hedgers always net short
Large Speculators
Commercials
Small Speculators

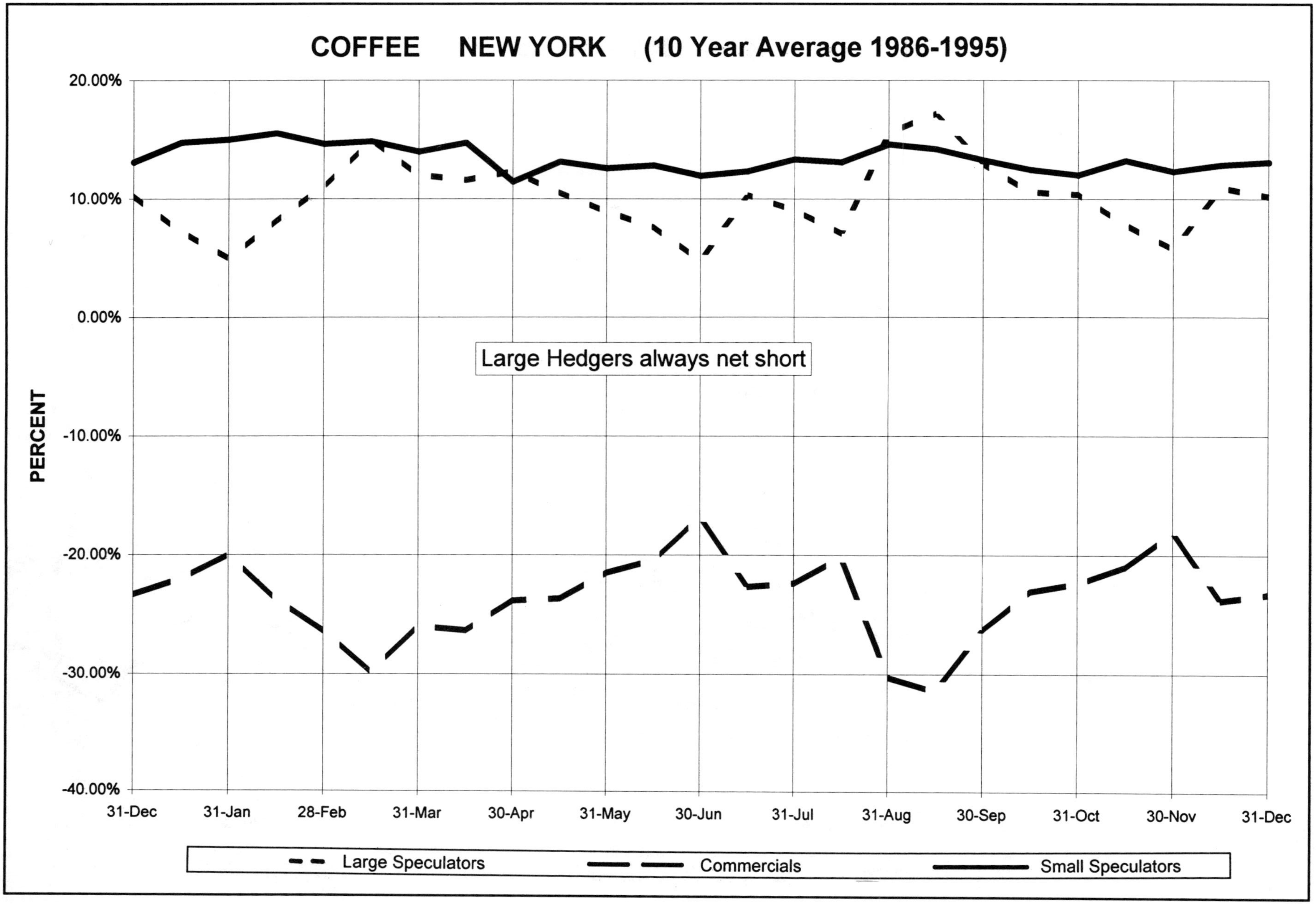
COFFEE NEW YORK (10 Year Average 1986-1995)
PERCENT
20.00%
10.00%
0.00%
-10.00%
-20.00%
-30.00%
-40.00%
Large Hedgers always net short
31-Dec
31-Jan
28-Feb
31-Mar
30-Apr
31-May
30-Jun
31-Jul
31-Aug
30-Sep
31-Oct
30-Nov
31-Dec
Large Speculators
Commercials
Small Speculators

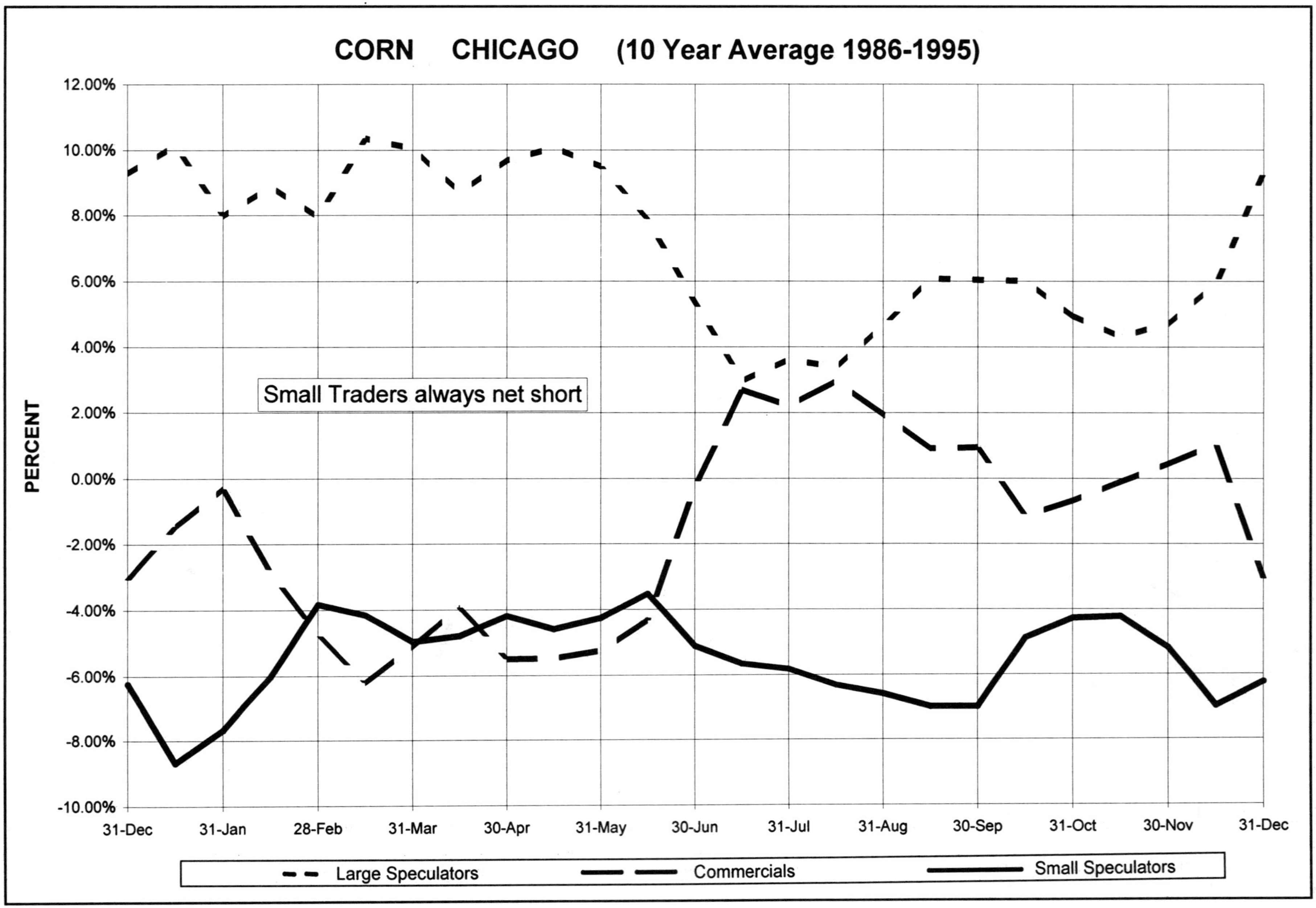
CORN CHICAGO (10 Year Average 1986-1995)
PERCENT
12.00%
10.00%
8.00%
6.00%
4.00%
2.00%
0.00%
-2.00%
-4.00%
-6.00%
-8.00%
-10.00%
31-Dec
31-Jan
28-Feb
31-Mar
30-Apr
31-May
30-Jun
31-Jul
31-Aug
30-Sep
31-Oct
30-Nov
31-Dec
Small Traders always net short
Large Speculators
Commercials
Small Speculators

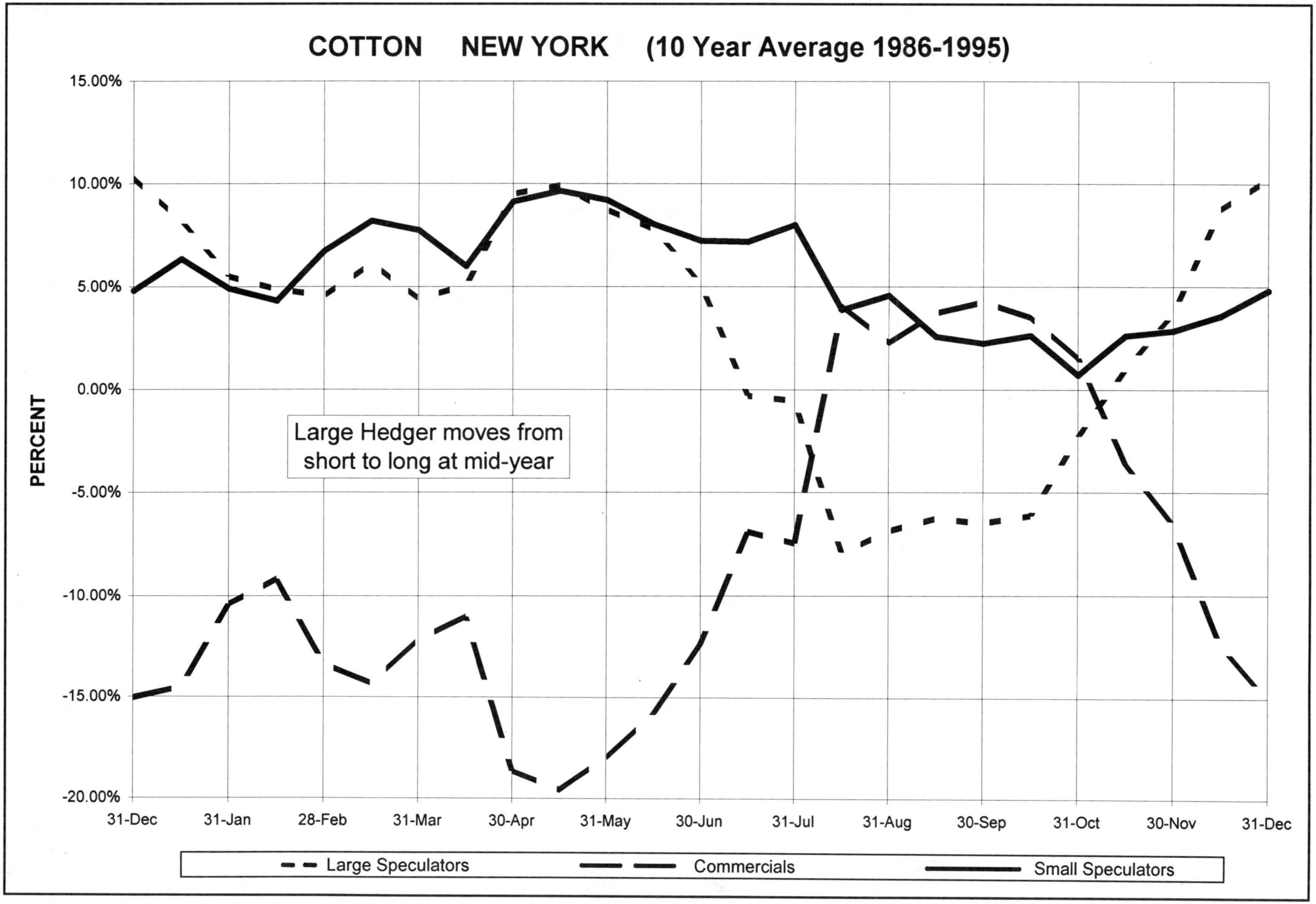
COTTON NEW YORK (10 Year Average 1986-1995)
PERCENT
15.00%
10.00%
5.00%
0.00%
-5.00%
-10.00%
-15.00%
-20.00%
31-Dec
31-Jan
28-Feb
31-Mar
30-Apr
31-May
30-Jun
31-Jul
31-Aug
30-Sep
31-Oct
30-Nov
31-Dec
Large Hedger moves from short to long at mid-year
Large Speculators
Commercials
Small Speculators

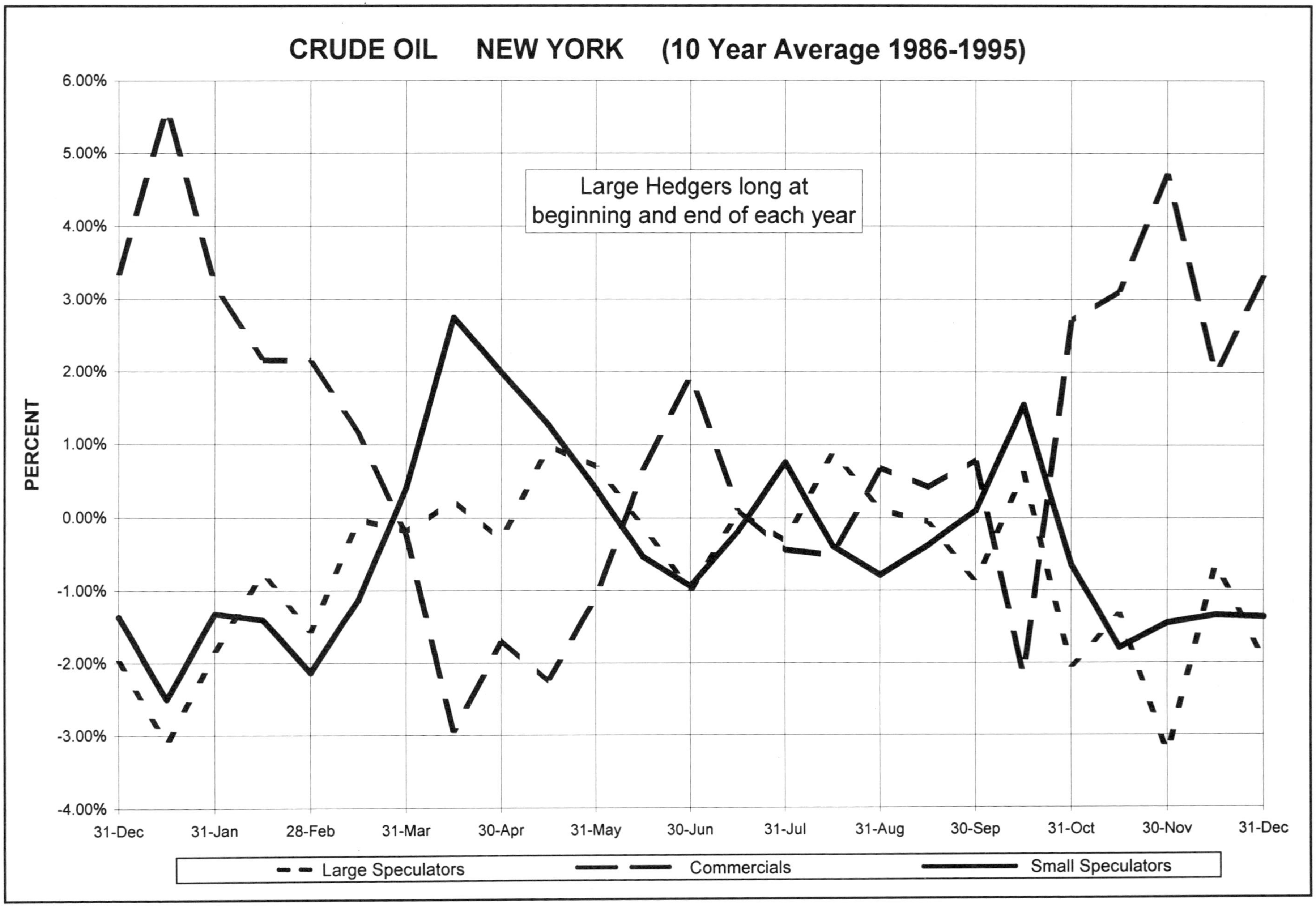
CRUDE OIL NEW YORK (10 Year Average 1986-1995)
PERCENT
6.00%
5.00%
4.00%
3.00%
2.00%
1.00%
0.00%
-1.00%
-2.00%
-3.00%
-4.00%
Large Hedgers long at beginning and end of each year
31-Dec
31-Jan
28-Feb
31-Mar
30-Apr
31-May
30-Jun
31-Jul
31-Aug
30-Sep
31-Oct
30-Nov
31-Dec
Large Speculators
Commercials
Small Speculators

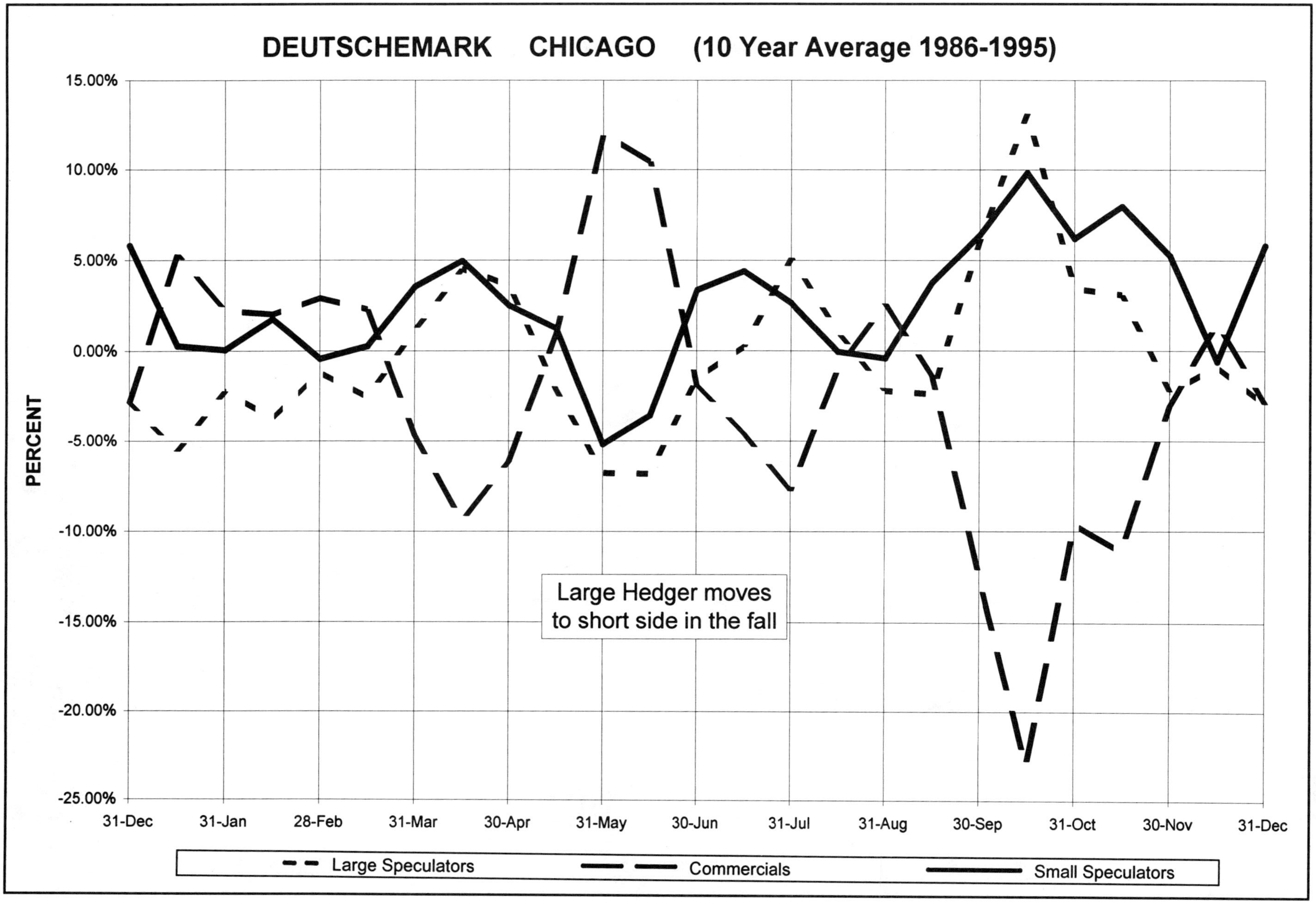

DEUTSCHEMARK CHICAGO (10 Year Average 1986-1995)
15.00%
10.00%
5.00%
0.00%
-5.00%
-10.00%
-15.00%
-20.00%
-25.00%
PERCENT
31-Dec
31-Jan
28-Feb
31-Mar
30-Apr
31-May
30-Jun
31-Jul
31-Aug
30-Sep
31-Oct
30-Nov
31-Dec
Large Hedger moves to short side in the fall
Large Speculators
Commercials
Small Speculators

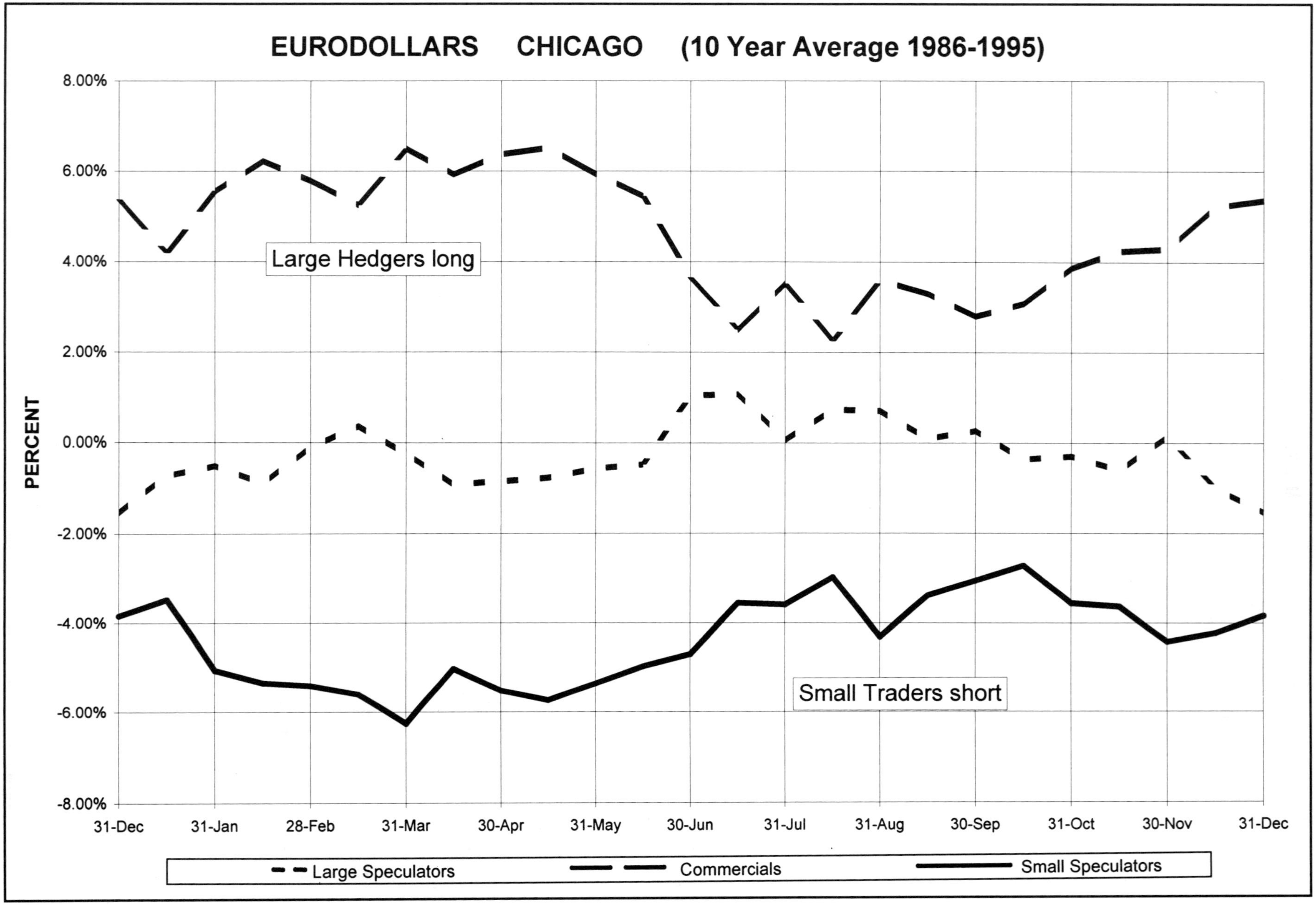
EURODOLLARS CHICAGO (10 Year Average 1986-1995)
PERCENT
8.00%
6.00%
4.00%
2.00%
0.00%
-2.00%
-4.00%
-6.00%
-8.00%
Large Hedgers long
Small Traders short
31-Dec
31-Jan
28-Feb
31-Mar
30-Apr
31-May
30-Jun
31-Jul
31-Aug
30-Sep
31-Oct
30-Nov
31-Dec
Large Speculators
Commercials
Small Speculators

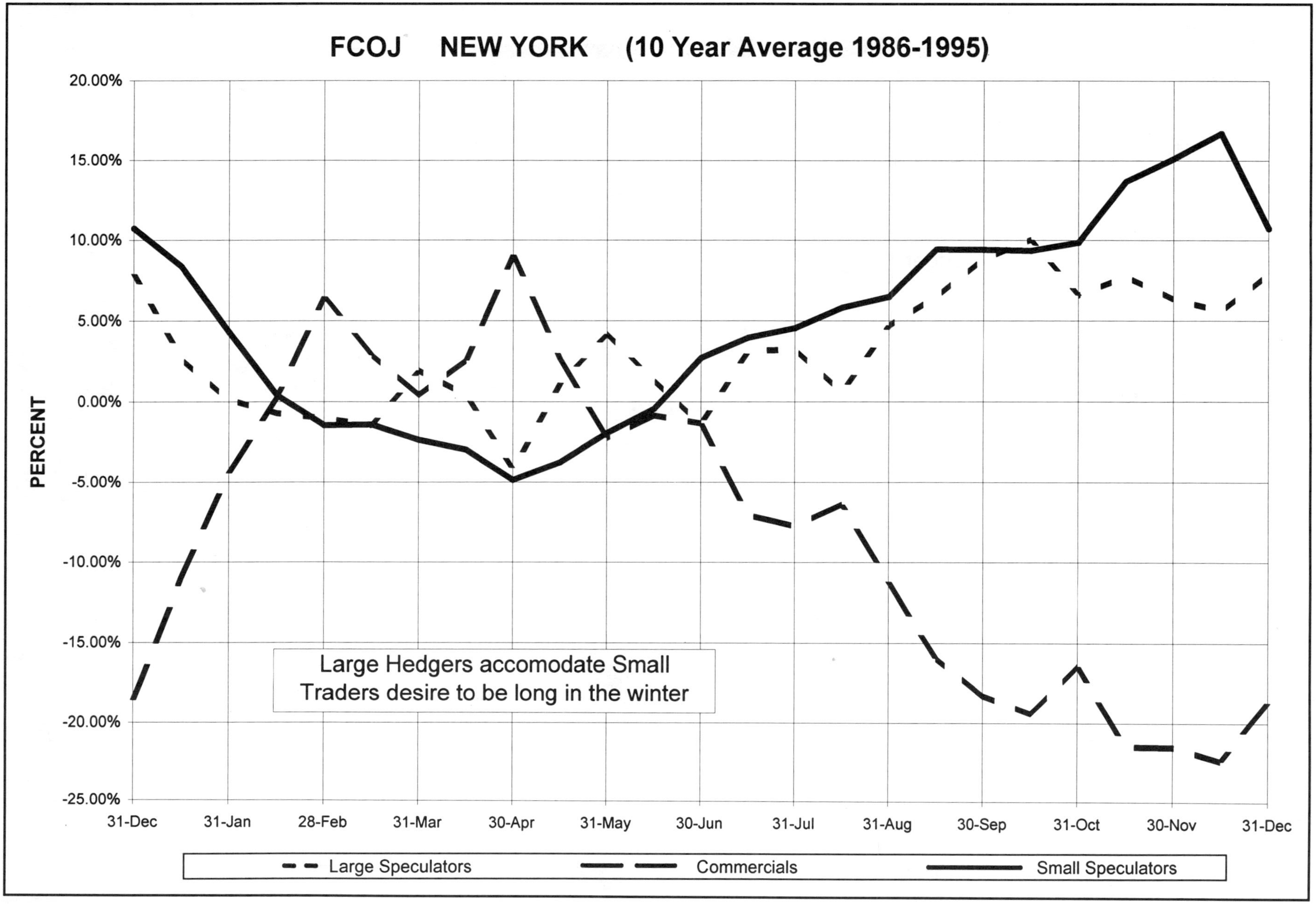
FCOJ NEW YORK (10 Year Average 1986-1995)
PERCENT
20.00%
15.00%
10.00%
5.00%
0.00%
-5.00%
-10.00%
-15.00%
-20.00%
-25.00%
31-Dec
31-Jan
28-Feb
31-Mar
30-Apr
31-May
30-Jun
31-Jul
31-Aug
30-Sep
31-Oct
30-Nov
31-Dec
Large Hedgers accomodate Small
Traders desire to be long in the winter
Large Speculators
Commercials
Small Speculators

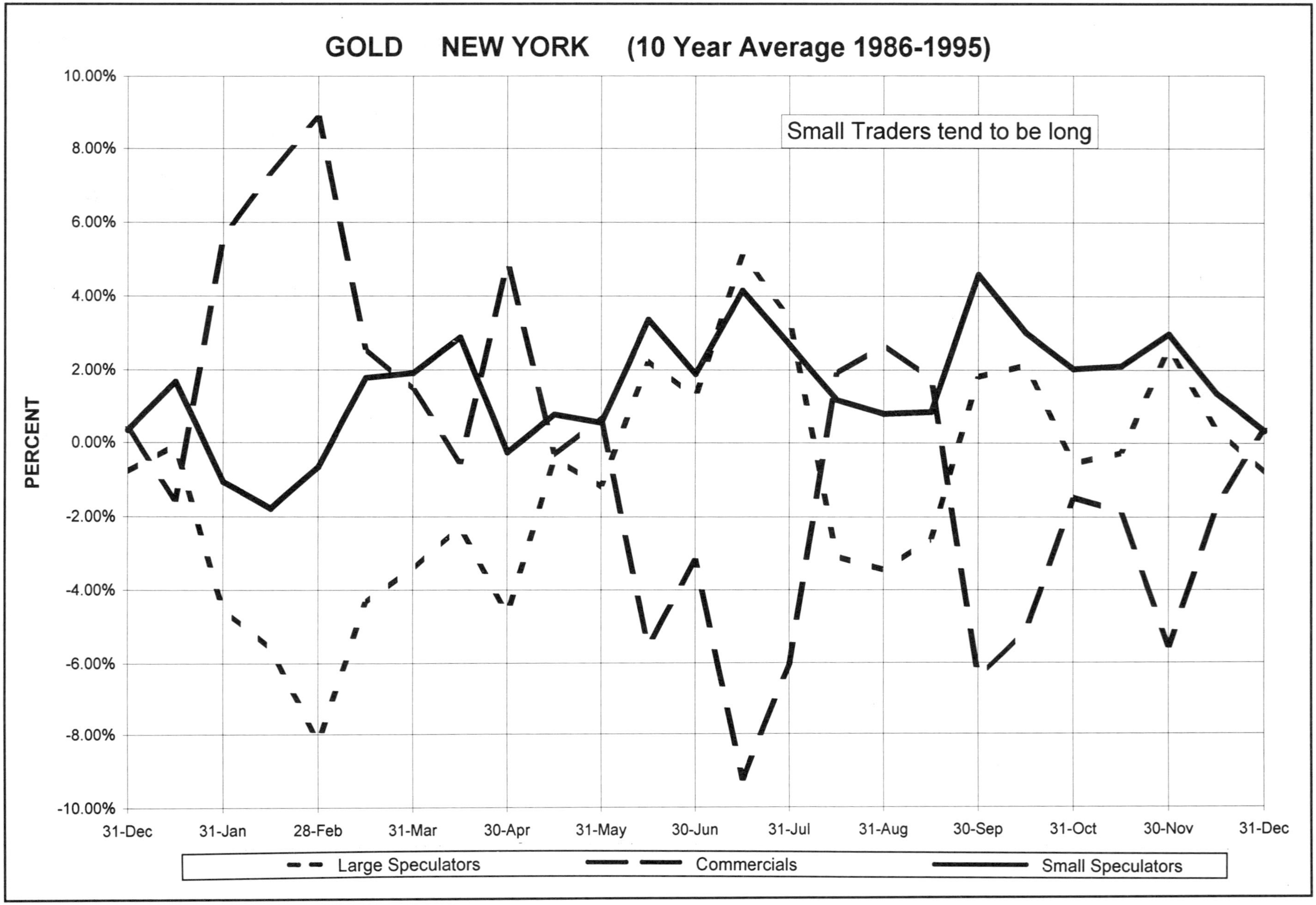
GOLD NEW YORK (10 Year Average 1986-1995)
Small Traders tend to be long
PERCENT
10.00%
8.00%
6.00%
4.00%
2.00%
0.00%
-2.00%
-4.00%
-6.00%
-8.00%
-10.00%
31-Dec
31-Jan
28-Feb
31-Mar
30-Apr
31-May
30-Jun
31-Jul
31-Aug
30-Sep
31-Oct
30-Nov
31-Dec
Large Speculators
Commercials
Small Speculators

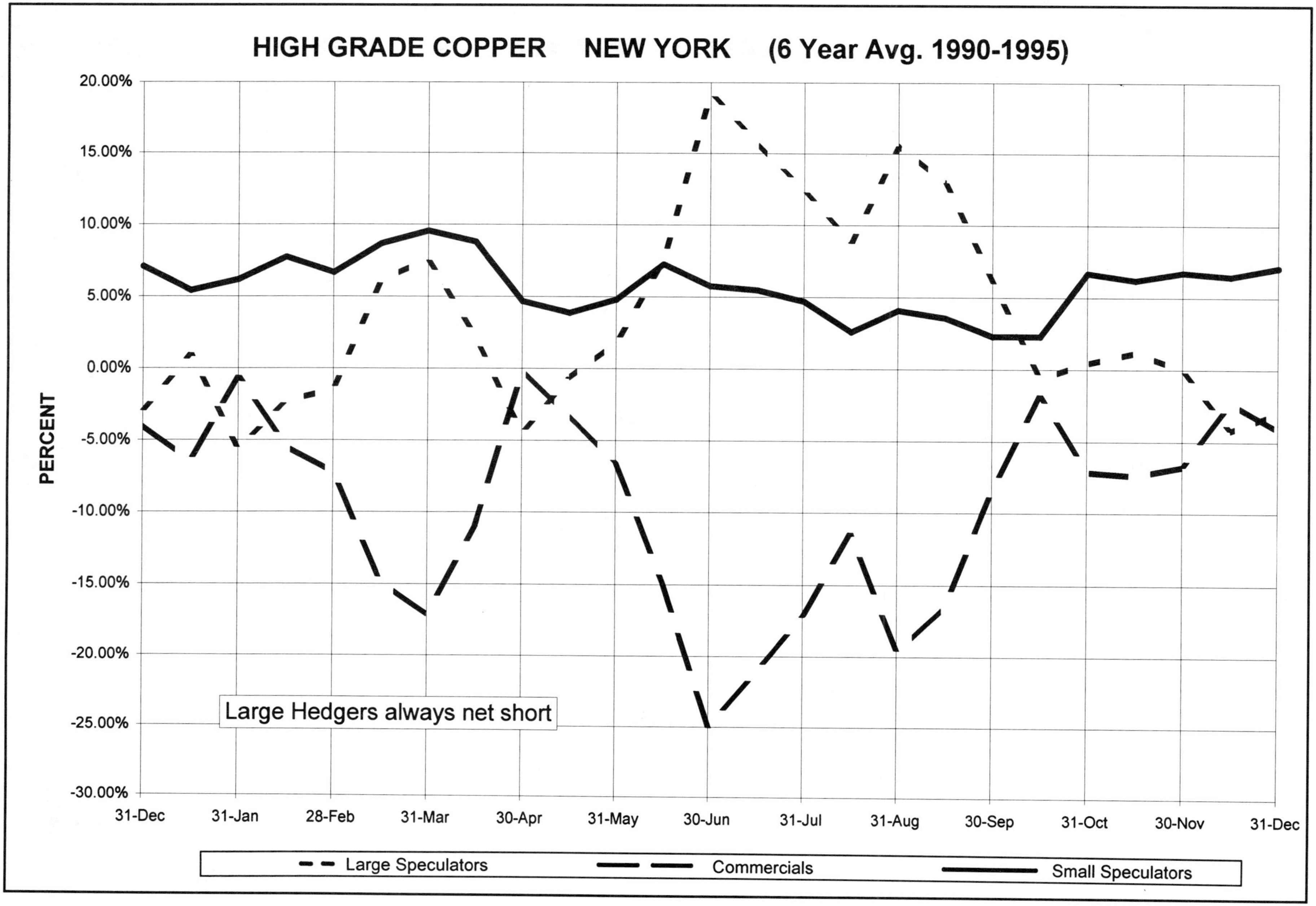

HIGH GRADE COPPER NEW YORK (6 Year Avg. 1990-1995)
PERCENT
20.00%
15.00%
10.00%
5.00%
0.00%
-5.00%
-10.00%
-15.00%
-20.00%
-25.00%
-30.00%
31-Dec
31-Jan
28-Feb
31-Mar
30-Apr
31-May
30-Jun
31-Jul
31-Aug
30-Sep
31-Oct
30-Nov
31-Dec
Large Hedgers always net short
Large Speculators
Commercials
Small Speculators

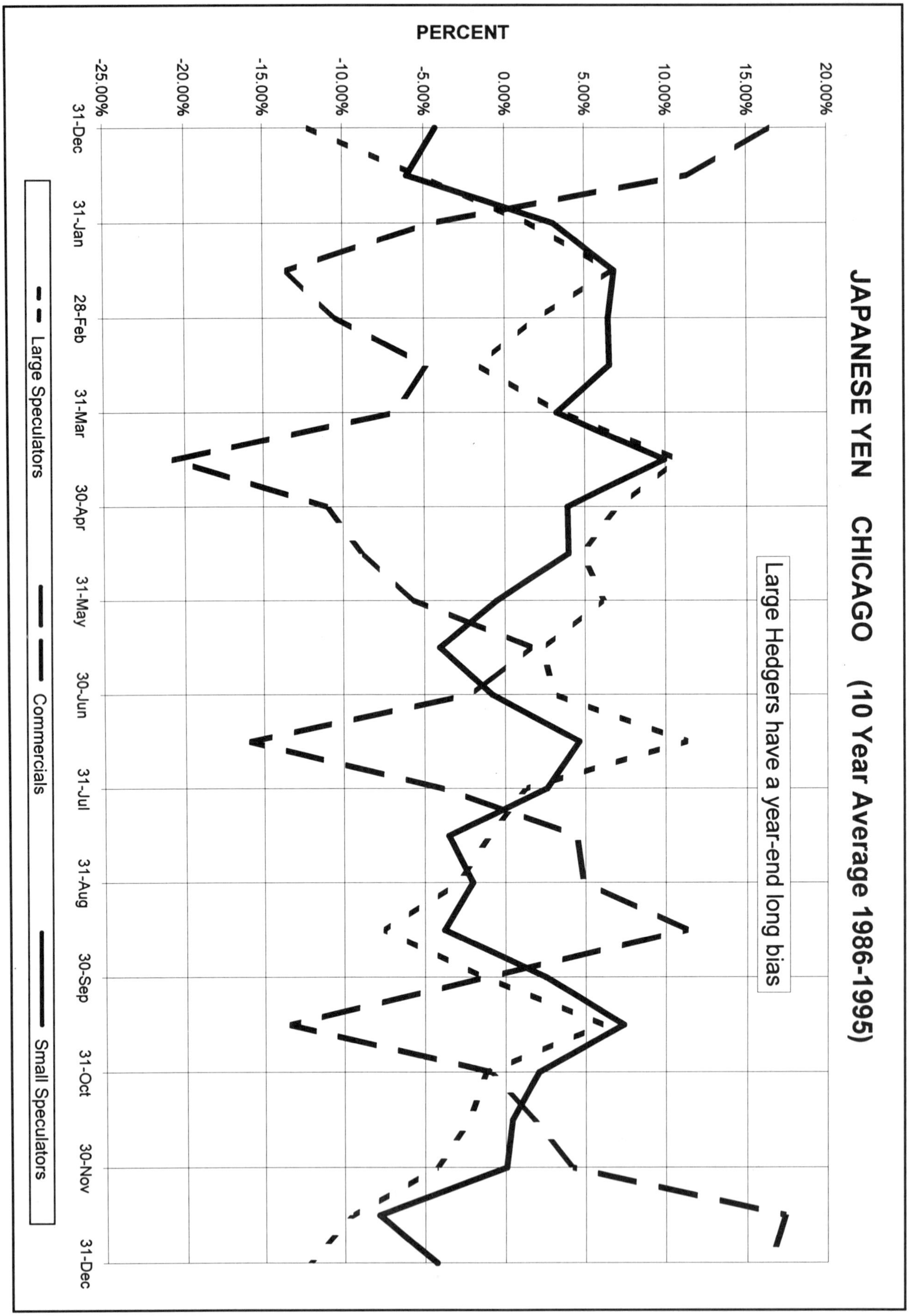

JAPANESE YEN CHICAGO (10 Year Average 1986-1995)
Large Hedgers have a year-end long bias
PERCENT
20.00%
15.00%
10.00%
5.00%
0.00%
-5.00%
-10.00%
-15.00%
-20.00%
-25.00%
31-Dec
31-Jan
28-Feb
31-Mar
30-Apr
31-May
30-Jun
31-Jul
31-Aug
30-Sep
31-Oct
30-Nov
31-Dec
Large Speculators
Commercials
Small Speculators

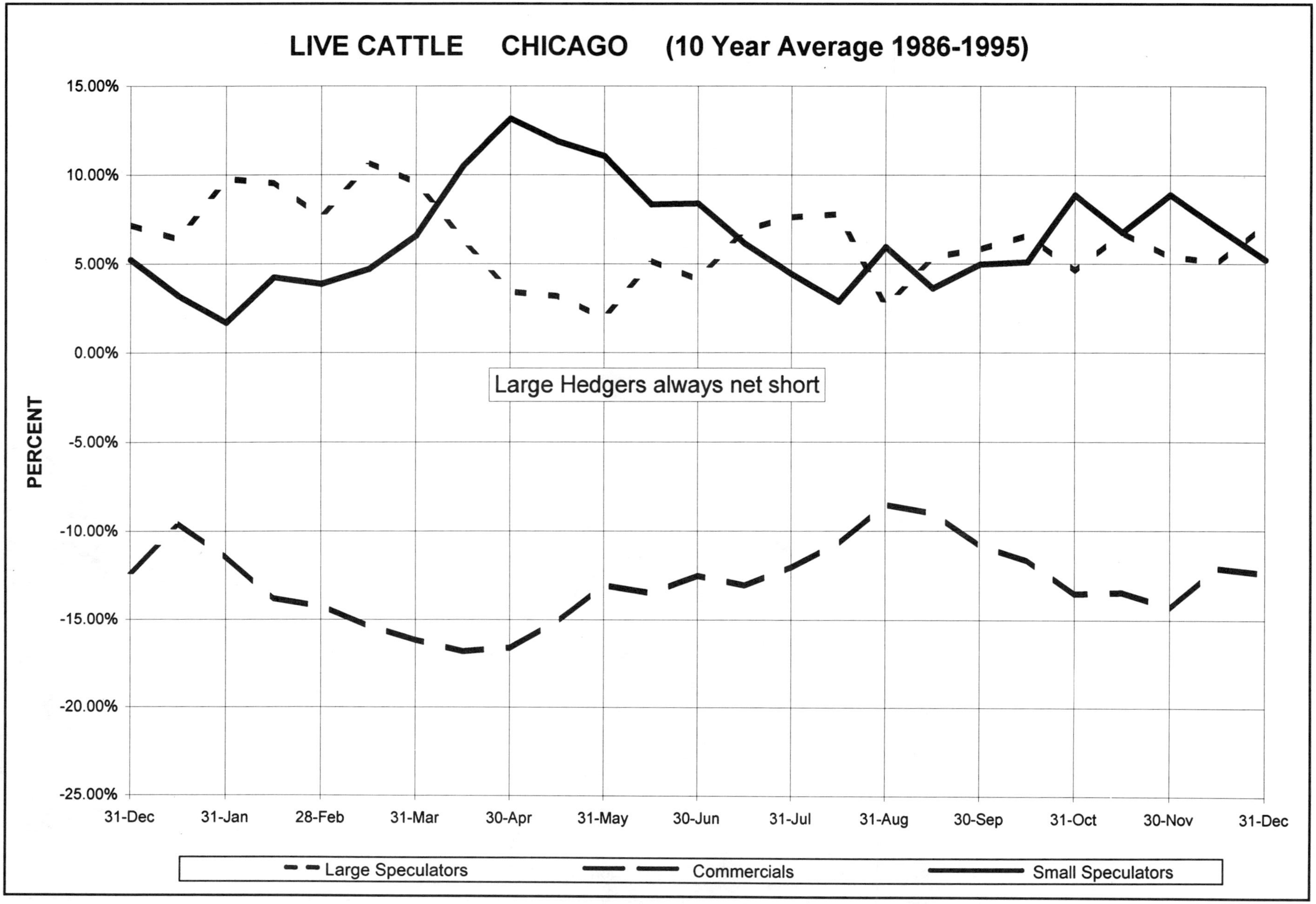
LIVE CATTLE CHICAGO (10 Year Average 1986-1995)
PERCENT
15.00%
10.00%
5.00%
0.00%
-5.00%
-10.00%
-15.00%
-20.00%
-25.00%
31-Dec
31-Jan
28-Feb
31-Mar
30-Apr
31-May
30-Jun
31-Jul
31-Aug
30-Sep
31-Oct
30-Nov
31-Dec
Large Hedgers always net short
Large Speculators
Commercials
Small Speculators

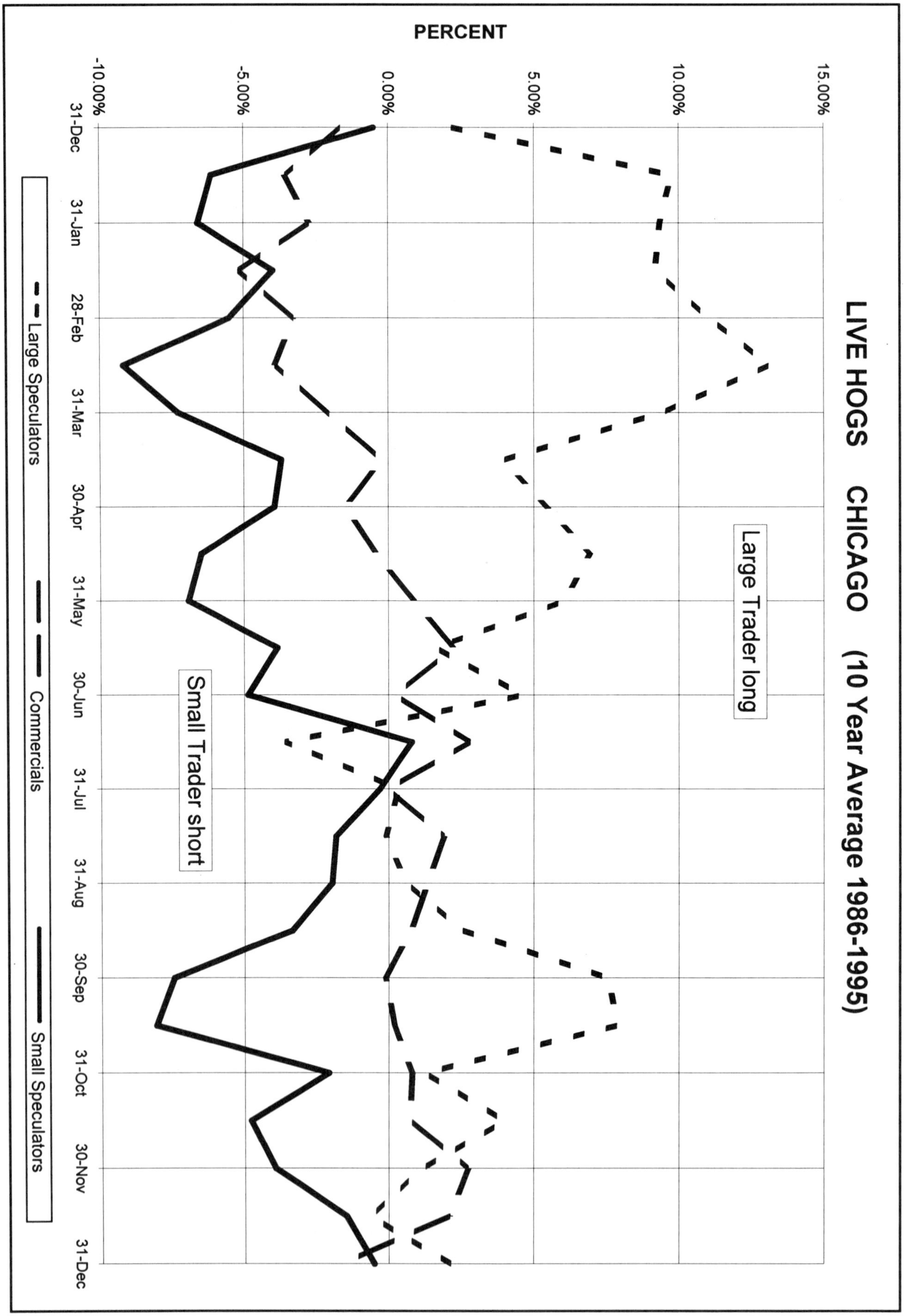
LIVE HOGS CHICAGO (10 Year Average 1986-1995)
PERCENT
15.00%
10.00%
5.00%
0.00%
-5.00%
-10.00%
31-Dec
31-Jan
28-Feb
31-Mar
30-Apr
31-May
30-Jun
31-Jul
31-Aug
30-Sep
31-Oct
30-Nov
31-Dec
Large Trader long
Small Trader short
Large Speculators
Commercials
Small Speculators

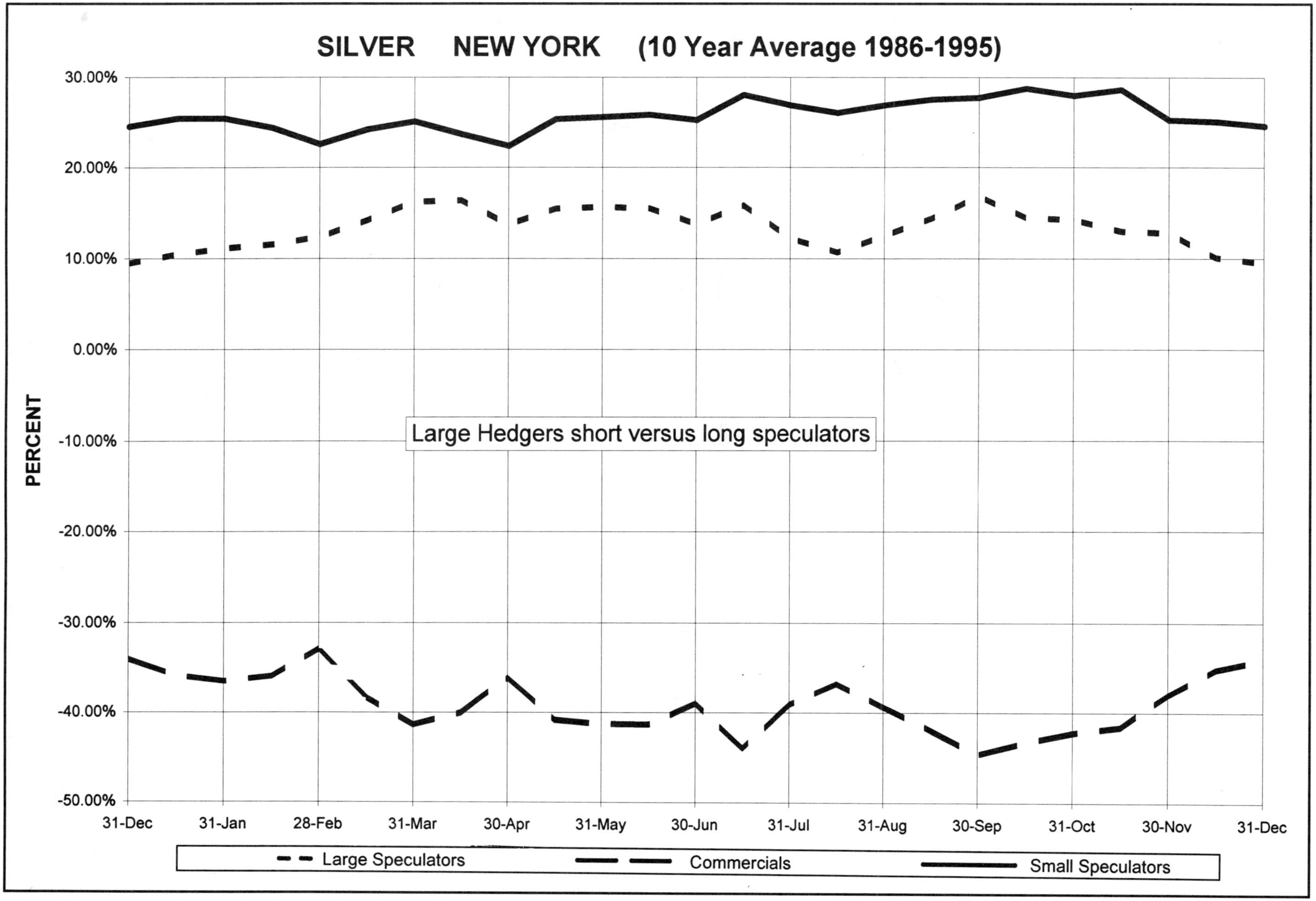
SILVER NEW YORK (10 Year Average 1986-1995)
PERCENT
30.00%
20.00%
10.00%
0.00%
-10.00%
-20.00%
-30.00%
-40.00%
-50.00%
Large Hedgers short versus long speculators
31-Dec
31-Jan
28-Feb
31-Mar
30-Apr
31-May
30-Jun
31-Jul
31-Aug
30-Sep
31-Oct
30-Nov
31-Dec
Large Speculators
Commercials
Small Speculators

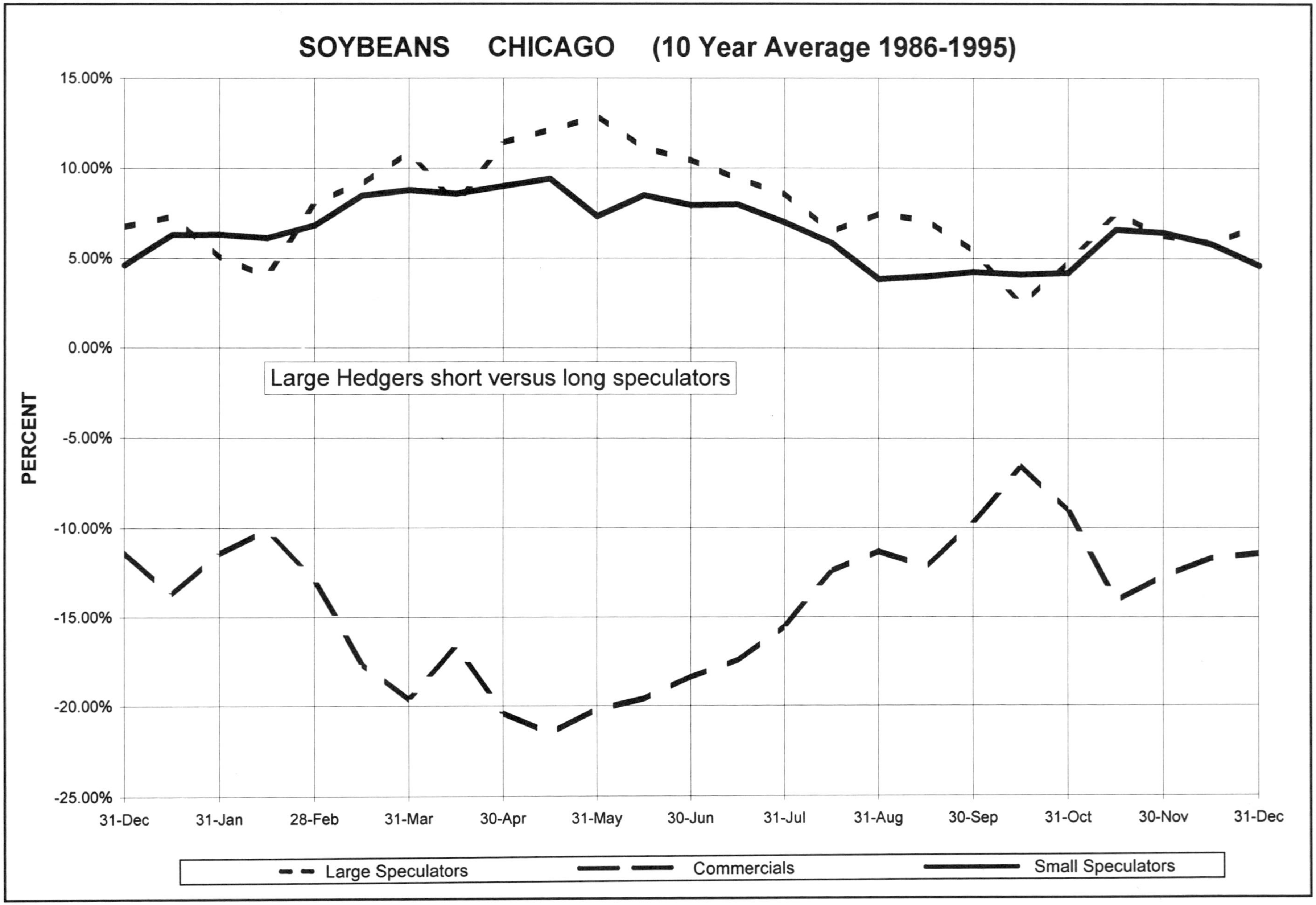
SOYBEANS CHICAGO (10 Year Average 1986-1995)
PERCENT
15.00%
10.00%
5.00%
0.00%
-5.00%
-10.00%
-15.00%
-20.00%
-25.00%
Large Hedgers short versus long speculators
31-Dec
31-Jan
28-Feb
31-Mar
30-Apr
31-May
30-Jun
31-Jul
31-Aug
30-Sep
31-Oct
30-Nov
31-Dec
Large Speculators
Commercials
Small Speculators

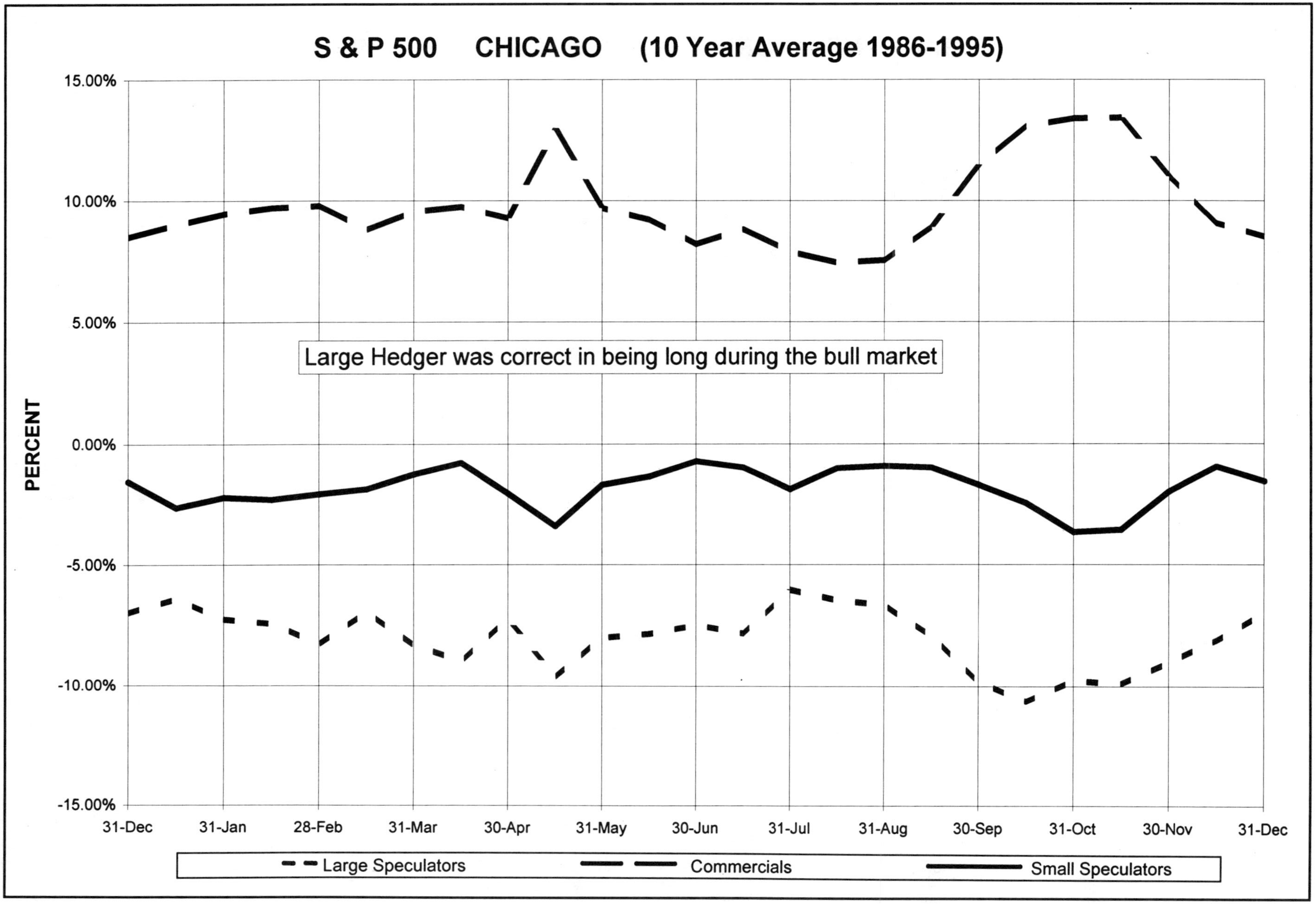
S & P 500 CHICAGO (10 Year Average 1986-1995)
PERCENT
15.00%
10.00%
5.00%
0.00%
-5.00%
-10.00%
-15.00%
Large Hedger was correct in being long during the bull market
31-Dec
31-Jan
28-Feb
31-Mar
30-Apr
31-May
30-Jun
31-Jul
31-Aug
30-Sep
31-Oct
30-Nov
31-Dec
Large Speculators
Commercials
Small Speculators

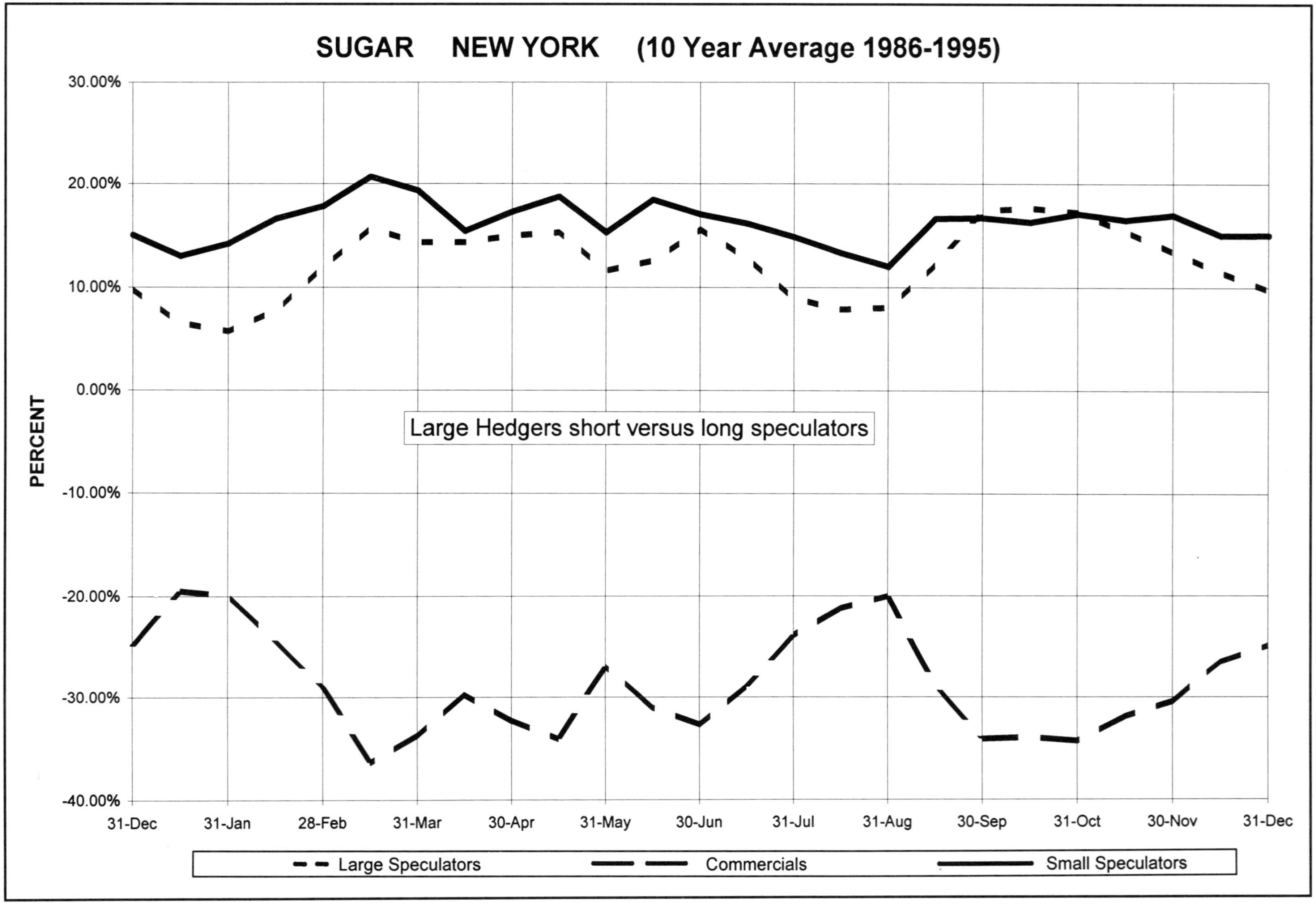
SUGAR NEW YORK (10 Year Average 1986-1995)
PERCENT
30.00%
20.00%
10.00%
0.00%
-10.00%
-20.00%
-30.00%
-40.00%
Large Hedgers short versus long speculators
31-Dec
31-Jan
28-Feb
31-Mar
30-Apr
31-May
30-Jun
31-Jul
31-Aug
30-Sep
31-Oct
30-Nov
31-Dec
Large Speculators
Commercials
Small Speculators

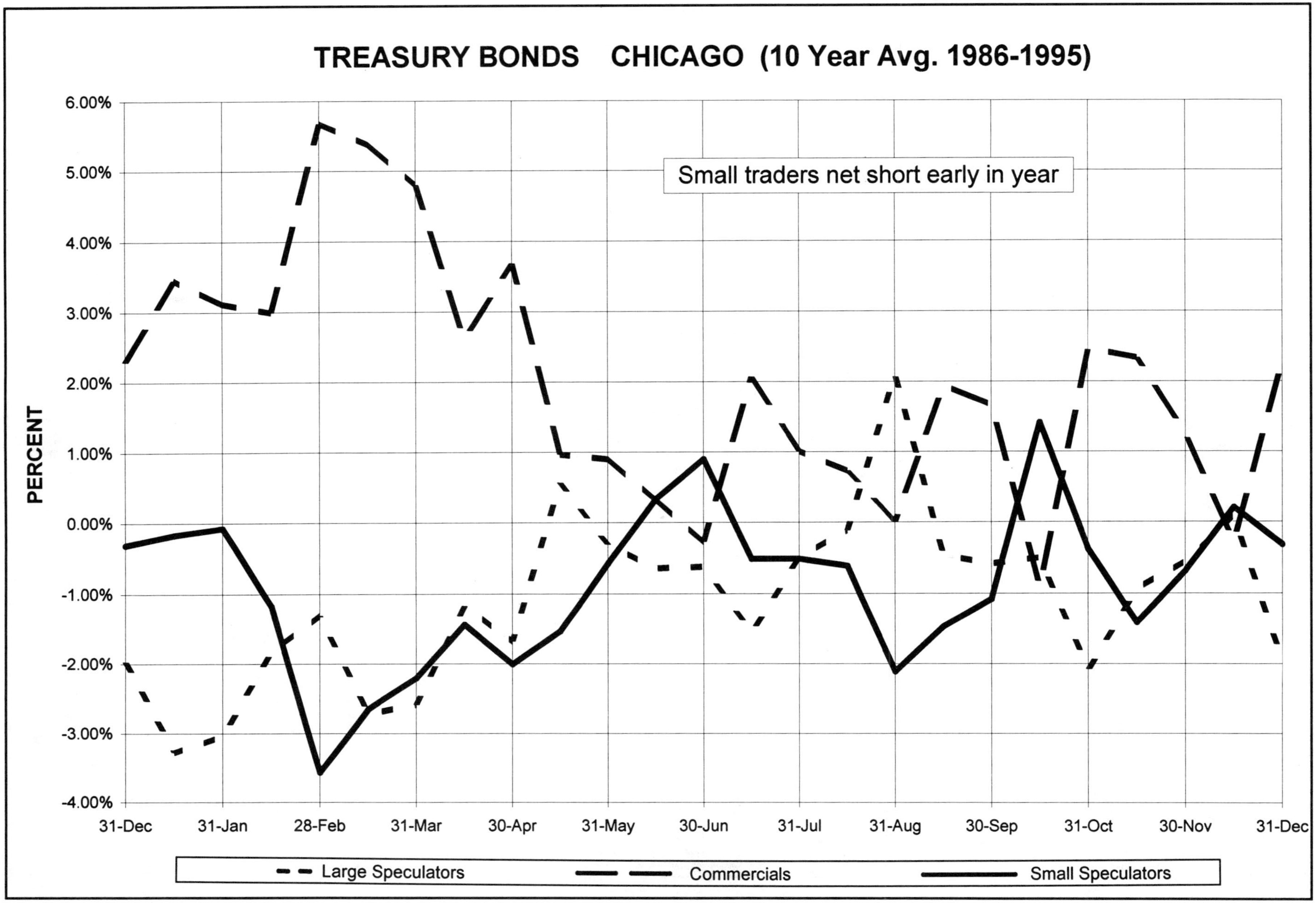

TREASURY BONDS CHICAGO (10 Year Avg. 1986-1995)
Small traders net short early in year
PERCENT
6.00%
5.00%
4.00%
3.00%
2.00%
1.00%
0.00%
-1.00%
-2.00%
-3.00%
-4.00%
31-Dec
31-Jan
28-Feb
31-Mar
30-Apr
31-May
30-Jun
31-Jul
31-Aug
30-Sep
31-Oct
30-Nov
31-Dec
Large Speculators
Commercials
Small Speculators

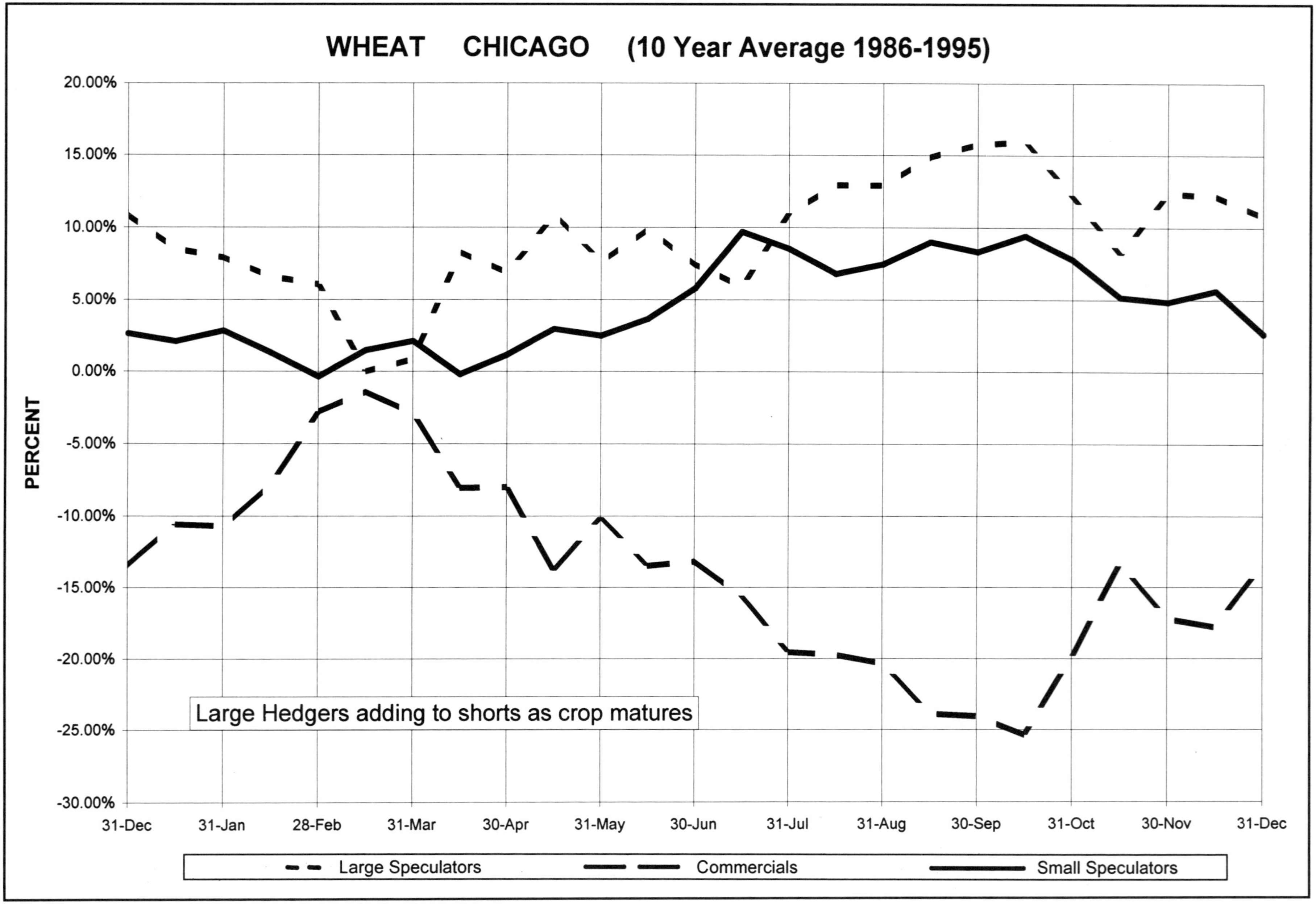
WHEAT CHICAGO (10 Year Average 1986-1995)
PERCENT
20.00%
15.00%
10.00%
5.00%
0.00%
-5.00%
-10.00%
-15.00%
-20.00%
-25.00%
-30.00%
31-Dec
31-Jan
28-Feb
31-Mar
30-Apr
31-May
30-Jun
31-Jul
31-Aug
30-Sep
31-Oct
30-Nov
31-Dec
Large Hedgers adding to shorts as crop matures
Large Speculators
Commercials
Small Speculators

UNDERSTANDING AND ANALYZING THE COTTON MARKET

by Walter Spilka

Cotton, a most familiar commodity, has a long history. Cotton appears to have its origins in China several thousand years ago. Because of its extensive use in apparel, household products, and industrial applications, it is a commodity in constant demand and therefore is grown in countries throughout the world. Among the major producers of cotton are the United States, China, India, and Pakistan, as well as the countries in Central Asia that were formerly part of the Soviet Union.

Most of the cotton that is grown in the world today is termed upland or *Gossypium hirstum*. This species of cotton was native to Mexico and Central America and it was from this cotton that American upland cotton was developed. The vast majority of the U.S. cotton crop is upland cotton and it accounts for most of the world's medium and medium long staple. Upland cotton has a staple length of between 1-3/32 inch and 1-3/16 inch. It can be rain grown and/or irrigated and finds widespread uses ranging from coarse industrial fabrics to fine broadcloths. Most discussions of the cotton market are about upland cotton.

A second species of cotton is *Gossypium barbadense* or long and extra long staple cotton (ELS). This cotton is a native of the West Indies and has numerous varieties including Egyptian, Sudanese, and some South American varieties. Egypt is the best known producer of long staple cotton. The U.S. produces smaller amounts of ELS which are known as "pima", a name given by the USDA to distinguish U.S. long staple from Egyptian cotton. Long staple cotton ranges in length from 1-1/8 to 1-5/16 inch, while extra long staple is 1-3/8 inch and longer. American pima cotton is found in staples of up to 1-1/2 inch while certain varieties of Egyptian long staple are longer than 1-1/2 inch. Long and extra long staple cotton are used primarily for very fine cloth and sewing thread.

The third species of cotton is *Gossypium herbaceum* which are primarily Asian cottons grown primarily in China and India. These cottons tend to be a shorter length, less than 3/4 inch. They find use in padding, wadding and blankets.

Cotton is classified using many different criteria, the primary ones being staple, grade, and micronaire. There are many combinations of these criteria. The USDA has administered official cotton grades since 1923 and U.S. cotton standards are used throughout the world. The grade of cotton is determined by color, foreign matter, and preparation. Color is described in terms of relative brilliance and it can range from white to spotted down to gray. Foreign matter refers to the amount of dirt, leaves, and other material in the cotton, a function of harvesting method and ginning. Machine picking results in more foreign matter than hand picking. Preparation refers to the relative roughness and uniformity of the fibers. Staple refers to the fiber length with short being under 13/16 inch, medium and medium long being 13/16 to 1-3/32 inch and long staple 1-1/8 inch to 1-5/16 inch. Extra long staple cotton is over 1-3/8 inch.

Micronaire is determined by an air-flow instrument which evaluates for the mill operator or merchant the spinnability and usefulness of the cotton by determining its fiber fineness and maturity in combination. The instrument subjects a cotton sample to standard air pressure and the amount of the air flow is indicated on the machine as a micronaire or "mike reading". A fine fibered, immature cotton causes more resistance to air flow, giving a low reading; a coarse and mature cotton causes less resistance, resulting in a high micronaire reading. Cotton that is immature or overmature is worth less to buyers than cotton that is properly matured.

To develop normally, cotton requires frost-free conditions and temperatures of at least 80 degrees. The cotton emerges about 7-10 days after seeding under normal conditions. For the next 45 days the plant forms buds or squares and about 21 days later the plant blooms. It takes approximately 180 days between the time the cotton is planted and a sufficient number of bolls have opened to begin harvesting or picking operations. While cotton thrives in hot weather, very hot temperatures for extended periods can damage the plant while low temperatures can hinder or retard proper development. In either case, the plant can be weakened making it vulnerable to disease and insect infestation. Weather affects the grade as well as the staple of the cotton.

Because the bolls mature at different intervals, a given cotton field may be harvested or picked several times. There are a number of picking techniques. Mechanical harvesters now pick the vast majority of cotton but there are machine pickers and strippers. The cotton plants are chemically defoliated prior to machine picking to reduce the amount of trash. About 1500 pounds of seed cotton needs to be picked to produce a 500 pound bale. The seed cotton moves from the field to a gin where moisture and trash are removed. The cotton lint is removed from the seed and the lint is pressed into gin bales, wrapped in jute bagging, and tied with steel ties. The average running bale is about 500 pounds with approximately 478 pounds of lint and 22 pounds of bagging and ties. The actual weight of the bagging and bands is termed the tare weight. At the gin, the cotton is usually sold to a shipper or merchant who in turn may put the cotton in storage, sell it to a domestic textile mill or to a foreign mill.

Production

Outside of the U.S., the major producers of cotton are China, India, Pakistan, Uzbekistan, Turkey, Turkmenistan, Brazil, and Egypt. China is usually the largest producer and a major factor in the market. China grows roughly a quarter of the world's cotton with an average crop of about 20 million bales though there is considerable variability. While China grows the most cotton, it is also the world's largest user. Consumption tends to exceed production in most years making the country a net importer. Because of government influence in the domestic market, the price the government pays cotton farmers for their crop largely determines how much cotton is available for domestic mills. Since the government price tends to be less than the world price, farmers are sometimes reluctant to sell to the government leading to imports. Pressure from land development and food crops could mean that China will devote less acreage to cotton in the future unless the government provides stronger incentives to grow the natural fiber.

India produces about 12 percent of the world's cotton. Production over the last few years is averaging ten million bales. The government allows unlimited imports but restricts exports. For the 1995-96 season, India will export perhaps 400,000 bales but generally production is about the same as consumption. Pakistan produces about nine percent of the world crop and at times is an important exporter. With the break up of the Soviet Union, two major cotton producing countries emerged: Uzbekistan and Turkmenistan. Uzbekistan produces about eight percent of world production and Turkmenistan two percent. These countries export virtually all of their production. Questions have arisen about the depletion of natural resources due to improper crop rotation in Uzbekistan's Aral Sea region and the possibility that yields will decline in the future. Infrastructure questions, such as the physical ability to deliver large amounts of high quality cotton for export, have also been raised.

The U.S. is one of the world's largest cotton producers and the largest exporter. Its advantages are many. High-quality cotton of various staple lengths and grades is grown in large amounts. The system of gathering, grading and selling cotton, i.e. merchandising, is highly efficient. Financial institutions, modern export facilities in New Orleans, LA; Charleston, SC; Galveston and Houston, TX; and the fact that efficient cotton futures and options markets are located in the U.S. make American cotton the fiber of choice for many of the world's textile mills. The U.S. Cotton Belt can be divided into four sections: the Southeast, the Delta, the Southwest, and the Far West.

The oldest cotton growing area is the Southeast which includes the Carolinas, Georgia, and Alabama with about 20 percent of the crop. Extra long staple cotton was first developed and grown for commercial consumption off the coast of South Carolina and almost all of the nation's textile mills are located here. Production in the Southeast has trended somewhat lower, the result of problems with disease and insects as well as acreage attrition to more profitable crops like soybeans. Planting generally begins in the March-April period with most harvesting finished by the beginning of November.

The Delta includes Mississippi, Arkansas, Tennessee, Louisiana, and Missouri. Delta production accounts for about a third of the national crop. Acreage devoted to cotton in this region has trended lower due in part to competition from more profitable crops like corn. The major growing area is the Yazoo Basin which runs from Jackson, MS, to Memphis, TN. Memphis is often called the cotton capital of the U.S. and is home to a number of major merchants. Planting in the Delta is usually completed by late May with most of the harvest finished in late November.

The Southwest region consists of Texas and Oklahoma with about 25 percent of the nation's pro-

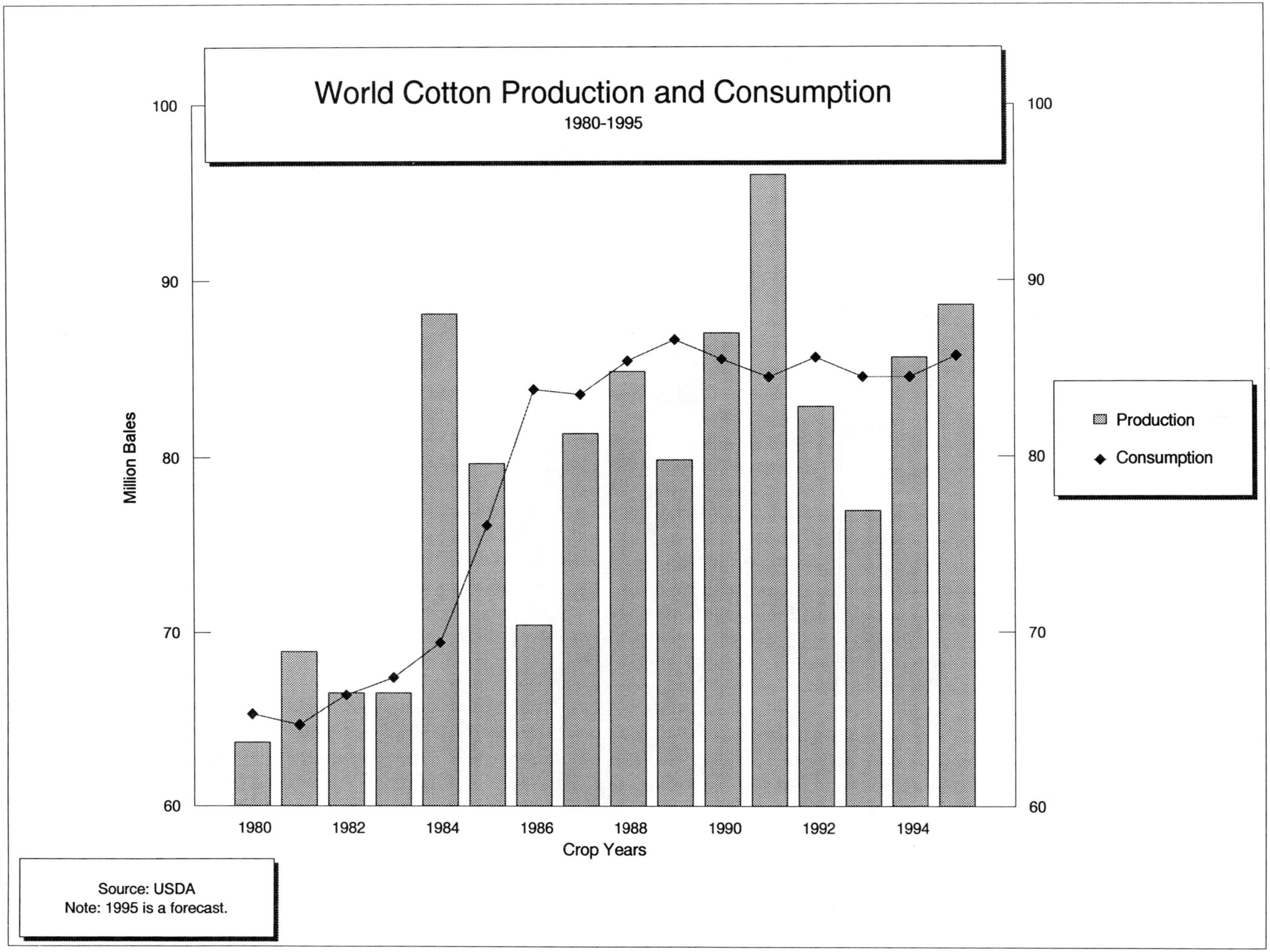
World Cotton Production and Consumption
1980-1995
Million Bales
100
90
80
70
60
1980
1982
1984
1986
1988
1990
1992
1994
Crop Years
Production
Consumption
Source: USDA
Note: 1995 is a forecast.

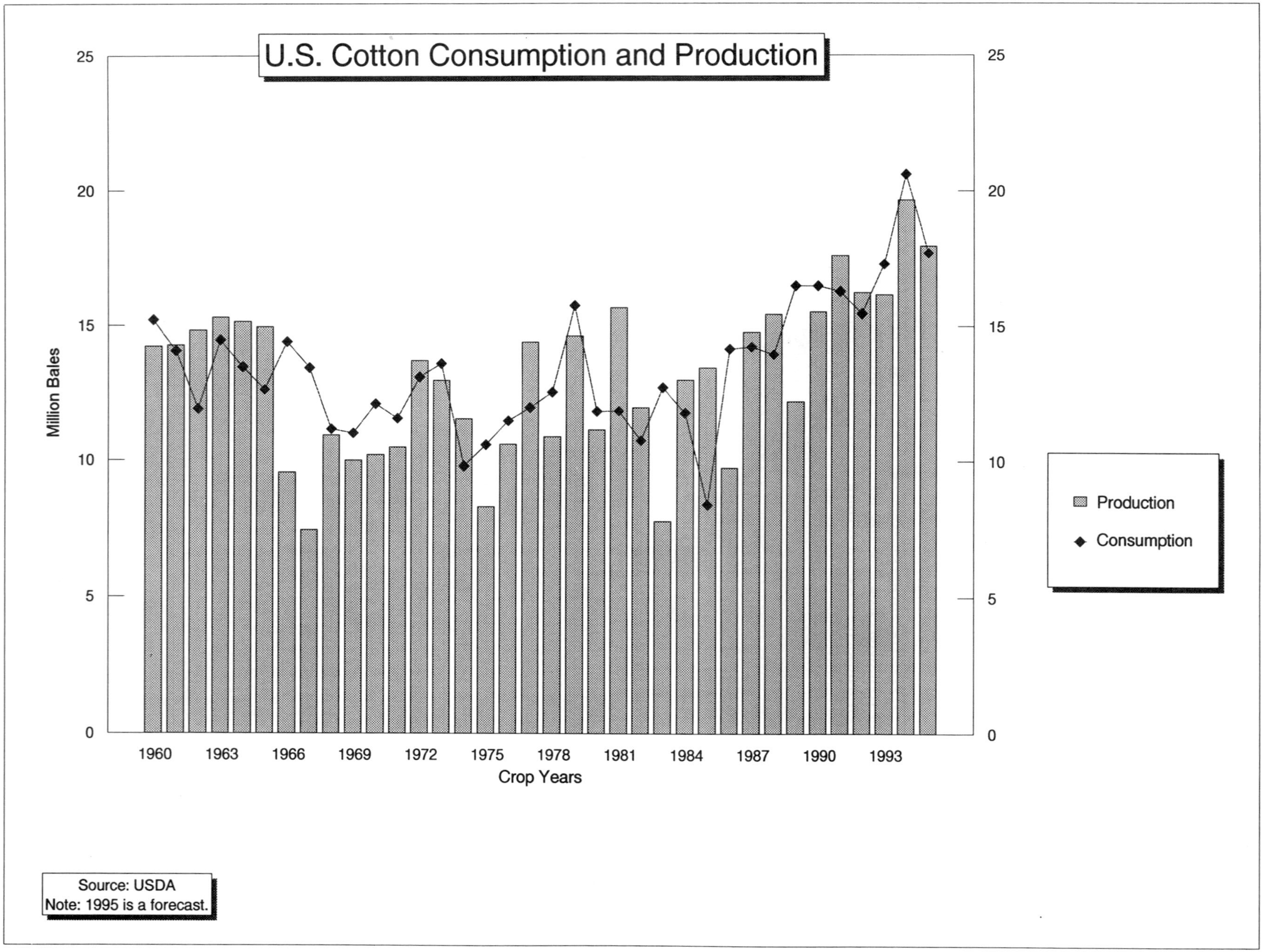
U.S. Cotton Consumption and Production
Million Bales
25
20
15
10
5
0
1960
1963
1966
1969
1972
1975
1978
1981
1984
1987
1990
1993
Crop Years
Production
Consumption
Source: USDA
Note: 1995 is a forecast.

duction. Texas is by far the largest producing state with a number of distinct production areas within the state. The lower Rio Grande Valley in the southernmost part of Texas is the earliest production region in the nation with planting underway in February and the harvest in July-August. Another important production area is the Coastal Bend of Texas around Corpus Christi. The Blacklands region, another area, extends from Austin to Dallas and has a growing season extending from April to September.

The nation's most concentrated production zone is the High Plains of Texas. This area encompasses the 25 counties surrounding the city of Lubbock. The land here is basically converted rangeland that is normally dry but through irrigation has become fertile. The High Plains are characterized by wide-ranging weather extremes including intense heat and drought as well as violent summer storms often containing hail which can reek extensive damage to the crop. Yields tend to be low and show wide variation. The staple length of the upland cotton grown in this region is about an inch putting it at a discount to other growths. The crop is planted in May-June and harvested in November.

The Far West includes California, Arizona and New Mexico and produces about 20 percent of the crop. The majority of the cotton is grown in California where irrigation and rich soils result in the highest yields in the country. The primary growing area is the San Joaquin Valley followed by the Imperial Valley. The upland cotton grown here has a longer-than-average staple length and trades at a premium to other growths. Planting occurs during March-May with the harvest during September-November. Much of this crop is exported to the Far East.

The major producers of extra long staple (ELS) cotton are Egypt, India, China, Central Asia, and the U.S. though other countries like Peru and Mexico grow high quality ELS. Egypt is by far the largest producer of this longest staple cotton. ELS production in Uzbekistan has fallen substantially as that country has shifted to upland cotton. U.S. production of ELS averages between 300,000 and 400,000 bales. California produces over half of the crop followed by Arizona, Texas, and New Mexico. Along with Egypt, the U.S. is the major supplier of ELS to foreign textile mills.

Consumption

After cotton is harvested, it is transported to a gin for cleaning, grading, and classing before being baled. A cotton shipper or merchant buys cotton from gins or producers. From the gin, the cotton can move to a number of other points such as a domestic textile mill or an export facility. Often the cotton may just be put in a warehouse for sale at a future date.

The most likely destination for raw cotton is a textile mill. While the textile industry had its beginnings in New England, the majority of U.S. textile mills are now located in the Southeast. Textile mills spin cotton into yarn and from there it is turned into weaving yarn which is made into knit goods, carpeting, and sewing thread. Weaving yarn also is turned into finished cloth and gray goods. The finished cloth is turned into clothing, household goods, and industrial products.

The major end use of cotton is in the apparel industry, mostly in men's and boy's clothing. Two important products, in which cotton finds extensive use, are denim and corduroy which together take about a quarter of the cotton that is consumed. In the household market, cotton finds extensive use in sheets, pillowcases, towels, draperies, and upholstery. Synthetic or manmade fibers, like polyester staple and rayon, have made significant inroads in the textile market over the last 20 years. Extensive promotional efforts by the cotton industry as well as consumer preference for products like denim, have allowed cotton to slow the loss of market share and even gain back some ground. One area of continued concern is in the finished textile export trade. On a cotton equivalent basis, textile imports into the U.S. are much larger than exports. In part, this development has been due to government policies which have encouraged the production and export of raw cotton which in turn is often used by foreign textile mills to produce textile products that are reexported to the U.S.

Domestic mill consumption of cotton has gone through some significant changes in the course of the last 25 years. In the 1970s mill consumption of cotton declined as consumers showed a marked preference for manmade fibers. In the 1980s, consumer preferences began to shift back to cotton away from manmade fibers. Cotton's share of the fibers consumed on the cotton textile system moved from about 75 percent at the beginning of the 1970s to about 60 percent a decade later, only to move back up toward 75 percent at the start of the current decade. In part, the change was a result of a strong consumer preference for fabrics like denim, which is usually constructed of 100 percent cotton yarn.

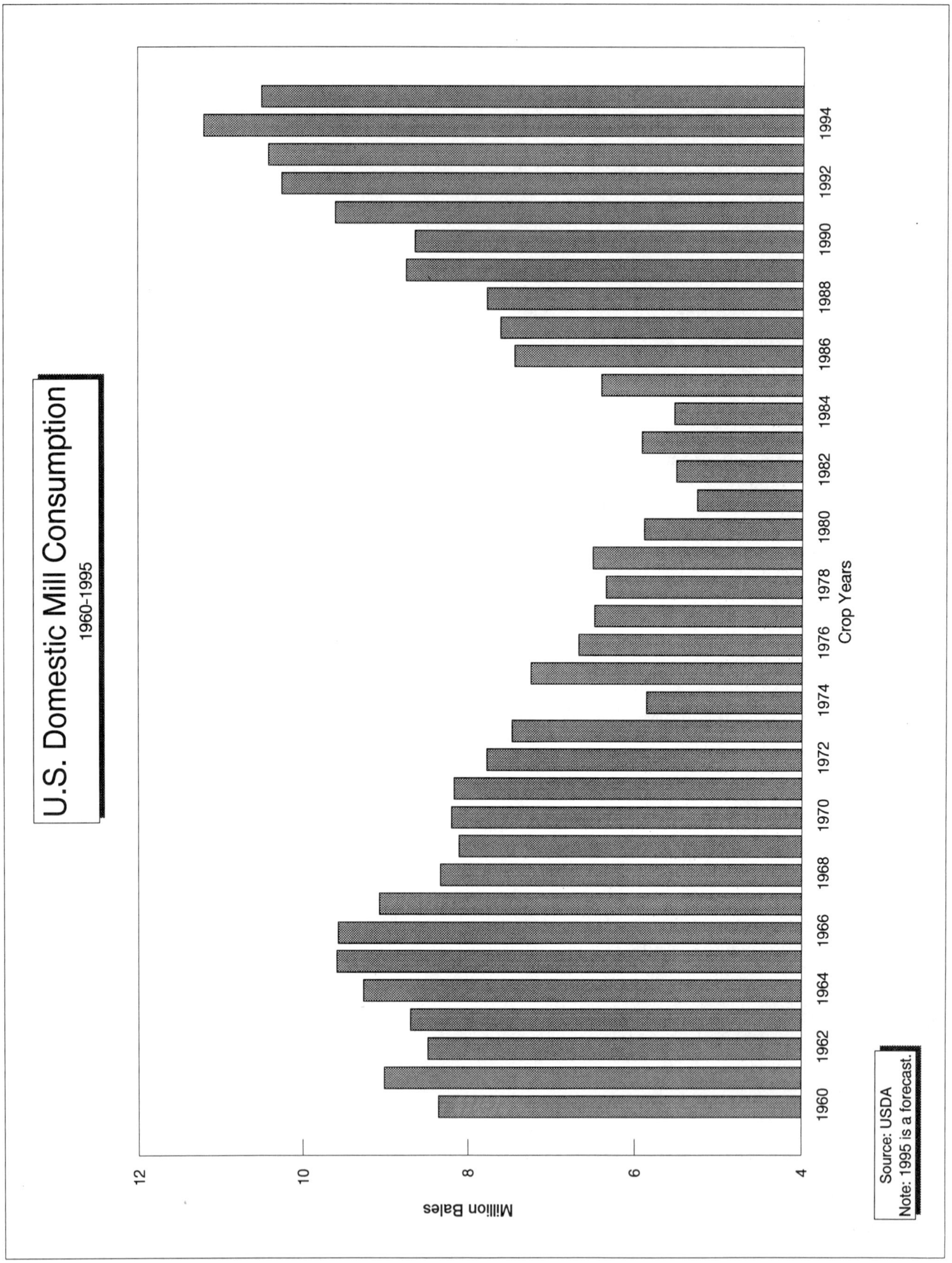
U.S. Domestic Mill Consumption
1960-1995
Million Bales
12
10
8
6
4
1960
1962
1964
1966
1968
1970
1972
1974
1976
1978
1980
1982
1984
1986
1988
1990
1992
1994
Crop Years
Source: USDA
Note: 1995 is a forecast.

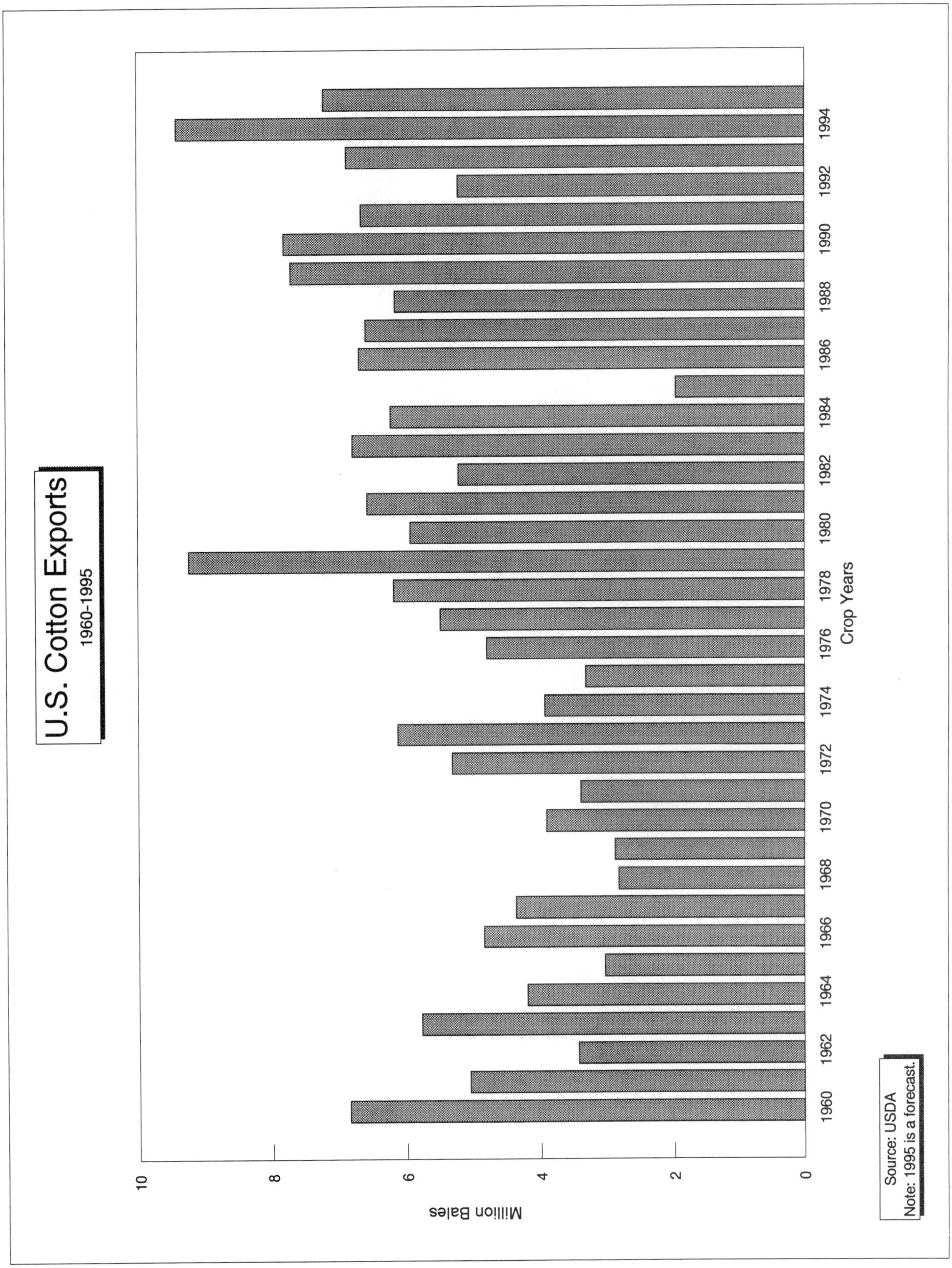
U.S. Cotton Exports
1960-1995
Million Bales
0
2
4
6
8
10
1960
1962
1964
1966
1968
1970
1972
1974
1976
1978
1980
1982
1984
1986
1988
1990
1992
1994
Crop Years
Source: USDA
Note: 1995 is a forecast.

There are numerous factors that affect how much cotton is used by textile mills and ultimately by consumers. Some of these variables are more statistically significant in explaining cotton use than others. Many economic studies have quantified the impact of these factors. The more important ones in explaining the level of cotton use are: growth rates of the economy or the level of economic activity, the prices of substitute fibers as well as cotton, consumer tastes and preferences, and the level of finished cotton textile imports and exports.

The prices of substitute fibers, particularly polyester staple, have a major impact on cotton use. Lower prices for polyester staple relative to cotton can lead to its direct substitution for cotton or increased blending ratios. Since polyester prices are highly related to the prices of the petroleum-based feedstocks used in their manufacture, higher prices for these chemicals can in turn lead to lower use of polyester and higher use of cotton.

Consumer tastes and preferences are very important in determining how much cotton is consumed. In the decade of the 1970s, polyester was a preferred fiber due to its characteristics such as durability, ability to hold colors and resistance to wrinkling. While these characteristics still exist, consumers have found other more compelling attributes in the natural fiber. In part this has been due to concerted promotional activity on the part of the cotton industry which has been particularly effective in pointing out cotton's advantages as a "breathable" fiber which imparts great comfort. Even fading, which at one time was considered a disadvantage, is now touted as an attribute. Consumers have shown a strong preference for 100 percent cotton products, especially apparel, as seen in stores that specialize in all cotton products. Apparel products such as denim pants and shirts, corduroy, printed undershirts, and sports clothing have been leading the way. Even in the market for sweaters, at one time dominated by wool, cotton sweaters have made inroads. To date, this preference for cotton has shown no sign of abating though there have been concerns about saturation i.e. just how much cotton clothing is enough to own.

A prime determinant of how much cotton is consumed is the level of national economic activity. There is a direct relationship between improvement in the general economy and increases in textile mill consumption. USDA analyses have shown that cotton use is most closely related to the level of personal consumption expenditures. As consumers have more income to spend, they tend to make more purchases of goods such as apparel products or clothing. At the same time, improvements in the general economy along with steady or declining interest rates results in heightened activity in the housing sector. This, in turn, results in increased purchases of household items like towels, rugs, bedding, curtains, and furniture, all of which contain large amounts of cotton. If one looks at periods of recessionary activity in the economy, one will see that use of cotton tends to decline in the 1-2 year period that follows. In particular, cotton use fell in 1974 and 1981, both years that were in or followed steep declines in the economy. With the general decline in interest rates since 1983, cotton consumption has increased on a fairly steady basis as the housing sector recovered and unemployment fell or remained steady. This was also a period when consumer preferences for cotton increased.

Price Seasonality

Research by Smith Barney indicates that cotton prices tend to exhibit fairly good seasonal patterns. As an agricultural commodity, cotton can be expected to display seasonality similar to other commodities, such as corn. For cotton, the harvest starts in August in the Lower Rio Grande Valley of Texas and extends into the late fall or early winter. The bulk of the harvesting activity, under normal conditions, usually occurs in October through December. That is usually the time of seasonal price weakness and prices typically make their lows in this period. Research indicates that cotton also exhibits bimodal seasonal price tendencies, i.e., it tends to make seasonal lows in either the July-August time period or in the October-November period. Lows occurring in July-August likely reflect expectations of a large crop. Research by Smith Barney reveals that in the past 93 years, 84 percent of the seasonal lows have been made in one of the two aforementioned time frames. In the 25 years starting with 1970, there have been 12 lows in the July-August period and nine lows in the October-December period. In looking at the 93 years of data, the nearby futures market contract posted the most seasonal lows in July (20), August (20), December (14) and October (10).

1995: A Record Year For The Cotton Market

The dynamics of the cotton market are best illustrated by looking at one season, albeit an interesting one, the year of 1995. This was a record season in a number of areas. The New York Cotton Exchange (NYCE), where cotton futures and options are traded, set several trading records. One was that total trading volume set a record of 6.348 million contracts, 14 percent higher than the previous record

U.S. Cotton Consumption and Recessions

1960-1995

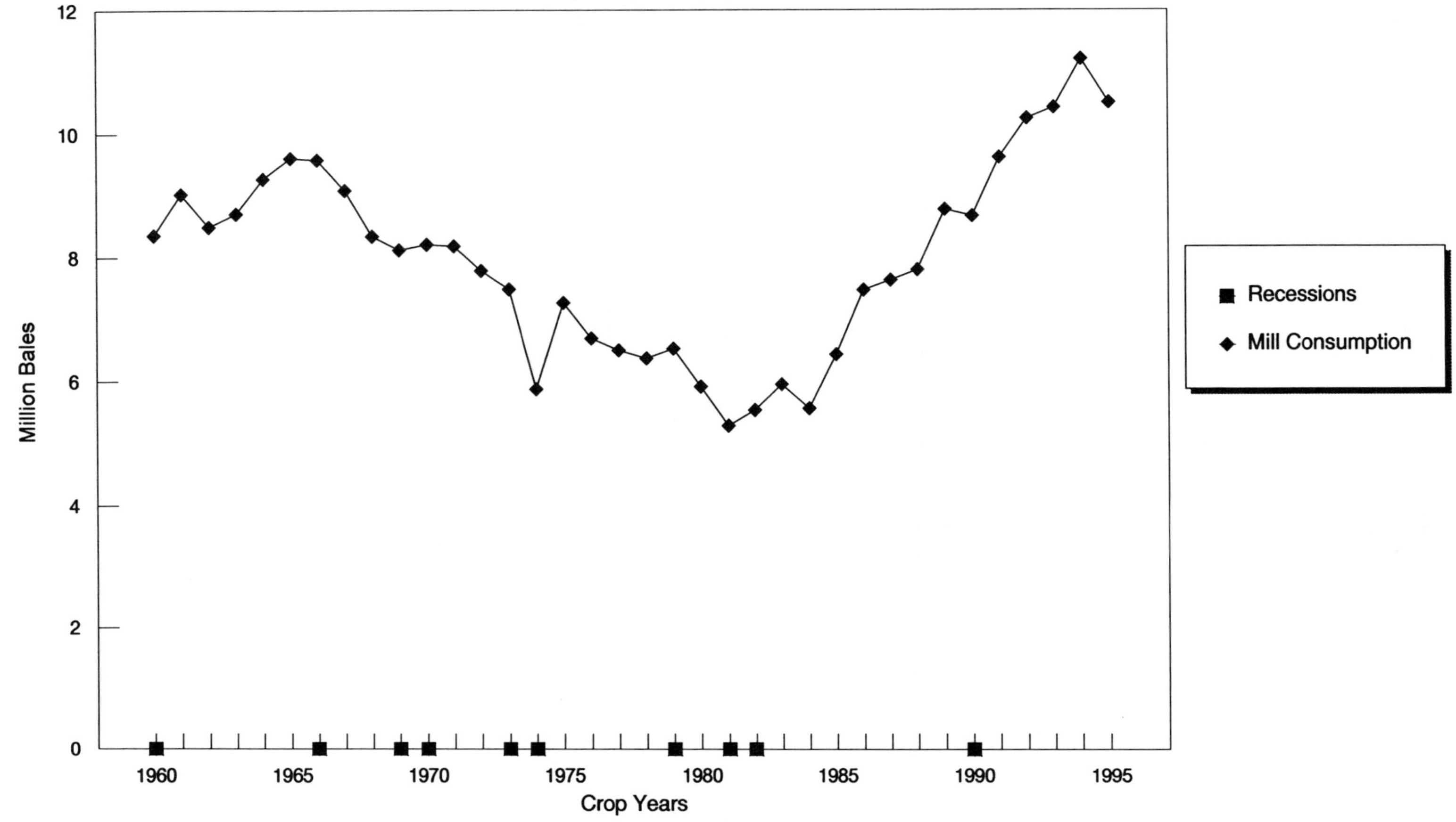

Source USDA, SB Inc. and National Bureau of Economic Research
Note: 1995 is a USDA forecast.

set in 1994 of 5.554 million contracts. The number of futures contracts traded was 2.525 million, a ten percent increase from the previous year. Cotton options also had a record year with a volume of 1.416 million contracts, up 74 percent from 1994. Cotton options set a volume record of 23,149 contracts on September 21, 1995, while the open interest, or number of contracts that had not been offset by an opposing transaction, set a record on April 4, 1995, of 229,564 contracts.

Perhaps most impressive in the 1995 market were the modern day price records that were posted. Indeed, if there was a most interesting feature of the 1994-95 season, it was the fact that the U.S. produced a record crop and witnessed record prices all within the same season. In the spring of 1994, cotton producers planted 13.7 million acres, harvested 13.3 million of them, and had a final record yield of 708 pounds per acre. The result was a record crop of 19.7 million bales. In October, based on USDA projections, the season's prospects did not appear that bullish as season-ending stocks of cotton were put at 4.9 million bales, not a tight situation. By December the situation had begun to change as USDA analysts overseas were reporting deteriorating conditions in some of the major cotton producing countries in Asia. While this is not unusual, what was startling was the fact that growing conditions were declining in virtually all of the major producers, the result of insect infestation, disease, and dry weather. While no changes were made to the Chinese crop forecast, then 20.7 million bales, Pakistan's crop estimate was lowered by 500,000 bales to 6.3 million, while India's was reduced 400,000 bales to 10.0 million. The Central Asian crops in Uzbekistan and Turkmenistan were lowered 250,000 bales. The reduced export availability from these foreign competitors subsequently caused USDA to raise the U.S. export projection by one million bales to 8.2 million. Projected U.S. ending stocks were lowered by a substantial 900,000 bales to four million.

By January the conditions overseas had deteriorated further allowing the USDA to increase the domestic export estimate an additional million bales to 9.2 million, while the Chinese crop estimate was lowered 1.2 million bales to 19.5 million. The Pakistani crop was reduced 300,000 bales while the Central Asian crops were lowered 210,000 bales. Reports from China indicated there continued to be spot shortages of cotton and soaring prices, leading many in the trade to question whether the crop might not be even smaller and reported stocks much less. In February the U.S. export forecast was raised 400,000 bales to 9.6 million.

While these bullish developments were occurring in the export sector, the Census Bureau was reporting that U.S. textile mills were consuming cotton at a near record pace as the economy improved. The rate of domestic use was approaching levels not seen since the Second World War. In February the USDA raised the domestic mill use forecast by 100,00 bales to 11.1 million, and then in March raised it another 200,000 bales to 11.3 million.

After a period where there was little new bullish news, the USDA in May increased the domestic mill consumption forecast another 100,000 bales to 11.4 million though there were some signs that the torrid pace of cotton use was starting to slow. Higher prices for raw cotton being paid by mills were not being reflected in the yarn market. In the export sector there were still a few bullish developments as the USDA concluded that Chinese cotton stocks were likely to be less than initially expected. The estimate of Chinese imports was raised by 400,000 bales, a significant increase. The U.S. export estimate was increased another 200,000 bales to 10.2 million. There was talk in the market that at current rates of use, the U.S. could possibly run out of cotton in late summer 1995. At about this time the bull market topped out as the futures market had served its function of discounting known and expected developments. The May futures contract set a modern day record high of $1.172 per pound on April 24, 1996. This was the highest price for cotton since the Civil War. On August 23, 1864, cotton prices reached their all time high of $1.89. As summer began, the record high prices started taking their toll as mills cut back on their purchases of cotton and foreign production showed some recovery.

Sources of Cotton Information

Information about the cotton market is available from a variety of sources. There are a number of informative reports published by the USDA, the New York Cotton Exchange (NYCE), as well as cotton trade organizations and other government agencies. While space considerations prevent a complete listing, some of the more useful reports are:

Monthly crop production, supply/demand estimates, and world crop production issued by the USDA. Perhaps the most important report in its scope. Issued around the 10th day of each month, crop production on a state-by-state basis comes out during the growing and harvesting season. Foreign production estimates are issued on a country-by-country basis. Supply/demand estimates provide USDA's opinion on the disposition of the crop (imports, exports, domestic use, stocks) both for the U.S. and major countries.

A weekly crop progress is issued by the USDA each Monday during the growing season providing an update on the U.S. crop. The report details on a state-by-state basis the condition of the crop.

Data on export sales and shipments of upland and ELS cotton by the U.S. is released on Thursday mornings. This report provides a detailed summary of export transactions on a country-by-country basis.

Domestic textile mill consumption is released by the Census Bureau around the 21st of each month providing the daily rate of cotton use as well as usage data on manmade fibers. This report is usually followed by the National Cotton Council's projections on annual rates of cotton use.

Daily international cotton prices provided by Cotlook Ltd. in London show the prices of various staples for different countries giving an idea of the price competitiveness between countries. The "A" and "B" indexes reflect a price average of the cheaper growths for two types of cotton. The "A" index represents middling 1-3/32 inch cottons, according to the Liverpool quality concept, while the "B" index represents coarse count cottons.

The daily certificated stocks of cotton at NYCE warehouses report shows the flow of cotton into and out of deliverable positions for the futures market.

The weekly hedging and speculation report from the NYCE indicates the percentage of long speculators and short speculators as well as long hedgers and short hedgers relative to the open interest in the futures market. This report provides a measure of the speculative sentiment in the market.

Every other week the Commitment of Traders report from the Commodity Futures Trading Commission provides a snapshot view of the positions of participants in the futures market including commercial and non-commercial interests.

The Cotton Futures Market

Trading of cotton futures and options takes place in New York City on the New York Cotton Exchange. The exchange was founded in 1870 by a group of cotton brokers and merchants and is the oldest commodity exchange in New York. The exchange also includes the Citrus Associates, an affiliate, where frozen concentrated orange juice futures and options are traded.

Trading in cotton futures takes place between 10:30 a.m. and 2:40 p.m. eastern time. The contract size is 50,000 pounds net weight or about 100 bales. The active trading months are March, May, July, October, and December, with December usually representing the new crop. Contract months extend out further into the future. The minimum price fluctuation is 1/100 of a cent per pound or $5.00. This is termed a point. A one cent move in futures prices would have a contract value of $500. The maximum daily price movement was increased on January 15, 1996, to 3 cents or 300 points above and below the previous session's settlement price. This was done partly in response to the bull market of 1995 when prices were "locked" the daily price limit for several sessions. The expanded daily price limits are expected to result in more trading activity when prices are extremely volatile. If any contract month is at or above $1.10, the price limit moves to 4 cents or 400 points and stays that way until no contract trades at or above $1.10.

The basis of the No. 2 cotton contract is termed strict low middling 1-1/16 inch cotton. The price difference for deliverable grades and staples above and below strict low middling 1-1/16 inch cotton are determined based on the average commercial difference for corresponding grades and staples quoted by the USDA Agricultural Marketing Service for Greenville, SC; Greenwood, MS; Memphis, TN; Dallas, TX; and Phoenix, AZ. The delivery points for the cotton contract are at approved warehouses in Galveston, TX; Houston, TX; New Orleans, LA; Memphis, TN; and Greenville, SC. First notice day on the contract occurs five business days from the end of the month preceding the spot month. The first delivery day is the first business day of the spot month. The last trading day is seventeen business days from the end of the spot month. The speculative position limit is 300 contracts in the delivery month and 1600 contracts in any other month. The limit in all months is 2500 contracts.

* * *

Walter Spilka is currently a cotton analyst with Smith Barney, Inc. in New York. He was formerly an economist with the USDA's Economic Research Service and a cotton trader. He received his Ph.D in agricultural economice from the Virginia Polytechnic Institute.

The CRB Futures Price Index, A Glimpse at Tomorrow...Today

The Commodity Research Bureau Futures Price Index was first calculated by Commodity Research Bureau, Inc. in 1957 and made its inaugural appearance in the 1958 CRB Commodity Year Book.

The Index was originally comprised of 28 commodities, 26 of which were traded on exchanges in the U.S. and Canada, and two cash markets. It included barley and flaxseed from the Winnipeg exchange; cocoa, coffee "B", copper, cotton, cottonseed oil, grease wool, hides, lead, potatoes, rubber, sugar #4, sugar #6, wool tops and zinc from New York exchanges; and corn, eggs, lard, oats, onions, rye, soybeans, soybean meal, soybean oil and wheat from Chicago exchanges. In addition to those 26 markets, the Index also included the spot New Orleans cotton and Minneapolis wheat markets which were added to balance some commodities repeated in the Index as by-products of other commodities.

The original base period was 1947-49, the same as the Bureau of Labor Statistics Spot Market Index.[1] This was purposely done to facilitate easy comparison of both spot and futures indices.

Like the Bureau of Labor Statistics spot index, the KR-CRB Futures Price Index is calculated to produce an unweighted geometric mean of the individual commodity price relatives. In other words, a ratio of the current price to the base year average price.

The KR-CRB Index was originally designed to provide dynamic representation of broad trends in overall commodity prices. In order to ensure that it continued to fulfill that role, its components and formula have been periodically adjusted to reflect changes in market structure and activity.

In the original calculation, all future deliveries up to a year ahead were averaged to calculate the current price. In 1987, the calculation was changed to only include deliveries nine months forward. In 1989, all non-cycle months were excluded from the calculation.

The 1995 revision lowers the number of forward deliveries included to those within six months of the current date, up to a maximum of five delivery months per commodity. However, a minimum of two delivery months must be used to calculate the cur-

Figure 1: Monthly history of the KR-CRB Futures Price Index

[1] 1957 Bureau of Labor Statistics Spot Market Index components: burlap, butter, cocoa beans, copper scrap, corn, cotton, cottonseed oil, hides, hogs, lard, lead scrap, printcloth, rosin, rubber, steel scrap, steers, sugar, tallow, tin, wheat, wool tops, and zinc.

rent price, even if the second contract is outside of the six month window.

There has also been a continuous adjustment of the individual components used in calculating the Index since the original 28 were chosen in 1957. All of these changes have been part of the continuing effort of Commodity Research Bureau and Knight-Ridder Financial to keep the KR-CRB Index "current," and to ensure that its value provides accurate representation of broad commodity price trends.

Since 1957, there have been nine revisions to Index components. The first was on April 3, 1961, and the latest on December 6, 1995. Pages 5-6 show a chronological listing of the revisions to the Index since its inception.

Current Construction and Calculation

The KR-CRB Index can be viewed as a three-dimensional index.[2] In addition to averaging prices across 17 commodities (two dimensions), the Index also incorporates an average of prices *across time,* within each commodity.

The KR-CRB Index is computed using a three-step process:

1) Each of the Index's 17 component commodities is arithmetically averaged using the prices for all of the designated contract months which expire on or before the end of the sixth calendar month from the current date, except that: a) no contract shall be included in the calculation while in delivery; b) there shall be a minimum of two contract months for each component commodity (adding contracts beyond the six month window, if necessary); c) there shall be a maximum of five contract months for each commodity (dropping the most deferred contracts to remain at five, if necessary).[3] The result is that the Index extends six to seven months into the future depending on where one is in the current month. For example, live cattle's average price on October 30, 1995 would be computed as follows:

$$\text{Cattle Average} = \frac{\text{Dec. '95} + \text{Feb. '96} + \text{Apr. '96}}{3}$$

Contract months eligible for inclusion in the Index:

Crude Oil:	All 12 Calendar Months
Heating Oil:	All 12 Calendar Months
Natural Gas:	All 12 Calendar Months
Corn:	March, May, July, September, December
Soybeans:	January, March, May, July, August, November
Wheat:	March, May, July, September, December
Copper:	March, May, July, September, December
Cotton:	March, May, July, December
Live Cattle:	February, April, June, August, October, December
Live Hogs:	February, April, June, July, August, October, Dec.
Gold:	February, April, June, August, December
Platinum:	January, April, July, October
Silver:	March, May, July, September, December
Cocoa:	March, May, July, September, December
Coffee:	March, May, July, September, December
Orange Juice:	January, March, May, July, September, November
Sugar:	March, May, July, October

Figure 2:

KR-CRB Component Commodities by Group

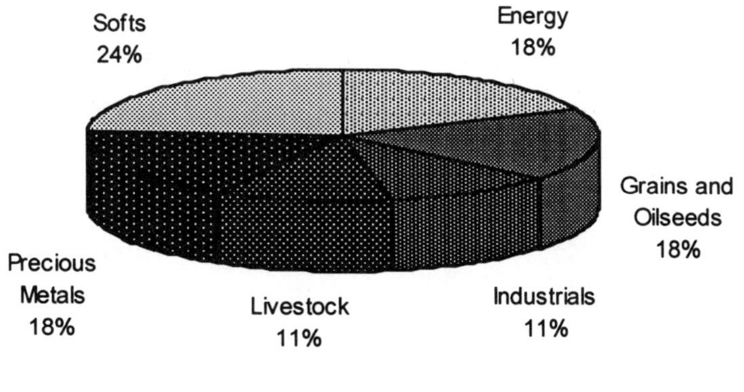

Groups:

Energy -	Crude Oil, Heating Oil, Natural Gas
Grains and Oilseeds-	Corn, Soybeans, Wheat
Industrials -	Copper, Cotton
Livestock -	Live Cattle, Live Hogs
Precious Metals -	Gold, Platinum. Silver
Softs -	Cocoa, Coffee, Orange Juice, Sugar

[2] An example of a one-dimensional product would be gold or corn; an example of a two-dimensional product would be the NYSE Composite Index®.

[3] It is important to note that certain commodity markets, like those for crude oil, heating oil, natural gas and sugar, cease trading the month prior to delivery (e.g. May Crude stops trading in April).

Soybean's average price on October 30, 1995 is:

$$\text{Soybean Average} = \frac{\text{Nov. '95} + \text{Jan. '96} + \text{Mar. '96}}{3}$$

2) These 17 component averages are then geometrically averaged by multiplying all of the numbers together and taking the 17th root.

Geometric Average =

$$\sqrt[17]{\text{Crude Avg. x Heating Avg. x ...Sugar Avg.}}$$

3) The resulting average is divided by 30.7766, the 1967 base-year average for these 17 commodities. That result is then multiplied by an adjustment factor of .8486. This adjustment factor is necessitated by the nine revisions to the Index since its inception in 1957. Finally, that result is multiplied by 100 in order to convert the Index into percentage terms:

KR-CRB Index =

$$\frac{\text{Current Geometric Average}}{\text{1967 Geometric Avg. (30.7766)}} \times .8486 \times 100$$

Arithmetic vs. Geometric Averaging

The KR-CRB Index involves both geometric and arithmetic averaging techniques. Geometric averaging has the statistically attractive property that successive percentage changes in a component's price do not alter that component's relative weight in the Index. Arithmetic averaging, on the other hand, causes the relative weight of a component to increase (or decrease) as that component appreciates (or depreciates) in value. The implications of these differences in index computation techniques may be seen in Figure 3, which reflects four different price scenarios. For convenience, assume that the index is comprised of only three components - X, Y, and Z - and that these components are equally weighted. The base period for each scenario is assumed to be 100.

Figure 3 demonstrates several important properties of geometric and arithmetic averages:

1) Equal component changes give equal index changes for both geometrically and arithmetically averaged indices.

2) Geometrically averaged indices rise slower and fall faster than arithmetically averaged indices.

3) The impact from equal, successive percentage changes in one element is constant for geometric averages, but increases with rising prices and decreases with falling prices for arithmetic averages.

Thus, a 10% increase in one of the Index's individual commodity averages, all others held constant, will *always* cause the KR-CRB Index itself to increase by 0.46%; and a 10% decrease in one of the Index's individual commodity averages, all others held constant, will *always* cause the KR-CRB Index itself to decrease by 0.50%. However, the impact on an indi-

Figure 3: Geometric Averaging vs. Arithmetic Averaging

	Variable Prices			Type of Index: Arithmetic Index Value/ % change	Type of Index: Geometric Index Value/ % change
	X	**Y**	**Z**		
Base Values:	100	100	100	100	100
Scenarios:					
1) Raise all prices by	110	110	110	110 (10%)	110 (10%)
10% for 2 periods	121	121	121	121 (10%)	121 (10%)
2) Lower all prices by	90	90	90	90 (-10%)	90 (-10%)
10% for 2 periods	81	81	81	81 (-10%)	81 (-10%)
3) Raise one price by	110	100	100	103.3 (3.3%)	103.2 (3.2%)
10% for 3 periods	121	100	100	107.0 (3.6%)	106.6 (3.2%)
	133	100	100	111.0 (3.7%)	110.0 (3.2%)
4) Lower one price by	90	100	100	96.7 (-3.3%)	96.5 (-3.5%)
10% for 3 periods	81	100	100	93.7 (-3.1%)	93.2 (-3.5%)
	73	100	100	91.0 (-2.9%)	90.0 (-3.5%)

vidual commodity *average* from a 10% increase or decrease on an *individual month* will vary according to the level of that month relative to the other months in the average of that commodity.

17 Commodity Components

The KR-CRB Index is widely viewed as a broad measure of overall commodity price trends because of the diverse nature of the 17 commodities of which it is comprised. As a broad measure of commodity price trends it serves as an excellent price measure for macro-economic analysis. This reflects the fact that a more diverse price index contains more information and, thus, can be used to better analyze economy-wide market forces.

Equal Weighting

Equal weighting is used for both arithmetic averaging of individual commodity months and for geometric averaging of these 17 commodity averages. From a pricing point of view, equal weighting is attractive because no single month or commodity has undue impact on the Index. This makes it harder to manipulate the Index and means that the Index is less subject to the discontinuities associated with temporary supply and demand imbalances in any one month or commodity.

Intra-Day Reporting of the KR-CRB Futures Price Index

Values of the underlying KR-CRB Index are computed by Knight-Ridder Financial Inc., and disseminated by the New York Futures Exchange every 15 seconds during the trading day.

Only settlement and last-sale prices are used in the Index's calculation, *bids and offers* are not recognized - including limit-bid and limit-offer price quotes. Where no last-sale price exists, typically in the more deferred contract months, the previous day's settlement price is used. This means that the underlying KR-CRB Index may lag its theoretical value. This tendency to lag is evident at the end of the day when the Index value is based on the settlement prices of the component commodities, and explains why the underlying KR-CRB Index often closes at or near the high or low for the day.

Futures Markets

In recent years investors have been seeking new asset classes in which to diversify their holdings, improve returns, reduce risk and hedge against inflation. Commodity futures qualify on all counts.

Futures markets have been transformed in recent years as new products have been developed, new markets opened in other countries and as government regulation has made them more acceptable.

Commodities As An Asset Class

As the world markets continue their evolution toward one global marketplace, the advent of financial futures trading has had much to do with that unification. The popularity of financial futures has removed some of the stigmas and fears that were associated with the perceived rough and tumble world of commodities. Previously, commodity futures were considered too risky for investors looking for the stability associated with a traditionally diversified portfolio. But now, with money managers searching the globe for additional investment opportunities, commodities have fallen under the spotlight. The advantages of asset diversification have uncovered this area of investment as the newest tool which will enable investors to better handle their long term exposure to the up and down movements inherent in today's markets. By allocating some of their investment dollars to commodities, investors are better able to obtain desirable long term results, while at the same time lowering the overall volatility of their portfolio.

Diversification into commodities allows the portfolio to attain a more balanced inventory of assets. Whether or not high levels of inflation resurface, the allocation of a percentage of investable funds into an asset that will successfully lower the overall volatility of a portfolio, while improving the annual performance, is every investors goal.

The counter-cyclic nature of commodities to financial assets makes commodities an ideal asset class to incorporate into a portfolio to achieve a more desirable return scenario. Should inflation remain under control, the commodity portion of a properly allocated portfolio may lag other asset classes, but that lag will indicate that the other non-commodity assets performed well. This is historically true because low to moderate inflation periods allow for the stable environment in which traditional financial assets have performed well. In such a case, the commodity allocation would have served its purpose as a counter-cyclic asset to the rest of the portfolio.

The KR-CRB Index and KR-CRB Index Futures

How is diversification into commodities best accomplished? Attempting to find the right combination of contracts in obscure markets such as soy-

KR-CRB FUTURES PRICE INDEX CHRONOLOGY

1957 26 futures, 2 spot	1961 25 futures, 2 spot	1967 26 futures, 2 spot	1971* 28 futures * Base Year to 1967	1973 28 futures

Futures Markets

Chicago

			Broilers	Broilers
		Cattle, Live	Cattle, Live	Cattle, Live
Corn	Corn	Corn	Corn	Corn
Eggs	Eggs	Eggs	Eggs	Eggs, Shell
			Hogs	Hogs, Live
Lard	Lard	Lard	Lard	
Oats	Oats	Oats	Oats	Oats
Onions				
			Plywood	Plywood
			Pork Bellies	Pork Bellies
Rye	Rye	Rye		
Soybean Meal	Soybean Meal	Soybean Meal	Soybean Meal	Soybean Meal
Soybean Oil	Soybean Oil	Soybean Oil	Soybean Oil	Soybean Oil
Soybeans	Soybeans	Soybeans	Soybeans	Soybeans
Wheat	Wheat	Wheat	Wheat	Wheat

Minneapolis

				Wheat

New York

Cocoa	Cocoa	Cocoa	Cocoa	Cocoa
Coffee "B"	Coffee "B"	Coffee "B"	Coffee "C"	Coffee "C"
Copper	Copper	Copper	Copper	Copper
Cotton	Cotton	Cotton	Cotton	Cotton "2"
Cottonseed Oil	Cottonseed Oil	Cottonseed Oil		
Grease Wool	Grease Wool	Grease Wool	Grease Wool	Grease Wool
Hides	Hides	Hides		
Lead	Lead	Lead		
			Orange Juice	Orange Juice
			Platinum	Platinum
Potatoes	Potatoes	Potatoes	Potatoes	Potatoes
Rubber	Rubber	Rubber		
			Silver	Silver
Sugar "4"	Sugar "4"	Sugar "4"	Sugar "4"	Sugar "10"
Sugar "6"	Sugar "6"	Sugar "6"	Sugar "6"	Sugar "11"
Wool Tops	Wool Tops	Wool Tops		
Zinc	Zinc	Zinc		

Winnipeg

Barley	Barley	Barley	Barley	Barley
Flaxseed	Flaxseed	Flaxseed	Flaxseed	Flaxseed
			Rapeseed	Rapeseed
			Rye	Rye

Spot Markets

New Orleans Cotton	New Orleans Cotton	New Orleans Cotton
Minneapolis Wheat	Minneapolis Wheat	Minneapolis Wheat

KR-CRB FUTURES PRICE INDEX CHRONOLOGY

1974 27 futures	1983 27 futures	1987 21 futures	1992 21 futures	1995 17 futures

Futures Markets

Chicago

1974	1983	1987	1992	1995
Broilers				
Cattle, Live	Cattle, Live	Cattle, Live	Cattle, Live	Cattle, Live
Corn	Corn	Corn	Corn	Corn
Eggs, Shell				
Hogs, Live	Hogs, Live	Hogs, Live	Hogs, Live	Hogs, Live
	Lumber	Lumber	Lumber	
Oats	Oats	Oats		
Plywood				
Pork Bellies	Pork Bellies	Pork Bellies	Pork Bellies	
Soybean Meal	Soybean Meal	Soybean Meal	Soybean Meal	
Soybean Oil	Soybean Oil	Soybean Oil	Soybean Oil	
Soybeans	Soybeans	Soybeans	Soybeans	Soybeans
Wheat	Wheat	Wheat	Wheat	Wheat

Minneapolis

1974	1983
Wheat	Wheat

New York

1974	1983	1987	1992	1995
Cocoa	Cocoa	Cocoa	Cocoa	Cocoa
Coffee "C"	Coffee "C"	Coffee "C"	Coffee "C"	Coffee "C"
Copper	Copper	Copper	Copper	Copper
Cotton	Cotton	Cotton	Cotton	Cotton
Grease Wool				
	Crude Oil	Crude Oil	Crude Oil	Crude Oil
	Gold	Gold	Gold	Gold
	Heating Oil	Heating Oil	Heating Oil	Heating Oil
				Natural Gas
Orange Juice	Orange Juice	Orange Juice	Orange Juice	Orange Juice
Platinum	Platinum	Platinum	Platinum	Platinum
Potatoes	Potatoes			
Silver	Silver	Silver	Silver	Silver
Sugar "11"	Sugar "11"	Sugar "11"	Sugar "11"	Sugar "11"
			Unleaded Gasoline	

Winnipeg

1974	1983
Barley	Barley
Flaxseed	Flaxseed
Rapeseed	Rapeseed
Rye	Rye

Figure 4:

KR-CRB Index Futures Contract Specifications

Contract:	KR-CRB Futures Price Index
Trading Symbol:	CR
Contract Quote:	Index points, e.g. 240.00, 240.05
Contract Size and Value:	$500 x Index Futures (e.g., futures at 240.00 valued at $120,000; $500 x 240.00)
Trading Cycle:	March, May, July, September, December
Trading Hours (Open/Close):	9:40 a.m. - 2:45 p.m. (N.Y. time) on all Exchange business days, except that trading in all contract months on the last trading day of each expiration month shall be from 9:40 a.m. to 3:15 p.m. (N.Y. time).
Minimum Price Fluctuation (Tick Size):	.05 (5 basis points) = $25.00, e.g. 240.05, 240.10, 240.15
Daily Price Limits:	None
Position Limits:	5,000 contracts net long or short
Last Trading Day:	The third business day of the expiration month.
Contract Settlement:	Settlement at contract maturity is by cash payment.

beans, gold, cattle, coffee, and crude oil would be difficult for a futures market professional and potentially disastrous for anyone else. Many mutual type commodity funds and money managers have surfaced, but most with unpredictable results, and very few offering the true commodity portfolio necessary for the proper asset diversification.

The KR-CRB Index has been recognized as the main barometer of commodity prices for many years. Globally, the CRB Index is the accepted standard for measuring the commodity futures price level. It is the most widely followed commodity index by the financial press around the world, and is found somewhere on almost every trader's quote terminal. This fact alone can cause changes in the price level of the Index to create an immediate impact on other markets such as stocks, bonds, and currencies.

To alleviate the need to choose individual commodities while facilitating the investment in a representative group, the New York Futures Exchange, Inc., began offering, in 1986, futures contracts on the KR-CRB Futures Price Index.

Buyers of the KR-CRB Index futures contract have direct participation in valuation changes of the component commodities. This 'long' position provides opportunities for obtaining a hedge against commodity inflation and reaping potentially extraordinary returns from commodity price appreciation.

The contract is traded on the NYFE from 9:40 A.M. to 2:45 P.M. New York time every business day.

CRB Index Portfolio Performance

In 1993, the New York Futures Exchange commissioned a study by Powers Research Associates L.P., to perform valuation and correlation studies on the KR-CRB Index and other asset classes and inflation indicators.

To measure the effect an investment in commodities would have on a typical portfolio the KR-CRB Index was used as a surrogate for a selection of individual commodity futures contracts. Since a futures contract has been trading on the KR-CRB Index since 1986, the commodities allocation of the portfolio (KR-CRB Account) was calculated at 10% cash for supporting a long position in KR-CRB Index futures, with the remaining 90% of the KR-CRB Index contract value invested in Treasury Bills. This two-part allocation simulates actual futures investment where excess margin funds are typically invested in interest bearing securities.

The results of the study indicated:

1) Adding a KR-CRB Account allocation to an efficient portfolio representative of existing institutional portfolios has a positive impact on the portfolio's Sharpe Ratio.

2) This positive impact is most clearly evident at KR-CRB Account allocations between 2.5% and 20% and clearly disappears at allocations above 40%.

3) This positive impact is seen if the KR-CRB Index contribution (not including T-Bill return from margin) is as small as 0.25%.

4) The KR-CRB Account was an excellent offset against inflation over the entire period and most shorter sub-periods studied.

5) A continuous fully collateralized buy and hold passive investment in KR-CRB Index futures, in the period June 1986 through December 1992, would have reaped a total return of 33.90%, or an annual return of 4.59%. The GDP Deflator as an indication of inflation during that same period averaged 3.10%.

The conclusion is that allocating KR-CRB Index futures to a typical institutional portfolio is beneficial to portfolio performance. Furthermore, even if KR-CRB Account return is low (perhaps as low as 0.25% annually) its inclusion is beneficial in improving the Sharpe ratio.

Figure 5: KR-CRB Indices (1967=100) compared with the Consumer Price Index (1982=100)
The chart shows the close correlation between the KR-CRB Futures Price Index (solid line), the CRB (BLS) Spot Market Index (dashed line), and the Consumer Price Index (dotted line). Notice that major trend changes in the KR-CRB Futures Price Index have consistently preceded slope changes in the Consumer Price Index trendline by approximately 12 months.

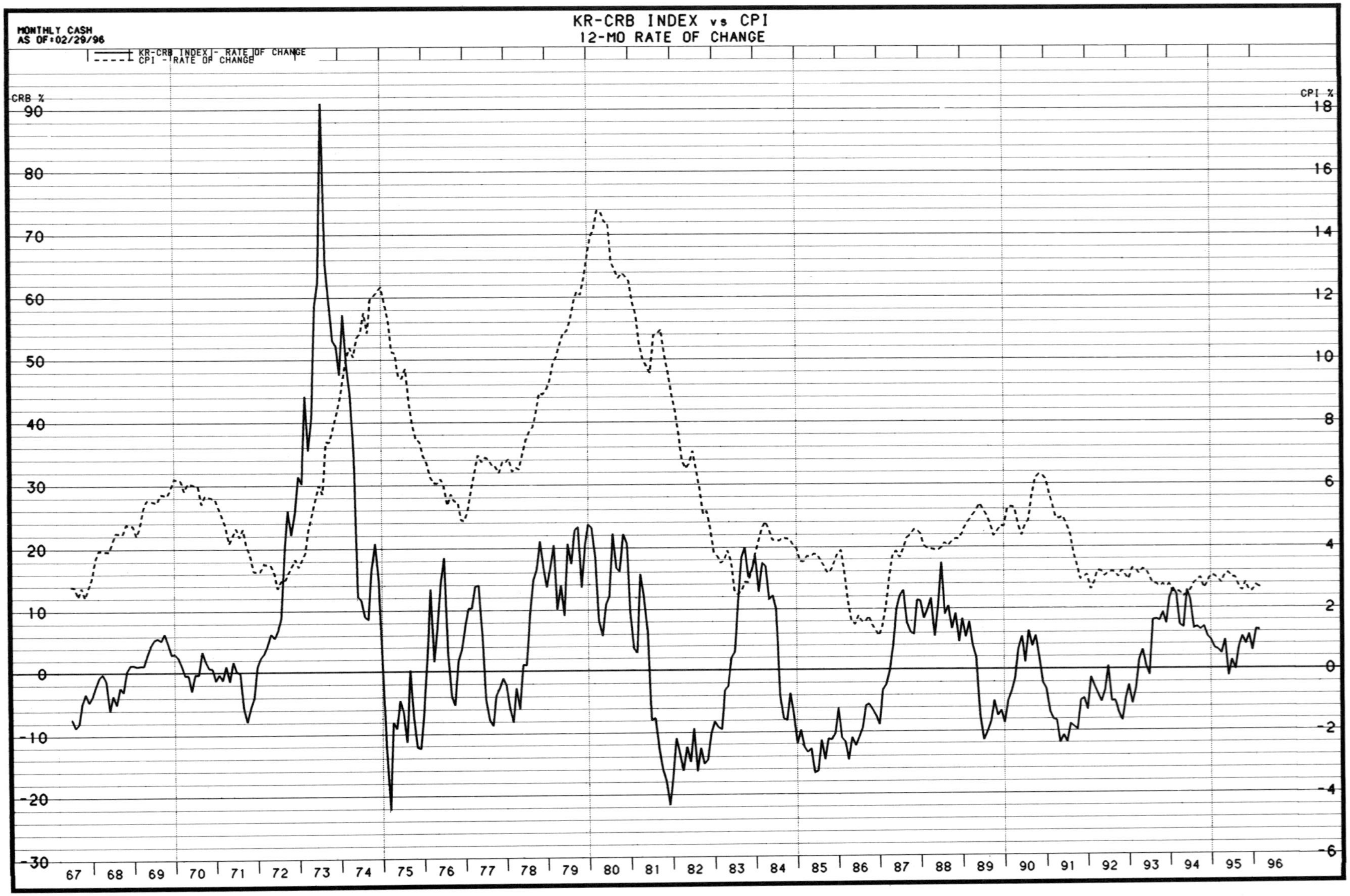

Figure 6: A comparison of the KR-CRB Futures Index and the CPI on a "rate of change" basis.
The strong correlation between the two indices is more dramatically demonstrated. Note that the major turns in the KR-CRB Index have consistently led those in the CPI.

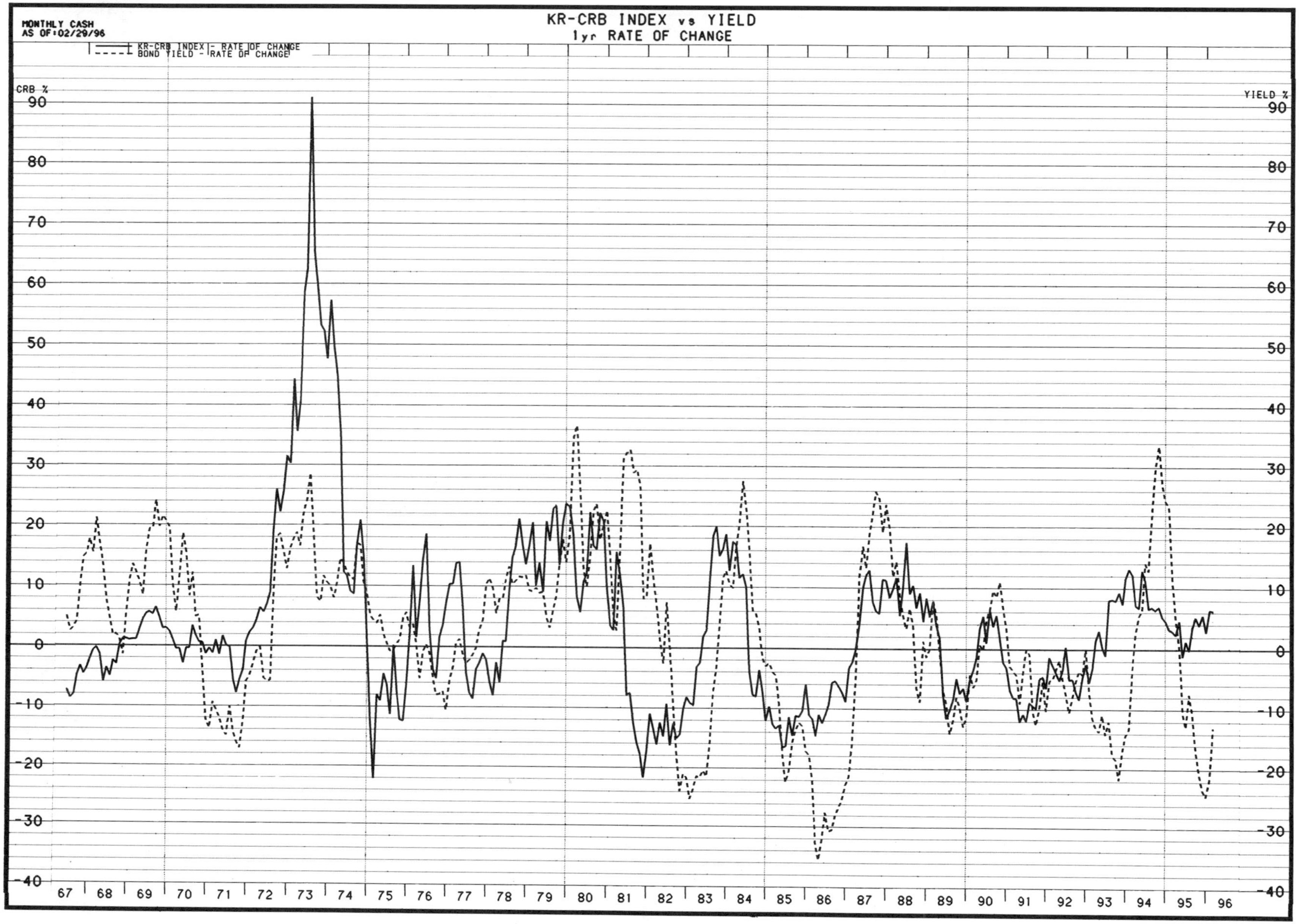

Figure 7: A "rate of change" chart comparing movement in the CRB Futures Price Index and long-term Treasury Bond yields. Besides the strong positive correlation, the CRB Index has often been a leading indicator of interest rate yields.

Volume U.S.

U.S. FUTURES VOLUME HIGHLIGHTS

1995 in Comparison with 1994

1995 Rank	Contracts with Volume Over 100,000 during 1995	1995 CONTRACTS	1995 %	1994 CONTRACTS	1994 %	1994 Rank
1	Eurodollar, CME	95,730,019	24.22%	104,823,245	24.59%	1
2	T-Bonds, CBOT	86,375,916	21.85%	99,959,881	23.45%	2
3	Crude Oil, NYMEX	23,613,994	5.97%	26,812,262	6.29%	3
4	T-Notes (10 Year), CBOT	22,445,356	5.68%	24,077,828	5.65%	4
5	S&P 500 Index, CME	18,852,149	4.77%	18,708,599	4.39%	5
6	Corn, CBOT	15,105,147	3.82%	11,529,884	2.70%	7
7	T-Notes (5 Year), CBOT	12,637,054	3.20%	12,462,838	2.92%	6
8	Soybeans, CBOT	10,611,534	2.68%	10,749,109	2.52%	9
9	#2 Heating Oil, NYMEX	8,266,783	2.09%	8,986,835	2.11%	10
10	Natural Gas, NYMEX	8,086,718	2.05%	6,357,560	1.49%	14
11	Gold (100 oz.), COMEX Div. of NYMEX	7,781,596	1.97%	8,503,366	1.99%	11
12	Deutschemark, CME	7,186,476	1.82%	10,956,479	2.57%	8
13	Unleaded Regular Gas, NYMEX	7,071,787	1.79%	7,470,836	1.75%	12
14	Japanese Yen, CME	5,630,053	1.42%	6,612,993	1.55%	13
15	Soybean Meal, CBOT	5,601,242	1.42%	4,593,814	1.08%	19
16	Silver (5,000 oz), COMEX Div. of NYMEX	5,183,236	1.31%	5,994,345	1.41%	15
17	Wheat, CBOT	4,955,067	1.25%	3,620,631	0.85%	20
18	Sugar #11, CSC	4,711,082	1.19%	4,719,218	1.11%	18
19	Soybean Oil, CBOT	4,611,336	1.17%	5,063,188	1.19%	17
20	Swiss Franc, CME	4,399,932	1.11%	5,217,236	1.22%	16
21	Live Cattle, CME	3,257,105	0.82%	3,580,896	0.84%	21
22	British Pound, CME	2,610,510	0.66%	3,562,865	0.84%	22
23	Cotton, NYCE	2,525,434	0.64%	2,289,998	0.54%	26
24	High Grade Copper, COMEX Div. of NYMEX	2,519,414	0.64%	2,737,967	0.64%	23
25	Cocoa, CSC	2,090,098	0.53%	2,417,006	0.57%	25
26	Coffee "C", CSC	2,003,014	0.51%	2,658,073	0.62%	24
27	Canadian Dollar, CME	1,756,569	0.44%	1,740,205	0.41%	28
28	One Month LIBOR, CME	1,707,062	0.43%	1,911,184	0.45%	27
29	Live Hogs, CME	1,699,680	0.43%	1,554,022	0.36%	30
30	Wheat, KCBT	1,560,538	0.39%	1,502,348	0.35%	31
31	T-Bonds, MIDAM	1,341,877	0.34%	1,385,904	0.33%	32
32	Municipal Bond Index, CBOT	1,169,470	0.30%	1,600,533	0.38%	29
33	Wheat, MGE	914,882	0.23%	737,089	0.17%	37
34	Soybeans, MIDAM	868,577	0.22%	797,803	0.19%	36
35	Platinum, NYMEX	846,693	0.21%	895,805	0.21%	35
36	T-Notes (2 Year), CBOT	744,866	0.19%	939,043	0.22%	34
37	Orange Juice (Frozen Conc.), NYCE	688,932	0.17%	653,824	0.15%	39
38	NYSE Composite Index, NYFE	685,922	0.17%	729,231	0.17%	38
39	30 Day Federal Funds, CBOT	643,717	0.16%	416,200	0.10%	45
40	T-Bills (90 Day), CME	620,223	0.16%	1,020,491	0.24%	33
41	Nikkei 225, CME	609,720	0.15%	548,233	0.13%	42
42	Pork Bellies, CME	561,913	0.14%	633,646	0.15%	40
43	Feeder Cattle, CME	511,895	0.13%	446,639	0.10%	44
44	Oats, CBOT	475,538	0.12%	492,504	0.12%	43
45	U.S. Dollar Index, NYCE	456,859	0.12%	558,439	0.13%	41
46	Australian Dollar, CME	346,823	0.09%	355,183	0.08%	46
47	Corn, MIDAM	305,347	0.08%	232,855	0.05%	48
48	Goldman Sachs Commodity Index, CME	270,504	0.07%	154,511	0.04%	50
49	S&P MidCap 400 Index, CME	253,741	0.06%	285,962	0.07%	47
50	Lumber, CME	179,538	0.05%	172,963	0.04%	49
	Top 50 Contracts	393,082,938		424,231,569		
	Contracts Below the Top 50	2,230,542	0.56%	2,076,373	0.53%	
	TOTAL	**395,313,480**	**100.00%**	**426,307,942**	**100.00%**	

Volume U.S.

U.S. FUTURES VOLUME HIGHLIGHTS

1995 in Comparison with 1994

1995 RANK	EXCHANGE	1995 CONTRACTS	1995 %	1994 CONTRACTS	1994 %	1994 RANK
1	Chicago Board of Trade (CBOT)	165,616,177	41.89%	175,697,680	41.21%	1
2	Chicago Mercantile Exchange (CME)	146,662,764	37.10%	162,696,029	38.16%	2
3	New York Mercantile Exchange (NYMEX) *	63,636,046	16.10%	68,010,380	15.95%	3
4	Coffee, Sugar & Cocoa Exchange (CSCE)	8,925,205	2.26%	9,947,040	2.33%	4
5	New York Cotton Exchange (NYCE) **	4,702,985	1.19%	4,501,842	1.06%	5
6	MidAmerica Commodity Exchange	3,047,982	0.77%	3,042,609	0.71%	6
7	Kansas City Board of Trade (KCBT)	1,747,664	0.44%	1,604,508	0.38%	7
8	Minneapolis Grain Exchange (MGE)	936,016	0.24%	765,508	0.18%	8
9	Philadelphia Board of Trade (PBOT)	38,641	0.01%	42,346	0.01%	9
	TOTAL	**395,313,480**	**100.00%**	**426,307,942**	**100.00%**	

* In August 1994, the Commodity Exchange and the New York Mercantile Exchange merged and is now listed as one exchange.
** The New York Cotton Exchange volume now includes the New York Futures Exchange volume.

U.S. FUTURES VOLUME 1991 - 1995

FUTURE	CONTRACT UNIT	1995	1994	1993	1992	1991
Wheat	5,000 bu	4,955,067	3,620,631	3,019,629	3,498,814	3,146,844
Corn	5,000 bu	15,105,147	11,529,884	11,462,618	10,356,632	10,852,909
Oats	5,000 bu	475,538	492,504	455,335	459,578	354,953
Soybeans	5,000 bu	10,611,534	10,749,109	11,649,333	9,000,169	9,013,739
Soybean Oil	60,000 lbs	4,611,336	5,063,188	4,612,229	4,282,678	4,018,544
Soybean Meal	100 tons	5,601,242	4,593,814	4,718,095	4,145,397	4,498,287
Rice	200,000 lbs	121,914	16,693			
Crop Yield	Crop yield estimate X 10	3,123				
Diammonium Phosphate	100 tons	6,755	15,588	45,314	34,465	10,931
Anhydrous Ammonia	100 tons	1,060	2,811	9,831	5,563	
Edible Oil Index	100 tons	21	298			
Barge Freight Index	%BF x $5/ton			6	20	
Structural Panel Index	100,000 sq. ft.	885	7,033			
Eastern Catastrophe Insurance	Loss/EP x $25,000			4,600	133	
Midwest Catastrophe Insurance	Loss/EP x $25,000			74		
National Catastrophe Insurance	Loss/EP x $25,000		4	4,782	79	
Silver	5,000 oz	8,617	10,278	1,022	472	640
Silver	1,000 oz	76,667	88,663	89,141	52,658	114,268
Gold	100 oz	647	984	778	56	825
Gold	Kilo	20,245	22,712	22,220	10,362	17,873
T-Bonds	$100,000	86,375,916	99,959,881	79,428,444	70,003,894	67,887,497
T-Notes (6 1/2-10 Year)	$100,000	22,445,356	24,077,828	16,601,258	11,217,938	6,341,432
T-Notes (5 Year)	$100,000	12,637,054	12,462,838	8,123,939	6,441,193	3,386,161
T-Notes (2 Year)	$200,000	744,866	939,043	532,203	445,394	285,567
Cash T-Note (2 Year)	$500,000					158
30-Day Federal Funds	$5,000,000	643,717	416,200	182,319	233,727	115,958
Mortgage Backed 7.5%	$100,000				44	
Mortgage Backed 8.0%	$100,000				96	291
Mortgage Backed 8.5%	$100,000					1,581
Mortgage Backed 9.0%	$100,000					2,744
Mortgage Backed 9.5%	$100,000					1,163
Municipal Bond Index	$1,000 x Index	1,169,470	1,600,533	1,120,510	776,205	549,135
Canadian Government Bonds	$100,000 C$		27,163			

Volume U.S.

FUTURE	CONTRACT UNIT	1995	1994	1993	1992	1991
3 Year Swap	25 million					1,231
5 Year Swap	25 million				2,389	5,675
US Dollar Index	$1,250 x Index			733		
MMI Maxi	$500 x Index			155,338	360,879	702,927
Wilshire Small Cap Index	$500 x Index			1,626		
CHICAGO BOARD OF TRADE (CBOT)		**165,616,177**	**175,697,680**	**157,697**	**363,268**	**709,833**
Live Hogs	40,000 lbs	1,669,680	1,554,022	1,401,754	1,556,092	1,582,234
Lean Hogs	40,000 lbs	984				
Pork Bellies, Frozen	40,000 lbs	561,913	633,646	698,799	784,152	1,005,196
Broilers	40,000 lbs				1,312	5,956
Live Cattle	40,000 lbs	3,257,105	3,580,896	3,306,952	3,319,618	3,792,824
Feeder Cattle	44,000 lbs	511,895	446,639	419,888	369,042	538,495
Lumber	160,000 bd ft	179,538	172,963	178,184	170,534	160,521
New Lumber	80,000 bd ft	3,148				
T-Bills (90-day)	$1,000,000	620,223	1,020,491	1,017,350	1,337,061	2,012,079
T-Bills (1 Year)	$500,000		586			
Eurodollar (3-month)	$1,000,000	95,730,019	104,823,245	64,411,394	60,531,066	37,244,223
Euromark (3-month)	$1,000,000		566	26,058		
Federal Funds Rate	$3,000,000	52,412				
Dollar/Pound Diff	$1,000,000					12
One Month LIBOR	$3,000,000	1,707,062	1,911,184	1,128,321	918,593	450,354
BP/DM Cross	50,000 x bp/dm X				15	3,605
DM/JY Cross (Old)	125,000 x dm/jy X				718	8,561
DM/JY Cross (New)	125,000 x dm/jy X	106		175	10,005	
DM/SF Cross	125,000 x dm/sf X				41	1,409
British Pound	62,500	2,610,510	3,562,865	3,701,427	3,053,428	3,745,617
Brazilian Real	100,000	20,364				
Canadian Dollar	100,000	1,756,569	1,740,205	1,410,818	1,171,640	1,139,397
Deutschemark	125,000	7,186,476	10,956,479	12,866,451	11,593,174	10,928,693
Japanese Yen	12,500,000	5,630,053	6,612,993	6,023,132	4,520,356	6,017,012
Mexican Peso	500,000	133,791				
Swiss Franc	125,000	4,399,932	5,217,236	5,604,841	5,134,717	5,835,480
Australian Dollar	100,000	346,823	355,183	198,954	89,784	76,016
French Franc	250,000	48,621	49,005	19,343		
Deutschemark Forward	$250,000	38,582	46,979			
Japanes Yen Forward	$250,000	16,898				
British Pound Rolling Spot	250,000 sterling			1,729		
Japanese Yen Rolling Spot	250,000 U.S.	15,310				
Deutschemark Rolling Spot	250,000 U.S.	44,013	126,994	28,936		
Nikkei 225	$5 x Index	609,720	548,233	356,523	383,755	246,948
S&P 500 Index	$500 x 500 Index	18,852,149	18,708,599	13,204,413	12,414,157	12,340,380
S&P 500 Barra Growth Index	$500 x 500 Index	1,240				
S&P 500 Barra Value Index	$500 x 500 Index	1,478				
S&P MidCap 400 Index	$500 x 400 Index	253,741	285,962	218,531	102,708	
FT-SE 100	50 x FTSE Index			94	1,057	
Major Market	$500 x Index	58,048	150,308	49,286		
Russell 2000	$500 x Index	43,857	36,239	19,479		
Goldman Sachs Commodity Index	$250 x GSCI	270,504	154,511	122,281	36,320	
CHICAGO MERCANTILE EXCHANGE (CME)		**146,632,764**	**162,696,029**	**116,415,113**	**107,499,345**	**87,135,012**
Coffee "C"	37,500 lbs	2,003,014	2,658,073	2,489,223	2,152,383	1,772,648
Sugar #11	112,000 lbs	4,711,082	4,719,218	4,285,945	3,667,481	4,268,546
Sugar #14	112,000 lbs	119,508	150,472	133,898	138,609	131,791
White Sugar	50 metric tons				10	20
Cocoa	10 metric tons	2,090,098	2,417,006	2,128,384	1,397,235	1,233,519
Euro-Diff Coffee	37,500 lbs					94
Brazil-Diff Coffee	37,500 lbs			11	359	
Cheddar Cheese	40,000 lbs	977	1,366	669		
Non Fat Dry Milk	44,000 lbs	90	905	1,276		
Milk	50,000 lbs	436				
COFFEE, SUGAR & COCOA EXCHANGE (CSCE)		**8,925,205**	**9,947,040**	**9,039,406**	**7,356,077**	**7,406,618**

Volume U.S.

FUTURE	CONTRACT UNIT	1995	1994	1993	1992	1991
Wheat	5,000 bu	1,560,538	1,502,348	1,348,500	1,339,842	1,412,510
Grain Sorghum	5,000 bu					1,064
Western Natural Gas	10,000 MMBtu	77,595				
Value Line Index	$500 x Index	35,185	50,259	45,806	46,195	57,705
Mini Value Line	$100 x Index	74,346	51,901	40,662	34,454	26,941
KANSAS CITY BOARD OF TRADE (KCBT)		**1,747,664**	**1,604,508**	**1,434,968**	**1,420,491**	**1,498,220**
Wheat	1,000 bu	137,573	102,145	101,353	239,180	153,949
Corn	1,000 bu	305,347	232,855	276,502	458,772	433,480
Oats	1,000 bu	5,846	5,208	4,555	8,008	4,681
Soybeans	1,000 bu	868,577	797,803	966,244	1,130,629	1,387,923
Soybean Meal New	20 tons	4,060	3,757	3,800	2,201	3,610
Soybean Oil	30,000 lbs	6,658				
Live Cattle	20,000 lbs	18,811	15,895	16,314	15,366	16,937
Live Hogs	20,000 lbs	24,059	19,614	17,841	17,597	19,388
Rice, Rough New	200,000 lbs		68,379	65,970	25,291	39,310
New York Silver	1,000 oz	13,320	17,170	10,986	8,888	13,106
New York Gold	33.2 oz	18,964	24,926	19,803	6,813	6,785
Platinum	25 oz	3,055	2,841	1,750	861	562
T-Bonds	$50,000	1,341,877	1,385,904	1,125,645	1,342,251	1,397,225
T-Bills	$500,000	754	826	1,129	2,017	1,297
T-Notes (10 Year)	$50,000	38,494	35,303	11,615		4
T-Notes (5 Year)	$50,000	37	4	39		
Eurodollars	$500,000	23,550	8,987	7,229	2,885	
U.S. Dollar Index	$1,250 x USDI			7	1,755	
Australian Dollar	50,000	221				
British Pound	12,500	23,620	66,162	67,208	44,120	30,019
Swiss Franc	62,500	50,201	64,501	73,532	62,788	74,349
Deutschemark	62,500	95,775	113,166	123,573	105,543	93,577
Japanese Yen	6,250,000	55,213	67,641	62,874	39,293	40,958
Canadian Dollar	50,000	11,970	9,522	8,505	4,802	4,030
MIDAMERICA COMMODITY EXCHANGE (MidAm)		**3,047,982**	**3,042,609**	**2,966,474**	**3,519,060**	**3,721,190**
Wheat	5,000 bu	914,882	737,089	822,898	742,703	624,826
White Wheat	5,000 bu	20,411	27,446	10,895	6,077	2,406
Oats	5,000 bu			4,025	118	116
White Shrimp	5,000 lbs	336	854	1,437		
Black Tiger Shrimp	5,000 lbs	387	119			
MINNEAPOLIS GRAIN EXCHANGE (MGE)		**936,016**	**765,508**	**839,255**	**748,898**	**627,348**
Cotton #2	50,000 lbs	2,525,434	2,289,998	1,603,027	1,701,258	1,614,244
Cotlook World Cotton	50,000 lbs X CWC		79	3,363	12,098	
Orange Juice Frozen Concentrate	15,000 lbs	688,932	653,824	640,131	339,230	287,538
European Currency Unit	$100,000				972	1,691
Mark Pound	$125,000 BP	32,804	12,351			
Mark Paris	$500,000 DM	36,649	10,295			
Dollar Mark	$125,000 DM	29,441	30,385			
Mark Yen	$125,000 DM	66,405	30,566			
Mark Lira	$250,000 DM	31,604	3,572			
Mark Swiss Franc	$125,000 DM	1,209				
U.S. Dollar/Swiss France	$125,000 SF	1,586	10			
U.S. Dollar/Japanese Yen	$12,500 Y	4,943	2			
U.S. Dollar/British Pound	$62,500 BP	3,021	2			
U.S. Dollar Index	$1,000 x Index	456,859	558,439	599,112	678,329	715,547
Emerging Markets Debt Index	$1,000 x Index	732				
T-Note (5 Year)	$100,000	44,959	69,858	50,200	80,186	71,220
T-Note (2 Year)	$200,000	11,072	3,233	734	892	9,931
NYSE Composite Index	$500 x Index	685,922	729,231	848,522	1,315,438	1,486,166
NYSE Utility Index	$500 x Index		11	10		
T-Bond (30 Year)	$100,000					21
Commodity Research Bureau Index	$500 x Index	81,413	109,986	91,908	56,255	61,185
NEW YORK FUTURES EXCHANGE (NYFE)*		**4,702,985**	**4,501,842**	**3,837,007**	**4,184,658**	**4,247,543**

Volume U.S.

FUTURE	CONTRACT UNIT	1995	1994	1993	1992	1991
High Grade Copper	25,000 lbs	2,519,414	2,737,967	2,064,629	1,674,163	1,640,065
Silver	5,000 oz	5,183,236	5,994,345	4,855,924	3,016,339	4,154,704
Gold	100 oz	7,781,596	8,503,366	8,916,195	6,002,009	6,799,917
Platinum	50 oz			342	9,963	
Paladium	100 oz			2	333	
Eurotop 100 Index	$100 x Price	49,328	62,231	56,497	26,453	
COMEX DIVISION		**15,533,574**	**17,297,909**	**15,893,589**	**10,729,260**	**12,594,686**
Palladium	100 oz	166,713	143,773	113,681	68,209	78,199
Platinum	50 oz	846,693	895,805	651,222	577,253	604,646
No. 2 Heating Oil, NY	1,000 bbl	8,266,783	8,986,835	8,625,061	8,005,462	6,680,171
Unleaded Gasoline, NY	1,000 bbl	7,071,787	7,470,836	7,407,809	6,674,757	5,509,926
Natural Gas	10,000 MMBTU	8,086,718	6,357 560	4,671,533	1,920,986	418,410
Gulf Coast Unleaded Gas	42,000 gal	252	300	510	4,902	
Propane	42,000 gal	49,532	45,100	44,923	50,601	55,854
Crude Oil	1,000 bbl	23,613,994	26,812,262	24,868,602	21,109,562	21,005,867
Sour Crude Oil	1,000 bbl				10,331	
NYMEX DIVISION		**48,102,472**	**50,712,471**	**46,383,341**	**38,422,063**	**34,353,073**
NEW YORK MERCANTILE EXCHANGE (NYMEX)**		**63,636,046**	**68,010,380**	**62,276,930**	**49,151,323**	**46,947,759**
Australian Dollar	100,000	1,716	265	142	132	
British Pound	62,500	4,147	2,485	1,493	234	2
Canadian Dollar	100,000	208	639			
ECU	125,000		1,768			
Deutschemark	125,000	17,121	21,661	11,469	60,647	350
Swiss Franc	125,000	3,915	3,038	614	130	66
French Franc	500,000	4,162	7,167	8,814	16,432	110
Japanese Yen	12,500,000	7,372	5,323	2,564	5,780	
PHILADELPHIA BOARD OF TRADE (PBOT)		**38,641**	**42,346**	**25,096**	**83,355**	**528**
TOTAL FUTURES		**395,313,480**	**426,307,942**	**339,075,626**	**295,292,042**	**262,895,551**
PERCENT CHANGE		**-7.27%**	**25.73%**	**14.83%**	**12.32%**	**-4.93%**

* The New York Cotton Exchange volume now includes the New York Futures Exchange.

** In August 1994, the Commodity Exchange and the New York Mercantile Exchange merged and is now listed as one exchange.

OPTIONS TRADED ON U.S. FUTURES EXCHANGES VOLUME HIGHLIGHTS

1995 in Comparison with 1994

1995 RANK	EXCHANGE	1995 CONTRACTS	1995 %	1994 CONTRACTS	1994 %	1994 RANK
1	Chicago Board of Trade (CBOT)	45,056,867	47.83%	43,806,394	43.42%	1
2	Chicago Mercantile Exchange (CME)	35,142,349	37.30%	42,489,574	42.12%	2
3	New York Mercantile Exchange (NYMEX) *	9,836,294	10.44%	10,651,003	10.56%	3
4	Coffee, Sugar & Cocoa Exchange (CSCE)	2,390,774	2.54%	2,717,012	2.69%	4
5	New York Cotton Exchange (NYCE) **	1,645,324	1.75%	1,051,795	1.04%	5
6	Kansas City Board of Trade (KCBT)	81,409	0.09%	93,364	0.09%	6
7	Minneapolis Grain Exchange (MGE)	32,666	0.03%	40,411	0.04%	7
8	MidAmerica Commodity Exchange (MidAm)	23,127	0.02%	31,953	0.03%	8
	TOTAL	**94,208,810**	**100.00%**	**100,881,506**	**100.00%**	

* In August 1994, the Commodity Exchange and the New York Mercantile Exchange merged and is now listed as one exchange.

** The New York Cotton Exchange volume now includes the New York Futures Exchange volume.

Volume U.S.

OPTIONS VOLUME ON U.S. FUTURES EXCHANGES 1991 - 1995

OPTION	CONTRACT UNIT	1995	1994	1993	1992	1991
Wheat	5000 bu	1,243,567	827,930	713,670	1,108,840	692,327
Corn	5000 bu	3,783,446	2,144,461	2,031,284	1,833,816	2,048,422
Oats	5000 bu	35,250	20,495	17,373	15,307	4,486
Soybeans	5000 bu	3,149,635	2,710,656	2,927,072	1,930,334	2,165,167
Soybean Oil	60,000 lbs	232,635	287,905	181,938	104,704	78,991
Soybean Meal	100 tons	304,835	263,734	306,523	152,394	116,433
Rice	200,000 lbs	14,336	1,750			
Crop Yield	Crop yield estimate X 10	3,519				
Eastern Catastrophe Insurance	Loss/EP x $25,000	3,274	7,742	2,482	28	
Midwest Catastrophe Insurance	Loss/EP x $25,000	50	44			
National Catastrophe Insurance	Loss/EP x $25,000		1,590	4,102	22	
Westerm Insurance-Annual	Loss/EP x $25,000		44			
PCS Castastrophe Insurance		1,064				
Silver	1,000 oz	1,476	5,952	12,423	20,105	2,804
T-Bonds	$100,000	25,639,950	28,142,549	23,435,164	20,258,740	21,925,578
T-Notes (10 Year)	$100,000	6,887,102	6,437,215	4,844,272	2,564,191	890,293
T-Notes (5 Year)	$100,000	3,619,462	2,675,097	1,976,924	665,587	129,389
T-Notes (2 Year)	$200,000	13,189	12,862	8,235	6,677	
Mortgage Backed 7.5%	$100,000				20	
Mortgage Backed 8.0%	$100,000				45	831
Mortgage Backed 8.5%	$100,000					5,079
Mortgage Backed 9.0%	$100,000					3,847
Mortgage Backed 9.5%	$100,000					160
3 Year Swap	25 million					530
5 Year Swap	25 million				400	5,877
Muni Bonds	$1,000 x Index	13,018	24,772	68,816	38,200	52,692
Canadian Government Bonds	$100,000 C$		1,385			
Flexible U.S. T-Bonds		59,804	174,295			
Flexible T-Notes (10 Year)		36,425	46,606			
Flexible T-Notes (5 Year)		14,730	19,060			
Flexible T-Notes (2 Year)		100	250			
Major Market Index	$500 x Index			1,368	2,215	3,059
Wilshire Small Cap Index	$500 x Index			52		
CHICAGO BOARD OF TRADE (CBOT)		**45,056,867**	**43,806,394**	**36,531,698**	**28,701,625**	**28,125,965**
Live Hogs	40,000 lbs	137,435	109,448	79,046	82,341	112,338
Pork Bellies, Frozen	40,000 lbs	21,156	24,173	32,698	32,507	32,780
Broilers	40,000 lbs				733	2,646
Live Cattle	40,000 lbs	463,455	519,813	500,664	561,058	776,624
Feeder Cattle	44,000 lbs	109,096	95,845	79,264	85,807	168,966
Lumber	160,000 bd ft	14,433	17,603	25,934	5,278	8,117
New Lumber	80,000 bd ft	491				
T-Bill (90-day)	$1,000,000	3,594	5,269	14,485	29,670	49,261
Eurodollar (3-month)	$1,000,000	22,363,853	28,145,929	17,008,764	13,762,628	7,874,551
Euromark (3-month)	$1,000,000			8,923		
One Month LIBOR	$3,000,000	54,219	79,172	90,604	98,839	74,805
BP/DM Cross	50,000 x bp/dm X				1	968
DM/JY Cross (Old)	125,000 x dm/jy X					3,373
DM/JY Cross (New)	125,000 x dm/jy X			82	29,106	
DM/SF Cross	125,000 x dm/sf X					756
British Pound	62,500	1,668,624	920,109	528,239	597,352	650,472
Brazilian Real	100,000	3,700				
Canadian Dollar	100,000	259,857	185,652	176,930	306,528	336,758
Deutschemark	125,000	2,642,904	4,793,639	5,916,463	6,354,248	5,643,031
Japanese Yen	12,500,000	2,141,043	2,946,432	2,261,977	1,518,409	2,397,141
Swiss Franc	125,000	630,016	767,583	627,923	1,026,974	998,002
Australian Dollar	100,000	9,892	7,800	3,482	13,132	37,519
French Franc	250,000	4,935	1,064	5,562		
Mexican Peso	500,000	1,114				
British Pound Rolling Spot	250,000 sterling			286		

Volume U.S.

OPTION	CONTRACT UNIT	1995	1994	1993	1992	1991
Deutschemark Rolling Spot	250,000 U.S.			420		
Nikkei 225	$5 x Index	8,986	7,982	9,684	13,971	12,378
S&P 500 Index	$500 x 500 Index	4,568,232	3,820,893	2,916,047	2,209,529	1,813,118
S&P 500 Barra Value Index	$500 x 500 Index	30				
S&P MidCap 400 Index	$500 x 400 Index	5,435	3,622	5,129	2,933	
FT-SE 100	50 x FTSE Index			2	73	
Major Market	$500 x Index	289	804	251		
Russell 2000	$500 x Index	1,532	2,793	1,428		
Goldman Sachs Commodity Index	$250 x GSCI	28,028	33,949	37,590	8,093	
CHICAGO MERCANTILE EXCHANGE (CME)		**35,142,349**	**42,489,574**	**30,331,877**	**26,739,210**	**20,993,604**
Coffee	37,500 lbs	867,303	1,208,925	1,022,017	860,943	411,550
Sugar	112,000 lbs	1,203,779	1,166,748	916,170	848,750	1,512,976
Cocoa	10 metric tons	319,513	341,131	326,760	209,938	163,610
Cheddar Cheese	40,000 lbs	76	150	174		
Non Fat Dry Milk	44,000 lbs		58	296		
Milk	50,000 lbs	103				
COFFEE, SUGAR & COCOA EXCHANGE (CSCE)		**2,390,774**	**2,717,012**	**2,265,417**	**1,919,631**	**2,088,136**
5 Day Copper	25,000 lbs	34	41	534		
High Grade Copper	25,000 lbs	134,212	184,125	146,060	87,324	97,163
Silver	5,000 oz	1,146,513	1,316,650	1,094,702	676,543	1,019,093
5 Day Silver	5,000 oz	221	368	1,262	9,606	798
Gold	100 oz	2,006,695	1,589,065	1,717,015	1,152,854	1,398,451
5 Day Gold	100 oz	688	911	418	17,233	13,464
Platinum	50 oz				359	
Eurotop 100 Index	$100 x Price			533		
COMEX DIVISION		**3,288,363**	**3,091,160**	**2,960,524**	**1,943,919**	**2,528,969**
Platinum	50 oz	43,601	90,556	62,661	39,458	27,989
Heating Oil	42,000 gal	703,388	699,325	803,216	1,247,891	863,143
Crude Oil	1,000 bbl	3,975,611	5,675,072	7,156,518	6,562,163	4,968,742
Unleaded Gasoline	1,000 bbl	766,557	573,502	660,886	860,086	573,767
Natural Gas	10,000 MMBTU	921,520	493,491	345,814	80,756	
Gas-Crude Oil Spread	1,000 bbl	64,285	13,932			
Heating Oil-Crude Oil Spread	1,000 bbl	72,969	13,965			
NYMEX DIVISION		**6,547,931**	**7,559,843**	**9,029,095**	**8,790,354**	**6,433,641**
NEW YORK MERCANTILE EXCHANGE (NYMEX)*		**9,836,294**	**10,651,003**	**11,989,619**	**10,734,273**	**8,962,610**
Wheat	5,000 bu	75,849	89,960	87,214	85,565	91,060
Western Natural Gas	10,000 MMBtu	2,546				
Mini Value Line	$100 x Index	3,014	3,404	1,797	918	
KANSAS CITY BOARD OF TRADE (KCBT)		**81,409**	**93,364**	**89,011**	**86,483**	**91,060**
Corn	1,000 bu	7,296	5,765	6,274	8,333	4,581
Soft Red Winter Wheat	5,000 bu	2,425	3,536	2,652	4,038	2,917
Soybeans	1,000 bu	11,908	13,498	19,062	15,786	19,797
Soybean Oil	30,000 lbs	5				
Rough Rice	200,000 lbs		5,588	6,013	6,121	
T-Bonds	$50,000	721	3,149	1,966	3,657	2,113
Gold	33.2 oz	772	417	39	289	255
MIDAMERICA COMMODITY EXCHANGE (MidAm)		**23,127**	**31,953**	**36,006**	**38,224**	**29,663**
American Spring Wheat	5,000 bu	26,893	26,441	27,822	13,556	5,132
European Spring Wheat	5,000 bu	184	284	48		
White Wheat	5,000 bu	5,333	13,556	9,009	3,273	990
Oats	5,000 bu			177		
White Shrimp	5,000 lbs	118	102	465		
Black Tiger Shrimp	5,000 lbs	138	28			
MINNEAPOLIS GRAIN EXCHANGE (MGE)		**32,666**	**40,411**	**37,521**	**16,829**	**6,122**

Volume U.S.

OPTION	CONTRACT UNIT	1995	1994	1993	1992	1991
Cotton	50,000 lbs	1,416,054	816,031	372,074	413,091	392,132
Cotlook World Cotton	50,000 lbs X CWC			206	1,188	
Orange Juice Frozen Concentrate	15,000 lbs	171,209	159,365	101,214	72,446	56,078
European Currency Unit	$100,000				4,570	
U.S. Dollar Index	$500 x Index	23,987	42,268	67,603	470,230	1,418,298
Mark Pound	$125,000 BP	116				
Mark Paris	$500,000 DM	570				
Mark Yen	$125,000 DM	160				
Mark Swiss Franc	$125,000 DM	33				
Mark Lira	$250,000 DM	354				
NYSE Composite Index	$500 x Index	26,457	26,636	29,571	43,386	34,570
Commodity Research Bureau Index	$500 x Index	6,384	7,495	6,818	3,589	3,667
NEW YORK COTTON EXCHANGE (NYCE)**		**1,645,324**	**1,051,795**	**577,486**	**1,008,500**	**1,904,745**
TOTAL OPTIONS		**94,208,810**	**100,881,506**	**81,858,635**	**69,244,775**	**62,201,905**
PERCENT CHANGE		**-6.61%**	**23.24%**	**18.22%**	**11.32%**	**-2.97%**

* In August 1994, the Commodity Exchange and the New York Mercantile Exchange merged and is now listed as one exchange.

** The New York Cotton Exchange volume now includes the New York Futures Exchange volume.

Volume Worldwide

	1995	1994	1993	1992
Live Hogs	30,877	41,382	46,117	
Piglets	1,047	3,417	3,358	
Potatoes	165,313	229,071	154,832	
Agricultural Futures Markets, Amsterdam	**197,237**	**273,870**	**204,307**	
Austrian Government Bond	176,527	124,070	43,410	
ATX Index	498,234	348,291	174,095	66,898
ATX Index Options	1,748,567	1,252,782	672,985	176,219
ATX LEOs (Long-term Equity Options)	71,555	9,077		
Australian Futures & Options Exchange	**2,494,883**	**1,734,220**	**890,490**	**243,117**
Belgian Government Bonds	507,254	687,987	584,970	263,832
BIBOR 3 Months	175,082	150,238	190,936	51,547
Bel 20 Index	187,686	154,574	12,281	
Belgian Government Bonds Options	4,504	51,989		
Bel 20 Index Options	862,492	561,012	345,510	
USO (Dollar/Belgian Franc)	108,471	29,546		
Gold Index Options	81,897			
BELFOX	**1,927,386**	**1,635,346**	**1,133,697**	**315,379**
R$/US$ Exchange Rate	22,948			
U.S. Denominated Arabica Coffee	6,733			
Long Term Interest Rate	20,422			
Average Interest Rate on Interbank Deposits	78,662	999,617		
R$ (Brazilian Real)/US$ Exchange Rate Options	89,700			
U.S. Denominated Arabica Coffee Options	591,752			
Average Interest Rate on Interbank Deposits Options	127,924,464	2,049,380		
BFF, Brazil	**128,734,681**	**3,048,997**		
Gold Options on Actuals	1,882,502	6,772,894	9,406,163	7,932,576
Gold Options Exercise	1,124,792	2,246,674	1,401,370	802,402
U.S. $ Denominated Arabica Coffee Futures	76,206	79,220	87,753	50,873
U.S. $ Denominated Arabica Coffee Options	2,810,322	3,290,667	1,504,776	2,491
U.S. $ Denominated Arabica Coffee Options Exercise	1,375,756	1,359,128	268,159	476
U.S. $ Denominated Robusta Coffee Futures			36	992
U.S. $ Denominated Cotton				2
U.S. $ Denominated Live Cattle	39,174	5,687	7,438	7,046
Live Cattle Options	34,240	88,428		
Live Cattle Options Exercise	38,504			
U.S. $ Denominated Sugar Crystal	4,301			
U.S. $ Denominated Soybean Futures	3,750	11	375	
U.S. $ Denominated Calf Futures				916
U.S. $ Denominated Gold Futures	607,288	132,240	11,720	
Bovespa Stock Index Futures	15,304,666	10,583,594	10,374,860	7,287,054
Bovespa Stock Options	74,469	11,875		
Bovespa Stock Options Exercise	1,765			
Interest Rate Futures	35,152,630	28,474,764	18,996,117	14,072,749
Interest Rate Options	42,200	320		
Interest Rate Options Exercise		120		
U.S. Dollar Futures	74,241,367	39,231,744	7,608,631	4,501,952
U.S. Dollar Options Exercise	403,456	80,703	50,190	38,176
U.S. Dollar Options on Actuals	3,338,020	588,911	359,411	374,441
Interest Rate Swap Futures	3,592,277	6,002,555	1,860,847	
Interest Rate x Exchange Rate Swap Futures	1,500,685	3,666,097	17,474	
Interest Rate x Reference Rate Swap Futures	127,796	119,229		
Interest Rate x Gold Price Variation Swap (Not Guaranteed) Futures		737		
Interest Rate x Inflation Index Swap	7,601			
Interest Rate x Basic Financial Rate Swap	2			
Central Bank Bills		10		
Exchange Rate Swap Futures	174,177	170,662		
Inflation Rate Future		75,513	258,352	
Reference Rate x Exchange Rate Swap	813			
Flexible Currency Options	6,097,019			
BM&F, Brazil	**148,055,778**	**102,981,783**	**52,213,672**	**35,072,146**

Volume Worldwide

	1995	1994	1993	1992
3 Month Hungarian T-Bills	6,333			
Budapest Stock Index (BUX) Futures	3,207			
DEM/HUF	1,407			
USD/HUF	940			
ECU/HUF	494			
Budapest Stock Exchange	**12,381**			
DAX	4,788,661	5,140,803	3,976,882	3,271,055
BUND	12,525,264	14,160,460	7,624,604	5,327,846
Medium Term Notional Bond (BOBL)	7,351,783	5,647,859	4,533,543	1,667,799
BULX	4,584	89,150		
FIBOR	99,809	428,516		
DAX Options	24,299,078	23,499,552	21,419,890	13,944,986
Medium Term Notional Bond (BOBL) Options	123,019	46,145	54,373	
BUND Options	194,036	261,110	251,859	498,324
Options on DAX Futures	21,073	49,642	62,976	136,439
Stock Options				9,996,329
DTB, Germany	**49,407,307**	**49,323,237**	**37,924,127**	**34,842,778**
High Grade Primary Aluminum	14,060,243	14,604,218	10,083,342	9,256,740
High Grade Primary Aluminum Options	1,241,596	1,231,794	900,266	
Aluminum Alloy	210,787	148,685	111,450	2,394
Aluminum Alloy Options	96			
Copper - Grade A	17,530,263	17,236,317	14,855,430	7,945,054
Copper - Grade A Options	2,212,821	2,155,587	1,156,352	
Standard Lead	1,758,742	1,942,234	1,020,579	986,000
Standard Lead Options	22,262	45,769	17,299	
Primary Nickel	3,319,697	3,404,942	2,118,710	1,485,064
Primary Nickel Options	83,637	142,107	70,607	
Special High Grade Zinc	5,241,931	5,303,060	4,167,832	4,527,594
Special High Grade Zinc Options	177,005	253,782	163,475	
Tin	1,275,718	1,192,735	613,952	534,074
Tin Options	15,532	26,487	10,638	
London Metal Exchange, UK	**47,150,330**	**47,687,717**	**35,289,932**	**24,736,920**
Copra	82,258	544,992		
Sugar	115,404	496,686		
Coffee	132,272	516,010		
Soybean	86,664	615,968		
Dry Cocoon	106,228	524,544		
Interest Rate		7,672		
US Dollar - Peso		2,356		
US Dollar - Deutschemark	95,554	43,280		
US Dollar - Yen	180,200	163,542		
British Pound - US Dollar	54,892	97,004		
US Dollar - Swiss Franc	98,772	79,840		
Manila International Futures Exchange	**952,244**	**3,091,894**		
CAC 40 Index	6,549,953	7,464,449	5,908,739	3,601,476
ECU Bond	657,152	618,715	873,002	1,354,012
ECU Bond Options		790	7,797	82,820
Notional Bond	33,610,221	50,153,150	36,804,824	31,062,844
Notional Bond Options	9,517,932	18,024,502	11,572,671	10,047,391
3 Month Pibor	15,488,076	13,176,354	11,863,798	6,436,765
3 Month Pibor Options	4,615,434	3,361,277	4,830,198	2,659,534
French Treasury Bond			29,213	
French Medium Term		63	99,260	
Potatoes	29,619	33,302	11,029	10,437
Rapseed	51,135	7,026		
Sugar	305,598	297,940	262,940	218,250
Coffee		170	490	608
U.S. Dollar/French Franc Options	67,286	75,436		
U.S. Dollar/Deutschemark Options	116,127	225,497		
Sterling/Deutschemark Options	35,734			
Deutschemark/Italian Lira Options	11,249			
Deutschemark/French Franc Options	34,491			
Sugar Option	505			
MATIF, Paris	**71,090,512**	**93,438,671**	**72,263,961**	**55,474,137**

Volume Worldwide

	1995	1994	1993	1992
MIBOR (90 Days)	3,153,112	3,730,008	2,319,132	747,191
90 Days MIBOR Plus	302,681			
360 Days MIBOR	177,964	446,160	44,130	
360 Days MIBOR Plus	15,403			
3 Year Notional Bond	456	12,112	15,585	235,804
5 Year Notional Bond				8,291
10 Year Notional Bond	13,035,805	13,191,835	4,537,765	770,480
Spanish Peseta/U.S. Dollar			26	12,215
Spanish Peseta/Deutschemark			3,172	54,635
3 Year Notional Bond Options				41,900
10 Year Notional Bond Options	1,888,547	2,047,754	1,087,972	339,877
90 Days MIBOR Plus Options	58,297			
MIBOR Options (90 Days)	450,310	307,460	139,550	8,300
MEFF RENTA FIJA, Spain	**19,082,575**	**19,735,329**	**8,147,332**	**2,218,693**
IBEX 35	28,096,699	27,020,886	10,856,012	
IBEX 35 Options	8,179,599	7,541,551	3,563,485	
MEFF RENTA VARIABLE, Spain	**36,276,298**	**34,562,437**	**14,419,497**	
10 Year BTP	2,636,161	3,702,802	2,776,992	
5 Year BTP	166,002	667,115	1,637,256	
10 Year BTP Options	113,665			
Mercato Italiano Dei Futures, Italy	**2,915,828**	**4,369,917**	**4,414,248**	
CAC 40 Index (Short Term) Options	2,425,363	2,755,289	2,451,512	3,170,782
CAC 40 Index (Long Term) Options	3,013,926	2,996,181	1,760,763	547,495
MONEP, Paris	**5,439,289**	**5,751,470**	**4,212,275**	**3,718,277**
Canadian Government Bond Options	40,147	51,305	61,455	50,955
Bankers Acceptance Futures 3 Month	2,326,709	1,918,976	724,158	419,765
Bankers Acceptance Futures 1 Month	7,225	12,172	24,552	23,502
10 Year Canadian Government Bond Futures	1,026,854	1,496,543	895,047	515,732
5 Year Canadian Government Bond Futures	63,842			
Options on Canadian Government Bond	2,191	6,363	9,489	5,195
Bankers Acceptance Futures 3 Month Options	51,855	29,464		
Equity Options				669,190
Montreal Exchange	**3,518,823**	**3,514,823**	**1,714,701**	**1,684,339**
U.S. Dollar	19	21	9	6
3 Year Government Stock	26,912	101,229	74,128	
3 Year Government Stock Options		80	1,000	
5 Year Government Stock			50,836	209,232
5 Year Government Stock Options			1,652	28,048
10 Year Government Stock	8,456	42,541	20,996	5
10 Year Government Stock Options	200	4,200	120	
90 Day Bank Bill	478,806	608,460	463,141	393,172
90 Day Bank Bill Options	18,221	6,870	8,193	38,258
New Zealand Wool				56
NZSE-40 Captial Share Price Index	3,936	7,397	3,633	4,620
NZSE-40 Captial Share Price Index Options	294	1,985	596	760
NZSE-10 Captial Share Price Index	2,971			
NZSE-10 Captial Share Price Index Options	24			
New Zealand Futures Exchange	**539,839**	**772,783**	**624,304**	**674,157**
EOE Stock Index (FTI)	1,004,005	1,031,333	811,882	510,517
Dutch Top 5 Index	63,751	61,957	58,483	51,896
Eurotop 100 Index	233	435	1,102	2,003
Deliverable Bond (FTO)	8,051	14,132	70,388	21,230
U.S. Dollar/Guilder (FUS)	14,663	13,395	22,000	11,101
Gold Options	45,283	133,412	284,040	72,815
Silver Options	5,704	5,100		
Dollar/Guilder Options	552,452	482,961	672,632	537,892
Dutch Government Bond Options	406,500	449,511	436,199	270,442
EOE Stock Index Options	3,681,781	2,851,170	2,694,680	2,452,238
Eurotop 100	5,204	853	2,647	10,424
Dutch Top 5 Index	561,611	393,584	411,757	493,466
Major Market Index Options		1,563	6,227	18,970
European Options Exchange	**6,349,238**	**5,439,406**	**5,472,037**	**4,452,994**

Volume Worldwide

	1995	1994	1993	1992
Finnish Government Bond	125,298			
FRA Interest Rate	4,375			
FOX Index	181,428			
Currency Options	9,669			
FOX Index Options	521,008			
Finnish Options Market Exchange	**841,778**			
Danish Government Bonds 9% 1995			480	117,684
Danish Government Bonds 9% 1998	8,395	103,103	185,953	7,356
Danish Government Bonds 9% 2000	14,520		1,250	396,181
Danish Government Bonds 8% 2003		343,101	391,969	27,235
Danish Government Bonds 8% 2006	7,679			
Danish Government Bonds 7% 2004	159,778	74,220		
6% 2026 Mortgage Bonds	54,885	172,239	28,618	
9% 2022 Mortgage Bonds			1,408	23,948
9% 2006 Mortgage Bonds				9,889
9% 2006 Mortgage Bonds Options				120
Danish Government Bonds 9% 2000 Options			170	144,962
Danish Government Bonds 8% 2003 Options		76,548	85,580	8,100
Danish Government Bonds 8% 2006 Options	1,204			
Danish Government Bonds 7% 2004 Options	77,767	24,045		
3 Month CIBOR	14,260	32,718	34,727	
KFX Stock Index	263,537	429,466	339,024	406,694
KFX Stock Index Options	51,053	79,952	87,246	193,598
Stock Options				186,992
FUTOP Clearing Centre, Denmark	**653,078**	**1,335,392**	**1,156,425**	**1,522,759**
Crude Oil	9,773,146	10,082,761	8,852,549	6,172,156
Crude Oil Options	571,308	531,742	1,059,222	791,810
Gasoil	4,491,463	3,779,064	3,608,637	3,452,643
Gasoil Options	116,424	136,859	217,508	199,256
Unleaded Gasoline Options				58,938
Unleaded Gasoline	3,030	3,977	32,062	
International Petroleum Exchange, UK	**14,955,371**	**14,534,403**	**13,769,978**	**10,674,803**
DIBOR	630	3,099	3,819	28,405
Long Gilt	1,717	12,123	9,888	3,900
Short Gilt		1,140	100	2,040
Medium Gilt	4,300			
Irish Futures & Options Exchange	**6,647**	**16,362**	**13,807**	**34,345**
MIB 30 Index	1,140,636			
MIB 30 Index Options	12,464			
Italian Derivative Market of the Italian Stock Exchange	**1,153,100**			
Crude Palm Oil	524,665	567,902	355,743	252,731
Crude Palm Kernel Oil (15 tonne)			4,474	
Crude Palm Kernel Oil (25 tonne)		230	2,741	2,721
Tin				18
Cocoa				519
Kuala Lumpur Commodity Exchange	**2,830,865**	**568,132**	**362,958**	**255,989**

Volume Worldwide

	1995	1994	1993	1992
Financial Time Index (FT-SE 100)	3,373,259	4,227,490	3,119,971	2,618,629
Short Sterling (3 Month)	15,314,576	16,603,52	12,135,981	11,296,327
Long Gilt	13,796,555	19,048,097	11,808,998	8,804,639
3 Month ECU	693,526	622,457	720,788	316,781
Eurodollar	2,720	91,738	244,728	709,305
U.S. T-Bond			4,660	272,077
Eurotrack 100				81
Japanses Government (Yen) Bond	845,329	610,925	421,454	221,370
Spanish Government Bond			28,318	
Italian Government Bond	9,612,899	11,823,741	6,344,233	3,773,105
3 Month Euroswiss	1,749,774	1,698,736	1,846,376	1,970,438
3 Month Eurolira	4,005,125	3,456,437	1,479,012	375,514
3 Month Euromark	25,737,379	29,312,222	21,318,942	12,173,431
ECU Bond				7,434
German BOBL		73,043	1,049,640	
German Government Bund	32,231,210	37,335,437	20,440,442	13,604,523
Financial Time Index (FT-SE Mid 250 Index)	35,068	40,674		
3 Month Eurodollar Options	2	12,400	20,015	72,906
3 Month Euromark Options	3,427,376	2,943,936	2,906,476	1,964,405
U.S. T-Bond Options			2,626	68,369
German Government Bond Options	6,988,655	8,574,137	4,416,480	2,749,670
Italian Government Bond Options	1,130,762	1,030,672	602,096	395,354
3 Month Euroswiss Options	33,781	19,245	32,163	17,412
3 Month Eurolira Options	100,129			
Long Gilt Options	1,756,533	2,357,348	2,059,142	1,812,576
Short Sterling Options	3,348,945	4,057,878	2,666,711	2,648,009
Equity (individual)				3,533,030
Financial Times Index Option (FT-SE 100)	4,434,086	4,786,656	3,439,460	2,571,640
Financial Times FLEX Index Option (FT-SE 100)	60,699			
LIFFE, UK	**128,678,388**	**148,726,421**	**97,108,712**	**71,977,025**
Barley	18,088	8,072	13,479	21,516
Barley Options	103	64	110	885
BIFFEX (Baltic Freight Index)	74,696	47,805	43,105	52,155
BIFFEX (Baltic Freight Index) Options	447	94	10	96
Cocoa	1,653,790	1,600,746	1,908,136	1,397,966
Cocoa Options	48,196	87,215	107,102	51,219
$ Coffee	1,062,744	1,269,477	908,963	876,687
$ Coffee Options	169,130	204,945	282,263	108,493
Hi Pro Soy			7,020	18,142
Hi Pro Soy Options			1	3,630
Lamb			110	650
Raw Sugar	34,219	30,959	14,898	
Pigs			2,291	8,749
Pigs Options			25	
Potatoes in Bulk	27,268	36,672	23,073	25,384
Sugar (FOB)		1,104		75,052
Wheat	101,025	84,212	62,546	63,202
Wheat Options	12,907	6,866	1,769	2,081
White Sugar	575,734	480,973	329,414	303,377
White Sugar Options	23,016	8,196		
London Commodity Exchange, UK	**3,801,363**	**3,867,400**	**3,704,315**	**3,009,284**
Hang Seng Index	4,546,613	4,192,574	2,415,739	1,089,037
Hang Seng Index Options	645,538	606,674	282,283	
Deutschemark Rolling Forex	12,633			
Japanes Yen Rolling Forex	8,688			
3 Month HIBOR				205
Soybeans				4,688
Sugar				8,598
Gold		490	972	1,000
Hang Seng Comm. & Ind. Sub-Index				205
Hang Seng Properties Sub-Index				205
Hang Seng Finance Sub-Index				205
Hang Seng Utilities Sub-Index				205
Hong Kong Futures Exchange	**5,213,472**	**4,799,738**	**2,698,994**	**1,104,348**

Volume Worldwide

	1995	1994	1993	1992
Domestic Soybeans		18	24	24
Red Beans	75,501	241,555	182,611	220,096
White Beans		18	24	24
Potato Starch		18	24	24
Imported Soybeans	24,912	89,916	106,152	255,198
***Hokkaido Grain Exchange**	**100,413**	**331,525**	**288,835**	**475,366**
Red Beans	237,745	492,294	579,751	488,167
Imported Soybeans	130,520	213,271	486,850	438,817
Refined Sugar	1,449	1,432	1,437	1,443
Corn	2,890,258	1,709,248	1,077,057	270,809
***Kanmon Commodity Exchange**	**3,259,972**	**2,416,245**	**2,145,095**	**1,199,236**
Red Beans	1,723,230	2,931,256	3,092,743	4,051,785
Imported Soybeans	1,695,414	1,298,180	2,113,812	2,340,144
Refined Sugar	2,886	2,864	2,874	2,880
Raw Sugar	730,582	664,683	1,063,480	648,833
Raw Sugar Options	79,365	63,789	26,793	95,802
***Kansai Ag. Commodities Exchange**	**4,231,477**	**4,960,772**	**6,299,702**	**7,139,444**
Raw Silk	591,922	695,172	687,723	195,037
***KOBE Raw Silk Exchange**	**591,922**	**695,172**	**687,723**	**195,037**
Rubber (RSS3)	3,810,938	2,933,883	1,275,051	791,948
Rubber Index	173,409			
KOBE Rubber Exchange	**3,984,347**	**2,933,883**	**1,275,051**	**791,948**
Dried Cocoon	443,411	475,978	1,782,394	492,494
***Maebashi Dried Cocoon Exchange**	**443,411**	**475,978**	**1,782,394**	**492,494**
Red Beans	502,369	919,371	1,217,337	1,376,017
Sweet Potato Starch	48	48	48	48
Imported Soybeans	307,451	177,513	287,612	348,733
Refined Sugar	1,449	1,789	2,874	2,886
***Nagoya Grain & Sugar Exchange**	**811,317**	**1,098,721**	**1,507,871**	**1,727,684**
Cotton Yarn (40S)	755,844	1,100,388	822,683	1,145,017
Staple Fiber Yarn (Dull)	9,967	13,114	18,279	29,614
Wool Yarn	53,811	87,240	79,114	123,570
***Nagoya Textile Exchange**	**819,622**	**1,200,742**	**920,076**	**1,298,201**
Nikkei 225 Index Futures	7,220,900	6,208,754	8,461,458	11,927,329
Nikkei 300 Index Futures	2,318,652	4,184,480		
Nikkei 225 Index Options	5,174,571	4,273,641	6,090,375	9,256,981
Nikkei 300 Index Options	122,084	269,067		
***Osaka Securities Exchange**	**14,836,207**	**14,935,942**	**14,551,833**	**21,184,310**
Staple Fiber Yarn (Bright)	4,128	3,507	2,928	2,940
Staple Fiber Yarn (Dull)	2,940	2,910	2,928	4,715
Wool Yarn	64,073	266,974	524,699	258,487
Cotton Yarn (20S)	2,151,580	2,000,530	648,345	652,535
Cotton Yarn (40S)	659,110	833,307	574,724	644,897
***Osaka Textile Exchange**	**2,881,831**	**3,107,228**	**1,753,624**	**1,563,574**
Gold	10,945,134	12,481,095	8,764,441	4,193,775
Silver	1,440,297	1,042,185	661,452	231,864
Palladium	629,034	774,284	2,275,843	404,091
Platinum	5,975,872	4,551,406	4,984,480	4,631,724
Rubber	14,287,783	9,021,881	2,973,241	1,726,487
Cotton Yarn	1,838,448	2,573,963	1,865,469	2,330,029
Woolen Yarn	8,859	36,499	32,869	67,409
***Tokyo Commodity Exchange Industry**	**35,125,427**	**30,481,313**	**21,557,795**	**13,585,379**

Volume Worldwide

	1995	1994	1993	1992
American Soybeans	2,699,926	2,559,288	3,750,291	4,000,410
Chinese Soybeans				208
Red Beans	3,384,267	5,122,015	6,353,667	7,804,868
Corn	6,899,593	3,053,244	1,263,357	556,501
Refined Sugar	2,898	2,864	2,874	2,886
Raw Sugar	1,291,441	1,220,931	2,218,688	1,279,354
American Soybean Options	206,993	96,505	60,420	54,684
Raw Sugar Options	158,044	67,636	38,450	43,203
***Tokyo Grain Exchange**	**14,643,162**	**12,122,483**	**13,687,747**	**13,742,114**
3 Month Euroyen	36,329,959	37,425,846	23,386,958	14,959,373
1 Year Euroyen	25,300	25,100	4,434	9,379
U.S. Dollar - Japanese Yen	5,037	13,770	48,241	86,008
Euroyen Options	361,920	570,237	686,514	485,727
***Tokyo International Financial Futures Exchange**	**36,722,216**	**38,034,953**	**24,126,147**	**15,540,487**
Yen Government Bond (10 Year)	14,010,374	12,999,698	15,162,159	11,868,414
Yen Government Bond (10 Year) Options	2,017,031	1,691,834	1,506,836	1,140,541
Yen Government Bond (20 Year)	2,734	3,194	3,106	3,972
TOPIX Stock Index Futures	2,745,614	2,623,067	2,156,960	1,358,723
TOPIX Options	16,742	20,078	37,831	48,576
U.S. T-Bond Futures	102,340	115,750	112,600	118,491
***Tokyo Stock Exchange**	**18,894,835**	**17,453,621**	**18,979,492**	**14,538,717**
OBr10	52,001	165,443	28,245	
OBr5	49,187	43,745		
OBX	18,615	4,151	16,650	
OBX Options	481,865	422,430	385,540	
OBX Long Options	12,100	1,370		
Oslo Stock Exchange	**613,768**	**637,139**	**430,435**	
Gold		26	436	667
Eurodollar	8,394,933	8,687,969	5,535,806	5,617,972
Deutschemark	66	8,727	16,368	44,990
Japanese Yen	106	16,825	21,009	19,921
British Pound	8	1,741	3,912	4,111
Deferred Spot US$/JY	58,922	68,605	13,182	
Deferred Spot US$/DM	109,181	131,210	26,298	
Nikkei Stock Average	6,456,984	5,801,098	5,162,199	3,349,243
Nikkei 300	174,234			
MSCI Hong Kong Index		317	80,245	
High Sulfur Fuel Oil	19,421	171,896	300,201	278,205
Brent Crude	73,445			
Gasoil			23,288	25,806
Euroyen	6,549,295	6,820,673	3,532,998	2,472,931
Euromark	1,800	231,068	23,127	4,940
Japanese Government Bond	297,426	443,564	29,253	
Eurodollar Options	5,247	13,545	6,525	11,534
Euroyen Options	128,944	126,280	57,395	80,815
Nikkei Options	1,943,096	1,496,922	897,545	269,039
Nikkei 300 Options	3,160			
Japanese Government Bond Options	35,071	39,808		
SIMEX, Singapore	**24,251,339**	**24,060,274**	**15,729,787**	**12,180,174**
Swiss Market Index	1,457,108	1,694,260	914,021	847,157
EUROTOP 100 Index				4
3 Month Euro Swiss Franc			353	184,084
5 Year Swiss Franc			28,548	199,829
Swiss Government Bond	955,895	949,657	270,653	233,761
Swiss Market Index Options	6,027,308	6,678,779	5,595,388	7,793,949
Swiss Government Bond Options	35,695	49,749		
EUROTOP 100 Index Options				75
SOFFEX, Switzerland	**8,476,006**	**9,372,445**	**6,808,963**	**9,258,859**

Volume Worldwide

	1995	1994	1993	1992
All Share Index Futures	1,816,846	2,185,672	1,670,540	
All Share Index Options	2,933,564	2,804,855	1,236,263	
Industrial Index Futures	1,030,714	920,786	422,203	
Industrial Index Options	494,227	377,593	148,101	
Financial Index	4,290			
Gold Index Futures	656,696	933,591	895,772	
Gold Index Options	175,332	132,230	102,136	
Krugerrand Futures	5,901	5,664		
Krugerrand Options	203	3,300		
3 Month Bank Bill Futures	5,564	3,901	2,135	
3 Month Bank Bill Options	820			
R 150 Futures	30,472	1,750		
R 150 Options	27,173			
E168 (Long Bond) Futures	530	8,495	6,903	
E168 (Long Bond) Options	60	100	920	
South African Futures Exchange (SAFEX)	**7,182,392**	**7,377,937**	**4,484,973**	
Interest Rate Options	42,783	86,410		19,584
Interest Rate Futures	10,949,860	14,123,881	11,272,285	7,420,164
OMX (Index) Options	6,067,268	5,812,435	4,073,852	5,605,059
OMX (Index) Futures	1,593,408	1,706,984	627,706	450,031
Financial Times Index (FT-SE Mid 250) Options		2,140		
Financial Times Index (FT-SE Mid 250) Futures		9,565		
Stockholm Options Exchange	**18,653,319**	**36,497,289**	**15,973,843**	**17,147,096**
All Ordinaries Share Price Index	2,476,331	2,552,546	980,866	342,013
Fifty Leaders Share Price Index		1	1	203
Bank Bills 90 Days	6,172,512	9,369,008	6,415,394	5,697,786
3 Year Treasury Bonds	8,820,651	9,709,791	6,939,811	5,434,795
10 Year Treasury Bonds	5,740,870	6,814,733	4,781,905	4,253,374
Wool (Cash Set)	1,221	4,833	3,271	1,259
Greasy Wool	4,799			
3 Year Treasury Bond Options	426,836	507,252	514,539	317,356
90 Day Bank Bills Options	712,834	943,749	663,317	610,458
10 Year Treasury Bonds Options	580,091	800,263	712,686	745,994
Overnight 3 Year Treasury Bond Options	7,443	2,078	320	
Overnight 10 Year Treasury Bond Options	24,419	18,656	2,082	
All Ordinaries Share Price Options	652,607	833,667	466,896	154,149
Sydney Futures Exchange	**25,620,614**	**31,556,584**	**21,481,096**	**17,557,685**
TSE 35 Index	110,011	104,209	69,058	59,049
TSE 35 Options	337,764	247,482	221,232	302,444
TSE 100 Index	2,963	10,819		
TSE 100 Index Options	7,824	13,200		
Silver Options	656	8,300	4,583	331
Toronto Futures Exchange	**459,218**	**384,010**	**294,877**	**361,824**
Wheat	155,699	191,696	210,074	199,060
Oats	32,761	52,550	59,244	45,913
Thunder Bay Barley		5,378	63,643	88,150
Cadadian Barley	18,523	31,600	4,150	
Rye	104	1,022	7,829	26,273
Flax Seed	132,525	105,338	104,110	144,581
Canola (Rapeseed)	1,075,683	1,167,447	972,354	839,715
Feed Peas	7,802			
Western Barley	172,733	115,376	40,248	22,655
Wheat Options	734	3,145	5,274	2,225
Flax Options	1,567	1,692	4,907	
Cadadian Barley Options	435		80	
Western Barley Options	274	1,716	10	
Canola Options	71,197	82,565	44,121	50,262
Winnipeg Commodity Exchange	**1,670,037**	**1,759,525**	**1,615,044**	**1,418,834**
Dried Cocoon	488,709	488,558	1,066,374	519,045
***Toyahashi Dried Cocoon Exchange**	**488,709**	**488,558**	**1,066,374**	**519,045**
Raw Silk	1,256,094	998,686	1,512,132	410,028
***Yokohama Raw Silk Exchange**	**1,256,094**	**998,686**	**1,512,132**	**410,028**

*Exchange located in Japan

Conversion Factors

Commonly Used Agricultural Weights and Measurements

Bushel Weights:
wheat and soybeans = 60 lbs.
corn, sorghum and rye = 56 lbs.
barley grain = 48 lbs.
barley malt = 34 lbs.
oats = 32 lbs.

Bushels to tonnes:
wheat and soybeans = bushels X 0.027216
barley grain = bushels X 0.021772
corn, sorghum and rye = bushels X 0.0254
oats = bushels X 0.014515

1 tonne (metric ton) equals:
2204.622 lbs.
1,000 kilograms
22.046 hundredweight
10 quintals
(continued above)

1 tonne (metric ton) equals:
36.7437 bushels of wheat or soybeans
39.3679 bushels of corn, sorghum or rye
45.9296 bushels of barley grain
68.8944 bushels of oats
4.5929 cotton bales (the statistical bale used by the USDA and ICAC contains a net weight of 480 pounds of lint)

Area Measurements:
1 acre = 43,560 square feet = 0.040694 hectare
1 hectare = 2.4710 acres = 10,000 square meters
640 acres = 1 square mile = 259 hectares

Yields:
wheat: bushels per acre X 0.6725 = quintals per hectare
rye, corn: bushels per acre X 0.6277 = quintals per hectare
barley grain: bushels per acre X 0.538 = quintals per hectare
oats: bushels per acre X 0.3587 = quintals per hectare

Commonly Used Weights

The troy, avoirdupois and apothecaries' grains are identical in U.S. and British weight systems, equal to 0.0648 gram in the metric system. One avoirdupois ounce equals 437.5 grains. The troy and apothecaries' ounces equal 480 grains, and their pounds contain 12 ounces.

Troy weights and conversions:
24 grains = 1 pennyweight
20 pennyweights = 1 ounce
12 ounces = 1 pound
1 troy ounce = 31.103 grams
1 troy ounce = 0.0311033 kilogram
1 troy pound = 0.37224 kilogram
1 kilogram = 32.1507 troy ounces
1 tonne = 32,151 troy ounces

Avoirdupois weights and conversions:
27 11/32 grains = 1 dram
16 drams = 1 ounce
16 ounces = 1 lb.
1 lb. = 7,000 grains
14 lbs. = 1 stone (British)
100 lbs. = 1 hundredweight (U.S.)
112 lbs. = 8 stone = 1 hundredweight (British)
2,000 lbs. = 1 short ton (U.S. ton)
2,240 lbs. = 1 long ton (British ton)
160 stone = 1 long ton
20 hundredweight = 1 ton
1 lb. = 0.4536 kilogram
1 hundredweight (cwt.) = 45.359 kilograms
1 short ton = 907.18 kilograms
1 long ton = 1,016.05 kilograms

Metric weights and conversions:
1,000 grams = 1 kilogram
100 kilograms = 1 quintal
1 tonne = 1,000 kilograms = 10 quintals
1 kilogram = 2.204622 lbs.
1 quintal = 220.462 lbs.
1 tonne = 2204.6 lbs.
1 tonne = 1.102 short tons
1 tonne = 0.9842 long ton

U.S. dry volumes and conversions:
1 pint = 33.6 cubic inches = 0.5506 liter
2 pints = 1 quart = 1.1012 liters
8 quarts = 1 peck = 8.8098 liters
4 pecks = 1 bushel = 35.2391 liters
1 cubic foot = 28.3169 liters

U.S. liquid volumes and conversions:
1 ounce = 1.8047 cubic inches = 29.6 milliliters
1 cup = 8 ounces = 0.24 liter = 237 milliliters
1 pint = 16 ounces = 0.48 liter = 473 milliliters
1 quart = 2 pints = 0.946 liter = 946 milliliters
1 gallon = 4 quarts = 231 cubic inches = 3.785 liters
1 milliliter = 0.033815 fluid ounce
1 liter = 1.0567 quarts = 1,000 milliliters
1 liter = 33.815 fluid ounces
1 imperial gallon = 277.42 cubic inches = 1.2 U.S. gallons = 4.546 liters

ENERGY CONVERSION FACTORS

U.S. Crude OIl (average gravity)
1 U.S. barrel = 42 U.S. gallons
1 short ton = 6.65 barrels
1 tonne = 7.33 barrels

Barrels per tonne for various origins

Abu Dhabi	7.624
Algeria	7.661
Angola	7.206
Australia	7.775
Bahrain	7.335
Brunei	7.334
Canada	7.428
Dubai	7.295
Ecuador	7.580
Gabon	7.245
Indonesia	7.348
Iran	7.370
Iraq	7.453
Kuwait	7.261
Libya	7.615
Mexico	7.104
Neutral Zone	6.825
Nigeria	7.410
Norway	7.444
Oman	7.390
Qatar	7.573
Romania	7.453
Saudi Arabia	7.338
Trinidad	6.989
Tunisia	7.709
United Arab Emirates	7.522
United Kingdom	7.279
United States	7.418
Former Soviet Union	7.350
Venezuela	7.005
Zaire	7.206

Barrels per tonne of refined products:

aviation gasoline	8.90
motor gasoline	8.50
kerosene	7.75
jet fuel	8.00
distillate, including diesel	7.46
residual feul oil	6.45
lubricating oil	7.00
grease	6.30
white spirits	8.50
paraffin oil	7.14
paraffin wax	7.87
petrolatum	7.87
asphalt and road oil	6.06
petroleum coke	5.50
bitumen	6.06
LPG	11.6

(continued above)

Approximate heat content of refined products:
(Million Btu per barrel, 1 British thermal unit is the amount of heat required to raise the temperature of 1 pound of water 1 degree F.)

Petroleum Product	Heat Content
asphalt	6.636
aviation gasoline	5.048
butane	4.326
distillate fuel oil	5.825
ethane	3.082
isobutane	3.974
jet fuel, kerosene	5.670
jet fuel, naptha	5.355
kerosene	5.670
lubricants	6.065
motor gasoline	5.253
natural gasoline	4.620
pentanes plus	4.620

Petrochemical feedstocks:

naptha less than 401°F	5.248
other oils equal to or greater than 401°F	5.825
still gas	6.000
petroleum coke	6.024
plant condensate	5.418
propane	3.836
residual fuel oil	6.287
special napthas	5.248
unfinished oils	5.825
unfractionated steam	5.418
waxes	5.537

Source: Department of Energy

Natural Gas Conversions

Although there are approximately 1,031 Btu in a cubic foot of gas, for most applications, the following conversions are sufficient:

Cubic Feet					MMBtu
1,000	(one thousand cubic feet)	=	1 Mcf	=	1
1,000,000	(one million cubic feet)	=	1 MMcf	=	1,000
10,000,000	(ten million cubic feet)	=	10 MMcf	=	10,000
1,000,000,000	(one billion cubic feet)	=	1 Bcf	=	1,000,000
1,000,000,000,000	(one trillion cubic feet)	=	1 Tcf	=	1,000,000,000

Cash Market Description for Monthly Charts

Aluminum
- Pig Ingots - New York from 1910 thru 1986
- Pig Ingots - Midwest from 11/14/86 to Date
- Cast Scrap - New York 1929 thru 1984
- Cast Scrap - Midwest (Chicago) 1985 to Date
- Clippings - New York 1929 thru 1984 (1950-1951 N/A)
- Clippings - Midwest (Chicago) 1985 to Date

Barley
- No. 2 Minneapolis 08/09 thru 06/25
- No. 3 Minneapolis (straight or better) 07/26 thru 06/76
- No. 2 Feed Minneapolis 07/26 thru 12/86
- No. 2 Feed Duluth 03/87 to Date

Beef Steers
- Chicago All Grades 1909 thru 1934
- Chicago Good 1935 thru 1939
- Chicago All Grades 1940 thru 1962
- Chicago Good - 1/2/48 to 12/31/64
- Chicago Choice - 1/2/65 to 7/30/71
- Omaha Choice Average - 8/2/71 to 8/25/87
- Texas-Oklahoma Cattle Average - 8/26/87 to Date

Cocoa
- Santos No. 4 NY - 1920 to 7/17/75
- Brazilian NY - 1/6/76 to Date
- Colombian Maniz NY - 1/2/48 to 7/6/53
- Colombian Medellin NY - 1/4/54 to 6/8/76; 10/8/76 to 12/27/77
- Colombian NY - 1/10/78 to 12/30/82; 1/2/83 to 7/1/83; 11/14/83 to 2/4/85; 8/29/85 to 10/15/87; 3/1/90 to Date

Copper
- Electrolytic NY - 1910 thru 1983
- Electrolytic US - 1984 to Date
- Scrap No. 1 NY - 1927 thru 1955
- Scrap No. 2 NY - 1956 thru 04/88
- Scrap No. 2 Chicago - 5/88 to Date

Corn
- No. 3 Yellow Chicago - 1901 to 04/47
- No. 2 Yellow Chicago - 5/5/47 to 3/28/82
- No. 2 Yellow Central Illinois - 3/29/82 to Date

Corn Oil
- FOB Midwestern Mills (Decatur) - 07/24 thru 06/85
- Wet Mill at Chicago - 10/85 to Date

Corporate AAA Bonds
- Federal Reserve Bank of St. Louis - 1919 to Date

Cotton
- 7/8" at Designated Mkts Middling - 08/15 thru 07/30
- 15/16" at Designated Mkts Middling - 08/30 thru 07/73
- 11/16" at Designated Mkts Middling - 08/73 to Date

Cottonseed Meal
- 36% Protein Memphis - 08/10 thru 09/20
- 41% Protein Memphis - 10/21 thru 09/46
- 41% Protein (Expeller) Memphis - 10/46 thru 12/81
- 41% Protein (Solvent) Memphis - 01/82 to Date

Cottonseed Oil
- FOB Southeastern Mills - 08/90 to Date

Discount Rate
- Federal Reserve Bank of St. Louis - 1934 to Date

Eggs
- NY Fresh Firsts - 1910 thru 1926
- Chicago Fresh Firsts - 1927 thru 06/43
- Chicago US Standards - 07/43 thru 1947
- Chicago Large - 1948 to Date

Feeder Cattle
- Oklahoma City - 1970 to Date

Five Year T-Bond Yield
- Federal Reserve Bank of St. Louis - 1953 to Date

Flaxseed
- No. 1 Minneapolis - 1901 thru 01/86
- US Farm Price - 1980 to Date

Gold
- NY Handy & Harman - 1968 to Date

Hides
- Chicago (Paker's Heavy Native Steers) - 1920 to Date
- Chicago (Light Native Steers) 1920 thru 1943

Hogs
- Top Chicago - 1909 to 4/1/68
- Live Hogs Farrowing Chicago - 4/2/68 to 5/15/70
- Live Hogs Average Omaha - 5/18/70 to Date

Lard
- Chicago - 1910 to Date

Lead
- Raw - 1910 to Date
- Scrap - 1985 to Date

Cash Market Description for Monthly Charts

Lumber
- White-Fir 2x4 - 1959 thru 1970
- Hem-Fir 2x4 - 1971 thru 03/80
- Spruce-Pine-Fir 2x4 - 03/80 to Date

Mercury
- N.Y. 75 pound Flask - 1920 thru 1931
- N.Y. 76 pound Flask - 1932 to Date

Molasses
- Blackstrap N.Y. - 1920 thru 1967
- Blackstrap (cane) New Orleans - 1968 to Date

Municipal Bonds
- Federal Reserve Bank of St. Louis - 1919 to Date

Oats
- No. 3 White Chicago - 1901 thru 1947
- Oats No. 2 White Chicago - 1/2/48 to 11/25/48
- Oats No. 1 White Hvy Chicago - 11/26/48 to 12/15/74
- Oats No. 2 White Hvy Chicago - 12/16/74 to Date

Pepper
- Black at N.Y. - 1920 to Date

Platinum
- N.Y. Producer Price - 1910 thru 1977
- N.Y. Merchants Price - 1978 to Date

Pork Bellies
- 12-14 Lbs Chicago - 1/2/49 to 10/3/75
- Pork Bellies 12-14 Lbs Midwest - 10/6/75 to Date

Potatoes
- N.Y. - U.S. No. 1 White - 1913 thru 1960
- U.S. Farmers Price - 1961 to Date

Prime Rate
- Federal Reserve Bank of St. Louis - 1930 to Date

Rice
- New Orleans Fancy (Honduras Grade) - 8/9 thru 1924
- New Orleans Fancy (Blue Rose Grade) - 1925-1933
- New Orleans Medium to Good (Blue Rose Grade) - 1934 thru 07/47
- New Orleans Fancy No. 2 Zenith Milled - 8/47-4/72
- Southwest Lousiana No. 2 Medium Grain - 5/72 to Date

Rubber
- N.Y. Plantation Smoked Sheets - 1908 to Date

Rye
- No. 2 Minneapolis - 07/09 to Date
- Winnipeg - 1950 thru 1982

Silver
- N.Y. Handy & Harman - 1910 to Date

Soybeans
- U.S. Farmers Price - 1913 thru 09/47
- No. 2 Yellow Chicago - 11/30/47 to 12/31/56
- No. 1 Yellow Chicago - 1/2/57 to 3/26/82
- No. 1 Yellow Central II - 3/29/82 to Date

Soybean Meal
- Chicago (Protein no specified) - 10/29 thru 10/36
- Chicago 41% Protein - 11/36 thru 06/50
- Chicago 44% Protein - 07/50 thru 09/65
- Decatur 44% Protein - 10/65 thru 11/16/92
- Decatur 48% Protein - 11/17/92 to Date

Soybean Oil
- N.Y. Crude (imported) - 1910 thru 09/29
- Decatur Crude - 10/29 to Date

Steel Scrap
- Chicago - 1929 to Date
- Pittsburg - 1910 to Date

Sugar
- N.Y. Raw-96 Centrifugal - 1980 to Date
- Raw (cif) NY Duty Pd #7 - 1/2/47 to 11/2/77
- #12 Raw New York - 8/20/79 to 12/30/82
- Spot Raw (cif) New York - 1/3/49 to 2/1/61
- No. 8 World Raw New York - 2/2/61 to 12/31/70
- No. 11 World Raw New York - 1/4/71 to 11/2/77
- No. 11 World Raw New York - 8/20/79 to Date
- Midwest Refined-Wholesale Beet - 1975 to Date

Tallow
- Chicago Inedible Prime - 1910 thru 1948
- Chicago Bleachable - 1949 to Date

Tin
- Staights - 1910 to Date

Wheat
- No. 2 Red Chicago - 1901 to 3/26/82
- No. 2 Red Spot St. Louis - 3/29/82 to Date

Wool
- Boston Territory Fine Scoured Staple - 1910 to 1971
- U.S. Mills Territory Fine Scoured Staple - 1972 to Date

Zinc
- East St. Louis Prime Western - 1910 to 1970
- U.S. Basis Prime Western - 1971 to Date

Aluminum

There were a number of developments in the aluminum market over the past year. The Japanese trading house Marubeni Corp. issued a forecast that global production of aluminum would increase sharply in 1996 as a result of the end of an agreement to curtail production by leading producers. The world's six largest aluminum producers, the U.S., European Union, Russia, Australia, Norway and Canada agreed in 1993 to lower production to draw down a large global oversupply. As a result of the agreement, global stocks of aluminum fell by one million tonnes in 1994 and by the same amount in 1995. Worldwide supplies of aluminum could increase by almost 8 percent in 1996.

The European Aluminum Association forecasts that European consumption of aluminum in 1995 would increase by 4 percent from 5.14 million tonnes in 1994. In the first seven months of 1995, European primary aluminum production rose less than 1 percent to 1.84 million tonnes. Primary aluminum consumption was expected to grow much faster in Europe than in North America and Japan. The Association predicted that Russian exports of aluminum in 1995 would total 2.4 million tonnes, unchanged from 1994, with Western Europe exports declining and exports to East Asia and China increasing.

Officials at Australia's Queensland Alumina Ltd. noted that because of a sixfold increase in caustic soda prices, it is much more expensive to produce alumina. Caustic soda is used to change bauxite to alumina.

Coca-Cola (Japan) Ltd. begun importing U.S.-made fruit juices packaged in aluminum cans in 1995. Coca-Cola is now test marketing its juices including orange juice, apple juice and combination fruit juices in Japan. The company intends to import a million cases of juice in 1995 and plans to import 20 million cases annually. Twenty million cases contain nearly 8,000 tonnes of aluminum.

Japanese carmakers are reported to be cutting the use of aluminum and other non-ferrous metals in a bid to reduce costs. Mazda has been substituting steel for aluminum in hood and trunk lids, cutting costs in half.

U.S. primary aluminum production in August 1995 was 286,000 tonnes. For the January-August 1995 period, primary aluminum production was 2.22 million tonnes which was about unchanged from the same period of 1994. Primary aluminum production for all of 1994 was 2.20 million tonnes. Secondary recovery of new aluminum for the first eight months of 1995 was 1.17 million tonnes compared to 968,000 tonnes in the same period of 1994. For all of 1994 production was 1.58 million tonnes.

In January-August 1995, secondary aluminum smelters consumed 902,000 tonnes of aluminum compared to 1.26 million tonnes for all of 1994. Aluminum metal recovery at secondary smelters from new and old aluminum scrap was 749,000 tonnes in the first eight months of 1995 compared to 1.04 million tonnes for all of 1994. Integrated aluminum companies consumed 956,000 tonnes of aluminum in the 1995 period and recovered 848,000 tonnes from scrap. Total consumption in the 1995 period was 2.57 million tonnes with metal recovery from scrap of 2.24 million tonnes.

U.S. imports for the January-July 1995 period of aluminum crude metals and alloys was 1.27 million tonnes. Imports of aluminum plates, sheets, bars and others was 416,000 tonnes while scrap imports were 249,000 tonnes. The major suppliers were Canada and Russia. U.S. January-July 1995 exports of crude metals and alloys were 194,000 tonnes, imports of plates, sheets, bars and others 501,000 tonnes and scrap 276,000 tonnes.

Futures Markets

Aluminum futures and options are listed on the London Metals Exchange (LME).

World Production of Primary Aluminum — In Thousands of Metric Tons

Year	Australia	Austria	Brazil	Canada	China	France	Germany	Italy	Japan	Norway	Russia[3]	Spain	Switzerland	United Kingdom	United States	Venezuela	World Total
1986	882	93	757	1,355	410	322	765	243	140	726	2,300	355	80	276	3,037	418	15,412
1987	1,004	93	843	1,540	615	323	793	233	41	853	2,400	341	73	294	3,343	428	16,514
1988	1,150	95	874	1,534	710	328	753	226	35	864	2,400	323	72	300	3,944	437	17,548
1989	1,244	93	890	1,555	750	335	796	219	35	863	3,300	352	71	297	4,030	540	19,010
1990	1,234	89	931	1,567	850	326	740	232	34	845	3,523	353	72	294	4,048	590	19,299
1991	1,228	80	1,140	1,822	963	286	690	206	32	833	3,251	355	66	294	4,121	601	19,575
1992	1,236	33	1,190	1,972	1,100	418	603	161	19	813	2,700	359	52	244	4,042	561	19,467
1993[1]	1,380	----	1,170	2,308	1,220	426	552	156	18	887	2,820	356	36	239	3,695	570	19,700
1994[2]	1,320	----	1,200	2,250	1,450	400	503	160	17	857	2,670	340	31	230	3,300	580	19,100

[1] Preliminary. [2] Estimate. [3] Formerly part of the U.S.S.R.; data not reported separately until 1992. *Source: U.S. Bureau of Mines*

U.S. Production of Primary Aluminum (Domestic & Foreign Ores) — In Thousands of Metric Tons

Year	Jan.	Feb.	Mar.	Apr.	May	June	July	Aug.	Sept.	Oct.	Nov.	Dec.	Total
1986	273	251	281	275	284	241	231	235	231	243	239	252	3,350
1987	262	238	266	263	275	272	282	286	286	301	301	316	3,349
1988	320	304	330	324	336	323	334	333	327	339	332	344	3,944
1989	346	312	347	334	347	335	346	341	323	328	328	343	4,030
1990	345	311	345	331	342	330	340	341	332	347	337	347	4,048
1991	349	317	352	340	353	343	354	350	336	347	337	343	4,121
1992	344	320	343	330	342	330	339	340	330	343	335	347	4,043
1993	335	292	323	313	325	315	316	302	291	303	287	294	3,696
1994[1]	292	261	286	269	277	268	275	274	267	277	270	280	3,296
1995[1]	281	253	280	272	285	277	288	286	280	289	270	280	3,296

[1] Preliminary. *Source: U.S. Bureau of Mines*

ALUMINUM

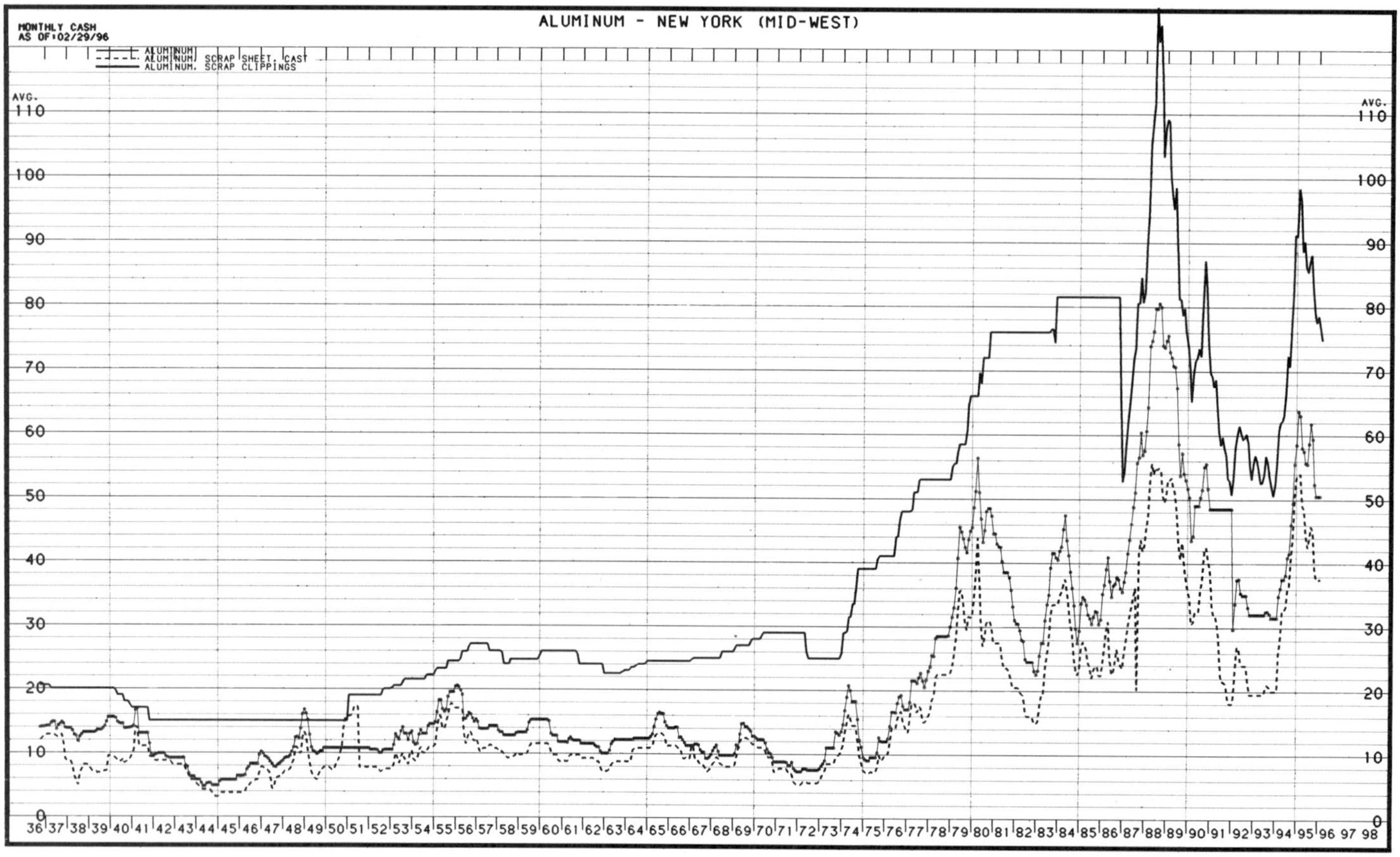

Salient Statistics of Aluminum in the U.S. In Thousands of Metric Tons

Year	Net Import Reliance as a % of Apparent Consumption	Production: Primary	Production: Secondary	Primary Shipments[2]	Recovery from Scrap: Old	Recovery from Scrap: New	Apparent Consumption	Net Shipments[5] by Producers — Wrought Products: Plate Sheet, Foil	Wrought: Rolled Structural Shapes[3]	Wrought: Extruded Shapes[4]	Wrought: All	Castings: Permanent Mold	Castings: Die	Castings: Sand	Castings: All	Total All Net Shipments
1986	26	3,037	1,773	6,545	784	989	5,143	3,397	337	1,335	5,179	155	749	77	1,032	6,211
1987	23	3,343	1,986	6,813	852	1,134	5,469	3,740	346	1,351	5,549	181	685	113	1,012	6,562
1988	7	3,944	2,122	6,851	1,045	1,077	5,373	3,787	343	1,341	5,589	201	700	115	1,055	6,621
1989	E	4,030	2,054	6,751	1,011	1,043	4,957	3,900	339	1,280	5,633	210	740	110	1,096	6,728
1990	E	4,048	2,393	6,592	1,359	1,034	5,264	3,799	301	1,211	5,425	208	620	103	968	6,393
1991	E	4,121	2,286	6,395	1,522	979	5,043	3,787	311	1,096	5,300	168	575	97	864	6,156
1992	1	4,042	2,756	6,809	1,612	1,145	5,725	4,097	303	1,186	5,691	198	595	99	804	6,609
1993[1]	19	3,695	2,944	7,300	1,648	1,310	6,600	4,030	297	1,294	5,770	225	645	103	994	6,770
1994[1]	31	3,299	3,080	8,160	1,500	1,580	6,880	4,740	356	1,440	6,700	NA	NA	NA	NA	NA

[1] Preliminary. [2] To domestic industry. [3] Also rod, bar & wire. [4] Also rod, bar, tube blooms & tubing. [5] Consists of total shipments less shipments to other mills for further fabrication. NA = Not available. E = Net exporter. *Source: U.S. Bureau of Mines*

U.S. Supply and Distribution of Aluminum In Thousands of Metric Tons

Year	Apparent Consumption	Production: Primary	Production: From Old Scrap	Imports	Exports	Inventories December 31: Private	Inventories December 31: Government[3]
1985	5,174	3,500	850	1,420	908	2,343	2
1986	5,143	3,037	784	1,967	753	2,235	2
1987	5,469	3,343	852	1,850	917	2,000	2
1988	5,373	3,944	1,045	1,620	1,247	1,883	2
1989	4,957	4,030	1,011	1,470	1,615	1,822	2
1990	5,264	4,048	1,359	1,514	1,659	1,820	2
1991	5,043	4,121	1,317	1,490	1,762	1,788	3
1992	5,725	4,042	1,612	1,725	1,453	1,875	-----
1993[1]	6,600	3,695	1,632	2,545	1,207	2,148	57
1994[2]	6,880	3,299	1,500	3,380	1,365	2,086	57

[1] Preliminary. [2] Estimate. *Source: U.S. Burea of Mines*

U.S. Aluminum Products Distribution of End-Use Shipments In Thousands of Metric Tons

Year	Building & Construction	Consumer Durables	Containers & Packaging	Electrical	Exports	Machinery & Equipment	Trans-portation	Other	Total
1984	1,300	502	1,828	681	488	377	1,375	279	7,040
1985	1,375	484	1,862	642	546	377	1,383	264	6,928
1986	1,432	540	1,926	626	413	383	1,372	252	6,958
1987	1,441	576	2,052	620	569	401	1,500	223	7,382
1988	1,316	588	2,036	671	787	435	1,536	269	7,638
1989	1,294	544	2,112	663	1,060	436	1,448	264	7,821
1990	1,208	509	2,157	594	1,131	452	1,388	261	7,700
1991	1,052	472	2,210	579	1,357	426	1,414	241	7,752
1992	1,144	523	2,259	587	1,236	448	1,591	256	8,045
1993[1]	1,237	563	2,181	609	1,092	477	1,970	259	8,390
1994[1]	1,400	647	2,280	677	1,200	572	2,310	276	9,360

[1] Prliminary. *Source: U.S. Bureau of Mines*

World Consumption of Primary Aluminum In Thousands of Metric Tons

Year	Aust-ralia	Belgium	Brazil	Canada	China	France	Ger-many	India	Italy	Japan	Rep. of Korea	Russia	Spain	United Kingdom	United States	World Total
1984	265.4	289.4	288.3	336.0	630.0	579.3	1,151.6	310.0	448.0	1,572.0	128.8	2,650.0	191.4	369.5	4,454.0	16,633.0
1985	288.4	267.7	323.1	345.0	720.0	586.1	1,160.9	297.6	470.0	1,694.8	145.6	2,700.0	211.0	350.4	4,282.0	16,919.2
1986	287.0	273.3	439.7	312.9	836.0	592.6	1,186.4	310.0	510.0	1,624.2	196.8	2,700.0	240.0	389.1	4,318.9	17,391.4
1987	318.7	284.7	430.3	423.1	727.0	615.6	1,185.7	326.0	548.0	1,696.8	207.9	2,830.0	25.7	383.6	4,546.2	18,137.5
1988	327.5	302.2	324.2	437.1	658.0	660.6	1,232.6	327.0	581.0	2,123.2	268.0	2,900.0	268.0	427.4	4,601.9	18,877.9
1989	323.9	302.1	420.1	450.2	920.0	685.5	1,289.1	420.0	607.0	2,211.6	287.6	2,700.0	273.4	454.7	4,381.4	19,281.1
1990	287.8	317.8	341.2	387.2	861.0	720.9	1,295.4	433.3	652.0	2,415.2	345.4	2,790.0	288.0	453.7	4,330.4	19,179.7
1991	298.0	323.0	354.2	408.2	938.0	734.2	1,360.9	430.2	670.0	2,431.6	383.3	2,409.0	297.0	412.4	4,137.2	18,717.4
1992	309.5	291.8	377.1	420.4	1,253.8	722.8	1,457.1	414.3	660.0	2,306.6	397.0	1,770.0	309.0	483.3	4,534.1	18,877.5
1993	339.5	270.0	383.7	492.5	1,318.0	665.0	1,159.2	475.3	554.0	2,115.0	557.9	1,185.0	291.9	477.3	4,877.1	18,466.5
1994[1]	369.3	270.0	457.0	123.0	1,318.0	623.7	1,499.3	433.1	447.5	2,320.5	559.9		285.4	576.0	4,908.1	18,818.6

[1] Preliminary. *Source: American Metal Market*

Salient Statistics of Recycling Aluminum in the U.S.

Year	Percent Recycled	New Scrap[1]	Old Scrap[2]	Recycled Metal[3]	Apparent Supply	New Scrap	Old Scrap	Recycled Metal	Apparent Supply
		In Thousands of Metric Tons				Value in Millions of Dollars			
1990	38	1,030	1,360	2,390	6,300	1,690	2,220	3,910	10,300
1991	38	969	1,320	2,290	6,010	1,270	1,730	3,000	7,880
1992	40	1,140	1,610	2,760	6,870	1,450	2,040	3,500	8,710
1993	37	1,310	1,630	2,940	7,920	1,540	1,920	3,460	9,300
1994	36	1,580	1,500	3,080	8,460	2,480	2,360	4,840	13,300

[1] Scrap that results from the manufacturing process. [2] Scrap that results from consumer products. [3] Metal recovered from new plus old scrap.
Source: U.S. Bureau of Mines

Producer Prices for Aluminum Used Beverage Can Scrap In Cents Per Pound

Year	Jan.	Feb.	Mar.	Apr.	May	June	July	Aug.	Sept.	Oct.	Nov.	Dec.	Average
1988	65.80	70.50	72.93	72.50	72.50	72.50	72.50	71.63	66.21	63.92	61.50	64.93	68.95
1989	72.64	73.76	73.15	69.50	71.55	66.59	57.92	55.50	54.68	55.50	54.30	51.50	63.05
1990	48.50	45.50	47.55	50.50	50.77	50.50	49.71	51.13	57.53	52.15	48.00	44.67	49.71
1991	49.00	49.11	48.67	42.09	37.86	37.00	39.79	37.50	37.50	35.76	35.18	34.50	40.33
1992	35.38	38.32	40.73	43.91	44.40	41.50	41.50	41.69	39.93	38.07	38.00	38.68	40.18
1993	41.00	41.00	38.04	36.63	35.00	35.00	37.52	37.59	36.50	34.19	33.60	34.78	36.74
1994	38.45	43.08	42.50	46.60	45.50	48.98	56.40	56.00	56.00	62.64	70.40	71.00	53.13

Source: American Metal Market

ALUMINUM

Average Price of Cast Aluminum Scrap (Crank Cases) in Chicago Area In Cents Per Pound

Year	Jan.	Feb.	Mar.	Apr.	May	June	July	Aug.	Sept.	Oct.	Nov.	Dec.	Average
1988	45.50	47.40	52.67	55.64	53.93	55.00	54.65	54.85	54.69	50.64	49.50	50.50	52.08
1989	53.02	52.97	53.41	51.90	51.14	47.59	42.97	40.63	43.30	40.14	37.75	35.65	45.87
1990	34.68	30.50	30.77	32.50	32.50	32.50	35.93	37.50	41.97	42.50	40.58	39.00	35.91
1991	33.50	32.00	32.00	30.64	28.45	22.40	21.50	21.50	21.13	19.00	18.11	18.00	24.85
1992	18.71	23.00	26.91	27.00	24.45	24.00	24.00	24.00	21.21	19.50	19.50	19.50	22.65
1993	19.50	19.50	19.50	19.50	19.50	19.50	20.79	21.00	20.62	20.00	20.00	20.00	19.95
1994	20.00	25.79	28.33	32.50	32.50	33.18	35.90	36.50	41.07	44.45	50.50	53.50	36.19
1995	53.53	54.08	49.02	48.50	44.41	42.50	43.76	45.80	45.05	39.27	37.50	37.50	45.08

Source: American Metal Market

Aluminum Products (Ingot & Mill Products) Shipments[1] in the U.S. In Million Pounds

Year	Jan.	Feb.	Mar.	Apr.	May	June	July	Aug.	Sept.	Oct.	Nov.	Dec.	Total
1988	1,186	1,199	1,402	1,246	1,331	1,416	1,214	1,357	1,334	1,293	1,322	1,155	15,453
1989	1,266	1,232	1,419	1,246	1,306	1,365	1,205	1,369	1,299	1,278	1,169	1,071	15,405
1990	1,234	1,154	1,313	1,224	1,355	1,318	1,257	1,272	1,224	1,247	1,098	1,120	14,761
1991	1,177	1,087	1,261	1,244	1,313	1,287	1,387	1,389	1,276	1,371	1,265	1,241	15,298
1992	1,324	1,280	1,376	1,298	1,277	1,339	1,330	1,333	1,361	1,453	1,333	1,360	16,081
1993	1,251	1,291	1,486	1,408	1,377	1,440	1,296	1,410	1,382	1,306	1,364	1,284	16,294
1994	1,611	1,640	2,039	1,708	1,918	1,792	1,708	1,960	1,779	1,786	1,893	1,833	21,666
1995	1,651	1,459	1,666	1,565	1,593	1,548	1,344	1,441	1,428	1,536	1,721	1,635	19,729

[1] Mills products & pig & ingot (net shipments). [2] Preliminary. *Source: Bureau of Census, U.S. Department of Commerce*

U.S. Aluminum Inventories, Total (Ingot, Mill Products & Scrap) In Million Pounds

Year	Jan. 1	Feb. 1	Mar. 1	Apr. 1	May 1	June 1	July 1	Aug. 1	Sept. 1	Oct. 1	Nov. 1	Dec. 1
1988	4,175	4,272	4,363	4,343	4,941	4,344	4,215	4,235	4,175	4,175	4,134	4,119
1989	4,151	4,189	4,163	4,160	4,246	4,224	4,289	4,373	4,253	4,158	4,064	3,991
1990	4,016	4,019	4,035	3,914	3,974	3,808	3,916	4,070	3,980	4,040	4,119	4,013
1991	4,013	4,068	4,169	4,256	4,212	4,135	4,044	3,990	4,028	4,008	3,992	3,923
1992	3,913	4,321	4,346	4,375	4,411	4,486	4,482	4,333	4,376	4,418	4,336	4,263
1993	4,131	4,059	4,091	4,146	4,216	4,241	4,294	4,357	4,374	4,345	4,318	4,251
1994[1]	4,093	4,646	4,759	4,778	4,785	4,791	4,725	4,660	4,637	4,606	4,540	4,552
1995[1]	4,573	4,726	4,849	4,664	4,714	4,717	4,585	4,637	4,556	4,436	4,293	4,345

[1] Preliminary. *Source: Bureau of Census, U.S. Department of Commerce*

Aluminum Exports (Metal & Alloys, Crude) from the U.S. In Cents Per Pound

Year	Jan.	Feb.	Mar.	Apr.	May	June	July	Aug.	Sept.	Oct.	Nov.	Dec.	Total
1988	18.4	13.7	19.8	20.9	34.5	43.4	41.6	44.3	39.0	25.7	47.5	51.3	400.1
1989	34.8	41.8	40.2	33.3	34.1	44.6	46.2	52.0	46.1	68.8	72.7	80.0	593.0
1990	79.0	65.1	55.3	61.4	41.4	48.6	41.5	39.0	53.6	59.6	62.2	76.0	679.8
1991	61.1	54.8	46.7	82.8	56.4	71.3	69.0	80.1	54.6	68.0	80.7	67.3	792.8
1992	50.8	43.8	49.7	38.6	33.6	39.8	50.0	50.3	40.4	82.1	50.5	73.5	603.1
1993	54.8	38.6	41.7	26.3	38.6	30.7	33.9	24.5	27.9	31.7	24.1	27.6	400.4
1994[1]	22.1	18.3	28.3	17.9	37.5	30.5	30.6	38.3	40.3	24.8	26.1	24.1	338.8
1995[1]	26.1	32.7	25.4	31.1	31.4	20.7	26.6	39.2	38.9	24.8	26.1	24.1	338.8

[1] Preliminary. *Source: U.S. Bureau of Mines*

Aluminum General Imports (Metal & Alloys, Crude) from the U.S. In Cents Per Pound

Year	Jan.	Feb.	Mar.	Apr.	May	June	July	Aug.	Sept.	Oct.	Nov.	Dec.	Total
1988	101.2	92.0	104.9	89.0	92.1	80.6	79.6	80.0	92.4	81.9	82.0	55.0	1,030.6
1989	99.4	78.6	83.3	92.4	75.5	73.9	71.8	91.9	83.6	65.2	53.9	54.2	923.0
1990	84.4	73.4	85.4	85.1	90.4	94.0	102.6	82.1	76.4	66.8	58.7	60.6	959.6
1991	79.5	79.4	84.3	88.2	85.1	75.9	97.3	89.0	86.6	90.4	81.0	88.0	1,024.7
1992	100.7	93.1	97.1	94.6	96.3	87.8	82.4	103.4	94.3	108.4	100.5	96.8	1,155.4
1993	120.8	123.9	165.8	172.0	152.1	152.6	125.1	162.7	173.5	149.4	182.9	155.6	1,836.4
1994[1]	200.2	157.8	282.0	206.9	251.9	179.3	202.8	198.3	160.0	183.4	240.1	222.2	2,484.8
1995[1]	214.0	168.0	204.0	195.0	184.0	172.0	136.0	134.0	117.0	183.4	240.1	222.2	2,484.8

[1] Preliminary. *Source: U.S. Bureau of Mines*

Antimony

Antimony is primarily a byproduct of mining, smelting and refining of other metals, usually lead and silver-copper ores. It is used in flame retardents, fabrics, plastics and ammunition. Reductions in the use of antimonial lead indicated that demand for antimony is shifting away from metal products and into plastics and pigments. Most antimony is found in Idaho, Nevada, Alaska and Montana.

Domestic consumption of primary antimony increased substantially in 1994 as did secondary production. Imports of and exports of antimony products increased markedly. Primary antimony metal and oxide were produced by six companies, operating six plants, using both foreign and domestic feed material. According to the U.S. Bureau of Mines, two plants were in Texas with one each in Idaho, Montana, Nebraska and New Jersey. Most domestic antimony smelter activity involved upgrading imported antimony oxide to higher purity. Small amounts of antimony were recovered as a byproduct from smelting lead and silver-copper ores, but most primary antimony metal and oxide produced domestically originated from imports. Secondary antimony produced from domestic scrap source materials was derived mostly from recycled lead-acid batteries.

Antimony was mined as a principal product and produced as a byproduct of the smelting of base metal ores in 18 countries. Of these, Bolivia, China, Russia and South Africa account together for more than 90 percent of the total world estimated mine antimony production.

U.S. production of primary smelter antimony in the second quarter of 1995 was 5,980 tonnes, up 12 percent from the first quarter. In 1994 total primary smelter antimony production was 25,000 tonnes. Production of secondary antimony in the second quarter of 1995 was 2,120 tonnes, down 11 percent from the first quarter. For 1994, secondary antimony production was 24,300 tonnes.

U.S. industrial consumption of primary antimony in the second quarter of 1995 was 4,770 tonnes, down 2 percent from the first quarter. In the second quarter, metal antimony consumption was 834 tonnes compared to 806 tonnes in the first quarter. For 1994, antimony metal consumption was 2,550 tonnes. Antimony oxide consumption in the second quarter of 1995 was 3,902 tonnes. For 1994, antimony oxide consumption was 12,100 tonnes.

For the January-May 1995 period U.S. imports of antimony were 16,900 tonnes. Imports of ore and concentrate were 2,870 tonnes while imports of antimony metal were 8,000 tonnes. Imports of antimony oxide were 5,930 tonnes. The major supplier of antimony ore and concentrate was Bolivia, while most antimony metal came from China.

World Mine Production of Antimony (Content of Ore) In Metric Tons

Year	Australia	Bolivia	Canada	China[2]	Czech Republic[3]	Guatemala	Kyrgyzstan[4]	Mexico[5]	Morocco	Peru[6]	Russia[4]	South Africa	Thailand	Turkey	United States	World Total[2]
1992	1,701	6,022	948	45,000	1,000	582	3,000	1,200	197	311	10,000	3,779	269	309	232	76,100
1993[1]	1,700	4,160	673	60,000	250	600	2,500	1,469	180	215	8,000	4,110	620	116	W	86,300
1994[2]	1,700	5,700	750	80,000	5	600	2,500	1,500	180	300	7,000	5,600	500	100	W	108,000

[1] Preliminary. [2] Estimate. [3] Formerly part of Czechoslovakia, data not reported separately until 1993. [4] Formerly part of the USSR; data not reported separately until 1992. [5] Includes antimony content of miscellaneous smelter products. [6] Recoverable W=Withheld proprietary data. *Source: U.S. Bureau of Mines*

Salient Statistics of Antimony in the United States In Metric Tons

Year	Avg. Price ¢ per lb. CIF U.S. Ports	Production[3]: Primary[2] Mine	Production[3]: Primary[2] Smelter	Production[3]: Secondary (Alloys)[2]	Imports[4]: Ore Gross Weight	Imports[4]: Ore Antimony Content	Imports[4]: Oxide (Gross Weight)	Exports (Oxide)	Industry Stocks, December 31[3]: Metallic	Oxide	Sulfide	Residues & Slag	Total[5]
1992	79.0	W	20,100	19,925	3,029	1,923	17,085	4,817	2,450	2,952	20	W	8,741
1993[1]	76.9	W	22,600	20,700	1,720	543	19,322	3,896	2,790	3,320	20	W	9,080
1994[2]	177.7	W	25,500	24,300	7,680	5,640	17,700	6,500	2,770	4,990	W	W	10,900

[1] Preliminary. [2] Estimate. [3] Antimony content. [4] Imports for consumption. [5] Including primary antimony residues & slag. W = Withheld proprietary data. *Source: U.S. Bureau of Mines*

Industrial Consumption of Primary Antimony in the United States In Metric Tons (Antimony Content)

Year	Metal Products: Ammunition	Antimonial Lead	Sheet & Pipe	Bearing Metal & Bearings	Solder	Type Metal	Total All Metal Products	Flame Retardents: Plastics	Flame Retardents: Total	Non-Metal Products: Ceramics & Glass	Rubber Products	Pigments	Plastics	Total	Grand Total
1992	W	1,642	W	36	248	W	3,297	5,113	6,826	928	W	314	717	2,102	12,225
1993	W	1,110	W	44	242	W	2,810	5,440	7,250	848	W	489	786	2,310	12,400
1994[1]	W	1,990	W	36	179	W	3,730	6,710	8,590	980	W	369	1,030	2,490	14,800

[1] Preliminary. [2] Estimated coverage based on 77% of the industry. W=Withheld proprietary data. *Source: U.S. Bureau of Mines*

United States Prices of Antimony[1] In Cents Per Pound

Year	January	February	March	April	May	June	July	August	September	October	November	December	Average
1993	133.00	133.00	133.00	133.00	133.00	133.00	74.00	74.00	74.00	74.00	74.00	73.15	104.00
1994	73.00	73.00	78.04	87.50	111.07	153.75	182.50	235.00	250.00	260.00	288.00	293.00	173.74
1995	293.00		284.00		201.00	142.00	188.00	240.00	244.00	213.00	170.00	170.00	214.50

[1] Prices thru June 1993 are for domestic refined antimony in alloy, content change only. From July 1993, prices are for antimony metal (99.65%) merchants, minimum 18-ton containers, c.i.f. U.S. Ports. *Source: American Metal Market*

Apples

World Production of Apples, Fresh (Dessert & Cooking) In Thousands of Metric Tons

Year	Argentina	Australia	Canada	France	Germany	Hungary	Italy	Japan	Mexico	Netherlands	Slovakia[4]	South Africa	Spain	Turkey	United States	World Total
1981	804	294	422	1,502	884	1,156	1,774	846	280	325	508	486	1,008	1,450	3,517	17,006
1982	817	301	478	1,978	2,637	1,278	2,642	924	394	490	746	519	860	1,600	3,684	21,626
1983	872	267	485	1,575	1,313	1,141	2,057	1,048	302	403	557	513	1,012	1,750	3,800	19,205
1984	922	352	434	2,005	1,799	1,088	2,241	812	486	431	584	557	970	1,900	3,776	20,701
1985	594	288	479	1,793	1,410	954	2,012	910	443	300	368	517	988	1,900	3,590	18,775
1986	1,078	362	388	1,867	2,180	1,253	2,020	986	629	445	637	470	829	1,860	3,565	21,098
1987	925	309	506	1,985	1,077	1,064	2,273	998	615	340	423	526	971	1,680	4,873	20,922
1988-9	1,030	350	501	1,935	2,467	1,131	2,443	1,042	624	383	518	534	845	1,950	4,140	22,662
1989-90	1,050	333	538	1,818	1,727	959	2,162	1,045	545	417	546	557	747	1,850	4,519	21,654
1990-1	950	292	540	1,895	2,222	945	2,102	1,053	520	431	523	542	635	1,900	4,398	21,224
1991-2	1,043	289	513	1,236	1,165	859	1,869	760	550	223	480	605	517	1,900	4,413	18,250
1992-3	947	336	564	2,398	3,228	666	2,394	1,039	580	640	112	633	1,095	2,100	4,798	35,443
1993-4	990	321	484	2,079	1,719	819	2,145	1,011	538	670	112	638	891	2,080	4,847	32,845
1994-5[1]	1,060	337	516	2,166	2,080	610	2,153	989	475	600	57	642	747	2,095	5,142	33,747
1995-6[2]	NA	NA	530	2,057	1,373	500	1,947	970	478	570	70	NA	708	2,100	5,051	33,073

[1] Preliminary. [2] Estimate. [3] Commercial crop. [4] Formerly part of Yugoslavia; data not reported separately until 1992. NA = Not available.
Source: Foreign Agicultural Service, U.S. Department of Agriculture

Salient Statistics of Apples[2] in the United States

Year	Production: Total	Production: Utilized	Growers Prices: Fresh ¢ Lb.	Growers Prices: Processing $ Ton	Utilization: Fresh	Processed[5]: Canned	Processed: Dried	Processed: Frozen	Processed: Juice & Cider	Processed: Other[3]	Avg. Farm Price ¢ Per Lb.	Farm Value Million $	Foreign Trade[4]: Domestic Exports Fresh	Domestic Exports Dried[5]	Imports Fresh & Dried[5]	Fresh Per Capita Consumption Lbs.
	Millions of Pounds												Metric Tons			
1981	7,740	7,693	15.4	102.0	4,442	1,002	190	173	1,798	87	11.1	851.1	269.2	8.3	128.3	16.9
1982	8,122	8,110	13.2	118.0	4,537	1,249	210	191	1,808	116	10.0	809.0	261.8	16.1	98.7	17.5
1983	8,379	8,358	14.8	104.0	4,621	1,204	283	170	1,985	95	10.5	879.0	228.7	12.0	126.0	18.3
1984	8,324	8,309	15.5	112.0	4,655	1,177	289	198	1,889	102	11.2	927.6	205.2	9.3	132.6	18.4
1985	7,915	7,827	17.3	103.0	4,222	1,255	242	194	1,839	74	11.7	914.3	147.1	5.5	152.6	17.3
1986	7,859	7,833	19.1	116.0	4,464	1,179	199	257	1,643	91	13.4	1,046.8	175.1	10.5	149.4	17.8
1987	10,742	10,451	12.7	79.3	5,610	1,306	284	249	2,929	74	8.6	903.1	296.2	7.7	132.7	20.8
1988	9,120	9,070	17.4	123.0	5,230	1,399	285	266	1,824	67	12.7	1,150.0	254.5	12.0	133.0	19.9
1989	9,917	9,871	13.9	107.0	5,822	1,320	282	322	2,068	57	10.4	1,034.4	357.4	23.7	119.7	21.2
1990	9,657	9,618	20.9	144.0	5,515	1,378	270	304	2,077	74	15.1	1,449.0	371.3	55.5	122.0	19.6
1991	9,707	9,637	25.1	171.0	5,447	1,311	299	286	2,194	100	17.9	1,733.1	530.1	44.2	143.9	18.2
1992	10,569	10,463	19.5	130.0	5,767	1,498	324	247	2,472	155	13.6	1,421.8	487.8	22.1	139.3	19.2
1993	10,685	10,574	18.4	107.0	6,124	1,335	366	282	2,382	85	12.9	1,557.4	505.8			19.2
1994[1]	11,336	11,168	18.2	112.0	6,353	1,396	395	304	2,587	133	12.8	1,426.6	719.6			19.6

[1] Preliminary. [2] Commercial crop. [3] Mostly crushed for vinegar, jam, etc. [4] Year beginning July. [5] Fresh weight basis. *Source: Economic Research Service, U.S. Department of Agriculture*

U.S. Prices of Apples Received by Growers (for Fresh Use) In Cents Per Pound

Year	Jan.	Feb.	Mar.	Apr.	May	June	July	Aug.	Sept.	Oct.	Nov.	Dec.	Average
1981	10.7	12.4	12.1	11.3	10.7	10.5	12.7	14.6	16.0	16.0	16.1	15.7	13.2
1982	14.1	15.7	16.0	14.5	16.2	17.7	15.3	12.8	16.3	14.5	13.9	13.0	15.0
1983	11.0	12.2	12.0	11.3	11.9	11.1	12.0	16.0	15.9	14.9	14.6	14.0	13.1
1984	14.3	15.1	15.2	14.8	15.0	14.6	14.9	16.5	18.5	17.4	16.4	15.6	15.7
1985	14.0	14.3	15.7	15.1	14.1	13.1	12.6	12.1	16.4	15.4	16.4	16.6	14.7
1986	16.6	17.2	17.2	17.2	20.7	21.0	28.5	27.6	20.9	18.0	17.3	16.5	19.9
1987	18.3	19.0	18.0	19.1	22.4	24.6	25.5	15.2	14.8	12.1	11.3	10.4	17.6
1988	11.1	12.9	12.5	11.0	10.9	10.4	22.8	27.7	23.7	18.5	17.5	17.4	16.4
1989	18.1	17.9	16.5	14.4	13.5	10.8	11.5	15.9	16.7	14.3	13.3	12.1	14.6
1990	12.2	12.4	12.3	12.0	12.6	13.7	20.3	22.3	22.2	19.3	19.6	20.9	16.7
1991	20.1	20.5	20.3	20.2	22.5	23.2	24.6	23.2	26.4	23.8	25.1	25.7	23.0
1992	24.6	24.8	24.3	24.1	25.0	25.2	28.6	33.3	27.1	21.2	19.4	19.9	19.5
1993	18.3	16.7	14.5	14.3	14.9	16.1	17.8	24.4	24.1	21.1	19.3	18.6	18.2
1994[1]	18.7	17.8	16.6	15.5	14.3	13.5	19.4	29.0	20.8	19.2	16.4	19.2	17.4
1995[1]	19.5	18.3	18.2	16.6	15.5	15.6	16.8	23.7	27.1	26.1	25.1	25.9	20.7

[1] Preliminary. *Source: Economic Research Service, U.S. Department of Agriculture*

Arsenic

Arsenic is a by-product of copper, lead, gold and zinc mining. With substantial quantities of these metals worldwide, availability of arsenic is ample. Arsenic is employed in a variety of products including laser materials and as a doping agent in the manufacturing of various solid state devices. Arsenic trioxide is imported and converted to arsenic acid for use in producing wood preservative. In addition to chromated copper arsenate being the most common arsenic-based wood preservative, ammoniacal copper arsenate and fluor chrome arsenate phenol are also used.

According to the U.S. Bureau of Mines, agricultural uses for arsenic were as herbicides for weed control; arsenic acid is used in the mechanical harvesting of cotton and in glass-making. Arsenilic acid is an arsenical drug used for growth, pigmentation and disease control. Commercial grade arsenic metal, 99 percent pure, is used in lead and copper-based alloys to increase strength in the posts and grids of lead-acid storage batteries, and to increase corrosion resistance in copper alloys. Very high purity arsenic metal is utilized in the manufacturing of crystalline gallium arsenide. This semiconduction material, which is faster but more costly than silicon products, is used in optoelectronic circuitry and high-speed computers.

According to the U.S. Bureau of Mines, the United States was the world's largest consumer of arsenic in 1994, accounting for about one-half of world demand. Domestic demand for arsenic was about unchanged in 1994. There was a decline in use for agricultural products but that was offset by increased use in wood preservatives and nonferrous alloys. All domestic arsenic requirements were met by imports, the last production of arsenic in the U.S. was in 1985. On a contained metal basis, arsenic trioxide accounted for 94 percent of imports.

U.S. imports of arsenic metal in 1994 were 1,330 tonnes, up sharply from the 1993 import total of 767 tonnes. Imports of arsenic compounds in 1994 were 20,300 tonnes, down three percent from the 1993 total of 20,900 tonnes. The total supply of arsenic in 1994 was therefore 21,600 tonnes.

Of the U.S. imports of arsenic metal in 1994, China was by far the largest supplier with 1,150 tonnes of the total of 1,330 tonnes. Imports of arsenic trioxide in 1994 were 26,800 tonnes, down from 27,500 tonnes in 1993. The value of these imports was $15.2 million. China supplied 15,300 tonnes, Mexico 3,440 tonnes, France 2,460 tonnes and Chile 3,720 tonnes. There were very minor imports of arsenic acid from Canada.

U.S. use of arsenic in 1994 was 21,500 tonnes. As estimated by the Bureau of Mines, agricultural chemicals took about six percent, glass manufacturing three percent, wood preservatives 84 percent, nonferrous alloys and electronics six percent, and other uses one percent. There were arsenic metal exports in 1994 of 79,000 tonnes.

World production of arsenic trioxide in 1994 was estimated at 43,000 tonnes, up close to four percent from 1993. The major producer was China with 13,000 tonnes, Chile 6,300 tonnes, France 6,000 tonnes, Mexico 4,400 tonnes, Namibia 2,300 tonnes, Philippines 2,000 tonnes, Belgium tonnes and Russia 1,500 tonnes.

Due to its toxicity there have been restrictions on the use of arsenic compounds. New Jersey has restricted the use of wood preservatives containing arsenic for use in marine applications as it is felt it could leach and be absorbed by invertebrate marine life.

World Production of White Arsenic (Arsenic Trioxide) In Metric Tons

Year	Belgium	Bolivia	Canada[4]	Chile	China	France	Germany	Japan	Mexico	Namibia[3]	Peru	Phillippines	Russia[5]	Sweden	World Total
1985	3,000	361	3,000	4,000	-------	8,000	360	500	4,782	2,471	1,257	5,000	8,100	10,000	53,235
1986	3,000	241	3,000	4,000	-------	10,000	360	500	5,315	2,208	1,273	5,000	8,100	10,000	53,173
1987	3,500	132	3,000	3,616	-------	10,000	360	500	5,304	1,864	1,757	5,000	8,100	10,000	52,351
1988	3,500	191	2,825	3,207	7,000	10,000	360	500	5,164	2,983	828	5,046	8,100	10,000	60,335
1989	3,500	338	1,825	5,000	7,000	10,000	360	500	5,551	2,399	563	4,652	8,100	10,000	61,026
1990	3,000	300	485	5,830	9,000	6,480	360	500	4,810	1,640	500	5,090	7,800	7,000	53,400
1991	2,500	463	236	6,820	10,000	2,000	300	500	4,920	1,800	661	5,000	7,000	2,500	46,000
1992	2,000	633	250	6,020	14,000	2,000	300	500	4,290	2,460	607	5,000	2,500	1,000	45,200
1993[1]	2,000	663	250	6,200	13,000	3,000	300	500	4,450	2,290	610	2,000	2,000	500	41,400
1994[2]	2,000	670	250	6,300	13,000	6,000	300	500	4,400	2,300	610	2,000	1,500		43,000

[1] Preliminary. [2] Estimate. [3] Output of Tsumeb Corp. Ltd. only. [4] Includes low-grade dusts that were exported to the U.S. for further refining. [5] Formerly part of the U.S.S.R.; reported seperately until 1992.

	Supply				Distribution		Estimated Demand Pattern						Average Price			
	Imports															
Year	Metal	Compounds	Industry Stocks Jan. 1	Total	Apparent Demand	Industry Stocks Dec. 31	Agricultural Chemicals	Glass	Wood Preservatives	Non-Ferrous Alloys & Electric	Other	Total	Trioxide Mexican (¢ Per Pound)	Metal Chinese (¢ Per Pound)	Imports Trioxide[3]	Exports
1989	928	21,498	100	22,526	22,300	100	4,900	900	15,600	700	200	22,300	27	47	28,348	126
1990	796	19,897	100	20,793	20,544	100	4,200	800	14,400	800	300	20,500	23	180	26,256	149
1991	1,008	20,741	100	21,849	21,615	-----	5,000	900	14,300	1,000	400	21,600	25	68	27,142	233
1992	740	23,256	-----	23,996	23,902	-----	3,900	900	17,900	800	400	23,900	29	56	30,671	94
1993[1]	767	20,900	-----	21,667	21,300	-----	3,000	900	16,200	800	400	21,300	33	44	27,500	364
1994[2]	1,330	20,300	-----	21,630	21,500	-----	1,200	700	18,000	1,300	300	21,500	32	40	26,800	79

Barley

Barley is the third largest produced feed grain in the U.S. Canada is the largest producer with a 1995/96 crop of 13 million tonnes. World production fell in 1995/96 to 160 million tonnes from the 165 million tonnes averaged during the first-half of the 1990s. Disappearance, however, also slipped to 165 million tonnes, nearly 5 million tonnes more than new supply, necessitating a drawdown on world stocks to about 20.4 million tonnes from the 1994/95 year-end 24.8 million tonnes. During the early-1990s, annual world supply/usage were about equal and carryover stocks averaged 32 million tonnes. Thus, a statistical imbalance exists for 1995/96 as evidenced by the 50 percent gain in Canadian futures prices during the second-half of calendar 1995.

In the U.S., the barley crop year begins June 1. Production has declined sharply since the mid-1980s when crops near 600 million bushels were realized. Production in 1995/96 of a record low 361 million bushels trailed initial forecasts owing largely to a decline in North Dakota's crop. Production in 1994/95 totaled 375 million bushels. Acreage planted to barley continues to slide, notably in the Northern plains states where returns to barley have generally been less favorable to producers than wheat and sunflower. North Dakota is usually the largest producing state.

The smaller barley crop and higher prices will dampen disappearance in 1995/96 to about 455 million bushels versus 470 million bushels in 1994/95. Barley's feed and residual use was estimated at 230 million bushels. Industrial use, mostly for beer and alcohol, should hold steady at 175 million bushels while exports fall to 50 million bushels, down 20 million bushels from 1994/95. Imports of about 70 million bushels, mostly of malting quality barley from Canada, will offset some of the reduced U.S. supply. Imports have risen sharply since the late-1980s when they averaged about 12 million bushels per season. If the 1995/96 forecasts prove correct, carryover stocks on May 31, 1996 of 104 million bushels will compare with the year earlier total of 109 million bushels.

World barley trade was forecast at about 17 millions tonnes in 1995/96 versus 15 million tonnes in 1994/95. The European Union exports more than one-third of the total with Canada and Australia much of the balance. Major importing countries are Saudi Arabia, China and Japan.

Farmers' barley prices were forecast to average between $2.20-2.60 per bushel in 1995/96, up sharply from the previous season's $2.01 per bushel.

U.S. Farm Program

For the 1995/96 marketing year, the national average loan rate has not been announced and the target price remained at $2.36 per bushel.

Futures Market

Barley futures and options are traded on the Winnipeg Commodity Exchange (WCE) and the London Commodity Exchange (LCE). Futures are traded on the Budapest Commodity Exchange.

World Barley Supply and Demand In Thousands of Metric Tons

	Exports						Imports			Utilization				Ending Stocks		
Crop Year	Australia	Canada	EC-12	Total Non-U.S.	U.S.	Total Exports	Saudi Arabia	Unaccounted	Total Imports	Production	Russia[3]	U.S.	Total Utilization	Canada	U.S.	Total Stocks
1986-7	2.2	6.0	6.2	15.6	3.0	18.6	9.0	NA	18.6	182.4	56.6	10.3	178.1	26.7	7.3	34.0
1987-8	1.6	3.5	7.0	13.1	2.9	16.0	4.8	NA	16.0	181.3	60.9	9.3	183.1	25.2	7.0	32.2
1988-9[4]	1,364	3,419	8,349	14,137	1,718	15,855	4,714	-12	15,855	162,722	44,245	7,540	162,536	2,800	4,276	30,674
1989-90	2,447	3,773	7,905	15,905	1,798	17,703	4,146	467	17,703	164,761	22,433	8,030	167,440	2,056	3,501	28,789
1990-1	2,683	4,460	7,053	17,016	1,507	18,523	4,342	742	18,523	178,056	29,156	8,283	174,898	2,646	2,948	32,317
1991-2	1,951	3,379	9,459	16,929	2,090	19,019	6,873	77	19,019	169,136	25,635	8,735	165,833	2,615	2,800	32,471
1992-3	2,600	2,859	5,816	15,084	1,611	16,695	3,917	769	16,695	165,680	28,368	7,916	166,092	3,271	3,292	31,809
1993-4	4,275	3,789	6,680	17,027	1,553	18,580	4,595	425	18,580	169,910	26,769	9,053	170,006	3,376	3,023	31,713
1994-5[1]	1,200	2,650	5,800	13,235	1,355	14,590	3,500	277	14,590	161,116	24,777	8,726	166,801	1,890	2,451	26,028
1995-6[2]	2,600	2,700	5,000	12,035	1,100	13,305	3,250	445	13,305	148,760	21,327	8,382	157,689	1,900	1,828	17,099

[1] Preliminary. [2] Estimate. [3] Formerly part of the U.S.S.R.; data not reported separately until 1989-90. [4] Prior to 1988-89, reported in millions of metric tons. NA = Not available. *Source: Foreign Agricultural Service, U.S. Department of Agriculture*

World Production of Barley In Thousands of Metric Tons

Year	Australia	Canada	China	Denmark	France	Germany	India	Japan	Kazakhstan[3]	Morocco	Saudi Arabia	Spain	Turkey	United Kingdom	United States	World Total
1986-7	3,611	14,634	5,632	5,134	9,950	9,377	1,962	344	53,900	3,563	12	7,431	6,300	10,015	13,293	182,428
1987-8	3,477	13,957	6,041	4,292	10,528	8,571	1,669	353	58,409	1,543	80	9,282	6,000	9,225	11,354	181,511
1988-9	3,306	10,212	6,041	5,419	9,800	9,587	1,577	399	44,500	3,454	200	12,070	6,000	8,775	6,314	167,302
1989-90	4,044	11,666	6,180	4,982	9,840	9,716	1,721	371	48,500	2,999	331	9,100	4,900	8,025	8,784	169,680
1990-1	4,184	13,441	3,930	4,990	10,150	13,990	1,490	346	8,500	2,138	372	9,410	6,600	7,900	9,192	178,056
1991-2	4,606	11,617	3,928	5,041	10,789	14,494	1,640	268	3,085	3,253	394	9,140	6,800	7,700	10,110	169,136
1992-3	5,460	10,919	4,000	2,974	10,580	12,196	1,700	286	8,511	1,081	406	6,105	6,500	7,350	9,908	165,680
1993-4	6,956	12,972	4,200	3,370	8,980	11,000	1,510	271	7,148	1,019	1,100	9,520	7,300	6,040	8,666	169,910
1994-5[1]	2,791	11,690	3,800	3,460	7,680	10,900	1,600	210	5,100	3,720	1,800	7,600	6,800	5,950	8,162	161,116
1995-6[2]	5,600	13,035	4,000	4,200	7,800	11,930	1,600	200	2,800	600	1,200	5,000	7,200	6,850	7,868	148,760

[1] Preliminary. [2] Estimate. [3] Formerly part of the U.S.S.R.; data not reported separately until 1990-91. *Source: Foreign Agricultural Service, U.S. Department of Agriculture*

U.S. Barley Acreage and Prices

Year Beginning-June 1	Acreage (1,000 Acres): Planted	Acreage (1,000 Acres): Harvested for Grain	Yield Per Harvested Acre (Bushels)	Received by Farmers[3]	Seasonal Prices: Minneapolis[4] or Better: Feed (No. 2)	Seasonal Prices: Minneapolis[4] or Better: Malting (No. 3)	Seasonal Prices: Portland No. 2 Western	Government Price Support Operations: National Average Loan Rate	Government Price Support Operations: Target Price	Government Price Support Operations: Put Under Support (Mil. Bu.)	Government Price Support Operations: % of Production
				Dollars per Bushel							
1988-9	9,831	7,636	38.0	2.80	2.32	4.11	2.74	1.44	2.51	21.9	7.6
1989-90	3,125	8,313	48.6	2.42	2.20	3.28	2.61	1.34	2.43	24.0	5.9
1990-1	8,221	7,529	56.1	2.14	2.13	2.42	2.65	1.28	2.36	33.8	8.0
1991-2	8,941	8,413	55.2	2.10	2.17	2.38	2.66	1.32	2.36	38.0	8.2
1992-3	7,762	7,285	62.5	2.04	2.11	2.37	2.57	1.40	2.36	42.9	9.4
1993-4	7,786	6,753	58.9	1.99	2.05	2.48	2.40	1.40	2.36	37.7	9.5
1994-5[1]	7,159	6,667	56.2	2.03	2.02	2.75	2.51	1.54	2.36	28.2	7.5
1995-6[2]	6,689	6,277	57.6	2.60-2.90	2.36	3.59	2.97	1.54	2.36	14.9	4.1

[1] Preliminary. [2] Estimate. [3] Excludes support payments. [4] Duluth beginning March 1987. [5] Available for total feed grains only.
Source: Economic Research Service, U.S. Department of Agriculture

Salient Statistics of Barley in the United States In Millions of Bushels

Year Beginning-June 1	Supply: Beginning Stocks	Supply: Production	Supply: Imports	Supply: Total Supply	Disappearance: Domestic Use: Food & Alcohol Beverages	Disappearance: Domestic Use: Seed	Disappearance: Domestic Use: Feed & Residual	Disappearance: Domestic Use: Total	Disappearance: Exports	Disappearance: Total Disappearance	Ending Stocks: Gov't Owned	Ending Stocks: Privately Owned[3]	Ending Stocks: Total Stocks
1988-9	321.1	290.0	10.5	621.6	160.4	15.0	170.9	346.3	78.9	425.2	30.4	166.0	196.4
1989-90	196.4	404.2	13.1	613.7	162.0	13.5	193.3	368.8	84.0	452.9	19.3	141.5	160.8
1990-1	160.8	422.2	13.5	596.5	161.1	14.6	204.8	380.5	80.6	461.1	8.4	127.0	135.4
1991-2	135.4	464.3	24.5	624.2	163.3	12.9	224.9	401.1	94.5	495.6	6.5	122.1	128.6
1992-3	128.6	455.1	11.4	595.1	158.4	13.1	192.1	363.6	80.3	443.9	5.4	145.8	151.2
1993-4	151.2	398.0	71.5	620.7	162.9	11.8	241.1	415.8	66.1	481.8	5.2	133.7	138.9
1994-5[1]	138.9	374.9	65.9	579.6	163.8	11.2	225.8	400.8	66.2	467.0	5.8	107.6	112.6
1995-6[2]	112.6	361.4	55.0	528.9	163.2	11.8	215.0	390.0	50.0	440.0	5.0	83.9	88.9

[1] Preliminary. [2] Estimate. [3] Uncommitted inventory. [4] Includes quantity under loan & farmer-owned reserves. *Source: Economic Research Service, U.S. Department of Agriculture*

BARLEY

Average Cash Prices of No. 2 (or Better) Feed Barley, in Duluth In Cents Per Bushel

Year	June	July	Aug.	Sept.	Oct.	Nov.	Dec.	Jan.	Feb.	Mar.	Apr.	May	Average
1986-7[2]	123	116	113	127	150	163	123	NQ	NQ	164	176	186	144
1987-8	173	159	160	176	178	182	174	172	177	188	194	198	178
1988-9	241	238	208	224	232	227	214	224	233	249	252	241	232
1989-90	212	211	217	213	216	215	223	228	220	227	227	233	220
1990-1	239	217	199	201	211	216	207	209	215	214	212	213	213
1991-2	202	189	192	208	218	223	218	220	228	230	235	238	217
1992-3	230	215	203	212	211	208	206	206	208	210	212	205	211
1993-4	199	196	189	189	201	216	214	215	216	207	208	211	205
1994-5	205	202	199	204	195	204	200	202	206	202	197	211	202
1995-6[1]	222	225	209	206	258	298	200	202					

[1] Preliminary. [2] Prior to March 1987, prices are at Minneapolis. NQ = No quote. *Source: Economic Research Service, U.S. Department of Agriculture*

Average Prices Received by Farmers for All Barley in the U.S. In Cents Per Bushel

Year	June	July	Aug.	Sept.	Oct.	Nov.	Dec.	Jan.	Feb.	Mar.	Apr.	May	Average
1990-1	229	216	213	213	204	216	213	214	213	215	210	205	214
1991-2	190	173	206	206	210	220	224	221	215	212	214	222	210
1992-3	209	226	216	184	192	205	195	207	200	200	209	197	204
1993-4	195	190	202	187	182	201	202	215	207	201	202	206	199
1994-5	191	192	207	193	193	209	199	205	213	213	215	220	203
1995-6[1]	225	243	263	257	282	309	315	323					

[1] Preliminary. *Source: National Agricultural Statistics Service, U.S. Department of Agriculture*

Average Open Interest of Western Feed Barley Futures at Winnipeg In Contracts -- 20 Tonnes

Year	Jan.	Feb.	Mar.	Apr.	May	June	July	Aug.	Sept.	Oct.	Nov.	Dec.
1991		869	997	1,242	1,156	1,027	1,234	1,158	1,371	1,514	919	1,065
1992	940	662	1,060	1,572	2,025	2,692	3,168	2,605	2,994	2,746	1,519	1,685
1993	1,471	1,000	1,369	2,318	2,818	3,500	2,287	2,016	2,580	3,643	4,743	5,946
1994	7,600	8,164	7,650	8,212	8,153	9,019	8,511	8,558	9,633	12,340	10,802	9,457
1995	8,900	9,295	9,965	8,657	7,279	8,731	9,297	9,770	10,704	12,043	10,324	12,089

Source: Winnipeg Commodity Exchange

Bauxite

Bauxite is the only raw material used in the production of alumina on a commercial scale in the U.S. However, production data for bauxite in the U.S. is withheld for proprietary reasons by the U.S. Bureau of Mines. U.S. bauxite production approximately doubled in 1994. It still amounted to just less than 1 percent of total world production and was used exclusively for nonmetal products such as abrasives, chemicals and refractories. The only active bauxite mines remaining in the U.S. are the surface operations in Alabama and Georgia that produce bauxitic materials, a natural mixture of bauxite clay and bauxite with a very low iron oxide content, used primarily for the production of alumina calcines. Demand for these domestic ores declined slightly in 1994.

U.S. consumption of bauxite in 1994 dropped by about 2 percent below 1993 levels, according to the U.S. Bureau of Mines. This downturn in domestic consumption was felt across all industrial sectors. Demand for alumina remained sluggish throughout the year, mainly in response to reduced primary aluminum smelter operating levels. U.S. production of smelter-grade alumina in 1994 decreased by 10 percent and shipments from domestic production facilities declined by a similar amount. This decrease in U.S. production and shipments of alumina, in combination with a decline in imports for consumption of alumina into the U.S., resulted in an approximate 1.2 million tonnes drop in domestic alumina supply compared to 1993.

Identified world bauxite resources (reserves plus subeconomic and undiscovered deposits) at year-end 1994 were estimated by the U.S. Geological survey to be 55-75 billion tonnes located in South America (33 percent), Africa (27 percent), Asia (17 percent) and Oceania (13 percent).

U.S. production of bauxite in the second-quarter of 1995 was 12 percent higher than in the first-quarter, but 6 percent below the second-quarter of 1994. U.S. imports of crude and dried bauxite during January-May 1995 were 3.99 million tonnes, decreasing 10 percent from the same period in 1994. Principal sources of these imports were Jamaica (39 percent), Guinea (37 percent), Brazil (16 percent) and Guyana (6 percent). Crude and dried bauxite exports in the period were 42,000 tonnes with most going to Canada. Calcine bauxite imports in the period were 173,000 tonnes, up 80 percent from a year earlier. Exports of calcined bauxite were 10,000 tonnes, up 43 percent. Alumina imports were 1.66 million tonnes in the period, up 22 percent. Most was from Australia. Alumina exports were 279,000 tonnes, down 38 percent with destinations primarily being Canada and Brazil.

World Production of Bauxite   In Thousands of Metric Tons

Year	Australia	Brazil	China	Ghana	Greece	Guinea	Guyana[2]	Hungary	India	Indonesia	Jamaica[3]	Russia[3,4]	Sierra Leone	Suriname	United States[3]	World Total
1984	31,537	6,433	2,500	49	2,296	14,738	2,485	2,994	2,078	1,003	8,735	6,200	1,041	3,375	856	92,502
1985	31,839	5,846	2,800	170	2,435	13,956	2,206	2,815	2,341	830	6,239	6,400	1,185	3,738	674	89,747
1986	32,384	6,446	2,900	204	2,231	14,835	2,600	3,022	2,322	650	6,964	6,275	1,242	3,731	510	92,534
1987	34,102	6,567	3,200	196	2,467	16,282	2,785	3,101	2,816	635	7,660	5,700	1,391	2,581	576	96,517
1988	36,192	8,083	2,300	285	2,433	15,624	1,339	2,593	3,961	513	7,305	5,500	1,403	3,434	588	103,105
1989	38,584	8,665	2,388	347	2,550	15,792	1,321	2,644	4,471	862	9,601	5,500	1,548	3,530	670	103,722
1990	41,391	9,678	2,400	381	2,496	15,772	1,424	2,559	4,852	1,206	10,921	5,500	1,430	3,283	495	113,000
1991	40,503	10,414	2,600	353	2,133	15,466	2,204	2,037	4,735	1,406	11,552	5,000	1,288	3,198	50	111,000
1992	39,746	9,366	2,700	338	2,042	13,773	2,376	1,721	4,898	804	11,302	4,580	1,246	3,250	50	105,000
1993[1]	41,300	9,410	3,500	424	1,700	14,100	2,126	1,560	5,223	1,320	11,400	4,260	1,170	3,400	40	108,000
1994[2]	41,700	8,120	3,700	426	1,600	14,400	2,100	900	5,400	1,300	11,700	3,000	735	3,440	40	107,000

[1] Preliminary. [2] Estimate. [3] Dry Bauxite equivalent of ore processed. [4] Formerly part of the U.S.S.R.; data not reported separetely until 1992.
Source: U.S. Bureau of Mines

U.S. Salient Statistics of Bauxite   In Thousands of Metric Tons

Year	Net Import Reliance as a % of Apparent Consumption	Average Price FOB Mine $ per Ton	Mine Production: Crude	Mine Production: Dried Equivalent	Consumption by Industry: Total	Alumina	Abrasive	Chemical	Refractory	Dry Equivalent: Imports[3] (for Consumption)	Dry Equivalent: Exports[3]	Dry Equivalent: Consumption	Stocks, December 31: Producers & Consumers	Government	Total
1983	96	13-20	826	679	9,100	8,275	135	281	362	7,601	104	9,100	5,613	16,326	21,939
1984	96	13-20	1,054	856	10,519	9,465	328	251	420	9,435	110	10,519	4,881	17,338	22,219
1985	96	13-20	787	674	8,206	7,219	305	219	408	7,158	69	8,206	3,643	18,357	22,000
1986	96	13-17	617	510	6,901	5,980	259	231	372	6,456	85	6,901	3,319	18,472	21,791
1987	96	13-17	689	576	9,548	8,601	224	243	422	9,156	231	9,548	3,019	18,472	21,491
1988	97	13-17	714	588	10,074	8,970	274	236	524	9,944	71	10,074	3,021	18,474	21,495
1989	96	15-20	W	670	11,810	10,782	275	223	407	10,893	44	11,810	2,891	18,474	21,365
1990	98	15-20	W	495	12,042	11,064	276	212	387	12,144	74	12,042	2,318	18,477	20,795
1991	100	15-18	W	50	12,204	11,383	204	218	328	11,871	51	12,204	2,620	18,477	21,097
1992	100	15-18	W	50	11,873	11,066	223	190	334	10,939	63	11,873	2,319	17,805	20,124
1993[1]	100	15-24	W	45	11,917	11,002	203	225	429	11,621	90	11,917	1,590	16,938	18,500
1994[2]	99	15-18	W	W	11,700	10,900	197	192	384	10,700	129	11,700	1,580	17,600	19,200

[1] Preliminary. [2] Estimate. [3] Including concentrates. W = Withheld proprietary data. *Source: U.S. Bureau of Mines*

Bismuth

Bismuth finds a wide variety of uses ranging from glass ceramics to pharmaceutical compounds to chemical and pigments. Bismuth is used for treating stomach ulcers and is found in household pharmaceuticals like Pepto Bismol. In recent years, bismuth has been of interest as a non-toxic substitute for lead in many metallurgical and chemical applications. Bismuth is being tested as an additive to brass for plumbing fixtures, and there has been research into using it for shotgun pellets for hunting water fowl. A study completed indicates that combinations of bismuth and selenium have good potential for replacing lead in certain brasses for many plumbing component applications.

The U.S. Fish and Wildlife Service approved the use of 97 percent bismuth, 3 percent tin shot for waterfowl hunting during the 1994-95 hunting season. The "conditional approval" was granted on the basis of initial testing which found that the shot was not toxic when ingested by waterfowl. The bismuth-tin shot is the first alternative to steel shot, which replaced lead for waterfowl hunting over the last few years. The approval may be extended, based on longer term toxicity tests. Because of the limited supply of bismuth, neither of these applications is likely to find extensive usage. The U.S. Bureau of Mines has estimated that world production of bismuth would have to double to meet the substitution for lead in plumbing fixtures.

Two companies have begun producing lead-free ceramic glazes containing bismuth for use on china and tableware. Glazes and enamel were also in use for decorative glass coatings for automobiles and buildings. The bismuth glazes were shown to have the same durability as those with lead, while the manufacturing waste would not have to be treated as hazardous.

Domestic consumption of bismuth increased moderately in 1994. The domestic use pattern was similar to that for 1993 but with increases in all three major categories: chemicals, fusible alloys and metallurgical additives. Chemical uses account for more than 50 percent of consumption. The best known chemical use is that of bismuth subsalicylate, the active ingredient in over-the-counter stomach remedies. Other bismuth pharmaceuticals are used to treat burns, stomach ulcers, intestinal disorders and in veterinary applications. Additional bismuth applications include use in fire assaying, ceramic glazes, pearlescent pigments in cosmetics and paints, varistors and superconductors.

Bismuth metal use is categorized by fusible alloys, metallurgical additives and other uses. Low melting point alloys are combinations of bismuth and other metals such as cadmium, lead and tin. Applications include holding parts or lenses for machining or grinding, solders, fire sprinklers triggering mechanisms and fuel tank safety plugs. Bismuth is added to aluminum, copper and steel to improve machinability.

According to the U.S. Bureau of Mines, the outlook for bismuth remains optimistic especially in the area of non-toxic replacements for lead. Still, demand has decreased in recent years. Since bismuth is a byproduct of lead, a rapid increase in supply is not likely.

U.S. bismuth consumption in the second quarter of 1995 was 410,000 kilograms. For the first half of 1995 it was 744,000 kilograms while for all of 1994 it was 1.47 million kilograms. Chemicals used 53 percent, fusible alloys 28 percent, metallurgical additives 17 percent while others were the remainder.

Major trade sources of bismuth (in all forms) for the U.S. included Belgium, Canada, China, Peru and the United Kingdom.

World Production of Bismuth In Metric Tons

	Mine Output, Metal Content								Refined Metal							
Year	Australia	Canada	China	Japan	Rep. of Korea	Mexico	Peru	Total	Belgium	China	Kazakhastan[3]	Japan	Mexico	Peru	U.K.	Total
1988	400	181	750	160	132	958	363	3,220	795	750	85	524	622	341	300	3,669
1989	500	205	850	150	96	883	687	3,750	800	850	85	502	597	646	200	3,970
1990	400	87	1,060	133	79	733	555	3,440	1,000	1,060	80	442	549	521	125	4,190
1991	400	65	1,040	138	42	651	610	3,230	800	1,260	70	461	500	576	100	4,010
1992	300	224	820	159	9	807	550	2,740	800	1,060	45	530	550	418	100	3,670
1993[1]	----	144	740	149	5	908	1,000	3,090	950	1,050	40	497	650	937	----	4,240
1994[2]	----	131	700	150	----	900	1,000	3,020	900	1,000	35	500	650	900	----	4,100

[1] Preliminary. [2] Estimate. [3] Formerly part of the U.S.S.R.; data not reported separately until 1992. *Source: U.S. Bureau of Mines*

U.S. Salient Statistics of Bismuth In Metric Tons

	Bismuth Consumed, By Uses							Imports of Metallic Bismuth from				
Year	Metallurgical Additives	Other Alloys & Uses	Fusible Alloys	Chemicals[3]	Total Consumption	Consumer Stocks Dec. 31	Exports of Metal & Alloys	Belgium	Mexico	Peru	Total	Dealer Price $ Per Pound
1985	303	19	277	601	1,199	230	122	209.0	307.6	78.6	907	5.18
1986	350	21	290	663	1,324	346	42	384.4	362.9	107.0	1,129	3.25
1987	494	22	334	748	1,597	294	38	435.0	391.3	440.4	1,581	3.65
1988	493	27	332	679	1,531	433	147	340.2	448.5	188.9	1,641	5.78
1989	396	25	272	659	1,352	440	122	835.7	390.8	271.4	1,880	5.76
1990	424	24	249	577	1,274	331	122	668.1	404.8	262.7	1,612	3.56
1991	341	26	271	789	1,427	247	75	345.1	535.0	169.8	1,411	3.00
1992	381	33	278	758	1,450	272	90	467.4	550.5	75.7	1,621	2.66
1993[1]	232	59	256	750	1,300	323	70	275.1	479.1	117.2	1,330	2.50
1994[2]	325	26	276	841	1,470	297	160	512.0	665.0	114.9	1,660	3.25

[1] Preliminary. [2] Estimate. [3] Includes pharmaceuticals. *Source: U.S. Bureau of Mines*

Broilers

U.S. broiler production continues to expand, reflecting strong domestic retail and food service demand, record high foreign demand and generally positive net returns to producers. In mid-1995, broiler net returns exceeded 10¢ per pound although higher feed costs trimmed the net return rate as the year progressed. Recording setting federally inspected production in 1995 of 25.1 billion pounds compares with 23.8 billion pounds in 1994. Another increase to almost 27 billion pounds is forecast for 1996. Retail per capita broiler consumption in 1995 of a record high 71.2 pounds compares with 69.8 pounds in 1994, and 1996 use is forecast at 74.8 pounds. Competition from red meat and seasonal factors (the Thanksgiving period, for example) pressures the domestic broiler market at times. The 12-city market average broiler price in 1995 of 55¢-56¢ compared with 55.69¢ in 1994 and 55.2¢ cents in 1993. Despite the expected record high broiler disappearance in 1996, the price average may slip to 50¢-54¢ per pound.

U.S. broiler exports moved at a record pace in the first-half of the 1990s. Export growth continues to be stimulated by attractive prices of U.S. broilers, notably leg quarters, and development of foreign markets by individual companies and via joint efforts of groups of companies to promote exports. Exports go to a number of nations. The 1995 total of 3.6 billion pounds compares with 2.9 billion pounds in 1994 and 2 billion pounds in 1993. An estimated 4 billion pounds may be shipped in 1996, about 15 percent of total U.S. production. Russia remains the largest single market, but shipments to China are growing rapidly in response to their growing economy and increased demand for poultry. The cumulative total to China through August of 467 millions pounds was 56 percent over 1994 period.

Broiler Supply and Prices in the United States

Year & Quarters	Federally Inspected Slaughter: Number (Millions)	Average Weight (Pounds)	Liveweight Pounds (Mil. Lbs.)	Certified RTC Weight (Mil. Lbs.)	Total Production RTC[3] (Mil. Lbs.)	Per Capita Consumption RTC Basis (Pounds)	Prices: Farm (Cents per Pound)	Georgia Dock[4] (Cents per Pound)
1990	5,841	4.37	25,550	18,555	18,430	69.1	32.38	51.39
1991	6,140	4.43	27,171	19,728	19,591	72.3	30.91	49.15
1992	6,425	4.51	28,998	21,052	20,904	75.7	31.85	50.21
1993	6,681	4.56	30,474	22,178	22,015	77.7	34.40	53.65
1994[1]	7,270	4.64	33,595	23,846	23,666	79.3	35.06	54.40
1995[2]	7,528	4.67	35,150	25,410	24,831	79.9	34.54	54.73
I	1,819	4.66	8,466	6,146	6,100	19.8	32.67	50.78
II	1,883	4.66	8,773	6,356	6,308	20.6	32.43	51.91
III	1,855	4.55	8,443	6,168	6,121	19.5	36.53	58.03
IV	1,835	4.76	8,723		6,302	20.0	36.53	58.20

[1] Preliminary. [2] Estimate. [3] Total production equals federally inspected slaughter plus other slaughter minus cut-up and futher processing condemnation. [4] Ready-to-cook-basis. *Source: Economic Research Service, U.S. Department of Agriculture*

Salient Broiler Statistics in the United States

Year	Commercial Production: Number (Millions)	Commercial Production: Liveweight (Mil. Lbs.)	Average Liveweight Per Bird (Pounds)	Average Price (¢/Pound)	Value of Production (Mil. $)	Total Chickens[3] Supply and Distribution — Production: Federally Inspected (In Millions of Pounds)	Production: Other Chickens	Production: Total	Storage Stocks January 1	Exports	Broiler Feed Ratio in Pounds	Consumption: Total (Mil. Lbs.)	Consumption: Per Capita[4] (in Lbs.)
1989	5,517	23,979	4.35	36.6	8,778	17,334	31	17,365	179	814	5.0	16,371	58.5
1990	5,864	25,631	4.37	32.6	8,365	18,555	29	18,583	221	1,143	4.9	17,266	60.9
1991	6,137	27,203	4.43	30.8	8,383	19,728	32	19,760	242	1,261	4.9	18,271	63.6
1992	6,402	28,829	4.50	31.8	9,174	21,052	36	21,088	300	1,489	5.1	19,347	66.6
1993	6,694	30,618	4.57	34.0	10,417	22,178	36	22,214	368	1,966	5.3	20,059	68.5
1994[1]	7,018	32,529	4.64	35.0	11,374	23,846	38	23,884	358	2,876	5.2	20,690	69.9
1995[2]						25,410	40	25,450	458	3,435		21,751	72.8

[1] Preliminary. [2] Estimate. [3] Ready-to-cook. [4] Retail weight basis. *Source: Economic Research Service, U.S. Department of Agriculture*

Average Wholesale Broiler Prices RTC (Ready-to-Cook)

Year	January	February	March	April	May	June	July	August	September	October	November	December	Average
1989	57.95	58.04	62.10	63.54	70.40	67.36	62.01	57.29	59.87	51.71	49.21	48.40	58.99
1990	51.70	57.37	60.39	55.28	57.93	56.44	59.47	54.89	57.35	48.79	48.02	49.63	54.77
1991	51.72	50.63	51.41	51.96	52.03	52.66	54.25	54.61	53.61	51.61	50.30	49.54	52.03
1992	50.14	50.28	50.24	49.45	55.06	52.38	56.04	56.13	51.29	53.67	54.98	51.17	52.57
1993	52.14	53.01	54.02	54.66	57.86	55.04	55.36	57.77	57.59	55.72	55.82	53.17	55.18
1994	52.67	55.22	57.51	57.80	61.39	60.71	57.34	54.65	55.80	54.02	50.50	50.87	55.71
1995[1]	51.14	51.73	52.32	51.51	52.94	55.88	58.76	61.74	61.48	58.79	61.10	58.90	56.36

[1] Preliminary. *Source: Economic Research Service, U.S. Department of Agriculture*

Butter

U.S. butter production peaked in 1992 when a record high 619,000 tonnes was produced. Production has since averaged 592,000 tonnes with about 595,000 tonnes produced in 1995 versus 588,000 tonnes in 1994. U.S. consumption of butter in the 1990s has maintained an upward trend; domestic use in 1995 was placed at 568,000 tonnes versus 570,000 tonnes in 1994, and an annual 1990-1993 average near 515,000 tonnes. Since the late-1980s new supply has consistently outpaced domestic demand. U.S. butter stocks, much of which has been government owned, have traversed a wide range in the past few years, from a high at the end of 1991 of 539.4 million pounds to only an estimated 17 million pounds at the end of 1995. U.S. per capita butter use in the first-half of the 1990s has averaged about 4.4 pounds versus 4.6 pounds in the 1980s.

Butter production is derived directly from milk production. In 1995, U.S. cow milk output was estimated at 71.3 million tonnes, the highest of the decade and up from 69.7 million tonnes in 1994. The increase largely reflects more milk output per cow. Butter manufacturing is the third largest use of milk production, the first being milk as a fluid and then its conversion into cheese. California is the largest producing state, accounting for nearly one-third of total U.S. production, followed by Wisconsin.

World butter production in 1995 of 5.2 million tonnes was slightly higher than in 1994, but still well under the annual 1990-1993 average of 5.7 million tonnes. Russia and the Ukraine combined are the world's largest producers, with about 15 percent of global output. Second is the U.S. with more than 10 percent. Statistically India is the largest producer with a record high 1.2 million tonnes in 1995, but their product is mostly Ghee, a butterlike substance consumed almost entirely in India. World consumption almost mirrors production: India is first, Russia and the Ukraine second, with Germany's usage at times contending with the U.S. for the third position. Global foreign trade in butter tends to be small. U.S. imports are insignificant at less than 2,000 tons, exports, however, show sharp variance, totaling 145,000 tons in 1993 and only 55,0000 tons in 1995. New Zealand was the largest exporter with 275,000 tonnes in 1995, 42 percent of the world total. Russia was the largest importer, demanding 180,000 tonnes of total world imports of 361,000 tonnes. Foreign demand for U.S. butter could quicken in 1996 as world stocks are low, with only 362,000 tonnes at the 1995 yearend versus 471,000 tonnes a year earlier. The key to increased world demand likely rests on Russia and how much it can afford to import.

World butter prices trended higher in 1995, nearing $2,400 per tonne in mid-year, basis mid-point F.O.B., Northern Europe, almost double the previous year's price and reflective of the low stocks. For a time U.S. butter was competitive on the export market, but recent strong domestic prices have limited exports. U.S. butter prices in early 1995 hovered near 65¢ per pound for salted (80%) AA butter. However, by early fall the price had soared to 85¢ per pound, and 93¢ per pound for unsalted (82%) butter. U.S. prices are expected to remain strong into 1996, but well under the 1980s average of more than $1.25 per pound.

Supply and Distribution of Butter in the United States In Millions of Pounds

	Supply				Distribution										
					Domestic Disappearance					Department of Agriculture				93 Score AA Wholesale Price	
Year	Production	Cold Storage Stocks[3] Jan. 1[6]	Imports	Total Supply	Total	Donated	Per Capita (Pounds)	Exports	Shipments[4]	Jan 1. Stocks[5]	Dec. 31 Stocks[5]	Removed by USDA Programs	Total Use	California ($ per Pound)	Chicago ($ per Pound)
1987	1,104	193	5	1,361	1,198	231	4.7	16	1	220	96	187.3	1,215	1.6748	1.4172
1988	1,208	143	5	1,359	1,131	195	4.5	15	1	96	173	312.6	1,147	1.6097	1.3412
1989	1,295	215	5	1,515	1,127	214	4.4	112	4	173	223	413.4	1,243	1.5660	1.2951
1990	1,302	256	5	1,582	1,039	182	4.4	126	2	223	373	400.3	1,167	1.3050	1.0346
1991	1,336	416	5	1,759	1,181	132	4.4	26	1	373	511	442.8	1,208	1.2856	1.0182
1992	1,365	539	4	1,919	1,323	119	4.4	142	1	511	430	439.5	1,466	1.1386	.8427
1993[1]	1,315	448	4	1,774	1,327	149	4.7	204	1	430	229	288.8	1,532	1.0612	.7693
1994[2]	1,296	235	3	1,543	1,362		4.8	101		229	67	204.3	1,464		

[1] Preliminary. [2] Estimates. [3] Includes butter equivalent. [4] Includes USDA shipments to territories. [5] Includes butteroil. [6] Includes stocks held by USDA.
Source: Economic Research Service, U.S. Department of Agriculture

Commercial Disappearance of Creamery Butter in the U.S. In Millions of Pounds

Year	First Quarter	Second Quarter	Third Quarter	Fourth Quarter	Total	Year	First Quarter	Second Quarter	Third Quarter	Fourth Quarter	Total
1984	194.0	241.3	215.6	251.9	902.7	1990	197.5	218.1	218.1	281.8	915.2
1985	200.0	203.9	241.5	272.9	918.2	1991	186.8	184.0	255.6	276.5	903.5
1986	198.6	220.1	234.4	269.8	922.9	1992	214.4	216.5	236.9	276.3	944.1
1987	222.7	222.1	218.4	239.3	902.5	1993	241.9	231.6	271.7	311.6	1,041.0
1988	194.5	221.6	219.7	274.0	909.8	1994[1]	261.7	254.9	285.0	298.3	1,097.0
1989	188.3	145.6	228.8	291.3	854.1	1995[1]	329.0	286.8	256.1		871.9

[1] Preliminary. *Source: Economic Research Service, U.S. Department of Agriculture*

World (Total) Butter[3] Production In Thousands of Metric Tons

Year	Argentina	Australia	Brazil	Canada	Former Czechoslovakia	Denmark	France	Germany[4]	India	Ireland	Japan	Netherland	New Zealand	Poland	Russia[5]	Sweden	Ukraine[5]	U.K.	United States
1985	32	114	70	108	150	110	595	515	700	163	89	306	293	308	------	74	1,596	202	566
1986	32	105	65	109	156	112	633	567	720	160	88	377	299	289	------	66	1,700	222	545
1987	34	104	65	95	149	96	569	553	750	150	69	234	248	293	------	64	1,742	174	501
1988	35	98	65	105	148	94	521	585	850	139	68	214	276	293	------	61	1,724	140	547
1989	45	96	65	99	156	92	525	711	880	156	78	213	246	325	820	70	441	130	588
1990	40	111	75	100	159	93	514	640	970	159	76	209	276	300	833	49	444	138	591
1991	38	111	70	97	136	71	496	555	1,020	146	76	196	269	220	729	38	376	132	606
1992	37	116	65	86	118	62	453	474	1,060	142	95	191	268	180	762	37	345	127	619
1993	36	131	65	83	115	59	444	480	1,110	135	108	184	276	180	716	39	325	152	596
1994[1]	39	147	60	89		59	439	460	1,150	135	80	159	297	145	490	32	320	178	588
1995[2]	43	142	65	90		58	440	475	1,200	135	70	168	284	140	446	30	310	185	595

[1] Preliminary. [2] Forecast. [3] Factory (including creameries and dairies) and farm. [4] Includes the former East Germany after 1988. [5] Formerly part of the U.S.S.R.; data not reported seperately until 1989. *Source: Foreign Agricultural Service, U.S. Department of Agriculture*

Production of Creamery Butter in Factories in the United States In Millions of Pounds

Year	January	February	March	April	May	June	July	August	September	October	November	December	Total
1985	116.8	104.6	105.9	111.4	112.9	95.6	92.4	92.1	92.1	109.3	99.4	115.4	1,247.9
1986	136.7	119.3	119.2	122.7	114.7	93.0	79.7	69.9	80.2	85.3	80.3	101.3	1,202.3
1987	111.9	97.4	105.4	102.6	98.2	81.5	75.2	66.4	77.9	91.2	87.9	108.5	1,104.1
1988	126.1	119.7	115.5	113.8	108.0	90.8	76.3	74.1	83.3	92.3	95.6	112.0	1,207.5
1989	129.0	124.7	135.7	124.7	122.5	95.3	72.2	80.1	81.6	95.1	94.4	107.4	1,262.7
1990	134.0	127.3	136.2	125.6	118.6	96.7	84.6	84.2	83.4	106.7	110.1	112.2	1,319.6
1991	142.1	126.3	131.6	133.7	126.0	98.3	88.9	85.0	84.7	105.2	108.5	130.1	1,360.4
1992	156.0	132.0	129.9	119.7	118.2	103.0	97.8	86.7	96.6	101.6	98.3	119.8	1,365.2
1993	147.3	127.2	131.6	121.8	116.4	102.3	86.2	80.7	86.3	97.8	97.3	120.3	1,315.2
1994[1]	135.3	118.4	118.0	119.4	118.2	99.2	84.2	88.2	91.2	101.8	100.7	121.4	1,295.9
1995[2]	132.0	120.3	125.7	119.3	116.5	99.5	82.9	78.6	82.2	94.4	91.5	111.2	1,254.1

[1] Preliminary. [2] Estimate. *Source: Economic Research Service, U.S. Department of Agriculture*

Cold Storage Holdings of Creamery Butter in the U.S. on First of Month In Millions of Pounds

Year	January	February	March	April	May	June	July	August	September	October	November	December
1985	296.6	277.3	289.4	291.7	272.7	283.2	286.8	280.7	264.6	247.0	231.6	206.9
1986	205.5	206.3	242.4	283.3	305.0	330.8	342.8	337.6	304.4	279.6	253.3	218.5
1987	193.0	206.6	231.6	254.0	247.9	251.1	237.9	211.2	187.3	176.2	165.6	158.5
1988	143.2	157.3	198.9	221.1	240.4	280.5	293.4	295.8	294.4	253.4	237.3	226.2
1989	214.7	246.6	314.4	341.9	377.2	438.3	464.1	461.3	439.7	407.9	370.6	294.1
1990	256.2	269.7	293.8	335.4	358.8	399.6	420.0	420.8	427.9	412.3	413.6	407.6
1991	416.1	470.8	524.8	555.9	620.5	646.7	662.7	659.8	629.4	597.2	567.1	539.4
1992	539.4	565.4	624.8	645.3	678.7	712.6	747.0	755.8	705.7	608.1	541.7	487.6
1993	447.7	489.1	492.5	515.6	552.7	559.0	569.0	516.4	473.3	395.4	341.1	276.3
1994	234.7	251.0	243.2	253.5	265.7	281.4	275.1	245.9	206.6	163.4	124.6	84.5
1995[1]	79.5	89.9	88.3	74.8	79.1	81.3	79.2	68.3	50.2	32.8	23.6	22.7

[1] Preliminary. *Source: Agricultural Statistics Board, U.S.Department of Agriculture*

Wholesale Price of 92 Score Creamery (Grade A) Butter at Chicago In Cents Per Pound

Year	January	February	March	April	May	June	July	August	September	October	November	December	Average
1985	141.5	141.3	141.3	141.9	141.9	141.9	141.5	140.7	141.2	141.6	139.5	139.1	141.1
1986	138.8	138.8	137.5	138.8	138.8	139.1	143.7	153.9	154.2	153.5	151.9	145.5	144.5
1987	137.3	136.8	137.8	138.8	138.4	144.6	149.0	148.1	145.3	136.8	135.6	134.0	140.2
1988	131.9	131.0	131.0	131.0	131.0	133.5	135.9	135.6	134.3	132.0	131.3	131.3	132.5
1989	131.0	131.0	131.0	131.0	131.0	131.0	130.3	132.8	125.1	120.5	120.5	120.0	127.9
1990	110.9	108.3	108.3	106.9	99.0	98.4	100.3	98.9	98.9	98.9	98.9	98.0	102.1
1991	97.3	97.3	97.3	97.3	97.3	98.6	98.9	98.9	100.7	106.3	104.6	98.4	99.3
1992	94.9	86.3	86.3	86.3	83.8	76.6	76.6	76.6	81.7	82.2	80.7	78.6	82.5
1993	75.3	75.3	75.3	75.3	75.3	76.2	73.5	74.6	74.3	74.2	73.6	69.7	74.4
1994	64.0	64.0	65.5	65.5	64.5	65.1	66.9	71.5	71.5	71.5	71.5	67.0	67.4
1995	64.0	65.5	66.5	66.5	66.5	66.9	74.5	79.5	80.9	95.4	103.5	74.4	75.3

Source: Economic Research Service, U.S. Department of Agriculture

Cadmium

Cadmium is a rare chemical element that's the by-product of the smelting and refining of zinc ores. It's used primarily for plating of iron and steel to protect them from corrosion. Due to the cost of waste disposal and assorted problems because of its toxicity, the use of cadmium in electroplating has decreased. Because of environmental concerns, the outlook for cadmium is not bright. Cadmium is highly toxic and its disposal is problematic. Approximately 71% of cadmium usage is in battery production with 8% used for coatings and plating, 10% in pigments, 6% in alloys, and 8% in plastics and synthetic products.

According to the U.S. Bureau of Mines, two companies, one in Illinois and one in Tennessee, recovered cadmium as a by-product of the smelting and refining of zinc concentrates. An extraction circuit located in Oklahoma and operated by a zinc producer was idle in 1994, and a company in Colorado which recovered cadmium from nonferrous sources halted operations in mid-1993.

U.S. refinery production of cadmium in 1994 was 1,000 tonnes, down 9 percent from 1993. Imports of cadmium metal in 1994 were 1,150 tonnes, down 19 percent from 1993. Since 1991, U.S. cadmium imports have fallen 44 percent. The major sources for U.S. imports are Canada, Mexico, Australia and Belgium.

U.S. exports of all forms of cadmium (cadmium content) were 490 tonnes in 1994, up from just 11 tonnes in 1993. Shipments of cadmium from Government excess stockpiles were 285 tonnes compared to 211 tonnes in 1993.

Cadmium recycling has been practical only for nickel-cadmium batteries, some alloys, and dust from electric arc furnaces operated by the steel industry. The recycled amount is unknown. The U.S. steel industry generated more than 500,000 tonnes of electric furnace dust in 1993. Collection networks recycle nickel-cadmium batteries.

U.S. apparent consumption of cadmium in 1994 was 2,020 tonnes, down 28 percent from 1993. The average price in 1-5 short tons, New York dealer, in 1994 was $1.03 per pound, up sharply from the 1993 average price of 45 cents. In 1990 the average price was $3.38.

Yearend stocks, producer and distributor, in 1994 were 700 tonnes, down from 770 tonnes in 1993. Net import reliance as a percent of apparent consumption was 50 percent in 1994, down from 61 percent in the prior year. The Government stockpile status as of September 30, 1994 was: uncommitted inventory 2,381 tonnes, committed inventory 95 tonnes, authorized for disposal 2,381 tonnes and January-September 1994 disposals 259 tonnes.

Demand for rechargeable nickel-cadmium batteries continues to grow in the Western World though the rate is slower than in the past. More than 60 percent of cadmium consumed by Western countries goes into batteries making batteries the principal end use for the metal. Japan is by far the largest refiner of cadmium and is also a net importer of cadmium metal. About 90 percent of Japanese consumption goes into batteries. Estimated world resources of cadmium are about six million tonnes.

World Refinery Production of Cadmium In Metric Tons

Year	Australia	Belgium	Canada	China	Finland	France	Germany	Italy	Japan	Kazakhstan[4]	Mexico	Norway	Poland	United Kingdom	United States[3]	Zaire	World Total
1985	910	1,252	1,717	540	565	337	1,095	526	2,535	3,000	734	159	600	370	1,603	296	18,924
1986	915	1,374	1,484	650	522	431	1,218	411	2,489	3,000	1,016	154	600	379	1,486	364	19,070
1987	944	1,308	1,481	680	690	457	1,125	320	2,450	3,000	935	147	600	498	1,515	299	19,066
1988	855	1,836	1,694	750	703	558	1,186	686	2,614	3,000	1,117	169	642	399	1,885	281	21,869
1989	696	1,764	1,620	800	612	170	1,234	776	2,694	3,000	976	207	555	395	1,550	224	20,873
1990	638	1,956	1,470	1,100	569	187	990	691	2,451	2,800	882	286	373	438	1,678	127	20,200
1991	1,076	1,807	1,829	1,200	593	271	1,050	658	2,889	2,500	688	227	364	449	1,676	65	20,900
1992	1,001	1,550	1,963	1,150	590	252	941	742	2,986	1,000	602	247	132	383	1,620	84	19,900
1993[1]	951	1,570	1,890	1,160	785	137	1,060	517	2,830	1,000	797	213	150	458	1,094	12	18,913
1994[2]	910	1,560	2,130	1,150	548	140	1,120	659	2,630	1,000	646	288	150	470	1,010	1	18,100

[1] Preliminary. [2] Estimate. [3] Primary and secondary metal. [4] Formerly part of the U.S.S.R.; data not reported separately until 1992.

Year	Net Import Reliance as a % of Apparent Consumption	Production (Metal)	Producer Shipments	Cadmium Sulfide Production	Production Other Compounds	Imports of Cadmium Metal[3]	Exports[4]	Apparent Consumption	Industry Stocks Dec. 31[5]	N.Y. Dealer Price $ per Pound[6]
1985	57	1,603	1,791	477	1,459	1,988	86	3,720	686	.92
1986	66	1,486	2,030	645	1,511	3,174	38	4,385	923	1.07
1987	64	1,515	1,916	540	1,497	2,701	241	4,178	720	1.60
1988	64	1,885	2,074	345	1,451	2,482	613	3,620	854	6.91
1989	48	1,550	2,015	267	1,451	2,787	369	4,096	726	6.28
1990	46	1,678	1,855	228	1,144	1,741	385	2,800	653	3.38
1991	50	1,676	1,736	263	1,089	2,040	158	3,080	835	2.01
1992	52	1,620	2,075	270	1,073	1,958	178	3,330	868	.91
1993[1]	61	1,094	1,320	303	731	1,415	38	2,940	582	.45
1994[2]	50	1,010	1,290	342	980	1,110	1,450	1,020	439	1.13

Cassava

Cassava, or tapioca root, is used primarily as an animal feed and as a foodstuff in tropical countries. Cassava is looked upon as a possible solution to world hunger problems, and advances in technology hold the promise of increasing yields substantially. Reports of new strains of cassava root being developed in Africa could eventually prove to be important weapons in the fight against hunger. The major producers of cassava are scattered around the world. The four largest producers are Brazil, Nigeria, Zaire and Thailand. These countries account for about half of world production. Other important producers include Indonesia, Tanzania, India and Uganda. Most of these countries have rapidly expanding populations so tapioca could prove to be a very important crop.

According to *Oil World*, world exports of cassava in the 1994-95 season plummeted to the lowest levels in more than 10 years. For the period of October 1994 to July 1995, world exports of cassava fell to only 3.35 million tonnes, down 41 percent from the 1993-94 season, and 56 percent less than in 1992-93. The world's largest exporter of cassava is Thailand. For the 1994-95 (October-July) period, Thailand exported 3.07 million tonnes of cassava. This was down 1.6 million tonnes from the 1993-94 period and significantly below 1992-93 exports of 6.29 million tonnes. Indonesia is the next largest exporter but its shipments also fell sharply in 1994-95 to only 200,000 tonnes. This was 74 percent less than the 1993-94 shipments of 777,000 tonnes. In 1992-93, Indonesia exported 977,000 tonnes of cassava. China, in recent years an important exporter of cassava, has also been shipping less. China is a small exporter, but it is an important importer. For the January-July 1995 period, *Oil World* reported that China imported 180,000 tonnes of cassava which set a new record. In 1993-94, (October-July), Chinese exports were 79,000 tonnes while in 1992-93 they were 246,000 tonnes and in 1991-92 351,000 tonnes. For the 1994-95 period, other exporters shipped 68,000 tonnes of tapioca which was down from 165,000 tonnes in 1993-94.

A major export market for cassava is the European Union (EU). Tapioca is used by feed compounders and is usually combined with soybean meal. Because of tightness in the market, European feed compounders have switched to other feeds and taken tapioca out of their rations.

Oil World reports that tapioca prices in the EU continued to rise in 1995 and were 30 percent above the prior year. Because of the tight supplies and high prices, tapioca usage in the EU is falling, especially in France, Germany and the Netherlands. Over the January-March 1995 period, EU tapioca imports from third-world countries fell by 50 percent from the previous year to only 750,000 tonnes, the lowest level in more than 10 years. A further reduction of EU imports has occurred from April 1995 onwards due to low supplies from Thailand and Indonesia. Exports of tapioca chips and pellets from Thailand to the EU in January-July 1995 fell by 30 percent to 2.06 million tonnes.

World Cassava Production In Thousands of Metric Tons

Year	Brazil	China	Columbia	Ghana	India	Indonesia	Madagascar	Mozambique	Nigeria	Paraguay	Phillippines	Tanzania	Thailand	Uganda	Viet Nam	Zaire	World Total
1989	23,668	3,320	1,509	3,327	4,833	17,117	2,277	4,000	15,425	3,978	1,873	7,792	15,128	3,568	2,585	17,400	151,773
1990	24,322	3,216	1,939	2,717	4,962	15,830	2,292	4,056	19,043	3,550	1,854	6,922	20,701	3,339	2,276	17,600	149,844
1991	24,538	3,310	1,645	3,600	5,416	15,954	2,307	3,690	20,000	2,585	1,816	7,460	20,356	3,229	2,455	19,500	153,562
1992	21,919	3,357	1,651	4,000	5,469	16,516	2,280	3,239	21,320	2,591	1,798	7,112	20,356	2,896	2,568	20,210	153,058
1993	21,865	3,403	1,723	4,200	5,340	16,799	2,350	3,511	21,000	2,680	1,844	6,833	20,203	3,137	2,631	20,835	154,328
1994[1]	24,009	3,503	2,000	4,378	5,340	15,000	2,260	3,294	21,000	2,550	1,850	7,209	19,091	3,420	2,631	19,600	152,473

[1] Estimate. *Source: Food and Agricultural Organization of the United Nations*

Prices of Tapioca, Hard Pellets, F.O.B. Rotterdam U.S. Dollars Per Tonne

Year	January	February	March	April	May	June	July	August	September	October	November	December	Average
1991	187	186	163	160	168	158	158	177	187	187	202	197	178
1992	197	184	179	177	179	181	184	192	195	187	172	170	183
1993	160	150	140	149	145	133	130	131	136	127	120	125	137
1994	122	123	128	133	138	141	147	154	158	161	161	161	144
1995	164	170	180	178	174	176	183	176	178	184	182	178	177

Source: Oil World

World Trade in Tapioca In Thousands of Metric Tons

	Exports					Imports						
Year	China	Indonesia	Thailand	Viet Nam	Total World Exports	China	EC-12[2]	Japan	Rep. of Korea	United States	Former U.S.S.R.	Total World Imports
1989	251	1,146	9,231	42	10,735	529	6,183	279	685	185	797	9,875
1990	198	1,271	7,556	20	9,135	573	4,947	221	763	179	855	8,598
1991	410	859	6,187	3	7,571	175	5,692	162	444	127	-----	7,353
1992	316	873	8,045	32	9,422	230	6,009	181	876	217	22	8,831
1993	269	936	6,707	29	8,089	149	6,449	151	658	60	8	8,417
1994[1]	82	740	4,703	38	5,713	86	5,246	94	122	18	-----	5,796
1995[1]	10	220	3,341	8	3,653	225	3,330	27	-----	-----	-----	3,712

[1] Estimate. [2] Excluding trade between the EEC members. *Source: Oil World*

Castor Beans

Oil World forecast world production of castorseed in 1994-95 at 1.23 million tonnes, up from 1.16 million tonnes in 1993-94 and 1.14 million tonnes in 1992-93. World yields were expected to increase by about two percent while harvested area was up almost four percent. India is by far the world's largest producer of castorseed with 1994-95 output forecast at 800,000 tonnes, up from 720,000 tonnes in 1993-94 and 620,000 tonnes in 1992-93. China was forecast to produce 280,000 tonnes, the same as in 1993-94 and down slightly from 290,000 tonnes in 1992-93. Brazilian production was estimated at 50,000 tonnes, unchanged from 1993-94 but down from output of 100,000 tonnes in 1992-93. The rest of the world was expected to produce 100,000 tonnes of castorseed in 1994-95, down from 110,000 tonnes the year before and 130,000 tonnes in 1992-93.

World castorseed crushings in 1994-95 were forecast by *Oil World* at 1.13 million tonnes, up from 1.08 million tonnes in 1993-94. World trade was put at 70,000 tonnes in the 1994-95 season. The major processors of castorseed in 1994-95 were India with 702,000 tonnes crushed, China with 225,000 tonnes and Brazil with 57,000 tonnes. Chinese exports were put at 38,000 tonnes while India was expected to export 15,000 tonnes.

For 1994-95, world castor oil production was forecast to be 465,000 tonnes, up from 448,000 tonnes in 1993-94. World use of castor oil was estimated at 453,000 tonnes, down from 455,000 tonnes the prior season. Global ending stocks were put at 72,000 tonnes.

World Production of Castorseed Beans In Thousands of Metric Tons

Crop Year	Brazil	China	Ecuador	Ethiopia	India	Mexico	Paraguay	Pakistan	Philip-pines	Romania	Sudan	Tanzania	Thailand	Former U.S.S.R.	World Total
1988-9	146	260	6	1	417	4	23	14	5	9	2	1	31	60	1,008
1989-90	128	270	7	1	517	4	41	10	7	7	2	2	29	43	1,099
1990-1	148	315	7	1	716	----	37	12	7	2	7	3	15	36	1,336
1991-2	133	310	5	1	575	1	33	13	7	1	6	3	13	32	1,163
1992-3	102	291	12	1	617	1	20	6	7	1	8	3	24	20	1,140
1993-4[1]	45	280	13	1	700	1	15	7	7	1	6	3	22	4	1,135
1994-5[2]	55	260	7	1	800	1	10	8	7	----	6	3	21	8	1,219

[1] Preliminary. [2] Estimate. *Sources: Foreign Agricultural Service, U.S. Department of Agriculture; Oil World*

Castor Oil Consumption[2] in the United States In Thousands of Pounds

Crop Year	October	November	December	January	February	March	April	May	June	July	August	September	Total
1989-90	4,325	4,570	3,568	4,268	4,487	4,724	4,385	4,436	4,092	3,847	5,156	3,833	51,691
1990-1	3,334	2,815	3,507	-----------	11,787	-----------	-----------	10,958	-----------	-----------	11,096	-----------	44,030
1991-2	-----------	12,073	-----------	3,877	2,914	3,766	2,806	3,516	3,606	3,203	3,708	3,019	42,488
1992-3	4,712	3,250	3,100	3,287	4,271	3,924	4,098	3,965	4,496	4,902	5,073	4,400	49,478
1993-4	5,046	5,649	5,092	5,510	4,982	5,766	4,548	6,335	5,258	4,603	4,929	4,543	62,261
1994-5[1]	5,032	4,204	5,092	6,001	5,179	4,911	4,722	3,740	5,067	4,891	6,452	4,834	60,125
1995-6[1]	5,228	5,463											

[1] Preliminary. [2] In inedible products (Resins, Plastics, etc.). *Source: Bureau of the Census, U.S. Department of Commerce*

Castor Oil Stocks in the United States In Thousands of Pounds

Crop Year	Oct. 1	Nov. 1	Dec. 1	Jan. 1	Feb. 1	Mar. 1	Apr. 1	May 1	June 1	July 1	Aug. 1	Sept. 1
1989-90	9,556	11,869	10,486	NA	NA	13,708	11,852	17,948	21,101	32,992	25,295	26,793
1990-1	18,819	18,118	25,245	-----------	17,198	-----------	-----------	21,714	-----------	-----------	14,417	-----------
1991-2	-----------	22,921	-----------	20,382	23,499	17,293	21,511	19,429	13,036	20,383	16,066	11,346
1992-3	7,158	5,383	5,364	4,124	10,076	13,154	19,345	14,983	17,094	24,652	20,616	25,070
1993-4	22,981	21,275	23,482	21,132	29,871	9,946	18,394	25,249	22,550	21,795	27,911	20,950
1994-5[1]	21,066	23,484	23,357	21,132	29,245	20,986	10,387	5,492	22,765	33,557	37,542	42,516
1995-6[1]	27,143	35,329	43,190									

[1] Preliminary. NA = Not available. *Source: Bureau of the Census, U.S. Department of Commerce*

Monthly Average Wholesale Prices of Castor Oil No. 1, Brazilian Tanks at New York In Cents Per Pound

Year	January	February	March	April	May	June	July	August	September	October	November	December	Average
1989	51.00	51.75	51.90	51.50	51.50	51.50	51.50	51.50	51.50	51.50	51.50	51.50	51.51
1990	54.50	53.50	52.60	52.00	51.20	51.00	51.00	51.00	45.00	43.40	39.63	39.63	48.70
1991	39.30	36.00	36.75	37.00	37.00	36.50	35.50	35.00	35.00	35.40	35.00	37.50	36.33
1992	37.50	37.50	37.50	36.00	34.50	34.50	34.50	34.50	34.50	34.00	34.00	34.00	35.21
1993	34.00	32.00	32.00	32.00	37.00	37.00	37.00	37.00	38.50	41.50	44.00	44.00	37.17
1994	44.00	41.75	41.00	41.00	46.00	45.00	45.00	45.00	45.00	45.00	45.00	45.00	44.06
1995	45.00	45.00	45.00	45.00	45.00	45.00							45.00

Source: Foreign Agricultural Service, U.S.D.A.

Cattle and Calves

The world cattle inventory on January 1, 1995, at slightly more than one billion head, was up slightly from a year earlier. Cattle herd developments in the Russian Federation and China dominated the world scene with Russia's herd being less than expected and China's cattle numbers expanding rapidly. In the U.S., the first half of the 1990s witnessed a steady increase in the total U.S. cattle inventory; from 95.8 million head on January 1, 1990, to 103.2 million five years later. An additional two million head were added during 1995, but the total yearend inventory was still well under the annual average of 110 million head during the first half of the 1980's. Still, the January 1, 1995 beef cow inventory of 36.1 million, coupled with an increase in the replacement heifer inventory, suggested that a rapid herd expansion was underway.

U.S. beef production reached a record high 25.1 billion pounds in 1995 versus 24.4 billion in 1994. The 1996 total may reach 26 billion pounds. However, total usage increased even faster in 1995, and carryover fell to 450 million pounds at yearend 1995 versus 548 million a year earlier. Despite the stronger beef demand during 1995, live cattle prices did not benefit as might have been expected. For much of 1995 prices pivoted around $.65 per pound, basis February 1996 futures, and then abetted by seasonal factors during the fourth quarter edged higher into yearend to $.68 per pound. Wholesale beef prices, however, fared better during 1995. Federally inspected slaughter in 1994 of 33.5 million head was up nearly a million head from 1993; through much of 1995 monthly slaughter was ahead of the year earlier pace.

The initial 1996 price outlook for the cattle industry was not encouraging. Large numbers of feeder cattle were moving off pasture and into feedlots in late 1995, suggesting hefty feedlot supplies in early 1996 and allowing more leverage for packers to dictate price levels. Moreover, a larger cattle inventory coupled with record supplies of competing meats could result in a sharp reduction in cow-calf revenues. Rising feed grain prices may further worsen the situation. The overall impact could prod producers into culling their herds which would add to near-term supplies. Or, producers may opt to finish more cattle on pasture rather than feed lots in an effort to contain costs. However, if the economy's growth proves lackluster consumer beef demand is apt to slip. The USDA's early estimate for choice steer prices in 1996 of $62-68 a cwt. compares with a $65-67 average in 1995, basis Nebraska; feeder steers were forecast at $63-68 a cwt. versus $67-68, basis Oklahoma city. Per capita beef usage in 1996 is expected to reach a record high 69 pounds in 1996 versus 68 pounds in 1995.

The dairy sector has become an increasingly important contributor to feeder cattle supplies and nearly every available young animal not retained for the breeding herd is now being placed on feed. Calf slaughter, meanwhile, declined sharply during the past decade partially due to the inelasticity of consumer demand to the higher retail priced veal. The 1995 calf crop was estimated at 42 million head, the largest since 1984, but less than 3 million head above the cyclical low of 39 million head in 1991.

The U.S. dominates world trade in beef. As a net importer, the U.S. generally purchases manufacturing-grade, grass-fed beef. U.S. beef imports in 1995 of 1.2 million tons were up 11 percent from 1994. As a part of the Uruguay Round, the U.S. committed itself to allow greater foreign access to the U.S. beef market which in the past was largely controlled by Australia and New Zealand. The U.S. also imports live cattle from Canada (slaughter ready) and Mexico (feeder cattle). It's only in the past decade that the U.S. became a major beef exporter, estimated at a record high 778,000 tons in 1995, up 7 percent from 1994's total of 731,000 tons which was up 26 percent from 1993. The growth has been fostered by higher quality grain-fed and competitively priced U.S. beef, and continued strong demand from Japan and Korea. World beef import demand was expected to jump in 1995, the increase paced by an estimated 35 percent rise in Russian beef imports.

Futures Markets

Live cattle futures and options are traded on the Chicago Mercantile Exchange (CME), the Bolsa de Mercadorias & Futuros (BM&F), and the MidAmerica Commodity Exchange (MidAm). Feeder cattle futures are traded on the CME and the BM&F, and feeder cattle options are traded on the CME.

World Cattle and Buffalo Numbers as of January 1 In Thousands of Head

Year	Agrentina	Australia	Brazil	Canada	China	Colombia	France	Germany[3]	India	Mexico	Russia[4]	South Africa	Turkey	Ukraine[4]	United Kingdom	United States	World Total (Mil Head)
1985	54,684	22,784	94,700	11,330	82,593	21,188	23,102	15,688	271,390	33,853	--------	12,000	15,500	121,055	12,985	109,582	1,041
1986	53,484	23,436	122,463	10,956	86,820	19,904	22,803	15,627	275,340	32,167	--------	11,750	15,000	120,888	12,695	105,378	1,067
1987	51,683	23,540	128,000	10,802	91,670	18,819	22,171	21,109	274,822	33,603	--------	12,002	14,450	122,103	12,476	102,118	1,073
1988	56,482	23,469	130,000	10,756	94,650	18,400	21,053	20,608	268,720	35,378	--------	12,187	14,000	115,824	11,849	99,622	1,070
1989	56,482	23,938	130,500	10,984	97,948	17,627	21,340	20,369	268,470	34,999	59,300	12,675	13,400	25,621	11,902	98,065	1,037
1990	56,482	24,673	140,400	11,220	100,752	16,835	21,394	20,287	270,070	31,747	58,800	13,398	12,700	25,195	11,922	95,816	1,035
1991	56,982	25,026	142,900	11,289	102,884	16,225	21,446	19,488	272,300	29,847	57,000	13,512	12,200	24,623	11,843	96,393	1,036
1992	55,229	25,857	141,800	11,713	104,592	16,008	20,970	17,134	271,200	30,232	54,700	13,311	12,000	23,728	11,623	97,556	1,029
1993	55,577	25,182	143,700	11,786	107,840	16,391	20,383	16,207	271,255	30,649	52,200	13,239	11,900	22,457	11,620	99,176	1,030
1994	54,875	25,732	144,900	12,251	113,157	16,614	20,112	15,897	272,655	30,702	48,900	12,506	11,800	21,607	11,709	100,988	1,034
1995[1]	54,207	26,000	148,100	12,726	123,300	16,868	20,470	15,962	274,155	30,191	73,900	12,632	11,700	19,624	11,868	103,265	1,043
1996[2]	53,687	26,400	151,800	13,106	133,000	17,075	20,270	15,800	276,105	27,841	39,700	12,900	11,700	17,700	11,810	105,407	1,052

[1] Preliminary. [2] Forecast. [3] Prior to 1987, data only reported for the Federal Republic of Germany. [4] Formerly part of the U.S.S.R.; country data not shown seperately prior to 1989. *Source: Foreign Agricultural Service, U.S. Department of Agriculture*

CATTLE AND CALVES

Cattle Supply and Distribution in the United States In Thousands of Head

Year	Cattle & Calves on Farms January 1	Imports	Calves Born	Total Supply	Livestock Slaughter - Cattle and Calves: Commercial: Federally Inspected	Other[3]	All Commercial	Farm	Total Slaughter	Deaths on Farms	Exports	Total Disappearance
1984	113,360	753	42,470	156,583	38,910	1,969	40,879	388	41,269	5,464	71	46,794
1985	109,582	836	41,050	151,468	37,933	1,745	39,678	370	40,048	5,046	125	45,219
1986	105,378	1,407	41,182	147,967	39,108	1,588	40,696	349	41,046	4,992	108	46,146
1987	102,118	1,200	40,152	143,470	37,148	1,314	38,462	330	38,792	4,800	131	43,723
1988	99,622	1,332	40,293	141,247	36,459	1,126	37,585	280	37,889	4,657	321	42,858
1989	98,065	1,459	40,102	139,626	35,110	980	36,089	240	36,329	4,452	169	40,950
1990	98,162	2,135	39,249	139,546	34,133	800	35,032	245	35,277	4,432	120	39,829
1991	98,896	1,939	39,026	139,861	33,285	841	34,126	242	34,368	4,347	311	39,027
1992	99,559	2,255	39,290	141,104	33,428	817	34,245	242	34,489	4,486	322	39,297
1993[1]	100,611	1,041	39,448	141,100	33,753	767	34,519	227	34,746	4,755	153	39,500
1994[1]	100,988	2,053	40,059	143,100	34,719	745	35,465	236	35,700	4,500	-----------	40,200
1995[2]	102,755	2,694	40,251	145,700	36,128	785	36,913	187	37,100	4,500	-----------	41,700

[1] Preliminary. [2] Estimate. [3] Wholesale and retail. *Source: Economic Research Service, U.S. Department of Agriculture*

United States Beef Supply and Utilization

Year/Quarter	Beginning Stocks	Production: Commercial	Production: Total	Imports	Total Supply	Exports	Ending Stocks	Total Disappearance	Per Capita Disappearance: Carcass Weight	Per Capita Disappearance: Retail Weight
	Million Pounds								Pounds	
1992	419	22,968	23,086	2,440	25,944	1,324	360	24,261	95.0	66.5
I	419	5,597	5,638	632	6,689	317	415	5,957	23.4	16.4
II	415	5,726	5,744	737	6,896	323	396	6,177	24.2	17.0
III	396	5,991	6,009	599	7,005	346	363	6,296	24.6	17.2
IV	363	5,654	5,695	471	6,529	338	360	5,831	22.7	15.9
1993	360	22,942	23,049	2,401	25,810	1,275	529	24,006	93.0	65.1
I	360	5,357	5,394	741	6,495	267	390	5,838	22.7	15.9
II	390	5,690	5,706	580	6,676	346	362	5,968	23.1	16.2
III	362	6,076	6,092	607	7,061	334	433	6,294	24.3	17.0
IV	433	5,819	5,857	473	6,763	328	529	5,906	22.8	15.9
1994	529	24,278	24,386	2,371	27,286	1,611	548	25,172	96.4	67.5
I[1]	529	5,745	5,783	682	6,994	359	562	6,073	23.4	16.4
II[1]	562	6,042	6,058	603	7,223	391	506	6,326	24.3	17.0
III[1]	506	6,377	6,393	587	7,486	416	543	6,527	25.0	17.5
IV[1]	543	6,114	6,152	499	7,194	445	548	6,201	23.7	16.6
1995	548	25,016	25,124	2,165	27,837	1,880	475	25,482	96.9	67.8
I[2]	548	5,877	5,915	572	7,035	368	515	6,152	23.5	16.4
II[2]	515	6,312	6,328	540	7,383	452	471	6,460	24.6	17.2
III[2]	471	6,602	6,618	570	7,659	520	459	6,680	25.4	17.8
IV[2]	459	6,225	6,263	483	7,205	540	475	6,190	23.4	16.4
1996	475	25,750	25,858	2,125	28,458	2,120	475	25,863	97.4	68.2
I[3]	475	6,125	6,163	545	7,183	450	500	6,233	23.6	16.5
II[3]	500	6,425	6,441	540	7,481	535	450	6,496	24.5	17.1
III[3]	450	6,775	6,791	540	7,781	560	425	6,796	25.6	17.9

[1] Preliminary. [2] Estimate. [3] Forecast. *Source: Economic Research Service, U.S. Department of Agriculture*

U.S. Cattle on Feed in 13 States, Quarterly In Thousands of Head

Year/Quarter	Number on Feed[3]	Placed on Feed	Marketings	Other Disappearance	Year/Quarter	Number on Feed[3]	Placed on Feed	Marketings	Other Disappearance
1992	10,135	24,251	21,981	1,431	1993	10,974	24,102	22,376	1,504
I	10,135	5,423	5,411	404	I	10,974	5,351	5,354	439
II	9,743	5,253	5,665	444	II	10,532	5,334	5,858	465
III	8,887	6,117	5,751	263	III	9,543	6,341	5,918	275
IV	8,990	7,458	5,154	320	IV	9,691	7,076	5,246	325
1994	11,196	23,449	22,979	1,060	1995	10,606			
I[1]	11,196	5,372	5,559	275	I[2]	10,606	5,914	5,545	287
II[1]	10,734	4,675	5,951	334	II[2]	10,688	5,249	6,107	272
III[1]	9,124	6,315	5,986	191	III[2]	9,558	6,233	6,196	192
IV[1]	9,252	7,087	5,483	260	IV[2]	9,403			

[1] Preliminary. [2] Estimate. [3] Beginning of Period. *Source: Economic Research Service, U.S.D.A.*

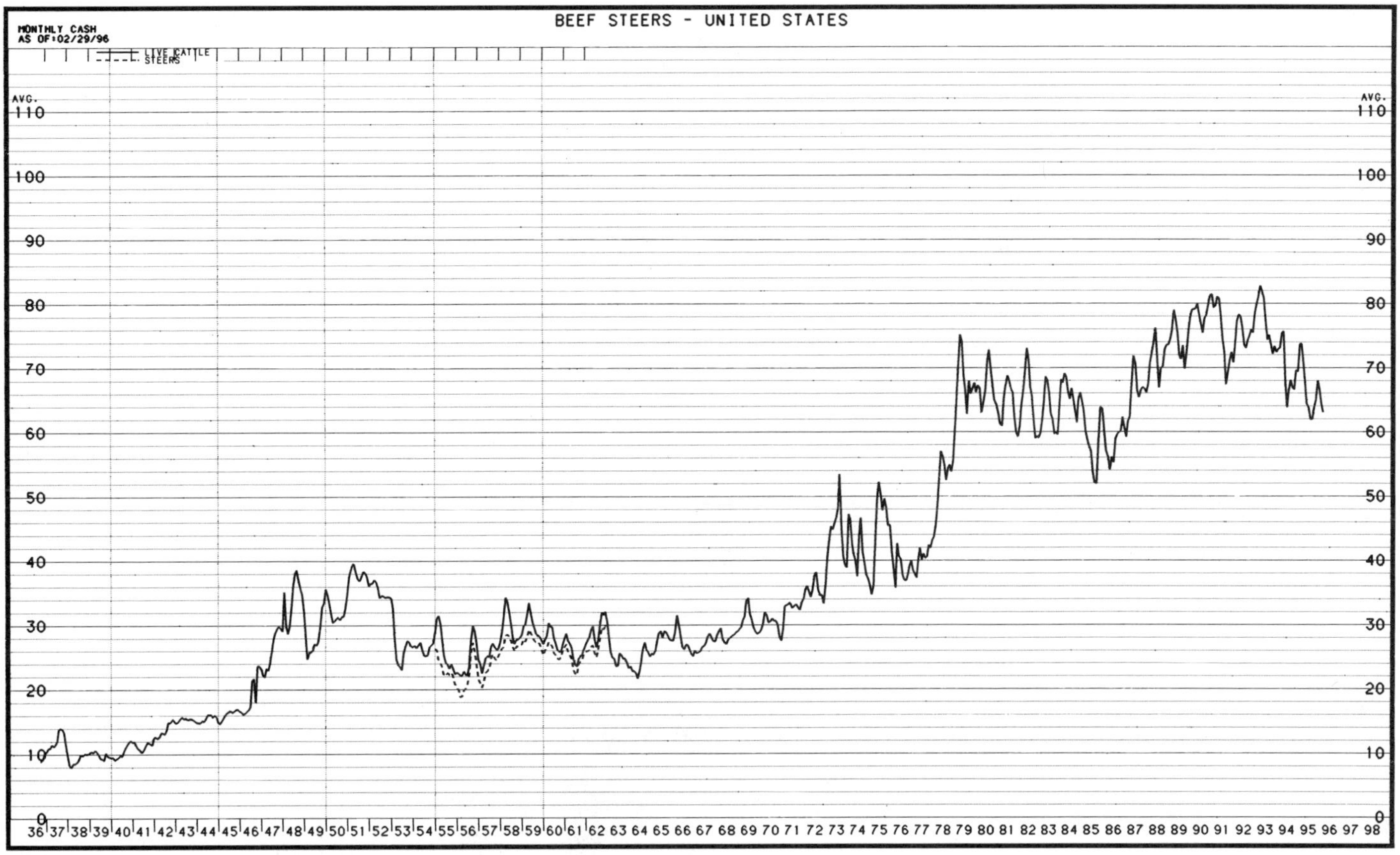

U.S. Cattle on Feed in 7 States In Thousands of Head

Year	January 1	February 1	March 1	April 1	May 1	June 1	July 1	August 1	Sept. 1	October 1	Nov.1	Dec.1
1984	8,006	7,917	7,515	7,568	7,391	7,333	7,155	6,851	6,787	7,482	8,251	8,554
1985	8,635	8,184	7,891	7,826	7,526	7,490	7,127	6,509	6,270	6,591	7,732	8,062
1986	8,150	7,894	7,552	7,523	7,337	7,326	6,773	6,561	6,619	7,031	7,796	8,101
1987	7,953	7,614	7,473	7,527	7,548	7,875	7,488	6,983	7,098	7,830	8,659	8,752
1988	8,411	8,204	7,912	8,056	7,829	8,134	7,736	7,140	6,944	7,404	8,194	8,255
1989	8,045	7,970	7,931	8,252	8,087	7,795	7,235	6,763	6,631	6,958	7,911	8,331
1990	8,378	8,526	8,319	8,483	8,181	7,867	7,310	6,998	6,975	7,635	8,669	9,039
1991	8,992	8,963	8,874	8,941	8,590	8,570	7,877	7,388	7,064	7,216	8,013	8,477
1992	8,397	8,223	8,195	8,058	7,868	7,876	7,377	7,050	7,018	7,565	8,704	8,984
1993	9,163	9,140	8,851	8,781	8,409	8,393	7,973	7,703	7,794	8,224	9,096	9,397
1994	9,370	9,232	9,011	8,977	8,701	8,325	7,654	7,463	7,486	7,840	8,629	8,914
1995[1]	8,870	8,866	8,926	8,992	8,790	8,630	8,113	7,699	7,453	7,968	8,707	9,074

[1] Preliminary. *Source: Economic Research Service, U.S. Department of Agriculture*

U.S. Cattle Placed on Feedlots in 7 States In Thousands of Head

Year	January	February	March	April	May	June	July	August	September	October	November	December	Total
1984	1,566	1,301	1,764	1,525	1,798	1,455	1,333	1,680	2,265	2,536	1,925	1,647	20,795
1985	1,449	1,341	1,592	1,436	1,691	1,296	1,098	1,520	2,000	2,829	1,801	1,590	19,643
1986	1,581	1,220	1,650	1,565	1,756	1,162	1,544	1,822	2,123	2,433	1,854	1,515	20,225
1987	1,581	1,442	1,719	1,701	1,984	1,432	1,289	1,915	2,474	2,614	1,676	1,390	21,217
1988	1,663	1,379	1,848	1,521	2,175	1,387	1,251	1,660	2,209	2,450	1,690	1,421	20,654
1989	1,706	1,610	1,975	1,539	1,624	1,293	1,291	1,638	1,953	2,652	2,001	1,537	20,819
1990	1,881	1,383	1,862	1,362	1,597	1,325	1,530	1,745	2,199	2,726	1,987	1,433	21,030
1991	1,721	1,455	1,703	1,427	1,772	1,102	1,327	1,459	1,826	2,539	1,917	1,456	19,704
1992	1,565	1,502	1,516	1,425	1,724	1,319	1,432	1,641	2,189	2,688	1,813	1,694	20,508
1993	1,641	1,262	1,626	1,326	1,801	1,430	1,513	1,865	2,148	2,494	1,878	1,490	20,474
1994	1,543	1,356	1,640	1,416	1,415	1,205	1,594	1,846	2,060	2,478	1,854	1,585	19,992
1995[1]	1,720	1,607	1,776	1,435	1,738	1,413	1,383	1,723	2,262	2,438	1,996	1,727	21,218

[1] Preliminary. *Source: Economic Research Service, U.S. Department of Agriculture*

CATTLE AND CALVES

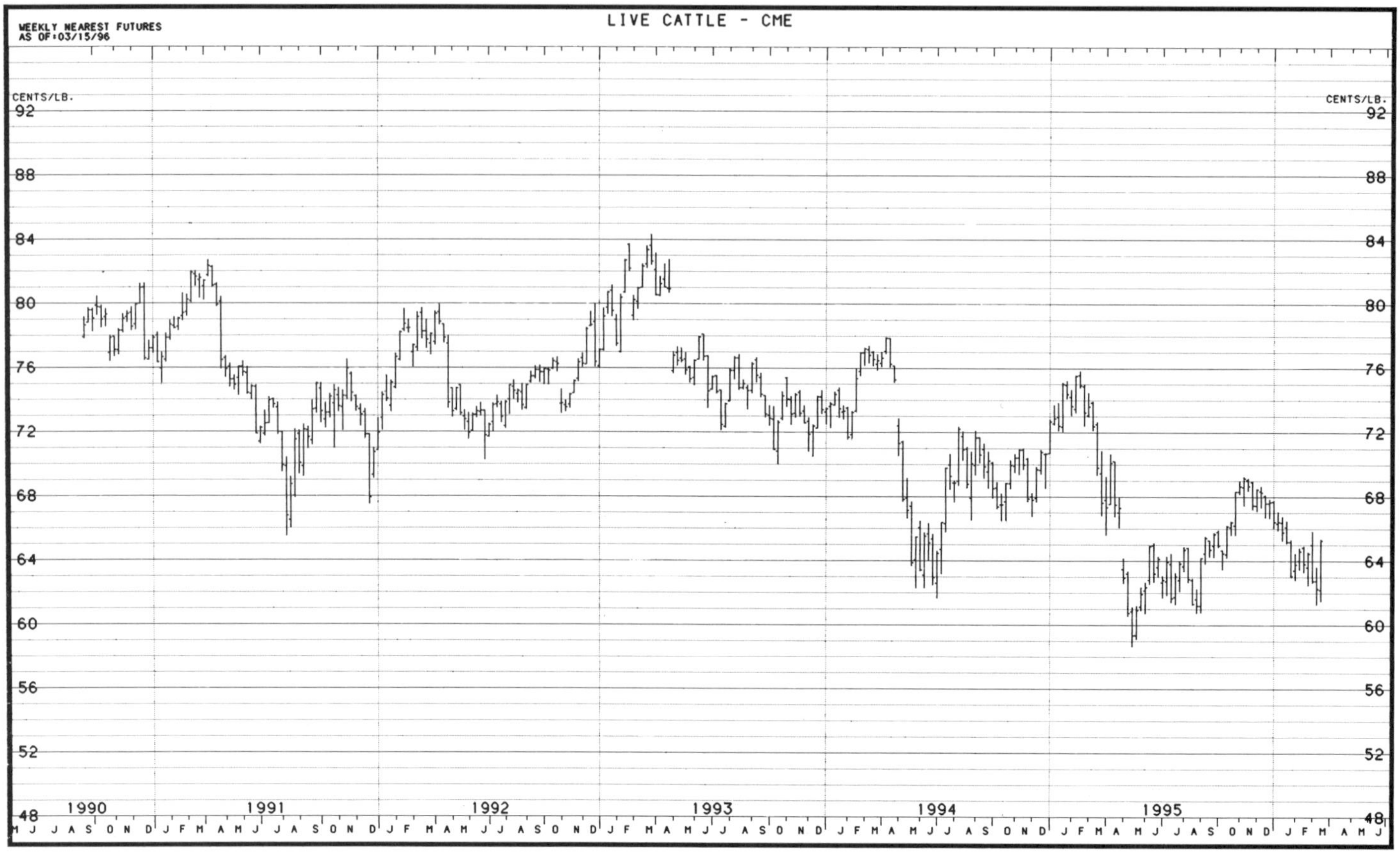

U.S. Cattle Marketings in 7 States In Thousands of Head

Year	January	February	March	April	May	June	July	August	September	October	November	December	Total
1985	1,782	1,540	1,559	1,603	1,604	1,577	1,655	1,697	1,598	1,603	1,395	1,401	19,014
1986	1,750	1,470	1,593	1,631	1,635	1,648	1,692	1,694	1,652	1,587	1,462	1,559	19,373
1987	1,793	1,478	1,571	1,541	1,514	1,732	1,723	1,732	1,671	1,700	1,478	1,612	19,545
1988	1,764	1,545	1,593	1,609	1,724	1,717	1,785	1,790	1,682	1,576	1,517	1,516	19,818
1989	1,677	1,534	1,579	1,580	1,752	1,791	1,700	1,694	1,579	1,628	1,490	1,403	19,407
1990	1,619	1,495	1,578	1,539	1,761	1,809	1,765	1,686	1,460	1,605	1,522	1,359	19,198
1991	1,632	1,431	1,499	1,650	1,651	1,681	1,724	1,716	1,598	1,665	1,376	1,443	19,066
1992	1,640	1,410	1,536	1,490	1,594	1,702	1,674	1,592	1,581	1,473	1,442	1,414	18,548
1993	1,534	1,441	1,585	1,572	1,681	1,743	1,702	1,692	1,652	1,546	1,469	1,431	19,048
1994	1,610	1,501	1,588	1,610	1,699	1,770	1,730	1,767	1,656	1,633	1,498	1,540	19,602
1995[1]	1,636	1,481	1,629	1,557	1,827	1,868	1,742	1,884	1,696	1,643	1,568	1,660	20,191

[1] Preliminary. *Source: Economic Research Service, U.S. Department of Agriculture*

Quarterly Trade of Live Cattle in the U.S. In Head

	Imports					Exports				
Year	First Quarter	Second Quarter	Third Quarter	Fourth Quarter	Annual	First Quarter	Second Quarter	Third Quarter	Fourth Quarter	Annual
1985	187,617	162,834	99,266	386,301	836,018	37,055	28,143	26,267	33,249	124,714
1986	375,446	265,978	174,834	590,266	1,406,524	20,054	23,377	28,558	35,858	107,847
1987	433,872	334,037	75,635	356,940	1,200,484	27,096	25,861	33,194	44,547	130,698
1988	731,806	216,269	131,503	252,628	1,332,206	22,563	28,008	157,642	113,236	321,449
1989	515,682	287,158	132,072	524,503	1,459,415	72,822	37,867	24,117	34,334	169,140
1990	566,516	577,328	301,668	689,488	2,135,000	33,929	28,384	23,335	34,266	119,914
1991	599,398	551,390	225,710	562,556	1,939,054	49,497	62,134	103,866	95,465	310,962
1992	599,255	505,568	389,417	801,025	2,255,265	97,683	100,282	74,827	48,998	321,790
1993	672,447	635,341	469,439	721,819	2,499,046	50,733	33,286	22,049	47,348	153,416
1994	569,466	540,845	386,596	585,597	2,082,504	51,803	43,115	62,729	73,144	230,791
1995[1]	868,694	804,686	488,515			26,597	18,441	19,794		

[1] Preliminary. *Source: Economic Research Service, U.S. Department of Agriculture*

Average Wholesale Prices of Slaughter Steers at Texas, Choice 2-4 (1100-1300 Lbs.[1]) In Dollars Per 100 Lbs.

Year	January	February	March	April	May	June	July	August	September	October	November	December	Average
1989	74.40	75.40	78.87	77.51	75.30	71.71	71.28	73.88	69.75	72.09	75.47	77.97	74.47
1990	79.02	78.62	79.31	80.00	78.14	76.73	75.07	77.61	78.05	79.82	81.12	81.26	78.73
1991	79.42	79.56	80.90	80.73	78.22	74.29	72.44	67.38	69.19	71.16	72.16	70.68	74.68
1992	73.88	77.21	78.18	77.83	75.98	73.55	73.02	74.26	75.04	75.97	75.29	78.35	75.71
1993	80.05	80.91	82.66	81.78	80.84	77.31	74.32	75.09	73.46	72.13	73.23	72.42	77.02
1994	72.88	73.03	75.41	75.48	68.12	63.60	66.58	68.04	66.79	66.51	69.43	69.35	73.78
1995	73.60	73.79	70.64	67.54	64.27	63.08	61.81	61.95	63.80	64.89	67.94	66.00	66.61

[1] Prior to 1986, 900-1100 lb. *Source: Economic Research Service, U.S.Department of Agriculture.*

Average Prices of Steers (Feeder) Oklahoma City In Dollars Per 100 Pounds

Year	January	February	March	April	May	June	July	August	September	October	November	December	Average
1989	93.94	92.49	92.02	88.67	86.26	90.16	93.52	92.18	90.19	89.58	90.78	90.52	90.86
1990	90.32	90.81	92.32	95.21	96.90	97.90	97.12	100.35	97.54	94.13	97.82	100.42	95.90
1991	99.22	101.01	101.50	103.00	101.22	104.05	102.32	96.09	94.62	92.90	89.93	86.69	97.71
1992	86.63	88.90	90.43	89.48	88.96	89.27	90.43	91.30	90.87	86.65	90.12	89.83	89.41
1993	93.59	93.80	95.82	97.65	96.85	100.09	98.58	96.48	94.78	91.82	90.57	91.04	95.09
1994	90.90	91.88	94.34	93.18	87.21	83.45	85.48	85.97	79.77	77.88	80.99	82.58	86.14
1995	83.41	83.05	79.50	76.62	73.69	72.89	70.09	69.62	66.71	68.60	63.45	64.44	72.67

Source: Chicago Mercantile Exchange

Federally Inspected Slaughter of Cattle in the United States In Thousands of Head

Year	January	February	March	April	May	June	July	August	September	October	November	December	Total
1989	2,711	2,500	2,744	2,576	2,947	2,951	2,730	2,975	2,706	2,876	2,694	2,600	33,010
1990	2,775	2,437	2,690	2,550	2,920	2,873	2,796	2,918	2,553	2,877	2,622	2,380	32,391
1991	2,809	2,408	2,444	2,674	2,786	2,650	2,784	2,843	2,634	2,855	2,508	2,491	31,887
1992	2,856	2,377	2,599	2,525	2,688	2,863	2,802	2,721	2,748	2,793	2,490	2,632	32,094
1993	2,601	2,411	2,712	2,623	2,720	2,957	2,811	2,883	2,810	2,729	2,632	2,706	32,593
1994[1]	2,679	2,501	2,799	2,656	2,780	2,984	2,770	3,001	2,885	2,878	2,744	2,806	33,483
1995[1]	2,802	2,524	2,890	2,591	3,064	3,187	2,878	3,160	3,019	2,982	2,897	2,741	34,735

[1] Preliminary. *Source: Agricultural Statistics Board, U.S. Department of Agriculture*

CATTLE AND CALVES

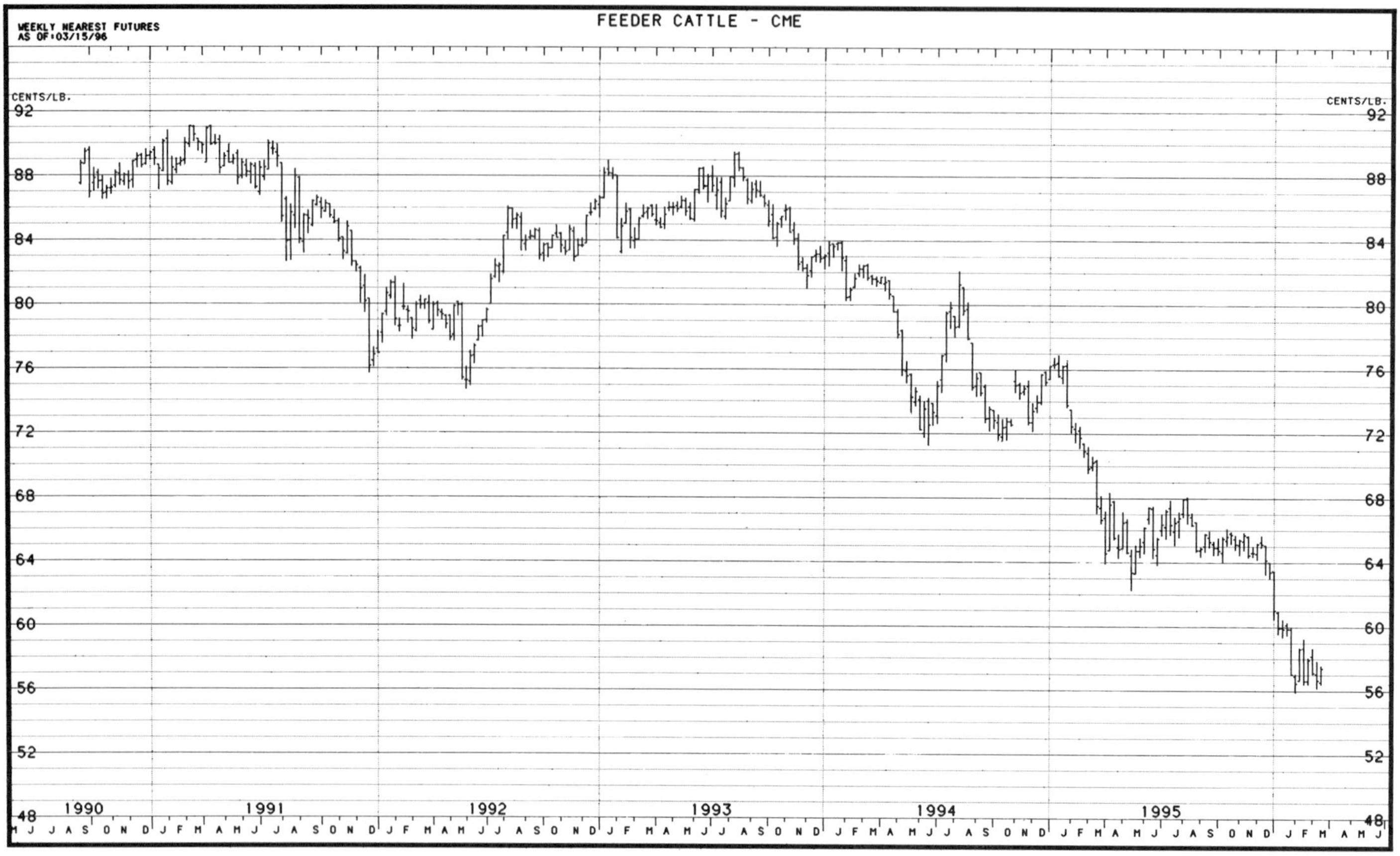

Average Open Interest of Live Cattle Futures at Chicago In Contracts

Year	January	February	March	April	May	June	July	August	September	October	November	December
1984	55,430	53,303	59,509	55,090	48,169	41,389	40,280	36,359	38,724	39,975	56,086	58,501
1985	58,544	57,763	60,999	59,309	53,332	48,603	49,092	43,730	49,443	55,616	67,849	63,076
1986	57,943	54,947	55,427	49,185	56,179	55,018	64,385	63,170	64,401	56,402	62,751	58,561
1987	62,770	83,958	91,018	89,818	98,350	86,144	81,399	81,315	90,915	80,156	75,379	74,839
1988	77,436	92,363	105,307	97,582	91,480	85,257	82,080	81,025	80,935	80,356	82,790	76,683
1989	80,464	84,909	93,240	82,267	81,588	69,981	78,045	76,582	73,530	65,807	73,962	71,508
1990	95,515	108,149	104,647	95,709	86,875	76,130	70,462	68,375	69,611	67,122	70,576	69,647
1991	74,392	79,695	84,574	83,322	78,284	70,107	67,868	68,359	74,483	70,395	75,788	74,687
1992	79,638	97,500	97,222	90,823	83,112	68,135	67,828	62,656	61,783	60,761	63,945	67,125
1993	78,481	79,256	88,113	78,144	72,183	68,287	66,617	66,560	70,275	70,559	73,571	76,042
1994	87,923	87,578	83,949	70,287	72,851	75,470	76,663	72,988	73,391	67,924	74,152	68,600
1995	80,306	78,793	76,821	64,763	61,460	56,783	58,077	55,511	58,319	62,222	69,495	69,065

Source: Chicago Mercantile Exchange

Volume of Trading of Live Cattle Futures at Chicago In Thousands of Contracts

Year	January	February	March	April	May	June	July	August	September	October	November	December	Total
1984	457.4	397.6	404.2	323.2	256.4	215.5	265.3	202.6	181.0	245.9	345.7	258.5	3,553.3
1985	340.7	290.3	327.9	304.3	412.0	317.2	440.5	370.2	400.2	445.3	405.0	383.8	4,437.3
1986	492.6	381.0	408.2	462.1	424.2	374.5	448.7	373.0	387.1	376.9	289.4	273.0	4,690.5
1987	376.6	426.7	474.2	456.6	523.7	357.8	394.8	412.7	485.8	580.4	363.1	377.0	5,229.3
1988	425.1	455.6	543.9	468.0	467.8	571.3	463.4	511.8	415.0	417.5	383.9	353.9	5,477.2
1989	452.9	357.7	409.0	404.2	382.9	370.3	327.9	331.9	376.9	345.4	266.2	240.2	4,265.7
1990	400.5	350.0	354.1	327.6	372.2	263.9	298.5	327.7	273.3	320.3	268.4	240.8	3,797.4
1991	344.2	252.1	288.9	300.4	247.2	254.8	311.2	406.1	321.2	386.3	327.7	352.8	3,792.9
1992	375.6	322.5	353.8	319.1	275.9	263.9	268.9	231.0	196.0	227.9	203.8	246.7	3,319.6
1993	328.8	294.2	363.4	263.5	199.7	255.4	269.3	226.0	269.5	297.6	248.4	291.1	3,307.0
1994	280.8	291.8	262.4	264.2	372.9	363.9	318.2	317.1	270.0	308.9	275.9	254.6	3,580.9
1995	289.6	259.0	391.7	287.2	285.7	290.2	245.3	266.8	233.4	220.1	246.7	241.1	3,257.1

Source: Chicago Mercantile Exchange

Beef Steer-Corn Price Ratio in the U.S.[1]

Year	January	February	March	April	May	June	July	August	September	October	November	December	Average
1988	39.0	39.0	39.0	39.0	38.0	29.2	24.7	26.4	27.6	28.1	29.1	28.9	32.33
1989	29.2	29.2	29.7	29.4	28.7	28.5	29.0	32.6	31.4	33.1	33.8	33.4	30.67
1990	34.1	33.8	32.9	31.5	29.9	29.4	29.2	31.5	34.0	36.6	37.6	36.6	33.09
1991	36.0	35.0	34.5	33.9	33.4	33.2	32.9	30.6	30.7	32.2	31.6	30.7	32.89
1992	30.3	31.0	30.7	30.8	30.2	29.8	31.7	34.7	35.0	37.3	38.2	38.7	33.20
1993	38.8	39.8	38.8	37.8	37.8	37.1	33.8	33.4	33.7	31.8	29.8	27.0	34.97
1994	27.1	26.3	27.5	28.5	26.8	24.0	28.4	31.6	30.2	32.1	34.4	31.9	29.07
1995[2]	32.6	32.4	30.5	28.4	26.4	25.2	23.2	23.5	23.0	21.0			26.62

[1] Bushels of corn equal in value to 100 pounds of steers and heifers. [2] Preliminary. *Source: Agricultural Statistics Board, U.S. Department of Agriculture.*

U.S. Farm Value, Income and Wholesale Prices of Cattle and Calves

	January 1		Gross Income	At Omaha[3]				Feeder Heifers at	Cows, Boning	Vealer, Choice	Cows, Com-	Wholesale Prices, Central U.S.		
			From	Steers[3]		Heifers		Oklahoma	Utility	Albany,	mercial	Choice,	Select,	Cow[6],
	Per Head	Total	C. & C.[2]	Choice	Select	Select	Choice	City[5]	Sioux Falls[6]	New York	Sioux Falls	700-850 lb.	700-850 lb.	Canner[7]
Year	Dollars	Million $	Million $	Dollars per 100 Pounds										
1988	523	52,148	36,810	69.58	67.06	65.35	68.16	77.11	47.21	95.82	49.46	NA	NA	88.61
1989	580	56,908	36,894	72.52	70.28	69.52	71.93	80.00	48.98	97.57	52.14	NA	NA	94.43
1990	614	60,285	39,945	77.40	75.24	73.94	76.82	85.31	53.60	97.61	57.13	123.11	116.49	99.96
1991	654	64,662	39,644	73.83	72.46	71.44	73.86	86.04	50.66	94.66	56.08	117.24	112.73	99.42
1992	629	62,656	37,958	74.65	73.65	72.88	74.91	78.41	44.84	87.01	51.22	116.02	111.66	93.85
1993[1]	649	65,287	39,750	75.60	74.80	74.76	75.90	82.79	47.52	89.11	56.47	117.71	113.53	95.43
1994[1]	659	66,968	36,802					74.55	42.51	88.01	48.28	106.73	102.08	84.39

[1] Preliminary. [2] Excludes interfarm sales and Government payments. Cash receipts from farm marketings and value of farm consumption. [3] 1,000 to 1,100 pound weight range. [4] 1,000 to 1,200 pound weight range. [5] 700 to 750 pound weight range. Prior to 1992, 600 to 700 pound weight range. [6] All weights. [7] & cutter. NA=Not available. *Source: Economic Research Service, U.S. Department of Agriculture*

Average Price Received by Farmers for Beef Cattle In Dollars Per 100 Pounds

Year	January	February	March	April	May	June	July	August	September	October	November	December	Average
1988	65.40	67.40	68.30	69.00	69.30	65.00	63.20	65.90	67.20	67.00	66.70	67.20	66.80
1989	70.60	71.60	72.00	70.10	68.80	67.60	68.00	69.70	68.20	68.70	69.80	71.00	69.68
1990	73.70	74.60	74.20	74.60	74.60	74.20	73.60	76.00	75.00	75.50	75.30	77.10	74.87
1991	76.60	77.00	78.50	78.20	75.90	73.60	71.60	68.80	68.70	70.40	67.90	67.40	72.88
1992	68.90	72.50	72.90	72.60	71.90	70.20	70.60	71.80	71.70	71.80	70.90	70.80	71.38
1993	73.20	75.80	77.30	77.30	77.10	74.50	72.50	72.70	71.40	69.10	69.30	68.50	73.23
1994	69.90	70.10	72.30	72.00	67.20	62.70	62.90	65.90	63.50	62.90	64.40	64.40	66.52
1995[1]	67.50	68.70	66.90	63.80	60.80	60.90	59.50	59.40	59.10	58.80	60.70	60.60	62.23

[1] Preliminary. *Source: Crop Reporting Board, U.S. Department of Agriculture*

Average Price Received by Farmers for Calves In Dollars Per 100 Pounds

Year	January	February	March	April	May	June	July	August	September	October	November	December	Average
1988	88.20	92.60	93.50	93.20	93.40	84.90	87.70	91.00	89.50	87.80	87.80	88.60	89.85
1989	92.80	95.90	94.00	90.40	91.10	94.10	94.60	94.20	91.10	88.10	86.70	89.10	91.84
1990	90.10	96.00	99.10	100.40	101.00	98.10	95.90	98.90	95.40	92.80	93.80	97.80	96.61
1991	98.00	104.00	107.00	104.00	107.00	106.00	103.00	98.30	96.20	93.90	90.20	87.60	99.60
1992	88.30	92.80	94.10	92.00	89.60	88.40	90.10	90.60	87.40	88.30	87.20	87.00	89.65
1993	91.40	95.90	98.20	99.60	99.20	99.10	96.90	95.10	93.50	93.90	91.60	92.80	95.60
1994	93.90	94.90	97.60	95.80	89.40	84.80	83.80	84.40	80.00	78.20	81.00	81.90	87.14
1995[1]	85.00	86.90	84.40	81.80	77.00	77.10	72.30	70.80	68.50	66.20	64.00	63.30	74.78

[1] Preliminary. *Source: Crop Reporting Board, U.S. Department of Agriculture*

Federally Inspected Slaughter of Calves and Vealers in the U.S. In Thousands of Head

Year	January	February	March	April	May	June	July	August	September	October	November	December	Total
1988	205	203	216	169	171	204	207	227	207	197	202	203	2,410
1989	196	175	194	152	157	161	169	189	173	191	175	167	2,137
1990	175	145	165	128	137	131	139	147	132	158	149	136	1,743
1991	150	120	119	105	102	90	108	108	115	127	125	131	1,408
1992	128	111	120	108	103	105	106	107	107	111	109	121	1,328
1993	101	97	116	96	82	91	90	95	94	94	101	103	1,159
1994	99	94	112	92	90	98	93	106	106	112	114	121	1,237
1995[1]	121	104	118	96	114	115	111	121	119	124	125	125	1,393

[1] Preliminary. *Source: Crop Reporting Board, U.S. Department of Agriculture*

Cement

Portland cement shipments in the U.S. and Puerto Rico in July 1995 were 7.91 million tonnes according to the U.S. Bureau of Mines. In June 1995 shipments were 8.64 million tonnes, while in July 1994 shipments were 7.77 million tonnes. For the first seven months of 1995, shipments of portland cement were 46.1 million tonnes for an average of 6.58 million tonnes a month. Foreign imports of cement in July 1995 were 1.11 million tonnes, while for the first seven months of 1995 they were 6.34 million tonnes. In July 1994 foreign imports were 895,150 tonnes.

Use of cement corresponds to areas where construction activity is increasing. The U.S. Bureau of Mines reports that from July 1994 to July 1995, portland cement shipments to the Northeast region declined 13 percent. Shipments to the South Atlantic region, which includes Florida, rose 10 percent. Shipments to the North Central region were up 2 percent. Shipments to the South Central region, which includes Texas, were up 6 percent. Cement shipments to the Mountain region were up 4 percent, while shipments to the Pacific region, including California, were down 1 percent.

For the first seven months of 1995, the leading producing districts for portland cement were Southern California with 3.74 million tonnes, Michigan with 2.67 million tonnes, Southern Texas with 2.57 million tonnes, and Alabama with 2.25 million tonnes.

Prepared masonry cement production in July 1995 was 288,045 tonnes, down 7 percent from June and down slightly from the June 1994 total of 293,016 tonnes. For the January-July 1995 period, masonry cement shipments were 1.86 million tonnes. For all of 1994, shipments were 3.32 million tonnes. Foreign imports of masonry in July 1995 were 4,345 tonnes, while for all of 1994 they were 42,092 tonnes. The leading producing states were Indiana, Florida, Michigan and Alabama.

White cement imported for consumption in the U.S. in June 1995 totaled 40,361 tonnes. For the first seven months of 1995, white cement imports were 231,788 tonnes with the leading sources being Canada, Denmark and Spain. Clinker cement imports in June 1995 were 319,501 tonnes, while for the January-June 1995 period they were 1.49 million tonnes. The major suppliers were Canada, Venezuela and Bulgaria.

World Production of Hydraulic Cement by Selected Countries In Thousands of Short Tons

Year	Brazil	Canada	China	France	Germany	India	Italy	Japan	Poland	Rep. of Korea	Russia[3]	Spain	Turkey	United Kingdom	United States	World Total
1988	27,922	13,267	231,000	27,888	42,694	44,864	41,760	85,489	18,722	31,961	153,771	28,000	24,995	18,195	78,252	1,232,686
1989	28,578	13,879	228,000	29,580	44,934	50,706	43,414	87,873	18,877	33,592	154,804	30,175	26,231	18,573	78,559	1,266,064
1990	25,848	11,745	210,000	26,388	37,684	49,000	39,975	84,445	12,518	33,600	151,371	28,092	24,500	14,700	71,407	1,160,000
1991	27,490	9,396	252,610	26,507	34,396	51,000	40,806	89,564	12,012	34,999	140,000	28,008	26,091	12,200	66,753	1,180,000
1992	24,920	5,698	308,000	21,165	37,529	50,000	41,347	88,253	11,908	44,400	64,000	25,067	28,607	11,000	71,426	1,240,000
1993[1]	25,900	6,672	368,000	19,300	36,600	53,800	42,000	88,000	12,228	47,300	60,000	26,000	31,400	11,200	75,117	1,300,000
1994[2]	26,000	10,600	400,000	20,200	40,400	54,000	40,000	91,500	13,900	52,100	50,000	26,000	30,600	11,500	77,900	1,370,000

[1] Preliminary. [2] Estimate. [3] Formerly part of the U.S.S.R.; data not reported separately until 1992. *Source: U.S. Bureau of Mines*

Salient Statistics of Cement in the United States

Year	Net Import Reliance as a % of Apparent Consumption	Production: Portland	Production: Others[3]	Production: Total	Capacity Used at (Portland Mills) %	Shipments From Mills: Total Mil. Tons	Shipments From Mills: Value[4] Mil. $	Average Value (F.O.B. Mill) $ per ton	Stocks at Mills Dec. 31	Exports[5]	Apparent Consumption	Imports for Consumption[5] by Country: Canada	Japan	Mexico	Spain	Total
		---- Thousand Tons ----							---- Million Tons ----			---- Thousands of Short Tons ----				
1988	19	73,272	3,595	76,867	74.3	89,460	4,370	48.85	5,997	101	93,256	3,628	1,758	4,992	1,857	17,488
1989	16	73,895	3,294	77,189	75.3	86,238	4,243	49.20	6,300	512	90,676	3,420	2,415	4,411	1,562	15,741
1990	14	67,044	2,911	69,955	76.3	78,199	4,280	54.73	5,637	503	81,305	2,918	1,906	2,093	1,188	12,041
1991	10	64,165	3,028	67,193	72.2	68,999	3,832	55.54	6,009	633	74,000	2,837	300	947	634	7,893
1992	7	66,841	2,744	69,585	76.0	69,203	3,779	54.61	5,272	746	75,400	2,997	278	825	446	6,166
1993[1]	8	70,845	2,962	73,807	79.1	74,079	4,175	56.36	4,788	625	80,514	3,629	43	783	597	7,060
1994[2]	12	74,335	3,613	77,948	82.3	80,490	4,981	61.88	4,805	633	91,160	4,268	14	640	1,342	11,303

[1] Preliminary. [2] Estimate. [3] Masonry, natural & pozzolan (slag-line). [4] Value received F.O.B. mill, excluding cost of containers. [5] Hydraulic & clinker cement. NA = Not available. *Source: U.S. Bureau of Mines*

Shipments of Finished Portland Cement from Mills in the U.S. In Thousands of Short Tons

Year	Jan.	Feb.	Mar.	Apr.	May	June	July	Aug.	Sept.	Oct.	Nov.	Dec.	Total
1991				38,750.1				7,382.0	6,780.3	7,586.8	5,310.9	4,434.4	70,245
1992	4,121.8	4,204.5	5,258.7	6,577.3	7,061.2	7,675.4	7,668.1	7,652.7	7,732.9	8,285.3	5,531.8	4,817.7	76,829
1993	3,715.7	4,039.0	5,381.5	6,375.9	7,294.4	8,079.0	7,936.4	8,330.6	8,747.2	8,920.2	7,463.4	5,968.1	86,386
1994	4,112.0	4,551.6	7,033.3	7,566.9	8,859.2	9,465.7	8,567.6	9,896.7	9,338.5	9,255.6	7,703.6	6,347.0	92,593
1995[1]	4,736.3	5,046.2	7,077.5	7,147.5	8,610.7	9,521.3	8,718.5	9,886.3	9,111.2	9,255.6	7,703.6	6,347.0	92,698

[1] Preliminary. *Source: U.S. Bureau of Mines*

Cheese

Each year of this decade saw world production and consumption of cheese setting new a record highs, with the U.S. the largest participant. World production in 1995 totaled 11.6 million metric tons versus 11.5 million in 1994; U.S. production totaled 3.2 million and 3.1 million, respectively. France, the second largest producer, turns out about half the U.S. total. World consumption of 11.2 million tons in 1995 compares with 11.1 million in 1994, with the U.S. totals, 3.3 million and 3.2 million. France and Italy combined consumed about 2.3 million tons in each year. Most of the world's cheese is consumed in the same country where it's produced, with total exports about 6 percent of production, two-thirds of which is exported from Europe. World stocks at the end of 1995 of 1.7 million tons were fractionally lower than a year earlier, with Italy's inventory, as usual, accounting for more than a third of the total.

Demand is sensitive to economic conditions and consumer disposable income. Changes in the U.S. dollar affect foreign trade. Following a rapid climb in prices in early 1995, world cheddar prices stabilized, but at historically high levels as the market adjusted to the dollar's value.

American cheese accounts for the largest individual variety of U.S. production. Since the late 1980's, however, other varieties—mostly Italian—have had a combined production that exceeds American cheese. U.S. per capita cheese consumption has shown irregular patterns in recent years. American cheese use peaked in the mid 1980s as Italian cheese varieties increased sharply. Mozzarella makes up the bulk of Italian cheese use. For most dairy products, statistical data is a product of the fat or skim solids content. Cheese is handled somewhat differently. Making cheese exhausts virtually all the value of the skim component of raw milk, even though most of the solids-not-fat are left in the liquid whey. To account for this, the factors used for cheese reflect the total skim solids needed to produce a pound, not just the casein and minerals in the cheese.

U.S. cheese prices have a seasonal pattern, generally strengthening in autumn. When counterseasonal price strength develops it usually reflects regional conditions more than national supply/demand factors. U.S. wholesale cheese prices (40-pound blocks, Wisconsin) averaged $1.315 per pound in 1994; the average for 1995 was expected to be higher.

Futures Markets

Cheddar Cheese futures and options are traded on the Coffee, Sugar & Cocoa Exchange, Inc. (CSCE)

World Cheese (Total[1]) Production In Millions of Metric Tons

Year	Agrentina	Australia	Brazil	Canada	Denmark	France	Germany	Italy	Mexico	Netherlands	New Zealand	Russia[3]	Sweden	Switzerland	Ukraine	United Kingdom	United States
1985	210	160	205	213	253	1,300	495	684	187	522	118	-----	109	126	809	260	2,305
1986	256	170	185	226	252	1,320	530	694	262	534	127	-----	106	131	844	256	2,363
1987	277	177	195	246	271	1,342	817	704	298	552	113	-----	107	128	861	263	2,424
1988	265	176	200	252	258	1,378	849	737	370	559	128	-----	115	134	895	299	2,527
1989	260	190	220	247	275	1,485	885	760	373	568	128	460	109	137	184	280	2,546
1990	270	175	200	255	293	1,471	749	811	384	593	122	458	108	138	184	316	2,749
1991	290	178	290	262	285	1,500	777	885	395	610	125	394	107	142	162	303	2,747
1992	310	197	296	262	290	1,489	783	890	390	634	142	299	117	141	160	324	2,943
1993	350	211	310	271	321	1,509	821	885	395	637	145	304	126	138	140	331	2,961
1994[1]	380	234	330	281	286	1,541	855	882	410	649	192	275	133	137	130	326	3,053
1995[2]	400	225	350	285	300	1,550	870	880	400	670	195	250	130	137	130	322	3,160

[1] Preliminary. [2] Estimate. [3] Formerly part of the U.S.S.R.; data not reported seperately prior to 1989. *Source: Foreign Agricultural Service, U.S. Department of Agriculture*

Supply and Distribution of All Cheese in the United States In Millions of Pounds

	Supply					Cheese	Distribution					Domestic Disapparence		
	Production							Government						
Year	Whole Milk[2]	All Cheese[3]	January 1 Commercial Stocks	Imports[4]	Total Supply	40-Lb. Blocks Wisconsin Assembly Points ¢ per lb.	Exports & Shipments[5]	January 1 Stocks	Dec. 31 Stocks	American Cheese Removed by USDA Programs	Total Disappearance	American Cheese Donated	Total	Per Capita
1984	2,648	4,674	1,266	306	6,246	137.96	108	793.0	621.0	447.3	5,184	560	5,118	21.48
1985	2,855	5,081	1,062	303	6,446	127.72	125	621.0	543.7	629.0	5,501	636	5,437	22.54
1986	2,798	5,209	945	295	6,449	127.30	97	543.7	420.1	468.4	5,660	560	5,602	23.11
1987	2,717	5,344	789	265	6,399	123.19	88	420.1	81.2	282.0	5,939	607	5,861	24.09
1988	2,757	5,572	460	252	6,284	123.80	76	81.2	36.7	238.1	5,886	257	5,801	23.70
1989	2,674	5,615	398	276	6,289	138.79	74	36.7	6.6	37.4	5,959	67	5,901	23.81
1990	2,894	6,059	330	298	6,689	136.69	75	6.6	8.2	21.5	6,231	21	6,168	24.64
1991	2,769	6,055	458	297	6,810	124.41	72	8.2	23.1	76.9	6,393	60	6,337	25.01
1992	2,937	6,488	393	285	7,191	131.91	78	23.1	16.5	14.4	6,698	0	6,661	26.01
1993[1]	2,376	6,528	454	320	6,719	131.52	87	16.5	2.2	8.3	6,829	0	6,789	26.24
1994[1]	2,345	6,730	464	332	7,526	131.45	55	2.2	.9	6.9	7,082		7,010	26.82

[1] Preliminary. [2] Whole milk American cheddar. [3] All types of cheese except cottage, pot and baker's cheese. [4] Imports for consumption. [5] Commercial.
Source: Economic Research Service, U.S. Department of Agriculture

CHEESE

Cheese Production in the United States   In Millions of Pounds

Year	American: Whole Milk	American: Part Skim	American: Total	Swiss, Including Block	Munster	Brick	Limburger	Cream & Neufchatel Cheese	Italian Varieties	Blue Mond	All Other Varieties	Total of All Cheese[2]	Cottage Cheese: Lowfat	Cottage Cheese: Curd[3]	Cottage Cheese: Creamed[4]
1984	2,649	2.7	2,652	208.0	76.0	16.0	1.2	276.5	1,318.8	34.1	92.2	4,674	229.3	606.2	736.1
1985	2,855	2.4	2,858	222.9	82.1	20.1	1.0	293.8	1,491.3	33.4	77.7	5,081	244.4	598.8	715.6
1986	2,798	2.1	2,800	227.3	88.5	20.4	1.1	321.5	1,632.9	34.2	82.1	5,209	265.5	600.1	704.8
1987	2,717	.9	2,718	227.2	92.6	28.9	1.1	342.2	1,799.8	35.9	99.1	5,344	270.5	573.8	674.8
1988	2,757	1.1	2,758	250.1	83.3	24.8	1.0	375.9	1,937.1	37.8	104.3	5,572	290.9	556.7	647.1
1989	2,674	.8	2,675	231.2	91.1	17.5	.9	401.0	2,042.9	34.6	121.2	5,615	300.9	526.9	572.3
1990	2,894	.8	2,895	261.1	100.2	17.3	.8	430.8	2,207.0	36.4	110.7	6,059	301.8	493.5	530.6
1991	2,769	.8	2,770	234.5	106.4	15.3	.7	446.7	2,328.6	34.3	118.5	6,055	321.1	490.9	497.9
1992	2,937	1.2	2,938	237.3	116.4	15.5	1.0	516.7	2,508.6	33.3	121.9	6,488	329.5	502.4	457.3
1993[1]	2,954	3.7	2,957	231.4	117.5	12.5	.9	539.9	2,621.5	33.3	137.2	6,730	321.0	471.4	410.0
1994[1]	2,952	24.7	2,977	221.2	111.8	12.2	8.5	573.4	2,610.2	36.5	150.8	6,713	311.0	463.3	411.8

[1] Preliminary. [2] Excludes full-skim cheddar and cottage cheese. [3] Includes cottage, pot, and baker's cheese with a butterfat content of less than 4%. [4] Includes cheese with a butterfat content of 4 to 19%. *Source: Economic Research Service, U.S. Department of Agriculture*

Wholesale Price of Cheese, 40-lb. Blocks, Wisconsin Assembly Points   In Cents Per Pound

Year	January	February	March	April	May	June	July	August	September	October	November	December	Average
1985	136.5	134.3	132.1	129.9	128.0	126.8	124.7	124.3	124.3	124.3	123.8	123.9	127.7
1986	123.8	124.5	123.2	125.0	126.0	125.4	126.7	129.5	129.7	130.2	133.4	130.4	127.3
1987	127.8	122.5	122.3	122.4	122.0	122.0	123.2	125.5	126.6	121.9	121.3	120.8	123.2
1988	118.4	116.1	115.6	115.1	115.0	116.2	118.3	127.6	134.6	136.4	136.3	136.0	123.8
1989	129.1	117.6	117.9	120.4	123.9	130.8	140.6	143.3	155.8	160.3	163.6	162.2	138.8
1990	152.3	131.6	130.7	140.5	145.8	149.5	151.0	150.3	142.6	114.9	112.0	112.7	136.2
1991	111.4	111.5	111.5	111.7	115.0	121.4	128.4	136.1	139.7	140.2	135.8	130.2	124.4
1992	125.4	119.0	119.8	131.9	140.0	141.3	141.8	142.0	136.9	132.4	129.4	123.2	131.9
1993	119.3	118.6	124.3	140.8	141.8	133.7	126.3	124.8	137.4	138.9	138.7	133.7	131.5
1994	132.2	134.2	140.0	143.3	125.7	120.2	129.1	132.2	135.6	135.4	127.9	121.3	131.5
1995[1]	124.5	130.4	131.1	122.8	122.1	126.9	126.7	132.2	141.3	145.0	145.8	144.6	132.8

[1] Preliminary. *Source: Economic Research Service, U.S. Department of Agriculture*

United States Total Cheese Production[1]   In Millions of Pounds

Year	January	February	March	April	May	June	July	August	September	October	November	December	Total
1985	395.0	361.5	416.0	435.3	461.1	447.2	443.8	427.3	403.6	432.9	415.4	441.8	5,081
1986	433.9	400.0	457.1	459.5	482.5	457.4	436.6	421.8	410.1	410.2	401.0	439.4	5,209
1987	422.0	398.6	457.4	462.1	477.8	465.6	453.8	426.0	430.7	448.6	431.8	469.7	5,344
1988	439.5	436.2	491.6	475.3	488.2	476.7	454.9	442.0	451.9	470.0	458.9	486.5	5,572
1989	456.6	419.5	488.4	472.6	494.9	485.5	464.6	460.4	448.5	464.0	453.0	489.5	5,614
1990	483.7	471.9	531.7	521.1	542.8	522.8	502.2	495.0	472.6	505.9	495.5	522.1	6,061
1991	501.7	458.0	530.1	515.4	532.3	509.0	499.5	498.2	485.0	521.0	502.3	533.7	6,061
1992	514.1	497.1	542.7	534.7	550.9	549.8	541.8	534.6	528.3	558.2	547.5	571.6	6,488
1993	517.3	492.5	563.2	561.4	576.9	563.2	537.9	525.8	531.1	560.0	540.1	558.9	6,528
1994	538.3	505.8	591.8	554.3	590.4	558.7	550.7	562.4	565.5	574.5	559.3	578.3	6,730
1995[2]	565.6	528.4	593.9	563.9	597.5	587.6	560.9	559.1	575.7	585.6	586.5	609.6	6,914

[1] Excludes cottage and full skim American. [2] Preliminary. *Source: National Agricultural Statistics Service, U.S. Department of Agriculture*

Cold Storage Holdings of All Varieties of Cheese in the U.S., on First of Month   In Millions of Pounds

Year	January	February	March	April	May	June	July	August	September	October	November	December
1985	986.2	968.9	944.4	907.7	898.6	911.0	954.2	963.5	962.9	941.0	891.8	877.5
1986	852.9	835.8	813.2	815.7	838.4	873.3	892.8	915.6	916.2	859.0	805.0	757.0
1987	693.6	683.9	652.4	646.5	645.1	666.8	659.0	642.5	606.6	580.8	538.0	495.9
1988	457.1	455.1	448.3	443.8	451.9	460.1	480.9	496.1	460.8	421.3	400.7	366.7
1989	388.1	395.3	404.4	396.6	412.1	431.9	429.6	430.4	419.8	370.2	331.4	330.6
1990	328.0	358.4	374.9	395.8	413.4	441.6	465.0	484.6	475.7	459.9	445.4	437.3
1991	457.8	483.9	475.1	492.4	510.3	512.1	521.5	511.5	494.1	477.9	429.3	409.0
1992	415.4	440.9	445.9	449.0	449.7	455.9	465.2	496.2	487.3	449.7	441.1	462.0
1993	462.0	476.1	454.4	460.0	453.6	480.5	541.2	533.3	517.7	500.1	471.9	462.4
1994	465.2	495.2	473.6	473.3	487.9	513.4	521.4	506.3	474.7	453.0	448.3	434.2
1995[1]	437.2	456.8	455.9	466.3	466.1	465.8	465.8	482.4	458.1	428.5	418.7	393.0

[1] Preliminary. [2] Quantities are given in "net weight." *Source: National Agricultural Statistics Service, U.S.Department of Agriculture*

Chromite

Chromite is the ore mineral of chromium. It is used in making stainless steel and other alloys for which resistance to oxidation and corrosion is important. Chromium is used for plating and as a tanning agent. The mineral chromite is made into refractory linings for steel-making furnaces. Since the U.S. mines no chromite ore, imports are essential. South Africa is the leading producer of ferrochromium, and its exports to the U.S. are for use in the defense industry. Outside of South Korea, the next largest chromite producers are Kazakhstan and Albania, and in the Western Hemisphere, Brazil and Cuba produce small amounts. Chromium is an essential trace element for human health. However, some chromium compounds are acutely toxic, chronically toxic or carcinogenic.

1994 chromium apparent consumption was 390,000 tonnes of contained chromium. U.S. supply consisted of recycled and imported chromium materials. The U.S. recycled about 582,000 tonnes of stainless steel scrap and imported about 567,000 tonnes of chromite ore, ferroalloys, chemicals and pigments. The U.S. exported about 90,300 tonnes of chromium materials. Compared to 1993, the quantity of chromium materials trade decreased in 1994.

The U.S. has no chromite ore reserves and a limited reserve base. As a result, domestic supply has been a concern during every national military emergency since World War I. World chromite resources, mining capacity and ferrochromium production capacity are concentrated in the Eastern Hemisphere. Recycling is the only domestic supply source of chromium. World chromite ore reserves are more than adequate to meet anticipated world demand.

In the Jan.-June 1995 period, U.S. production of chromium ferroalloys and metal were 26,800 tonnes. For all of 1994, production was 45,800 tonnes. Stainless steel production in the period was 520,000 tonnes, while for all of 1994 it was 1.83 million tonnes.

U.S. consumption of chromium ferroalloys and metal is primarily by the steel industry. In the Jan.-June 1995 period, stainless and heat resisting steel used 104,000 tonnes. Full alloy steel production consumed 16,900 tonnes while carbon steel production used 3,760 tonnes. Use in the production of superalloys was 5,130 tonnes while tool steel used 3,220 tonnes.

For the Jan.-June 1995 period, U.S. imports for consumption of chromite ore were 66,000 tonnes while for all of 1994 they were 201,000 tonnes. Imports of chromium ferroalloys were 200,000 tonnes compared to the 1994 total of 317,000 tonnes. Chromium metal imports were 3,670 tonnes while for all of 1994 they were 6,520 tonnes.

U.S. exports of chromite ore over the Jan.-May 1995 period were 8,180 tonnes, gross weight. For all of 1994, chromite ore exports were 47,100 tonnes. Exports of chromium ferroalloys in the first five months of 1995 were 4,020 tonnes, gross weight, and for all of 1994 were 12,000 tonnes. Chromium metal exports for the same periods were 263 tonnes, gross weight, and 446 tonnes, respectively.

In June 1995, the U.S. stockpile of chromite ore was 1.41 million tonnes, chromium ferroalloy stocks were 1.07 million tonnes and chromium metal stocks were 7,690 tonnes.

World Mine Production of Chromite   In Thousands of Metric Tons (Gross Weight)

Year	Albania	Brazil	China	Cuba	Finland	Greece	India	Iran	Kazak-hstan[3]	Mada-gascar	Philip-pines	South Africa	Sudan	Turkey	Zim-babwe	World Total[1]
1985	825	190	------	38	506	59	565	56	3,360	127	272	3,699	10	589	536	10,945
1986	850	223	50	50	678	62	638	56	3,640	83	174	3,907	9	543	533	11,555
1987	1,075	338	32	52	543	64	624	92	3,570	107	188	3,789	13	762	570	11,919
1988	1,109	410	26	52	700	50	821	60	3,700	64	129	4,245	8	851	561	12,896
1989	900	476	25	51	513	62	1,003	73	3,800	63	217	4,951	25	1,077	627	14,006
1990	950	263	25	50	504	35	1,050	77	3,800	151	183	4,620	13	836	573	13,200
1991	587	340	25	50	473	37	940	90	3,800	149	191	5,100	10	940	564	13,320
1992	322	449	25	50	499	4	1,150	130	3,500	161	66	3,360	10	531	522	10,993
1993[1]	282	308	54	50	511	3	1,000	130	2,900	144	68	2,830	10	570	252	9,301
1994[2]	223	360	50	50	573	4	909	129	2,020	90	69	3,590	10	790	517	9,600

[1] Estimate. [2] Preliminary. [3] Formerly part of the U.S.S.R.; data not reported seperately until 1992. *Source: U.S. Bureau of Mines*

U.S. Salient Statistics of Chromite   In Thousands of Metric Tons (Gross Weight)

Year	% Net Import Reliance of Apparent Con-sumption	Production of Ferro-chromium	Exports	Imports for Con-sumption	Reexports	Consumption by Primary Consumer Groups: Total	Metal-lurgical & Chemical	Refractory	Consumer Stocks, Dec. 31: Metal-lurgical & Chemical	Refractory	Total Stocks	$ per Metric Ton: South Africa[3]	Turkish[4]
1985	75	100	91	376	3	508	449	59	228	44	272	42	125
1986	79	95	84	443	1	388	342	45	249	35	285	42	125
1987	75	107	1	490	5	506	459	48	309	23	332	46	115
1988	78	120	4	615	1	551	495	56	366	23	390	56	180
1989	78	147	40	525	2	561	517	44	368	24	392	65	185
1990	71	109	6	306	4	405	361	44	333	21	355	55	135
1991	72	68	9	212	-----	375	339	36	310	11	321	50	130
1992	76	61	7	219	-----	362	335	27	308	13	321	60	110
1993[1]	74	63	10	255	2	337	314	23	259	16	275	60	110
1994[2]	75	67	47	201	-----	322	302	20	250	17	266	55	108

[1] Preliminary. [2] Estimate. [3] Cr_2O_3, 44% (Transvaal). *Source: U.S. Bureau of Mines*

Coal

U.S. coal production in the first quarter of 1995 reached a record 265 million short tons, up from 254 million tons in the first quarter of 1994 and 260 million tons in the fourth quarter of 1994. A major reason for the increase in coal use has been rising demand by electric utilities which accounted for 88% of U.S. coal production in 1994. For all of 1994, coal production was 1.03 billion tons. Wyoming produced nearly 86 million tons in the first quarter 1995, up 15% from the same period of 1994, West Virginia production was 42.1 million tons, up 11%, and Kentucky production at 40 million tons was up almost 2%.

U.S. coal exports in the first quarter 1995 totaled 19 million tons, up 28 percent from the same quarter of 1994. Exports of steam coal were 7 million tons while exports of metallurgical coal were 12 million tons. There were increased shipments of steam coal to Italy, Germany, the Netherlands and Denmark. The increases in metallurgical coal went to Canada, Japan and South Korea.

U.S. coal imports in the first quarter of 1995 were 1.8 million short tons, down slightly from the fourth quarter of 1994. The major sources were Colombia and Venezuela.

Domestic coal consumption in the January-March 1995 period totaled 228 million tons, down 4% from the previous year. Electric utilities used 199 million tons in the first quarter 1995, down 4%. Coal consumption at coke plants rose 5% to just over 8 million tons while consumption at other industrial plants fell 5% to 19 million tons.

At the end of first quarter 1995, coal stocks held by producers and distributors were just over 42 million tons, versus 33 million tons held at the end of the previous quarter. Consumer stocks rose 5% to 144 million tons. Total stocks of coal on March 31, 1995 were 186 million tons.

World Coal Production (Monthly Average)[3] In Thousands of Metric Tons

Year	Australia	Canada	China	Czech Rep.[4]	France	Germany	India	Indonesia	Kazakhstan[5]	Rep. of Korea	Poland	Romania	Russia[5]	Ukraine[5]	United Kingdom	United States
1987	12,309	2,721	74,910	2,145	1,124	6,865	14,748	157	------	1,920	16,084	733	43,257	------	8,703	63,528
1988	11,234	3,215	78,872	2,159	1,012	6,610	15,692	238	------	1,889	16,085	742	43,587	------	8,649	65,405
1989	12,317	3,233	87,833	2,089	1,025	6,454	16,569	380	------	1,583	14,830	691	48,083	------	8,190	67,608
1990	13,236	3,139	90,000	1,842	879	6,363	16,819	611	------	1,328	12,306	319	39,300	------	7,442	71,137
1991	13,720	3,326	88,212	1,623	842	6,063	18,905	1,143	------	1,148	11,698	270	33,769	------	8,028	68,755
1992	14,594	2,693	91,278	NA	790	6,013	19,490	1,760	10,546	928	10,960	292	16,123	NA	7,273	75,413
1993	14,711	2,943	96,177	1,574	790	5,347	20,503	2,299	9,323	737	10,937	331	16,200	9,545	5,282	71,473
1994[1]	19,442	3,028	100,508	1,530	829	4,802	20,679	2,644	8,696	595	10,963	377	14,300	9,222	3,976	78,102
1995[2]	19,658	NA	104,098	1,563	NA	4,911	27,723	2,174	6,358	478	11,382	346	14,157	NA	4,099	85,960

[1] Preliminary. [2] Estimate. [3] All grades of anthracite and bituminous coal, but excludes recovered slurries, lignite and brown coal. [4] Formerly part of Czechoslovakia; data not reported separately until 1993. [5] Formerly part of the U.S.S.R.; data not reported separately until 1992. NA = Not available.
Source: United Nations

United States Production of Coal by Principal States In Thousands of Short Tons

	Bituminous & Lignite													
Year	Alabama	Colorado	Illinois	Indiana	Kentucky	Montana	Ohio	Pennsylvania	Texas	Virgina	West Virgina	Wyoming	Total	Total U.S.
1986	25,826	15,237	61,866	32,852	153,933	33,978	36,441	67,356	48,590	41,178	129,907	136,826	886,023	890,315
1987	25,540	14,420	59,155	34,208	165,192	34,399	35,788	66,863	50,529	44,543	136,676	146,850	915,202	918,762
1988	26,518	15,913	58,594	31,271	157,852	38,881	34,043	67,091	52,281	45,886	145,005	164,014	946,711	950,265
1989	27,992	17,123	59,267	33,641	167,389	37,742	33,689	67,248	53,854	43,006	153,580	171,558	980,729	980,729
1990	29,030	18,910	60,393	35,907	128,396	37,616	35,252	67,008	55,755	46,917	169,205	184,249	1,025,569	1,029,076
1991	27,269	17,834	60,258	31,468	158,980	38,237	30,569	61,936	53,825	41,954	167,352	193,854	992,539	995,984
1992	25,796	19,226	59,857	30,466	161,068	38,889	30,403	65,498	55,071	43,024	162,164	190,172	994,062	997,545
1993[1]	24,768	21,886	41,098	29,295	156,299	35,917	28,816	55,394	21,847	39,317	130,525	210,129	941,119	945,424
1994[1]	23,285	25,249	52,981	31,025	160,605	41,676	29,121	57,452	52,450	38,448	161,476	236,077	1,025,893	1,030,649
1995[2]	26,087	24,447	47,900	25,682	150,598	37,442	23,541	57,851	49,537	34,506	162,920	263,683	1,016,960	1,021,119

[1] Preliminary. [2] Estimate. *Source: Energy Information Administration, U.S. Department of Energy*

Bituminous Coal Production[1] in the United States In Thousands of Short Tons

Year	Jan.	Feb.	Mar.	Apr.	May.	June	July	Aug.	Sept.	Oct.	Nov.	Dec.	Total
1986	78,282	72,686	77,569	74,894	73,137	72,671	67,818	76,549	75,022	76,832	68,671	70,264	886,023
1987	74,256	71,253	75,396	70,524	70,256	76,555	69,207	80,087	81,854	85,335	78,677	79,275	915,202
1988	75,325	76,757	83,943	75,324	73,981	76,443	69,176	88,175	83,196	80,799	82,925	80,260	946,711
1989	81,969	75,040	88,981	77,233	82,486	78,544	66,269	90,824	84,618	87,657	85,043	72,554	980,729
1990	90,304	81,796	91,357	83,350	86,615	84,720	79,585	91,558	83,107	93,418	86,772	75,676	1,029,076
1991	85,810	82,592	85,012	79,324	79,917	76,896	79,745	88,851	81,533	90,307	81,730	79,383	995,984
1992	87,979	82,102	85,835	82,364	80,197	79,968	80,768	84,401	83,555	86,265	80,240	83,021	997,545
1993	80,508	76,341	84,782	79,329	73,759	80,949	70,771	76,209	79,705	80,628	79,404	79,905	945,424
1994	76,578	81,569	95,969	87,534	82,105	86,223	77,421	93,881	88,346	85,085	86,317	87,856	1,033,504
1995[2]	88,029	83,587	92,666	80,054	83,253	84,169	79,759	87,776	88,214	87,525	83,866	78,526	1,016,960

[1] Includes small amounts of lignite. [2] Preliminary. *Source: Energy Information Administration, U.S. Department of Energy*

Pennsylvania Anthracite Coal Production[1] In Thousands of Short Tons

Year	Jan.	Feb.	Mar.	Apr.	May	June	July	Aug.	Sept.	Oct.	Nov.	Dec.	Total
1986	261	243	260	300	294	297	298	330	333	431	373	340	4,292
1987	256	264	305	339	333	359	426	441	441	371	331	310	3,560
1988	215	268	279	265	296	282	246	360	315	377	302	253	3,555
1989	281	282	337	273	280	256	197	311	299	373	339	291	3,519
1990	237	221	259	297	329	327	225	280	323	354	310	183	3,506
1991	248	243	259	230	224	235	253	313	285	346	299	238	3,445
1992	247	257	279	296	274	287	305	337	311	322	321	306	3,483
1993	272	266	290	175	305	358	222	277	351	603	315	271	4,306
1994	318	335	415	380	375	379	346	457	412	453	452	395	4,756
1995[2]	304	304	372	332	335	353	307	396	376	407	355	317	4,159

[1] Represents production in Pennsylvania only.. [2] Preliminary. *Source: Energy Information Administration, U.S. Department of Energy*

Salient Statistics of Coal in the United States In Thousands of Short Tons

Year	Production	Imports	Consumption	Exports					Total Ending Stocks[2]	Losses & Unaccounted For[3]
				Brazil	Canada	Europe	Asia	Total		
1986	890,315	2,212	804,231	5,720	14,774	42,552	19,639	85,518	207,319	-1,175
1987	918,762	1,747	836,941	5,830	16,464	34,159	20,206	79,607	213,780	-2,499
1988	950,265	2,134	883,642	5,252	19,232	45,137	23,075	95,023	188,831	-1,316
1989	980,729	2,851	889,699	5,681	16,777	51,604	22,734	100,815	178,087	6,811
1990	1,029,076	2,699	895,480	5,847	15,511	58,382	22,725	105,804	201,629	3,949
1991	995,984	3,390	887,621	7,052	11,178	65,520	21,788	108,969	200,682	3,731
1992	997,545	3,803	892,421	6,370	15,140	57,255	20,540	102,516	197,685	9,407
1993	945,424	7,309	925,944	5,197	8,889	37,575	19,500	74,519	145,742	4,213
1994[1]	1,033,504	7,584	930,201	5,482	9,193	35,825	17,957	71,359	169,358	13,037

[1] Preliminary. [2] Producer & distributor and consumer stocks, excludes stocks held by retail dealers for consumption by the residential and commercial secor. [3] Equals production plus imports minus the change in producer & distributor and consumer stocks minus consumption minus exports.
Source: Energy Information Administration, U.S. Department of Energy

U.S. Consumption and Stocks of Total Coal In Thousands of Short Tons

Year	Consumption								Stocks, Dec. 31[3]			
	Electric Utilities				Industrial		Residential and Commercial	Total	Consumer			Producers and Distributors
	Anthracite	Bituminous	Lignite	Total	Coke Plants	Other Industrial[2]			Electric Utilities	Coke Plants	Other Industrials	
1986	829	616,134	69,093	685,056	35,924	75,583	7,667	804,231	161,806	2,992	10,429	32,093
1987	972	647,824	69,098	717,894	36,957	75,175	6,914	836,941	170,797	3,884	10,777	28,321
1988	1,063	681,048	76,260	758,372	41,888	76,252	7,130	883,642	146,507	3,137	8,768	30,418
1989	1,049	688,504	77,335	766,888	40,508	76,134	6,167	889,699	135,860	2,864	7,363	29,000
1990	1,031	694,317	78,201	773,549	38,877	76,330	6,724	895,480	156,166	3,329	8,716	33,418
1991	994	691,275	79,999	772,268	33,854	75,405	6,094	887,621	157,876	2,773	7,061	32,971
1992	986	698,626	80,248	779,860	32,366	74,042	6,153	892,421	154,130	2,597	6,965	33,993
1993	951	732,736	79,821	813,508	31,323	74,892	6,221	925,944	111,341	2,401	6,716	25,284
1994[1]	1,123	737,102	79,045	817,270	31,740	75,179	6,013	930,201	126,897	2,657	6,585	33,219

[1] Preliminary. [2] Including transportation. [3] Excludes stocks held at retail dealers for consumption by the residential and commercial sector.
Source: *Energy Information Administration, U.S. Department of Energy*

Average U.S. Price of Coal In Dollars Per Short Ton

Year	End-Use Sector			Imports[4]	Exports			Year	End-Use Sector			Imports[4]	Exports		
	Electric Utilities	Coke Plants	Other Indust-rial[3]		Steam	Metal-lurgical	Total Average[4]		Electric Utilities	Coke Plants	Other Indust-rial[3]		Steam	Metal-lurgical	Total Average[4]
1986	33.30	50.83	35.84	36.02	43.37	47.14	45.95	1991	30.02	48.88	33.54	33.12	36.91	46.15	42.39
1987	31.83	46.55	33.71	32.04	39.22	44.49	42.77	1992	29.36	47.92	32.78	33.46	35.73	45.41	41.34
1988	30.64	47.70	33.43	29.96	38.59	44.17	42.23	1993	28.58	47.44	32.23	29.89	36.03	44.11	41.41
1989	30.15	47.50	33.03	34.14	37.64	45.19	42.52	1994[1]	28.03	46.56	32.54	30.21	34.34	42.77	39.93
1990	30.45	47.73	33.59	34.45	36.81	46.51	42.63	1995[2]	27.39	47.38	32.47	34.25	34.29	43.44	39.73

[1] Preliminary. [2] Estimate. [3] Manufacturing plants only. [4] Based on the free alongside ship (F.A.S) value. NA = Not available.
Source: Energy Information Administration, U.S. Department of Energy

COAL

U.S. Trends in Bituminous Coal, Lignite and Pennsylvania Anthracite   In Thousands of Short Tons

	Bituminous Coal and Lignite							Pennsylvania Anthracite					All Mines
	Production				Labor Productivity							Labor	Labor
Year	Under-ground	Surface	Total	Miners[1] Employed	Under-ground -Short Tons	Surface Per Miner	Average Per Hour-	Under-ground	Surface	Total	Miners[1] Employed	Product. Short Tons Miner/Hr.	Product. Short Tons Miner/Hr.
1980	336,925	486,719	823,644	224,938	1.21	3.27	1.94	583	5,473	6,056	3,631	1.11	1.93
1981	315,875	502,477	818,352	226,250	1.29	3.50	2.11	621	4,802	5,423	3,052	.92	2.10
1982	338,572	494,951	833,523	214,400	1.37	3.48	2.14	579	4,009	4,588	2,717	.59	2.11
1983	299,882	478,111	778,003	173,543	1.62	3.87	2.52	487	3,602	4,089	2,099	1.01	2.50
1984	351,474	540,285	891,759	175,746	1.72	4.10	2.65	576	3,586	4,162	2,102	1.02	2.64
1985	350,073	528,856	878,930	167,009	1.79	4.32	2.76	727	3,982	4,708	2,272	1.05	2.74
1986	359,800	526,223	886,023	152,668	2.00	4.69	3.04	638	3,654	4,292	1,977	1.03	3.01
1987	372,238	542,963	915,202	141,065	2.21	5.06	3.32	636	2,925	3,560	1,602	1.13	3.30
1988	381,546	565,164	946,710	133,913	2.38	5.41	3.58	610	2,945	3,555	1,453	1.21	3.55
1989	393,322	584,058	977,381	130,103	2.46	5.70	3.73	513	2,835	3,348	1,394	1.12	3.70
1990	424,119	601,449	1,025,570	129,619	2.54	6.07	3.86	427	3,080	3,506	1,687	1.03	3.83
1991	406,901	585,638	992,539	119,441	2.70	6.51	4.12	324	3,121	3,445	1,161	1.39	4.09
1992	406,815	587,248	994,062	108,979	2.95	6.73	4.41	424	3,058	3,483	1,217	1.33	4.36
1993	350,637	590,482	941,119	100,099	3.24	7.84	4.74	416	3,889	4,306	1,124	1.85	4.70

[1] Excludes miners employed at mines producing less than 10,000 tons. *Source: Energy Information Adminstration, U.S. Department of Energy*

U.S. Average Mine Prices of Coal   In Dollars Per Short Ton

	Average Mine Price by Method			Average Mine Prices by Rank				Bituminous		All Coal
Year	Under-ground	Surface	Total	Lignite	Sub-bituminous	Bituminous	Anthracite[1]	& Lignite FOB Mines[2]	Anthracite FOB Mines[2]	CIF[3] Electric Utility Plants
1980	33.50	18.78	24.65	W	11.08	29.17	42.51	24.52	42.51	28.76
1981	35.78	20.60	26.40	W	12.18	31.51	44.28	26.29	44.28	32.32
1982	35.78	21.46	27.25	W	13.37	32.15	49.85	27.14	49.85	34.91
1983	34.47	20.68	25.98	W	13.03	31.11	59.29	25.85	52.29	34.99
1984	33.36	20.59	25.61	10.45	12.41	30.63	48.22	25.51	48.22	35.12
1985	32.91	20.13	25.20	10.68	12.57	30.78	45.80	25.10	45.80	34.53
1986	30.33	19.34	23.79	10.64	12.26	28.84	44.12	23.70	44.12	33.30
1987	29.63	18.58	23.07	10.85	11.32	28.19	43.65	23.00	43.65	31.83
1988	28.97	17.43	22.07	10.06	10.45	27.66	44.16	22.00	44.16	30.64
1989	28.44	17.38	21.82	9.91	10.16	27.40	42.93	21.76	42.93	30.15
1990	28.58	16.98	21.76	10.13	9.70	27.43	39.40	21.71	39.40	30.45
1991	28.56	16.60	21.49	10.89	9.68	27.49	36.34	21.45	36.34	30.02
1992	27.83	16.34	21.03	10.81	9.68	26.78	34.24	20.98	34.24	29.36
1993	26.92	15.67	19.85	11.11	9.33	26.15	32.94	20.56	37.80	28.64

[1] Produced in Pennsylvania. [2] FOB = free on board. [3] CIF = cost, insurance and freight. W = Withheld data. *Source: Energy Information Administration, U.S. Department of Energy*

Cobalt

Cobalt is a strategic metal used in many diverse industrial and military applications. It is found widely in the ores of iron and copper. The largest use of cobalt is in superalloys, which are alloys designed to resist stress and corrosion at high temperatures. Superalloys are used in turbine engine parts for aircraft jet engines and industrial gas turbines. Cobalt, because of its properties is used in heavy-wear, high-temperature and magnetic applications. It is used to make magnets for a wide range of motors, meters and devices; corrosion and wear-resistant alloys for hard facing and castings; and high speed steels for cutting tools. Cobalt metal powder acts as a binder in cemented carbides and diamond tools, which are used for metal cutting and forming, mining and oil and gas drilling. Cobalt compounds are used in catalysts for the petroleum and chemical industries; drying agents for paints, varnishes and inks; pigments for ceramics, paints and plastics; battery electrodes; steel-belted radial tires; and magnetic recording media. Cobalt salt is used for electroplating baths and the radioactive isotope of cobalt has medical uses. Recently Japan's Sony Corporation announced that it had developed a new car battery using lithium and cobalt that it says will allow electric cars to run nearly three times as long as conventional lead-acid batteries. the battery is reported to still be too large and too expensive for mass production.

The U.S. is the world's largest consumer of cobalt, but has no domestic production and therefore relies on imports. There are significant stocks of cobalt metal in the National Defense Stockpile for use during a national emergency.

The world cobalt supply and demand were in close balance during 1994. World production increased, reversing a trend of decreasing production that started in 1991. Cobalt sales from the National Defense Stockpile and exports from Russia contributed to the supply. World cobalt demand increased as economies improved.

U.S. reported consumption of cobalt materials for the January-July 1995 period were 3,670 tonnes of contained cobalt. For the same period of 1994, consumption was 3,880 tonnes while for all of 1994 it was 6,870 tonnes. U.S. reported consumption of cobalt metal for the first seven months of 1995 was 1,760 tonnes compared to 1,710 tonnes in 1994. For 1994, consumption was 3,360 tonnes. Consumption of cobalt oxide and other chemical compounds over the first seven months of 1995 was 974 tonnes, down significantly from the first seven months of 1994's total of 1,230 tonnes. For all of 1994, consumption was 2,000 tonnes. Consumption of cobalt scrap was 945 tonnes in the seven months of 1995 compared to 929 tonnes in 1994. For calendar year 1994, scrap consumption was 1,510 tonnes.

In terms of end use, for the January-July 1995 period, superalloys consumed 40 percent, magnetic alloys 10 percent, cemented carbides 13 percent, chemical catalysts 11 percent, chemical paint driers or related usage 12 percent and miscellaneous 14 percent.

U.S. reported stocks of cobalt materials as reported by cobalt processors and consumers in July 1995 were 772 tonnes. Metal stocks were 362 tonnes, cobalt oxide and other chemical compounds 275 tonnes, and cobalt scrap 135 tonnes. At year end 1994, cobalt stocks were 926 tonnes.

For the January-June 1995 period, U.S. imports for consumption of cobalt materials was 3.5 million kilograms. For the same period of 1994 it was 3.75 million kilograms. The major suppliers were Norway, Finland, Canada, Russia, Zaire, Zambia and Belgium.

World Mine Production of Cobalt In Metric Tons (Cobalt Content)

Year	Albania	Australia	Botswana	Brazil	Canada	Cuba	Finland (Refinary)	France (Refinary)	Japan (Refinary)	Morocco	New Caledonia	Norway (Refinary)	Russia[3]	South Africa	Zaire	Zambia	World Total
1986	600	1,237	163	150	2,297	1,553	1,348	158	1,338	-----	700	1,574	2,800	690	33,373	5,869	50,199
1987	600	1,261	181	150	2,490	1,566	1,234	136	124	224	750	1,576	2,800	380	23,200	7,365	41,245
1988	600	1,200	291	150	2,398	1,783	1,132	176	109	253	800	1,951	2,850	300	26,000	7,090	43,819
1989	600	1,100	215	300	6,167	1,825	1,295	165	99	121	800	1,946	5,700	300	18,400	7,255	42,873
1990	600	1,200	205	400	5,470	1,460	1,300	150	199	194	800	1,830	5,500	350	19,000	6,999	42,300
1991	600	1,400	208	400	5,274	1,120	1,503	123	185	325	800	1,983	5,000	300	9,900	6,994	32,500
1992	20	1,600	208	400	5,102	1,150	2,100	150	105	461	800	2,293	4,000	350	5,700	6,910	26,800
1993[1]	10	1,700	205	400	5,110	1,030	2,200	150	190	397	800	2,414	3,300	350	2,459	4,750	20,600
1994[2]	10	2,100	200	400	4,330	1,000	3,000	600	480	440	800	2,900	3,300	350	2,500	3,500	18,500

[1] Preliminary. [2] Estimate. [3] Formerly part of the U.S.S.R.; data not reported seperately until 1992. *Source: U.S. Bureau of Mines*

U.S. Salient Statistics of Cobalt In Metric Tons (Cobalt Content)

Year	Net Import Reliance as a % of Apparent Consumption	Cobalt Secondary Production	Processors and Consumer Stocks Dec. 31	Imports for Consumption	Consumption by End Uses: Ground Coat Frit	Stainless & Heat Resisting	Catalysts	Super-Alloys	Tool Steel	Magnetic Alloys	Pigments	Drier in Paints, etc.[3]	Cutting & Wear-Resistant Material	Welding Materials	Total Apparent Uses	Price $ Per Pound[4]
1987	87	1,025	2,043	8,832	360	26	497	2,873	174	666	258	799	654	W	7,986	6.56
1988	87	1,018	1,766	7,051	332	26	617	2,865	180	878	378	892	522	206	7,824	7.09
1989	83	1,184	1,456	5,793	366	74	819	2,860	219	870	319	718	538	136	7,172	7.64
1990	84	1,225	1,853	6,529	357	41	W	3,345	123	710	W	751	541	180	7,512	10.09
1991	80	1,578	1,622	6,924	W	51	W	3,066	W	713	W	781	525	135	7,240	16.92
1992	75	1,613	840	5,757	257	26	949	2,697	47	670	197	745	522	128	6,471	22.93
1993[1]	79	1,566	819	5,945	W	41	935	2,530	59	569	193	732	569	171	6,420	13.79
1994[2]	79	1,600	926	6,780	W	28	871	2,760	81	693	198	809	598	W	6,870	24.66

[1] Preliminary. [2] Estimate. [3] Or related usage. [4] Annual spot for cathodes. W = Witheld proprietary data. *Source: U.S. Bureau of Mines*

Cocoa

World cocoa prices drifted lower during 1995 despite a lower carryover at the September 30th close of the 1994/95 crop year and prospects of a further drawdown of perhaps 50,000 tons during 1995/96. Apparently, the bearish bias reflected the size of the carryover rather than the net change; the 1994/95 carryover of about 1.1 million tons represented about a six month cocoa supply at current annual grinding rates and timewise may be about the same at the end of 1995/96. However, cocoa's initial statistical data tends to have a wide margin of error.

World cocoa bean production for 1995/96 was forecast at a record large 2.6 million metric tons, 4 percent over 1994/95. The Ivory Coast (Cote d' Ivoire), the largest producer, placed production at a record 970,000 tons versus 905,000 in 1994/95; a decade earlier the Ivory Coast annual output totaled about 550,000 tons. The Ivory Coast formally opened its 1995/96 marketing season on October 7. Due to the political tensions in the country, the government left the farmer price unchanged from a year earlier, but cocoa export taxes were reduced by 20 percent. Brazil's crop of 276,000 tons compares with 234,000 tons in 1994/95, and Indonesia forecast 290,000 tons versus 280,000 in 1994/95. Brazil's 1995/96 crop, however, has been hit by a fungus disease that could easily cut production to well under initial forecasts. Still, If the overall upward trend persists as seems likely, world production could top 3 million tons by the end of the 1990's. In Indonesia, for example, the government appears committed to stimulating cocoa production with various incentives to growers, which if successful could see crops of about 450,000 tons by the year 2000. In Malaysia, whose production topped Indonesia in the early 1990's, the acreage under cultivation for cocoa continues to drop and production in 1995/96 of only 150,000 tons is the lowest since 1985/86.

World cocoa bean grindings in 1994/95, at a record high 2.53 million tons, compare with 2.48 million in 1993/94. From 1984/85 through 1990/91, world production exceeded consumption, resulting in large global stocks. Since then consumption has exceeded production, necessitating a draw upon world stocks which in 1994/95 were a record high 218,000 tons. However, any bullish effect on prices has been evasive at best. The International Cocoa Organization (ICCO) continues its controlled liquidation of the buffer stock inventory which is being sold in monthly installments of 4,250 tons over a four and a half year period in order to check bearish pressure on prices. ICCO sales in the first nine months of 1995 totaled 38,245 tons leaving 128,813 tons in the ICCO's stockpile; about 60 percent of the sales in 1995 were of Brazilian origin. The new International Cocoa Agreement (ICCA) is based on production management and consumption promotion rather than on a buffer stock mechanism to stabilize prices; the agreement's success still remains uncertain as some producing nations are reluctant to voluntarily limit their production.

Raw cocoa consumption (absorption) is reflected by grindings, most of which occurs in the U.S. and Europe. A broader analysis of total consumption picks up quarterly net imports of cocoa beans adjusted for changes in stocks. Based on the latter, the U.S. is the largest consumer but at times has trailed the Netherlands. The U.S. grind in 1994/95 of a record large 347,000 tons compares with 317,000 in 1993/94. Germany's 1994/95 grind of 278,000 tons compares with 304,000, respectively. The Netherlands grind of a record high 355,000 tons was up 24.000 tons from 1993/94.

The U.S. imported 672,000 tons of cocoa beans and products in 1994 versus 801,000 tons in 1993. Through the first half of 1995, imports were running about 40,000 tons under the like 1994 period. Cocoa products include butter, liquor and powder. Seasonally, the Halloween period is the largest for confectionery and gum sales, followed by Christmas. Cocoa products command a higher price than the beans with cocoa butter the most expensive. Generally, Norfolk, Virginia is the major port of entry for beans, while processed cocoa products come primarily through Philadelphia. Cocoa products come mostly from Canada. The U.S. exports cocoa products and re-exports a small quantity of beans, most of which goes to Canada and Mexico. The U.S. is the world's largest total cocoa importer, but per capita consumption of cocoa (bean equivalent) tends to lag a number of European nations.

Futures Markets

Cocoa futures and options are traded on the Coffee, Sugar, and Cocoa Exchange (CSCE) and the London Commodity Exchange (LCE). Futures are traded on the Kuala Lumpur Commodity Exchange (KLCE).

World Cocoa Supply and Demand In Thousands of Metric Tons

Crop Year Beginning October	Stock Oct. 1	Net World Production[4]	Total Availability	Seasonal Grindings	Closing Stocks	Stock Change	Crop Year Beginning October	Stock Oct. 1	Net World Crop[4]	Total Availability	Seasonal Grindings	Closing Stocks	Stock Change
1980-1	562	1,664	2,225	1,583	643	+81	1988-9	813	2,436	3,250	2,125	1,125	+312
1981-2	643	1,712	2,354	1,606	749	+106	1989-90	1,125	2,394	3,519	2,222	1,297	+172
1982-3	749	1,533	2,281	1,635	646	-102	1990-1	1,297	2,473	3,770	2,343	1,426	+130
1983-4	646	1,524	2,169	1,726	444	-195	1991-2	1,426	2,212	3,638	2,297	1,341	-86
1984-5	444	1,920	2,370	1,862	501	+63	1992-3	1,341	2,410	3,750	2,427	1,323	-18
1985-6	501	1,942	2,455	1,877	567	+67	1993-4[1]	1,323	2,387	3,710	2,480	1,230	-93
1986-7	567	1,968	2,548	1,896	639	+72	1994-5[2]	1,230	2,298	3,528	2,517	1,011	-219
1987-8	639	2,172	2,811	1,998	813	+174	1995-6[3]	1,011	2,526	3,538	2,592	946	-65

[1] Preliminary. [2] Estimate. [3] Forecast. [4] Obtained by adjusting the Gross World Crop for one percent loss in weight. *Source: E D & F Man Cocoa, Ltd.*

World Production of Cocoa Beans in Principal Producing Countries — In Thousands of Metric Tons

Crop Year Beginning October	Brazil	Cameroon	Colombia	Dominican Republic	Ecuador	Ghana	Indonesia	Ivory Coast	Malaysia	Mexico	Nigeria	Papua New Guinea	Peru	Philippines	Togo	Venezuela	World Total
1985-6	380	119	45.6	39.0	112.0	219	34.3	555	130	39.2	130	32.7	10	6.5	12.8	11.2	1,946.1
1986-7	365	123	52.0	45.2	77.0	228	167.0	620	167	37.9	100	34.0	10	6.6	15.7	13.9	2,013.5
1987-8	400	133	53.8	50.0	76.0	188	70.0	674	227	47.5	145	35.0	10	7.2	12.0	12.5	2,214.2
1988-9	334	124	56.3	44.3	82.0	300	98.0	849	225	41.0	160	48.0	10	7.8	10.0	11.5	2,471.3
1989-90	356	122	58.0	57.0	102.0	295	135.0	710	240	38.5	155	41.0	10	9.0	7.6	14.4	2,419.1
1990-1	375	100	60.0	42.3	104.0	293	165.0	804	235	38.9	160	34.0	10	9.0	6.8	16.5	2,525.5
1991-2	301	107	60.5	48.8	82.4	243	200.0	747	217	41.5	110	41.0	10	9.0	8.0	16.0	2,301.0
1992-3	330	100	60.0	50.8	76.0	312	240.0	700	225	43.5	140	39.0	10	9.0	6.0	16.5	2,418.5
1993-4[1]	281	105	60.0	58.7	80.0	312	280.0	850	204	34.0	130	35.0	10	9.0	4.0	16.0	2,525.2
1994-5[2]	234	100	60.0	55.5	81.0	315	280.0	905	162	38.5	130	32.0	10	9.0	4.0	16.0	2,488.6
1995-6[3]	276	100	60.0	56.5	85.0	315	290.0	970	150	40.5	130	30.0	10	9.0	4.0	16.0	2,598.7

[1] Preliminary. [2] Estimate. [3] Forecast. *Source: Foreign Agricultural Service, U.S. Department of Agriculture*

World Absorption (Consumption) of Cocoa[1] — In Thousands of Metric Tons

Crop Year Beginning October	Belgium	Brazil	Canada	Colombia	Cote d'Ivoire	France	Germany	Italy	Japan	Malaysia	Netherlands	Singapore	Spain	United Kingdom	United States	Former USSR	World Total
1985-6	34	240	20	51	117	41	218	45	35	27	176	30	31	83	193	144	1,875
1986-7	34	233	19	48	89	35	225	43	36	36	190	33	33	94	228	164	1,896
1987-8	35	241	21	46	102	40	245	46	40	40	215	40	43	100	241	132	1,998
1988-9	41	210	22	41	110	44	265	46	40	47	234	46	40	112	237	201	2,124
1989-90	47	243	24	45	111	59	287	51	47	72	241	52	42	120	265	106	2,220
1990-1	49	283	25	47	115	70	295	56	52	77	268	51	45	145	265	83	2,347
1991-2	46	216	31	44	108	67	306	62	49	87	294	50	46	153	307	25	2,297
1992-3	47	218	41	45	100	80	311	58	39	99	309	46	46	169	326	95	2,427
1993-4[2]	52	224	32	42	110	95	304	65	38	103	331	51	49	170	317	90	2,480
1994-5[3]	55	194	35	45	108	108	279	70	39	100	350	57	48	154	352	80	2,517
1995-6[4]	57	189	36	45	120	112	259	70	43	100	363	60	49	163	362	80	2,592

[1] Figures represent the "grindings" of cocoa beans in each country. [2] Preliminary. [3] Estimate. [4] Forecast. *Source: Foreign Agricultural Service, U.S. Department of Agriculture*

Raw Cocoa Grindings in Selected Countries — In Metric Tons

Year	Total	First Quarter	Second Quarter	Third Quarter	Fourth Quarter	Total	First Quarter	Second Quarter	Third Quarter	Fourth Quarter
			Germany[2]					Netherlands		
1985	206,806	57,042	51,722	44,047	53,995	167,353	44,633	41,690	36,970	44,060
1986	201,037	53,643	50,641	42,589	54,164	182,570	46,200	45,050	40,290	51,030
1987	208,684	55,190	49,224	46,424	57,846	195,627	49,141	47,399	42,772	56,315
1988	232,794	60,039	53,990	53,008	65,757	216,499	56,074	51,712	50,539	58,174
1989	245,997	61,960	59,211	56,994	67,832	233,529	61,071	56,392	55,129	60,937
1990	281,855	69,125	64,613	70,994	77,123	247,590	62,243	58,817	58,702	67,828
1991	290,703	73,172	72,396	70,934	73,661	274,741	64,299	71,643	63,973	74,826
1992	319,251	78,661	73,797	80,111	86,682	293,157	77,954	71,537	69,871	73,795
1993	298,681	74,119	69,805	74,010	80,747	320,060	78,338	75,548	81,183	84,991
1994	296,219	80,242	68,033	67,706	80,238	334,384	83,963	78,055	84,249	88,117
1995[1]		69,441	56,478	61,523			91,314	85,248	85,311	
			United Kingdom					United States[3]		
1985	91,295	26,547	24,435	19,981	20,332	153,911	38,970	37,519	40,549	36,873
1986	87,243	21,109	21,998	20,088	24,048	153,621	33,761	37,014	42,264	40,582
1987	95,396	24,469	22,941	22,405	25,581	180,811	39,665	45,930	49,864	45,352
1988	100,507	26,309	24,997	22,407	26,794	186,885	45,197	47,327	48,376	45,985
1989	114,669	28,506	30,113	26,873	29,177	192,837	43,802	49,185	47,071	52,779
1990	124,791	32,116	29,322	29,419	33,934	216,740	51,559	51,683	58,278	55,220
1991	148,191	32,902	36,016	41,863	37,410	255,781	51,191	64,365	66,544	73,681
1992	159,284	39,831	37,903	37,120	44,430	313,921	70,335	74,515	84,109	84,962
1993	171,343	44,575	41,975	37,496	47,297	321,905	78,968	77,720	84,593	80,624
1994	163,170	44,131	39,063	39,591	40,385	320,106	71,398	76,282	86,247	86,179
1995[1]		43,410	35,348	34,431			83,170	87,805	94,485	

[1] Preliminary. [2] Beginning October 1990, includes former East Germany. [3] Data incomplete January 1984-March 1991, excludes one major processor.
Source: Foreign Agricultural Service, U.S. Department of Agriculture

COCOA

Imports of Cocoa Butter--Selected Countries In Metric Tons

Year	Australia	Austria	Belgium	Canada	Finland	France	Germany	Greece	Italy	Japan	Netherlands	Norway	Russia[2]	Sweden	Switzerland	United Kingdom	United States
1983	6,067	3,535	12,128	5,313	2,428	16,690	30,581	1,788	2,151	9,947	20,224	1,892	NA	7,404	10,224	31,581	47,981
1984	6,445	3,763	13,451	5,437	2,156	17,325	35,241	1,561	2,337	8,346	25,072	2,139	4,200	5,103	9,798	30,203	51,711
1985	8,538	3,682	15,416	5,535	2,039	19,908	33,378	1,225	3,056	8,632	24,595	1,957	7,150	4,920	11,175	31,372	70,146
1986	8,204	4,387	13,795	5,377	1,966	19,397	25,513	1,557	3,246	8,474	14,925	2,295	3,450	4,866	11,369	32,669	70,264
1987	8,370	3,879	14,312	5,833	1,971	23,704	27,436	1,860	3,509	9,330	16,152	2,734	1,000	5,272	11,932	29,689	79,773
1988	9,405	4,315	12,869	7,371	2,246	24,562	33,590	2,812	4,731	12,497	20,431	2,523	1,008	5,596	12,821	34,329	78,285
1989	10,291	4,599	17,748	8,224	2,469	26,597	41,765	2,806	5,932	15,280	22,924	2,706	2,500	5,735	16,276	35,045	64,353
1990	10,025	6,047	22,125	8,830	2,536	28,539	49,999	2,891	6,187	15,686	34,529	2,897	4,750	5,855	16,306	34,604	92,165
1991	11,218	5,171	24,795	8,682	2,744	28,628	54,452	3,203	7,813	15,245	29,729	3,027	610	6,299	16,544	26,876	90,004
1992	10,697	5,249	31,836	10,706	3,451	28,560	44,906	2,284	8,431	15,835	29,999	2,962	870	5,885	17,422	26,300	99,509
1993	13,129	5,417	28,989	10,225	4,530	30,611	37,269	2,448	9,851	16,422	51,559	3,566	1,308	6,390	16,711	25,941	85,400
1994[1]	13,030	5,410	34,061	11,551	4,563	36,698	59,170	-----	9,173	15,937	43,192	2,799	-----	7,079	17,242	35,453	54,550

[1] Preliminary. [2] Formerly part of the U.S.S.R.; data not reported separately until 1992. NA = Not available. *Source: Food and Agricultural Organization of the United Nations*

Imports of Cocoa Liquor and Cocoa Powder (Selected Countries) In Metric Tons

	Cocoa Liquior						Cocoa Powder								
Year	France	Germany	Netherlands	Japan	United Kingdom	United States	Former U.S.S.R.	Belgium	France	Germany	Italy	Japan	Netherlands	Sweden	United Kingdom	United States
1984	20,268	3,075	13,622	2,928	2,184	45,457	32,000	4,204	9,652	13,554	7,462	3,260	3,574	3,996	3,654	89,978
1985	24,031	3,570	14,822	2,792	3,400	53,042	37,510	4,586	8,269	16,624	8,313	3,841	4,669	3,928	2,591	81,775
1986	28,426	2,006	10,915	3,346	4,091	50,705	30,110	4,844	8,984	15,654	9,059	4,844	4,669	3,980	3,258	89,454
1987	31,171	391	8,805	3,402	1,870	38,105	21,680	5,229	8,967	16,989	9,330	5,517	3,624	3,982	3,897	103,455
1988	31,157	793	9,014	3,445	3,022	34,454	21,000	5,572	9,750	16,455	9,498	6,470	3,432	4,330	3,576	91,337
1989	29,257	1,040	9,315	3,451	2,524	27,556	31,504	6,138	10,920	18,470	10,233	6,033	5,862	4,125	3,255	53,736
1990	35,146	1,860	9,875	3,123	1,713	25,047	18,580	6,235	12,244	21,294	11,418	6,284	6,446	4,357	3,619	58,280
1991	40,251	3,242	7,443	2,057	1,918	25,320	NA	6,665	12,215	25,315	12,189	6,557	6,239	4,314	4,315	55,636
1992	45,056	2,540	7,130	2,246	3,611	24,255	NA	6,700	14,896	27,745	14,469	6,067	9,412	3,533	3,548	56,089
1993	41,999	1,694	15,543	2,468	1,490	31,641	NA	6,600	16,773	25,732	13,221	5,771	5,626	4,292	2,882	66,533
1994[1]	42,392	2,682	14,913	2,312	4,443	26,846	NA	8,748	19,215	28,806	12,884	6,461	10,078	5,015	2,661	67,207

[1] Preliminary. NA = Not available. *Source: E D & F Man Cococa, Ltd.*

United States Imports of Cocoa and Products In Thousands of Metric Tons

Year	Jan.	Feb.	Mar.	Apr.	May	June	July	Aug.	Sept.	Oct.	Nov.	Dec.	Total
1983	46	43	19	36	14	11	10	7	6	5	8	8	214
1984[3]	16	21	29	17	25	15	13	11	10	5	11	18	191
1985	43	44	40	10	31	16	14	13	11	10	13	25	270
1986	30	17	15	9	19	16	22	23	12	8	15	18	209
1987	27	28	23	31	21	10	11	14	6	23	24	45	263
1988	27	31	27	19	15	21	15	20	9	9	14	31	237
1989	44	24	30	29	25	18	18	23	14	20	10	10	266
1990[2]	72	53	70	110	83	60	NA	61	41	NA	72	49	716
1991	70	53	51	74	62	66	65	59	53	NA	NA	73	761
1992	83	66	62	55	50	60	52	60	67	67	64	69	755
1993	67	57	56	61	58	61	77	58	59	71	71	88	801
1994	67	68	56	61	49	51	49	58	58	61	45	77	672
1995[1]	68	54	44	48	47	48	48	51	53	49			

[1] Preliminary. [2] Prior to 1990, data for cocoa bean imports only. [3] Prior to 1984, data are in thousands of long tons. NA = Not available. *Source: Foreign Agricultural Service, U.S. Department of Agriculture*

Visible Stocks of Cocoa at Port of Hampton Road Warehouses[1], End of Month In Thousands of Bags

Year	Jan.	Feb.	Mar.	Apr.	May	June	July	Aug.	Sept.	Oct.	Nov.	Dec.
1989	528.4	653.3	777.7	775.0	875.0	741.6	655.8	583.2	509.1	594.2	567.0	552.3
1990	403.6	445.9	583.2	674.3	807.4	1,064.7	917.2	67.2	1,046.5	19.0	996.5	958.2
1991	946.5	953.3	910.1	946.0	906.1	1,036.6	1,174.5	1,291.2	1,386.2	1,429.0	1,426.0	1,502.9
1992	1,588.3	1,892.1	2,233.1	2,236.2	2,236.9	2,204.8	2,150.8	2,087.4	1,982.4	2,018.6	2,043.9	2,188.5
1993	2,209.9	2,497.3	2,443.9	2,676.8	2,771.8	2,689.7	2,920.0	2,708.6	2,740.1	2,418.7	2,328.3	2,356.9
1994	2,329.6	2,441.1	2,443.9	2,522.9	2,533.1	2,460.2	2,445.4	2,335.0	2,308.4	2,360.2	2,306.9	2,253.7
1995	2,152.7	2,098.6	2,195.7	2,212.3	2,120.2	2,016.0	1,919.8	1,786.6	1,713.1	1,598.2	1,463.9	1,470.3

[1] Licensed and unlicensed warehouses approved by the CSCE. *Source: Coffee, Sugar & Cocoa Exchange, Inc. (CSCE)*

Visible Stocks of Cocoa in Philadelphia (Delaware River) Warehouses[1], End of Month In Thousands of Bags

Year	Jan.	Feb.	Mar.	Apr.	May	June	July	Aug.	Sept.	Oct.	Nov.	Dec.
1985	221.3	282.0	333.6	420.9	416.4	389.1	315.9	323.9	320.7	316.3	289.1	280.6
1986	281.3	276.4	258.8	255.8	237.9	201.3	208.7	182.0	209.5	137.1	136.7	188.5
1987	209.8	210.8	228.9	224.1	243.6	276.2	291.4	259.7	236.6	177.9	189.6	206.3
1988	164.6	149.2	154.9	211.1	227.3	232.0	238.1	193.3	185.5	157.6	123.4	112.0
1989	86.0	67.5	88.7	96.2	114.0	112.5	100.3	100.0	54.6	46.1	51.9	53.5
1990	35.1	61.1	87.5	107.9	120.5	204.4	297.1	231.2	185.9	193.0	195.3	215.1
1991	216.2	226.9	249.3	254.9	309.2	376.8	382.8	376.8	375.5	355.1	280.5	282.7
1992	344.6	345.5	412.1	547.6	576.7	632.0	637.7	654.0	616.4	606.0	565.8	612.4
1993	562.2	589.8	603.9	606.0	653.1	678.0	665.7	648.9	600.6	611.5	685.2	781.8
1994	831.5	937.7	1,004.2	1,010.9	1,055.4	1,095.2	1,076.0	1,029.8	968.5	857.1	843.9	818.9
1995	807.5	1,034.3	1,038.9	1,020.2	963.7	924.3	860.7	759.2	852.2	727.0	666.0	735.6

[1] Licensed and unlicensed warehouses approved by the CSCE. *Source: Coffee, Sugar & Cocoa Exchange, Inc. (CSCE)*

Visible Stocks of Cocoa in New York Warehouses[1], End of Month In Thousands of Bags

Year	Jan.	Feb.	Mar.	Apr.	May	June	July	Aug.	Sept.	Oct.	Nov.	Dec.
1985	34.7	22.0	13.2	36.4	167.8	170.9	161.3	155.7	164.6	150.6	131.8	107.1
1986	99.2	96.9	95.6	89.7	87.4	90.3	88.9	103.6	102.1	87.5	70.6	59.9
1987	51.9	43.5	40.0	39.4	55.2	46.1	58.7	43.5	49.4	44.8	107.7	149.1
1988	138.7	115.4	100.1	96.8	102.8	135.4	140.8	146.8	114.3	105.8	73.7	59.8
1989	65.0	81.9	47.3	82.2	214.8	245.3	274.2	215.6	181.3	247.7	313.6	293.5
1990	288.4	267.5	311.9	335.3	294.8	359.2	431.3	409.0	442.2	406.3	413.4	397.2
1991	355.6	219.6	295.9	294.1	250.4	292.6	313.3	317.1	271.5	253.9	292.9	282.4
1992	321.2	303.7	278.7	302.6	273.4	287.8	329.7	301.5	280.5	252.3	212.7	183.3
1993	150.9	144.1	122.0	125.0	119.8	119.8	119.8	119.8	119.8	118.6	132.4	187.7
1994	271.0	275.0	280.8	296.6	358.6	394.1	447.5	447.5	467.3	427.3	407.2	556.1
1995	560.5	634.5	559.2	539.4	510.4	561.1	579.3	595.4	459.9	598.7	679.7	598.7

[1] Licensed and unlicensed warehouses approved by the CSCE. *Source: Coffee, Sugar & Cocoa Exchange, Inc. (CSCE)*

COCOA

U.S. Spot Cocoa Prices[1] for Selected Origins of Cocoa Beans and Products   Dollars Per Metric Ton

Crop Year Beginning October	Cocoa Beans Brazil	Cocoa Beans Cote d'Ivoire	Cocoa Beans Dominican Republic	Cocoa Beans Ecuador	Cocoa Beans Malaysia	Chocolate Liquor Brazil	Chocolate Liquor Ecuador	Cocoa Butter African	Cocoa Butter Other	Cocoa Cake 10-12% Fat
1985-6	2,207	2,281	2,020	2,048	NA	2,720	2,552	4,940	4,897	825
1986-7	2,087	2,155	1,942	1,975	NA	2,634	2,554	4,643	4,608	965
1987-8	1,807	1,952	1,664	1,700	NA	2,280	2,216	4,001	3,919	916
1988-9	1,669	1,773	1,442	1,466	1,364	2,136	1,912	3,543	3,515	945
1989-90	1,259	1,307	1,142	1,250	1,162	1,775	1,640	3,176	3,151	666
1990-1	1,222	1,289	1,091	1,168	1,131	1,704	1,646	3,232	3,199	394
1991-2	1,234	1,262	1,051	1,136	1,111	1,656	1,540	2,763	2,815	393
1992-3	1,109	1,199	969	1,123	1,020	1,571	1,513	2,517	2,572	539
1993-4	1,378	1,560	1,277	1,393	1,326	2,076	2,028	3,348	3,393	649
1994-5	1,547	1,596	1,347	1,436	1,434	2,202	2,105	3,730	3,737	560

[1] All prices are nominal and are net ex-dock or ex-warehouse, U.S. eastern seaboard north of Hatteras, for merchandise physically available in interstate commerce, in truckload and regular commercial quantities. NA = Not available. *Source: Foreign Agricultural Service, U.S. Department of Agriculture*

Average Open Interest of Cocoa Futures at New York   In Contracts

Year	Jan.	Feb.	Mar.	Apr.	May	June	July	Aug.	Sept.	Oct.	Nov.	Dec.
1986	18,507	19,543	20,841	21,267	22,520	23,172	24,287	24,376	25,795	24,769	23,678	24,576
1987	25,412	23,578	24,541	23,372	24,869	26,115	32,859	32,063	30,946	32,643	29,666	27,674
1988	27,704	28,713	32,178	33,589	35,239	36,444	37,772	38,841	38,762	38,222	37,834	36,697
1989	36,747	35,492	32,917	36,597	41,341	45,016	47,222	45,700	42,731	46,366	48,062	49,553
1990	52,094	52,599	55,796	51,299	51,076	50,385	49,603	49,083	47,332	50,084	44,944	41,955
1991	42,446	38,205	40,198	45,250	47,764	49,111	53,153	53,886	53,974	54,854	53,390	53,412
1992	54,464	54,797	52,110	49,904	48,076	47,690	49,924	50,532	51,706	56,101	57,426	60,521
1993	64,886	68,307	69,464	68,533	71,802	71,792	87,011	83,057	88,000	94,844	96,507	91,573
1994	89,174	87,349	91,715	82,500	82,970	72,288	72,249	69,614	73,436	74,163	72,232	75,995
1995	78,873	80,786	82,299	78,435	80,547	75,496	74,975	65,794	68,547	72,758	76,680	79,844

Source: Coffee, Sugar & Cocoa Exchange, Inc.

Volume of Trading of Cocoa Futures at New York   In Contracts

Year	Jan.	Feb.	Mar.	Apr.	May	June	July	Aug.	Sept.	Oct.	Nov.	Dec.	Total
1986	52,774	61,836	70,859	74,249	57,525	77,335	79,029	65,963	75,673	64,729	54,090	43,703	777,765
1987	67,268	61,641	73,341	67,954	68,521	93,849	111,728	66,990	71,591	70,164	81,605	60,813	895,465
1988	84,590	83,826	92,644	85,144	111,277	121,184	128,859	106,031	87,684	137,635	142,016	87,160	1,268,050
1989	138,883	122,374	116,082	132,208	135,783	129,943	98,922	137,879	73,741	95,531	101,152	59,352	1,341,850
1990	121,610	128,357	166,277	191,007	194,759	181,377	126,596	143,323	75,757	120,689	116,175	69,990	1,635,917
1991	94,609	92,450	104,973	99,176	76,435	104,327	96,840	146,379	104,136	135,677	106,888	72,629	1,234,519
1992	122,576	119,375	94,131	116,804	66,185	135,373	104,660	145,815	113,589	109,888	137,815	95,024	1,397,235
1993	145,378	139,932	111,751	149,771	82,961	189,474	225,901	215,044	240,371	217,697	229,752	183,352	2,128,384
1994	178,303	190,804	205,623	188,004	267,188	251,300	193,883	241,340	142,589	183,975	210,635	164,917	2,417,006
1995	197,032	183,784	191,328	208,707	169,061	199,211	140,789	205,169	120,433	149,810	211,171	113,603	2,090,098

Source: Coffee, Sugar & Cocoa Exchange, Inc.

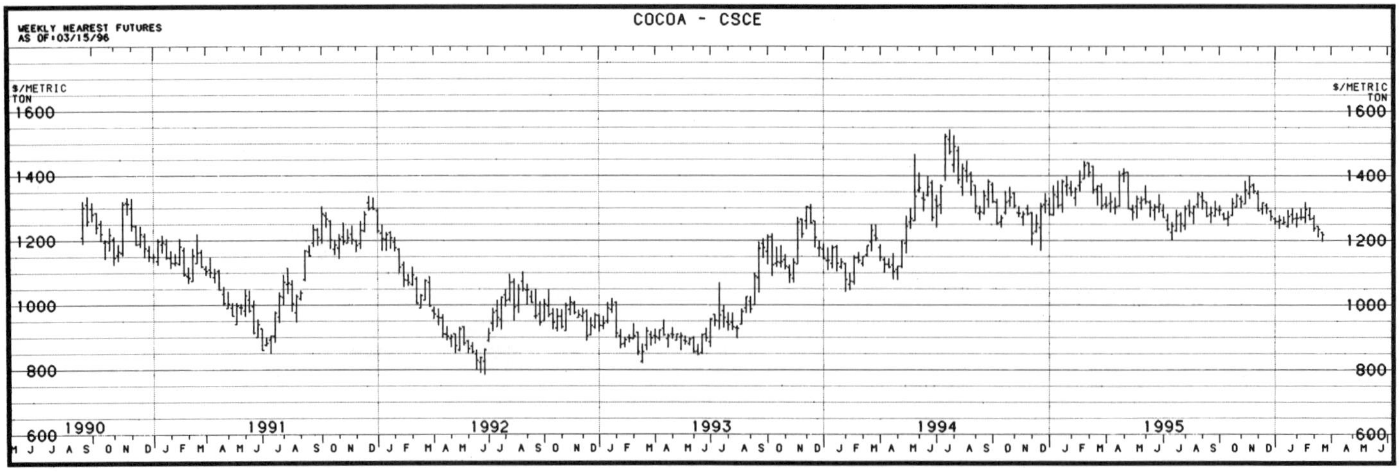

Coconut Oil and Copra

Copra, dried coconut meat, is crushed or processed to yield coconut oil and copra meal. Coconut oil is an important ingredient in cosmetics and soap, and is also used as a food ingredient. However, as an edible oil used in a variety of foods, its continued use is questionable because the oil has a high level of saturated fats (92 percent). More than three-fourths of U.S. coconut oil imports are now processed into inedible products. Its use in food products has stagnated, dropping from over 300,000 tons in the 1980's to less than 200,000 tons in the 1990s.

World copra production is small. Most of the crop is processed into oil. In 1995/96 oil production totaled 3.1 million metric tons versus 3.4 million in 1994/95. Copra meal production totaled 1.7 million tons in 1995/96 versus 2 million in 1994/95. The Philippines account for at least 40 percent of world copra output and Indonesia about 25 percent. Copra production is not only dependent on the weather, but also subject to a biological cycle making fluctuations in output more violent than most annual crops. The Philippine's copra production appears to be developing cycles of 4 to 5 years with annual fluctuations of up to 30 percent. Production in calendar year 1996 was forecast at 1.9 million metric tons versus nearly 2.5 million in 1995 and 1.9 million in 1994. On balance, however, Philippine production has trended lower since the mid-1980's. Foreign trade in copra products is small: coconut oil exports in 1995/96 were estimated at 1.5 million tons versus 1.9 million in 1994/95; copra meal exports were placed at 1 million and 1.2 million tons, respectively.

U.S. imports of coconut oil in 1995/96 were estimated at 1,047 million pounds, down from 1,069 million in 1994/95. Stocks as of October 31, 1995 were estimated at 163 million pounds, unchanged from a year earlier. Manufacturers are not adverse to switching to palm oil when necessary, especially if coconut oil's premium to palm oil widens too far.

Crude coconut oil prices, New York, trended higher in 1995. During the first half of the year prices averaged about 32.00 cents per pound versus 29.20 cents in the like 1994 period. The price outlook into 1996 was less optimistic due to large world supplies of competing oils.

World Copra Production by Principal Countries   In Thousands of Metric Tons

Year	India	Indonesia	Ivory Coast	Malaysia	Mexico	Mozambique	New Guinea	Philippines	Solomon Islands	Sri Lanka	Thailand	Vanuatu	Vietnam	World Total
1982-3	300	1,225	36	214	100	55	158	1,237	43	62	35	47	60	3,781
1983-4	360	1,260	60	166	100	55	176	1,813	45	240	93	39	65	4,681
1984-5	380	1,250	53	162	100	55	160	2,500	31	242	65	41	70	5,306
1985-6	320	1,270	48	97	115	65	149	2,100	28	125	74	36	70	4,709
1986-7	434	1,195	64	81	201	68	136	1,700	29	62	49	30	118	4,450
1987-8	487	1,021	52	97	203	70	134	1,710	35	130	62	24	139	4,444
1988-9	470	1,381	70	96	202	70	117	2,345	30	128	59	45	188	5,488
1989-90	450	1,392	75	76	175	72	91	1,950	24	61	62	28	192	4,933
1990-1	440	1,110	79	82	175	72	110	1,845	29	70	65	27	220	4,612
1991-2	440	1,110	65	82	200	72	117	1,845	23	70	65	24	220	4,624
1992-3	445	1,100	60	65	173	73	120	1,950	23	60	68	26	200	4,648
1993-4[1]	455	1,270	65	60	170	74	115	1,930	28	48	64	26	200	4,798
1994-5[2]	470	1,170	68	55	169	74	110	2,460	30	50	65	28	215	5,260
1995-6[3]	490	1,280	69	52	168	74	115	1,900	30	53	65		218	4,840

[1] Preliminary. [2] Estimate. [3] Forecast. *Source: The Oil World*

World Coconut Oil Supply and Distribution   In Thousands of Metric Tons

	Production							Consumption						Ending Stocks		
Year	India	Indonesia	Malaysia	Philippines	Total	Exports	Imports	EC-12	India	Indonesia	Philippines	United States	Total	Philippines	United States	Total
1984-5	226	708	104	919	2,607	1,186	1,102	410	226	574	253	386	2,553	115	59	223
1985-6	236	720	86	1,587	3,296	1,613	1,523	575	236	710	286	461	3,040	178	140	389
1986-7	198	731	56	1,320	2,934	1,487	1,340	553	198	610	257	488	2,800	187	123	375
1987-8	253	721	38	1,141	2,851	1,451	1,490	535	246	479	304	416	2,891	122	151	589
1988-9	285	669	40	957	2,685	1,219	1,287	473	282	517	297	396	2,911	100	68	432
1989-90	284	782	34	1,314	3,212	1,587	1,554	521	284	576	278	386	3,039	115	128	571
1990-1	273	843	31	1,283	3,175	1,525	1,563	639	278	682	278	402	3,317	52	127	467
1991-2	267	701	29	1,110	2,841	1,341	1,325	490	280	380	257	409	2,872	115	85	417
1992-3	267	681	30	1,294	2,996	1,643	1,581	491	280	430	249	492	2,977	38	114	374
1993-4[1]	271	746	24	1,051	2,793	1,358	1,442	546	275	379	266	483	2,931	50	74	319
1994-5[2]	280	708	22	1,647	3,371	1,863	1,843	654	284	503	269	498	3,264	82	74	405
1995-6[3]	291	768	21	1,255	3,056	1,561	1,565	570	293	440	282	480	3,092	70	74	360

[1] Preliminary. [2] Estimate. [3] Forecast. *Source: The Oil World*

COCONUT OIL AND COPRA

Supply and Distribution of Coconut Oil in the United States In Millions of Pounds

	---- Rotterdam ----						--------- Disappearance ---------			-------- Production of Coconut Oil (Refined) --------				
Year	Copra Tonne ------- $ U.S. -------	Coconut Oil, CIF	Imports For Consumption	Stocks Oct. 1	Total Supply	Exports	Total Domestic	Edible Products	Inedible Products	Total	Oct. - Dec.	Jan. - March	April - June	July - Sept.
1983-4	707	1,123	917	145	1,061	37	915	299	602	688.7	172.5	163.1	186.0	167.1
1984-5	476	746	891	112	1,001	20	851	275	376	658.5	176.4	161.3	175.7	145.1
1985-6	200	304	1,217	132	1,347	22	1,019	333	683	546.3	134.1	130.7	133.9	147.6
1986-7	285	413	1,087	308	1,395	49	1,076	319	720	685.5	151.8	197.9	180.4	155.4
1987-8	385	547	1,074	271	1,344	77	935	233	700	786.1	181.7	194.2	214.9	195.3
1988-9	371	545	778	332	1,111	55	904	211	713	712.7	199.3	165.1	182.0	166.3
1989-90	251	371	1,038	152	1,190	44	866	161	705	703.1	195.4	163.8	187.3	156.6
1990-1	247	364	946	279	1,216	51	897	169	742	754.6	196.8	150.8	141.8	265.2
1991-2	397	605	838	277	1,000	22	906	164	699	733.9	145.3	158.8	159.3	270.5
1992-3	292	446	1,162	187	NA	15	1,082	202	692	650.5	156.0	158.8	166.6	169.1
1993-4	388	564	999	251	NA	11	1,076	234	716	536.2	155.6	129.0	131.8	119.8
1994-5[1]	432	656	1,069	163	NA	9	1,091	247	844	546.8	137.5	142.7	144.3	122.3

[1] Preliminary. NA = Not available. *Source: Bureau of Census, U.S. Department of Commerce*

U.S. Consumption of Coconut Oil in End Products (Edible and Inedible) In Millions of Pounds

Year	January	February	March	April	May	June	July	August	September	October	November	December	Total
1985	53.4	57.1	46.1	52.5	51.7	52.8	53.2	57.2	61.2	53.0	57.7	50.0	645.9
1986	67.7	43.8	44.7	52.5	45.7	50.0	49.5	67.2	52.8	78.7	65.9	52.2	670.7
1987	63.7	58.0	76.2	74.1	72.8	81.4	73.8	79.1	82.5	89.6	70.0	72.8	894.0
1988	76.1	71.2	59.1	59.6	66.8	65.8	55.1	53.8	48.7	65.2	57.8	57.9	737.1
1989	52.6	51.6	64.3	55.0	65.9	58.0	60.5	51.3	48.7	55.1	49.7	39.6	652.3
1990	45.4	44.9	44.3	44.6	43.2	39.4	39.8	39.5	39.2	49.7	41.0	43.9	514.9
1991	------------	137.6	------------	------------	150.6	------------	------------	134.4	------------	------------	122.1	------------	544.7
1992	72.5	70.6	76.5	70.7	78.7	74.8	65.2	70.6	77.4	75.8	76.2	66.4	875.4
1993	74.4	75.9	81.3	77.6	72.1	71.0	73.6	78.2	72.6	85.9	90.9	84.6	938.1
1994	74.4	77.4	77.5	80.4	86.6	88.8	76.0	88.4	65.1	74.6	85.1	95.0	969.2
1995[1]	78.2	79.5	86.5	81.0	79.7	82.0	76.5	71.4	61.6	62.1	64.0		

[1] Preliminary. *Source: Bureau of Census, U.S. Department of Commerce*

Stocks of Coconut Oil (Crude and Refined) in the United States In Millions of Pounds

Year	Jan. 1	Feb. 1	Mar. 1	Apr. 1	May 1	June 1	July 1	Aug.1	Sept.1	Oct. 1	Nov. 1	Dec. 1
1985	121.4	128.0	91.9	81.3	75.9	86.0	116.0	121.7	140.5	130.0	177.4	162.8
1986	206.5	259.0	262.1	285.1	247.4	289.3	275.0	273.4	273.8	308.0	295.5	320.5
1987	323.3	323.6	355.7	318.1	336.9	271.2	203.6	243.9	240.8	270.2	288.5	370.9
1988	367.7	358.8	370.7	371.1	356.0	353.6	336.6	290.2	287.5	335.0	332.7	307.0
1989	275.7	278.9	247.4	205.3	167.7	134.7	189.9	177.5	149.8	150.8	218.6	238.5
1990	297.3	304.4	307.0	348.0	305.6	306.6	292.2	264.3	315.4	281.1	309.3	304.6
1991	-------	--------	359.0	--------	--------	364.3	--------	--------	279.3	--------	--------	298.0
1992	-------	266.3	274.2	239.7	211.2	173.7	178.3	141.1	187.1	187.7	225.1	278.8
1993	355.7	406.7	418.9	348.7	338.3	305.2	257.2	233.8	321.4	250.8	335.0	299.1
1994	291.7	316.5	284.5	251.5	237.6	199.9	151.4	163.7	156.0	164.1	166.2	152.9
1995[1]	155.6	173.6	168.1	163.7	148.5	183.5	163.8	136.9	124.1	162.9	199.7	187.7

[1] Preliminary. *Source: U.S. Department of Commerce*

Average Price of Coconut Oil (Crude) Tank Cars at New York In Cents Per Pound

Year	January	February	March	April	May	June	July	August	September	October	November	December	Average
1985	42.20	40.20	41.00	41.00	NA	NA	31.70	27.50	25.00	24.00	22.80	17.40	31.30
1986	20.60	18.00	15.60	15.50	13.80	13.90	13.80	13.00	13.30	16.80	19.80	20.70	16.20
1987	21.40	20.88	19.30	20.38	21.44	24.25	25.75	25.13	24.40	24.69	24.50	27.15	23.27
1988	28.81	26.06	25.45	25.25	26.50	30.45	31.88	28.30	27.38	27.44	28.06	27.81	27.80
1989	26.75	27.63	27.90	28.94	29.90	29.56	28.94	27.75	28.63	27.25	26.35	24.75	27.86
1990	24.31	23.69	22.10	21.63	21.15	20.31	19.16	18.58	18.26	18.18	20.45	20.13	22.69
1991	20.22	20.31	20.50	19.38	19.69	21.69	26.19	25.63	25.63	28.50	31.50	32.38	24.72
1992	39.33	36.00	34.57	34.75	33.56	32.13	29.63	27.31	27.88	26.94	27.00	25.50	31.33
1993	24.94	24.33	23.65	23.25	24.13	24.95	25.50	25.75	24.25	23.75	26.50	32.00	25.25
1994	30.30	29.69	27.31	28.19	29.45	30.25	29.56	30.35	30.63	30.60	34.19	33.69	30.35
1995[1]	32.50	32.00	31.13	31.00	30.50	35.00							32.02

[1] Preliminary. NA = Not available. *Source: Economic Research Service, U.S. Department of Agriculture*

Coffee

Coffee prices drifted lower during 1995, but the bearish trend was occasionally interrupted when the market attempted to digest (1) seemingly conflicting crop reports, mostly focusing on Brazil's production, and (2) the supporting effect of round number price levels such as $1.25 per pound in mid-year and again in late summer, and a $1.00 per pound at the end of the year. For the 1995 calendar year prices had a range of about $.94 per pound, basis nearest futures contracts. The price action was in sharp contrast to the volatility seen in 1994 when prices surged from $.70 per pound up to $2.60 by mid-year, and fell back to about $1.50 by yearend. During the past twenty years the coffee market has witnessed dramatic price swings: In the late 1970s prices surged from 75 cents per pound to a record high $3.25; in the mid-1980's prices doubled from a base of $1.25; by the close of the 1980's prices were under $1.00 per pound. Perhaps the relative lethargy of 1995 may prove only a temporary respite for gyrating prices in the late 1990s.

World green coffee production in 1995/96 was forecast at 97.4 million bags (60 kilograms each), the smallest crop since 1986/87, (79.5 million bags) and compares with 1994/95 production of 93.8 million and the record high 104 million in 1991/92. Crop forecasts, however, are often suspect and/or questioned even if the source is considered reliable. A case in point are the USDA's coffee crop and/or exportable estimates, which if too high, are disputed by producing nations as, not surprisingly, Brazil did in 1995. And if world prices are too low, producing nations voice their ire and reluctance to participate in any international agreement designed to limit their exports.

Global green coffee exportable production in 1994/95 (total harvested production less domestic consumption in producing countries) was forecast at 72 million bags compared with 70 million in 1993/94. World coffee consumption has been basically flat in recent years in importing nations owing largely to strong competition from other beverages. Usage in producing nations has shown somewhat better growth. Producer stocks at the beginning of the 1994/95 marketing year of about 35.5 million bags were expected to slide to a record low 31 million by the end of the season. U.S. stocks in mid-1995 of about 3 million bags were nearly 50 percent under a year earlier and continuing a downward trend dating back to mid-1993. On the surface, the relatively low U.S. stock level, compounded by the anticipated production losses, would have been expected to be supportive to coffee's price. However, the marketplace thought otherwise. Stocks in the key importing nations are apparently seen as adequate. Moreover, 1994's high prices likely encouraged producers to plant more trees and implement better cultural practices that with normal crop weather should lead to record large coffee production in the late 1990s.

Brazil is the world's leading producer of green coffee, with Columbia holding the second spot. In the 1980's Brazil's production varied from 38 million bags in 1987/88 to 13.9 million in 1986/87. In the first half of the 1990s Brazil's production averaged about 27 million bags. The USDA estimated 17.6 million bags for 1995/96; Brazilian estimates ranged from 11.5 to 14 million bags. The decline largely reflects reduced acreage as farmers uprooted over one billion coffee trees between 1991-1993, the equivalent of one-quarter of Brazil's coffee tree population. This should result in reducing Brazil's annual production to a maximum of 27-30 million bags under optimum crop conditions and normal crop weather. Brazil's 1994 exports of green and roasted coffee totaled 14.5 million bags; for 1995 less than 14 million is likely. Columbia's 1995/96 production of 12.5 million bags compares with 11.8 million in 1994/95. Indonesia is the world's largest producer of Robusta coffee and third largest producer of all coffees. Java is the Indonesian synonym for coffee. Mexico is the fourth largest producer with 4.4 million bags in 1995/96 versus 3.9 million in 1994/95.

The U.S. is the world's largest consumer of coffee, importing the equivalent of 16.2 million bags in 1994 versus 19.3 million in 1993. The largest exporters to the U.S. in 1994 were Brazil (20 percent), Mexico (16 percent) and Columbia (15 percent). Much of the world's Robusta coffee goes to Europe and Japan. New Orleans is the major port of entry for U.S. green coffee followed by New York. U.S. per capita coffee consumption has been dropping while use of soft drinks has been expanding. In 1970, U.S. per capita coffee use totaled 35.7 gallons. By 1990 per capita use had dropped to 26.4 gallons and was estimated at 23.4 gallons in 1993. Bottled water use is also expanding rapidly and may be having some adverse effect on coffee use. The U.S. retail price for roasted coffee in 1994 averaged about $3.40 per pound, buoyed by a $4.48 high in November; prices trended lower in 1995. Retail soluble prices are generally at least twice as high as roasted coffee.

An International Coffee Agreement (ICA) that runs to September 30, 1999 attempts to take measures—usually export quotas when needed—that are designed to balance world supply and demand for coffee.

Futures Markets

Coffee futures are traded on the Bolsa de Mercadorias & Futuros (BM&F), the Manila International Futures Exchange Inc. (MIFE), the Singapore Commodity Exchange Ltd., the London Commodity Exchange (LCE), and the Coffee, Sugar and Cocoa Exchange Inc. (CSCE). Options are traded on the BM&F, the LCE, and the CSCE.

COFFEE

World Coffee Supply and Distribution — In Thousands of 60 Kilogram Bags (132.276 Lbs. Per Bag)

Crop Year	Beginning Stocks	Production	Imports	Supply	Total Exports	Bean Exports	Rst/Grn Exports	Soluble Exports	Domestic Use	Ending Stocks
1981-2	32,122	98,152	755	131,029	65,340	61,037	235	4,068	21,056	44,633
1982-3	44,633	82,074	733	127,440	65,454	62,739	220	2,495	20,620	41,366
1983-4	41,366	88,975	606	130,947	68,202	65,080	351	2,771	21,080	41,665
1984-5	41,665	90,508	456	132,629	72,140	68,493	306	3,341	22,968	37,521
1985-6	37,521	95,837	397	133,755	70,121	67,367	248	2,506	21,386	42,248
1986-7	42,248	79,549	262	122,059	66,408	63,777	298	2,333	22,201	33,450
1987-8	33,450	103,285	296	137,031	67,150	64,484	337	2,329	23,074	46,807
1988-9	46,807	94,363	415	141,585	70,892	67,874	162	2,856	22,165	48,528
1989-90	48,528	97,286	258	146,072	83,321	79,953	129	3,239	21,536	41,215
1990-1	41,215	100,417	352	141,984	76,957	73,898	83	2,976	21,806	43,221
1991-2	46,096	104,049	349	150,494	80,495	77,410	53	3,032	22,098	47,901
1992-3	47,901	92,925	770	141,596	77,337	73,240	113	3,984	21,698	42,561
1993-4[1]	42,561	93,237	1,002	136,800	77,261	72,494	108	4,659	23,964	35,575
1994-5[2]	35,575	95,993	765	132,333	68,596	64,118	159	4,319	23,558	40,179
1995-6[3]	40,179	88,226	840	129,245	72,104	67,505	128	4,471	24,802	32,339

[1] Preliminary. [2] Estimate. [3] Forecast. *Source: Foreign Agricutural Service, U.S. Department of Agriculture*

World Green Coffee (Total) Production — In Thousands of 60 Kilogram Bags (132.276 Lbs. Per Bag)

Crop Year	Brazil	Cameroon	Colombia	Costa Rica	El Salvador	Ethiopia	Guatemala	India	Indonesia	Ivory Coast	Mexico	Papua New Guinea	Uganda	Zaire	World Total
1981-2	33,000	1,850	14,342	1,782	2,886	3,212	2,653	2,540	5,785	4,160	3,900	910	2,885	1,425	98,189
1982-3	17,750	1,830	13,300	2,300	3,100	3,670	2,530	2,170	4,750	4,510	4,530	640	3,000	1,354	82,778
1983-4	30,000	1,000	13,000	2,070	2,400	3,300	2,340	1,667	5,515	4,120	4,530	925	2,700	1,350	88,595
1984-5	27,000	2,316	11,000	2,516	2,680	2,587	2,703	3,250	5,600	4,609	4,250	775	2,800	1,540	90,266
1985-6	33,000	2,067	12,000	1,514	2,300	2,833	2,650	2,033	5,800	4,420	4,826	860	2,700	1,610	95,934
1986-7	13,900	2,191	11,000	2,566	2,275	2,700	2,843	3,350	5,900	4,405	5,297	756	2,700	1,875	79,549
1987-8	38,000	1,251	13,000	2,375	2,538	3,200	3,020	2,050	5,965	3,103	4,717	1,100	2,600	2,000	103,231
1988-9	25,000	1,760	10,700	2,758	1,492	3,400	3,022	3,590	6,750	3,989	5,500	1,175	3,300	1,750	94,363
1989-90	26,000	1,440	13,300	2,453	2,787	3,400	3,472	2,150	7,100	4,734	5,100	1,092	2,500	2,000	97,286
1990-1	31,000	1,450	14,500	2,565	2,603	3,500	3,282	2,970	7,480	3,300	4,550	964	2,700	1,695	100,417
1991-2	28,500	1,920	17,980	2,530	2,357	3,000	3,549	3,200	7,100	3,967	4,620	841	2,900	1,500	104,245
1992-3	24,000	837	14,950	2,620	2,894	2,800	3,584	2,700	7,350	2,500	4,180	1,030	2,800	1,790	92,841
1993-4[1]	28,500	1,250	11,400	2,475	2,361	3,000	3,078	3,465	7,400	2,700	4,200	1,080	2,700	1,100	93,697
1994-5[2]	26,000	1,300	13,000	2,492	2,314	3,500	3,500	3,185	6,000	3,733	4,030	1,100	3,000	1,300	95,808
1995-6[3]	16,800	1,300	13,500	2,500	2,425	3,500	3,622	3,500	5,800	3,000	4,600	1,000	3,000	1,000	87,527

[1] Preliminary. [2] Estimate. [3] Forecast. *Source: Foreign Agricultural Service, U.S. Department of Agriculture*

World Green Coffee (Exportable)[4] Production — In Thousands of 60 Kilogram Bags (132.276 Lbs. Per Bag)

Crop Year	Brazil	Cameroon	Colombia	Costa Rica	El Salvador	Ethiopia	Guatemala	Indonesia	Ivory Coast	Kenya	Mexico	Papua New Guinea	Uganda	Zaire	World Total
1981-2	24,500	1,815	12,492	1,539	2,686	1,596	2,328	4,630	4,095	1,434	2,450	901	2,840	1,240	77,311
1982-3	9,750	1,785	11,445	2,077	2,900	2,108	2,195	3,636	4,445	1,501	2,830	631	2,954	1,159	62,366
1983-4	21,500	945	11,140	1,837	2,200	1,728	2,000	4,375	1,395	1,938	3,030	923	2,653	1,150	67,676
1984-5	16,500	2,261	9,135	2,281	2,480	1,087	2,373	4,590	4,582	1,488	2,635	762	2,752	1,340	67,449
1985-6	24,000	1,987	10,130	1,276	2,120	1,293	2,350	4,800	4,391	1,951	3,326	842	2,650	1,410	74,841
1986-7	4,900	2,058	9,000	2,324	2,095	1,034	2,543	4,950	4,375	1,591	3,797	738	2,649	1,670	57,786
1987-8	28,000	1,206	10,980	2,140	2,369	1,756	2,720	4,915	3,071	1,985	3,137	1,087	2,547	1,791	80,390
1988-9	15,500	1,725	8,891	2,508	1,332	1,767	2,717	5,478	3,957	1,787	3,880	1,160	3,250	1,530	71,891
1989-90	17,000	1,405	11,538	2,198	2,607	2,239	3,162	5,820	4,700	1,665	3,650	1,081	2,450	1,780	75,944
1990-1	22,000	1,420	12,885	2,305	2,423	1,800	2,972	6,185	3,264	1,433	3,150	954	2,650	1,480	78,814
1991-2	19,500	1,895	16,580	2,270	2,173	1,300	3,239	5,550	3,929	1,483	3,170	832	2,845	1,300	82,147
1992-3	15,500	812	13,647	2,365	2,677	1,100	3,274	5,570	2,461	1,195	2,880	1,021	2,745	1,615	71,620
1993-4[1]	18,500	1,225	9,700	2,225	2,131	1,200	2,777	5,535	2,661	1,208	2,900	1,071	2,640	950	69,625
1994-5[2]	16,000	1,275	11,600	2,252	2,079	1,700	3,220	4,040	3,694	1,550	3,030	1,091	2,940	1,150	72,717
1995-6[3]	5,800	1,275	12,050	2,265	2,183	1,900	3,322	3,750	2,961	1,578	3,580	891	2,940	850	63,607

[1] Preliminary. [2] Estimate. [3] Forecast. [4] Marketing year begins in October in some countries and April or July in others. Exportable production represents total harvested production minus estimated domestic consumption. *Source: Foreign Agricultural Service, U.S. Department of Agriculture*

Origin of Green Coffee Imports (for Consumption) into the U.S. In Thousands of 60 Kilogram Bags[2]

Year	Brazil	Colombia	Costa Rica	Domin. Republic	Ecuador	El Salvador	Ethiopia	Guate-mata	Indonesia	Ivory Coast	Mexico	Peru	Philip-pines	Uganda	Vene-zuela	Grand Total
1981	3,243	1,727	226	359	701	779	547	645	1,516	602	1,393	439	270	863	27	16,555
1982	3,372	1,710	248	500	773	919	578	844	1,118	998	1,377	513	308	1,229	16	17,416
1983	3,417	1,755	226	430	857	1,214	519	887	1,079	674	1,495	439	276	729	26	16,449
1984	3,866	2,170	258	447	961	1,052	423	1,118	1,030	1,144	1,553	557	296	570	88	17,734
1985	4,148	2,554	360	438	974	1,366	195	1,054	1,041	951	1,812	543	407	739	107	18,698
1986	2,200	2,629	413	488	1,371	1,108	243	1,658	1,346	694	2,125	675	440	739	224	19,483
1987	3,928	2,549	551	446	1,285	1,117	421	1,439	911	476	2,764	573	105	587	163	19,906
1988	4,213	2,235	233	366	811	829	218	609	731	654	1,719	436	298	481	72	15,348
1989	4,155	2,413	393	402	1,137	790	432	1,404	635	335	3,937	673	362	458	87	19,377
1990	3,633	2,771	403	445	876	843	234	1,871	830	54	3,305	473	107	246	222	19,566
1991	5,335	3,048	603	343	785	868	31	1,489	536	54	2,993	610	61	287	108	18,849
1992	4,253	4,852	662	254	753	1,344	23	1,812	581	407	3,042	526	13	223	104	21,673
1993	3,376	2,957	437	213	671	1,274	192	1,815	542	273	2,947	158	6	163	444	18,023
1994	2,850	2,372	325	207	969	376	215	1,403	558	114	2,516	249	78	191	295	14,872
1995[1]	2,302	2,485	388	266	745	284	109	1,637	513	129	2,887	621	3	61	89	15,886

[1] Preliminary. [2] 132.276 pounds per bag. *Source: Bureau of Census, U.S. Department of Commerce*

Total Coffee (Green) Imports (for Consumption) into the U.S. In Thousands of 60 Kilogram Bags[2]

Year	Jan.	Feb.	Mar.	Apr.	May	June	July	Aug.	Sept.	Oct.	Nov.	Dec.	Total
1981	1,858	1,738	1,395	1,299	1,356	1,026	922	1,213	1,150	1,487	1,565	1,547	16,555
1982	1,287	1,195	1,490	1,147	1,476	1,335	1,282	1,602	1,640	2,005	1,356	1,602	17,416
1983	1,556	1,332	1,373	1,253	1,502	1,034	1,319	1,230	1,532	1,685	1,380	1,253	16,449
1984	1,598	1,299	1,440	1,905	1,615	1,059	1,722	1,735	1,432	1,614	1,127	1,187	17,734
1985	1,622	1,681	1,702	1,430	1,324	1,751	1,217	1,757	1,773	1,385	1,272	1,785	18,698
1986	2,360	1,836	1,645	1,667	1,810	1,286	1,549	1,513	1,641	1,535	1,449	1,192	19,483
1987	1,092	1,218	1,841	1,789	1,883	2,181	1,717	1,481	1,770	2,631	1,246	1,056	19,906
1988	1,175	1,683	1,427	1,179	1,141	832	1,543	1,621	1,238	1,272	1,195	1,040	15,348
1989	1,646	1,323	1,368	1,398	1,296	1,199	1,634	1,974	1,951	2,180	1,748	1,660	19,337
1990	1,950	1,989	2,358	1,783	1,658	1,548	1,451	1,261	1,229	1,611	1,140	1,591	19,566
1991	2,106	1,946	1,590	1,748	1,556	984	1,056	1,335	1,424	1,368	1,616	2,122	18,849
1992	2,262	1,944	2,125	1,698	1,534	1,795	1,806	1,692	1,644	1,615	1,508	2,050	21,673
1993	1,782	1,663	2,012	1,481	1,631	1,253	1,442	1,344	1,374	1,464	1,018	1,561	18,023
1994	1,538	1,152	1,409	1,077	1,082	1,151	1,195	1,560	1,266	1,127	1,103	1,213	14,872
1995[1]	1,469	1,253	1,702	1,221	1,190	1,240	1,117	1,094	1,220	1,326	1,492	1,563	15,886

[1] Preliminary. [2] 132.276 pounds per bag. *Source: Bureau of Census, U.S. Department of Commerce*

Average Spot Price of Coffee (Brazilian[1]) at New York In Cents Per Pound

Year	Jan.	Feb.	Mar.	Apr.	May	June	July	Aug.	Sept.	Oct.	Nov.	Dec.	Average
1981	221.72	NA	218.58	218.50	NA	224.76	169.43	143.05	137.50	149.18	158.56	154.21	181.54
1982	148.95	153.11	143.70	143.86	141.33	144.42	138.17	142.05	142.92	141.31	141.63	142.69	143.68
1983	140.73	142.29	142.02	140.86	141.51	142.81	142.51	138.70	136.65	145.31	146.88	152.76	142.75
1984	155.15	155.38	152.82	149.80	145.91	149.45	146.99	150.62	151.55	147.63	144.93	145.59	149.65
1985	152.10	157.25	155.56	146.33	143.84	136.71	130.81	133.25	139.03	150.27	174.28	201.70	151.76
1986	303.42	276.26	286.68	288.55	280.24	229.10	183.40	190.43	210.36	187.89	175.58	162.40	231.19
1987	119.75	114.42	97.41	101.68	111.96	98.34	89.95	91.40	100.67	111.68	122.05	117.09	106.37
1988	117.35	130.40	126.21	123.30	121.02	122.81	120.01	111.89	118.79	115.65	118.53	136.10	121.84
1989	145.29	128.72	128.06	131.45	128.94	115.02	78.75	67.32	67.75	60.32	65.53	67.93	98.76
1990	70.36	77.59	86.17	87.45	86.31	82.94	78.94	90.25	92.20	85.78	77.46	80.17	82.97
1991	75.59	79.39	83.83	81.58	75.56	72.44	69.24	68.15	75.08	65.91	66.03	62.14	72.91
1992	62.03	58.05	59.60	54.94	51.11	49.08	48.53	46.40	49.43	59.64	64.64	74.39	56.49
1993	67.13	66.34	62.60	54.92	57.26	55.70	65.76	73.25	75.58	71.65	74.20	74.51	66.58
1994	71.42	80.14	84.72	87.14	118.37	136.43	211.81	192.38	212.73	191.21	172.83	159.73	143.24
1995	162.81	161.07	171.48	166.54	161.72	145.22	139.68	149.54	130.26	127.23	125.33	110.46	145.95

[1] And other Arabicas. NA = Not available. *Source: Foreign Agricultural Service, U.S. Department of Agriculture*

COFFEE

U.S. Prices of Coffee In Cents Per Pound

Year	Jan.	Feb.	Mar.	Apr.	May	June	July	Aug.	Sept.	Oct.	Nov.	Dec.	Average
Average Monthly Retail[1]													
1991	294.5	297.1	289.4	292.4	287.9	286.6	280.5	272.4	269.2	270.6	267.3	262.5	280.9
1992	266.8	268.8	263.1	261.2	266.0	262.5	265.2	261.3	253.7	249.2	239.1	236.4	257.8
1993	235.2	245.2	246.2	247.7	251.4	253.3	254.8	250.0	249.3	241.5	243.3	248.0	247.2
1994	253.0	252.9	251.5	251.6	253.5	259.8	334.1	448.0	445.8	445.0	448.2	438.2	340.1
1995	439.8	423.4	410.8	408.4	406.7	405.9	402.7	405.1	399.6				
Colombian Mild Arabicas[2]													
1991	91.55	94.23	99.36	97.27	91.51	90.18	88.02	88.09	91.95	82.88	82.43	79.70	89.76
1992	78.40	71.75	73.67	69.55	64.93	64.10	62.50	56.49	56.18	64.77	71.72	81.52	67.97
1993	71.61	72.45	67.07	59.77	67.35	68.13	76.40	84.18	86.58	83.02	85.56	87.33	75.79
1994	85.85	93.04	93.23	97.53	133.90	151.85	222.75	210.57	231.52	206.07	186.96	173.94	157.27
1995	177.23	175.07	185.75	180.30	177.18	170.89	157.22	163.21	141.49	132.08	129.09	110.47	158.33
Other Mild Arabicas[2]													
1991	86.32	89.57	93.72	91.73	87.50	85.50	82.73	81.63	87.45	79.87	78.46	75.11	84.97
1992	72.99	67.88	69.96	65.23	60.14	58.38	57.68	52.42	52.73	61.40	67.36	77.46	63.64
1993	68.66	67.46	62.77	56.88	61.48	61.61	71.46	76.56	79.87	75.05	77.07	80.00	69.91
1994	77.21	82.69	85.57	89.23	121.97	142.57	217.67	198.07	220.10	199.06	180.76	167.47	148.53
1995	171.74	168.71	178.22	172.81	168.63	151.56	143.83	151.41	131.87	125.38	123.23	103.99	149.28
Robustas 1976[2]													
1991	53.92	52.46	52.13	52.38	48.22	47.10	46.49	46.57	48.11	47.31	51.47	51.45	49.80
1992	49.44	43.22	43.08	42.32	38.79	38.07	39.60	39.92	42.39	45.50	49.08	52.09	43.63
1993	48.13	48.25	46.86	45.51	46.91	47.65	50.39	59.29	63.44	60.05	62.53	62.90	53.49
1994	60.91	62.25	66.46	72.64	96.05	113.31	164.65	162.68	182.95	170.09	154.19	130.48	119.72
1995	132.26	135.22	146.83	145.47	141.89	129.53	120.89	131.28	116.41	114.15	112.79	94.72	126.79
Composite 1979 ICA[2]													
1991	69.39	70.55	72.47	71.45	67.47	65.58	64.31	63.38	66.86	62.83	64.30	63.07	66.81
1992	61.12	55.51	56.48	53.64	49.27	48.13	48.70	45.89	47.11	52.88	57.49	64.00	53.35
1993	58.14	57.32	54.76	51.38	54.18	54.54	60.61	67.69	71.64	67.78	70.03	71.53	61.63
1994	69.17	72.37	76.11	81.19	108.42	127.91	191.44	181.53	202.39	185.64	168.12	149.14	134.45
1995	152.08	152.24	162.73	159.59	155.96	141.66	132.71	141.70	124.75	120.02	117.99	99.57	138.42

[1] Roasted in 13.1 to 20 ounce cans. [2] ICO monthly and composite indicator prices on the New York Market, 1979 ICA Agreement basis.

Source: Foreign Agricultural Service, U.S. Department of Agriculture

Average Open Interest of Coffee Futures at New York In Contracts

Year	Jan.	Feb.	Mar.	Apr.	May	June	July	Aug.	Sept.	Oct.	Nov.	Dec.
1984	7,928	9,664	11,925	12,058	11,343	9,844	9,969	9,776	9,347	10,696	10,192	11,320
1985	13,493	13,291	12,952	12,885	12,811	12,393	11,722	11,015	10,198	10,504	11,652	13,287
1986	13,104	14,391	15,714	15,972	16,684	15,712	15,917	16,374	16,798	18,079	16,995	14,905
1987	15,317	16,034	17,415	20,445	22,455	21,160	22,536	23,943	25,857	26,418	22,757	21,064
1988	22,581	26,100	24,591	21,413	22,228	23,346	21,570	24,525	22,460	21,961	19,424	20,356
1989	24,544	23,684	23,246	25,870	23,663	24,716	27,184	31,410	32,404	35,019	32,687	32,096
1990	37,352	43,516	46,187	43,978	41,756	40,464	39,856	41,428	39,278	39,523	43,750	41,365
1991	42,320	41,326	39,948	39,410	41,726	43,717	42,037	40,661	42,126	43,940	41,819	40,628
1992	47,042	51,183	48,961	51,979	59,275	58,304	59,096	58,401	56,446	59,808	57,527	58,257
1993	59,193	54,249	53,618	55,578	51,797	50,918	53,871	48,541	47,649	49,809	46,901	48,812
1994	54,796	50,230	53,713	57,226	58,574	54,589	43,056	35,052	35,800	34,258	31,046	31,134
1995	34,455	35,391	36,925	34,387	34,615	34,462	30,156	27,448	27,800	28,408	24,505	26,412

Source: Coffee, Sugar & Cocoa Exchange, Inc.

Volume of Trading of Coffee "C" Futures at New York In Contracts

Year	Jan.	Feb.	Mar.	Apr.	May	June	July	Aug.	Sept.	Oct.	Nov.	Dec.	Total
1984	33,327	44,890	46,793	46,833	51,174	42,891	34,956	48,979	43,159	29,703	37,457	36,094	499,133
1985	48,733	54,809	52,365	58,531	38,755	54,725	42,222	39,425	23,615	58,870	83,845	94,671	650,768
1986	113,305	95,509	76,787	82,308	75,176	87,323	78,670	106,366	93,465	112,685	89,713	61,835	1,073,142
1987	69,564	81,427	78,671	104,350	71,189	86,564	77,621	106,182	77,207	85,315	72,846	53,650	964,586
1988	67,955	119,075	85,154	80,772	73,379	125,684	91,569	118,956	88,460	83,713	85,366	129,627	1,149,710
1989	141,903	106,019	102,594	129,018	95,902	134,848	100,700	122,207	97,744	104,100	111,434	82,484	1,328,953
1990	130,223	174,115	211,105	144,641	128,121	147,605	127,767	172,947	119,088	113,569	175,067	119,802	1,774,050
1991	138,642	174,688	188,842	153,436	103,344	135,887	107,058	170,113	180,017	148,640	159,099	112,882	1,772,648
1992	153,332	199,420	174,662	188,232	156,944	164,586	177,493	182,741	163,214	108,707	211,678	199,374	2,152,383
1993	290,120	214,771	183,354	209,607	176,559	197,761	193,002	233,479	202,363	187,763	217,947	182,486	2,489,223
1994	188,508	219,455	208,113	284,734	380,119	304,542	210,479	196,685	159,574	177,424	184,172	142,713	2,658,073
1995	169,250	191,352	213,326	156,191	163,248	186,550	162,562	161,076	165,337	152,959	157,240	123,923	2,003,014

Source: Coffee, Sugar & Cocoa Exchange, Inc.

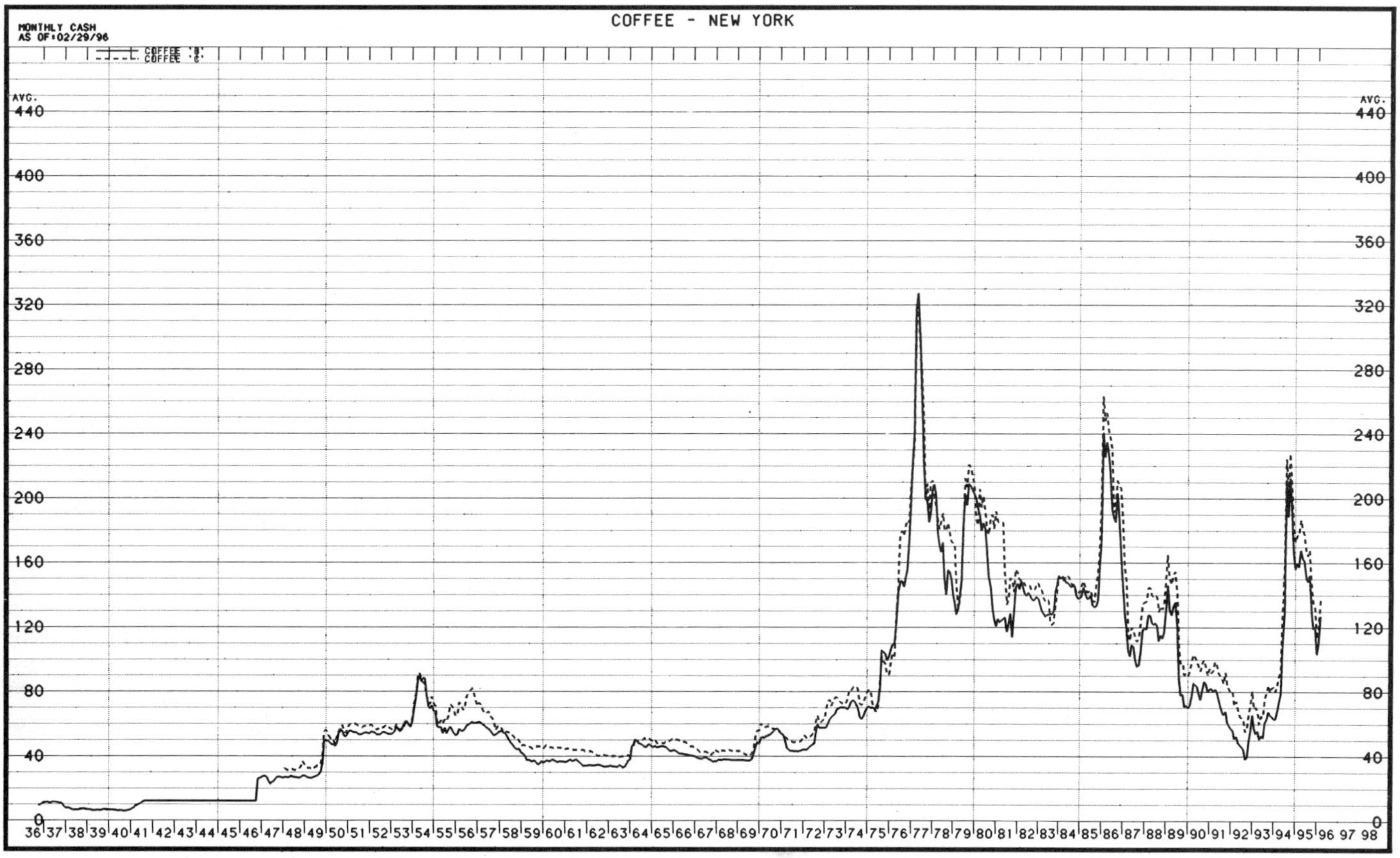

Coke

U.S. Salient Statistics of Coke   In Thousands of Short Tons

	Production at Coke Plants						Exports			Producer & Distributor	Avg. Price of Coal
Year	Merchant Coke Plants	Furance Coke Plants	Total Coke	Breeze	Imports	Consumption[2]	Total	Canada	Mexico	Ending Stocks	Receipts at Coke Plants
1987	3,551	24,486	26,304	2,252	922	27,654	574	248	106	1,064	46.55
1988	3,868	28,536	28,945	2,478	2,688	30,021	1,093	348	101	1,583	47.70
1989	------------	28,045	------------	2,342	2,311	28,935	1,085	644	157	1,919	47.50
1990	3,724	23,892	27,617	1,736	765	27,811	572	376	94	1,918	47.73
1991	3,251	20,795	24,046	1,734	1,099	24,216	740	239	98	2,107	48.95
1992	3,248	20,162	23,410	1,721	1,739	24,731	642	310	76	1,883	47.92
1993	3,209	19,973	23,182	3,424	1,534	24,303	835	417	92	1,461	47.44
1994[1]	3,244	19,443	22,686	1,392	1,612	24,163	660	371	94	936	46.56

[1] Preliminary. [2] Equal to production plus imports minus the change in producer and distributor stocks minus exports.
Source: Energy Information Administration, U.S. Department of Energy

Petroleum Coke Production in the United States   In Thousands of Barrels[2]

Year	Jan.	Feb.	Mar.	Apr.	May	June	July	Aug.	Sept.	Oct.	Nov.	Dec.	Total
1986	3,161	2,825	3,027	2,865	3,191	3,176	3,059	3,230	3,171	3,066	2,925	3,206	36,903
1987	3,228	2,960	3,034	2,794	3,087	3,121	3,190	3,138	3,047	3,060	3,158	3,384	37,380
1988	3,436	3,171	3,415	3,164	3,367	3,282	3,333	3,347	3,205	3,281	3,347	3,462	39,811
1989	3,505	2,931	3,201	3,200	3,337	3,406	3,509	3,447	3,255	3,252	3,104	3,227	39,533
1990	3,336	3,142	3,329	3,278	3,357	3,291	3,437	3,617	3,304	3,366	3,351	3,502	40,332
1991	3,518	3,056	3,276	3,303	3,527	3,404	3,537	3,575	3,410	3,501	3,505	3,808	41,493
1992	3,710	3,266	3,565	3,523	3,692	3,737	3,866	3,656	3,569	3,533	3,540	3,877	43,599
1993	18,551	17,289	19,226	18,200	18,587	18,715	20,196	19,319	18,547	18,695	18,954	19,737	226,016
1994	19,170	16,873	18,695	18,454	19,748	19,325	20,008	19,473	17,868	18,753	18,995	19,697	227,059
1995[1]	19,079	17,117	18,556	18,519	19,774	19,993	19,660	19,178	19,178	19,266			

[1] Preliminary. [2] Prior to 1993, data shown in thousands of short tons (5 barrels = 1 short ton). *Source: Energy Information Administration, U.S. Department of Energy*

Coal Receipts and Carbonization at Coke Plants in the U.S.   In Thousands of Short Tons

	Coal Receipts at Coke Plants							Coal Carbonized at Coke Plants						
	By State					By Plant Type		By State					By Plant Type	
Year	Alabama	Indiana	Ohio	Pennsylvania	Total	Merchant Coke Plants	Furance Coke Plants	Alabama	Indiana	Ohio	Pennsylvania	Total	Merchant Coke Plants	Furance Coke Plants
1987	3,250	9,774	5,770	8,504	37,744	4,660	33,084	3,150	9,791	5,361	8,395	36,957	4,536	32,422
1988	3,313	11,251	5,041	10,179	41,115	5,008	36,107	3,383	11,287	5,448	10,146	41,910	5,034	36,876
1989	3,330	10,558	5,143	9,822	41,019	4,959	36,060	3,314	10,568	5,265	9,877	41,369	5,010	36,876
1990	3,304	10,497	5,021	10,604	40,736	4,988	35,749	3,288	8,867	4,949	10,456	38,877	4,950	33,927
1991	3,114	8,141	3,595	8,912	33,090	4,399	28,692	3,166	8,234	3,698	8,812	33,854	4,482	29,371
1992	3,334	6,894	3,717	9,761	32,027	4,295	27,732	3,297	7,153	3,755	9,868	32,366	4,316	28,050
1993	3,184	6,515	2,853	10,424	31,104	4,184	26,921	3,206	6,591	2,892	10,333	31,323	4,267	27,056
1994[1]	3,242	5,023	3,064	10,776	31,719	4,205	27,514	3,253	4,841	3,092	10,849	31,740	4,218	27,522

[1] Preliminary. *Source: Energy Information Administration, U.S. Department of Energy*

United States Coke Distribution and Stocks   In Thousands of Short Tons

	Distribution							Coke Plant Stocks, Dec. 31			
	By Plant Type		By Consumer Category						By Plant Type		
Year	Merchant Coke Plants	Furance Coke Plants	Blast Furance	Foundries	Other Industrial Plants	Total Coke	Breeze	Total Coke	Merchant Coke Plants	Furance Coke Plants	Breeze
1987	3,639	26,163	27,236	1,552	1,014	29,802	2,151	1,064	218	846	332
1988	3,953	29,758	30,499	1,630	1,581	33,710	2,448	1,583	163	1,420	189
1989	3,755	30,286	30,676	1,535	1,830	34,041	2,251	1,919	216	1,703	179
1990	3,724	29,564	30,877	1,437	974	33,289	1,882	1,918	244	1,674	228
1991	3,246	24,267	25,669	1,213	630	27,513	2,057	2,107	252	1,856	259
1992	3,253	26,718	28,075	1,290	606	29,971	2,255	1,883	267	1,616	215
1993	3,226	27,009	28,295	1,373	567	30,235	3,563	1,461	272	1,189	486
1994[1]	3,400	25,949	27,248	1,480	621	29,349	1,735	936	122	814	105

[1] Preliminary. *Source: Energy Information Administration, U.S. Department of Energy*

Copper

Copper metal and copper alloy have considerable commercial importance due to their electrical, mechanical and physical properties. Copper for commercial purposes is obtained by the reduction of copper compounds in ores, followed by electrolytic refining. Copper is used largely in alloys such as brass, which is composed of copper and zinc.

The principal mining states for copper are Arizona, New Mexico, Utah, Michigan and Montana. 14 mines account for over 95 percent of U.S. production. The U.S. Bureau of Mines indicated that U.S. production of recoverable mine copper for the Jan.-July 1995 period was 1.08 million tonnes. Production was around record levels as several mines in Arizona increased production. For all of 1994, mine production of copper was 1.8 million tonnes. Arizona copper production over the first seven months of 1995 was 677,000 tonnes. The other states produced 400,000 tonnes. In 1994, Arizona produced 1.12 million tonnes of mine copper with the other states producing 676,000 tonnes.

Smelter production of copper (from domestic and foreign ores) in the first seven months of 1995 was 732,000 tonnes. For all of 1994, smelter production was 1.31 million tonnes. Smelter production of copper from scrap for the Jan.-July 1995 period was 190,000 tonnes. In 1994, copper production at smelters from scrap was 397,000 tonnes.

Refinery production of copper during Jan.-July 1995 was 1.08 million tonnes. In 1994 it totaled 1.83 million tonnes. There are also significant amounts of copper produced from secondary recoverable sources. These include refineries, ingot makers, brass and wire-rod mills and foundries.

U.S. consumption of refined copper in the first seven months of 1995 was 1.51 million tonnes. Consumption by wire-rod mills was 1.17 million tonnes while brass mills used 317,000 tonnes and other plants (ingot makers, chemical plants, foundries) used 23,800 tonnes. For all of 1994, consumption of refined copper was 2.68 million tonnes.

Crude copper stocks at the end of July 1995 were 180,000 tonnes compared to stocks at the end of 1994 of 171,000 tonnes. For refined copper, stocks at the end of July 1995 were: refineries 37,500 tonnes, wire-rod mills 25,500 tonnes, brass mills 13,800 tonnes, other 3,650 tonnes and the Commodity Exchange, Inc. in New York 15,100 tonnes. In Jan.-July 1995, copper cathode prices averaged $1.40 per pound compared to the 1994 average of $1.11. The average price of copper wirebar was $1.48 versus $1.19.

In the first half of 1995, U.S. imports of copper ore and concentrate were 59,600 tonnes with major sources being Chile and Mexico. Imports of copper blister and anodes were 44,300 tonnes supplied primarily by Canada. Imports of refined copper were 213,000 tonnes with most coming from Canada, Mexico and Russia. Imports of unalloyed scrap were 38,500 tonnes, mostly from Mexico and Canada.

For the first half of 1995, U.S. exports of refined copper were 141,000 tonnes while copper ore and concentrate exports were 128,000 tonnes. Exports of unalloyed copper scrap were 115,000 tonnes while copper-base scrap was 42,600 tonnes.

Futures Markets

High-grade copper futures and options are traded on the Commodity Exchange (COMEX), a division of the New York Mercantile Exchange. Cash copper futures and options are listed on the London Metals Exchange (LME).

World Mine Production of Copper (Content of Ore) In Thousands of Metric Tons

Year	Australia	Canada[3]	Chile	China	Indonesia	Mexico	Mongolia	Peru	Philippines	Poland	Russia[4]	South Africa	United States[3]	Zaire	Zambia	World Total[2]
1985	259.8	738.6	1,359.8	200	88.7	171.3	128.0	400.8	222.2	432.0	600	203.2	1,102.6	525.2	519.6	7,988
1986	248.4	698.6	1,398.8	185	95.8	189.1	136.0	399.9	222.6	434.0	620	184.2	1,144.2	527.8	462.4	7,939
1987	232.7	802.2	1,418.1	250	102.1	252.7	120.8	417.6	216.1	438.0	630	188.1	1,243.6	515.6	463.2	8,243
1988	238.3	776.5	1,451.0	282	121.5	284.9	121.7	337.5	218.1	437.0	1,000	168.5	1,419.7	495.8	456.6	8,727
1989	296.0	723.1	1,609.3	276	144.0	264.2	123.6	387.9	193.0	384.0	1,000	181.9	1,507.3	466.2	466.3	9,058
1990	330.0	793.7	1,588.4	285	164.1	293.9	123.9	339.3	182.1	330.0	950	178.7	1,587.8	356.0	421.0	8,950
1991	311.0	811.3	1,814.3	304	211.7	292.1	90.1	399.9	148.3	320.3	900	184.6	1,631.0	237.5	391.0	9,140
1992	378.0	769.1	1,932.7	334	281.0	290.9	105.1	367.7	123.5	332.0	699	197.8	1,765.1	144.0	430.0	9,500
1993[1]	402.0	733.7	2,060.0	345	299.0	304.0	96.9	393.3	136.5	383.0	584	166.0	1,786.6	46.4	396.0	9,480
1994[2]	416.0	626.0	2,220.0	350	322.0	295.0	99.6	399.0	110.0	328.0	573	165.0	1,808.0	40.0	385.0	9,430

[1] Preliminary. [2] Estimate. [3] Recoverable. [4] Formerly part of the U.S.S.R.; data not reported separately until 1992. NA = Not available.
Source: U.S. Bureau of Mines

Commodity Exchange, Inc. (COMEX) Warehouse Stocks of Copper In Thousands of Short Tons

Year	Jan. 1	Feb. 1	Mar. 1	Apr. 1	May 1	June 1	July 1	Aug. 1	Sept. 1	Oct. 1	Nov. 1	Dec. 1
1986	120.3	120.1	118.5	116.4	114.5	108.5	103.4	95.7	90.6	86.6	81.0	84.0
1987	93.3	102.8	108.9	97.5	88.4	71.4	65.3	69.0	73.5	89.2	66.2	33.7
1988	18.5	16.9	16.8	11.8	10.2	19.0	16.9	24.6	22.3	13.6	9.5	5.9
1989	13.4	14.9	17.3	29.7	21.2	25.2	23.0	20.4	15.2	11.4	10.4	9.1
1990	16.3	7.2	4.1	4.5	6.0	14.7	18.1	11.5	8.9	6.7	8.3	9.3
1991	20.2	14.7	16.4	30.2	30.9	25.0	25.1	35.9	33.6	24.4	26.8	29.3
1992	33.7	34.8	29.5	28.2	30.3	32.4	31.8	36.0	40.4	51.7	70.1	73.8
1993	105.9	124.0	114.8	107.6	110.8	108.3	105.5	113.8	100.1	94.1	96.6	80.5
1994	74.0	56.7	49.8	37.2	31.6	30.4	36.0	37.4	28.5	17.9	20.3	21.5
1995	26.7	18.7	17.7	9.0	11.5	7.0	13.1	16.7	16.5	11.2	6.0	5.0

Source: Commodity Exchange, Inc. of New York (COMEX)

COPPER

U.S. Salient Statistics of Copper In Thousands of Metric Tons

	New Copper Produced						Imports[3]		Exports		Stocks, Dec. 31			Apparent Consumption	
	From Domestic Ores														
Year	Mines	Smelters	Refineries	From Foreign Ores[3]	Total New	Secondary Recovered[4]	Unmanufactured	Refined	Ore, Concentrate[6]	Refined[7]	COMEX	Primary Producers (Refined)	Blister & Material in Solution	Refined Copper (Reported)	Primary & Old Copper[8]
1984	1,103	990	1,090	75	1,165	461	552	445	69	91	251	125	245	2,123	2,107
1985	1,105	939	1,004	54	1,057	503	444	378	116	38	109	320	146	1,976	2,144
1986	1,144	908	1,033	41	1,074	479	597	502	174	12	84	225	136	2,097	2,138
1987	1,244	972	1,127	W	1,127	498	568	469	125	9	17	113	150	2,127	2,197
1988	1,417	1,043	1,282	124	1,406	518	513	332	211	58	12	97	121	2,210	2,214
1989	1,498	1,120	1,352	125	1,477	548	515	300	267	130	15	107	132	2,203	2,185
1990	1,588	1,158	1,502	75	1,577	537	512	262	258	211	18	101	119	2,150	2,168
1991	1,631	1,123	1,501	77	1,577	518	512	289	253	263	31	132	135	2,048	2,105
1992	1,765	1,180	1,615	96	1,711	555	593	289	266	177	96	205	166	2,178	2,311
1993[1]	1,801	1,265	1,214	89	1,793	543	637	343	227	217	67	153	146	2,364	2,510
1994[2]	1,810	1,310	1,280	64	1,840	500	763	470	261	157	24	119	171	2,680	2,680

[1] Preliminary. [2] Estimate. [3] Also from matte, etc., refinery reports. [4] From scrap only. [5] For consumption. [6] Blister (copper content). [7] Ingots, bars, etc. [8] Old scrap only. *Source: U.S. Bureau of Mines*

Consumption of Refined Copper[3] in the United States In Thousands of Metric Tons

	By-Products						By Class of Consumer						Total
Year	Cathodes	Wire Bars	Ingot & Ingot Bars	Cakes & Slabs	Billets	Other	Wire Rod Mills	Brass Mills	Chemical Plants	Ingot Makers	Foundries	Miscellaneous	Consumption
1984	1,635.1	72.1	74.4	127.7	118.5	8.2	1,401.7	514.0	.7	5.3	19.8	34.6	1,976.0
1985	1,563.4	70.3	64.2	115.8	139.6	22.8	1,401.7	564.9	.9	1.4	20.6	22.9	2,101.5
1986	1,717.7	52.5	105.9	81.6	127.9	16.9	1,491.9	564.9	.9	1.4	20.6	22.9	2,102.6
1987	1,852.9	13.8	74.0	71.9	92.7	20.3	1,593.9	488.6	1.1	1.4	14.2	26.4	2,125.7
1988	1,967.4	14.0	54.2	63.0	99.0	12.7	1,667.2	493.2	1.0	2.6	14.5	31.9	2,210.4
1989	1,981.6	6.1	34.4	64.9	104.9	11.2	1,698.4	461.0	.9	1.3	14.9	26.5	2,203.1
1990	1,922.4	6.6	50.5	57.9	---- 113.0 ----		1,653.5	445.2	1.1	4.5	14.6	31.6	2,150.4
1991	1,854.9	W	24.7	33.3	---- 135.4 ----		1,591.8	458.5	.9	3.4	12.7	25.3	2,048.3
1992	1,974.9	W	20.0	43.7	---- 139.6 ----		1,675.0	458.5	.9	3.0	15.0	25.8	2,178.2
1993[1]	2,130.0	W	37.7	55.5	---- 136.0 ----		1,819.1	503.0	.9	2.2	10.2	27.6	2,360.0
1994[2]	2,410.0	W	37.3	73.2	---- 164.0 ----		2,060.0	568.0	1.1	4.5	11.1	30.4	2,680.0

[1] Preliminary. [2] Estimate. [3] Primary & secondary. *Source: U.S. Bureau of Mines*

London Metals Exchange (LME) Warehouse Stocks of Copper (End of Period) In Thousands of Metric Tons

Year	Jan.	Feb.	Mar.	Apr.	May	June	July	Aug.	Sept.	Oct.	Nov.	Dec.
1987	213.2	170.6	159.9	176.0	133.5	126.4	118.3	139.6	128.0	82.9	69.1	64.3
1988	59.6	74.4	69.4	54.8	86.8	109.1	145.8	148.4	122.4	86.2	78.3	79.9
1989	96.6	104.2	117.4	138.7	125.2	99.2	96.1	100.8	126.7	117.8	142.2	131.2
1990	121.5	106.8	71.9	67.0	92.8	67.7	126.8	161.1	227.1	221.1	199.9	220.6
1991	189.0	202.8	213.9	237.9	275.0	264.9	266.5	307.1	308.4	291.7	308.3	332.3
1992	308.6	302.7	296.4	279.7	265.4	259.1	246.8	275.2	299.7	317.8	327.0	315.8
1993	313.5	333.1	365.8	403.5	429.1	446.9	464.3	521.7	600.7	612.3	590.9	599.5
1994	597.6	554.5	504.3	446.4	379.0	350.9	338.9	367.8	359.3	333.1	318.4	301.8
1995[1]	309.7	281.0	244.7	208.6	198.0	175.8	151.2	162.8	178.4	193.4	217.8	296.5

[1] Preliminary. *Source: American Bureau of Metal Statistics*

U.S. Copper Refined from Scrap In Thousands of Metric Tons

Year	Jan.	Feb.	Mar.	Apr.	May	June	July	Aug.	Sept.	Oct.	Nov.	Dec.	Total
1985	29.5	29.5	32.0	31.6	31.2	34.7	32.0	30.0	29.6	25.9	28.7	28.5	377.5
1986	42.5	44.9	45.2	42.6	42.4	40.8	39.1	37.4	43.9	43.5	36.0	36.7	405.9
1987	28.7	31.6	40.1	44.3	34.0	35.1	39.5	33.2	34.5	35.8	30.8	37.1	414.7
1988	34.2	35.2	42.9	38.1	38.0	38.4	30.4	37.9	42.3	37.0	37.5	40.2	453.3
1989	37.4	40.8	47.0	40.1	40.8	41.1	36.6	41.4	40.6	41.3	35.9	37.1	479.9
1990	37.3	35.2	37.1	38.5	39.3	38.1	34.6	39.2	29.9	34.3	31.9	32.0	440.8
1991	35.4	32.8	40.5	39.6	38.2	35.7	32.6	33.0	28.5	37.3	32.1	32.6	417.7
1992	27.8	34.1	39.8	34.8	36.7	39.4	27.8	35.4	39.8	40.0	34.3	35.8	433.2
1993	38.1	45.9	38.9	37.8	36.4	41.1	35.0	37.6	37.4	43.0	35.4	32.2	459.8
1994	33.3	28.3	37.9	30.7	37.1	28.7	26.9	33.0	38.7	27.0	34.3	37.3	391.7
1995[1]	30.9	30.6	36.0	32.7	33.7	28.2	18.7	25.1	25.4				

[1] Preliminary. *Source: U.S. Bureau of Mines*

Average Open Interest of Copper Futures[1] at COMEX In Contracts

Year	Jan.	Feb.	Mar.	Apr.	May	June	July	Aug.	Sept.	Oct.	Nov.	Dec.
1986	87,280	83,713	86,713	79,370	71,169	68,505	63,529	61,827	62,779	65,073	73,414	78,164
1987	77,851	77,433	76,967	70,108	74,628	84,725	85,391	75,725	65,678	59,073	47,279	41,781
1988	43,177	41,220	35,505	34,787	31,410	35,949	31,750	29,520	34,946	35,724	36,607	33,094
1989	33,397	33,756	34,664	35,694	30,459	27,606	24,462	25,128	23,742	19,439	14,955	2,898
1990	31,401	33,908	34,654	34,405	31,552	30,113	32,780	31,515	32,578	36,145	35,088	30,128
1991	34,927	35,978	35,026	34,096	44,153	39,879	33,100	33,333	40,347	42,028	41,618	44,283
1992	47,109	47,929	48,700	45,114	39,986	48,129	47,065	38,397	37,041	41,658	44,927	45,541
1993	47,433	48,707	48,220	51,217	52,762	56,856	54,861	54,571	54,929	57,406	63,632	69,311
1994	65,518	65,446	66,177	59,346	63,825	60,383	51,616	46,855	56,344	59,060	59,158	51,078
1995	52,632	50,770	47,267	47,793	50,089	48,200	40,968	37,744	33,709	36,476	38,475	35,996

[1] High grade copper contracts from 1990. *Source: New York Mercantile Exchange, COMEX Division*

Volume of Trading of Copper Futures[1] at COMEX In Contracts

Year	Jan.	Feb.	Mar.	Apr.	May	June	July	Aug.	Sept.	Oct.	Nov.	Dec.	Total
1983	306,001	381,645	230,574	278,655	226,482	309,540	213,832	295,470	188,201	230,063	289,111	147,340	3,186,914
1984	199,461	259,881	217,635	269,765	196,382	223,551	152,424	215,226	149,465	170,568	279,151	172,856	2,514,311
1985	254,052	261,784	167,686	310,487	215,079	209,506	146,396	195,882	138,803	178,728	200,142	166,007	2,444,552
1986	190,983	206,513	197,818	240,770	106,750	200,547	89,818	145,468	123,779	121,361	162,963	85,439	1,872,209
1987	124,845	178,598	165,216	170,827	208,696	306,029	272,794	214,181	193,035	276,491	278,985	179,481	2,569,178
1988	210,209	222,625	194,722	151,177	130,289	179,991	120,088	142,945	141,899	186,220	258,725	173,569	2,112,459
1989	216,828	200,945	226,425	201,677	193,956	174,055	132,793	173,273	151,097	176,822	154,241	93,243	2,096,547
1990	152,156	148,766	179,445	181,726	164,489	163,372	141,602	154,383	156,924	161,814	133,718	114,790	1,853,185
1991	159,621	131,044	108,191	150,390	148,777	139,207	110,025	149,702	132,354	125,757	153,910	135,132	1,643,310
1992	145,245	168,015	105,003	157,473	77,722	182,091	138,225	177,581	137,423	121,392	146,062	117,931	1,674,163
1993	152,387	148,388	132,705	212,086	160,751	181,427	165,727	169,428	222,099	133,364	203,729	182,538	2,064,629
1994	197,959	233,016	231,239	207,963	247,143	297,393	188,644	242,393	219,788	208,957	290,585	178,887	2,737,967
1995	242,760	267,883	232,229	242,302	195,554	274,587	167,836	213,110	169,689	181,945	185,141	146,378	2,519,414

[1] Beginning May 1989 thru December 1989, high grade contracts are included (May total was 353 contracts). *Source: New York Mercantile Exchange, COMEX Division*

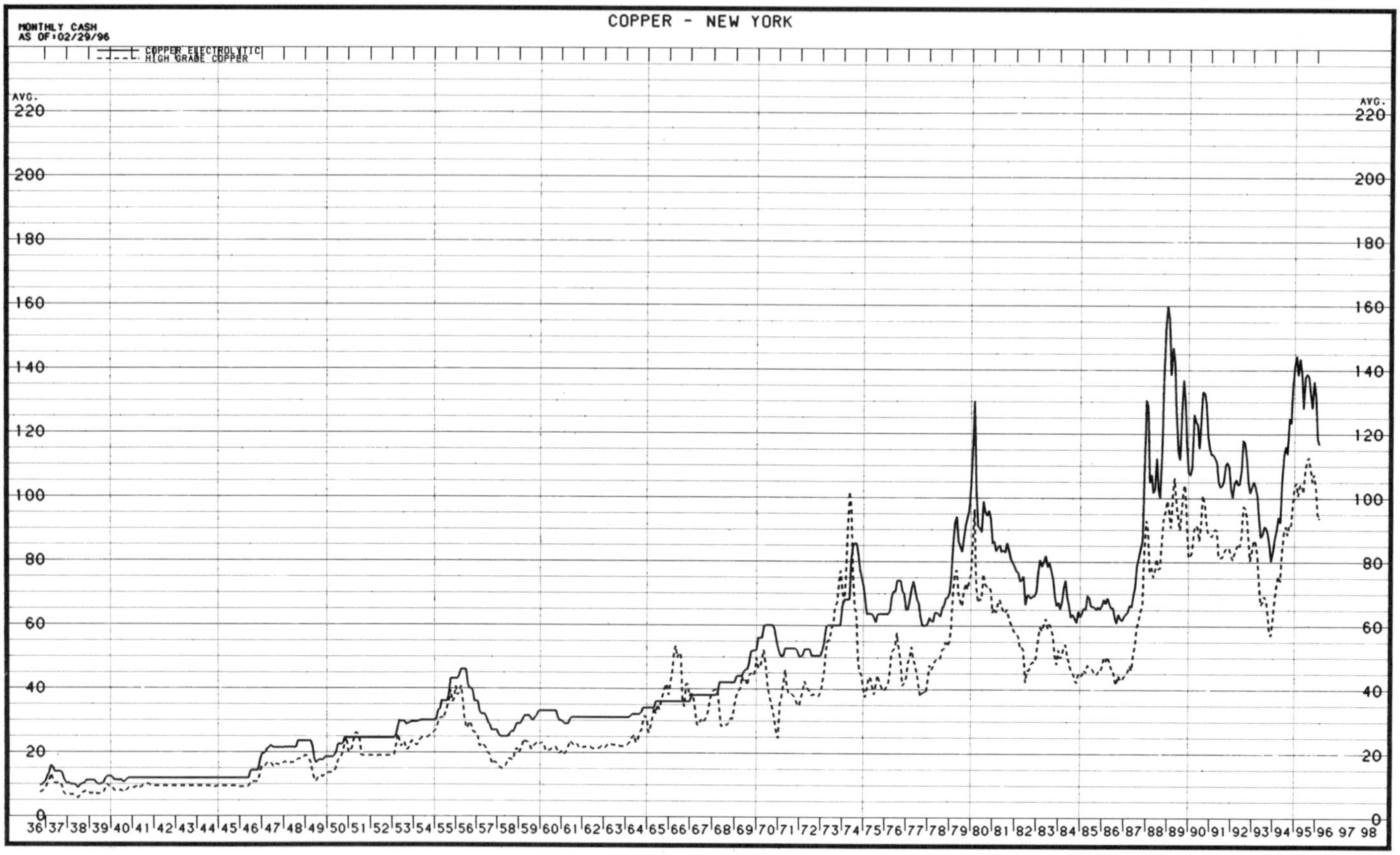

Producers' Prices of Electrolytic (Wirebar) Copper, Delivered U.S. Destinations In Cents Per Pound

Year	Jan.	Feb.	Mar.	Apr.	May	June	July	Aug.	Sept.	Oct.	Nov.	Dec.	Average
1985	66.23	68.32	67.19	72.17	71.89	68.86	68.53	68.32	67.66	68.60	68.37	70.10	68.85
1986	71.57	70.21	71.78	70.55	68.69	69.15	65.47	64.12	66.82	65.61	65.06	65.91	67.91
1987	67.29	67.87	70.50	69.83	73.54	76.71	83.10	84.94	88.04	91.52	109.59	134.71	84.80
1988	135.63	110.58	111.99	107.51	106.91	116.46	107.90	103.62	118.04	126.38	159.08	167.80	122.66
1989	164.21	146.17	154.89	150.26	132.72	121.45	119.27	133.75	143.60	137.61	123.59	115.64	136.93
1990	116.36	119.35	136.22	134.38	132.32	124.93	133.91	142.53	142.45	138.41	127.76	124.39	131.08
1991	122.59	122.73	121.24	120.35	133.11	111.72	111.90	113.48	118.92	118.90	117.26	110.33	118.54
1992	108.16	112.52	113.56	112.35	112.56	116.74	125.66	124.30	119.39	112.09	108.23	111.13	114.72
1993	112.57	110.26	107.80	99.03	92.35	94.98	93.41	97.06	92.36	81.69	86.07	91.08	96.56
1994	95.65	99.13	101.76	99.87	112.30	120.58	123.68	121.38	132.53	130.91	141.92	148.86	119.05
1995	152.02	146.00	151.14	146.03	139.80	149.51	150.00	149.77	144.14	140.00	148.48	143.78	146.72

Source: American Metal Market

Dealers' Buying Price of No. 2 Heavy Copper Scrap In the Chicago Area[1] In Cents Per Pound

Year	Jan.	Feb.	Mar.	Apr.	May	June	July	Aug.	Sept.	Oct.	Nov.	Dec.	Average
1983	42.55	46.71	51.50	51.50	53.74	54.50	54.50	53.54	51.74	48.12	43.30	42.50	49.52
1984	41.17	40.60	43.59	44.50	43.30	42.21	39.36	38.50	38.08	36.20	34.50	35.67	39.81
1985	37.50	37.50	37.50	37.50	37.50	37.50	37.50	37.50	37.50	37.50	37.50	37.50	37.50
1986	38.23	39.50	39.50	39.50	39.50	39.50	39.50	37.79	37.50	37.50	37.50	37.50	38.59
1987	37.50	37.50	37.86	39.50	41.15	42.50	44.68	49.07	49.50	53.32	55.39	64.73	46.06
1988[1]	77.10	68.00	63.50	63.12	70.07	70.59	69.80	69.54	72.36	78.93	83.66	85.50	72.68
1989	89.83	87.13	95.33	95.95	91.14	80.27	74.45	75.54	86.50	90.32	86.00	80.25	86.06
1990	78.27	71.00	78.73	88.00	88.00	84.38	84.00	85.50	91.84	89.50	86.48	83.00	84.06
1991	83.00	79.50	82.21	82.50	78.66	72.40	71.00	71.00	72.05	75.39	75.08	74.50	76.44
1992	73.21	73.37	75.23	75.16	74.00	74.27	77.18	78.38	75.38	70.27	69.00	67.18	73.55
1993	67.95	67.00	67.00	62.95	55.12	53.59	56.33	54.18	52.67	49.10	47.00	48.00	56.74
1994	50.80	56.11	59.61	62.00	64.86	72.32	76.40	74.30	75.69	76.45	78.10	82.95	69.13
1995	89.48	90.79	89.39	91.75	85.91	88.73	92.32	92.65	92.70	90.64	92.00	92.00	90.70

[1] Prior to May 1988, prices are for the New York area. *Source: American Metal Market*

U.S. Foreign Trade of Refined Copper In Thousands of Metric Tons

Year		Jan.	Feb.	Mar.	Apr.	May	June	July	Aug.	Sept.	Oct.	Nov.	Dec.	Total
1987	Imports	34.4	38.7	55.8	38.9	60.2	69.3	37.0	45.0	28.6	35.9	40.8	31.1	515.6
	Exports	.8	1.9	2.4	2.8	.8	1.1	.6	.5	.8	.7	2.3	3.2	17.9
1988	Imports	49.4	38.0	39.0	33.7	25.9	25.1	22.3	27.7	25.7	44.2	39.2	20.2	390.4
	Exports	4.9	2.0	3.8	5.7	7.7	9.5	3.5	4.4	14.3	2.3	4.0	4.5	66.5
1989	Imports	32.7	24.8	18.7	20.9	24.1	25.9	20.9	24.4	28.1	30.5	32.3	16.9	300.1
	Exports	6.2	4.8	5.9	13.5	4.3	6.6	21.4	15.8	23.4	13.7	6.3	12.1	130.2
1990	Imports	24.7	15.8	26.5	25.3	31.3	24.0	20.6	18.0	21.4	18.4	20.8	16.7	263.6
	Exports	18.1	20.8	12.2	7.6	15.6	12.2	23.9	20.1	22.4	21.5	17.2	19.8	211.3
1991	Imports	22.7	27.1	21.7	30.9	17.5	23.6	23.7	17.4	22.9	36.3	26.8	18.0	288.6
	Exports	33.6	21.4	37.4	16.8	31.5	23.9	20.6	20.9	17.9	13.4	15.4	17.9	270.7
1992	Imports	22.6	24.5	31.9	25.2	25.3	26.1	24.7	25.3	24.0	19.6	20.3	20.8	289.1
	Exports	21.7	18.4	10.8	12.3	11.7	12.0	9.3	13.0	13.6	24.1	14.1	16.1	176.9
1993	Imports	21.8	25.6	28.2	35.9	29.5	26.9	30.6	28.3	22.5	31.6	32.2	30.5	343.4
	Exports	14.0	24.9	23.6	16.3	15.4	13.1	10.7	10.1	19.5	19.5	14.9	14.5	216.7
1994[1]	Imports	28.7	33.6	49.8	36.8	36.1	46.8	35.6	34.4	34.7	62.4	35.9	36.2	470.0
	Exports	13.0	10.2	10.7	6.8	14.8	9.1	15.6	10.9	15.4	15.9	13.1	21.1	157.0
1995[1]	Imports	34.9	30.0	37.1	36.9	36.5	37.9	31.5						
	Exports	11.1	24.0	25.6	18.2	23.4	38.9	16.3						

[1] Preliminary. *Source: U.S. Bureau of Mines*

Refined Copper Stocks in the U.S.A. In Thousands of Short Tons (Recoverable Copper Content)

Year	Jan. 1	Feb. 1	Mar. 1	Apr. 1	May 1	June 1	July 1	Aug. 1	Sept. 1	Oct. 1	Nov. 1	Dec. 1
1980	186.3	203.5	228.2	237.1	269.1	277.3	295.7	310.6	301.0	274.6	265.0	246.0
1981	253.0	261.6	249.4	236.8	245.5	243.4	264.7	276.9	276.0	275.5	281.6	301.2
1982	338.6	351.9	375.9	387.3	409.8	422.5	448.1	463.7	449.9	436.2	438.2	470.8
1983	484.5	489.6	501.6	508.9	524.1	519.4	498.7	509.0	522.7	509.1	514.2	505.2
1984	475.3	497.8	499.6	483.3	478.3	463.4	483.2	493.4	490.7	467.1	475.2	457.3
1985	469.7	452.9	380.9	368.2	358.4	363.2	344.1	331.4	310.9	275.7	257.3	264.1
1986	270.7	271.0	261.6	242.0	231.1	201.4	188.0	209.6	214.4	188.1	189.0	211.3
1987	238.4	211.5	206.8	170.1	175.7	161.6	136.4	141.0	140.4	151.3	121.1	86.7
1988	81.4	79.8	81.6	89.0	83.1	75.7	42.0	48.8	52.5	42.9	40.6	39.8
1989	56.3	67.5	56.3	60.6	54.3	54.4	49.1	61.8	66.1	42.3	48.1	48.2
1990	72.7	42.4	38.6	45.2	55.9	60.2	67.5	67.2	67.6	27.4	27.9	45.4
1991	72.3	72.8	53.2	68.6	63.2	52.8	52.4	71.4	64.4	48.5	48.3	63.1
1992	75.3	76.3	67.2	69.7	75.9	65.0	62.2	71.2	87.1	99.5	110.3	107.1
1993	135.4	152.7	144.3	132.3	146.0	153.6	137.1	151.0	128.4	117.2	124.6	107.1
1994	103.0	87.7	83.6	72.8	70.7	70.4	73.3	81.1	74.6	66.5	52.7	53.6
1995[1]	51.5	54.7	52.2	36.3	45.3	51.4	50.2	54.7	56.1	43.6	43.1	41.4

[3] Preliminary. *Source: American Bureau of Metal Statistics*

Refined Copper Stocks Outside the U.S.A. In Thousands of Short Tons (Recoverable Copper Content)

Year	Jan. 1	Feb. 1	Mar. 1	Apr. 1	May 1	June 1	July 1	Aug. 1	Sept. 1	Oct. 1	Nov. 1	Dec. 1
1980	619.5	598.3	560.9	534.6	516.5	525.9	531.2	530.9	553.2	527.9	489.1	472.6
1981	476.2	485.2	471.0	463.0	458.8	449.8	446.0	454.9	454.7	433.4	419.4	403.0
1982	432.5	466.3	448.4	459.6	452.0	458.7	479.3	492.0	503.6	522.7	575.1	642.9
1983	699.9	760.8	766.4	759.1	795.5	780.0	722.2	683.0	757.4	767.2	765.2	810.4
1984	832.8	817.5	730.0	653.0	618.5	519.3	551.9	526.5	516.0	493.9	483.9	430.0
1985	425.0	420.7	385.7	361.9	364.6	380.4	368.8	464.0	546.7	558.4	533.6	486.6
1986	502.8	501.5	451.8	435.7	422.6	418.7	396.8	430.4	455.1	455.4	458.5	464.8
1987	473.7	467.5	410.5	397.5	387.4	348.5	337.8	336.8	341.1	314.7	254.9	269.6
1988	260.9	292.1	301.1	290.2	277.4	317.9	329.9	374.7	348.7	310.9	282.8	272.2
1989	337.5	325.7	341.0	350.3	406.5	385.7	374.2	389.8	335.8	368.7	348.1	358.3
1990	362.3	382.0	335.6	320.0	332.6	356.3	291.8	370.9	417.9	484.6	483.0	447.6
1991	439.5	464.2	447.1	501.1	559.5	595.4	593.1	605.4	664.7	653.5	644.9	676.9
1992	640.4	718.1	704.2	715.7	714.9	723.2	726.4	737.9	816.5	822.5	873.8	896.1
1993	757.1	765.9	789.6	817.2	885.1	912.2	910.4	943.8	1,040.3	1,124.3	1,133.9	1,106.1
1994	1,075.0	1,095.5	1,046.8	984.9	913.7	859.5	843.7	839.7	874.6	870.7	835.1	818.4
1995[1]	804.6	800.6	748.6	718.2	701.4	709.0	718.5	703.7	706.2	728.7	754.0	786.6

[1] Preliminary. *Source: American Bureau of Metal Statistics*

COPPER

Refined Copper Production in the U.S.A. In Thousands of Short Tons (Recoverable Copper Content)

	Refined													
Year	Jan.	Feb.	Mar.	Apr.	May	June	July	Aug.	Sept.	Oct.	Nov.	Dec.	Total	**Crude**
1985	113.5	101.2	118.8	122.4	124.1	100.8	99.9	96.8	93.0	112.9	119.7	106.7	1,310	1,387
1986	109.5	98.3	103.5	115.0	122.4	112.1	109.3	108.9	106.7	114.4	116.6	138.1	1,355	1,323
1987	118.0	110.5	105.4	127.7	118.5	95.5	107.7	106.4	121.8	131.3	123.3	127.7	1,394	1,308
1988	124.5	127.2	145.6	122.5	133.7	116.7	112.7	146.0	133.8	121.1	137.7	131.8	1,553	1,527
1989	129.5	128.1	137.2	118.3	132.2	142.6	121.3	150.8	116.5	137.0	127.4	130.7	1,572	1,555
1990	136.0	122.0	150.4	140.1	147.5	136.1	125.5	132.5	130.1	141.6	141.0	125.5	1,628	1,630
1991	129.0	127.7	134.9	119.7	137.1	124.8	136.8	142.7	135.6	153.1	141.0	149.7	1,632	1,393
1992	139.9	135.6	150.6	142.8	123.0	138.5	140.3	150.1	146.9	155.3	156.8	153.7	1,734	1,503
1993	153.9	153.8	173.2	166.0	160.3	177.0	151.4	153.7	160.2	157.3	157.2	166.2	1,930	1,269
1994	160.9	150.0	167.8	157.2	165.5	160.4	148.9	165.6	162.1	157.3	153.3	159.8	1,909	1,473
1995[1]	158.4	140.3	165.0	150.5	180.0	157.9	152.3	166.5	147.2	163.3	168.9	159.4	1,910	1,584

[1] Preliminary. *Source: American Bureau of Metal Statistics*

Refined Copper Production Outside the U.S.A. In Thousands of Short Tons (Recoverable Copper Content)

	Refined													
Year	Jan.	Feb.	Mar.	Apr.	May	June	July	Aug.	Sept.	Oct.	Nov.	Dec.	Total	**Crude**
1985	371.6	338.8	388.5	376.1	377.4	351.4	384.2	385.6	380.4	387.6	385.5	394.9	4,522	5,217
1986	366.5	351.5	401.7	409.7	373.1	361.2	361.7	374.8	400.3	407.4	396.4	403.6	4,608	5,132
1987	385.8	375.4	410.6	412.2	399.9	403.6	393.3	370.6	391.2	402.7	402.5	407.5	4,755	5,233
1988	397.7	387.8	434.2	370.6	389.4	391.5	366.6	386.9	365.9	412.8	417.0	414.9	4,735	5,210
1989	387.8	372.7	411.9	404.3	430.1	388.7	409.5	413.5	421.7	436.1	434.0	402.7	4,913	5,439
1990	423.7	396.7	424.6	412.8	414.1	395.6	372.6	407.1	404.6	422.6	417.4	411.0	4,902	5,278
1991	416.5	381.1	427.7	405.5	425.3	404.5	375.1	378.7	411.4	411.8	409.2	424.5	4,871	5,533
1992	441.2	412.6	447.0	418.0	438.7	449.5	418.5	425.8	418.7	438.9	431.3	426.1	5,166	5,730
1993	429.2	405.6	475.1	426.2	440.9	447.5	421.6	449.4	448.0	425.9	447.2	436.5	5,253	5,378
1994	432.5	390.8	432.7	400.6	432.9	421.1	387.8	413.8	421.5	416.3	437.4	428.8	5,016	5,970
1995[1]	419.7	414.4	466.1	452.2	457.4	455.0	444.1	454.6	450.0	486.9	458.6	451.1	5,410	6,334

[1] Preliminary. *Source: American Bureau of Metal Statistics*

Refined Copper Deliveries to Fabricators Outside the U.S.A. In Thousands of Short Tons[2]

Year	Jan.	Feb.	Mar.	Apr.	May	June	July	Aug.	Sept.	Oct.	Nov.	Dec.	Total
1985	170.2	188.7	159.8	153.0	144.3	135.2	122.3	130.0	93.0	151.5	137.9	120.7	1,767
1986	123.8	120.1	150.5	155.3	164.5	131.5	113.1	127.1	106.7	141.1	114.7	128.4	1,631
1987	160.2	138.7	166.9	152.3	165.6	152.3	131.6	127.2	121.8	188.3	192.7	168.2	1,885
1988	152.0	151.5	162.5	149.6	150.1	161.2	116.5	164.7	133.8	148.2	159.1	139.0	1,824
1989	127.8	147.7	148.4	141.1	153.2	168.4	131.4	173.2	116.5	156.8	149.2	121.9	1,781
1990	167.4	132.8	163.3	156.6	153.3	144.5	129.5	132.5	130.1	140.9	130.7	108.6	1,733
1991	128.4	153.3	125.3	126.7	152.7	115.0	125.4	152.8	135.6	167.7	130.4	132.9	1,684
1992	144.9	159.0	165.9	155.5	149.4	161.4	145.8	144.1	146.9	150.4	166.2	130.0	1,813
1993	142.9	165.3	201.6	170.4	162.5	209.6	144.8	191.4	178.9	164.3	194.8	182.7	2,109
1994	193.3	168.6	204.6	178.3	187.8	171.9	154.3	194.6	188.2	188.7	167.5	175.1	2,173
1995[1]	168.6	159.5	200.5	158.0	191.1	165.8	165.3	177.6	174.2	180.3	188.8	148.8	2,079

[1] Preliminary. [2] Recoverable copper content. *Source: American Bureau of Metal Statistics*

Refined Copper Deliveries to Fabricators Outside the U.S.A. In Thousands of Short Tons[2]

Year	Jan.	Feb.	Mar.	Apr.	May	June	July	Aug.	Sept.	Oct.	Nov.	Dec.	Total
1985	356.6	372.1	408.2	369.8	379.8	395.9	300.4	319.9	384.6	422.0	419.6	375.9	4,505
1986	364.5	396.9	403.4	403.2	375.6	387.9	331.0	334.1	376.2	384.9	380.9	380.8	4,519
1987	386.0	413.0	413.9	406.8	426.7	401.8	384.1	359.4	416.4	468.8	377.1	396.8	4,851
1988	359.6	375.2	448.7	385.1	366.8	403.2	340.9	405.9	401.8	437.4	455.6	356.6	4,737
1989	426.0	369.9	411.8	360.9	459.0	398.0	386.8	464.2	393.2	456.9	423.0	399.1	4,949
1990	419.9	466.3	436.7	392.9	408.3	466.7	303.7	373.5	370.8	448.9	469.1	420.7	4,972
1991	405.0	404.4	391.5	361.2	406.3	433.5	368.5	323.4	420.7	499.1	391.4	483.4	4,807
1992	453.7	408.9	441.8	416.4	413.4	432.4	410.4	364.7	432.6	403.5	406.1	461.3	5,045
1993	427.9	392.9	452.3	361.7	422.2	442.6	384.4	347.9	387.5	414.8	463.4	458.5	4,956
1994	399.8	429.5	481.2	466.5	468.9	428.1	387.9	369.2	423.5	448.9	457.1	436.0	5,197
1995[1]	380.7	454.4	477.3	452.5	432.6	439.0	441.5	441.6	413.2	446.1	405.7	327.0	5,112

[1] Preliminary. [2] Recoverable copper content. *Source: American Bureau of Metal Statistics*

Corn

The U.S. 1995/96 corn crop fell to 7.4 billion bushels from the record large 10.1 billion in 1994/95 and compares with average annual production of about 8.2 billion bushels in the first half of the 1990's. In October alone the USDA's estimate was lowered 167 million bushels as the average yield fell to 113.7 bushels per acre, down nearly 3 bushels due to adverse weather. Hardest hit were the western sections of the Corn Belt causing heavy damage to fields that were ready to be harvested. However, the sharp October drop was partially offset by a downward revision in projected domestic 1995/96 use, but export demand was likely to be higher than expected. Despite the flux in the early 1995/96 statistical data there was little doubt that carryover stocks as of August 31, 1996 will be well under the 1.6 billion carryin a year earlier, perhaps by as much as one billion bushels. The stock-to-use ratio was forecast at a low 6.1 percent versus 16.6 percent a year earlier.

The impact of the smaller crop was decisively manifested in futures values as prices surged $.90 a bushel in five months time, from $2.80 in August, 1995 to $3.70 by the end of the year, basis March '96 futures. The contra-seasonal price action was somewhat analogous to 1993 when futures soared nearly $.60 per bushel during the second half of the year. In 1993/94 the average price received by farmers for corn was $2.50 per bushel; in 1994/95 it was $2.26 and for 1995/96 was forecast within a range of $2.95-$3.35 per bushel which, if realized, could best the record high of $3.21 per bushel in 1983/84.

Corn is the leading U.S. feed grain with 4.6 billion bushels allocated to this usage in 1995/96 versus the 1994/95 record high of 5.5 billion. Food, seed, and industrial use (FSI) was estimated at 1.7 billion bushels, only marginally higher than in 1994/95 and the first season since the 1970s to witness little, if any, year to year gain in the FSI sector. This growth was paced by increasing demand for corn as a fuel alcohol and as the sweetener High Fructose corn syrup (HFCS). However, some older, less efficient fuel ethanol producing plants have shut down while some manufactures have apparently postponed planned expansions due to cost considerations.

The U.S. exported 1.5 billion bushels of corn on average in the early 1990's, but a record large 2.2 billion bushels were exported in 1994/95. Increasing worldwide demand suggests an equal or greater amount may be shipped in 1995/96. World demand is growing and the U.S. remains without any doubt the primary export source. World foreign trade in corn in 1995/96 of about 63 million tons compares with 70 million in 1994/95, of which the U.S. accounts for about 51 million and 58 million, respectively. The second largest exporter is Argentina with about 6 million tons. Importers are scattered: Japan and Korea are the leaders with about 16 and 9 million tons, respectively, but the key variable in the late 1990's is likely to be China.

Total world corn production in 1995/96 of 501 million metric tons compares with the record large 555 million in 1994/95. The decrease was due largely to the 50 plus million ton drop in the United States. China, since 1987/88 the second largest producer, harvested a record large 108 million tons in 1995/96 versus 100 million 1994/95. The U.S. and China produced about 60 percent of the world's corn in 1995/96; Brazil and Mexico combined produced about 10 percent. China's production has jumped 50 percent since the mid-1980's as increases in per capita income and meat consumption have led to a large increase in China's corn demand for feed. Global consumption in 1995/96 is forecast marginally higher than the record large 537 million tons of 1994/95, the gain largely attributed to China's demand for 110 million tons versus 100 million in 1994/95. The U.S. is the largest consumer of corn at almost a third of total production. The Russian Federation is in second place, but if the usage trends from the first half of the 1990's are maintained, China will replace the Russian federation by the end of the 1990s. World stocks are forecast to decrease in 1995/96 by almost 30 million tons, ending the season near 62 million tons. This is in sharp contrast to the gain during 1994/95 of 18 million tons which raised the carryin to 91 million tons. The drop in 1995/96 largely reflects a 20 million ton fall in U.S. stocks. The world's statistical setting for corn prices in 1995/96 is bullish, but what actually happens to prices as 1995/96 marketing progresses is also dependent on the quality and availability of other coarse grains from local harvests, especially wheat.

U.S. #2 yellow corn prices vary with the location. Typically, Gulf port prices are about 30¢ per bushel higher than prices in Central Illinois, while quotes at St. Louis run about 10¢-12¢ higher than Illinois prices.

U.S. Farm Program

Washington D.C. legislators are currently rewriting the entire U.S Farm Program. Target prices and price support loan rates are unavailable. The target price for corn in the previous five years was $2.75. The price support loan rate in 1994/95 was $1.89. Government controlled corn stocks are now insignificant.

Futures Markets

Corn futures are traded on the Beijing Commodity Exchange (BCE), the Budapest Commodity Exchange, the Tokyo Grain Exchange, (TGE), the Chicago Board of Trade (CBOT), and the Mid-American Commodity Exchange (MidAm). Corn options are traded on the CBOT and the MidAm.

CORN

World Production of Corn or Maize In Thousands of Metric Tons

Crop Year	Agrentina	Brazil	Canada	China	France	Hungry	India	Indo-nesia	Italy	Mexico	Romania	South Africa	Ukraine[4]	United States	Yugo-slavia	World Total
1981-2	9,600	22,932	6,673	59,205	8,956	6,998	6,897	4,509	8,197	12,500	11,892	8,355	8,000	208,330	9,807	441,237
1982-3	9,000	19,500	6,513	60,295	10,400	7,800	6,594	3,235	6,847	7,000	12,620	4,083	13,500	209,181	11,126	438,354
1983-4	9,200	21,000	5,933	68,210	10,400	6,426	7,922	5,087	6,669	9,300	11,982	4,405	12,000	106,042	10,719	345,817
1984-5	11,500	22,000	7,024	73,410	10,384	6,686	8,356	5,288	6,776	9,900	13,274	7,755	12,500	194,929	11,293	456,959
1985-6	12,400	21,000	6,970	63,830	12,567	8,818	6,643	4,330	6,357	10,500	11,000	8,078	14,400	225,479	9,896	479,797
1986-7	9,250	26,500	5,912	70,856	11,470	7,261	7,457	5,000	6,401	10,000	15,000	7,150	12,479	209,556	12,526	477,912
1987-8	9,000	24,790	7,015	79,150	12,454	7,234	5,721	4,800	5,762	9,900	10,500	7,075	14,808	181,143	8,863	448,762
1988-9	5,000	26,050	5,369	77,350	14,578	6,028	8,229	5,200	6,318	10,100	10,000	12,384	16,030	125,194	7,697	401,962
1989-90	5,200	22,300	6,571	78,928	13,400	6,747	9,409	5,000	6,359	9,750	6,760	8,900	7,026	191,156	9,415	460,484
1990-1	7,600	24,330	7,067	96,820	9,500	4,317	8,962	5,000	5,864	14,100	6,800	8,300	4,737	201,534	6,724	477,855
1991-2	10,600	30,800	7,413	98,770	12,930	7,745	8,060	5,400	6,240	14,689	10,500	3,125	4,747	189,868	11,500	487,307
1992-3	10,200	29,200	4,883	95,380	14,870	4,301	10,200	5,650	7,410	18,631	6,829	9,985	2,851	240,719	6,650	534,635
1993-4[1]	10,000	32,934	6,501	102,700	14,840	4,012	9,480	5,400	8,030	19,141	8,000	12,875	3,786	160,954	5,912	470,999
1994-5[2]	10,900	36,943	7,043	99,280	12,640	4,300	9,300	5,200	7,480	18,200	8,500	4,650	1,537	256,629	6,760	555,430
1995-6[3]	12,000	33,000	7,250	108,000	12,500	4,500	9,800	5,300	8,500	16,500	9,700	9,000	3,200	187,301	7,500	501,568

[1] Preliminary. [2] Estimate. [3] Forecast. [4] Formerly part of the U.S.S.R.; data not reported separately until 1989.
Source: Foreign Agricultural Service, U.S. Department of Agriculture

World Course Grains Supply & Demand In Millions of Metric Tons/Hectares

Crop Year Beginning Oct. 1	Area Harvested	Yield	Pro-duction	World Trade	Total Con-sumption	Ending Stocks	Stocks as % of Consump-tion[3]
1981-2	348.5	2.18	758.8	97.4	734.1	151.1	20.6
1982-3	337.8	2.29	775.2	89.8	744.0	182.3	24.5
1983-4	332.7	2.04	677.5	93.1	748.8	111.1	14.8
1984-5	334.3	2.41	805.8	100.0	772.2	144.7	18.7
1985-6	339.9	2.45	832.3	82.7	767.8	209.3	27.3
1986-7	336.0	2.45	822.4	82.9	796.5	235.2	29.5
1987-8	323.3	2.43	784.2	88.3	807.2	215.1	26.7
1988-9	323.4	2.23	721.0	95.5	784.6	151.5	19.3
1989-90	321.1	2.46	791.2	103.9	814.2	128.5	15.8
1990-1	314.4	2.61	821.5	89.5	809.3	134.5	16.6
1991-2	318.2	2.53	805.0	96.1	804.9	134.6	16.7
1992-3	318.8	2.71	865.3	91.3	836.9	162.9	19.5
1993-4[1]	311.7	2.53	790.1	85.6	830.9	122.1	14.7
1994-5[1]	315.2	2.74	862.8	95.8	850.4	134.5	15.8
1995-6[2]	303.4	2.59	786.9	87.3	832.3	89.1	10.7

[1] Preliminary. [2] Estimate. [3] Represents the ratio of marketing year ending stocks to total consumption. *Source: Foreign Agricultural Service, U.S. Department of Agriculture*

Acreage and Supply of Corn in the United States In Millions of Bushels

Crop Year Beginning Sept. 1[3]	Planted	------ Harvested -------- For Grain	For Silage	Yield Per Harvested Acre Bushels	Carry-over, Sept. 1 On Farms[3]	Off Farms[3]	Supply Beginning Stocks	Pro-duction	Imports	Total Supply
	------- In Thousands of Acres ---------									
1984-5	80,517	71,897	7,535	106.7	347.9	375.4	1,006	7,672	2	8,680
1985-6	83,398	75,209	7,155	118.0	678.9	701.8	1,648	8,875	10	10,534
1986-7	76,580	68,907	6,418	119.4	NA	NA	4,040	8,226	2	12,267
1987-8	66,200	59,505	5,994	119.8	2,284.5	2,597.2	4,882	7,131	3	12,016
1988-9	67,717	58,250	8,294	84.6	2,002.8	2,256.3	4,259	4,929	3	9,191
1989-90	72,221	64,703	6,606	116.3	967.5	962.9	1,930	7,525	2	9,458
1990-1	74,171	66,952	6,124	118.5	754.8	589.7	1,344	7,934	3	9,282
1991-2	75,951	68,847	6,101	108.6	691.2	830.0	1,521	7,475	20	9,016
1992-3	79,340	72,162	6,069	131.4	605.0	494.8	1,100	9,482	7	10,589
1993-4[1]	73,235	62,921	6,831	100.7	1,070.7	1,042.0	2,113	6,336	21	8,470
1994-5[1]	79,175	72,887	5,601	138.6	395.4	454.7	850	10,103	10	10,963
1995-6[2]	71,245	64,995	5,295	113.5	740.0	816.9	1,558	7,374	10	8,942

[1] Preliminary. [2] Estimate. [3] Data prior to 1986-87 are as of October 1. NA = Not available. *Source: Economic Research Service, U.S. Department of Agriculture*

U.S. Corn Supply and Disappearance In Millions of Bushels

Crop Year Beginning Sept. 1	Supply: Beginning Stocks	Supply: Production	Supply: Imports	Supply: Total Supply	Disappearance, Domestic Use: Food, Alcohol & Industrial	Seed	Feed & Residual	Total	Exports	Total Disappearance	Ending Stocks: Gov't Owned[3]	Privately Owned[4]	Total
1992-3/1	1,100	9,477	7.1	10,584	1,493	18.7	5,296	6,807	1,663	8,471	56	2,058	2,113
Sept.-Nov.	1,100	9,477	1.3	10,578	360	0	1,825	2,185	488	2,672	87	7,819	7,906
Dec.-Feb.	7,906	--------	1.0	7,907	350	0	1,416	1,766	463	2,229	87	5,591	5,678
Mar.-May	5,678	--------	2.0	5,680	387	16.4	1,157	1,560	411	1,971	64	3,645	3,709
June-Aug.	3,709	--------	2.8	3,712	396	2.3	899	1,298	301	1,599	56	2,058	2,113
1993-4[1]	2,113	6,337	20.8	8,470	1,568	20.1	4,704	6,292	1,328	7,620	45	805	850
Sept.-Nov.	2,113	6,337	5.2	8,455	378	0	1,705	2,083	435	2,518	53	5,884	5,937
Dec.-Feb.	5,937	--------	8.0	5,945	371	0	1,248	1,619	330	1,949	50	3,946	3,996
Mar.-May	3,996	--------	6.3	4,002	399	19.5	954	1,372	270	1,642	48	2,312	2,360
June-Aug.	2,360	--------	1.4	2,361	420	.6	798	1,218	293	1,511	45	805	850
1994-5[2]	850	10,103	9.6	10,963	1,675	18.4	5,534	7,227	2,178	9,404	42	1,516	1,558
Sept.-Nov.	850	10,103	2.1	10,955	410	0	2,015	2,425	449	2,875	55	8,026	8,081
Dec.-Feb.	8,081	--------	3.7	8,084	403	0	1,499	1,902	590	2,493	50	5,542	5,592
Mar.-May	5,592	--------	3.0	5,595	432	16.0	1,164	1,612	568	2,180	50	3,365	3,415
June-Aug.	3,415	--------	.8	3,416	430	2.4	856	1,288	570	1,857	42	1,516	1,558
1995-6[2]	1,558	7,374	10.0	8,942	1,685	20.2	4,600	6,305	2,200	8,485	42	575	457
Sept.-Nov.	1,558	7,374	2.0	8,934	402	0	1,771	2,173	660	2,833			6,101

[1] Preliminary. [2] Estimate. [3] Uncommitted inventory. [4] Includes quantity under loan and farmer-owned reserves. *Source: Economic Research Service, U.S. Department of Agriculture*

Corn Production Estimates and Cash Prices in the U.S.

Crop Year	Corn for Grain Production Estimates (In Thousands of Bushels): Aug. 1	Sept. 1	Oct. 1	Nov. 1	Final	St. Louis No. 2 Yellow (Dollar Per Bushel)	Omaha No. 2 Yellow	Los Angeles No. 2 Yellow	Kansas City No. 2 White	Chicago No. 2 Yellow	Average Farm Price[2]	Value of Production (Million Dollars)
1990-1	7,850,164	8,118,117	8,021,697	7,934,892	7,934,028	2.49	2.28	3.33	2.98	2.41	2.28	18,192
1991-2	7,474,480	7,295,071	7,479,421	7,485,901	7,475,480	2.53	2.36	3.39	3.06	2.52	2.37	17,864
1992-3	8,762,060	7,873,436	8,592,821	9,328,850	9,476,698	2.25	2.10	3.12	2.49	2.22	2.07	19,723
1993-4	7,423,142	7,229,427	6,961,902	6,503,237	6,336,470	2.67	2.56			2.68	2.50	16,032
1994-5[1]	9,214,420	9,257,170	9,602,340	10,010,310	10,102,735	2.51	2.33			2.43	2.26	
1995-6[1]	8,121,520	7,832,140	7,541,400	7,373,700	7,373,876						2.95-3.35	

[1] Preliminary. [2] Season-average price based on monthly weighted by monthly marketings. *Source: Economic Research Service, U.S. Department of Agriculture*

Production of Corn (for Grain) in the United States In Millions of Bushels

Year	Colorado	Illinois	Indiana	Iowa	Kansas	Michigan	Minnesota	Missouri	Nebraska	Ohio	Pennslvania	South Dakota	Texas	Wisconsin
1989	134.9	1,322.3	691.6	1,445.5	155.0	222.6	700.0	219.8	847.0	342.2	98.9	190.8	148.4	310.8
1990	128.7	1,320.8	703.1	1,562.4	188.5	238.1	762.6	205.8	934.4	417.5	109.6	234.0	130.5	354.0
1991	128.5	1,177.0	510.6	1,427.4	206.3	253.0	720.0	213.4	999.6	326.4	68.4	240.5	165.0	380.8
1992	130.2	1,646.5	877.6	1,903.7	259.5	241.5	741.0	324.0	1,066.5	507.7	118.8	277.2	202.5	306.8
1993	106.8	1,300.0	712.8	880.0	216.0	225.5	322.0	166.5	785.2	360.8	93.1	160.7	212.8	216.2
1994	133.5	1,786.2	858.2	1,930.4	304.6	260.9	915.9	273.7	1,153.7	486.5	123.6	367.2	238.7	437.1
1995[1]	92.1	1,130.0	598.9	1,402.2	244.3	249.6	731.9	149.9	854.7	375.1	94.1	193.6	216.6	347.7

[1] Preliminary. *Source: National Agricultural Statistics Service, U.S. Department of Agriculture*

Distribution of Corn in the United States In Millions of Bushels

Year Crop Beginning Sept. 1	Food, Seed and Industrial Use: HFCS	Glucose & Dextrose	Starch	Alcohol: Fuel	Alcohol: Beverage[3]	Seed	Cereal & Other Products	Total	Livestock Feed[4]	Exports (Including Grain Equiv. of Products)	Domestic Disappearance	Total Utilization
1989-90	368	193	230	321	109	19	115	1,355	4,389	2,368	5,745	8,113
1990-1	379	200	232	349	80	19	114	1,373	4,663	1,725	6,036	7,761
1991-2	392	210	237	398	81	20	116	1,454	4,878	1,584	6,332	7,916
1992-3	414	215	238	426	83	19	117	1,493	5,296	1,663	6,826	8,471
1993-4[1]	442	223	244	458	83	20	118	1,568	4,704	1,328	6,292	7,620
1994-5[2]	462	231	247	533	84	18	118	1,674	5,534	2,178	7,227	9,404
1995-6[2]	470	235	245	515	82	20	118	1,665	4,575	2,050	6,275	8,325

[1] Preliminary. [2] Estimate. [3] Also includes nonfuel industrial alcohol. [4] Feed and waste (residual, mostly feed). *Source: Economic Research Service, U.S. Department of Agriculture*

CORN

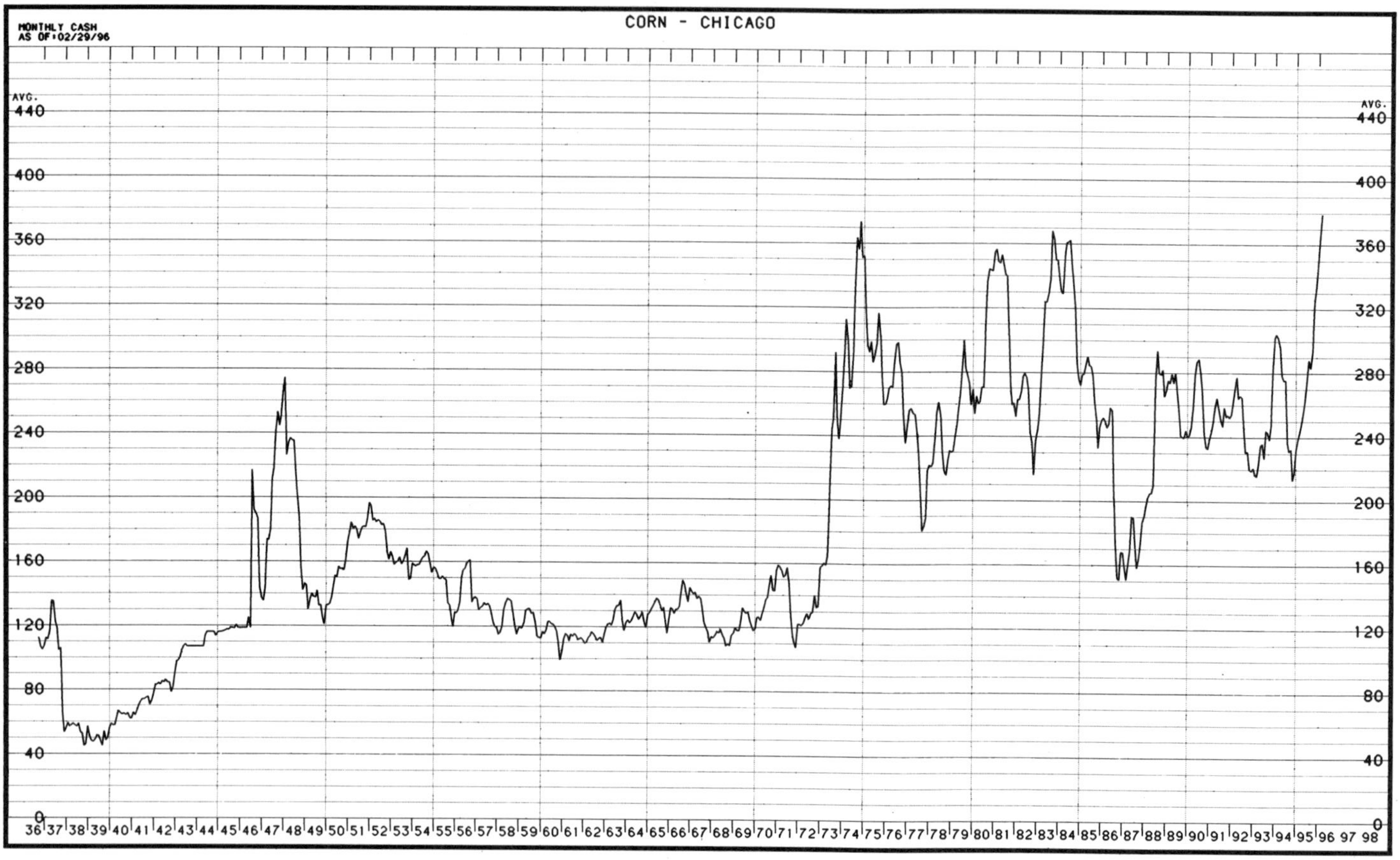

Average Cash Price of Corn, No. 2 Yellow in Central Illinois[2] In Dollars Per Bushel

Crop Year	Sept.	Oct.	Nov.	Dec.	Jan.	Feb.	Mar.	Apr.	May	June	July	Aug.	Average
1984-5	2.95	2.81	2.79	2.72	2.79	2.79	2.84	2.90	2.95	2.83	2.76	2.50	2.80
1985-6	2.28	2.10	2.32	2.38	2.36	2.33	2.29	2.31	2.42	2.41	1.93	1.52	2.22
1986-7	1.34	1.34	1.55	1.52	1.44	1.38	1.46	1.56	1.75	1.74	1.60	1.46	1.51
1987-8	1.50	1.64	1.74	1.78	1.84	1.90	1.92	1.92	1.97	2.66	2.85	2.70	2.04
1988-9	2.68	2.70	2.54	2.56	2.62	2.60	2.64	2.58	2.64	2.53	2.44	2.30	2.57
1989-90	2.35	2.25	2.29	2.29	2.29	2.34	2.44	2.64	2.73	2.70	2.68	2.54	2.46
1990-1	2.25	2.18	2.20	2.27	2.31	2.36	2.45	2.50	2.41	2.34	2.34	2.45	2.34
1991-2	2.39	2.41	2.41	2.42	2.49	2.58	2.64	2.50	2.51	2.51	2.31	2.17	2.45
1992-3	2.13	1.97	1.99	2.05	2.07	2.05	2.16	2.23	2.20	2.09	2.25	2.27	2.12
1993-4	2.22	2.27	2.63	2.81	2.89	2.83	2.76	2.61	2.58	2.61	2.19	2.13	2.54
1994-5[1]	2.08	1.92	2.04	2.17	2.22	2.27	2.36	2.41	2.50	2.65	2.79	2.68	2.34
1995-6[1]	2.83	3.12	3.22										

[1] Preliminary. [2] Data prior to 1985-86 are for Omaha. *Source: Economic Research Service, U.S. Department of Agriculture*

Average Cash Price of Corn, No. 2 Yellow at Gulf Ports[2] In Dollars Per Bushel

Crop Year	Sept.	Oct.	Nov.	Dec.	Jan.	Feb.	Mar.	Apr.	May	June	July	Aug.	Average
1984-5	3.31	3.08	2.98	2.90	3.03	3.04	3.05	3.05	2.96	2.95	2.92	2.67	2.99
1985-6	2.59	2.50	2.69	2.75	2.72	2.63	2.56	2.57	2.68	2.63	2.12	1.85	2.52
1986-7	1.68	1.66	1.83	1.81	1.73	1.70	1.83	1.89	2.06	2.06	1.95	1.81	1.83
1987-8	1.86	1.99	2.08	2.11	2.20	2.23	2.29	2.28	2.29	3.05	3.22	3.02	2.39
1988-9	3.08	3.07	2.89	2.99	3.01	2.99	3.02	2.93	2.99	2.87	2.73	2.57	2.93
1989-90	2.60	2.40	2.75	2.75	2.69	2.70	2.72	3.01	3.08	3.05	2.92	2.79	2.79
1990-1	2.59	2.55	2.54	2.60	2.68	2.70	2.77	2.80	2.69	2.65	2.67	2.79	2.67
1991-2	2.76	2.76	2.72	2.71	2.70	2.89	2.96	2.77	2.77	2.80	2.61	2.48	2.74
1992-3	2.50	2.40	2.42	2.39	2.39	2.40	2.48	2.55	2.50	2.36	2.59	2.55	2.46
1993-4	2.57	2.68	2.94	3.08	3.22	3.14	3.05	2.88	2.81	2.85	2.51	2.44	2.85
1994-5	2.48	2.44	2.43	2.61	2.72	2.72	2.79	2.79	2.84	3.04	3.23	3.21	2.78
1995-6[1]	3.32	3.57	3.63										

[1] Preliminary. [2] Barge delivered to Louisiana Gulf. *Source: Economic Research Service, U.S. Department of Agriculture*

Weekly Outstanding Export Sales & Cumulative Exports -- U.S. Corn   In Thousands of Metric Tons

1993/94			1994/95			1995/96		
Marketing Year 1993/94 Week Ending	Out-standing Sales	Cumu-lative Exports	Marketing Year 1994/95 Week Ending	Out-standing Sales	Cumu-lative Exports	Marketing Year 1995/96 Week Ending	Out-standing Sales	Cumu-lative Exports
Sept. 2, 1993	6,624	176	Sept. 1, 1994	5,728	53	Sept. 7, 1995	16,892	985
9	6,623	708	8	6,210	510	14	16,576	2,354
16	7,332	1,456	15	6,370	1,162	21	16,456	3,898
23	7,610	2,246	22	6,681	1,805	28	16,176	5,244
30	7,881	3,122	29	6,923	2,622	Oct. 5	15,798	6,510
Oct. 7	7,873	4,029	Oct. 6	7,460	3,151	12	15,721	7,720
14	7,601	4,882	13	7,974	3,840	19	16,208	8,956
21	7,385	5,744	20	8,053	4,522	26	16,757	9,979
28	7,395	6,518	27	8,350	5,308	Nov. 2	3,548	17,182
Nov. 4	7,230	7,315	Nov. 3	8,164	6,332	9	17,351	12,478
11	7,031	8,204	10	7,955	7,453	16	17,785	13,428
18	6,918	9,072	17	8,745	8,317	23	17,387	14,508
25	6,567	9,784	24	9,147	9,478	30	16,881	15,973
Dec. 2	6,392	10,609	Dec. 1	10,437	10,991	Dec. 7	16,754	17,103
9	6,059	11,689	8	10,953	12,089	14	16,717	17,910
16	5,647	12,544	15	10,669	13,218	21	17,474	18,962
23	5,122	13,362	22	13,065	14,097	28	17,362	20,299
30	4,921	13,950	29	13,403	15,185	Jan. 4, 1996	17,975	21,154
Jan. 6, 1994	4,975	14,348	Jan. 5, 1995	13,278	16,408	11	18,538	22,389
13	5,278	15,153	12	13,973	17,460	18		
20	5,490	15,771	19	13,531	18,815	25		
27	5,521	16,399	26	13,347	19,938	Feb. 1		
Feb. 3	5,306	17,036	Feb. 2	12,613	21,330	8		
10	5,289	17,361	9	11,853	22,750	15		
17	5,044	17,940	16	11,409	23,896	22		
24	4,724	18,564	23	11,190	24,789	29		
Mar. 3	4,664	19,005	Mar. 2	10,699	26,039	Mar. 7		
10	4,271	19,633	9	10,305	27,263	14		
17	3,719	20,411	16	10,639	28,335	21		
24	3,637	20,814	23	11,670	30,483	28		
31	3,312	21,440	30	11,670	30,454	Apr. 4		
Apr. 7	3,103	21,891	Apr. 6	11,223	31,342	11		
14	3,339	22,277	13	11,325	32,644	18		
21	3,097	22,817	20	11,337	33,647	25		
28	2,796	23,292	27	11,409	34,430	May 2		
May 5	2,690	23,668	May 4	11,251	35,469	9		
12	2,863	24,124	11	10,531	36,642	16		
19	2,944	24,701	18	9,971	37,669	23		
26	3,161	25,053	25	9,499	38,866	30		
June 2	3,230	25,334	June 1	9,272	40,109	June 6		
9	3,452	25,716	8	10,061	40,867	13		
16	3,510	26,096	15	10,374	41,562	20		
23	3,770	26,604	22	10,848	42,584	27		
30	3,727	27,179	29	10,265	43,832	July 4		
July 7	3,995	27,489	July 6	9,617	44,737	11		
14	4,089	27,854	13	8,807	46,220	18		
21	3,721	28,409	20	8,133	47,295	25		
28	3,434	28,895	27	7,373	48,328	Aug. 1		
Aug. 4	3,228	29,375	Aug. 3	6,290	49,649	8		
11	2,848	30,146	10	5,123	50,993	15		
18	2,598	30,723	17	4,245	52,180	22		
25	3,802	0	24	3,263	53,446	29		
			31	2,023	54,742			

Source: Foreign Agricultural Service, U.S. Department of Agriculture

CORN

U.S. Exports[1] of Corn (Including Seed), by Country of Destination In Thousands of Metric Tons

Year Beginning Oct.	Algeria	Brazil	Canada	Dominican Republic	Egypt	Israel	Japan	Mexico	Rep. of Korea	Russia[3]	Saudi Arabia	Spain	Taiwan	Vene-zuela	Total
1986-7	974	1,162	428	341	2,055	401	12,459	3,256	4,080	3,907	301	468	3,184	0	39,297
1987-8	1,113	0	158	394	1,078	415	14,816	2,900	4,411	5,585	545	1,836	4,169	0	43,955
1988-9	973	20	896	392	1,014	304	13,016	3,113	4,591	15,573	616	1,280	3,625	0	50,676
1989-90	1,146	12	637	421	1,135	250	13,885	4,585	5,680	16,371	707	1,712	5,009	593	59,854
1990-1	1,328	393	302	442	1,756	299	13,639	1,901	1,982	9,077	725	1,434	5,086	321	44,497
1991-2	827	148	314	531	1,058	369	13,481	1,041	1,508	6,533	602	1,273	4,998	552	40,693
1992-3	1,224	71	1,189	614	1,543	539	14,235	396	1,021	3,380	787	1,075	5,450	777	41,766
1993-4	1,182	0	640	604	1,437	268	12,032	1,678	631	2,337	851	1,116	4,955	751	33,057
1994-5[2]	846	0	1,135	633	2,608	671	16,107	3,166	8,921	9	864	2,497	6,210	886	58,645

[1] Excludes exports of corn by-products. [2] Preliminary. [3] Formerly part of the U.S.S.R.; data not reported separately until 1992.
Source: Economic Research Service, U.S. Department of Agriculture

Corn (Shelled & Ear) Stocks in the United States In Millions of Bushels

	On Farms				Off Farms				Total Stocks			
Year	Mar. 1	June 1	Sept. 1	Dec. 1	Mar. 1	June 1	Sept. 1	Dec. 1	Mar. 1	June 1	Sept. 1	Dec. 1
1985[2]	2,833.8	2,007.8	NA	NA	1,131.7	827.7	NA	NA	3,965.5	2,835.5	1,648.2	8,614.7
1986	NA	3,143.1	2,049.4	6,795.5	NA	1,847.0	1,990.1	3,510.0	6,587.1	4,990.0	4,039.5	10,305.5
1987	5,024.0	3,491.8	2,284.5	6,100.0	3,224.2	2,840.4	2,597.2	3,668.5	8,248.2	6,332.2	4,881.7	9,768.5
1988	4,421.0	3,241.0	2,002.8	4,280.2	3,214.6	2,594.5	2,256.3	2,791.4	7,635.6	5,835.5	4,259.1	7,071.6
1989	3,021.0	2,022.0	967.5	4,698.8	2,182.9	1,397.3	962.9	2,383.3	5,203.9	3,419.3	1,930.4	7,082.1
1990	2,910.5	1,623.5	754.8	4,874.0	1,901.9	1,219.7	589.7	2,066.3	4,812.4	2,843.2	1,344.5	6,940.3
1991	3,064.5	1,755.0	691.2	4,294.5	1,724.5	1,237.0	830.0	2,246.6	4,789.0	2,992.0	1,521.2	6,541.1
1992	2,610.2	1,517.5	605.5	5,736.9	1,950.8	1,221.1	494.8	2,169.5	4,561.0	2,738.6	1,100.3	7,906.4
1993	3,630.0	2,216.5	1,070.7	3,803.0	2,048.2	1,492.9	1,042.3	2,133.5	5,678.2	3,709.4	2,113.0	5,936.5
1994	2,210.0	1,203.0	395.4	5,417.5	1,785.5	1,156.9	454.7	2,663.0	3,995.7	2,359.9	850.1	8,080.5
1995[1]	3,502.0	2,072.0	740.9	3,690.0	2,089.7	1,342.9	816.9	2,140.9	5,591.7	3,414.9	1,557.8	6,100.9

[1] Preliminary. [2] April 1 stocks. NA = Not available. *Source: National Agricultural Statistics Service, U.S. Department of Agriculture*

Volume of Trading of Corn Futures at Chicago In Millions of Bushels

Year	Jan.	Feb.	Mar.	Apr	May	June	July	Aug.	Sept.	Oct.	Nov.	Dec.	Total
1985	2,406	2,369	2,746	2,608	2,346	2,494	3,231	2,743	2,629	2,597	3,545	2,248	31,964
1986	2,629	2,153	2,203	2,840	3,029	2,390	2,605	2,217	2,486	3,103	2,591	2,555	30,801
1987	2,343	2,901	3,088	3,646	3,579	3,984	2,978	2,498	2,620	3,380	2,923	2,327	36,266
1988	3,040	3,333	3,212	3,478	4,235	7,898	6,818	5,352	4,353	4,661	5,597	3,549	55,528
1989	4,170	3,384	3,818	4,138	3,930	4,485	4,323	3,433	2,827	4,702	4,352	2,793	46,354
1990	3,248	3,991	4,623	5,742	7,146	6,767	5,509	4,541	3,028	3,939	5,682	2,899	57,114
1991	4,284	3,484	4,663	5,205	4,227	5,064	6,268	5,486	3,462	4,420	4,539	3,161	54,264
1992	4,506	5,013	4,761	4,343	4,691	5,076	4,328	3,975	3,443	3,442	4,981	3,222	51,783
1993	2,588	3,182	3,870	4,474	3,440	5,237	6,978	5,071	4,480	5,180	7,872	4,941	57,313
1994	6,257	5,178	5,228	5,544	5,396	7,275	3,738	3,009	3,075	3,515	5,127	4,307	57,649
1995	3,936	4,162	4,868	4,939	6,069	8,798	6,469	6,593	6,101	8,066	8,716	6,780	75,526

Source: Chicago Board of Trade

Average Open Interest of Corn Futures at Chicago In Thousands of Bushels

Year	Jan.	Feb.	Mar.	Apr.	May	June	July	Aug.	Sept.	Oct.	Nov.	Dec.
1985	667,033	655,735	592,298	630,084	525,072	513,082	549,368	627,919	639,756	637,095	716,065	656,807
1986	603,350	562,749	545,073	572,669	548,970	586,031	574,077	607,718	621,703	712,114	773,156	590,845
1987	651,105	708,597	692,102	706,486	650,705	632,792	568,933	591,430	593,557	689,305	690,809	631,781
1988	728,517	759,008	787,238	813,253	826,970	1,072,313	1,229,357	1,174,962	1,164,763	1,236,846	1,211,708	1,112,098
1989	1,081,102	994,058	963,200	917,720	819,439	783,908	719,030	727,027	706,896	857,567	971,254	839,719
1990	890,470	1,014,224	1,149,729	1,260,776	1,250,101	1,212,310	1,063,743	1,039,755	1,033,015	1,056,112	1,151,665	1,019,404
1991	1,050,031	1,096,179	1,145,049	1,147,020	1,024,140	1,010,500	992,637	1,098,500	1,077,634	1,212,331	1,285,325	1,141,737
1992	1,270,977	1,474,784	1,427,144	1,302,633	1,151,794	1,160,944	1,056,106	1,098,981	1,043,064	1,199,439	1,311,724	1,224,013
1993	1,280,564	1,304,929	1,243,192	1,249,999	1,145,079	1,162,948	1,328,361	1,324,688	1,219,460	1,378,962	1,662,225	1,636,129
1994	1,730,383	1,681,711	1,637,696	1,528,608	1,313,103	1,231,541	1,075,406	1,044,950	1,064,915	1,218,389	1,314,246	1,253,229
1995	1,460,450	1,556,861	1,682,163	1,777,215	1,841,903	2,138,722	2,069,193	2,092,251	2,195,849	2,368,488	2,454,850	2,439,887

Source: Chicago Board of Trade

Corn Price Support Data in the United States

Crop Year Beginning Sept. 1	National Average Loan Rate[3]	Target Price	Placed Under Loan	% of Production	Acquired by CCC	Owned by CCC Aug. 31	CCC Inventory As of Dec. 31: CCC Owned	CCC Inventory As of Dec. 31: Under CCC Loan	Quantity Pledged	Face Amount
	$ Per Bushel		Millions of Bushels						Ths. Bu	Ths. $
1984-5	2.55	3.03	1,100	14.3	65	225	296	1,056	2,290	627
1985-6	2.55	3.03	3,163	35.6	580	546	477	2,811	56,868	156,478
1986-7	1.92	3.03	4,894	59.5	1,332	1,443	1,265	4,905	59,188	114,611
1987-8	1.82	3.03	4,186	58.7	787	835	1,843	4,436	4,186,077	7,514,145
1988-9	1.77	2.93	756	15.3	151	363	679	982	755,895	1,313,581
1989-90	1.65	2.84	920	12.2	361	233	679	1,110	920,068	1,487,026
1990-1	1.57	2.75	1,071	13.5	285	371	214	1,071	1,071,040	1,616,948
1991-2	1.62	2.75	1,006	13.5	291	113	265	678	26,636	45,609
1992-3	1.72	2.75	1,646	17.4	0	56	125	1,646	15,245	28,947
1993-4[1]	1.72	2.75	618	9.7	0	45	50	-----		
1994-5[1]	1.89	2.75	2,002	19.8	0			2,002		
1995-6[2]	1.89	2.75	390	5.3	0			390		

[1] Preliminary. [2] Estimate. [3] Finley or announced loan rate. *Source: National Agricultural Statistics Service, U.S. Department of Agriculture*

Average Price Received by Farmers for Corn in the U.S. In Dollars Per Bushel

Crop Year	Sept.	Oct.	Nov.	Dec.	Jan.	Feb.	Mar.	Apr.	May	June	July	Aug.	Average
1985-6	2.29	2.11	2.21	2.29	2.33	2.32	2.29	2.30	2.39	2.32	2.00	1.73	2.23
1986-7	1.45	1.40	1.47	1.50	1.48	1.42	1.47	1.52	1.66	1.69	1.60	1.47	1.50
1987-8	1.49	1.55	1.61	1.72	1.77	1.83	1.86	1.88	1.94	2.41	2.72	2.65	1.94
1988-9	2.60	2.58	2.51	2.53	2.60	2.59	2.60	2.56	2.58	2.52	2.47	2.27	2.54
1989-90	2.29	2.22	2.24	2.27	2.31	2.32	2.37	2.51	2.62	2.63	2.62	2.51	2.36
1990-1	2.32	2.19	2.16	2.22	2.27	2.32	2.39	2.42	2.38	2.31	2.27	2.33	2.28
1991-2	2.33	2.31	2.29	2.33	2.40	2.46	2.49	2.48	2.49	2.47	2.33	2.15	2.37
1992-3	2.16	2.05	1.98	1.97	2.03	2.00	2.10	2.16	2.14	2.09	2.22	2.25	2.07
1993-4	2.21	2.28	2.45	2.67	2.70	2.79	2.74	2.65	2.60	2.61	2.29	2.16	2.50
1994-5[1]	2.19	2.06	1.99	2.13	2.19	2.23	2.30	2.36	2.42	2.51	2.63	2.63	2.26
1995-6[1]	2.69	2.95	2.87	3.08									

[1] Preliminary. *Source: Economic Research Service, U.S. Department of Agriculture*

Corn Oil

Supply & Distribution of Corn Oil In Millions of Pounds

Crop Year Beginning Oct. 1	Supply: Stocks Oct. 1	Supply: Production	Supply: Imports	Supply: Total Supply	Disappearance: Baking and Frying Fats	Disappearance: Salad and Cooking Oil	Disappearance: Margarine	Disappearance: Total Edible Products	Disappearance: Domestic Disappearance	Disappearance: Exports	Disappearance: Total Disappearance
1985-6	74	1,253	-----	1,327	W	524	200	837	863	344	1,207
1986-7	120	1,400	-----	1,520	W	491	248	934	1,143	268	1,411
1987-8	109	1,435	-----	1,546	W	555	212	946	1,065	370	1,435
1988-9	111	1,415	2.0	1,528	227	615	218	1,060	1,073	356	1,429
1989-90	99	1,470	-----	1,569	W	659	218	1,129	1,028	414	1,442
1990-1	127	1,656	1.8	1,785	304	589	195	1,143	1,149	498	1,647
1991-2	138	1,821	5.1	1,965	411	565	185	1,085	1,202	566	1,768
1992-3	196	1,878	7.2	2,081	241	547	W	945	1,220	712	1,931
1993-4[1]	150	1,906	6.6	2,062	86	412	W	648	1,228	717	1,944
1994-5[1]	118	2,215	10.1	2,343	100	446	W	636	1,237	865	2,103
1995-6[2]	241	2,175	14.0	2,430					1,255	1,000	2,255

[1] Preliminary. [2] Estimate. W = Withheld proprietary data. *Source: Economic Research Service, U.S. Department of Agriculture*

Crude Corn Oil Production in the United States[2] In Millions of Pounds

Year	Oct.	Nov.	Dec.	Jan.	Feb.	Mar.	Apr.	May	June	July	Aug.	Sept.	Total
1984-5	88.8	75.5	89.6	87.7	84.2	107.3	107.0	110.1	107.7	130.1	101.9	104.0	1,194
1985-6	114.2	101.5	97.1	72.8	97.9	102.2	109.8	118.4	106.3	108.6	119.9	104.1	1,253
1986-7	134.6	120.2	114.0	100.1	102.2	119.3	111.2	123.8	117.5	123.0	114.7	119.5	1,400
1987-8	121.5	115.9	110.6	107.1	110.2	113.4	117.3	125.6	125.4	131.7	132.1	124.5	1,435
1988-9	123.8	107.5	127.8	125.5	108.6	128.9	122.0	125.1	119.9	118.6	98.7	108.5	1,415
1989-90	130.2	106.1	128.6	127.7	122.0	131.4	135.6	115.5	140.7	150.4	145.2	132.2	1,566
1990-1	142.0	129.4	129.3		405.0			422.3			427.6		1,656
1991-2		436.7		138.1	137.5	164.5	153.3	150.2	160.0	165.0	162.4	153.6	1,821
1992-3	168.1	151.8	151.6	135.5	139.0	165.6	153.5	161.6	164.5	163.0	158.5	165.1	1,878
1993-4	160.8	153.4	162.5	140.6	138.6	166.9	155.3	164.2	171.8	164.8	162.3	165.1	1,906
1994-5[1]	175.5	165.3	180.9	163.2	161.8	232.7	188.4	191.2	193.6	193.6	180.3	188.5	2,215

[1] Preliminary. [2] Not seasonally adjusted. *Source: Bureau of Census, U.S. Department of Commerce*

U.S. Corn Oil Consumption in Refining In Millions of Pounds

Year	Oct.	Nov.	Dec.	Jan.	Feb.	Mar.	Apr.	May	June	July	Aug.	Sept.	Total
1984-5	82.1	86.7	91.0	84.0	71.3	89.4	75.5	106.0	97.4	109.1	96.2	90.8	1,080
1985-6	106.0	95.8	87.1	94.1	87.8	100.9	95.1	103.4	91.2	105.2	97.4	98.1	1,162
1986-7	101.2	98.9	98.3	95.7	98.4	104.0	88.7	83.1	90.9	82.6	77.1	92.3	1,111
1987-8	99.2	90.5	78.3	77.7	93.4	90.0	91.7	103.6	104.1	100.6	119.0	110.6	1,159
1988-9	100.8	101.2	107.9	116.5	98.6	118.0	89.5	110.1	106.2	100.1	107.5	98.0	1,254
1989-90	119.8	99.2	105.2	109.1	94.3	96.9	99.8	102.2	105.6	118.3	107.6	102.2	1,260
1990-1	115.4	100.0	108.2		330.2			287.2			293.5		1,235
1991-2		287.2		138.1	137.5	164.5	153.3	150.2	160.0	165.0	162.4	153.6	1,672
1992-3	168.1	151.8	151.6	81.2	93.6	110.5	102.4	85.8	99.9	88.0	90.9	96.4	1,320
1993-41	106.7	101.7	114.3	71.8	76.5	92.6	79.4	91.5	91.7	90.6	106.4	109.1	1,132
1994-5[1]	103.5	107.2	116.9	100.7	92.3	109.9	97.3	95.6	108.9	97.2	78.2	95.5	1,203

[1] Preliminary. *Source: Bureau of Census, U.S. Department of Commerce*

Corn Oil Spot Price, Wet Mill at Chicago In Cents Per Pound

Year	Oct.	Nov.	Dec.	Jan.	Feb.	Mar.	Apr.	May	June	July	Aug.	Sept.	Average
1985-6[2]	20.90	20.20	20.10	20.80	18.70	17.10	17.90	18.00	17.30	17.00	16.70	16.70	18.45
1986-7	19.60	20.47	21.48	22.45	24.61	22.65	20.94	21.43	22.90	21.48	20.00	19.14	21.43
1987-8	20.68	20.69	21.49	23.09	22.46	21.26	20.44	21.61	26.43	29.56	26.58	24.94	23.27
1988-9	23.35	21.78	21.22	20.65	20.30	21.61	21.40	21.75	21.44	20.05	19.21	19.39	21.01
1989-90	20.84	22.67	23.25	22.61	23.57	24.96	26.05	24.99	26.56	25.09	28.49	28.00	24.76
1990-1	26.61	24.24	22.15	25.89	27.29	28.50	29.98	28.87	29.61	29.76	29.55	28.50	27.58
1991-2	27.75	27.25	28.75	29.00	28.45	27.19	26.75	26.04	24.75	22.48	20.40	21.00	25.82
1992-3	20.43	20.60	20.75	20.75	20.87	20.79	20.80	20.75	20.60	20.67	21.50	22.23	20.90
1993-4	22.25	23.06	26.93	28.00	29.89	30.30	29.63	29.48	29.43	27.20	25.02	24.87	27.17
1994-5[1]	24.73	24.75	24.75	28.01	27.26	28.17	27.30	26.42	26.61	27.38	26.35	25.93	26.47

[1] Preliminary. [2] Prior to October 1985, prices are for F.O.B. Decatur (Tank Cars). *Source: Economic Research Service, U.S. Department of Agriculture*

Cotton

World cotton production in 1995/96 (August to July) totaled 89.3 million bales (480 pounds/bale), slightly more than expected and 4 percent above 1994/95's crop of 85.5 million. The increase was due to a near record harvested acreage of 34.8 million hectares. Average yield fell to 558 kilos per hectare versus the 1994/95 yield of 582 kg. The record for production occurred in 1991/92 when 96 million bales were produced on yields averaging 600kg/ha.

China, the world's largest producer, harvested 19.5 million bales in 1995/96, below the upward trend set in the preceding five years. Pest problems cut China's production, suggesting an entrenched problem that might affect future production. The U.S. 1995/96 crop of 18.8 million bales compares with the previous year's record of 19.7 million. Poor growing conditions accounted for the lower production as planted acreage increased significantly. However, drought struck the Delta cotton crop as well as the Rio Grande Valley crop in South Texas. Heavy rains delayed planting in California and slowed initial development. Some of the heaviest infestation by insects in recent years occurred in Texas and the Delta. The biggest production change in 1995/96 versus a year earlier occurred in Pakistan, whose 8.5 million bale crop was up 2 million bales.

The larger 1995/96 crop will top world consumption by 3 million bales. Usage is estimated at 86 million bales, up 1.6 million from 1994/95. Although world consumption in the first half of the 1990's has trended irregularly higher, carryover supplies have a less discernible trend, estimated at 32.8 million bales as of July 31, 1996, versus 29.9 million a year earlier, and 37.4 million 4 years earlier. The most favorable factor for increased cotton usage is improved economic growth overseas, notably in Asia. China accounts for nearly a fourth of world consumption and at times has been forced to import large quantities of cotton. China's use in 1995/96 is expected to be up 4 percent to 20.5 million bales, the first increase in 3 years. Consumption in India is estimated at a record 10.5 million bales, the fourth consecutive annual increase. Similarly, Pakistan's domestic 1995/96 use was put at a record 6.8 million bales.

World trade during 1995/96 was lower than expected at 27.5 million bales versus 28.8 million in 1994/95. The U.S. share of world exports is expected to be near 25 percent of the total, with 6.8 million bales versus the extraordinarily high 9.4 million in 1994/95. The drop in U.S. 1995/96 exports reflects the larger world crop, increased foreign competition and reduced import demand from China whose 1995/96 imports may drop two million bales as their stock rebuilding program appears to have ended.

The USDA's November 1995/96 cotton crop estimate of 18.8 million bales reflected a 306,000 bale reduction from the October forecast and the third consecutive cut from the initial record high estimate in August. Production in 1994/95 totaled 19.7 million bales. Planted acreage in 1995 increased 23 percent to 16.8 million acres, the most since 1956, but average yield of 567 pounds per acre was 20 percent under 1994/95 and the lowest since 1986. Total U.S. 1995/96 supplies of 21.5 million bales included a carryin of 2.7 million. Mill use in 1995/96 at 11 million bales was down from 11.2 million in 1994/95, but the aforementioned drop in exports placed the marketing year's total use at 17.8 million bales versus 20.6 million in 1994/95. Carryover stocks were estimated at 3.7 million bales as of July 31, 1996.

World and U.S. cotton prices began the 1995/96 season nearly ten cents above a year earlier. Domestically, nearby futures began the season around $0.79 per pound, but by yearend March 1996 futures were at $0.81. The USDA, by law, cannot publish a cotton price forecast, but based on the early months of the 1995/96 season the average for the year should top the 1994/95 average farm price of $0.73 cents a pound for all cotton; $0.72 cents for upland.

U.S. Government Program

The 1995/96 price support loan rate for 1-1/16" cotton was 51.92 cents per pound and the target price 72.90 cents. The 1994/95 prices were 50.00 cents and 72.90 cents, respectively. USDA cotton programs cover a wide spectrum of requirements and grades. Shorter staple grades have lower loan rates than longer lengths.

Futures Market

Cotton futures and options are traded on the New York Cotton Exchange (NYCE). Cotton futures are traded on the Bolsa de Mercadorias & Futuros (BM&F). Cotton Yarn futures are traded on the Nagoya Textile Exchange, the Osaka Textile Exchange, and the Tokyo Commodity Exchange (TOCOM).

Supply and Distribution of All Cotton in the United States — In Thousands of 480-Pound Bales

Crop Year Beginning Aug. 1	Area: Planted (1,000 acres)	Area: Harvested (1,000 acres)	Yield Lbs./acre	Supply: Beginning Stocks[3]	Supply: Production[4]	Supply: Imports	Supply: Total	Disappearance: Mill Use	Disappearance: Exports	Disappearance: Total	Unaccounted	Ending Stocks	Farm Price[5] (Cents Per Lb.)	"A" Index Price[6] (Cents Per Lb.)	Value of Production Million $
1986	10,045	8,468	552	9,348	9,731	3	19,082	7,452	6,684	14,136	80	5,026	52.4	61.98	2,449
1987	10,397	10,030	706	5,026	14,760	2	19,788	7,617	6,582	14,199	182	5,771	64.3	72.26	4,555
1988	12,515	11,948	619	5,771	15,411	5	21,187	7,785	6,148	13,930	-165	7,092	56.6	66.42	4,190
1989	10,587	9,538	614	7,092	12,196	2	19,290	8,759	7,694	16,453	163	3,000	66.2	82.40	3,878
1990	12,348	11,732	634	3,000	15,505	4	18,509	8,657	7,793	16,450	285	2,344	67.1	82.90	5,076
1991	14,052	12,960	652	2,344	17,614	13	19,971	9,613	6,646	16,259	-8	3,704	58.1	63.05	4,728
1992	13,240	11,143	699	3,704	16,218	1	19,923	10,250	5,201	15,451	190	4,662	54.9	57.74	4,082
1993[1]	13,438	12,783	606	4,662	16,134	6	20,802	10,418	6,862	17,280	8	3,530	58.4	70.69	4,342
1994[1]	13,720	13,322	708	3,530	19,662	20	23,212	11,198	9,402	20,600	38	2,650	73.0	91.82	
1995[2]	16,932	15,986	540	2,650	17,971	15	21,503	11,000	6,800	17,800	-3	3,700	59.0	89.70	

[1] Preliminary. [2] Estimate. [3] Excludes preseason ginnings (adjusted to 480-lb. bale net weight basis). [4] Includes preseason ginnings. [5] Marketing year average price. [6] Average of 5 cheapest types of SLM 1 3/32" staple length cotton offered on the European market. *Source: Economic Research Service, U.S. Department of Agriculture*

World Production of Cotton (All Types) In Thousands of 480-Lb. Bales

Crop Year Beginning Aug. 1	Argentina	Brazil	China	Colombia	Egypt	India	Iran	Israel	Mexico	Pakistan	Sudan	Turkey	United States	Uzbekistan[3]	World Total
1981-2	696	2,941	13,632	404	2,293	6,559	356	423	1,440	3,435	712	2,242	15,641	11,267	68,892
1982-3	515	2,976	16,526	151	2,115	6,755	431	400	840	3,783	944	2,246	11,963	10,380	66,472
1983-4	826	3,423	21,298	352	1,838	6,122	420	427	1,038	2,271	1,021	2,398	7,771	9,976	66,460
1984-5	786	4,423	28,700	575	1,840	7,925	512	402	1,240	4,628	945	2,664	12,982	11,876	88,146
1985-6	547	3,812	19,000	531	1,999	8,355	482	455	970	5,669	652	2,379	13,432	12,777	79,613
1986-7	482	3,008	16,300	493	1,822	7,418	510	308	630	6,060	757	2,376	9,731	12,157	70,447
1987-8	1,295	3,514	19,500	614	1,614	7,388	487	271	1,010	6,741	612	2,465	15,411	11,491	81,349
1988-9	896	3,376	19,100	554	1,405	8,276	551	285	1,416	6,547	700	2,985	12,196	12,621	84,774
1989-90	1,272	3,030	17,400	481	1,324	10,599	524	212	769	6,687	584	2,835	12,196	7,605	79,780
1990-1	1,355	3,215	20,700	581	1,378	9,135	553	236	813	7,522	380	3,007	15,505	7,317	86,980
1991-2	1,148	3,445	26,100	724	1,338	9,430	543	101	831	10,000	386	2,578	17,614	6,790	95,992
1992-3	666	2,113	20,700	290	1,620	10,931	465	133	138	7,073	276	2,635	16,218	6,000	82,709
1993-4[1]	1,075	1,860	17,200	244	1,882	9,400	310	120	110	6,024	250	2,666	16,145	6,240	76,049
1994-5[2]	1,608	2,526	19,900	230	1,225	10,845	542	142	458	6,500	400	2,886	19,662	5,570	85,610
1995-6[2]	1,900	2,300	20,000	330	1,200	11,000	700	200	860	8,500	550	3,850	17,971	5,650	89,121

[1] Preliminary. [2] Estimate. [3] Formerly part of the U.S.S.R.; data not reported separately until 1989. *Source: Foreign Agricultural Service, U.S. Department of Agriculture*

Cotton World Supply and Demand In Thousands of 480-Lb. Bales

Crop Year Beginning Aug. 1	Beginning Stocks				Production				Consumption				Exports			
	United States	Uzbekistan[3]	China	World Total	United States	Uzbekistan[3]	China	World Total	United States	Russia[3]	China	World Total	United States	Uzbekistan[3]	China	World Total
1981-2	2,668	2,585	2,392	20,455	15,641	11,267	13,632	68,892	5,264	7,855	16,285	64,666	6,567	4,295	0	20,239
1982-3	6,632	2,527	1,892	25,181	11,963	10,380	16,526	66,472	5,513	7,600	16,822	66,412	5,207	3,890	75	19,452
1983-4	7,937	1,900	3,101	25,198	7,771	9,976	21,298	66,460	5,926	7,900	15,714	67,353	6,786	3,202	760	19,166
1984-5	2,775	707	8,305	23,952	12,982	11,928	28,720	88,364	5,540	8,630	16,002	69,392	6,215	2,994	944	20,206
1985-6	4,102	1,460	20,146	43,246	13,432	12,778	19,046	79,863	6,399	9,200	18,909	76,070	1,960	3,170	2,799	20,299
1986-7	9,348	2,260	16,848	47,026	9,731	12,217	16,261	70,107	7,452	9,400	20,976	83,793	6,684	3,462	3,169	26,014
1987-8	5,026	2,031	10,795	35,926	14,760	11,345	19,500	81,109	7,617	9,000	20,065	83,500	6,582	3,457	2,322	23,227
1988-9	5,771	1,302	7,559	32,850	15,412	12,704	19,056	84,423	7,782	9,200	20,533	85,352	6,148	3,656	1,636	25,869
1989-90	7,092	473	5,971	31,423	12,196	7,605	17,400	79,741	8,759	5,831	20,000	86,579	7,694	6,810	865	31,275
1990-1	3,000	460	4,379	25,771	15,505	7,317	20,700	86,964	8,657	5,469	20,000	85,492	7,793	5,393	928	29,678
1991-2	2,344	1,555	5,956	27,073	17,614	6,790	26,100	95,983	9,613	4,539	20,500	86,136	6,646	5,200	602	28,115
1992-3	3,704	2,295	12,284	37,403	16,218	6,000	20,700	82,741	10,250	2,200	21,500	85,770	5,201	5,500	684	25,517
1993-4[1]	4,662	1,845	10,442	35,121	16,134	6,240	17,200	76,988	10,418	2,200	21,200	85,325	6,862	6,100	749	27,197
1994-5[2]	3,530	737	6,101	26,507	19,662	5,570	19,900	85,610	11,198	1,300	20,200	84,574	9,402	5,100	183	28,772
1995-62	2,650	462	9,678	28,889	17,971	5,650	20,000	89,121	10,700	1,500	20,800	86,080	7,000	4,800	400	27,762

[1] Preliminary. [2] Estimate. [3] Formerly part of the U.S.S.R.; data not reported separately until 1989. *Source: Foreign Agricultural Service, U.S. Department of Agriculture*

World Consumption of All Cottons in Specific Countries In Thousands of 480-Lb. Bales

Crop Year Beginning Aug. 1	Agrentina	Brazil	China	Egypt	France	Germany	India	Italy	Japan	Mexico	Pakistan	Poland	United Kingdom	United States	Uzbekistan[3]	World Total
1981-2	360	2,600	15,700	1,341	743	745	5,843	1,024	3,426	620	2,238	711	207	5,264	9,400	65,647
1982-3	460	2,600	16,400	1,370	765	928	6,250	1,030	3,290	625	2,450	650	230	5,513	9,200	67,862
1983-4	514	2,435	16,000	1,310	745	976	6,531	1,170	3,300	528	2,030	650	234	5,921	9,300	68,612
1984-5	464	2,665	15,500	1,367	724	1,000	7,117	1,200	3,187	550	2,264	712	248	5,538	9,500	69,401
1985-6	551	3,100	19,500	1,550	672	1,000	7,191	1,170	3,146	670	2,342	750	248	6,413	9,600	76,888
1986-7	575	3,285	20,200	1,290	710	1,100	7,847	1,419	3,445	580	2,990	600	225	7,452	9,350	82,239
1987-8	575	3,399	20,000	1,334	690	1,110	7,612	1,381	3,477	600	3,600	715	216	7,617	9,300	83,499
1988-9	551	3,766	20,500	1,300	640	910	8,139	1,424	3,408	650	3,904	725	193	7,782	9,100	85,565
1989-90	533	3,445	20,000	1,352	600	1,435	8,667	1,450	3,229	725	4,801	650	170	8,759	9,200	86,579
1990-1	597	3,215	20,000	1,457	530	955	9,018	1,470	3,027	712	5,648	410	140	8,657	8,700	85,492
1991-2	606	3,215	19,000	1,465	484	830	8,674	1,447	2,783	772	6,482	275	100	9,613	860	86,136
1992-3	588	3,445	21,500	1,640	470	680	9,761	1,400	2,301	740	6,634	390	85	10,250	950	85,770
1993-4[1]	550	3,675	20,900	1,530	500	750	9,950	1,375	2,060	825	6,500	400	85	10,418	925	85,325
1994-5[2]	459	4,000	20,200	1,350	500	660	10,334	1,525	1,800	800	6,750	400	90	11,198	750	84,574
1995-6[2]	450	3,900	20,800	1,300	480	700	10,550	1,550	1,700	925	6,800	450	90	10,700	800	86,080

[1] Preliminary. [2] Estimate. [3] Formerly part of the U.S.S.R.; data not reported separately until 1991. *Source: Foreign Agricultural Service, U.S. Department of Agriculture*

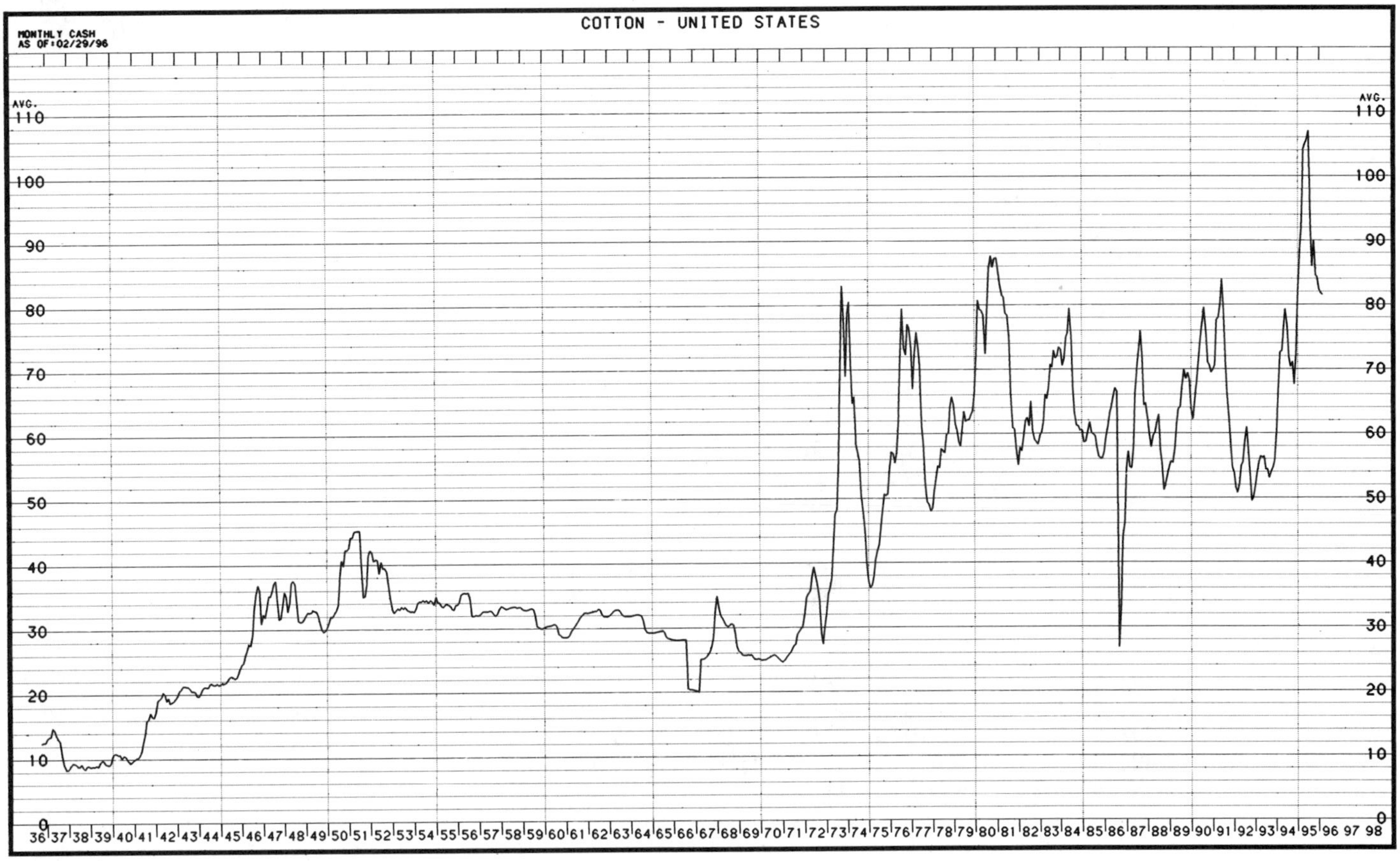

Average Spot Cotton Prices[2], C.I.F. Northern Europe   In U.S. Cents Per Pound

Crop Year Beginning Aug. 1	Argentina "C"[3] 1 1/16"	Australia M 1 3/32"	Central America[4] M 1 3/32"	China Type 329	Cotlook Index A	Cotlook Index B	Egypt Giza[5] 81	Greece M 1 3/32"	Mexico M 1 3/32"	Pakistan Sind/ Punjab[6]	Tanzania AR[7] Type 3	Turkey Izmir[8] 1 3/32"	U.S. Calif. ACALA SJV[9]	U.S. Memphis Terr.[10] M 1 3/32"	U.S. Orleans/ Texas[11] M 1 1/32"
	M & SM 1" - 1 3/32"														
1978-9	71.60	------	74.42	------	76.05	67.95	------	82.44	76.02	66.99	90.13	77.38	82.96	76.27	67.22
1979-80	75.04	------	83.46	------	85.40	74.55	136.37	84.00	77.87	75.45	84.01	------	90.69	78.47	75.36
1980-1	82.06	------	98.25	------	94.20	84.20	137.66	100.41	95.48	85.11	103.78	97.43	101.85	99.99	89.14
1981-2	63.55	------	72.99	------	73.80	64.40	115.73	81.06	75.36	65.56	87.92	77.65	79.79	75.87	66.76
1982-3	62.63	------	76.13	------	76.65	66.60	110.07	85.25	76.37	65.58	87.19	83.28	84.94	77.95	68.11
1983-4	83.32	90.83	86.86	------	87.65	80.40	134.07	94.42	87.54	75.51	95.23	92.64	94.90	87.23	78.41
1984-5	60.95	60.33	67.22	62.50	69.15	59.55	134.01	76.14	70.10	56.20	77.29	75.92	76.20	73.88	65.95
1985-6	49.42	50.05	42.39	42.39	49.00	40.95	111.40	50.98	53.16	37.92	55.81	57.06	59.43	65.01	52.26
1986-7	68.97	66.59	62.76	62.11	62.05	55.05	112.59	63.53	64.64	55.11	67.41	64.63	74.27	61.96	56.38
1987-8	64.13	76.14	71.94	71.94	72.30	67.50	145.11	83.85	73.75	65.88	87.96	86.43	81.17	74.24	72.07
1988-9	64.11	72.14	60.69	60.69	66.35	61.30	176.85	63.07	61.54	56.98	69.09	68.98	77.13	69.00	63.92
1989-90	77.05	84.16	80.63	85.92	82.40	77.40	189.54	83.76	82.50	76.75	86.68	90.49	88.59	83.90	78.93
1990-1	77.06	85.58	83.28	87.45	82.90	77.80	177.43	84.24	84.46	77.19	89.62	81.32	92.84	88.13	80.35
1991-2	55.08	65.97	68.40	71.72	63.05	58.50	128.10	65.90	68.19	58.14	68.90	74.66	74.47	66.35	63.41
1992-3	64.31	64.01	NA	61.59	57.70	53.70	99.24	56.92	NA	52.66	62.24	------	68.37	63.08	58.89
1993-4	80.20	72.81	NA	73.49	70.60	67.30	88.35	58.81	NA	54.42	69.83	59.80	77.55	72.80	69.78
1994-5[1]	101.88	81.05	NA	NA	92.75	92.40	93.70	88.64	82.65	73.75	NA	NA	106.40	98.67	95.70

[1] Preliminary. [2] Generally for prompt shipment. [3] 1 1/32 inches prior to January 20, 1984; 1 1/16 inches since. [4] Guatemala SM 1 1/16 inches 1971/72 through 1985/86; Central American Middling 1 3/32 inches since. [5] Giza 67 1969/70 until December 1983; Giza 69/75/81 until November 1990; Giza 81 since. [6] Punjab until 1979/80; Sind SG until June 1984; Sind/Punjab SG until January 1985; Afzal 1 inch until January 1986; Afzal 1 1/32 inches since. [7] No. 1 until 1978/79; No. 1/2 until January 1987; Izmir/Antalya ST 1 White 1 3/32 inches RG since. [9] SM 1 1/8 inches. [10] SM 1 1/16 inches prior to 1981-82; Middling 1 3/32 inches since. [11] Middling 1 inch prior to 1988/89; Middling 1 1/32 inches since. NA = Not available. *Source: International Cotton Advisory Committee*

COTTON

Average Price of Strict Low Middling 1 1/16", Cotton at Designated U.S. Markets ¢ Per Pound (Net Weight)

Year	Aug.	Sept.	Oct.	Nov.	Dec.	Jan.	Feb.	Mar.	Apr.	May	June	July	Average
1985-6	57.87	56.38	56.14	56.03	56.25	58.39	59.81	61.75	62.62	63.95	65.24	65.73	60.01
1986-7	26.81	33.56	43.95	45.74	54.19	57.17	54.75	54.60	57.72	65.94	70.42	73.07	53.16
1987-8	75.89	71.41	64.30	64.66	62.26	59.69	57.83	59.64	60.07	61.55	62.86	57.40	63.13
1988-9	55.20	51.25	52.20	53.40	54.80	55.67	55.37	57.59	61.43	63.70	64.06	67.39	57.67
1989-90	69.88	68.46	69.40	68.33	63.56	62.21	64.95	68.06	71.31	74.61	77.06	79.53	69.78
1990-1	76.27	71.01	70.54	69.48	69.92	70.50	77.69	77.92	79.94	83.94	79.05	71.33	74.80
1991-2	66.44	62.39	58.28	54.70	53.89	51.54	50.76	52.01	54.97	55.45	58.82	60.93	56.68
1992-3	57.56	53.49	49.47	49.98	51.85	53.72	55.38	56.45	56.17	56.37	54.38	54.35	54.10
1993-4	53.04	54.01	54.58	55.61	60.29	66.53	72.69	72.74	76.12	79.30	76.85	71.71	66.12
1994-5	70.32	71.10	67.58	72.00	81.92	88.11	91.89	104.20	104.94	105.38	106.96	93.26	88.14
1995-6[1]	85.90	90.00	84.65	84.16	82.18								

[1] Preliminary. Note: Grade 41, staple 34 cotton. *Source: Agricultural Marketing Service, U.S Department of Agriculture*

Average Spot Cotton, 1 3/32", Price (SLM) at Designated U.S. Markets In Cents Per Pound (Net Weight)

Year	Aug.	Sept.	Oct.	Nov.	Dec.	Jan.	Feb.	Mar.	Apr.	May	June	July	Average	1 1/32"	1"
1985-6	57.40	55.89	55.66	55.55	55.77	57.92	59.34	61.28	62.15	63.48	64.77	66.20	59.62	57.87	55.81
1986-7	27.39	35.56	44.53	46.27	54.71	57.70	55.26	55.12	58.24	66.46	70.94	73.59	53.81	50.78	47.77
1987-8	76.42	71.99	64.84	65.17	62.76	60.14	58.28	60.12	60.55	62.03	63.34	57.88	63.63	60.81	59.33
1988-9	55.69	51.80	52.66	53.80	55.20	56.07	55.77	58.04	61.94	64.21	64.57	67.92	58.14	53.99	52.32
1989-90	70.42	69.00	69.89	68.75	63.99	62.63	65.37	68.48	71.73	75.03	77.48	79.95	70.23	66.02	64.89
1990-1	76.69	71.43	70.97	69.97	70.43	71.09	78.45	78.63	80.65	84.60	79.69	71.99	75.38	71.52	69.15
1991-2	66.88	62.75	58.63	55.04	54.23	51.92	51.16	52.41	55.37	55.85	59.22	61.33	57.07	54.15	53.23
1992-3	57.96	53.88	49.99	50.65	52.49	54.43	56.09	57.23	56.95	57.15	55.16	55.13	54.76	52.42	52.46
1993-4	54.89	55.90	56.46	57.34	61.76	67.97	73.99	74.15	77.55	80.42	78.01	72.97	67.62	64.28	63.91
1994-5	71.46	72.42	68.82	73.38	83.41	89.92	94.25	106.66	107.50	107.93	109.52	96.31	90.13	85.13	84.47
1995-6[1]	88.31	92.71	87.06	86.43	84.25	84.32									

[1] Preliminary. *Source: Economic Research Service, U.S. Department of Agriculture*

Average Spot Prices of U.S. Cotton,[1] Base Quality--(SLM) at Designated Markets In Cents Per Pound

Crop Year Beginning Aug. 1	Dallas (East Tex.-Okl.)	Fresno (San Joaquin Valley)	Greenville (South-east)	Green-wood (South Delta)	Lubbock (West Texas)	Memphis (North Delta)	Phoenix Desert (South-west)	Average
1985-6	58.96	60.35	60.52	60.69	59.17	60.40	59.84	60.01
1986-7	51.03	60.97	51.66	51.99	51.20	51.70	55.38	53.16
1987-8	61.14	66.02	63.37	62.41	61.09	62.54	65.69	63.13
1988-9	55.88	63.30	57.26	56.67	55.77	56.71	59.67	57.90
1989-90	67.11	73.47	70.64	69.50	67.06	69.51	71.19	69.78
1990-1	71.40	78.30	75.90	75.53	71.09	75.49	75.90	74.80
1991-2	55.63	57.50	57.70	56.21	55.79	56.18	57.77	56.68
1992-3	53.78	52.84	56.73	55.03	53.53	55.03	51.61	54.10
1993-4	66.22	65.04	67.46	67.04	65.92	67.04	64.16	66.12
1994-5	86.96	93.73	87.17	87.25	86.66	87.25	87.96	88.14

[1] Prices are for mixed lots, net weight, uncompressed in warehouse. [2] 1993 prices are for mixed lots, net weight, compressed, F.O.B. car/truck.
Source: Agricultural Marketing Service, U.S. Department of Agriculture

Average Price[1] Received by Farmers for Upland Cotton in the U.S. In Cents Per Pound

Year	Aug.	Sept.	Oct.	Nov.	Dec.	Jan.	Feb.	Mar	Apr.	May	June	July	Average
1985-6	56.6	55.9	57.3	56.5	53.7	54.0	56.9	58.1	59.2	58.5	58.5	61.5	56.8
1986-7	46.8	48.6	50.0	52.6	52.7	52.1	46.4	47.5	50.4	60.0	66.2	68.3	51.5
1987-8	63.8	65.4	65.1	65.6	64.6	61.7	57.0	57.9	59.9	58.3	62.0	59.5	63.7
1988-9	53.9	51.9	55.1	57.5	55.3	54.7	52.8	55.6	58.7	58.3	57.2	59.5	55.6
1989-90	60.4	63.8	65.8	65.6	61.9	60.2	61.0	63.9	65.8	66.2	64.0	63.9	63.6
1990-1	64.6	65.1	67.7	68.4	67.1	64.9	67.9	68.9	69.5	70.1	67.5	66.3	67.1
1991-2	66.3	64.9	62.9	61.2	55.7	51.7	49.8	50.3	53.1	53.2	58.0	56.3	56.8
1992-3	52.7	52.8	53.9	52.7	54.3	53.0	53.8	56.3	55.1	54.4	53.6	53.7	53.7
1993-4	52.4	51.4	52.4	53.3	56.5	62.7	65.7	66.6	67.5	69.0	63.3	58.7	58.1
1994-5	66.8	65.9	66.2	68.5	73.3	79.7	81.6	86.5	84.5	82.6	86.3	86.6	72.0
1995-6[2]	75.2	75.2	75.0	75.6	76.6	79.7	81.0						

[1] Weighted average by sales. [2] Preliminary. *Source: Agricultural Marketing Service, U.S. Department of Agriculture*

Purchases Reported by Exchanges in Designated U.S. Spot Markets[1] In Running Bales

Year Beginning Aug. 1	Aug.	Sept.	Oct.	Nov.	Dec.	Jan.	Feb.	Mar.	Apr.	May	June	July	Market Total
1985	166,725	152,795	258,891	395,097	570,460	671,758	389,436	416,654	487,813	626,319	968,185	690,947	7,250,658
1986	585,628	638,356	392,451	422,542	1,353,241	1,055,081	633,852	354,643	501,265	354,008	163,307	160,474	6,614,848
1987	152,935	252,669	650,349	718,829	1,065,457	622,727	571,851	463,739	266,545	572,702	336,191	117,645	5,791,639
1988	288,187	166,692	230,724	163,642	323,025	383,699	811,630	388,169	307,937	282,564	261,958	282,288	3,890,515
1989	119,516	49,237	89,853	214,910	258,849	388,519	333,417	206,528	157,187	86,966	42,299	46,312	1,993,593
1990	36,735	53,948	154,499	376,790	600,752	516,421	180,949	66,869	138,503	101,180	45,731	40,551	2,312,928
1991	50,469	55,637	179,671	347,393	776,233	1,043,190	1,063,959	699,026	302,102	110,764	134,500	105,795	4,868,739
1992	81,778	233,424	325,600	853,846	1,049,780	1,321,861	317,451	330,381	224,874	208,962	189,401	231,390	5,368,748
1993	143,237	173,896	321,119	1,071,518	1,213,655	500,246	602,766	318,008	234,331	318,244	83,083	40,699	5,020,802
1994	92,401	98,251	426,371	1,075,829	1,491,429	608,701	233,159	149,762	49,192	44,228	43,821	13,244	4,326,388
1995	60,442	38,855	73,857	209,279	381,943								

[1] Commencing March 28, 1983, spot transactions are for eight markets; and commencing September 1, 1988, spot transactions are for seven months.
Source: Agricultural Marketing Service, U.S. Department of Agriculture

Average Open Interest of Cotton Futures at New York In Contracts

Year	Jan.	Feb.	Mar.	Apr.	May	June	July	Aug.	Sept.	Oct.	Nov.	Dec.
1986	23,451	21,654	20,686	20,088	22,473	23,566	22,399	26,058	26,379	24,227	22,056	22,320
1987	25,196	25,048	22,482	23,760	26,074	27,996	32,012	37,426	39,204	39,912	38,017	33,888
1988	35,240	35,974	30,507	29,933	29,753	31,804	28,307	34,637	38,453	37,162	33,210	30,682
1989	31,415	30,978	36,725	36,657	40,761	38,693	40,059	45,894	49,629	49,072	48,136	42,349
1990	40,237	36,291	36,073	37,829	37,908	38,556	36,083	34,042	35,250	40,431	43,997	40,241
1991	43,003	46,793	44,001	43,957	50,086	46,637	40,924	39,616	38,252	39,772	39,295	36,066
1992	38,097	40,095	38,592	36,228	37,839	36,861	35,891	42,241	46,168	46,577	40,425	38,487
1993	41,946	38,657	38,576	33,641	33,012	34,057	32,118	33,872	37,393	36,479	38,567	45,975
1994	54,424	55,558	53,724	54,670	52,830	51,001	52,357	50,597	50,955	51,561	53,563	59,065
1995	71,353	75,100	79,090	71,488	71,714	68,159	65,656	69,653	69,528	65,768	38,475	35,996

Source: New York Cotton Exchange

Volume of Trading of Cotton Futures at New York In Contracts

Year	Jan.	Feb.	Mar.	Apr.	May	June	July	Aug.	Sept.	Oct.	Nov.	Dec.	Total
1986	73,576	77,152	57,433	74,520	57,479	64,742	75,545	94,025	130,898	111,359	113,812	84,618	1,015,392
1987	110,165	106,520	88,621	106,620	110,303	132,180	98,339	127,048	131,214	124,319	126,582	107,124	1,395,980
1988	114,672	119,832	97,533	118,614	127,880	149,303	89,907	100,447	108,285	135,221	124,221	84,334	1,370,249
1989	124,764	135,963	113,028	118,573	135,044	167,442	91,381	151,034	165,255	143,713	178,889	124,034	1,649,120
1990	135,260	116,806	126,820	121,203	139,489	135,040	132,329	129,081	103,936	142,670	150,958	98,895	1,534,611
1991	133,415	179,656	148,918	156,978	174,690	122,242	116,458	115,175	107,742	125,558	150,545	82,867	1,614,244
1992	134,531	134,184	149,711	167,778	173,128	153,194	105,534	142,323	144,844	129,680	161,194	105,157	1,701,258
1993	171,180	135,400	136,965	135,300	105,920	128,985	130,886	122,280	110,989	107,571	178,350	139,344	1,603,027
1994	210,011	207,421	210,363	252,614	178,942	208,945	161,688	128,879	140,574	179,604	205,936	203,021	2,289,998
1995	223,073	290,600	286,098	219,187	214,052	185,276	183,171	199,050	191,534	196,676	195,601	141,116	2,525,434

Source: New York Cotton Exchange

United States Government Crop Forecasts and Actual Cotton Crops

	Forecast of Production (1,000 Bales of 480 Lbs.[1])						Actual	Forecasts of Yields (Lbs. Per Harvested Acre)						Actual
Year	Aug.1	Sept.1	Oct. 1	Nov. 1	Dec. 1	Jan. 1	Crop	Aug.1	Sept.1	Oct. 1	Nov. 1	Dec. 1	Jan. 1	Yield
1981	14,789	15,507	15,476	15,560	15,733	------	15,646	515	540	540	543	546	------	542
1982	11,143	11,029	11,365	11,947	12,102	------	11,963	563	569	587	605	613	------	590
1983	7,810	7,776	7,550	7,497	7,725	------	7,771	503	501	487	504	506	------	508
1984	12,569	13,276	13,272	13,271	13,292	------	12,982	583	615	620	613	610	------	600
1985	13,780	13,655	13,638	13,875	13,810	13,534	13,432	638	632	633	644	644	630	630
1986	10,676	10,506	10,006	9,875	9,792	9,785	9,731	573	565	539	546	539	553	552
1987	12,907	12,846	13,336	13,936	14,281	14,724	14,760	615	616	640	671	695	703	706
1988	14,934	14,709	14,714	14,837	15,197	15,446	15,411	616	605	605	612	627	623	619
1989	11,834	12,279	11,991	12,102	12,083	11,233	12,196	618	603	607	608	619	619	614
1990	14,864	14,722	14,540	14,905	15,399	15,617	15,499	622	616	609	622	640	640	634
1991	17,648	17,868	17,614	13,429	14,052	17,542	17,614	630	638	620	635	630	656	652
1992	16,533	17,943	15,885	16,204	16,259	16,260	16,219	696	685	694	698	696	700	699
1993	18,545	17,867	17,014	16,297	16,284	16,176	16,134	668	645	614	594	597	607	606
1994	19,195	19,025	19,303	19,453	19,573	19,728	19,662	690	690	690	695	699	710	708
1995	21,811	20,266	18,771	18,838	18,236	17,971	17,971	663	615	574	567	551	540	540

[1] Net weight bales. *Source: Agricultural Statistics Board, U.S. Department of Agriculture*

COTTON

U.S. Production of Cotton (Upland) & American-Pima In Thousands of 480-Pound Bales

	Upland														
Year	Alabama	Arizona	Arkansas	California	Georgia	Louisiana	Mississippi	Missouri	New Mexico	North Carolina	Oklahoma	South Carolina	Tennessee	Texas	Total American-Pima
1978	291	1,068	660	1,940	111	478	1,378	188	101	45	355	115	235	3,792	93.4
1979	324	1,280	606	3,408	152	690	1,437	157	104	43	522	116	171	5,515	98.6
1980	275	1,354	444	3,109	86	460	1,143	177	107	52	205	77	200	3,320	104.2
1981	422	1,556	604	3,535	159	742	1,565	168	141	95	440	164	315	5,663	79.6
1982	460	1,095	534	3,073	235	870	1,760	204	78	102	238	155	339	2,700	98.7
1983	183	725	323	1,971	112	532	900	73	70	43	145	53	151	2,380	94.7
1984	447	1,097	612	2,913	281	1,056	1,650	187	87	120	183	170	337	3,680	130.4
1985	545	928	703	3,114	370	742	1,655	204	71	117	285	180	419	3,910	155.1
1986	330	675	602	2,245	185	673	1,190	196	62	109	210	87	396	2,535	205.9
1987	397	849	901	2,989	338	977	1,745	330	89	98	346	106	634	4,635	284.6
1988	380	865	1,044	2,824	370	948	1,825	306	102	133	303	140	584	5,215	334.2
1989	383	649	851	2,661	342	868	1,555	269	80	141	173	154	476	2,870	691.7
1990	375	811	1,081	2,734	405	1,177	1,850	314	95	263	382	145	495	4,965	358.5
1991	553	898	1,576	2,548	722	1,414	2,275	429	63	640	240	344	701	4,710	398.4
1992	621	725	1,681	2,817	744	1,299	2,131	541	48	468	210	226	834	3,265	508.3
1993	469	790	1,094	2,918	733	1,105	1,550	376	78	429	270	204	545	5,095	369.3
1994	726	782	1,772	2,717	1,537	1,512	2,132	615	75	829	247	393	885	4,915	337.7
1995[1]	460	790	1,460	2,300	1,970	1,375	1,845	525	79	830	125	390	730	4,500	361.0

[1] Preliminary. *Source: Agricultural Statistics Board, U.S. Department of Agriculture*

Supply and Distribution of Upland Cotton in the United States — In Thousands of 480-Pound Bales

Crop Year Beginning Aug. 1	Area: Planted (1,000 Acres)	Area: Harvested (1,000 Acres)	Yield Lbs./Acre	Supply: Beginning Stocks[3]	Supply: Production[4]	Supply: Imports	Supply: Total	Disappearance: Mill Use	Disappearance: Exports	Disappearance: Total	Ending Stocks	Farm Price[5] Cents/Lb.
1982	11,275	9,663	589	6,567	11,864	12	18,443	5,457	5,194	10,651	7,844	59.5
1983	7,863	7,285	506	7,844	7,676	8	15,528	5,853	6,750	12,603	2,693	65.3
1984	11,065	10,300	599	2,693	12,851	21	15,566	5,490	6,125	11,615	4,024	58.7
1985	10,601	10,145	628	4,024	13,277	33	17,334	6,352	1,855	8,207	9,289	56.8
1986	9,933	8,357	547	9,289	9,525	3	18,817	7,385	6,570	13,955	4,942	51.5
1987	10,259	9,894	702	4,942	14,475	2	19,419	7,565	6,345	13,910	5,718	63.7
1988	12,325	11,759	615	5,718	15,077	5	20,800	7,711	5,883	13,594	7,026	55.6
1989	10,210	9,166	602	7,026	11,504	2	18,532	8,686	7,242	15,928	2,798	63.6
1990	12,117	11,505	632	2,798	15,147	4	17,949	8,592	7,378	15,970	2,262	67.1
1991	13,802	12,716	650	2,262	17,216	13	19,491	9,548	6,348	15,896	3,583	56.8
1992	12,977	10,863	694	3,583	15,710	1	19,294	10,190	4,869	15,059	4,456	53.7
1993[1]	13,248	12,594	601	4,456	15,764	6	20,226	10,346	6,555	16,901	3,303	58.1
1994[1]	13,552	13,156	705	3,303	19,324	18	22,645	11,096	8,978	20,074	2,591	72.0
1995[2]	16,718	15,775	536	2,591	17,610	10	21,082	10,915	6,500	17,415	3,664	

[1] Preliminary. [2] Estimate. [3] Excludes preseason ginnings (adjusted to 480-lb. bale net weight basis). [4] Includes preseason ginnings. [5] Marketing year average price. [6] Average of 5 cheapest types of SLM 1 3/32" staple length cotton offered on the European market. *Source: Economic Research Service, U.S. Department of Agriculture*

U.S. Daily Rate of Upland Cotton Mill Consumption[2] on Cotton-System Spinning Spindles — In Thousands of Running Bales

Crop Year Beginning Aug. 1	Aug.	Sept.	Oct.	Nov.	Dec.	Jan.	Feb.	Mar.	Apr.	May.	June	July	Average
1981-2	21.4	20.7	22.4	20.1	16.0	18.9	19.9	19.7	20.5	19.6	18.4	16.0	19.5
1982-3	19.3	19.0	20.8	19.5	17.0	20.2	21.5	22.0	21.5	22.0	21.7	18.4	20.2
1983-4	22.6	22.4	22.9	22.3	18.7	23.5	22.4	21.9	21.5	22.1	20.1	17.7	21.6
1984-5	21.4	20.4	21.4	19.5	16.9	20.0	20.9	20.8	21.0	21.9	21.0	18.5	20.3
1985-6	22.9	22.5	24.6	23.9	19.5	23.8	24.9	24.6	24.8	25.2	24.4	20.9	23.4
1986-7	26.7	26.2	27.3	26.5	23.1	27.3	28.1	29.4	28.7	29.3	28.3	27.0	27.3
1987-8	30.3	30.1	31.0	30.3	24.4	28.4	29.5	29.5	27.8	27.6	26.5	21.7	28.1
1988-9	28.8	27.7	27.6	26.1	22.9	28.3	29.2	30.0	31.2	32.2	31.9	27.9	28.6
1989-90	32.9	32.8	33.0	30.6	25.9	29.9	31.4	31.5	30.9	31.8	32.8	27.8	30.9
1990-1	33.8	41.4	33.2	30.2	29.7	---	32.3	---	---	34.0	---	---	33.5
1991-2	33.6	---	---	33.1	---	34.6	36.3	35.7	35.6	37.3	35.2	33.9	35.0
1992-3	38.5	37.8	39.7	37.6	31.5	39.1	39.5	38.8	38.7	39.4	37.8	34.5	37.8
1993-4	39.8	38.4	39.4	36.4	31.4	36.9	39.0	39.7	40.0	41.1	41.0	36.9	38.3
1994-5[1]	43.2	42.5	43.3	41.6	35.6	42.5	43.4	43.4	41.9	41.7	39.5	33.7	41.0
1995-6[1]	41.1	40.4	39.5	37.7									

[1] Preliminary. [2] Not seasonally adjusted. *Source: Bureau of Census, U.S. Department of Commerce*

Consumption of American and Foreign Cotton in the United States — In Thousands of Running Bales

Year	Aug.	Sept.	Oct.	Nov.	Dec.	Jan.	Feb.	Mar.	Apr.	May	June	July	Total
1981-2	429	517	448	403	400	378	398	493	410	392	460	317	5,038
1982-3	386	474	416	391	425	404	430	549	431	441	543	369	5,259
1983-4	453	560	459	446	468	469	448	548	430	442	503	354	5,628
1984-5	428	509	428	390	423	399	418	519	419	439	525	369	5,268
1985-6	458	562	493	477	486	595	499	492	620	503	489	522	6,198
1986-7	534	523	683	529	576	546	562	734	573	586	708	540	7,096
1987-8	606	753	621	606	610	568	590	738	556	551	662	433	7,294
1988-9	577	693	552	523	572	568	584	751	623	645	798	559	7,444
1989-90	689	860	690	642	685	630	658	826	650	667	826	559	8,383
1990-1	680	835	671	610	601	---	2,068	---	---	2,212	---	---	8,367
1991-2	2,215	---	---	2,199	---	870	730	898	718	752	885	682	9,949
1992-3	776	950	799	756	792	788	796	976	778	792	951	694	9,846
1993-4	801	965	792	731	790	743	785	999	806	830	1,032	744	10,019
1994-5[1]	870	1,070	873	838	897	858	878	1,097	847	842	999	681	10,750
1995-6[1]	829	1,020	798	762									

[1] Preliminary. *Source: Bureau of Census, U.S. Department of Commerce*

COTTON

Exports of All Cotton from the United States   In Thousands of Running Bales

Year	Aug.	Sept.	Oct.	Nov.	Dec.	Jan.	Feb.	Mar.	Apr.	May	June	July	Total
1981-2	233	198	211	545	698	669	756	793	765	450	560	386	6,263
1982-3	348	304	248	442	357	472	355	435	557	511	381	467	4,961
1983-4	369	329	308	438	566	821	737	783	839	494	429	370	6,419
1984-5	454	249	340	472	712	755	705	692	556	435	359	299	5,943
1985-6	166	218	180	198	236	189	202	206	125	69	68	19	1,875
1986-7	374	496	489	525	664	591	518	750	500	465	554	439	6,366
1987-8	355	304	316	612	536	698	879	649	565	537	486	359	6,297
1988-9	248	173	292	352	524	756	514	597	575	795	515	649	5,987
1989-90	431	384	507	469	516	909	840	882	818	495	510	550	7,310
1990-1	480	355	433	591	639	1,112	950	804	960	488	404	273	7,488
1991-2	219	126	239	396	674	961	725	791	787	535	430	466	6,386
1992-3	252	263	277	342	528	501	502	533	639	401	317	395	4,950
1993-4	246	299	317	385	557	522	598	841	623	727	855	614	6,584
1994-5[1]	430	523	238	503	952	991	1,307	1,565	1,010	741	604	305	9,169
1995-6[1]	251	222	706	820									

[1] Preliminary. *Source: Foreign Agricultural Service, U.S. Department of Agriculture*

U.S. Exports of American Cotton to Countries of Destination   In Thousands of 480-Pound Bales

Crop Year Beginning Aug. 1	Canada	China	Egypt	Germany	Hong Kong	Indonesia	Italy	Japan	Rep. of Korea	Mexico	Philippines	Sweden	Taiwan	Thailand	United Kingdom	Former USSR	Total
1981-2	167	847	0	119	243	243	106	1,626	1,412	-----	58	17	777	167	43	0	6,567
1982-3	238	20	0	163	158	268	105	1,286	1,322	-----	72	23	378	197	50	192	5,207
1983-4	227	12	0	195	283	320	252	1,709	1,269	-----	59	28	495	244	67	351	6,785
1984-5	195	6	126	195	125	258	301	1,464	1,257	-----	58	22	513	139	72	329	6,211
1985-6	98	0	120	85	1	105	91	520	513	-----	8	15	46	17	35	0	1,958
1986-7	70	0	68	263	52	324	263	1,723	1,330	-----	153	15	907	239	56	0	6,685
1987-8	153	0	93	376	88	287	406	1,569	1,450	-----	135	19	424	248	69	98	6,582
1988-9	148	793	102	255	108	307	239	1,381	1,302	-----	50	16	254	172	37	2	6,147
1989-90	197	670	242	368	244	499	431	1,594	1,365	117	134	22	320	375	74	5	7,694
1990-1	191	1,233	243	214	306	561	425	1,437	1,168	202	132	22	358	317	36	5	7,793
1991-2	181	792	339	101	335	739	240	1,107	1,024	213	181	18	380	368	60	0	6,646
1992-3	154	1	170	74	100	429	144	839	1,031	557	117	20	279	150	65	0	5,201
1993-4[1]	165	1,183	0	50	314	653	96	790	976	653	168	12	356	277	65	0	6,862
1994-5[2]	253	2,257	162	30	347	925	83	1,061	951	558	173	25	352	441	89	0	9,402

[1] Preliminary. [2] Estimate. *Source: Foreign Agricultural Service, U.S. Department of Agriculture*

Cotton[1] Government Loan Program in the United States

Crop Year Beginning Aug. 1	Support Price	Target Price	Put Under Support	% of Production	Acquired	Owned July 31	Crop Year Beginning Aug. 1	Support Price	Target Price	Put Under Support	% of Production	Acquired	Owned July 31
	--- ¢ per Pound ---		Ths Bales		----- Ths. Bales -----			--- ¢ per Pound ---		Ths Bales		---- Ths. Bales ----	
1984-5	55.00	81.00	2,957	23.0	649	123	1990-1	50.27	72.90	3,205	21.1	1	4
1985-6	57.30	81.00	7,287	54.9	161	792	1991-2	50.77	72.90	6,312	36.6	8	1
1986-7	55.00	81.00	6,170	64.8	12	24	1992-3	52.35	72.90	8,302	52.9	[3]	8
1987-8	52.25	79.40	5,362	37.0	131	3	1993-4	52.35	72.90	7,721	49.0	[3]	0
1988-9	51.80	75.90	11,231	74.5	66	35	1994-5[2]	50.00	72.90	4,716	24.4	[3]	0
1989-90	50.00	73.40	3,732	32.4	2	27	1995-6[2]	51.92	72.90	2,640	15.1	0	NA

[1] Upland. [2] Preliminary. [3] Less than 500 bales. NA = Not available. *Source: Economic Research Service, U.S. Department of Agriculture*

Cotton Cloth[1] Production in the United States   In Millions of Square Yards

Year	First Quarter	Second Quarter	Third Quarter	Fourth Quarter	Total Year	Year	First Quarter	Second Quarter	Third Quarter	Fourth Quarter	Total Year
1984	1,069	1,031	947	955	4,002	1990	1,202	1,127	1,087	1,048	4,463
1985	1,030	1,002	933	955	3,921	1991	1,081	1,148	1,082	1,093	4,404
1986	1,037	1,103	1,095	1,129	4,364	1992	1,154	1,172	1,130	1,144	4,600
1987	1,158	1,217	1,219	1,178	4,772	1993	1,150	1,144	1,071	1,039	4,403
1988	1,252	1,255	1,072	1,052	4,632	1994[2]	1,073	1,125	1,131	1,143	4,473
1989	1,157	1,192	1,134	1,106	4,589	1995[2]	1,169	1,137	1,083		

[1] Cotton broadwoven goods over 12 inches in width. [2] Preliminary. *Source: Bureau of Census, U.S. Department of Commerce*

United States Cotton Ginnings[1] To: In Thousands of Running Bales

Crop Year	Aug. 1	Aug. 15	Sept. 1	Sept. 15	Oct. 1	Oct. 15	Nov. 1	Nov. 15	Dec. 1	Dec. 15	Jan. 1	Jan. 15	Feb. 1	Total Crop
1983-4	2	NA	315	397	763	1,748	3,348	4,638	6,003	6,880	7,209	7,389	7,476	7,665
1984-5	163	NA	634	780	1,175	2,277	4,321	7,025	8,972	10,478	11,079	11,682	12,319	12,452
1985-6	70	NA	681	1,073	2,431	4,342	6,246	8,216	10,052	11,372	12,365	12,776	12,948	13,063
1986-7	145	NA	624	1,022	2,407	3,618	5,292	6,369	7,491	8,263	8,588	9,093	9,270	9,294
1987-8	1	NA	429	1,242	3,196	5,359	7,531	9,135	11,082	12,588	13,276	13,733	14,177	14,493
1988-9	136	NA	804	1,147	2,279	4,116	6,922	9,535	11,845	13,257	14,248	14,686	14,904	14,939
1989-90	90	NA	382	523	981	2,772	5,948	8,388	10,353	11,246	11,548	11,681	11,771	11,884
1990-1	120	NA	583	1,090	2,616	4,739	7,955	10,207	12,428	13,863	14,516	14,809	14,963	15,064
1991-2	------------	699	------------	983	2,467	4,955	8,351	10,752	13,260	15,067	15,888	16,402	16,765	17,146
1992-3	14	NA	446	740	1,664	4,046	7,584	10,296	12,597	14,083	14,944	15,311	15,527	15,786
1993-4	95	NA	435	748	1,846	4,471	7,975	10,952	13,244	14,695	15,321	15,517	15,590	15,675
1994-5[2]	113	NA	680	943	2,324	5,002	8,878	12,479	15,587	17,465	18,438	18,842	19,028	19,127
1995-6[2]	17	NA	472	898	2,455	4,864	8,454	11,259	14,164	16,071	17,002	17,299	17,402	

[1] Excluding linters. [2] Preliminary. NA = Not available. *Source: National Agricultural Statistics Service, U.S. Department of Agriculture*

U.S. Fiber Prices In Cents Per Pound

Year		Cotton[1]		Rayon[2]		Polyester[3]		Price Ratios[4] in Percent	
		Actual	Raw[5] Equivalent	Actual	Raw[5] Equivalent	Actual	Raw[5] Equivalent	Cotton/ Rayon	Cotton/ Polyester
1983		77.72	86.36	80.25	83.59	73.00	76.04	1.03	1.14
1984		76.06	84.51	84.00	87.50	78.83	82.12	.97	1.03
1985		65.83	73.15	78.83	82.12	66.33	69.10	.89	1.06
1986		60.99	67.77	75.75	78.91	62.33	64.93	.86	1.04
1987		72.71	80.79	81.00	84.38	65.75	68.49	.96	1.18
1988		64.89	72.10	90.67	94.44	73.83	76.91	.77	.94
1989		71.99	79.99	109.75	114.32	85.67	89.24	.70	.90
1990		79.29	88.10	119.92	124.91	82.58	86.02	.71	1.03
1991		79.05	87.83	122.00	127.08	73.50	76.56	.69	1.15
1992		61.92	68.80	114.08	118.84	73.50	76.56	.58	.90
1993		62.43	69.37	111.42	116.06	72.50	75.52	.60	.92
1994		78.69	87.43	103.00	107.29	74.92	78.04	.82	1.12
1995	Jan.	95.17	105.74	104.00	108.33	82.00	85.42	.98	1.24
	Feb.	100.06	111.18	104.00	108.33	86.00	89.58	1.03	1.24
	Mar.	111.91	124.34	104.00	108.33	86.00	89.58	1.15	1.39
	Apr.	113.17	125.74	104.00	108.33	86.00	89.58	1.16	1.40
	May	113.94	126.60	119.00	123.96	86.00	89.58	1.02	1.41
	June	117.65	130.72	119.00	123.96	92.00	95.83	1.06	1.36
	July	100.04	111.16	125.00	130.21	92.00	95.83	.85	1.16
	Aug.	89.71	99.68	125.00	130.21	92.00	95.83	.77	1.04
	Sept.	96.34	107.04	125.00	130.21	92.00	95.83	.82	1.12

[1] SLM-1 1/16" at group B Mill points, net weight. [2] 1.5 and 3.0 denier, regular rayon staples. [3] Reported average market price for 1.5 denier polyester staple for cotton blending. [4] Raw fiber equivalent. [5] Actual prices converted to estimated raw fiber equivalent as follows: cotton, divided by 0.90, rayon and polyester, divided by 0.96. *Source: Economic Research Service, U.S. Department of Agriculture*

Average Producer Price Index of Gray Cotton Boardwovens Index 1982=100

Year	Jan.	Feb.	Mar.	Apr.	May	June	July	Aug.	Sept.	Oct.	Nov.	Dec.	Average
1986	101.6	101.2	100.8	100.7	101.0	101.0	101.2	101.0	101.3	101.2	101.5	101.2	101.1
1987	101.8	101.8	101.9	102.5	103.0	103.3	106.0	103.9	107.1	109.5	110.6	111.5	105.2
1988	112.7	114.3	114.5	115.9	116.2	116.1	115.9	115.6	114.8	111.9	112.5	112.3	114.4
1989	112.4	111.3	110.9	110.9	110.5	110.1	109.4	109.8	109.8	110.8	110.9	113.5	110.9
1990	113.7	113.8	113.8	114.0	114.1	109.9	115.1	115.1	112.3	112.5	116.1	116.4	113.8
1991	113.3	113.6	114.1	114.5	114.9	115.2	115.3	115.3	115.3	115.4	115.7	115.6	114.9
1992	116.9	116.8	116.7	116.7	116.8	117.5	117.3	117.3	117.2	116.9	117.1	117.2	117.0
1993	117.0	116.8	115.9	116.3	115.7	115.7	115.2	115.2	112.5	114.1	114.1	114.9	115.3
1994[1]	109.9	110.8	115.4	115.7	114.9	114.9	115.0	117.5	117.6	118.9	117.2	118.0	115.5
1995[1]	117.8	120.2	120.7	121.6	123.4	123.6	124.0	125.3	125.1	123.4			

[1] Preliminary. *Source: Bureau of Labor Statistics (0337-01), U.S. Department of Commerce*

Cottonseed and Products

Cottonseed production is directly related to the amount of cotton produced. In the 1994-95 season, U.S. cotton production was very large and production of cottonseed rose by 20 percent from 1993-94. The 1995-96 season started off with expectations of a record cotton crop as cotton producers had numerous reasons to expand the acreage they seed to the natural fiber. While acreage increased substantially, it was a poor growing season almost from the start. What initially looked like a crop of 22 million bales turned out closer to 18 million bales, forcing the U.S.D.A. to lower projections of cottonseed production.

USDA estimated cottonseed stocks at the beginning of the 1995-96 season at 551,000 short tons, up 28 percent from the 1994-95 season. Cottonseed production was put at 7.37 million tons, down 3 percent from 1994-95. The total supply of cottonseed was therefore 7.93 million tons, down 1 percent. The cottonseed crush was estimated at 4.1 million short tons, up close to 4 percent from 1994-95. Exports of cottonseed were 150,000 tons, down over 35 percent from the previous season. Cottonseed used for other purposes, mostly whole-seed feeding, was 3.4 million tons, up just over 2 percent. Total use of cottonseed was forecast at 7.5 million tons, up 19 percent. Projected stocks of cottonseed on July 31, 1996 were projected to fall over 45 percent to 300,000 tons.

U.S. stocks of cottonseed oil on October 1, 1995 were 90 million pounds. For 1995-96, cottonseed oil production was put at 1.31 billion pounds, down marginally from the previous year. Domestic use of cottonseed oil was put at 975 million pounds, about the same as in 1994-95. Exports were forecast to be 340 million pounds. Stocks of cottonseed oil on September 30, 1996 were projected at 90 million pounds.

U.S. cottonseed meal stocks on October 1, 1995 were 95,000 short tons with production put at 1.85 million tons. Domestic use was 1.7 million tons, up close to 2 percent from the prior season. Exports were projected to be 115,000 tons with stocks on September 30, 1996 being 95,000 tons.

World Production of Cottonseed   In Thousands of Metric Tons

Crop Year	Argentina	Australia	Brazil	China	Colombia	Egypt	Greece	India	Mexico	Pakistan	South Africa	Spain	Turkey	United States	Former U.S.S.R.	World Total
1987-8	467	445	1,620	7,853	235	584	255	3,110	414	2,936	97	138	859	5,234	4,446	31,759
1988-9	367	449	1,338	7,676	229	532	390	3,600	491	2,852	119	195	920	5,499	4,779	32,699
1989-90	495	493	1,255	7,008	201	498	440	4,610	255	2,911	99	100	987	4,243	4,600	31,242
1990-1	538	686	1,352	8,340	265	504	365	3,980	294	3,275	108	139	977	5,415	4,550	33,919
1991-2	435	724	1,313	10,499	298	491	355	4,090	307	4,352	87	137	878	6,283	4,283	37,691
1992-3	275	528	800	8,340	178	571	410	4,740	52	3,080	36	104	905	5,652	3,557	32,196
1993-4[1]	390	466	920	6,655	107	655	460	4,120	31	2,740	26	47	892	5,754	3,600	29,688
1994-5[1]	610	447	1,020	7,727	90	430	656	4,590	140	2,958	48	59	956	6,898	3,360	32,892
1995-6[2]	770	417	1,000	7,500	-----	415	640	4,750	270	3,650	42	38	1,150	6,585	3,350	34,160

[1] Preliminary. [2] Estimate. *Source: The Oil World*

Salient Statistics of Cottonseed in the United States

Crop Year Beginning Aug. 1	Supply: Stocks	Supply: Production	Total Supply	Disappearance: Crush	Disappearance: Exports	Disappearance: Other	Total Disappearance	Farm Price $/Ton	Value of Production Mil. $	Products Produced: Oil Millions Lbs.	Products Produced: Meal Thousand Sh. Tons
	In Thousands of Short Tons										
1987-8	189	5,769	5,958	3,396	50	2,153	5,599	83.0	474.7	1,204	1,647
1988-9	359	6,062	6,421	3,730	39	1,987	5,756	118.0	718.3	1,243	1,689
1989-90	665	4,677	5,342	2,974	46	1,957	4,977	105.0	492.7	1,039	1,327
1990-1	366	5,969	6,337	3,369	53	2,264	5,686	121.0	722.3	1,154	1,691
1991-2	651	6,926	7,579	3,981	161	2,977	7,119	71.0	492.3	1,279	1,765
1992-3	460	6,230	6,690	3,629	192	2,504	6,325	98.0	608.4	1,137	1,533
1993-4	365	6,343	6,708	3,470	157	2,649	6,276	113.0	714.4	1,119	1,563
1994-5[1]	432	7,604	8,036	3,947	232	3,306	7,485	101.0	768.0	1,312	1,830
1995-6[2]	551	7,374	7,475	3,950	100	3,200	7,250	105-118		1,265	1,780

[1] Preliminary. [2] Estimate. *Source: Economic Research Service, U.S. Department of Agriculture*

Average Wholesale Price of Cottonseed Meal (41% Solvent) at Memphis   In Dollars Per Short Ton

Year	Jan.	Feb.	Mar.	Apr.	May	June	July	Aug.	Sept.	Oct.	Nov.	Dec.	Average
1987	146.25	138.10	128.00	133.75	149.60	154.50	166.90	163.80	141.50	150.60	177.50	195.00	153.79
1988	187.50	160.00	141.00	143.10	147.50	230.00	223.75	181.00	205.00	212.50	293.00	199.40	193.65
1989	200.50	191.25	196.25	184.40	161.50	163.30	157.50	172.00	190.00	181.25	180.00	180.00	179.83
1990	160.00	150.00	146.25	150.00	155.00	147.50	161.50	169.50	178.75	163.00	147.50	141.25	155.85
1991	125.00	118.10	125.00	122.50	118.10	117.20	127.50	130.90	133.10	131.00	144.40	162.00	129.57
1992	156.25	140.10	124.25	121.25	127.50	132.50	133.75	146.90	163.00	154.40	157.50	174.50	144.33
1993	164.40	149.40	153.50	149.00	143.10	153.00	170.30	178.50	193.75	173.10	181.00	180.00	165.75
1994	170.30	173.10	174.00	166.25	157.75	154.10	152.50	144.50	145.00	134.40	120.50	114.20	150.55
1995[1]	106.75	97.50	100.30	98.10	92.75	108.75	116.90	116.50	137.60	153.25	165.00	185.83	123.27

[1] Preliminary. *Source: Economic Research Service, U.S. Department of Agriculture*

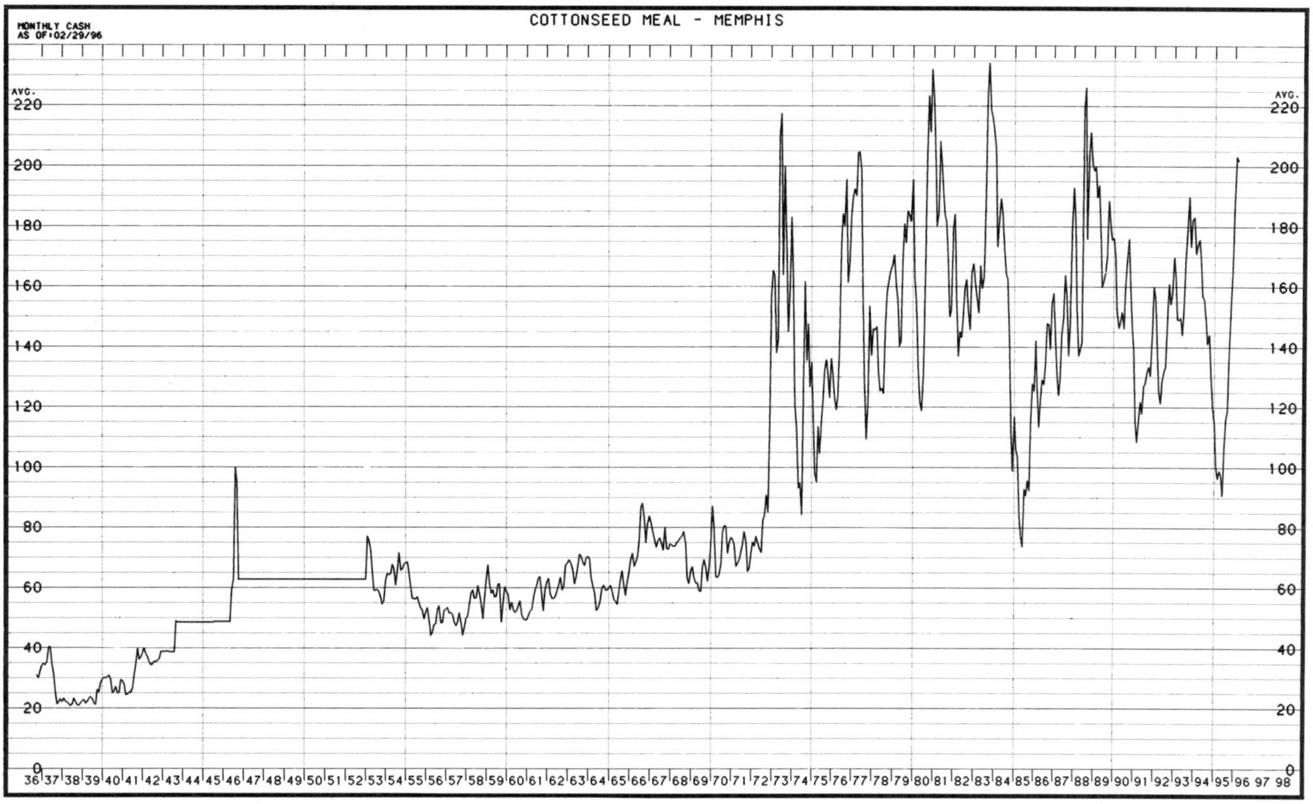

Supply & Distribution of Cottonseed Oil in the United States In Millions of Pounds

Crop Year Beginning Oct. 1	Supply: Stocks	Supply: Production	Supply: Imports	Supply: Total Supply	Disappearance: Domestic	Disappearance: Exports	Disappearance: Total	Per Capita Consump. of Salad & Ck. Oils -- In Lbs.--	Utilization Food Uses: Shortening	Utilization Food Uses: Salad & Cooking Oils	Utilization Food Uses: Total	Prices U.S.[3] (Crude) $/Tonne	Prices Rott[4] (Cif) $/Tonne
1989-90	147	1,039	13	1,199	765	354	1,119	24.0	235	507	801	514	650
1990-1	80	1,154	3	1,237	851	249	1,100	24.2	272	438	777	492	614
1991-2	137	1,279	18	1,434	1,075	281	1,356	25.2	247	375	685	443	545
1992-3	78	1,137	38	1,253	995	177	1,172	25.6	238	353	640	550	688
1993-4	81	1,119	26	1,226	873	248	1,121	25.1	217	289	558	613	749
1994-5[1]	106	1,312	0	1,417	998	338	1,335	24.4	217	262	532	568	671
1995-6[2]	82	1,265	8	1,355	980	295	1,275					607	645

[1] Preliminary. [2] Estimate. [3] Valley Points F.O.B.; Tank Cars. [4] Rotterdam;US PBY *Source: Economic Research Service, U.S. Department of Agriculture.*

U.S. Consumption of Crude Cottonseed Oil in Refining In Millions of Pounds

Year	Oct.	Nov.	Dec.	Jan.	Feb	Mar.	Apr.	May	June	July	Aug.	Sept.	Total
1989-90	87.5	121.1	121.6	133.7	103.4	114.2	83.8	79.1	68.0	53.3	62.2	56.5	1,084.4
1990-1	79.4	99.7	92.8		264.7			265.9			227.7		1,030.2
1991-2		265.0		104.6	108.9	101.3	88.7	76.0	84.2	84.6	72.7	48.6	1,034.6
1992-3	75.7	93.3	95.5	107.3	85.1	77.5	92.8	79.3	74.7	65.1	68.6	57.6	972.5
1993-4	82.7	113.0	103.8	110.8	96.7	111.5	69.6	74.8	73.2	74.6	88.4	64.2	1,063.3
1994-5	81.9	97.2	109.8	107.7	87.1	96.2	87.2	72.8	73.4	76.0	83.3	71.6	1,044.4
1995-6[1]	76.1	91.8											

[1] Preliminary. *Source: Bureau of Census, U.S. Department of Commerce*

U.S. Exports of Cottonseed Oil (Crude & Refined) In Thousands of Pounds

Year	Jan.	Feb.	Mar.	Apr.	May	June	July	Aug.	Sept.	Oct.	Nov.	Dec	Total
1989	47,178	41,019	49,938	11,840	16,583	14,094	38,654	63,633	72,349	49,077	17,030	40,066	461,461
1990	34,922	37,220	39,152	14,018	39,665	35,560	16,860	21,412	8,721	18,285	9,452	46,463	321,730
1991		55,378			67,155			52,469			38,291		213,293
1992	68,977	69,631	19,704	19,753	13,071	13,443	16,027	7,947	13,090	8,101	4,625	17,308	271,677
1993	23,904	14,238	6,294	27,370	25,849	17,685	5,066	7,065	19,246	7,079	15,103	14,075	182,974
1994	32,011	11,093	21,156	26,595	34,775	11,023	24,000	24,000	24,250	17,487	33,385	36,613	296,388
1995[1]	18,808	43,454	48,471	34,500	28,775	22,692	18,490	11,973	NA	9,896	30,268		

[1] Preliminary. NA = Not available. *Source: Economic Research Service, U.S. Department of Agriculture*

COTTONSEED AND PRODUCTS

Cottonseed Crushed (Consumption) in the United States   In Thousands of Short Tons

Year	Aug.	Sept.	Oct.	Nov.	Dec.	Jan.	Feb.	Mar.	Apr.	May	June	July	Total
1987-8	71.4	137.7	251.8	344.2	363.2	373.4	352.4	340.1	310.7	312.5	275.5	263.6	3,397
1988-9	216.8	179.5	299.3	375.3	376.7	399.7	325.4	383.3	336.6	321.7	287.0	228.9	3,730
1989-90	218.8	150.6	273.4	338.3	335.1	346.6	285.1	254.8	245.5	201.5	194.9	129.3	2,974
1990-1	157.3	176.1	274.9	339.4	320.8	------------	973.0	------------	------------	864.5	------------	--------	3,106
1991-2	813.6	------------	---------	1,145.2	------------	420.6	378.3	381.3	297.8	245.4	292.1	270.2	4,245
1992-3	245.7	162.9	323.2	353.3	372.1	413.3	334.6	324.1	323.8	296.4	242.7	237.2	3,629
1993-4	182.9	162.6	300.4	391.4	375.0	391.0	335.2	358.6	265.7	257.7	239.4	210.2	3,470
1994-5[1]	192.1	195.5	343.9	386.2	397.5	404.6	360.5	391.0	345.4	304.0	316.5	310.0	3,947
1995-6[1]	264.4	245.5	337.1	386.7	362.4								

[1] Preliminary.   *Source: Economic Research Service, U.S. Department of Agriculture*

Production of Cottonseed Cake and Meal in the United States   In Thousands of Short Tons

Year	Aug.	Sept.	Oct.	Nov.	Dec.	Jan.	Feb.	Mar.	Apr.	May	June	July	Total
1987-8	32.2	58.3	121.7	156.9	169.3	169.4	160.2	155.7	144.0	144.0	124.7	120.6	1,557
1988-9	100.7	80.1	135.4	170.0	172.5	183.2	151.6	175.3	152.7	157.6	126.7	106.1	1,712
1989-90	98.5	69.3	126.1	154.9	152.6	157.1	130.6	116.6	111.9	90.7	86.6	56.6	1,352
1990-1	68.7	77.4	128.2	160.1	148.8	------------	456.2	------------	------------	409.1	------------	-------	1,449
1991-2	388.6	------------	------------	533.9	------------	192.6	170.5	173.5	138.2	111.7	129.9	127.8	1,967
1992-3	111.2	76.0	143.7	150.2	160.5	176.2	146.6	136.4	140.9	126.1	103.0	101.0	1,572
1993-4	76.7	71.5	130.1	172.2	166.6	161.8	151.8	164.0	119.6	116.1	106.9	93.4	1,531
1994-5[1]	90.6	89.4	154.2	171.5	176.9	184.1	162.2	174.3	154.2	137.4	143.9	137.2	1,776
1995-6[1]	120.1	113.6	159.9	178.2	162.9								

[1] Preliminary.   *Source: Bureau of Census, U.S. Department of Commerce*

U.S. Production of Crude Cottonseed Oil[2]   In Millions of Pounds

Year	Aug.	Sept.	Oct.	Nov.	Dec.	Jan.	Feb.	Mar.	Apr.	May	June	July	Total
1987-8	22.6	46.9	84.0	118.2	124.8	125.7	115.8	113.2	104.4	105.8	91.2	91.0	1,144
1988-9	72.7	56.9	98.6	125.3	125.0	129.3	106.0	127.1	111.7	109.7	94.5	76.6	1,233
1989-90	81.9	56.8	97.6	115.3	117.4	118.4	98.2	89.4	88.8	74.7	75.4	48.0	1,062
1990-1	58.7	57.6	86.2	104.0	102.3	------------	309.9	------------	------------	283.0	------------	------	1,002
1991-2	263.7	-----------	------------	398.9	------------	137.4	127.2	121.5	97.5	79.3	91.8	91.3	1,409
1992-3	77.8	56.8	99.5	110.2	117.6	134.7	107.2	104.9	101.7	96.1	77.7	76.5	1,161
1993-4	59.1	51.7	93.5	122.2	117.5	124.7	99.9	119.6	85.3	85.2	78.4	69.8	1,107
1994-5[1]	61.7	61.0	109.8	122.6	125.6	133.4	115.6	125.2	110.4	97.7	102.4	96.6	1,262
1995-6[1]	87.8	84.3	105.2	121.6	111.7								

[1] Preliminary.   [2] Not seasonally adjusted.   *Source: Bureau of Census, U.S. Department of Commerce*

United States Production of Refined Cottonseed Oil   In Millions of Pounds

Year	Aug.	Sept.	Oct.	Nov.	Dec.	Jan.	Feb.	Mar.	Apr.	May	June	July	Total
1987-8	45.8	56.9	71.5	110.3	120.9	119.9	117.8	132.6	116.5	119.2	103.3	109.6	1,224
1988-9	83.2	61.7	94.1	124.8	127.8	139.7	121.9	137.0	116.3	119.1	102.8	71.6	1,300
1989-90	86.6	69.1	79.8	111.8	111.6	122.3	94.4	109.7	80.4	74.8	65.0	50.8	1,056
1990-1	57.8	53.7	75.4	96.0	90.0	------------	253.9	------------	------------	256.3	------------	-------	883
1991-2	209.3	------------	------------	205.0	------------	103.2	105.6	97.9	85.6	73.4	82.1	81.1	1,043
1992-3	69.3	46.3	72.6	90.2	91.9	103.1	82.0	74.5	88.8	75.6	70.8	62.4	928
1993-4	65.1	54.6	79.4	109.1	100.6	107.2	93.4	107.8	66.9	71.6	70.0	72.2	998
1994-5[1]	86.3	62.9	80.0	94.4	106.2	104.2	94.4	92.6	84.2	70.1	70.7	72.6	1,019
1995-6[1]	80.5	69.0	74.0	89.5									

[1] Preliminary.   *Source: Bureau of Census, U.S. Department of Commerce*

U.S. Stocks of Cottonseed Oil (Crude & Refined) at End of Month   In Millions of Pounds

Year	Aug.	Sept.	Oct.	Nov.	Dec.	Jan.	Feb.	Mar.	Apr.	May	June	July
1987-8	127.3	90.2	107.2	136.1	169.8	210.0	197.6	184.7	177.2	197.8	175.6	176.0
1988-9	172.9	160.4	163.9	188.6	206.1	266.3	274.0	276.6	263.7	249.2	266.7	247.6
1989-90	191.4	147.3	138.3	163.2	189.6	186.8	180.9	174.8	168.8	156.1	135.6	111.8
1990-1	75.9	80.4	83.0	93.5	102.7	------------	145.8	------------	------------	124.3	------------	-------
1991-2	136.3	------------	------------	163.3	------------	193.1	183.6	180.3	171.5	154.0	139.9	119.8
1992-3	94.3	81.0	98.4	101.7	123.2	148.4	152.6	167.1	157.0	159.2	144.8	143.8
1993-4	85.8	54.6	79.4	109.1	100.6	107.2	93.4	107.8	66.9	71.6	70.0	72.1
1994-5[1]	112.4	105.6	103.5	117.0	114.7	122.2	150.5	129.9	120.8	95.7	96.9	92.2
1995-6[1]	87.8	82.1	82.6	89.9								

[1] Preliminary.   *Source:Bureau of Census, U.S. Department of Commerce*

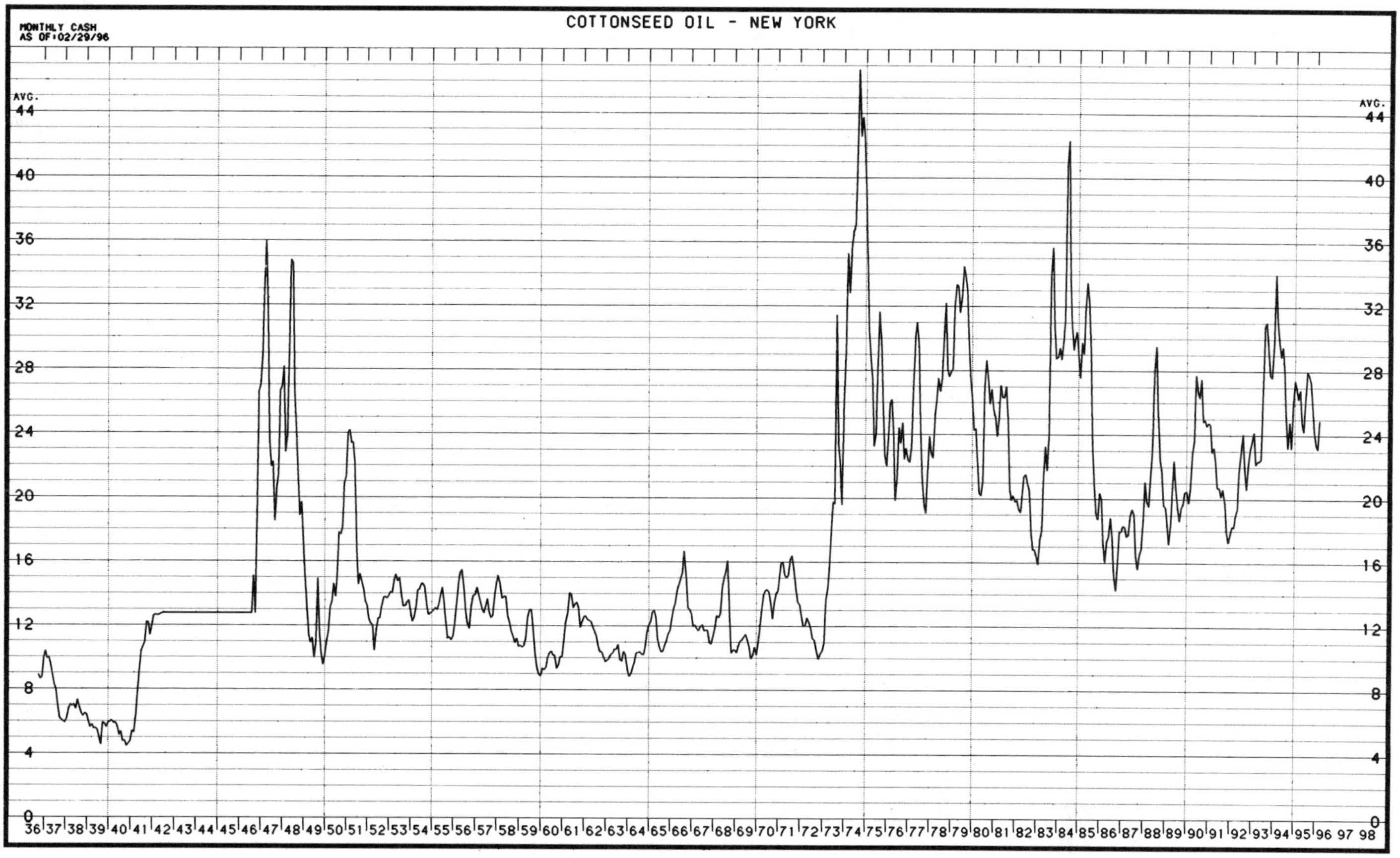

Average Price of Crude Cottonseed Oil, F.O.B. Valley Points[1] (Tank Cars) In Cents Per Pound

Year	Jan.	Feb.	Mar.	Apr.	May	June	July	Aug.	Sept.	Oct.	Nov.	Dec.	Average
1985	27.30	30.10	30.10	32.30	33.30	32.50	29.10	23.70	20.60	18.25	18.88	20.60	26.39
1986	19.88	17.63	15.75	17.50	17.69	17.90	15.38	17.44	14.25	15.38	17.44	17.75	17.00
1987	18.38	18.56	17.85	17.88	18.94	19.25	19.00	16.70	15.44	16.75	17.00	18.35	17.84
1988	21.31	20.19	19.60	21.00	22.88	26.65	30.25	15.00	23.00	21.44	19.70	19.94	21.75
1989	19.19	17.56	20.25	21.06	21.80	20.25	19.63	18.60	19.75	19.95	20.81	20.50	19.95
1990	19.95	20.19	22.88	22.83	26.90	26.94	26.00	24.60	24.88	24.80	24.19	24.75	24.08
1991	23.75	22.88	23.00	22.13	20.67	20.31	20.50	21.00	19.88	17.98	17.41	18.07	20.63
1992	18.50	18.13	19.25	19.38	21.38	22.58	24.45	21.86	21.04	22.17	22.96	23.91	21.30
1993	24.09	22.03	22.24	22.55	22.70	26.76	30.74	30.45	28.98	24.79	26.69	30.39	26.03
1994	33.16	29.96	29.60	29.06	29.66	27.55	24.29	23.71	24.51	23.64	24.85	25.50	27.12
1995	26.41	25.63	26.41	24.00	24.24	26.72	28.26	27.09	26.50	28.12	26.88	26.10	26.36

[1] Southeastern mills. *Source: Economic Research Service, U.S Department of Agriculture*

U.S. Exports of Cottonseed Oil to Important Countries In Thousands of Metric Tons

Year	Canada	Dominican Republic	Egypt	Guat-emala	Japan	Mexico	Nether-lands	Salvador	South Korea	Turkey	Venez-uela	Total
1984	3.8	4.5	50.3	-----	11.7	.2	3.1	5.2	2.3	-----	79.0	171.3
1985	2.5	7.6	57.1	9.8	24.9	.3	5.8	19.4	2.3	-----	51.9	191.4
1986	2.9	2.2	16.5	11.6	27.3	9.3	8.0	25.9	5.7	-----	50.9	173.7
1987	3.2	5.0	1.9	2.4	15.7	3.1	2.9	15.6	7.8	-----	47.3	109.9
1988	4.8	3.1	29.6	.5	21.5	8.2	2.7	26.3	7.7	13.5	46.2	167.8
1989	6.6	5.1	39.4	6.0	34.3	3.2	3.4	30.5	21.0	2.0	53.7	209.4
1990	6.8	6.0	14.7	.4	36.7	1.4	2.9	21.0	36.0	-----	9.2	136.3
1991	7.8	2.1	14.7	-----	24.1	4.8	3.4	13.0	13.0	5.5	4.2	97.0
1992	11.3	1.0	8.2	3.2	15.3	8.5	17.4	26.5	10.9	7.0	3.7	123.3
1993	10.9	-----	-----	.5	17.6	5.8	.2	30.8	6.6	.5	1.5	83.1
1994[1]	10.8	-----	7.5	12.3	29.8	10.3	1.9	26.1	16.9	-----	4.5	135.7

[1] Prelminary. *Source: The Oil World*

Currencies

The world's major currencies generally strengthened against the U.S. Dollar during the first half of 1995, reaching a high in early spring, then weakening in the second half with the lows set in mid-summer. On balance, however, prices traversed relatively narrow trading ranges during much of the year, with the exception of the Japanese Yen. The U.S. Dollar Index began the year with a value near 90, basis nearby futures on FINEX, and closed 1995 around 85. The year's range was 90 to 80, but for much of 1995 the index traded between 80 and 85.

The dominant economic feature in the FOREX market in the closing months of 1995 was the shrinking U.S. trade deficit which helped buoy the Dollar's value. During the fourth quarter, the monthly trade deficit averaged $8 billion versus an $11.2 billion monthly average in the second and third quarters. Exports were strong despite slowing economies in Europe, Canada, Mexico and Japan. Exports to Western Europe were up 13 percent, and up nearly 20 percent to Japan even though their economy on a year-over-year basis was the weakest among the industrialized nations. U.S. exports also moved at a hefty pace to Latin America and Asia. Imports, meanwhile, fell due to the slowing U.S. economy. Imports have generally accounted for about 12 percent of U.S. demand for goods and services.

The U.S. budget deficit erodes confidence in the Dollar's value, but when seen as a percentage of GDP, the U.S. deficit is the lowest among the G-7 nations. Still, the budget impasse between the U.S. Congress and the President in late 1995 triggered a partial shutdown of the federal government and pressured the Dollar's value.

The D-Mark closed 1995 at $.6988, basis nearby futures, with the year's high and low of $.7443 and $.6402 both registered by April 19. Germany's economy slowed and the Bundesbank responded with cuts in key lending rates. German exports dropped, partially due to high manufacturing production costs that damaged competitiveness, but while the D-Mark slipped against the U.S. Dollar in late 1995, its value held firm against other EC countries which may see exports drop further. The Swiss-Franc tends to mirror the action in the D-Mark. The Swiss economy also slowed in 1995, primarily due to a perception that the Franc was overvalued on a trade-weighted basis. This served to hurt both exports and tourism. The odds favor increased pressure on the S-Franc against the Dollar in 1996.

The British-Pound closed 1995 at $1.5514 against the U.S. Dollar, basis nearby futures. This was near the low end of 1995's $1.6570 to $1.5200 trading range. The U.K.'s economy slowed in 1995 while the trade deficit widened sharply. Contributing to the late 1995 pressure on the B-Pound was the market's perception that the U.K.'s government 1996 economic projections were overly optimistic.

Although the Canadian-Dollar moved within a 3 cent range during the second half of 1995, the volatility was pronounced. The economy slowed, but the FOREX market's attention was focused on the nation's political troubles, notably the Quebec separatism movement which was defeated in an election. The economic outlook seems to favor some improvement in 1996, which if realized may stabilize the C-Dollar's value.

The Japanese-Yen was the most volatile of the major currencies in 1995. Using nearest futures against the U.S. Dollar it moved from .9925¢ on January 5 to 1.2625¢ on April 19. The entire gain was then erased by September 15 when the market bottomed at .9610¢. The Yen ended 1995 at .9773¢ against the Dollar, but fared better against the European currencies. Still, the outlook for the Yen against the Dollar was not promising as 1996 unfolded: Japan's trade surplus is declining, the economy has slowed and capital is flowing out of the country as interest rates are low. Also, Japan's banks are very slowly writing off a series of bad loans, the impact of which suggests the banks will play a diminished role in revitalizing the economy.

Futures Markets

The Chicago Mercantile Exchange's International Monetary Market (IMM) trades futures and options on the British Pound, Swiss Franc, Deutsche Mark, Japanese Yen, Canadian Dollar, Australian Dollar, and the Mexican Peso. The exchange also lists a D-Mark rolling spot contract and a D-Mark forward contract. Additional currency futures are likely to begin trading there in 1996. Chicago's MidAmerica Commodity Exchange (MidAm) trades smaller futures contracts on many of the IMM's currencies. The FINEX division of the New York Cotton Exchange (NYCE) trades futures and options on a composite Dollar Index and also offers crossrate futures contracts: D-Mark/J-Yen, D-Mark/French Franc and D-Mark/B-Pound. Currency futures and options are also traded on the Philadelphia Board of Trade (PBOT).

Monthly Close of the Knight-Ridder CRB Currency Futures Index 1977 = 100

Year	January	February	March	April	May	June	July	August	September	October	November	December
1985	81.6	78.0	84.2	83.4	84.8	85.5	91.4	90.3	93.9	95.9	98.7	98.8
1986	99.5	103.9	103.3	108.5	104.3	109.6	112.4	113.2	112.3	109.2	112.0	114.4
1987	118.5	119.5	123.3	125.7	123.4	122.9	120.6	123.8	122.6	128.7	134.8	141.3
1988	134.0	133.6	138.3	137.0	134.5	129.2	127.1	125.1	126.7	131.3	136.3	133.7
1989	128.2	130.0	126.0	125.5	119.3	120.2	125.2	119.7	123.6	122.6	123.9	126.1
1990	127.3	126.3	124.9	125.8	127.5	129.1	134.8	136.6	137.4	141.5	141.8	140.8
1991	142.8	139.8	129.3	130.6	129.0	125.5	128.0	128.3	132.4	132.5	134.5	138.8
1992	134.4	132.0	129.8	130.2	134.0	137.9	140.6	145.6	141.1	132.7	128.9	127.6
1993	127.4	127.2	130.2	133.5	134.7	129.4	129.6	130.7	131.8	129.3	128.6	127.7
1994	129.6	131.0	131.8	133.2	132.3	137.1	136.3	136.9	140.2	143.2	138.2	138.7
1995	139.4	142.8	151.4	152.3	150.2	151.4	150.3	143.9	146.2	146.3	142.9	144.1

Source: Knight-Ridder Financial

WEEKLY NEAREST FUTURES
AS OF:03/15/96
BRITISH POUND - IMM
USD/GBP
2.2
2.1
2.0
1.9
1.8
1.7
1.6
1.5
1.4
1.3
1.2
1.1
1990
1991
1992
1993
1994
1995

WEEKLY NEAREST FUTURES
AS OF:03/15/96
CANADIAN DOLLAR - IMM
USD/CAD
.88
.86
.84
.82
.80
.78
.76
.74
.72
.70
.68
.66
1990
1991
1992
1993
1994
1995

CURRENCIES

DEUTSCHE MARK - IMM
WEEKLY NEAREST FUTURES
AS OF:03/15/96
USD/DEM
.88
.84
.80
.76
.72
.68
.64
.60
.56
.52
.48
.44
1990
1991
1992
1993
1994
1995

JAPANESE YEN - IMM
WEEKLY NEAREST FUTURES
AS OF:03/15/96
USD/JPY
1.25
1.20
1.15
1.10
1.05
1.00
.95
.90
.85
.80
.75
.70
1990
1991
1992
1993
1994
1995

WEEKLY NEAREST FUTURES
AS OF:03/15/96
SWISS FRANC - IMM
USD/CHF
1.00
.96
.92
.88
.84
.80
.76
.72
.68
.64
.60
.56
1990
1991
1992
1993
1994
1995
M J J A S O N D J F M A M J J A S O N D J F M A M J J A S O N D J F M A M J J A S O N D J F M A M J J A S O N D J F M A M J J A S O N D J F M A M J

WEEKLY CASH
AS OF:03/15/96
KR-CRB CURRENCY INDEX
(1967=100)
KR-CRB Currencies Index
5 Futures Markets
(1977=100)
British Pound
Canadian Dollar
Deutsche Mark
Japanese Yen
Swiss Franc
INDEX
VALUE
170
165
160
155
150
145
140
135
130
125
120
115
1990
1991
1992
1993
1994
1995
M J J A S O N D J F M A M J J A S O N D J F M A M J J A S O N D J F M A M J J A S O N D J F M A M J J A S O N D J F M A M J J A S O N D J F M A M J

CURRENCIES

Canadian Dollars per U.S. Dollar

Year	January	February	March	April	May	June	July	August	September	October	November	December	Average
1988	1.284	1.268	1.249	1.235	1.237	1.217	1.208	1.224	1.227	1.206	1.218	1.196	1.231
1989	1.191	1.189	1.195	1.189	1.193	1.199	1.189	1.176	1.192	1.202	1.169	1.161	1.187
1990	1.172	1.197	1.180	1.168	1.170	1.170	1.160	1.150	1.160	1.160	1.164	1.160	1.168
1991	1.156	1.155	1.157	1.154	1.150	1.144	1.124	1.145	1.139	1.121	1.131	1.145	1.143
1992	1.157	1.218	1.192	1.187	1.199	1.196	1.192	1.191	1.221	1.244	1.268	1.271	1.211
1993	1.277	1.260	1.247	1.262	1.269	1.279	1.282	1.308	1.321	1.325	1.316	1.331	1.290
1994	1.318	1.342	1.365	1.382	1.381	1.383	1.382	1.378	1.354	1.350	1.365	1.390	1.366
1995	1.412	1.400	1.407	1.375	1.361	1.377	1.361	1.355	1.350	1.345	1.353	1.369	1.372

Source: Knight-Ridder Financial

German (Deutsche) Marks per U.S. Dollar

Year	January	February	March	April	May	June	July	August	September	October	November	December	Average
1988	1.654	1.697	1.676	1.671	1.693	1.757	1.846	1.888	1.867	1.817	1.748	1.756	1.756
1989	1.836	1.851	1.869	1.869	1.946	1.979	1.889	1.927	1.949	1.866	1.766	1.736	1.874
1990	1.692	1.677	1.704	1.688	1.660	1.680	1.640	1.570	1.570	1.540	1.486	1.498	1.617
1991	1.509	1.481	1.612	1.703	1.718	1.782	1.783	1.743	2.122	1.686	1.620	1.561	1.693
1992	1.580	1.619	1.659	1.649	1.621	1.572	1.489	1.446	1.449	1.486	1.587	1.583	1.562
1993	1.614	1.643	1.646	1.594	1.605	1.654	1.714	1.693	1.620	1.640	1.700	1.711	1.653
1994	1.742	1.734	1.691	1.697	1.656	1.627	1.571	1.564	1.549	1.519	1.541	1.571	1.622
1995	1.531	1.500	1.404	1.379	1.409	1.399	1.387	1.446	1.460	1.413	1.418	1.440	1.432

Source: Knight-Ridder Financial

Japanese Yen per U.S. Dollar

Year	January	February	March	April	May	June	July	August	September	October	November	December	Average
1988	127.6	129.1	127.0	124.9	124.7	127.4	133.0	133.8	134.3	128.7	123.2	123.6	128.1
1989	127.4	127.7	130.6	132.0	137.9	144.0	140.4	141.4	144.9	141.4	143.4	143.7	137.9
1990	145.0	145.7	153.2	158.4	156.2	153.8	149.0	147.4	138.5	129.6	128.2	133.9	144.9
1991	133.7	130.5	137.4	137.1	138.0	139.6	137.6	136.9	134.8	130.5	129.7	128.0	134.5
1992	125.3	127.7	132.8	133.5	130.7	126.7	125.7	126.1	122.6	121.2	123.8	123.9	126.7
1993	124.9	120.8	117.0	112.2	110.1	107.3	107.6	103.7	105.4	107.0	107.8	109.9	111.1
1994	111.3	106.2	105.0	103.4	103.8	102.4	98.7	99.9	98.8	98.4	98.1	100.1	102.2
1995	99.7	98.1	90.4	83.6	85.0	84.6	87.2	94.7	100.5	100.8	101.9	101.8	94.0

Source: Knight-Ridder Financial

Swiss Francs per U.S. Dollar

Year	January	February	March	April	May	June	July	August	September	October	November	December	Average
1988	1.349	1.393	1.387	1.383	1.413	1.463	1.534	1.584	1.575	1.539	1.463	1.480	1.464
1989	1.562	1.574	1.611	1.647	1.729	1.706	1.629	1.663	1.687	1.632	1.618	1.567	1.635
1990	1.518	1.489	1.513	1.485	1.420	1.425	1.391	1.309	1.306	1.281	1.256	1.280	1.389
1991	1.271	1.269	1.389	1.438	1.456	1.530	1.551	1.520	1.482	1.480	1.436	1.383	1.434
1992	1.403	1.457	1.507	1.518	1.490	1.423	1.332	1.295	1.276	1.319	1.428	1.423	1.406
1993	1.478	1.520	1.520	1.457	1.447	1.477	1.514	1.495	1.416	1.442	1.497	1.463	1.477
1994	1.471	1.456	1.430	1.436	1.412	1.372	1.326	1.318	1.290	1.264	1.297	1.328	1.366
1995	1.287	1.269	1.169	1.136	1.168	1.156	1.154	1.196	1.187	1.144	1.144	1.162	1.181

Source: Knight-Ridder Financial

British Pounds per U.S. Dollar

Year	January	February	March	April	May	June	July	August	September	October	November	December	Average
1988	1.799	1.757	1.834	1.877	1.868	1.777	1.704	1.696	1.684	1.738	1.812	1.824	1.781
1989	1.774	1.753	1.713	1.701	1.628	1.554	1.626	1.593	1.572	1.586	1.573	1.597	1.639
1990	1.651	1.696	1.625	1.638	1.678	1.711	1.810	1.901	1.880	1.948	1.964	1.921	1.785
1991	1.935	1.964	1.821	1.751	1.726	1.649	1.648	1.684	1.725	1.721	1.778	1.831	1.769
1992	1.811	1.778	1.725	1.756	1.810	1.856	1.919	1.945	1.851	1.655	1.527	1.550	1.765
1993	1.533	1.438	1.462	1.547	1.549	1.509	1.497	1.493	1.525	1.503	1.481	1.490	1.502
1994	1.493	1.479	1.492	1.483	1.504	1.526	1.545	1.542	1.565	1.607	1.586	1.558	1.532
1995	1.574	1.573	1.600	1.609	1.589	1.596	1.596	1.567	1.560	1.578	1.561	1.541	1.579

Source: International Monetary Market (Chicago)

Average Open Interest of Canadian Dollar Futures in Chicago In Contracts

Year	January	February	March	April	May	June	July	August	September	October	November	December
1988	22,411	24,244	22,965	24,095	27,747	35,787	33,207	28,513	22,645	23,138	19,548	24,844
1989	24,221	27,726	23,102	21,146	24,900	24,807	20,007	31,041	27,206	25,903	29,645	29,116
1990	26,426	29,204	23,848	24,048	33,823	30,809	39,843	42,092	34,998	29,434	31,250	25,272
1991	29,072	28,214	25,550	24,894	29,310	33,136	25,113	25,310	30,909	28,805	27,453	22,311
1992	19,724	24,020	24,118	21,354	24,020	22,860	24,773	27,665	28,221	27,827	28,025	24,923
1993	20,410	24,376	25,877	23,639	27,438	29,784	29,385	45,397	40,639	43,476	32,469	28,879
1994	28,277	38,157	48,411	42,730	44,363	42,845	35,370	39,582	49,312	40,706	42,353	59,763
1995	55,863	44,677	33,706	45,394	47,832	36,677	44,930	42,629	49,526	43,032	40,047	40,592

Source: International Monetary Market (Chicago)

Average Open Interest of Deutsche Mark Futures in Chicago In Contracts

Year	January	February	March	April	May	June	July	August	September	October	November	December
1988	32,849	45,974	42,134	37,759	53,511	60,575	48,574	60,803	48,777	46,456	53,695	46,461
1989	51,439	65,251	52,869	52,693	70,062	72,766	62,365	66,520	65,666	70,976	91,393	93,491
1990	63,745	73,216	72,357	63,058	70,475	65,113	64,765	72,684	58,241	61,839	76,650	67,322
1991	51,211	73,463	72,824	71,737	79,162	80,318	68,046	73,860	70,525	59,236	85,248	77,632
1992	60,390	69,246	76,614	74,945	85,123	74,761	79,297	93,027	82,287	87,679	126,380	132,676
1993	134,432	140,184	126,046	118,747	131,816	159,334	165,356	147,140	108,958	103,720	135,960	145,414
1994	146,742	144,594	118,301	99,177	125,321	108,586	94,767	106,647	108,742	88,784	101,376	101,548
1995	79,425	92,975	79,700	61,954	71,050	60,698	46,832	63,789	63,820	53,300	59,123	70,267

Source: International Monetary Market (Chicago)

Average Open Interest of Japanese Yen Futures in Chicago In Contracts

Year	January	February	March	April	May	June	July	August	September	October	November	December
1988	48,680	54,426	54,728	45,399	49,150	45,113	49,300	51,337	49,228	45,162	54,522	47,509
1989	39,467	48,400	53,654	52,013	67,213	73,355	48,261	30,235	71,230	50,594	60,283	57,748
1990	60,012	67,723	82,783	71,709	79,850	62,252	62,760	65,050	77,686	74,890	77,115	65,365
1991	43,552	64,694	57,115	49,060	52,964	55,727	53,045	56,496	66,174	74,353	74,585	64,219
1992	63,856	67,714	71,702	63,938	63,079	64,596	56,465	58,353	53,462	44,488	45,941	46,887
1993	50,066	70,195	81,979	76,696	82,028	81,103	72,186	80,780	73,002	83,097	84,812	95,817
1994	101,792	94,470	73,286	57,281	65,835	70,759	73,734	72,798	63,419	63,091	80,053	92,834
1995	86,569	86,852	77,649	63,379	67,644	56,285	48,680	63,463	73,830	67,336	73,335	70,268

Source: International Monetary Market (Chicago)

Average Open Interest of Swiss Franc Futures in Chicago In Contracts

Year	January	February	March	April	May	June	July	August	September	October	November	December
1988	25,852	32,781	26,245	25,640	36,244	33,748	28,750	33,839	29,886	25,733	37,820	29,276
1989	27,442	31,287	34,749	34,074	42,256	36,445	35,625	41,613	38,429	31,432	39,757	47,927
1990	36,339	42,435	34,953	32,853	45,464	42,862	39,769	48,544	40,269	37,216	44,166	37,220
1991	31,489	36,483	49,061	40,026	38,601	43,476	36,031	35,881	29,833	24,949	32,342	32,439
1992	24,653	33,640	42,825	36,230	38,269	36,668	30,159	33,707	33,167	34,767	45,428	44,901
1993	52,713	49,472	48,002	43,514	47,832	42,343	40,703	44,329	60,446	49,320	58,406	49,670
1994	41,914	46,280	44,134	37,450	42,071	49,162	45,223	43,746	44,495	39,587	51,539	55,424
1995	39,726	44,364	39,358	30,270	30,586	26,766	23,121	30,267	34,228	34,889	38,033	44,741

Source: International Monetary Market (Chicago)

Average Open Interest of British Pound Futures in Chicago In Contracts

Year	January	February	March	April	May	June	July	August	September	October	November	December
1988	29,433	40,278	41,665	43,291	45,745	29,892	18,052	18,917	18,149	17,930	21,850	23,829
1989	22,870	24,705	27,436	21,170	25,871	26,512	22,899	22,559	27,661	21,971	24,850	26,124
1990	23,272	30,729	26,219	23,909	33,355	35,528	37,898	41,820	33,458	32,213	39,623	32,790
1991	23,686	34,680	33,558	29,900	30,697	33,792	26,443	21,578	28,215	22,882	31,792	26,443
1992	21,578	28,215	22,882	31,595	36,426	35,529	27,160	28,041	30,137	30,330	33,121	27,935
1993	26,614	41,752	40,238	38,544	39,654	34,953	26,056	32,446	33,560	29,733	37,246	33,606
1994	39,223	43,878	35,554	44,725	46,577	41,801	37,633	34,988	40,751	42,648	49,684	65,834
1995	47,740	44,935	36,805	23,161	26,571	28,402	22,662	34,932	38,900	34,485	43,634	49,804

Source: International Monetary Market (Chicago)

CURRENCIES

United States Merchandise Trade Balance In Millions of Dollars

Year	January	February	March	April	May	June	July	August	September	October	November	December	Total
1986	-12,166	-9,027	-9,961	-11,618	-10,706	-10,212	-13,056	-12,157	-13,144	-12,470	-13,140	-10,623	-145,081
1987	-13,453	-10,956	-10,628	-11,613	-12,410	-13,721	-14,431	-13,747	-12,484	-15,298	-11,932	-11,445	-159,557
1988	-9,874	-11,179	-7,656	-8,233	-7,915	-11,738	-10,211	-11,006	-9,237	-10,251	-10,824	-10,402	-126,959
1989	-8,639	-8,622	-6,954	-7,191	-9,463	-8,724	-10,582	-11,034	-8,971	-11,780	-10,754	-6,687	-115,249
1990	-9,640	-6,150	-6,369	-6,527	-7,308	-6,476	-10,759	-10,509	-9,157	-12,805	-10,529	-6,211	-109,033
1991	-7,079	-4,201	-1,889	-3,411	-4,158	-3,948	-7,894	-7,450	-7,111	-8,735	-4,942	-5,908	-74,068
1992	-5,470	-2,178	-3,527	-5,772	-5,409	-6,718	-9,893	-10,218	-9,693	-9,706	-8,644	-7,276	-96,106
1993	-6,113	-5,905	-8,886	-8,428	-6,542	-11,749	-12,609	-11,949	-12,516	-12,638	-11,120	-7,322	-132,618
1994	----------	-31,544	----------	----------	-38,148	----------	----------	-49,935	----------	----------	-46,472	----------	-166,099
1995	----------	-39,144	----------	----------	-45,475	----------							

Not seasonally adjusted. *Source: Bureau of Economic Analysis, U.S. Department of Commerce*

Index of Real Trade-Weighted Dollar Exchange Rates for Total Agricultural[2] 1985 = 100

Year	January	February	March	April	May	June	July	August	Sept.	October	Nov.	Dec.
1989 U.S. Markets	77.2	77.5	79.4	79.1	81.0	82.1	79.5	80.6	81.4	79.5	79.5	78.5
U.S. Competitors	82.1	81.4	81.9	85.0	88.7	88.7	86.8	85.7	85.2	83.7	82.4	83.9
1990 U.S. Markets	78.3	78.1	79.3	79.4	78.5	78.9	79.2	79.1	78.5	76.6	74.7	75.3
U.S. Competitors	80.1	81.2	79.6	79.2	77.8	77.5	76.4	76.1	76.3	75.0	75.3	73.5
1991 U.S. Markets	75.8	75.0	78.4	79.4	79.7	80.8	80.5	79.8	78.4	78.3	77.1	76.3
U.S. Competitors	75.3	75.1	76.4	77.0	77.3	77.8	77.8	76.9	75.8	77.0	76.4	76.2
1992 U.S. Markets	75.5	76.4	80.9	78.2	76.5	76.0	74.7	74.2	74.2	75.2	77.6	77.3
U.S. Competitors	76.2	76.8	81.1	76.6	77.4	76.6	75.6	75.1	77.2	75.7	77.7	77.4
1993 U.S. Markets	78.2	78.4	78.3	77.0	77.3	76.0	77.1	76.8	76.0	76.6	77.4	77.9
U.S. Competitors	78.3	78.6	79.1	78.4	78.9	77.7	78.5	78.7	78.0	78.3	78.6	78.1
1994 U.S. Markets	77.0	77.0	97.1	97.4	97.0	96.9	95.3	95.2	94.3	93.8	94.2	96.7
U.S. Competitors	78.3	78.3	107.3	107.6	105.7	104.5	101.5	101.2	100.1	98.4	99.1	100.5
1995[1] U.S. Markets	99.2	98.6	96.8	92.4	91.9	92.0	92.3	95.3	96.9	96.7		
U.S. Competitors	98.9	98.0	95.6	93.8	94.3	93.8	92.8	94.7	95.4	93.8		

[1] Preliminary. [2] Real indexes adjust nominal exchange rates for differences in rates of inflation to avoid the distortion caused by high-inflation countries. A higher value means the dollar has appreciated. Federal Reserve Board Index of trade-weighted value of the U.S. Dollar against ten major currencies. Weights are based on relative importance in world financial markets. *Source: Economic Research Service, U.S.D.A.*

United States Balance on Current Account In Millions of Dollars

Year	1st Quarter	2nd Quarter	3rd Quarter	4th Quarter	Annual
1986	-31,159	-37,629	-42,687	-39,726	-151,201
1987	-35,631	-42,034	-46,171	-43,261	-167,097
1988	-28,905	-31,188	-34,381	-33,721	-128,194
1989	-21,184	-25,207	-30,244	-26,186	-102,820
1990	-16,468	-19,511	-30,311	-25,458	-91,748
1991	15,825	2,722	-16,526	-9,445	-7,424
1992	-1,420	-13,926	-22,247	-23,956	-61,549
1993	-11,035	-23,293	-32,625	-32,972	-99,925
1994	-23,880	-36,151	-45,384	-45,830	-151,245
1995	-31,787	-41,658			

Not seasonally adjusted. *Source: Bureau of Economic Analysis, U.S. Department of Commerce*

Merchandise Trade and Account Balances In Billions of Dollars

	Merchandise Trade Balance					Current Account Balance				
Year	Canada	Germany	Japan	Switzerland	U.K.	Canada	Germany	Japan	Switzerland	U.K.
1987	9.0	67.7	96.4	-3.1	-18.9	-11.8	46.1	87.0	7.6	-8.1
1988	8.1	76.4	95.0	-3.2	-38.2	-17.1	49.5	79.6	9.0	-29.6
1989	6.0	75.1	76.9	-4.1	-40.4	-22.8	57.2	57.2	7.0	-36.8
1990	8.3	69.4	63.5	-3.2	-33.4	-21.6	48.9	35.8	8.6	-33.8
1991	3.9	18.0	103.0	-2.1	-18.1	-23.6	-19.2	72.9	10.6	-14.4
1992	5.8	26.5	132.3	2.7	-23.0	-21.4	-21.6	117.6	15.1	-17.3
1993	7.9	39.7	141.5	5.1	-20.1	-22.3	-15.6	131.4	18.3	-17.7
1994[1]	12.2	50.3	145.9	5.5	-16.1	-16.3	-21.1	129.1	18.1	-0.3
1995[2]	18.5	73.7	138.4	3.9	-17.1	-14.1	-18.9	112.1	19.3	-12.1
1996[2]	25.7	76.5	122.5	3.1	-20.0	-11.6	-23.3	92.9	19.0	-17.4

[1] Estimate. [2] Projections. *Source: Organization for Economic Cooperation and Development*

WEEKLY CASH
AS OF:03/15/96
DEUTSCHE MARK / SWISS FRANC
CASH
CHF/DEM
.96
.94
.92
.90
.88
.86
.84
.82
.80
.78
.76
.74
1993
1994
1995
1996
M A M J J A S O N D J F M A M J J A S O N D J F M A M J J A S O N D J F M A M J J

WEEKLY CASH
AS OF:03/15/96
BRITISH POUND / DEUTSCHE MARK
CASH
DEM/GBP
2.65
2.60
2.55
2.50
2.45
2.40
2.35
2.30
2.25
2.20
2.15
2.10
1993
1994
1995
1996
M A M J J A S O N D J F M A M J J A S O N D J F M A M J J A S O N D J F M A M J J

WEEKLY CASH
AS OF:03/15/96
JAPANESE YEN / BRITISH POUND
CASH
JPY/GBP
175
170
165
160
155
150
145
140
135
130
125
120
1993
1994
1995
1996
M A M J J A S O N D J F M A M J J A S O N D J F M A M J J A S O N D J F M A M J J

WEEKLY CASH
AS OF:03/15/96
DEUTSCHE MARK / JAPANESE YEN
CASH
JPY/DEM
76
74
72
70
68
66
64
62
60
58
56
54
1993
1994
1995
1996
M A M J J A S O N D J F M A M J J A S O N D J F M A M J J A S O N D J F M A M J J

Diamonds

World Production of Natural Gem Diamonds In Thousands of Carats

Year	Angola	Australia	Botswana	Brazil	Central African Republic	China	Ghana	Guinea	Namibia	Russia[3]	Sierra Leone	South Africa	Tanzania	Zaire	World Total
1985	464	4,242	6,318	233	190	200	60	123	865	4,400	243	4,550	165	4,032	26,233
1986	240	13,145	9,590	310	259	200	88	190	970	7,400	215	4,473	133	4,661	42,038
1987	180	13,650	9,368	300	304	200	65	163	971	7,400	150	4,063	87	3,885	41,024
1988	950	17,413	10,660	350	284	200	55	136	925	11,000	12	3,800	105	2,724	49,206
1989	1,165	17,540	10,680	350	334	200	395	137	910	11,500	90	4,000	105	2,663	50,665
1990	1,060	17,331	12,150	600	303	200	520	119	750	12,000	66	3,900	60	2,914	52,600
1991	899	17,978	11,550	600	296	200	560	91	1,170	10,000	160	3,800	70	3,000	51,090
1992	1,100	18,100	11,160	653	307	200	570	90	1,520	9,000	180	4,600	48	8,934	57,300
1993[1]	130	18,800	10,300	600	370	230	570	90	1,120	8,000	90	4,600	48	2,010	47,700
1994[2]	270	19,500	11,000	600	370	230	580	-----	1,280	8,500	155	5,000	-----	4,000	52,300

[1] Preliminary. [2] Estimate. [3] Formerly part of the U.S.S.R.; data not reported separately until 1992. *Source: U.S. Bureau of Mines*

World Production of Natural Industrial Diamonds In Thousands of Carats

Year	Angola	Australia	Botswana	Brazil	Central African Republic	China	Ghana	Liberia	Russia[3]	Sierra Leone	South Africa	Tanzania	Venezuela	Zaire	World Total
1984	250	2,277	7,104	550	101	800	311	132	6,400	105	5,627	84	232	13,290	37,359
1985	250	2,828	6,317	217	87	800	576	72	6,400	106	5,652	71	180	16,127	39,785
1986	10	16,066	3,500	315	99	800	498	189	7,400	100	5,755	57	165	18,643	53,702
1987	10	16,683	3,840	200	108	800	400	183	7,400	75	4,990	37	68	15,540	50,464
1988	50	17,413	4,570	180	59	800	465	100	11,000	6	4,700	45	75	15,439	55,122
1989	80	17,540	4,570	150	81	800	99	93	11,500	39	5,100	45	185	15,092	55,562
1990	73	17,331	5,200	900	78	800	130	60	12,000	12	4,800	25	248	16,513	58,452
1991	62	17,978	4,950	900	82	800	140	60	10,000	83	4,600	30	112	14,814	54,737
1992	80	22,100	4,790	665	107	800	140	93	9,000	116	5,600	20	176	4,567	48,500
1993[1]	15	23,000	4,420	900	125	850	140	90	8,000	68	5,700	20	155	13,600	57,300
1994[2]	30	23,800	5,000	900	125	850	145	-----	8,500	100	5,800	-----	175	13,000	58,700

[1] Preliminary. [2] Estimate. [3] Formerly part of the U.S.S.R.; data not reported separately until 1992. *Source: U.S. Bureau of Mines*

World Production of Synthetic Diamonds In Thousands of Carats

Year	Belarus[3]	China	Czech Republic[4]	France	Greece	Ireland	Japan	Russia[3]	South Africa	Sweden	Ukraine[3]	United States	World Total
1989	------	15,000	10,000	4,000	1,000	60,000	25,000	120,000	60,000	25,000	------	W	325,000
1990	------	15,000	10,000	5,000	1,000	60,000	25,000	120,000	60,000	25,000	------	W	329,000
1991	------	15,000	10,000	4,000	1,000	60,000	30,000	120,000	60,000	25,000	------	90,000	423,000
1992	30,000	15,000	10,000	3,500	750	60,000	30,000	80,000	60,000	25,000	10,000	90,000	424,000
1993[1]	30,000	15,500	5,000	3,500	1,000	66,000	32,000	80,000	60,000	25,000	10,000	103,000	446,000
1994[2]	25,000	15,500	5,000	3,500	1,100	65,000	32,000	80,000	60,000	25,000	8,000	104,000	439,000

[1] Preliminary. [2] Estimate. [3] Formerly part of the U.S.S.R.; data not reported separately until 1992. [4] Formerly part of Czechoslovakia; data not reported separately until 1993. W = Withheld proprietary data. *Source: U.S. Bureau of Mines*

U.S. Salient Statistics of Industrial Diamonds In Millions of Carats

	Bort, Grit & Powder & Dust — Natural and Synthetic								Stones (Natural)						
	--- Production ---														
Year	Manufactured Diamond	Secondary	Imports for Consumption	Exports & Reexports	In Manufactured Products	Gov't Sales	Apparent Consumption	Price Value of Imports $ Per Carat	Secondary Production	Imports for Consumption	Exports & Reexports	Gov't Sales	Apparent Consumption	Price Value of Imports $ Per Carat	Net Import Reliance % of Consumption
1987	W	3.0	45.0	56.8	.6	-----	W	1.28	.3	3.9	3.0	2.0	1.2	10.86	75
1988	W	6.6	64.3	74.5	.6	-----	W	1.03	.6	6.9	3.0	1.8	4.5	9.31	87
1989	W	3.0	61.6	78.2	.6	-----	75.8	.72	.6	8.8	2.8	-----	6.6	6.94	91
1990	90.0	5.9	85.4	71.0	.6	3.0	112.7	.76	.5	11.0	1.7	-----	9.8	6.57	95
1991	90.0	3.5	70.0	78.8	.6	5.0	89.1	.83	.3	7.6	2.9	-----	5.0	6.68	94
1992	95.0	3.4	97.3	83.6	.6	10.4	121.9	.70	.1	9.8	5.6	-----	4.3	4.56	98
1993[1]	100.3	15.8	133.0	96.1	.6	-----	134.4	.61	.1	5.5	3.7	1.3	1.8	6.85	95
1994[2]	108.0	41.1	140.0	110.0	.4	2.0	181.0	.62	.1	3.0	1.0	3.1	2.0	6.90	95

[1] Preliminary. [2] Estimate. W = Withheld proprietary data. *Source: U.S. Bureau of Mines*

Eggs

U.S. annual egg production has increased about 10 percent since the mid-1980's, but the U.S. remains the world's second largest producer. China, both the largest producer and consumer of eggs, has doubled output since the early 1990's with the 290 million eggs produced in 1995 accounting for more than a third of the world total. A major difference persists between the two nations in respect to utilization. Much of China's production is directly consumed as fresh brown eggs, whereas in the U.S. about a third of production is processed and white eggs are the favored table use variety.

However, a change in attitude towards egg use may have taken hold in the U.S.. Per capita egg consumption in 1995 is forecast at 239 eggs, of which shell egg use accounted for about 178 eggs, marginally higher than in 1994 but still supporting an upward trend that began in 1991. During the 1980's per capita use declined with the drop mostly in shell eggs. Although usage will likely continue to favor egg products relative to shell eggs, U.S. consumers now appear less concerned about the connection between the cholesterol content of eggs and heart disease, perhaps because the cause and effects are seen as questionable. Per capita egg usage remains much higher abroad than in the U.S.; Japan's per capita egg use is the world's highest.

Foreign trade in eggs is widespread, but small. The net totals gives an edge to exports. Trade within the EC accounts for half of the world's egg trade. The U.S. is a consistent net exporter. Japan is a net importer with a breakdown that includes hatched, table, dried and preserved eggs as well as egg albumen. Japan is generally the largest buyer of U.S. egg yolks. U.S. egg and egg product exports in 1995 totaled a record 192 million dozen versus 188 million in 1994.

There are definitive seasonal swings in U.S. egg production and table consumption. The table egg flocks typically reach a low in mid-summer and then increase throughout the year with monthly production peaking during the winter. Table egg consumption tends to be highest when consumers have more time for leisurely meals, generally in the summer. Wholesale prices (Chicago) lack a clear seasonality, but on balance appear highest during the winter months. U.S. egg production in 1994 of 74.4 billion eggs compares with 70.7 billion in 1993. Higher production during the first half of 1995 relative to 1994 suggests a total for the year around a record high 76 billion, the increase reflecting larger numbers of hens and pullets of laying age, and more eggs laid per hundred layers.

The average wholesale price of large shell eggs (delivered, Chicago) in 1994 of $.602 per dozen was the lowest since 1988. In the first half of 1995, prices were about 5 cents lower than a year earlier, strengthening during the summer to 10 cents a dozen over the previous year.

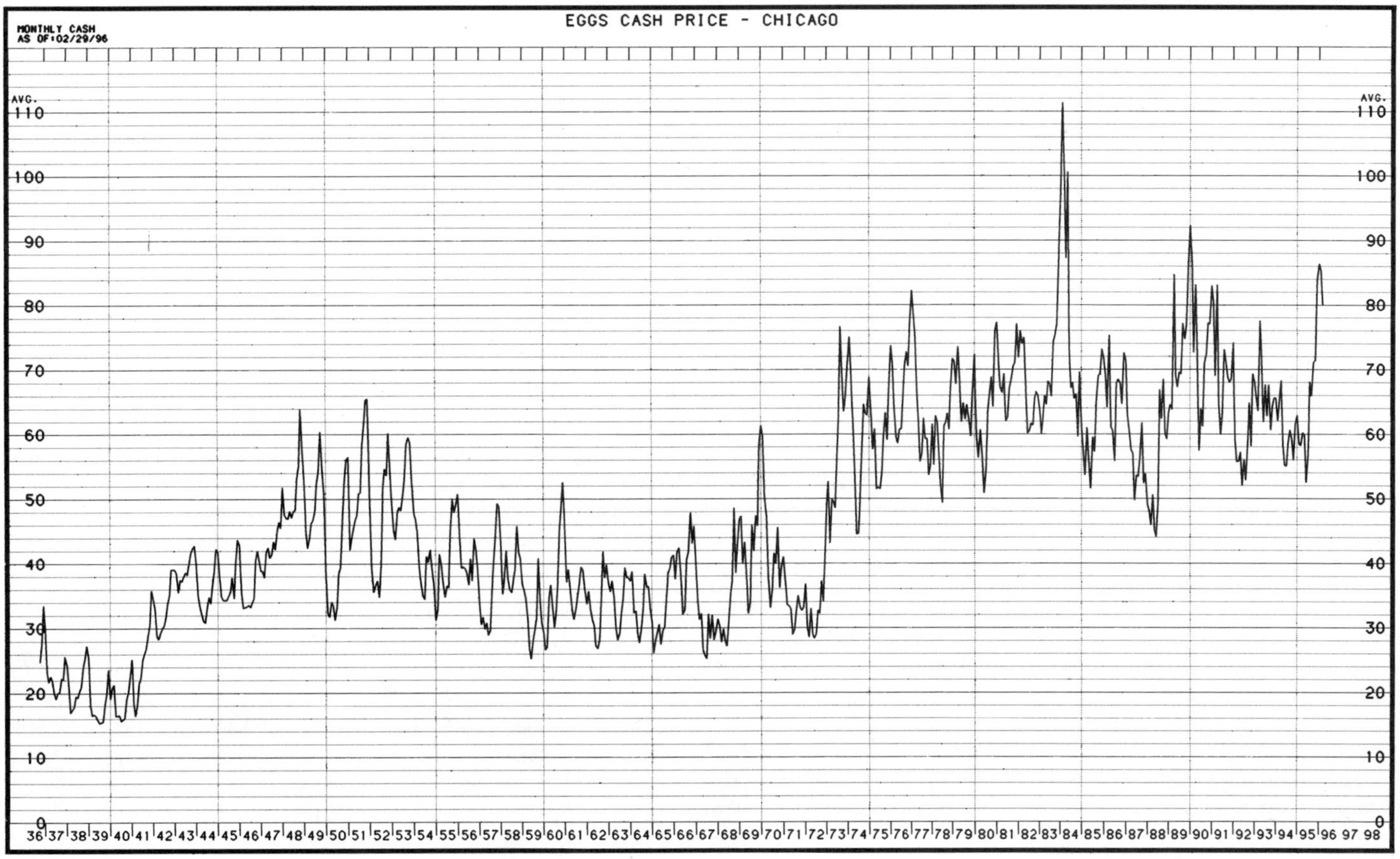

EGGS

World Production of Eggs   In Millions of Eggs

Year	Brazil	Canada	China	France	Germany	Italy	Japan	Rep. of Korea	Mexico	Netherlands	Poland	Russia[4]	Spain	Ukraine[4]	United Kingdom	United States
1986	13,000	5,898	111,000	14,970	12,765	10,300	37,080	6,011	18,563	10,930	8,303	------	10,877	79,892	13,150	69,196
1987	15,400	5,706	118,000	14,540	17,995	10,743	39,567	6,574	18,039	10,930	7,966	47,447	10,500	17,425	13,300	70,418
1988	12,174	5,719	139,100	15,050	17,960	11,234	40,383	7,204	17,950	10,660	8,220	49,144	10,856	17,672	13,500	67,174
1989	12,174	5,719	140,900	15,050	17,794	11,223	40,356	6,919	17,950	10,660	8,200	49,042	10,140	17,393	10,547	67,178
1990	13,454	5,661	158,920	14,629	16,800	11,454	40,318	7,145	18,040	10,801	7,649	47,470	10,659	16,287	10,658	67,987
1991	13,655	5,666	184,400	15,300	15,525	11,568	41,638	7,770	19,840	10,762	6,500	46,900	10,184	15,188	11,006	69,352
1992	14,190	5,670	230,980	15,375	15,165	11,454	42,911	7,750	19,650	10,458	6,300	42,900	8,675	13,445	10,699	70,860
1993	12,700	5,689	235,960	15,355	13,678	11,502	43,252	8,200	20,140	10,019	5,450	40,300	8,454	11,766	10,645	72,036
1994[1]	13,460	5,736	284,423	16,200	13,960	11,599	43,047	8,100	22,150	10,164	6,100	37,400	9,670	10,145	10,670	74,124
1995[2]	14,940	5,795	285,000	15,800	13,800	11,655	42,850	8,300	21,200	9,950	6,700	35,100	9,700	9,500	10,600	74,400
1996[3]	16,434	5,800	290,000	15,600	13,700	11,600	42,700	8,400	21,620	9,750	6,700	33,300	9,000	9,000	10,600	75,840

[1] Preliminary. [2] Estimate. [3] Forecast. [4] Formerly part of the U.S.S.R.; data not reported separately until 1987. *Source: Foreign Agricultural Service, U.S. Department of Agriculture*

Salient Egg Statistics in the United States

	Hens & Pullets			Eggs							Consumption	
Year	On Farm Dec. 1[3]	Average Number During Year	Rate of Lay Per Layer During Year[4]	Total Produced	Price in ¢ Per Dozen	Value of Production[5]	Total Egg Production	Imports[6]	Exports[6]	Used for Hatching	Total	Per Capita Eggs[6]
	Thousands		(Number)	Millions		Million $	Million Dozen					(Number)
1986	283,193	279,046	248	69,196	61.5	3,543	5,766	13.7	101.6	566.8	5,112	254.9
1987	288,320	283,872	248	70,418	54.7	3,209	5,868	5.6	111.2	599.1	5,159	255.0
1988	275,447	277,781	251	69,410	52.8	3,067	5,784	5.3	141.8	606.0	5,041	246.8
1989	271,064	269,347	250	67,178	68.9	3,861	5,598	25.2	91.6	641.8	4,894	237.4
1990	271,963	269,862	251	67,987	70.9	4,010	5,666	9.1	100.8	678.5	4,894	235.0
1991	279,325	274,287	252	69,352	67.8	3,909	5,779	2.3	154.5	708.6	4,917	233.5
1992	282,034	278,830	254	70,860	57.6	3,387	5,885	4.3	157.0	732.0	5,000	234.9
1993[1]	290,626	284,776	253	72,037	63.4	3,800	5,960	4.7	158.9	769.3	5,039	234.2
1994[2]	298,509	291,018	254	73,911	61.4	3,777	6,177	3.7	187.6	803.0	5,186	238.7
1995[2]	297,332	293,648	253	74,258			6,180	4.3	190.1	836.5	5,160	235.4

[1] Preliminary. [2] Estimate. [3] All layers of laying age. [4] Number of eggs produced during the year divided by the average number of all layers of laying age on hand during the year. [5] Value of sales plus value of eggs consumed in households of producers. [6] Shell-egg equivalent of eggs and egg products.
Source: National Agricultural Statistics Service, U.S. Department of Agriculture

Average Wholesale Prices of Shell Eggs (Large) Delivered, Chicago   In Cents Per Dozen

Year	Jan.	Feb.	Mar.	Apr.	May	June	July	Aug.	Sept.	Oct.	Nov.	Dec.	Average
1986	70.6	65.7	76.9	62.6	62.0	57.3	69.4	70.0	69.4	66.3	74.1	72.8	68.1
1987	64.4	62.0	59.2	59.0	51.8	55.6	55.4	58.7	64.8	55.5	56.3	52.1	57.9
1988	51.2	48.9	53.6	47.9	47.1	52.8	69.8	65.4	71.4	63.1	62.2	66.1	58.3
1989	67.8	66.6	91.0	71.6	69.8	72.0	71.8	79.6	77.2	79.4	89.1	94.3	77.5
1990	88.6	75.1	86.1	78.6	60.3	66.9	64.2	73.9	75.4	80.0	80.0	83.1	76.0
1991	86.0	72.0	85.8	67.6	60.9	63.4	73.1	71.3	68.8	67.9	68.7	73.9	71.6
1992	59.1	55.7	55.7	57.4	52.0	56.0	53.0	57.9	64.9	58.2	69.4	68.0	58.9
1993	65.7	63.6	77.5	70.9	61.9	67.6	62.8	67.6	60.6	64.2	65.6	65.5	66.1
1994	62.1	64.9	68.3	58.3	55.1	55.1	58.8	60.6	59.2	55.9	61.5	62.9	60.2
1995[1]	58.6	58.2	60.2	59.9	52.5	56.8	68.1	65.9	71.1	71.3	83.9	86.4	66.1

[1] Preliminary. *Source: National Agricultural Statistics Service, U.S. Department of Agriculture*

Total Egg Production in the United States   In Cents Per Dozen

Year	Jan.	Feb.	Mar.	Apr.	May	June	July	Aug.	Sept.	Oct.	Nov.	Dec.	Total
1986	5,904	5,340	5,943	5,698	5,844	5,655	5,763	5,766	5,613	5,865	5,783	6,022	69,196
1987	5,989	5,417	6,093	5,864	5,925	5,685	5,863	5,861	5,756	6,008	5,873	6,084	70,418
1988	6,047	5,667	6,050	5,767	5,839	5,575	5,740	5,762	5,589	5,838	5,697	5,839	69,410
1989	5,758	5,182	5,782	5,569	5,696	5,498	5,648	5,613	5,450	5,658	5,543	5,781	67,178
1990	5,708	5,172	5,838	5,655	5,769	5,533	5,703	5,718	5,533	5,783	5,696	5,879	67,987
1991	5,865	5,316	5,935	5,666	5,796	5,643	5,840	5,855	5,675	5,915	5,811	6,035	69,352
1992	5,951	5,558	6,042	5,832	5,918	5,693	5,908	5,919	5,753	6,019	5,913	6,112	70,618
1993	6,030	5,432	6,067	5,861	6,009	5,816	5,992	6,015	5,876	6,144	6,085	6,296	71,623
1994[1]	6,186	5,598	6,320	6,073	6,189	5,992	6,205	6,272	6,125	6,377	6,265	6,516	74,118
1995[2]	6,369	5,714	6,448	6,177	6,251	6,010	6,145	6,146	5,990	6,260	6,232	6,534	74,276

[1] Preliminary. [2] Estimate. *Source: National Agricultural Statistics Service, U.S. Department of Agriculture*

Shell Eggs: Per Capita Disappearance in the United States In Number of Eggs

Year	Jan.	Feb.	Mar.	Apr.	May	June	July	Aug.	Sept.	Oct.	Nov.	Dec.	Total	Total Consumption (Million Dozen)
1984	19.4	17.2	19.2	18.8	18.5	17.7	18.7	18.4	18.3	18.8	18.8	20.2	224.0	4,412
1985	19.5	17.0	19.5	17.9	17.7	17.4	17.6	18.0	17.6	18.1	18.3	19.2	217.9	4,331
1986	18.9	17.0	19.3	17.5	18.0	17.2	17.5	17.8	17.3	17.9	18.5	18.8	215.8	4,327
1987	18.6	16.5	18.5	17.8	17.8	16.6	17.3	17.6	17.3	18.1	17.5	18.1	211.6	4,282
1988	18.4	16.8	18.0	17.0	16.7	15.6	16.9	16.4	16.1	16.8	16.6	17.3	202.6	4,138
1989	16.8	15.1	17.3	16.1	15.9	15.2	16.2	15.8	15.5	16.0	15.9	17.1	192.2	3,978
1990	16.2	14.5	16.3	15.9	15.5	14.9	15.4	15.3	15.3	15.6	15.5	16.6	186.8	3,891
1991	15.9	14.4	16.4	14.6	14.8	14.4	15.0	15.2	14.9	15.1	15.7	16.2	182.6	3,844
1992	15.4	14.3	15.4	15.1	15.0	14.0	14.7	15.2	14.5	15.3	15.5	15.9	180.3	3,838
1993	15.9	14.0	15.6	14.8	14.7	13.9	14.6	14.6	14.1	15.0	15.0	15.6	177.8	3,825
1994[1]	---------	45.0	---------	--------	43.0	--------	--------	43.9	--------	--------	46.0	--------	177.9	3,864
1995[2]	---------	43.9	---------	--------	42.6	--------	--------	42.1	--------				171.8	3,769

[1] Preliminary. [2] Estimate. *Source: Economic Research Service, U.S. Department of Agriculture*

Egg-Feed Ratio[1] in the United States

Year	Jan.	Feb.	Mar.	Apr.	May	June	July	Aug.	Sept.	Oct.	Nov.	Dec.	Average
1984	12.4	12.2	9.8	11.3	7.9	6.9	7.2	7.5	8.0	7.9	9.4	8.9	9.1
1985	7.2	7.5	8.4	7.4	7.0	7.8	7.9	9.4	10.8	11.8	12.0	11.6	9.1
1986	11.1	10.3	11.7	9.4	9.1	8.0	10.8	12.6	14.0	13.3	15.4	14.6	11.7
1987	13.1	13.0	11.7	11.2	9.0	9.0	9.4	10.0	12.2	9.8	10.3	8.3	10.6
1988	8.2	7.5	8.0	6.9	6.0	5.5	6.9	7.1	8.3	7.7	8.0	8.2	7.3
1989	8.3	8.2	11.1	9.0	8.4	8.8	9.2	11.6	11.8	12.1	13.6	14.3	10.5
1990	14.3	11.5	13.0	11.0	8.5	9.0	7.9	9.9	10.9	12.1	12.4	12.3	11.1
1991	13.2	11.1	12.6	10.0	8.6	8.8	10.4	9.8	9.4	9.7	9.9	11.2	10.4
1992	8.4	7.8	7.4	7.6	6.7	7.0	7.3	8.1	9.6	9.3	11.2	11.1	8.5
1993	10.5	10.3	11.7	10.6	9.2	9.8	8.2	8.9	8.1	8.8	8.8	8.3	9.4
1994	7.9	8.0	8.6	7.7	8.6	7.1	7.9	9.0	9.2	9.0	10.3	10.2	8.6
1995[2]	9.7	9.6	9.2	9.2	7.8	7.8	8.0	8.7	9.0	8.4	10.2	10.4	9.0

[1] Pounds of laying feed equivalent in value to one dozen eggs. [2] Preliminary. *Source: Economic Research Service, U.S. Department of Agriculture*

Total Eggs -- U.S. Supply and Distribution In Millions of Dozen

	Supply				Utilization			Consumption	
Year & Quarters	Beginning Stocks	Production	Imports[4]	Total Supply	Exports[4]	Eggs Used for Hatching	Ending Stocks	Total	Per Capita (Number)
1991 I	11.6	1,422	.2	1,434	34.9	174.9	11.1	1,213	57.9
II	11.1	1,420	.3	1,432	38.0	182.2	11.2	1,200	57.1
III	11.2	1,441	.7	1,453	38.8	176.6	12.9	1,224	58.1
IV	12.9	1,475	.5	1,488	42.7	174.3	13.0	1,258	59.6
1992 I	13.0	1,464	.8	1,477	40.5	180.0	15.8	1,241	58.5
II	15.8	1,454	1.0	1,471	36.1	186.9	17.0	1,231	57.9
III	17.0	1,464	1.3	1,482	34.5	180.6	15.8	1,251	58.7
IV	15.8	1,501	1.2	1,518	45.9	178.9	13.5	1,280	59.8
1993 I	13.5	1,461	.9	1,475	37.1	187.3	11.9	1,237	57.7
II	11.9	1,474	1.5	1,487	34.5	196.6	11.7	1,244	57.9
III	11.7	1,490	1.4	1,503	42.0	192.4	11.4	1,258	58.4
IV	11.4	1,535	.9	1,548	45.3	191.4	10.7	1,300	60.2
1994[1] I	10.7	1,509	1.0	1,520	40.2	195.3	12.1	1,273	58.8
II	12.1	1,521	1.1	1,535	45.5	205.3	11.9	1,272	58.6
III	11.9	1,550	1.0	1,563	49.3	202.8	13.8	1,297	59.6
IV	13.8	1,597	.6	1,611	52.6	199.6	14.9	1,344	61.6
1995[2] I	14.9	1,545	1.1	1,561	45.5	206.2	14.2	1,295	59.3
II	14.2	1,535	1.2	1,550	50.1	213.4	17.6	1,269	58.0
III	17.6	1,520	1.0	1,538	45.5	211.9	12.9	1,268	57.8
IV	12.9	1,580	1.0	1,594	49.0	205.0	12.0	1,328	60.4
1996[3] I	12.0	1,555	1.0	1,568	42.0	215.0	12.0	1,299	58.9
II	12.0	1,565	1.0	1,578	49.0	225.0	12.0	1,292	58.5
III	12.0	1,575	1.0	1,588	52.0	215.0	12.0	1,309	59.1

[1] Preliminary. [2] Estimate. [3] Forecast. [4] Shell-egg equivalent of eggs and egg products. *Source: Economic Research Service, U.S. Department of Agriculture*

EGGS

Hens and Pullets of Laying Age (Layers) in the U.S., First of Month In Thousands

Year	Jan. 1	Feb. 1	Mar. 1	Apr. 1	May 1	June 1	July 1	Aug. 1	Sept. 1	Oct. 1	Nov. 1	Dec. 1
1987	285,939	287,082	285,877	285,536	282,109	280,642	278,452	280,232	282,032	285,954	286,409	288,320
1988	286,470	285,670	283,225	279,221	277,449	272,482	270,282	271,220	273,136	275,191	276,415	275,447
1989	272,243	272,780	271,590	269,278	267,269	267,239	267,088	266,253	267,656	267,919	270,006	271,064
1990	271,164	272,826	271,921	272,813	270,664	269,040	265,647	266,767	267,004	268,835	270,274	271,963
1991	273,917	275,533	274,446	272,541	272,150	272,944	272,779	272,998	274,277	276,187	278,433	279,325
1992	280,697	279,274	279,117	279,009	276,757	275,645	275,179	275,091	274,010	279,233	280,183	282,034
1993	281,639	282,933	282,005	282,480	281,468	280,795	280,517	282,201	282,341	284,771	285,298	290,626
1994	290,413	289,625	290,416	290,979	289,125	288,398	287,454	288,484	292,116	294,576	295,719	298,509
1995[1]	300,331	298,202	297,689	296,290	294,697	290,806	289,028	286,519	289,595	290,889	294,486	298,293

[1] Preliminary. *Source: National Agricultural Statistics Service, U.S. Department of Agriculture*

Eggs Laid Per Hundred Layers in the United States In Number of Eggs

Year	Jan.	Feb.	Mar.	Apr.	May	June	July	Aug.	Sept.	Oct.	Nov.	Dec.	Average
1987	2,126	1,919	2,166	2,103	2,137	2,060	2,123	2,114	2,053	2,129	2,078	2,157	2,097
1988	2,154	2,027	2,189	2,103	2,150	2,081	2,150	2,150	2,073	2,152	2,105	2,179	2,126
1989	2,154	1,937	2,178	2,111	2,165	2,089	2,148	2,135	2,071	2,142	2,099	2,182	2,118
1990	2,150	1,940	2,185	2,120	2,173	2,105	2,179	2,181	2,104	2,189	2,149	2,208	2,140
1991	2,186	1,978	2,218	2,124	2,168	2,108	2,186	2,189	2,106	2,175	2,134	2,206	2,148
1992	2,174	2,036	2,216	2,148	2,186	2,110	2,196	2,204	2,125	2,201	2,156	2,227	2,165
1993	2,138	1,923	2,149	2,078	2,137	2,072	2,130	2,131	2,073	2,155	6,085	2,169	2,437
1994	2,133	1,930	2,174	2,094	2,143	2,081	2,155	2,160	2,088	2,160	2,113	2,176	2,117
1995[1]	2,130	1,919	2,173	2,092	2,137	2,075	2,137	2,135	2,065	2,140	2,109	2,185	2,108

[1] Preliminary. *Source: National Agricultural Statistics Service, U.S. Department of Agriculture*

Egg-Type Chicks Hatched by Commercial Hatcheries in the United States In Thousands

Year	Jan.	Feb.	Mar.	Apr.	May	June	July	Aug.	Sept.	Oct.	Nov.	Dec.	Total
1987	34,156	35,815	41,708	42,356	40,858	37,256	33,375	34,667	31,800	33,959	30,593	31,242	427,785
1988	29,274	28,433	35,615	34,749	35,984	33,049	24,876	27,838	30,918	31,007	27,181	27,311	366,235
1989	26,602	27,271	32,597	36,135	38,376	34,708	29,828	32,217	32,862	33,456	29,666	29,284	383,002
1990	32,004	32,107	36,509	36,915	37,895	34,471	31,582	32,949	31,219	32,926	29,809	31,046	398,432
1991	34,487	34,837	37,041	39,775	38,404	36,227	33,696	33,656	34,007	34,307	30,400	32,717	419,554
1992	32,496	31,950	36,490	35,755	38,513	34,568	32,265	28,349	28,760	32,843	27,718	31,612	391,319
1993	34,885	34,009	38,264	37,163	36,742	35,587	33,980	31,455	31,775	31,634	30,074	30,448	405,986
1994	33,212	31,086	33,492	35,668	35,336	31,986	29,613	31,295	30,873	31,766	25,475	29,072	378,874
1995[1]	31,527	31,693	34,806	34,101	36,335	33,392	28,682	30,399	32,112	31,682	28,539	30,012	383,280

[1] Preliminary. *Source: National Agricultural Statistics Service, U.S. Department of Agriculture*

U.S. Cold Storage Holdings of Shell Eggs, First of Month In Thousands Cases (One Case = 30 Dozen)

Year	Jan.	Feb.	Mar.	Apr.	May	June	July	Aug.	Sept.	Oct.	Nov.	Dec.
1987	22	20	25	22	28	38	32	34	32	33	51	40
1988	43	67	53	32	14	21	30	28	25	23	24	26
1989	9	12	7	33	18	26	27	12	17	23	6	11
1990	12	22	16	16	12	21	22	29	19	18	11	16
1991	15	17	9	23	12	15	13	13	10	13	12	13
1992	21	20	25	14	27	34	30	29	23	22	17	15
1993	15	12	12	15	6	6	7	6	6	15	13	6
1994	10	7	8	9	8	8	8	14	14	9	7	3
1995[1]	4	12	14	7	8	5	6	8	19	24	28	13

[1] Preliminary. *Source: National Agricultural Statistics Service, U.S. Department of Agriculture*

U.S. Cold Storage Holdings of Frozen Eggs, First of Month In Millions of Pounds[1]

Year	Jan.	Feb.	Mar.	Apr.	May	June	July	Aug.	Sept.	Oct.	Nov.	Dec.
1987	12.8	14.3	13.5	14.5	14.9	17.4	16.9	17.3	17.5	16.5	17.9	17.4
1988	17.3	18.3	18.3	14.1	17.3	20.3	25.3	22.9	24.5	22.2	20.0	17.9
1989	19.6	19.7	19.0	14.8	15.3	16.2	15.1	16.5	15.0	14.4	14.9	13.4
1990	13.6	14.2	15.2	16.8	19.7	16.8	18.1	17.1	17.1	16.6	16.8	17.2
1991	14.7	14.8	14.0	14.1	13.0	13.5	14.2	18.1	16.3	16.5	17.0	15.1
1992	16.0	20.0	19.2	19.7	18.8	18.9	21.1	19.5	20.2	20.0	21.7	18.7
1993	17.2	16.7	16.9	15.1	14.3	15.5	15.1	17.6	18.1	14.4	14.0	13.5
1994	13.7	14.8	15.8	15.6	16.3	15.2	15.4	19.0	19.7	17.8	20.0	19.1
1995[2]	19.5	19.5	18.3	18.5	17.3	18.1	22.9	20.6	18.0	16.2	14.4	12.5

[1] Converted on basis 39.5 pounds frozen eggs equal 1 case [2] Preliminary. *Source: National Agricultural Statistics Service, U.S. Department of Agriculture*

Electric Power

U.S. net generation of electricity in June 1995 was 256 billion kilowatt-hours, down three percent from the amount reported for June 1994. Of that total, the energy sources were as follows: coal generated 53.9 percent, nuclear 22 percent, hydroelectric 11.1 percent, gas 11.1 percent, petroleum 1.7 percent and other (geothermal, wood, wind, waste and solar) .2 percent. For the first six months of 1995, total net generation of electricity was 1.43 trillion kilowatt-hours, virtually unchanged from the first half of 1994. In June 1995, coal generated electricity amounted to 138 billion kilowatt-hours, down six percent from June 1994. For the first half of 1995, coal generated 781 billion kilowatt-hours of electricity, down almost four percent from 1994. Nuclear power generated 56 billion kilowatt-hours in June 1995, up seven percent from 1994, while for the first half of 1995 nuclear power generated 327 billion kilowatt-hours, up over nine percent from 1994. Gas generated 28 billion kilowatt-hours of electricity in June 1995, down 10 percent, while for the first half of 1995 it produced almost 135 billion kilowatt-hours, up over 11 percent. For first half of 1995, hydroelectric power generated 154 billion kilowatt-hours, up 15 percent from 1994.

Retail sales of electricity in June 1995 to residential customers in the U.S. was 84.3 billion kilowatt-hours. For the first half of 1995, residential customers consumed 486 billion kilowatt-hours of electricity, down almost two percent from 1994. Sales to commercial customers in June 1995 were 74.2 billion kilowatt-hours. For the January-June 1995 period, commercial customers purchased nearly 402 billion kilowatt-hours, up just over one percent from the same period of 1994. Industrial purchases of electricity in June 1995 were 87.3 billion kilowatt-hours. For the first half 1995, industrial purchases were 497 billion kilowatt-hours, up almost three percent from 1994. Other users in the first half of 1995, which include public street, highway lighting and railroads, purchased almost 47 billion kilowatt-hours, up one percent from 1994.

The average cost of electricity for residential users in June 1995 was 8.74¢ per kilowatt-hour, down from 8.79¢ in June 1994. For the first half of 1995, the average cost was 8.26¢ per kilowatt-hour, up almost one percent from 1994. The average cost to commercial users in June 1995 was 7.97¢ compared to 7.99¢ per kilowatt-hour in June 1994. For the first half of 1995, the average cost was 7.60¢, unchanged from 1994. For industrial users, the average cost in June 1995 was 4.85¢ per kilowatt-hour, down slightly from 4.88¢ in June 1994. For the first six months of 1995, the average cost was 4.61¢, down from 4.68¢ in first half 1994. For all users of electricity, the average cost in first half 1994 was 6.75¢, down from 6.78¢ in first half 1994.

The New York Mercantile Exchange proposed two electricity futures contracts, one delivering on the California-Oregon border and one at Palo Verde in Arizona. Approval to start trading was pending from the CFTC.

World Electricity Production (Monthly Average) In Millions of Kilowatt Hours

Year	Australia	Canada	China	France	Germany	India	Italy	Japan	Poland	Rep. of Korea	Russia[3]	South Africa	Sweden	Ukraine[3]	United Kingdom	United States
1985	10,083	38,254	34,225	27,144	43,379	14,186	15,190	55,996	11,476	4,834	128,676	10,125	11,378	------	24,477	214,027
1986	10,518	39,049	37,458	28,586	43,474	15,626	15,749	55,981	11,691	4,167	133,244	12,210	11,502	------	24,846	216,610
1987	11,027	41,361	41,442	29,383	34,873	16,824	16,748	58,248	12,153	6,166	138,744	12,550	10,802	------	25,161	226,561
1988	11,592	42,164	49,460	30,456	35,228	18,427	16,931	62,811	12,028	7,122	142,090	13,062	12,451	------	25,761	239,875
1989	12,316	41,628	49,549	33,908	36,716	20,428	17,570	66,563	12,124	7,873	143,500	13,527	11,992	------	25,153	246,659
1990	12,923	40,169	51,500	35,011	37,433	22,025	18,074	71,439	11,361	8,972	139,455	12,270	12,204	------	26,581	250,979
1991	13,071	42,326	55,918	37,846	44,949	23,893	18,503	74,007	11,225	9,885	136,156	14,026	12,282	------	26,900	254,818
1992	13,260	41,803	61,562	38,522	44,761	25,081	18,854	74,611	11,070	10,914	84,038	14,008	12,187	------	27,240	256,209
1993	13,482	42,591	67,723	35,728	37,722	26,961	18,566	75,559	11,156	12,036	79,716	14,572	11,883	19,083	26,834	262,158
1994[1]	13,708	50,495	75,312	42,420	37,786	29,250	19,435	62,902	10,984	13,754	75,740	15,204	11,449	15,431	27,637	243,585
1995[2]	13,465	------	79,719	------	32,964	31,169	20,079	58,310	11,364	14,853	69,122	15,748	11,988	------	28,146	233,830

[1] Preliminary. [2] Estimate. [3] Formerly part of the U.S.S.R.; data not reported separately until 1992. *Source: United Nations*

Installed Capacity, Capability & Peak Load of the U.S. Electric Utility Industry In Millions of Kilowatt Hours

	Installed Generating Capacity at Dec. 31															
		Type of Prime Mover				Type of Ownership										
Year	Total Electric Utility Industry	Hydro	Gas Turbine & Steam	Nuclear Power	Internal Combustion	Investor Owned	Cooperative	Sub-total Gov't.	Municipal Utilities	Federal	Power Districts, State Projects	Capability at Winter Peak Load	Non-Co incident Winter Peak Load	Capacity Margin Non-Co incident Peak Load (%)	Total Electric Utility Industry Generation	Annual Peak Load Factor (%)
1985	688.7	83.0	520.3	80.4	5.0	530.4	24.6	133.8	37.0	63.7	33.0	636.5	423.7	25.9	2,470	62.0
1986	707.7	85.2	524.1	92.4	5.9	544.2	26.4	137.1	38.6	63.9	34.6	646.7	422.9	24.8	2,487	60.7
1987	718.1	85.9	524.3	101.6	6.2	552.8	26.4	138.9	39.4	64.7	34.9	663.0	448.3	23.4	2,572	60.8
1988	723.9	86.9	526.6	103.4	7.0	557.8	26.4	139.7	40.4	64.8	34.5	676.9	466.5	20.0	2,704	59.5
1989	730.9	87.5	529.1	106.7	7.5	562.1	26.4	142.4	40.7	67.2	34.5	685.2	496.4	22.3	2,784	62.2
1990	735.1	87.2	531.1	108.0	8.7	568.8	26.3	139.9	40.1	65.4	34.4	696.8	484.0	20.4	2,808	60.4
1991	740.0	88.7	534.1	108.4	8.8	573.0	26.5	140.5	40.4	65.6	34.5	703.2	485.4	20.2	2,825	60.9
1992	741.7	89.7	534.5	107.9	9.6	572.9	26.0	142.7	41.6	66.1	35.0	707.8	493.0	21.1	2,797	61.1
1993[1]	744.7	90.2	536.9	107.8	9.8	575.2	26.1	143.4	41.8	66.1	35.5	712.0	521.7	17.1	2,883	61.0
1994[1]	746.0	90.3	537.9	107.9	9.9	574.8	26.4	144.7	42.0	66.3	36.4	715.1	518.3	16.7	2,911	61.2

[1] Preliminary. *Source: Edison Electric Institute*

ELECTRIC POWER

Available Electricity & Energy Sales in the United States   In Billions of Kilowatt Hours

	Net Generation									Sales to Ultimate Customers							
	Electric Utility Industry																
Year	Total[2]	Hydro	Natural Gas	Coal	Fuel Oil	Nuclear	Other Sources[3]	Total	Total Million $	Total	Residential	Inter-Departmental	Commercial	Industrial	Street & Highway Lighting	Other Public Auth.	Railways & Railroads
1981	2,295	261	346	1,204	206	273	6.1	2,359	111,001	2,151	730.5	6.2	521.7	819.6	14.7	53.7	4.2
1982	2,241	309	305	1,192	146	283	5.2	2,302	121,584	2,100	732.7	5.4	517.0	770.4	14.2	55.7	4.3
1983	2,310	332	274	1,259	144	294	6.5	2,368	129,589	2,160	750.3	5.4	545.6	783.0	13.9	57.3	4.3
1984	2,416	321	297	1,342	120	328	8.6	2,488	143,093	2,281	782.6	5.8	578.1	835.5	14.2	59.9	4.5
1985	2,470	281	292	1,402	100	384	10.7	2,568	149,162	2,306	792.9	5.3	605.9	820.3	14.6	62.2	4.7
1986	2,487	291	249	1,386	137	414	11.5	2,599	152,467	2,355	820.0	5.2	629.0	819.0	15.0	61.9	4.7
1987	2,572	250	273	1,464	118	455	12.3	2,719	155,700	2,435	846.5	4.5	658.4	843.7	14.4	63.0	4.9
1988	2,704	223	253	1,541	149	527	12.0	2,879	162,388	2,554	886.1	4.2	697.8	881.8	14.6	64.6	5.1
1989	2,784	265	267	1,554	158	529	11.3	2,985	169,627	2,621	898.8	4.3	715.9	912.8	14.6	69.3	5.3
1990	2,808	280	264	1,560	117	577	10.7	3,041	176,468	2,684	915.8	4.2	738.9	931.9	15.2	72.8	5.3
1991	1,825	276	264	1,551	111	613	10.1	3,100	185,118	2,764	948.8	2.6	753.3	934.9	15.6	76.1	5.3
1992	2,797	240	264	1,576	89	619	10.2	3,107	187,283	2,735	929.3	2.6	755.7	949.3	15.8	77.2	5.2
1993[1]	2,883	265	259	1,639	100	610	9.6	3,210	196,410	2,836	989.9	2.4	781.8	975.6	16.2	64.7	5.1
1994[1]	2,911	244	291	1,635	91	640	8.9	2,911	201,183	2,895	995.7	2.3	814.3	989.5	16.9	69.3	7.1

[1] Preliminary. [2] Includes internal combustion. [3] Includes electricity produced from geothermal, wood, waste, wind, solar, etc.
Source: Edison Electric Insititute

Electric Power Production by Electric Utilities in the U.S.   In Millions of Kilowatt Hours

Year	Jan.	Feb.	Mar.	Apr.	May	June	July	Aug.	Sept.	Oct.	Nov.	Dec.	Total
1981	206,467	179,613	185,553	172,545	177,806	202,702	220,373	210,403	186,838	181,352	175,570	195,590	2,294,812
1982	209,403	180,299	187,687	172,580	177,147	186,128	210,584	205,656	180,662	172,966	173,377	184,722	2,241,211
1983	195,579	172,479	182,488	170,372	174,392	191,048	220,165	229,957	195,604	182,931	183,949	212,319	2,310,285
1984	216,632	189,564	200,107	181,084	192,217	209,648	221,245	229,296	195,198	190,936	190,380	199,996	2,416,304
1985	227,856	198,242	194,970	184,877	196,790	205,363	226,722	226,050	202,499	194,789	192,427	219,255	2,469,841
1986	217,470	192,336	196,834	186,074	197,315	215,015	242,672	225,166	206,692	197,754	196,432	213,551	2,487,310
1987	222,749	194,034	201,849	189,496	206,074	225,589	247,915	247,645	213,008	203,009	200,258	220,500	2,572,127
1988	237,897	216,937	214,013	196,000	208,371	232,747	257,461	267,693	220,179	210,608	209,593	232,752	2,704,250
1989	232,747	219,826	226,742	208,042	220,124	235,689	257,050	258,687	227,150	219,910	219,300	259,038	2,784,304
1990	237,289	212,880	226,034	211,070	222,908	249,175	266,375	268,527	237,017	224,694	213,748	237,434	2,808,151
1991	248,455	210,821	221,400	209,004	234,373	248,427	271,976	268,115	233,885	223,430	221,377	233,760	2,825,023
1992	243,970	217,761	224,665	210,837	220,355	236,842	266,148	255,203	234,760	221,289	221,263	244,126	2,797,219
1993	245,782	224,617	234,801	211,374	222,396	249,633	282,292	279,132	236,603	223,629	225,855	246,412	2,882,525
1994	261,697	225,011	231,544	214,817	227,703	263,859	278,149	274,645	237,663	227,972	224,745	242,906	2,910,712
1995[1]	253,085	228,594	233,689	217,408	236,375	256,066	292,550	304,620	245,580	234,416			

[1] Preliminary. *Source: Energy Information Administration, U.S. Department of Energy*

Use of Fuels for Electric Generation in the United States

	Consumption of Fuel									
Year	Coal (Thousand Short Tons)	Fuel Oil (Thousand Barrels)[2]	Gas (Million Cubic Feet)	Total Fuel in Coal Equivalent[3] (Thousand Short Tons)	Net Generation by Fuels[4] (Million Kw. Hr.)	Pounds of Coal Per Kw. Hr. (Pounds)	Cost of Fossil-Fuel at Elec. Util. ¢ Mil. BTU	Average Cost of Fuel Per Kw. Hr. (¢)	Heat Rate BTU Per Kw. Hr.	Cost Per Million BTU Consumed (¢)
1981	596,936	351,111	3,640,154	922,133	1,755,401	.992	225.6	2.42	10,506	230.2
1982	593,666	249,771	3,225,518	858,869	1,644,062	.996	224.9	2.46	10,517	234.0
1983	625,211	245,497	2,910,767	867,621	1,678,021	.993	220.6	2.40	10,547	227.1
1984	664,399	204,479	3,111,342	909,156	1,758,882	.990	219.1	2.41	10,385	232.0
1985	693,841	173,414	3,044,083	926,793	1,794,276	.990	209.4	2.27	10,429	217.7
1986	685,056	230,482	2,602,370	907,720	1,770,925	.989	175.0	1.92	10,423	184.5
1987	717,894	199,378	2,844,051	944,420	1,854,895	.981	170.6	1.84	10,354	177.7
1988	758,372	248,096	2,635,613	984,969	1,942,353	.984	164.3	1.76	10,328	170.7
1989	766,888	267,451	2,787,012	1,004,964	1,978,577	.987	167.5	1.79	10,312	174.0
1990	773,549	196,054	2,787,332	988,300	1,940,712	.997	168.9	1.80	10,366	174.1
1991	772,268	184,886	2,789,014	987,469	1,926,801	.996	160.3	1.75	10,322	169.6
1992	779,860	147,335	2,765,608	983,484	1,928,683	.990	159.0	1.72	10,340	166.6
1993	813,508	162,454	2,682,440	1,017,086	1,997,605	.993	159.5	1.72	10,351	166.6
1994[1]	817,270	151,004	2,987,146	1,033,575	2,017,646	.999	152.6	1.59	10,425	152.6

[1] Preliminary. [2] 42-gallon barrels. [3] Beginning in 1980, coal equivalents are calculated on the basis of Btu instead of generation data. [4] Excludes wood & waste fuels. *Source: Edison Electric Institute*

Fertilizer

The three primary fertilizer chemicals in the U.S. are nitrogen, phosphorus and potassium. These chemicals provide the basic nutrients to plants. The basic nitrogen fertilizer is ammonia, which is comprised of natural gas and nitrogen. Ammonia can be applied in liquid form below the surface of the soil or converted into solid nitrogenous fertilizers. Made from phosphate rock and sulfuric acid, phosphoric acid is the source of most phosphatic acid fertilizer. Diammonium phosphate is the only major fertilizer containing the two basic nutrients, nitrogen and phosphatic fertilizer. Potassium chloride, or potash, is the major potassium fertilizer. Nitrogen-based fertilizers account for more than one-half of total fertilizer consumption.

Potash is primarily a fertilizer that has slowed the conversion of fragile and marginal lands to crop lands, while allowing human populations to continue increasing by providing low cost food. Fixed nitrogen water-soluble phosphorus and water-soluble potassium are the main fertilizers. Potassium chloride accounted for about 70 percent of potash sales by domestic producers; potassium sulfate was more than 15 percent of sales by domestic producers. It is estimated that 10 percent of total sales went to non-agricultural end uses. Apparent domestic consumption of potash increased in 1994 by nearly six percent from 1993.

Three potash mines have closed since 1978. U.S. production of potash in 1994 was 2.83 million tonnes, down eight per cent from 1993. Sales by producers were 2.97 million tonnes compared to 3.03 million tonnes in 1993. Total sales of North American potash for agriculture in 1994 were 4.94 million tonnes, up fourteen percent from 1993. By state destination, Illinois took 607,000 tonnes, Iowa 455,000 tonnes, Ohio 447,000 tonnes and Indiana 403,000 tonnes. Non-agricultural potash sales were 592,000 tonnes with the major states of destination being Ohio 86,800 tonnes, Wisconsin 69,800 tonnes, Alabama 201,000 tonnes and Mississippi 53,300 tonnes.

U.S. exports of potassium chloride in 1994 were 419,000 tonnes, up 16 percent from 1993. Major destinations were Mexico, Chile, Ecuador and France. Exports of potassium sulfate in 1994 were 563,000 tonnes, up one percent. Major destinations were Japan and China. U.S. imports for consumption of potash were 7.92 million tonnes, up 10 percent. Canada was by far the major supplier.

Phosphate rock is produced mostly in Florida and North Carolina. In 1994, marketable phosphate rock production and consumption increased because of record diammonium phosphate export shipments to China, as well as rising domestic fertilizer demand due to an increase in feedgrain and cotton acreage. Economic recovery in the U.S. led to additional increases in the production of phosphate rock for industrial products. In 1994, U.S. production of phosphate rock was 157 million tonnes, up 47 percent from 1993. U.S. exports of phosphate rock in 1994 were 3.31 million tonnes, down seven percent from 1993. The major destination was South Korea. U.S. exports of superphosphates was 801,000 tonnes, up five percent. exports of diammonium phosphates was 9.19 million tonnes, up 25 percent as China imported 5.41 million tonnes. Exports of monoammonium phosphate were 1.48 million tonnes, up 36 percent.

Futures Market

Diammonium phosphate futures are traded on the Chicago Board of Trade (CBOT).

World Production of Ammonia In Thousands of Metric Tons of Contained Nitrogen

Year	Bulgaria	Canada	China	France	Germany	India	Indonesia	Italy	Japan	Mexico	Netherlands	Poland	Romania	Russia[3]	United Kingdom	United States	Total
1988	1,342	3,289	16,500	1,832	2,980	6,205	2,367	1,561	1,524	2,067	2,695	2,338	2,795	20,200	1,105	12,544	99,265
1989	1,326	3,339	17,000	1,476	2,932	6,661	2,526	1,446	1,539	2,100	2,901	2,360	2,736	19,400	1,037	12,280	99,331
1990	1,309	3,054	17,500	1,586	2,690	7,010	2,789	1,197	1,531	2,164	3,188	1,962	1,785	18,200	1,148	12,680	97,160
1991	1,093	3,016	18,000	1,604	2,123	7,132	2,706	1,147	1,553	2,221	3,033	1,531	1,130	17,100	1,011	12,803	97,500
1992	905	3,104	18,000	1,848	2,113	7,450	2,688	1,098	1,602	2,203	2,588	1,490	1,420	8,786	869	13,400	93,800
1993[1]	750	3,410	19,000	1,870	2,100	7,350	2,888	729	1,447	1,758	2,470	1,420	1,400	8,138	873	12,600	91,700
1994[2]	800	3,470	19,000	1,800	2,130	7,400	2,800	800	1,450	2,030	2,500	1,500	1,400	7,500	900	13,400	91,600

[1] Preliminary. [2] Estimate. [3] Formerly part of the U.S.S.R.; data not reported separately until 1992. *Source: U.S. Bureau of Mines*

U.S. Salient Statistics of Nitrogen[3] (Ammonia) In Thousands of Metric Tons

Year	Net Import Reliance as a % of Apparent Consumption	Production[3] (Fixed): Fertilizer	Production[3] (Fixed): Non-fertilizer	Production[3] (Fixed): Total	Imports[4] (Fixed)	Exports	Nitrogen[5] Compounds: Produced	Nitrogen[5] Compounds: Consumption	Stocks, Dec. 31: Ammonia	Stocks, Dec. 31: Fixed Nitrogen Compounds	Ammonia Consumption (Apparent)	Average Price ($ Per Tonne): Urea F.O.B. Gulf/6 Coast	Urea F.O.B. Corn Belt	Ammonium Nitrate: F.O.B. Corn Belt	Ammonia F.O.B. Gulf Coast
1986[7]	13	10,852	1,057	11,909	2,048	531	8,100	8,147	1,507	NA	13,714	75-78	90-110	100-120	75
1987	13	10,903	1,101	12,004	2,138	769	8,468	8,514	955	NA	13,783	114-117	125-135	100-120	95
1988	14	11,400	1,144	12,544	2,751	582	9,279	9,333	925	705	14,742	139-145	150-155	128-135	109
1989	17	11,131	1,148	12,280	2,861	346	9,634	9,687	849	787	14,871	139-145	110-120	105-115	104
1990	15	11,573	1,107	12,680	2,673	482	9,851	9,902	797	1,451	14,923	155-156	155-165	120-125	106
1991	14	11,559	1,244	12,803	2,742	580	9,770	9,815	936	1,607	14,826	142-143	146-160	108-130	117
1992	14	12,000	1,349	13,400	2,690	354	10,404	10,448	1,059	1,789	15,600	142-146	149-160	138-149	106
1993[1]	17	11,300	1,320	12,600	2,657	378	10,000	10,100	852	1,600	15,100	139-141	141-165	138-149	121
1994[2]	18	11,600	1,750	13,400	3,450	215	10,200	10,200	956	1,650	16,500	219-226	204-215	165-176	211

[1] Preliminary. [2] Estimate. [3] Anhydrous ammonia, synthetic. [4] For consumption. [5] Major downstream nitrogen compounds. [6] Granular. [7] Reported in short tons before 1987. NA = Not available. *Source: U.S. Bureau of Mines*

FERTILIZER

World Production of Phosphate Rock, Basic Slag & Guano   In Thousands of Metric Tons (Gross Weight)

Year	Algeria	Brazil	China	Egypt	Israel	Jordan	Morocco	Nauru Island	Russia[3]	Senegal	Syria	Togo	Tunisia	United States	World Total
1985	1,207	4,214	6,970	1,074	4,076	6,067	20,737	1,508	33,750	1,814	1,270	2,452	4,530	50,835	148,849
1986	1,203	4,509	6,700	1,271	3,673	6,249	21,178	1,494	33,900	1,850	1,606	2,314	5,951	38,710	138,869
1987	1,073	4,777	15,000	1,175	3,798	6,800	21,300	1,376	34,100	1,874	1,986	2,644	6,390	40,954	151,962
1988	1,332	4,672	17,000	1,154	3,479	6,611	25,015	1,541	37,000	2,326	2,186	3,464	6,103	45,389	166,436
1989	1,124	3,655	20,000	1,355	3,922	6,900	18,067	1,181	37,500	2,273	2,256	3,355	6,610	49,817	167,342
1990	1,128	2,968	21,550	1,151	3,516	6,082	21,396	926	36,800	2,147	1,633	2,314	6,258	46,343	162;783
1991	1,090	3,280	22,000	1,660	3,370	4,433	17,900	530	28,400	1,741	1,359	2,965	6,352	48,096	150,731
1992	1,136	2,850	23,000	2,008	3,595	4,296	19,146	747	11,500	2,284	1,266	2,080	6,400	46,965	141,000
1993[1]	718	3,420	24,000	1,590	3,590	3,570	18,305	634	9,400	1,670	931	1,750	5,500	35,494	121,000
1994[2]	725	3,400	24,000	1,500	3,600	3,500	18,000	613	8,000	1,600	900	1,800	5,500	41,100	124,000

[1] Preliminary. [2] Estimate. [3] Formerly part of the U.S.S.R.; data not reported separately until 1992. *Source: U.S. Bureau of Mines*

U.S. Salient Statistics of Phosphate Rock   In Thousands of Metric Tons

Year	Mine Production	Marketable Production	Value Million $	Imports for Consumption	Exports	Apparent Consumption	Stocks, Dec. 31 (Producer)	Price - $ Avg. Per Metric Ton (F.O.B. Mine)	**Avg. Price of Florida & North Carolina - $ Tonne - F.O.B. Mine (-60% to +74%) -** Domestic	Export	Average
1985	175,227	50,835	1,236	34	9,136	37,532	15,534	24.31	23.08	26.72	23.81
1986	135,683	40,320	897	528	7,848	34,456	13,277	22.25	21.64	25.02	22.31
1987	148,426	40,954	793	464	8,454	35,683	10,884	19.37	18.93	22.87	19.77
1988	162,299	45,389	888	676	8,092	41,025	9,323	19.56	18.29	25.24	19.56
1989	170,268	49,817	1,084	705	7,842	42,143	11,027	21.76	20.65	28.67	21.76
1990	151,277	46,343	1,075	451	6,238	43,967	8,912	23.20	22.44	30.43	23.55
1991	154,485	48,096	1,109	552	5,082	40,177	10,168	23.06	22.67	31.69	23.69
1992	154,936	46,965	1,058	1,530	3,723	42,920	12,612	22.53	22.47	31.69	23.32
1993[1]	106,790	35,494	759	534	3,198	38,287	9,215	21.38	21.26	28.11	21.89
1994[2]	157,000	41,100	839	620	2,800	43,100	5,980	20.42	21.79	25.60	22.08

[1] Preliminary. [2] Estimate. *Source: U.S. Bureau of Mines*

World Production of Marketable Potash   In Thousands of Metric Tons (K_2O Equivalent)

Year	Belarus[3]	Brazil	Canada	Chile	China	France	Germany	Israel	Italy	Jordan	Russia[3]	Spain	United Kingdom	United States	World Total
1985	------	------	6,661	21	40	1,750	6,048	1,200	205	561	10,367	659	343	1,296	29,151
1986	------	18	6,753	20	40	1,617	5,646	1,255	158	660	10,228	795	396	1,202	28,788
1987	------	62	7,668	23	40	1,539	5,709	1,253	178	734	10,888	741	429	1,262	30,526
1988	------	54	8,154	25	22	1,502	5,800	1,244	95	785	11,301	855	460	1,521	31,820
1989	------	97	7,333	45	42	1,195	5,388	1,273	112	792	10,200	741	462	1,595	29,276
1990	------	66	6,989	45	29	1,292	4,960	1,311	68	841	9,000	686	488	1,713	27,493
1991	------	101	7,406	55	32	1,129	3,855	1,320	31	818	8,560	585	495	1,749	26,136
1992	3,311	85	7,270	55	21	1,141	3,460	1,300	86	808	3,454	594	529	1,705	23,900
1993[1]	1,947	173	6,841	55	25	890	2,860	1,310	0	822	2,597	661	550	1,506	20,300
1994[2]	2,510	240	8,040	70	25	870	3,290	1,260	0	930	2,480	684	580	1,400	22,500

[1] Preliminary. [2] Estimate. [3] Formerly part of the U.S.S.R.; data not reported separately until 1992. *Source: U.S. Bureau of Mines*

U.S. Salient Statistics of Potash   In Thousands of Metric Tons (K_2O Equivalent)

Year	Net Import as % of Consumption	Production	Sales by Producers	Value Million $	Imports for Consumption	Exports	Apparent Consumption	Producer Stocks, Dec. 31	-------- **$ Per Ton** -------- Avg. Value Per Ton of Product - $	Avg. Value of K2O Equiv.	Avg. Price[3] $ Per Tonne
1986	75	1,202	1,147	144.9	4,212	547	4,843	378	63.24	126.28	82
1987	75	1,262	1,485	197.7	4,073	470	5,088	155	67.98	131.73	93
1988	71	1,521	1,427	240.3	4,217	380	5,264	248	85.75	168.37	132
1989	65	1,595	1,536	271.5	3,410	446	4,500	307	90.28	176.74	137
1990	68	1,713	1,716	303.3	4,164	470	5,410	303	89.46	176.80	130
1991	69	1,749	1,709	304.5	4,158	624	5,243	343	91.52	178.20	131
1992	68	1,705	1,766	334.4	4,248	663	5,351	283	96.45	189.36	134
1993	72	1,506	1,484	286.0	4,363	415	5,432	305	94.36	192.72	131
1994[1]	74	1,420	1,390	270.0	4,570	399	5,560	213	94.83	193.88	125
1995[2]		1,430	1,430	289.0	4,720	462	5,690	218	99.20	202.50	139

[1] Preliminary. [2] Estimate. [3] Unit of K_2O, standard 60% muriate F.O.B. mine. *Source: U.S. Bureau of Mines*

Fish

Domestic fish supplies come mainly from landings by the wild catch industry and imports. Aquaculture or domestically raised fish have become an increasingly important industry in the U.S. The Commerce Department's National Marine Fisheries Service reported that the U.S. appetite for seafood is increasing. The latest data for 1994 shows that average per capita consumption of seafood is 15.2 pounds a year, up two percent. Per capita consumption of shrimp reached a record 2.6 pounds. Imports accounted for 54 percent of the seafood consumed in the U.S. Americans consumed 3.93 billion pounds of fish and shellfish in 1994 compared to 3.85 billion pounds the year before. Per capita consumption rose by .2 pounds. U.S. per capita consumption of seafood has averaged about 15 pounds since 1985 with the record set in 1987 at 16.2 pounds. Of the 1994 total of 15.2 pounds per capita, there were 10.4 pounds of fresh or frozen fish and shellfish, up .2 pounds, 4.5 pounds of canned seafood, up .2 pounds and .3 pounds of cured seafood. Consumption of canned tuna was down slightly.

The USDA reported that as of July 1, 1995 catfish growers reported they had 158,800 acres of ponds in production. This was two percent above the previous two years but still less than the July 1991 total of 166,000 acres. Most of the increase was in Alabama, Arkansas and Louisiana with Mississippi acreage increasing only slightly. Over 10,000 acres of ponds were under construction or being renovated. While farm prices for catfish are strong, acreage costs are high also. Because of the high cost of constructing catfish ponds, producers responses to high prices will be muted but acreage will stay in production as prices fall. In 1995, the number of catfish operations was 1,267. The USDA notes that the catfish industry is following the path of other livestock industries toward fewer but larger production units. There are economies of size for feed purchases, harvesting and pond management.

Grower inventories of food-size fish on July 1, 1995 were down one percent but inventories of stockers were up 13 percent. Farm level catfish sales were expected to reach 455-465 million pounds, up 4-6 percent from 1994. During the first eight months of 1995, catfish sales totaled 304 million pounds, four percent more than in 1994.

Over the first six months of 1995, Atlantic salmon imports reached 51.4 million pounds with a value of $128 million, both 32 percent above 1994. Imports of Atlantic salmon have almost doubled in the last four years as farm-raised product (almost all Atlantic salmon) continues to displace fresh Pacific salmon products. Fresh Atlantic salmon is available year round which has probably expanded the market. Salmon farming is one of the world's largest aquaculture industries and second only to shrimp in trade value. World farm-raised salmon production in 1995 is estimated at over 500,000 tonnes and is forecast to soon surpass wild harvests. Norway is by far the largest producer of farm-raised salmon.

U.S. Fishery Products -- Supply In Millions of Pounds[2]

					Domestic Catch					Imports				
	Grand	-For Human Food-		For Industrial		% of Grand	-For Human Food-		For Industrial		% of Grand	-For Human Food-		For Industrial
Year	Total	Finfish	Shellfish[3]	Use[4]	Total	Total	Finfish	Shellfish[3]	Use[4]	Total	Total	Finfish	Shellfish[3]	Use[4]
1983	12,252	6,358	2,055	3,939	6,439	52.1	2,351	887	3,201	5,913	47.9	4,007	1,168	738
1984	12,552	6,303	2,195	4,054	6,438	51.3	2,348	972	3,118	6,114	48.7	3,955	1,223	936
1985	15,150	6,991	2,346	5,813	6,258	41.3	2,273	1,021	2,964	8,892	58.7	4,718	1,325	2,849
1986	14,368	7,087	2,533	4,748	6,031	42.0	2,240	1,153	2,638	8,337	58.0	4,847	1,380	2,110
1987	15,744	7,919	2,642	5,183	6,896	43.8	2,769	1,177	2,950	8,848	56.2	5,150	1,465	2,233
1988	14,628	7,786	2,719	4,123	7,192	49.2	3,306	1,282	2,604	7,436	50.8	4,480	1,437	1,519
1989	15,485	9,735	2,533	3,217	8,463	54.7	4,897	1,307	2,259	7,022	45.3	4,838	1,226	958
1990	16,349	10,120	2,542	3,687	9,404	57.5	5,747	1,294	2,363	6,945	42.5	4,373	1,248	1,324
1991	16,364	10,186	2,834	3,344	9,484	58.0	5,564	1,467	2,453	6,879	42.0	4,622	1,367	890
1992	16,106	10,297	2,945	2,864	9,637	59.8	6,182	1,436	2,019	6,469	40.2	4,115	1,509	845
1993[1]	20,334	10,796	3,025	6,513	10,467	51.5	6,746	1,468	2,253	9,867	48.5	4,026	1,581	4,260

[1] Preliminary. [2] Live weight, except percent. [3] For univalue and bivalues mollusks (conchs, clams, oysters, scallops, etc.) the weight of meats, excluding the shell is reported. [4] Fish meal and sea herring. *Source: Fisheries Statistics Division, U.S. Department of Commerce*

U.S. Fisheries -- Landings of Principal Species In Millions of Pounds

	Fish									Shellfish					
Year	Cod, Atlantic	Flounder	Halibut	Herring, Sea	Men-haden	Pollock	Salmon, Pacific	Tuna	Whiting	Clams (Meats)	Crabs	Lobsters (American)	Oysters (Meats)	Scallops (Meats)	Shrimp
1986	61	169	78	210	2,391	185	659	88	40	145	356	46	41	22	400
1987	59	200	76	207	2,712	598	562	100	35	134	386	46	40	41	363
1988	76	229	82	222	2,086	1,290	606	111	36	132	456	49	32	43	331
1989	78	202	75	209	1,989	2,385	786	89	39	138	458	53	30	41	352
1990	96	255	70	221	1,962	3,129	733	62	44	139	499	61	29	42	346
1991	93	405	66	230	1,977	2,873	783	36	37	134	650	63	32	40	320
1992	62	646	67	282	1,644	2,952	716	57	36	142	624	56	36	34	338
1993[1]	51	599	63	216	1,983	3,258	888	55	36	148	604	57	34	19	293
1994[1]	NA	427	NA	214	2,324	3,133	901	72	NA	131	447	75	38	25	283

[1] Preliminary. NA = Not available. *Source: Fisheries Statistics Division, U.S. Department of Commerce*

FISH

U.S. Fisheries: Quantity & Value of Domestic Catch & Consumption & World Fish Oil Production

Year	Disposition: Fresh & Frozen	Canned	Cured	For Meal, Oil, Etc.	Total	For Human Food	For Industrial Products	Ex-vessel Value[3] Million $	Average Price ¢ Lb.	Fish Per Capita Consumption Lbs.	World[2] Fish Oil Production 1,000 Tonnes
	Millions Pounds										
1983	2,304	1,087	80	2,968	6,439	3,238	3,201	2,355	36.6	13.3	1,482
1984	2,336	1,128	82	2,892	6,438	3,320	3,118	2,350	36.5	14.1	1,369
1985	2,725	749	70	2,714	6,258	3,294	2,964	2,326	37.2	15.0	1,517
1986	2,487	1,134	60	2,350	6,031	3,393	2,638	2,763	45.8	15.4	1,384
1987	3,157	1,009	89	2,641	6,896	3,946	2,950	3,115	45.2	16.1	1,544
1988	3,813	1,017	86	2,276	7,192	4,588	2,604	3,520	48.9	15.1	1,613
1989	5,585	798	128	1,952	8,463	6,204	2,259	3,238	38.3	15.6	1,393
1990	6,501	751	126	2,026	9,404	7,041	2,363	3,522	37.4	15.0	1,406
1991	6,541	674	119	2,150	9,484	7,031	2,453	3,308	34.9	14.8	1,105
1992	7,288	543	110	1,696	9,637	7,618	2,019	3,678	38.2	14.7	1,187
1993[1]	7,744	649	115	1,959	10,467	8,214	2,253	3,471	32.6	14.9	1,224

[1] Preliminary. [2] Crop year on a marketing year basis. [3] At the Dock Prices. *Source: Fisheries Statistics Division, U.S. Department of Commerce*

Imports of Seafood Products into the U.S. In Thousands of Pounds

Year	Fresh: Atlantic Salmon	Fresh: Pacific Salmon	Fresh: Shrimp	Frozen: Trout	Frozen: Atlantic Salmon	Frozen: Pacific Salmon	Frozen: Shrimp	Oysters[1]	Mussels[2]	Clams[3]	Canned Salmon	Prepared Shrimp[4]
1990	35,948	43,296	11,193	4,866	6,362	10,293	464,529	18,971	5,853	10,267	1,371	25,622
1991	39,709	47,487	12,206	3,331	3,687	8,245	499,859	17,914	6,595	6,975	990	27,531
1992	48,843	40,075	8,348	6,197	5,302	10,199	558,580	16,800	7,657	6,192	2,671	36,782
1993	62,860	33,920	11,649	4,741	7,714	11,659	556,213	17,293	9,658	5,818	2,053	44,765
1994	68,254	31,952	NA	3,878	7,851	11,210	580,010	15,415	11,032	8,265	3,190	47,910
1995[5]	47,284	10,406	NA	1,775	4,127	4,786	232,837	5,359	7,758	2,789	1,404	20,304

[1] Oysters fresh or prepared. [2] Mussels fresh or prepared. [3] Clams, fresh or prepared. [4] Shrimp, canned, breaded or prepare. [5] January to June trade figures. NA = Not available. *Source: Bureau of Census, U.S. Department of Commerce*

Exports of Seafood Products into the U.S. In Thousands of Pounds

Year	Fresh: Atlantic Salmon	Fresh: Pacific Salmon	Fresh: Shrimp	Frozen: Trout	Frozen: Atlantic Salmon	Frozen: Pacific Salmon	Frozen: Shrimp	Oysters[1]	Mussels[2]	Clams[3]	Canned Salmon	Prepared Shrimp[4]
1990	0	22,372	1,971	1,336	112	281,289	18,071	1,010	1,508	3,893	49,401	11,601
1991	473	14,389	2,927	1,040	123	195,821	14,980	929	1,665	4,405	66,025	9,937
1992	1,396	20,655	3,558	1,201	406	240,072	18,082	1,105	2,317	4,999	85,369	11,134
1993	4,018	24,275	2,776	955	373	257,751	16,524	1,454	2,291	4,217	84,520	11,539
1994	1,184	22,483	NA	1,958	384	260,469	13,622	2,634	1,935	3,785	90,393	15,778
1995[5]	2,802	5,595	NA	774	119	31,887	7,584	1,171	941	1,739	38,552	7,138

[1] Oysters fresh or prepared. [2] Mussels fresh or prepared. [3] Clams, fresh or prepared. [4] Shrimp, canned, breaded or prepare. [5] January to June trade figures. NA = Not available. *Source: Bureau of Census, U.S. Department of Commerce*

World Production of Fish Meal In Thousands of Metric Tons

Year	Chile	Spain	Denmark	EC-12	FSU-12	Iceland	Japan	Mexico	Norway	Peru	South Africa	Thailand	United States	World Total
1983-4	943.8	84.8	322.9	542.9	659.0	132.3	1,174.3	58.2	307.5	423.8	130.4	220.1	417.8	5,630.2
1984-5	1,056.2	87.5	290.7	508.9	658.6	166.9	1,181.6	73.0	263.0	567.7	120.0	221.6	410.9	6,064.8
1985-6	1,169.0	88.7	316.7	523.1	725.3	181.3	1,132.9	84.2	200.2	965.0	122.2	215.9	366.3	6,526.5
1986-7	1,073.2	88.7	268.0	469.1	761.1	202.0	1,073.0	100.3	164.0	1,008.4	260.7	219.9	389.4	6,554.4
1987-8	1,066.0	83.4	306.0	538.9	768.8	184.3	1,042.5	84.1	193.2	892.6	215.7	237.2	346.1	6,436.7
1988-9	1,305.2	128.0	340.6	579.5	754.1	181.4	977.4	86.4	196.3	1,405.9	151.7	260.8	338.8	7,002.9
1989-90	1,124.6	129.6	256.4	499.0	705.0	140.9	1,000.8	85.0	166.8	1,180.4	103.8	284.9	299.5	6,341.2
1990-1	1,144.2	116.6	302.6	535.8	643.9	87.1	841.8	80.1	220.8	1,308.5	87.9	291.9	310.4	6,300.7
1991-2	1,322.1	108.3	351.7	575.0	547.1	158.9	509.6	49.8	239.9	1,095.6	150.3	264.2	312.2	5,971.9
1992-3[1]	1,091.2	94.0	300.1	509.4	480.0	197.3	395.0	36.4	250.8	1,767.3	128.3	254.5	352.5	6,201.0
1993-4[2]	1,526.1	85.0	352.7	551.7	370.0	183.0	335.0	39.0	216.8	2,210.0	75.4	245.0	478.4	6,966.5
1994-5[3]	1,430.0	83.0	330.0	525.5	340.0	175.0	260.0	38.0	220.0	2,060.0	115.0	245.0	400.0	6,552.2

[1] Preliminary. [2] Estimate. [3] Forecast. *Source: The Oil World*

Monthly Production of Catfish--Round Weight Processed--in the U.S. In Thousands of Pounds (Live Weight)

Year	Jan.	Feb.	Mar.	Apr.	May	June	July	Aug.	Sept.	Oct.	Nov.	Dec.	Total
1986	19,761	19,083	18,664	16,354	16,013	15,951	17,036	18,663	18,859	20,453	17,107	15,812	213,756
1987	20,988	22,163	27,583	26,781	21,623	19,581	21,638	24,403	26,577	27,920	20,684	20,555	280,496
1988	26,018	27,786	28,179	20,805	20,351	22,839	23,687	26,941	24,611	26,221	25,037	22,634	295,109
1989	26,948	28,559	29,458	27,310	28,892	27,598	27,827	28,371	30,366	31,670	29,096	25,805	341,900
1990	33,066	31,884	33,120	30,980	31,542	28,967	29,540	31,108	27,566	29,211	27,913	25,538	360,435
1991	32,206	33,036	35,951	31,205	31,322	31,588	32,720	32,912	33,244	35,400	31,114	30,172	390,870
1992	36,200	39,228	45,048	41,177	39,111	36,813	36,128	37,958	37,857	39,212	35,073	33,562	457,367
1993	40,327	40,277	43,521	39,920	37,030	35,496	37,086	37,706	37,072	39,472	36,557	34,549	459,013
1994	36,714	35,035	40,446	34,494	34,163	34,595	35,901	39,813	38,716	39,072	36,054	34,266	439,269
1995[1]	38,807	38,515	42,200	36,588	37,030	36,047	35,800	38,827	37,634	39,456	34,119	31,863	446,886

[1] Preliminary. *Source: Economic Research Service, U.S. Department of Agriculture*

U.S. Average Price Paid to Producers for Farm-Raised Catfish In Cents Per Pound (Live Weight)

Year	Jan.	Feb.	Mar.	Apr.	May	June	July	Aug.	Sept.	Oct.	Nov.	Dec.	Average
1986	70.0	70.0	72.0	74.0	72.0	68.0	66.0	63.0	63.0	62.0	61.0	61.0	66.8
1987	60.0	57.0	59.0	65.0	69.0	64.0	61.0	60.0	60.0	61.0	62.0	64.0	61.8
1988	68.0	72.0	75.0	75.0	75.0	78.0	80.0	80.0	79.0	79.0	78.0	78.0	76.4
1989	78.0	78.0	77.0	76.0	76.0	75.0	71.0	68.0	65.0	64.0	64.0	68.0	71.7
1990	72.0	74.0	78.0	78.0	78.0	78.0	76.0	76.0	76.0	76.0	75.0	72.0	75.8
1991	69.0	69.0	69.0	69.0	66.0	65.0	63.0	60.0	59.0	58.0	57.0	53.0	63.1
1992	53.0	56.0	60.0	63.0	63.0	61.0	59.0	58.0	59.0	61.0	62.0	63.0	59.8
1993	63.0	67.0	70.0	71.0	72.0	72.0	72.0	73.0	73.0	73.0	73.0	73.0	71.0
1994	74.0	77.0	79.0	80.0	80.0	80.0	80.0	80.0	80.0	77.0	77.0	77.0	78.4
1995[1]	78.0	79.0	79.0	79.0	79.0	79.0	79.0	79.0	78.0	78.0	78.0	78.0	78.6

[1] Preliminary. *Source: Economic Research Service, U.S. Department of Agriculture*

U.S. Sales and Prices of Fresh Catfish

Year	Jan.	Feb.	Mar.	Apr.	May	June	July	Aug.	Sept.	Oct.	Nov.	Dec.	Total/Avg.
						In Thousands of Pounds							
SALES--Whole													
1992	4,462	4,793	4,928	4,156	3,631	3,999	3,937	4,223	4,164	4,102	3,522	3,570	49,487
1993	4,363	4,385	4,073	3,730	3,399	3,278	3,281	3,424	3,457	3,305	3,224	3,277	43,196
1994	3,664	3,677	3,752	3,192	3,176	2,892	3,036	3,173	3,179	3,197	2,888	2,862	38,688
1995[1]	3,221	3,373	3,856	3,086	2,997	2,903	2,951	3,184	3,108	3,166	2,962	2,847	37,654
Fillets[2]													
1992	3,410	3,608	4,316	3,426	3,203	3,155	3,219	3,408	3,507	3,461	2,924	2,788	40,425
1993	3,743	3,732	3,893	3,535	3,362	3,200	3,194	3,290	3,311	3,291	2,996	3,050	40,597
1994	3,101	3,204	3,550	3,061	3,103	3,015	3,046	3,383	3,183	3,212	2,784	2,665	37,307
1995[1]	3,054	3,281	3,646	3,369	3,350	3,246	3,115	3,348	3,162	3,295	2,897	2,845	38,608
Other[3]													
1992	839	920	978	877	789	799	822	847	850	873	726	693	10,013
1993	965	915	1,068	824	761	734	751	707	824	842	771	803	9,965
1994	967	926	1,019	912	1,079	907	914	959	965	965	821	790	11,224
1995[1]	998	1,115	1,437	1,328	1,234	1,172	934	1,035	1,067	1,166	1,049	938	13,473
						In Dollars Per Pound							
PRICE--Whole													
1992	1.23	1.31	1.33	1.36	1.40	1.33	1.35	1.31	1.30	1.33	1.33	1.32	1.33
1993	1.35	1.41	1.51	1.52	1.54	1.54	1.56	1.54	1.52	1.55	1.52	1.53	1.51
1994	1.54	1.62	1.71	1.73	1.73	1.74	1.76	1.76	1.72	1.72	1.70	1.66	1.70
1995[1]	1.69	1.69	1.68	1.69	1.69	1.71	1.70	1.69	1.68	1.67	1.63	1.65	1.68
Fillets[2]													
1992	2.38	2.42	2.48	2.50	2.55	2.52	2.51	2.46	2.44	2.45	2.48	2.47	2.47
1993	2.48	2.56	2.62	2.64	2.65	2.65	2.65	2.63	2.65	2.67	2.67	2.66	2.63
1994	2.69	2.73	2.86	2.91	2.91	2.92	2.93	2.94	2.93	2.93	2.91	2.91	2.88
1995[1]	2.89	2.90	2.92	2.93	2.90	2.90	2.91	2.90	2.91	2.92	2.90	2.89	2.91
Other[3]													
1992	1.66	1.69	1.77	2.01	1.90	1.85	1.82	1.77	1.75	1.78	1.83	1.77	1.80
1993	1.70	1.80	1.93	1.94	1.92	1.90	1.89	1.91	1.94	1.90	1.92	2.00	1.90
1994	1.92	1.82	1.90	1.93	2.02	2.02	1.95	1.95	1.92	1.89	1.91	1.87	1.93
1995[1]	1.82	1.80	1.93	1.99	1.99	1.97	1.81	1.86	1.84	1.84	1.87	1.81	1.88

[1] Preliminary. [2] Includes regular, shank and strip fillets; excludes breaded products. [3] Includes steaks, nuggets and all other products not reported.
Source: Economic Research Service, U.S. Department of Agriculture

Flaxseed and Linseed Oil

The USDA lists flaxseed as a minor U.S. oilseed. U.S. production in recent years has averaged 3.0-3.5 million bushels. Linseed oil is derived from flaxseed, with annual production averaging 170 million pounds since 1990.

The area planted to U.S. flaxseed production has been trending irregularly lower for many years. Planted acreage for the 1995/96 crop of 213,000 compares with 178,000 in 1994/95. The mid-1980's average of 600,000 acres was less than half the acreage of the 1970's. Production in 1995/96 of 3.7 million bushels compares with 2.9 million in 1994/95. Annual production in the mid-1980's averaged about 8 million bushels and over 15 million in the early 1970's. The U.S crop is produced mostly in the Northern Plains states with North Dakota the largest producer. The crop year begins on June 1.

Imports of flaxseed come mostly from Canada, the world's largest producer. A dramatic shift in U.S. foreign trade of flaxseed has developed since the 1970's when the U.S. was net exporter of flaxseed, at times by a substantial margin. The U.S. has been a net flaxseed importer since 1978. The U.S. imports no linseed oil or meal.

U.S. domestic demand for linseed oil in 1995/96 of 170 million pounds compares with 168 million in 1994/95, while exports were put at 8 million pounds versus 24 million, respectively. Linseed oil is used as a drying agent in paint. Although its use has fallen in line with the acceptance of water based latex paints, overall demand for paint tends to reflect the strength or weakness in housing starts. U.S. demand for linseed oil for domestic usage and export apparently peaked years ago. Annual disappearance in the first half of the 1990's averaged about 175 million pounds and carryover stocks near 50 million pounds. Linseed meal production in 1995/96 of 162,000 short tons compares with 158,000 in 1994/95. Disappearance was nearly equal in both years at 164,000 tons, with slightly less than half the total exported.

The average price received by U.S. farmers for flaxseed in 1995/96 was expected to average between $4.75-$5.25 per bushel versus the year earlier average of $4.65. Linseed oil prices in 1995/96 were forecast between $.30-.36 per pound versus $.338 in 1994/95, basis Minneapolis. Linseed meal prices, basis 34 percent protein, Minneapolis, in 1995/96 were forecast between $107-147 per ton versus $97.50 in 1994/95.

Futures Markets

Flaxseed futures are traded on the Winnipeg Commodity Exchange (WPG). Prices are quoted in Canadian dollars per metric ton.

World Production of Flaxseed In Thousands of Metric Tons

Crop Year	Argentina	Australia	Bangladesh	Canada	China	Czechoslovakia	Egypt	France	Hungary	India	Poland	Romania	Turkey	United States	Uruguay	Former USSR	World Total
1985-6	460	12	8	902	535	15	22	34	7	380	18	36	5	211	6	201	2,350
1986-7	622	9	8	1,026	485	15	19	24	6	317	15	32	4	293	3	233	2,658
1987-8	535	8	43	701	400	10	29	21	20	393	11	38	4	189	5	228	2,755
1988-9	446	3	43	328	490	12	28	32	11	361	12	38	3	41	5	220	2,215
1989-90	526	2	47	498	400	16	21	31	11	326	12	49	3	31	4	227	2,352
1990-1	458	4	48	889	535	16	28	34	10	339	11	53	2	97	6	197	2,923
1990-1	458	4	48	889	535	16	28	34	10	339	11	53	2	97	6	197	2,923
1991-2	341	5	55	635	410	14	24	26	13	292	5	23	1	158	8	140	2,458
1992-3[1]	177	5	49	334	430	14	21	29	10	268	2	18	1	84	4	130	1,969
1993-4[2]	112	8	49	627	430	12	22	27	11	330	2	28	1	88	2	120	2,197
1994-5[3]	129	6	50	960	420	12	23	35	11	345	2	27	1	74	3	115	2,435

[1] Preliminary. [2] Estimate. [3] Forecast. *Source: The Oil World*

U.S. Supply and Distribution of Flaxseed In Thousands of Bushels

Crop Year Beginning June	Planted (1,000 Acres)	Harvested (1,000 Acres)	Yield Per Acre Bushels	Supply: Beginning Stocks	Supply: Production	Supply: Imports	Supply: Total Supply	Distribution: Seed	Distribution: Crush	Distribution: Exports	Distribution: Residual	Distribution: Total Distribution
1985-6	620	584	14	1,649	8,293	2,927	12,869	517	10,313	250	160	11,240
1986-7	720	683	17	1,629	11,538	2,224	15,391	362	10,000	1,448	280	12,090
1987-8	470	463	16	3,301	7,444	2,925	13,671	223	10,800	156	167	11,346
1988-9	275	226	7	2,325	1,615	6,730	10,670	158	8,500	764	-59	9,363
1989-90	195	163	8	1,307	1,215	7,260	9,782	211	8,250	1,054	23	9,538
1990-1	260	253	15	244	3,812	6,715	10,771	288	8,800	549	163	9,800
1991-2	356	342	18	971	6,200	4,371	11,542	139	9,050	541	256	9,986
1992-3	171	165	20	1,556	3,288	6,035	10,879	167	8,600	230	337	9,334
1993-4[1]	206	191	18	1,545	3,480	5,110	10,135	144	8,650	126	60	8,980
1994-5[2]	178	171	17	1,155	2,922	6,005	10,082	173	8,550	72	117	8,912
1995-6[3]	213	206	18	1,170	3,710	5,505	10,385	174	8,750	100	111	9,135

[1] Preliminary. [2] Estimate. [3] Forecast. *Source: Economic Research Service, U.S. Department of Agriculture*

U.S. Production of Flaxseed, by States In Thousands of Bushels

Crop Year	Minne-sota	North Dakota	South Dakota	Other States	Total	Crop Year	Minne-sota	North Dakota	South Dakota	Other States	Total
1986	544	9,538	1,456	------	11,538	1991	640	4,860	578	122	6,200
1987	224	6,518	702	------	7,444	1992	220	2,730	322	16	3,288
1988	110	1,295	210	------	1,615	1993	170	2,886	323	101	3,480
1989	95	980	140	------	1,215	1994	126	2,450	304	42	2,922
1990	238	3,118	456	------	3,812	1995[1]	171	1,725	260	55	2,211

[1] Preliminary. *Source: National Agricultural Statistics Service, U.S. Department of Agriculture*

Average Price Received by Farmers for Flaxseed in the U.S. In Dollars Per Bushel

Year	July	Aug.	Sept.	Oct.	Nov.	Dec.	Jan.	Feb.	Mar.	Apr.	May	June	Average
1986-7	4.39	3.80	3.69	3.46	3.39	3.41	3.18	3.13	3.04	3.15	3.35	3.44	3.47
1987-8	3.47	3.33	3.15	3.07	3.03	3.20	3.45	3.80	3.95	4.11	4.19	5.28	3.39
1988-9	6.29	7.19	7.67	7.85	8.09	8.34	8.34	8.70	8.09	7.78	7.54	6.79	7.56
1989-90	5.90	6.49	7.07	7.09	7.15	7.14	7.24	7.69	8.03	8.60	8.23	8.31	7.20
1990-1	7.56	5.86	5.36	5.15	5.16	5.15	5.12	4.80	4.90	4.66	4.33	3.98	5.32
1991-2	3.91	3.68	3.55	3.40	3.31	3.46	3.39	3.43	3.52	3.53	3.61	3.67	3.50
1992-3	3.70	3.71	4.12	4.09	4.10	4.21	4.12	4.47	4.54	4.41	4.37	4.44	4.19
1993-4	4.29	3.79	4.24	4.09	4.05	4.18	4.38	4.61	4.64	4.60	4.43	4.25	4.30
1994-5[1]	4.28	4.52	4.54	4.49	4.51	4.71	4.75	4.94	5.15	5.10	4.93	5.13	4.75
1995-6[1]	5.20	5.16	5.11	5.11	5.13	5.03	5.12						

[1] Preliminary. *Source: National Agricultural Statistics Service, U.S. Department of Agriculture*

United States Linseed Oil Consumption in Inedible Products In Millions of Pounds

Crop Year	July	Aug.	Sept.	Oct.	Nov.	Dec.	Jan.	Feb.	Mar.	Apr.	May	June	Total
1990-1	9.5	10.2	6.8	8.3	6.3	4.7		19.4			24.2		89.4
1991-2		29.0			23.2		15.5	15.5	13.0	15.0	15.3	11.4	137.9
1992-3	16.3	14.8	11.5	11.2	6.9	8.0	8.3	8.5	11.8	10.5	12.6	13.0	133.4
1993-4	14.9	8.1	11.2	9.0	7.2	10.7	10.2	7.5	9.9	8.5	11.5	11.7	120.4
1994-5	10.7	10.8	12.3	12.2	9.0	10.0	12.6	8.2	11.4	8.1	10.0	9.7	124.9
1995-6[1]	8.8	10.0	9.4	10.6	7.8								76.6

[1] Preliminary. *Source: Bureau of Census, U.S. Department of Commerce*

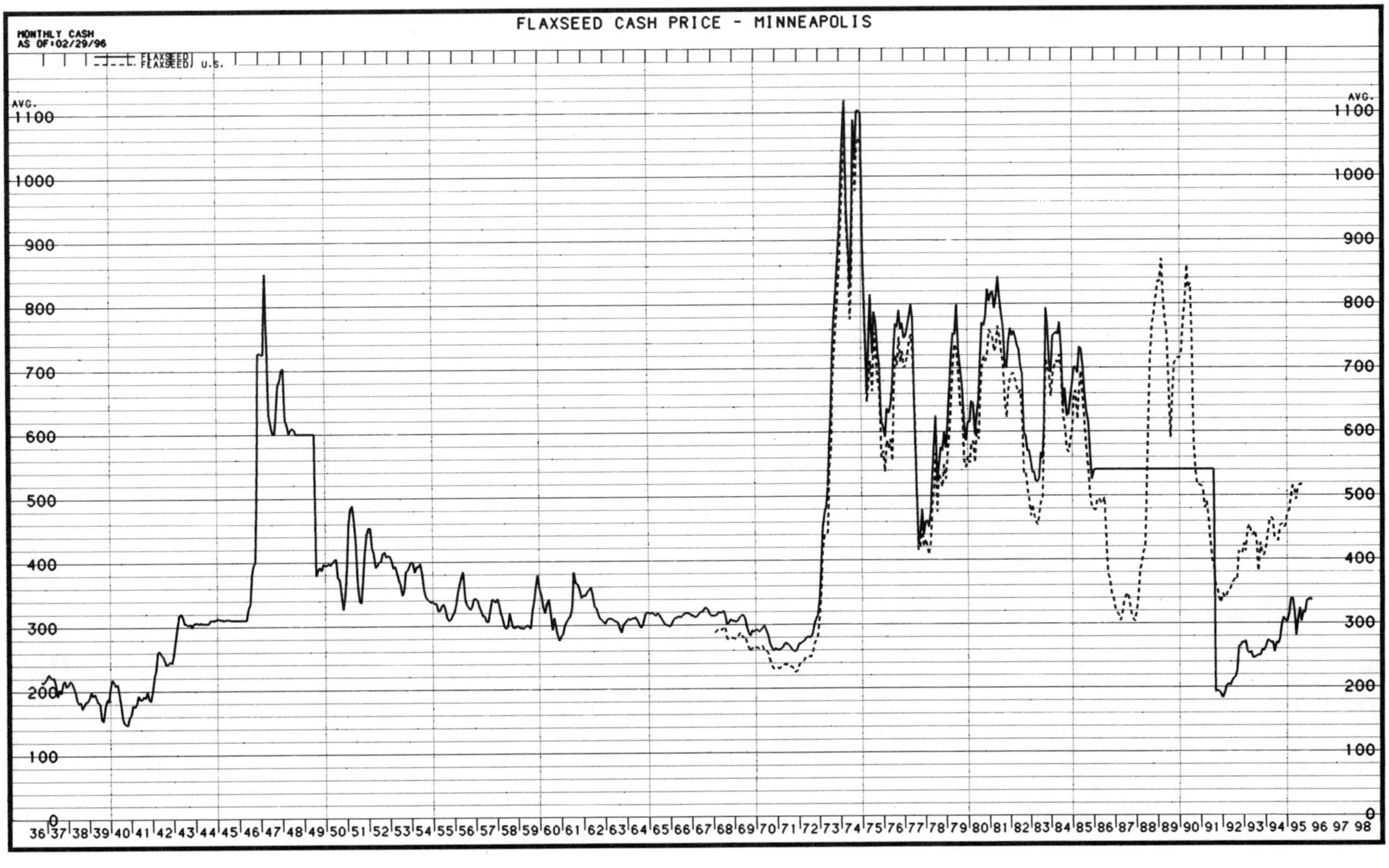

FLAXSEED AND LINSEED OIL

Supply and Distribution of Linseed Oil in the U.S. In Millions of Pounds

Crop Year Beginning June	Supply: Stocks June 1	Supply: Production	Supply: Total	Disappearance: Exports	Disappearance: Domestic	Disappearance: Total Disappearance	Average Price at Minneapolis Cents/Lb.
1985-6	33	205	238	15	184	199	30.80
1986-7	39	201	240	6	183	189	26.40
1987-8	51	217	268	8	219	227	24.70
1988-9	41	170	211	12	151	163	39.50
1989-90	48	165	213	12	164	176	40.20
1990-1	37	176	213	6	167	173	38.00
1991-2	40	182	222	12	170	182	32.10
1992-3	40	172	212	8	150	158	31.00
1993-4	54	174	228	7	159	166	32.50
1994-5[1]	63	172	237	24	169	192	34.10
1995-6[2]	45	175	223	8	170	178	30.0-34.0

[1] Preliminary. [2] Forecast. *Source: Economic Research Service, U.S. Department of Agriculture*

World Production and Price of Linseed Oil In Thousands of Metric Tons

Year	Argentina	Bangladesh	Belgium	China	Egypt	Ethiopia	Germany	India	Japan	United Kingdom	United States	Former U.S.S.R.	World Total	Price Rotterdam Ex-Tank $ Tonne
1985-6	143.7	------	7.1	139.7	13.0	13.3	113.1	104.7	36.5	14.0	90.8	7.3	784.2	475
1986-7	198.5	9.2	6.2	125.2	12.3	12.7	135.3	90.8	31.6	17.1	97.3	11.8	837.0	319
1987-8	175.5	10.3	8.3	111.3	11.1	10.5	81.1	105.7	33.6	13.5	82.4	12.6	734.9	441
1988-9	137.7	10.8	9.6	127.5	11.8	8.2	41.6	103.4	33.2	12.2	76.0	10.5	658.3	716
1989-90	158.8	11.6	12.9	104.1	11.7	6.6	44.9	92.9	31.4	11.4	76.1	11.5	646.6	756
1990-1	141.5	12.0	12.2	126.9	12.3	12.1	57.5	94.2	34.7	16.8	84.0	10.1	685.8	502
1991-2	114.0	13.5	14.7	115.5	11.3	11.7	56.1	83.8	31.9	27.0	87.9	9.1	642.9	377
1992-3	62.3	12.6	25.5	109.5	8.1	10.5	56.8	78.0	28.4	27.2	80.0	9.6	566.8	450
1993-4[1]	32.2	12.7	26.7	109.5	7.8	10.1	77.2	90.7	30.7	35.2	78.7	9.9	601.4	476
1994-5[2]	39.8	13.0	28.5	108.0	8.4	10.1	87.0	96.7	30.3	30.8	83.3	10.2	642.7	636

[1] Preliminary. [2] Forecast. *Source: The Oil World*

Factory Shipments of Paints, Varnish and Lacquer in the U.S. In Millions of Dollars

Year	Jan.	Feb.	Mar.	Apr.	May	June	July	Aug.	Sept.	Oct.	Nov.	Dec.	Total
1985	630.5	621.2	754.3	865.3	930.1	880.5	862.2	864.3	805.9	820.4	673.6	571.0	9,279
1986	698.6	681.1	760.0	903.9	913.8	891.0	862.7	856.3	841.5	863.4	660.1	614.3	9,547
1987	696.7	754.6	849.5	903.2	916.0	933.0	906.6	890.8	879.6	895.4	751.7	681.3	10,168
1988	751.5	822.3	958.0	970.1	1,034.0	1,067.0	937.5	1,000.0	932.6	908.1	819.7	751.5	10,783
1989	820.5	841.3	952.6	985.7	1,072.7	1,091.5	965.9	1,114.4	1,019.7	995.9	914.3	755.5	11,239
1990	853.2	881.1	1,020.4	1,035.1	1,076.3	1,077.2	1,032.7	1,084.3	963.1	1,046.8	854.9	730.9	11,762
1991		2,498.4			3,158.7			3,123.0			2,611.2		11,707
1992		2,852.3			3,464.1			3,308.7			2,816.4		12,441
1993		2,894.1			3,600.5			3,448.9			2,993.7		12,937
1994[1]		3,143.7			3,862.8			3,781.6			3,282.0		14,070
1995[1]		3,358.2			3,863.7			3,840.0					

[1] Preliminary. *Source: Bureau of Census, U.S. Department of Agriculture*

U.S. Stocks of Linseed Oil (Crude & Refined) at Factories & Warehouses In Millions of Pounds

Year	July 1	Aug. 1	Sept. 1	Oct. 1	Nov. 1	Dec. 1	Jan. 1	Feb. 1	Mar. 1	Apr. 1	May 1	June 1
1985-6	32.7	36.9	25.4	47.0	62.3	55.2	60.6	62.7	64.6	66.0	56.1	40.1
1986-7	46.0	45.3	40.4	40.0	50.3	68.0	60.0	68.0	60.0	64.6	55.0	51.1
1987-8	52.2	45.9	40.2	52.1	54.3	50.4	50.8	56.0	39.0	35.5	35.6	40.8
1988-9	35.6	36.0	44.8	24.4	33.5	36.6	46.8	54.6	47.6	49.1	54.6	47.5
1989-90	48.4	43.8	23.2	21.5	23.9	30.3	29.9	39.5	36.7	39.1	38.3	36.8
1990-1	28.2	21.9	17.2	41.8	41.4	47.5		61.7			75.4	
1991-2		60.6			64.2		73.1	51.2	62.3	45.6	45.7	41.4
1992-3	34.6	35.5	29.7	41.3	49.1	47.7	39.9	44.2	45.1	49.1	42.8	43.1
1993-4	45.2	39.0	42.1	47.0	27.9	19.3	22.5	38.0	42.0	49.4	52.0	62.6
1994-5[1]	60.3	56.5	49.4	60.6	48.1	39.3	38.6	38.9	31.0	35.7	37.9	44.8
1995-6[1]	39.5	44.6	37.4	46.0	48.0	46.9						

[1] Preliminary. *Source: Bureau of Census, U.S. Department of Commerce*

Wholesale Price of Raw Linseed Oil at Minneapolis in Tank Cars In Cents Per Pound

Year	July	Aug.	Sept.	Oct.	Nov.	Dec.	Jan.	Feb.	Mar.	Apr.	May	June	Average
1984-5	33.40	38.00	31.00	28.80	28.50	30.00	31.20	32.00	NA	NA	NA	NA	31.60
1985-6	34.60	33.30	33.00	30.00	30.00	27.60	30.00	30.00	30.00	30.00	30.00	29.40	30.70
1986-7	29.00	29.00	29.00	25.00	25.00	25.00	25.00	25.00	25.00	25.00	25.00	25.00	26.00
1987-8	25.00	25.00	25.00	22.75	24.25	25.00	25.00	25.00	25.00	24.75	24.75	28.20	24.98
1988-9	35.00	37.00	41.50	42.00	42.00	41.50	41.00	41.00	41.40	42.00	42.00	39.75	40.51
1989-90	39.00	39.00	39.50	40.00	40.00	40.00	40.00	40.00	41.60	42.00	42.00	43.00	40.51
1990-1	44.00	40.40	39.75	36.80	36.00	36.00	36.00	36.00	36.00	36.00	36.50	36.00	37.45
1991-2	36.00	36.00	36.00	30.00	30.00	30.00	30.00	30.00	30.00	30.00	30.00	30.00	31.50
1992-3	30.00	30.00	32.00	32.00	32.00	32.00	32.00	32.00	32.00	32.00	32.00	28.50	31.38
1993-4	32.00	32.00	32.00	32.00	32.00	32.00	32.00	32.00	32.00	32.00	32.00	32.00	32.00
1994-5[1]	30.31	32.00	32.00	33.50	35.00	35.00	35.00	35.00	35.00	35.00	35.00	35.00	33.98
1995-6[1]	35.00	35.50	37.00	37.00	37.00								

[1] Preliminary. *Source: Economic Research Service, U.S. Department of Agriculture*

Average Open Interest of Flaxseed Futures in Winnipeg In Contracts

Year	Jan.	Feb.	Mar.	Apr.	May	June	July	Aug.	Sept.	Oct.	Nov.	Dec.
1986	4,960	5,417	4,631	6,212	6,244	6,440	5,403	6,150	6,910	4,986	4,860	4,662
1987	4,356	4,284	4,034	5,665	6,938	6,932	6,348	6,953	7,901	5,880	5,705	5,210
1988	5,838	6,341	5,583	6,189	6,089	7,219	5,964	7,018	7,791	8,777	10,662	7,621
1989	7,864	7,875	5,422	6,038	6,479	8,297	8,609	9,234	8,191	5,120	4,613	3,349
1990	3,812	5,165	5,701	5,790	4,839	4,985	4,950	4,908	4,651	4,477	5,079	4,502
1991	4,033	4,140	4,175	4,861	4,137	4,642	5,317	6,106	6,173	5,733	5,669	5,333
1992	5,620	6,772	7,864	7,984	7,786	7,321	6,299	6,553	5,623	4,860	6,734	5,979
1993	7,810	8,052	6,203	5,672	5,505	5,321	4,246	5,777	5,923	3,568	3,763	3,922
1994	6,118	6,201	5,946	5,519	4,683	3,945	4,301	4,654	4,997	3,077	4,888	5,251
1995	6,242	8,731	7,505	7,121	8,107	7,212	6,436	5,557	6,230	5,245	5,937	4,414

Source: Winnipeg Commodity Exchange

Fruits

The USDA reported that fresh fruit consumption reached a new record in 1994, but a decline in processed non-citrus fruit consumption resulted in total per capita fruit consumption declining slightly for the year. For 1995, per capita consumption was not likely to post a substantial gain. Near-record output of oranges has been boosting juice consumption to record levels. California stonefruits, pears and strawberries were damaged by storms in 1995, reducing shipments but increasing prices. Fresh-market apple consumption was expected to decline in 1995 due to a smaller crop in Washington and higher export demand. Strong export demand for fresh grapefruit and oranges was expected to continue.

Total U.S. fruit consumption in 1994 was estimated at 276.5 pounds per person (fresh-weight equivalent), down from 278.2 pounds in 1993. Declines were registered in non-citrus fruit, about 60 percent of the total, as well as citrus fruit.

Total citrus fruit consumption rose to 115 pounds per person in 1994. Fresh use declined to 25 pounds, while processed fruit consumption, including oranges at 75 pounds and grapefruit at 8.8 pounds, rose to 90 pounds (fresh-weight equivalent). Total consumption of other citrus fruit rose in 1994.

Non-citrus fruit consumption fell to 161.5 pounds in 1994 (fresh-weight equivalent). Total apple consumption rose slightly to 49.3 pounds but grape consumption dropped to 41.6 pounds. Fresh grape consumption was higher in 1994, but processed use (raisins, wine, juice) fell to 34.3 pounds from 37.9 pounds in 1993.

U.S. per capita fresh-market fruit consumption set a record in 1994 of over 100 pounds. Non-citrus fruit consumption rose to 75.65 pounds in 1994. Fresh citrus fruit consumption declined to 24.93 pounds. Banana consumption rose to a record 28.1 pounds per person. Apples were the second most popular fresh-market fruit in 1994 with per capita consumption of 19.55 pounds.

The USDA forecast 1995 U.S. apple production at 11.19 billion pounds, down from 11.34 billion in 1993. The Washington crop was expected to be 5.2 billion pounds. The Michigan crop was forecast to be 19 percent higher at 1.21 billion pounds, while New York was forecast to increase three percent to 1.13 billion pounds. California production was estimated at 1.0 billion pounds, down five percent.

The 1995 U.S. grape crop was forecast to decline two percent to 11.55 billion pounds. California production was put at 10.18 billion pounds, down three percent. Raisin grapes were down six percent at 4.5 billion pounds with wine grapes down three percent at 4.4 billion pounds.

U.S. pear production in 1995 was 1.93 billion pounds, down eight percent from 1994. Sweet cherry production in 1995 was estimated at 271.4 billion pounds, down 35 percent due to heavy rains during pollination on the West Coast.

U.S. Commercial Production for Selected Fruits In Thousands of Short Tons

Year	Apples	Cherries[2]	Cranberries	Grapes	Grapefruit	Lemons	Nectarines	Oranges	Peaches	Pears	Pineapples	Prunes & Plums	Strawberries	Tangelos	Tangerines	Total All Fruits
1990	4,828	261	170	5,660	1,978	706	232	7,745	1,121	962	575	734	628	132	164	26,472
1991	4,853	244	211	5,556	2,256	719	215	7,848	1,348	903	555	831	683	119	166	27,110
1992	5,284	373	208	6,052	2,224	766	236	8,909	1,336	923	550	829	668	117	260	29,482
1993	5,342	331	196	6,023	2,791	942	205	10,992	1,330	948	370	588	724	137	247	31,742
1994[1]	5,668	351	227	5,871	2,661	984	242	10,329	1,253	1,046	365	878	813	150	318	31,746
1995[1]	4,856			5,777	2,809	1,045		11,659	1,247	964			727	113	317	

[1] Preliminary. [2] Sweet and tart. *Source: Economic Research Service, U.S. Department of Agriculture*

U.S. Commercial Production of Selected Fruits In Thousands of Short Tons

Year	Utilizated Production: Citrus[1]	Utilizated Production: Noncitrus[2]	Utilizated Production: Total	Value of Production: Citrus[1]	Value of Production: Noncitrus[2]	Value of Production: Total
	In Thousands of Short Tons			In Thousands of Dollars		
1989	13,186	16,345	29,531	2,663,248	5,279,382	7,942,630
1990	10,860	15,640	26,500	2,242,862	5,525,279	7,768,141
1991	11,285	15,740	27,025	2,414,933	6,021,210	8,436,143
1992	12,452	17,124	29,576	2,401,351	3,036,615	8,437,966
1993	15,274	16,555	31,829	2,151,173	6,133,463	8,284,636
1994[3]	14,561	17,217	31,778	2,245,415	6,159,422	8,404,837

[1] Year harvest was completed. [2] Includes bushberries (beginning 1992), cranberries and strawberries. [3] Preliminary. *Source: Economic Research Service, U.S. Department of Agriculture*

U.S. Annual-Average Retail Prices for Selected Fruits In Dollars Per Pound

Year	Red Delicious Apples	Bananas	Anjou Pears	Thompson Seedless Grapes	Lemons	Grapefruit	Oranges: Navel	Oranges: Valencias
1990	.719	.463	.763	1.256	1.074	.657	.570	.558
1991	.885	.481	.840	1.400	1.227	.618	.784	.925
1992	.890	.458	.830	1.288	1.007	.607	.586	.559
1993	.834	.439	.846	1.465	1.084	.529	.557	.654
1994	.803	.462	.802	1.642	1.090	.513	.545	.587
1995[1]	.829	.499	.774	1.525	1.111	.541	.597	.642

[1] Estimate. *Source: Economic Research Service, U.S. Department of Agriculture*

U.S. Utilization of Fruit Production, and Value In Thousands of Short Tons (Fresh Equivalent)

Year	Utilized Pro-duction	Fresh	Processed Canned	Dried	Juice	Frozen	Wine	Other	Value of Utilized Production $1,000
1986	13,874	4,896	2,211	1,668	1,135	286	2,909	259	4,203,597
1987	16,012	5,943	2,369	2,367	1,893	475	2,647	317	4,420,956
1988	15,911	5,909	2,374	2,546	1,415	459	2,983	224	5,102,962
1989	16,345	6,104	2,266	2,857	1,580	479	2,869	190	5,279,382
1990	15,640	6,093	2,244	2,440	1,448	506	2,717	192	5,525,279
1991	15,740	6,215	2,119	2,417	1,583	501	2,739	167	6,021,210
1992	17,124	6,522	2,386	2,369	1,743	584	3,256	264	6,036,615
1993	16,555	6,590	2,040	2,339	1,743	627	3,029	186	6,133,463
1994[1]	17,217	6,913	2,090	2,794	1,822	669	2,711	217	6,159,422

[1] Preliminary. *Source: Economic Research Service, U.S. Department of Agriculture*

U.S. Average Price Indexes for Fruits

Year	Index of all Fruit and Nut Prices Received by Growers (1990-92 = 100)	Producer Price Index (1982 = 100) Fresh Fruit	Dried Fruit	Canned Fruits and Juices	Frozen Fruits and Juices	Consumer Price Index (1982-84 = 100) Fresh Fruit	Processed Fruit
1986	83	112.9	91.9	111.0	103.0	118.7	106.3
1987	93	112.0	95.0	115.4	113.3	132.0	110.6
1988	96	112.8	98.9	120.3	130.0	143.0	121.9
1989	99	110.4	103.1	122.6	124.5	152.4	125.9
1990	97	116.1	107.0	126.9	138.9	170.9	136.6
1991	112	129.4	111.5	128.6	115.1	193.9	131.8
1992	99	83.2	114.3	134.6	125.7	184.2	137.7
1993	92	84.3	117.6	126.1	110.9	188.8	132.3
1994	90	82.2	120.9	124.5	111.9	201.2	133.1
1995[1]	92	85.0	121.0	128.4	115.3	216.6	137.0

[1] Estimate. *Source: Economic Research Service, U.S. Department of Agriculture*

U.S. Fresh Fruit: Per Capita Consumption[1] In Pounds

Year	Citrus Fruit Oranges	Tangerines & Tangelos	Lemons	Grapefruit	Total	Noncitrus Fruit Apples	Apricots	Avocados	Bananas	Cherries	Cran-berries
1986	12.81	1.78	2.48	6.32	23.90	17.84	.10	1.51	25.82	.49	.14
1987	13.90	1.77	2.47	6.66	25.36	20.83	.08	2.35	25.02	.72	.13
1988	12.17	1.71	2.39	6.58	23.54	19.84	.15	1.58	24.29	.53	.11
1989	12.38	1.31	2.60	4.43	21.37	21.22	.10	1.54	24.71	.62	.20
1990	8.46	1.38	2.60	5.87	19.07	19.60	.16	1.07	24.36	.39	.24
1991	12.91	1.94	2.54	5.95	24.36	18.18	.13	1.41	25.13	.40	.26
1992	14.24	1.87	2.65	6.23	25.95	19.24	.15	1.43	27.26	.53	.24
1993	13.07	2.11	2.68	6.09	24.93	19.16	.13	2.17	26.79	.43	.19
1994[2]	11.81	1.95	2.46	6.04	23.45	19.55	.18	1.32	28.06	.53	.31

[1] All data on calendar-year basis except for citrus fruits; apples, August; grapes and pears, July; grapefruit, September; lemons, August of prior year; all other citrus, November. [2] Preliminary. *Source: Economic Research Service, U.S. Department of Agriculture*

U.S. Fresh Fruit: Per Capita Consumption[1] In Pounds

Year	Noncitrus - Continued Grapes	Kiwifruit	Mangos	Nectarines & Peaches	Pears	Pine-apples	Papaya	Plums & Prunes	Straw-berries	Total Noncitrus	Total Fruit
1986	7.10	.15	.49	5.84	2.97	1.75	.18	1.29	2.89	68.56	92.77
1987	7.05	.25	.56	6.05	3.51	1.70	.19	1.91	3.12	73.47	97.40
1988	7.70	.25	.38	6.75	3.22	1.81	.16	1.72	3.33	71.82	97.21
1989	7.94	.33	.51	5.86	3.20	2.04	.14	1.41	3.25	73.07	96.63
1990	7.92	.49	.54	5.54	3.22	2.05	.18	1.55	3.24	70.55	91.92
1991	7.26	.44	.85	6.43	3.15	1.92	.17	1.42	3.58	70.73	89.80
1992	7.19	.33	.68	6.02	3.14	2.00	.24	1.78	3.61	73.84	98.20
1993	7.04	.53	.90	5.95	3.38	2.05	.28	1.28	3.64	73.92	99.87
1994[2]	7.33	.50	.98	5.46	3.48	2.04	.30	1.61	4.00	75.65	100.58

[1] All data on calendar-year basis except for citrus fruits; apples, August; grapes and pears, July; grapefruit, September; lemons, August of prior year; all other citrus, November. [2] Preliminary. *Source: Economic Research Service, U.S. Department of Agriculture*

Gas

U.S. demand for natural gas in the first quarter of 1995 fell relative to 1994 due to a very mild winter. Total annual gas demand in 1995 was projected to increase by 2.7 percent if gas prices remain as low as expected and if normal weather conditions prevail through the fall. The summer of 1995 proved to be very hot which increased the use of natural gas in air conditioning, while the fall of 1995 was colder than normal. Into 1996, it appeared the winter would be colder than normal which would increase natural gas use. In 1996, a record high 21.8 trillion cubic feet of total natural gas demand is projected, growing by 2.5 percent. This expected growth, which would bring natural gas demand to levels last seen in 1973, is dependent on normal weather and somewhat slower economic growth.

Residential gas demand growth in the fourth quarter of 1994 was negative due to the mild winter weather. This carried over into the first quarter of 1995 and was expected to result in negative residential gas demand growth for the entire year. For 1996, with more normal weather, residential demand is expected to rise 5.2 percent. This rate of growth also reflects the addition of new natural gas customers.

The Energy Information Administration reported that the preliminary data for 1994 showed surprising weakness in natural gas demand, but was expected to be reversed in 1995. Relatively low natural gas prices were expected to result in an increase in industrial gas use in 1995. For 1996, industrial natural gas demand was expected to slow in line with the economy.

Growth in gas-powered electricity generation by utilities was expected to increase by 2.4 percent in 1995 as lower-priced natural gas edges out oil generation. Demand in 1996 was expected to be at about the level of 1995.

Total U.S. dry gas production in 1995 was put at 18.85 trillion cubic feet, the same level as in 1994. For 1996, dry natural gas production was forecast at 19.34 trillion cubic feet. Net imports of natural gas were put at 2.56 trillion cubic feet in 1995, up close to seven percent from the 1994 total of 2.4 trillion. For 1996, net imports of gas are expected to be 2.75 trillion cubic feet. The total new supply of natural gas in 1995 was 21.54 trillion cubic feet, up less than one percent from 1994. For 1996, the supply of natural gas was expected to be 22.20 trillion cubic feet.

In terms of demand, for 1995, lease and plant fuel were expected to take 1.24 trillion cubic feet, while pipeline use took .66 trillion. Residential use of natural gas was expected to be 4.80 trillion cubic feet, while commercial demand was 2.97 trillion feet. Electric utilities were expected to take 3.13 trillion cubic feet. Total demand for natural gas in 1995 was expected to be 21.30 trillion cubic feet.

Futures Market

Natural gas futures and options are traded on the New York Mercantile Exchange (NYMEX).

World Natural Gas Production (Average Monthly Marketed Production[3]) In Terajoule[4]

Year	Australia	Canada	China	France	Germany	Indonesia	India	Italy	Mexico	Netherlands	Romania	Russia[5]	United Kingdom	United States	Venezuela
1982	36,000	235,377	38,696	21,417	48,360	7,386	53,862	48,621	136,482	211,053	129,070	1,451,200	123,574	1,471,285	56,870
1983	36,939	228,371	39,597	24,725	52,899	8,881	64,428	41,240	121,028	224,209	128,083	1,553,149	127,258	1,332,128	55,640
1984	39,195	247,646	39,824	20,562	51,422	10,450	78,373	43,706	92,630	226,410	127,167	1,705,724	124,522	1,445,086	61,718
1985	51,070	265,709	41,834	18,067	48,670	12,196	78,115	44,956	89,002	236,580	126,833	1,845,787	138,724	1,491,513	60,574
1986	47,591	248,984	45,600	13,713	38,755	17,467	93,305	45,105	82,043	212,582	112,177	1,974,833	145,609	1,454,350	67,116
1987	49,077	271,207	45,063	17,172	48,527	89,971	24,374	46,133	82,603	195,827	106,431	2,107,896	140,085	1,506,613	66,607
1988	50,286	313,592	46,331	10,104	45,312	101,638	28,441	47,009	79,163	173,213	102,977	2,184,357	134,778	1,550,343	68,799
1989	51,406	331,923	48,816	6,774	44,734	121,871	33,715	49,618	75,131	210,184	92,312	2,245,667	143,708	1,569,198	69,877
1990	66,445	342,826	49,380	6,450	44,162	131,545	36,795	54,389	79,594	211,717	79,931	2,311,092	158,628	1,614,310	79,683
1991	69,105	362,029	49,955	7,739	52,460	158,214	43,284	53,037	79,009	239,349	68,977	2,286,626	176,344	1,609,083	83,097
1992	75,218	397,229	50,052	7,470	51,911	165,761	43,297	57,117	77,934	240,043	67,900	------	176,661	1,614,941	79,784
1993[1]	80,907	437,922	52,297	10,125	47,904	171,828	44,475	60,792	81,417	244,205	68,891	2,068,113	196,792	1,667,401	85,907
1994[2]	89,732	499,337	55,230	10,500	50,535	268,017	47,219	64,638	138,977	207,317	65,057	1,932,514	203,875	1,700,081	120,882
1995[2]	85,258	------	55,165	------	59,425	------	46,487	65,810	138,213	265,125	62,101	1,337,108	223,304	1,714,632	------

[1] Preliminary. [2] Estimate. [3] Compares all gas collected & utilized as fuel or as a chemical industry raw material, including gas used in oilfields as a fuel by producers. [4] Terajoule = 10 to the 12th power Joule = approximately 10 to the 9th power BTU. [5] Formerly part of the U.S.S.R., data not reported separately until 1992. *Source: United Nations*

Marketed Production of Natural Gas by Important States in the U.S. In Million of Cubic Feet

Year	Alaska	California	Colorado	Kansas	Louisiana	Michigan	Mississippi	New Mexico	Oklahoma	Texas	Wyoming	Total
1989	393,729	362,860	216,737	601,196	5,078,125	155,988	102,645	854,615	2,237,037	6,241,425	665,699	18,095,147
1990	402,907	362,748	242,997	573,603	5,241,989	172,151	94,616	965,104	2,258,471	6,343,146	735,728	18,593,792
1991	437,822	378,384	285,961	628,459	5,034,361	195,749	108,031	1,038,284	2,153,852	6,280,654	776,528	18,532,439
1992	443,597	365,632	323,041	658,007	4,914,300	194,815	91,697	1,268,863	2,017,356	6,145,862	842,576	18,711,808
1993	430,350	315,851	400,985	686,347	4,991,138	204,635	80,695	1,409,429	2,049,942	6,249,624	634,957	18,981,915
1994[1]	453,425	309,427	453,207	712,730	5,169,705	222,657	63,448	1,557,689	1,934,864	6,353,844	696,018	19,635,495

[1] Preliminary. *Source: Energy Information Administration, U.S. Department of Energy*

World Natural Gas Plant Liquids Production   Thousand Barrels Per Day

Year		Algeria	Canada	Mexico	Saudi Arabia	Former USSR	United States	Persian Gulf[2]	OAPEC[3]	OPEC[4]	World
1980	Average	36	331	193	369	285	1,573	534	618	732	3,444
1981	Average	49	330	241	433	300	1,609	599	691	825	3,625
1982	Average	58	318	255	430	315	1,550	612	721	842	3,626
1983	Average	56	309	265	330	330	1,559	552	655	780	3,635
1984	Average	105	336	257	355	340	1,630	604	761	869	3,869
1985	Average	120	337	271	375	350	1,609	645	808	892	3,938
1986	Average	120	328	352	385	440	1,551	700	860	969	4,150
1987	Average	140	367	338	418	495	1,595	721	900	1,006	4,344
1988	Average	120	381	370	499	525	1,625	808	979	1,077	4,556
1989	Average	130	410	384	503	515	1,546	851	1,041	1,188	4,593
1990	Average	130	426	428	620	520	1,559	930	1,107	1,281	4,735
1991	Average	140	431	457	680	420	1,659	950	1,132	1,318	4,843
1992	Average	140	460	454	713	390	1,697	1,003	1,185	1,364	4,953
1993	Average	145	503	457	704	380	1,736	1,092	1,270	1,455	5,157
1994[1]	Average	145	538	461	698	400	1,727	1,083	1,260	1,453	5,280
1995[1]	Average	145	575	452	703	410	1,762	1,088	1,265	1,458	5,439

[1] Preliminary. [2] Bahrain, Iran, Iraq, Kuwait, Qatar, Saudi Arabia and the United Arab Emirates. [3] Organization of Arab Petroleum Exporting Countries. [4] Organization of Petroleum Exporting Countries. *Source: Energy Information Administration, U.S. Department of Energy*

United States Recoverable Reserves and Deliveries of Natural Gas   In Billions of Cubic Feet

Year	Gross Withdrawals Natural Gas	Recoverable Reserves of Natural Gas Dec. 31[2]	Deliveries: Residential	Commercial	Electric Utility Plants[3]	Industrial	Total Deliveries	Consumption: Lease & Plant Fuel	Used as Pipline Fuel	Heating Value BTU per Cubic Foot
1982	20,272	201,512	4,633	2,606	3,226	5,831	16,295	1,109	596	1,028
1983	18,659	200,247	4,381	2,433	2,911	5,643	15,367	978	490	1,031
1984	20,267	197,463	4,555	2,524	3,111	6,154	16,345	1,077	529	1,031
1985	19,607	193,369	4,433	2,432	3,044	5,901	15,811	966	504	1,032
1986	19,131	191,586	4,314	2,318	2,602	5,579	14,814	923	485	1,030
1987	20,140	187,211	4,315	2,430	2,844	5,953	15,542	1,149	519	1,031
1988	20,999	168,024	4,630	2,670	2,636	6,383	16,320	1,096	614	1,029
1989	21,074	167,116	4,781	2,718	2,787	6,816	17,102	1,070	629	1,031
1990	21,523	169,346	4,391	2,623	2,786	7,018	16,820	1,236	660	1,031
1991	21,750	167,062	4,556	2,729	2,789	7,231	17,305	1,129	601	1,030
1992	22,132	165,015	4,690	2,803	2,766	7,527	17,896	1,171	588	1,030
1993	22,726	162,415	4,956	2,862	2,682	7,981	18,483	1,172	624	1,027
1994[1]	23,609	163,837	4,848	2,895	2,987	8,178	18,910	1,161	685	1,028

[1] Preliminary. [2] Estimated proved recoverable reserves of dry natural gas. [3] Figures include gas other than natural (impossible to segregate); therefore, shown separately from other consumption. *Source: Energy Information Administration, U.S. Department of Energy*

Gas Utility Sales in the United States by Types & Class of Service   In Trillions of BTU's

Year	Total Utility Sales	Number of Customers (Millions)	Class by Service: Residential	Commercial	Industrial	Electric Generation	Other	Revenue -- Million $ From Sales to Customers: Total	Residential	Commercial	Industrial	Electric Generation	Other
1981	15,375	46.5	4,610	2,375	5,977	2,262	150	56,110	19,180	9,286	19,796	7,328	520
1982	14,183	45.4	4,770	2,471	4,861	1,933	147	63,200	23,700	11,666	19,292	7,908	634
1983	12,858	46.8	4,450	2,298	4,364	1,606	140	65,837	26,173	12,659	19,576	6,739	690
1984	13,162	47.2	4,628	2,396	4,241	1,750	146	67,496	27,485	13,205	18,705	7,389	713
1985	12,615	47.3	4,513	2,338	3,686	1,949	130	63,293	26,864	12,723	15,658	7,428	620
1986	11,125	52.0	4,381	2,239	2,891	1,447	167	51,201	24,759	11,274	10,546	3,949	673
1987	10,543	53.6	4,385	2,156	2,339	1,509	155	45,492	23,622	10,271	7,279	3,789	530
1988	10,705	52.1	4,695	2,306	2,208	1,336	160	46,162	24,828	10,681	6,713	3,400	538
1989	10,551	47.2	4,798	2,322	1,963	1,280	188	47,493	26,172	11,074	9,217	3,449	582
1990	9,842	47.8	4,468	2,192	1,890	1,120	171	45,153	25,000	10,604	6,034	2,962	553
1991	9,601	55.2	4,546	2,198	1,743	888	226	44,647	25,729	10,669	5,326	2,250	674
1992	9,907	56.1	4,694	2,209	1,959	813	231	46,178	26,702	10,865	5,837	2,077	698
1993	10,151	57.0	5,054	2,397	2,009	524	168	50,137	29,787	12,076	6,162	1,480	632
1994[1]	9,584	58.0	4,972	2,355	1,690	420	148	50,087	30,563	12,252	5,529	1,170	572
1995[2]	10,034	NA	4,696	2,202	1,938	913	185	50,913	29,558	11,957	6,349	2,213	664

[1] Preliminary. [2] Estimate. NA = Not available. *Source: American Gas Association*

GAS

Salient Statistics of Gas in the United States

	Supply						Disposition				Average Price Delivered to Consumers						
Year	Marketed Production	Extraction Loss	Dry Production	Storage Withdrawals	Imports (Consumed)	Total Supply	Consumption	Exports	Added to Storage	Total Disposition	Wellhead Price	Imports	Exports	Residential	Commercial	Industrial	Electric Utilities
	In Billions of Cubic Feet										$ Per Thousand Cubic Feet						
1980	20,180	777	19,403	1,972	985	21,875	19,877	49	1,949	21,875	1.59	4.28	4.70	3.68	3.39	2.56	2.27
1981	19,956	775	19,181	1,930	904	21,691	19,404	59	2,228	21,691	1.98	4.88	5.90	4.29	4.00	3.14	2.89
1982	18,520	762	17,820	2,164	933	20,525	18,001	52	2,472	20,525	2.46	5.03	5.81	5.17	4.82	3.87	3.48
1983	16,822	790	16,094	2,270	920	18,712	16,835	55	1,822	18,712	2.59	4.78	5.10	6.06	5.59	4.18	3.58
1984	18,230	838	17,466	2,908	843	20,300	17,953	55	2,295	20,300	2.66	4.08	4.92	6.12	5.55	4.22	3.70
1985	17,198	816	16,454	2,397	950	19,499	17,281	55	2,163	19,499	2.51	3.19	4.77	6.12	5.50	3.95	3.55
1986	16,791	800	16,059	1,837	750	18,266	16,221	61	1,984	18,266	1.94	2.53	2.81	5.83	5.08	3.23	2.43
1987	17,349	812	16,621	1,905	993	19,176	17,211	54	1,911	19,176	1.67	2.17	3.07	5.54	4.77	2.94	2.32
1988	17,918	816	17,103	2,270	1,294	20,315	18,030	74	2,211	20,315	1.69	1.84	2.74	5.47	4.63	2.95	2.33
1989	18,095	785	17,311	2,854	1,382	21,435	18,801	107	2,528	21,435	1.69	1.82	2.51	5.64	4.74	2.96	2.43
1990	18,594	784	17,810	1,986	1,532	21,302	18,716	86	2,499	21,300	1.71	1.94	3.10	5.80	4.83	2.93	2.38
1991	18,532	835	17,698	2,752	1,773	21,836	19,035	129	2,672	21,836	1.64	1.82	2.59	5.82	4.81	2.69	2.18
1992	18,712	872	17,840	2,772	2,138	22,360	19,544	216	2,599	22,360	1.74	1.85	2.25	5.89	4.88	2.84	2.36
1993[1]	18,982	886	18,095	2,799	2,350	23,253	20,278	140	2,835	23,253	2.04	2.03	2.59	6.16	5.22	3.07	2.61
1994[2]	19,635	889	18,747	2,562	2,624	23,780	20,754	162	2,865	23,780	1.88	1.87	2.50	6.41	5.44	3.05	2.28

[1] Preliminary. [2] Estimate. *Source: Energy Information Administration, U.S. Department of Energy*

Gasoline

During the peak 1995 driving season (April-September), motor gasoline demand was projected at 7.9 million barrels per day, an increase of 140,000 barrels per day or 1.8 percent compared to the previous summer driving season. In the third quarter (July-September) of 1995, average gasoline demand was expected to approach eight million barrels per day. Primarily because of increases in real personal disposable income, highway travel activity was expected to increase by 2.8 percent from 1994. While increased highway travel activity will result in an increase in consumption, this will be partially offset by increased fuel efficiency which was expected to increase by one percent from the previous summer. The impact of higher gasoline prices was expected to be slight with projections of an average $1.24 per gallon, five cents higher than in 1994. The implementation of reformulated gasoline regulations accounts for 1-2 cents of this increase. Adjusting for inflation, that increase amounts to only 1.2 percent. Real fuel costs remain unchanged on a cost-per-mile basis.

Domestic fuel and refinery production was estimated at 7.5 million barrels per day during the summer, an increase of 160,000 barrels per day from 1994. Refinery utilization rates were estimated at 94.3 percent and gasoline yields 46.1 percent. Potential refinery output could be larger than that. Recent refinery activity has shown that after years of upgrading, utilization rates have averaged 95.8 percent while the gasoline yield is 47.2 percent. Including field production, total output could be 7.86 million barrels per day. The recent record average, set in November 1994, was 7.85 million barrels per day.

Net imports for the 1995 summer season were expected to be 370,000 barrels per day, about the same as in 1994. In the summer of 1988, net imports averaged a record 420,000 barrels per day, and in May 1990 a record 560,000 barrels per day were imported. Atlantic Basin refineries, especially those in the Caribbean, have added substantial catalytic cracking capacity during the last two years. There is also surplus European production which can be imported.

At the beginning of the season, gasoline stocks (including blending components and oxygenates) were estimated at 230 million barrels, up from 227 million barrels last year. This was the equivalent of 30 days forward supply. Season ending stocks were 230 million barrels, the same as in 1994.

For the January-July 1995 period, finished motor gasoline production averaged 7.53 million barrels per day. This compares with the average daily production in 1994 of 7.15 million barrels in the same period, and the 1993 average of 7.23 million barrels. For the first seven months of 1995, gasoline imports averaged 279,000 barrels per day, down substantially from the daily average over the same period of 1994 of 389,000 barrels, but up from the 1993 average of 246,000. Exports over the first seven months of 1995 averaged 95,000 barrels, up from the 1994 average of 81,000 barrels, but down from the 1993 average of 104,000 barrels.

At the end of July 1995, motor gasoline stocks were 206,000 barrels. In July 1994, they were 208,000 barrels while in July 1993 they were 215,000. These stocks included gasoline blending components and gasohol but excluded oxygenates. Finished gasoline stocks at the end of July 1994 were 164,000 barrels compared to 173,000 in July 1994 and 177,000 in July 1993.

Futures Markets

Unleaded gasoline futures and options are traded on the New York Mercantile Exchange (NYMEX).

Average Spot Prices of Unleaded Gasoline In Cents Per Gallon

Year	Jan.	Feb.	Mar.	Apr.	May	June	July	Aug.	Sept.	Oct.	Nov.	Dec.	Average
1986	67.71	46.38	40.65	47.18	55.10	42.01	33.84	42.51	42.02	41.04	41.08	43.12	45.22
1987	49.23	47.64	51.13	50.54	54.18	55.75	55.78	52.43	51.71	54.03	51.68	45.58	51.64
1988	45.14	45.79	45.25	50.89	52.20	51.70	55.12	48.18	46.40	51.15	52.39	47.22	49.29
1989	50.24	48.47	54.91	69.98	67.97	63.75	56.34	52.81	59.29	55.76	50.80	53.94	57.02
1990	64.20	59.59	56.15	61.86	64.24	64.55	65.25	89.61	99.85	95.68	88.10	68.07	73.10
1991	68.88	65.82	74.25	72.07	70.28	63.59	65.23	69.90	62.17	64.41	65.10	55.55	66.44
1992	53.04	55.14	54.10	59.75	63.48	64.51	59.94	62.06	61.63	60.81	58.22	53.24	58.83
1993	52.96	52.54	54.33	59.35	59.37	54.78	51.80	53.13	48.61	50.22	44.30	37.68	51.59
1994	42.40	43.75	44.04	48.98	50.62	52.84	54.52	55.61	46.53	51.14	52.32	46.87	49.14
1995	50.99	51.43	50.74	61.01	64.76	59.47	51.45	53.45	56.10	48.89	51.15	53.44	54.41

Source: New York Mercantile Exchange

Average Open Interest of Unleaded Regular Gasoline Futures in New York In Contracts

Year	Jan.	Feb.	Mar.	Apr.	May	June	July	Aug.	Sept.	Oct.	Nov.	Dec.
1987	28,026	32,240	41,440	40,630	37,152	32,453	28,977	27,463	27,522	29,271	31,998	38,327
1988	39,887	43,055	44,006	46,094	46,517	50,754	57,897	51,064	49,636	49,649	49,877	50,893
1989	55,838	57,011	59,012	69,547	68,478	61,519	56,913	52,158	51,910	55,312	65,392	71,464
1990	77,580	80,425	75,368	71,132	62,121	72,105	68,826	59,528	60,558	61,253	56,332	56,569
1991	54,807	75,337	81,393	74,801	71,900	73,633	74,503	87,073	90,680	100,606	111,745	125,578
1992	124,896	117,155	108,388	89,775	79,680	80,394	81,110	76,741	71,264	68,059	71,110	77,508
1993	80,610	93,630	100,657	96,607	88,311	94,926	104,260	103,371	100,921	107,339	126,649	150,359
1994	135,366	120,204	118,977	122,092	96,525	89,854	86,401	76,213	67,881	70,258	71,245	63,679
1995	61,015	67,631	65,201	76,323	76,269	69,676	64,379	58,426	62,089	58,782	57,902	70,098

Source: New York Mercantile Exchange

GASOLINE

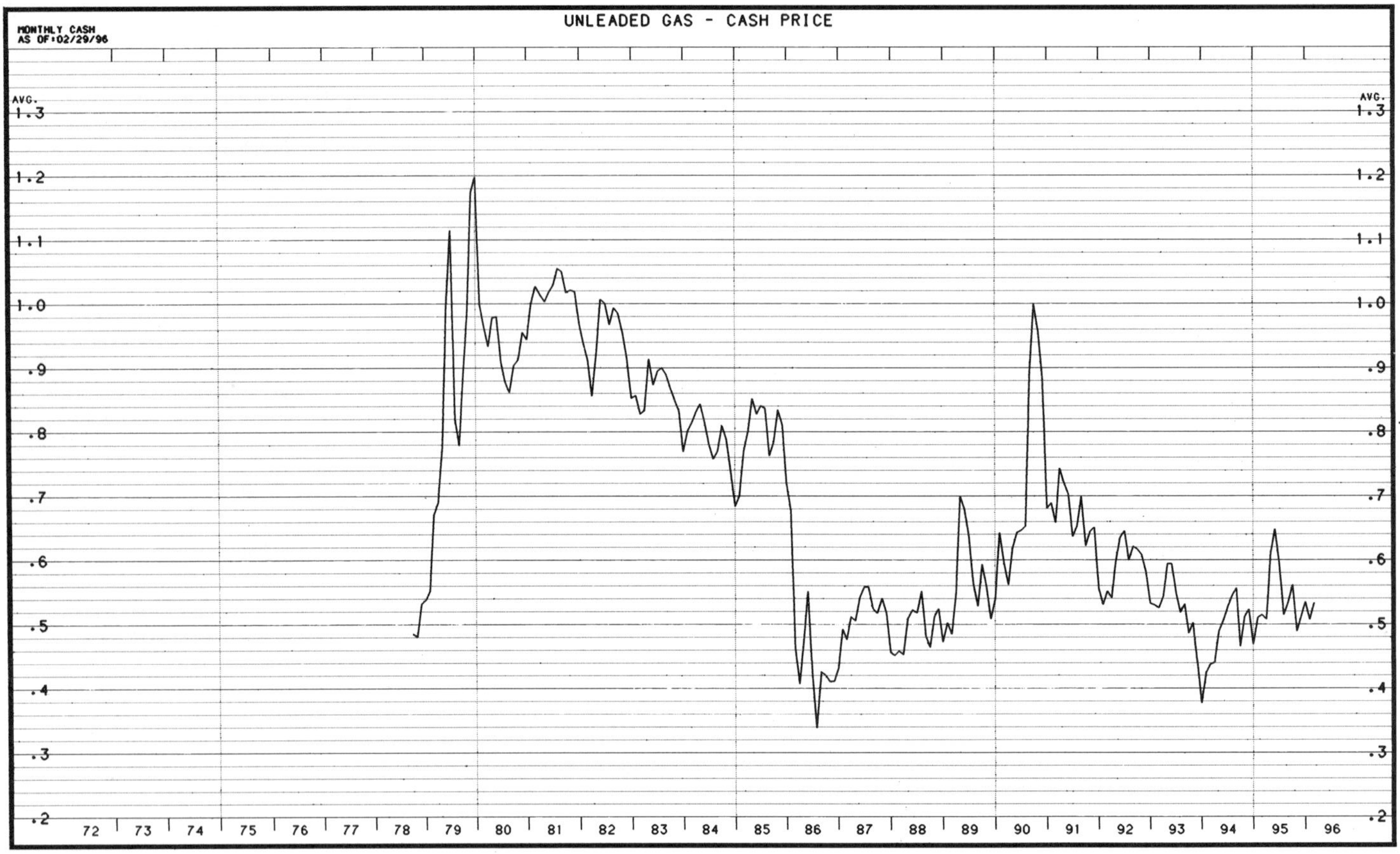

Volume of Trading of Unleaded Regular Gasoline Futures in New York In Contracts

Year	Jan.	Feb.	Mar.	Apr.	May	June	July	Aug.	Sept.	Oct.	Nov.	Dec.	Total
1987	135,208	139,885	211,590	214,982	178,735	175,585	182,661	154,685	155,352	166,365	152,176	190,014	2,056,238
1988	196,616	191,231	245,019	217,139	257,507	330,009	401,196	254,010	294,512	355,982	308,438	240,366	3,292,055
1989	354,167	258,669	373,936	510,964	407,445	443,205	356,939	310,546	412,753	375,489	328,277	352,168	4,484,558
1990	540,633	349,439	461,438	481,665	527,637	472,377	456,342	549,702	373,102	386,472	314,051	248,137	5,205,995
1991	366,772	351,188	525,432	541,073	482,943	446,350	396,429	562,085	386,421	477,111	537,834	529,940	5,594,915
1992	565,922	558,476	604,678	668,490	580,088	620,114	600,897	545,520	469,844	563,856	435,847	461,025	6,674,757
1993	531,780	558,770	584,899	539,785	571,860	611,951	594,740	721,852	642,959	629,733	674,814	729,717	7,407,809
1994	634,027	526,505	615,594	677,891	636,990	673,034	601,980	783,181	569,384	684,670	582,359	519,987	7,470,836
1995	592,329	506,640	736,704	663,743	780,568	680,792	565,655	556,589	573,551	473,014	480,507	461,695	7,071,787

Source: New York Mercantile Exchange

United States Production of Finished Motor Gasoline Thousand Barrels Per Day

Year	Jan.	Feb.	Mar.	Apr.	May	June	July	Aug.	Sept.	Oct.	Nov.	Dec.	Average
1983	6,065	5,848	5,906	6,201	6,397	6,655	6,707	6,537	6,611	6,188	6,634	6,308	6,340
1984	6,036	6,317	6,359	6,525	6,650	6,619	6,450	6,405	6,516	6,388	6,709	6,478	6,453
1985	5,926	5,914	6,072	6,344	6,564	6,780	6,788	6,814	6,299	6,356	6,480	6,651	6,419
1986	6,522	6,302	6,061	6,498	7,095	7,101	6,956	7,092	6,891	6,616	6,895	6,970	6,752
1987	6,714	6,365	6,569	6,850	6,991	7,089	7,043	6,933	6,921	6,668	6,907	7,015	6,841
1988	6,730	6,736	6,715	6,907	6,851	6,983	7,159	7,209	6,948	6,858	7,060	7,303	6,956
1989	6,937	6,650	6,612	6,811	6,894	7,275	7,360	7,155	7,069	6,845	7,046	6,884	6,963
1990	6,879	6,989	6,613	6,775	6,610	7,101	7,238	7,326	7,274	6,880	6,940	6,887	6,959
1991	6,629	6,573	6,643	6,742	7,063	7,351	7,274	7,247	7,030	6,749	7,018	7,354	6,975
1992	7,013	6,726	6,683	6,954	7,092	7,198	7,195	6,817	7,071	7,198	7,323	7,411	7,058
1993	7,228	7,144	6,904	7,126	7,446	7,442	7,337	7,335	7,573	7,394	7,652	7,725	7,360
1994	7,097	6,790	6,760	7,195	7,348	7,455	7,380	7,432	7,385	7,151	7,849	7,867	7,312
1995[1]	7,317	7,250	7,171	7,547	7,697	7,866	7,718	7,634	7,785	7,522	7,716	7,664	7,575

[1] Preliminary. *Source: Energy Information Adminstration, U.S. Department of Energy*

United States Disposition of Finished Motor Gasoline, Total Product Supplied   Thousand Barrels Per Day

Year	Jan.	Feb.	Mar.	Apr.	May	June	July	Aug.	Sept.	Oct.	Nov.	Dec.	Average
1986	6,502	6,469	6,955	7,105	7,106	7,209	7,436	7,435	6,864	7,250	6,879	7,143	7,034
1987	6,535	6,796	6,964	7,314	7,460	7,539	7,581	7,338	7,205	7,305	7,151	7,251	7,206
1988	6,693	7,039	7,323	7,430	7,303	7,817	7,482	7,556	7,404	7,271	7,379	7,344	7,336
1989	6,745	7,119	7,421	7,157	7,381	7,780	7,296	7,717	7,240	7,302	7,353	7,410	7,328
1990	6,643	7,179	7,338	7,121	7,358	7,519	7,496	7,796	6,914	7,226	7,241	6,978	7,235
1991	6,645	6,838	7,017	7,137	7,437	7,456	7,561	7,528	7,083	7,281	7,008	7,224	7,188
1992	6,869	6,963	7,137	7,238	7,328	7,460	7,639	7,380	7,344	7,338	7,102	7,396	7,268
1993	6,639	7,112	7,389	7,435	7,585	7,700	7,785	7,864	7,607	7,382	7,533	7,661	7,476
1994	6,980	7,275	7,395	7,564	7,644	7,922	7,884	7,975	7,615	7,548	7,464	7,924	7,601
1995[1]	7,157	7,505	7,780	7,670	7,898	8,243	7,854	8,151	7,788	7,770	7,878	7,674	7,782

[1] Preliminary. *Source: Energy Information Adminstration, U.S. Department of Energy*

Stocks of Finished Gasoline[2] on Hand in the United States   In Millions of Barrrels

Year	Jan.	Feb.	Mar.	Apr.	May	June	July	Aug.	Sept.	Oct.	Nov.	Dec.
1986	203.2	207.8	186.2	176.0	189.8	197.8	192.0	189.7	198.5	187.0	193.0	196.4
1987	213.0	209.0	207.2	202.9	197.7	194.5	190.8	190.0	193.4	184.1	190.2	191.1
1988	203.1	205.1	196.4	192.1	190.8	176.7	181.2	185.4	184.6	182.3	185.8	192.0
1989	207.8	205.7	191.1	190.6	185.8	180.1	192.1	183.8	187.5	184.8	187.1	179.1
1990	197.6	203.3	187.9	186.3	180.3	177.7	182.0	175.4	190.5	181.9	178.7	182.4
1991	189.1	182.7	174.4	171.9	173.7	178.5	173.5	172.8	179.1	168.3	173.3	183.3
1992	192.8	191.4	182.9	185.0	187.4	189.5	182.0	168.2	170.0	168.7	178.2	179.1
1993	197.8	201.9	189.0	184.0	186.8	184.2	176.8	166.7	171.2	175.6	182.6	187.1
1994	194.1	186.2	175.6	176.5	179.0	176.9	173.0	167.6	168.9	154.2	134.8	132.7
1995[1]	140.8	138.5	127.5	127.8	128.8	129.4	128.0	121.3	124.1	119.5	119.8	

[1] Preliminary. [2] Includes oxygenated and other finished. *Source: Energy Information Administration, U.S. Department of Energy*

Refiner Sales Prices of Finished Motor Gasoline to End Users (Excluding Taxes)[1]   In Cents Per Gallon

Year	Jan.	Feb.	Mar.	Apr.	May	June	July	Aug.	Sept.	Oct.	Nov.	Dec.	Average
1986	89.3	80.5	65.4	59.1	63.8	64.9	58.0	55.5	56.2	53.2	53.2	54.2	62.4
1987	59.7	62.1	62.7	64.9	66.3	67.7	69.6	71.6	70.5	69.7	69.4	67.4	66.9
1988	64.9	63.3	62.5	66.0	68.4	68.1	69.9	71.8	70.0	68.0	67.6	66.1	67.3
1989	65.6	66.1	68.4	81.7	85.5	84.5	82.0	76.6	74.9	74.7	72.7	72.1	75.6
1990	78.8	76.5	75.1	77.9	80.2	81.5	80.8	92.4	101.2	108.7	107.2	98.4	88.3
1991	88.8	79.5	74.0	77.0	82.0	81.9	78.9	81.1	80.2	77.9	79.1	76.0	79.7
1992	71.2	70.2	71.0	74.6	80.3	84.0	83.5	82.3	82.3	81.3	81.4	78.5	78.4
1993	76.9	76.1	75.7	77.8	80.1	79.8	77.6	76.2	74.9	75.3	72.5	68.0	75.9
1994	66.7	67.6	67.3	69.5	71.1	74.1	77.0	81.5	79.6	76.9	77.5	74.9	73.7
1995[2]	74.5	73.3	73.1	77.3	83.4	83.9	80.0	76.9	75.8	73.6	71.9		

[1] Excludes aviation. [2] Preliminary. *Source: Energy Information Administration, U.S. Department of Energy*

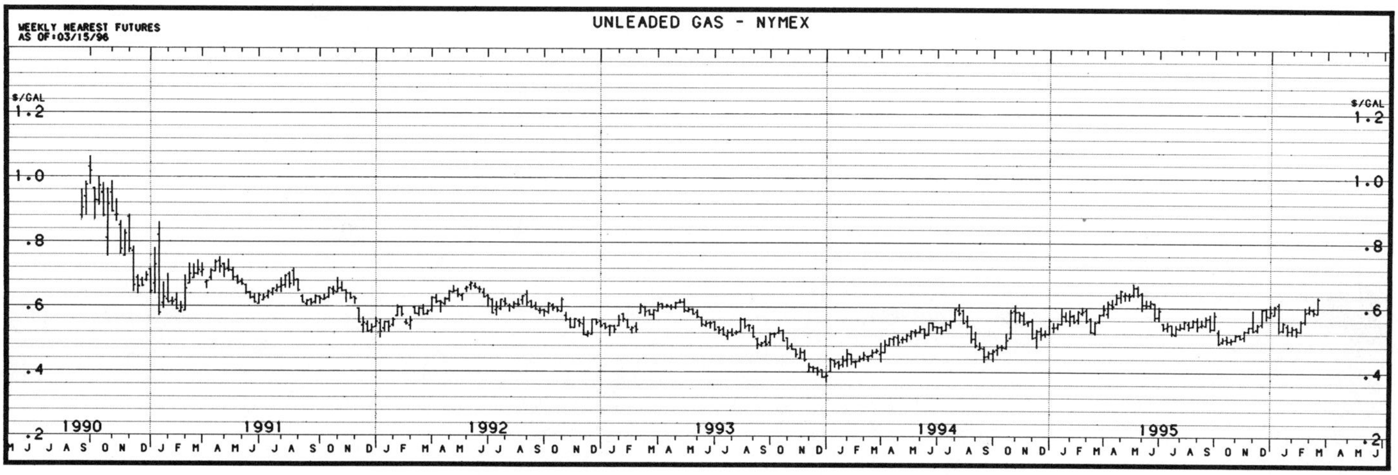

GASOLINE

U.S. Average Retail Selling Prices of Motor Gasoline (Including Taxes) In Cents Per Gallon

Year	Jan.	Feb.	Mar.	Apr.	May	June	July	Aug.	Sept.	Oct.	Nov.	Dec.	Average
							Unleaded Premium						
1983	137.6	133.8	130.8	136.0	139.7	141.1	142.1	141.9	141.0	139.5	138.4	137.6	138.3
1984	136.9	136.1	136.2	137.5	138.0	137.7	137.0	135.5	136.0	136.5	136.4	135.4	136.6
1985	130.4	129.0	131.0	134.0	136.0	137.1	136.7	135.9	134.9	134.2	133.9	134.4	134.0
1986	133.6	128.2	116.0	106.1	107.5	110.0	104.5	99.9	101.0	98.7	98.0	98.4	108.5
1987	100.7	104.7	105.2	107.3	107.9	109.8	111.5	113.9	113.6	112.8	112.5	111.9	109.3
1988	109.5	108.2	107.4	108.8	110.5	111.1	112.3	113.8	113.0	111.9	111.6	110.1	110.7
1989	109.1	110.0	111.5	122.1	127.8	127.8	126.4	123.3	121.3	120.9	118.7	117.0	119.7
1990	123.0	122.7	121.8	123.3	124.8	127.1	127.2	136.9	146.7	155.4	155.9	153.7	134.9
1991	143.1	132.1	126.4	128.1	133.1	133.8	131.3	131.8	132.4	130.7	131.8	130.9	132.1
1992	126.7	124.8	125.0	126.8	131.7	135.9	136.3	134.8	134.6	134.5	135.1	133.0	131.6
1993	131.3	130.1	129.4	130.4	131.9	132.1	130.5	129.4	128.2	132.3	130.5	126.8	130.2
1994	124.0	124.5	124.3	126.0	127.4	130.0	132.7	136.7	136.4	134.5	135.4	133.7	130.5
1995[1]	132.4	131.6	130.6	132.5	138.3	141.1	138.4	135.2	133.2	131.5	129.2	129.0	133.6
							Unleaded Regular						
1983	123.0	118.7	115.2	121.5	125.9	127.7	128.8	128.5	127.4	125.5	124.1	123.1	124.1
1984	121.6	120.9	121.0	122.7	123.6	122.9	121.2	119.6	120.3	120.9	120.7	119.3	121.2
1985	114.8	113.1	115.9	120.5	123.1	124.1	124.2	122.9	121.6	120.4	120.7	120.8	120.2
1986	119.4	112.0	98.1	88.8	92.3	95.5	89.0	84.3	86.0	83.1	82.1	82.3	92.7
1987	86.2	90.5	91.2	93.4	94.1	95.8	97.1	99.5	99.0	97.6	97.6	96.1	94.8
1988	93.3	91.3	90.4	93.0	95.5	95.5	96.7	98.7	97.4	95.7	94.9	93.0	94.6
1989	91.8	92.6	94.0	106.5	111.9	111.4	109.2	105.7	102.9	102.7	99.9	98.0	102.1
1990	104.2	103.7	102.3	104.4	106.1	108.8	108.4	119.0	129.4	137.8	137.7	135.4	116.4
1991	124.7	114.3	108.2	110.4	115.6	116.0	112.7	114.0	114.3	112.2	113.4	112.3	114.0
1992	107.3	105.4	105.8	107.9	113.6	117.9	117.5	115.8	115.8	115.4	115.9	113.6	112.7
1993	111.7	110.8	109.8	111.2	112.9	113.0	110.9	109.7	108.5	112.7	111.3	107.0	110.8
1994	104.3	105.1	104.5	106.4	108.0	110.6	113.6	118.2	117.7	115.2	116.3	114.3	111.2
1995[1]	112.9	112.0	111.5	114.0	120.0	122.6	119.5	116.4	114.8	112.7	110.1	110.1	114.7
							All-Types[2]						
1983	121.4	117.0	113.5	119.8	124.3	126.1	127.2	126.9	125.7	123.9	122.4	121.5	122.5
1984	120.0	119.3	119.4	121.1	122.1	121.4	119.7	118.4	118.9	119.5	119.3	117.9	119.8
1985	114.5	112.8	115.5	119.9	122.3	123.3	123.3	122.2	120.9	119.8	120.1	120.3	119.6
1986	119.0	111.9	98.3	89.5	92.7	95.8	89.5	84.8	86.4	83.7	82.7	83.0	93.1
1987	86.8	91.1	91.8	94.0	94.8	96.6	98.0	100.4	100.0	98.8	98.7	97.5	95.7
1988	94.7	92.8	92.0	94.6	97.0	97.1	98.4	100.4	99.2	97.6	97.2	95.3	96.3
1989	94.4	95.5	97.4	109.8	115.2	115.0	113.2	109.6	107.3	107.1	104.6	103.0	106.0
1990	109.0	108.6	107.6	109.6	111.4	114.0	113.9	124.6	134.7	143.1	143.2	141.0	121.7
1991	130.4	119.8	113.8	115.9	120.9	121.4	118.5	119.6	119.9	118.0	119.3	118.2	119.6
1992	113.5	111.7	112.2	114.3	119.7	123.9	123.8	122.1	122.2	121.9	122.3	120.1	119.0
1993	118.2	117.2	116.3	117.5	119.3	119.4	117.4	116.3	115.1	119.3	117.8	113.6	117.3
1994	110.9	111.4	110.9	112.8	114.3	116.7	119.9	124.3	123.7	121.2	122.2	120.3	117.4
1995[1]	119.0	118.1	117.3	119.7	125.6	128.1	125.2	122.2	120.6	118.5	116.1	116.0	120.5

[1] Preliminary. [2] Also includes types of motor oil not shown separately. *Source: Energy Information Administration, U.S. Department of Energy*

U.S. Refiner Sales Prices of Finished Aviation Gasoline to End Users[2] In Cents Per Gallon

Year	Jan.	Feb.	Mar.	Apr.	May	June	July	Aug.	Sept.	Oct.	Nov.	Dec.	Average
1983	129.2	127.2	126.6	125.2	125.4	125.6	125.1	125.9	124.2	124.7	124.5	124.4	125.5
1984	123.9	123.7	123.8	124.4	123.9	124.6	124.3	123.2	123.7	123.3	119.3	121.9	123.4
1985	121.7	121.1	121.4	121.2	121.9	121.7	120.2	118.9	119.5	118.9	118.3	117.0	120.1
1986	116.2	117.2	111.5	104.3	102.2	101.0	98.2	94.9	93.2	91.2	87.2	88.8	101.1
1987	87.9	89.7	90.3	89.8	90.6	91.3	91.5	92.4	91.9	91.4	91.0	90.0	90.7
1988	88.4	88.2	87.7	87.6	89.2	87.2	89.7	92.2	90.8	88.7	89.2	89.2	89.1
1989	89.2	89.7	90.6	99.1	107.0	107.1	105.5	101.9	100.7	100.4	98.6	97.3	99.5
1990	102.0	102.4	100.9	101.4	103.6	104.2	103.9	112.8	125.6	134.4	131.7	122.5	112.0
1991	112.1	106.4	101.3	101.2	105.3	105.2	103.6	105.8	105.7	104.6	104.3	102.0	104.7
1992	98.5	98.5	98.0	99.1	102.4	106.4	106.8	105.7	104.9	104.3	103.4	101.3	102.7
1993	100.3	99.9	99.4	100.7	102.2	102.5	99.7	98.8	98.2	98.0	95.7	91.2	99.0
1994	88.6	88.4	89.0	91.3	92.3	95.6	95.9	101.7	101.1	100.0	100.0	99.2	95.6
1995[1]	99.6	99.8	99.0	101.3	105.8	106.4	101.8	99.2	101.3	98.6	95.4		

[1] Preliminary. [2] Excluding taxes. *Source: Energy Information Administration, U.S. Department of Energy*

Gold

Gold's price drifted sideways during 1995 within a range defined by a high of $401.00 on March 31, and a low of $371.20 on January 6, basis Comex nearby futures.

Gold's world production costs apparently average in the low $200 an ounce range, suggesting that much of the metal's market price above costs and profit margins is a speculative based premium and impossible to quantify. As usual, a tug of war persisted between the confirmed gold bull who believed that gold would see $500 an ounce during 1995, and the less dogmatic bear who saw little reason for gold to strengthen. It's evident that the psychology towards gold changed, and other than the occasional technically motivated price swings, trading enthusiasm for gold turned lethargic early in 1994. Perhaps gold's luster as the one true hedge has diminished now that world financial markets offer so many alternatives for hedging against economic and/or political uncertainties.

During 1995, U.S. equities, interest rate markets and economists all ignored the threat of rising inflation, real or perceived, and were ultimately proven correct. Without a perception of inflation it was difficult for gold to sustain any price rally. The bull move in equities surely siphoned capital away from gold, a non-interest bearing asset that was going nowhere. Moreover, the world's usual military and/or political flareups were seen as having little adverse effect on the major industrialized nations, and when they did it was the FOREX markets that reacted, not gold.

World mined gold production accelerated in the first half of the 1990's, averaging 2.25 million kilograms versus 1.5 million in the 1980's. Percentagewise, some nations—notably Australia, Canada and China—show dramatic gains in gold output during the past decade. However, world production in 1994 of 2.3 million kg was marginally under 1993's. This was primarily due to a drop in South Africa's production to 580,000 kg from 619,201 in 1993. This was the lowest output from the world's largest producer in years. The U.S., the world's second largest provider since 1991, produced 326,000 kg versus 331,013 in 1993. The Soviet Union formerly accounted for 12 percent of world production, and the new component nations may still be doing so, but the known new supply data suggests otherwise. Identified world gold resources at yearend 1994 were estimated at 75,000 tons, of which 15 percent to 20 percent were byproduct resources. South Africa had one-half of the resources and the U.S. 12 percent. Of the estimated 116,000 tons mined from historical times through 1994, about 15 percent is believed to have been lost or unaccounted for. Of the remaining 99,000 tons, central banks hold about 35,000 tons and the balance is privately held in the form of coin, jewelry and bullion.

Nevada accounts for nearly two-thirds of U.S. mine production with California a distant second. Through the first half of 1995, production was ahead of 1994's rate. Secondary production (old scrap) has also been trending higher, totaling a record high 74,332 kg in 1994 versus less than 60,000 in the late 1980's. However, imports for consumption have no apparent pattern, totaling 140,000 kg in 1994 versus 97,519 in 1990 and a high of 489,863 in 1986.

U.S. consumption of gold for industry and arts totaled 76,100 kg in 1994 versus 91,400 in 1993, and an annual average of more than 110,000 kg in the late 1980's. Industrial and dental usage fell to 22,443 kg in 1994 from 25,836 in 1993, both half the demand of 1985. Jewelry demand also fell, from 65,600 kg in 1993 to 53,700 in 1994. U.S. exports of refined and unrefined gold in 1994 totaled 471,000 kg versus 792,680 in 1993.; in the first half of 1995 about 245,000 kg were exported. Most of the U.S. exports are refined bullion with Hong Kong and the U.K. the primary importers. U.S. Treasury yearend gold stocks during the past decade have held near 8,150,000 kg; Commodity exchange stocks at yearend 1994 totaled 49,063 kg.

Futures Markets

Gold futures are traded on the Bolsa de Mercadorias & Futuros (BM&F), The Hong Kong Futures Exchange Ltd. (HKFE), the Tokyo Commodity Exchange (TOCOM), the Singapore International Monetary Exchange Ltd. (SIMEX), the Chicago Board of Trade (CBOT), the Mid America Commodity Exchange, (MidAm), and the New York Mercantile Exchange, COMEX division (COMEX). Gold options are traded on the the Vancouver Stock Exchange (VSE), the European Options Exchange (EOE-Optiebeurs), the MidAm, and the COMEX. Futures and options on Krugerrands are traded on the South Africa Futures Exchange (SAFEX).

World Mine Production of Gold In Kilograms (1 Kilogram = 32.1507 Troy Ounces)

Year	Australia	Brazil	Canada	Chile	China	Colombia	Ghana	Indonesia	Mexico	Papua N.Guinea	Philippines	Russia[3]	South Africa	United States	Uzbekistan[3]	World Total
1982	26,961	46,655	64,734	16,907	55,986	14,702	10,295	2,236	6,667	18,328	25,954	266,000	664,219	45,588	------	1,340,730
1983	30,591	57,542	73,510	17,759	57,542	13,266	8,585	2,391	6,164	18,022	25,397	267,000	679,528	62,286	------	1,404,737
1984	40,309	61,585	83,444	16,829	59,097	22,726	8,927	2,447	8,429	25,971	25,727	269,000	679,952	64,839	------	1,459,671
1985	58,521	72,160	87,561	17,240	61,000	35,532	9,322	2,619	8,264	36,908	33,063	270,000	670,754	75,495	------	1,531,858
1986	75,079	67,500	102,899	17,947	66,000	39,995	8,931	3,304	7,795	35,075	40,322	275,000	638,047	116,297	------	1,606,570
1987	110,696	83,700	115,818	17,035	72,000	26,546	10,201	3,643	7,988	33,250	32,599	260,000	607,000	153,870	------	1,660,535
1988	156,950	112,159	134,813	20,614	78,000	29,014	11,601	4,738	9,098	38,129	30,482	277,600	621,000	200,914	------	1,873,803
1989	203,563	52,527	159,527	22,559	90,000	29,506	13,358	6,155	10,000	27,538	30,040	304,000	607,460	265,731	------	2,013,913
1990	244,137	101,913	169,412	27,503	100,000	29,352	16,840	11,158	9,682	31,938	24,591	302,000	605,100	294,189	------	2,180,000
1991	234,218	89,369	176,552	28,879	120,000	34,844	26,311	16,879	10,142	60,780	25,916	260,000	601,110	294,062	------	2,190,000
1992	243,400	85,862	161,402	33,774	140,000	32,118	31,032	37,983	9,891	71,190	22,702	146,000	614,071	330,212	75,000	2,290,000
1993[1]	247,196	74,200	152,929	33,600	160,000	27,500	39,235	42,097	11,100	60,587	15,826	149,500	619,201	331,013	75,000	2,310,000
1994[2]	256,000	76,000	146,000	38,600	160,000	27,500	44,500	45,000	13,900	59,300	14,600	147,000	580,000	326,000	75,000	2,290,000

[1] Preliminary. [2] Estimate. [3] Formerly part of the U.S.S.R.; data not reported separately until 1992. *Source: U.S. Bureau of Mines*

GOLD

Salient U.S. Gold Statistics In Kilograms (1 Kilogram = 32.1507 Troy Ounces)

Year	Mine Production	Value Million $	Refinery Production: Domestic & Foreign Ores	Refinery Production: Secondary (Old Scrap)	Exports (Excluding Coinage)	Imports for Consumption	Stocks, Dec. 31: Treasury Department[3]	Stocks, Dec. 31: Futures Exch.	Stocks, Dec. 31: Industry	Official World Reserves[4]	Consumption: Dental	Consumption: Industrial[5]	Consumption: Jewelry & Arts	Consumption: Total
1985	75,495	771.0	64,583	49,824	123,378	255,857	8,170,019	65,628	18,538	35,616	9,309	35,828	50,951	96,318
1986	155,365	1,819.0	75,618	47,266	155,365	489,863	8,149,938	87,370	28,771	35,743	7,921	36,858	65,827	110,795
1987	153,870	2,216.0	112,368	63,843	119,630	119,539	8,160,251	81,647	23,390	35,655	6,944	35,245	71,024	113,319
1988	200,914	2,831.3	137,829	61,391	328,237	92,457	8,145,696	44,634	38,360	35,829	7,576	37,226	67,027	111,836
1989	265,731	3,268.6	183,685	51,943	211,091	152,504	8,147,169	69,727	30,462	35,603	7,927	37,621	69,524	115,078
1990	294,189	3,640.8	225,183	43,980	296,397	97,519	8,146,432	50,881	37,065	35,572	8,700	30,996	78,514	118,216
1991	294,062	3,434.7	224,675	48,088	284,127	178,749	8,145,696	49,893	39,411	35,501	8,485	21,793	84,096	114,375
1992	330,212	3,662.4	283,951	53,396	368,851	174,341	8,145,000	46,453	36,713	35,199	6,543	20,360	83,508	110,410
1993[1]	331,013	3,840.9	243,135	65,964	792,680	169,305	8,143,000	78,514	34,400	34,700	6,173	19,663	65,600	91,400
1994[2]	326,000	4,040.0	240,584	74,332	471,000	140,000	8,142,000	49,063	32,700	34,500	5,430	17,013	53,700	76,100

[1] Preliminary. [2] Estimate. [3] Includes gold in Exchange Stabilization Fund. [4] Held by market economy country central banks and governments and international monetary organizations. [5] Including space and defense. *Source: U.S. Bureau of Mines*

Monthly Average Gold Price (Handy & Harman at New York) Dollars Per Troy Ounce

Year	Jan.	Feb.	Mar.	Apr.	May	June	July	Aug.	Sept.	Oct.	Nov.	Dec.	Average
1983	479.9	490.4	419.7	432.2	437.6	412.8	423.1	416.3	411.5	393.2	382.3	387.1	423.83
1984	370.9	386.0	394.4	381.7	377.3	377.7	346.4	347.7	340.9	340.1	340.9	319.0	360.23
1985	302.8	298.8	303.9	324.9	316.1	316.5	317.8	330.2	322.6	326.2	325.5	322.4	317.31
1986	345.5	339.3	345.4	304.6	340.5	342.8	348.9	376.9	419.0	423.6	398.8	391.2	367.70
1987	408.3	401.3	408.9	438.7	460.1	449.6	450.8	460.9	460.2	465.5	466.5	486.0	446.40
1988	476.6	441.9	443.6	451.8	450.8	451.3	437.6	431.3	412.8	406.8	420.1	418.5	436.93
1989	404.0	387.8	390.1	384.4	371.3	367.6	394.7	364.9	361.9	366.9	392.3	408.1	382.92
1990	410.1	416.8	393.1	374.3	369.2	352.3	362.5	395.0	389.5	380.7	381.7	378.2	383.61
1991	383.6	363.8	363.4	358.4	356.8	366.7	367.5	356.2	348.8	358.7	359.5	361.1	362.18
1992	354.5	353.9	344.3	338.5	337.2	340.8	353.0	343.0	345.4	344.4	335.1	334.7	343.74
1993	329.0	329.4	330.1	341.9	366.7	371.9	392.4	378.5	354.9	364.2	373.5	383.7	359.67
1994[1]	387.0	382.0	384.1	378.2	381.2	385.6	385.4	380.4	391.8	389.8	349.4	379.6	384.14
1995[1]	378.6	376.5	382.1	391.1	385.5	387.6	386.4	383.6	382.2	383.1	385.5		

[1] Preliminary. *Sources: U.S. Bureau of Mines; American Metal Market*

Gold Average Open Interest at New York (COMEX) In Thousands of Contracts

Year	Jan.	Feb.	Mar.	Apr.	May	June	July	Aug.	Sept.	Oct.	Nov.	Dec.
1986	147,771	139,118	141,941	137,748	130,605	116,896	121,769	133,225	149,013	140,621	145,940	135,533
1987	137,650	134,151	146,896	172,605	169,606	147,703	147,005	149,345	147,346	139,482	137,383	154,110
1988	147,067	152,789	158,224	154,788	153,465	145,951	147,822	140,311	153,556	160,591	153,497	144,839
1989	162,226	166,455	167,419	160,215	180,709	164,196	154,517	150,414	151,836	146,262	154,927	151,788
1990	147,884	132,400	126,890	118,750	117,707	113,958	105,496	120,579	116,331	113,873	111,638	110,343
1991	104,666	98,000	98,429	101,266	100,341	88,961	94,467	99,790	105,053	96,302	109,030	109,004
1992	106,110	103,319	109,796	106,485	109,947	98,127	111,039	102,239	102,376	102,232	109,965	100,328
1993	112,420	109,093	115,505	142,208	172,491	170,829	200,168	180,509	166,201	152,531	152,853	154,730
1994	156,045	139,354	146,269	144,386	147,738	146,255	148,915	155,641	167,981	166,041	166,536	178,998
1995	184,549	170,972	168,651	191,667	173,805	174,075	175,727	176,135	185,128	185,854	170,674	141,751

Source: New York Mercantile Exchange, COMEX Division

Total Volume of Trading of Gold Futures at New York (COMEX) In Thousands of Contracts

Year	Jan.	Feb.	Mar.	Apr.	May	June	July	Aug.	Sept.	Oct.	Nov.	Dec.	Total
1986	1,126.2	574.2	703.9	617.9	482.2	451.6	527.6	711.1	1,054.7	846.9	724.3	579.6	8,400
1987	936.4	706.9	794.9	1,135.2	1,021.2	793.4	796.9	760.3	747.9	951.3	847.1	748.2	10,240
1988	815.0	778.7	965.0	637.7	866.2	946.3	884.2	587.5	790.9	694.5	895.5	634.9	9,496
1989	900.4	800.0	993.8	682.4	932.0	936.6	756.1	591.1	630.0	681.2	1,228.4	876.4	9,989
1990	1,327.1	885.1	975.6	472.4	745.2	541.0	747.4	1,191.5	729.4	879.9	705.3	530.1	9,730
1991	957.3	497.8	617.7	446.1	584.4	520.0	551.4	457.2	429.1	551.0	677.3	510.6	6,771
1992	729.8	388.4	607.3	425.4	485.4	427.2	734.6	500.2	465.3	414.1	504.1	320.1	6,002
1993	506.0	446.2	661.4	640.4	1,140.7	809.6	1,171.7	808.8	728.9	565.2	892.3	533.2	8,916
1994	981.8	584.0	889.5	589.2	922.6	749.2	723.8	626.0	645.6	651.2	687.8	461.5	8,503
1995	881.9	420.0	1,087.5	613.0	777.0	588.1	669.9	500.5	495.5	387.7	982.5	378.1	7,782

Source: New York Mercantile Exchange, COMEX Division

GOLD

Commodity Exchange, Inc. (COMEX) Depository Warehouse Stocks of Gold In Thousands of Troy Ounces

Year	Jan. 1	Feb. 1	Mar. 1	Apr. 1	May 1	June 1	July 1	Aug. 1	Sept. 1	Oct. 1	Nov. 1	Dec. 1
1983	2,247	2,621	2,754	2,645	2,636	2,723	2,630	2,648	2,570	2,538	2,500	2,485
1984	2,481	2,472	2,408	2,452	2,412	2,426	2,376	2,395	2,387	2,391	2,349	2,366
1985	2,308	2,308	2,273	2,109	2,136	2,142	2,133	2,107	2,119	2,083	2,099	2,105
1986	2,109	2,352	2,580	2,593	2,567	1,986	1,992	1,621	1,664	1,726	1,787	2,193
1987	2,890	2,798	2,817	2,903	2,628	2,665	2,614	2,624	2,670	2,636	2,644	2,645
1988	2,624	2,605	2,586	1,596	1,566	1,675	1,834	2,099	2,189	1,949	1,629	1,267
1989	1,434	1,408	1,454	1,532	1,606	1,634	1,602	1,602	1,433	1,483	1,731	2,263
1990	2,241	2,225	2,245	2,220	2,048	1,809	1,582	1,530	1,539	1,564	1,585	1,347
1991	1,636	1,686	1,540	1,298	1,458	1,711	1,772	1,875	1,220	1,342	1,302	1,479
1992	1,605	1,362	1,435	1,411	1,591	1,618	1,605	1,733	1,688	1,947	1,766	1,524
1993	1,507	1,340	1,365	1,426	1,383	2,231	2,247	2,448	2,437	2,425	2,349	2,552
1994	2,524	2,955	2,958	2,862	2,802	2,434	2,665	2,574	2,030	1,904	1,843	1,867
1995	1,577	1,498	1,386	1,360	1,391	1,488	1,505	1,608	1,448	1,745	1,395	1,315

Source: New York Mercantile Exchange, COMEX division

Central Gold Bank Reserves In Millions of Troy Ounces

	Industrial Countries															
Year	Belgium	Canada	France	Germany	Italy	Japan	Netherlands	Switzerland	United Kingdom	United States	Industrial Total	Developing Oil	Developing Non-Oil	IMF[2]	Bank for Int'l Settlements	World Total
1985	34.2	20.1	81.9	95.2	66.7	24.2	43.9	83.3	19.0	262.7	896.5	43.8	94.7	103.4	6.7	1,145.2
1986	34.2	19.7	81.9	95.2	66.7	24.2	43.9	83.3	19.0	262.0	895.6	43.7	100.3	103.4	6.4	1,149.5
1987	33.6	18.5	81.9	95.2	66.7	24.2	43.9	83.3	19.0	262.4	894.3	43.6	99.1	103.4	6.1	1,146.5
1988	33.7	17.1	81.9	95.2	66.7	24.2	43.9	83.3	19.0	261.9	895.1	42.0	99.1	103.4	6.4	1,146.1
1989	30.2	16.1	81.9	95.2	66.7	24.2	43.9	83.3	19.0	261.9	891.5	42.1	103.3	103.4	6.1	1,146.4
1990	30.2	14.8	81.9	95.2	66.7	24.2	43.9	83.3	18.9	261.9	889.4	41.5	101.3	103.4	6.6	1,142.2
1991	30.2	13.0	81.9	95.2	66.7	24.2	43.9	83.3	18.9	261.9	887.3	42.0	101.6	103.4	6.6	1,141.0
1992	25.0	9.9	81.9	95.2	66.7	24.2	43.9	83.3	18.6	261.8	877.4	42.0	101.7	103.4	6.8	1,131.3
1993	25.0	6.1	81.9	95.2	66.7	24.2	35.1	83.3	18.5	261.8	860.4	42.0	100.1	103.4	8.6	1,114.6
1994[1]	25.0	4.0	81.9	95.2	66.7	24.2	34.8	83.3	18.4	261.8	867.3	42.0	99.7	103.4	7.3	1,109.6

[1] Thru October only. [2] International Monetary Fund. *Source: American Metal Market*

U.S. Mine Production of Recoverable Gold In Kilograms

Year	Arizona	California	Idaho	Montana	Nevada	Alaska	Colorado	South Dakota	New Mexico	Utah	Other States	Total
1987	1,791	18,277	3,041	7,143	83,342	3,812	5,561	------ 30,903 ------				153,870
1988	4,549	22,442	3,218	9,175	114,322	4,210	5,126	13,981	------ 23,891 ------			200,914
1989	2,768	29,804	3,057	12,434	153,995	5,756	3,448	16,123	1,076	----- 37,270 -----		265,731
1990	5,000	29,607	W	13,012	179,078	3,232	2,357	17,870	888	----- 43,145 -----		294,189
1991	6,195	30,404	3,348	13,715	180,382	3,200	3,181	16,371	------ 39,161 ------			295,957
1992	6,656	33,335	3,177	13,994	203,165	5,003	3,763	18,681	------ 41,350 ------			329,124
1993	3,042	35,356	4,324	20,265	206,304	------ 62,803 ------						332,091
1994[1]	2,476	28,846	3,608	13,300	203,000	------ 55,600 ------						306,000

[1] Preliminary. W = Withheld proprietary data, included in "Other States." *Source: U.S. Bureau of Mines*

U.S. Consumption of Gold, by End-Use In Kilograms

	Jewelry and the Arts					Industrial				
Year	Gold-filled & Other	Electroplating	Karat Gold	Total	Dental	Gold-filled & Other	Electroplating	Karat Gold	Total	Grand Total
1987	9,256	3,133	58,635	71,024	6,944	21,010	12,343	1,892	35,245	113,319
1988	7,598	1,469	57,959	67,027	7,576	21,034	15,088	1,104	37,226	111,836
1989	7,364	1,283	60,877	69,524	7,927	15,723	20,684	1,215	37,621	115,078
1990	8,132	429	69,952	78,514	8,700	12,725	17,251	1,020	30,996	118,216
1991	3,848	373	79,875	84,096	8,485	8,102	12,624	1,068	21,793	114,375
1992	3,546	581	79,381	83,508	6,543	8,802	10,476	1,082	20,360	110,410
1993	3,532	373	61,700	65,600	6,173	9,474	9,094	1,095	19,663	91,400
1994[1]	3,652	369	49,700	53,700	5,430	7,447	9,471	97	17,013	76,100

[1] Preliminary. *Source: U.S. Bureau of Mines*

GOLD IN BRITISH POUNDS
WEEKLY CASH
AS OF:03/15/96
RATIO
310
300
290
280
270
260
250
240
230
220
210
200
1993
1994
1995
1996
M A M J J A S O N D J F M A M J J A S O N D J F M A M J J A S O N D J F M A M J J

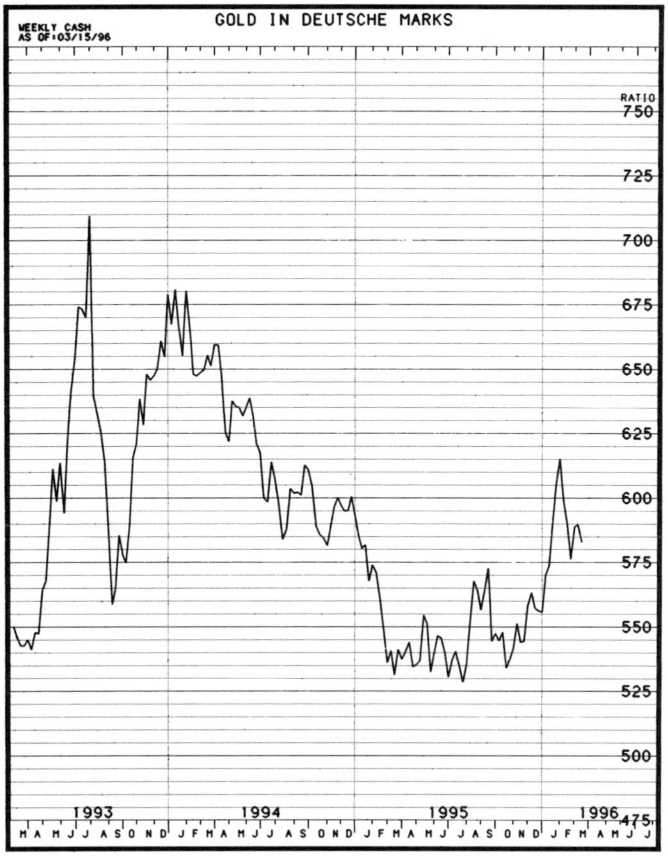
GOLD IN DEUTSCHE MARKS
WEEKLY CASH
AS OF:03/15/96
RATIO
750
725
700
675
650
625
600
575
550
525
500
475
1993
1994
1995
1996
M A M J J A S O N D J F M A M J J A S O N D J F M A M J J A S O N D J F M A M J J

GOLD IN JAPANESE YEN
WEEKLY CASH
AS OF:03/15/96
RATIO
480
460
440
420
400
380
360
340
320
300
280
260
1993
1994
1995
1996
M A M J J A S O N D J F M A M J J A S O N D J F M A M J J A S O N D J F M A M J J

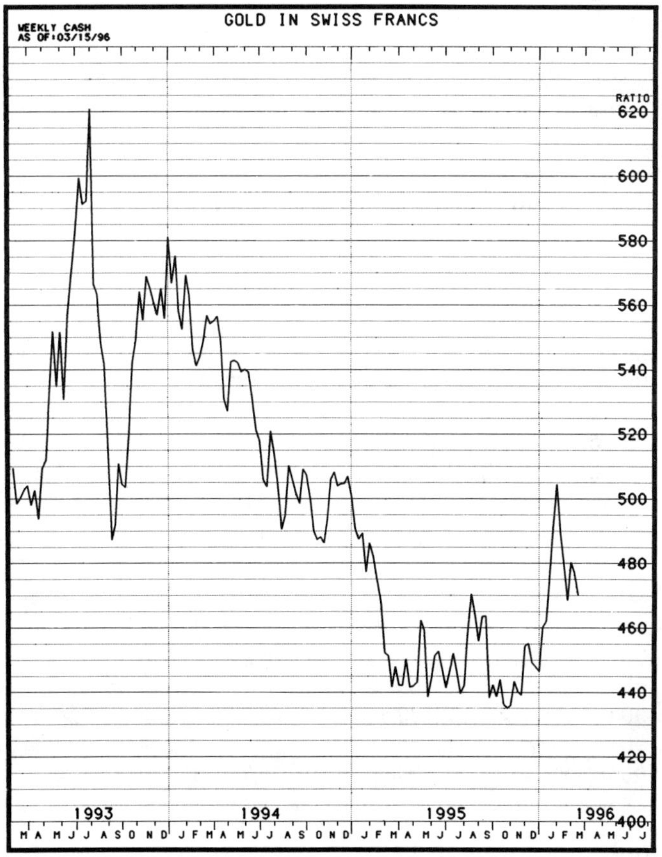
GOLD IN SWISS FRANCS
WEEKLY CASH
AS OF:03/15/96
RATIO
620
600
580
560
540
520
500
480
460
440
420
400
1993
1994
1995
1996
M A M J J A S O N D J F M A M J J A S O N D J F M A M J J A S O N D J F M A M J J

Grain Sorghum

The U.S. accounts for nearly a quarter of 1995/96 world sorghum (milo) production of 53 million metric tons versus 57 million in 1994/95. The U.S. share was 12.5 million and 16.6 million, respectively. Despite the decline it was still enough for domestic use, but afforded a relatively small margin of longer term safety in the event the 1996 crop runs into trouble. India, the second largest producer at 11 million tons in 1995/96, consumes virtually all its production and at times relies on imports to fulfill demand. Based on the trend of the first half of the 1990's, India will soon be both the largest producer and consumer of sorghum. World trade is small. The U.S. is the largest exporter, mostly to Mexico and Japan. Argentina is the second largest exporter.

In the U.S. the sorghum crop year begins September 1. Kansas and Texas are the largest producing states. Unfavorable weather in the summer of 1995 sharply reduced yield to less than 60 bushels per acre versus 73 bushels in 1994/95. Weather problems aside, harvested acreage continues to slide, declining to 8.3 million acre from 9 million in 1994/95 and well under the 12 million acres harvested in 1992/93. Production in 1995/96 of 492 million bushels was the lowest since the drought year of 1983 and compares with 655 million in 1994/95.

Total supplies in 1995/96 of 563 million bushels including a 71 million carryin (the U.S. imports no sorghum) would be the lowest total since the 1970's. The smaller sorghum supply is expected to force a reduction in use of more than 100 million bushels, placing disappearance around a near record low 522 million bushels. Still, carryover stocks as of August 31, 1996 were forecast to total only 41 million bushels versus 71 million a year earlier. Carryover at the end of the 1992/93 crop year totaled 175 million bushels. Export demand for U.S. sorghum, although falling in recent years, still accounts for nearly a third of total disappearance. Exports were estimated at 180 million bushels in 1995/96 versus 220 million in 1994/95. Domestic 1995/96 usage was placed at 335 million bushels versus 404 million in 1994/95.

Sorghum prices received by farmers during 1994/95 averaged $2.13 versus $2.31 per bushel the previous year. The average, however, is somewhat misleading as it masks the price surge in the summer of 1995 when prices averaged $2.64. Strong prices were expected to persist into the 1995/96 marketing year with prices averaging between $2.60 to $3.00 per bushel, the strength partially reflecting the anticipated drop in carryover, assuming prices do not push higher than expected and dampen usage.

Government Program

Washington D.C. legislators are currently rewriting the entire U.S Farm Program. Target prices and price support loan rates are unavailable. The levels in 1994/5 were $2.61 per bushel and $1.80, respectively.

World Sorghum Supply and Demand — In Thousands of Metric Tons

Crop Year	Exports: Argentina	Exports: Non-U.S.	Exports: U.S.	Exports: Total	Imports: Japan	Imports: Mexico	Imports: Unaccounted	Imports: Total	Total Production	Utilization: China	Utilization: Japan	Utilization: Mexico	Utilization: U.S.	Utilization: Total	Ending Stocks: Non-U.S.	Ending Stocks: U.S.	Ending Stocks: Total
1991-2	1,300	1,907	7,457	9,364	3,247	4,996	22	9,364	53,162	4,851	3,217	9,399	9,717	54,820	4,592	1,351	5,943
1992-3	1,023	2,005	6,634	8,639	3,221	3,951	12	8,639	65,048	4,597	3,210	7,339	12,091	61,491	5,054	4,446	9,500
1993-4[1]	426	1,561	5,318	6,879	2,852	3,089	327	6,879	52,806	4,906	3,000	6,307	11,687	58,221	2,877	1,208	4,085
1994-5[2]	300	550	5,653	6,203	2,341	2,544	114	6,203	54,141	5,318	2,400	5,644	10,380	53,674	2,743	1,809	4,552
1995-6[3]	300	850	4,600	5,450	2,000	2,350	100	5,450	50,753	5,000	2,050	6,550	7,798	52,245	1,971	1,089	3,060

[1] Preliminary. [2] Estimate. [3] Forecast. *Source: Foreign Agricultural Service, U.S. Department of Agriculture*

Salient Statistics of Grain Sorghum in the United States

Year	Acreage Planted[4] for All Purposes (1,000 Acres)	For Grain: Acreage Harvested (1,000 Acres)	For Grain: Production 1,000 Bushels	For Grain: Yield Per Harvested Acre Bushels	For Grain: Price in Cents Per Bushel	For Grain: Value of Production Million $	For Silage: Acreage Harvested 1,000 Acres	For Silage: Production 1,000 Tons	For Silage: Yield Per Harvested Acre Tons	Sorghum Grain Stocks (1,000 Bushels): Dec. 1 On Farms	Dec. 1 Off Farms	June 1 On Farms	June 1 Off Farms
1990-1	10,535	9,089	573,303	63.1	212	1,220.5	527	5,377	10.2	NA	NA	43,750	178,250
1991-2	11,064	9,870	584,860	59.3	225	1,331.3	483	4,846	10.0	140,000	372,340	34,140	76,247
1992-3	13,177	12,050	875,022	72.6	189	1,666.9	453	5,468	12.1	110,200	340,262	58,465	206,348
1993-4[1]	9,882	8,916	534,172	59.9	231	1,234.5	351	3,914	11.2	105,950	340,198	32,075	96,035
1994-5[2]	9,827	8,917	649,206	73.0	213	1,323.8	329	3,932	12.0	126,650	295,809	44,570	114,212
1995-6[3]	9,454	8,278	460,373	56.4	315	1,408.5	368	3,652	9.9	79,090	222,796		

[1] Preliminary. [2] Estimate. [3] Forecast. NA = Not available. *Source: Economic Research Service, U.S. Department of Agriculture*

Production of All Sorghum for Grain in the United States, by States — In Thousands of Bushels

Year	Alabama	Arkansas	Colorado	Illinois	Kansas	Louisiana	Mississippi	Missouri	Nebraska	New Mexico	North Carolina	Oklahoma	South Dakota	Texas
1990	990	18,150	10,340	14,625	184,800	8,320	5,525	42,640	108,750	3,250	1,840	16,450	14,300	135,200
1991	1,265	15,390	10,800	13,840	176,400	10,120	4,760	37,440	90,450	10,200	1,250	13,800	13,020	176,900
1992	1,250	31,160	6,660	26,780	244,000	15,232	10,500	62,080	143,820	12,300	1,000	17,490	14,060	279,000
1993	817	12,470	7,140	17,430	176,400	7,200	4,225	39,420	73,750	7,425	675	14,500	10,500	156,750
1994	900	18,375	7,140	17,820	231,000	8,364	5,250	49,500	117,600	7,410	1,100	14,000	11,375	153,400
1995[1]	320	13,135	4,620	11,730	173,600	5,880	2,665	35,770	56,840	3,380	650	12,800	4,800	129,600

[1] Preliminary. *Source: National Agricultural Statistics Service, U.S Department of Agriculture*

U.S. Grain Sorghum Quarterly Supply and Disappearance In Millions of Bushels

Crop Year Beginning Sept. 1	Supply: Beginning Stocks	Supply: Production	Supply: Imports	Supply: Total Supply	Disappearance – Domestic Use: Food, Alcohol & Industrial	Disappearance – Domestic Use: Seed	Disappearance – Domestic Use: Feed & Residual	Disappearance – Domestic Use: Total	Disappearance: Export	Disappearance: Total	Ending Stocks: Gov't. Owned[3]	Ending Stocks: Privately Owned[4]	Ending Stocks: Total Stocks
1992-3	53.2	875.0	0	928.2	6.1	1.4	468.5	476.0	277.2	753.2	3.9	171.1	175.0
Sept.-Nov.	53.2	875.0	0	928.2	1.5	0	266.0	267.5	56.4	323.9	2.5	601.8	604.3
Dec.-Feb.	605.3	------	0	604.3	1.2	0	67.2	69.4	101.5	169.9	4.0	430.4	434.4
Mar.-May	434.4	------	0	434.4	1.8	.7	79.7	82.2	87.4	169.6	3.9	260.9	264.8
June-Aug.	264.8	------	0	264.8	1.6	.7	55.6	57.9	31.9	89.8	3.9	171.1	175.0
1993-4[1]	175.0	534.2	0	709.2	6.3	1.2	452.6	460.1	201.6	661.6	1.0	46.9	47.6
Sept.-Nov.	175.0	534.2	0	709.2	1.7	0	222.1	223.8	39.2	263.0	1.9	444.2	446.1
Dec.-Feb.	446.1	------	0	446.2	1.5	0	108.0	109.5	60.4	169.9	2.0	274.2	276.2
Mar.-May	276.2	------	0	276.2	1.7	.8	81.9	84.4	63.7	148.1	2.0	126.1	128.1
June-Aug.	128.1	------	0	128.1	1.4	.4	40.5	42.3	38.2	80.5	1.0	46.9	47.6
1994-5[2]	47.6	655.0	0	702.6	5.8	1.2	401.7	408.7	222.7	631.4	1.0	70.2	71.2
Sept.-Nov.	47.6	655.0	0	702.6	1.7	0	214.4	216.1	64.1	280.1	3.0	419.5	422.5
Dec.-Feb.	422.5	------	0	422.5	1.4	0	79.2	80.6	60.9	141.5	2.0	278.9	280.9
Mar.-May	280.9	------	0	280.9	1.5	.4	65.9	67.8	54.4	122.2	1.0	157.8	158.8
June-Aug.	158.8	------	0	158.8	1.2	.8	42.2	44.2	43.3	87.6	1.0	70.2	71.2
1995-6[2]	71.2	463.6	0	534.9	5.8	1.2	315.0	322.0	170.0	492.0	1.0	40.0	42.9

[1] Preliminary. [2] Forecast. [3] Uncommitted inventory. [4] Includes quantity under loan & farmer-owned reserve. *Source: Economic Research Service,*

Average Price of Sorghum Grain, No. 2, Yellow at Kansas City In Dollars Per Hundred Pounds (Cwt.)

Year	Sept.	Oct.	Nov.	Dec.	Jan.	Feb.	Mar.	Apr.	May	June	July	Aug.	Average
1987-8	2.64	2.75	2.90	2.95	3.05	3.24	3.27	3.16	3.21	4.58	4.79	4.28	3.40
1988-9	4.27	4.17	4.00	4.23	4.24	4.26	4.32	4.17	4.29	4.15	3.96	3.92	4.17
1989-90	4.73	3.91	4.00	3.98	3.91	3.84	4.01	4.32	4.47	4.54	4.48	4.27	4.21
1990-1	3.89	3.79	3.85	3.97	4.12	4.21	4.35	4.34	4.13	4.02	4.05	4.22	4.08
1991-2	4.24	4.30	4.27	4.35	4.44	4.62	4.78	4.41	4.54	4.51	4.05	3.77	4.36
1992-3	3.76	3.60	3.61	3.70	3.70	3.66	3.70	3.72	3.82	3.58	3.99	4.01	3.74
1993-4	3.89	4.03	4.60	4.91	4.93	4.81	4.64	4.33	4.38	4.43	3.79	3.73	4.37
1994-5[1]	3.72	3.55	3.60	3.81	3.92	3.90	4.01	4.08	4.27	4.50	4.93	4.85	4.10
1995-6[1]	5.08	5.45											5.27

[1] Preliminary. *Source: Economic Research Service, U.S. Department of Agriculture*

U.S. Exports of Grain Sorghum, by Country of Destination In Metric Tons

Year Beginning October	Canada	Ecuador	Ethiopia	Israel	Japan	Jordon	Mexico	South Africa	Spain	Sudan	Turkey	World Total
1989-90	1,167	29,999	8,497	347,639	3,028,529	254,907	3,022,079	0	233,080	0	52,150	7,240,836
1990-1	1,325	33,060	0	165,906	1,853,079	20,500	3,015,944	0	181,501	91,400	114,636	5,778,792
1991-2	1,613	36,000	42,150	104,952	1,738,075	120,001	4,956,607	19,031	174,758	122,183	99,394	7,454,616
1992-3	1,795	9,501	0	217,110	1,933,012	0	3,970,069	56,186	188,893	4,287	132,182	6,651,528
1993-4[1]	1,699	0	86,697	66,264	1,681,976	0	3,118,139	0	169,454	48,042	0	5,245,524
1994-5[2]			0	214,073	1,987,738		2,543,696		398,339			5,652,585

[1] Preliminary. [2] Estimate. *Source: Economic Research Service, U.S. Department of Agriculture*

Grain Sorghum Price Support Program and Market Prices

Year	Price Support Operations: Put Under Price Support: Quantity (Million Cwt.)	Price Support Operations: Put Under Price Support: % of Production	Price Support Operations: Aquired by CCC (Million Cwt.)	Price Support Operations: Owned by CCC at Year End (Million Cwt.)	Basic Loan Rate ($ Per Bushel)	Target Price ($ Per Bushel)	Findley Loan Rate ($ Per Bushel)	Effective Base[3] Mil. Acres	Participation Rate[4] % of Base	No. 2 Yellow ($ Per Cwt.): Kansas City	No. 2 Yellow ($ Per Cwt.): Texas High Plains	No. 2 Yellow ($ Per Cwt.): Los Angeles	No. 2 Yellow ($ Per Cwt.): Gulf Ports
1987-8	201.3	49.2	119.7	259.6	2.17	2.88	1.82	17.4	84	3.40	3.81	5.18	3.96
1988-9	22.7	7.0	17.0	190.9	2.10	2.78	1.74	16.8	82	4.17	4.66	6.08	4.81
1989-90	11.7	3.4	10.1	91.3	1.96	2.70	1.57	16.2	71	4.21	4.38	5.53	4.76
1990-1	12.1	3.8	5.0	36.4	1.86	2.61	1.49	15.4	70	4.08	4.48	5.52	4.65
1991-2	9.5	2.9	5.4	4.5	1.80	2.61	1.54	13.5	77	4.36	4.78	5.69	4.86
1992-3	27.2	5.5	0	2.2	1.91	2.61	1.63	13.6	79	3.74	4.06	5.11	4.27
1993-4	8.2	2.6	0	1.1	1.89	2.61	1.63	13.5	82	4.37	4.95		4.90
1994-5[1]	25.2	6.9	0		1.89	2.61	1.80	13.5	81	4.10	4.75		4.73
1995-6[2]	1.5	.6	0		-----	2.61	1.80	13.4	77	5.27	5.95		5.94

[1] Preliminary. [2] Estimate. [3] National effective crop acreage base as determined by ASCS. [4] Percentage of effective base acres enrolled in acreage reduction programs. *Source: Economic Research Service, U.S. Department of Agriculture*

Hay

U.S. hay production of 157 million tons in 1995/96 was five percent over 1994/95 with the gain reflecting increased acreage and higher yield. Alfalfa and alfalfa mixtures production was up two percent and all other hay was up three percent. Annual production since the mid-1980's has averaged close to 145 million tons. California and Texas are the largest producing states, generally accounting for nearly 15 percent of total production. Total hay supplies in 1995/96 were estimated three percent higher than a year earlier and about equal to disappearance.

The index of roughage consuming animal units (RCAU) in 1995/95 was up two percent from 1994/95; reflecting the increase in the number of beef cattle. On July 1, 1995 beef cow numbers were up three percent from a year earlier. Disappearance of hay per RCAU during 1995/96 was likely to rebound somewhat from 1994/95 to about two tons per animal unit. The key to hay prices rests largely on the number of dairy cows and producer intentions to plant acreage to hay for forage. Much depends on the dairy cow inventory in California and Wisconsin. If the 1995/96 demand proves to match supply, the average farm price for hay is expected to hold in the $80-85/ton range, a shade higher than 1994/95.

Salient Statistics of All Hay in the United States

Year Crop Beginning May	Acres Harvested 1,000 Acres	Yield Per Acre Tons	Production (Millions of Tons)	Carryover May 1 (Millions of Tons)	Disappearance (Millions of Tons)	Supply Per Animal Unit (In Tons)	Disappearance Per Animal Unit (In Tons)	Animal Units Fed[3] Millions	Farm Price $ Per Ton	Farm Production Value Million $	Retail Price Paid by Farmers for Seed, April 15: Alfalfa (Certified) (Dollars Per Cwt.)	Timothy	Red Clover	Sudan-Grass
1989-90	63,300	2.30	145.5	17.5	135.9	2.20	1.83	77.4	85.40	11,197	249.00	132.00	143.00	45.30
1990-1	61,407	2.39	146.8	27.1	146.9	2.36	1.99	80.1	80.60	10,462	253.00	82.10	145.00	47.70
1991-2	62,475	2.45	153.3	27.0	152.0	2.40	2.02	80.8	71.20	10,006	266.00	66.40	134.00	48.10
1992-3	58,903	2.49	146.9	28.6	156.4	2.33	2.05	82.7	72.10	10,436	252.00	66.30	122.00	47.10
1993-4[1]	59,679	2.46	146.8	21.0	147.3	2.20	1.91	84.0	84.70	10,957	269.00	80.60	148.00	45.20
1994-5[2]	58,735	2.55	150.1	22.1		2.20	1.93	84.6	86.70	11,114	266.00	76.00	148.00	47.90
1995-6[2]	59,779	2.59	154.8	20.8		2.22		86.7	85.00	10,977	274.00	71.00	134.00	51.80

[1] Preliminary. [2] Estimate. [3] Roughage-consuming animal units fed annually. *Source: Economic Research Service, U.S. Department of Agriculture*

Production of All Hay in the United States by Important States In Thousands of Tons

Year	California	Idaho	Illinois	Iowa	Michigan	Minnesota	Missouri	Nebraska	New York	North Dakota	Ohio	Oklahoma	Pennsylvania	South Dakota	Texas	Wisconsin
1990	8,307	4,084	2,220	7,095	5,335	6,560	6,865	7,205	4,377	3,745	4,620	3,926	4,719	6,300	8,000	9,120
1991	8,610	4,294	3,162	6,285	5,255	8,090	7,110	7,473	4,102	4,780	3,150	4,360	4,026	8,045	9,700	9,060
1992	7,755	3,655	3,316	6,615	4,280	6,550	6,780	7,793	3,590	3,515	4,240	4,750	4,740	6,780	9,800	6,090
1993	7,590	4,844	4,106	4,803	5,370	5,970	7,335	7,323	3,605	5,043	3,475	4,248	4,352	8,190	7,506	6,260
1994	8,210	4,438	3,175	5,775	4,865	7,530	6,770	7,415	3,961	4,510	4,384	4,198	4,528	7,330	8,455	6,550
1995[1]	9,000	5,080	3,598	5,665	5,025	6,943	6,818	6,975	3,448	5,095	4,035	4,174	4,409	9,050	8,136	6,820

[1] Preliminary. *Source: Agricultural Statistics Board, U.S. Department of Agriculture*

U.S. Types of Hay Production & Farm Stocks In Thousands of Short Tons

Year	Production: Alfalfa & Mixtures	All Others	All Hay	Corn for Silage[1]	Sorghum Silage[1]	Farm Stocks: May 1	Dec. 1
1990	83,555	63,265	146,820	86,844	5,377	26,993	104,701
1991	83,795	69,530	153,325	80,543	4,846	26,974	111,123
1992	79,140	67,763	146,903	87,663	5,468	28,216	105,290
1993	80,305	66,494	146,799	81,829	3,914	21,010	100,953
1994	81,336	68,724	150,060	88,588	3,932	22,096	104,406
1995[2]	84,980	69,806	154,789	77,867	3,652	20,786	

[1] Not included in all tame hay. [2] Preliminary. *Source: Agricultural Statistics Board, U.S. Department of Agriculture*

Mid-Month Price Received by Farmers of All Hay (Baled) In Dollars Per Ton

Year	May	June	July	Aug.	Sept.	Oct.	Nov.	Dec.	Jan.	Feb.	Mar.	Apr.	Average[2]
1989-90	100.00	90.20	83.40	81.60	85.70	83.20	83.20	83.50	84.90	85.70	87.50	95.00	85.40
1990-1	96.00	85.00	81.60	81.00	83.20	84.00	81.40	78.70	77.90	77.80	80.50	85.50	80.60
1991-2	81.10	75.20	71.80	70.80	69.80	68.50	68.20	68.90	68.70	71.10	69.90	70.90	71.20
1992-3	79.50	75.80	69.70	71.90	70.10	70.30	71.00	73.50	76.10	78.00	80.50	83.60	74.30
1993-4	86.60	79.60	76.90	77.50	78.80	82.30	84.20	83.50	85.70	86.90	90.80	98.20	84.70
1994-5[1]	100.00	88.70	82.50	83.10	82.40	86.80	86.60	85.50	84.80	85.00	86.70	90.30	86.00
1995-6[1]	90.40	83.90	80.60	81.10	80.30	83.00	81.00	80.30					82.58

[1] Preliminary. [2] Marketing year average. *Source: Economic Research Service, U.S. Department of Agriculture*

Heating Oil

Heating oil use in the U.S. is concentrated in the Northeastern states where it is primarily used for residential heating. There continues to be a vigorous competition between heating oil distributors and regulated natural gas distributors, who are primarily utilities. The trend in recent years has been for consumers to initially choose natural gas or switch to gas from heating oil when their oil furnaces expire. Natural gas pipelines are now widespread in residential neighborhoods allowing consumers to easily switch from oil to gas. Heating oil distributors have met the competition head on by using the commodity futures markets to lock in "guaranteed" low prices. Natural gas is promoted as being the cleaner and environmentally safer of the fuels, but heating oil burners are now designed to be safer and more efficient, while requiring less fuel to operate.

The trend appears to be going against heating oil. In many residential neighborhoods restrictions govern its use. Oil tanks are now required to be above ground which many homeowners find unacceptable. Natural gas travels through underground pipelines. While heating oil distributors often cite potential safety problems with natural gas, there have been few incidents of residential natural gas accidents. The trend appears to be toward heating with natural gas instead of heating oil.

In December 1995, heating oil prices, as measured on the New York Mercantile Exchange, reached their highest levels since the winter of 1992/93. Behind the price rise was cold weather in both the U.S. and Europe. Below-normal temperatures, along with heavier than normal snowfall, resulted in increased residential heating needs. While the Northeastern U.S. was cold, the market was finding its strength from the European market for gasoil which staged a strong price rally. Gasoil prices were outpacing U.S. heating oil gains which provided a premium for spot cargoes and prevented European supplies from reaching the U.S. That compounded an already tight distillate stock situation in the U.S. and set the stage for still higher prices if the colder-than-normal winter persisted.

For the first seven months of 1995, distillate fuel oil production averaged 3.08 million barrels per day. For the same period of 1994 the average daily production of distillate fuel oil was 3.18 million barrels per day, while for the like period of 1993 it was 3.0 million barrels. Average daily imports of fuel oil in the January-July 1995 period averaged 198,000 barrels, down from 218,000 barrels in 1994 and 185,000 barrels in 1993. Exports of distillate fuel oil just about offset imports. For the first seven months of 1995, the average daily exports were 185,000 barrels. This was down substantially from the 1994 average of 246,000 barrels and the 1993 average of 256,000 barrels. Total distillate fuel oil supplied in the first seven months averaged 3.21 million barrels per day. This was marginally above the 1994 supply level of 3.19 million barrels and the 1993 average of 3.02 million barrels. At the end of July, stocks of distillate fuel oil were 124,000 barrels. In July 1994, they were 134,000 barrels while in July 1993 stocks were 121,000 barrels. Of the stocks in July 1994, 60,000 barrels had .05 percent or less sulfur content while 64,000 had sulfur content greater than .05 percent.

Residual fuel oil production over the January-July 1995 period averaged 789,000 barrels per day. This was down five percent from the daily average production in the same period of 1994 and down from the 1993 average of 834,000 barrels. For the first seven months of 1995, imports of residual fuel oil averaged 179,000 barrels per day. This was down substantially from the average daily imports in 1994 of 378,000 barrels and 1993's daily imports of 345,000 barrels. Residual fuel oil production and imports have declined in the last several years. The highest production was in 1979 when daily output averaged 1.69 million barrels while in 1973 daily imports were 1.85 million barrels.

For January-July 1995, average daily exports of residual fuel oil were 154,000 barrels. This was up from the same period in 1994 when daily exports averaged 116,000 barrels and the 1993 average of 139,000 barrels. Total residual fuel oil supplied in the first seven months of 1995 averaged 838,000 barrels per day. Stocks at the end of July 1995 were 36,000 barrels, down from 40,000 barrels in July 1994 and 43,000 barrels in July 1993.

Refiner prices of No. 2 fuel oil to end users for the first five months of 1995 averaged 55.56 cents per gallon (excluding taxes). Refiner prices of No. 2 fuel oil for resale averaged 49.88 cents per gallon (excluding taxes).

Futures Markets

Heating oil futures and options are traded on the New York Mercantile Exchange (NYMEX). In London, gasoil futures and options are listed on the International Petroleum Exchange (IPE).

Average Spot Prices of Heating Oil #2 In Cents Per Gallon

Year	Jan.	Fe.	Mar.	Apr.	May	June	July	Aug.	Sept.	Oct.	Nov.	Dec.	Average
1985	74.28	75.88	80.57	79.24	72.63	70.31	68.80	72.90	78.97	83.72	86.94	81.45	77.14
1986	66.81	53.31	59.69	43.70	46.90	37.84	33.33	40.93	40.31	39.47	42.17	44.52	45.49
1987	52.34	47.36	49.18	48.58	51.75	52.30	54.62	52.46	52.33	56.14	55.84	53.75	52.22
1988	51.73	48.10	47.43	51.46	50.82	44.76	42.79	43.41	40.71	40.52	44.84	50.91	46.46
1989	54.35	51.47	56.86	53.98	50.76	48.51	49.35	49.75	55.78	58.80	59.20	80.91	55.81
1990	73.26	57.48	57.93	58.51	53.99	48.22	53.14	75.23	88.82	93.95	87.51	79.73	68.98
1991	74.96	70.80	61.92	56.36	55.04	53.67	57.74	60.48	61.54	66.58	64.33	53.35	61.31
1992	51.72	53.39	52.49	56.22	57.38	61.26	60.24	58.29	61.90	62.72	56.52	54.98	57.25
1993	53.14	56.02	58.13	55.49	54.53	52.62	49.74	50.70	51.96	54.00	50.30	43.47	52.51
1994	49.93	55.81	49.18	48.01	47.98	49.37	49.93	49.51	47.90	48.23	49.62	48.41	49.49
1995	47.98	47.64	45.95	49.40	50.31	47.75	46.65	49.14	50.21	48.89	51.89	57.76	49.46

Source: New York Mercantile Exchange

HEATING OIL

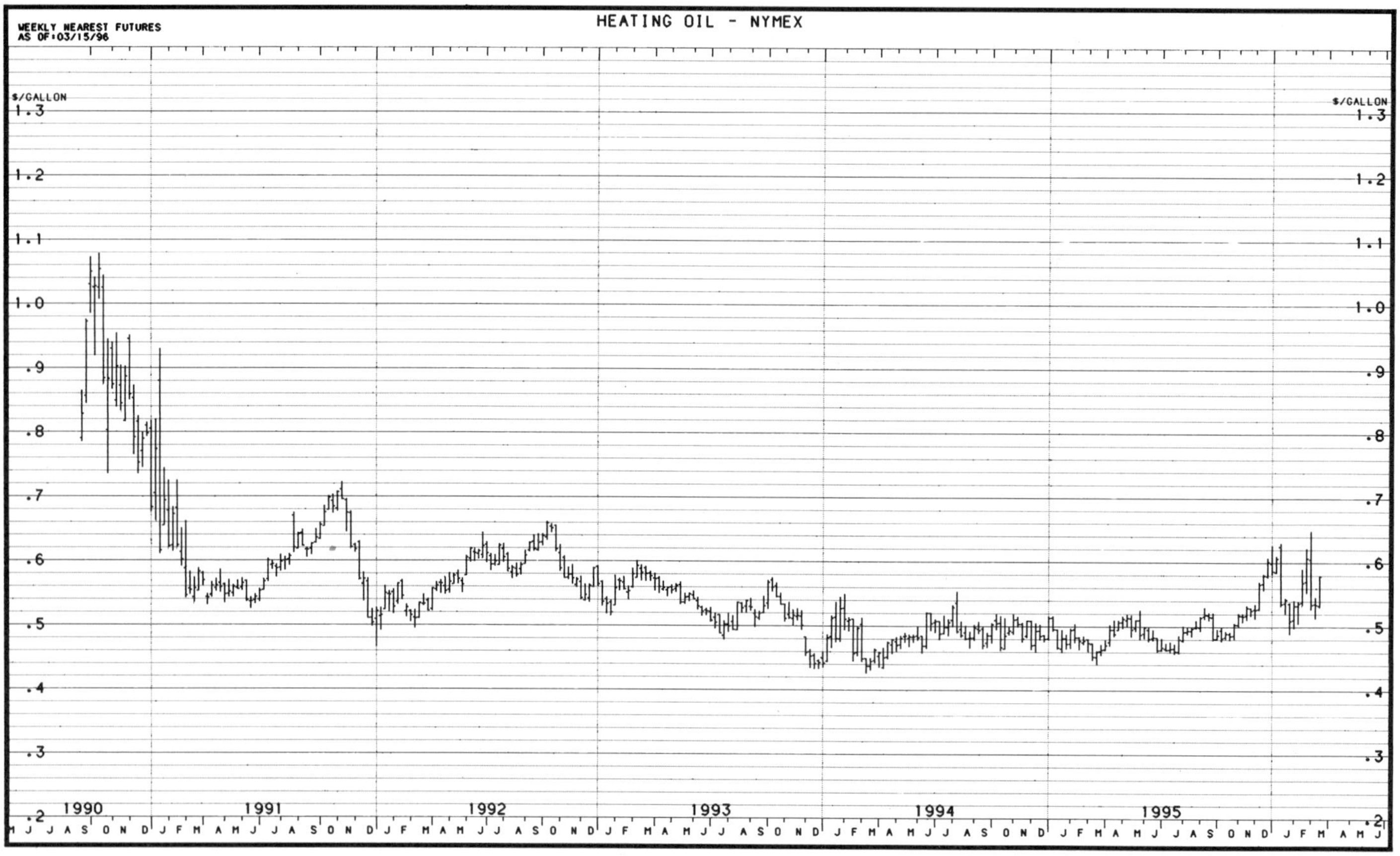

Average Open Interest of Heating Oil Futures (No. 2) in New York In Contracts

Year	Jan.	Feb.	Mar.	Apr.	May	June	July	Aug.	Sept.	Oct.	Nov.	Dec.
1984	31,359	24,817	17,751	17,421	17,818	17,491	18,646	20,928	23,968	28,550	26,520	25,306
1985	23,197	16,243	16,881	17,196	16,970	20,150	21,419	25,061	29,626	31,726	35,062	33,275
1986	28,866	29,476	32,783	33,841	37,897	50,299	63,935	65,337	70,994	79,030	75,477	70,723
1987	66,228	60,479	47,798	45,494	40,865	44,530	52,480	54,696	65,781	70,167	74,093	74,945
1988	59,605	51,640	49,705	44,674	49,155	58,960	77,018	77,777	87,942	93,762	85,350	80,093
1989	75,038	63,791	60,455	57,533	49,174	49,527	59,799	69,578	88,642	97,064	99,293	105,240
1990	83,020	68,065	67,389	76,954	85,349	112,506	116,108	103,280	97,589	93,631	92,399	81,864
1991	74,216	81,742	81,103	82,419	89,482	102,887	115,896	125,463	135,804	144,026	128,330	117,182
1992	108,337	96,543	91,508	90,816	87,459	101,185	98,623	109,787	119,595	129,951	140,952	135,380
1993	130,536	125,603	130,438	107,363	102,708	113,898	131,816	142,054	166,253	172,940	175,781	199,299
1994	196,390	185,607	186,539	164,417	140,658	129,005	124,764	149,571	172,071	165,475	152,570	148,298
1995	128,664	112,508	118,700	121,974	115,501	122,163	136,722	140,214	149,934	152,244	139,232	138,596

Source: New York Mercantile Exchange

Volume of Trading of Heating Oil Futures[1] In New York In Contracts

Year	Jan.	Feb.	Mar.	Apr.	May	June	July	Aug.	Sept.	Oct.	Nov.	Dec.	Total
1984	254,788	209,802	144,326	144,041	161,689	144,182	120,668	153,913	137,011	281,183	182,005	163,938	2,091,546
1985	286,264	149,403	162,503	137,064	122,699	133,339	148,117	157,552	202,785	246,558	219,126	242,323	2,207,733
1986	274,057	221,156	214,501	207,748	223,943	247,552	309,662	282,636	285,246	387,054	271,497	349,992	3,275,044
1987	399,813	328,327	348,204	282,109	238,048	273,708	329,078	343,355	347,152	437,157	422,982	543,462	4,293,395
1988	506,182	377,379	403,181	267,233	286,365	380,550	431,231	363,276	441,939	578,648	475,675	423,356	4,935,015
1989	534,041	422,660	430,447	372,640	334,973	445,822	372,388	402,420	475,402	554,733	574,693	820,748	5,740,967
1990	754,945	415,420	462,479	451,708	516,989	463,263	518,993	723,152	505,810	612,310	521,969	429,833	6,376,871
1991	603,683	523,870	392,484	387,232	399,919	425,082	507,755	595,913	538,240	689,143	781,291	835,559	6,680,165
1992	815,199	574,007	550,113	592,056	586,707	601,067	645,020	663,743	625,675	709,532	808,201	807,142	8,005,462
1993	829,340	660,546	747,299	537,543	481,957	543,356	632,168	721,852	833,800	761,764	886,565	988,871	8,625,061
1994	1,085,683	875,714	766,788	631,664	629,295	723,677	612,316	783,181	706,822	721,375	652,257	798,063	8,986,835
1995	779,827	608,691	715,968	622,810	729,753	618,812	612,683	563,605	714,239	650,809	659,518	990,068	8,266,783

[1] No. 2 heating oil. *Source: New York Mercantile Exchange*

Stocks of Distillate Fuel in the U.S., First of the Month In Millions of Barrels

Year	Jan.	Feb.	Mar.	Apr.	May	June	July	Aug.	Sept.	Oct.	Nov.	Dec.	Residual Fuel ---- Oil Stocks ---- Jan. 1	July 1
1985	161.1	142.4	121.4	99.3	96.8	104.4	109.7	115.7	113.8	117.4	123.4	139.7	53.0	39.6
1986	143.7	136.5	112.4	98.8	95.9	98.9	107.9	118.9	137.7	152.4	151.6	158.3	50.4	42.8
1987	155.1	141.3	123.7	109.3	100.3	101.3	104.4	114.6	124.7	126.8	121.0	128.0	47.4	41.4
1988	134.5	128.1	110.3	89.8	95.0	104.9	110.4	120.0	125.7	131.5	128.2	128.8	47.4	42.2
1989	123.5	120.3	107.5	96.6	98.4	99.3	99.6	115.0	116.3	123.2	121.7	119.8	44.6	44.1
1990	105.7	118.0	112.2	99.7	99.5	102.8	109.4	125.2	136.0	136.3	132.4	132.2	43.8	46.8
1991	112.1	111.7	101.6	98.2	102.9	106.9	113.7	124.7	131.4	140.1	138.3	144.5	47.6	43.7
1992	143.5	126.7	108.8	97.7	92.1	96.4	104.5	114.6	122.8	127.8	136.8	146.3	49.9	40.9
1993	140.6	130.7	110.4	97.3	99.5	102.8	110.0	120.7	128.2	131.3	145.3	149.2	42.6	45.7
1994	140.9	117.5	102.9	99.4	102.6	112.4	119.5	134.2	138.6	144.7	146.0	147.3	44.2	39.4
1995[1]	145.2	140.4	121.9	115.5	114.6	118.8	114.8	125.1	130.9	131.7			41.9	36.1

[1] Preliminary. *Source: Energy Information Administration, U.S. Department of Energy*

U.S. Production of Distillate Fuel Oil Thousand Barrels Per Day

Year	Jan.	Feb.	Mar.	Apr.	May	June	July	Aug.	Sept.	Oct.	Nov.	Dec.	Average
1985	2,631	2,504	2,267	2,490	2,686	2,647	2,646	2,592	2,594	2,902	3,102	3,176	2,687
1986	2,899	2,563	2,643	2,788	2,858	2,729	2,710	2,922	2,865	2,717	2,917	2,943	2,798
1987	2,759	2,556	2,421	2,553	2,563	2,689	2,700	2,706	2,748	2,780	3,035	3,242	2,731
1988	3,010	2,667	2,706	2,867	2,936	2,893	2,784	2,848	2,778	2,827	2,909	3,068	2,859
1989	2,974	2,797	2,713	2,789	2,750	2,809	2,848	2,907	2,952	2,906	3,063	3,266	2,899
1990	3,130	2,753	2,657	2,803	2,874	2,996	3,008	3,131	2,968	2,928	2,915	2,917	2,925
1991	2,845	2,870	2,865	2,819	2,929	2,941	2,998	2,961	3,055	3,040	3,103	3,107	2,962
1992	2,818	2,661	2,749	2,930	2,933	2,995	3,067	2,865	2,983	3,251	3,240	3,179	2,974
1993	2,914	2,815	2,919	3,047	2,994	3,093	3,186	3,100	3,205	3,432	3,474	3,382	3,132
1994	3,114	3,018	3,096	3,249	3,317	3,285	3,191	3,187	3,285	3,203	3,270	3,232	3,205
1995[1]	3,055	2,954	3,156	3,125	3,111	3,114	3,041	3,130	3,288	3,176	3,357		3,138

[1] Preliminary. *Source: Energy Information Administration, U.S. Department of Energy*

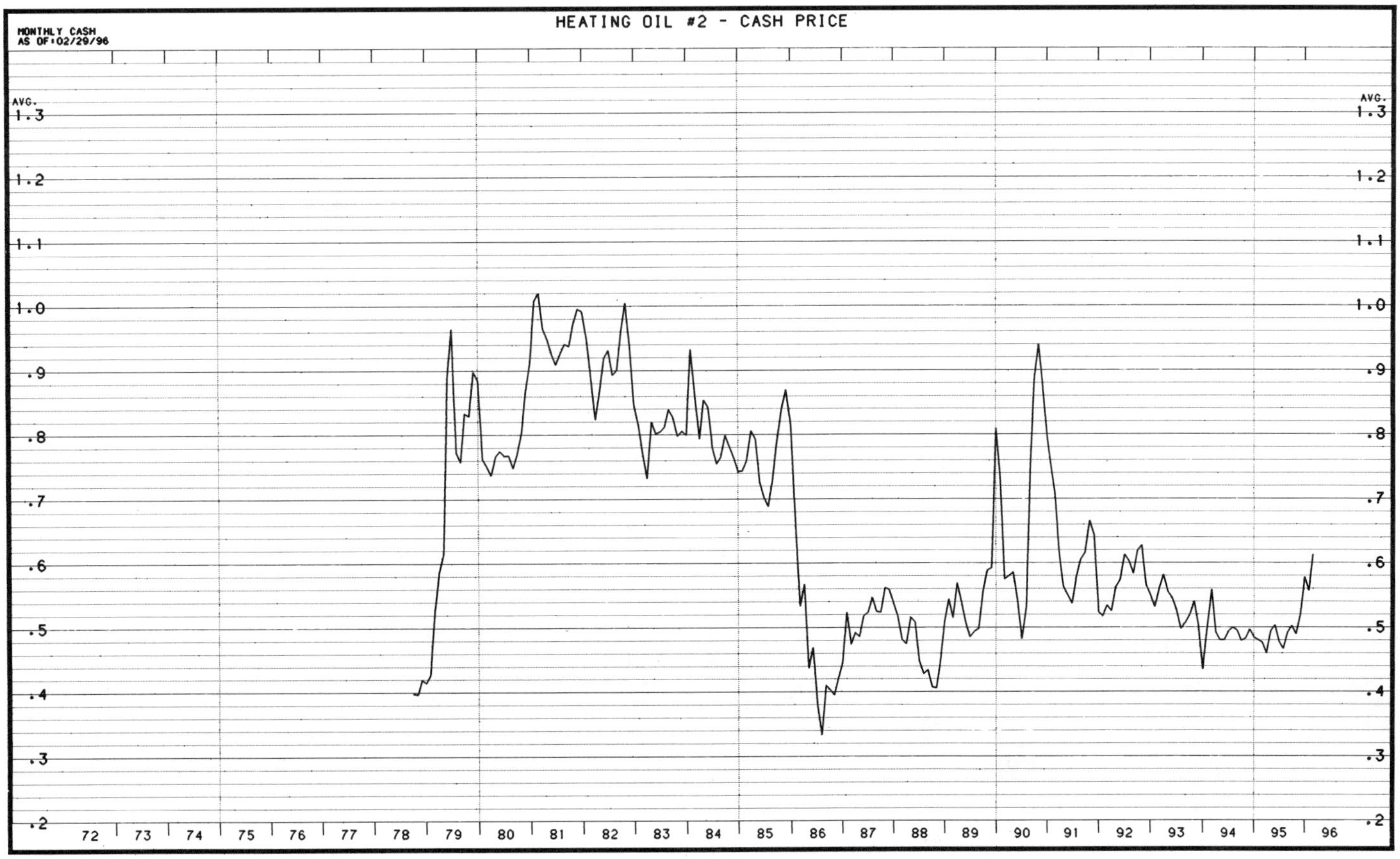

HEATING OIL

U.S. Imports of Distillate Fuel Oil Thousand Barrels Per Day

Year	Jan.	Feb.	Mar.	Apr.	May	June	July	Aug.	Sept.	Oct.	Nov.	Dec.	Average
1985	272	143	156	253	197	152	95	81	222	262	280	287	200
1986	325	169	217	147	149	169	313	370	262	243	254	339	247
1987	222	253	297	192	203	265	381	222	222	237	187	378	255
1988	424	383	247	210	253	222	222	279	307	336	327	409	302
1989	346	331	439	301	290	233	334	254	249	261	307	324	306
1990	505	357	281	308	209	257	236	293	226	190	238	239	278
1991	192	139	206	258	186	209	155	168	237	207	249	252	205
1992	232	217	238	202	179	157	172	229	237	263	236	229	216
1993	182	224	235	209	153	168	130	159	137	242	214	160	184
1994	161	276	318	226	202	182	164	211	193	159	166	187	203
1995[1]	270	287	188	125	108	176	157	171	142	162	212		181

[1] Preliminary. *Source: Energy Information Administration, U.S. Department of Energy*

U.S. Disposition of Distillate Fuel Oil, Total Product Supplied Thousand Barrels Per Day

Year	Jan.	Feb.	Mar.	Apr.	May	June	July	Aug.	Sept.	Oct.	Nov.	Dec.	Average
1985	2,465	3,330	3,093	2,398	2,607	2,594	2,436	2,636	2,575	2,901	2,747	3,254	2,868
1986	3,330	3,416	3,168	2,904	2,762	2,544	2,592	2,621	2,540	2,912	2,877	3,329	2,914
1987	3,310	3,345	3,116	2,991	2,684	2,790	2,713	2,553	2,838	3,151	2,932	3,318	2,976
1988	3,558	3,557	3,539	2,864	2,765	2,854	2,640	2,873	2,821	3,218	3,183	3,560	3,122
1989	3,303	3,427	3,428	2,975	2,954	3,002	2,596	2,966	2,889	3,127	3,311	3,914	3,157
1990	3,185	3,260	3,277	3,043	2,900	2,923	2,726	3,218	2,864	2,960	3,094	2,816	3,021
1991	3,367	2,976	2,984	2,839	2,765	2,775	2,648	2,770	2,865	3,047	2,921	3,087	2,921
1992	3,231	3,219	3,207	3,039	2,753	2,679	2,710	2,705	2,908	3,056	2,929	3,316	2,979
1993	3,128	3,465	3,420	2,943	2,685	2,863	2,674	2,820	2,973	2,983	3,218	3,357	3,041
1994	3,698	3,581	3,307	3,116	2,912	3,062	2,663	3,063	3,133	3,066	3,180	3,203	3,162
1995[1]	3,335	3,689	3,336	3,108	2,883	3,284	2,718	3,031	3,286	3,102	3,304		3,184

[1] Preliminary. *Source: Energy Information Administration, U.S. Department of Energy*

U.S. Production of Residual Fuel Oil Thousand Barrels Per Day

Year	Jan.	Feb.	Mar.	Apr.	May	June	July	Aug.	Sept.	Oct.	Nov.	Dec.	Average
1985	1,004	1,040	963	912	793	702	732	742	808	912	932	1,055	882
1986	940	856	813	933	913	818	850	896	854	827	975	987	889
1987	920	825	863	831	813	864	901	882	904	887	928	1,001	885
1988	1,002	994	948	960	862	880	906	866	852	852	916	1,069	926
1989	949	930	937	904	934	953	862	903	856	1,001	1,075	1,140	954
1990	1,163	1,060	976	882	884	926	987	944	909	799	846	1,021	950
1991	1,001	1,050	995	916	929	933	871	925	838	814	896	1,051	934
1992	965	957	990	900	964	894	838	815	810	818	895	862	892
1993	820	840	818	896	908	795	762	752	822	841	899	869	835
1994	809	852	859	846	860	779	807	838	800	755	835	871	826
1995[1]	909	776	778	789	749	749	798	799	810	722	701		780

[1] Preliminary. *Source: Energy Information Adminstration, U.S. Department of Energy*

United States Residual Fuel Oil Supply and Disposition

	Supply		Disposition				
Year	Total Production	Imports	Stock Change	Exports	Product Supplied	Ending Stocks	Average Sales to End Users[3]
	Thousand Barrels per Day					Mil. Barrels	¢ per Gallon
1985	852	699	-55	185	1,421	49	61.0
1986	891	681	12	190	1,369	53	34.3
1987	882	510	-7	197	1,202	50	42.3
1988	889	669	-8	147	1,418	47	33.4
1989	885	565	[2]	186	1,264	47	38.5
1990	950	504	13	211	1,229	49	44.4
1991	934	453	4	226	1,158	50	34.0
1992	892	375	-20	193	1,094	43	33.6
1993	835	373	4	123	1,080	44	33.7
1994	826	314	-6	125	1,021	42	35.2
1995[1]	780	177	-17	145	829	37	39.3

[1] Preliminary. [2] Less than +500 barrels per day and greater than -500 barrels per day. [3] Refiner price excluding taxes.
Source: Energy Information Administration, U.S. Department of Energy

Hides and Leather

World bovine production of hides and skins fell by two percent in 1994 to 3.82 million tonnes. The largest decline occurred in Russia where hide production fell 13 percent to 400,000 tonnes. South American production fell three percent and Eastern European output was down eight percent. In North America, production rose three percent. For 1995, hide production was forecast to decline less than one percent as continued declines in Russia were expected to be offset by increased output in North and South America.

Utilization of hides declined marginally in 1994. Utilization in the European Union (EU) rose 14 percent but that was more than offset by a decline in Russia of 40 percent. In Asia there has been a shifting in tanning facilities. Utilization in Korea and Japan continued to decline slowly while there was impressive growth in China and Taiwan. For 1995, hide utilization was expected to decline further with reductions in Russia.

World trade in hides increased by five percent in 1994 on larger exports by the U.S., Russia and Brazil. U.S. exports of hides and skins rebounded strongly after three years of decline. On a value basis, U.S. exports rose by 18 percent. EU exports were lower as domestic tanners and processors bid up for material. The combination of strong demand for hides by EU leather manufacturers and declining EU hide production led to record EU imports in 1994 including an increase of 87 percent in imports of U.S. hides. World trade in 1995 is projected to increase y as demand remains strong.

U.S. hides and skins production continued to trend higher in 1994 to 1.109 million tonnes, the highest output since 1987. 1995 production was forecast to increase two percent.

U.S. hides and skins utilization has been steadily recovering from its recent 1990 low. This is attributable in part to major restructurings in U.S. tanneries. Between 1982 and 1993, the number of U.S. tanneries has declined from 384 to 110. Many tanneries have been unable to continue to operate under more stringent environmental regulations. Those that did invest in modernization have managed to increase efficiency while at the same time reducing labor costs. The U.S, tanning industry has been operating at close to peak capacity for two years. Utilization for 1993 was estimated at 554,000 tonnes while for 1994 it is put at 560,000 tonnes. According to the USDA, for 1995 utilization is estimated at 553,000 tonnes. The growth in the U.S. tanning industry is attributable to large supplies of domestic hides and skins as well as strong export demand for luxury leather products in Asia, such as auto and furniture upholstery leather. In 1994, for example, U.S. leather exports were a record $815 million, with more than 17 percent accounted for by automobile leather upholstery exports.

U.S. exports of hides and skins were also strong in 1994. After three straight years of decline, U.S. hide exports reached 305,000 tonnes. On a value basis, exports increased 18 percent to $1,265 million. For 1995, the USDA estimates that U.S. hide exports will increase 630,000 tonnes. For 1994, exports to Asia were up 17 percent while the EU imported 87 per cent more U.S. hides, the most since 1989.

World Production of Bovine Hides and Skins In Thousands of Metric Tons

Year	Agrentina	Australia	Brazil	Canada	Colombia	France	Germany	Italy	Mexico	New Zealand	Russia[3]	South Africa	Turkey	United Kingdom	United States
1986	332	131	324	92	92	186	209	95	120	36	1,022	59	62	104	1,115
1987	314	144	350	85	86	193	203	91	122	54	1,060	59	62	101	1,128
1988	303	139	390	82	93	185	191	89	176	41	1,089	51	63	90	1,022
1989	304	137	429	84	97	170	228	88	222	35	1,090	55	65	91	1,086
1990	307	149	447	78	105	175	247	92	181	40	503	55	67	92	1,057
1991	308	153	448	75	104	182	251	95	155	44	502	54	64	93	1,061
1992	298	162	442	77	88	180	205	98	160	44	466	57	66	88	1,073
1993	303	154	455	73	79	160	175	95	161	46	460	54	65	77	1,078
1994[1]	305	152	448	74	77	151	160	93	166	46	350	51	64	81	1,106
1995[1]	302	140	465	76	78	154	160	91	172	50	320	48	61	83	1,153
1996[2]	308	161	470	83	79	153	157	90	162	50	300	49	61	85	1,180

[1] Preliminary. [2] Forecast. [3] Formerly part of the U.S.S.R.; data not reported separately until 1990. *Source: Foreign Agricultural Service, U.S. Department of Agriculture*

Salient Statistics of Hides & Leather in the United States

	New Supply of Cattle Hides				Wholesale					Wholesale Leather			
	Domestic Slaughter				Prices - ¢ Lb.		Production			Indexes		Footwear	
										Upper			
Year	Federally Inspected	Uninspected[4]	Total Production	Net Exports	Heavy Native Cows[2]	Heavy Native[3] Steers	All U.S. Tanning	Cattle-Hide	Value of Leather Exports	Men	Women	Production[5]	Export
	Thousands of Equivalent Hides						In 1,000 Equiv. Hides		$1,000	1982 = 100		Mil. Pairs	
1985	34,765	1,528	36,293	24,398	57.55	54.0	15,280	12,616	283,704	104.2	103.6	265,098	11,320
1986	35,913	1,375	37,288	26,522	68.06	63.7	14,510	12,598	313,408	107.2	104.3	241,273	12,452
1987	34,468	1,179	35,647	24,007	83.43	79.9	14,750	12,754	395,536	111.4	107.2	225,888	14,575
1988	34,048	1,031	35,079	24,527	86.50	87.3	13,300	11,475	506,483	121.3	112.5	234,852	18,394
1989	33,010	907	33,917	22,500	83.16	89.4	12,932	11,242	624,925	127.5	116.2	221,790	14,358
1990	32,391	851	33,242	20,920	92.58	92.0	14,820	13,018	750,836	135.8	120.9	184,568	15,174
1991	31,887	803	32,690	18,636	76.92	78.9	14,800	13,021	680,348	141.0	124.0	167,386	18,109
1992	32,094	780	32,874	17,810	81.71	75.9	15,900	14,474	705,038	145.0	126.4	168,451	21,401
1993[1]	32,593	731	33,324	17,117	82.16	78.9	18,057	16,931	764,120	145.3	129.3	171,733	20,700
1994[1]	33,483	713	34,196	16,259		87.3	18,842	18,117	811,951			156,712	22,505

[1] Preliminary. [2] Central U.S., heifers. [3] FOB, Chicago. [4] Includes farm slaughter; diseased and condemned animals and hides taken off fallen animals. [5] Other than rubber. *Sources: Leather Industries of America; U.S. Department of Commerce*

HIDES AND LEATHER

U.S. Production of All Footwear (Shoes, Sandals, Slippers, Athletic, Etc.) In Millions of Pairs

Year	Jan.	Feb.	Mar.	Apr.	May	June	July	Aug.	Sept.	Oct.	Nov.	Dec.	Total
1984	27.3	29.1	30.2	27.7	28.6	24.6	20.7	26.0	21.9	25.2	22.3	19.6	303.2
1985	22.5	21.0	22.2	22.2	24.9	21.1	19.7	24.5	22.4	24.8	21.1	18.7	265.1
1986	22.5	21.6	21.3	21.2	20.8	18.4	18.4	20.8	19.7	21.4	18.4	16.6	240.9
1987	18.2	19.2	20.7	20.0	19.7	20.7	16.1	20.6	20.9	20.6	18.2	15.2	230.0
1988	16.7	20.8	21.6	19.3	20.2	19.7	14.0	21.4	21.3	21.2	21.3	17.6	234.8
1989	18.1	18.5	19.6	16.6	18.7	17.5	13.7	19.7	17.4	19.0	17.5	14.3	221.9
1990	17.8	17.2	18.5	16.7	18.9	16.7	14.3	18.8	16.5	18.2	15.4	12.6	184.6
1991	----------	48.1	----------	----------	37.8	----------	----------	41.8	----------	----------	41.2	----------	169.0
1992	----------	41.1	----------	----------	40.8	----------	----------	43.6	----------	----------	39.3	----------	164.8
1993	----------	43.3	----------	----------	44.6	----------	----------	42.8	----------	----------	41.0	----------	171.7
1994	----------	42.2	----------	----------	40.5	----------	----------	39.8	----------	----------	39.2	----------	161.8
1995[1]	----------	42.9	----------	----------	38.5	----------	----------	37.4	----------				

[1] Preliminary. *Source: U.S. Department of Commerce*

Average Factory Price[2] of Footwear in the United States In Dollars Per Pair

Year	Jan.	Feb.	Mar.	Apr.	May	June	July	Aug.	Sept.	Oct.	Nov.	Dec.	Average
1984	14.95	14.19	14.00	14.99	15.20	14.43	14.88	14.59	15.11	14.56	15.00	15.62	14.79
1985	15.24	14.97	14.10	14.87	14.86	15.35	14.24	14.55	14.12	13.71	13.56	15.13	14.56
1986	14.60	13.86	13.82	14.22	15.00	14.98	15.53	14.38	14.64	14.38	14.40	16.50	14.69
1987	15.09	14.58	14.05	15.15	15.89	15.63	16.47	15.60	15.63	15.23	15.89	17.96	15.60
1988	16.57	14.80	13.88	15.97	13.77	14.46	17.27	14.92	15.32	15.18	14.98	16.73	15.32
1989	15.94	15.35	15.00	16.90	15.77	16.45	16.36	17.17	17.38	17.20	17.73	18.68	16.98
1990	----------	18.04	----------	----------	18.65	----------	----------	19.91	----------	----------	20.72	----------	19.37
1991	----------	22.14	----------	----------	20.40	----------	----------	19.74	----------	----------	18.52	----------	20.14
1992	----------	20.19	----------	----------	22.21	----------	----------	21.15	----------	----------	20.46	----------	20.96
1993	----------	21.62	----------	----------	21.67	----------	----------	21.37	----------	----------	21.79	----------	21.61
1994	----------	26.47	----------	----------	24.25	----------	----------	22.08	----------	----------	23.05	----------	23.86
1995[1]	----------	21.18	----------	----------	23.79	----------	----------	22.94	----------				

[1] Preliminary. [2] Average value of factory shipments per pair. *Source: U.S. Department of Commerce*

U.S. Imports and Exports of All Cattle Hides In Thousands of Hides

	----- Imports -----		------ U.S. Exports -- By Country of Destination ------													
Year	Total	From Canada	Total	Canada	France	Germany	Italy	Japan	Rep. of Korea	Mexico	Netherlands	Portugal	Romania	Spain	Taiwan	Thailand
1984	711	669	25,889	1,145	316	256	1,243	7,394	5,447	1,888	257	202	1,088	540	2,765	2
1985	1,044	883	25,428	796	220	125	1,169	6,835	6,453	2,309	82	180	1,168	340	2,831	17
1986	761	594	26,963	714	275	85	1,553	6,626	9,324	1,042	156	247	688	255	3,579	20
1987	490	338	24,235	924	158	56	394	5,998	10,077	1,437	85	82	308	200	3,184	37
1988	642	481	24,687	759	93	97	319	7,140	9,986	1,865	100	44	624	142	2,493	35
1989	901	1,043	23,401	614	17	68	343	6,268	10,322	1,284	132	46	1,154	64	1,886	70
1990	661	678	21,582	674	28	78	136	6,802	9,839	1,438	99	29	253	175	1,476	91
1991	1,549	1,088	20,185	561	4	52	138	4,662	9,300	2,702	65	7	-----	39	2,058	123
1992	1,536	1,457	19,347	684	2	-----	107	4,647	8,589	2,729	56	100	4	30	1,823	160
1993	1,660	1,597	18,777	965	8	1	354	4,167	7,919	2,217	9	79	1	60	1,950	386
1994	1,731		17,990	995	15	2	309	3,133	7,472	1,553	8	168	72	141	2,491	332

[1] Preliminary. *Source: Leather Industries of America*

Foreign Trade of Bovine Hides and Skins by Selected Countries In Metric Tons

	------ Imports ------								------ Exports ------							
Year	Hong Kong	Italy	Japan	Mexico	Rep. of Korea	Spain	Taiwan	United States	Australia	Canada	Germany	Hong Kong	Netherlands	New Zealand	Russia	United States
1990	54	383	236	52	373	96	73	24	134	88	129	53	105	23	16	693
1991	67	156	206	70	392	39	100	67	149	90	63	69	70	33	22	637
1992	80	131	188	71	385	26	91	65	144	74	38	75	66	31	28	610
1993	81	141	188	71	372	35	94	57	142	87	40	76	35	21	150	581
1994	95	243	139	60	356	29	112	56	96	79	24	93	37	22	215	602
1995[1]	96	255	125	45	350	30	114	55	100	81	20	94	40	22	200	626
1996[2]	97	260	125	45	350	30	115	55	121	88	20	96	40	23	190	640

[1] Preliminary. [2] Forecast. *Source: Foreign Agricultural Service, U.S. Department of Agriculture*

Utilization of Bovine Hides and Skins by Selected Countries In Metric Tons

Year	Argentina	Brazil	Colombia	Germany	Italy	Japan	Mexico	Poland	Portugal	Rep. of Korea	Russia	Spain	Taiwan	Turkey	United States
1990	307	395	100	176	425	261	233	60	67	380	487	129	74	74	388
1991	308	396	98	143	435	253	225	70	67	400	480	119	101	78	491
1992	298	382	97	129	435	229	231	64	65	400	438	98	91	90	528
1993	302	400	94	100	435	226	232	81	62	385	315	98	94	95	554
1994	304	380	95	85	550	200	226	75	80	374	140	94	112	85	560
1995[1]	301	388	98	120	570	165	217	73	70	361	125	100	114	90	582
1996[2]	307	390	101	117	570	165	207	69	75	354	115	101	115	90	595

[1] Preliminary. [2] Forecast. *Source: Foreign Agricultural Service, U.S. Department of Agriculture*

Wholesale Price of Hides (Packer Native Steer) F.O.B. Chicago In Cents Per Pound

Year	Jan.	Feb.	Mar.	Apr.	May	June	July	Aug.	Sept.	Oct.	Nov.	Dec.	Average
1982	42.3	40.5	41.4	44.5	46.0	42.8	43.3	44.5	44.5	44.5	42.7	38.8	43.0
1983	37.1	37.7	40.4	46.0	50.8	51.8	59.2	57.3	53.3	53.8	56.7	54.8	49.9
1984	54.8	56.0	62.0	61.7	64.5	64.7	66.5	69.2	68.9	61.7	52.5	47.9	60.9
1985	46.0	41.7	45.5	54.7	57.0	53.1	54.0	55.7	57.1	57.6	63.5	60.8	53.9
1986	57.7	58.4	57.7	63.1	68.6	68.7	68.3	69.9	64.5	65.9	65.2	61.8	64.2
1987	61.8	64.2	69.7	82.4	83.5	81.7	82.5	83.8	89.0	89.9	85.4	83.7	79.8
1988	82.9	86.3	97.4	100.0	99.2	87.6	84.2	93.7	87.3	80.5	77.1	76.7	87.7
1989	84.0	87.4	94.6	87.5	85.2	85.0	90.3	91.7	95.9	94.7	92.9	90.9	90.0
1990	92.7	92.8	95.5	100.0	99.6	97.9	96.7	91.7	87.5	84.6	83.0	84.4	92.2
1991	81.6	76.4	75.7	86.3	88.8	86.7	84.1	77.2	74.1	75.4	75.4	71.3	79.4
1992	70.6	67.8	69.9	76.0	80.0	76.8	76.5	72.8	77.6	81.2	80.1	81.0	75.9
1993	79.8	81.8	81.5	81.4	80.4	76.9	76.6	79.3	80.5	81.8	80.8	79.8	80.1
1994	75.1	75.1	79.0	84.8	87.3	88.8	90.4	89.8	93.9	93.7	93.2	91.1	86.9
1995	90.1	91.4	98.0	102.3	99.6	92.5	85.7	82.5	82.5	82.2	78.0	73.0	88.1

Source: Knight-Ridder Financial

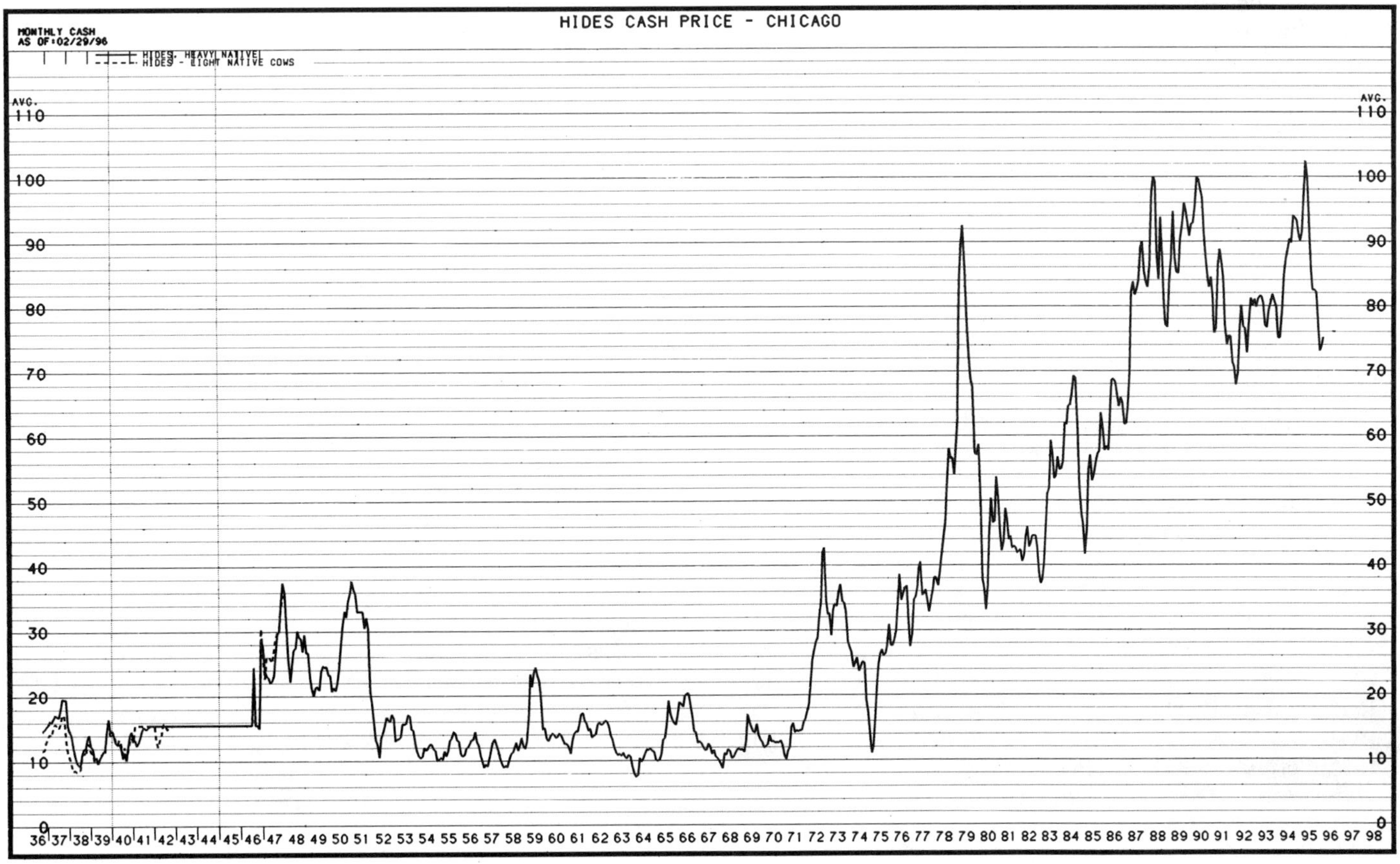

Hogs

The share of U.S. hog marketings from contract hog operations has risen dramatically in recent years as evidence by the fact that farms with hog sales have fallen more than 50 percent since the late 1970s, while the number of hogs marketed has increased nearly 25 percent, reflecting increased concentration of production on fewer and larger farms. In a contractual agreement, the contractor provides the hogs, feed, medication and supplies, while the contractee provides the housing, utilities and labor. Most hog production still occurs in Corn Belt states. Iowa is the leading producing state, where ample feed supplies provide a low-cost feed source. However, southern states, led by North Carolina, have seen a dramatic growth in contractual operations in recent years. Still, over 70 percent of U.S. producers continue to raise hogs in farrow-to-finish operations, but areas of the greatest structural change now account for more than 20 percent of marketings. Despite the contraction, the U.S. hog population has steadily pushed to new highs. The U.S., with about 60 million head, is the world's second largest hog producer; China, with about 425 million head, is first.

On September 1, 1995 the U.S. total market hog inventory of 51.9 million head compared with the year earlier total of 54.9 million; in the sixteen major producing states the totals were 47.2 million and 49.9 million, respectively. Despite the decline, the farrowing intentions into the first quarter of 1996 were unchanged indicating that producers were still on a course of gradual expansion. If realized, the ratio of sows farrowing to breeding herd would climb to 42.4 percent versus the previous five year average of 41.1 percent. First half 1996 hog slaughter is expected to be large relative to any period prior to 1994 but many producers will barely cover cash operating expenses, due to higher feed costs, unless cash hog prices remain in the mid $40's or higher per cwt.

The USDA expects pork supplies to stay at near record levels into the late 1990s. Commercial 1995 hog slaughter was estimated at a record 96.7 million head year versus 95.7 million in 1994. Pork production totaled 17.9 billion pounds versus 17.7 billion in 1994. Estimates for 1996 place slaughter at 99.6 million head and pork production at 18.3 billion pounds, both record highs. Dress weight averaged about 185 pounds in 1995, the same as in 1994.

Per capita pork consumption continues to grow on a pace to reach 60 pounds by the late 1990s, partly due to the industry's strong marketing approach that stresses pork as a white meat rather than red.

The U.S. is a net importer of pork products and hogs. Canada is the largest supplier. U.S. pork exports have gone largely to Japan and Mexico. However, sales to Russia surged in 1995 but were generally limited to lower value products and the pace appeared sustainable only at lower prices. Total U.S. exports in 1995 were estimated at 728 million pounds, up 37 percent from 1994. Canada is the sole exporter of live hogs to the U.S. and Mexico is the largest importer of U.S. hogs. Feeder pigs account for almost half of all hogs imported from Canada.

Wholesale hog prices during the first quarter of 1995 trailed 1994, but strengthened in the second half. The USDA initially forecast the 1995 average price at $38.52 per cwt, basis Sioux City, versus a 1994 average of $39.75. However, the final average is likely to top $40/cwt.

Futures Markets

Live hog futures and options are traded on the Chicago Mercantile Exchange (CME) and the Mid American Commodity Exchange (MidAm). Live hog futures are traded on the Budapest Commodity Exchange.

World Hog Numbers in Specified Countries as of January 1 In Thousands of Head

Year	Brazil	Canada	China	Denmark	France	Germany	Italy	Japan	Meixco	Philippine	Poland	Russia	Spain	Ukraine	United Kingdom	United States
1991	32,550	10,468	362,408	9,282	12,013	30,818	8,837	11,355	8,593	8,007	19,739	38,500	16,001	19,427	7,380	54,477
1992	33,050	10,498	369,646	9,767	12,067	26,063	8,549	10,966	9,928	8,022	20,725	35,400	17,209	17,839	7,519	57,469
1993	31,050	10,577	384,211	10,345	13,015	26,514	8,307	10,783	11,298	7,954	21,059	31,500	18,260	16,175	7,705	58,202
1994[1]	31,200	10,851	393,000	10,870	14,291	26,075	8,348	10,622	12,083	8,227	17,422	28,600	18,234	15,298	7,869	57,904
1995[2]	32,100	11,181	414,620	10,864	14,593	24,698	8,000	10,250	12,513	8,941	19,138	25,000	18,400	13,946	7,879	59,992
1996[3]	32,400	11,100	426,000	11,190	14,773	24,134	7,900	10,100	11,053	8,950	20,000	22,100	18,000	12,300	7,870	59,063

[1] Preliminary. [2] Estimate. [3] Forecast. *Source: Foreign Agricultural Service, U.S. Department of Agricultures*

Salient Statistics of Pigs and Hogs in the U.S.

	Pig Crop						Value of Hogs on Farms, Dec. 1					Hogs Slaughtered in Thousand Heads				
	Spring[3]			Fall[4]								Commercial				
Year	Sows Farrowed - 1,000s of Head -	Pig Crop - 1,000s of Head -	Pigs Per Liter	Sows Farrowed - 1,000s of Head -	Pig Crop - 1,000s of Head -	Pigs Per Liter	$ Per Head	Total Million $	Hog Marketings Thousand Head	Quantity Produced (Live Wt.) Mil. Lbs.	Value of Production Mil. $	Federally Inspected	Other	Total	Farm	Total
1988	6,041	47,238	7.82	6,036	46,000	7.62	66.30	3,678	90,334	21,670	9,145	85,517	2,278	87,795	341	88,136
1989	5,745	45,321	7.89	5,775	44,836	7.76	79.10	4,256	92,550	21,942	9,294	86,328	2,364	88,692	315	89,007
1990	6,001	47,507	7.92	5,717	44,939	7.86	85.40	4,655	89,373	21,347	11,376	82,901	2,235	85,136	296	85,431
1991	6,275	50,577	8.06	6,074	47,926	7.89	68.90	3,972	92,351	22,809	11,104	85,952	2,217	88,169	266	88,445
1992	6,004	48,806	8.13	6,006	48,626	8.10	71.60	4,281	98,688	24,014	9,879	92,611	2,278	94,888	268	95,157
1993	6,028	49,006	8.13	5,954	48,044	8.07	74.90	4,338	97,911	23,595	10,582	90,933	2,135	93,068	229	93,296
1994[1]	6,274	51,344	8.18	6,102	50,056	8.20	53.20	3,172				93,435	2,261	95,696		
1995[2]	6,146	50,980	8.29	5,992	49,914	8.33						94,203	2,125	96,328		

[1] Preliminary. [2] Estimate. [3] December-May. [4] June-November. *Source: Economic Research Service, U.S. Department of Agriculture*

Hogs and Pigs on U.S. Farms on December 1 In Thousands of Head

Year	Georgia	Illinois	Indiana	Iowa	Kansas	Kentucky	Minne-sota	Missouri	Nebraska	North Carolina	Ohio	Penn-slvanyia	South Dakota	Wis-consin	Total
1988	1,210	5,600	4,300	14,000	1,500	1,090	4,690	2,850	4,150	2,700	2,210	970	1,810	1,275	55,469
1989	1,200	5,700	4,350	13,500	1,450	975	4,450	2,700	4,200	2,570	2,080	975	1,720	1,150	53,821
1990	1,100	5,700	4,400	13,800	1,500	920	4,500	2,800	4,300	2,800	2,000	920	1,770	1,200	54,477
1991	1,130	5,900	4,600	15,000	1,430	950	4,900	2,700	4,500	3,650	1,925	920	1,950	1,180	57,684
1992	1,100	5,900	4,600	16,400	1,440	870	4,700	2,850	4,650	4,500	1,800	950	1,830	1,210	59,815
1993	1,000	5,450	4,300	15,000	1,350	850	4,750	3,000	4,300	5,400	1,630	1,060	1,750	1,170	57,904
1994	1,020	5,350	4,500	14,500	1,310	780	4,850	3,500	4,350	7,000	1,800	1,090	1,740	1,040	59,992
1995[1]	930	4,900	4,150	14,400	1,250	800	5,050	3,600	4,100	8,300	1,850	1,040	1,500	930	60,190

[1] Preliminary. *Source: National Agricultural Statistics Service, U.S. Department of Agriculture*

Quarterly 10 -- U.S. State Hogs & Pigs Report In Thousands of Head

Year[2]	Inventory[3]	Breeding[3]	Market[3]	Farrowings	Pig Crop	Year[2]	Inventory[3]	Breeding[3]	Market[3]	Farrowings	Pig Crop
1990	42,200	5,275	36,925	8,960	70,589	1993	58,202	7,109	51,093	11,982	97,050
I	42,200	5,275	36,925	2,013	15,748	I	58,202	7,109	51,093	3,665	29,739
II	40,190	5,245	34,945	2,458	19,576	II	47,145	5,735	41,410	2,363	19,267
III	42,630	5,405	37,225	2,236	17,684	III	58,395	7,320	51,075	2,972	24,041
IV	44,120	5,300	38,820	2,238	17,459	IV	59,030	7,130	51,900	2,982	24,003
1991	42,900	5,257	37,643	9,516	75,330	1994[1]	57,904	7,130	50,739	12,376	101,400
I	42,900	5,257	37,643	2,129	16,700	I	57,904	7,130	50,739	2,296	18,607
II	41,990	5,450	36,540	2,577	20,555	II	57,350	7,210	50,140	3,389	27,976
III	44,520	5,700	38,820	2,413	19,260	III	60,715	7,565	53,150	3,107	25,547
IV	46,950	5,685	41,265	2,433	18,551	IV	62,320	7,415	54,905	2,995	24,509
1992	45,735	5,610	40,125	10,202	82,497	1995[1]	59,992	7,061	52,932	12,151	80,020
I	45,735	5,610	40,125	2,296	18,532	I	59,992	7,061	52,932	2,886	23,860
II	44,800	5,555	39,245	2,663	21,570	II	58,465	6,998	51,467	3,260	27,120
III	47,255	5,845	41,410	2,501	20,395	III	60,160	7,245	52,915	3,006	25,000
IV	49,175	5,840	43,335	2,398	19,351	IV	61,060	7,068	53,992	2,999	

[1] Preliminary. [2] Quarters are December preceding year-February (I), March-May (II), June-August (III) and September-November (IV). [3] Beginning of period. *Source: National Agricultural Statistics Service, U.S.Department of Agriculture*

Hog-Corn Price Ratio[1] in the U.S.

Year	Jan.	Feb.	Mar.	Apr.	May	June	July	Aug.	Sept.	Oct.	Nov.	Dec.	Average
1985	19.0	18.4	17.6	17.3	19.2	22.7	29.5	35.9	17.3	20.4	19.5	19.8	22.5
1986	31.9	33.9	32.2	33.4	32.8	35.0	37.3	39.9	40.2	37.9	35.9	33.7	34.6
1987	24.3	25.0	22.7	22.3	23.9	19.5	16.2	16.9	36.4	31.5	25.2	23.4	21.4
1988	15.7	15.6	15.1	14.4	16.1	17.9	18.6	20.1	15.7	15.0	14.4	15.7	16.7
1989	20.5	20.8	21.6	21.4	23.4	22.9	23.2	23.3	19.0	21.0	20.1	21.2	22.1
1990	22.0	22.5	21.5	21.0	22.7	23.7	23.9	22.0	22.3	23.3	25.9	21.5	22.4
1991	22.0	22.5	21.5	21.0	22.7	23.7	23.9	22.0	19.9	18.9	16.6	16.6	20.9
1992	15.3	16.3	15.7	16.5	18.1	18.9	19.1	20.5	19.5	20.5	20.8	21.2	18.5
1993	20.3	22.0	22.1	21.0	21.9	23.0	20.6	21.0	21.6	20.6	17.3	15.2	20.6
1994	16.1	17.2	16.2	16.1	16.4	16.3	18.6	19.4	16.2	15.4	14.1	14.5	16.4
1995[2]	16.8	17.5	16.4	15.1	15.4	16.9	17.6	18.5	18.0	15.8	13.9	14.4	16.4

[1] Bushels of corn equal in value to 100 pounds of hog, live weight [2] Preliminary. *Source: Economic Research Service, U.S. Department of Agriculture*

Cold Storage Holdings of Frozen Pork[1] in the U.S., on First of Month In Millions of Pounds

Year	Jan.	Feb.	Mar.	Apr.	May	June	July	Aug.	Sept.	Oct.	Nov.	Dec.
1985	274.3	291.9	286.3	314.1	368.2	410.3	385.0	343.1	294.7	277.0	277.5	265.0
1986	229.4	235.4	239.1	253.5	282.0	275.6	247.7	214.9	184.7	185.9	215.8	206.2
1987	197.1	217.7	228.5	221.8	217.8	218.8	189.2	181.1	175.1	186.2	212.2	251.7
1988	285.4	291.5	308.2	345.8	397.3	388.6	362.8	337.2	287.0	288.0	320.8	361.3
1989	357.9	377.6	393.5	392.8	432.6	428.1	380.1	342.6	277.9	278.0	275.8	279.2
1990	255.8	272.5	303.9	294.6	320.3	320.3	292.6	256.4	224.7	225.8	231.9	221.5
1991	233.6	247.0	281.2	289.0	340.0	333.3	312.3	277.9	282.4	280.5	299.7	308.0
1992	311.1	341.2	364.0	372.2	362.6	344.9	319.0	307.0	266.7	297.3	306.8	316.7
1993	314.5	329.5	344.4	330.4	378.5	371.6	351.3	342.5	308.9	311.2	324.8	313.0
1994	299.2	348.8	356.9	393.1	429.7	437.6	410.8	393.7	364.0	352.7	385.4	383.2
1995[2]	365.3	389.6	395.1	416.8	422.3	434.9	431.1	408.1	536.0	332.6	321.7	347.1

[1] Excludes lard. [2] Preliminary. *Source: Economic Research Service, U.S. Department of Agriculture*

HOGS

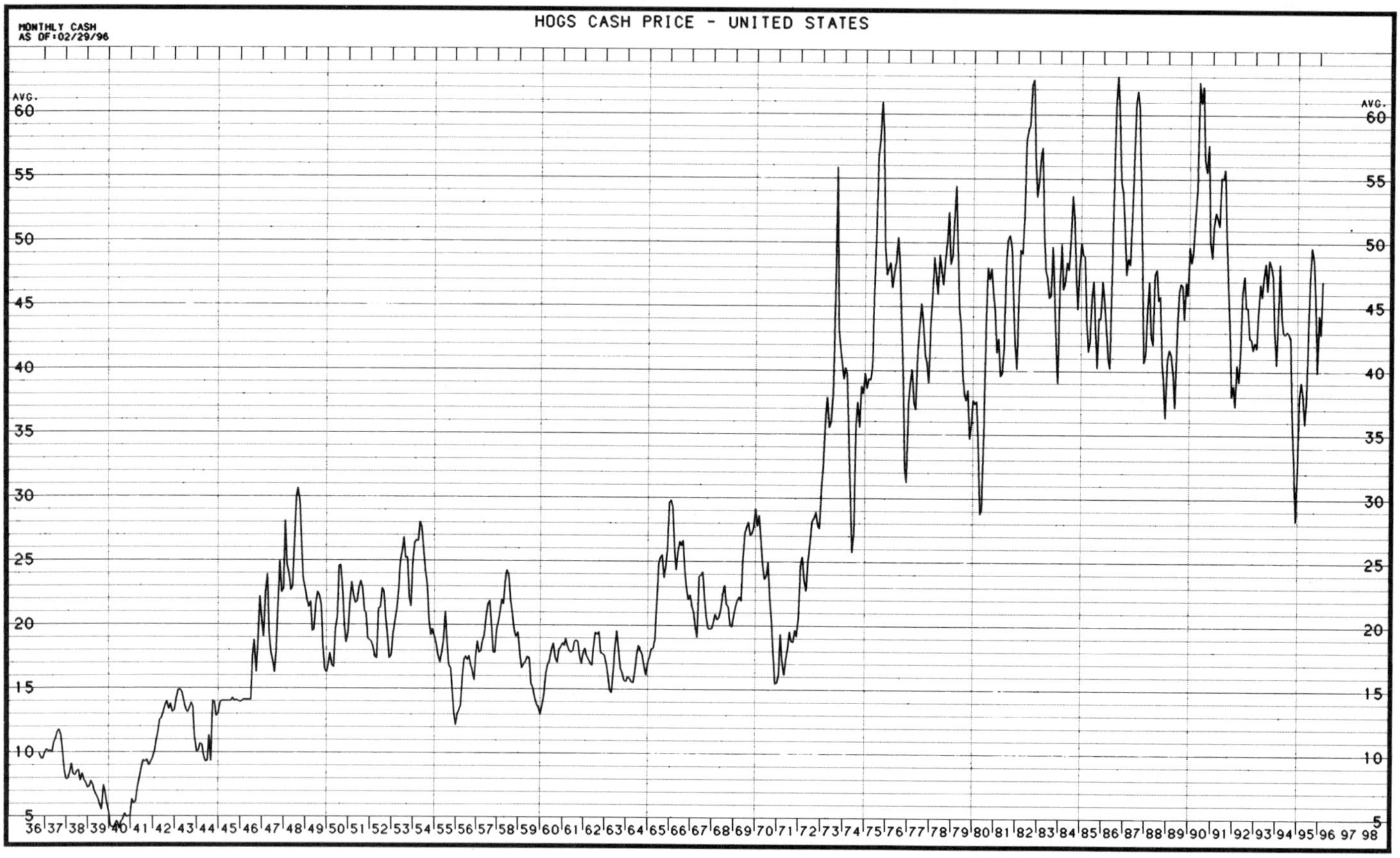

Average Wholesale Price of Hogs, Average (All Weights) at Sioux City In Dollars Per Hundred Pounds (Hwt.)

Year	Jan.	Feb.	Mar.	Apr.	May	June	July	Aug.	Sept.	Oct.	Nov.	Dec.	Average
1987	47.56	49.08	48.67	52.10	55.79	61.37	62.69	50.56	55.19	49.28	40.74	41.56	51.22
1988	44.59	47.45	43.19	42.28	47.75	48.26	45.60	45.98	41.28	38.92	36.52	40.58	43.53
1989	41.64	41.11	39.88	37.22	42.40	46.24	47.26	47.04	44.58	47.49	47.21	49.65	44.31
1990	48.41	49.48	52.56	54.63	62.80	61.34	62.54	56.37	55.64	58.02	50.17	48.96	55.08
1991	51.32	52.31	51.92	51.42	54.83	54.79	55.74	51.11	46.76	43.51	38.29	38.93	49.24
1992	37.15	40.45	39.09	42.01	45.90	47.59	44.98	44.88	42.50	42.57	41.98	42.12	42.60
1993	41.66	44.57	46.76	45.46	47.10	48.52	46.38	48.67	48.40	47.27	42.76	40.38	45.66
1994	43.99	48.12	44.30	42.72	42.27	42.76	42.62	42.37	35.49	32.56	28.25	31.59	39.75
1995[1]	37.82	39.09	37.94	35.88	37.35	43.03	47.18	49.46	48.67	45.42	40.02	43.80	42.14

[1] Preliminary. *Source: Economic Research Service, U.S. Department of Agriculture*

Average Price Received by Farmers for Hogs in the U.S. In Cents Per Pound

Year	Jan.	Feb.	Mar.	Apr.	May	June	July	Aug.	Sept.	Oct.	Nov.	Dec.	Average
1987	47.20	48.20	47.40	50.80	54.40	59.20	59.60	58.60	54.30	48.90	40.60	40.30	50.79
1988	43.00	45.80	42.20	41.90	46.30	47.10	44.10	44.70	40.70	38.70	36.20	39.70	42.53
1989	40.90	40.40	39.30	36.90	41.60	45.10	45.90	45.60	43.40	46.60	45.00	48.20	43.24
1990	47.30	48.20	51.30	53.80	61.20	60.30	60.80	55.90	54.30	56.80	50.20	47.80	53.99
1991	50.00	52.20	51.50	50.90	54.10	54.70	54.20	51.20	46.40	43.60	38.00	38.60	48.78
1992	36.40	40.20	39.10	41.00	45.10	46.40	44.40	43.90	41.90	42.60	40.90	41.80	41.98
1993	41.20	44.00	46.50	45.40	46.90	48.10	45.70	47.30	47.80	46.90	42.50	40.40	45.23
1994	43.50	47.90	44.40	42.70	42.70	42.70	42.20	41.80	35.40	31.80	28.00	30.80	39.49
1995[1]	36.90	39.10	37.80	35.70	37.20	42.30	46.20	48.60	48.30	45.60	39.90	44.30	41.83

[1] Preliminary. *Source: Economic Research Service, U.S. Department of Agriculture*

U.S. Federally Inspected Hog Slaughter   In Thousands of Head

Week Ended	1993	1994	1995
January[1]			
7	1,943	1,777	1,822
14	1,944	1,857	1,994
21	1,812	1,601	1,628
28	1,824	1,732	1,791
February			
4	1,784	1,731	1,752
11	1,771	1,643	1,781
18	1,652	1,698	1,810
25	1,715	1,714	1,887
March			
4	1,750	1,756	1,908
11	1,780	1,826	1,888
18	1,725	1,769	1,808
25	1,735	1,751	1,876
April			
1	1,697	1,799	1,837
8	1,745	1,729	1,788
15	1,773	1,817	1,819
22	1,857	1,810	1,824
29	1,823	1,802	1,859
May			
6	1,803	1,796	1,867
13	1,719	1,767	1,876
20	1,701	1,749	1,774
27	1,670	1,729	1,769
June			
3	1,488	1,489	1,603
10	1,701	1,731	1,762
17	1,618	1,675	1,722
24	1,666	1,634	1,702

Week Ended	1993	1994	1995
July			
1	1,544	1,644	1,735
8	1,422	1,444	1,466
15	1,621	1,752	1,687
22	1,654	1,652	1,702
29	1,642	1,713	1,683
August			
5	1,679	1,680	1,733
12	1,698	1,773	1,704
19	1,747	1,757	1,780
26	1,712	1,780	1,817
September			
2	1,743	1,819	1,795
9	1,577	1,638	1,650
16	1,846	1,973	1,896
23	1,834	2,000	1,888
30	1,853	1,976	1,888
October			
7	1,861	1,969	
14	1,877	1,984	
21	1,843	2,037	
28	1,822	2,027	
November			
4	1,874	2,053	
11	1,825	1,985	
18	1,936	2,059	
25	1,606	1,697	
December			
2	1,960	2,086	
9	1,947	2,087	
16	1,847	2,002	
23	1,545	1,796	

[8] Corresponding dates to 1995: 1993, January 9; 1994, January 8.   *Source: Economic Research Service, U.S. Department of Agriculture*

Federally Inspected Hog Slaughter in the United States   In Thousands of Head

Year	Jan.	Feb.	Mar.	Apr.	May	June	July	Aug.	Sept.	Oct.	Nov.	Dec.	Total
1988	6,803	6,518	7,505	6,929	6,713	6,715	6,199	7,101	7,534	7,887	7,908	7,703	85,516
1989	7,116	6,619	7,569	7,199	7,277	6,881	6,131	7,392	7,493	7,823	7,815	7,012	86,328
1990	7,407	6,643	7,279	6,785	6,799	6,152	5,938	7,110	6,716	7,546	7,334	7,140	82,901
1991	7,461	6,469	7,044	7,320	6,948	6,296	6,557	7,098	7,177	8,292	7,744	7,708	85,951
1992	8,144	7,153	7,934	7,610	6,897	7,166	7,461	7,494	8,217	8,599	7,796	8,142	92,613
1993	7,649	6,921	7,958	7,840	6,988	7,338	7,010	7,473	7,763	7,857	7,952	8,184	90,993
1994	7,285	6,783	8,148	7,609	7,383	7,452	6,941	7,997	8,192	8,585	8,516	8,547	93,435
1995[1]	7,882	7,157	8,628	7,379	8,012	7,732	6,918	8,083	7,752	8,358	8,424	7,881	94,203

[1] Preliminary.   *Source: National Agricultural Statistics Service, U.S. Department of Agriculture*

Average Live Weight of all Hogs Slaughtered Under Federal Inspection   In Pounds Per Head

Year	Jan.	Feb.	Mar.	Apr.	May	June	July	Aug.	Sept.	Oct.	Nov.	Dec.	Average
1985	245	242	242	245	247	248	245	243	242	246	248	247	245
1986	246	244	244	246	246	246	245	244	245	248	250	252	246
1987	251	248	246	247	247	248	246	244	246	249	252	250	248
1988	248	247	247	249	250	250	249	247	248	251	253	251	249
1989	249	247	247	251	251	251	247	247	246	248	251	250	249
1990	249	248	248	250	251	252	249	249	248	250	253	252	250
1991	251	250	250	252	254	253	251	250	251	253	256	255	252
1992	255	253	252	253	254	254	251	250	252	252	255	255	253
1993	254	253	253	254	254	256	254	252	252	254	257	258	254
1994	254	254	254	256	255	256	252	252	255	259	261	260	256
1995[1]	258	256	257	258	258	258	256	253	252	255	259	258	257

[1] Preliminary.   *Source: Economic Research Service, U.S. Department of Agriculture*

HOGS

Average Open Interest of Live Hogs Futures at Chicago In Contracts

Year	Jan.	Feb.	Mar.	Apr.	May	June	July	Aug.	Sept.	Oct.	Nov.	Dec.
1984	33,760	32,849	34,212	33,930	35,009	33,006	27,643	23,016	22,755	20,871	24,145	23,141
1985	26,589	29,408	27,125	24,248	24,019	23,545	20,878	18,894	19,799	21,567	27,843	24,852
1986	22,480	21,273	19,769	17,522	23,209	25,855	30,480	31,697	34,611	28,256	30,491	27,062
1987	26,275	28,125	30,794	30,195	32,431	32,889	30,752	31,553	34,197	28,562	25,138	24,440
1988	26,681	30,532	31,329	28,156	31,801	31,221	27,466	26,476	31,507	30,092	34,251	31,458
1989	31,923	30,853	29,014	30,414	29,646	27,353	25,375	25,345	28,308	33,936	35,913	29,693
1990	30,335	31,018	37,789	39,257	47,291	43,631	32,942	29,964	26,982	25,691	27,648	25,757
1991	22,742	24,798	24,449	22,400	25,871	21,275	18,154	16,771	17,281	18,462	21,572	19,167
1992	23,854	31,545	32,441	32,430	30,947	26,362	24,935	24,535	27,535	32,555	32,738	30,468
1993	27,210	25,620	28,264	24,139	22,581	19,840	19,026	20,761	20,544	20,051	21,167	24,096
1994	31,899	32,123	31,012	31,713	30,889	27,327	26,414	25,335	28,957	32,077	36,304	33,516
1995	36,705	30,958	30,736	28,035	28,294	28,729	29,959	31,599	34,183	31,312	31,519	35,127

Source: Chicago Mercantile Exchange

Volume of Trading of Live Hogs Futures at Chicago In Thousands of Contracts

Year	Jan.	Feb.	Mar.	Apr.	May	June	July	Aug.	Sept.	Oct.	Nov.	Dec.	Total
1984	232.2	212.7	243.8	172.3	211.0	192.6	189.2	143.9	109.1	140.7	181.0	140.5	2,169.0
1985	155.0	128.3	160.2	141.7	156.2	141.9	134.7	120.2	136.1	156.8	145.2	143.5	2,719.9
1986	156.3	108.5	113.7	153.6	157.4	160.8	224.3	168.8	196.5	183.4	171.0	142.5	1,936.7
1987	159.2	138.5	172.7	190.3	189.7	212.1	219.5	169.8	174.0	175.5	121.1	118.0	2,040.5
1988	172.9	143.0	172.4	137.6	169.6	267.0	171.4	140.3	160.7	150.3	166.8	156.7	2,008.8
1989	188.2	135.0	152.8	130.7	175.2	147.5	141.9	131.8	149.6	181.5	205.9	151.6	1,891.9
1990	181.0	119.9	189.7	188.8	278.3	277.0	212.5	170.4	147.0	160.3	186.1	130.4	2,241.3
1991	177.9	150.3	148.0	157.0	155.7	120.8	131.1	120.9	102.9	118.4	104.5	94.8	1,695.8
1992	135.2	137.0	140.4	138.2	116.7	131.2	148.8	102.2	116.6	149.5	117.0	123.3	1,556.1
1993	131.5	101.9	160.0	131.0	120.2	121.1	112.5	91.5	109.4	102.7	116.1	103.0	1,401.8
1994	144.8	97.6	146.9	93.1	127.4	144.4	116.2	122.1	110.7	129.0	150.7	172.1	1,554.0
1995	155.8	115.8	181.9	116.8	145.4	155.3	139.0	144.6	135.3	132.1	142.1	135.5	1,699.7

Source: Chicago Mercantile Exchange

Honey

Honey production in the world's key producing countries declined 7 percent in 1995, totaling 450,000 tonnes versus 480,000 in 1994. Production in other countries is small with the cumulative total under 50,000 tonnes. Annual world production during the 1980s averaged nearly 700,000 tonnes. China is the world's largest producer with as estimated 165,000 tonnes in 1995, the lowest output since 1988, but still almost one-third of the world total. U.S. production of 90,000 tonnes was a distant second. Several factors influence a country's annual honey production. In 1995, almost all producing countries experienced adverse weather that hampered production, ranging from hot and dry to excessively wet. However, another factor remains the displacement of honey producing bees by more aggressive and less productive bees, notably Africanized bees. The latter have virtually wiped out honey production in some parts of the world.

China's annual honey production continues to fall from the early 1990's when production averaged 200,000 tonnes. Poor weather in 1995 contributed to the decline which also had the secondary impact of hindering the transportation of the crop from the interior to marketing centers. The nation's high inflation rate has apparently caused many beekeepers to leave the industry. Reports of government intervention may help to hinder downsizing of China's bee colonies. Approximately 50 percent of China's production is exported.

Mexico's colony numbers have declined sharply; from a record 2.5 million in 1987 to an estimated 2.0 million in 1995, primarily due to rising costs and the presence of Africanized honeybees.

The first official estimate of U.S. 1995 honey production is not released until after this book's publication date, but unofficial estimates put production down 7-8 percent from 1994's 98,500 tonnes due to variable weather patterns and steady declines in colony numbers.

World Production of Honey In Metric Tons

Year	Agrentina	Australia	Brazil	Canada	China	Germany[2]	Japan	Mexico	Russia[3]	United States	Total[4]
1982	33,000	22,400	25,000	30,500	136,000	18,000	7,400	45,000	186,000	104,300	-----
1983	30,000	24,963	22,000	38,771	138,000	19,000	6,869	68,000	210,000	93,000	650,603
1984	35,000	27,997	25,000	43,298	140,000	16,000	6,798	60,000	193,000	75,000	622,093
1985	45,000	26,871	28,000	36,120	150,000	11,000	7,225	56,000	204,000	68,000	632,216
1986	36,000	25,077	27,000	34,041	160,000	16,000	5,553	54,000	210,000	90,900	658,571
1987	44,000	28,000	30,500	39,776	204,000	16,000	6,023	47,850	219,245	102,875	738,269
1988	46,000	27,622	30,000	37,105	156,000	18,000	4,870	46,140	243,000	97,114	705,851
1989	40,000	26,198	32,000	27,815	189,000	29,000	5,343	48,530	225,000	80,266	703,152
1990	47,000	27,561	30,000	32,115	193,000	23,000	4,854	51,000	236,219	89,717	732,466
1991	54,000	20,604	32,300	31,606	206,000	25,000	4,202	58,770	240,000	99,414	714,790
1992	61,000	18,948	18,841	30,339	178,000	24,677	3,800	48,852	47,000	100,055	531,512
1993	59,000	22,556	19,000	30,760	176,000	26,360	3,500	48,000	49,600	104,620	539,396
1994	64,000	22,600	19,000	32,920	177,000	22,230	3,500	41,500	43,899	98,500	525,149
1995[1]	55,000			31,250	165,000	25,000		38,000	43,900	98,000	456,150

[1] Preliminary. [2] Data prior to 1989 are for West Germany. [3] Formerly part of the U.S.S.R.; data not reported separately until 1992. [4] Only for countries listed. *Source: Foreign Agricultural Service, U.S. Department of Agriculture*

Salient Statistics of Honey in the United States In Millions of Pounds

Year	Number of Colonies (1,000)	Yield Per Colony Pounds	Stocks Jan. 1	Total U.S. Production	Imports for Consumption	Domestic Disappearance	Exports	Total Supply	Program Activity: Placed Under Loan	Program Activity: CCC Take Over	Program Activity: Net Gov't. Expenditure[3] Mil. $	Domestic Avg. Price All Honey (¢ Lb.)	National Avg. Price Support (¢ Lb.)	Per Capita Consumption Lbs.
1980	4,141	48.2	37.7	199.8	49.0	226.2	8.5	286.5	41.1	6.0	8.7	61.5	50.3	.8
1981	4,213	44.1	51.8	185.9	77.3	232.0	9.2	315.0	55.2	35.2	8.4	63.2	57.4	.8
1982	4,250	54.1	73.8	230.0	92.0	250.8	8.5	395.8	88.4	74.5	27.4	56.8	60.4	.9
1983	4,275	48.0	136.5	205.0	109.8	269.0	7.5	451.3	113.6	106.4	48.0	54.4	62.2	1.0
1984	4,300	38.4	174.8	165.1	128.7	251.7	7.5	468.6	107.5	105.8	90.2	49.5	65.8	.9
1985	4,325	34.7	209.4	150.1	138.2	256.9	6.5	497.7	102.0	98.0	80.8	45.5	65.3	.9
1986	3,205	62.5	234.3	200.4	120.0	282.9	9.2	554.7	180.4	41.0	89.4	51.3	64.0	1.0
1987	3,190	71.1	262.6	226.8	58.3	320.9	12.4	547.7	218.0	52.7	72.6	50.3	61.0	1.1
1988	3,219	66.3	214.4	214.1	55.9	278.0	14.0	484.4	209.5	32.0	100.1	50.0	59.1	.9
1989	3,443	51.4	192.4	177.0	77.3	292.0	10.0	446.7	161.7	2.8	41.7	49.8	56.4	1.0
1990	3,210	61.6	144.7	197.8	77.0	303.4	12.4	419.5	183.5	1.1	46.7	53.7	53.8	1.0
1991	3,181	68.9	103.7	219.2	92.2	303.4	9.6	415.1	112.9	3.2	18.6	55.6	53.8	1.0
1992	3,030	72.8	102.1	220.6	114.6	298.2	10.4	437.3	122.7	4.1	16.6	55.0	53.8	1.0
1993	2,876	80.1	128.7	230.4	133.6	304.2	8.5	492.7	136.8	16.4	22.1	54.4	53.8	1.0
1994[1]	2,770	78.4	59.8	217.2	123.2	292.0	8.3	400.2	73.4	0	0	51.2	50.0	1.0
1995[2]	2,647	89.5	47.0	210.4	46.3	170.9	4.6	201.4	48.0					

[1] Preliminary. [2] Forecast. [3] Fiscal year. *Source: Economic Research Service, U.S. Department of Agriculture*

Interest Rates, U.S.

The Federal Reserve seemed to follow rather than lead the financial markets during 1995. The year began with the Fed lifting short term rates a notch in late January, the seventh increase in less than a year. Then the evidence of a slowing economy began filtering into the market with the consensus forecast calling for a "soft landing", i.e. a GDP growth rate of about 2 1/2 percent with little inflationary pressures. The Fed seemed to have the leeway to ease without fanning inflation fears, but instead opted to hold monetary policy steady. Their concern may have focused on the dollar's slide against the key currencies, notably the J-Yen, which lower U.S. interest rates would have intensified. Indeed, in the spring, the world's major central banks took steps to bolster the dollar. By September, the dollar's weakness had apparently been checked and the evidence of a slowing U.S. economy was mounting.

The Fed eased short term rates in late summer, dropping the Fed funds rate to 5 3/4 percent, the first cut since 1992. The marketplace thought the Fed action was "too little-too late" and the pressure mounted steadily for another easing. The Fed found itself in a quandary; the economy probably needed a shot in the arm which another easing might do, but a political impasse was taking hold in Washington on how and when to balance the federal budget deficit. Moreover, a surge in grain prices during the fourth quarter could reawaken food inflationary fears. The timing was not good for the Fed to act. Outside events resolved the Fed's dilemma. On December 18, the closely watched Dow-Jones 30 stock index broke 101 points, the largest one-day decline in four years and while it may have been an overdue correction to a very powerful equities market, it also signaled deepening concern about the economy. The Fed's window of opportunity had opened and the year's second easing of monetary policy followed. At yearend the average Fed funds rate was 5.40 percent versus a high for the year of 6 percent. The discount rate was 5.25 percent versus 4.75 percent in late 1994 and the prime rate was 8.5 percent, unchanged from a year earlier. Long-term rates worked steadily lower during the second half of 1995: the 30 year T-bond was hovering near 6 percent at yearend versus 7.8 percent a year earlier; the ten-year T-note was at 5.65 percent versus 7.79 percent, and 3-month T-bills were yielding 4.89 percent, 50 basis points under late 1994.

Consumer confidence showed signs of breaking in late 1995. Retail sales during the important yearend holiday period were routine and consumer credit card debt was topping a record $1 trillion with delinquencies on the debt at the second highest level of the 1990's. Housing starts were flat towards yearend and the inventory of unsold houses was expanding. The good news was that November's consumer prices, seasonally adjusted, were unchanged for the first time since the 1990-91 recession. For the September-November period the CPI was up a 1.8 percent annual rate versus a 2.7 percent increase in 1994. Although inflation may prove higher in 1996, the marketplace is anticipating at least one more easing going into the first quarter. Clouding the picture is whether Fed Chairman Alan Greenspan will be renominated in the spring of 1996 for another four term.

Futures Markets

A futures (and options) contract exists for almost every maturity on the yield curve, as well as for municipal and commercial credit risks. Major U.S. contracts include T-bills and Eurodollars on Chicago's International Monetary Market (IMM), and T-bonds and municipal bonds on the Chicago Board of Trade (CBOT). Futures are also traded in Chicago on two, five, and ten year T-notes, 30 day fed funds and one month LIBOR. Smaller size contracts on interest rate instruments are listed at the MidAmerica Commodity Exchange (MidAm).

U.S. Producer Commodity Price Index (Wholesale, All Commodities) 1982 = 100

Year	Jan.	Feb.	Mar.	Apr.	May	June	July	Aug.	Sept.	Oct.	Nov.	Dec.	Average
1987	100.5	101.0	101.2	101.9	102.6	103.0	103.5	103.8	103.7	104.1	104.2	104.2	102.8
1988	104.6	104.8	104.9	105.8	106.5	107.2	107.9	108.0	108.1	108.2	108.3	109.0	106.9
1989	110.5	110.8	111.5	112.3	113.2	112.9	112.8	112.0	112.3	112.7	112.7	113.0	112.2
1990	114.9	114.4	114.2	114.1	114.6	114.3	114.5	116.5	118.3	120.8	120.1	118.7	116.3
1991	119.0	117.2	116.2	116.0	116.5	116.4	116.1	116.2	116.1	116.4	116.4	115.9	116.5
1992	115.6	116.0	116.1	116.3	117.2	118.0	117.9	117.7	118.0	118.1	117.8	117.6	117.2
1993	118.0	118.4	118.7	119.3	119.7	119.5	119.2	118.7	118.7	119.1	119.0	118.6	118.9
1994[1]	119.1	119.3	119.7	119.7	119.9	120.5	120.7	121.2	120.9	120.9	121.5	121.9	120.4
1995[1]	122.9	123.5	123.9	124.6	124.9	125.3	125.3	125.0	125.2	125.0			

[1] Preliminary. *Source: Bureau of Labor Statistics, U.S. Department of Commerce*

U.S. Consumer Price Index[2] (Retail Price Index for All Items: Urban Consumers) 1982-1984 = 100

Year	Jan.	Feb.	Mar.	Apr.	May	June	July	Aug.	Sept.	Oct.	Nov.	Dec.	Average
1987	111.2	111.6	112.1	112.7	113.1	113.5	113.8	114.4	115.0	115.3	115.4	115.4	113.6
1988	115.7	116.0	116.5	117.1	117.5	118.0	118.5	119.0	119.8	120.2	120.3	120.5	118.3
1989	121.1	121.6	122.3	123.1	123.8	124.1	124.4	124.6	125.0	125.6	125.9	126.1	124.0
1990	127.4	128.0	128.7	128.9	129.2	129.9	130.4	131.6	132.7	133.5	133.8	133.8	130.7
1991	134.6	134.8	135.0	135.2	135.6	136.0	136.2	136.6	137.2	137.4	137.8	137.9	136.2
1992	138.1	138.6	139.3	139.5	139.7	140.2	140.5	140.9	141.3	141.8	142.0	141.9	140.3
1993	142.6	143.1	143.6	144.0	144.2	144.4	144.4	144.8	145.1	145.7	145.8	145.8	144.5
1994[1]	146.2	146.7	147.2	147.4	147.5	148.0	148.4	149.0	149.4	149.5	149.7	149.7	148.2
1995[1]	150.3	150.9	151.4	151.9	152.2	152.5	152.9	153.2					

[8] Preliminary. [2] Not seasonally adjusted. *Source: Bureau of Labor Statistics, U.S. Department of Commerce*

Average Open Interest of 13 Week[1] Treasury Bill Futures in Chicago In Thousands of Contracts

Year	Jan.	Feb.	Mar.	Apr.	May	June	July	Aug.	Sept.	Oct.	Nov.	Dec.
1983	48,730	47,608	39,257	42,777	44,259	42,574	43,574	44,782	42,656	49,731	51,947	45,577
1984	44,814	50,417	47,490	51,299	58,668	47,626	45,713	43,931	42,313	42,337	48,923	42,866
1985	47,022	47,171	40,954	40,069	39,624	33,712	35,817	37,911	35,473	36,887	40,830	35,963
1986	37,365	43,008	48,572	51,145	43,394	36,479	40,676	40,819	37,532	36,107	37,940	36,271
1987	40,710	48,375	39,691	35,671	32,202	23,431	24,077	25,454	20,539	26,014	24,222	20,989
1988	19,571	22,956	21,460	26,134	28,166	19,081	21,812	21,626	21,374	21,930	24,711	26,923
1989	29,023	26,612	25,672	20,433	21,864	19,934	20,950	22,687	25,216	29,118	34,224	33,469
1990	39,168	38,358	27,668	31,274	25,128	21,171	26,524	37,903	35,723	46,974	53,284	50,146
1991	55,371	53,484	38,259	43,538	53,941	51,178	55,514	55,999	47,509	50,865	57,680	51,750
1992	51,312	45,902	35,539	44,757	47,734	41,091	38,399	35,638	29,781	32,556	35,379	29,566
1993	32,544	35,756	32,556	39,115	40,724	34,614	30,895	34,177	28,983	30,121	33,800	30,996
1994	36,456	41,150	43,243	51,485	41,164	34,580	32,572	29,559	24,522	32,325	30,077	22,322
1995	21,065	26,289	33,420	35,873	34,608	25,930	20,534	19,195	18,929	16,781	16,384	11,279

[1] 90-day U.S. Treasury Bill. *Source: International Monetary Market (Chicago Mercantile Exchange)*

Volume of Trading of 13 Week[1] Treasury Bill Futures in Chicago In Thousands of Contracts

Year	Jan.	Feb.	Mar.	Apr.	May	June	July	Aug.	Sept.	Oct.	Nov.	Dec.	Total
1983	302.2	337.9	361.4	308.5	331.4	366.2	283.9	371.1	273.5	309.8	275.7	268.5	3,790.0
1984	200.0	213.4	304.9	300.2	489.1	342.8	315.1	242.5	201.6	203.6	264.0	215.5	3,293.0
1985	231.3	245.4	314.5	217.9	206.2	205.6	180.6	165.8	206.8	159.9	142.1	138.1	2,413.0
1986	175.0	215.4	149.5	212.8	169.7	152.9	117.8	135.7	160.8	114.2	106.3	105.1	1,815.2
1987	137.9	218.8	151.8	197.6	207.8	125.5	97.5	125.4	110.1	262.2	161.0	131.6	1,927.0
1988	103.2	111.6	129.2	125.6	163.4	105.3	84.3	117.9	97.9	101.6	129.1	104.5	1,373.6
1989	109.6	146.5	143.2	119.2	126.3	101.4	89.3	126.9	135.9	149.1	130.1	124.9	1,502.4
1990	169.3	153.6	118.5	120.3	102.4	96.7	138.1	206.6	168.9	178.5	223.7	193.1	1,869.6
1991	252.9	197.9	166.8	164.0	188.2	173.3	141.7	223.2	111.0	110.8	140.8	141.6	1,912.2
1992	143.8	137.9	145.0	115.9	106.5	106.1	85.8	76.2	103.0	127.0	106.5	83.4	1,337.1
1993	86.1	100.4	97.0	65.6	103.2	106.0	71.7	75.7	89.3	69.1	87.4	66.0	1,071.3
1994	59.8	137.5	115.9	104.4	99.4	89.4	53.7	60.9	77.6	57.4	81.2	83.8	1,020.5
1995	72.2	80.0	90.3	37.4	58.7	49.9	28.1	41.5	44.4	36.9	46.6	34.2	620.2

[1] 90-day U.S. Treasury Bill. *Source: International Monetary Market (Chicago Mercantile Exchange)*

Average Open Interest of U.S. Treasury Bond Futures in Chicago   In Thousands of Contracts

Year	Jan.	Feb.	Mar.	Apr.	May	June	July	Aug.	Sept.	Oct.	Nov.	Dec.
1984	174,827	163,119	168,705	168,980	193,248	198,144	193,662	205,630	209,920	223,808	244,596	217,550
1985	196,826	223,282	224,553	215,742	224,351	209,985	209,823	229,284	229,382	279,083	315,082	307,137
1986	320,040	317,197	266,005	253,991	237,236	212,415	203,921	207,524	196,672	223,588	241,717	239,695
1987	256,822	286,198	237,005	285,491	297,998	250,315	272,633	303,192	336,976	383,640	337,855	293,160
1988	296,133	328,081	307,004	317,891	366,723	406,493	441,064	489,339	475,841	478,585	472,628	411,888
1989	395,874	366,704	303,891	308,850	330,016	312,318	325,851	321,493	283,133	301,719	355,555	314,252
1990	315,671	324,954	294,968	280,745	303,544	278,889	285,934	317,197	297,075	286,291	288,581	254,775
1991	257,229	279,378	250,028	283,473	279,443	254,983	273,774	325,303	310,110	304,198	317,445	301,604
1992	343,156	353,782	318,737	313,742	346,542	347,293	370,850	427,723	385,645	364,250	362,231	321,706
1993	336,327	375,435	361,675	362,404	370,485	349,285	361,393	396,411	388,188	360,859	359,739	337,575
1994	380,057	422,902	454,539	500,790	497,296	421,286	441,884	451,462	447,924	436,684	449,642	397,554
1995	384,356	389,908	369,989	367,964	399,500	421,234	438,267	381,237	361,394	395,346	447,409	426,384

Source: Chicago Board of Trade

Volume of Trading of Treasury Bond Futures in Chicago   In Thousands of Contracts

Year	Jan.	Feb.	Mar.	Apr.	May	June	July	Aug.	Sept.	Oct.	Nov.	Dec.	Total
1984	1,476	1,891	2,629	2,069	3,374	2,594	2,692	2,792	2,557	2,924	2,781	2,185	29,963
1985	2,974	3,250	2,906	2,272	3,339	3,755	3,308	3,409	3,149	3,558	4,118	3,965	40,448
1986	4,640	5,220	4,445	5,115	4,783	4,486	4,114	4,175	4,638	3,853	3,595	3,534	52,599
1987	4,188	4,308	4,128	7,110	6,120	5,518	4,839	6,185	7,769	7,388	4,861	4,428	66,841
1988	5,550	5,765	6,088	4,984	5,570	7,495	5,133	6,346	5,641	6,136	6,431	5,171	70,307
1989	5,806	6,300	5,605	4,858	6,673	7,995	5,231	7,640	4,792	6,329	5,828	3,244	70,303
1990	7,215	7,438	7,175	5,653	6,189	5,279	4,895	8,855	4,939	6,659	6,570	4,691	75,559
1991	5,804	5,717	5,658	5,957	6,186	5,582	4,293	6,592	4,765	6,450	6,239	4,643	67,886
1992	7,523	6,270	6,793	4,810	5,418	4,829	6,081	6,085	5,953	6,871	5,288	4,083	70,005
1993	5,577	6,483	7,903	6,156	6,800	5,817	6,218	6,914	7,444	6,537	8,193	5,385	79,428
1994	7,288	8,430	10,837	9,557	9,999	9,804	6,987	7,910	7,913	7,004	8,533	5,699	99,960
1995	7,058	7,714	9,624	5,835	8,722	8,447	5,790	7,084	7,317	6,927	6,626	5,232	86,376

Source: Chicago Board of Trade

Average Open Interest of Eurodollar Futures in Chicago In Contracts

Year	Jan.	Feb.	Mar.	Apr.	May	June	July	Aug.	Sept.	Oct.	Nov.	Dec.
1985	93,554	105,150	107,654	105,703	122,952	120,183	118,905	129,144	125,433	127,799	154,873	144,419
1986	135,703	151,853	148,114	157,288	171,319	164,950	163,345	186,915	213,502	219,995	228,157	219,868
1987	232,311	267,832	229,482	263,086	291,824	269,490	279,309	316,878	361,431	379,188	354,892	323,502
1988	317,384	358,496	340,855	375,951	422,663	421,907	440,567	510,188	509,180	477,860	519,843	566,951
1989	574,799	672,315	731,344	749,690	756,850	720,434	690,204	713,979	637,947	591,502	663,588	661,925
1990	638,515	662,860	653,188	616,948	662,787	676,324	690,639	740,018	697,837	678,167	728,362	664,136
1991	630,859	722,741	741,075	767,644	857,350	835,233	797,940	883,085	916,708	949,479	1,054,742	1,067,187
1992	1,129,756	1,213,739	1,244,564	1,269,120	1,377,229	1,382,685	1,434,127	1,549,891	1,537,036	1,537,640	1,546,965	1,418,669
1993	1,429,428	1,586,690	1,643,285	1,653,433	1,782,750	1,739,140	1,777,713	1,918,439	1,940,677	2,026,541	2,148,959	2,150,194
1994	2,300,466	2,529,469	2,568,095	2,627,293	2,734,294	2,565,180	2,599,129	2,703,830	2,699,588	2,561,170	2,660,339	2,606,336
1995	2,443,647	2,535,403	2,463,879	2,447,444	2,503,283	2,390,765	2,279,486	2,374,569	2,347,247	2,290,304	2,405,451	2,480,455

Source: International Monetary Market (Chicago Mercantile Exchange)

Volume of Trading of Eurodollar Futures in Chicago In Thousands of Contracts

Year	Jan.	Feb.	Mar.	Apr.	May	June	July	Aug.	Sept.	Oct.	Nov.	Dec.	Total
1985	525	724	877	765	754	892	798	698	769	694	695	711	8,901
1986	889	825	628	934	983	1,018	755	847	1,289	1,047	836	775	10,825
1987	1,072	1,472	1,197	2,562	1,825	1,760	1,292	1,514	2,495	2,849	1,202	1,177	20,416
1988	1,466	1,681	1,635	1,575	1,830	2,288	1,604	1,893	1,957	1,586	2,236	1,952	21,705
1989	2,257	3,107	3,848	4,471	3,941	4,116	3,193	3,980	2,977	3,971	2,914	2,043	40,818
1990	3,244	2,459	2,727	2,566	3,132	2,473	2,947	3,857	2,730	2,898	2,982	2,680	34,696
1991	2,859	2,635	3,445	3,208	2,458	2,972	2,629	4,035	3,000	3,505	3,301	3,196	37,243
1992	5,366	4,419	5,583	4,942	4,819	4,603	5,358	4,016	4,705	6,692	5,461	4,568	60,531
1993	5,557	5,004	6,014	4,059	5,978	5,673	5,657	4,494	6,341	4,888	6,270	4,477	64,411
1994	6,538	9,394	9,469	9,639	11,494	9,348	7,810	7,128	7,641	7,992	9,715	9,766	104,823
1995	10,305	10,396	9,549	6,069	9,897	10,105	6,670	7,013	7,171	6,478	6,055	5,952	95,730

Source: International Monetary Market (Chicago Mercantile Exchange)

INTEREST RATES

Average Open Interest of U.S. Treasury Note (10-year) Futures in Chicago In Contracts

Year	Jan.	Feb.	Mar.	Apr.	May	June	July	Aug.	Sept.	Oct.	Nov.	Dec.
1985	38,462	44,251	49,909	42,744	48,416	52,963	55,676	62,118	59,587	66,796	70,300	69,603
1986	76,661	78,528	75,024	63,804	70,568	72,565	67,048	62,122	60,839	56,955	64,397	58,763
1987	58,926	56,177	55,093	64,924	68,797	71,033	72,033	78,281	88,939	82,672	75,139	77,631
1988	76,066	75,884	73,083	75,836	78,038	84,349	84,612	101,470	96,821	91,811	89,307	74,602
1989	76,964	84,605	78,966	86,661	88,511	76,364	77,211	76,538	71,138	82,844	82,149	72,238
1990	73,155	82,211	76,939	76,030	82,174	78,498	71,413	75,644	72,900	67,309	73,744	76,697
1991	72,621	79,355	79,413	71,451	84,203	81,884	85,527	94,379	96,836	93,187	95,450	87,063
1992	119,739	114,521	106,497	102,862	112,666	126,228	143,924	158,831	179,045	191,725	199,990	195,705
1993	190,018	206,852	198,653	209,221	229,378	217,521	233,458	238,189	237,243	237,877	273,336	262,831
1994	264,848	258,643	300,080	328,821	294,091	254,612	232,373	253,233	273,564	277,313	301,000	271,992
1995	282,978	285,187	265,747	263,816	273,945	289,052	306,046	323,078	277,011	278,832	270,527	249,073

Source: Chicago Board of Trade

Volume of Trading of U.S. Treasury Note (10-year) Futures in Chicago In Thousands of Contracts

Year	Jan.	Feb.	Mar.	Apr.	May	June	July	Aug.	Sept.	Oct.	Nov.	Dec.	Total
1985	171.8	216.0	215.9	175.8	274.9	266.9	219.4	282.9	212.7	234.3	297.5	292.5	2,860
1986	269.7	401.4	383.1	381.7	434.8	470.3	309.7	363.1	459.5	319.9	328.1	305.2	4,426
1987	304.9	358.3	347.6	643.8	541.3	405.1	269.6	446.0	512.9	662.0	369.4	392.8	5,254
1988	335.3	462.8	420.6	298.8	467.8	469.6	327.4	566.0	455.4	383.2	537.4	476.7	5,201
1989	450.5	547.9	468.3	431.6	625.6	637.3	453.0	629.6	465.8	555.8	516.7	327.4	6,110
1990	491.3	650.5	480.9	381.1	638.7	427.4	415.0	703.0	399.3	449.6	574.3	442.6	6,054
1991	507.7	519.6	508.3	466.5	566.9	456.6	318.9	705.9	467.2	573.2	661.3	591.4	6,342
1992	929.6	866.4	824.9	531.2	758.9	683.3	859.4	1,047.7	1,138.5	1,300.2	1,225.8	1,052.1	11,218
1993	1,134.6	1,286.3	1,763.1	1,089.5	1,341.4	1,390.6	1,147.0	1,390.7	1,523.7	1,279.5	1,926.6	1,328.2	16,601
1994	1,484.3	1,935.7	2,572.4	2,213.5	2,399.4	2,250.2	1,621.8	2,028.7	1,932.9	1,635.1	2,253.6	1,750.2	24,078
1995	1,752.6	1,978.8	2,458.7	1,368.2	2,236.5	2,495.8	1,588.9	2,028.7	1,859.0	1,459.7	1,730.8	1,487.6	22,445

Source: Chicago Board of Trade

Average Open Interest of 5-Year Treasury Notes Futures in Chicago In Contracts

Year	Jan.	Feb.	Mar.	Apr.	May	June	July	Aug.	Sept.	Oct.	Nov.	Dec.
1988					2,545	5,292	10,584	11,424	12,677	18,403	24,569	34,267
1989	34,728	40,203	45,320	46,371	48,195	42,496	44,985	34,675	37,474	42,669	57,901	73,798
1990	81,705	74,568	74,999	60,841	59,417	56,485	54,004	64,100	75,955	78,370	82,981	93,549
1991	80,059	82,666	83,109	74,612	75,799	65,543	72,197	86,981	85,794	91,096	102,890	99,291
1992	116,322	121,667	125,155	130,826	135,111	144,386	143,928	143,203	127,418	122,113	129,548	127,690
1993	139,207	150,443	152,711	158,607	169,234	152,262	152,403	160,258	159,754	154,501	181,492	206,914
1994	200,812	213,037	200,626	185,083	192,659	186,026	189,828	182,027	181,518	181,578	176,322	205,150
1995	206,539	210,192	199,357	200,087	213,531	189,332	176,329	173,897	163,419	162,121	177,915	171,023

Source: Chicago Board of Trade

Volume of Trading of 5-Year Treasury Notes Futures in Chicago In Thousands of Contracts

Year	Jan.	Feb.	Mar.	Apr.	May	June	July	Aug.	Sept.	Oct.	Nov.	Dec.	Total
1988					20.6	56.5	45.6	66.4	73.8	54.8	97.1	91.8	244
1989	91.1	156.8	128.1	89.2	167.3	162.0	142.3	205.2	121.2	148.3	253.4	116.9	519
1990	184.5	277.5	164.9	107.6	266.6	140.8	131.6	320.4	189.0	197.9	305.7	40.8	544
1991	220.5	318.5	252.3	181.4	307.6	232.4	179.7	385.4	243.9	291.5	419.9	353.1	1,065
1992	498.6	543.8	560.0	322.2	590.1	551.5	484.2	565.7	582.1	539.0	640.8	563.2	1,743
1993	539.5	673.1	886.0	447.6	755.9	753.8	506.4	711.3	753.8	472.6	908.0	715.8	2,096
1994	695.9	1,235.1	1,295.4	917.1	1,202.0	1,154.9	834.8	944.9	1,107.3	840.6	1,156.7	1,078.0	12,463
1995	988.5	1,296.2	1,386.9	783.4	1,291.1	1,402.9	828.6	1,100.5	1,008.7	769.6	996.0	784.7	12,637

Source: Chicago Board of Trade

INTEREST RATES

U.S. Federal Funds Rate In Percent

Year	Jan.	Feb.	Mar.	Apr.	May	June	July	Aug.	Sept.	Oct.	Nov.	Dec.	Annual
1976	4.87	4.77	4.84	4.82	5.29	5.48	5.31	5.29	5.25	5.03	4.95	4.65	5.05
1977	4.61	4.68	4.69	4.73	5.35	5.39	5.42	5.90	6.14	6.47	6.51	6.56	5.54
1978	6.70	6.78	6.79	6.89	7.36	7.60	7.81	8.04	8.45	8.96	9.76	10.03	7.93
1979	10.07	10.06	10.09	10.01	10.24	10.29	10.47	10.94	11.43	13.77	13.18	13.78	11.19
1980	13.82	14.13	17.19	17.61	10.98	9.47	9.03	9.61	10.87	12.81	15.85	18.90	13.36
1981	19.08	15.93	14.70	15.72	18.52	19.10	19.04	17.82	15.87	15.08	13.31	12.37	16.38
1982	13.22	14.78	14.68	14.94	14.45	14.15	12.59	10.12	10.31	9.71	9.20	8.95	12.26
1983	8.68	8.51	8.77	8.80	8.63	8.98	9.37	9.56	9.45	9.48	9.34	9.47	9.09
1984	9.56	9.59	9.91	10.29	10.32	11.06	11.23	11.64	11.30	9.99	9.43	8.38	10.23
1985	8.35	8.50	8.58	8.27	7.97	7.53	7.88	7.90	7.92	7.99	8.05	8.27	7.41
1986	8.14	7.86	7.48	6.99	6.85	6.92	6.56	6.17	5.89	5.85	6.04	6.91	6.81
1987	6.43	6.10	6.13	6.37	6.85	6.73	6.58	6.73	7.22	7.29	6.69	6.77	6.66
1988	6.83	6.58	6.58	6.87	7.09	7.51	7.76	8.01	8.19	8.30	8.35	8.76	7.57
1989	9.12	9.36	9.85	9.84	9.81	9.53	9.24	8.99	9.02	8.84	8.55	8.45	9.22
1990	8.23	8.24	8.28	8.26	8.18	8.29	8.15	8.13	8.20	8.11	7.81	7.31	8.10
1991	6.91	6.25	6.12	5.91	5.78	5.90	5.82	5.66	5.45	5.21	4.81	4.43	5.69
1992	4.03	4.06	3.98	3.73	3.82	3.76	3.25	3.30	3.22	3.10	3.09	2.92	3.52
1993	3.02	3.03	3.07	2.96	3.00	3.04	3.06	3.03	3.09	2.99	3.02	2.96	3.02
1994	3.05	3.25	3.34	3.56	4.01	4.25	4.26	4.47	4.73	4.76	5.29	5.45	4.20
1995	5.53	5.92	5.98	6.05	6.01	6.01	6.00	5.74	5.80				

Source: Bureau of Economic Analysis, U.S. Department of Commerce

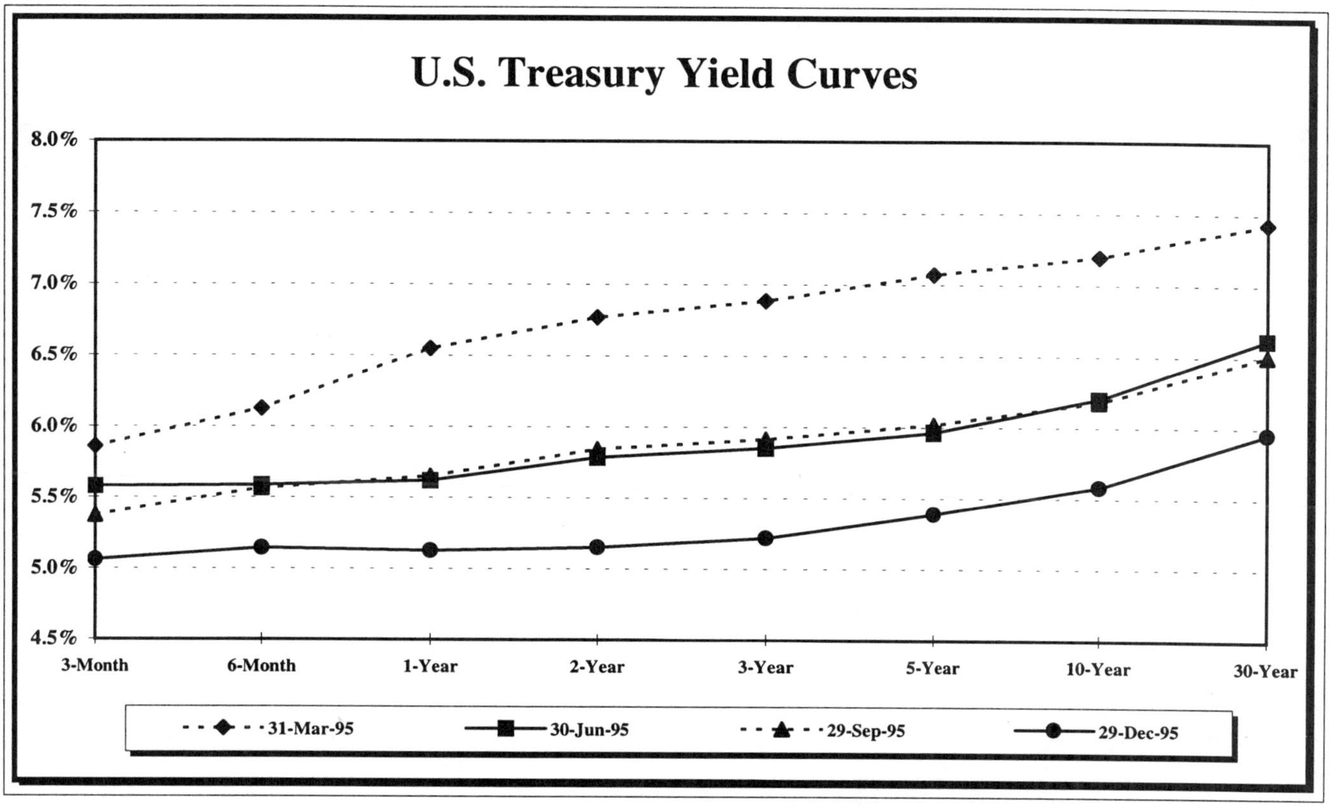

U.S. Industrial Production Index[1] (Seasonally Adjusted) 1987 = 100

Year	Jan.	Feb.	Mar.	Apr.	May	June	July	Aug.	Sept.	Oct.	Nov.	Dec.	Average
1984	91.0	90.9	91.9	92.4	93.0	93.5	93.9	94.0	93.9	93.2	93.3	92.8	92.8
1985	93.1	93.8	94.1	94.5	94.7	94.4	94.1	94.5	95.0	94.2	94.6	95.6	94.4
1986	96.1	95.5	94.6	94.8	94.8	94.4	94.8	95.0	95.1	95.6	96.2	96.7	95.3
1987	96.5	97.6	98.2	98.3	99.2	100.1	100.8	101.0	100.9	102.3	102.2	102.6	100.0
1988	103.5	103.5	103.9	104.3	104.8	105.0	106.1	106.4	106.2	106.5	106.9	107.4	105.4
1989	107.7	107.6	107.7	108.6	108.3	108.4	107.8	108.2	108.2	107.7	108.1	108.6	108.1
1990	107.5	108.5	108.9	108.8	109.4	110.1	110.4	110.5	110.4	109.9	108.3	107.2	109.2
1991	106.6	105.7	105.0	105.5	106.4	107.3	108.1	108.0	108.4	108.4	108.1	107.4	107.1
1992	106.6	107.2	105.6	106.3	106.7	106.0	106.8	106.6	106.2	107.5	108.4	108.9	106.9
1993	109.2	109.9	110.0	110.5	110.0	110.4	110.9	111.1	112.5	112.7	113.7	114.7	112.0
1994	114.7	115.6	116.6	116.7	117.4	118.0	118.2	119.1	119.0	119.5	120.3	121.7	118.1
1995[2]	122.0	122.1	122.0	121.2	121.4	121.4	121.4	121.5	122.9	122.6			

[1] Total Index of the Federal Reserve Index of Quantity Output. [2] Preliminary. *Source: Bureau of Economic Analysis, U.S. Department of Commerce*

U.S. Gross National Product, National Income, and Personal Income In Billions of Current Dollars[1]

	Gross Domestic Product					National Income					Personal Income				
Year	I	II	III	IV	Annual Average	I	II	III	IV	Annual Average	I	II	III	IV	Annual Average
1985	3,926	3,979	4,047	4,108	4,015	3,162	3,209	3,252	3,313	3,234	3,263	3,308	3,332	3,399	3,325
1986	4,181	4,195	4,253	4,297	4,232	3,363	3,395	3,419	3,473	3,413	3,457	3,510	3,540	3,598	3,526
1987	4,412	4,498	4,578	4,691	4,545	3,572	3,646	3,722	3,829	3,692	3,716	3,760	3,814	3,919	3,802
1988	4,764	4,863	4,952	5,054	4,908	3,889	3,966	4,028	4,128	4,003	3,968	4,038	4,103	4,195	4,076
1989	5,144	5,218	5,280	5,351	5,248	4,203	4,231	4,245	4,301	4,245	4,304	4,352	4,391	4,474	4,380
1990	5,433	5,506	5,577	5,583	5,525	4,396	4,461	4,475	4,507	4,460	4,581	4,655	4,719	4,765	4,680
1991	5,615	5,674	5,726	5,764	5,695	4,493	4,529	4,555	4,599	4,544	4,753	4,807	4,846	4,907	4,828
1992	5,897	5,971	6,044	6,169	6,020	4,752	4,807	4,794	4,965	4,830	5,032	5,102	5,148	5,335	5,154
1993	6,240	6,300	6,359	6,478	6,343	5,031	5,094	5,139	5,262	5,131	5,256	5,365	5,396	5,485	5,375
1994[2]	6,575	6,690	6,792	6,897	6,738	5,309	5,431	5,495	5,599	5,458	5,556	5,660	5,735	5,857	5,702
1995[2]	6,977	7,030	7,113			5,688	5,688	5,719			5,962	6,008	6,076		

[1] Seasonally adjusted at annual rates. [2] Preliminary *Source: Bureau of Economic Analysis, U.S. Department of Commerce*

U.S. Money Supply M1 in 1987 Dollars[3] In Billions of Dollars

Year	Jan.	Feb.	Mar.	Apr.	May	June	July	Aug.	Sept.	Oct.	Nov.	Dec.	Average
1985	507.8	511.4	512.0	513.3	517.1	523.0	527.3	534.1	539.6	540.4	541.7	546.7	526.2
1986	545.5	551.3	562.1	569.4	577.7	583.2	591.5	599.0	603.5	609.0	618.0	633.0	585.4
1987	632.7	631.0	630.7	636.8	635.9	629.8	629.5	629.2	629.5	635.3	630.9	628.0	632.7
1988	630.4	630.8	631.8	634.7	632.0	634.4	636.7	634.5	633.0	631.4	630.8	631.7	632.7
1989	625.0	622.9	619.0	612.0	605.0	601.6	604.0	603.0	605.5	606.7	605.4	607.2	609.9
1990	600.8	602.6	602.4	603.4	601.0	600.9	598.4	598.6	598.8	594.2	593.6	593.4	599.6
1991	591.8	598.7	601.6	600.6	605.2	608.0	609.5	611.9	613.7	618.6	623.8	627.2	609.2
1992[2]	635.2	644.1	647.6	650.0	656.7	655.6	661.2	668.2	677.2	685.2	692.3	696.5	664.2
1993	823.1	822.4	824.2	827.1	841.4	847.7	854.4	859.1	866.1	869.8	874.1	876.8	848.9
1994[1]	880.0	880.7	881.8	881.8	881.0	881.0	882.2	877.8	876.0	872.4	871.4	869.7	878.0
1995[1]	867.7	863.8	862.4	860.6	860.6	853.6	853.0	852.0	850.3	846.5			

[1] Preliminary. [2] Prior to 1993, shown in 1982 dollars. [3] M1--This measure is currency, travelers checks, plus demand deposits at commercial banks and interest-earning checkable deposits at all depository institutions. *Source: Bureau of Economic Analysis, U.S. Department of Commerce*

U.S. Money Supply M2 in 1987 Dollars[2] In Billions of Dollars

Year	Jan.	Feb.	Mar.	Apr.	May	June	July	Aug.	Sept.	Oct.	Nov.	Dec.	Average
1985	2,582.3	2,594.7	2,594.7	3,591.5	2,600.6	2,624.2	2,636.3	2,648.9	2,662.4	2,661.8	2,664.3	2,671.2	2,627.7
1986	2,668.3	2,682.2	2,719.3	2,753.8	2,772.9	2,787.0	2,812.1	2,832.7	2,844.2	2,863.0	2,873.4	2,891.2	2,791.7
1987	2,889.9	2,881.9	2,874.2	2,875.2	2,871.2	2,862.9	2,860.4	2,862.8	2,866.7	2,876.7	2,867.7	2,868.4	2,871.5
1988	2,881.2	2,896.8	2,905.6	2,910.0	2,918.3	2,917.4	2,913.9	2,909.3	2,895.7	2,895.9	2,899.5	2,898.6	2,903.5
1989	2,886.2	2,877.2	2,870.4	2,852.7	2,838.8	2,852.2	2,864.1	2,880.0	2,893.2	2,892.5	2,902.0	2,910.3	2,876.6
1990	2,893.6	2,893.0	2,888.0	2,892.3	2,889.5	2,887.1	2,880.6	2,871.7	2,865.1	2,848.0	2,837.0	2,837.6	2,873.6
1991	2,827.7	2,835.9	2,852.7	2,851.4	2,853.6	2,856.4	2,849.0	2,845.1	2,836.6	2,835.5	2,834.8	2,838.4	2,843.1
1992	2,833.3	2,840.0	2,830.9	2,821.5	2,819.1	2,807.8	2,801.9	2,801.8	2,803.4	2,801.0	2,799.2	2,795.8	2,813.0
1993	2,791.1	2,775.4	2,769.3	2,763.0	2,775.3	2,778.5	2,778.1	2,773.4	2,777.7	2,772.0	2,772.8	2,772.3	2,774.9
1994[1]	2,788.7	2,777.8	2,780.1	2,781.9	2,780.0	2,769.0	2,768.9	2,757.4	2,750.4	2,743.2	2,742.4	2,740.0	2,765.0
1995[1]	2,740.8	2,729.4	2,729.0	2,728.7	2,735.0	2,757.9	2,766.0	2,783.0	2,789.9				

[1] Preliminary. [2] M2--This measure adds to M1 overnight repurchase agreements (RPs) issued by commercial banks and certain overnight Eurodollars (those issued by Caribbean branches of member banks) held by U.S. nonbank residents, general purpose and broker/dealer money market mutual shares (MMMF), and savings and small-denomination time deposits. *Source: Bureau of Economic Analysis, U.S. Department of Commerce*

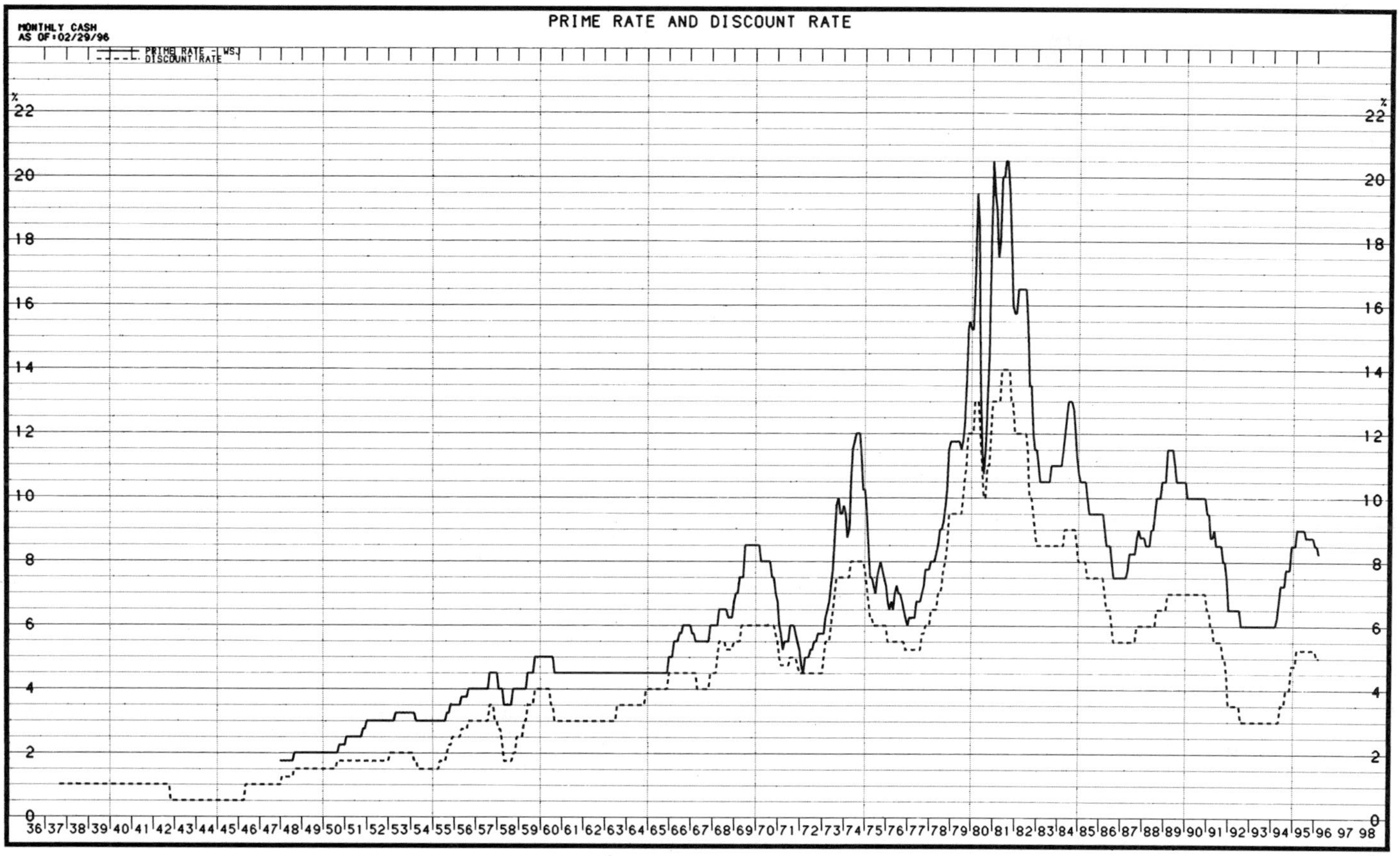
PRIME RATE AND DISCOUNT RATE
MONTHLY CASH
AS OF:02/29/96
PRIME RATE - WSJ
DISCOUNT RATE
%
22
20
18
16
14
12
10
8
6
4
2
0
36 37 38 39 40 41 42 43 44 45 46 47 48 49 50 51 52 53 54 55 56 57 58 59 60 61 62 63 64 65 66 67 68 69 70 71 72 73 74 75 76 77 78 79 80 81 82 83 84 85 86 87 88 89 90 91 92 93 94 95 96 97 98

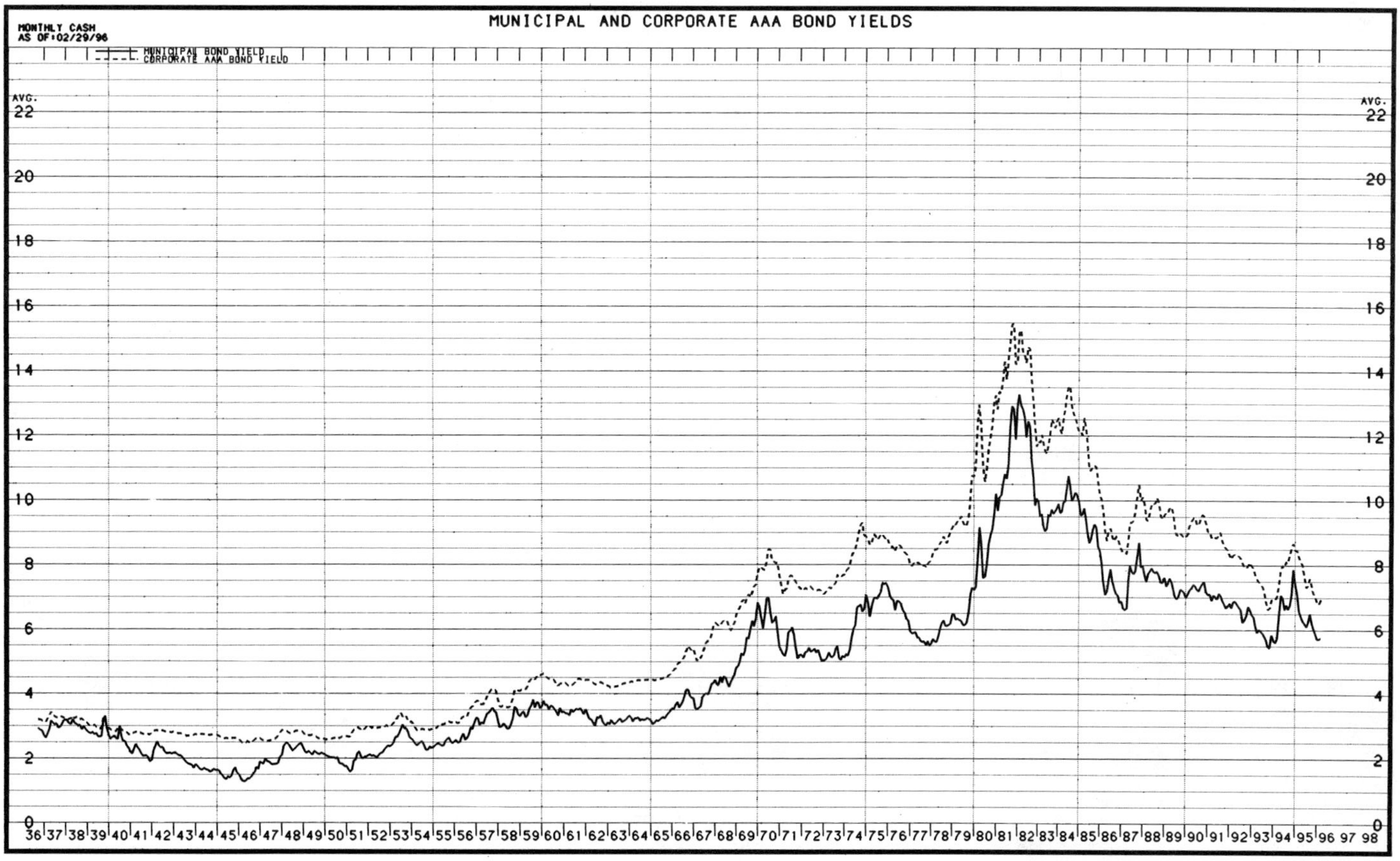
MUNICIPAL AND CORPORATE AAA BOND YIELDS
MONTHLY CASH
AS OF:02/29/96
MUNICIPAL BOND YIELD
CORPORATE AAA BOND YIELD
AVG.
22
20
18
16
14
12
10
8
6
4
2
0
36 37 38 39 40 41 42 43 44 45 46 47 48 49 50 51 52 53 54 55 56 57 58 59 60 61 62 63 64 65 66 67 68 69 70 71 72 73 74 75 76 77 78 79 80 81 82 83 84 85 86 87 88 89 90 91 92 93 94 95 96 97 98

INTEREST RATES

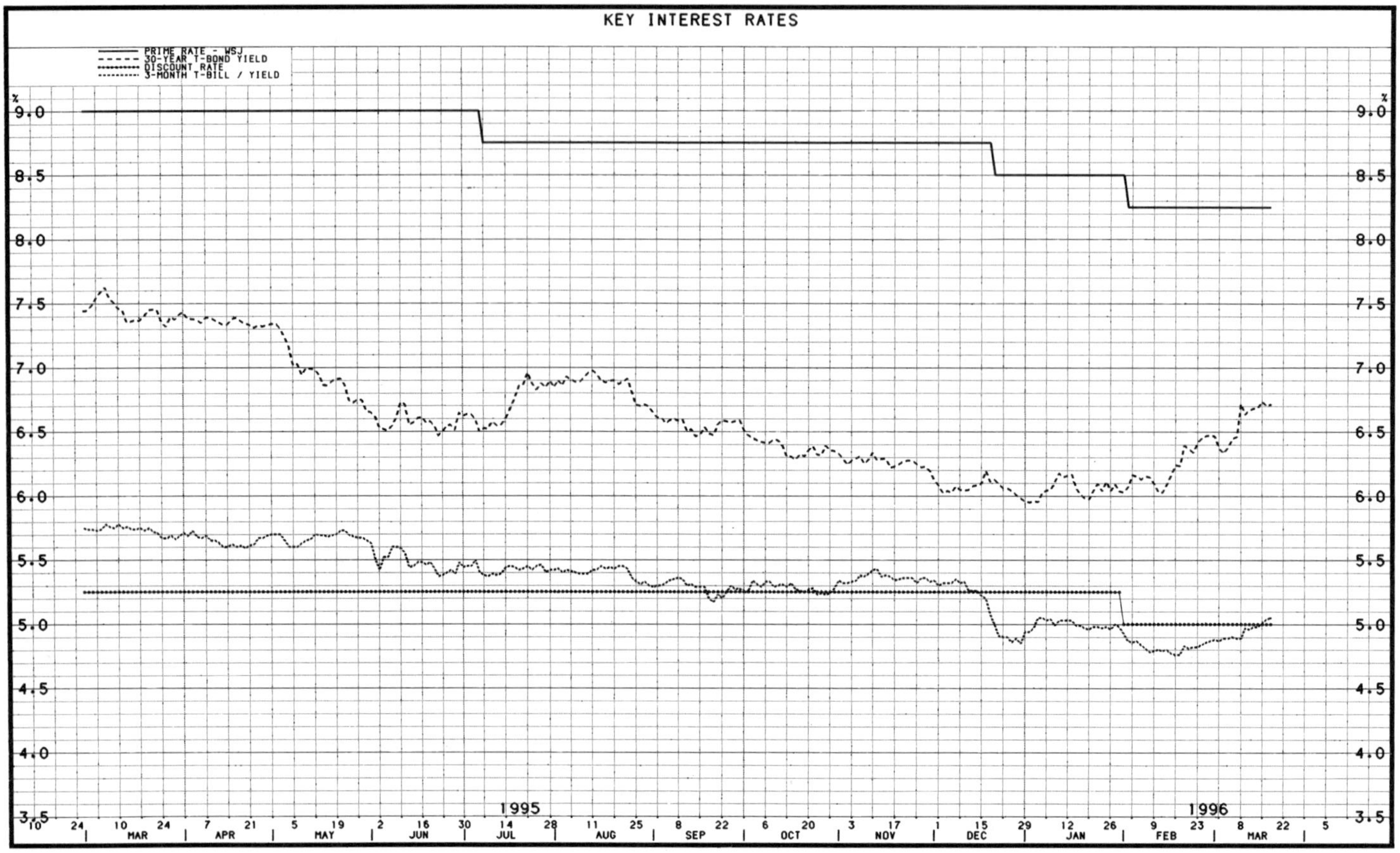

Interest Rates, Worldwide

Slow growth was the feature of the world's leading economies in 1995. The good news was that inflationary pressures were contained and likely to remain so, enabling the major central banks to continue easier monetary polices. The more important question may focus on how much the financial markets have already anticipated new rate cuts. In the U.S., for example, as 1995 came to a close, it was widely assumed that in early 1996 the federal Reserve would trim short term rates at least 25 basis and cut again in the second quarter. However, 1996 fiscal policies in a number of countries may tighten in an effort to rein in growing debt burdens which have caused real interest rates to be higher than they should be and economic growth lower. Japan may be the exception to a tighter fiscal policy as that country attempts to avoid a repeat of 1995's flirtation with a debt/deflation tailspin. Japan's expansionary monetary and fiscal policy during 1995 failed to provide an acceptable cure for what now seem to be deep rooted structural economic problems.

In Europe, the strains imposed on many of the continent's economies by the EMU convergence criteria of the Maastricht Treaty have kept both monetary and fiscal policies tighter than they should be. Justified or not, the marketplace appeared to impose in 1995 an EMU risk factor on European debt obligations; for example, the decline in the German ten-year Government bond lagged the comparable U.S. Treasury market by almost 100 basis points. In mid-December, Germany's Bundesbank cut its two key interest rates, the discount and Lombard rate, a half point each to 3 percent and 5 percent respectively. It was the Bundesbank's third cut of the year and left rates at the lowest level since mid-1988. Similar cuts followed in a number of European countries. The action was deemed necessary to spur sluggish economies, but for Germany it may have also been aimed to ease the pressure on the French franc. The French economy was in turmoil due to widespread labor strife and latent fears that France might fail to meet the EMU's criteria towards attaining a single European currency.

In Germany, prospects for continued low inflation, a strong D-Mark and mild economic recovery in 1996 auger well for the Bundesbank keeping interest rates low. However, further rate cuts by the Bundesbank are not likely unless prospects for the EMU treaty deteriorate. In the U.K. inflation remains subdued. In November 1995 the U.K.'s annualized inflation was 2.9 percent, the 38th consecutive month in which inflation was under 4 percent and the longest peacetime run under 4 percent since the 1930's. The odds favor low U.K. inflation in 1996, even if the Bank of England cuts its base lending rate, as seems likely, another 25 to 50 basis points from the late 1995 level of 6 1/2 percent.

In France, the Bank of France confirmed a shift towards an aggressive easy monetary policy when they quickly followed the German's Bundesbank cut in late December, despite the country's labor unrest. Indeed, across much of Europe, almost all the key economic indicators in late 1995 pointed toward slowing economies and the need for still lower interest rates. There are exceptions: Italy's central bank apparently feels that accelerating labor costs may hold inflation at a higher than desired level, suggesting little if any change in monetary policy through the first half of 1996. In Sweden, however, economic growth in 1995 of almost 4 percent is expected to be cut in half during 1996 suggesting favorable prospects for short term rates to ease in the first quarter of the year. The same expectations exist in Spain.

Japan has economic problems; dealing with them effectively is the enigma. Changes in the GDP calculations in 1995 suggest that growth in business investment may be less sensitive to interest rate changes than previously thought. If so, the potential adverse impact to investment spending in 1996 from higher interest rates may be softer than expected, enabling the Bank of Japan to nudge short term rates higher as seems likely in 1996. Moreover, consumer disposable income is expected to increase in 1996 at a faster rate than seen in 1995 and offset the impact of higher interest rates. Of course, realization of this theory is far from certain.

In Canada, inflationary pressure was minimal in 1995. Unemployment ran near 10 percent and economic growth was well under potential with forecasts calling for lackluster real GDP growth in the fourth quarter at an estimated 1.25 percent. However, the Bank of Canada in late 1995 appeared reluctant to ease interest rates due to the fact that any fresh easing could have an adverse impact on the Canadian-Dollar's value. This stance will likely persist into 1996.

Futures Markets

A number of actively traded interest rate futures markets are traded worldwide. The London International Financial Futures Exchange (LIFFE) trades contracts on 3-month Sterling prices and British government bonds, called long gilts. LIFFE also offers futures on Euromarks, Euroswiss, Italian government bonds, the FT-SE 100 index and German government bonds, called bunds. The latter is also traded in Frankfurt. Canadian Bankers Acceptances are traded on the Montreal Exchange. Notional bond and PIBOR futures are traded on the Paris MATIF. Euroyen futures and Japanese yen government bonds are traded in Tokyo. Libor and eurodollars are traded on Chicago's Mercantile Exchange, with the latter also on the Mid-America Exchange. A Eurotop 100 is traded on New York's Commodity Exchange.

INTEREST RATES, WORLDWIDE

10-YR YEN BOND - TSE
WEEKLY NEAREST FUTURES
AS OF:03/15/96
% NOMINAL VALUE
128
124
120
116
112
108
104
100
96
92
88
84
1990
1991
1992
1993
1994
1995
M J J A S O N D J F M A M J J A S O N D J F M A M J J A S O N D J F M A M J J A S O N D J F M A M J J A S O N D J F M A M J J A S O N D J F M A M J

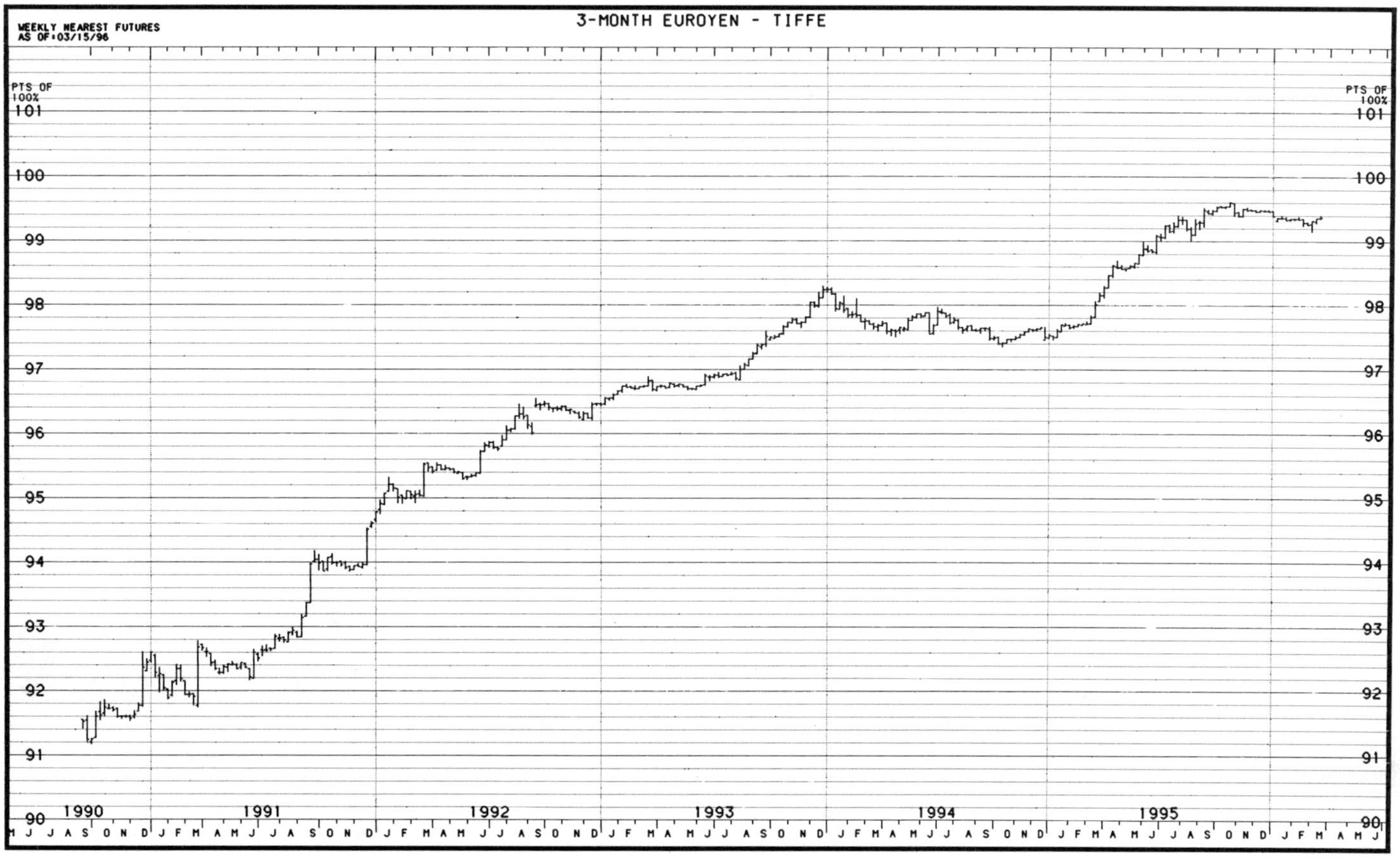

3-MONTH EUROYEN - TIFFE
WEEKLY NEAREST FUTURES
AS OF:03/15/96
PTS OF 100%
101
100
99
98
97
96
95
94
93
92
91
90
1990
1991
1992
1993
1994
1995
M J J A S O N D J F M A M J J A S O N D J F M A M J J A S O N D J F M A M J J A S O N D J F M A M J J A S O N D J F M A M J J A S O N D J F M A M J

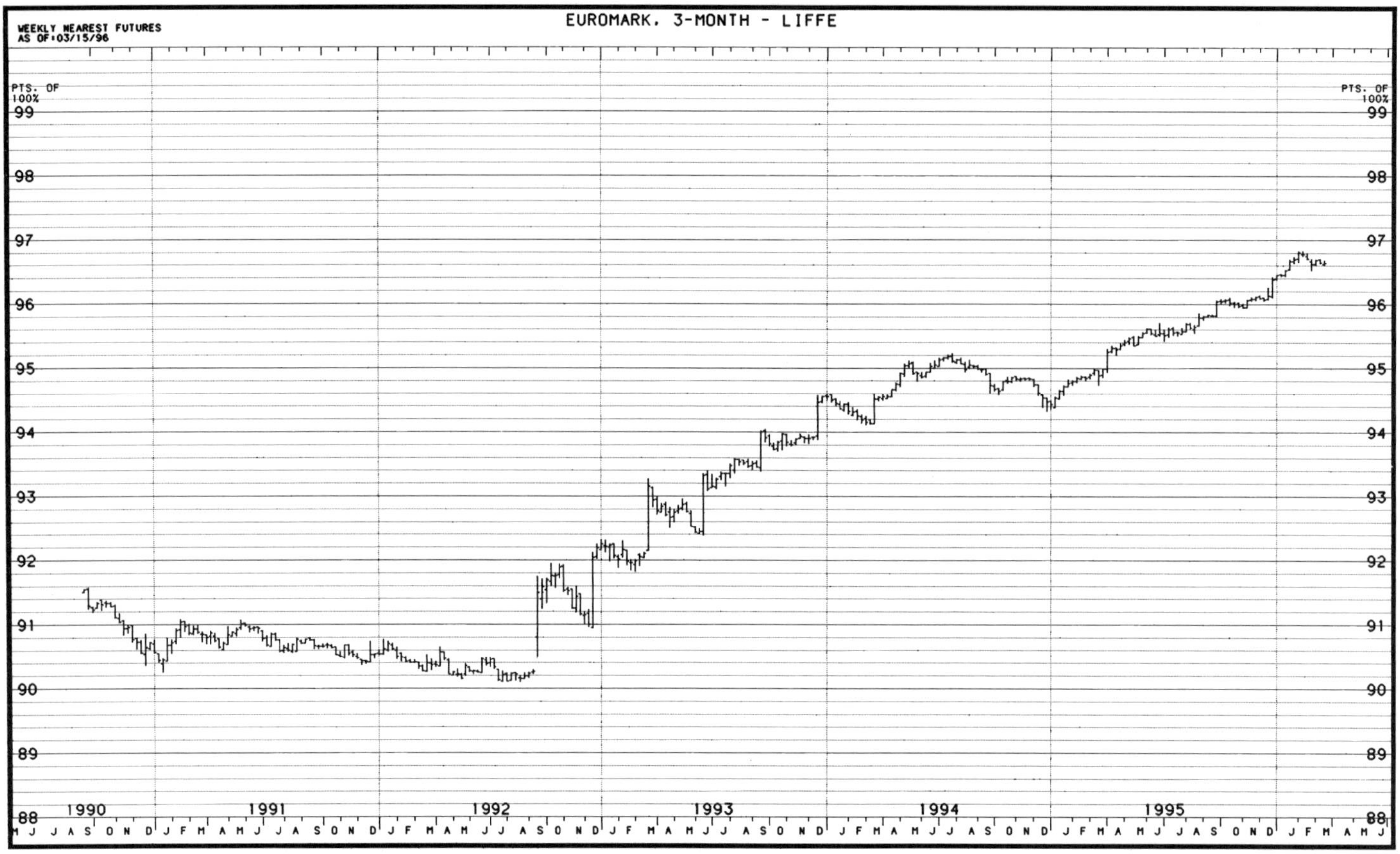
WEEKLY NEAREST FUTURES
AS OF:03/15/96
EUROMARK, 3-MONTH - LIFFE
PTS. OF 100%
99
98
97
96
95
94
93
92
91
90
89
88
1990
1991
1992
1993
1994
1995
M J J A S O N D J F M A M J J A S O N D J F M A M J J A S O N D J F M A M J J A S O N D J F M A M J J A S O N D J F M A M J J A S O N D J F M A M J

WEEKLY NEAREST FUTURES
AS OF:03/15/96
GERMAN BOND, BUND - LIFFE
% NOMINAL VALUE
102
100
98
96
94
92
90
88
86
84
82
80
1990
1991
1992
1993
1994
1995
M J J A S O N D J F M A M J J A S O N D J F M A M J J A S O N D J F M A M J J A S O N D J F M A M J J A S O N D J F M A M J J A S O N D J F M A M J

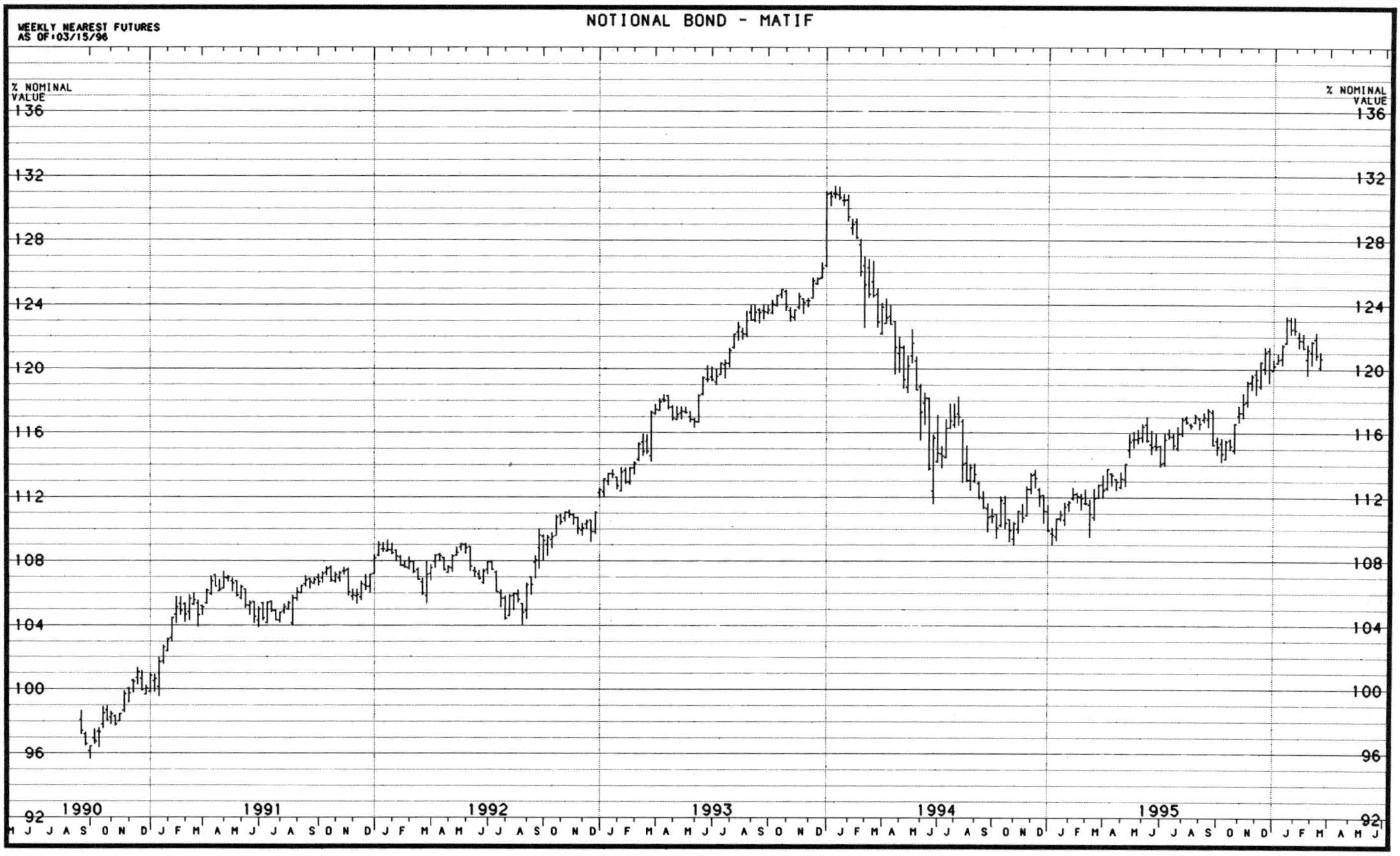
WEEKLY NEAREST FUTURES
AS OF:03/15/96
NOTIONAL BOND - MATIF
% NOMINAL VALUE
136
132
128
124
120
116
112
108
104
100
96
92
1990
1991
1992
1993
1994
1995

WEEKLY NEAREST FUTURES
AS OF:03/15/96
3-MONTH PIBOR - MATIF
PTS. OF 100%
97
96
95
94
93
92
91
90
89
88
87
86
1990
1991
1992
1993
1994
1995

INTEREST RATES, WORLDWIDE

Japan--Economic Statistics   Percentage Change from Previous Period

Year	Real GDP	Nominal GDP	Real Private Consump-tion	Real Public Consump-tion	Grossed Fixed Investment	Real Total Domestic Demand	Real Exports of Goods & Services	Real Imports of Goods & Services	Consumer Prices[1]	Unem-ployment Rate
1987	4.1	4.1	4.2	.4	9.6	5.1	.1	7.8	.1	2.9
1988	6.2	6.6	5.2	2.2	11.9	7.6	7.0	18.7	.7	2.5
1989	4.7	6.7	4.3	2.0	9.3	5.8	9.0	17.6	2.3	2.3
1990	4.8	7.2	3.9	1.9	8.8	5.0	7.	8.6	3.1	2.1
1991	4.3	6.3	2.2	1.6	3.7	2.9	5.2	-4.1	3.3	2.1
1992	1.1	2.6	1.7	2.7	-1.1	.3	5.2	-.4	1.7	2.2
1993	-.2	.6	1.0	1.7	-1.8	0	1.3	2.7	1.3	2.5
1994	.5	.7	2.2	2.8	- .3	1.0	5.0	8.4	.7	2.9
1995[2]	.3	-.5	.9	2.6	.6	1.0	6.0	10.7	NA	3.1
1996[2]	2.0	1.5	1.9	2.1	4.2	2.6	5.8	9.4	NA	3.4

[1] National accounts implicit private consumption deflator. [2] Forecast. *Source: Organization for Economic Co-operation and Development (OECD)*

United Kingdom--Economic Statistics   Percentage Change from Previous Period

Year	Real GDP	Nominal GDP	Real Private Consump-tion	Real Public Consump-tion	Grossed Fixed Investment	Real Total Domestic Demand	Real Exports of Goods & Services	Real Im orts of Goods & Services	Consumer Prices[1]	Unem-ployment Rate
1987	4.8	10.0	5.3	1.0	10.3	5.3	5.8	7.8	4.1	9.8
1988	5.0	11.3	7.5	.7	13.9	7.9	.5	12.6	4.9	7.8
1989	2.2	9.4	3.2	1.4	6.0	2.9	4.7	7.4	7.8	6.1
1990	.4	6.8	.6	2.5	-3.5	-.6	5.0	.5	9.5	5.9
1991	-2.0	4.4	-2.2	2.6	-9.5	-3.1	-.7	-5.3	5.9	8.2
1992	-.5	3.8	0	-.1	-1.5	.2	4.0	6.5	3.7	9.9
1993	2.3	5.6	2.6	.3	.6	2.1	3.3	2.8	1.6	10.2
1994	3.8	6.1	3.0	2.0	3.7	3.3	8.2	6.1	2 5	9.2
1995[2]	2.7	4.6	2.0	.7	2.2	1.9	4.9	2.2	NA	8.4
1996[2]	2.4	5.0	2.3	1.4	4.8	2.5	6.2	6.5	NA	8.2

[1] National accounts implicit private consumption deflator. [2] Forecast. *Source: Organization for Economic Co-operation and Development (OECD)*

France--Economic Statistics   Percentage Change from Previous Period

Year	Real GDP	Nominal GDP	Real Private Consump-tion	Real Public Consump-tion	Grossed Fixed Investment	Real Total Domestic Demand	Real Exports of Goods & Services	Real Imports of Goods & Services	Consumer Prices[1]	Unem-ployment Rate
1987	2.3	5.3	2.9	2.8	4.8	3.3	3.1	7.7	3.1	10.5
1988	4.5	7.5	3.3	3.4	9.6	4.7	8.1	8.6	2.7	10.0
1989	4.3	7.4	3.1	.5	7.9	3.9	10.2	8.1	3.6	9.4
1990	2.5	5.7	2.7	2.1	2.8	2.8	5.4	6.1	3.4	8.9
1991	.8	4.1	1.4	2.8	0	.6	4.1	3.0	3.2	9.4
1992	1.3	3.5	1.4	3.4	-3.1	.4	4.9	1.1	2.4	10.3
1993	-1.5	1.0	.2	3.3	-5.8	-2.3	-.4	-3.4	2.1	11.7
1994	2.9	4.2	1.5	1.1	1.6	3.1	5.8	6.8	1.7	12.2
1995[2]	2.7	4.8	2.0	1.5	3.0	2.1	6.8	4.6	NA	11.5
1996[2]	2.2	4.3	2.0	.9	3.8	2.3	5.0	5.6	NA	11.3

[1] National accounts implicit private consumption deflator. [2] Forecast. *Source: Organization for Economic Co-operation and Development (OECD)*

Germany[2]--Economic Statistics   Percentage Change from Previous Period

Year	Real GDP	Nominal GDP	Real Private Consump-tion	Real Public Consump-tion	Gr ssed Fixed Investment	Real Total Domestic Demand	Real Exports of Goods & Services	Real Imports of Goods & Services	Consumer Prices[1]	Unem-ployment Rate
1987	1.5	3.4	3.4	1.5	1.8	2.4	.4	4.2	.2	7.6
1988	3.7	5.3	2.7	2.1	4.4	3.6	5.5	5.1	1.3	7.6
1989	3.6	6.1	2.8	-1.6	6.3	2.9	10.2	8.3	2.8	6.9
1990	5.7	9.1	5.4	2.2	8.5	5.2	11.0	10.3	2.7	6.2
1991	5.0	9.1	5.6	.5	6.0	4.8	12.3	12.8	3.6	6.7
1992	2.2	7.8	2.6	5.0	3.5	2.8	-.3	2.2	4.0	7.7
1993	-1.2	2.6	.5	-.5	-5.6	-1.3	-4.7	-5.2	3.6	8.9
1994	2.9	5.	.9	1.2	4.3	2.8	7.5	7.1	2.6	9.6
1995[3]	2.1	4.5	1.8	2.1	2.2	2.0	3.8	3.1	NA	9.3
1996[3]	2.4	4.5	2.4	2.0	3.6	2.5	6.5	6.7	NA	9.3

[1] National accounts implicit private consumption deflator. [2] Data are for Western Germany only, except for foreign trade statistics. [3] Forecast.
Source: Organization for Economic Co-operatio and Development (OECD)

Iron and Steel

Iron and steel scrap is the vital raw material for the production of new steel and cast iron products. Since scrap is readily available from manufacturing operations and from the recovery of products that have reached the end of their useful lives, the steel industry and the foundry industry in the U.S. has been structured efficiently to recyle scrap and as a result is highly dependent on scrap.

According to the U.S. Bureau of Mines, the recycling of steel scrap plays an important role in the conservation of energy because remelting scrap requires much less energy than the production of steel or iron products from iron ore. In addition, the consumption of iron and steel scrap by remelting reduces the burden on landfill disposal facilities and prevents the accumulation of abandoned steel products in the environment.

Iron and steel slags are byproducts of the iron and steel industry. They are used not only in construction and roadbuilding, but also in other ways such as waste stabilization. Slags are used in road bases, concrete aggregates, fill, glass manufacturing, mineral wool, railroad ballast and soil conditioning.

Current research has focused on blast furnace slags incorporated into blended cements and used in oil well drilling and waste stabilization as well as various uses of steel slags. Most slag is used within about 50 kilometers from its source. Trucking costs make slag noncompetitive with mined aggregates at distances beyond that point.

Many of the projects involving slag in 1994 were related to highway repaving projects. Steel slag was principally used for highly skid-resistant asphalt road surfaces, road-bases and asphalic aggregates. In 1994, steel slag consumption increased by 17 percent from 1993. The National Rock and Roll Hall of Fame, located in Cleveland, Ohio, utilized ground granulated blast furnace slag as a replacement for portland cement throughout the structure's concrete.

For the January-June 1995 period, raw steel production in the U.S. was 47 million tonnes according to the American Iron and Steel Institute. Year-to-date raw steel capability utilization was 93.3 percent. For all of 1994, raw steel production in the U.S. was 91.2 million tonnes with raw steel capability utilization 93 percent. The American Metal Market reported that for the first seven months of 1995, the average composite price of no.1 heavy melting steel scrap was $134.19 per tonne while Iron Age reported the average price was $131.90 per tonne.

U.S. production of Iron Ore for the first seven months of 1995 was 35.6 million tonnes, virtually all of it from the Lake Superior district. For all of 1994, iron ore production was 58.2 million tonnes. Shipments of iron ore in the January-July 1995 period were 31.3 million tonnes. For all of 1994, shipments were 57.9 million tonnes. In July 1995, U.S. iron ore production was 5.69 million tonnes compared to 5.06 million tonnes in July 1994. Shipments were 5.87 million tonnes compared to 5.89 million in 1994. Stocks of iron ore were 7.05 million tonnes, up sharply from 5.61 million in July 1994.

U.S. imports of iron ore and agglomerates for the first half of 1995 were 7.31 million tonnes compared to 6.58 million in 1994. The major sources were Canada, Brazil, Venezuela and Australia.

World Production of Raw Steel (Ingots & Castings) In Thousands of Metric Tons

Year	Belgium	Brazil	Canada	China	Czech Republic[4]	France	Germany	Italy	Japan	Rep. of Korea	Russia[3]	Spain	Ukraine[3]	United Kindom	United States	World Total
1985	10,683	20,456	14,600	46,720	15,036	18,833	48,350	23,898	105,281	13,539	154,670	14,235	------	15,723	80,069	718,131
1986	9,771	21,234	14,101	52,070	15,112	17,624	45,101	22,883	98,277	14,554	160,553	11,976	------	14,811	74,033	712,704
1987	9,787	22,231	14,737	56,280	15,356	17,693	44,491	22,859	98,513	16,782	161,887	11,691	------	17,425	80,877	734,319
1988	11,222	24,657	14,866	59,430	15,319	19,122	49,154	23,760	105,681	19,117	163,037	11,685	------	19,013	90,650	780,318
1989	10,952	25,055	15,458	61,200	15,465	19,335	48,902	25,213	107,908	21,873	160,096	12,684	------	18,813	88,852	786,712
1990	11,419	20,567	12,281	66,100	14,877	19,032	43,981	25,439	110,339	23,125	154,414	12,705	------	17,908	89,726	771,169
1991	11,334	22,617	12,987	70,570	12,133	18,437	42,169	25,046	109,649	26,001	77,093	12,933	45,002	16,511	79,738	736,007
1992	10,332	23,939	13,840	80,953	10,846	17,965	39,720	24,843	98,100	28,061	67,018	12,111	41,768	16,215	84,323	722,000
1993[1]	10,173	25,160	14,297	88,696	6,730	17,200	37,633	25,695	99,645	33,023	58,300	12,600	32,400	16,629	88,794	728,000
1994[2]	11,200	25,700	13,900	91,500	7,090	18,000	40,800	26,100	98,300	33,700	48,800	13,600	23,800	17,400	91,200	726,000

[1] Preliminary. [2] Estimate. [3] Formerly part of the U.S.S.R.; data not reported separately until 1992. [4] Formerly part of Czechoslovakia; data not reported separately until 1993. *Source: U.S. Bureau of Mines*

Average Wholesale Prices of Iron and Steel in the U.S.

Year	No. 1 Heavy Melting Steel Scrap: Pittsburgh ($ Per Gross Ton)	No. 1 Heavy Melting Steel Scrap: Chicago ($ Per Gross Ton)	Pittsburgh Prices: Hot Rolled Sheet[2] (Cents Per Pound)	Sheet Bars: Hot Rolled	Sheet Bars: Cold Finished	Hot Rolled Strip	Carbon Steel Plates	Cold Rolled Strip	Galvanized Sheets	Rail Road Steel Scrap[3] ($ Per Gross Ton)	Used Steel Cans[4] ($ Per Gross Ton)
1985	77.43	72.89	23.60	24.10	32.00	23.49	24.50	37.24	30.15	98.03	NA
1986	74.87	73.49	21.15	24.10	32.00	23.30	18.27	37.24	27.89	94.07	NA
1987	90.58	87.22	21.92	17.12	21.23	22.50	19.29	37.24	29.97	117.65	NA
1988	113.78	113.47	21.50	17.25	21.23	22.10	21.64	37.24	31.05	150.25	NA
1989	106.80	108.33	22.21	19.60	25.21	22.10	23.50	37.24	32.48	145.23	60.18
1990	106.61	108.62	22.25	20.43	25.37	22.10	23.75	37.24	33.55	131.59	77.16
1991	95.18	95.19	22.88	20.60	25.75	23.15	24.50	38.86	35.35	129.69	89.00
1992	88.72	88.52	19.13	17.48	24.03	23.50	24.50	39.40	30.88	117.40	88.73
1993	116.30	115.26	17.25	18.44	23.83	23.50	25.12	39.40	30.90	142.18	91.79
1994[1]	136.76	131.91	17.25	NA	25.70	23.50	27.61	39.40	32.24	169.00	102.33

[1] Preliminary. [2] 10 gauge. [3] Specialties scrap. [4] Consumer buying prices. NA = Not available. *Source: American Metal Market*

IRON AND STEEL

Salient Statistics of Steel in the United States In Thousands of Net Tons

Year	Pig Iron Production	Producer Price Index for Steel Mill Products (1982=100)	Raw Steel Production — By Type of Furnace — Basic Oxygen	Open Hearth	Electric[2]	Stainless	Carbon	Alloy	Total	Net Shipments Steel Mill Products	Total — Steel Products — Exports	Imports
1986	43,952	99.7	47,885	3,330	30,390	1,689	71,413	8,505	81,606	70,263	1,215	22,355
1987	48,410	102.3	52,496	2,666	33,989	2,028	77,976	9,147	89,151	76,654	1,647	22,005
1988	55,745	110.7	57,960	5,118	36,846	2,199	86,823	10,902	99,924	83,840	2,469	22,989
1989	55,873	114.5	58,348	4,442	35,154	1,926	86,230	9,786	97,943	84,100	5,098	19,699
1990	54,750	112.1	58,471	3,496	36,939	2,037	86,590	10,279	98,606	84,981	5,001	19,401
1991	48,637	109.5	52,714	1,408	33,774	1,878	77,879	8,139	87,896	78,846	7,112	17,743
1992	52,224	106.4	57,642	NA	35,308	1,993	82,458	8,498	92,949	82,241	5,016	19,033
1993	53,082	108.2	59,353	NA	38,524	1,956	86,865	9,056	97,877	89,022	4,727	21,796
1994[1]	54,426	113.4	61,028	NA	39,551	2,023	89,535	9,022	100,579	95,084	4,852	32,705

[1] Preliminary. [2] Includes crucible sheets. NA = Not available. *Sources: American Iron & Steel Institute; U.S. Bureau of Mines*

U.S. Production of Steel Ingots, Rate of Capability Utilization[1] In Percents

Year	Jan.	Feb.	Mar.	Apr.	May	June	July	Aug.	Sept.	Oct.	Nov.	Dec.	Average
1986	69.4	71.8	71.9	73.5	69.5	63.5	59.2	52.8	54.3	56.8	56.5	54.9	63.8
1987	65.5	69.5	77.3	80.3	80.2	79.7	77.3	79.1	83.9	84.4	85.2	82.8	79.5
1988	88.1	89.7	92.2	91.4	93.1	87.4	88.0	86.6	90.1	87.7	85.8	83.8	89.2
1989	88.2	89.8	90.9	92.2	88.1	86.2	80.8	79.2	80.0	83.0	77.4	73.3	84.5
1990	83.1	85.1	85.7	85.2	85.7	84.5	82.0	85.5	84.6	85.1	83.8	75.0	84.0
1991	74.6	73.1	71.7	72.5	70.0	71.7	74.8	75.2	78.5	78.0	78.0	74.4	74.2
1992	80.5	82.4	83.5	85.3	83.5	82.1	78.9	78.7	78.3	80.9	80.4	77.7	82.2
1993	84.8	89.0	87.0	87.4	88.3	87.5	86.9	86.2	87.7	90.2	86.3	85.9	89.1
1994	87.7	92.2	91.3	91.4	91.2	88.7	87.1	87.7	90.0	92.0	92.6	94.3	93.0
	93.8	95.6	96.0	92.9	91.6	90.1	86.8	88.3					

[1] Based on tonnage capability to produce raw steel for a full order book. [2] Preliminary. *Sources: American Iron and Steel Institute; U.S. Bureau of Mines*

United States Production of Steel Ingots In Thousands of Short Tons

Year	Jan.	Feb.	Mar.	Apr.	May	June	July	Aug.	Sept.	Oct.	Nov.	Dec.	Total
1986	7,666	7,171	7,947	7,787	7,616	6,730	6,352	5,668	5,644	6,087	5,860	5,877	81,606
1987	6,248	5,992	7,375	7,402	7,641	7,349	7,324	7,494	7,694	8,073	7,882	7,916	89,151
1988	8,380	7,984	8,763	8,398	8,832	8,031	8,313	8,181	8,237	8,332	7,883	7,954	99,924
1989	8,729	8,022	8,997	8,738	8,633	8,171	7,955	7,790	7,617	8,175	7,386	7,222	97,943
1990	8,241	7,624	8,505	8,209	8,529	8,142	8,101	8,452	8,094	8,424	8,021	7,422	98,906
1991	7,577	6,608	7,283	7,089	7,076	7,017	7,338	7,386	7,457	7,711	7,461	7,348	87,896
1992	7,754	7,432	8,043	7,875	7,968	7,584	7,542	7,526	7,249	7,742	7,449	7,438	92,949
1993	7,942	7,528	8,148	7,926	8,278	7,937	8,066	8,001	7,878	8,409	7,786	8,008	97,877
1994[1]	8,003	7,598	8,323	8,180	8,437	7,941	7,996	8,053	7,993	8,477	8,256	8,684	100,579
1995[1]	8,918	8,211	9,131	8,548	8,696	8,286	8,308	8,455	8,668	8,685			

[1] Preliminary. *Source: American Iron and Steel Institute*

Shipments of Steel Products[1] by Market Classifications in the United States In Thousands of Net Tons

Year	Appliances Utensils & Cutlery	Auto-motive	Con-tainers, Packaging & Shipping Materials	Cons-truction Including Maint.	Con-tactors Products	Electrical Equip-ment	Export	Machinery, Industrial Equipment & Tools	Oil and Gas	Rail Trans-portation	Steel for Converting & Pro-cessing[2]	Steel Service Center & Dis-tributors	All Other[3]	Total Ship-ments
1986	1,648	11,889	4,113	7,336	3,278	2,113	495	2,076	1,023	798	5,635	17,478	12,381	70,263
1987	1,633	11,343	4,372	7,681	3,337	2,373	515	2,277	1,489	758	7,195	19,840	13,841	76,654
1988	1,638	12,555	4,421	8,607	3,495	2,459	1,233	2,798	1,477	1,146	8,792	21,037	14,182	83,840
1989	1,721	11,763	4,459	8,318	3,182	2,449	3,183	2,409	1,203	1,229	8,235	20,769	15,180	84,100
1990	1,540	11,100	4,474	9,245	2,870	2,453	2,487	2,388	1,892	1,080	9,441	21,111	14,900	84,981
1991	1,388	10,015	4,278	9,161	2,306	2,102	4,476	1,982	1,425	999	8,265	19,464	12,985	78,846
1992	1,503	11,092	3,974	9,536	2,694	2,136	2,650	1,951	1,454	1,052	9,226	21,328	13,645	82,241
1993	1,592	12,719	4,355	10,516	2,913	2,213	2,110	2,191	1,526	1,223	9,451	23,714	14,499	89,022
1994	1,736	14,753	4,495	10,935	3,348	2,299	1,710	2,427	1,703	1,248	10,502	24,153	15,775	95,084

[1] All grades including carbon, alloy and stainless steel. [2] Net total after deducting shipments to reporting companies for conversion or resale. [3] Includes agricultural; bolts, nuts, rivets and screws; forgings (other than automotive); shipbuilding and marine equipment; aircraft; mining, quarrying and lumbering; other domestic and commercial equipment machinery; ordnance and other direct military; seven shipments of non-reporting companies.
Source: American Iron and Steel Institute

Net Shipments of Steel Products in the United States[1] In Thousands of Net Tons

Year	Cold Finished Bars	Rails & Acces-sories	Wire Drawn	Tin Mill Products	Plates (Cut & Coils)	Sheet & Strip Galv. (Hot Dipped)	Hot Rolled Bars	Pipe & Tubing	Structural Shapes & Steel Piling	Rein-forcing Bars	Hot Rolled Sheets	Cold Rolled Sheets	Carbon	Alloy	Stain-less
1985	1,255	121	874	3,773	4,327	6,850	5,698	4,096	4,373	4,326	12,952	13,574	64,360	7,432	1,251
1986	1,257	101	802	3,801	3,565	7,224	5,648	2,836	4,233	4,299	12,167	13,250	62,520	6,556	1,187
1987	1,361	62	800	3,988	4,048	7,660	6,048	3,569	4,839	4,918	13,048	13,859	68,116	7,120	1,418
1988	1,499	118	1,073	4,069	7,328	8,115	6,460	4,443	4,860	5,091	12,969	13,871	77,702	4,552	1,586
1989	1,472	562	1,002	4,126	7,384	8,543	6,301	4,011	4,987	5,015	13,281	13,854	78,485	4,143	1,472
1990	1,486	519	918	4,031	7,945	7,878	6,655	4,652	5,670	5,305	13,388	13,199	78,818	4,647	1,516
1991	1,341	486	865	4,041	6,942	6,910	5,431	4,488	5,245	4,859	13,161	11,532	73,480	3,917	1,449
1992	1,458	562	900	3,927	7,102	8,199	5,806	4,198	5,081	4,781	13,361	12,692	76,625	4,101	1,514
1993	1,580	679	802	4,123	7,538	9,712	6,339	4,445	4,973	5,033	14,873	12,758	83,106	4,381	1,534
1994	1,786	631	788	4,137	8,556	10,943	7,088	4,965	5,506	4,929	15,654	13,016	88,505	4,859	1,720

[1] All grades, including carbon, alloy and stainless steel. *Source: American Iron and Steel Institute*

World Production of Pig Iron (Excludes Ferro-Alloys) In Thousands of Metric Tons

Year	Australia	Belgium	Brazil	Canada	China	Czech Repub.[3]	France	Ger-many	India	Italy	Japan	Poland	Russia[4]	Ukraine[4]	United Kindom	United States	World Total
1986	5,890	8,052	20,350	9,938	50,640	9,573	13,982	31,926	10,679	11,916	74,653	10,547	113,954	------	9,685	40,032	507,900
1987	5,569	8,244	21,509	10,446	55,030	9,788	13,449	31,272	11,083	11,335	73,418	10,476	115,038	------	12,017	44,034	522,720
1988	5,730	9,147	23,649	10,245	57,040	9,706	14,786	34,676	11,925	11,349	79,295	10,264	116,158	------	13,056	50,861	553,395
1989	6,094	8,868	24,621	10,849	58,200	9,911	15,071	35,197	12,420	11,795	80,197	9,488	116,628	------	12,638	50,977	561,762
1990	6,125	9,416	21,360	8,080	62,380	9,667	14,415	32,058	13,395	11,883	80,229	8,658	111,763	------	12,277	50,058	549,000
1991	5,647	9,354	22,926	8,823	67,700	8,479	13,646	30,868	15,356	10,856	79,985	6,355	90,900	------	11,883	44,510	528,000
1992	6,390	8,530	23,430	9,259	75,900	8,039	13,051	28,788	16,540	10,462	73,144	6,351	47,380	34,700	11,500	47,790	524,000
1993[1]	6,770	8,180	24,240	9,388	87,400	4,670	12,700	27,250	17,710	11,100	73,738	6,180	42,440	27,005	11,500	48,640	530,000
1994[2]	7,470	9,030	25,420	8,920	96,400	5,290	13,300	30,100	20,420	11,200	73,800	6,800	37,810	20,000	12,000	49,880	540,000

[1] Preliminary. [2] Estimate. [3] Formerly part of Czechoslovakia; data not reported separately until 1993. [4] Formerly part of the U.S.S.R.; data not reported separately until 1992. *Source: U.S. Bureau of Mines*

U.S Pig Iron Production (Excluding Production of Ferro-Alloys) In Thousands of Short Tons

Year	Jan.	Feb.	Mar.	Apr.	May	June	July	Aug.	Sept.	Oct.	Nov.	Dec.	Total
1987	3,214	3,069	3,891	4,048	4,256	4,079	4,235	4,165	4,208	4,407	4,351	4,447	48,137
1988	4,683	4,443	4,842	4,699	4,932	4,497	4,762	4,584	4,612	4,646	4,455	4,712	55,745
1989	4,964	4,654	5,112	4,990	4,917	4,707	4,604	4,172	4,403	4,692	4,322	4,202	55,873
1990	4,638	4,221	4,681	4,549	4,746	4,530	4,656	4,788	4,629	4,673	4,523	4,264	54,925
1991	4,077	3,470	4,047	3,830	3,885	3,830	4,179	4,121	4,175	4,251	4,300	4,338	48,503
1992	4,390	4,175	4,524	4,400	4,444	4,232	4,347	4,299	4,065	5,329	4,268	4,306	52,224
1993	4,503	4,503	4,454	4,328	4,555	4,351	4,522	4,504	4,367	4,652	4,218	4,514	53,103
1994[1]	3,970	3,858	3,957	4,099	4,394	4,519	4,518	4,446	4,320	4,564	4,618	4,928	54,431
1995[1]	4,820	4,453	4,916	4,568	4,674	4,499	4,576	4,688	4,727	4,687			

[1] Preliminary. *Source: American Iron and Steel Institute*

Salient Statistics of Ferrous Scrap & Pig Iron in the U.S. In Thousands of Metric Tons

	Consumption: Ferrous Scrap & Pig Iron Charged To												Stocks--Dec. 31 Ferrous Scrap & Pig Iron at Consumers		
	Mfg. of Pig Iron & Steel Ingots & Castings			Iron Foundries & Misc. Users			Mfg. of Steel Castings	All Uses			Imports of	Exports of			
Year	Scrap	Pig Iron	Total	Scrap	Pig Iron	Total	(Scrap)	Ferrous Scrap	Pig Iron	Grand Total	Scrap[2]	Scrap[3]	Scrap	Pig Iron	Total Stocks
1986	45,053	40,211	85,264	13,034	1,113	14,147	1,657	59,745	41,372	101,117	657	10,618	3,941	171	4,112
1987	46,870	44,421	91,291	13,371	955	14,326	1,723	61,964	45,387	107,351	765	9,405	4,394	255	4,649
1988	51,054	52,163	103,217	16,513	1,393	17,906	2,126	69,692	53,567	123,259	942	9,161	4,131	188	4,319
1989	52,733	50,210	102,943	13,270	892	14,162	1,894	67,897	51,122	119,019	1,016	11,149	4,293	246	4,539
1990	54,361	49,337	103,698	13,085	835	13,920	1,850	69,296	50,193	119,489	1,324	11,580	4,292	147	4,439
1991	48,778	44,095	92,873	11,126	656	11,782	1,609	61,513	44,765	106,278	1,073	9,502	4,072	190	4,262
1992	50,144	47,263	97,407	11,444	619	12,063	1,640	63,228	47,894	111,122	1,316	9,262	3,752	181	3,933
1993	53,084	48,092	101,176	12,658	676	13,334	1,900	68,000	48,777	116,777	1,390	9,805	3,725	220	3,945
1994[1]	53,801	50,257	104,057	14,000	1,000	15,000	2,000	70,000	51,000	121,000	1,710	8,813	4,100	400	4,500

[1] Preliminary. [2] Includes tinplate and terneplate. [3] Excludes used rails for rerolling and other uses and ships, boats, and other vessels for scrapping.
Source: U.S. Bureau of Mines

IRON AND STEEL

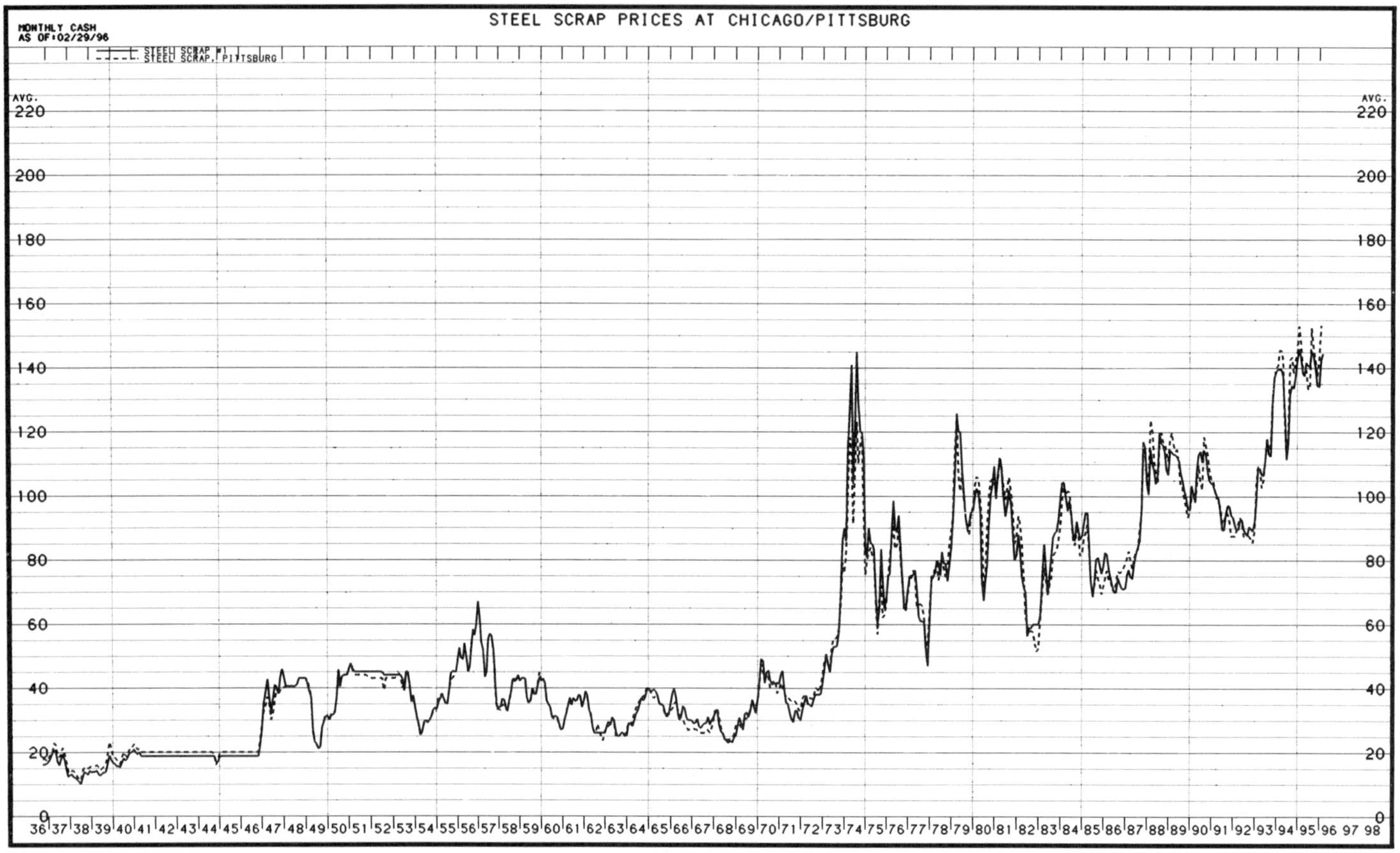

Consumption of Pig Iron in the U.S. by Type of Furance or Equipment In Thousands of Metric Tons

Year	Open Hearth	Electric	Cupola	Basic Oxygen Process	Air & Other Furnace	Direct Casting	Total
1983	3,554	309	386	40,216	83	875	45,424
1984	5,187	334	425	41,324	83	909	48,265
1985	4,297	456	455	40,384	51	998	46,640
1986	2,109	284	388	37,723	53	816	41,372
1987	1,866	1,322	336	38,468	51	891	39,790
1988	3,500	1,269	679	47,199	40	879	53,567
1989	1,582	1,051	389	49,380	30	536	52,969
1990	2,072	982	332	47,307	19	387	51,100
1991	997	574	265	42,955	13	106	44,911
1992	------	429	215	47,194	7	49	47,894
1993[1]	------	519	292	47,848	34	84	48,777
1994[2]	------	1,700	520	49,138	4	39	51,000

[1] Preliminary. [2] Estimate. *Source: U.S. Bureau of Mines*

Wholesale Price of No. 1 Heavy Melting Steel Scrap at Chicago In Dollars Per Gross Ton

Year	Jan.	Feb.	Mar.	Apr.	May	June	July	Aug.	Sept.	Oct.	Nov.	Dec.	Average
1983	56.14	67.00	77.70	70.33	65.00	70.52	70.08	74.00	78.00	78.00	78.30	84.00	72.42
1984	88.29	89.00	87.09	85.14	85.00	84.71	79.00	78.00	81.00	81.09	83.00	76.00	83.12
1985	78.86	82.16	84.76	79.59	68.00	62.00	64.24	73.00	72.00	71.87	69.00	69.19	72.89
1986	74.23	76.89	74.05	74.00	74.00	71.00	71.00	76.71	73.14	70.87	73.00	73.00	73.49
1987	78.00	78.00	73.00	72.00	74.15	77.00	78.73	84.00	96.52	116.00	115.47	103.73	87.22
1988	100.80	119.43	119.02	117.24	111.38	108.55	120.00	119.78	115.00	115.00	109.16	106.33	113.47
1989	114.10	118.32	113.00	113.00	113.00	113.00	108.00	108.00	108.00	101.09	96.00	94.50	108.33
1990	104.00	102.29	98.00	109.43	114.55	111.67	108.50	116.00	113.76	112.50	107.73	105.00	108.62
1991	104.76	100.74	98.00	97.80	93.18	87.50	87.74	94.14	98.50	97.50	91.97	90.50	95.19
1992	90.50	90.50	90.50	90.50	89.70	87.68	87.50	87.55	88.50	85.50	85.50	88.36	88.52
1993	98.34	109.50	109.50	106.50	106.50	111.27	118.50	114.18	113.50	125.88	131.50	138.00	115.26
1994	138.00	138.00	138.00	138.00	123.64	110.50	117.20	133.63	134.50	132.50	137.50	141.50	131.91
1995	152.05	147.50	140.20	141.50	144.50	141.64	141.50	149.76	144.90	141.50	136.50	136.50	143.17

Source: American Metal Market

World Production of Iron Ore[3], by Specific Countries — In Thousands of Metric Tons (Gross Weight)

Year	Australia	Brazil	Canada	Chile	China	France	India	Maur-itania	Mexico	North Korea	Russia[4]	South Africa	Sweden	Ukraine[4]	United States	Vene-zula	World Total
1984	89,046	113,132	39,930	6,685	75,000	14,839	41,026	9,527	8,317	8,000	247,104	24,647	18,123	------	52,092	13,054	829,349
1985	97,447	128,251	39,502	6,534	80,000	14,447	42,545	9,333	7,820	8,000	247,639	24,414	20,454	------	49,533	14,710	860,556
1986	94,015	129,405	36,167	6,981	90,000	12,437	47,800	9,170	7,298	8,500	249,959	24,483	20,475	------	39,486	16,753	863,650
1987	101,748	134,497	37,702	6,637	113,000	11,267	51,018	9,002	7,523	8,500	250,874	22,008	19,636	------	47,648	17,782	902,737
1988	99,450	146,008	39,934	7,710	154,380	9,872	49,961	10,004	8,431	9,000	249,754	25,248	20,440	------	57,515	18,932	967,218
1989	105,810	157,900	40,509	9,030	171,850	9,368	53,418	12,110	15,000	9,500	241,348	29,958	21,763	------	59,032	18,053	1,013,383
1990	110,508	152,300	34,855	7,903	168,300	8,729	53,700	11,590	15,000	10,000	236,000	30,291	19,877	------	56,408	20,119	983,000
1991	117,134	152,000	36,383	8,692	176,070	7,472	56,900	10,246	13,000	10,000	199,000	29,100	19,328	------	56,800	21,296	956,000
1992	112,000	146,000	32,697	7,640	197,600	5,707	54,900	8,202	15,000	10,500	82,100	28,226	19,277	75,700	55,593	18,070	949,000
1993[1]	120,534	159,000	30,568	6,520	234,600	3,520	55,800	9,300	15,000	10,500	76,100	29,385	18,728	65,000	55,651	16,851	983,000
1994[2]	128,000	166,000	36,600	6,400	240,000	2,550	57,000	9,000	15,000	11,000	73,300	32,300	19,700	51,300	58,400	16,100	995,000

[1] Preliminary. [2] Estimate. [3] Iron ore, iron ore concentrates and iron ore agglomerates. [4] Formerly part of the U.S.S.R.; data not reported separately until 1992. *Source: U.S. Bureau of Mines*

Salient Statistics of Iron Ore[3] in the U.S. — In Thousands of Metric Tons

Year	Net Import Reliance % of Apparent Consumption	Production: Total	Production: Lake Superior	Production: Other Regions	Ship-ments	Value Million $ (at Mine)	Average Value $ at Mine Per Ton	Stocks--Dec. 31: Mines	Stocks--Dec. 31: Con-suming Plants	Stocks--Dec. 31: Lake Erie Docks	Imports	Exports	Con-sumption	Value Million $ Imports
1984	19	52,092	50,476	1,616	51,700	2,247.7	43.48	5,349	24,403	2,989	17,463	5,073	73,678	529.1
1985	21	49,533	48,148	1,385	50,204	2,076.7	41.37	6,046	21,631	2,442	16,024	5,114	71,708	452.3
1986	33	39,486	38,203	1,283	41,991	1,472.5	35.07	3,307	17,439	2,019	17,011	4,553	62,097	460.6
1987	22	47,648	46,756	892	47,983	1,503.1	31.33	2,402	16,565	2,056	16,849	5,093	67,768	408.8
1988	18	57,515	56,038	1,477	57,113	1,716.7	30.06	2,957	18,005	2,537	20,183	5,285	83,694	484.5
1989	22	59,032	56,981	2,052	58,299	1,939.9	33.27	4,575	15,730	2,171	19,596	5,365	80,447	522.3
1990	21	56,408	54,628	1,780	57,010	1,570.0	27.52	4,795	15,911	2,273	18,054	3,199	76,855	559.5
1991	11	56,761	55,636	1,124	56,775	1,530.0	26.91	4,853	17,612	2,981	13,335	4,045	66,366	436.8
1992	12	55,593	55,018	575	55,569	1,550.0	27.81	3,783	16,093	2,981	12,504	5,055	75,067	395.8
1993[1]	14	55,661	54,814	848	56,251	1,510.0	26.87	2,504	16,548	2,288	14,097	5,061	76,800	419.0
1994[2]	18	58,215	57,848	367	57,917	1,580.0	27.44	2,750	16,300	2,230	17,513	4,975	76,900	499.0

[1] Preliminary. [2] Estimate. [3] Usable iron ore exclusive of ore containing 5% or more manganese and includes byproduct ore. *Source: U.S. Bureau of Mines*

U.S. Imports (for Consumption) of Iron Ore[2] from Principal Countries — In Thousands of Metric Tons

Year	Australia	Brazil	Canada	Chile	Maur-itania	Peru	Sweden	Vene-zuela	Total
1984	-----	2,298	10,152	-----	-----	6	76	1,383	15,592
1985	-----	2,304	7,763	149	-----	110	59	1,876	14,307
1986	10	3,752	8,836	94	66	92	106	2,346	17,011
1987	194	3,698	7,981	636	412	84	139	2,622	16,849
1988	1,076	4,935	9,157	139	522	181	88	3,568	20,183
1989	394	5,169	8,538	61	594	186	57	4,232	19,596
1990	14	4,276	9,344	138	666	59	54	3,503	18,054
1991	-----	2,481	7,299	103	459	157	51	2,763	13,335
1992	163	2,442	6,834	107	280	70	64	2,540	12,504
1993	254	2,872	7,442	68	206	1	60	3,170	14,097
1994[1]	675	3,610	10,073	134	124	0	45	2,780	17,513

[1] Preliminary. [2] Including agglomerates. *Source: U.S. Bureau of Mines*

Total[1] Iron Ore Stocks at End of Month in the U.S. — In Thousands of Metric Tons

Year	Jan.	Feb.	Mar.	Apr.	May	June	July	Aug.	Sept.	Oct.	Nov.	Dec.
1986	26,829	25,770	24,743	23,618	24,652	24,677	24,546	23,047	23,331	23,251	22,336	21,783
1987	21,472	21,406	20,580	19,571	18,875	19,008	19,235	19,085	19,343	19,994	20,264	20,613
1988	20,997	20,925	20,041	20,119	19,789	19,341	19,835	20,801	22,210	22,140	22,485	22,755
1989	23,189	23,252	22,685	21,145	21,670	21,544	22,286	22,275	22,588	21,429	21,448	22,476
1990	22,088	21,986	20,958	20,609	20,501	21,019	21,863	22,110	22,268	22,027	22,042	22,978
1991	22,572	22,218	21,316	20,757	21,756	23,174	23,319	24,329	25,148	25,117	25,358	25,445
1992	24,527	23,162	20,922	20,550	21,501	22,492	23,046	21,721	22,735	23,190	23,433	22,856
1993	21,296	20,806	19,235	18,996	19,180	22,036	22,905	21,575	22,629	21,355	21,615	21,341
1994[2]	19,013	17,816	15,953	14,883	15,251	16,592	17,864	18,931	20,554	20,760	21,552	21,339
1995[2]	20,316	19,330	18,200	18,340	19,369	20,905	22,336	23,668				

[1] All stocks at mines, furnance yards and at U.S. docks. [2] Preliminary. *Source: U.S. Bureau of Mines*

KR-CRB Futures Index

The Commodity Research Bureau Futures Price Index was first calculated by Commodity Research Bureau, Inc. in 1957 and made its innaugural appearance in the 1958 CRB Commodity Year Book.

The Index was originally comprised of two cash markets and 26 futures markets which were traded on exchanges in the U.S. and Canada. It included barley and flaxseed from the Winnipeg exchange; cocoa, coffee "B", copper, cotton, cottonseed oil, grease wool, hides, lead, potatoes, rubber, sugar #4, sugar #6, wool tops and zinc from New York exchanges; and corn, oats, wheat, rye, soybeans, soybean oil, soybean meal, lard, onions, and eggs from Chicago exchanges. In addition to those 26, the Index also included the spot New Orleans cotton and Minneapolis wheat markets.

Like the Bureau of Labor Statistics spot index, the CRB Futures Price Index is calculated to produce an unweighted geometric mean of the individual commodity price relatives. In other words, a ratio of the current price to the base year average price. Currently, 1967 is the base year the Index is calculated against (1967 = 100.00).

The formula considers all future delivery contracts which expire on or before the end of the sixth calendar month from the current date, up to a maximum of five delivery months per commodity. However, a minimum of two delivery months must be used to calculate the current price, even if the second contract is outside of the six month window. Contracts are excluded from the calculation when in their delivery period.

The 1995 closing Index value of 243.18 was 2.76 percent higher than 1994's close of 236.64 and marked the third consecutive annual increase. Six of the eight sub-indices advanced in 1995, led by a 47.71 percent rise in grains.

Futures Markets

Futures and options on the KR-CRB Index are traded on the New York Futures Exchange (NYFE).

KR-CRB Component Commodities by Group

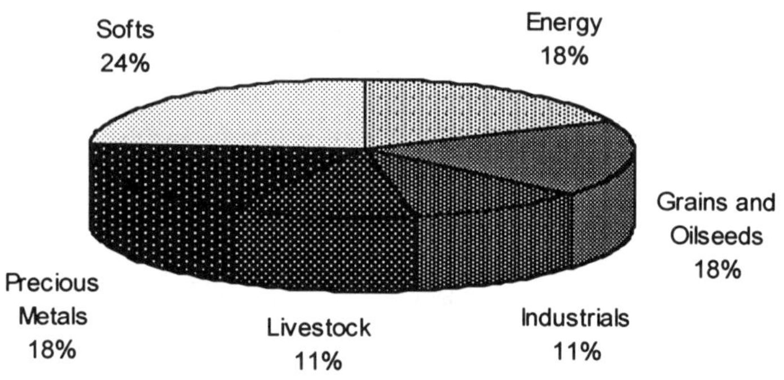

Groups:	*Components:*
Energy -	Crude Oil, Heating Oil, Natural Gas
Grains and Oilseeds-	Corn, Soybeans, Wheat
Industrials -	Copper, Cotton
Livestock -	Live Cattle, Live Hogs
Precious Metals -	Gold, Platinum. Silver
Softs -	Cocoa, Coffee, Orange Juice, Sugar

The KR-CRB Index is computed using a three-step process:

1) Each of the Index's 17 component commodities is arithmetically averaged using the prices for all of the designated contract months which expire on or before the end of the sixth calendar month from the current date, except that: a) no contract shall be included in the calculation while in delivery; b) there shall be a minimum of two contract months for each component commodity (adding contracts beyond the six month window, if necessary); c) there shall be a maximum of five contract months for each commodity (dropping the most deferred contracts to remain at five, if necessary). The result is that the Index extends six to seven months into the future depending on where one is in the current month. For example, live cattle's average price on October 30, 1995 would be computed as follows:

$$\text{Cattle Average} = \frac{\text{Dec. '95 + Feb. '96}}{2}$$

2) These 17 component averages are then geometrically averaged by multiplying all of the numbers together and taking the 17th root.

$$\text{Geometric Average} = 17\ \sqrt{\text{Crude Avg. x Heating Avg. x ...Sugar Avg.}}$$

3) The resulting average is divided by 30.7766, the 1967 base-year average for these 17 commodities. That result is then multiplied by an adjustment factor of .8486. This adjustment factor is necessitated by the nine revisions to the Index since its inception in 1957. Finally, that result is multiplied by 100 in order to convert the Index into percentage terms:

$$\text{KR-CRB Index} = \frac{\text{Current Geometric Average}}{\text{1967 Geometric Avg. (30.7766)}} \text{ x .8486 x 100}$$

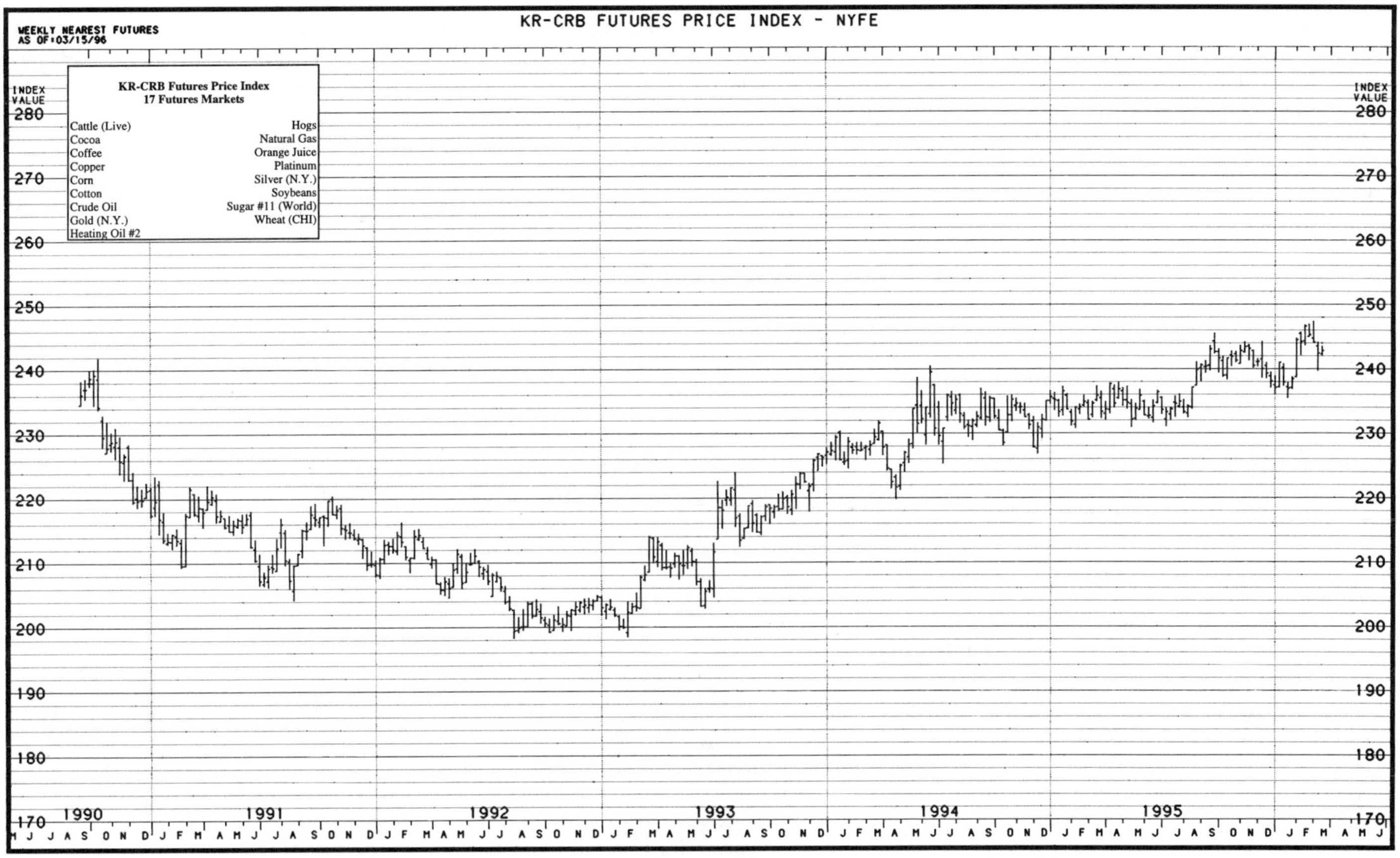

Average Open Interest of Knight-Ridder CRB Futures at New York In Contracts

Year	Jan.	Feb.	Mar.	Apr.	May	June	July	Aug.	Sept.	Oct.	Nov.	Dec.
1988	2,597	2,607	2,682	2,819	3,592	3,934	2,846	2,795	2,659	2,419	2,529	2,556
1989	2,679	3,008	2,491	2,274	2,117	2,104	1,891	1,992	1,861	1,907	2,215	2,209
1990	1,889	1,229	1,476	1,858	1,499	1,459	1,289	1,286	1,181	1,247	1,505	1,530
1991	1,443	1,593	1,524	1,620	1,511	1,524	1,168	1,071	1,045	1,172	1,357	1,383
1992	1,435	1,472	1,185	1,347	1,311	1,087	951	1,179	1,075	1,226	1,283	1,406
1993	1,969	1,984	1,842	2,201	2,564	2,947	2,616	2,409	2,128	2,383	2,432	2,351
1994	2,607	3,146	2,680	2,691	2,339	2,698	3,838	5,146	4,562	4,942	4,535	2,800
1995	2,144	2,164	2,147	2,370	2,016	2,144	2,053	2,070	2,062	1,942	2,003	1,640

Source: New York Futures Exchange

Volume of Trading of Knight-Ridder CRB Futures at New York In Contracts

Year	Jan.	Feb.	Mar.	Apr.	May	June	July	Aug.	Sept.	Oct.	Nov.	Dec.	Total
1988	9,557	10,726	13,841	9,480	20,299	43,591	31,043	22,020	15,615	9,044	9,691	11,044	205,951
1989	8,805	10,045	12,035	11,437	13,145	13,824	11,917	9,846	7,918	7,412	9,613	8,551	124,548
1990	6,505	5,829	7,042	6,670	7,191	6,687	6,477	6,415	4,096	4,744	4,409	3,842	69,907
1991	5,835	5,391	6,715	6,432	3,671	5,557	4,853	5,876	4,414	3,766	4,132	4,543	61,185
1992	4,895	6,031	4,136	5,697	5,496	4,487	4,162	4,617	3,874	3,183	5,277	4,400	56,255
1993	3,620	5,720	8,050	7,340	8,680	10,722	12,418	8,590	6,192	4,350	8,535	6,954	91,908
1994	6,956	7,473	10,085	10,274	11,298	14,652	10,560	8,967	7,445	6,575	10,186	5,515	109,986
1995	6,151	5,545	5,763	7,955	7,877	7,573	6,875	10,094	7,376	5,030	5,865	5,309	81,413

Source: New York Futures Exchange

Lard

Production of lard is directly related to commercial pork production. *Oil World*, a trade publication, indicated that world production of lard, tallow and greases was projected to increase by two percent in 1994-95 (October-September). This compared with an expansion of 2.5 percent in 1994-94. Due to lower stocks at the beginning of the season, world disappearance of lard, tallow and greases was expected to slow to one percent from three percent in 1993-94. It was expected that the growth in lard and tallow output would occur primarily in the U.S. and China, whereas production in Western and Eastern Europe will probably stagnate, while output in the former Soviet Union would decline. World production of red meats was expected to reach record levels in calendar year 1995 with growth accelerating from 1994.

Oil World indicated that world disappearance of lard was expected to rise by two percent to 5.68 million tonnes in the 1994-95 (October-September) year. Most of the increase was expected to occur in China and the U.S., whereas usage in the European Community was expected to hold about steady at 1.23 million tonnes.

The U.S. Department of Agriculture estimates that 1995 beginning stocks of lard were 40 million pounds, up 16 percent from 1994. U.S. production of lard in 1995 was forecast at 1.045 billion pounds, down three percent versus a year ago. Imports of lard were expected to be minimal at two billion pounds, leaving total supply at 1.087 billion pounds.

Domestic disappearance of lard was projected to be 910 million pounds, unchanged from 1994. Use has been rising for several years. Exports of lard were expected to decline to 135 million pounds, down 16 percent from 1994. Total disappearance was put at 1.045 million pounds, down about two percent from last season. Ending stocks were projected to remain at 40 million pounds. Per capita consumption of lard has been running between three and four pounds.

World Production of Lard In Thousands of Metric Tons

Year Beginning Oct. 1	Brazil	Canada	China	Czecho-slovak	France	Germany	Italy	Japan	Poland	Romania	Spain	Taiwan	United States	Former U.S.S.R.	World Total
1988-9	147.5	79.0	1,438.3	124.6	126.5	518.7	181.0	91.0	137.7	130.4	154.8	54.9	426.2	852.1	5,382.8
1989-90	151.0	75.6	1,519.5	123.9	129.2	534.4	178.5	91.0	136.8	130.1	156.1	59.1	412.3	844.4	5,441.8
1990-1	158.6	75.6	1,605.6	112.4	137.3	476.3	187.6	87.0	150.1	129.0	169.7	65.5	415.0	762.8	5,448.1
1991-2	165.7	76.9	1,710.2	111.0	140.4	411.3	188.0	85.0	156.9	117.7	170.6	66.7	447.7	653.6	5,368.3
1992-3[1]	175.5	77.0	1,813.1	96.8	150.4	418.2	192.0	85.8	148.7	113.7	185.8	68.9	445.0	567.9	5,427.0
1993-4[2]	186.2	76.0	2,020.9	88.0	155.6	409.6	190.4	82.4	122.6	114.3	186.6	69.9	451.0	509.6	5,562.5
1994-5[3]	199.3	78.3	2,104.0	87.8	156.2	404.1	192.3	81.0	134.7	114.6	185.6	71.6	475.0	454.9	5,644.6

[1] Preliminary. [2] Estimate. [3] Forecast. *Source: Oil World*

Supply and Distribution of Lard in the United States In Millions of Pounds

Year	Supply: Production	Supply: Stocks Oct. 1	Supply: Total Supply	Disappearance: Domestic	Disappearance: Baking or Frying Fats	Disappearance: Margarine[2]	Disappearance: Exports	Disappearance: Total Disappearance	Disappearance: Direct Use	Disappearance: Per Capita (Lbs.)
1987	915	29	885	787	224	22	120	852	441	3.1
1988	940	39	965	811	265	35	127	928	433	3.2
1989	909	42	972	845	295	32	85	940	442	3.3
1990	934	23	960	825	264	35	110	936	439	3.3
1991	1,016	24	1,043	885	274	43	131	1,016	424	3.3
1992	1,011	27	1,041	886	310	37	129	1,015	439	3.5
1993	1,015	26	1,044	890	296	31	119	1,009	573	3.4
1994[1]	1,053	34	1,089	924	306	42	140	1,065	585	3.4
1995[1]	1,025	24	1,061	908			113	1,021		

[1] Preliminary. [2] Includes edible tallow. *Source: Economic Research Service, U.S. Department of Agriculture*

Consumption (Edible & Inedible) of Lard in the United States In Millions of Pounds

Year	Jan.	Feb.	Mar.	Apr.	May	June	July	Aug.	Sept.	Oct.	Nov.	Dec.	Total
1987	20.2	22.1	25.9	21.3	18.5	28.0	26.8	22.3	33.0	27.4	26.3	32.4	304.2
1988	25.6	27.7	31.1	29.3	28.5	27.4	25.9	28.0	37.9	34.6	36.3	35.3	367.6
1989	28.9	27.5	34.0	31.1	33.5	32.2	28.9	33.5	34.1	39.0	42.5	32.7	397.9
1990	27.0	27.3	30.9	26.3	32.1	29.2	22.8	32.0	31.3	34.6	33.8	30.6	384.9
1991	----------	97.3	----------	----------	94.7	----------	----------	95.2	----------	----------	105.9	----------	393.1
1992	33.9	31.6	39.9	40.0	38.7	39.6	42.9	41.1	47.6	46.4	41.0	37.2	479.7
1993	40.1	34.4	45.9	36.8	38.2	38.8	32.6	38.4	41.8	44.0	43.0	40.3	474.3
1994	33.5	33.9	36.2	34.6	35.9	34.4	32.4	37.5	43.4	43.8	44.7	41.7	452.0
1995[1]	37.5	34.7	41.2	36.2	42.2	44.4	34.9	35.9	35.9	40.1	38.9		

[1] Preliminary. *Source: Bureau of Census, U.S. Department of Commerce*

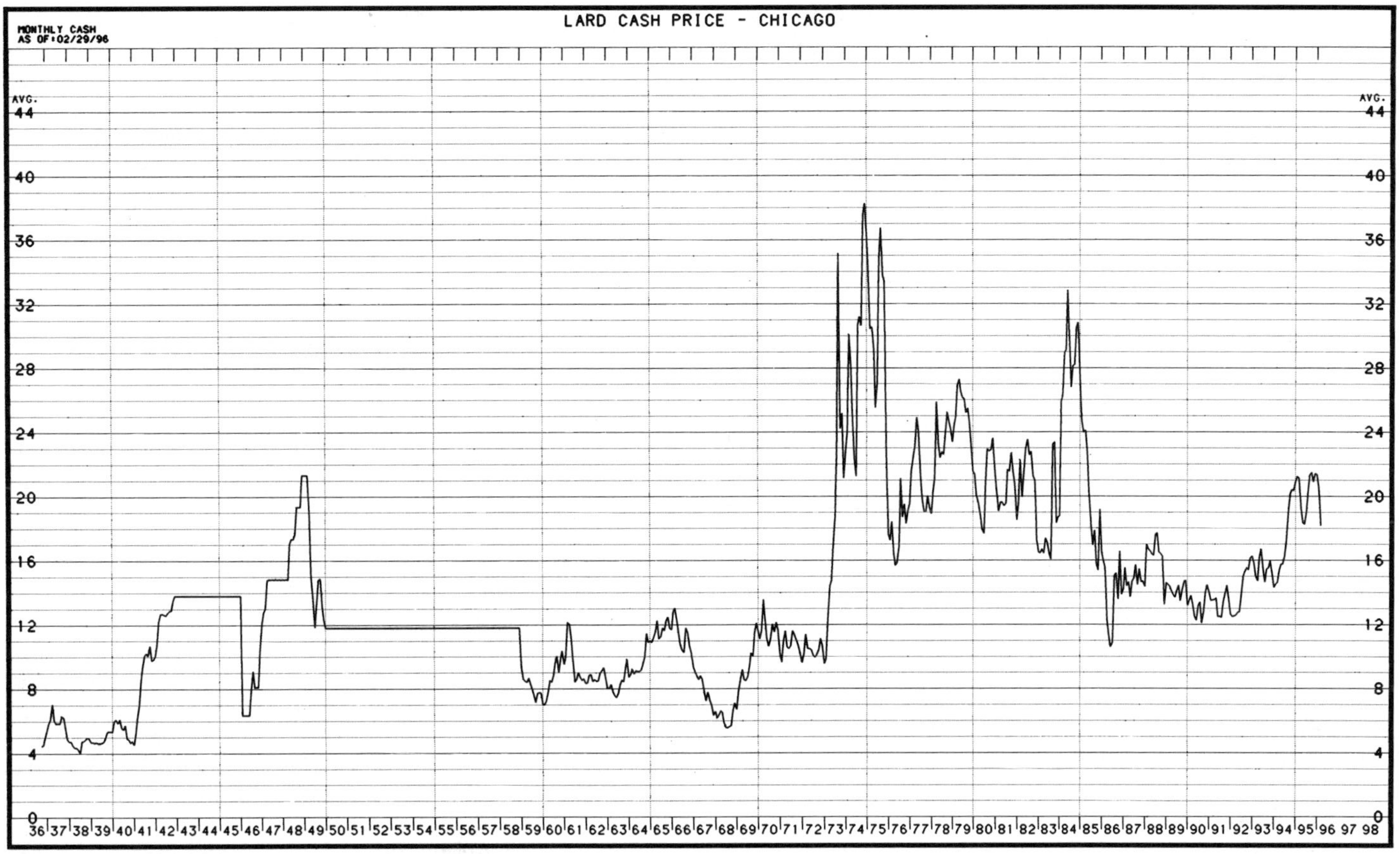

Average Wholesale Price of Lard--Loose, Tank Cars, Chicago In Cents Per Pound

Year	Jan.	Feb.	Mar.	Apr.	May	June	July	Aug.	Sept.	Oct.	Nov.	Dec.	Average
1986	16.00	15.50	12.30	11.30	10.60	11.30	14.90	15.20	13.60	16.50	13.90	14.20	13.78
1987	15.50	14.40	14.60	13.70	14.70	14.90	15.70	14.50	15.50	14.70	14.70	14.40	14.78
1988	17.00	16.70	16.60	16.40	16.30	17.60	17.70	16.50	16.40	16.30	13.20	14.60	16.28
1989	14.50	14.40	14.10	13.80	13.70	14.10	14.40	13.50	14.20	14.60	14.80	13.20	14.11
1990	13.50	13.80	13.20	12.50	12.30	13.20	13.40	12.10	12.70	14.00	14.50	14.10	13.28
1991	13.50	13.50	13.50	13.70	12.50	12.50	12.40	13.40	14.00	14.40	13.60	12.20	13.27
1992	12.50	12.50	12.60	12.60	13.90	15.00	15.00	15.30	15.50	15.40	16.10	16.30	14.39
1993	15.80	15.00	14.70	16.20	16.70	15.50	14.60	15.40	15.50	15.90	15.30	14.30	15.41
1994	14.50	14.60	15.40	15.70	15.80	16.30	17.20	18.90	20.10	20.40	20.40	20.90	17.52
1995	21.21	21.13	19.25	18.34	18.25	19.02	20.25	21.30	21.48	20.90	21.38	21.35	20.32

Source: Knight-Ridder Financial

United States Cold Storage Holdings of all Lard[1], on First of Month In Millions of Pounds

Year	Jan.	Feb.	Mar.	Apr.	May	June	July	Aug.	Sept.	Oct.	Nov.	Dec.
1986	35.4	37.6	36.4	40.8	39.8	35.5	27.3	32.1	28.3	21.6	30.6	28.9
1987	21.9	31.5	30.9	27.2	28.9	29.9	27.4	27.8	28.9	28.8	38.2	36.2
1988	33.0	37.2	33.8	37.1	31.2	31.9	37.8	41.1	30.1	39.0	41.7	36.7
1989	37.4	38.2	37.1	27.3	34.2	37.6	41.3	32.4	28.9	41.6	29.0	36.6
1990	32.0	33.7	37.6	28.5	31.6	27.4	25.2	25.9	22.8	22.9	22.2	30.3
1991	----------	24.4	----------	----------	28.3	----------	----------	24.0	----------	----------	24.1	----------
1992	37.4	27.2	28.9	28.3	26.7	23.2	24.8	29.2	26.9	27.2	22.2	24.8
1993	22.7	25.9	27.2	24.0	22.8	25.8	31.1	27.4	23.6	26.2	24.6	30.1
1994	37.7	38.0	31.8	28.8	25.1	27.4	27.0	25.5	29.7	34.4	34.0	35.8
1995[2]	40.6	50.3	46.4	43.0	36.8	27.1	25.8	22.1	30.2	24.3	19.9	20.6

[1] Stocks in factories and warehouses (except that in hands of retailers). [2] Preliminary. *Source: Bureau of Census, U.S. Department of Commerce*

Lead

Lead finds widespread use in batteries, fuel tanks, ammunition, building construction, electrical equipment, cans and containers, and as solder for pipes and plumbings. Lead and compounds that contain lead are very toxic. As a result, there has been a concerted effort to reduce the use of lead, especially in areas where humans are exposed to it. Substitutes for lead include plastic, aluminum, tin and iron. There has been research into the use of bismuth as a non-toxic substitute for lead in a variety of uses from solder to ceramic glazes. There continues to be extensive research into the use of other materials to make automobile batteries, a major user of lead. Research is currently focusing on substituting lithium-polymer materials for lead which would provide distinct advantages. Lithium is the lightest metal on the atomic chart while lead is one of the heaviest. Other components of these new batteries are plastics and hydrocarbons, also light materials.

There were several proposed rules issued by Government agencies during 1994 which would impact the regulation of new and existing uses and clean-up activities in lead. There were also proposed rules about the disclosure of information regarding the potential risks of lead. A final rule was issued on containment level goals and regulations for drinking water. There were two reports completed that concluded the need for additional protection from lead risk for children in tenant-based housing and the need for standards to ensure availability of lead-based paint hazard insurance for property owners and for contractors involved in lead abatement activities.

The Environmental Protection Agency issued a proposed rule in March 1994 that would effectively ban the use of certain lead and zinc fishing sinkers. The proposed rule would ban the manufacture, import and processing of fishing sinkers containing lead or zinc which are one inch or less in any dimension for use in the U.S. The rule would not prohibit manufacturing these sinkers solely for export.

U.S. lead mine production increased by 2 percent in 1994, following a three year decline. Missouri was the dominant producing state with an 80 percent share, followed by Alaska, Idaho and Montana. Lead was produced at 16 mines which employed about 1,300 people. Primary lead was processed at two smelter-refineries in Missouri, a smelter in Montana and a refinery in Nebraska.

Lead was consumed in 200 plants in the manufacture of end-use products, including batteries, ammunition, covering for power and communication cable, building construction materials, solder for motor vehicles, metal containers and electrical components.

Lead-acid batteries continued to be the dominant user of lead, accounting for about 84 percent of lead consumption in 1994. The Battery Council International reported that in 1994 starting-lighting-ignition battery production of 97.5 million units. An estimated 1.031 million tonnes of lead were consumed in these batteries in 1994.

U.S. mine production in the January-July 1995 period was 224,000 tonnes, up from 212,000 tonnes in the same period of 1994. For all of 1994, production was 363,000 tonnes. Primary refinery lead production in the period was 222,000 tonnes compared to 215,000 tonnes in the first half of 1994. Secondary refinery production was 547,000 tonnes compared to 553,000 tonnes in 1994.

U.S. consumption of lead in January-July 1995 was 806,000 tonnes, up 1 percent from the same period of 1994. For all of 1994, lead consumption was 1.38 million tonnes.

World Smelter (Primary & Secondary) Production of Lead In Thousands of Metric Tons

Year	Australia[3]	Belgium[4]	Bulgaria	Canada[3]	China[2]	France	Germany	Italy	Japan	Kazakhstan[5]	Mexico[3]	Peru[3]	Spain	United Kingdom[3]	United States	World Total
1987	220.7	89.6	100.6	230.7	246.4	245.5	340.4	168.3	338.5	750.0	253.6	71.4	122.7	347.0	1,042.0	5,411
1988	185.0	105.2	101.0	268.1	241.4	255.7	345.1	177.7	340.0	727.0	250.0	53.6	110.8	373.8	1,090.5	5,518
1989	205.0	109.4	101.5	242.8	260.0	427.6	184.2	186.2	332.4	745.0	235.0	78.4	114.5	350.5	1,287.8	6,077
1990	229.0	105.8	66.6	183.6	296.0	432.7	177.9	166.8	327.4	700.0	232.2	74.3	110.0	329.4	1,330.0	5,950
1991	239.4	110.7	56.2	212.4	330.0	439.0	161.0	209.0	332.4	630.0	161.8	79.5	169.0	311.0	1,230.3	5,770
1992	231.8	116.3	53.1	253.0	365.0	444.6	175.3	186.3	330.2	210.0	177.0	87.5	120.0	346.8	1,220.0	5,430
1993[1]	243.0	127.0	55.0	220.0	412.0	438.0	175.0	183.0	309.0	195.0	188.0	92.4	125.0	364.0	1,230.0	5,450
1994[2]	226.0	135.0	55.0	220.0	407.0	444.0	189.0	180.0	292.0	170.0	190.0	92.0	140.0	343.0	1,260.0	5,380

[1] Preliminary. [2] Estimate. [3] Refined & bullion. [4] Includes scrap. [5] Formerly part of the U.S.S.R.; data not reported separately until 1992.
Source: U.S. Bureau of Mines

Consumption of Lead in the United States by Products In Metric Tons

Year	Ammunition	Bearing Metals	Pipes, Traps & Bends[2]	Cable Covering	Calking Lead	Casting Metals	Other Metal Products[3]	Total Other Oxides[4]	Sheet Lead	Solder	Storage Battery: Grids, Post, etc.	Storage Battery: Oxides	Brass and Bronze	Total Consumption
1986	44,382	5,525	12,542	17,061	1,833	10,268	7,481	69,527	17,275	21,302	488,932	364,878	9,057	1,125,521
1987	46,835	5,260	11,532	20,140	1,893	19,909	7,119	68,094	17,400	19,758	529,362	424,236	9,868	1,230,373
1988	52,708	6,034	11,193	16,170	1,618	15,872	7,614	62,524	17,458	19,064	514,694	454,964	9,994	1,245,170
1989	57,310	2,586	9,818	22,605	1,831	16,175	6,850	57,984	20,987	17,009	552,308	459,847	9,610	1,283,234
1990	58,210	5,212	9,281	18,253	1,688	14,843	3,812	56,484	21,013	16,490	571,187	448,450	9,943	1,275,226
1991	58,458	3,669	8,975	17,472	1,074	14,141	3,254	59,617	22,334	14,750	591,884	415,233	8,997	1,246,337
1992	64,845	4,785	11,652	15,992	1,045	17,111	3,024	63,225	21,006	13,518	629,147	373,185	9,175	1,236,571
1993	65,100	4,830	5,740	17,165	961	18,500	5,360	63,600	21,200	14,400	677,000	374,000	5,750	1,290,000
1994[1]	62,400	5,560	3,370	16,000	764	18,900	5,330	62,700	21,500	12,400	802,000	419,000	6,320	1,450,000

[1] Preliminary. [2] Including building. [3] Including terne metal, type metal, and lead consumed in foil, collapsible tubes, annealing, plating, galvanizing and fishing weights. [8] Includes paints, glass and ceramic products, and other pigments and chemicals. W = Withheld proprietary data.
Source: U.S. Bureau of Mines

Salient Statistics of Lead in the United States In Thousands of Metric Tons

Year	Net Import Reliance as a % of Apparent Consumption	Production of Refined Lead from Domestic Ores[3]	Production of Refined Lead from Foreign Ores[3]	Production of Refined Lead from Total Primary	Total Value of Refined Million $	Secondary Lead Recovered As Soft Lead	Secondary Lead Recovered In Antimonial Lead	Secondary Lead Recovered In Other Alloys	Secondary Lead Recovered Total	Total Value of Secondary Million $	Stocks, Dec. 31 Primary	Stocks, Dec. 31 Consumer[4]	Average Price ¢ Per Pound New York	Average Price ¢ Per Pound London[5]
1978	12	501.6	63.5	565.2	419.3	282.6	409.9	76.5	769.2	570.7	98.7	125.2	33.65	29.86
1979	5	530.0	45.6	575.6	668.0	352.2	378.8	70.3	801.4	930.0	89.3	153.2	52.64	54.52
1980	E	508.2	39.4	547.6	512.6	315.2	306.7	53.7	675.6	632.4	126.0	126.2	42.46	41.21
1981	1	440.2	55.1	495.3	398.9	282.2	304.4	54.6	641.1	516.3	140.2	123.2	36.53	33.30
1982	11	459.9	52.3	512.2	288.4	240.5	284.4	46.4	615.7	321.7	125.5	97.2	25.54	24.66
1983	20	463.9	55.2	519.2	248.1	189.6	271.6	42.3	503.5	240.7	53.4	100.8	21.68	19.27
1984	20	324.0	65.4	389.4	219.3	263.4	327.8	42.1	633.4	266.3	45.1	97.1	25.55	20.12
1985	12	422.7	71.4	494.0	207.7	273.7	299.3	42.7	615.7	258.9	84.5	93.1	19.07	17.84
1986	20	348.2	22.1	370.3	180.0	289.5	291.9	43.3	624.8	303.7	20.4	83.8	22.05	18.43
1987	17	336.5	37.1	373.6	296.0	345.1	323.3	41.7	710.1	562.6	21.6	88.6	35.94	26.99
1988	13	371.3	20.7	392.1	321.0	367.1	331.3	38.0	736.4	603.0	15.4	89.9	37.14	29.73
1989	8	379.0	17.4	396.5	343.9	438.0	418.6	34.7	891.3	773.3	15.6	82.4	39.35	30.63
1990	3	385.6	18.0	403.7	409.5	461.4	425.4	35.6	922.2	935.6	25.5	86.3	46.02	37.05
1991	6	323.9	21.9	345.7	255.2	421.9	426.9	35.8	884.6	652.9	9.1	71.7	33.48	25.30
1992	10	284.0	20.8	304.8	235.9	452.9	424.5	23.1	916.3	709.1	20.5	82.3	35.10	24.50
1993[1]	15	310.7	24.9	335.6	234.4	444.0	417.0	17.0	893.0	625.0	14.3	80.5	31.74	18.42
1994[2]	17	328.0	23.4	351.4	288.0	510.0	371.0	16.1	913.0	748.0	9.3	67.5	37.17	24.83

[1] Preliminary. [2] Estimate. [3] And base bullion. [4] Also at secondary smelters. [5] LME data in dollars per metric ton beginning July 1993. E = Net exporter. *Source: U.S. Bureau of Mines*

U.S. Mine Production of Recoverable Lead In Metric Tons

Year	Total	Missouri	Missouri's % of Total	Year	Total	Missouri	Missouri's % of Total
1983	449,295	409,280	91%	1989	410,915	366,931	89%
1984	322,677	278,329	86%	1990	483,704	380,781	79%
1986	413,955	371,008	90%	1991	465,931	351,995	76%
1986	339,793	319,900	94%	1992	397,923	300,589	76%
1987	311,381	W	NA	1993[1]	353,607	276,569	78%
1988	384,983	353,194	92%	1994[2]	363,443	290,738	80%

1 Preliminary. 2 Estimate. W = Withheld. NA = Not available. *Source: U.S. Bureau of Mines*

U.S. Foreign Trade of Lead In Thousands of Metric Tons

Year	Exports: Ore Concentrate	Exports: Unwrought Lead[3]	Exports: Wrought Lead[4]	Exports: Scrap	Exports: Ash & Residues[5]	Imports for Consumption: Ores, Flue Dust or Fume & Mattes	Imports for Consumption: Base Bullion	Imports for Consumption: Pigs & Bars	Imports for Consumption: Reclaimed Scrap, Etc.	Imports for Consumption: Value Million $	General Imports From: Ore, Flue Dust & Matte: Australia	Ore, Flue Dust & Matte: Canada	Ore, Flue Dust & Matte: Peru	Pigs & Bars: Australia	Pigs & Bars: Canada	Pigs & Bars: Mexico	Pigs & Bars: Peru
1978	54.2	3.2	5.1	98.6	-----	61.9	4.3	225.4	3.3	203.0	6.5	19.6	6.3	16.3	70.4	80.2	25.7
1979	32.9	7.4	3.3	119.7	-----	44.4	1.7	182.6	4.0	248.3	1.9	12.8	12.4	17.3	-----	73.6	17.9
1980	27.6	156.5	8.0	119.7	-----	29.6	.3	81.3	2.9	116.5	3.0	8.5	18.0	11.3	34.9	28.6	3.3
1981	33.0	16.8	6.5	59.4	-----	27.2	.4	100.1	2.7	110.5	2.2	23.5	14.1	10.9	50.8	33.7	2.9
1982	29.1	51.0	4.6	51.8	-----	18.9	-----	94.9	4.8	69.9	7.7	4.8	14.5	7.3	49.8	23.5	8.3
1983	20.1	17.7	2.8	50.9	-----	19.8	.1	134.4	4.2	89.9	10.0	6.1	22.7	10.9	72.7	34.9	10.1
1984	11.9	5.0	2.5	45.1	9.1	29.9	-----	161.5	5.0	104.2	17.0	14.1	22.7	10.9	94.9	39.5	9.2
1985	10.0	25.4	2.0	59.9	10.0	2.6	.8	131.4	3.2	56.5	12.3	5.2	15.2	3.6	90.1	33.8	5.2
1986	4.4	11.2	1.4	59.0	7.2	4.6	.1	140.2	3.3	62.1	11.5	62.9	8.4	-----	105.3	29.5	1.1
1987	8.8	4.4	5.8	52.8	3.5	.9	10.8	185.7	6.6	133.8	1.7	201.2	19.1	.1	92.6	42.6	.4
1988	20.9	7.5	6.0	81.9	15.5	20.6	4.0	148.6	7.3	124.8	1.4	221.8	11.4	6.7	104.8	30.9	-----
1989	57.0	28.5	5.4	59.9	10.0	5.1	5.8	115.7	.7	95.7	1.9	189.9	12.9	-----	90.5	19.2	2.3
1990	56.6	57.2	6.8	75.0	13.0	10.7	2.7	90.6	.3	91.2	1.2	124.3	7.1	6.9	70.7	25.0	1.0
1991	88.0	94.4	7.6	72.0	11.0	12.4	.4	116.5	.1	82.6	1.0	226.7	3.9	8.0	83.6	11.9	.5
1992	72.3	64.3	5.3	63.2	2.1	5.3	.2	190.7	.2	120.6	-----	239.9	21.2	-----	124.7	56.1	9.8
1993[1]	41.8	51.4	7.1	54.1	1.7	.5	0	195.6	.1	99.4	-----	55.7	13.6	1.0	130.8	40.3	18.3
1994[2]	38.7	48.2	5.3	88.1	20.6	.5	.6	230.8	.1	146.6	-----	.3	11.7	.5	159.0	31.9	25.6

[1] Preliminary. [2] Estimate. [3] And lead alloys. [4] Blocks, pigs, etc. [5] Formerly drosses and flue dust. *Source: U.S. Bureau of Mines*

LEAD

Average Price of Pig Lead, U.S. Primary Producers (Common Corroding)[1] In Cents Per Pound

Year	Jan.	Feb.	Mar.	Apr.	May	June	July	Aug.	Sept.	Oct.	Nov.	Dec.	Average
1984	26.38	26.00	26.45	27.00	26.55	29.00	32.14	30.13	25.68	24.04	26.42	23.11	26.91
1985	20.45	19.76	19.24	20.48	20.50	20.00	19.88	19.32	19.44	18.97	19.06	19.05	19.68
1986	18.70	18.41	18.55	18.93	19.58	22.41	22.63	22.52	23.43	25.53	27.23	28.37	22.25
1987	27.75	26.03	26.00	27.01	35.10	36.77	41.82	42.00	42.00	42.00	42.00	42.00	35.95
1988	38.00	34.83	34.00	34.00	34.67	36.59	37.00	37.04	38.81	39.58	40.75	42.04	37.28
1989	40.22	37.00	35.00	35.03	36.14	38.82	39.97	41.30	43.00	43.00	40.55	38.55	39.05
1990	39.73	41.74	54.45	48.10	45.00	45.14	50.62	51.00	49.08	44.52	41.33	37.03	45.63
1991	34.18	33.00	33.00	33.00	32.00	31.80	33.00	33.00	33.70	35.00	35.00	35.00	33.47
1992	35.00	35.00	35.00	35.00	35.00	35.00	36.91	40.00	40.00	36.64	32.63	32.00	35.68
1993	32.00	32.00	32.00	32.00	32.00	32.00	32.00	32.00	32.00	32.00	32.00	33.00	32.08
1994	34.00	34.00	34.00	34.00	34.00	35.73	37.70	38.00	40.00	42.00	43.70	44.00	37.59
1995	44.00		42.00		42.00	42.00	42.00	43.65	44.00	44.00	46.10	48.00	43.78

[1] New York Delivery. *Source: American Metal Market*

Refiners Production[1] of Lead in the United States In Metric Tons

Year	Jan.	Feb.	Mar.	Apr.	May	June	July	Aug.	Sept.	Oct.	Nov.	Dec.	Total
1984	46,721	46,630	39,010	36,288	35,562	23,769	25,764	26,400	22,952	37,014	25,402	24,041	389,398
1985	39,100	45,632	51,075	47,809	48,444	46,176	29,484	42,276	40,733	35,653	27,307	40,370	494,003
1986	43,001	37,740	44,816	36,469	36,469	24,041	15,332	28,395	24,948	25,946	25,855	27,307	370,288
1987	35,199	30,482	32,659	30,119	31,026	26,762	26,127	28,032	30,300	34,111	35,834	33,113	373,610
1988	31,117	32,115	35,472	31,117	32,841	31,571	28,849	22,952	29,121	44,997	36,288	35,653	392,087
1989	37,195	32,659	35,381	30,845	32,841	32,206	32,387	34,474	35,653	31,480	32,024	29,303	396,455
1990	34,927	34,383	33,476	35,018	33,022	30,210	30,845	34,474	33,929	38,375	33,476	31,571	403,657
1991	30,763	30,863	33,771	30,248	27,031	22,371	27,973	28,204	29,411	29,846	26,428	28,813	345,714
1992	29,121	27,691	33,366	27,456	26,742	22,441	24,993	21,587	19,365	22,945	23,674	25,414	304,791
1993	29,627	26,693	30,197	27,578	29,814	28,253	16,734	22,817	32,725	31,220	27,953	31,312	335,014
1994	29,908	30,685	31,420	29,059	31,588	31,707	30,661	27,335	31,185	32,874	29,301	30,447	366,170
1995[2]	32,100	29,100	32,600	32,300	32,600	28,300	31,000	29,300	30,600				

[1] Represents refined lead produced from domestic ores by primary smelters plus small amounts of secondary material passing through these smelters. Includes GSA metal purchased for remelt. [2] Preliminary. *Source: U.S. Bureau of Mines*

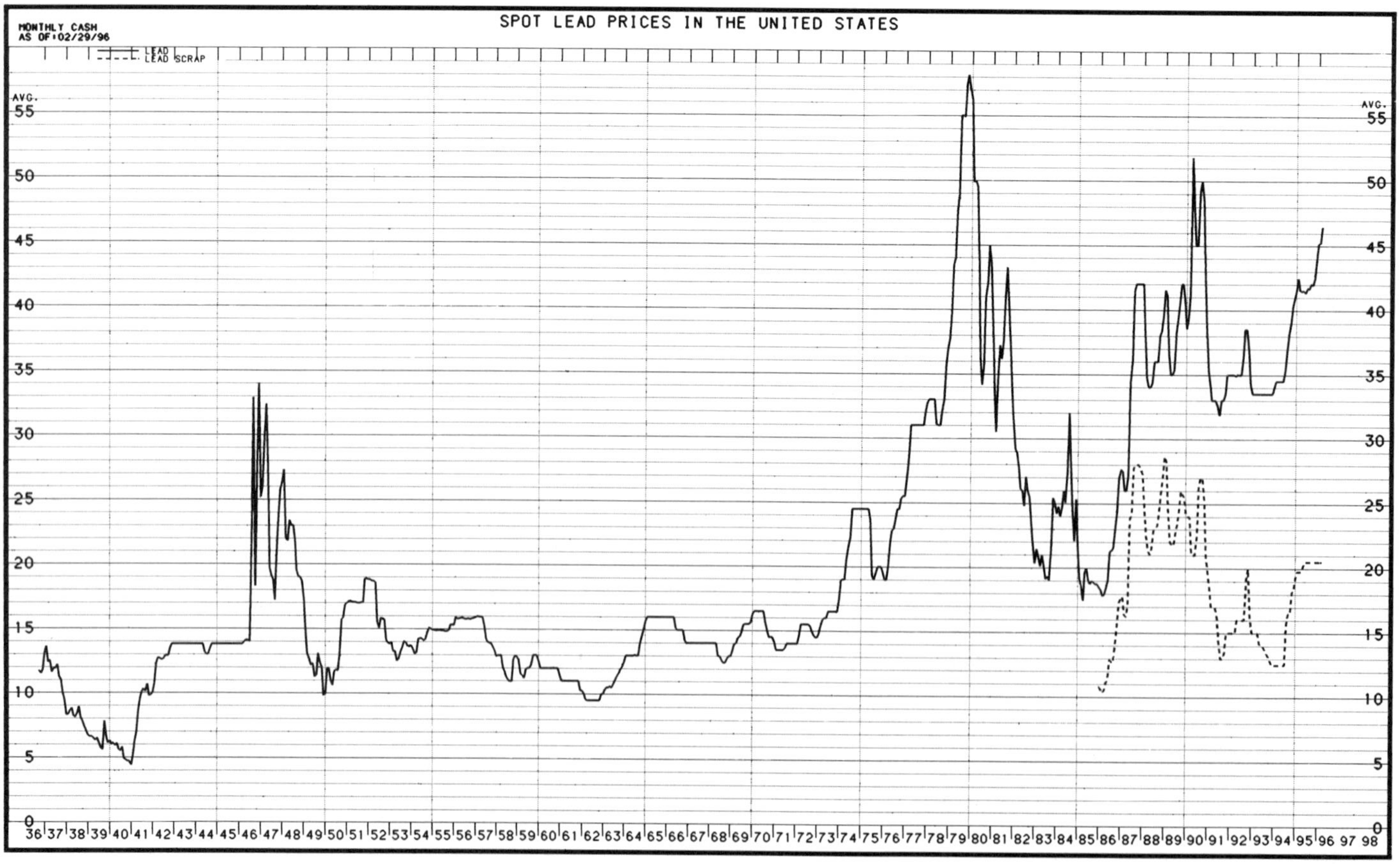

U.S. Mine Production of Recoverable Lead In Thousands of Metric Tons

Year	Jan.	Feb.	Mar.	Apr.	May	June	July	Aug.	Sept.	Oct.	Nov.	Dec.	Total
1987	24.2	23.9	27.9	23.6	27.0	26.3	29.0	24.1	28.2	28.4	23.2	25.5	311.4
1988	27.9	28.2	36.0	32.7	30.3	32.5	30.4	36.3	33.1	34.4	31.1	31.8	385.0
1989	33.3	31.0	34.4	33.2	33.8	36.1	33.2	38.6	34.3	35.1	32.9	30.1	410.9
1990	42.4	39.0	39.9	37.4	40.8	38.8	42.3	47.2	37.9	43.0	38.5	36.6	483.7
1991	41.5	41.1	41.6	37.8	43.5	36.4	47.5	41.1	36.1	38.9	28.0	26.1	465.9
1992	36.0	34.0	34.0	31.2	31.5	32.4	33.8	32.5	32.5	33.3	30.8	31.7	392.7
1993	33.3	30.5	34.2	30.6	28.5	29.5	25.8	27.5	28.4	27.3	29.5	28.5	355.2
1994	27.6	28.8	33.0	31.3	32.4	29.1	29.4	30.4	31.2	28.0	31.7	29.9	363.4
1995[1]	29.6	30.3	35.2	28.9	32.7	34.8	32.5	33.5	29.9				

[1] Preliminary. *Source: U.S. Bureau of Mines*

Total Stocks of Lead[1] in the United States at Refiners, at End of Month In Metric Tons

Year	Jan.	Feb.	Mar.	Apr.	May	June	July	Aug.	Sept.	Oct.	Nov.	Dec.
1987	31,026	33,839	35,653	28,577	29,575	18,598	10,614	10,977	11,521	14,878	18,053	21,591
1988	22,408	27,670	27,397	28,849	24,041	15,060	14,697	5,988	4,627	10,524	11,884	15,422
1989	26,037	32,931	39,191	37,558	29,665	28,940	31,389	27,942	27,488	18,779	14,606	15,604
1990	14,697	18,325	16,420	21,138	19,323	19,596	20,775	19,958	20,593	23,769	22,771	25,492
1991	24,177	24,333	26,990	21,261	17,474	16,195	15,362	9,072	6,608	4,091	4,491	9,089
1992	9,774	15,785	21,682	25,220	28,940	26,490	26,634	22,347	17,736	14,971	14,796	20,543
1993	28,069	33,338	34,058	34,306	35,775	32,162	22,753	14,797	15,086	14,408	13,456	14,289
1994	11,964	12,633	12,048	11,445	11,598	10,251	12,368	9,256	8,897	10,659	9,060	9,271
1995[2]	8,200	9,750	11,500	14,500	16,700	16,200	21,300	14,000	12,800			

[1] Primary refineries. [2] Preliminary. *Source: U.S. Bureau of Mines*

Total[1] Lead Consumption in the United States In Thousands of Metric Tons

Year	Jan.	Feb.	Mar.	Apr.	May	June	July	Aug.	Sept.	Oct.	Nov.	Dec.	Total
1987	96.5	91.1	103.0	101.0	101.4	103.5	97.4	103.2	108.5	119.1	105.8	100.1	1,230
1988	99.8	101.4	116.0	99.3	104.0	103.6	92.1	102.5	103.0	110.6	103.4	95.1	1,231
1989	104.7	98.3	101.2	99.2	101.3	101.6	95.2	102.7	105.9	114.0	106.2	97.3	1,283
1990	104.1	106.7	111.9	101.1	106.2	103.2	97.7	112.4	104.6	109.0	104.3	97.3	1,275
1991	101.3	105.3	101.2	101.3	98.4	92.4	90.8	101.9	102.7	106.9	102.4	92.7	1,246
1992	102.5	99.3	108.3	98.5	96.0	103.5	94.8	104.8	106.6	105.4	98.2	92.9	1,215
1993	108.9	107.5	112.3	104.6	109.2	113.8	106.8	112.6	117.1	113.2	109.3	102.2	1,357
1994	107.0	115.2	112.8	111.6	113.5	115.2	114.3	115.5	115.9	121.2	118.7	113.0	1,384
1995[2]	119.0	119.0	119.0	109.0	110.0	113.0	115.0	105.0	115.0				

[1] Represents total consumption of primary and secondary lead as metal, in chemicals, or in alloys. [2] Preliminary. *Source: U.S. Bureau of Mines*

U.S. Lead Recovered from Scrap In Thousands of Metric Tons (Lead Content)

Year	Jan.	Feb.	Mar.	Apr.	May	June	July	Aug.	Sept.	Oct.	Nov.	Dec.	Total
1987	50.0	49.9	54.4	55.6	59.3	53.9	59.9	63.4	53.3	67.3	55.9	55.1	710.2
1988	52.2	57.5	60.1	55.9	52.2	59.4	55.3	56.3	60.7	61.8	61.6	59.7	737.0
1989	62.1	58.6	67.5	64.1	65.3	66.3	61.6	65.9	64.4	73.5	67.1	66.9	808.6
1990	68.7	69.6	73.0	69.4	66.9	67.9	67.0	71.8	71.0	77.5	72.3	77.3	923.0
1991	79.0	74.4	71.0	72.0	72.0	70.7	69.8	70.0	72.3	74.6	70.7	75.9	883.7
1992	76.1	71.5	66.5	71.0	73.3	72.3	71.1	77.7	77.5	79.6	76.9	74.3	888.5
1993	71.1	76.8	71.7	80.2	78.9	72.5	70.3	76.6	76.3	77.0	77.9	79.3	903.6
1994	74.0	76.0	84.2	81.7	81.1	79.0	78.9	79.8	78.4	76.4	81.0	80.4	949.0
1995[1]	82.5	80.8	84.4	72.8	73.7	72.5	79.9	71.5	82.3				

[1] Preliminary. *Source: U.S. Bureau of Mines*

Domestic Shipments[1] of Lead in the United States by Refiners In Thousands of Short Tons

Year	Jan.	Feb.	Mar.	Apr.	May	June	July	Aug.	Sept.	Oct.	Nov.	Dec.	Total
1987	27.0	30.5	34.1	41.1	34.8	40.0	37.8	30.1	33.1	33.8	35.7	32.7	410.7
1988	33.5	29.5	39.2	33.0	41.4	44.7	32.0	34.7	33.7	43.0	38.5	35.5	438.7
1989	29.3	28.5	32.2	35.7	45.1	36.4	32.8	41.5	40.0	44.2	40.2	31.1	437.1
1990	39.3	33.9	39.1	33.5	38.4	32.9	32.6	38.9	36.6	38.9	37.9	31.7	433.7
1991	35.4	33.8	34.3	39.8	33.9	26.0	31.8	37.9	35.1	35.7	28.7	26.7	399.2
1992	31.3	23.9	30.4	26.3	25.6	27.2	27.3	28.7	26.3	28.5	26.3	21.7	323.5
1993	24.6	23.6	32.5	30.0	31.3	35.1	28.9	34.0	35.5	35.5	31.7	33.5	376.2
1994	35.9	32.8	35.2	32.7	34.7	36.6	31.6	33.4	34.8	34.3	34.0	33.3	409.2

[1] Includes GSA metal. *Source: American Metal Market*

Lumber & Plywood

The American Forest and Paper Association reported that for the first three quarters of 1995, U.S. softwood production was 24.4 billion board feet. For all of 1994, U.S. production was 34.1 billion board feet. In the first nine months of 1995, California redwood production was one billion board feet while for all of 1994 it was 1.5 billion board feet. Inland region softwood production was 5.3 billion board feet which compares with total 1994 production of 8.1 billion board feet. Southern pine softwood production for the January-September 1995 period was 11.2 billion board feet. For all of 1994 it was 15 billion board feet. West Coast softwood production in the first three quarters of 1995 was 5.6 billion board feet. In 1994, it was 7.9 billion board feet. Total hardwood production over the first nine months of 1995 was 10.1 billion board feet. For all of 1994, total hardwood production was 13 billion board feet.

In the first three quarters of 1995, total U.S. softwood consumption was 35.8 billion board feet while for all of 1994 it was 48.1 billion board feet. Consumption of inland region softwood in the first nine months of 1995 was 5.3 billion board feet. For 1994 it was 7.9 billion board feet. Southern pine softwood consumption was 11 billion board feet. For all of 1994 it was 14.6 billion board feet. West Coast softwood consumption was 4.8 billion board feet. For all of 1994, consumption was 6.8 billion board feet. U.S. softwood imports over the first nine months of 1995 were 13 billion board feet. For 1994, U.S. softwood imports were 16.4 billion board feet. U.S. hardwood consumption in the first three quarters of 1995 was 9.2 billion board feet. For 1994 hardwood consumption was 11.8 billion board feet.

U.S. imports of softwood in the January-September 1995 period were 13 billion board feet. For the first three quarters of 1995, imports of cedar were 592 million board feet. Imports of Douglas fir were 317 million board feet. Hemlock imports were 189.1 million board feet. Spruce imports were 2.2 billion board feet. Total hardwood imports were 272.2 billion board feet. Pine imports were 72.5 million board feet. Total lumber imports in the January-September 1995 period were 13.3 billion board feet.

The U.S. also exports softwoods and hardwoods. Total lumber imports over the first nine months of 1995 were 2.5 billion board feet. For all of 1994, lumber imports were 3.3 billion board feet. Total softwood imports in the first three quarters of 1995 were 1.6 billion board feet. For 1994 they were 2.2 billion board feet. Total hardwood imports were 843.2 billion board feet while for all of 1994 they were a billion board feet. Stocks (gross) of softwood lumber on October 1, 1995 were 4.3 billion board feet, down 4 percent from stocks on October 1, 1994.

U.S. exports of softwood logs in the January-September 1995 period were 8.8 million cubic meters, up 9 percent from 1994. Exports of hardwood logs in the first nine months of 1995 were 948,000 cubic meters, up 9 percent from 1994. Exports of poles, piles and posts were 1.1 million units, down 33% from the same period of 1994. Exports of softwood chips were 1.4 million tonnes, down 5%. Hardwood chip exports were 2.4 million tonnes, up 6%.

Exports of softwood lumber were 3.5 million cubic meters, down 6 percent from 1994. Hardwood lumber exports were 1.9 million cubic meters, up 8 percent from 1994. Softwood flooring exports were 515,768 square feet, a substantial increase of 43 percent from the first three quarters of 1994. Hardwood flooring exports were put at 871,593 square meters, some 21 percent more than in 1994.

Softwood molding exports were 276 million meters in the January-September 1995 period, down 33 percent from 1994. Hardwood molding exports were 23.1 million meters, down 9 percent from the previous year. Treated lumber exports were 146,288 cubic meters, up 6 percent from 1994. Railroad tie exports in January-September 1995 were 187,351 cubic meters, unchanged from 1994.

Softwood plywood exports were 762,274 cubic meters, down 3 percent. Particle board exports in the first part of 1995 were 269,948 cubic meters, up 8 percent from 1994.

Japan is by far the leading export market purchasing about half of U.S. wood products. The next leading market is Canada followed by Germany, Korea, Mexico, the U.K, Italy and Taiwan.

In terms of market developments, on November 21, 1995, the U.S. submitted to Japan a list of areas where it would like to see specific deregulation reforms. In the wood products sector, the U.S. requested that Japan increase acceptance and use of foreign building materials and construction methods. The U.S. requested that Japan simplify and expedite the process for gaining approval to use new or innovative building materials and construction methods. One reform would be to revise the requirements for three-story wood-frame structures to allow increased wood utilization.

Futures Markets

Lumber futures and options are traded on the Chicago Mercantile Exchange (CME).

U.S. Housing Starts: Seasonally Adjusted Annual Rate In Thousands (Total is Actual Starts)

Year	Jan.	Feb.	Mar.	Apr.	May	June	July	Aug.	Sept.	Oct.	Nov.	Dec.	Average
1987	1,840	1,787	1,715	1,622	1,607	1,583	1,592	1,587	1,685	1,535	1,659	1,391	1,621
1988	1,391	1,511	1,528	1,576	1,392	1,463	1,478	1,459	1,463	1,532	1,567	1,577	1,488
1989	1,678	1,465	1,409	1,343	1,308	1,414	1,424	1,325	1,263	1,423	1,347	1,273	1,376
1990	1,568	1,488	1,307	1,216	1,206	1,189	1,153	1,131	1,107	1,026	1,130	971	1,207
1991	844	1,008	918	978	983	1,036	1,053	1,053	1,022	1,085	1,085	1,118	1,113
1992	1,180	1,285	1,318	1,095	1,197	1,141	1,106	1,229	1,218	1,226	1,226	1,286	1,200
1993	1,170	1,194	1,092	1,232	1,241	1,238	1,245	1,319	1,359	1,409	1,406	1,612	1,293
1994[1]	1,266	1,318	1,499	1,463	1,489	1,370	1,440	1,463	1,511	1,451	1,536	1,527	1,444
1995[1]	1,359	1,315	1,231	1,255	1,264	1,293	1,390	1,392	1,389	1,343	1,420		

[1] Preliminary. Total privately owned. *Source: American Forest & Paper Association*

World Production of Industrial Roundwood by Selected Countries In Thousands of Cubic Meters

Year	Austria	Canada	Czech[3] Republic	Finland	France	Germany	Japan	Norway	Poland	Russia[4]	Spain	Sweden	Switzer-land	Turkey	United Kingdom	United States
1989	13,575	170,625	16,856	42,670	34,276	41,806	31,202	10,590	18,980	305,300	15,691	51,430	3,729	5,728	6,207	416,900
1990	14,160	173,897	16,398	40,196	34,913	40,934	29,300	10,900	15,549	305,300	13,790	49,071	5,383	5,960	6,125	430,200
1991	12,535	159,039	13,770	31,616	33,754	29,823	27,938	10,345	14,334	275,300	12,988	47,600	3,751	5,502	6,122	388,310
1992	9,255	165,436	8,820	35,279	52,854	29,159	26,934	9,200	15,720	164,000	12,614	49,720	3,638	8,458	5,740	403,100
1993[1]	9,107	173,133	9,706	37,758	29,566	29,357	25,570	9,253	15,940	136,030	11,477	50,200	3,501	9,408	7,185	401,520
1994[2]	11,101	NA	11,400	43,502	33,050	33,217	NA	8,274	16,621	94,700	NA	52,700	NA	9,211	7,915	399,725

[1] Preliminary. [2] Estimate. [3] Formerly part of Czechoslovakia; data not reported separately until 1992. [4] Formerly part of the U.S.S.R.; data not reported separately until 1992. NA = Not available. *Source: Food and Agricultural Organization of the United Nations*

United States Lumber Production and Consumption In Millions of Board Feet

	Production						Domestic Consumption							
	Softwood						Softwood							
Year	California Redwood	Inland Region	Southern Pine	West Coast	Total	Total Hardwood	Inland Region	Southern Pine	West Coast	Softwood Imports	Total	U.S. Hardwood	Hardwood Imports	Total Lumber
1984	1,664	8,992	10,674	8,329	31,174	9,865	8,764	10,401	7,551	13,270	42,832	9,501	328	52,661
1985	1,730	9,276	10,730	8,062	31,321	8,866	8,977	10,480	7,250	14,608	44,240	8,864	364	53,468
1986	2,021	10,482	11,678	9,412	35,273	10,877	10,273	11,383	8,377	14,238	47,492	10,469	347	58,308
1987	2,181	11,407	12,473	10,354	38,235	11,695	11,008	12,240	9,117	14,680	50,558	11,235	511	62,304
1988	2,214	11,395	12,676	10,029	38,130	12,170	11,180	12,108	8,096	13,806	48,513	10,636	390	59,539
1989	2,053	11,348	12,544	9,811	37,545	12,415	11,134	12,125	7,950	13,638	47,966	11,970	375	60,311
1990	1,972	10,452	12,911	8,751	35,791	12,660	10,390	12,388	7,184	12,148	45,003	11,070	255	56,328
1991	1,657	9,510	12,507	7,908	33,161	11,633	9,302	12,147	6,454	11,742	42,225	10,278	226	52,730
1992	1,571	9,263	14,106	7,948	34,526	12,109	9,107	13,893	6,709	13,381	45,737	11,330	276	57,343
1993	1,354	8,312	14,392	7,319	32,947	12,300	8,129	14,020	6,043	15,260	45,810	10,932	335	57,078
1994[1]	1,474	8,097	15,010	7,902	34,107	13,012	7,856	14,618	6,833	16,380	48,104	11,825	394	60,323
1995[1] I	342	1,844	3,712	2,020	8,314	3,295	1,742	3,554	1,692	3,910	11,448	3,031	96	14,575
II	341	1,705	3,824	1,797	8,050	3,331	1,694	3,773	1,580	4,560	12,200	3,131	86	15,418
III	343	1,777	3,695	1,806	8,002	3,443	1,870	3,651	1,553	4,518	12,189	3,045	90	15,325

[1] Preliminary. *Source: American Forest & Paper Association*

Stocks (Gross) of Softwood Lumber in the United States, Beginning of Month In Millions of Board Feet

Year	Jan.	Feb.	Mar.	Apr.	May	June	July	Aug.	Sept.	Oct.	Nov.	Dec.
1984	4,606	4,424	4,494	4,602	4,717	4,715	4,658	4,560	4,509	4,573	4,515	4,590
1985	4,594	4,533	4,637	4,733	4,508	4,415	4,633	4,680	4,687	4,699	4,850	4,870
1986	4,765	4,842	4,959	4,846	4,886	4,748	4,605	4,615	4,722	4,840	4,929	5,038
1987	5,040	5,039	5,112	5,203	5,181	5,097	4,927	4,928	4,755	4,855	4,787	4,823
1988	4,771	4,867	4,950	4,994	4,939	4,894	4,685	4,677	4,765	4,823	4,951	4,979
1989	4,999	4,896	4,818	4,837	4,810	4,740	4,746	4,748	4,797	4,762	4,908	4,934
1990	4,898	5,022	5,022	5,020	4,961	5,043	4,831	4,783	4,752	4,810	4,834	4,809
1991	4,734	4,925	4,949	4,946	4,849	4,600	4,699	4,684	4,793	4,786	4,741	4,710
1992	4,616	4,603	4,567	4,608	4,730	4,731	4,678	4,606	4,418	4,419	4,365	4,263
1993	4,669	4,217	4,166	4,239	4,490	4,618	4,599	4,526	4,418	4,445	4,282	4,298
1994	4,207	4,512	4,656	4,816	4,883	4,649	4,738	4,432	4,349	4,539	4,235	4,294
1995[1]	4,403	4,336	4,344	4,653	4,352	4,663	4,508	4,323	4,342	4,359	4,361	4,335

[1] Preliminary. *Source: American Forest & Paper Association*

Lumber Production in the United States In Millions of Board Feet

Year	Jan.	Feb.	Mar.	Apr.	May	June	July	Aug.	Sept.	Oct.	Nov.	Dec.	Total
1984	2,740	2,678	3,104	2,983	2,828	2,968	2,685	2,933	2,776	3,154	2,814	2,295	41,039
1985	2,727	2,718	3,085	3,296	3,256	3,101	3,034	3,299	3,196	3,387	2,851	2,649	40,187
1986	3,092	3,046	3,347	3,362	3,405	3,355	2,961	3,441	3,397	3,820	3,496	3,623	46,150
1987	3,293	3,307	3,742	3,616	3,518	3,905	3,662	3,737	3,617	3,942	3,458	3,829	49,930
1988	3,814	4,042	4,389	4,247	4,245	4,137	3,671	4,056	4,180	4,040	3,715	3,641	50,300
1989	3,849	3,311	3,758	3,773	4,025	4,273	3,683	4,023	3,787	4,172	3,811	3,615	49,960
1990	4,160	3,862	4,300	4,121	4,084	3,944	3,976	4,060	3,602	4,015	3,412	2,914	48,451
1991	3,534	3,410	3,661	3,958	3,837	3,762	3,664	3,808	3,682	3,933	3,473	3,254	44,794
1992	3,836	3,628	4,121	3,862	3,632	3,911	3,882	3,746	3,736	4,048	3,617	3,425	46,635
1993	3,545	3,596	3,954	3,809	3,555	3,787	3,685	3,930	3,824	4,103	3,883	3,576	45,247
1994	3,839	3,662	4,097	3,735	3,972	4,113	3,785	4,124	4,135	4,145	3,636	3,851	47,094
1995[1]	4,084	3,577	3,931	3,675	3,805	3,897	3,641	3,866	3,757	4,105	3,589		

[1] Preliminary. *Source: American Forest & Paper Association*

LUMBER

United States Lumber Shipments In Millions of Board Feet

Year	Jan.	Feb.	Mar.	Apr.	May	June	July	Aug.	Sept.	Oct.	Nov.	Dec.	Total
1984	2,589	2,603	3,002	2,875	2,852	2,993	2,756	2,950	2,688	3,154	2,922	2,397	40,693
1985	2,666	2,602	3,013	3,496	3,349	3,031	2,944	3,294	3,162	3,221	2,828	2,809	39,784
1986	2,955	2,899	3,478	3,321	3,538	3,498	2,979	3,344	3,291	3,689	3,480	3,791	46,099
1987	3,350	3,302	3,735	3,686	3,656	4,039	3,671	3,812	3,540	4,034	3,470	3,865	50,311
1988	3,790	4,092	4,320	4,257	4,261	4,309	3,688	3,929	4,038	3,871	3,656	3,649	49,839
1989	3,914	3,417	3,877	3,846	4,163	4,420	3,760	3,977	3,823	4,081	3,854	3,626	50,476
1990	4,035	3,870	4,317	4,173	3,952	4,176	3,912	3,987	3,453	3,890	3,357	2,873	47,773
1991	3,240	3,301	3,617	4,037	4,028	3,764	3,412	3,926	3,676	4,012	3,477	3,370	44,559
1992	3,912	3,693	4,078	3,682	3,565	3,936	3,884	3,878	3,692	4,147	3,745	3,491	47,314
1993	3,575	3,649	3,852	3,563	3,402	3,759	3,721	3,997	3,724	4,211	3,798	3,617	44,868
1994	3,576	3,663	3,912	3,761	4,192	4,091	4,039	4,163	3,914	4,321	3,603	3,696	46,931
1995[1]	3,971	3,584	3,855	3,831	3,765	4,026	3,826	3,870	3,760	4,055	3,509		

[1] Preliminary. *Source: American Forest & Paper Association*

United States Trade of Lumber by Type In Millions of Board Feet

	Imports[2]								Exports[2]						
	Softwood								Softwood						
Year	Cedar	Douglas Fir	Hemlock	Pine	Spurce	Total	Total Hardwood	Total Lumber	Douglas Fir	Hemlock	Pond-erosa/ White Pine	Southern Pine	Total	Total Hardwood	Total Lumber
1984	704.1	603.0	514.9	901.6	9,471.4	13,270.2	327.7	13,622.2	532.1	337.4	174.1	172.4	1,599.3	466.5	2,150.4
1985	807.9	765.1	643.9	817.2	10,393.4	14,607.8	363.6	14,999.1	475.6	364.4	167.7	164.4	1,515.4	397.1	1,945.3
1986	800.6	686.2	488.4	668.7	10,389.1	14,238.2	346.9	14,608.2	512.4	532.0	209.4	178.6	1,877.0	498.3	2,398.6
1987	792.2	631.4	553.6	499.6	10,964.4	14,680.4	511.0	15,219.3	660.8	663.9	269.1	247.5	2,423.3	775.1	3,216.9
1988	786.8	721.4	539.7	332.3	10,284.5	13,806.0	390.1	14,225.3	888.6	714.9	233.4	492.3	3,263.9	1,232.0	4,528.0
1989	786.0	603.4	469.5	335.8	7,387.4	13,638.4	375.1	14,022.5	1,018.2	670.9	197.0	442.3	3,319.1	856.0	4,213.1
1990	652.8	375.4	362.4	87.6	3,535.7	12,148.2	255.4	12,429.4	818.5	549.4	215.2	374.7	2,970.4	877.7	3,900.0
1991	700.6	354.1	287.8	55.7	2,248.3	11,741.5	226.2	11,998.2	798.1	497.7	222.9	396.0	2,863.2	934.3	3,858.9
1992	666.4	355.3	300.0	91.4	2,410.5	13,380.5	276.4	13,681.9	735.0	396.7	308.7	440.5	2,650.7	977.2	3,687.1
1993	615.3	327.6	354.9	84.6	3,104.1	15,259.9	335.0	15,625.4	664.9	340.4	273.3	339.6	2,376.4	1,008.9	3,468.9
1994	702.6	336.2	399.2	97.2	2,948.5	16,380.3	394.4	16,787.1	591.9	283.2	157.2	356.7	2,186.6	1,040.9	3,333.4
1995[1] I	196.7	67.7	78.2	24.6	648.3	3,909.5	95.8	4,007.6	178.0	61.0	39.6	69.7	525.6	286.8	827.2
II	212.2	112.6	57.1	23.2	769.8	4,560.3	86.0	4,650.2	171.4	70.9	26.4	90.8	555.0	300.5	888.3
III	182.9	136.4	53.8	24.7	798.5	4,517.6	90.4	4,611.2	156.7	55.0	18.6	91.1	479.6	255.9	767.4

[1] Preliminary. [2] Includes sawed timber, board planks and scantings, flooring, box shook and railroad ties. *Source: American Forest & Paper Association*

Average Open Interest of Lumber Futures at Chicago In Contracts

Year	Jan.	Feb.	Mar.	Apr.	May	June	July	Aug.	Sept.	Oct.	Nov.	Dec.
1984	7,907	8,295	8,592	9,082	8,305	7,628	7,426	7,822	8,094	8,354	9,197	9,605
1985	9,953	9,704	8,102	9,115	9,115	10,038	8,823	8,672	7,672	7,247	6,819	6,567
1986	5,486	6,121	8,866	9,287	8,171	6,112	5,441	5,197	5,701	5,262	5,275	5,732
1987	6,077	7,330	6,406	6,950	6,019	6,770	6,563	7,439	6,961	7,247	6,579	6,572
1988	6,212	6,701	5,791	6,395	5,548	5,644	5,586	6,272	5,527	5,697	5,368	5,919
1989	7,982	7,484	7,436	8,244	7,363	7,921	8,248	8,055	7,065	7,192	6,600	6,167
1990	6,078	6,061	4,991	4,957	4,538	4,359	3,570	3,028	2,881	3,105	2,632	2,001
1991	1,922	2,003	2,023	2,354	2,076	2,601	2,571	2,181	2,276	2,480	2,206	1,606
1992	1,969	2,651	2,743	2,467	1,900	1,774	1,338	1,369	1,507	1,441	1,745	2,155
1993	2,194	2,432	2,163	2,055	2,302	2,658	2,254	2,141	2,011	2,080	2,140	2,721
1994	2,571	2,814	2,638	2,563	1,936	1,838	1,705	1,854	2,102	2,169	1,702	1,967
1995	1,757	1,923	2,142	2,509	2,742	3,252	2,896	2,918	2,809	3,039	2,626	2,940

Source: Chicago Mercantile Exchange

Volume of Trading of Lumber Futures at Chicago In Contracts

Year	Jan.	Feb.	Mar.	Apr.	May	June	July	Aug.	Sept.	Oct.	Nov.	Dec.	Total
1984	51,170	70,031	57,075	68,314	88,009	59,592	60,156	65,739	60,035	61,012	52,496	59,939	753,568
1985	71,719	55,737	56,718	65,762	62,766	57,422	43,525	39,151	36,517	34,703	29,556	27,972	581,548
1986	29,570	34,647	61,718	64,176	44,778	49,929	35,203	42,212	44,961	35,847	28,912	30,577	502,530
1987	40,351	49,167	40,504	39,211	27,954	33,505	31,345	38,876	34,039	39,437	32,052	30,648	437,089
1988	35,451	32,410	32,886	30,386	28,100	37,508	27,550	33,454	29,743	24,632	26,131	23,238	371,489
1989	29,963	25,857	23,947	31,427	26,789	26,712	20,258	19,514	18,790	18,965	17,286	14,395	273,903
1990	27,416	21,914	20,948	18,362	19,053	16,084	16,465	13,446	8,914	11,839	15,794	11,749	201,984
1991	10,535	13,460	10,326	11,309	15,135	19,029	19,350	14,912	12,214	14,054	10,295	9,902	160,521
1992	17,073	16,778	17,557	13,713	14,059	13,807	12,177	13,043	12,127	11,261	11,514	17,425	170,534
1993	14,915	15,080	14,808	14,661	14,241	15,308	13,287	13,358	12,400	13,248	18,150	18,728	178,184
1994	16,837	15,204	17,323	17,380	14,996	14,348	11,542	13,327	14,856	13,032	10,997	13,121	172,963
1995	12,150	12,909	15,088	12,139	14,536	20,126	13,757	16,714	15,504	18,580	14,997	13,038	179,538

Source: Chicago Mercantile Exchange

Production of Plywood by Selected Countries In Thousands of Cubic Meters

Year	Austria	Canada	Czech Republic[2]	Finland	France	Germany	Italy	Japan	Poland	Romania	Russia[3]	Slovenia[4]	Spain	Sweden	Turkey	United States
1989	111	2,165	245	657	498	439	445	6,707	154	181	2,298	138	150	68	65	19,700
1990	120	2,228	234	643	518	436	445	6,738	126	123	1,744	79	141	68	65	18,771
1991	140	1,927	157	477	470	424	450	6,588	111	51	1,548	71	140	67	65	16,508
1992	150	1,838	87	462	484	429	427	5,954	132	100	1,268	65	120	55	74	17,109
1993	150	1,824	75	621	460	416	415	5,263	133	100	1,042	63	200	73	77	17,093
1994[1]	150	1,834	80	700	485	416	427	NA	143	NA	870	64	210	85	77	17,500

[1] Preliminary. [2] Formerly part of Czechoslovakia; data not reported separately until 1992. [3] Formerly part of the U.S.S.R.; data not reported separately until 1992. [4] Formerly part of Yugoslavia; data not reported separately until 1992. NA = Not available.
Source: Food and Agricultural Organization of the United Nations

Imports of Plywood by Selected Countries In Thousands of Cubic Meters

Year	Austria	Belgium	Belarus[2]	Canada	Denmark	France	Germany	Italy	Japan	Netherlands	Norway	Sweden	Switzerland	United Kingdom	United States
1989	58	325	28	135	173	376	574	188	3,098	582	62	143	149	1,643	1,790
1990	61	361	22	231	206	442	706	212	2,941	655	68	158	137	1,454	1,493
1991	76	385	14	262	161	414	664	204	3,046	619	51	131	121	1,271	1,338
1992	79	300	157	242	198	423	879	216	3,003	583	58	106	110	1,397	1,649
1993	77	436	127	288	152	341	865	241	4,105	612	57	98	118	1,157	1,630
1994[1]	104	NA	NA	288	171	304	967	257	NA	560	71	126	144	1,202	1,547

[1] Preliminary. [2] Formerly part of the U.S.S.R.; data not reported separately until 1992. NA = Not available.
Source: Food and Agricultural Organization of the United Nations

Exports of Plywood by Selected Countries In Thousands of Cubic Meters

Year	Austria	Baltic States[2]	Belgium	Canada	Czech Republic[3]	Finland	France	Germany	Italy	Netherlands	Poland	Russia[2]	Spain	United Kingdom	United States
1989	105	419	145	310	55	512	210	83	160	51	30	-------	44	26	931
1990	128	361	133	391	72	515	210	83	94	50	44	-------	41	40	1,563
1991	130	240	169	288	35	347	222	81	95	63	49	-------	39	45	1,374
1992	119	25	132	412	12	348	228	122	90	72	56	226	32	25	1,618
1993	129	90	87	416	69	542	252	110	104	99	43	464	60	13	1,562
1994[1]	158	133	NA	416	55	627	250	131	108	102	NA	650	67	23	1,346

[1] Preliminary. [2] Formerly part of the U.S.S.R.; data not reported separately until 1992. [3] Formerly part of Czechoslovakia; data not reported separately until 1992. NA = Not available. *Source: Food and Agricultural Organization of the United Nations*

Selected World Prices of Plywood

Year	Jan.	Feb.	Mar.	Apr.	May	June	July	Aug.	Sept.	Oct.	Nov.	Dec.	Average
Philippines, Lauan, Wholesale Price, Spot Tokyo In U.S. Cents Per Sheet[1]													
1992	403.7	396.0	380.6	370.7	338.5	347.6	350.2	348.4	358.5	414.4	419.8	446.8	381.3
1993	512.0	611.8	700.4	708.0	712.0	715.0	696.2	703.8	664.8	617.3	644.3	630.7	659.7
1994	610.4	625.0	639.4	654.9	655.7	606.8	631.9	600.4	545.6	564.3	578.3	543.5	604.7
1995	557.5	622.5	712.1	715.4	629.7	629.8	595.3	563.1	597.9				624.8
Canada, Export Unit Value, F.O.B. In Canadian Dollar Per Cubic Meter													
1992	426.14	409.62	373.22	396.94	387.59	395.95	354.61	373.58	385.20	395.29	410.59	353.95	388.56
1993	392.59	396.65	393.73	424.19	515.51	448.76	408.39	435.72	505.58	517.58	494.52	476.08	450.78
1994	442.04	574.74	553.92	553.81	542.95	458.48	472.29	510.01	526.42	454.20	462.90	499.71	504.29
Finland, Export Unit Value, F.O.B. In Markka Per Cubic Meter													
1992	4,548	4,501	4,523	4,425	4,488	4,474	4,532	4,399	4,807	4,465	4,662	3,999	4,485
1993	4,135	3,939	4,088	3,752	3,876	3,906	3,962	3,817	3,914	4,046	3,890	3,719	3,920
1994	3,758	3,518	3,829	3,822	3,800	4,029	3,963	3,916	4,041	3,680	3,631	3,569	3,796
United Kingdom, Import Unit Value, C.I.F. In Pound Sterling Per Cubic Meter													
1992	143.52	182.04	215.30	230.92	204.20	156.32	229.29	202.98	215.69	255.57	252.41	266.59	212.90
1993	227.26	255.36	269.62	204.76	270.40	249.27	265.25	273.33	291.90	261.68	328.13	304.04	266.75
1994	256.36	252.50	263.47	299.61	291.19	209.08	275.85	272.06	294.44	276.46	213.94	247.54	262.71

[1] Sheet measurement = 1.2cm X 90.0cm X 1.8cm. *Source: Food and Agricultural Organization of the United Nations*

Magnesium

The year of 1994 was characterized by tight magnesium supplies in the U.S. While the U.S. is the world's largest producer of magnesium, domestic production fell as one producer closed nearly one-third of its annual capacity while domestic demand rose for aluminum alloying. As a result of the tight stock situation, prices for primary metal increased by more than $1,000 per tonne during 1994 while producer's inventories fell by 35 percent.

With a density only two-thirds that of aluminum, magnesium finds use in applications where weight is a consideration. Magnesium alloys find widespread use in aircraft and automobile parts, photo optical instruments, engines, luggage pipelines, water heaters and dry-cell batteries. Among the magnesium compounds, magnesium sulfate is consumed in explosives, fertilizers and paper production. Magnesium oxide is used in water treatment, household cleaners and pharmaceuticals. Demand for magnesium is expected to rise further as U.S. automobile manufacturers introduce new magnesium compounds in the 1996, 1997 and 1998 models. More diecasting facilities are scheduled to be constructed to handle the increased demand.

The tight supply situation that affected the U.S. was also seen in other parts of the world. Japan closed its last magnesium plant and there was a temporary shutdown in France. New magnesium extraction facilities were being planned in Australia, Canada and Israel, but the first of these facilities (Israel) was not expected to come on line until 1996. New production in other countries was not expected to start until the end of the 1990's.

In 1994, world primary production of magnesium was estimated by the Bureau of Mines to be 267,000 tonnes, down 7 percent from 1993. The U.S. produced about half of the total followed by Canada, Norway, Russia and Kazakhstan. World secondary production of magnesium was 88,200 tonnes, up almost 10 percent from 1993. The U.S. produced 62,100 tonnes while Japan produced 19,000 tonnes. On December 31, 1994, world annual primary magnesium production capacity was 500,000 tonnes. U.S. production capacity was 141,000 tonnes.

U.S. exports of magnesium metal in 1994 were 25,600 tonnes while exports of magnesium alloy were 5,630 tonnes. The major markets for magnesium metal were Belgium, Japan and the Netherlands. The major market for alloy was Canada.

In the U.S., consumption was primarily for aluminum alloys and for iron and steel desulfurization.

World Production of Magnesium (Primary and Secondary) In Metric Tons

	Primary Production											Secondary Procuction			
Year	Brazil	Canada	China	France	Italy	Japan	Kazakhstan[3]	Norway	Russia[4]	United States	World Total[2]	Japan	United Kingdom	United States	Former USSR
1983	551	6,600	7,700	12,208	8,473	6,643	-----	32,897	91,000	115,431	286,755	14,343	1,900	46,329	9,000
1984[3]	1,323	8,800	7,700	14,299	8,257	7,830	-----	54,343	94,000	159,207	360,459	17,258	1,102	48,357	9,000
1985	2,615	7,200	3,000	13,639	7,863	8,456	-----	54,704	87,000	135,728	325,183	20,894	900	41,298	8,000
1986	4,356	5,100	3,000	13,361	12,417	8,116	-----	56,522	89,000	125,639	322,408	13,400	1,000	41,807	8,000
1987	5,488	8,800	3,000	13,601	7,626	8,180	-----	56,907	90,000	124,396	323,930	10,124	1,000	45,165	8,000
1988	5,865	7,600	3,200	13,776	5,436	9,012	-----	50,317	91,000	141,983	334,348	15,099	1,000	50,207	8,000
1989	6,200	7,000	3,500	14,600	5,768	8,381	-----	49,827	91,000	152,066	344,447	20,270	1,000	51,200	8,000
1990	8,700	25,300	5,900	14,000	5,725	12,843	-----	48,222	88,000	139,333	354,000	23,308	900	54,808	7,500
1991	7,800	35,512	8,600	14,000	3,919	11,559	-----	44,322	80,000	131,288	342,000	17,158	800	50,543	7,000
1992	7,300	25,800	10,600	13,700	1,211	7,119	20,000	30,404	40,000	136,947	307,000	12,978	800	57,045	6,500
1993[1]	9,700	23,000	11,800	10,900	-----	7,470	20,000	27,300	30,000	132,144	281,000	13,215	500	58,890	6,000
1994[2]	9,700	28,900	11,000	8,800	-----	3,410	15,000	27,600	25,000	128,000	267,000	19,000	500	62,100	5,000

[1] Preliminary. [2] Estimate. [3] Data prior to 1985 reported in short tons. [4] Formerly part of the U.S.S.R.; data not reported separately until 1992.
Source: U.S. Bureau of Mines

Salient Statistics of Magnesium in the United States In Metric Tons

	Production								Domestic Consumption of Primary Magnesium					
		Secondary							Structural Products					
Year	Primary (Ingot)	New Scrap	Old Scrap	Total	Exports[3]	Imports for Consumption	Stocks Dec. 31[4]	$ Price per Pound[5]	Castings	Wrought	Total	Aluminum Alloys	Other Uses[6]	Total
1982	102,197	19,801	23,431	43,232	39,613	4,784	46,000	1.34	3,600	10,128	13,728	39,878	20,993	74,599
1983	115,431	21,591	24,738	46,329	46,690	6,350	28,000	1.38	3,341	11,435	14,776	46,026	21,174	81,976
1984[7]	159,207	21,594	26,763	48,357	48,337	9,381	35,000	1.43-1.48	4,193	10,246	14,439	48,673	26,775	89,887
1985	135,728	19,579	25,944	41,298	36,680	8,411	39,000	1.48-1.53	4,536	10,840	15,376	31,059	31,317	83,752
1986	125,639	18,813	22,994	41,807	39,909	8,355	39,000	1.53	5,767	7,737	13,504	39,290	26,167	78,961
1987	134,396	21,712	23,452	45,164	44,182	10,851	28,000	1.53	6,285	8,300	14,585	52,172	27,863	94,620
1988	141,983	22,567	27,640	50,207	49,802	14,407	25,000	1.58-1.63	7,069	10,138	17,207	53,671	29,915	100,793
1989	152,066	23,229	27,971	51,200	56,631	12,289	26,000	1.63	7,455	9,653	17,108	53,821	34,297	88,118
1990	139,333	23,424	31,384	54,808	51,834	26,755	26,000	1.43-1.63	9,078	10,944	20,022	45,060	31,026	76,086
1991	131,288	23,059	27,484	50,543	55,160	31,863	27,000	1.43	8,857	8,802	17,659	45,809	28,404	74,213
1992	136,947	26,191	30,854	57,045	51,951	11,844	13,000	1.46-1.53	10,223	8,843	19,066	41,003	33,758	74,761
1993[1]	132,144	28,313	30,577	58,890	38,815	37,248	26,000	1.43-1.46	12,543	9,870	22,413	46,498	32,202	78,700
1994[2]	128,000	32,500	29,600	62,100	45,200	29,100	20,000	1.63	15,076	7,690	22,766	61,100	27,900	89,000

[1] Preliminary. [2] Estimate. [3] Metal & alloys in crude form & scrap. [4] Estimate of Industry Stocks, metal. [5] Magnesium (99.8%), F.O.B. Valasco, Texas.
[6] Distributive or sacrificial purposes. [7] Data prior to 1985 reported in short tons. *Source: U.S. Bureau of Mines*

Manganese

Manganese finds its primary use in the steel industry, where it is used as an alloy. Virtually all steel contains some amount of manganese, which increases hardness. Manganese is essential to iron and steel production due to its sulfur-fixing, deoxidizing and alloying properties. No practical approach currently exists for replacing it with other materials or for obtaining the bulk of U.S. requirements from domestic sources. Manganese ore, when converted to a metallic alloy with iron, forms the compound known as ferromanganese. Nonmetallurgical uses for manganese include plant fertilizer and animal feed. Manganese is a key component of some widely used aluminum alloys and is used in oxide form in dry cell batteries. The use of manganese in batteries has been denoted by the expansion of domestic production of electrolytic manganese dioxide as well as record imports of manganese dioxide.

The world's largest producers of manganese include countries that made up the former Soviet Union, such as the Ukraine, China, South Africa and Brazil. In the U.S., manganese ore was consumed by approximately 20 firms located principally in the Eastern and Midwestern states. Most ore consumption is directly related to steel production. The U.S. Bureau of Mines reported that U.S. imports of manganese for consumption over the January-June 1995 period were 298,000 tonnes, down 16 percent from the same period of 1994. Imports of manganese ore and manganese dioxide over the 1995 period were 79,700 tonnes, down 2 percent, while imports of ferroalloy and manganese metal were 220,000 tonnes, down 20 percent. The U.S. exports minor amounts of manganese. For the January-June 1995 period, manganese ore exports were 3,840 tonnes, up 28 percent on 1994, while ferroalloy and manganese metal exports were up 19 percent at 10,800 tonnes.

In June 1995, U.S. imports of silicomanganese had a manganese content of 15,300 tonnes. For the January-June 1995 period, these imports had a manganese content of 88,200 tonnes. The major suppliers were the Republic of South Africa, 32,300 tonnes, Australia 13,000 tonnes, India 12,500 tonnes and Mexico 9,310 tonnes.

In January-June 1995. U.S. imports of low carbon ferromangenese were 5,680 tonnes. Medium carbon ferromangenese imports were 17,200 tonnes. High carbon ferromanganese imports in January-June 1995 were 129,000 tonnes. The major suppliers were South Africa, France and Australia.

World Production of Manganese Ore   In Thousands of Metric Tons (Gross Weight)

Year	Australia[2] 37-53[4]	Brazil 30-50	Bulgaria 29	China 30	Gabon 50-53	Georgia[5] 29-30	Ghana 30-50	Hungary[3] 30-33	India 10-54	Iran 25-35	Mexico 27-50	Morocco 50-53	South Africa 30-48 +	Ukraine[5] 29-30	World Total
1984	2,038	2,969	50	1,760	2,336	-----	296	74	1,246	73	525	65	3,361	11,100	26,100
1985	2,208	2,781	42	2,900	2,579	-----	351	69	1,367	61	437	48	3,969	10,900	27,948
1986	1,818	2,973	41	3,000	2,767	-----	335	69	1,337	37	506	44	4,100	10,300	27,523
1987	2,043	2,279	42	2,900	2,649	-----	303	86	1,435	69	425	47	3,631	10,313	26,404
1988[6]	1,985	1,991	34	3,212	2,254	-----	260	81	1,333	75	444	30	4,023	9,108	25,013
1989	2,124	1,904	32	3,200	2,592	-----	297	84	1,334	81	394	32	4,884	9,141	26,260
1990	1,920	2,300	39	4,080	2,423	-----	247	60	1,385	54	451	49	4,402	8,500	26,108
1991	1,482	2,000	34	5,150	1,620	-----	320	30	1,401	48	254	59	3,146	7,240	22,937
1992	1,210	1,990	29	5,300	1,556	1,200	276	18	1,810	40	407	44	2,464	5,819	22,400
1993	2,090	1,840	-----	5,860	1,290	1,000	295	59	1,660	55	363	43	2,507	3,800	21,200
1994[1]	2,000	2,300	-----	5,900	1,440	800	270	55	1,600	40	307	31	2,850	2,980	20,900

[1] Preliminary. [2] Metallurgical Ore. [3] Concentrate. [4] Range of percentage of manganese. [5] Formerly part of the U.S.S.R.; data not reported separately until 1992. [6] Data reported in short tons prior to 1988. *Source: U.S. Bureau of Mines*

Salient Statistics of Manganese in the United States   In Thousands of Metric Tons (Gross Weight)

Year	Net Import Reliance as a % of Apparent Consumption	Manganese Ore (35% or More Manganese): Imports for Consumption	Exports	Consumption	Stocks, Dec. 31[3]	Ferromanganese: Imports for Consumption	Exports	Consumption	Avg. Price Mn. Metallurgical Ore $ Lg. Ton Unit[4]	Silicomanganese: Exports	Imports
1984	98	338	238	615	582	409	7	492	1.42	5.3	138.5
1985	100	387	56	545	589	367	7	466	1.43	3.1	165.5
1986	100	463	42	500	455	396	4	376	1.34	2.0	198.6
1987	100	341	63	533	456	368	3	409	1.27	.7	191.4
1988[5]	100	464	62	503	415	482	3	425	1.75	8.3	256.0
1989	100	580	52	559	470	432	8	399	2.76	6.5	281.5
1990	100	307	70	497	379	380	7	413	3.78	1.8	224.5
1991	100	234	66	473	275	320	15	346	3.72	2.9	258.3
1992	100	247	13	438	276	304	13	339	3.25	9.2	257.2
1993[1]	100	232	16	389	302	347	18	341	2.60	9.4	316.0
1994[2]	100	331	15	449	269	336	11	347	2.40	6.8	273.0

[1] Preliminary. [2] Estimate. [3] Including bonded warehouses; excludes Government stocks; also excludes small tonnages of dealers' stocks. [4] 46-48% Mn, C.I.F., U.S. Ports. [5] Data reported in short tons prior to 1988. *Source: U.S. Bureau of Mines*

U.S. Consumption of Manganese by End Uses In Thousands of Metric Tons

Year	Appliances & Equipment	Batteries	Cans & Containers	Chemicals	Construction	Machinery	Oil & Gas Industry	Transportation	Other	Total
1979	59	17	61	59	291	217	70	296	180	1,250
1980	49	17	49	50	243	167	79	214	161	1,029
1981[3]	46	15	42	45	229	155	81	194	125	932
1982	27	19	28	26	138	83	36	104	147	610
1983	30	23	25	20	137	82	25	117	147	606
1984	33	31	34	31	154	88	33	126	39	569
1985	29	35	32	20	149	71	31	112	154	633
1986	24	39	28	21	134	59	23	86	248	662
1987	28	39	32	40	150	70	27	95	153	634
1988	17	44	28	42	221	100	19	93	119	682
1989	11	41	21	39	138	75	9	49	340	723
1990	9	42	22	36	138	74	14	45	250	630
1991[1]	8	52	20	33	122	45	10	47	260	598
1992[2]	8	50	20	34	101	63	10	60	250	596

[1] Preliminary. [2] Estimate. [3] Data reported in short tons prior to 1981. *Source: U.S. Bureau of Mines*

Manganese Ore (20% or More Mn) Imported[3] into the U.S. In Metric Tons (Mn Content)

Year	Australia	Brazil	Gabon	Mexico	Morocco	South Africa	Total	Customs Value Thous. $
1979	55,316	51,660	49,222	2,059	10,719	52,117	243,553	27,485
1980	106,043	33,648	79,858	18,568	5,260	86,373	329,750	46,413
1981	34,259	38,909	90,629	25,813	13,594	97,536	300,740	42,643
1982	18,842	2,962	23,156	1,492	4,996	57,873	111,054	16,160
1983	15,118	39,112	85,509	25,598	20	12,703	178,060	19,867
1984	21,005	44,259	66,135	16,298	39	17,286	165,023	16,024
1985	43,104	59,816	64,093	21,761	65	-----	188,840	22,561
1986	35,539	38,728	119,068	14,771	186	13,988	225,608	23,122
1987	48,747	29,673	88,413	3,712	30	-----	170,576	15,079
1988[4]	39,324	27,004	146,654	35,490	94	-----	248,566	29,074
1989	60,436	93,283	109,637	9,828	20	21,618	298,485	43,794
1990[5]	35,873	22,776	74,766	3,012	20	10,977	164,180	40,054
1991	16,485	2,583	79,997	4,673	44	-----	117,255	40,332
1992	25,519	15,541	75,354	3,930	56	-----	120,400	29,967
1993[1]	30,171	5,573	66,659	7,317	43	6,006	115,770	24,927
1994[2]	23,200	4,530	112,000	13,700	56	7,780	116,100	29,800

[1] Preliminary. [2] Estimate. [3] Imports for consumption. [4] Manganese content of 35% or more prior to 1989. [5] Data reported in short tons prior to 1991.
Source: U.S. Bureau of Mines

Average Price of Ferromanganese[1] (High Carbon[2] - F.O.B. Plant) In Dollars Per Gross Ton -- Carloads

Year	Jan.	Feb.	Mar.	Apr.	May	June	July	Aug.	Sept.	Oct.	Nov.	Dec.	Average
1976	432.50	432.50	432.50	432.50	432.50	432.50	432.50	432.50	432.50	432.50	425.00	417.50	430.63
1977	417.50	417.50	417.50	399.50	399.50	399.50	399.50	399.50	399.50	399.50	399.50	399.50	404.00
1978	399.50	399.50	399.50	399.50	422.17	425.00	425.00	425.00	425.00	425.00	425.00	425.00	416.26
1979	440.00	440.00	440.00	465.00	490.00	490.00	490.00	490.00	490.00	493.00	510.00	510.00	479.04
1980	510.00	510.00	510.00	510.00	510.00	510.00	510.00	510.00	510.00	510.00	510.00	510.00	510.00
1981	510.00	510.00	510.00	510.00	510.00	510.00	510.00	510.00	510.00	510.00	510.00	510.00	510.00
1982	510.00	510.00	510.00	510.00	510.00	510.00	510.00	510.00	510.00	510.00	510.00	510.00	510.00
1983	510.00	510.00	510.00	510.00	510.00	510.00	510.00	510.00	510.00	510.00	510.00	510.00	510.00
1984	510.00	510.00	510.00	510.00	510.00	510.00	510.00	510.00	510.00	NQ	NQ	NQ	510.00
1985	NQ	NQ	NQ	NQ	NQ	NQ	NQ	NQ	NQ	NQ	NQ	NQ	NQ
1986	NQ	NQ	NQ	NQ	NQ	NQ	NQ	NQ	NQ	NQ	NQ	NQ	NQ
1987	NQ	NQ	NQ	NQ	326.25	331.88	339.50	345.00	355.00	358.00	363.00	373.00	348.95
1988	382.50	382.50	414.50	422.50	435.63	440.00	457.50	475.00	530.00	550.00	550.00	550.00	465.84
1989	550.00	550.50	573.75	597.50	640.00	640.00	640.00	634.00	610.00	610.00	610.00	610.00	605.48
1990	610.00	610.00	610.00	610.00	610.00	610.00	610.00	610.00	610.00	610.00	610.00	610.00	610.00
1991	610.00	610.00	610.00	610.00	610.00	610.00	610.00	610.00	610.00	610.00	610.00	610.00	610.00
1992	610.00	610.00	610.00	610.00	610.00	610.00	610.00	610.00	610.00	610.00	610.00	610.00	610.00
1993	610.00	610.00	610.00	610.00	610.00	610.00	610.00	610.00	610.00	610.00	610.00	610.00	610.00

[1] Domestic standard. [2] Prior to May 1987, prices are for 78% Mn-F.O.B. plant. NQ = No quote. *Source: American Metal Market*

Meats

U.S. commercial red meat production continues to set new annual production records; the combined total of beef, veal, lamb and pork in 1995 of 43.6 billion pounds compares with the previous record of 42.5 billion in 1994. Forecasts for 1996 place total production at 44.7 billion pounds. Red meat accounts for almost 60 percent of total meat production, with poultry contributing the balance. Beef accounted for more than half of 1995 red meat output at 25 billion pounds. Pork output totaled 18 billion pounds. On a world basis, China is the largest red meat producing nation with a record high 43.5 million metric tons in 1995. The U.S. was second at 20 million tons.

U.S. per capita red meat usage (carcass weight) has shown a mixed pattern in recent years, slipping for beef and rising for pork. Beef use in 1995 of 97.3 pounds compares with 96.4 pounds in 1994, but during the 1980's per capita use averaged about 105 pounds. Pork use continues to set new highs with 69 pounds in 1995, up from 68.4 in 1994 and a 1980's average of 65 pounds. Forecasts for 1996 put per capita beef use at 98.5 pounds and pork at a record high 69.7 pounds. The divergence largely reflects a shift in consumer food preferences which favor lean products and the aggressive advertising by the pork industry emphasizing pork as a white meat. Also, U.S. consumer meat demand is sensitive to the nation's economic strength and level of disposable income, and beef's higher retail can abet demand for pork.

Large supplies pressured beef prices in 1995: Choice steers (basis Nebraska) averaged $65-67/cwt. versus $68.84 1994 and forecasts for 1996 ranged from $62 to $68. Midwest barrow prices of $42-43/cwt. compare with $40.06/cwt. in 1994, but estimates for 1996 point to increased pressure with a $37-41/cwt. range.

The U.S. is a net red meat importer, but if poultry is included in the foreign trade totals, the U.S. is a net meat exporter. Red meat imports in 1995 of 1.5 million metric tons (carcass weight) compares with 1.4 million in 1994 and a record high 1.6 million in 1988. (Japan is the world's largest red meat importer with almost 1.7 million tons in 1995). Total 1995 exports of 1 million tons were a record high and almost three times the pace of the 1980's. (The world's largest exporter is the Netherlands with 1.4 million tons in 1995). The U.S. imports live cattle from Canada and Mexico, while beef and veal are mostly imported from Australia and New Zealand. U.S. pork trade is small by comparison.

World Total Meat Production[4] In Thousands of Metric Tons

Year	Agrentina	Australia	Brazil	Canada	China[5]	Denmark	France	Germany	Italy	Japan	Mexico	New Zealand	Poland	Russia[6]	Ukraine[6]	United Kingdom	United States
1987	2,782	2,423	3,450	2,108	19,859	1,385	3,605	4,565	2,428	2,146	2,228	1,190	2,609	------	15,517	2,410	17,547
1988	2,697	2,377	3,600	2,161	21,870	1,386	3,532	4,477	2,378	2,147	2,791	1,811	2,635	------	15,893	2,314	18,146
1989	2,696	2,452	4,750	2,164	23,262	1,372	3,670	6,006	2,515	2,142	3,125	1,168	2,621	------	16,501	2,326	17,963
1990	2,738	2,683	4,650	2,022	25,132	1,100	3,816	6,111	2,583	2,104	2,658	1,014	2,736	8,204	3,608	2,331	17,597
1991	2,735	2,704	5,513	2,022	27,238	1,485	3,963	5,552	2,608	2,057	2,535	1,053	2,768	7,526	3,339	2,389	17,956
1992	2,602	2,810	5,620	2,107	29,406	1,600	3,997	4,994	2,648	2,024	2,626	1,036	2,708	6,748	2,874	2,297	18,589
1993	2,630	2,780	5,795	2,052	32,254	1,727	3,901	4,796	2,642	2,026	2,718	1,095	2,022	6,260	2,419	2,236	18,488
1994[1]	2,682	2,763	5,775	2,137	36,957	1,729	3,872	4,518	2,618	1,992	2,852	1,085	1,799	5,670	2,371	2,323	19,361
1995[2]	2,630	2,612	6,050	2,215	43,500	1,707	3,959	4,464	2,596	1,951	2,948	1,100	1,937	4,950	2,213	2,346	19,778
1996[3]	2,650	2,681	6,200	2,300	46,500	1,725	3,974	4,406	2,596	1,914	2,780	1,085	1,984	4,480	2,110	2,353	20,325

[1] Preliminary. [2] Estimate. [3] Forecast. [4] Includes beef, veal, pork, sheep and goat meat. [5] Predominately pork production. [6] Formerly part of the U.S.S.R.; data not reported separately until 1990. *Source: Foreign Agricultural Service, U.S. Department of Agriculture*

Production and Consumption of Red Meats in the United States (Carcass Weight)

	Beef			Veal			Lamb & Mutton			Pork (Excluding Lard)			All Meats		
	Commercial Production	Consumption		Commercial Production	Consumption		Commercial Production	Consumption		Commercial Production	Consumption		Commercial Production	Consumption	
Year	-- Million Pounds --	Total	Per Capita Lb.[4]	- Million Pounds -	Total	Per Capita Lb.[4]	- Million Pounds -	Total	Per Capita Lb.[4]	-- Million Pounds --	Total	Per Capita Lb.[4]	-- Million Pounds --	Total	Per Capita Lb.[4]
1985	23,557	25,523	107.0	515	499	2.2	352	389	1.6	14,728	15,865	66.5	39,136	42,311	177.4
1986	24,213	25,257	108.0	524	509	2.3	331	378	1.6	13,998	15,135	62.9	39,051	42,051	174.7
1987	23,405	25,252	104.0	430	417	1.9	309	362	1.5	14,311	15,352	63.2	38,442	41,422	170.6
1988	23,424	24,330	103.1	396	387	1.7	329	387	1.6	15,623	16,549	67.5	39,763	42,599	173.9
1989	22,974	24,030	98.4	355	344	1.4	341	386	1.6	15,759	16,571	67.0	39,418	41,644	168.4
1990	22,634	24,114	96.2	327	316	1.3	358	397	1.6	15,300	16,030	64.1	38,608	40,782	163.2
1991	22,800	24,261	95.4	306	296	1.2	358	397	1.6	15,948	16,399	64.9	39,402	41,214	163.1
1992	22,968	24,261	95.0	310	299	1.2	343	388	1.5	17,185	17,475	68.4	40,795	42,437	166.1
1993	22,942	24,006	93.0	267	286	1.1	329	381	1.5	17,030	17,419	67.5	40,568	42,092	163.1
1994[1]	24,278	25,127	96.4	283	291	1.2	304	345	1.3	17,658	17,829	68.4	42,523	43,592	167.3
1995[2]	25,016	25,482	96.9	310	321	1.2	280	337	1.2	17,822	17,768	67.5	43,428	43,908	166.8
1996[3]	25,750	25,863	97.4	316	326	1.2	262	310	1.2	18,325	19,413	68.2	44,653	45,912	168.0

[1] Preliminary. [2] Estimate. [3] Forecast. [4] Carcass Weight. *Source: Economic Research Service, U.S. Department of Agriculture*

Total Red Meat Imports (Carcass Weight Equivalent) of Principal Countries In Thousands of Metric Tons

Year	Belgium & Lux.	Canada	Czecho-slovakia	France	Ger-many	Greece	Hong Kong	Italy	Japan	Rep. of Korea	Nether-lands	Russia[3]	Singa-pore	Spain	Switzer-land	United Kingdom	United States
1981	88	110	21	579	687	80	------	690	612	45	146	786	------	16	31	1,072	1,058
1982	79	112	29	618	692	157	68	824	546	82	119	679	3	28	25	1,137	1,175
1983	107	121	25	676	728	216	82	832	599	78	108	779	24	26	27	1,072	1,212
1984	79	130	15	711	796	194	238	823	636	39	105	691	22	36	21	1,015	1,280
1985	79	132	15	760	843	208	296	948	647	19	116	587	0	36	15	955	1,476
1986	77	130	15	841	837	221	300	961	712	14	104	537	38	92	16	1,007	1,506
1987	78	157	15	829	880	246	281	952	869	16	109	495	42	90	20	1,036	1,602
1988	76	170	15	869	940	232	313	906	994	45	132	353	40	93	18	1,081	1,630
1989	81	175	25	908	952	239	292	974	1,150	111	119	355	47	127	14	1,033	1,421
1990	110	198	15	967	1,033	209	311	1,025	1,153	120	143	545	43	971	17	76	1,503
1991	71	232	0	1,035	1,240	179	306	1,106	1,206	201	181	740	41	140	13	896	1,463
1992	81	237	108	1,033	1,431	248	265	1,235	1,388	187	203	292	44	121	14	885	1,423
1993	76	305	44	1,093	1,389	246	246	1,242	1,482	142	177	140	56	129	16	889	1,449
1994[1]	108	313	25	1,013	1,312	230	294	1,125	1,628	191	233	584	50	147	18	838	1,435
1995[2]	123	250	40	1,032	1,337	238	296	1,136	1,775	280	190	700	54	134	20	869	1,308

[1] Preliminary. [2] Estimate. [3] Formerly part of the U.S.S.R.; data not reported separately until 1992. *Source: Foreign Agricultural Service, U.S. Department of Agriculture*

Total Red Meat Exports (Carcass Weight Equivalent) of Principal Countries In Thousands of Metric Tons

Year	Agren-tina	Aust-ralia	Brazil	Canada	China	Den-mark	France	India	Ireland	Nether-lands	New Zealand	Poland	Romania	Ukraine[3]	United Kingdom	United States	Uruguay
1981	508	966	281	207	------	905	415	59	324	932	817	60	245	53	243	240	185
1982	546	1,184	361	247	230	909	401	62	311	879	846	52	160	32	194	213	182
1983	438	947	404	242	264	945	387	83	341	957	938	93	185	25	296	225	236
1984	266	747	483	280	273	952	489	88	301	1,066	815	68	177	27	344	227	142
1985	272	860	540	313	278	958	503	65	370	1,158	876	13	265	30	284	210	131
1986	261	1,031	355	376	222	1,007	649	64	473	1,216	863	122	280	353	306	279	198
1987	294	1,122	304	394	238	986	604	79	496	1,265	922	128	310	1,157	313	327	104
1988	464	1,102	567	405	227	1,005	630	69	431	1,309	901	131	305	747	270	402	142
1989	369	1,069	304	407	261	990	586	70	478	1,357	908	140	320	704	301	606	177
1990	461	1,312	243	424	395	995	644	133	469	1,395	794	107	25	545	188	565	192
1991	402	1,391	290	375	494	1,097	757	151	529	1,438	845	31	31	740	299	669	117
1992	288	1,496	390	453	195	1,173	864	91	643	1,485	884	34	40	291	348	787	125
1993	281	1,478	335	490	264	1,257	913	104	736	1,538	931	25	3	236	398	779	104
1994[1]	378	1,473	383	518	295	1,349	1,042	118	613	1,454	894	41	60	181	430	976	152
1995[2]	463	1,329	315	520	310	1,313	999	129	372	1,425	923	39	47	167	430	1,211	150

Preliminary. [2] Estimate. [3] Formerly part of the U.S.S.R.; data not reported separately until 1992. *Source: Foreign Agricultural Service, U.S. Department of Agriculture*

U.S. Exports and Imports of Meats into the United States (Carcass Weight Equivalent)[3]

	Exports				Imports			
Year	Beef and Veal	Lamb and Mutton	Pork[4]	All Meat	Beef and Veal	Lamb and Mutton	Pork[4]	All Meat
	In Millions of Pounds							
1981	221	2	307	531	1,761	31	541	2,333
1982	254	2	214	470	1,958	21	612	2,591
1983	276	1	219	497	1,974	18	707	2,717
1984	335	2	164	500	1,847	20	954	2,821
1985	332	1	128	461	2,091	36	1,128	3,255
1986	526	1	86	613	2,156	41	1,122	3,319
1987	611	1	109	722	2,293	44	1,195	3,533
1988	690	1	195	887	2,406	51	1,137	3,594
1989	1,023	5	262	1,290	2,178	46	896	3,120
1990	1,006	6	238	1,250	2,356	41	898	3,295
1991	1,188	10	283	1,481	1,406	41	775	3,223
1992	1,324	8	407	1,739	2,440	50	645	3,135
1993	1,275	8	435	1,718	2,401	53	740	3,194
1994[1]	1,611	9	531	2,151	2,371	49	743	3,163
1995[2]	1,880	7	785	2,672	2,165	59	655	2,879
1996[2]	2,120	8	900	3,028	2,125	53	650	2,828

[1] Preliminary. [2] Estimate. [3] Includes meat content of minor meats and of mixed products. *Source: Economic Research Service, U.S. Department of Agriculture*

MEATS

United States Meat Imports by Type of Product In Metric Tons

Year	Beaf and Veal: Fresh, Chilled & Frozen	Beaf and Veal: Canned, including Sausage	Beaf and Veal: Other Prepared or Preserved	Lamb Mutton and Goat, Except Canned	Pork: Fresh and Frozen	Pork: Canned[2]	Pork: Other Prepared or Preserved	Sausage, all Types	Mixed Sausage	Other Meats[3]	Variety Meats, Fresh or Frozen	Total
1982	607,184	37,747	17,402	8,649	125,282	96,831	1,547	2,372	2,242	4,408	2,823	906,487
1983	565,997	59,073	16,766	8,752	121,707	125,593	2,300	2,176	1,911	3,606	3,935	911,814
1984	516,960	57,863	19,864	8,693	207,703	142,423	3,372	2,243	2,121	5,088	5,707	972,037
1985	594,476	64,277	19,314	15,565	254,538	160,802	6,312	2,192	2,672	5,305	5,622	1,130,075
1986	637,718	45,779	20,778	16,596	263,488	151,730	8,221	2,640	2,849	4,621	6,475	1,160,895
1987	671,152	56,653	17,450	17,204	302,392	145,464	9,387	2,688	4,222	4,126	9,590	1,240,328
1988	703,415	66,919	10,367	19,239	282,728	139,847	10,214	2,906	2,732	3,977	8,905	1,251,249
1989	638,999	68,710	1,434	20,917	225,304	107,267	8,651	2,656	2,620	3,509	11,102	1,091,169
1990	694,163	67,054	1,520	19,056	232,253	98,479	10,055	3,421	1,874	1,239	11,423	1,140,537
1991	709,997	71,570	1,870	19,100	215,933	72,666	11,760	2,144	1,533	3,904	18,266	1,128,744
1992	728,922	72,631	2,112	23,853	185,672	54,114	13,104	2,453	1,674	1,607	20,059	1,106,201
1993[1]	720,079	71,351	2,995	24,468	207,652	70,577	14,295	2,695	1,368	2,274	25,298	1,143,052
1994[1]	714,445	------ 74,905 ------		23,282	209,024	------ 87,674 ------		2,237	1,899	1,689	27,789	1,149,851

[1] Preliminary. [2] Includes canned hams, shoulders and bacon. [3] Mostly mixed lucheon meats. *Source: Foreign Agricultural Service, U.S. Department of Agriculture*

United States Meat Exports by Type of Product In Metric Tons

Year	Beef and Veal: Fresh, Chilled & Frozen	Beef and Veal: Prepared and Preserved	Lamb and Mutton, Fresh or Frozen	Pork: Fresh, Chilled & Frozen	Pork: Hams & Shoulders, Cured	Pork: Bacon	Pork: Other Pork Prepared or Preserved: Not Canned	Pork: Other Pork Prepared or Preserved: Canned	Sausage, Bologna & Frankfurters	Variety Meats, Fresh, Chilled & Frozen	Other Meats[2]	Total
1982	71,621	14,046	676	58,541	1,358	774	7,514	1,289	3,404	222,688	48,924	416,095
1983	80,976	12,070	632	62,141	1,794	601	5,581	695	3,139	213,155	36,176	416,960
1984	99,208	12,322	878	46,098	1,474	621	3,837	513	2,603	213,180	35,457	416,191
1985	99,923	9,605	460	34,394	1,175	450	4,066	638	2,908	239,451	38,395	431,465
1986	173,884	10,519	558	20,969	650	474	4,796	349	3,214	241,051	46,760	503,224
1987	200,180	10,789	668	29,145	1,227	617	3,597	376	4,582	222,342	61,812	535,335
1988	214,530	14,083	619	54,598	2,138	1,045	4,924	268	8,439	302,087	75,084	677,815
1989	373,110	8,810	2,076	79,318	6,101	3,788	2,204	1,395	11,968	245,235	78,550	812,555
1990	339,925	7,783	2,490	66,756	5,567	4,518	4,310	1,036	14,208	226,623	70,558	731,566
1991	395,697	10,248	3,790	76,193	4,702	5,443	6,133	1,278	24,025	280,721	61,440	869,670
1992	436,455	12,064	3,278	116,496	8,181	7,396	5,812	2,352	22,796	303,295	57,154	975,279
1993[1]	411,003	14,464	3,608	129,240	5,208	7,092	4,579	2,349	34,198	338,689	45,905	996,335
1994[1]	517,481	13,539	3,763	149,311	8,476	12,062	4,455	2,973	46,912	371,816	70,625	1,406,499

[1] Preliminary. [2] Includes sausage ingredients, cured (excluding canned); meat and meat products canned; and baby food, canned.
Source: Foreign Agricultural Service, U.S. Department of Agriculture

Average Wholesale Prices of Meats In Cents Per Pound

Year	Composite Retail Price: of Beef, Choice, Grade 3	Composite Retail Price: of Pork[3]	Wholesale Value[4]: Beef	Wholesale Value[4]: Pork	Net Farm Value of Pork[5]	Cow Beef Canner & Cutter, Central US	Boxed Beef Cut-out, Choice 1-3, Central US, 550-700 lbs.	Pork Carcass Cut-out, U.S., No. 2	Lamb Carcass, Choice-Prime, East Coast, 55-65 lbs.	Pork[6] Loins, Central US, 14-18 lbs.	Skinned Ham, Central US, 17-20 lbs.	Pork Bellies, Central US, 12-14 lbs.
1982	238.40	175.40	165.90	121.80	87.00	------	105.69	71.41	121.86	111.51	90.22	76.54
1983	234.10	169.80	160.10	108.90	76.50	78.48	101.96	59.91	125.86	97.30	73.99	61.69
1984	235.50	162.00	162.50	110.10	77.40	74.70	103.80	61.35	130.99	96.36	75.41	60.31
1985	228.60	162.00	148.80	101.10	71.50	74.13	97.95	50.38	140.23	91.51	67.27	59.51
1986	226.80	178.40	146.50	110.90	80.60	71.31	94.61	69.05	140.32	104.78	77.96	65.82
1987	238.40	188.40	160.00	113.00	82.70	85.26	103.85	69.40	150.41	106.23	79.29	63.11
1988	250.30	183.40	169.40	101.00	69.40	87.77	110.35	59.57	137.81	97.49	69.05	41.25
1989	265.70	182.90	176.80	99.20	70.40	94.43	114.78	60.62	131.35	101.11	69.25	34.14
1990	281.00	212.60	189.60	118.30	87.20	102.41	123.21	74.00	121.47	117.52	84.87	53.80
1991	288.30	211.90	182.50	108.90	78.40	99.42	118.31	67.02	117.33	108.39	75.68	47.79
1992	284.60	198.00	179.60	98.90	67.80	93.85	116.73	58.37	131.66	101.41	67.42	30.39
1993[1]	293.40	197.60	182.50	102.80	72.50	95.43	118.74	62.19	143.97	107.47	67.85	41.62
1994[2]	283.40	199.80	170.80	104.00	62.80	84.39	108.47	57.28	147.62	101.50	58.29	40.00

[1] Preliminary. [2] Estimate. [3] Sold as retail cuts (ham, bacon, loin, etc.). [4] Quantity equivalent to 1 pound of retail cuts. [5] Portion of gross farm value minus farm by-product allowance. [6] Prior to 1983, 8-14 pounds. *Source: Economic Research Service, U.S. Department of Agriculture*

Average Wholesale Price of Boxed Beef Cut-Out[1], Choice, at Central Markets   In Cents Per Pound

Year	Jan.	Feb.	Mar.	Apr.	May	June	July	Aug.	Sept.	Oct.	Nov.	Dec.	Average
1985	105.48	102.77	98.73	96.40	97.31	94.89	91.02	91.48	91.83	97.37	105.12	103.03	97.95
1986	96.70	91.22	89.02	88.17	90.56	90.37	96.05	98.40	98.48	98.00	101.41	96.95	94.61
1987	96.71	98.56	98.40	106.45	114.03	113.18	104.55	101.52	104.33	103.97	102.62	101.82	103.85
1988	102.55	105.94	108.50	110.79	116.73	111.96	107.09	110.37	112.72	112.74	112.37	112.45	110.35
1989	113.62	114.30	117.09	118.58	118.53	114.53	113.17	112.83	110.08	110.04	115.06	119.52	114.78
1990	121.75	120.97	122.10	123.62	124.56	121.53	118.54	121.52	121.18	124.96	128.32	129.48	123.21
1991	125.04	123.24	125.45	125.96	123.76	120.61	115.82	111.54	110.61	113.04	113.43	111.18	118.31
1992	114.38	119.65	119.14	118.66	119.18	117.53	112.79	114.36	114.40	115.51	115.26	119.95	116.73
1993	122.69	122.13	124.80	126.12	127.19	120.52	114.48	116.73	114.65	111.52	113.26	110.83	118.74
1994	112.11	112.23	115.03	114.98	108.85	102.92	104.19	108.38	105.49	103.63	106.66	107.22	108.47
1995[2]	112.17	111.12	107.87	103.03	104.21	107.90	103.03	102.55	105.82	108.80	108.88	106.08	106.79

[1] Choice 1-3, 550-700 pounds. [2] Preliminary. *Source: Economic Research Service, U.S. Department of Agriculture*

Production (Commercial) of All Red Meats in the U.S.   In Millions of Pounds (Carcass Weight)

Year	Jan.	Feb.	Mar.	Apr.	May	June	July	Aug.	Sept.	Oct.	Nov.	Dec.	Total
1985	3,421	2,938	3,163	3,296	3,489	3,084	3,277	3,403	3,251	3,545	3,123	3,146	39,136
1986	3,483	2,942	3,133	3,476	3,388	3,157	3,281	3,179	3,260	3,505	2,986	3,261	39,051
1987	3,410	2,875	3,198	3,161	2,976	3,103	3,158	3,135	3,330	3,521	3,197	3,378	38,442
1988	3,246	3,071	3,355	3,158	3,206	3,319	3,170	3,507	3,462	3,512	3,399	3,358	39,763
1989	3,265	3,004	3,325	3,131	3,397	3,343	3,048	3,483	3,317	3,523	3,411	3,171	39,418
1990	3,354	2,972	3,259	3,049	3,320	3,175	3,100	3,431	3,096	3,499	3,273	3,080	38,608
1991	3,430	2,954	3,081	3,285	3,291	3,059	3,253	3,425	3,308	3,708	3,324	3,284	39,402
1992	3,623	3,090	3,376	3,259	3,237	3,423	3,441	3,406	3,560	3,656	3,289	3,434	40,794
1993	3,304	3,012	3,396	3,299	3,212	3,481	3,342	3,504	3,516	3,499	3,449	3,554	40,568
1994	3,367	3,125	3,591	3,383	3,429	3,616	3,361	3,683	3,721	3,799	3,666	3,714	42,531
1995[1]	3,560	3,210	3,751	3,304	3,758	3,798	3,424	3,860	3,697	3,795	3,748	3,553	43,549

[1] Preliminary. *Source: Economic Research Service, U.S. Department of Agriculture*

Cold Storage Holdings of All[1] Meat in the United States, at End of Month   In Millions of Pounds

Year	Jan.	Feb.	Mar.	Apr.	May	June	July	Aug.	Sept.	Oct.	Nov.	Dec.
1985	735.0	702.9	721.2	772.7	784.9	758.6	738.2	677.1	654.2	645.2	633.0	607.4
1986	616.8	615.3	622.5	658.2	667.2	638.8	618.6	572.0	541.1	572.4	564.3	566.2
1987	597.6	599.0	598.2	590.8	560.2	498.7	515.6	495.9	523.0	575.6	613.8	622.9
1988	664.6	689.5	716.6	759.4	721.2	670.7	670.7	633.9	644.3	644.0	701.5	716.4
1989	745.0	758.7	474.5	747.5	763.7	683.5	652.0	576.3	557.0	538.2	554.2	536.0
1990	564.7	609.6	637.5	653.0	632.8	591.6	565.9	507.4	507.5	536.7	536.7	536.4
1991	566.2	588.6	606.2	597.7	640.1	614.1	589.7	593.2	592.8	594.7	650.2	644.9
1992	707.9	690.5	725.4	706.8	692.2	665.3	646.0	595.6	613.4	637.8	626.6	615.1
1993	649.4	654.6	652.9	692.0	671.0	660.8	664.2	650.7	671.7	702.4	720.3	726.7
1994	807.7	800.5	842.5	858.0	837.5	822.6	816.2	771.9	788.5	822.7	827.5	802.0
1995[2]	838.8	834.9	837.6	852.7	831.2	820.8	802.7	802.7	733.4	711.3	731.6	756.3

[1] Includes beef and veal, mutton and lamb, pork and products, rendered pork fat, and miscellaneous meats. Excludes lard. [2] Preliminary.
Source: Economic Research Service, U.S. Department of Agriculture

Cold Storage Holdings of Frozen Beef in the United States   In Millions of Pounds

Year	Jan. 1	Feb. 1	Mar. 1	Apr. 1	May 1	June 1	July 1	Aug. 1	Sept. 1	Oct. 1	Nov. 1	Dec. 1
1985	357.7	375.1	347.0	334.0	328.0	300.9	295.5	319.7	310.6	308.4	294.9	302.3
1986	317.4	318.4	302.3	297.1	301.2	318.5	321.6	337.0	319.4	291.6	292.3	297.5
1987	310.6	320.6	306.0	311.1	312.3	280.1	252.7	278.7	269.3	286.5	307.6	304.3
1988	288.7	316.7	325.4	313.2	305.0	275.1	248.4	269.6	294.9	307.6	296.5	300.4
1989	317.5	315.1	313.4	298.9	275.4	244.1	241.8	249.2	242.4	231.8	220.7	237.6
1990	251.7	259.8	267.6	304.3	293.3	270.4	256.5	265.4	240.5	243.0	267.4	277.2
1991	300.4	298.9	271.3	276.9	265.6	234.7	247.1	273.2	259.4	276.7	298.2	306.3
1992	315.9	329.1	298.9	313.7	302.1	303.5	299.4	294.1	288.9	275.2	291.2	275.9
1993	272.8	286.4	279.9	293.9	276.7	262.1	271.7	285.3	307.5	326.8	344.4	376.3
1994	401.0	430.2	414.4	423.2	399.5	367.9	379.4	388.9	377.2	406.8	410.6	419.5
1995[1]	411.2	420.3	407.7	385.4	392.2	359.2	352.3	358.7	344.9	347.7	380.8	390.7

[1] Preliminary. *Source: Economic Research Service, U.S. Department of Agriculture*

Mercury

Mercury's use is declining due to the metal's toxicity to the environment which has eliminated several former uses. In the U.S., strict environmental legislation has limited the use and disposal of mercury, effectively confining the metal to products only where its use is still necessary, such as thermostats. The trend has been to substitute other materials for mercury rather than develop large-scale recycling programs. Secondary mercury now accounts for a large part of the world mercury supply as more chlor-alkali plants are dismantled and recycling of other products increases.

Mercury is a unique metal. At ordinary temperatures it's a liquid with a high specific value and good electrical conductivity. In the U.S., the last producing primary mercury mine (in Nevada) closed in 1990. Since then, the only prime virgin mercury produced in the U.S. has been recovered as a by-product of gold mining operations in California, Nevada and Utah; the recovery is required to prevent contamination of the environment.

World production of mercury is limited to a few countries. China and Algeria produced 975 metric tons in 1994, 55 percent of the world total of 1,760 and the lowest total in the first half of the 1990's. (One ton equals 29 flasks of 76 pounds each.) Spain, once the world's largest producer, output 300 tons in 1994 versus 643 tons in 1993. In 1986-87 Spain produced 4,100 tons. World reserves and reserve base (mostly in Spain) are estimated at 130,000 and 240,000 tons, respectively. Mercury occurs with gold ores and must be recovered to avoid contamination, but recovery restrictions are lax in some countries.

Mercury is a recoverable metal. In the U.S., secondary production totaled 466 tons in 1994 versus 350 tons in 1993, and a combined 1990-92 total of 449 tons. The larger secondary production in 1993-94 largely reflected new EPA restrictions banning landfill disposal and/or transport of mercury-containing wastes, which in turn encouraged more efficient recovery methods, especially from fluorescent lamps. Stockpiled mercury is another source of world supply. Industry stocks at U.S. sites in late 1994 totaled 368 metric tons versus 384 tons a year earlier. The U.S. government has a mercury stockpile but tight restrictions are in place as to how much can be sold each year and the stated goal is to reduce the inventory to zero. The Defense Logistics Agency (DLA) sold 86 tons from the National Defense Stockpile in 1994 before suspending sales in July. The DLA had authorization to sell 690 tons in fiscal 1995 and proposed to sell another 690 tons in fiscal 1996; whether these totals are realized is questionable.

U.S. mercury consumption totaled 483 tons in 1994, down from 558 tons in 1993. In 1984, battery production consumed almost 30,000 tons of mercury; the total in 1994 was only 6 tons. Domestic battery manufacturers now produce alkaline and zinc-carbon batteries without any added mercury. Chlorine and caustic soda manufacture is now the largest domestic use for mercury; 135 metric tons in 1994 versus 180 tons in 1993. Substitutes for mercury include lithium and composite ceramic materials.

U.S. foreign trade in mercury is small, but exports are usually well in excess of imports; totaling 316 metric tons and 129 tons, respectively, in 1994. In 1993, exports were 389 tons and imports 40 tons. India was the largest importer with 149 tons in 1994, while Russia was the major exporter to the U.S at 117 tons. The foreign trade totals sharply contrast 1993 when the Netherlands imported 108 tons and Russian exports to the U.S. were zero.

Mercury is usually sold in 34.5 kilogram flasks. The U.S. average price in 1994 was $194.450/flask (N.Y.) versus $187.00 in 1993. Prices during the 1980's averaged near $300/fl. European prices are generally lower than in the U.S. and considered more reflective of true market values.

World Mine Production of Mercury In Metric Tons (1 tonne = 29.008216 flasks)

Year	Algeria	China	Finland	Kyrgyzstan[3]	Mexico	Spain	Tajikistan[3]	Turkey	Ukraine[3]	United States	World Total
1986	759	700	146	------	104	2,757	------	291	2,250	NA	7,247
1987	705	700	144	------	124	1,395	------	211	2,300	100	5,810
1988	662	940	130	------	345	1,716	------	97	850	378	5,357
1989	587	1,200	159	------	651	1,224	------	197	850	414	5,464
1990	637	1,000	141	------	735	425	------	60	800	562	4,100
1991	431	760	74	------	340	100	------	25	750	58	2,540
1992	476	580	85	300	21	56	100	5	100	64	1,890
1993[1]	475	520	98	250	12	643	80	5	80	70	2,290
1994[2]	475	500	100	200	10	300	55	NA	50	NA	1,760

[1] Preliminary. [2] Estimate. [3] Formerly part of the U.S.S.R.; data not reported separately until 1992. NA = Not available. *Source: U.S. Bureau of Mines*

Salient Statistics of Mercury in the U.S. In Metric Tons

Year	Producing Mines	Secondary Production: Industrial	Secondary Production: Government[3]	N.D.S.[4] Shipments	Consumer & Dealer Stocks, Dec. 31	Industrial Demand	Exports	Imports
1988	10	278	214	52	338	1,503	NA	329
1989	10	137	180	170	217	121	221	131
1990	9	108	193	52	197	720	311	15
1991	8	165	215	103	313	554	786	56
1992	9	176	103	267	436	621	977	92
1993[1]	9	350	----	543	384	558	389	40
1994[2]	7	466	----	86	368	483	316	129

[1] Preliminary. [2] Estimate. [3] Secondary mercury shipped from the Department of Energy. [4] National Defense Stockpile. NA = Not available.
Source: U.S. Bureau of Mines

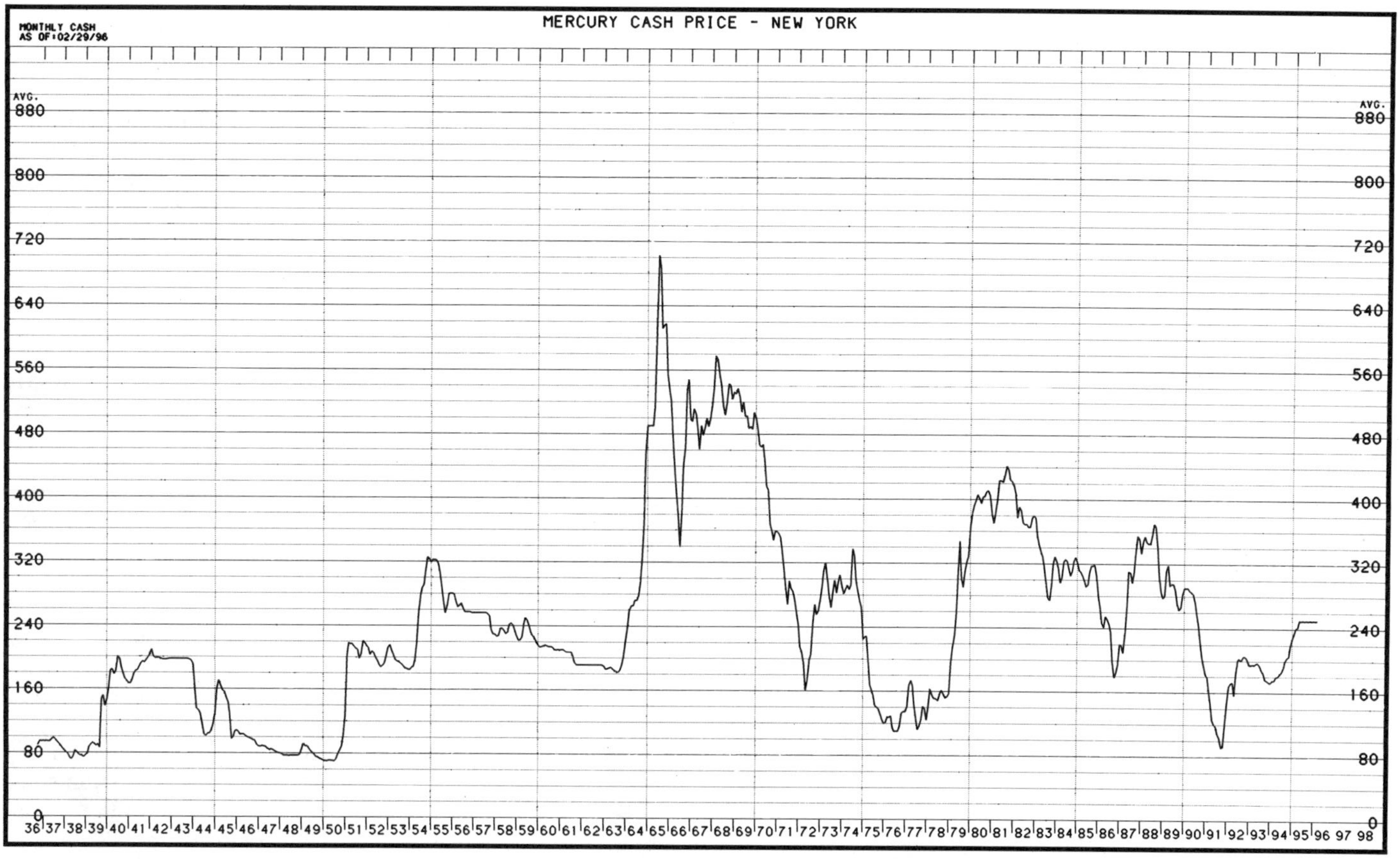

Average Price of Mercury in New York In Dollars Per Flask of 76 Pounds (34.5 Kilograms)

Year	Jan.	Feb.	Mar.	Apr.	May	June	July	Aug.	Sept.	Oct.	Nov.	Dec.	Average
1985	317.30	315.00	314.38	309.34	297.27	309.05	316.74	324.61	325.00	325.00	325.00	325.00	316.97
1986	285.68	261.97	252.44	272.05	277.50	276.07	260.00	218.10	181.91	193.80	215.19	219.43	242.85
1987	216.70	211.03	223.73	260.00	297.63	297.73	286.82	306.55	337.86	345.91	348.95	342.27	289.60
1988	354.00	357.00	350.00	337.14	326.90	352.28	367.13	360.43	349.29	322.74	299.34	293.45	339.14
1989	292.50	318.42	330.00	327.50	315.68	308.86	293.03	273.80	265.13	267.61	282.50	292.50	297.29
1990	292.50	292.50	287.84	285.00	285.00	285.00	281.45	262.50	259.34	235.54	198.75	182.50	262.33
1991	181.55	169.08	150.36	140.68	129.77	119.75	110.36	102.50	98.00	94.02	127.50	150.12	131.14
1992	162.86	177.24	180.00	180.00	190.63	202.50	202.50	203.45	207.50	207.50	207.50	207.50	194.10
1993	207.50	207.50	207.50	207.50	207.50	201.30	191.00	191.00	185.00	185.00	181.00	175.00	195.57
1994	175.00	175.00	179.78	180.00	180.95	186.64	196.50	200.00	203.10	205.00	217.50	230.71	194.18
1995	235.00		241.30		250.00	250.00	250.00	250.00	250.00	250.00	250.00	250.00	247.63

Source: American Metal Market

Mercury Consumed in the United States In Metric Tons

Year	Batteries	Chlorine & Caustic Soda	Catalysts, Misc.	Dental Equip.	Electrical Lighting	General Lab Use	Measuring Control Instrument	Paints	Wiring Devices & Switches	Other Uses	Grand Total
1984[3]	29,700	7,347	359	1,432	1,487	269	2,856	4,651	2,730	1,404	54,669
1985	952	235	61	50	40	14	79	169	95	20	1,718
1986	750	259	90	52	41	20	63	179	103	31	1,588
1987	533	311	59	56	45	20	59	198	131	34	1,446
1988	448	354	86	53	31	26	77	197	176	55	1,503
1989	250	379	40	39	31	18	87	192	141	32	1,212
1990	106	247	29	44	33	32	108	14	70	38	720
1991	18	184	26	41	39	30	90	6	71	49	554
1992	13	209	20	42	55	28	80	NA	82	92	621
1993[1]	10	180	18	35	38	26	65	NA	83	103	558
1994[2]	6	135	25	24	27	24	53	NA	79	110	483

[1] Preliminary. [2] Estimate. [3] Data reported in flasks prior to 1985. NA = Not available. *Source: U.S. Buraeu of Mines*

Milk

U.S. milk production in the first half of 1995 was hampered by adverse weather that put dairy cows under stress and slowed milk per cow. Conditions improved during the second half and 1995's estimated total output of a record high 71.4 million metric tons compares with 69.7 million in 1994. Although cow numbers in 1996 are expected to be marginally below 1995, milk production in 1996 is projected up 2-3 percent on milk-per-cow increases of three percent.

About 87 percent of U.S. milk output is produced in 22 states. Dairy cow numbers in mid-1995 totaled 8.1 million head; the number of cows in the U.S. averaged 9.5 million.

Seasonally, milk production is highest during the April-June quarter and this pattern basically held in 1995 as 40.5 billion pounds were produced, up 1 percent from a year earlier. During the third quarter 38.5 billion pounds were produced, also up 1 percent.

Since 1992, returns to milk production have neither encouraged rapid expansion by producers nor brought large additional numbers of farms under financial stress. What appears to have occurred are structural industry changes that released long standing pent-up pressures as reflected by the recent stability in cow numbers. Any erosion of returns by projected higher feed costs and lower milk prices are not expected to affect milk cow numbers much in 1996. Moreover, recent milk and feed price changes probably have not significantly altered longer prospects that may increase the number of new or expanding dairy farms. Similarly, the expected slippage in returns should not push the number of existing farms to the levels of the early 1990's.

The U.S. is the world's largest fluid milk producer. 1995 U.S. production of 71.4 million metric tons accounted for 20 percent of the world total. The USSR was the largest world producer until that country's breakup. Now, Russia is second with 1995 output of 41 million tons, down from 42.6 million in 1994. The Ukraine produced 17.5 million tons versus 18.2 million in 1994. Their combined total of 58.5 million tons was 2.3 million lower than 1994. Other major producers include India, Germany and France, each producing in excess of 25 million tons annually in the 1990's.

The U.S. also holds the top rank in world fluid milk consumption, but just barely. Consumption of 26.7 million tons in both 1995 and 1994 compares with India's two year average of 26.3 million. Russia is third at about 15 million.

Pricewise, U.S. fluid milk prices are lower than abroad but dried milk prices tend to be higher. This is largely due to the government's support program which has pegged nonfat dry milk (extra grade) at nearly $2300 per metric ton. Comparable dry milk in Europe in mid-1995 was generally closer to $2000 per ton. The international price differential was even larger for whole milk powder prices (26 percent butter fat) during much of 1995, but narrowed late in the year because of low world stocks. The average U.S. producer price for milk eligible for fluid use in 1995 was expected to dip about 3 percent from the $13.03 per cwt. in 1994. Generally, fluid milk prices average near $20/cwt. in Europe and even higher in Japan. Despite the seemingly favorable U.S. milk prices, U.S. per capita consumption at less than 230 pounds compares with an average near 240 pounds in the 1980's.

Average U.S. milk prices in 1996 are expected to dip slightly from 1995. In both years, the growth in skim solid sales was not likely to match the expansion in milk production and offset gains in milkfat values.

Futures Markets

Nonfat dry milk futures and options are traded on the Coffee, Sugar, & Cocoa Exchange Inc. (CSCE).

World Fluid Milk Production (Cow's Milk) In Thousands of Metric Tons

Year	Australia	Brazil	Canada	France	Germany	India	Italy	Japan	Mexico	Netherlands	New Zealand	Poland	Russia[3]	Ukraine[3]	United Kingdom	United States
1988	6,297	13,200	8,229	26,000	32,000	22,000	10,671	7,607	8,830	11,406	7,936	15,450	------	106,622	14,880	65,840
1989	6,465	13,400	7,980	26,150	32,400	24,000	10,828	8,059	8,970	11,321	7,406	16,371	55,742	24,237	14,647	65,424
1990	6,435	14,500	7,975	26,400	31,200	27,500	11,491	8,190	9,330	11,285	7,746	15,801	55,715	24,360	14,952	67,005
1991	6,578	14,200	7,790	25,700	28,916	28,200	11,400	8,260	10,200	11,047	8,122	14,504	51,971	22,409	14,503	66,994
1992	6,918	15,000	7,633	25,315	28,106	29,400	11,300	8,581	10,700	10,901	8,603	13,060	47,237	19,114	14,428	68,440
1993	7,530	15,300	7,500	25,049	28,080	30,600	10,400	8,627	10,720	10,953	8,735	12,650	46,524	18,148	14,645	68,303
1994[1]	8,300	15,700	7,640	25,319	28,050	30,000	10,180	8,383	11,010	10,873	9,719	11,920	42,811	18,200	14,920	69,682
1995[2]	8,427	16,100	7,950	25,800	28,700	31,200	9,980	8,500	11,120	10,900	9,540	11,600	40,500	17,500	14,600	71,350

[1] Preliminary. [2] Estimate. [3] Formerly part of the U.S.S.R.; data not reported separately until 1989. *Source: Foreign Agricultural Service, U.S. Department of Agriculture*

U.S. Milk-Feed Price Ratio[1] In Pounds

Year	Jan.	Feb.	Mar.	Apr.	May	June	July	Aug.	Sept.	Oct.	Nov.	Dec.	Average
1988	3.34	3.14	2.98	2.80	2.57	2.28	2.11	2.23	2.40	2.50	2.59	2.59	2.63
1989	2.51	2.45	2.30	2.26	2.25	2.38	2.52	2.83	2.97	3.22	3.34	3.39	2.70
1990	3.25	3.02	2.84	2.59	2.54	2.72	2.79	2.92	2.93	2.82	2.83	2.59	2.82
1991	2.57	2.52	2.42	2.34	2.41	2.54	2.73	2.82	2.94	3.14	3.25	3.19	2.74
1992	3.04	2.86	2.77	2.79	2.68	2.81	3.06	3.20	3.22	3.23	3.23	3.13	3.01
1993	2.96	2.87	2.77	2.79	2.81	2.91	2.78	2.70	2.80	2.79	2.77	2.65	2.80
1994	2.62	2.51	2.51	2.50	2.36	2.44	2.61	2.74	2.81	2.92	2.96	2.81	2.65
1995[2]	2.73	2.69	2.67	2.56	2.53	2.47	2.44	2.52	2.56	2.48	2.64	2.55	2.57

[1] Pounds of 16% protein mixed dairy feed equal in value to one pound of whole milk. [2] Preliminary. *Source: Economic Research Service, U.S. Department of Agriculture*

Salient Statistics of Milk in the United States In Millions of Pounds

Year	Number of Milk Cows on Farms[3] (Thousands)	Supply: Production: Per Cow[4] (Pounds)	Supply: Production: Total[4]	Supply: Beginning Stocks[5]	Supply: Imports	Supply: Total Supply	Utilization: Exports[5]	Utilization: Domestic: Fed to Calves	Utilization: Domestic: Humans	Utilization: Total Use	Average Farm Price Received Per Cwt.: All Milk, Wholesale	Average Farm Price Received Per Cwt.: Milk Eligible for Fluid Market	Average Farm Price Received Per Cwt.: Milk, Manufacturing Grade	Per Capita Consumption[6] (Fluid Milk in Lbs.)
1987	10,327	13,819	142,709	12,922	2,490	158,121	2,446	1,599	146,001	150,648	12.54	12.66	11.37	239
1988	10,224	14,185	145,034	7,473	2,394	155,019	1,582	1,620	142,824	146,641	12.26	12.36	11.15	235
1989	10,046	14,323	143,893	8,378	2,498	155,115	3,995	1,503	139,802	146,079	13.56	13.66	12.38	236
1990	9,993	14,782	147,721	9,036	2,690	160,039	1,886	1,517	142,626	146,680	13.74	13.89	12.34	233
1991	9,826	15,031	147,697	13,359	2,625	164,461	3,673	1,511	142,818	148,621	12.27	12.30	11.05	233
1992	9,688	15,574	150,885	15,840	2,522	170,008	8,532	1,454	145,230	155,794	13.15	13.19	11.91	231
1993[1]	9,589	15,704	150,582	14,214	2,806	167,974	8,643	1,450	147,733	158,404	12.86	12.88	11.80	227
1994[2]	9,525	16,128	153,626	9,570	2,871	159,300		1,400			13.04	13.08	11.87	

[1] Preliminary. [2] Estimate. [3] Average number on farms during year including dry cows, excluding heifers not yet fresh. [4] Excludes milk sucked by calves. [5] Government and commercial. [6] Product pounds of commercial sales and on farm consumption. *Source: Economic Research Service, U.S. Department of Agriculture*

Utilization of Milk in the United States In Millions of Pounds (Milk Equivalent)

Year	Butter from Whey Cream	Creamery Butter[2]	Cheese[3]	Cottage Cheese (Creamed)	Canned Milk[4]	Bulk Condensed Whole Milk: Unsweetened	Bulk Condensed Whole Milk: Sweetened	Dry Whole Milk Products	Ice Cream[5]	Other Frozen Dairy Products	Other Manufactured Products[6]	Used on Farms: Farm-Churned Butter	Used on Farms: Total
1990	4,348	29,391	47,368	672	1,332	351	243	1,292	2,014	12,307	332	522	2,039
1991	4,296	30,039	46,769	644	1,194	364	236	785	2,092	12,726	356	508	2,019
1992	4,150	30,478	49,458	592	1,872	417	301	1,227	2,367	11,825	188	470	1,925
1993	4,500	29,493	49,871	559	1,178	374	324	1,130	1,995	12,063	199	446	1,896
1994[1]		29,127	51,115	410	1,184	205	277	1,227	----- 14,540 -----		740		

[1] Preliminary. [2] Excludes whey butter. [3] American and other. [4] Includes evaporated and sweetened condensed. [5] Milk equivalent of butter and condensed milk used in ice cream. [6] Whole milk equivalent of dry cream, malted milk powder, part-skim milk, dry or concentrated ice cream mix, dehydrated butterfat and other miscellaneous products using milkfat. *Source: National Agricultural Statistics Service, U.S. Department of Agriculture*

Milk Production[1] in the United States In Millions of Pounds

Year	Jan.	Feb.	Mar.	Apr.	May	June	July	Aug.	Sept.	Oct.	Nov.	Dec.	Total
1989	12,296	11,412	12,733	12,582	12,973	12,147	11,981	11,838	11,338	11,657	11,380	11,902	144,239
1990	12,283	11,491	12,988	12,749	13,256	12,635	12,562	12,312	11,737	12,098	11,831	12,372	148,314
1991	12,587	11,732	13,106	12,888	13,268	12,477	12,348	12,202	11,705	12,102	11,763	12,347	148,477
1992	12,671	12,132	13,155	12,838	13,346	12,893	12,844	12,577	12,094	12,476	12,064	12,626	150,886
1993	10,728	9,908	11,060	10,927	11,410	12,957	12,894	12,492	11,978	12,272	11,872	12,427	150,582
1994	12,721	11,662	13,209	13,118	13,719	13,079	13,020	12,837	12,360	12,732	12,330	12,871	153,626
1995[2]	13,147	12,169	13,634	13,323	13,856	13,305	13,176	12,848	12,430	12,758	12,318	12,851	155,803

[1] Excludes milk sucked by calves. [2] Preliminary. *Source: Economic Research Service, U.S. Department of Agriculture*

Average Price Received by U.S. Farmers for All Milk (Sold to Plants) In Dollars Per Hundred Pounds (Cwt.)

Year	Jan.	Feb.	Mar.	Apr.	May	June	July	Aug.	Sept.	Oct.	Nov.	Dec.	Average
1989	13.50	13.20	12.70	12.40	12.30	12.40	12.60	13.20	14.00	14.80	15.60	16.00	13.56
1990	15.50	14.50	13.90	13.40	13.50	13.80	14.00	14.20	13.90	13.10	12.70	11.70	13.74
1991	11.70	11.60	11.40	11.30	11.30	11.40	11.80	12.40	12.80	13.50	13.90	13.80	12.27
1992	13.40	12.90	12.50	12.60	12.80	13.20	13.40	13.50	13.50	13.40	13.10	12.80	13.15
1993	12.50	12.20	12.20	12.60	12.90	13.00	12.80	12.40	12.80	13.10	13.60	13.50	12.86
1994	13.60	13.40	13.50	13.40	12.80	12.60	12.20	12.40	12.80	13.00	13.10	12.80	12.97
1995[1]	12.60	12.60	12.70	12.40	12.40	12.10	12.10	12.40	12.80	13.40	13.70	13.90	12.76

[1] Preliminary. *Source: Economic Research Service, U.S. Department of Agriculture*

Farm Price of Milk Eligible for Fluid Market In Dollars Per Hundred Pounds (Cwt.)

Year	Jan.	Feb.	Mar.	Apr.	May	June	July	Aug.	Sept.	Oct.	Nov.	Dec.	Average
1989	13.60	13.40	12.90	12.50	12.40	12.50	12.70	13.30	14.10	14.90	15.60	16.10	13.66
1990	15.60	14.70	14.00	13.40	13.60	13.90	14.10	14.30	14.00	13.30	12.90	11.80	13.89
1991	11.80	11.70	11.50	11.40	11.40	11.50	11.90	12.40	12.90	13.60	13.90	13.90	12.30
1992	13.50	13.00	12.50	12.60	12.90	13.30	13.40	13.50	13.60	13.50	13.20	12.90	13.19
1993	12.60	12.30	12.20	12.70	13.00	13.10	12.80	12.50	12.80	13.10	13.60	13.60	12.88
1994	13.60	13.50	13.50	13.50	12.90	12.70	12.20	12.50	12.80	13.10	13.10	12.90	13.03
1995[1]	12.70	12.60	12.70	12.40	12.40	12.20	12.10	12.50	12.80	13.50	13.70	14.00	12.80

[1] Preliminary. *Source: Economic Research Service, U.S. Department of Agriculture*

Molasses

U.S. supplies of molasses (including production and imports) amount to about three million tonnes a year. Of this total, about a third comes from mainland sugar mills, a quarter from beet sugar refiners, smaller amounts from Hawaiian cane and cane refiner's blackstrap, and the remainder from imports. Beet molasses is used primarily as a livestock feed and as a yeast by the pharmaceutical industry.

According to the USDA, molasses production from cane from mainland mills in 1994 was 824,453 tonnes, down slightly from the 1993 total of 831,661 tonnes. Cane refiners blackstrap molasses production in 1994 was 114,000 tonnes, up from 113,000 tonnes in 1993. Shipments of molasses from Hawaii to the U.S. mainland in 1994 were 151,172 tonnes, down over 20 percent from the 1993 total of 190,371 tonnes. Production of molasses from beets in 1994 was 1.2 million tonnes, up 73 percent from the 1993 total of only 692,465 tonnes. Estimated domestic supplies of molasses in 1994 were 2.29 million tonnes, 25 percent higher than in 1993. Hawaiian production in 1994 was 180,884 tonnes.

U.S. imports of molasses in 1994 were 1.66 million tonnes, up 59 percent from 1993. Major sources of molasses to the U.S. were Australia, Mexico, Guatemala, Colombia, Venezuela and the Dominican Republic. U.S. mainland exports were 277,098 tonnes, up 8 percent from 1993. Total available supplies of molasses were 3.67 million tonnes, up 41 percent.

In terms of utilization, distilled use of molasses in 1994 was estimated to be 192,000 tonnes, down 14 percent from 1993. Industrial use of molasses (includes lysine, yeast, citric acid, edible molasses and pharmaceuticals) was 605,000 tonnes, up one percent from 1993. Desugarization molasses was 615,000 tonnes, up 37 percent from the year before. Molasses used in mixed feeds was 2.6 million tonnes, up 69 percent from 1993. Total utilization of molasses in the U.S. in 1994 was 3.67 million tonnes, up 41 percent from 1993.

World Production of Sugarcane and Sugarbeets by Selected Countries — In Thousands of Metric Tons

	Sugarcane								Sugerbeets							
Crop Year	Australia	Brazil	China	Cuba	India	Indonesia	Pakistan	Thailand	China	France	Germany	Poland	Russia[3]	Turkey	Ukraine[3]	United States
1984-5	25,513	98,000	39,519	75,000	173,569	21,141	14,692	25,053	8,284	26,803	20,024	16,048	------	11,108	85,251	20,080
1985-6	24,402	247,199	58,711	67,400	170,319	22,621	27,856	25,055	8,919	29,977	28,210	14,664	------	9,830	82,392	20,438
1986-7	25,413	238,493	56,483	68,500	170,648	26,208	29,926	24,093	8,306	25,830	28,007	14,217	------	10,662	79,299	22,827
1987-8	2,960	268,741	52,526	70,800	182,480	26,131	29,910	24,450	8,140	26,471	26,732	13,987	------	12,717	90,405	25,466
1988-9	3,185	258,449	55,847	73,700	196,723	24,825	32,970	27,191	13,290	28,606	23,215	14,069	------	11,534	87,855	22,507
1989-90	26,940	252,643	55,423	81,003	203,040	29,421	36,976	36,668	9,243	27,694	20,767	14,374	------	10,929	97,414	22,798
1990-1	24,370	262,674	63,451	76,230	225,569	27,980	35,494	33,561	14,525	31,735	23,310	16,721	32,327	13,986	44,265	24,959
1991-2	20,640	260,888	72,695	71,000	241,046	28,133	35,989	47,480	16,289	29,520	25,926	11,412	24,280	15,474	36,168	25,585
1992-3	27,958	271,475	78,869	58,000	249,256	32,000	38,865	39,827	15,069	31,685	27,150	11,052	25,548	15,126	28,783	26,438
1993-4[1]	30,710	244,304	68,997	44,000	227,850	33,000	38,059	37,823	12,048	31,805	28,606	15,621	25,468	15,621	33,717	23,812
1994-5[2]	32,700	279,768	65,660	39,000	231,000	31,500	44,427	37,569	12,530	28,997	24,848	11,676	13,900	13,690	28,138	29,037

[1] Preliminary. [2] Estimate. [3] Formerly part of the U.S.S.R.; data not reported separately until 1990. *Source: Food and Agriculture Organization of the United Nations*

U.S. Annual Average Prices of Molasses, by Types (F.O.B. Tank Car or Truck) — In Dollars Per Short Ton[2]

	Blackstrap							Beet Molasses	
Year	New Orleans	South Florida	Baltimore	Upper Mississippi[3]	Savannah[4]	California Ports[5]	Houston[6]	Montana/ Wyoming & Nebraksa	Red River Valley[7]
1979	82.95	85.50	91.20	107.90	107.75	84.05	85.30	82.65	NA
1980	96.50	96.80	106.75	124.45	128.85	101.70	95.60	96.55	NA
1981	84.90	90.00	99.30	111.20	119.40	89.20	85.30	95.20	NA
1982	48.00	56.55	64.15	70.85	81.90	60.50	69.40	63.70	44.50
1983	56.50	63.10	73.05	76.90	91.90	70.40	79.45	65.95	60.55
1984	61.50	71.00	77.65	81.00	94.45	71.95	82.50	79.15	70.65
1985	50.28	59.79	64.66	72.83	85.00	61.89	NA	67.50	57.33
1986	69.61	78.10	83.05	92.03	NA	73.26	80.33	73.75	68.44
1987	53.23	61.96	72.83	80.05	NA	67.17	60.31	54.69	62.22
1988	64.89	74.54	82.93	90.07	NA	74.61	72.95	69.94	55.71
1989	55.63	65.31	75.15	81.12	NA	70.36	79.94	74.50	55.00
1990	61.70	68.37	80.59	88.48	76.13	75.40	64.26	75.00	58.33
1991	67.02	74.58	89.15	94.78	82.52	80.00	69.52	71.92	66.16
1992	61.27	68.36	80.41	92.95	76.70	78.43	63.75	67.81	57.50
1993	55.48	62.36	76.03	89.26	70.00	74.24	57.12	72.63	64.44
1994[1]	65.53	72.23	85.94	91.97	79.23	83.31	69.86	NA	NA

[1] Preliminary. [2] To convert dollars per short ton to cents per gallon divide by 171. [3] Prior to 1989, prices are for Minneapolis. [4] Prior to 1989, prices are for Omaha. [5] Los Angeles and Stockton. [6] Prior to 1990, prices are for Colorado. [7] North Dakota and Minnesota. NA = Not available.
Source: Agricultural Marketing Service, U.S. Department of Agriculture

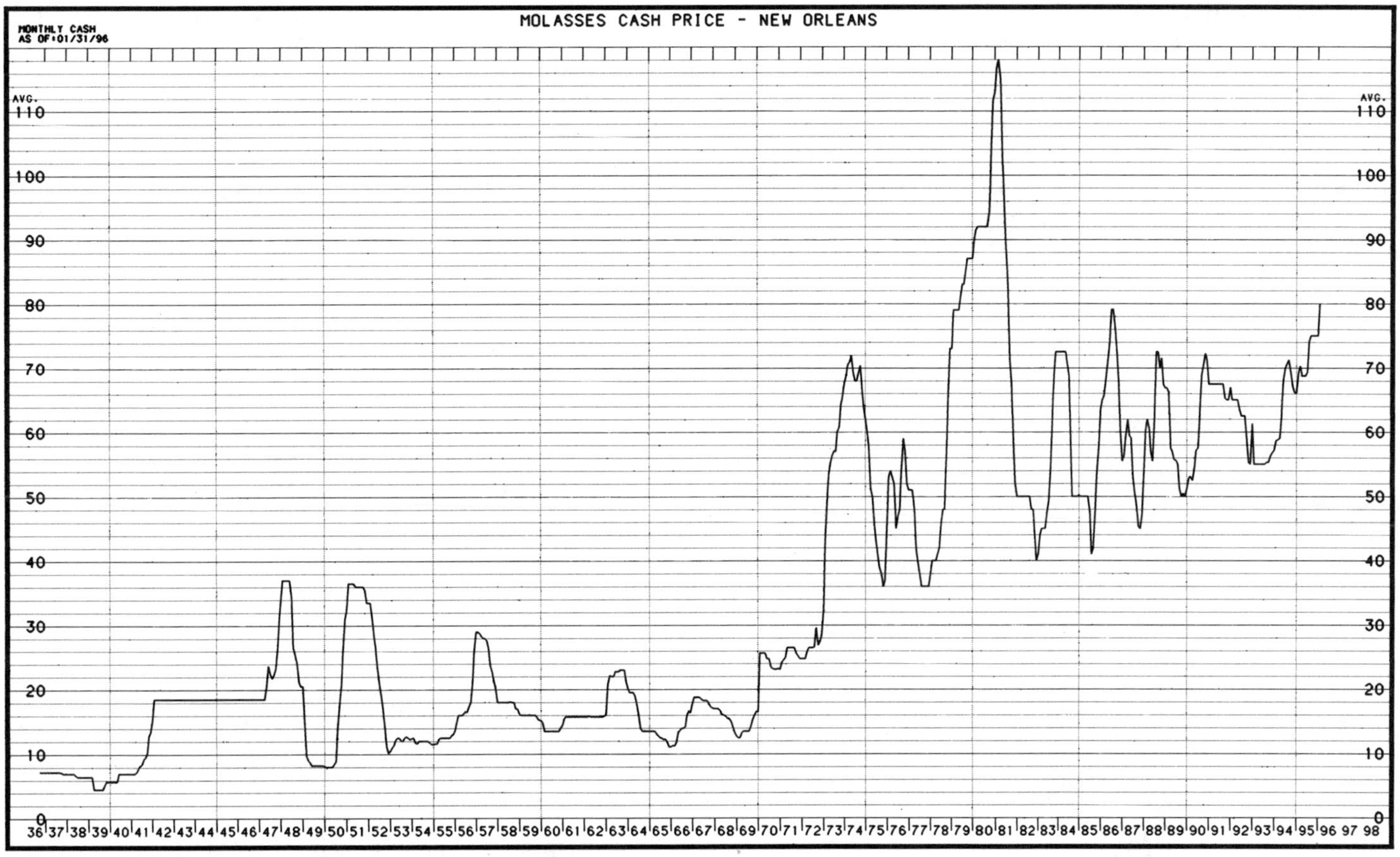

Salient Statistics of Molasses[3] in the United States In Metric Tons

	Production						Inedible Imports From						Pro-duction of
		Mainland				In Ship-ments							Edible
			Refiners									Total	Molasses
		Mainland	Black-		Puerto	From	Total		Dominican		Mainland	U.S.	(1,000
Year	Hawaii	Mills[4]	strap	Beet	Rico	Hawaii	Imports	Brazil	Republic	Mexico	Exports[5]	Supply	Gallons)
1986	268,305	731,056	136,184	879,019	31,354	273,683	123,055	309,340	136,687	97,436	329,936	3,058,167	1,700
1987	260,930	726,854	110,784	1,137,014	35,385	152,087	962,151	95,004	123,619	183,525	366,957	2,721,954	1,630
1988	252,516	775,936	101,257	1,006,353	40,694	178,476	969,870	142,897	102,792	93,605	299,217	2,749,692	1,925
1989	218,009	808,355	122,786	974,179	34,864	169,270	926,870	107,109	147,235	75,634	293,535	2,707,925	1,990
1990	228,968	741,749	105,124	948,820	24,959	214,045	1,078,924	70,986	145,543	88,401	212,263	2,876,399	1,405
1991	188,252	807,652	126,000	1,165,962	27,882	184,337	1,258,637	10,342	137,271	235,244	242,635	3,299,953	1,825
1992	182,849	782,566	123,000	950,312	25,097	183,657	1,115,863	0	127,500	117,722	282,098	2,873,300	1,460
1993[1]	187,915	831,661	113,000	692,465	22,802	190,371	1,040,858	0	163,180	47,596	255,907	2,612,448	1,480
1994[1]	180,884	824,453	114,000	1,200,000	18,531	151,172	1,659,309	0	121,320	197,753	277,098	3,671,836	

[1] Preliminary. [2] Estimate. [3] Feed and industrial molasses. [4] Includes high-test milasses from frozen cane. [5] Excluding exports from Hawaii and Puerto Rico. NA = Not available. *Source: Agricultural Marketing Service, U.S. Department of Agriculture*

Wholesale Price of Blackstrap Molasses (Cane) at New Orleans In Dollars Per Short Ton

Year	Jan.	Feb.	Mar.	Apr.	May	June	July	Aug.	Sept.	Oct.	Nov.	Dec.	Average
1986	65.00	65.60	68.50	71.00	73.75	79.00	79.13	76.60	72.30	68.10	60.25	55.50	69.56
1987	56.25	59.40	62.00	59.40	59.10	53.00	50.60	48.60	45.30	45.00	47.00	53.10	53.23
1988	60.30	62.00	60.60	56.90	55.50	62.50	72.50	72.50	70.00	71.50	67.50	66.90	64.89
1989	66.90	66.25	57.50	56.90	55.75	55.60	55.00	51.25	50.00	50.50	50.00	51.25	55.58
1990	52.75	53.13	52.50	54.25	57.19	57.50	62.75	68.75	70.63	72.25	71.25	67.50	61.70
1991	67.50	67.50	67.50	67.50	67.50	67.50	67.50	67.50	65.25	65.00	65.00	65.00	67.02
1992	65.00	65.00	65.00	65.00	63.75	62.50	62.50	62.50	58.75	55.31	55.00	55.00	61.27
1993	55.00	55.00	55.00	55.00	55.00	55.00	55.00	55.25	55.31	56.25	56.75	57.19	55.48
1994	57.75	57.50	59.38	62.50	68.00	70.00	70.63	71.25	69.38	67.50	66.25	66.25	65.53
1995[1]	69.00	70.31	68.75	68.75	68.75	69.38	74.25	75.00	75.00	75.00	75.00	75.00	72.02

[1] Preliminary. *Source: Agricultural Marketing Service, U.S. Department of Agriculture*

Molybdenum

Molybdenum is a silver-gray metal which is strong at high temperatures, hard and resistant to corrosion. It is a refractory metallic element used principally as an alloying agent in steels, cast irons and superalloys to enhance strength, toughness and wear resistance. Primarily added in the form of molybdic oxide or ferromolybdenum, it is frequently used in combination with chromium, manganese nickel, tungsten or other alloy metals to achieve desired metallurgical properties. Molybdenum's versatility ensures a significant role in contemporary technology and industry. Molybdenum finds significant usage as a refractory metal in numerous chemical applications, including catalysts, lubricants and pigments. The variety of uses for molybdenum materials, few of which afford acceptable substitutions, has resulted in a demand that is expected to increase at a greater rate than most other ferrous metals.

Distribution of molybdenum reserves and productive capacity is concentrated in a few countries of the world. In 1994, the Bureau of Mines estimated world mine output at 104,000 tonnes. The major producers are Canada, Chile, China and the U.S. These countries possess about 90 percent of the estimated 12 million tonnes of world reserve base.

The world demand for molybdenum is expected to increase 4-6 percent in 1995. It's estimated that the growth in demand will drop 3-5 percent in 1996.

U.S. production of molybdenum concentrate for the first six months of 1995 was 29,900 tonnes. For 1994, production was 48,300 tonnes.

Domestic shipments of molybdenum concentrate for the first half of 1995 were 6,560 tonnes. U.S. exports of molybdenum ore and concentrate in May 1995 were 5.94 million kilograms, up sharply from 2.69 million kilograms in April. For the first five months of 1995 exports were 20.8 million kilograms, while for all of 1994 they were 33.6 million kilograms. The major destinations for U.S. exports are Belgium, the Netherlands, Japan, Great Britain and Chile. U.S. exports of ferromolybdenum in May 1995 were 49,000 kilograms, while for the first five months of 1995 they were 324,000 kilograms. For all of 1994, exports were 479,000 kilograms. The major markets were Canada, Mexico, Japan and the Netherlands.

U.S. imports of molybdenum products (contained molybdenum) over the January-May 1995 period were 3.95 million kilograms. For all of 1994, imports were 6.52 million kilograms.

World Mine Production of Molybdenum In Metric Tons (Contained Molybdenum)

Year	Bulgaria	Canada[3]	Chile	China	Iran	Kazakhstan[4]	Mexico	Mongolia	Peru	Russia[4]	United States	Uzbekisten[4]	World Total
1984	420	25,479	37,172	4,400	1,100	------	8,938	2,200	6,557	24,700	103,664	------	214,275
1985[5]	420	17,311	40,541	4,400	1,100	------	8,292	2,200	8,393	24,900	108,409	------	216,959
1986	190	11,251	16,581	2,000	900	------	3,350	1,100	3,484	11,400	42,627	------	93,218
1987	200	14,771	16,941	12,000	500	------	4,400	1,400	3,353	11,500	34,063	------	89,871
1988	200	13,535	15,515	14,400	700	------	4,456	1,400	2,444	17,000	43,051	------	112,860
1989	190	14,073	16,550	15,700	785	------	4,189	1,580	3,177	17,000	63,105	------	136,494
1990	150	11,994	13,830	15,700	542	------	2,000	1,578	2,510	17,000	61,611	------	127,028
1991	120	11,329	14,434	13,200	395	------	1,716	1,716	3,031	16,000	53,364	------	115,000
1992	120	9,405	14,840	19,200	847	700	1,458	1,522	3,220	5,000	49,725	700	108,000
1993[1]	120	9,700	14,900	18,300	1,000	600	1,705	1,500	2,980	4,800	36,803	700	93,600
1994[2]	100	9,540	16,000	17,500	1,000	500	2,610	1,500	3,000	4,500	46,800	700	104,000

[1] Preliminary. [2] Estimate. [3] Shipments. [4] Formerly part of the U.S.S.R.; data not reported separately until 1992. [5] Data reported in thousands of pounds prior to 1986. *Source: U.S. Bureau of Mines*

U.S. Salient Statistics of Molybdenum In Metric Tons (Contained Molybdenum)

	Concentrate							Primary Products[4]							
		Shipments						Net Production				Shipments			
Year	Production	Total (Includes Exports)	Value Mil. $	For Exports	Consumption	Imports for Consumption	Stocks, Dec. 31[3]	Grand Total	Molybdic Oxide[5]	Molybdenum Metal Powder	Price Avg. Value $ Kl.[6]	To Domestic Destinations	Oxide for Exports (Gross Weight)	Consumption	Producer Stocks, Dec. 31
1984	103,664	102,405	326.8	41,687	54,843	28	12,450	53,353	40,186	4,302	3.56	65,527	24,553	34,792	22,155
1985	108,409	111,936	347.8	38,646	W	112	9,322	61,901	48,750	3,734	3.33	73,861	36,268	33,451	21,014
1986[7]	93,976	95,006	240.5	18,267	53,061	1,120	8,715	17,953	6,147	4,256	2.92	57,855	21,325	31,898	20,699
1987	34,073	31,692	179.3	18,377	16,983	2,954	6,841	11,257	7,076	4,181	7.28	18,447	5,567	14,800	10,055
1988	43,051	45,240	266.9	23,500	35,690	514	4,777	29,782	25,404	4,378	7.61	20,535	W	17,422	7,116
1989	63,105	61,733	421.4	51,232	41,877	238	6,969	16,545	16,545	W	8.05	18,277	1,391	17,204	6,675
1990	61,611	61,580	346.3	41,380	35,455	478	7,672	15,727	15,727	W	7.39	17,983	787	18,060	5,919
1991	53,364	53,607	249.9	22,424	32,998	161	5,291	20,782	18,739	2,043	5.27	19,105	1,571	16,901	9,422
1992	49,725	45,098	189.9	33,439	15,243	831	11,905	13,880	11,916	1,964	4.85	17,305	557	17,200	7,480
1993[1]	36,803	39,209	165.1	28,280	13,794	3,398	11,200	11,989	10,697	1,292	5.13	15,981	1,042	17,700	6,150
1994[2]	46,800	46,000	284.0	14,568	17,200	2,280	5,510	16,000	14,900	1,070	7.70	21,400	2,240	19,100	3,940

[1] Preliminary. [2] Estimate. [3] At mines and at plants making molybdenum products. [4] Comprises ferromolybdenum, molybdic oxide, and molybdenum salts and metal. [5] Includes molybdic oxide briquets, molybdic acid, molybdenum trioxide, and all others. [6] U.S. producer price per kilogram of molybdenum contained in technical-grade molybdic oxide. [7] Data reported in thousands of pounds and dollars per pound prior to 1987. W = Withheld proprietary data.
Source: U.S. Bureau of Mines

Nickel

Most commercial nickel is used in stainless steel and other corrosion-resistant alloys. Approximately one-fifth of the nickel produced in the U.S. is used in plating to give hard, tarnish-resistant, polishable surfaces. Plating techniques, like electroless coating or single-slurry coating, are employed for such applications as helicopter rotors, turbine blades, extrusion dies and rolled steel strip. Nickel finds use in coins to replace silver and has been utilized in ceramics, rechargeable batteries and electronic circuitry. Nickel-base alloys are consumed in wire, bars, sheets and tubular forms fabricated into finished products.

U.S. consumption of nickel in the January-July 1995 period was 60,200 tonnes, 15 percent more than in the same period of 1994. Over the January-July 1995 period, the form of nickel consumption was cathodes, pellets, briquets and powder 49,200 tonnes; ferronickel 7,810 tonnes; and oxide-sinter, salts and other forms 3,200 tonnes.

U.S. ending stocks of nickel-containing products at the end of July 1995 were 5,550 tonnes. Stocks of cathodes, pellets, briquets and powder were 5,200 tonnes; ferronickel stocks were 194 tonnes; while oxide-sinter, salts and other forms of nickel were 157 tonnes.

U.S. consumption of secondary nickel over the January-July 1995 period was 35,800 tonnes. Consumption of ferrous scrap was 30,400 tonnes and nonferrous scrap 5,450 tonnes. For all of 1994, U.S. consumption of secondary nickel was 53,200 tonnes. At the end of July 1995, stocks of ferrous scrap were 2,040 tonnes, while stocks of nonferrous scrap were 107 tonnes.

Imports for consumption of nickel for the first six months of 1995 were 83,300 tonnes, up 18 percent from the same period of 1994. For all of 1994, U.S. imports were 133,000 tonnes. The major sources were Canada, Russia, Norway and Australia.

U.S. exports of nickel for the January-June 1995 period were 25,300 tonnes, up 35 percent from the same period of 1994. Stainless steel scrap exports were 13,700 tonnes, waste and scrap 6,710 tonnes, chemicals 1,820 tonnes, metallurgical grade oxide 1,690 tonnes, and powder and flakes 516 tonnes. The major countries of destination were Canada, South Korea, Japan and Spain.

Nickel prices soared during 1995 as stocks of nickel were drawn down. It was reported that physical nickel was in limited supply with very little western material for sale and limited Russian supplies. The combination of declining stocks on the London Metals Exchange, very high stainless steel production, and delayed exports from Russia caused prices to move sharply higher. Nickel consumption continued to grow faster than production leading to a deficit.

Futures Markets

Nickel futures are traded on the London Metals Exchange.

World Mine Production of Nickel In Metric Tons (Contained Nickel)

Year	Australia[3]	Botswana	Brazil	Canada	China	Dominican Republic	Finland[3]	Greece	Indonesia	New Caledonia	Philippines	Russia[4]	South Africa	United States	Zimbabwe	World Total
1985	85,759	26,301	16,473	169,974	25,000	25,394	8,547	22,045	40,337	72,395	28,159	185,000	25,039	5,558	11,116	812,622
1986	76,740	25,583	21,103	163,642	25,000	21,878	11,886	14,424	53,680	61,780	12,791	259,000	31,026	1,066	3,720	852,151
1987	74,554	25,900	22,092	189,086	25,000	32,521	10,557	9,202	57,764	56,850	7,819	270,000	34,300	------	6,300	890,539
1988	62,358	26,000	18,677	216,589	32,700	29,345	11,699	13,131	57,982	71,200	10,349	280,000	30,000	------	12,600	952,215
1989	67,041	23,700	18,826	200,899	34,250	31,264	10,480	16,097	62,987	96,200	15,380	280,000	28,900	------	12,721	984,078
1990	67,000	23,200	24,100	196,225	33,000	28,700	11,524	18,500	68,308	85,100	15,818	280,000	29,000	330	12,654	974,000
1991	69,000	23,500	26,400	192,259	31,000	29,062	9,900	19,300	71,681	114,492	13,658	245,000	27,700	5,523	12,371	991,000
1992	64,000	23,500	29,400	192,086	37,000	25,000	9,171	17,000	77,600	113,100	13,000	280,000	28,400	6,671	12,200	981,000
1993[1]	64,717	23,000	32,200	188,378	30,700	23,863	8,290	12,940	65,800	97,100	7,660	243,000	30,000	2,464	12,769	905,000
1994[2]	71,900	23,000	32,000	150,000	33,000	30,500	7,250	19,000	81,100	96,000	9,800	240,000	31,000	------	13,500	895,000

[1] Preliminary. [2] Estimate. [3] Content of nickel and sulfate and concentrates. *Source: U.S. Bureau of Mines*

Salient Statistics of Nickel in the United States In Metric Tons (Contained Nickel)

Year	Net Import Reliance as a % of Apparent Consumption	Production: Plant[4]	Production: Secondary[5]	Nickel Consumed[1], By Uses: Alloy Steels	Cast Irons	Copper Base Alloys	Electroplating Anodes	Nickel Alloys	Stainless & Heat Resisting Steels	Super Alloys	Chemicals	Apparent Consumption	Stocks, Dec. 31: At Consumers' Plants	At Producer Plants	Primary & Secondary Nickel: Exports	Imports	Avg. Price LME[6] $ Lb.
1985	71	33,006	32,332	8,712	2,820	13,488	22,560	22,927	61,668	12,351	1,863	198,818	23,050	15,785	31,974	143,056	2.26
1986	73	1,498	41,039	7,458	2,370	9,609	19,050	18,086	54,580	11,563	1,692	164,483	19,256	9,344	19,586	117,114	1.76
1987	79	------	32,331	8,139	1,591	10,169	20,548	17,377	71,797	16,605	1,765	183,397	13,474	6,191	20,951	134,511	2.19
1988	74	------	49,371	7,330	2,359	6,890	19,520	19,046	80,107	13,537	1,816	159,156	15,081	6,967	27,916	127,680	6.25
1989	71	347	42,565	6,094	2,318	9,928	21,604	18,757	68,866	10,956	1,164	147,059	15,403	6,326	31,460	137,017	6.04
1990	64	3,701	57,367	7,007	2,646	7,594	15,550	16,315	96,120	15,713	1,500	170,042	13,971	8,065	37,057	145,600	4.02
1991	61	7,065	53,521	5,536	1,185	6,938	15,474	16,882	84,292	13,787	1,363	156,663	15,940	11,794	36,902	138,210	3.70
1992	59	8,962	55,871	4,988	1,202	6,313	16,538	15,946	83,460	10,872	51	159,373	17,480	10,140	33,867	128,510	3.18
1993[2]	63	4,878	54,702	4,940	805	6,078	16,611	17,004	87,300	10,783	1,170	158,000	14,430	15,700	33,199	132,710	2.40
1994[3]	66	-----	-----	5,930	499	7,940	15,500	20,500	88,700	11,700	2,670	164,000	10,200	10,200	41,940	133,060	2.88

[1] Exclusive of scrap. [2] Preliminary. [3] Estimate. [4] Smelter & refinery. [5] From purchased scrap (ferrous & nonferrous). [6] London Metal Exchange
W = Withheld proprietary data. *Source: U.S. Bureau of Mines*

Oats

Within the U.S. feed grain complex oats production is the smallest. The 1995/96 crop (June to May) totaled a record low 163 million bushels due largely to the continued decline in planted acreage. Since 1991/92, planted acreage has averaged less than 8 million acres versus an average of about 15 million in the first half of the 1980's. Production in 1995/96 totaled 229 million bushels; the high for the 1990s was 358 million in 1990/91. Generally the Dakotas are the largest producing region followed by Iowa and Minnesota. The small 1995/96 crop is expected to lift imports to a near record 105 million bushes versus 93 million in 1994/95. The bulk of this supply will come from Canada, with the balance from Finland and Sweden. A decade earlier, U.S. oat imports were considerably smaller.

1995/96 carryin stocks of 101 million bushels were down five million from a year earlier and the lowest since 1989/90 when carryin was 98 million bushels. Total supply for 1995/96 of 369 million bushels compares with 428 million in 1994/95, while disappearance was estimated at 281 million versus 327 million, respectively. Feed use was forecast at 155 million bushels versus 201 million in 1994/95, and feed/seed/industrial use placed at 125 million, unchanged from 1994/95. If the 1995/96 totals are realized, carryover stocks will fall to a record low 88 million bushels, prospects of which—along with higher corn prices—helped strengthen oat prices in the second half of 1995. Nearby oat futures rose from $1.34/bushel in June 1995, to $2.42/bushel by year-end. The average farm price for 1995/96 was forecast at $1.55-1.65/bushel versus $1.22 in 1994/95, and the highest since 1987/88. Despite the price strength in the first half of the 1995/96 crop year doubts persisted as to whether it carried far enough to induce a curtailment of usage and/or trigger greater demand for Canadian oats. U.S. Government owned oats stocks are an insignificant part of total carryover. U.S. oats exports are also minimal, averaging about 2 million bushels per year since 1990/91.

The former USSR is the world's largest oats producing region with virtually all the crop consumed domestically. World trade in oats in 1995/96 was forecast at 2.1 million tons, a shade under 1994/95. Canada is the single largest exporter with more than half the world total, 1.2 million tons. Australia was expected to ship 300,000 tons. The U.S. is consistently the world's largest importer, taking almost 80 percent of the world total in 1995/96, about the same as in 1994/95.

U.S. Farm Program

Washington D.C. legislators are currently rewriting the entire U.S Farm Program. Target prices and price support loan rates are unavailable. The national average loan rate for 1994/95 oats was .97¢ per bushel and the target price was $1.45 per bushel.

Futures Markets

Oat futures and options are traded on the Chicago Board of Trade (CBOT) and the Winnipeg Commodity Exchange (WCE). Oat futures are traded on the Mid America Commodity Exchange (MidAm).

World Production of Oats In Thousands of Metric Tons

Crop Year	Agrentina	Australia	Canada	China	Denmark	France	Germany	Italy	Poland	Spain	Sweden	Turkey	United Kingdom	United States	Former U.S.S.R.	World Total
1980-1	433	1,128	3,028	1,800	160	1,927	3,249	450	2,245	680	1,567	355	601	6,652	15,544	44,543
1981-2	339	1,617	3,188	1,700	176	1,774	3,200	422	2,731	445	1,816	325	620	7,391	15,000	45,343
1982-3	637	848	3,637	1,660	178	1,802	3,777	359	2,608	443	1,663	330	575	8,602	15,500	47,866
1983-4	593	2,296	2,773	1,650	86	1,374	2,489	307	2,377	464	1,268	310	465	6,923	17,000	45,115
1984-5	610	1,367	2,670	780	150	1,892	2,973	433	2,604	780	1,904	300	516	6,875	19,200	48,391
1985-6	400	1,339	2,997	664	152	1,803	3,278	363	2,682	719	1,668	314	615	7,559	20,500	50,062
1986-7	400	1,584	3,251	599	111	1,007	2,687	397	2,486	433	1,486	300	505	5,608	21,929	47,471
1987-8	650	1,738	2,995	642	94	1,045	2,406	361	2,428	502	1,440	310	450	5,424	18,495	43,270
1988-9	451	1,867	2,993	670	202	984	2,941	383	2,222	537	1,330	300	545	3,158	15,287	37,506
1989-90	620	1,640	3,546	622	125	970	2,010	296	2,186	494	1,455	270	530	5,423	14,972	39,554
1990-1	434	1,530	2,692	685	121	830	2,104	298	2,119	512	1,584	270	550	5,189	15,081	39,042
1991-2	400	1,690	1,794	650	125	740	1,867	359	1,873	410	1,426	280	545	3,534	12,342	32,785
1992-3	450	1,937	2,823	640	93	700	1,314	333	1,229	320	807	280	525	4,298	13,974	33,587
1993-4[1]	440	1,652	3,550	640	150	710	1,730	370	1,500	400	1,295	280	500	2,994	14,422	35,162
1994-5[2]	350	900	3,640	640		680	1,660	370	1,240		990	300	600	3,320	13,900	33,420
1995-6[3]	350	1,700	2,860	640		650	1,430	360	1,550		1,100	280	600	2,370	11,130	29,570

[1] Preliminary. [2] Estimate. [3] Forecast. *Source: Foreign Agricultural Service, U.S. Department of Agriculture*

United States Official Oats Crop Production Reports In Thousands of Bushels

Year	July 1	Aug. 1	Sept. 1	Oct. 1	Dec.	Final	Year	July 1	Aug. 1	Sept. 1	Oct. 1	Dec.	Final
1984	454,747	455,190	472,460	------	471,921	473,661	1990	374,457	365,337	365,337	358,288	------	357,524
1985	498,953	519,028	537,443	------	518,626	520,800	1991	280,016	259,666	259,666	242,526	------	243,451
1986	------	443,183	413,025	------	383,553	386,356	1992	256,381	276,381	------	------	------	294,229
1987	------	392,843	------	------	------	373,713	1993	262,860	249,830	249,830	208,138	------	206,770
1988	------	206,330	206,330	210,766	------	217,600	1994	248,151	247,753	247,753	229,717	------	229,008
1989	387,593	380,690	380,690	370,693	------	373,587	1995	181,508	186,167	186,167	------	------	161,847

Source: National Agricultural Statistics Service, U.S. Department of Agriculture

Oat Stocks in the United States In Thousands of Bushels

Year	On Farms				Off Farms				Total Stocks			
	Mar. 1	June 1	Sept. 1	Dec. 1	Mar. 1	June 1	Sept. 1	Dec. 1	Mar. 1	June 1	Sept. 1	Dec. 1
1990	140,000	82,850	234,700	194,700	74,749	74,062	117,009	99,398	214,749	156,912	351,709	294,098
1991	138,600	92,400	173,600	148,100	90,659	78,831	110,487	96,508	229,259	171,231	284,087	244,608
1992	98,150	61,000	199,900	161,200	76,735	66,721	94,717	81,292	174,885	127,721	294,617	242,492
1993	110,250	66,130	161,000	124,200	64,875	47,063	58,004	69,517	175,125	113,193	219,004	193,717
1994	85,050	53,940	144,300	113,400	61,502	51,583	75,551	78,664	146,552	105,523	219,851	192,064
1995[1]	78,400	46,750	107,200	87,000	70,575	53,848	72,967	65,744	148,975	100,598	180,167	152,944

[1] Preliminary. Source: National Agriucultural Statistics Service, U.S. Department of Agriculture

Oats Supply and Utilization in the United States

Crop Year Beginning June 1	Acreage — 1,000 Acres — Planted	Harvested	Yield Per Acre (Bushels)	Production	Imports	Total Supply	Feed & Residual	Food, Alcohol & Industrial	Seed	Exports	Total Use	Ending Stocks	Farm Price	Findley Loan Rate	Target Price
				In Millions of Bushels									Dollars Per Bushel		
1980-1	13,381	8,657	53.0	458.8	1.1	696.3	436.5	41.0	33.0	8.8	519.3	177.0	1.72	1.16	0
1981-2	13,632	9,407	54.2	509.5	1.5	688.0	458.0	41.2	34.2	2.7	536.1	151.9	1.88	1.24	0
1982-3	13,951	10,258	57.8	592.6	3.5	748.0	442.4	41.7	43.3	.8	528.2	219.8	1.49	1.31	1.50
1983-4	20,289	9,062	52.6	476.5	29.9	726.2	474.0	40.9	29.5	.9	545.3	180.9	1.62	1.36	1.60
1984-5	12,414	8,163	58.0	473.7	33.6	688.2	435.6	41.0	31.2	.5	508.3	179.9	1.67	1.31	1.60
1985-6	13,235	8,147	63.6	518.5	27.2	725.6	464.2	44.0	32.5	1.2	541.9	183.7	1.23	1.31	1.60
1986-7	14,671	6,840	56.3	385.0	32.4	601.0	384.4	45.0	38.0	.9	468.3	132.7	1.21	.99	1.60
1987-8	17,907	6,888	54.3	373.7	45.7	552.1	358.2	49.8	31.6	.5	440.1	112.0	1.56	.94	1.60
1988-9	13,910	5,533	39.3	217.6	62.9	392.5	193.8	72.7	27.1	.6	294.2	98.3	2.61	.90	1.55
1989-90	12,085	6,882	54.3	373.6	66.4	538.3	265.6	91.6	23.4	.8	381.4	156.9	1.49	.85	1.50
1990-1	10,423	5,945	60.1	357.5	63.4	578.0	286.1	100.9	19.1	.6	406.7	171.2	1.14	.81	1.45
1991-2	8,654	4,806	50.7	243.5	74.8	489.4	235.2	107.2	17.8	1.9	362.1	127.7	1.21	.83	1.45
1992-3	7,961	4,492	65.6	294.8	55.0	476.9	233.0	107.2	17.8	5.7	363.7	113.2	1.32	.88	1.45
1993-4	7,937	3,803	54.4	206.8	106.8	426.8	193.3	110.0	15.0	3.0	321.3	105.5	1.36	.88	1.45
1994-5[1]	6,639	4,010	57.1	229.0	93.2	427.7	201.1	111.0	14.0	1.0	327.1	100.6	1.22	.97	1.45
1995-6[2]	6,336	2,959	55.2	163.2	105.0	368.8	155.0	110.2	14.8	1.0	281.0	87.8	1.30-1.70	.97	1.45

[1] Preliminary. [2] Forecast. Source: Economic Research Service, U.S. Department of Agriculture

Production of Oats in the United States by States In Thousands of Bushels

Year	California	Illinois	Indiana	Iowa	Michigan	Minnesota	Missouri	Nebraska	New York	North Dakota	Ohio	Oregon	Pennsylvania	South Dakota	Texas	Wisconsin
1980	4,340	14,030	5,850	62,010	20,100	82,650	1,978	15,580	17,920	13,500	19,430	4,140	19,040	66,000	12,580	58,743
1981	3,600	13,530	5,525	59,520	21,080	90,090	4,590	15,800	17,920	44,160	17,010	4,550	20,010	70,520	18,860	52,606
1982	3,350	11,800	6,720	54,150	28,350	97,920	3,276	26,680	18,200	55,650	23,460	6,375	19,765	123,540	10,730	49,290
1983	2,925	12,600	4,560	38,250	15,600	76,950	2,538	13,640	11,400	63,630	15,360	6,000	16,200	79,200	24,000	45,050
1984	3,450	11,385	4,960	47,360	21,700	78,000	1,584	15,680	10,620	49,980	13,860	6,600	15,960	86,800	8,750	53,320
1985	3,015	12,480	7,590	57,760	26,130	77,000	5,775	25,620	17,710	44,520	26,350	9,200	21,000	79,520	15,000	51,480
1986	3,150	14,400	6,390	39,060	17,010	43,350	5,000	21,240	12,920	38,500	12,160	7,600	16,120	46,200	8,400	52,700
1987	2,800	13,110	6,365	35,750	17,100	45,600	3,420	17,640	12,000	36,400	17,500	5,200	14,820	52,900	9,900	43,200
1988	2,730	9,180	3,000	25,000	6,000	24,750	1,520	12,160	7,540	7,200	9,000	6,500	13,000	20,000	9,000	46,860
1989	3,375	16,000	6,840	54,000	20,100	46,750	3,600	8,640	9,145	20,150	15,750	6,860	13,770	44,000	6,600	46,860
1990	3,375	11,560	4,830	40,800	13,050	48,180	2,226	13,440	8,235	16,100	2,280	4,590	15,840	53,200	9,225	47,570
1991	3,375	6,600	2,565	21,250	5,400	22,800	1,632	11,880	5,000	10,200	1,292	4,725	8,400	38,500	7,200	26,500
1992	2,800	7,930	2,800	25,125	8,400	35,000	2,430	15,400	7,700	37,400	12,070	4,230	13,735	42,900	5,720	34,410
1993	2,400	4,590	2,240	9,000	7,150	23,750	686	6,880	6,510	37,100	9,000	3,000	10,000	26,520	7,420	24,150
1994	2,400	5,490	1,855	26,660	6,270	24,750	1,768	7,500	7,040	33,550	6,720	4,500	8,480	31,360	5,200	25,380
1995[1]	2,550	5,360	2,040	14,625	5,130	18,000	1,363	4,500	5,310	21,600	6,900	3,395	9,440	11,500	5,040	18,700

[1] Preliminary. Source: National Agricultural Statistics Service, U.S. Department of Agriculture

OATS

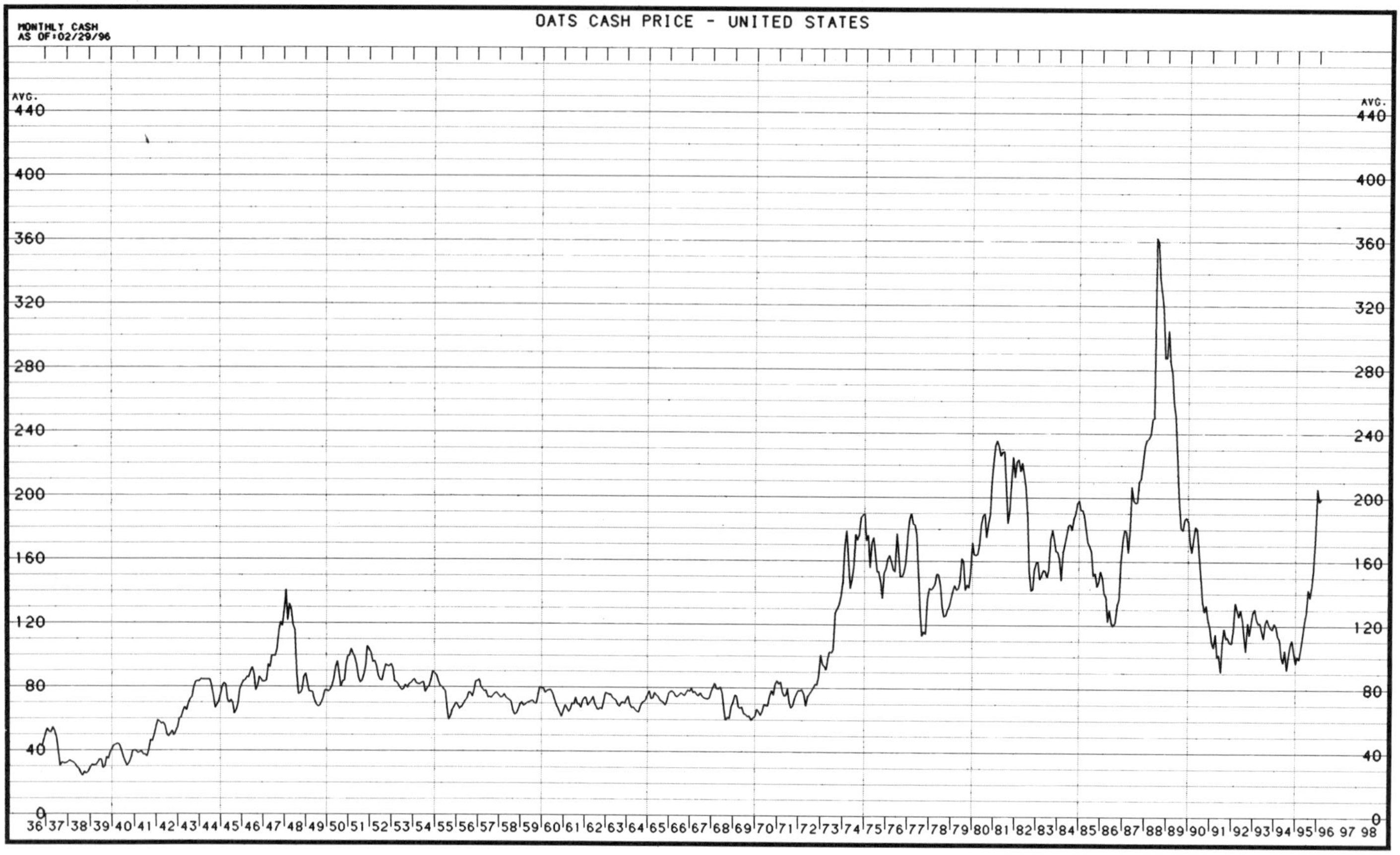

Volume of Trading in Oat Futures at the Chicago Board of Trade In Millions of Bushels

Year	July	Aug.	Sept.	Oct.	Nov.	Dec.	Jan.	Feb.	Mar.	Apr.	May	June	Total
1987-8	103.7	153.6	109.4	135.4	139.4	116.6	92.1	121.2	146.6	162.1	162.6	267.1	1,709.8
1988-9	160.3	121.1	107.6	108.1	183.0	141.1	168.5	136.6	150.7	188.7	138.7	195.2	1,799.6
1989-90	148.7	174.9	104.2	86.7	191.9	64.5	123.3	158.7	169.4	225.7	270.0	231.8	1,949.8
1990-1	160.2	248.0	126.0	139.0	236.9	77.8	100.2	151.4	151.6	213.6	102.9	224.7	1,932.3
1991-2	185.5	205.3	89.3	101.5	172.8	76.0	155.1	420.1	211.3	235.3	210.1	272.7	2,335.0
1992-3	111.0	200.8	125.5	82.9	176.1	97.0	102.4	132.5	130.3	315.7	167.1	215.6	1,856.9
1993-4	166.5	160.4	134.4	203.9	361.6	186.3	239.9	285.3	199.0	269.1	171.5	348.8	2,726.7
1994-5	103.8	196.7	144.2	124.5	284.7	98.4	67.6	185.1	147.5	227.7	170.6	535.4	2,286.1
1995-6	149.3	228.4	158.4	193.2	261.6	235.0							

Source:Chicago Board of Trade

Average Open Interest of Oats at the Chicago Board of Trade In Thousands of Bushels

Year	Jan.	Feb.	Mar.	Apr.	May	June	July	Aug.	Sept.	Oct.	Nov.	Dec.
1987	31,648	36,004	33,508	30,655	26,271	24,536	28,090	36,166	35,212	35,173	28,988	29,724
1988	35,008	42,084	39,209	43,132	43,594	48,130	40,230	35,936	34,095	35,978	45,844	46,842
1989	50,341	51,226	50,761	50,283	47,606	48,831	48,967	47,272	48,824	55,834	59,311	56,240
1990	56,134	59,043	56,777	61,213	62,563	54,455	53,714	60,559	64,824	74,022	75,574	58,791
1991	59,450	64,161	69,476	78,100	71,117	65,457	55,584	54,469	51,842	57,798	56,284	46,776
1992	47,776	77,496	76,797	75,261	76,646	73,863	63,793	55,501	49,345	45,889	43,906	36,433
1993	36,990	38,696	38,274	57,897	66,783	60,098	54,472	56,906	55,855	70,578	100,285	102,734
1994	105,964	100,687	100,971	99,412	91,561	72,873	58,550	69,616	73,715	81,330	76,768	66,882
1995	65,665	66,155	65,001	77,131	80,272	68,054	55,096	56,741	55,059	59,848	62,710	65,016

Source: Chicago Board of Trade

Average Cash Price of No. 2 Heavy White Oats at Minneapolis   In Dollars Per Bushel

Year	June	July	Aug.	Sept.	Oct.	Nov.	Dec.	Jan.	Feb.	Mar.	Apr.	May	Average	No. 2 – Heavy, White – Portland	No. 2 – Heavy, White – Toledo
1983-4	1.67	1.60	1.79	1.94	2.00	1.97	1.94	1.98	1.82	1.88	1.89	1.96	1.87	1.95	2.01
1984-5	1.92	1.84	1.77	1.79	1.84	1.92	1.87	1.81	1.82	1.79	1.73	1.65	1.81	2.12	1.92
1985-6	1.59	1.44	1.23	1.24	1.19	1.32	1.39	1.37	1.30	1.27	1.16	1.22	1.31	1.60	1.08
1986-7	1.18	1.05	1.12	1.29	1.39	1.72	1.66	1.64	1.56	1.46	1.59	1.83	1.46	1.53	1.20
1987-8	1.64	1.61	1.77	1.85	1.97	2.05	2.02	2.10	2.06	1.93	1.94	2.12	1.92	1.76	1.68
1988-9	3.26	3.25	3.09	3.07	2.99	2.71	2.74	2.87	2.59	2.49	2.30	2.22	2.80	2.24	2.26
1989-90	1.97	1.72	1.59	1.58	1.61	1.68	1.70	1.56	1.48	1.57	1.63	1.68	1.65	1.63	1.40
1990-1	1.52	1.37	1.25	1.23	1.29	1.30	1.24	1.22	1.18	1.27	1.32	1.36	1.30	1.58	1.17
1991-2	1.25	1.33	1.38	1.35	1.41	1.42	1.49	1.50	1.68	1.66	1.57	1.59	1.47	1.60	1.37
1992-3	1.55	1.49	1.45	1.58	1.52	1.59	1.63	1.66	1.63	1.63	1.66	1.57	1.58	1.73	1.51
1993-4	1.54	1.63	1.63	1.66	1.56	1.51	1.56	1.57	1.52	1.55	1.46	1.37	1.55	NQ	1.40
1994-5	1.47	1.36	1.44	1.44	1.44	1.41	NQ	1.46	1.42	1.54	1.62	1.76	1.36	NQ	1.37
1995-6[1]	1.73	1.92	1.96	2.04	2.11	2.63									

[1] Preliminary. NQ = No quote. Source: Economic Research Service, U.S. Department of Agriculture

Average Price Received by U.S. Farmers for Oats   In Dollars Per Bushel

Year	Jan.	Feb.	Mar.	Apr.	May	June	July	Aug.	Sept.	Oct.	Nov.	Dec.	Marketing Year Average
1983	1.51	1.46	1.45	1.55	1.62	1.67	1.73	1.81	1.88	1.81	1.82	1.84	1.62
1984	1.80	1.68	1.62	1.60	1.69	1.64	1.72	1.74	1.69	1.68	1.68	1.60	1.67
1985	1.59	1.31	1.16	1.10	1.08	1.17	1.20	1.18	1.16	1.14	1.13	1.21	1.23
1986	1.10	.90	.86	.99	1.10	1.32	1.44	1.46	1.47	1.45	1.50	1.57	1.21
1987	1.52	1.29	1.40	1.49	1.60	1.62	1.76	1.79	1.84	1.78	1.82	1.84	1.56
1988	2.63	2.86	2.54	2.57	2.56	2.41	2.47	2.52	2.46	2.41	2.24	2.13	2.61
1989	2.52	2.46	2.41	2.24	2.13	1.82	1.53	1.47	1.38	1.47	1.48	1.53	1.49
1990	1.47	1.43	1.39	1.44	1.45	1.33	1.15	1.06	1.09	1.14	1.16	1.17	1.14
1991	1.13	1.13	1.16	1.16	1.16	1.08	1.08	1.09	1.12	1.21	1.25	1.25	1.21
1992	1.31	1.44	1.44	1.46	1.43	1.38	1.32	1.23	1.28	1.31	1.35	1.36	1.32
1993	1.42	1.42	1.43	1.45	1.51	1.43	1.36	1.32	1.31	1.33	1.39	1.42	1.36
1994	1.42	1.42	1.39	1.32	1.49	1.31	1.20	1.16	1.18	1.21	1.18	1.18	1.22
1995[1]	1.22	1.22	1.33	1.36	1.39	1.38	1.53	1.47	1.43	1.50	1.69	1.74	

[1] Preliminary. Source: National Agricultural Statistics Service, U.S. Department of Agriculture

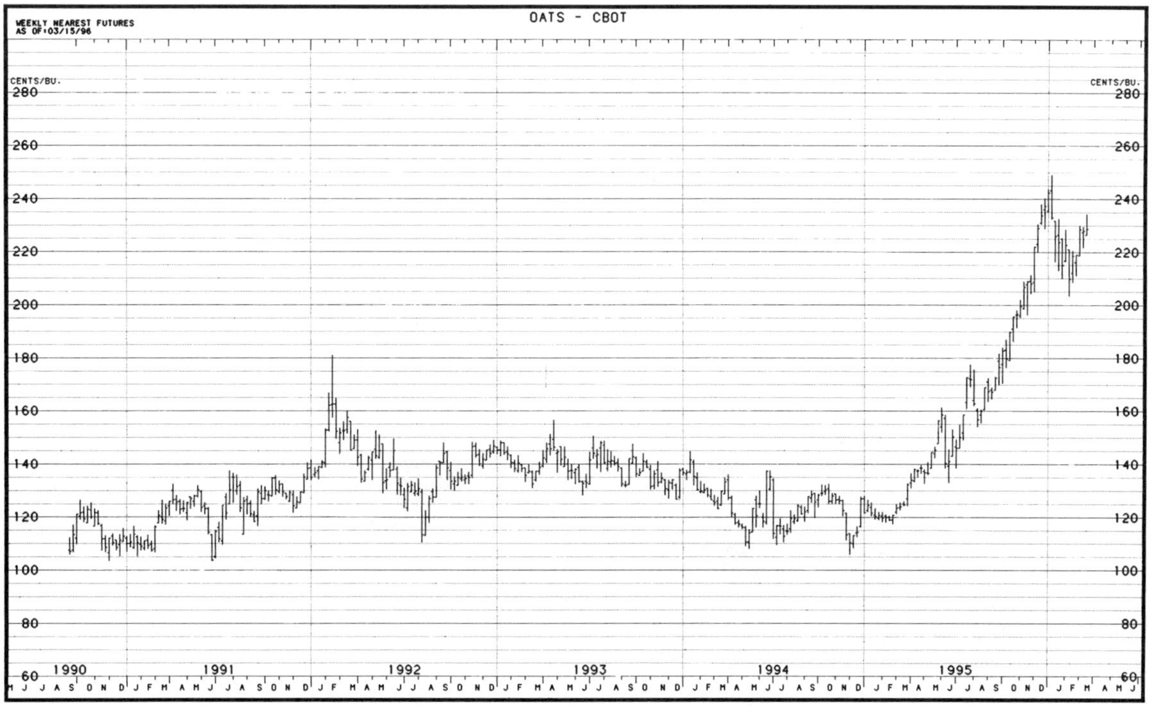

Olive Oil

Despite its steep price premium to other cooking oils, olive oil remains the oil of choice for many due to its taste and health benefits. Perhaps due to its higher price, olive oil consumption has shown virtually no growth in recent years. The olive harvest begins in the northern Mediterranean region in mid-November and moves south, ending in March. The main producers are Italy, Spain and Greece, with Tunisia, Turkey and Morocco accounting for smaller amounts. Tunisia has emerged in recent seasons as a more important supplier. Between 1990-91 and 1994-95, average olive oil production by Spain was 578,000 tonnes, Italy 418,000 tonnes, Greece 293,000 tonnes and Tunisia 181,000 tonnes. As a tree crop, olive oil production is cyclical with large crops typically followed by smaller ones.

The USDA forecasts that world olive oil production will fall substantially in 1995-96 (Aug.-Sept.). Production is estimated at 1.47 million tonnes, down 12.5 percent from the previous season's output of 1.68 million tonnes. *Oil World* estimates that production by the fifteen nations of the European Union will fall to a five year low in 1995/96, down 130,000 tonnes from the 1994-95 season and 170,000 tonnes below the recent five year average. A serious drought took a toll on the Spanish olive oil industry insuring that Spain's olive oil output will be the lowest in 20 years. This in turn could force Spain to increase imports of olive oil from Italy, Greece and North Africa to 150,000-200,000 tonnes to cover domestic and export requirements according to *Oil World*. Olive oil stocks were estimated at 200,000 tonnes at the start of the new season, a four year low. Somewhat offsetting the smaller Spanish crop will be larger crops in Italy and Greece.

Much of the world's olive oil is consumed where it is grown. It is expected the steep production decline and very tight stocks could increase prices substantially. This could cause a switch by consumers to other cooking oils such as soybean oil or corn oil. The U.S., a major importer of olive oil, forecast 1995 usage at 289 million pounds, a four percent increase from 1994. On a net basis. U.S. imports of olive oil were forecast at 287 million pounds versus 276 million in 1994.

World Production of Olive Oil (Pressed Oil) In Thousands of Metric Tons

Crop Year	Algeria	Argentina	Greece	Israel	Italy	Jordan	Lebanon	Libya	Morocco	Portugal	Spain	Syria	Tunisia	Turkey	World Total
1984-5	15.0	9.7	266.0	4.0	371.8	7.1	7.0	12.0	28.5	48.0	724.2	66.6	99.8	91.0	1,769.8
1985-6	18.0	9.5	386.4	2.0	656.0	9.1	5.0	9.0	43.4	36.0	432.2	52.0	114.7	81.0	1,870.3
1986-7	15.0	7.5	257.0	3.0	383.1	15.4	6.0	7.4	38.0	44.0	529.8	81.0	127.5	138.0	1,670.2
1987-8	10.0	9.5	322.0	3.0	742.5	3.1	5.0	6.5	41.5	38.0	792.0	36.0	101.5	63.0	2,198.0
1988-9	10.0	11.0	319.2	4.0	390.0	13.0	8.0	6.0	31.5	24.6	431.4	100.0	61.0	102.0	1,552.0
1989-90	16.0	10.5	316.3	2.5	624.2	7.5	5.5	8.0	70.0	44.3	594.9	33.0	137.0	39.0	1,938.6
1990-1	6.0	11.0	187.0	7.5	176.4	9.0	6.5	7.0	40.0	22.0	690.6	92.0	189.0	92.0	1,579.1
1991-2	37.0	9.5	423.5	2.5	727.9	5.5	5.0	10.0	55.5	72.7	640.5	51.0	264.0	72.0	2,394.0
1992-3	26.5	10.5	339.0	7.5	469.8	15.5	8.0	6.0	43.0	26.9	672.8	95.0	133.0	65.0	1,974.0
1993-4[1]	21.0	8.5	275.0	1.5	451.5	9.5	2.0	8.0	45.5	36.0	593.0	71.0	251.0	55.0	1,875.0
1994-5[2]	14.0	10.0	390.0	8.0	464.0	16.5	8.5	6.5	50.0	36.0	520.0	101.5	108.0	184.0	1,965.0
1995-6[3]	18.0	12.0	378.0		626.0	15.0		4.0	34.0	36.0	284.0	75.0	85.0	60.0	1,682.0

[1] Preliminary. [2] Estimate. [3] Forecast. *Source: The Oil World*

Average Unit Value of U.S. Olive Oil Imports In Dollars Per Metric Ton

Year	Jan.	Feb.	Mar.	Apr.	May	June	July	Aug.	Sept.	Oct.	Nov.	Dec.	Average
1986	1,402	1,400	1,402	1,469	1,492	1,495	1,587	1,554	1,751	1,572	1,732	1,589	1,537
1987	1,690	1,763	1,652	1,726	1,635	1,577	1,588	1,608	1,563	1,646	1,609	1,696	1,646
1988	1,682	1,694	1,736	1,699	1,701	1,669	1,465	1,562	1,691	1,582	1,493	1,606	1,632
1989	1,642	1,642	1,890	1,930	2,005	1,981	1,919	1,919	1,862	1,917	1,910	2,017	1,886
1990	1,892	1,940	1,931	2,034	2,047	2,047	2,044	2,169	2,142	2,029	2,245	2,170	2,058
1991	2,195	2,213	2,355	2,188	2,283	2,274	2,281	2,282	2,401	2,250	2,417	2,523	2,305
1992	2,448	2,365	2,317	2,271	2,270	2,267	2,299	2,302	2,206	2,204	2,189	2,295	2,286
1993	2,132	2,071	1,853	1,823	1,779	1,820	1,805	1,815	1,836	1,788	1,885	1,852	1,872
1994[1]	1,838	1,752	1,891	1,850	1,872	1,889	1,943	2,001	2,032	2,141	2,215	2,126	1,963
1995[1]	2,245	2,316	2,470	2,629	2,794	2,857	3,032	3,112	3,110				

[1] Preliminary. *Source: Foreign Agricultural Service, U.S. Department of Agriculture*

World Olive Oil Supply and Distribution In Thousands of Metric Tons

Crop Year	Production	Exports	Imports	Consumption	Ending Stocks	Crop Year	Production	Exports	Imports	Consumption	Ending Stocks
1984-5	1,600	484	503	1,729	799	1990-1	1,579	821	801	1,868	394
1985-6	1,626	367	500	1,718	839	1991-2	2,394	357	342	1,947	713
1986-7	1,670	746	730	1,849	764	1992-3	1,974	362	365	2,040	650
1987-8	2,095	509	519	1,929	1,936	1993-4[1]	1,875	421	420	2,027	498
1988-9	1,552	558	575	1,870	634	1994-5[2]	1,965	424	428	2,000	466
1989-90	1,939	579	573	1,861	706	1995-6[3]	1,682	350	350	1,900	247

[1] Preliminary. [2] Estimate. [3] Forecast. *Source: The Oil World*

Onions

Salient Statistics of Onions in the United States

Crop Year	Harvested Acres	Yield Per Acre	Production 1,000 Cwt.	Price Per Cwt.	Farm Value $1,000	Jan. 1 Stocks Frozen	Annual Pack Frozen	Imports Canned	Exports (Fresh)	Imports (Fresh)	Per Capita[3] Utilization --Lbs., Farm Weight-- All	Fresh
						Millions of Pounds						
1986	115,540	375	43,615	11.10	439,239	27.4	185.5	12.3	261.1	247.7	15.6	13.7
1987	123,720	364	45,113	12.50	505,163	35.7	185.2	13.0	282.0	371.2	14.9	13.4
1988	128,950	362	46,733	9.75	413,996	29.6	198.9	14.1	322.9	407.0	16.2	14.5
1989	132,660	361	47,902	11.40	496,971	33.4	208.8	3.3	250.0	359.7	16.4	14.8
1990	138,340	382	52,781	10.50	488,786	39.6	243.1	3.7	370.8	377.0	17.1	15.1
1991	133,970	378	50,702	12.50	582,556	34.4	226.5	3.4	339.0	491.7	17.3	15.7
1992	141,730	386	54,731	13.00	629,019	32.1	202.3	3.4	355.9	417.3	17.6	16.2
1993	152,580	380	57,956	16.80	831,986	34.2	213.7	4.7	301.5	504.1	18.1	16.0
1994[1]	160,750	396	63,621	10.90	628,025	36.1	241.3	4.2	341.8	539.2	17.5	16.3
1995[2]	163,800	391	64,046	11.10	634,344	51.2			600.0	490.0	18.2	16.6

[1] Preliminary. [2] Forecast. [3] Includes fresh and processing. *Source: Economic Research Service, U.S. Department of Agriculture*

Production of Onions in the United States In Thousands of Hundred Pounds (Cwt.)

Year	Spring: Arizona	California	Texas	Total (All)	Summer: California	Colorado	Idaho	Michigan	Minnesota	New Mexico	New York	Oregon (Malheur)	Texas	Total (All)	Grand Total
1986	660	2,886	3,600	7,146	9,953	4,590	3,710	1,653	208	1,810	3,456	5,945	1,537	36,155	43,301
1987	585	3,198	2,750	6,533	10,730	4,688	4,620	1,900	195	2,106	3,132	7,032	799	39,334	45,867
1988	450	3,315	3,220	6,985	10,512	5,535	4,028	2,000	126	2,752	2,925	6,649	861	39,748	46,733
1989	440	3,080	3,225	7,380	10,125	5,520	3,996	2,212	161	3,000	2,912	6,710	1,040	40,516	47,902
1990	473	3,570	2,520	7,655	12,675	5,130	4,180	2,442	208	2,870	5,120	6,865	1,377	45,853	53,508
1991	441	3,160	3,264	7,093	11,250	4,953	4,543	2,044	294	2,960	3,510	7,588	960	42,017	49,110
1992	450	3,600	2,793	8,229	10,313	5,460	5,063	2,448	285	3,200	4,392	6,649	740	46,502	54,213
1993	631	3,300	2,768	8,193	13,035	5,735	4,698	2,201	22	4,074	3,720	5,940	936	49,763	57,956
1994	688	2,948	4,704	10,297	12,710	6,125	5,547	2,308	312	3,318	3,844	7,378	837	53,324	63,621
1995[1]	672	3,300	3,763	10,110	12,658	6,141	5,481	2,001	125	4,095	4,032	7,134	658	53,936	64,046

[1] Preliminary. *Source: Agricultural Statistics Board, U.S. Department of Agriculture*

Cold Storage Stocks of Fresh Onions in the United States In Thousands of Pounds

Year	Jan. 1	Feb. 1	Mar. 1	Apr. 1	May 1	June 1	July 1	Aug. 1	Sept. 1	Oct. 1	Nov. 1	Dec. 1
1986	5,171	5,325	2,572	1,573	545	1,769	1,627	1,001	346	2,116	4,693	7,784
1987	6,773	5,330	2,710	1,883	1,560	2,403	1,181	137	1,276	2,500	3,823	6,641
1988	4,406	1,982	192	35	575	2,551	1,587	268	3,508	7,453	10,499	9,018
1989	7,608	4,914	2,348	70	462	670	184	140	2,133	13,283	16,492	16,000
1990	11,858	12,787	7,282	5,226	2,633	3,346	2,394	984	2,296	13,927	23,224	21,731
1991	17,030	14,387	5,918	2,885	995	1,957	2,225	1,695	2,164	26,746	35,362	29,414
1992	9,894	7,717	5,799	595	357	2,072	1,882	951	6,476	22,115	28,573	16,839
1993	12,032	5,196	3,536	1,642	733	600	747	1,270	16,948	11,735	19,967	16,875
1994	6,353	2,668	1,678	1,390	838	2,973	2,106	2,060	1,631	3,858	6,300	4,058
1995[1]	2,520	907	561	150	237	1,861	747	385	485	2,227	4,149	3,722

[1] Preliminary. *Source: National Agricultural Statistics Service, U.S. Department of Agriculture*

F.O.B. Price Received by Growers for Onions in the U.S. In Dollars Per Hundred Pounds (Cwt.)

Year	Jan.	Feb.	Mar.	Apr.	May	June	July	Aug.	Sept.	Oct.	Nov.	Dec.	Season Average
1986	7.84	6.89	7.26	9.71	9.45	10.80	11.20	9.72	10.30	11.10	11.50	12.40	11.10
1987	16.50	18.30	20.60	26.30	22.30	16.80	14.90	10.60	9.71	8.77	9.38	10.60	12.50
1988	15.70	15.70	15.00	16.80	8.90	8.52	10.40	8.97	12.50	12.10	12.20	12.00	9.75
1989	11.50	10.90	9.70	10.90	9.47	12.90	16.90	16.00	11.20	10.10	9.62	9.70	11.40
1990	10.90	15.70	18.40	19.40	13.40	10.50	9.49	10.80	9.01	8.29	9.54	10.90	10.50
1991	13.80	10.20	11.90	18.40	21.50	14.10	17.70	12.90	11.20	10.00	10.60	10.40	12.50
1992	10.70	12.80	20.80	23.60	12.40	10.00	12.20	13.80	12.40	11.60	12.00	14.80	13.00
1993	16.60	14.00	17.30	31.00	23.60	10.40	12.70	14.80	13.30	12.10	18.70	24.50	16.70
1994	29.80	32.10	17.90	10.70	8.64	8.54	12.80	9.44	9.14	10.40	12.00	12.10	10.50
1995[1]	13.80	17.10	16.90	23.70	15.50	10.10	12.80	10.40	10.00	10.60			

[1] Preliminary. *Source: Economic Research Service, U.S. Department of Agriculture*

Oranges and Orange Juice

1994-95 U.S. orange juice production is forecast at a record 1.27 billion single-strength gallons, up 13 percent from 1993-94. Florida's crop was 205.4 million 90-pound boxes of oranges. This was up almost 18 percent from the previous crop of 174.4 million boxes. The Florida juice yield was 1.50 gallons (42 degree brix) per box, a decline of 4 percent from the prior year. About 95 percent of Florida's oranges were processed, slightly higher than 1993-94.

Imports of juice into the U.S. fell in 1994-95 to the lowest levels in 10 years. Most U.S. imports originate in Brazil. Brazilian prices were above that of Florida, leading to the reduced imports. Brazil has been concentrating on building its market share in Europe as well as Asia. This trend is expected to continue into the 1995-96 season. Imports of juice were 225 million single-strength equivalents in 1994-95, down 44 percent from 1993-94. Season beginning stocks were 269 million gallons for a supply of 1.76 billion gallons. In terms of use, exports of juice were 120 million gallons, up from 107 million the prior season. Europe takes half of U.S. exports. Domestic consumption of juice was estimated at 1.39 billion gallons, unchanged from 1993-94. Ending stocks were put at 255 million gallons.

Brazil is the world's largest producer of oranges and orange juice. The season in Brazil starts in July. The 1995-96 season got off to a slow start as a drought delayed the crop. For 1995-96, Brazilian orange juice production was forecast at 1.41 billion gallons, single-strength equivalent, down 9 percent. Exports were projected to be 1.36 billion gallons, down 10 percent. Brazilian consumption of processed orange juice is minimal; they prefer to buy fresh oranges and squeeze them at home. About 30 percent of the Brazilian orange crop is sold for fresh consumption.

The 1995-96 season in Florida got off to a good start. Heavy rains may have caused some reduction in yields but overall the season was good, if not excellent. The number of bearing orange trees in 1994-95 was 70 million and was estimated at 76 million in 1995-96.

In December 1995, the USDA estimated the Florida citrus crop at 204 million boxes, down 1 percent from 1994-95. Early mid-season and navel oranges were estimated at 124 million boxes, up 4 percent from the prior season. Valencia orange production was estimated at 80 million boxes, down 7 percent from 1994-95. Temple orange production was put at 2.2 million boxes, down 14 percent. All U.S. orange production was put at 272.15 million boxes, up 1 percent from 1993-94. California orange production was put at 66 million boxes, up from 61 million in 1994-95. The Texas orange crop was estimated at 1.05 million boxes, about the same as the previous season. The Arizona crop was estimated at 1.1 million boxes, up nearly 5 percent from 1994-95.

Consumption of orange juice is at record levels. The Florida Department of Citrus reported that October 1995 U.S. orange juice consumption was a record. Premium orange juice (not from concentrate) was rising the most.

Futures Market

Frozen concentrated orange juice futures and options are traded on the Citrus Associates of the New York Cotton Exchange (NYCE).

World Production of Oranges In Thousands of Metric Tons

Season	Argentina	Australia	Brazil	Cuba	Cyprus	Egypt	Greece	Israel	Italy	Mexico	Morocco	South Africa	Spain	Turkey	United States	Grand Total
1986-7	621	475	10,650	496	204	1,235	881	815	2,424	1,683	650	577	2,059	750	7,122	31,196
1987-8	650	394	10,400	508	138	1,387	462	627	1,343	1,942	891	681	2,442	700	7,903	30,990
1988-9	620	544	14,150	474	170	1,199	770	546	2,170	2,000	994	629	2,216	740	8,272	35,835
1989-90	750	458	12,036	604	223	1,397	932	877	2,067	1,900	775	697	2,400	740	7,083	33,361
1990-1	600	485	12,362	600	169	1,574	819	567	1,760	2,300	1,103	648	2,590	735	7,222	33,938
1991-2	640	595	14,974	428	168	1,694	820	513	1,842	2,100	780	680	2,651	830	8,175	38,193
1992-3	660	578	14,484	379	160	1,771	1,042	377	2,111	2,913	874	712	2,926	820	10,074	41,582
1993-4[1]	746	588	13,710	350	160	1,324	854	365	2,100	3,174	916	770	2,509	840	9,462	39,563
1994-5[2]	720	470	15,710	350	166	1,513	865	405	1,710	3,300	657	770	2,644	920	10,641	42,591
1995-6[3]	NA	NA	NA	350	252	1,360	870	460	1,770	2,700	870	NA	2,481	880	10,741	NA

[1] Preliminary. [2] Estimate. [3] Forecast. NA = Not available. *Source: Foreign Agricultural Service, U.S. Department of Agriculture*

U.S. Salient Statistics of Oranges & Orange Juice

Season	Production[4] California (Million Boxes)	Production[4] Florida (Million Boxes)	Production[4] Total U.S. (Million Boxes)	Farm Price $ Per Box	Farm Value Million $	Florida Crop Processed: Frozen Concentrates (Million Boxes)	Florida Crop Processed: Chilled Products (Million Boxes)	Florida Crop Processed: Total Processed (Million Boxes)	Yield Per Box Gallons[5]	Frozen Concentrated Orange Juice-Florida: Carry-in (In Million Gallons (42° Brix))	Frozen Concentrated Orange Juice-Florida: Pack	Frozen Concentrated Orange Juice-Florida: Total Supply	Frozen Concentrated Orange Juice-Florida: Total Season Movement	Brazilian U.S. Imports of Frozen Concentrated OJ: Pack	Brazilian Exports: Total	Brazilian Exports: To U.S.
1985-6	53.9	119.2	175.7	6.18	1,090.4	96.1	17.3	114.7	1.4	48.3	215.1	263.4	226.4	285.9	190.7	112.2
1986-7	57.9	119.7	181.2	7.29	1,322.5	96.2	19.7	116.8	1.5	37.0	227.9	264.9	225.1	210.4	277.8	139.8
1987-8	59.0	138.0	200.3	8.52	1,773.7	110.2	23.3	134.4	1.6	39.8	240.9	280.7	238.5	244.8	254.5	120.5
1988-9	58.9	146.6	207.2	8.90	1,848.5	113.7	29.9	144.8	1.5	42.1	239.1	281.2	235.0	245.8	243.8	123.1
1989-90	71.4	110.2	184.5	7.96	1,465.1	73.6	33.8	108.1	1.2	46.3	184.7	231.0	191.1	362.0	330.7	132.4
1990-1	25.6	151.6	179.0	8.70	1,584.7	104.1	38.4	143.1	1.5	40.0	221.2	261.2	229.2	294.8	284.5	87.7
1991-2	67.4	139.8	209.6	7.43	1,545.2	93.9	37.3	131.7	1.6	31.8	211.7	243.5	212.6	274.1	279.3	107.8
1992-3	66.8	186.6	255.8	5.77	1,489.9	132.2	47.4	180.0	1.6	31.0	292.0	322.9	269.4	394.8	418.2	103.1
1993-4[1]	63.6	174.4	240.5	6.37	1,541.3	116.2	52.9	169.4	1.6	53.5	182.2	303.2	244.5	388.2	387.5	102.0
1994-5[2]	61.0	205.4	268.5	5.76	1,563.5	144.7	54.7	199.7	1.5	58.6	216.5	320.1	269.0	356.9	370.7	
1995-6[3]	66.0	202.0	270.3			134.7	56.0	202.0								

[1] Preliminary. [2] Estimate. [3] Forecast. [4] Fruit ripened on trees, but destroyed prior to picking in not included. [5] 42° Brix equivalent.
Sources: Economic Research Service, U.S. Department of Agriculture; Florida Department of Citrus

U.S. Cold Storage Stocks of Orange Juice Concentrate[2] In Millions of Pounds

Year	Jan. 1	Feb. 1	Mar. 1	Apr. 1	May 1	June 1	July 1	Aug. 1	Sept. 1	Oct. 1	Nov. 1	Dec. 1
1986	679.2	888.4	966.8	911.5	1,031.6	1,047.5	1,056.9	920.3	855.3	715.4	577.8	524.8
1987	621.2	874.8	1,012.7	933.8	999.0	1,109.1	1,105.1	942.1	792.6	840.0	652.8	569.0
1988	662.4	903.8	1,072.9	1,004.1	1,019.0	1,122.1	1,171.8	998.5	827.0	693.3	638.7	589.5
1989	721.6	980.9	1,155.9	1,087.0	1,144.8	1,296.1	1,324.8	1,167.5	932.6	808.4	725.7	669.7
1990	749.6	926.6	1,046.5	1,119.2	980.9	1,148.2	1,074.8	1,008.1	901.4	797.1	802.0	871.3
1991	1,031.6	1,195.8	1,199.5	1,236.9	1,363.2	1,304.7	1,110.6	1,007.5	876.9	765.2	617.3	655.4
1992	828.4	1,130.7	1,150.0	1,102.9	1,269.3	1,294.8	1,143.8	978.0	874.9	741.9	665.5	638.0
1993	892.9	1,135.9	1,282.8	1,297.5	1,440.9	1,462.3	1,351.8	1,147.0	1,029.6	875.7	813.3	890.9
1994	955.5	1,248.9	1,429.0	1,273.8	1,499.6	1,615.2	1,521.8	1,449.1	1,257.5	1,119.6	1,026.1	1,055.9
1995[1]	1,353.1	1,704.0	1,685.1	1,752.0	1,864.6	1,833.8	1,631.6	1,424.1	1,233.7	1,038.3	830.3	883.9

[1] Preliminary. *Source: Agricultural Statistics Board, U.S. Department of Agriculture*

Average Open Interest of Frozen Concentrated Orange Juice Futures In Contracts

Year	Jan.	Feb.	Mar.	Apr.	May	June	July	Aug.	Sept.	Oct.	Nov.	Dec.
1986	10,440	8,532	7,986	7,010	6,909	6,860	7,198	6,669	6,924	8,287	9,270	10,849
1987	11,222	10,283	10,031	9,206	8,658	8,104	6,994	6,665	7,229	8,810	9,000	10,212
1988	11,683	14,089	16,708	14,576	11,861	11,427	11,235	11,192	9,708	6,564	9,170	8,697
1989	7,169	6,959	7,009	7,821	8,374	9,767	8,340	7,531	6,857	7,218	7,029	9,887
1990	9,667	11,067	11,877	11,952	10,528	10,229	9,413	7,485	6,867	5,939	5,802	6,983
1991	6,773	6,457	5,739	6,255	5,762	6,338	5,653	6,556	9,854	11,924	9,877	9,101
1992	9,095	10,033	9,872	11,309	10,791	9,776	10,109	12,132	11,910	14,224	16,669	17,455
1993	17,733	18,199	19,030	20,210	18,525	19,267	20,000	18,899	18,287	18,825	18,422	20,367
1994	17,544	18,137	19,073	21,607	21,450	23,530	24,829	21,874	22,739	23,385	26,859	26,413
1995	27,439	25,885	26,407	30,172	27,057	26,844	23,537	17,881	20,918	22,460	26,303	24,202

Source: Citrus Association of the New York Cotton Exchange

ORANGES AND ORANGE JUICE

Volume of Trading of Frozen Concentrated Orange Juice Futures In Contracts

Year	Jan.	Feb.	Mar.	Apr.	May	June	July	Aug.	Sept.	Oct.	Nov.	Dec.	Total
1986	39,756	24,971	21,413	13,209	13,909	14,979	10,469	9,887	10,940	17,513	9,551	24,946	211,543
1987	28,566	24,342	27,999	19,569	10,651	15,470	8,805	10,710	12,330	20,321	20,724	26,758	266,641
1988	40,976	42,153	37,295	28,937	22,931	36,877	23,752	27,118	26,228	26,922	19,399	25,451	358,039
1989	26,156	26,419	28,501	26,855	30,272	32,051	23,403	19,698	17,119	18,069	15,893	39,668	304,104
1990	53,133	32,035	31,676	28,025	23,656	45,028	21,302	24,029	13,131	21,793	16,473	30,739	342,574
1991	35,037	28,221	17,298	17,116	17,991	20,956	14,905	20,187	26,412	42,016	23,228	24,171	287,076
1992	30,508	28,177	21,371	31,725	21,253	22,473	21,877	27,208	26,912	29,604	33,133	44,979	339,230
1993	43,634	46,067	58,298	52,554	53,566	60,330	49,415	52,381	56,838	63,808	44,167	58,073	640,131
1994	46,166	51,123	43,075	55,955	48,236	60,110	37,069	55,711	52,209	73,155	54,978	76,037	653,824
1995	50,875	66,370	51,292	78,288	32,607	80,165	41,357	67,528	38,781	64,904	45,688	71,077	688,932

Source: Citrus Association of the New York Cotton Exchange

U.S Retail and Nonretail Sales of Orange Juice In Millions of SSE Gallons

Crop Year	Retail Sales	% Change[2]	Nonretail Sales	% Change[2]	Apparent Con-sumption	% Change[2]	Per Capita Con-sumption	% Change[2]
1983-4	856	-.8	218	-50.6	1,074	-17.6	4.5	-19.6
1984-5	817	-4.6	376	72.5	1,193	11.1	5.0	11.1
1985-6	884	8.2	321	-14.6	1,205	1.0	5.0	0
1986-7	701	-20.7	385	19.9	1,243	3.2	5.1	2.0
1987-8	667	-4.9	432	12.2	1,229	-1.1	5.0	-2.0
1988-9	690	3.4	401	-7.2	1,238	.7	5.0	0
1989-90	628	-9.0	317	-20.9	1,079	-12.8	4.3	-14.0
1990-1	701	11.6	296	-6.6	1,146	6.2	4.5	4.7
1991-2	689	-1.7	268	-9.5	1,112	-3.0	4.3	-4.4
1992-3	748	8.6	371	38.4	1,328	19.4	5.1	18.6
1993-4	740	-1.1			1,368	3.0	5.2	2.0
1994-5[1]	740	0			1,355	-1.0	5.1	-1.9
1995-6[1]	726-713	-1.9 to -3.6			1,309	-3.4	4.9	-3.9

[1] Estimate. [2] Percentage change from previous period. *Source: Florida Department of Citrus*

Producer Price Index of Frozen Orange Concentrate 1982 = 100

Year	Jan.	Feb.	Mar.	Apr.	May	June	July	Aug.	Sept.	Oct.	Nov.	Dec.	Average
1986	328.5	321.7	307.2	297.0	296.3	296.7	296.5	296.7	295.0	302.1	310.4	319.2	305.6
1987[2]	106.9	106.9	107.4	109.5	109.7	110.0	110.1	111.0	110.6	110.6	117.2	129.9	111.7
1988	132.1	140.1	142.4	140.5	142.0	141.1	141.6	142.0	141.7	140.7	140.8	139.1	140.3
1989	136.4	127.7	126.5	126.5	131.7	139.2	140.6	140.3	134.0	131.6	123.1	121.7	131.6
1990	137.6	162.4	162.8	159.9	159.7	160.0	160.4	160.8	150.9	147.2	120.9	117.8	150.0
1991	114.4	114.4	111.7	111.7	111.0	111.0	111.0	107.2	107.4	116.0	127.3	131.5	114.5
1992	135.1	134.7	134.7	134.3	126.2	118.5	115.5	114.5	112.5	106.5	104.2	98.8	119.6
1993	91.6	88.8	88.2	89.0	89.3	97.5	104.5	104.5	104.7	104.7	107.9	107.9	98.2
1994	107.9	104.8	104.2	104.2	102.7	101.2	100.2	100.1	99.9	99.8	100.7	100.5	102.2
1995[1]	107.4	105.4	107.6	107.6	109.1	109.1	109.1	104.5	100.1	100.9	104.1		

[1] Preliminary. [2] Prior to 1987, price index shown as 1967 = 100. *Source: Bureau of Labor Statistics, U.S. Department of Commerce*

Average Price of Oranges (Equivalent On-Tree) Received by Growers In Dollar Per Box

Year	Jan.	Feb.	Mar.	Apr.	May	June	July	Aug.	Sept.	Oct.	Nov.	Dec.	Average
1986	4.20	4.01	4.07	3.76	4.24	4.18	3.58	3.91	4.59	6.50	6.46	4.79	4.52
1987	4.64	4.80	4.96	5.40	5.99	6.40	6.02	5.41	7.43	10.43	9.10	6.35	6.41
1988	6.43	6.59	6.87	7.76	8.79	8.78	6.47	5.44	5.56	3.39	6.15	6.76	6.58
1989	6.51	6.45	6.26	7.28	8.39	8.51	7.27	6.52	6.54	6.29	7.34	6.34	6.98
1990	5.92	5.82	6.00	6.47	6.97	6.61	5.74	4.38	4.48	5.04	5.78	5.76	5.75
1991	5.64	6.28	6.94	7.09	7.95	19.43	17.40	18.45	21.39	9.87	6.27	5.79	11.04
1992	5.90	6.02	5.81	6.14	6.16	4.26	1.85	1.02	1.05	2.43	4.10	3.67	4.03
1993	3.37	3.21	3.41	4.00	4.03	4.09	5.02	7.25	11.85	11.44	5.95	3.81	5.62
1994	3.76	3.90	4.66	4.83	5.04	4.94	4.08	4.24	3.44	2.50	2.74	3.01	3.93
1995[1]	3.21	3.51	4.11	4.70	4.96	5.11	6.04	4.25	7.21	6.90	3.36	3.39	4.73

[1] Preliminary. *Source: Economic Research Service, U.S. Department of Agriculture*

Palm Oil

World palm oil production and consumption is second only to soybean oil, but it is the leading vegetable oil in foreign trade. Statistically, production and disappearance doubled between 1985/86 and 1995/96, the fastest growth rate of the major edible oils. Palm oil is a tropical oil, but competes directly with other cooking oils that are grown in more temperate climates. Almost all the world's production comes from Malaysia and Indonesia.

Production in 1994/95 of a record large 15.4 million metric tons compares with 13.8 million in 1993/94. Much of the production is exported to meet world consumption, estimated at 14.7 million tons in 1994/95 versus 14.4 million in 1993/94 and an early 1990's average of about 11.5 million tons. However, consumption in 1994/95 trailed expectations, necessitating sharp price discounts at times to maintain palm oil's competitiveness against other oils, notably in Europe, the world's largest net importer of crude vegetable oils. World palm oil stocks increased to a record large 2.64 million tons at yearend 1994/95 (September) from 2.08 million a year earlier.

Malaysia's 1994/95 production of 8 million tons was up 11 percent from 1993/94, reflecting increased acreage and higher yields. Indonesia's crop of 4.3 million tons compares with 3.9 million the previous year. Higher oil prices have contained demand, even in producing countries; in the first quarter of 1995 world exports, mostly from Malaysia, fell 21 percent from the previous quarter and 10 percent from a year earlier. Still, total palm oil exports in 1994/95 of 10.48 million tons compare with 10.19 million in 1993/94. In calendar year 1994, China was the biggest player in palm oil foreign trade as import demand increased sharply, as it did also for competing oils. The reason was apparently to increase stocks as a way to contain inflation. China's import demand slackened in 1995 as edible oil stocks were at a record high.

The outlook for palm oil prices is mixed. On the positive side is the expected strong growth in consumption from Eastern and Western Europe, together with China and India. However, large world stocks, hefty production growth and the availability of competing oils could prove more important price influencing factors on palm oil in 1995/96.

Futures Markets

Crude Palm Oil and Crude Palm Kernal Oil are traded on the Kuala Lumpur Commodity Exchange (KLCE).

World Palm Oil Statistics In Thousands of Metric Tons

Crop Year	Production: Colombia	Ecuador	Indonesia	Ivory Coast	Malaysia	Nigeria	Papua/ N.Guinea	Thailand	World Total	Imports: China	Pakistan	Singapore	World Total	Exports: Indonesia	Malaysia	Singapore	World Total
1989-90	230	119	2,272	264	6,418	592	135	225	11,164	988	721	790	8,044	1,033	5,817	673	8,135
1990-1	251	127	2,574	277	6,036	631	184	234	11,255	1,291	818	848	8,570	1,626	5,717	644	8,617
1991-2	281	139	2,803	278	6,224	633	195	254	11,782	877	1,002	696	8,340	1,267	5,783	572	8,291
1992-3	303	146	3,355	310	7,122	640	232	289	13,396	1,162	1,102	745	9,325	1,733	6,212	501	9,304
1993-4[1]	346	176	3,630	314	7,103	640	249	311	13,818	1,684	1,080	469	10,355	1,965	6,737	346	10,357
1994-5[2]	386	170	4,185	336	7,771	655	258	350	15,218	1,782	1,270	568	10,847	2,110	6,692	400	10,821
1995-6[3]	380	197	4,700	348	8,031	660	267	375	16,122	1,400	1,240	570	10,770	2,370	6,520	375	10,838

[1] Preliminary. [2] Estimate. [3] Forecast. *Source: The Oil World*

Palm Oil--U.S. Supply and Distribution In Thousands of Metric Tons

Year Beginning Oct.	Stocks Oct. 1	Imports	Total Supply	Consumption: Edible Products (In Millions of Pounds)	Inedible Products	Total End Products	Total Disappearance	Exports	Prices: U.S. Import Value[4] (U.S. $ Per Metric Ton)	Malaysia, F.O.B., RBD	Palm Kernel Oil, Malaysia, C.I.F. Rotterdam
1990-1	12.8	129.0	141.8	97.8	71.1	168.9	115.0	3.1	323	318	362
1991-2	23.7	100.1	123.8	98.6	101.5	200.1	100.4	3.3	347	365	586
1992-3	20.1	120.6	140.7	83.5	113.5	197.0	122.5	3.3	377	382	439
1993-4[1]	14.9	167.0	181.9	86.2	118.2	204.4	162.0	3.6	370	445	566
1994-5[2]	16.4	102.0	118.4	38.1	113.6	151.7	105.0	4.3	538	651	680
1995-6[3]	15.0	130.0	145.0				116.0			592	711

[1] Preliminary. [2] Estimate. [3] Forecast. [4] Market value in the foreign country, excluding import duties, ocean freight and marine insurance.
Sources: The Oil World; Economic Research Service, U.S. Department of Agriculture

Average Wholesale Palm Oil Prices, CIF, Bulk, U.S. Ports In Cents Per Pound

Year	Jan.	Feb.	Mar.	Apr.	May	June	July	Aug.	Sept.	Oct.	Nov.	Dec.	Average
1989	19.27	19.45	19.20	18.79	20.37	20.26	18.88	15.31	15.82	16.10	16.05	15.16	17.89
1990	15.14	13.94	14.53	14.68	13.91	14.98	14.16	15.04	14.63	15.21	16.24	15.73	14.85
1991	19.49	19.50	19.25	19.18	19.05	19.40	20.32	19.14	18.86	20.63	21.63	18.99	19.62
1992	21.91	21.05	21.92	22.05	21.51	21.77	21.19	21.00	21.50	21.86	22.18	22.24	21.68
1993	23.18	23.09	22.99	22.26	21.95	21.01	20.31	19.84	19.43	18.83	19.74	21.90	21.21
1994	21.91	21.67	21.72	23.08	26.27	28.94	27.44	30.18	32.15	31.93	34.95	36.83	28.09
1995[1]	34.26	33.82	36.18	35.56	32.80	33.06							34.28

[1] Preliminary. *Source: Economic Research Service, U.S. Department of Agriculture*

Paper

Canada is the world's largest producer of newsprint, followed by the U.S. Domestic U.S. production of newsprint in 1994 was 6.34 million tonnes, down just over 1 percent from 1993. Production was also slightly less than in 1992. Shipments of newsprint were 6.36 million tonnes, down marginally from 1993 and 2 percent less than 1992. Stocks at the end of December 1994 were just under 60,000 tonnes, down 26 percent from stocks at the end of December 1993, but just above the stocks on December 31, 1992.

5.69 million tonnes of newsprint went to the U.S., an increase of just over 1 percent from 1993. Shipments to other markets were 672,000 tonnes, down over 12 percent from 1993. Shipments of newsprint to the U.S. from overseas for the first 11 months of 1994 were 84,700 tonnes, down over 34 percent from 1993.

Canadian production of newsprint in 1994 was 9.32 million tonnes, up close to 2 percent from 1993. Shipments of newsprint in 1994 were 9.44 million tonnes, up nearly 4 percent. Newsprint stocks at the end of December 1994 were 242,100 tonnes, down just over 34 percent from 1993. In terms of distribution, 5.91 million tonnes went to the U.S., up nearly 2 percent. Some 1.11 million tonnes went to Canada, down less than 1 percent. Shipments to other markets were 2.42 million tonnes, up over 10 percent.

The American Forest and Paper Association provided estimates on annual newsprint capacity. For 1994, the U.S. newsprint production capacity was 6.56 million tonnes, while for 1995 it was 6.57 million. 1996 was estimated at 6.58 million tonnes and in 1997 it was 6.58 million tonnes. For Canada, 1994 production capacity was put at 9.70 million tonnes while for 1995 it was 9.69 million tonnes. In 1996 it was projected to be 9.64 million tonnes while for 1997 Canadian newsprint capacity was forecast to be 9.60 million tonnes.

Production of Paper and Paperboard by Selected Countries In Thousands of Metric Tons

Year	Austria	Canada	Czech Republic[2]	Finland	France	Germany	Italy	Japan	Netherlands	Norway	Russia[3]	Spain	Sweden	Switzerland	United Kingdom	United States
1990	2,932	16,466	1,300	8,967	7,049	12,759	5,587	28,088	2,770	1,820	10,718	3,446	8,419	1,295	4,824	71,965
1991	3,090	16,559	1,087	8,776	7,190	12,904	5,795	29,056	2,862	1,784	9,590	3,579	8,349	1,259	4,951	72,724
1992	3,252	16,585	688	9,147	7,690	13,214	6,040	28,324	2,835	1,684	5,765	3,449	8,378	1,305	5,151	75,161
1993	3,300	17,528	643	9,990	7,975	13,034	6,019	27,764	2,855	1,968	4,459	3,348	8,781	1,332	5,406	77,167
1994[1]	3,603	18,342	735	10,909	8,481	14,457	6,705	-----	3,011	-----	3,407	3,503	9,283	-----	5,829	80,911

[1] Preliminary. [2] Formerly part of Czechoslovakia; data not reported separately until 1992. [3] Formerly part of the U.S.S.R.; data not reported separately until 1992. *Source: Food and Agricultural Organization of the United Nations*

Production of Newsprint by Selected Countries (Monthly Average) In Thousands of Metric Tons

Year	Australia	Brazil	Canada	China	Finland	France	Germany	India	Japan	Rep. of Korea	Norway	Russia[3]	Sweden	United Kingdom	United States
1990	32.6	20.5	755.7	33.3	119.1	35.2	92.7	23.3	289.9	44.3	82.4	143.5	212.3	58.0	500.0
1991	33.2	21.3	748.1	36.5	108.8	34.8	94.1	24.3	292.9	47.4	79.6	128.6	192.3	56.0	517.2
1992	33.6	18.9	729.0	40.8	104.8	55.8	94.2	24.7	271.1	50.2	77.9	78.6	147.5	58.3	535.3
1993	33.1	22.2	761.0	48.3	118.7	66.7	105.4	23.5	243.1	61.9	83.9	70.4	193.8	61.7	534.3
1994[1]	33.5	22.1	776.8	52.6	119.4	43.4	119.0	22.3	247.7	72.3	-----	86.5	201.3	64.1	528.3
1995[2]	38.6	21.6	767.8	64.1	115.0	56.4	141.6	23.9	259.5	79.3	-----	-----	200.6	-----	526.5

[1] Preliminary. [2] Estimate. [3] Formerly part of the U.S.S.R.; data not reported separately until 1992. *Source: Statistical Division, United Nations*

Salient Stastistics of Newsprint in the the United States and Canada In Thousands of Metric Tons

	United States													Canada		
			Imports by Countries of Origin									-Stocks, Dec. 31-				
Year	Production	Exports	Canada	Finland	Italy	Norway	South Africa	Sweden	United Kingdom	Total	Consumption	At Mills	At Publishers	Production	Exports	Stocks at Mills
1990	5,997	427	6,423	30	0	33	0	96	0	7,528	12,126	46	801	9,068	7,999	315
1991	6,206	570	5,623	22	0	29	0	46	0	6,795	11,268	98	932	8,855	9,165	565
1992	6,424	753	5,690	14	0	25	0	38	0	6,658	11,505	59	938	8,753	7,924	351
1993	6,412	768	5,805	14	0	37	0	54	6	7,061	11,535	81	956	9,130	8,003	362
1994[1]	6,336	672	5,906	12	0	28	1	30	1	7,150	11,695	60	879	9,321	8,326	246
1995[1]	6,352	642										76	1,133	9,252	8,062	252

[1] Preliminary. Not seasonally adjusted. *Source: Newsprint Division, American Forest & Paper Association*

Index Price of Paperboard 1982 = 100

Year	Jan.	Feb.	Mar.	Apr.	May	June	July	Aug.	Sept.	Oct.	Nov.	Dec.	Average
1989	137.7	138.7	140.4	142.3	142.5	141.0	139.5	140.0	139.7	139.8	139.7	140.0	140.1
1990	139.2	138.9	138.9	137.6	136.0	135.5	135.0	133.4	133.1	134.3	134.2	132.8	135.9
1991	132.6	132.0	129.6	128.4	127.0	127.2	127.1	127.8	131.8	132.7	132.8	132.9	130.2
1992	133.4	133.6	133.4	134.3	134.3	134.3	134.2	134.6	135.9	135.7	133.9	133.6	134.3
1993	133.0	131.6	131.3	130.6	129.9	128.9	128.6	128.0	128.0	129.7	130.2	130.5	130.0
1994	130.2	130.1	131.1	133.4	133.1	133.5	137.8	143.5	146.9	153.6	156.0	156.7	140.5
1995[1]	165.3	171.2	172.3	183.8	188.2	188.4	189.9	190.5	190.1	188.5	185.9		

[1] Preliminary. *Source: Bureau of Labor Statistics, U.S. Department of Commerce*

Index Price of Wood Pulp, Bleached Suphate Softwood 1982 = 100

Year	Jan.	Feb.	Mar.	Apr.	May	June	July	Aug.	Sept.	Oct.	Nov.	Dec.	Average
1989	176.2	176.9	178.1	180.7	184.8	184.8	184.4	184.4	184.4	185.8	185.8	184.0	182.5
1990	183.2	183.0	180.9	179.3	177.1	174.9	174.5	173.5	173.5	170.2	170.9	170.4	176.0
1991	152.2	150.0	143.6	142.1	136.8	132.4	126.2	124.2	123.2	120.0	120.7	114.8	132.2
1992	121.6	123.7	125.2	131.8	132.1	131.4	134.2	136.1	135.1	133.7	132.0	132.8	130.8
1993	121.6	118.1	112.7	112.3	112.7	112.7	110.7	108.9	108.6	107.1	105.5	104.0	111.2
1994	106.7	106.9	109.6	113.5	113.4	118.0	119.4	124.3	130.3	137.1	141.4	142.2	121.9
1995[1]	150.9	153.0	187.5	193.0	202.4	215.2	217.8	217.5	223.1	225.1	229.0		

[1] Preliminary. *Source: Bureau of Labor Statistics, U.S. Department of Commerce*

Index Price of Shipping Sack Paper[2] 1982 = 100

Year	Jan.	Feb.	Mar.	Apr.	May	June	July	Aug.	Sept.	Oct.	Nov.	Dec.	Average
1989	133.2	144.4	144.4	144.4	144.4	144.4	144.4	144.4	144.4	144.4	144.4	144.4	143.5
1990	144.4	144.4	144.4	144.4	144.4	144.4	144.4	144.4	NA	NA	NA	NA	144.4
1991	148.9	148.9	148.9	148.9	148.9	148.9	148.9	148.9	148.9	148.9	148.9	148.9	148.9
1992	148.9	148.9	154.0	154.0	154.0	148.9	148.9	148.9	155.7	155.7	155.7	155.7	152.4
1993	155.7	155.7	155.7	155.7	151.8	151.8	151.8	151.8	151.8	151.8	152.5	152.5	153.3
1994	151.3	150.9	154.3	154.5	159.3	163.9	169.9	170.3	176.6	178.2	184.9	185.5	166.6
1995[1]	190.4	204.5	209.5	212.0	221.5	224.2	224.2	224.2	224.0	223.1	210.1		

[1] Preliminary. *Source: Bureau of Labor Statistics, U.S. Department of Commerce*

Producer Price Index of Standard Newsprint 1982 = 100

Year	Jan.	Feb.	Mar.	Apr.	May	June	July	Aug.	Sept.	Oct.	Nov.	Dec.	Average
1989	126.5	126.0	126.6	126.5	123.2	122.0	121.3	120.7	120.4	119.3	119.0	118.3	122.5
1990	116.8	115.4	115.6	115.5	116.6	121.6	122.2	122.2	121.8	122.5	122.3	122.7	119.5
1991	126.8	127.2	127.1	121.7	121.4	120.1	119.5	118.8	118.1	117.3	116.4	115.8	120.9
1992	115.3	114.8	112.3	108.8	108.3	106.6	106.6	106.7	109.5	109.2	110.6	109.6	109.9
1993	110.4	111.2	114.1	113.9	113.0	113.1	112.7	112.6	111.3	111.2	111.0	111.0	112.1
1994	109.9	109.5	110.7	110.6	112.2	113.8	116.9	116.9	121.7	123.8	126.8	127.3	116.7
1995[1]	135.8	134.6	140.1	147.4	152.3	164.8	166.1	165.6	181.0	187.6	185.3		

[1] Preliminary. *Source: Bureau of Labor Statistics, U.S. Department of Commerce*

Index Price of Coated Printing Paper, No. 3 1982 = 100

Year	Jan.	Feb.	Mar.	Apr.	May	June	July	Aug.	Sept.	Oct.	Nov.	Dec.	Average
1989	127.8	127.8	129.3	130.3	130.5	130.7	130.5	130.5	130.3	130.2	130.3	130.1	129.9
1990	130.3	130.2	130.2	130.3	130.3	130.3	130.2	130.2	130.2	130.2	130.2	130.2	130.2
1991	129.3	129.4	129.4	129.1	128.7	128.1	128.1	128.1	128.1	128.7	128.7	127.8	128.6
1992	126.8	123.6	123.7	123.7	122.3	121.7	122.1	121.7	121.7	124.2	123.4	123.3	123.2
1993	123.4	123.3	123.3	123.4	123.4	123.3	123.0	123.0	123.2	122.9	122.9	122.9	123.2
1994	122.0	122.1	121.8	122.2	121.6	121.6	121.6	125.2	130.7	131.7	132.9	136.3	125.8
1995[1]	139.5	145.8	150.2	153.1	147.7	152.0	159.3	161.5	161.2	161.0	161.0		

[1] Preliminary. *Source: Bureau of Labor Statistics, U.S. Department of Commerce*

International Paper Prices--Export Unit Value

Year	Jan.	Feb.	Mar.	Apr.	May	June	July	Aug.	Sept.	Oct.	Nov.	Dec.	Average
NEWSPRINT - Canada	In Canadian Dollars Per Metric Ton												
1992	658	668	662	659	655	654	676	652	647	671	663	682	662
1993	687	676	668	690	692	690	676	674	664	666	658	642	674
1994	634	618	638	657	656	642	663	672	658	657	749	755	667
NEWSPRINT - Finland	In Markka Per Metric Ton												
1992	2,516	2,317	2,327	2,276	2,283	2,276	2,221	2,208	2,364	2,458	2,286	2,322	2,321
1993	2,362	2,414	2,415	2,461	2,324	2,336	2,265	2,371	2,386	2,437	2,376	2,371	2,377
1994	2,339	2,273	2,320	2,366	2,349	2,364	2,318	2,360	2,295	2,262	2,236	2,275	2,313
PRINTING AND WRITING - Canada	In Canadian Dollars Per Metric Ton												
1992	843	856	850	861	866	844	874	858	859	887	898	864	863
1993	885	861	860	891	902	920	923	921	924	919	927	931	905
1994	910	920	925	923	915	922	955	978	987	1,024	1,078	1,127	972
PRINTING AND WRITING - Finland	In Markka Per Metric Ton												
1992	3,138	3,122	3,173	3,174	3,196	3,244	3,196	3,082	3,388	3,404	3,418	3,454	3,249
1993	3,510	3,580	3,652	3,652	3,668	3,536	3,522	3,587	3,568	3,576	3,517	3,500	3,572
1994	3,471	3,290	3,370	3,375	3,484	3,507	3,524	3,490	3,498	3,472	3,501	3,666	3,471

Source: Food and Agricultural Organization of the United Nations

Peanuts and Peanut Oil

World peanut (groundnut) production fell to 18.7 million metric tons (shelled) in 1995/96, down 2 percent from 19.2 million tons in 1994/95. This compares with the most recent 5-year average of 17.5 million tons. (Shelled production runs about 75 percent of raw production.) Groundnuts are the world's fifth largest oilseed crop, but in the first half of the 1990's showed the least increase in production as allotted acreage has been stagnant. India and China produce more than half the world's crop; the U.S. is a distant third with less than 10 percent. It's in Asia, paced by Indonesia, that demand is greatest as evidenced by the fact that Asia now accounts for nearly a third of world imports versus less than a fourth during the 1980's. Foreign trade in groundnuts, however, is small as most of the crop is consumed locally. World imports during 1995/96 were estimated at 1.3 million metric tons, marginally under 1994/95 but higher than the average of the late 1980's of less than a million tons. More of the world's groundnut crop is allocated to meal production than oil. World production and use of groundnut meal was estimated at 6.1 million tons, down slightly from 1994/95 and in line with lower crushing, notably in India and the U.S. World consumption of groundnut oil in 1995/96 may increase one percent to 4.8 million tons, with only China showing some gain while oil use stagnates in the rest of the world.

Despite relatively small foreign trade, world prices of edible groundnuts turned higher in volatile trading in late summer 1995. The strength largely reflected adverse weather in key U.S. producing states, which not only reduced production, but perhaps more importantly raised concern about the crop's quality. In Rotterdam, U.S. prices in September rose to more than $1000 per metric ton, up 13 percent in less than a month and the highest in more than a year. U.S. peanut production in 1995/96 (August to July) was initially estimated at 3.9 million pounds, down about 10 percent from the 4.2 billion produced in 1994/95; later estimates placed the crop down about 16 percent which if realized would place production close to the 3.4 billion produced in 1993/94. U.S. peanut production tends to be erratic: a record large 4.9 billion pounds were produced in 1991/92, while the low since the mid-1970s was 2.3 billion in 1980/81.

U.S. peanut production is largely concentrated in the Southeast. Peanuts are also grown in the Southern Plains States, although irrigation may be needed and production costs run higher. Georgia is the largest producing state with at least a third of total production followed by North Carolina and Alabama. Total supplies in 1995/96, initially estimated at 5 billion pounds, included a 1.1 billion pound carryin as of August 1, 1995, and imports of 100 million pounds. Total 1994/95 supplies of 5.4 billion pounds also included a near 1.1 billion carryin and 100 million pound imports. Although small in total, imports have increased dramatically from recent years when a season total of 2 million pounds was not unusual. By contrast, in the short 1980 crop, 401 million pounds were imported.

Although higher prices will likely dampen disappearance, the 1995/96 crush was placed at 890 million pounds versus 1.1 billion in 1994/95; exports were at 825 million versus 900 million. U.S. crude peanut oil production in 1995/96 was estimated at 254 million pounds versus 224 million in 1994/95. In the U.S., peanuts are mostly used as a foodstuff, estimated at 2 billion pounds in 1995/96, about the same as in 1994/95. Peanut usage, however, as a direct food has gained very little during the past decade. In fact, there's been some slippage. Total 1995/96 disappearance of about 4 billion pounds will lag 1994/95 by at least 300 million pounds but should necessitate some draw of stocks.

The average peanut price received by farmers in 1994/95 was 29.0 cents per pound compared with 30.4 cents in 1993/94; for the 1995/96 season the average price was initially forecast between 29-31 cents, with the higher end more likely.

U.S. Government Program

For quota peanuts, the 1995 price support was maintained at 33.92 cents per pound. There is also an additional 6.6 cents allotted, the same as in the previous three crop years.

Futures Markets

Peanut futures are traded on the Beijing Commodity Exchange (BCE).

World Production of Peanuts (in the Shell) In Thousands of Metric Tons

Crop Year	Agrentina	Brazil	Burma	China	India	Indonesia	Mali	Nigeria	Senegal	South Africa	Sudan	Taiwan	Thailand	United States	Zaire	World Total
1983-4	329	220	532	3,951	7,086	747	50	591	72	568	413	87	147	1,495	367	18,738
1984-5	270	337	667	4,815	6,436	755	45	500	196	560	390	89	172	1,998	375	19,683
1985-6	439	216	560	6,664	5,120	780	90	400	111	587	275	77	172	1,870	375	19,900
1986-7	518	195	544	5,882	5,875	750	90	400	235	817	350	83	169	1,677	380	20,383
1987-8	450	170	519	6,170	5,854	786	100	475	204	932	435	100	162	1,640	380	20,863
1988-9	243	156	438	5,693	9,000	843	115	350	163	350	450	74	164	1,806	380	23,279
1989-90	336	137	459	5,365	8,088	875	90	350	113	350	400	58	161	1,810	380	22,059
1990-1	574	157	440	6,368	7,514	860	100	250	703	112	325	73	162	1,634	380	22,206
1991-2	400	160	440	6,300	7,065	890	95	220	724	114	400	83	160	2,235	380	22,138
1992-3	225	150	425	5,953	8,850	890	95	250	580	172	390	65	162	1,943	380	23,050
1993-4[1]	210	150	390	8,420	7,660	870	-----	250	620	150	390	-----	170	1,540	380	23,950
1994-5[1]	280	150	450	9,680	8,560	880	-----	250	740	80	390	-----	170	1,930	380	26,590
1995-6[2]	300	-----	500	9,630	7,400	890	-----	250	770	140	400	-----	170	1,590	380	25,270

[1] Preliminary. [2] Estimate. *Source: Foreign Agricultural Service, U.S. Department of Agriculture*

PEANUTS AND PEANUT OIL

Salient Statistics of Peanuts in the United States

Crop Year	Acreage Planted (1,000 Acres)	Acreage Harvested for Nuts (1,000 Acres)	Average Yield Per Acre In Lbs.	Production 1,000 Lbs.	Season Farm Price ¢ Lb.	Farm Value Million Dollars	Thousand Pounds (Year Beg. August) Exports Unshelled	Exports Shelled	Imports Unshelled	Imports Shelled
1982-3	1,311.4	1,277.4	2,693	3,440,255	25.1	862.7	51,321	473,416	844	1,323
1983-4	1,411.0	1,373.5	2,399	3,295,530	24.7	814.6	39,509	529,949	298	1,715
1984-5	1,558.6	1,528.0	2,883	4,405,745	27.9	1,230.8	72,907	592,333	79	2,167
1985-6	1,490.4	1,467.4	2,810	4,122,787	24.3	1,003.4	83,747	721,690	1,493	1,942
1986-7	1,564.7	1,535.2	2,408	3,700,745	29.2	1,073.3	75,687	441,954	328	1,598
1987-8	1,567.4	1,547.4	2,337	3,619,440	28.0	1,021.9	76,345	407,557	880	1,949
1988-9	1,657.4	1,628.4	2,445	3,980,917	27.9	1,115.2	105,746	437,867	650	2,094
1989-90	1,665.2	1,644.7	2,426	3,989,995	28.0	1,116.5	126,682	577,807	55	1,477
1990-1	1,840.0	1,809.5	1,991	3,602,770	34.7	1,257.2	250,851	401,149	6,429	20,571
1991-2	2,039.2	2,015.7	2,444	4,926,570	28.3	1,392.0	997,000		5,000	
1992-3	1,686.6	1,669.1	2,567	4,284,416	30.0	1,285.4	951,000		2,000	
1993-4	1,733.5	1,689.8	2,008	3,392,415	30.4	1,030.9	555,000		2,000	
1994-5[1]	1,641.0	1,618.5	2,624	4,247,455	29.0	1,230.0	878,000		74,000	
1995-6[2]	1,538.5	1,516.0	2,294	3,477,760	28.5-30.0	1,146.0	825,000		104,000	

[1] Preliminary. [2] Estimate. *Source: Economic Research Service, U.S. Department of Agriculture*

Peanut Supply and Disposition (Farmer's Stock Basis) & Support Program in the United States

Crop Year Beginning Aug. 1	Supply: Production	Supply: Imports	Supply: Stocks Aug. 1	Supply: Total	Disposition: Exports	Disposition: Crushed for Oil	Disposition: Seed, Loss & Residual	Disposition: Food	Total Disappearance	Government Support Program: Support Price (¢ per Lb.)	Additional (¢ per Lb.)	Amount Put Under Support: Quantity Mil. Lbs.	% of Prod.
	Million Pounds												
1982-3	3,440	2	757	4,199	681	342	463	1,849	3,335	27.50	10.0	539	15.7
1983-4	3,296	2	864	4,162	744	387	564	1,856	3,551	27.50	9.3	367	11.1
1984-5	4,406	2	611	5,019	860	625	199	1,911	3,595	27.50	9.3	1,370	30.9
1985-6	4,123	2	1,424	5,549	1,043	812	826	2,023	4,704	27.95	7.4	1,359	33.0
1986-7	3,697	2	845	4,544	663	514	291	2,073	3,541	30.37	7.5	290	7.8
1987-8	3,616	2	1,003	4,621	618	560	539	2,071	3,788	30.41	7.5	700	19.3
1988-9	3,981	2	833	4,816	688	814	217	2,254	3,974	30.76	7.5	540	13.6
1989-90	3,990	2	843	4,835	989	624	211	2,312	4,136	30.79	7.5	401	10.0
1990-1	3,603	27	701	4,331	652	689	288	2,020	3,649	31.57	7.5	576	16.0
1991-2	4,927	5	683	5,615	997	1,103	254	2,207	4,561	32.14	7.5	1,070	21.7
1992-3	4,284	2	1,055	5,341	951	891	227	2,122	3,991	33.75	6.6	436	10.2
1993-4	3,392	2	1,350	4,745	555	670	371	2,088	3,684	33.75	6.6	324	9.6
1994-5[1]	4,247	74	1,061	5,382	878	982	317	2,009	4,184	33.92	6.6		
1995-6[2]	3,478	104	1,198	4,779	825	867	244	1,950	3,959	33.92	6.6		

[1] Preliminary. [2] Estimate. *Source: Economic Research Service, U.S. Department of Agriculture*

U.S. Production of Peanuts (Harvested for Nuts) by States   In Thousands of Pounds

Crop Year	Alabama	Florida	Georgia	New Mexico	North Carolina	Oklahoma	South Carolina	Texas	Virgina	Total
1982	522,150	153,000	1,517,480	25,220	417,200	174,580	30,000	325,125	275,500	3,440,255
1983	454,500	166,800	1,567,980	25,630	318,255	176,540	25,000	362,275	198,550	3,295,530
1984	648,550	246,400	2,160,000	32,190	449,500	189,000	39,150	371,295	269,660	4,405,745
1985	590,000	216,000	1,921,320	31,992	451,990	170,980	34,200	422,625	283,680	4,122,787
1986	494,940	233,160	1,632,575	28,700	440,440	184,500	25,530	385,000	275,900	3,700,745
1987	465,300	215,800	1,575,000	29,760	392,200	222,750	31,200	441,000	243,000	3,616,010
1988	561,680	228,600	1,801,550	30,552	419,985	225,040	32,110	417,500	263,900	3,980,917
1989	537,750	214,890	1,849,500	43,680	370,120	210,700	32,500	484,700	246,155	3,989,995
1990	386,560	233,120	1,347,500	50,000	475,600	235,320	30,105	534,650	309,915	3,602,770
1991	638,485	279,660	2,228,550	51,075	461,700	243,800	33,600	682,500	307,200	4,926,570
1992	591,180	202,510	1,820,465	58,236	406,980	236,180	32,500	680,150	256,215	4,284,416
1993	473,220	194,880	1,383,545	56,680	299,585	233,580	24,500	550,175	176,250	3,392,415
1994	446,220	207,480	1,862,630	51,660	485,465	261,000	36,250	605,570	291,180	4,247,455
1995[1]	483,360	196,800	1,421,900	43,000	352,800	200,900	29,700	553,500	195,800	3,477,760

[1] Preliminary. *Source: Agricultural Statistics Board, U.S. Department of Agriculture*

PEANUTS AND PEANUT OIL

Supply and Reported Uses of Shelled Peanuts and Products in the U.S. In Thousands of Pounds

Crop Year Beginning Aug. 1	Shelled Peanuts -- Stocks Aug.1 --- Edible	Oil Stock[2]	Shelled Peanuts ----- Production ----- Edible	Oil Stock[2]	Reported Used (Shelled Peanuts--Raw Basis) Edible Grades Used in: Candy[3]	Snacks[4]	Sandwich Spread	Butter[5]	Other Products	Total	Shelled Peanuts Crushed[6]	Crude Oil Production	Cake & Meal Production
1983-4	537,855	19,208	1,776,069	342,477	298,065	301,971	24,279	671,430	15,469	1,311,214	291,084	119,008	159,340
1984-5	402,449	33,063	2,414,852	422,026	290,318	309,050	26,240	697,137	19,201	1,341,945	470,264	187,283	264,658
1985-6	860,508	30,407	2,238,427	496,928	313,836	358,542	24,623	701,289	23,515	1,421,805	610,897	256,545	336,232
1986-7	559,256	4,734	2,123,054	299,651	321,191	384,286	33,858	679,373	41,065	1,459,773	386,388	152,423	214,526
1987-8	683,622	21,300	2,015,144	301,379	325,583	373,773	45,808	701,436	37,791	1,484,391	421,214	168,263	247,851
1988-9	565,779	22,647	2,095,351	406,626	326,907	381,481	28,373	831,928	35,978	1,604,667	612,200	250,498	348,662
1989-90	513,679	44,397	2,319,780	374,859	330,158	392,811	-----	897,318 -----	36,682	1,656,969	469,351	193,000	261,465
1990-1	455,586	15,194	1,836,052	330,102	305,324	355,258	-----	742,384 -----	37,888	1,440,854	517,712	213,112	299,820
1991-2	386,155	65,950	2,538,398	616,170	327,617	346,255	-----	886,367 -----	34,173	1,594,412	828,986	356,276	459,457
1992-3	871,207	57,829	2,376,782	533,641	328,324	352,775	-----	797,910 -----	24,981	1,503,990	669,942	285,904	377,301
1993-4	679,639	42,054	1,748,734	425,710	362,418	348,867	-----	727,006 -----	36,301	1,474,592	503,674	212,216	292,093
1994-5[1]	732,272	57,188	1,741,824	511,635	349,630	301,548	-----	709,823 -----	36,854	1,397,855	739,221	314,189	415,394

[1] Preliminary. [2] Includes straight run oil stock peanuts. [3] Includes peanut butter made by manufacturers for own use in candy. [4] Formerly titled "Salted Peanuts." [5] Includes peanut butter made by manufacturers for own use in cookies and sandwiches, but excludes peanut butter used in candy. [6] All crushings regardless of grade. *Source: National Agricultural Statistics Service, U.S. Department of Agriculture*

Shelled Peanuts (Raw Basis) Used in Primary Products by Type In Thousands of Pounds

Crop Year Beginning Aug. 1	Virginia: Candy[2]	Snack Peanuts	Peanut Butter[3]	Total	Runner: Candy[2]	Snack Peanuts	Peanut Butter[3]	Total	Spanish: Candy[2]	Snack Peanuts	Peanut Butter[3]	Total
1983-4	15,402	101,980	44,091	163,268	237,075	164,389	600,226	1,032,248	45,588	35,602	33,263	115,698
1984-5	31,276	96,181	46,735	176,237	209,765	175,404	620,057	1,050,877	49,276	37,466	26,896	114,831
1985-6	32,900	113,577	54,794	206,557	240,198	207,503	648,566	1,091,850	40,739	37,463	43,159	123,400
1986-7	27,591	171,679	61,405	280,765	261,630	169,715	633,307	1,053,159	31,970	42,892	48,706	125,849
1987-8	40,251	120,084	42,841	216,987	249,673	220,511	613,231	1,152,848	35,659	33,178	43,224	114,556
1988-9	37,145	112,101	75,436	241,130	259,680	237,008	644,555	1,256,252	30,082	32,372	43,668	107,285
1989-90	28,701	130,000	90,622	263,014	278,062	234,661	773,985	1,306,810	23,395	28,150	32,711	87,145
1990-1	26,043	142,113	101,069	286,242	259,995	189,254	580,691	1,049,423	19,286	23,841	60,624	105,189
1991-2	51,312	142,514	89,045	297,570	244,815	180,609	759,747	1,203,233	31,490	23,132	37,575	93,609
1992-3	49,223	124,875	92,355	275,895	259,498	203,732	674,962	1,152,775	19,603	24,168	30,593	75,320
1993-4	44,889	99,381	63,270	222,641	298,325	227,286	365,047	1,179,396	19,204	22,200	28,689	72,555
1994-5[1]	27,425	97,277	51,354	191,372	302,131	185,460	642,893	1,149,809	20,078	18,806	13,756	54,853

[1] Preliminary. [2] Includes peanut butter made by manufacturers for own use in candy. [3] Includes peanut butter made by manufacturers for own use in cookies and sandwiches, but excludes peanut butter used in candy. *Source: National Agricultural Statistics Service, U.S. Department of Agriculture*

Production, Consumption, Stocks and Foreign Trade of Peanut Oil in the U.S. In Millions of Pounds

Crop Year Beginning Aug. 1	Production: Crude	Refined	Consumption: In Refining	In End Products	Stocks Dec. 31: Crude	Refined	Imports for Consumption	Exports
1982-3	106.9	168.8	133.5	174.0	NA	3.9	3.7	5
1983-4	119.0	139.6	183.9	132.9	17.9	4.0	.6	7
1984-5	187.3	119.9	148.4	NA	9.6	4.8	2.2	29
1985-6	256.5	139.7	124.6	NA	64.9	4.0	.5	93
1986-7	152.4	160.0	145.7	153.2	17.0	3.6	2.4	6
1987-8	168.3	199.6	169.0	179.3	10.9	3.8	33.1	7
1988-9	250.5	185.5	207.5	NA	18.6	4.4	1.9	11
1989-90	193.0	212.5	192.4	NA	17.6	4.1	5.0	19
1990-1	213.1	131.7	229.1	169.0	19.3	5.8	10.0	25
1991-2	261.5	125.6	132.3	141.0	27.5	3.1	1.0	151
1992-3	285.9	181.1	188.4	182.1	46.2	5.3	0	59
1993-4	212.2	155.2	163.7	149.1	6.5	3.9	11.0	61
1994-5[1]	194.1	119.9	126.2	107.8	5.0	2.8	4.0	97

[1] Preliminary. NA = Not available. Source: Bureau of Census, U.S. Department of Commerce

Average Price Received by Producers in U.S. for Peanuts in the Shell In Cents Per Pound

Crop Year	Aug.	Sept.	Oct.	Nov.	Dec.	Jan.	Feb.	Mar.	Apr.	May.	June	July	Average[1]
1980-1	NQ	22.5	23.2	27.9	37.3	47.7	NQ	NQ	NQ	NQ	NQ	NQ	31.7
1981-2	25.7	28.9	26.7	25.1	25.8	24.9	NQ	NQ	NQ	NQ	NQ	NQ	26.2
1982-3	27.1	25.1	24.9	25.3	26.1	22.9	NQ	NQ	NQ	NQ	NQ	NQ	25.2
1983-4	NQ	25.2	24.3	24.5	26.0	27.8	NQ	NQ	NQ	NQ	NQ	NQ	25.6
1984-5	NQ	29.9	27.1	25.6	26.3	NQ	NQ	NQ	NQ	NQ	NQ	NQ	27.2
1985-6	24.7	24.4	24.3	24.6	23.3	20.6	NQ	NQ	NQ	NQ	NQ	NQ	23.7
1986-7	29.6	27.0	28.8	29.8	32.5	24.5	NQ	NQ	NQ	NQ	NQ	NQ	28.7
1987-8	29.7	29.2	27.9	27.4	27.6	28.5	NQ	NQ	NQ	NQ	NQ	NQ	28.4
1988-9	20.0	29.9	28.0	26.4	25.8	27.8	NQ	NQ	NQ	NQ	NQ	NQ	26.3
1989-90	28.4	28.2	27.7	26.9	28.2	24.6	NQ	NQ	NQ	NQ	NQ	NQ	27.3
1990-1	26.5	32.2	34.0	40.1	43.6	44.8	NQ	NQ	NQ	NQ	NQ	NQ	34.7
1991-2	30.4	29.3	28.1	24.4	25.1	NQ	NQ	NQ	NQ	NQ	NQ	NQ	28.3
1992-3	NQ	31.3	29.9	28.2	25.7	29.5	NQ	NQ	NQ	NQ	NQ	NQ	30.0
1993-4	NQ	32.0	30.0	29.5	29.7	36.1	NQ	NQ	NQ	NQ	NQ	NQ	30.4
1994-5[2]	NQ	30.6	28.6	25.9	25.8	25.7	NQ	NQ	NQ	NQ	NQ	NQ	27.3
1995-6[2]	30.7	29.7	28.8	29.5	28.3	29.3							29.4

[1] Weighted average by sale. [2] Preliminary. NQ = No quote. *Source: National Agricultural Statistics Service, U.S. Department of Agriculture*

Crude Peanut Oil Produced in the United States In Millions of Pounds

Year	Jan.	Feb.	Mar.	Apr.	May	June	July	Aug.	Sept.	Oct.	Nov.	Dec.	Total
1980	6.2	15.1	16.7	25.9	30.7	22.9	23.5	21.2	5.9	2.1	6.3	5.9	182.4
1981	6.1	6.0	10.5	17.3	19.1	19.5	13.6	9.8	5.3	9.7	12.0	12.7	141.6
1982	11.3	11.1	19.4	26.3	22.3	19.0	15.0	11.8	NA	NA	NA	NA	NA
1983	NA	NA	NA	NA	NA	NA	NA	NA	NA	NA	NA	NA	NA
1984	12.1	13.3	10.8	12.5	10.1	8.9	5.1	5.3	4.3	9.9	8.6	7.3	108.2
1985	9.8	13.9	15.8	15.5	14.5	12.4	10.4	10.0	10.1	9.2	10.2	14.9	146.7
1986	19.2	21.1	19.9	20.8	24.0	26.4	14.2	9.6	NA	4.1	11.9	10.7	181.9
1987	9.8	13.6	20.5	11.6	17.8	15.8	14.5	9.7	4.2	7.5	13.7	13.1	151.8
1988	13.8	14.9	10.1	8.3	19.5	12.5	17.0	11.4	2.8	9.7	17.0	18.4	155.4
1989	10.5	20.8	27.8	24.3	19.0	33.4	26.6	22.4	NA	7.4	11.6	9.8	213.6
1990	11.1	15.8	14.2	22.2	24.9	24.1	14.0	8.5	2.1	14.4	12.5	15.9	179.7
1991		70.8			71.1			59.5			60.1		261.5
1992	28.0	26.8	42.5	40.9	39.8	40.6	37.3	31.3	35.1	24.2	19.2	15.6	381.5
1993	16.9	17.0	24.1	28.8	23.3	29.0	25.6	22.5	3.6	8.6	16.4	14.6	233.8
1994	18.1	18.3	21.2	18.7	25.6	15.4	21.7	15.9	16.5	11.4	18.0	23.6	224.4
1995[1]	27.1	29.4	41.7	36.3	38.8	28.7	26.9	26.3	17.4	13.2	19.5	24.3	329.4

[1] Preliminary. NA = Not available. *Source: Bureau of Census, U.S. Department of Commerce*

Average Price of Domestic Crude Peanut Oil (in Tanks) F.O.B. Southeast Mills In Cents Per Pounds

Year	Oct.	Nov.	Dec.	Jan.	Feb.	Mar.	Apr.	May	June	July	Aug.	Sept.	Average
1980-1	35.8	48.7	49.1	47.7	39.3	34.1	34.0	37.1	38.0	38.1	43.2	40.3	40.5
1981-2	34.5	34.5	30.9	27.3	31.4	23.3	29.1	29.9	26.2	24.7	22.7	22.5	28.1
1982-3	22.9	25.2	26.1	25.6	25.7	24.1	25.1	26.4	26.4	26.7	30.7	50.5	28.0
1983-4	50.7	48.8	48.1	47.3	46.5	48.4	52.6	58.2	59.1	57.7	54.8	39.2	47.3
1984-5	36.7	41.2	41.4	39.2	38.8	40.3	49.6	46.2	40.7	39.7	37.6	33.9	40.4
1985-6	38.3	42.2	36.1	29.5	22.6	21.5	24.4	27.6	28.0	27.5	30.5	28.3	29.7
1986-7	27.80	29.80	26.50	25.10	25.00	23.75	24.00	26.15	25.68	25.27	24.61	26.74	25.87
1987-8	33.48	31.50	32.10	35.73	32.40	29.61	29.50	30.02	34.00	39.80	37.86	36.00	33.50
1988-9	42.50	36.75	34.25	26.50	25.09	29.98	32.39	36.25	39.80	NA	35.75	34.40	33.97
1989-90	39.06	41.50	41.60	43.25	46.00	43.40	41.25	45.25	46.90	46.88	49.05	51.13	44.61
1990-1	48.13	44.20	43.00	41.00	42.83	47.60	46.75	43.33	42.25	41.50	35.33	30.66	45.50
1991-2	34.33	27.67	23.50	23.50	23.63	23.17	25.00	27.88	25.60	26.19	23.88	22.00	27.30
1992-3	23.63	25.58	30.30	30.88	27.17	26.00	27.50	30.00	30.20	33.00	39.50	35.93	27.40
1993-4	40.20	43.33	43.17	46.10	46.12	44.50	43.40	44.25	43.75	44.00	45.00	43.10	43.20
1994-5[1]	46.00	50.88	53.80	50.25	41.83	41.00	41.25	40.25	39.00	39.13	41.50	41.30	44.30
1995-6[1]	42.50	41.63	39.20										

[1] Preliminary. *Source: Agricultural Marketing Service, U.S. Department of Agriculture*

Pepper

Pepper prices increased in 1994 reflecting lower world production and a drawdown of global stocks to meet increasing consumption. Much of the statistical data on pepper is laggard. Production estimates are further complicated by the tendency of third-world producing countries to hold stocks in lieu of local currency in hopes of avoiding inflation and currency risk. Additionally, pepper can be stored for long periods, so actual world stocks are likely to be underestimated. Countries experiencing high inflation are likely to build stocks as a hedge against inflation.

World production of pepper has not kept pace with consumption for a number of reasons. For one, prices for pepper have been low in the past. this in turn has caused farmers to stop plantings and reduce maintenance. Additionally, low prices for one crop lead producers to plant other more profitable crops. New York spot prices for Indonesian Lampong black pepper averaged 95 cents per pound in 1994, up from 62 cents a year earlier and up from 56 cents in 1992. Prices in 1995 were expected to remain firm as supplies were expected to stay tight. Actual spot prices for pepper made their recent high in 1987 and trended lower until last year. Over the first quarter of 1995 pepper prices averaged over $1.00 per pound.

U.S. imports of black pepper in 1994 rose nearly 20 percent as importers and processors replenished stocks which were drawn down in the previous year. The higher prices in 1994 met resistance from consumers who utilized stocks from previous years. Those drawn down stocks are now being rebuilt. India was the largest source of the black pepper imports accounting for nearly half of the total. Most of the remainder was imported from Indonesia and Brazil. White pepper imports were also higher in 1994 with nearly two thirds of the total supplied by Indonesia. Shipments from China rose sharply as they have become the second largest source of U.S. white pepper imports.

World exports of black and white pepper by major producing countries in 1993 totaled 149,000 tons, down 10 percent from 1992. Exports by Indonesia fell sharply to only 27,684 tons from 1992 shipments of 61,438 tons. India's shipments more than doubled to 47,228 tons to offset the Indonesian shipments. Exports from Malaysia and Vietnam were lower. European buyers have hesitated to buy black pepper from Vietnam because of inconsistent quality. Traders had estimated that over the first six months of 1995 Vietnam had shipped about 5,000 tonnes of black pepper including more than 1,000 tonnes to China. Vietnam's black pepper exports were forecast at 15,000 tonnes.

The Indian Cabinet approved a proposal to set up an international pepper futures exchange. It was decided to upgrade the domestic pepper futures commodity exchange into an international exchange. The Indian Pepper and Spice Trade Association will upgrade the existing domestic futures exchange at Cochin in southern Kerala state. The Indian pepper exchange will reportedly be linked to the Malaysian Kuala Lumpur Commodities Exchange. One plan is for trading to take place in both Cochin, India and in Kuala Lumpur, Malaysia, with the settlement done in Cochin, India.

World Exports of Pepper (Black & White) and U.S. Prices

	Exports (In Metric Tons)									New York Spot Prices (¢ Per Pound)				
										Indonesian			Indian	
Year	Brazil	India	Indonesia	Madagascar	Malaysia	Mexico	Sri Lanka	Thailand	Vietnam	Lampong Black	Muntok White	Brazilian Black	Malabar Black	Tellicherry[2]
1985	24,676	19,538	26,202	2,002	19,070	2,283	1,260	1,785	1,335	169.6	190.6	167.4	169.6	185.3
1986	22,069	49,808	29,566	972	15,380	1,794	1,286	1,816	3,133	215.0	275.3	212.5	214.6	235.1
1987	26,260	32,971	29,995	1,851	14,185	2,125	2,014	1,477	4,275	237.1	267.7	235.9	236.0	262.8
1988	24,393	47,258	41,568	2,497	19,190	2,602	2,714	910	2,612	173.9	243.4	170.3	170.3	220.6
1989	27,717	25,120	42,138	1,417	26,260	2,388	1,576	2,077	7,551	138.2	146.2	136.2	135.9	174.8
1990	28,014	34,429	47,675	1,222	27,706	2,663	2,609	4,042	1,288	99.1	90.3	97.1	97.1	139.1
1991	47,553	18,735	49,667	1,844	25,458	1,861	2,058	3,838	16,252	71.1	70.1	67.1	67.1	117.8
1992	25,702	19,399	61,438	1,948	21,932	3,441	2,127	6,158	22,347	56.1	70.8	54.7	54.7	86.1
1993[1]	26,254	47,228	27,684	2,001	16,700	2,430	5,032	4,422	14,801	62.5	114.6	62.3	62.3	84.0
1994[1]										95.3	151.9	95.0	95.0	110.7

[1] Preliminary. [2] Extra bold. *Sources: Foreign Agricultural Service, U.S. Department of Agriculture; Food and Agricultural Organization of the United Nations*

United States Imports of Unground Pepper from Specified Countries In Metric Tons

	Black Pepper										White Pepper						
Year	Brazil	China	India	Indonesia	Malaysia	Mexico	Singapore	Spain	Sri Lanka	Total	Brazil	China	Germany	Indonesia	Malaysia	Singapore	Total
1985	12,227	378	4,024	9,814	131	3	322	34	158	27,421	246	260	10	3,805	100	100	4,762
1986	9,416	243	20,976	5,980	634	7	120	1	255	38,063	134	171	7	2,846	65	140	3,578
1987	11,981	107	9,341	6,958	1,667	23	379	-----	388	31,372	65	6	1	4,238	22	110	4,533
1988	6,033	14	7,481	11,131	1,400	119	104	-----	344	26,939	20	2	25	4,169	12	26	4,326
1989	11,038	109	1,272	11,016	6,732	20	324	-----	375	31,819	37	38	1	5,272	63	90	5,549
1990	8,778	70	6,679	8,444	6,768	20	457	20	644	32,980	17	15	1	5,506	24	86	5,721
1991	15,069	4	2,308	11,330	8,154	20	391	-----	396	38,860	2	7	1	4,938	37	96	5,174
1992	6,601	1	9,892	20,768	2,073	160	52	1	310	40,590	51	2	-----	5,089	29	261	5,544
1993	4,580	6	21,985	7,666	209	-----	-----	-----	539	35,969	322	114	3	4,304	137	363	5,481
1994[1]	8,215	1	21,097	11,877	829	-----	90	1	386	43,011	312	756	58	3,974	228	302	6,102

[1] Preliminary. *Source: Foreign Agricultural Service, U.S. Department of Agriculture*

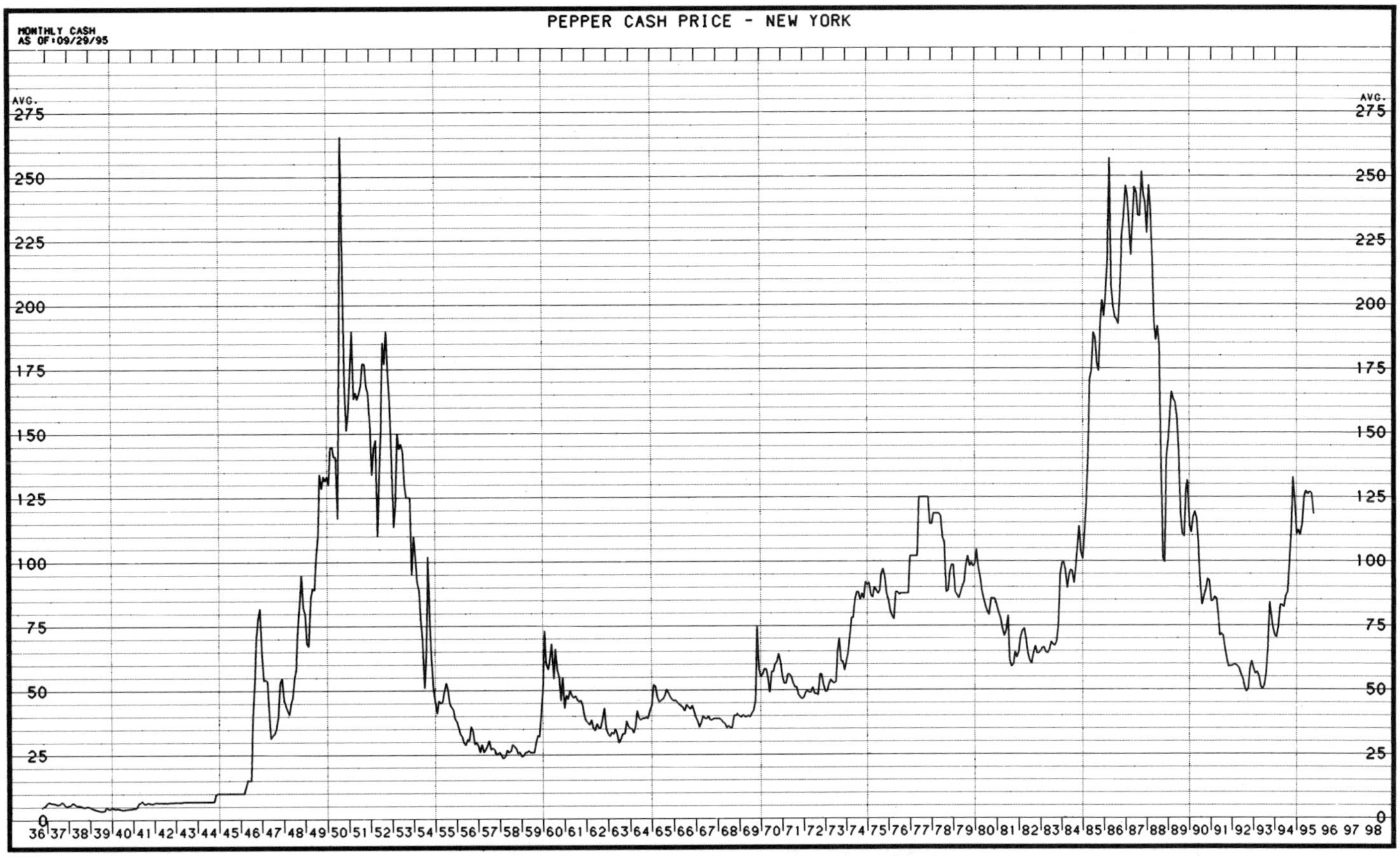

Average Black Pepper Prices in New York In Cents Per Pound

Year	Jan.	Feb.	Mar.	Apr.	May	June	July	Aug.	Sept.	Oct.	Nov.	Dec.	Average
1974	64.0	70.0	78.0	78.0	85.0	88.0	88.0	85.0	87.5	85.5	92.0	91.0	82.7
1975	91.5	87.0	86.0	90.0	89.0	87.5	88.5	95.0	97.0	94.0	87.5	85.0	89.8
1976	81.0	79.0	77.5	88.0	88.0	87.0	87.5	87.5	NA	NA	NA	102.0	86.4
1977	102.0	102.0	102.0	102.0	125.0	125.0	125.0	125.0	125.0	125.0	114.5	NA	115.7
1978	118.5	118.5	118.5	118.5	117.5	109.0	107.5	88.0	88.5	95.5	98.5	98.5	106.4
1979	105.0	NA	130.0	NA	NA	95.0	97.0	110.0	108.0	108.0	102.0	101.3	106.3
1980	108.0	101.0	96.3	93.0	87.0	84.3	82.8	79.0	79.0	88.0	86.5	89.3	89.5
1981	88.5	93.3	92.0	81.0	83.0	82.3	84.0	82.5	82.3	82.3	82.5	82.5	84.7
1982	82.5	82.5	75.0	75.0	70.0	69.0	67.0	63.0	69.0	70.5	68.5	68.3	71.7
1983	68.3	66.5	66.3	65.5	65.5	65.5	75.0	69.3	76.3	77.3	83.5	83.5	71.9
1984[1]	99.5	96.5	89.4	93.9	96.4	96.2	89.3	94.8	104.0	110.5	100.0	97.5	97.3
1985	108.0	119.3	137.6	167.5	170.4	188.0	186.0	175.8	172.5	190.8	199.8	192.5	167.4
1986	197.6	210.5	250.0	206.0	198.2	193.8	193.8	190.8	204.8	226.0	232.0	246.2	212.5
1987	241.4	231.0	218.8	232.5	245.2	241.8	232.6	232.5	251.5	241.4	238.5	233.8	236.8
1988	233.3	228.8	210.5	190.3	184.3	190.5	182.8	141.5	100.2	99.5	138.3	143.0	170.3
1989	156.8	161.8	159.0	160.0	154.5	141.8	115.5	108.0	108.2	124.7	131.3	112.4	136.2
1990	107.0	110.8	115.4	115.0	106.0	91.0	82.3	85.8	88.5	92.3	89.6	81.8	97.1
1991	79.0	78.5	78.6	74.5	66.8	70.0	68.8	61.6	59.5	56.8	55.8	55.0	67.1
1992	55.6	54.5	56.0	55.3	54.0	54.0	50.8	49.0	50.0	57.8	61.0	58.0	54.7
1993	56.0	56.5	54.3	51.2	50.0	51.5	55.8	64.8	84.0	79.0	74.2	70.8	62.3
1994	69.3	74.3	82.0	82.8	82.0	86.5	87.8	97.8	112.2	131.5	123.5	110.4	95.0
1995	111.0	110.0	114.2	124.8	127.3	126.0	127.0	126.3	118.2	113.5	104.8		

[1] Brazilian Black since 1984. NA = Not available. *Source: Foreign Agricultural Service, U.S. Department of Agriculture*

Petroleum

According to the U.S. Department of Energy world oil demand is expected to increase by one million barrels per day in 1995, and an additional 1.1 million barrels per day in 1996, after an increase of 900,000 barrels per day in 1994. This development is the result of continued oil demand growth in the developing world and smaller demand declines by the former Soviet Union. After declining by 900,000 barrels per day in 1994, oil demand in the former Soviet Union was expected to decline by 400,000 barrels per day or less in 1995 and 1996. It's expected that as these countries move toward Western-style economies, oil demand will decline by a smaller amount in each succeeding year.

Oil demand in the countries of the Organization for Economic Cooperation and Development (OECD) is forecast to increase by nearly 500,000 barrels per day in 1995, with nearly all of the increase coming from outside the U.S. In 1996, OECD demand is expected to grow by an additional 600,000 barrels per day with over half of the increase coming from the U.S..

Oil demand in China and other Asian countries is expected to increase 5-6 percent in 1995 and 1996 as the economies of many of these countries grow by 6-10 percent per year. In Africa and Latin America, oil demand is projected to grow by 1.5-2.5 percent in 1995 and 1996 while in the Middle East, oil demand is expected to rise by four percent in 1995 and four percent in 1996.

After increasing by 800,000 barrels per day in 1994, oil demand in the non-OECD countries, excluding the former Soviet Union and non-OECD Europe, is expected to increase by an average of 900,000 barrels per day in 1995 and 1996. These countries continue to have strong economic growth. The Energy Information Administration reports that in 1994, world supplies of petroleum increased by 500,000 barrels per day. In 1995, the world oil supply was expected to increase by another 400,000 barrels per day, with the increase in 1996 expected to be 700,000 barrels per day. More than half of the increase between 1994 and 1996 will come from the Organization of Petroleum Exporting Countries (OPEC). OPEC production was expected to increase by about 200,000 barrels per day in 1995 and by about 500,000 barrels per day in 1996.

Petroleum production in the North Sea was expected to increase by over 300,000 barrels per day in 1995 and by another 400,000 barrels per day in 1996. Production by non-OPEC developing countries was expected to increase by over 300,000 barrels per day in 1995 and another 300,000 barrels per day in 1996. U.S. production was forecast to continue to decline by about 300,000 barrels per day between 1994 and 1996.

In the former Soviet Union, petroleum production was expected to continue in decline but at a slower rate. In 1994 the decrease was 1.1 million barrels per day but in 1995 and 1996 the decline is expected to be 400,000 barrels per day.

Average OPEC excess production capacity (excluding Iraq) is expected to be three million barrels per day in 1995 and 2.8 million barrels in 1996. Most of the excess capacity is from Saudi Arabia which has 1.9 million barrels per day, Kuwait with 200,000 barrels per day, Iran with 200,000 barrels per day, and the United Arab Emirates with 200,000 barrels per day.

U.S. petroleum demand is expected to rise by 90,000 barrels per day in 1995 and another 200,000 barrels per day in 1996. In the first half of 1995, oil demand declined by 190,000 barrels per day primarily due to mild weather in the Northeast. For the rest of 1995, growth will come from strength in transportation fuels and a recovery in residual fuel oil demand. Oil demand growth in 1996 is expected to exceed 1995 due to strength in transportation fuels and a recovery in residual fuel oil demand. Oil demand growth in 1996 was expected to exceed 1995 due to strength in transportation fuels and more normal weather patterns.

Futures Markets

Futures and options contracts on light sweet crude oil, heating oil and unleaded gasoline are traded on the New York Mercantile Exchange (NYMEX). Propane and natural gas futures also are traded there. London's International Petroleum Exchange (IPE) trades Brent crude oil futures and options on those futures. The IPE also trades heating oil futures and options (termed gas oil) and unleaded gasoline futures. High-sulfur fuel oil futures are traded on the SIMEX in Singapore.

World Production of Crude Petroleum, by Specified Countries In Thousands of Barrels Per Day

Year	Algeria	Canada	China	Libya	Indonesia	Iran	Iraq	Kuwait	Mexico	Nigeria	Russia[3]	Saudi Arabia	United Kingdom	United States	Venezuela	Total World
1983	968	1,356	2,120	1,105	1,343	2,440	1,005	1,064	2,689	1,241	11,972	5,086	2,291	8,688	1,801	53,255
1984	1,014	1,438	2,296	1,087	1,412	2,174	1,209	1,157	2,780	1,388	11,861	4,663	2,480	8,879	1,798	54,488
1985	1,037	1,471	2,505	1,059	1,325	2,250	1,433	1,023	2,745	1,495	11,585	3,388	2,530	8,971	1,677	53,981
1986	945	1,474	2,620	1,034	1,390	2,035	1,690	1,419	2,435	1,467	11,895	4,870	2,539	8,680	1,787	56,227
1987	1,048	1,535	2,690	972	1,343	2,298	2,079	1,585	2,548	1,341	12,050	4,265	2,406	8,349	1,752	56,666
1988	1,040	1,616	2,730	1,175	1,342	2,240	2,685	1,492	2,512	1,450	12,053	5,086	2,232	8,140	1,903	58,737
1989	1,095	1,560	2,757	1,150	1,409	2,810	2,897	1,783	2,520	1,716	11,715	5,064	1,802	7,613	1,907	59,863
1990	1,175	1,553	2,774	1,375	1,462	3,088	2,040	1,175	2,553	1,810	10,975	6,410	1,820	7,355	2,137	60,566
1991	1,230	1,548	2,835	1,483	1,592	3,312	305	190	2,680	1,892	9,992	8,115	1,797	7,417	2,375	60,207
1992	1,217	1,605	2,845	1,433	1,504	3,429	425	1,058	2,669	1,943	7,632	8,332	1,825	7,171	2,371	60,213
1993	1,190	1,680	2,911	1,377	1,528	3,650	512	1,872	2,671	2,050	6,890	8,198	1,915	6,847	2,450	60,640
1994[1]	1,170	1,743	2,939	1,378	1,514	3,635	553	2,034	2,689	2,037	5,821	8,147	2,375	6,662	2,514	60,916
1995[2]	1,190	1,799	2,991	1,390	1,510	3,629	555	2,060	2,689	2,002	5,795	8,259	2,425	6,541	2,714	62,040

Includes lease condensate. [1] Preliminary. [2] Estimate. [3] Formerly part of the U.S.S.R.; data not reported separately until 1992.

Source: Energy Information Administration, U.S. Department of Energy

Refiner Sales Prices of Petroleum Products for Resale (Excluding Taxes) In Cents Per Gallon

Year	Jan.	Feb.	Mar.	Apr.	May	June	July	Aug.	Sept.	Oct.	Nov.	Dec.	Average
						Residual Fuel Oil (Sulfur 1% or less)							
1989	38.8	37.0	38.8	44.1	43.6	39.3	39.0	37.3	38.2	40.2	40.5	47.7	40.7
1990	56.0	44.4	39.7	36.1	34.5	31.1	33.2	49.1	56.4	64.1	63.3	57.6	47.2
1991	52.1	36.5	36.0	33.6	36.6	32.1	32.6	33.4	33.7	34.1	36.6	34.8	36.4
1992	30.3	32.7	30.8	31.6	33.1	35.9	38.0	37.7	37.9	41.4	39.2	35.9	35.1
1993	36.8	35.5	39.1	38.4	34.8	33.7	32.7	31.6	31.9	32.1	30.7	27.5	33.7
1994	33.8	39.3	30.0	29.4	31.7	35.8	37.8	37.1	32.6	32.6	35.7	36.9	34.5
1995[1]	38.4	37.1	38.3	36.8	40.4	39.9	36.8	35.2	36.4	35.2			
						No. 2 Fuel Oil							
1989	53.2	51.1	54.4	56.5	52.6	49.6	50.4	51.2	56.4	60.1	60.4	72.8	56.5
1990	73.8	57.8	57.9	57.4	54.5	49.4	51.9	72.1	85.3	95.0	90.6	80.9	69.7
1991	76.6	67.9	59.6	57.2	56.0	54.0	56.7	60.6	62.1	66.3	66.6	55.9	62.2
1992	51.9	54.0	53.7	56.5	58.8	61.7	61.3	60.1	62.7	64.6	58.8	55.7	57.9
1993	54.4	56.9	59.0	57.5	56.9	55.0	51.0	51.0	54.8	58.1	53.1	45.1	54.4
1994	50.8	54.1	49.7	48.9	48.9	49.8	50.9	51.4	50.1	50.8	51.0	49.5	50.6
1995[1]	49.4	49.1	48.1	50.4	52.4	49.3	48.1	51.0	52.0	50.5			
						No. 2 Diesel Fuel							
1989	51.1	52.8	56.0	59.5	54.0	50.8	50.5	52.4	58.5	62.2	62.0	68.4	56.7
1990	69.3	57.1	57.6	57.6	55.4	50.5	52.0	73.7	87.2	99.4	93.6	79.8	69.4
1991	75.5	67.4	57.7	57.4	57.2	54.5	57.1	61.9	62.9	65.6	66.5	55.6	61.5
1992	51.4	54.1	54.0	57.0	60.1	62.7	61.8	60.4	63.3	65.5	60.4	56.4	59.1
1993	54.9	57.4	60.0	59.8	59.6	57.2	53.2	53.2	58.9	65.8	58.9	46.8	57.0
1994	49.1	52.8	52.9	52.3	51.7	52.2	53.7	54.1	54.2	55.2	55.1	50.8	52.9
1995[1]	50.1	50.6	51.2	54.8	55.9	52.6	51.4	54.2	55.7	54.6			
						Kerosine-Type Jet Fuel							
1989	56.2	55.4	56.5	59.5	56.6	54.4	53.5	54.5	58.6	63.2	63.4	67.3	58.3
1990	76.6	66.7	61.6	59.5	57.1	54.6	55.5	71.4	92.9	114.7	107.0	90.1	77.3
1991	82.0	74.0	62.4	58.9	60.8	58.8	59.4	63.3	65.9	67.1	68.2	60.1	65.0
1992	53.9	55.2	54.6	56.9	60.8	63.3	64.8	63.9	64.3	66.0	61.5	58.9	60.5
1993	57.7	60.4	60.3	59.8	60.1	58.5	55.1	55.1	56.6	60.5	58.7	51.0	57.7
1994	52.6	56.0	52.4	50.8	50.6	51.5	53.8	54.4	54.0	54.4	56.3	53.1	53.4
1995[1]	52.3	52.1	50.1	52.6	54.7	53.1	51.3	53.1	55.2	54.1			
						Propane (Consumer Grade)							
1989	24.0	22.7	22.5	22.7	22.1	21.4	20.7	21.7	23.1	24.4	24.3	36.4	24.7
1990	54.4	34.1	27.1	25.2	24.0	24.9	27.3	36.3	43.5	53.5	50.5	44.6	38.6
1991	42.2	31.6	31.3	31.8	31.9	29.3	27.6	29.6	34.9	40.2	43.0	37.7	34.9
1992	30.9	30.2	29.5	29.0	29.4	31.6	31.5	32.9	35.4	36.6	36.2	36.3	32.8
1993	40.2	36.7	38.2	36.2	34.0	33.8	33.3	33.3	34.1	34.7	33.6	30.9	35.1
1994	32.3	34.0	31.8	30.5	30.4	29.9	29.8	31.0	31.7	33.5	35.0	35.8	32.5
1995[1]	35.6	34.5	34.3	33.0	33.2	32.6	32.1	33.2	33.8	34.4			

[1] Preliminary. *Source: Energy Information Administration, U.S. Department of Energy*

United States Crude Oil Supply & Disposition

Yearly Average	Supply: Field Production: Total Domestic	Supply: Field Production: Alaskan	Supply: Imports: Total	Supply: Imports: SPR[2]	Supply: Imports: Other	Unaccounted for Crude Oil	Stock Withdrawal[3]: SPR[2]	Stock Withdrawal[3]: Other	Disposition: Refinery Inputs	Disposition: Exports	Ending Stocks: Total	Ending Stocks: SPR[2]	Ending Stocks: Other Primary
	Thousands of Barrels Per Day										Million of Barrels		
1986	8,680	1,867	4,178	48	4,130	139	50	28	12,716	154	843	512	331
1987	8,349	1,962	4,674	73	4,601	145	80	49	12,854	151	890	541	349
1988	8,140	2,017	5,107	51	5,055	196	52	-51	13,246	155	890	560	330
1989	7,613	1,874	5,843	56	5,787	200	56	30	13,401	142	921	580	341
1990	7,355	1,773	5,894	27	5,867	258	16	-51	13,409	109	908	586	323
1991	7,417	1,798	5,782	0	5,782	195	-47	5	13,301	116	893	569	325
1992	7,171	1,714	6,083	10	6,073	258	17	-18	13,411	89	893	575	318
1993	6,847	1,582	6,787	15	6,772	168	34	47	13,613	98	922	587	335
1994	6,662	1,559	7,063	12	7,051	266	13	5	13,866	99	929	592	337
1995[1]	6,530	1,487	7,261	0	7,261	201	0	-96	13,987	93	896	592	305

[1] Preliminary. [2] Strategic Petroleum Reserve. [3] A negative number indicates a decrease in stocks and a positive number indicates an increase. Note: Crude oil includes lease condensate. Stocks of Alaskan crude oil in transit were included beginning in January 1981. *Source: Energy Information Administration, U.S. Department of Energy*

PETROLEUM

Crude Petroleum Refinery Operations Ration[1] In Percent of Capacity

Year	Jan.	Feb.	Mar.	Apr.	May	June	July	Aug.	Sept.	Oct.	Nov.	Dec.	Average
1985	74	74	74	76	78	79	81	78	77	79	80	81	78
1986	81	78	76	82	86	86	84	87	86	83	84	84	83
1987	82	80	79	81	82	85	87	87	86	83	82	84	83
1988	83	81	83	84	86	86	86	87	84	83	84	85	84
1989	86	83	84	84	86	90	89	89	88	86	86	84	86
1990	88	88	84	85	87	89	93	91	91	84	84	83	87
1991	83	84	83	85	87	90	89	89	88	83	84	87	86
1992	83	81	85	86	89	92	92	89	91	89	90	88	88
1993	87	87	89	91	93	95	95	93	93	92	92	91	92
1994	90	89	88	92	95	96	96	96	94	90	93	93	93
1995[2]	90	88	88	90	94	96	94	93	95				

[1] Based on the ration of the daily average crude runs to stills to the rated capacity of refineries per day. [2] Preliminary.
Source: Energy Information Administration, U.S. Department of Energy

United States Crude Oil Refinery Inputs In Thousands of Barrels Per Day

Year	Jan.	Feb.	Mar.	Apr.	May	June	July	Aug.	Sept.	Oct.	Nov.	Dec.	Average
1985	11,445	11,367	11,372	11,805	12,094	12,292	12,445	12,045	11,925	12,209	12,410	12,570	12,002
1986	12,374	11,918	11,652	12,512	13,279	13,261	12,917	13,287	13,097	12,636	12,831	12,777	12,716
1987	12,570	12,290	12,081	12,512	12,653	13,202	13,430	13,380	13,168	12,733	12,981	13,212	12,854
1988	12,920	12,644	13,016	13,135	13,425	13,487	13,617	13,752	13,261	13,126	13,156	13,381	13,246
1989	13,330	12,765	12,963	12,956	13,405	13,905	13,848	13,861	13,791	13,360	13,420	13,165	13,401
1990	13,491	13,487	12,876	13,051	13,386	13,689	14,212	14,142	14,104	12,825	12,953	12,708	13,409
1991	12,735	13,046	12,839	13,042	13,539	13,918	13,703	13,800	13,694	12,896	12,929	13,465	13,301
1992	12,923	12,486	13,083	13,260	13,679	14,059	13,953	13,426	13,714	13,584	13,547	13,194	13,411
1993	12,938	12,865	13,200	13,538	13,829	14,129	14,136	13,844	13,841	13,729	13,686	13,571	13,613
1994	13,286	13,130	12,985	13,809	14,272	14,351	14,344	14,491	14,234	13,529	13,968	13,951	13,866
1995[1]	13,610	13,367	13,478	13,816	14,299	14,568	14,380	14,245	14,402	13,626	13,812		

[1] Preliminary. *Source: Energy Information Administration, U.S. Department of Energy*

Production of Major Refined Petroleum Products in the Continental U.S. In Millions of Barrels

Year	Asphalt	Aviation Gasoline	Fuel Oil Distillate	Fuel Oil Residual	Gasoline	Jet Fuel	Kerosene	Natural Gas Plant Liquids	Lubri-cants	Liquefied Gases Total	Liquefied Gases at L.P.G.[2]	Liquefied Gases at L.P.G.[3]
1985	146.3	9.3	980.9	322.0	2,352	433.9	34.5	607.5	53.1	622.0	479.3	142.6
1986	149.7	11.7	1,021.2	324.3	2,476	472.0	32.6	587.1	58.2	618.5	466.2	152.3
1987	158.4	9.1	996.6	323.2	2,506	490.1	28.7	605.6	60.9	638.2	474.5	163.7
1988	162.1	9.3	1,046.3	338.7	2,555	501.3	28.8	614.2	62.3	665.2	482.6	182.6
1989	154.9	9.2	1,152.2	500.1	2,684	543.6	30.8	586.1	58.1	653.5	451.3	202.2
1990	164.0	8.5	1,067.5	346.6	2,650	555.6	15.5	598.3	59.7	638.4	456.2	182.2
1991	156.8	8.0	1,081.0	341.1	2,554	525.0	14.0	639.2	57.0	683.1	487.5	195.6
1992	153.0	7.9	1,088.4	326.1	2,591	512.0	14.8	668.0	57.5	738.7	499.7	222.2
1993	165.6	7.9	1,139.7	303.9	2,644	518.8	17.5	631.2	58.4	849.4	633.5	215.9
1994[1]	164.8	7.9	1,169.7	301.4	2,621	528.4	21.1	630.2	62.1	734.3	511.1	223.2

[1] Preliminary. *Source: Energy Information Administration, U.S. Department of Energy*

Stocks of Petroleum & Products in the United States on January 1 In Millions of Barrels

Year	Crude Petroleum	Strategic Reserve	Refined Products Total	Asphalt	Aviation Gasoline	Fuel Oil Distillate	Fuel Oil Residual	Finished Gasoline	Jet Fuel	Kero-sene	Liquefied Gases[2]	Lubricants	Motor Gasoline Total	Motor Gasoline Finished[3]
1985	795.9	450.5	620.6	17.2	2.7	161.1	53.0	207.9	42.0	11.9	100.8	12.7	243	205
1986	814.2	493.3	556.6	21.2	2.1	143.7	50.4	192.4	40.5	7.5	73.5	11.8	223	190
1987	842.8	511.6	609.4	17.7	2.2	155.1	47.4	196.4	49.7	8.4	102.7	14.2	233	194
1988	889.6	540.6	579.5	18.8	2.3	134.5	47.4	191.1	49.9	8.4	97.1	13.3	226	189
1989	889.9	559.5	561.6	20.8	2.1	123.5	44.6	192.0	43.8	7.3	97.3	13.3	228	190
1990	921.1	579.9	508.3	20.6	2.1	105.7	43.8	179.1	40.9	5.1	80.2	13.8	213	177
1991	908.4	585.7	566.8	18.7	1.7	132.2	48.6	182.4	52.1	5.6	97.9	12.4	220	181
1992	893.1	568.5	576.7	22.3	1.6	143.5	49.9	183.3	48.8	5.8	92.3	12.3	219	182
1993	892.9	574.7	549.1	17.7	1.6	140.6	42.6	179.1	43.1	5.7	88.7	13.3	216	178
1994	922.5	587.1	465.8	19.1	1.8	140.9	44.2	185.7	40.4	4.1	106.6	11.8	226	187
1995[1]	928.9	591.7	468.0	18.6	2.3	145.2	41.9	175.9	46.8	8.0	108.0	11.5	215	176

1 Preliminary. [2] Includes ethane and ethylene at plants and refineries. [3] Includes oxygenated. *Source: Energy Information Administration, U.S. Department of Energy*

Stocks of Crude Petroleum in the United States at the Beginning of the Month   In Millions of Barrels

Year	Jan.	Feb.	Mar.	Apr.	May	June	July	Aug.	Sept.	Oct.	Nov.	Dec.
1985	795.9	793.5	781.6	791.2	806.8	828.6	820.6	810.5	805.6	806.6	803.6	812.4
1986	814.2	826.1	827.1	837.8	836.6	828.5	828.4	845.2	837.7	844.2	851.4	848.6
1987	842.8	847.9	848.6	852.4	850.9	849.8	854.8	853.8	864.4	871.1	891.5	902.2
1988	889.6	888.3	892.2	898.9	904.6	907.6	908.9	900.8	885.7	883.2	895.6	895.7
1989	889.9	894.8	896.6	892.5	907.4	915.7	903.0	907.6	916.3	912.0	914.3	930.5
1990	921.1	932.9	924.0	955.9	953.1	968.7	970.9	966.2	959.2	932.7	935.7	924.7
1991	908.4	905.3	912.8	905.3	907.2	924.3	915.3	910.6	913.8	909.1	910.7	912.0
1992	893.1	909.7	914.8	907.1	916.5	912.0	894.6	902.2	898.3	893.5	906.2	899.4
1993	892.9	902.0	908.1	914.7	930.4	935.0	935.1	935.2	919.6	906.4	916.5	924.1
1994	922.5	925.3	922.6	932.6	930.6	922.7	919.6	924.2	920.2	927.0	934.9	938.0
1995[1]	928.9	920.1	918.8	929.4	926.4	923.0	918.9	906.1	898.4	896.6		

[1] Preliminary. *Source: Energy Information Administration, U.S. Department of Agriculture*

Production of Crude Petroleum in the United States   In Thousands of Barrels Per Day

Year	Jan.	Feb.	Mar.	Apr.	May	June	July	Aug.	Sept.	Oct.	Nov.	Dec.	Average
1985	8,740	9,025	9,095	9,043	9,132	9,022	8,949	8,803	8,954	8,970	8,902	9,030	8,971
1986	9,137	9,173	9,013	8,864	8,838	8,623	8,660	8,374	8,328	8,419	8,412	8,352	8,680
1987	8,480	8,389	8,464	8,498	8,336	8,279	8,251	8,210	8,205	8,364	8,397	8,318	8,349
1988	8,250	8,374	8,374	8,288	8,229	8,170	8,040	8,079	7,895	8,023	8,023	7,942	8,140
1989	7,937	7,788	7,575	7,772	7,816	7,624	7,444	7,544	7,548	7,453	7,536	7,337	7,613
1990	7,546	7,497	7,433	7,407	7,328	7,106	7,173	7,287	7,224	7,542	7,387	7,338	7,355
1991	7,500	7,637	7,546	7,509	7,409	7,320	7,347	7,316	7,368	7,437	7,328	7,299	7,417
1992	7,361	7,389	7,348	7,293	7,169	7,167	7,131	6,922	7,030	7,126	7,024	7,103	7,171
1993	6,961	6,943	6,974	6,881	6,847	6,795	6,688	6,758	6,712	6,839	6,912	6,858	6,847
1994[1]	6,817	6,770	6,746	6,612	6,688	6,611	6,501	6,544	6,609	6,658	6,628	6,760	6,662
1995[2]	6,596	6,703	6,606	6,561	6,572	6,540	6,449	6,481	6,462	6,380	6,441		

[1] Preliminary. [2] Estimate. *Source: Energy Information Administration, U.S. Department of Energy*

U.S. Foreign Trade of Petroleum and Products   In Thousands of Barrels Per Day

	Exports		Imports						Exports		Imports				
Year	Total[2]	Petroleum Products	Crude	Petroleum Products	Distillate Fuel Oil	Residual Fuel Oil	Net Imports[3]	Year	Total[2]	Petroleum Products	Crude	Petroleum Products	Distillate Fuel Oil	Residual Fuel Oil	Net Imports[3]
1976	223	215	5,287	2,026	146	1,413	7,090	1986	785	631	4,178	2,045	247	669	5,439
1977	243	193	6,615	2,193	250	1,359	8,565	1987	764	613	4,674	2,004	255	565	5,914
1978	362	204	6,356	2,008	173	1,355	8,002	1988	815	661	5,107	2,295	302	644	6,587
1979	471	236	6,519	1,937	193	1,151	7,985	1989	859	717	5,843	2,217	306	629	7,202
1980	544	258	5,263	1,646	142	939	6,365	1990	857	748	5,894	2,123	278	504	7,161
1981	595	367	4,396	1,599	173	800	5,401	1991	1,001	885	5,782	1,844	205	453	6,626
1982	815	579	3,488	1,325	93	776	4,298	1992	950	861	6,083	1,805	216	375	6,938
1983	739	575	3,329	1,722	174	699	4,312	1993	1,003	904	6,787	1,833	184	373	7,618
1984	722	541	3,426	2,011	272	681	4,715	1994	942	843	7,063	1,933	203	314	8,054
1985	781	577	3,201	1,866	200	510	4,286	1995[1]	909	816	7,261	1,558	178	182	7,910

[1] Preliminary. [2] Includes crude oil. [3] Equals imports minus exports. *Source: Energy Information Administration, U.S. Department of Energy*

Domestic First Purchase Price of Crude Petroleum at Wells[1]   In Dollars Per Barrel

Year	Jan.	Feb.	Mar.	Apr.	May	June	July	Aug.	Sept.	Oct.	Nov.	Dec.	Average
1985	24.26	23.64	23.89	24.19	24.18	24.07	24.04	23.99	23.96	24.10	24.27	24.51	24.09
1986	23.12	17.65	12.62	10.68	10.75	10.68	9.25	9.77	11.09	11.00	11.05	11.73	12.51
1987	13.79	14.51	14.54	14.95	15.29	15.95	16.88	17.06	16.25	15.95	15.46	14.27	15.40
1988	13.64	13.43	12.96	13.92	14.12	13.59	12.38	12.22	11.63	10.62	10.31	11.99	12.58
1989	13.80	14.24	15.65	17.04	16.76	16.42	16.32	15.01	15.58	16.25	16.30	17.01	15.86
1990	18.49	18.16	16.57	14.52	13.82	12.79	14.03	21.87	28.46	30.86	27.53	22.63	20.03
1991	19.60	16.28	15.13	16.16	16.44	15.58	16.36	16.60	16.71	17.72	17.12	14.68	16.54
1992	13.99	14.04	14.12	15.36	16.38	17.96	17.80	17.07	17.20	17.16	16.00	14.94	15.99
1993	14.70	15.53	15.94	16.15	16.03	15.06	13.83	13.75	13.39	13.72	12.45	10.38	14.25
1994	10.51	10.73	10.81	12.33	14.03	14.95	15.31	14.50	13.62	13.84	14.14	13.43	13.19
1995[2]	14.00	14.69	14.68	15.84	15.85	15.02	14.01	14.13	14.49	13.67			

[1] Buyers posted prices. [2] Preliminary. *Source: Energy Information Adiministration, U.S. Department of Energy*

PETROLEUM

Volume of Trading of Crude Oil Futures in New York   In Thousands of Contracts

Year	Jan.	Feb.	Mar.	Apr.	May	June	July	Aug.	Sept.	Oct.	Nov.	Dec.	Total
1986	520	491	560	691	677	613	861	702	667	986	604	942	8,314
1987	873	968	1,199	1,059	937	1,196	1,412	1,505	1,126	1,205	1,287	1,813	14,582
1988	1,626	1,336	1,809	1,352	1,205	1,507	1,754	1,219	1,956	2,040	1,609	1,450	18,859
1989	1,919	1,524	2,053	2,070	1,911	2,082	1,663	1,343	1,541	1,521	1,425	1,483	20,535
1990	2,164	1,790	1,794	1,813	1,945	1,839	2,046	2,716	2,073	2,437	1,769	1,302	23,687
1991	1,997	1,478	1,605	1,885	1,741	1,411	1,675	1,598	1,543	2,064	2,051	1,960	21,008
1992	2,097	1,630	1,620	1,889	1,885	2,006	1,796	1,531	1,541	1,797	1,542	1,778	21,110
1993	2,139	1,886	1,895	1,459	1,641	2,018	2,616	2,200	2,679	1,945	2,378	2,122	24,869
1994	2,296	1,933	2,228	2,382	2,602	2,576	2,186	2,544	1,897	2,195	2,196	1,778	16,812
1995	2,133	1,657	2,290	2,220	2,409	2,172	1,749	1,794	1,968	1,835	1,739	1,647	23,614

Source: New York Mercantile Exchange

Average Open Interest of Crude Oil Futures in New York   In Contracts

Year	Jan.	Feb.	Mar.	Apr.	May	June	July	Aug.	Sept.	Oct.	Nov.	Dec.
1986	69,614	66,811	73,167	88,203	100,012	103,300	122,760	113,286	104,874	117,423	113,077	113,250
1987	127,129	144,569	160,668	155,686	143,305	147,501	177,760	195,468	197,623	183,276	165,489	199,806
1988	202,830	200,813	210,878	192,074	177,155	180,019	177,978	177,879	220,973	221,628	196,454	196,109
1989	204,066	210,299	224,322	248,032	231,390	222,748	221,389	209,702	230,990	235,716	242,677	257,974
1990	273,193	300,069	287,013	287,538	278,600	285,384	275,771	262,746	266,313	269,167	242,500	232,405
1991	249,759	272,396	285,417	303,942	286,159	277,587	278,704	267,186	264,223	298,434	292,889	284,453
1992	310,763	331,050	316,544	340,315	335,545	364,155	331,972	316,066	314,446	301,381	308,467	330,134
1993	352,316	369,180	385,768	381,954	384,309	396,832	423,041	428,418	404,172	397,121	404,046	427,756
1994	427,705	438,929	424,462	410,974	427,071	414,257	409,251	396,657	395,194	413,206	388,932	391,151
1995	373,798	379,329	353,805	364,929	350,826	346,051	357,718	343,636	342,360	334,170	329,786	348,954

Source: New York Mercantile Exchange

Plastics

Plastics find wide use in a variety of products ranging from packaging materials to replacement material for wood, metals, glass and paper. A major concern of the industry has been the environmental impact of the disposal of items containing plastic material. The recycling of plastic material has taken on increasing importance in many communities and there are concerted efforts under way to gather and then recycle plastic materials. The American Plastics Council has published the following facts about plastics. They note that without plastics packaging weight would increase fourfold, and the volume of packaging would more than double. Plastics are the most efficient packaging material because they have the highest package-to-product ratio compared to other materials. One ounce of plastic typically delivers 38.8 ounces of food and beverage.

One area where plastic is making an important contribution is the automobile industry. This has been attributed to the need by automakers to keep the prices of cars down, while at the same time increasing gasoline efficiency by making vehicles lighter. New high-temperature plastics continue to find increasing use in a variety of products and have many applications in the aviation and aerospace industries. In automobile production, these new products find use in bumpers, gas tanks, hoods and fenders. Some of the fastest growing segments of the plastics industry include engineering resin, high-density polyethylene polyvinyl chloride, and polyolefins.

For 1994, total plastic production in the U.S. was estimated by the Society of Plastics Industry, Inc. at 76 billion pounds, a 10 percent increase from 1993. Thermoplastic polyester production was estimated at 3.2 billion pounds, up 25 percent from 1993. Polyvinyl chloride production was put at 11.7 billion pounds, up 14 percent from 1993. Polystyrene production was estimated at 5.8 billion pounds, up nearly 9 percent from 1993. Polypropylene production was put at 9.5 billion pounds, up close to 11 percent. Nylon production was put at 943 million pounds, 23 percent more than 1993. Total thermoplastic production in 1994 was estimated at 56.8 million pounds, up 11 percent. Total thermoset plastic production was estimated at 7.5 billion pounds, up over 9 percent.

In terms of use by market, plastics resins are used in a number of important industries. Total use of plastic resins in 1994 was 70.8 billion pounds, up over 11 percent. By far the dominant use is in packaging materials. In 1994, packaging used 19.6 billion pounds (dry weight) of plastic resins, virtually unchanged from 1993. The next largest use is in building and construction. In 1994, that category used 14.7 billion pounds, up 14 percent. Consumption of plastic resin for consumer and industrial uses was 9.3 billion pounds in 1994, up 54 percent from the previous year. Plastic resin used in electrical and electronic applications in 1994 totaled 3.3 billion pounds, up close to 12 percent. Resins consumed in furniture and furnishings were 3.2 billion pounds, up 13 percent. Plastic resins used in adhesives, inks and coatings were 1.8 billion pounds, up 14 percent. Resins used in the transportation industry were 3.8 billion pounds, up 18 percent. Industrial and machinery applications used 836 million pounds, up almost 9 percent. Exports of plastic resins in 1994 totaled 6.9 billion pounds, up almost 4 percent from 1993.

Plastics Production by Resin in the United States In Millions of Pounds

	Thermosets				Thermoplastics										
Year	Polyester Unsaturated	Phenolic	Epoxy	Total Thermosets	Thermoplastic Polyester	Polyvinyl Chloride	Polystyrene	Polypropylene	Nylon	Low Density Polyethylene[1]	High Density Polyethylene	Total Thermoplastics	Total Selected Plastics	Other Plastics	Total Plastics
1985	1,223	2,640	385	5,631	965	6,772	4,054	5,139	399	8,889	6,671	34,004	39,635	8,311	47,946
1986	1,271	2,735	398	5,848	1,175	7,256	4,470	5,812	465	8,903	7,182	36,447	42,295	8,554	50,849
1987	1,367	2,869	433	6,263	1,394	7,971	4,780	6,647	507	9,599	7,995	40,194	46,457	9,294	55,751
1988	1,404	3,066	486	6,588	1,652	8,350	5,187	7,274	566	10,397	8,400	43,251	49,839	9,923	59,762
1989	1,319	2,879	510	6,407	1,630	8,478	5,104	7,238	569	9,695	8,102	42,189	48,596	9,933	58,529
1990	1,221	2,946	499	6,364	1,879	9,096	5,021	8,310	558	11,148	8,337	45,646	52,010	9,950	61,960
1991	1,075	2,658	497	5,909	2,115	9,164	4,954	8,330	576	11,582	9,213	47,146	53,055	9,731	62,786
1992	1,175	2,923	457	6,335	2,413	9,989	5,096	8,421	668	11,917	9,808	49,751	56,086	10,285	66,371
1993	1,264	3,078	512	6,868	2,549	10,257	5,382	8,628	768	12,067	9,941	51,159	58,027	10,777	68,854
1994	1,468	3,229	601	7,513	3,196	11,712	5,848	9,539	943	12,600	11,117	56,794	64,307	11,664	75,971

[1] Includes LDPE and LLDPE. *Source: The Society of the Plastics Industry, Inc.*

Total Resin Sales and Captive Use by Important Markets In Millions of Pounds (Dry Weight Basis)

Year	Adhesive, Inks & Coatings	Building & Construction	Consumer & Industrial	Electrical & Electronics	Exports	Furniture & Furnishings	Industrial & Machinery	Packaging	Transportation	Other	Total
1989	1,211	11,096	6,217	3,145	[1]	2,285	475	14,711	2,547	10,911	52,598
1990	1,373	11,803	5,861	3,165	[1]	2,190	636	16,568	2,504	11,811	55,910
1991	1,391	10,650	5,689	2,896	7,418	2,255	587	16,723	2,328	6,616	56,553
1992	1,723	11,876	6,093	2,766	6,950	2,559	617	18,284	2,817	6,877	60,562
1993	1,572	12,885	6,015	2,981	6,632	2,759	768	19,569	3,221	7,234	63,636
1994	1,789	14,715	9,266	3,325	6,889	3,118	836	19,551	3,795	7,515	70,799

[1] Included in other. *Source: The Society of the Plastics Industry, Inc.*

PLASTICS

Average Producer Price Index of Plastic Materials in the United States 1982 = 100

Year	Jan.	Feb.	Mar.	Apr.	May	June	July	Aug.	Sept.	Oct.	Nov.	Dec.	Average
Plastic Resins and Materials (066)													
1987	102.6	102.4	103.2	106.3	107.0	109.7	112.8	113.1	114.2	116.8	117.4	117.7	110.3
1988	121.5	123.5	124.4	127.6	130.1	131.2	134.8	136.9	138.9	139.8	140.2	140.1	132.4
1989	140.3	141.1	140.6	140.7	139.8	138.0	135.3	127.7	126.1	124.7	123.7	123.3	133.4
1990	122.2	121.6	122.2	123.0	123.5	123.0	122.1	122.3	123.6	125.1	128.6	131.2	124.0
1991	131.1	128.7	125.4	122.9	120.6	117.0	115.0	114.9	114.9	116.4	116.7	116.0	120.0
1992	115.4	115.6	114.2	114.2	114.7	115.2	115.9	117.7	117.5	118.2	118.1	118.1	116.2
1993	118.3	118.0	117.6	117.1	116.3	116.9	116.9	117.6	117.4	116.9	116.2	116.2	117.1
1994	115.0	114.7	114.5	116.5	117.7	119.1	119.6	121.5	126.3	131.9	134.1	138.1	122.4
1995[1]	142.5	144.1	145.9	148.5	149.0	148.9	147.0	145.8	143.3	140.5	137.1		
Thermoplastic Resins (0662)													
1987	102.3	102.1	103.1	107.3	107.9	111.1	113.9	114.1	115.3	118.5	119.3	119.7	111.2
1988	124.4	126.7	127.8	131.1	133.7	134.9	139.0	141.2	143.5	144.3	144.4	144.2	136.3
1989	114.5	145.2	144.4	143.9	143.2	141.1	137.7	128.5	126.7	125.1	124.0	124.0	133.2
1990	122.9	121.9	122.5	123.5	124.1	123.4	122.4	122.5	124.1	125.8	130.5	134.0	124.8
1991	132.1	129.4	125.5	122.9	120.2	116.2	113.8	113.7	114.6	115.5	116.0	115.3	119.6
1992	114.7	114.7	113.0	112.9	113.4	114.1	114.8	117.1	116.8	117.6	117.6	117.5	115.4
1993	117.5	117.1	116.3	115.8	114.8	115.4	115.5	116.4	116.4	116.4	115.5	114.6	116.0
1994	113.0	112.7	112.5	115.0	116.2	117.9	118.4	120.1	125.4	131.6	133.9	138.4	121.3
1995[1]	143.1	145.0	147.1	150.3	151.0	151.2	148.7	147.3	144.4	141.0	136.8		
PE Resin, Low, Film & Sheeting (0662-0301)													
1987	112.3	113.1	110.5	113.9	114.6	121.5	123.9	127.8	127.9	131.9	138.8	140.7	123.1
1988	145.9	150.3	153.8	157.9	171.4	172.0	178.3	192.3	201.3	203.5	202.7	201.6	177.6
1989	202.0	206.6	206.0	204.0	200.8	195.3	191.9	151.5	150.3	150.9	152.3	153.0	180.4
1990	151.9	145.3	146.1	145.9	152.5	151.7	144.9	141.9	152.3	145.6	149.8	157.4	148.8
1991	158.1	150.7	142.6	135.8	130.1	121.9	117.8	114.8	113.9	123.2	131.3	124.6	130.4
1992	126.5	130.9	126.7	121.3	123.5	122.4	132.9	138.9	145.2	149.3	148.6	150.6	134.7
1993	NA	151.4	145.6	141.8	135.5	137.1	132.2	136.6	129.2	128.4	127.6	127.4	135.7
1994	121.6	119.4	119.3	120.8	127.6	134.5	136.3	140.8	146.6	155.4	172.8	182.2	139.8
1995[1]	188.5	196.0	202.0	210.6	215.4	211.1	205.7	194.8	186.0	176.9	169.7		
Styrene Plastics Materials (0662-06)													
1987	96.0	96.1	101.3	108.3	110.0	116.8	119.6	115.4	117.6	116.6	119.5	119.7	111.4
1988	122.2	125.2	127.0	128.9	129.0	131.7	133.6	134.1	134.1	135.4	134.7	134.8	130.9
1989	135.3	136.3	134.4	135.8	135.1	133.1	124.6	119.5	119.0	116.8	114.2	114.4	126.5
1990	113.1	114.7	117.2	116.8	116.8	115.2	113.7	113.7	116.8	123.4	127.8	124.2	117.8
1991	123.3	122.7	115.4	115.5	112.4	121.9	109.2	107.7	108.3	113.0	113.0	111.5	114.5
1992	109.5	109.6	109.1	109.1	110.3	109.4	110.4	112.6	111.2	112.5	111.7	111.5	110.6
1993	110.7	110.5	110.0	110.4	111.0	111.3	111.2	111.1	110.6	109.1	106.5	106.4	109.9
1994	105.8	104.1	104.1	108.1	108.3	109.2	110.4	110.6	116.0	123.3	125.3	126.2	112.6
1995[1]	129.0	127.0	132.5	134.7	135.9	137.5	135.1	132.7	131.7	130.4	129.3		
Thermosetting Resins (0663)													
1987	101.5	101.4	101.9	102.2	103.6	105.5	110.6	111.1	111.8	111.8	111.3	111.0	107.0
1988	110.2	110.4	110.7	113.5	115.4	115.7	116.8	118.4	119.2	120.0	122.4	122.7	116.3
1989	122.4	124.0	124.9	127.9	126.6	126.5	126.8	127.5	126.9	126.6	125.9	123.8	125.8
1990	122.8	124.0	124.1	124.4	124.3	124.7	124.7	124.8	125.0	125.6	124.0	126.6	124.6
1991	130.1	129.1	128.9	127.1	126.3	125.2	124.9	124.9	123.9	124.5	123.8	123.1	126.0
1992	123.1	124.1	123.9	124.3	124.4	124.4	124.7	125.0	125.0	125.3	125.1	125.2	124.5
1993	126.1	126.5	127.4	127.5	127.8	128.0	127.7	127.7	127.9	127.8	127.8	128.3	127.5
1994	128.2	128.1	128.1	127.8	128.7	129.1	129.7	132.1	134.9	137.7	140.1	141.5	132.2
1995[1]	144.3	145.1	145.4	145.2	144.7	143.5	144.0	143.8	143.3	142.7	142.9		
Phenolic & Tar Acid Resins (0663-02)													
1987	103.7	103.0	105.1	104.8	111.8	117.9	127.1	129.7	132.8	132.1	130.6	129.8	119.0
1988	126.8	126.2	126.4	128.8	135.4	136.2	141.6	143.6	147.1	150.9	154.8	157.1	139.6
1989	156.7	158.9	162.6	166.8	164.2	164.4	166.2	159.5	158.6	158.0	156.9	152.3	160.4
1990	148.2	149.4	149.1	148.7	148.5	147.3	143.9	142.5	141.5	139.0	138.2	143.7	145.0
1991	146.4	147.3	142.4	140.7	138.3	132.8	131.6	131.5	128.3	129.7	126.5	125.5	135.1
1992	125.4	126.4	125.1	124.7	125.6	125.6	127.7	127.6	127.9	129.7	128.8	128.5	126.9
1993	128.5	130.3	130.5	131.4	133.7	134.1	133.9	132.8	133.1	132.1	132.0	132.9	132.1
1994	133.0	130.9	129.7	131.3	134.1	135.9	139.2	143.7	147.2	154.7	161.0	161.5	141.9
1995[1]	164.6	166.4	165.1	162.5	158.6	15.5	152.0	149.6	148.1	147.0	144.7		

[1] Preliminary. NA = Not available. *Source: Bureau of Labor Statistics, U.S. Department of Commerce*

Platinum-Group Metals

Platinum prices traded in a narrow $25 per ounce range during the first quarter, then spiked higher early in the second quarter in sympathy with higher prices for gold and silver. The price rally carried to $478.50 per troy ounce, basis nearby futures, the metal's highest level since 1990. Palladium's price followed, but due to that market's smaller liquidity and greater volatility the advance carried nearby futures to more than $180 per troy ounce, extending a three year bull move that started in mid-1992 under $80 per troy ounce However, both metals trended lower during the second half of 1995 with platinum finishing at $398.20 per troy ounce, and palladium at $129.65 per troy ounce.

The upward push partially reflected hopes for a protracted strong U.S. economy that would enhance the demand for the metals. Palladium, meanwhile, had been buoyed by latent expectations that the automotive industry would find increased use for the metal. The price erosion that followed mirrored ideas that the economy's strength was fading and was coupled with weakness in gold and silver. Moreover, the surging equity markets likely siphoned speculative capital away from the precious metals complex. Adding to the bearish pressure was the absence of any serious problems in South Africa which could have hindered mine production and/or shipments of the metals. Generally, the short term variables effecting price are more supply sensitive.

Six metals make up the platinum group (PGM). However, reasonably up to date statistical data is limited to platinum and palladium; for iridium, osmium, rhodium (the most expensive) and ruthenium (the least expensive) the data is spotty at best. Minable deposits of the PGM's are very rare, production occurs as a byproduct of other metals, usually nickel or copper. The world's annual platinum group metal production trended downward during the first half of the 1990's, totaling about 250,000 kilograms in 1994 versus a high of 291,015 kilograms in 1990. However, a shift may have developed in the production breakdown. Until 1991, more palladium was produced than platinum, generally by about 10,000 kilograms. However, in 1992 platinum's output was higher by 8,000 kilograms, and in 1993 the difference exceeded 16,000 kilograms. Identified world PGM resources at yearend 1994 were estimated at 100 million kilograms, of which 90 percent were in South Africa, 9 percent in Russia and 1 percent in the U.S. At yearend 1994, accountable PGM stocks in the U.S. Government's National Defense Stockpile totaled 14,100 kilograms of platinum, 39,300 kilograms of palladium and 920 kilograms of iridium. The next largest stockpile of accountable supplies were held in approved futures exchange vaults.

South Africa is the largest producer with about 146,000 kilograms in 1994, down from a record high 157,000 kilograms in 1993. Generally, platinum production is twice that of palladium. In the late 1980's The USSR's annual production averaged about 125,000 kilograms; production has since fallen sharply. Russia's production is now estimated at only 55,000 kilograms in 1994, most of which was palladium. However, the mine data is suspect, but by how much and where it was produced is not readily known. Canada's recent annual production has averaged about 11,500 kilograms, but a record high 13,000 kilograms were produced in 1994, with palladium accounting for 7,000 kilograms. U.S. production is growing, but is well under demand leaving the U.S. highly dependent on imports. The Stillwater Mine in Montana accounts for nearly all domestic PGM production; reportedly there are large deposits of PGM in the Montana region, but the extracting costs exceed the metals' value. The U.S. produced 2,000 kilograms of platinum in 1994 and 6,400 kilograms of palladium, about the same as in 1993 and compares with 1,810 and 5,930 kilograms, respectively, in 1990.

The U.S. imports half the world's production, but re-exports a portion as refined platinum. In 1994, U.S. apparent platinum metal consumption totaled a record high 127,000 kilograms versus 123,273 kilograms in 1993. Apparent is defined by the U.S. Bureau of Mines as: mine production + non-toll production + refined imports - refined exports + beginning stocks - ending stocks. The automotive industry is the largest consumer as the metal(s) are used as an emission control catalyst, demand for which will grow as more stringent standards for automobile emissions are adopted. The electrical industry takes less than a third of the automotive needs and the jewelry industry less than 10 percent.

U.S. imports of platinum group metals in 1994 totaled 170,901 kilograms, of which palladium accounted for 92,500 kilograms; 1993 imports totaled 153,165 kilograms. South Africa was the largest supplier to the U.S. with more than half being platinum. Next in line was Russia, most of which was palladium. Most of U.S. exports are relegated to the category known as waste and scrap, 42,100 kilograms in 1994, of which Belgium took almost half with Japan and the U.K. accounting for most of the balance.

Producers maintain an artificial price for the platinum group metals, but dealer or market prices are generally much lower. Platinum averaged $401 per ounce in 1994 versus $370 in 1993; palladium averaged $142 in 1994 and $120 in 1993. Through 1995 platinum maintained a premium to gold, as it usually does, with the differential at yearend averaging about $25 per ounce.

Futures Markets

Platinum and palladium futures and options are traded on the New York Mercantile Exchange (NYMEX). In Japan, platinum and palladium futures a listed on the Tokyo Commodity Exchange (TOCOM).

PLATINUM-GROUP METALS

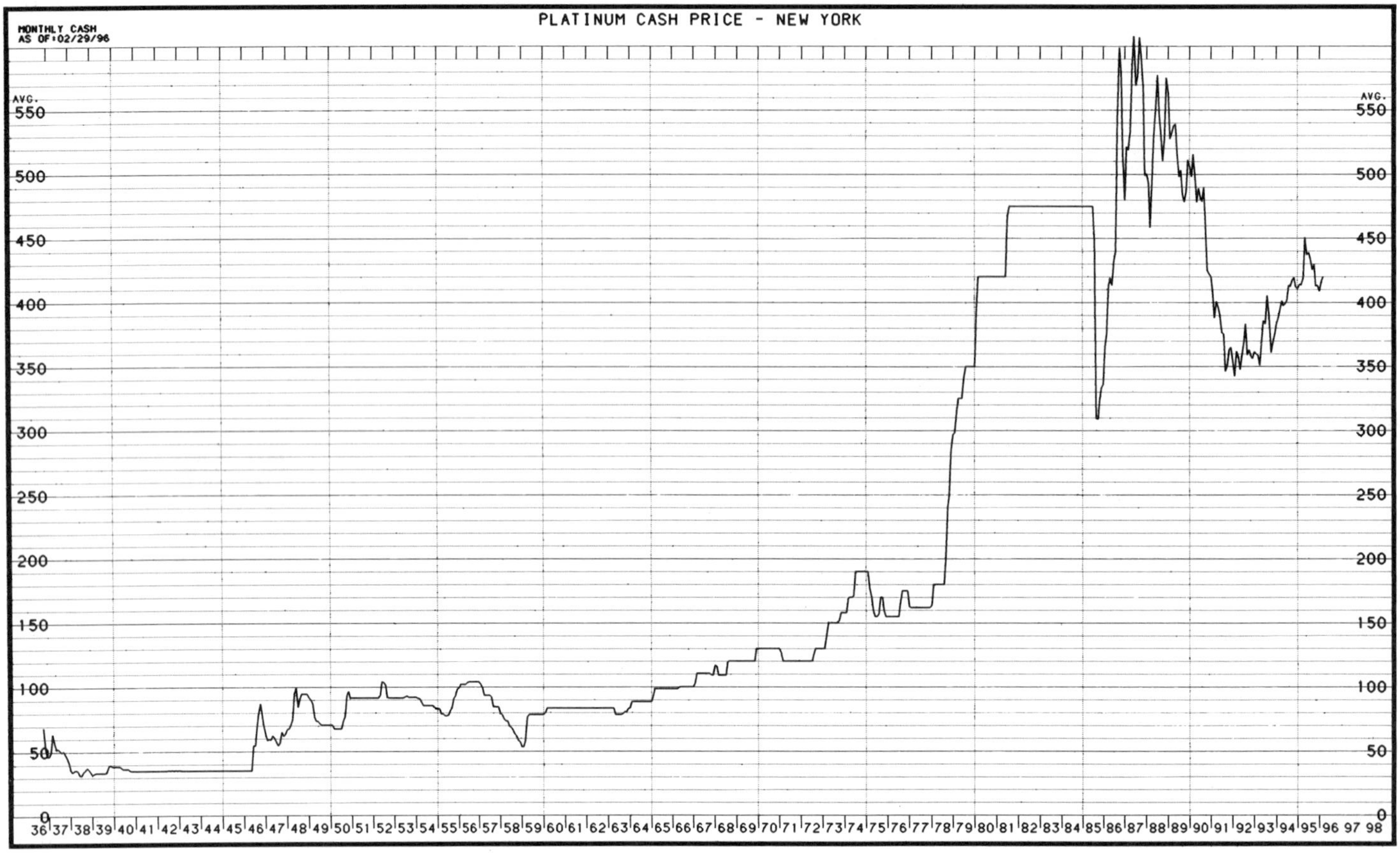

World Mine Production of Platinum--Group Metals In Kilograms

Year	Australia	Canada Platinum	Canada Palladium	Canada Total	Colombia[3]	Japan Platinum	Japan Palladium	Russia[4] Platinum	Russia[4] Palladium	Russia[4] Total	South Africa Platinum	South Africa Palladium	South Africa Total	United States Platinum	United States Palladium	World Total
1985	571	-----	-----	10,485	362	691	1,359	-----	-----	118,200	-----	-----	115,100	W	W	246,988
1986	543	5,242	5,486	12,190	447	663	1,453	30,000	81,000	121,300	73,100	32,300	123,200	W	W	260,193
1987	620	4,354	5,910	10,930	638	753	1,417	31,000	83,000	124,400	78,400	33,900	128,000	780	2,330	270,281
1988	517	5,393	5,643	12,541	815	647	1,170	32,000	85,000	127,500	80,322	34,400	131,722	1,240	3,730	280,282
1989	500	4,467	4,676	10,389	973	1,031	821	32,000	85,000	127,500	82,884	35,800	133,684	1,430	4,850	281,629
1990	500	5,044	5,269	11,709	1,316	1,425	1,047	31,000	84,000	125,000	87,813	38,300	141,913	1,810	5,930	291,015
1991	500	4,683	6,439	11,708	1,603	988	1,053	30,000	82,000	121,500	88,861	38,000	142,861	1,730	6,050	288,343
1992	500	4,800	5,800	11,907	1,956	629	986	28,000	70,000	104,000	94,891	41,000	152,891	1,840	6,470	282,000
1993[1]	500	5,000	6,000	11,000	1,720	661	1,180	20,000	50,000	70,000	109,000	48,000	157,000	1,800	6,500	275,000
1994[2]	500	6,000	7,000	13,000	1,800	700	1,200	15,000	40,000	55,000	102,000	44,000	146,000	2,000	6,400	250,000

[1] Preliminary. [2] Estimate. [3] Placer platinum. [4] Formerly part of the U.S.S.R.; data not reported separately until 1992 W = Withheld proprietary data.
Source: U.S. Bureau of Mines

Salient Statistics of Platinum and Allied Metals[3] in the U.S. In Kilograms

Year	Net Import Reliance as a % of Apparent Consumption	Mine Production Platinum	Mine Production Palladium	Refinery Production (Secondary)	Total Refined	Refiner, Importer & Dealer Stocks as of Dec. 31 Platinum	Stocks Palladium	Stocks Other[4]	Stocks Total	Imports for Consumption Refined	Imports for Consumption Total	Exports Refined	Exports Total	Apparent Consumption
1985	92	W	W	40,336	40,563	17,783	14,152	3,171	35,106	106,928	124,090	16,369	27,640	104,511
1986	90	W	W	46,939	47,074	20,426	16,958	2,803	40,187	115,925	139,256	11,880	23,349	109,904
1987	91	780	2,330	50,053	50,243	19,004	17,356	2,052	38,412	98,878	118,397	13,423	22,031	95,458
1988	91	1,240	3,730	51,190	51,488	18,438	14,837	2,239	35,514	110,947	124,324	20,301	28,787	103,302
1989	90	1,430	4,850	50,186	50,525	14,791	15,182	2,570	32,543	111,107	113,278	23,082	38,301	101,209
1990	88	1,810	5,930	71,248	71,312	13,421	14,425	2,478	30,324	120,631	125,354	20,148	55,044	117,043
1991	90	1,730	6,050	72,349	72,564	10,349	12,263	1,701	24,313	121,741	125,661	27,401	39,624	111,798
1992	87	1,840	6,470	64,309	64,309	14,187	10,641	2,118	26,946	129,419	132,006	31,060	57,830	109,469
1993[1]	89	1,800	6,500	65,792	65,792	10,263	8,324	176	18,763	148,790	153,165	43,798	78,486	123,273
1994[2]	91	2,000	6,400	63,000	63,000	10,304	9,345	123	19,772	167,681	170,907	46,259	88,561	127,000

[1] Preliminary. [2] Estimate. [3] Includes platinum, palladium, iridium, osmium, rhodium, and ruthenium. [4] Includes iridium, osmium, rhodium, and ruthenium. W = Withheld proprietary data. *Source: U.S. Bureau of Mines*

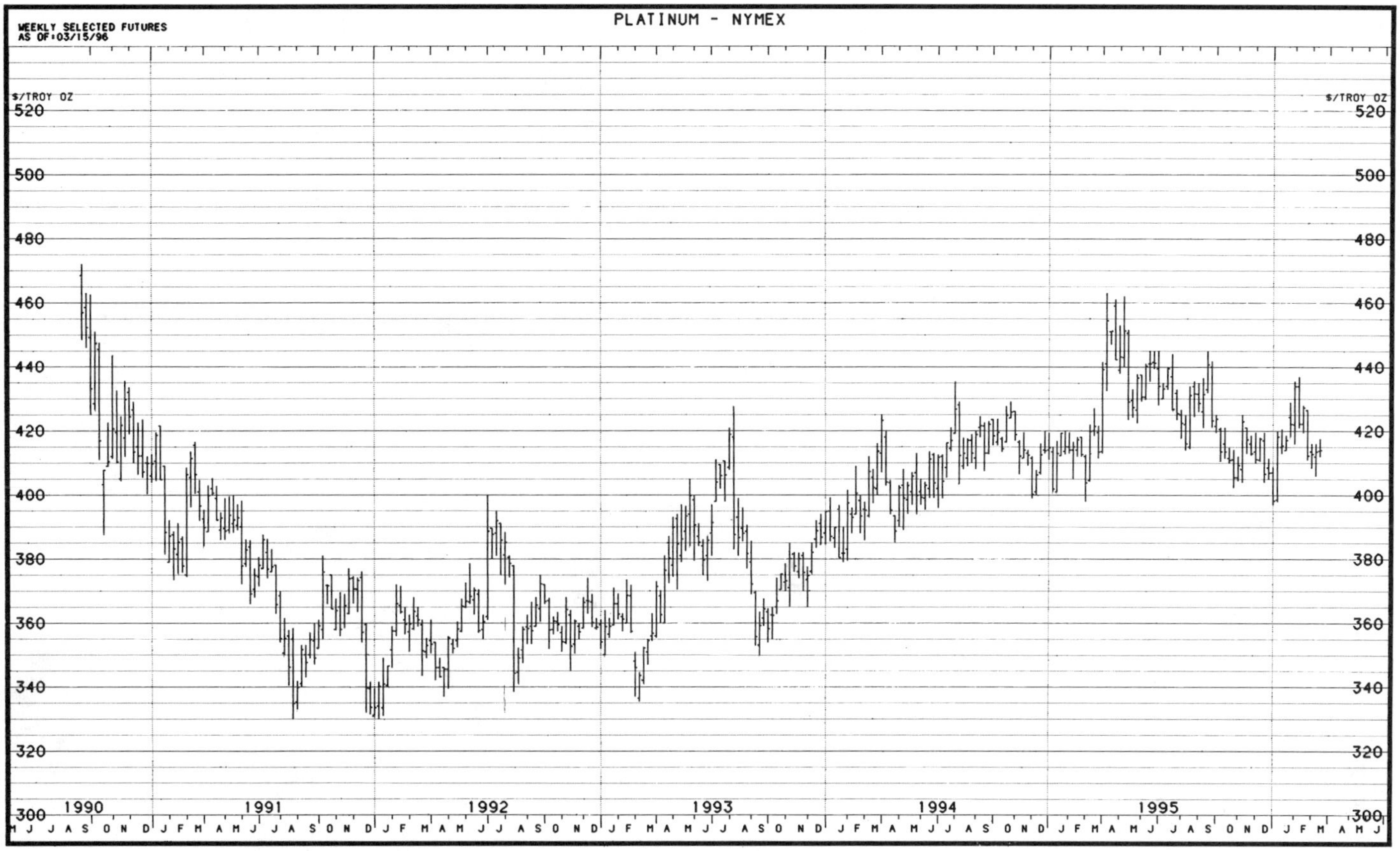

Average Merchant's Price of Platinum in the U.S. In Dollars Per Troy Ounce

Year	Jan	Feb	Mar	Apr	May	Jun	Jul	Aug	Sep	Oct	Nov	Dec	Average
1975	195.00	180.53	175.00	163.06	160.00	160.00	162.73	175.00	175.00	172.17	160.00	160.00	169.87
1976	160.00	160.00	160.00	160.00	160.00	163.54	175.60	182.50	182.50	182.50	167.00	167.00	168.39
1977	167.00	167.00	167.00	167.00	167.00	167.00	167.00	167.00	167.00	167.00	167.65	174.81	167.71
1978[1]	186.55	206.58	217.07	220.00	220.00	227.73	237.89	241.74	250.23	253.18	284.00	300.00	237.08
1979	303.41	325.00	325.00	327.38	350.00	350.00	350.00	357.83	380.00	380.00	380.00	393.33	351.83
1980	420.00	420.00	420.00	420.00	420.00	420.00	420.00	425.24	475.00	475.00	475.00	475.00	436.77
1981	475.00	475.00	475.00	475.00	475.00	475.00	475.00	475.00	475.00	475.00	475.00	475.00	475.00
1982	369.26	361.95	322.46	338.95	314.43	278.26	286.90	290.41	334.98	324.58	346.65	370.95	328.32
1983	441.07	468.34	400.17	410.38	446.69	420.23	431.63	438.30	431.93	399.87	389.33	399.70	423.14
1984	375.11	391.38	398.47	395.17	388.95	386.31	345.55	336.03	327.36	324.65	328.45	309.11	358.83
1985	275.76	274.37	255.36	287.23	273.24	267.94	269.52	303.91	304.59	321.73	334.53	327.75	291.33
1986	362.77	377.74	412.48	422.93	415.52	431.23	436.50	526.52	597.92	578.50	524.65	480.14	463.91
1987	520.08	518.30	533.27	587.38	607.08	569.14	573.57	610.12	590.55	568.65	500.02	479.29	554.79
1988	494.14	458.64	496.49	527.73	548.91	581.32	548.51	532.80	513.16	527.35	577.74	567.36	531.18
1989	528.69	532.66	538.26	539.96	517.20	498.81	503.16	485.20	479.29	485.48	508.73	507.24	510.39
1990	949.93	517.34	500.32	478.33	485.89	486.60	476.93	492.02	463.87	423.78	424.12	446.94	474.26
1991	408.92	385.53	403.12	398.16	373.06	374.25	375.38	351.68	348.01	362.52	364.01	356.65	375.11
1992	341.88	362.97	356.84	347.73	354.75	368.17	378.89	360.20	361.60	359.75	355.81	361.98	359.21
1993	359.99	361.53	349.31	365.98	385.50	384.54	401.10	394.69	365.29	369.19	376.98	383.85	374.75
1994	390.30	393.95	398.29	400.38	395.41	401.42	408.25	411.91	415.93	421.11	415.73	408.83	405.13

[1] Prior to 1978 prices are for producer prices. *Source: American Metal Market*

PLATINUM-GROUP METALS

Platinum–Group Metals Sold to Consuming Industries in the United States In Kilograms

Year	Automotive		Chemical		Electrical		Dental & Medical		Jewelry & Decorative		Petroleum		All Platinum–Group Metals			
	Platinum	Other[3]	Platinum	Other[3]	Platinum	Other[3]	Platinum	Other[3]	Platinum	Other[3]	Platinum	Other[3]	Platinum	Palladium	Other[3]	Total
1985	19,251	7,785	2,651	2,718	3,603	11,169	762	10,576	499	397	895	2,518	31,901	32,976	5,765	70,642
1986	19,438	7,234	2,416	2,346	3,219	11,082	645	8,363	352	304	951	1,896	30,509	27,677	6,511	64,698
1987	18,816	6,935	1,919	1,283	1,821	10,879	479	10,526	177	478	543	1,286	25,469	30,953	3,851	60,273
1988	19,346	7,186	3,184	4,499	3,494	14,429	581	6,650	385	407	1,027	1,560	31,125	34,241	5,632	70,998
1989	18,774	6,869	2,424	2,233	3,894	19,514	632	8,601	418	396	2,859	2,570	33,698	39,273	5,512	78,483
1990	20,967	5,990	2,080	2,574	3,907	19,791	687	6,287	431	387	3,274	1,488	36,055	35,116	6,316	77,487
1991	18,643	5,338	861	1,749	3,910	14,428	598	4,918	626	500	3,163	181	31,112	25,747	5,738	62,597
1992	20,290	5,789	1,716	2,297	2,922	15,738	640	5,386	881	1,417	1,036	790	31,095	28,935	6,816	66,846
1993[1]	19,444	10,123	2,364	3,121	2,125	12,699	687	5,562	1,024	1,422	1,204	709	29,879	26,840	8,544	65,063
1994[2]	21,754	11,412	3,104	1,889	2,790	7,961	902	5,092	1,345	824	1,581	422	34,044	21,509	7,387	62,940

[1] Preliminary. [2] Estimate. [3] Includes palladium, iridium, osmium, rhodium, and ruthenium. *Source: U.S. Bureau of Mines*

Average Open Interest of Platinum Futures in New York In Contracts

Year	Jan.	Feb.	Mar.	Apr.	May	June	July	Aug.	Sept.	Oct.	Nov.	Dec.
1984	12,460	12,838	14,246	14,544	15,827	15,911	15,768	15,743	16,556	15,305	14,885	15,651
1985	15,107	14,770	14,307	12,934	11,787	11,844	11,585	14,225	15,229	12,615	14,618	16,534
1986	17,496	18,587	20,993	17,591	16,007	18,867	17,473	20,989	27,426	19,825	20,256	17,485
1987	16,641	16,544	18,629	20,777	19,675	17,977	17,290	22,890	24,421	22,631	20,458	19,756
1988	17,133	18,080	16,737	16,718	18,643	22,735	19,668	17,671	19,936	19,097	22,022	24,384
1989	19,334	18,648	19,736	19,895	19,661	20,597	17,310	19,121	19,165	16,981	19,934	20,392
1990	19,510	17,970	15,888	15,915	16,688	15,652	15,496	17,254	18,494	17,472	16,313	16,994
1991	15,497	16,043	16,083	14,334	15,779	18,273	17,503	19,214	18,611	15,933	13,579	14,533
1992	15,464	14,231	14,272	14,130	15,353	19,070	20,402	18,444	17,574	14,079	13,532	14,282
1993	11,889	14,315	12,990	15,490	19,641	17,919	20,931	18,892	16,883	15,690	16,658	19,633
1994	18,779	19,655	21,673	22,834	21,880	22,835	24,804	25,049	24,245	24,159	26,287	26,661
1995	23,285	23,058	23,470	23,657	20,984	21,533	20,801	25,288	23,489	24,498	22,137	21,534

Source: New York Mercantile Exchange

Volume of Trading of Platinum Futures in New York In Thousands of Contracts

Year	Jan.	Feb.	Mar.	Apr.	May	June	July	Aug.	Sept.	Oct.	Nov.	Dec.	Total
1984	44.7	43.7	68.9	54.5	44.9	53.8	55.2	38.4	52.2	35.9	38.3	40.7	571.1
1985	41.0	26.2	53.5	48.8	43.1	42.2	40.3	98.1	82.7	68.6	64.8	84.0	693.3
1986	101.3	114.7	139.8	100.3	77.0	122.2	75.4	189.8	289.4	164.8	136.6	113.3	1,624.6
1987	117.2	85.7	134.1	149.3	110.8	116.5	87.1	133.2	122.7	127.2	88.6	89.2	1,361.5
1988	82.8	77.6	119.2	74.3	123.3	182.2	111.5	105.8	125.1	114.6	164.8	179.2	1,460.5
1989	113.6	96.6	148.5	107.3	111.6	126.9	69.8	86.8	85.1	56.4	99.8	88.1	1,190.5
1990	85.6	80.9	81.3	55.3	65.2	70.1	52.7	73.8	77.2	68.0	50.1	56.8	817.1
1991	50.8	42.3	72.7	43.0	51.1	55.7	40.6	45.7	55.8	42.9	41.9	60.3	598.6
1992	47.9	38.3	54.1	29.3	37.7	82.0	61.0	50.6	51.8	28.5	42.3	53.8	577.3
1993	29.4	55.6	61.4	50.6	65.8	72.5	59.8	56.4	58.6	37.0	44.0	60.3	651.2
1994	18.8	19.7	21.7	22.8	21.9	22.8	24.8	25.0	24.2	24.2	26.3	81.6	895.8
1995	61.4	38.6	131.3	69.9	60.4	75.4	53.4	62.5	98.8	55.9	56.3	82.8	846.7

Source: New York Mercantile Exchange

Average Open Interest of Palladium Futures in New York In Contracts

Year	Jan.	Feb.	Mar.	Apr.	May	June	July	Aug.	Sept.	Oct.	Nov.	Dec.
1988	6,094	6,434	6,194	6,269	6,419	7,038	7,330	7,160	6,360	6,263	6,188	6,289
1989	6,460	6,758	6,636	9,082	9,173	9,116	8,307	7,616	7,105	6,847	7,123	6,660
1990	6,296	6,350	5,276	5,359	5,476	5,361	5,493	5,717	5,165	5,100	5,316	4,565
1991	4,658	4,559	4,319	4,686	4,559	4,302	4,454	4,429	4,429	4,384	4,337	4,042
1992	3,984	4,071	4,101	4,206	4,137	3,852	3,762	3,362	3,041	2,982	2,901	3,246
1993	3,718	4,213	4,365	4,897	5,312	4,513	4,655	5,080	4,360	4,495	4,472	4,484
1994	4,626	4,995	4,672	4,303	5,116	4,530	5,807	6,851	6,625	6,511	7,726	6,917
1995	7,484	7,579	7,102	7,231	6,519	6,413	6,739	6,852	5,950	6,120	6,486	6,090

Source: New York Mercantile Exchange

Volume of Trading of Palladium Futures in New York In Contracts

Year	Jan.	Feb.	Mar.	Apr.	May	June	July	Aug.	Sept.	Oct.	Nov.	Dec.	Total
1987	9,870	14,469	9,849	19,005	22,323	7,728	9,660	18,270	6,741	17,514	17,724	9,303	162,456
1988	12,348	16,065	8,673	11,970	15,435	15,456	15,393	11,781	6,363	7,077	14,973	11,739	147,273
1989	12,852	16,296	12,978	48,699	28,266	13,062	15,477	15,351	11,235	8,862	17,745	10,836	211,659
1990	4,893	19,026	6,930	5,355	13,104	5,670	4,452	11,130	5,407	7,150	9,592	3,178	95,887
1991	5,017	10,542	5,380	7,245	10,521	4,447	5,230	10,114	2,914	5,668	8,150	2,971	78,199
1992	7,217	7,323	3,429	2,833	8,011	2,881	4,965	6,752	5,066	5,359	6,461	7,912	68,209
1993	7,708	14,461	8,057	10,034	12,190	7,368	7,043	13,356	6,977	9,220	12,477	4,790	113,681
1994	8,250	14,953	6,067	6,676	15,481	6,514	9,024	21,741	15,690	9,603	21,384	8,390	143,773
1995	10,684	17,092	21,001	12,775	17,413	9,615	11,816	18,948	9,754	9,320	16,662	11,633	166,713

Source: New York Mercantile Exchange

Average Dealer[1] Price of Palladium in the United States In Dollars Per Troy Ounce

Year	Jan.	Feb.	Mar.	Apr.	May	June	July	Aug.	Sept.	Oct.	Nov.	Dec.	Average
1986	101.83	103.18	110.62	110.64	109.23	110.40	112.00	127.05	142.30	136.68	125.36	118.15	117.29
1987	124.13	121.32	122.74	136.58	146.55	140.00	141.34	143.32	137.93	132.72	113.42	121.99	131.84
1988	125.26	120.40	122.67	123.62	124.06	128.77	126.25	123.84	121.04	122.59	126.80	133.30	124.89
1989	135.74	141.79	152.84	165.46	155.17	152.92	151.36	135.97	137.85	137.84	139.35	139.75	145.50
1990	135.80	136.63	131.25	128.18	120.08	117.40	116.60	116.17	106.62	96.12	94.84	90.93	115.89
1991	86.61	85.11	86.44	95.25	96.61	97.39	95.57	84.55	82.49	81.87	85.96	82.72	88.38
1992	82.96	86.04	84.50	83.71	82.90	80.98	86.49	86.04	90.67	95.07	95.01	104.88	88.27
1993	110.39	112.57	106.22	113.79	119.94	125.36	139.74	137.37	121.95	130.04	123.62	125.60	122.22
1994	124.40	130.92	132.43	133.22	135.76	137.03	145.28	151.83	152.99	154.90	158.10	153.80	142.56
1995[2]	157.86	158.53	164.65	172.05	163.09								

[1] Based on wholesale quantities, prompt delivery. [2] Estimate. *Sources: American Metal Market; U.S. Bureau of Mines*

Pork Bellies

Pork bellies, the source of bacon, are obtained from the underside of a hog. A hog has two bellies, generally weighing about 8-18 pounds, depending on the hog's commercial slaughter weight. Slaughter weights now generally average 250 pounds per head, equal to a dressed weight of about 185 pounds. Bellies account for about 12 percent of a hog's live weight, but represent a somewhat larger percentage of the total cutout value of the realized pork products. Bellies deliverable against futures generally weigh around 12-14 pounds.

Definitive seasonal trends for pork bellies exist. Bellies are storable and the movement into cold storage builds early in the calendar year and peaks about mid-year. Net withdrawals from storage then carry stocks to a low around October. Then the cycle begins anew. Retail bacon demand also follows a well established pattern. Demand is strongest in the summer when consumer preference shifts to lighter foods, and then tapers off to a low during the winter.

Pricewise, a weak seasonality is evident if the swings in futures values serve as a clue. Demand patterns would suggest the highest prices in the summer and the lowest in the winter. Just the opposite is not unusual. Such contra-seasonal price moves can be partially attributed to supply logistics; notably, the availability of storage stocks deliverable against futures at exchange approved warehouses. When it happens, underlying demand factors for bacon are on the backburner as a market making variable. The fact that there are no futures contracts between August and the following February adds to the price distortion and one should be aware of the gap when analyzing pork belly futures continuation charts.

Belly prices (cash and futures) are sensitive to the inventory in cold storage during the year and to the weekly net movement in and out of storage. Storage movements can afford a clue to demand although a better measure is the weekly quantity of bellies being sliced into bacon.

Belly prices began an advance in mid-1995 that ended in October, but in the interim carried prices to a five year high. A sharp drawdown in freezer stocks during August left September 1, 1995, inventories at the lowest level for the date since 1982. Strong commercial use was apparently a primary factor for the large disappearance. Prices then retreated about ten percent from their high, partly in anticipation of a seasonal gain in hog slaughter which was expected to take some of the pressure off the tightness in nearterm supplies. Retail bacon prices held firm most of 1995, averaging around $1.90/pound, lower than the 1994 average, but the year's monthly high topped the 1994 high. Still, retail prices are likely to have difficulty matching the levels of the early 1990's when retial prices averaged near $2.20/lb. Bacon is not a food necessity and consumer demand for the product is sensitive to trends in disposable income and the state of the economy. The slackening economy in 1995 likely held retail prices in check as may occur in 1996. Also, changes in consumer food preferences persist with the emphasis away from fatty foods and/or those requiring chemicals in their processing, as bacon does.

Futures Markets

Pork belly futures and options are traded on the Chicago Mercantile Exchange (CME).

Average Bureau of Labor Statistics Retail Price of Bacon, Sliced In Dollars Per Pound

Year	Jan.	Feb.	Mar.	Apr.	May	June	July	Aug.	Sept.	Oct.	Nov.	Dec.	Average
1987	2.12	2.09	2.10	2.08	2.11	2.13	2.23	2.28	2.28	2.19	2.07	2.02	2.14
1988	1.95	1.94	1.92	1.91	1.90	1.90	1.91	1.88	1.84	1.86	1.80	1.79	1.88
1989	1.80	1.80	1.79	1.75	1.68	1.69	1.71	1.72	1.72	1.77	1.82	1.96	1.77
1990	1.97	2.01	1.99	1.98	2.04	2.15	2.21	2.24	2.18	2.21	2.24	2.28	2.13
1991	2.26	2.30	2.32	2.27	2.31	2.31	2.31	2.22	2.16	2.12	2.07	1.99	2.22
1992	1.96	1.95	1.92	1.92	1.90	1.93	1.95	1.94	1.93	1.89	1.85	1.86	1.92
1993	1.87	1.84	1.80	1.89	1.91	1.95	2.00	1.95	1.98	1.99	2.01	2.02	1.93
1994	2.04	2.02	2.02	2.06	1.99	1.99	2.00	1.99	1.97	1.97	1.92	1.89	1.99
1995[1]	1.93	1.93	1.91	1.89	1.92	1.90	1.91	1.97	2.04	2.12	2.16	2.12	1.98

[1] Preliminary. *Source: Economic Research Service, U.S. Department of Agriculture*

Year	Jan.	Feb.	Mar.	Apr.	May	June	July	Aug.	Sept.	Oct.	Nov.	Dec.
1984	78,648	71,568	78,169	95,009	112,205	127,527	115,034	85,630	43,626	22,321	24,048	38,333
1985	57,361	53,623	51,633	68,315	83,836	96,040	88,367	61,397	35,764	20,158	29,787	47,427
1986	51,314	47,633	51,218	62,508	68,325	65,895	61,547	40,333	20,797	12,941	17,022	24,528
1987	37,771	34,900	34,717	41,821	50,482	58,245	47,367	28,649	18,938	12,620	14,850	35,487
1988	62,089	62,996	67,035	90,347	102,543	111,484	103,401	73,747	42,623	31,054	49,550	93,254
1989	113,137	116,191	121,556	127,617	143,751	142,340	126,676	94,107	49,083	32,031	39,358	67,489
1990	85,026	77,255	85,789	96,945	102,899	105,482	87,983	55,859	23,352	4,785	5,506	24,044
1991	46,998	48,750	54,529	68,094	80,382	79,936	72,032	45,915	29,832	15,944	25,558	48,311
1992	71,318	76,894	75,925	85,095	96,653	92,677	78,646	54,544	26,854	21,973	26,044	49,970
1993	70,576	65,280	65,919	66,064	79,430	77,903	70,251	46,630	20,811	10,964	14,345	33,563
1994	53,168	55,999	54,921	63,099	72,230	79,018	73,583	57,747	30,636	18,260	22,656	40,725
1995[1]	61,073	62,819	64,229	78,976	78,539	77,919	67,607	47,055	17,435	6,255	13,478	37,092

[1] Preliminary. *Source: National Agricultural Statistics Service, U.S. Department of Agriculture*

Weekly Pork Belly Storage Movement

1994 Week Ending		In	Out	On Hand	Net Move-ment	1995 Week Ending		In	Out	On Hand	Net Move-ment
		Stocks[1] in Thousands of Pounds						Stocks[1] in Thousands of Pounds			
Jan.	1	3,017	78	43,348	+2,939	Jan.	7	748	287	44,157	+461
	8	1,522	153	44,717	+1,369		13	294	790	43,661	-496
	15	1,250	142	45,825	+1,108		21	939	953	43,647	-14
	22	670	124	46,370	+546		28	289	570	43,366	-281
	29	274	369	46,276	-95	Feb.	4	627	846	43,147	-219
Feb.	5	103	859	45,520	-756		11	579	613	43,113	-34
	12	626	576	45,570	+50		18	1,300	1,047	43,366	+253
	19	394	135	45,829	+259		25	735	732	43,369	+3
	26	1,077	39	46,867	+1,038	Mar.	4	1,511	933	43,947	+578
Mar.	5	833	615	47,085	+218		11	2,698	242	46,403	+2,456
	12	2,004	577	48,512	+1,427		18	2,329	479	48,253	+1,850
	19	2,369	495	50,386	+1,874		25	2,380	399	50,234	+1,981
	26	1,519	276	51,629	+1,243	Apr.	1	2,207	132	52,309	+2,075
Apr.	2	1,794	198	53,225	+1,596		8	1,137	287	53,159	+850
	9	2,410	140	55,495	+2,270		15	779	210	53,728	+569
	16	1,467	227	56,735	+1,240		22	1,331	272	54,787	+1,059
	23	2,256	553	58,438	+1,703		29	660	384	55,063	+276
	30	2,322	456	60,304	+1,866	May	6	922	262	55,723	+660
May	7	1,055	735	60,624	+320		13	1,411	60	57,074	+1,351
	14	1,138	1,364	60,398	-221		20	1,366	113	58,326	+1,253
	21	1,104	1,063	60,439	+41		27	870	384	58,812	+486
	28	798	366	60,891	+432	June	3	247	528	58,531	-281
June	4	473	741	60,603	-268		10	18	623	57,926	-605
	11	66	1,020	59,649	-954		17	199	1,219	56,906	-1,020
	18	369	1,742	58,276	-1,373		24	16	3,034	53,888	-3,018
	25	24	1,457	56,843	-1,433	July	1	293	2,788	51,393	-2,495
July	2	71	1,516	55,398	-1,445		8	235	1,192	50,436	-957
	9	231	2,834	52,795	-2,603		15	95	2,966	47,565	-2,871
	16	0	3,878	48,917	-3,878		22	54	5,607	42,012	-5,553
	23	77	3,554	45,440	-3,477		29	26	5,122	36,916	-5,096
	30	67	3,529	41,978	-3,462	Aug.	5	297	4,688	32,525	-4,391
Aug.	6	10	4,178	37,810	-4,168		12	382	4,021	28,913	-3,639
	13	41	4,915	32,936	-4,874		19	188	5,199	23,875	-5,011
	20	2	4,188	28,750	-4,186		26	0	6,061	17,814	-6,061
	27	8	4,875	23,883	-4,867	Sept.	2	41	4,978	12,836	-4,978
Sept.	3	161	4,391	19,653	-4,230		9	19	3,202	9,675	-3,161
	10	699	2,920	17,432	-2,221		16	43	3,381	6,313	-3,362
	17	1,621	2,972	16,081	-1,351		23	304	2,249	4,107	-2,206
	24	276	2,075	14,282	-1,799		30	80	1,249	3,162	-945
Oct.	1	121	2,517	11,886	-2,396	Oct.	7	86	121	3,121	-41
	8	255	1,956	10,185	-1,701		15	149	214	2,993	-128
	15	897	1,023	10,059	-126		21	2,850	776	2,366	-627
	22	2,119	266	11,912	+1,853		28	3,748	203	5,013	+2,647
	29	1,669	110	13,471	+1,559	Nov.	4	3,837	39	8,804	+3,791
Nov.	5	2,310	659	15,122	+1,651		11	4,404	40	12,525	+3,721
	12	3,455	529	18,048	+2,926		18	4,503	207	17,010	+4,191
	19	4,633	698	21,983	+3,935		25	4,028	43	21,219	+4,503
	26	5,028	122	26,889	+4,906	Dec.	2	3,024	123	25,081	+3,862
Dec.	3	4,043	287	30,645	+3,756		9	1,478	368	27,737	+2,656
	10	4,516	447	34,714	+4,069		16	1,772	128	29,101	+1,364
	17	4,059	488	38,285	+3,571		23	1,988	41	30,938	+1,837
	24	3,333	162	41,456	+3,171		30	42	0	32,848	+1,910
	31	2,605	365	43,696	+2,240						

[1] 57 Chicago and Outside Combined Chicago Mercantile Exchange approved warehouses. *Source: Chicago Mercantile Exchange*

PORK BELLIES

Average Open Interest of Pork Bellies Futures at Chicago   In Contracts

Year	Jan.	Feb.	Mar.	Apr.	May	June	July	Aug.	Sept.	Oct.	Nov.	Dec.
1984	19,762	16,732	16,932	18,932	17,465	17,397	13,661	7,781	7,845	9,297	11,583	12,769
1985	13,804	14,545	13,138	12,356	11,526	11,315	9,770	6,878	6,710	7,507	8,481	9,018
1986	8,313	7,969	7,357	8,635	9,509	10,781	9,135	7,462	8,515	8,287	10,412	11,440
1987	11,617	10,159	10,936	13,586	14,277	12,863	11,291	8,940	8,301	9,550	9,924	11,846
1988	11,250	10,942	13,421	16,229	17,887	18,428	15,782	11,874	14,678	15,860	19,292	19,723
1989	20,453	20,444	21,897	22,117	24,931	25,898	20,053	12,724	11,916	12,501	14,802	13,844
1990	12,885	12,114	13,017	15,338	14,513	13,038	11,146	6,104	6,059	7,851	11,419	12,589
1991	11,777	10,187	9,776	11,509	10,436	10,111	7,356	6,176	7,532	10,813	13,173	12,844
1992	12,521	12,195	11,901	12,345	12,497	13,598	12,623	7,149	6,540	7,033	9,251	10,953
1993	10,623	9,244	8,283	8,626	10,096	11,092	9,031	5,427	4,644	7,241	8,701	9,121
1994	11,053	10,426	9,375	9,894	8,092	8,248	7,836	7,841	8,398	10,072	10,141	10,216
1995	10,294	9,080	7,809	7,367	8,017	7,036	5,666	4,271	6,246	7,007	7,103	7,282

Source: Chicago Mercantile Exchange

Volume of Trading of Pork Bellies Futures at Chicago   In Contracts

Year	Jan.	Feb.	Mar.	Apr.	May	June	July	Aug.	Sept.	Oct.	Nov.	Dec.	Total
1984	221,795	182,080	186,817	159,774	207,820	173,066	187,619	119,469	77,028	121,926	148,940	121,711	1,908,045
1985	173,488	137,334	133,509	148,489	149,809	135,139	136,026	89,784	77,326	99,291	85,377	91,634	1,457,386
1986	92,033	81,768	75,830	96,642	106,958	100,331	109,981	78,967	91,470	87,712	91,779	86,868	1,100,339
1987	104,134	95,108	92,707	118,107	112,112	120,598	118,996	89,564	60,670	66,423	53,903	64,688	1,097,010
1988	70,150	76,741	85,947	99,754	116,780	179,505	112,356	90,371	79,667	94,646	84,236	96,446	1,186,599
1989	107,577	89,922	84,768	90,353	145,975	152,207	119,733	91,200	75,155	106,389	141,983	105,714	1,310,976
1990	109,036	100,813	129,476	133,946	165,880	143,663	122,187	74,653	53,428	76,549	112,752	80,746	1,303,129
1991	106,078	89,975	88,056	111,195	119,773	96,273	74,255	59,176	65,604	80,707	63,331	50,773	1,005,196
1992	80,697	79,700	67,470	57,565	73,137	73,081	78,588	54,663	39,839	64,248	60,724	54,440	784,152
1993	77,380	62,871	63,988	62,403	62,400	70,124	65,496	42,613	37,992	47,780	60,163	49,099	698,799
1994	60,316	67,250	58,183	53,839	56,575	58,424	50,450	47,626	38,375	45,525	49,280	47,803	633,646
1995	62,918	54,312	59,324	43,501	49,453	53,571	45,869	36,623	31,112	35,444	47,061	42,631	561,913

Source: Chicago Mercantile Exchange

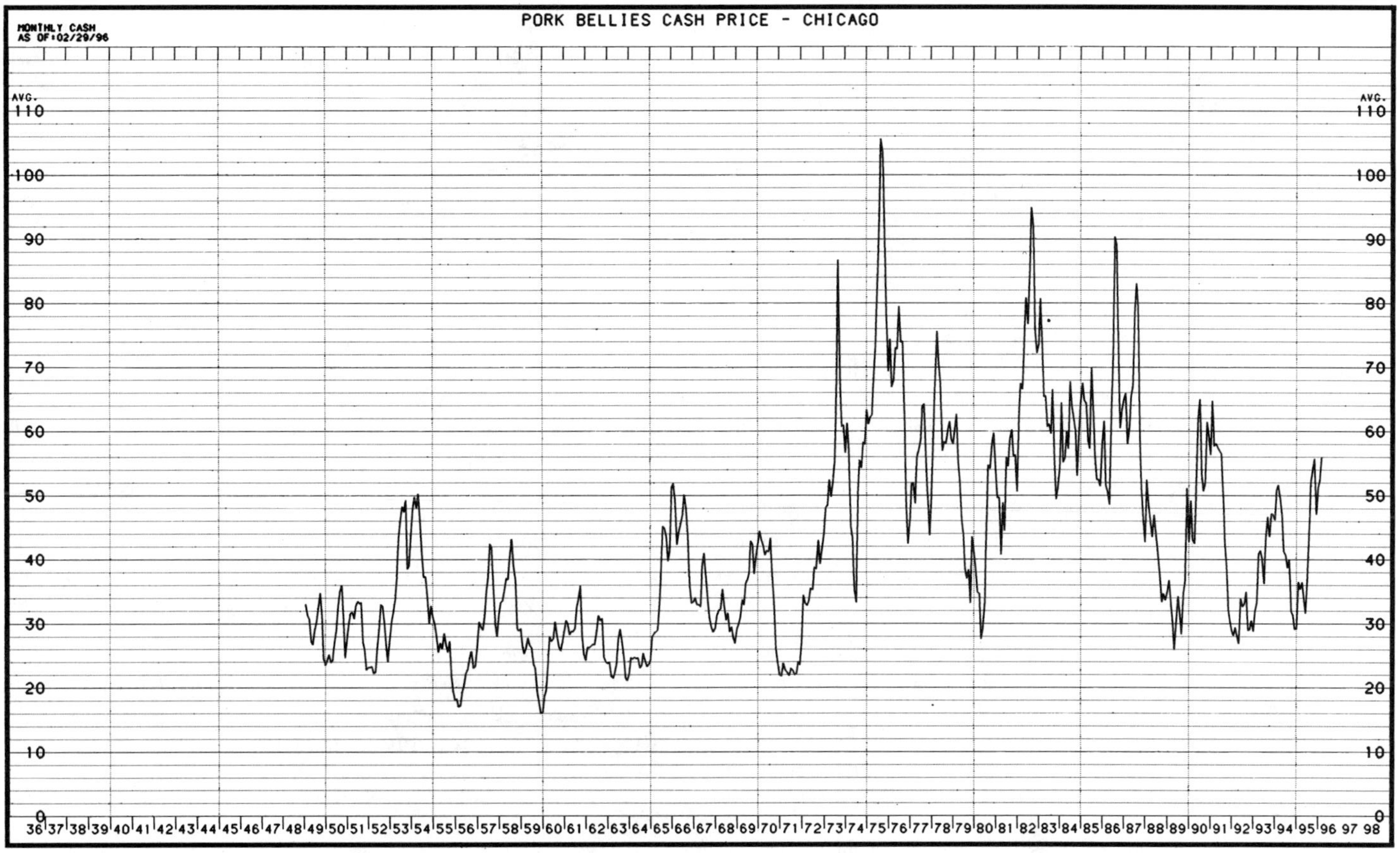

Average Price of Pork Bellies (12-14 Pounds) Midwest In Cents Per Pound

Year	Jan.	Feb.	Mar.	Apr.	May	June	July	Aug.	Sept.	Oct.	Nov.	Dec.	Average
1982	62.22	67.84	66.67	74.38	80.82	76.72	84.50	93.50	90.70	75.20	71.86	74.02	76.54
1983	80.91	73.88	65.11	64.71	60.81	60.19	59.06	65.72	55.25	49.10	50.96	54.59	61.69
1984	65.03	54.68	56.04	59.53	57.38	67.12	64.75	62.17	58.00	52.80	61.88	64.31	60.31
1985	67.50	64.14	64.25	58.83	58.64	70.15	62.53	54.17	51.40	52.09	51.73	58.63	59.51
1986	61.27	51.50	50.80	49.45	61.82	71.83	90.08	89.10	75.64	60.32	63.29	64.72	65.82
1987	66.32	57.81	60.02	65.79	67.21	78.44	83.62	80.46	59.74	49.39	45.87	42.60	63.11
1988	51.82	48.40	45.32	43.13	46.09	45.51	40.84	37.46	33.05	34.97	33.64	34.82	41.25
1989	36.91	31.41	30.19	25.49	29.11	32.90	31.52	28.82	34.23	36.88	49.96	42.23	34.14
1990	48.65	42.53	42.60	52.60	61.48	65.15	53.18	51.08	51.31	59.83	60.57	56.58	53.80
1991	64.11	57.20	58.52	57.25	57.50	56.48	50.40	42.01	38.97	32.26	30.04	28.79	47.79
1992	28.05	29.44	28.01	26.93	34.09	32.78	32.77	35.13	29.09	29.13	30.48	28.80	30.39
1993	31.97	33.22	41.28	41.19	39.86	36.24	44.51	46.68	43.82	47.25	47.21	46.21	41.62
1994	50.63	51.66	49.68	46.84	41.40	40.39	38.64	39.60	31.50	31.33	29.09	29.29	40.00
1995[1]	36.03	35.80	36.30	33.83	31.70	37.94	43.10	52.42	54.43	56.20	47.28	51.45	43.04

[1] Preliminary. *Source: Economic Research Service, U.S. Department of Agriculture*

Potatoes

U.S. annual potato production has trended higher in the 1990s due largely to record high yields. On the consumption side a year to year uptrend remains solidly in place, paced by the allocation of the crop into processed potatoes. The latter topped 261 million cwt. in 1994, up 8 percent and 14 percent from 1993 and 1992, respectively. Tablestock (fresh potatoes) use also gained 11 million cwt. in 1994 to 135 million cwt., following little gain is usage during 1991-93.

Potatoes are grown in all fifty states. However, the crop is divided into four seasonal groups based on the time of harvest. The fall crop accounts for 85-90 percent of total production and is harvested September through November in two dozen states. The winter crop is the smallest and harvested only in Florida and California from January to March. Spring and summer crop production tends to be fairly close in size. The pronounced seasonal disparities reflect major differences in planted acreage and realized yield which is consistently higher in the fall producing states. The marketing season follows the harvest, but the movement of the fall crop can extend into the following July with supplies drawn from storage. The inventoried fall crop, however, can serve as a supply buffer in the event the spring and summer crops are short. Generally about 30 percent of farm marketings occur in September/October and 15 percent in March/April.

A record large 468 million cwt. crop was produced in 1994, up 10 percent from 1993. Harvested acreage increased to 1.38 million acres from 1.32 million in 1993 on which a record high average yield of 338 cwt/acre was realized, 12 cwt above 1993. The 1994 production and yield totals reflected the fourth consecutive year of record highs. The fall crop of 421 million cwt. compares with 386 million in 1993, as yield averaged 354 cwt/acre versus 341 cwt., respectively. Idaho was the largest producer at 139 million cwt. with Washington a distant second at 89 million cwt. Washington's average yield of 585 cwt./acre was the nation's highest while Idaho's yield averaged 340 cwt./acre. However, within Idaho, sharp variations in yield occur with counties in the southern part of the state realizing higher yields. The value of the 1994 crop was estimated at $2.6 billion, down 2 percent from 1993, but 11 percent above 1992. The average price received by farmers in 1994 was $5.58 per cwt. versus $6.17 from the 1993 crop.

Almost 60 percent of U.S. production is processed, either into frozen products or as a direct consumer food such as chips. Frozen french fries account for most of all frozen use—137 million cwt in 1994. Chips and shoestrings generally account for 20 percent of total processing use; in 1994 there were 132 chip producing plants in the U.S. versus 141 in 1993. Per capita use of potatoes, the largest U.S. vegetable crop, totals 135 pounds; tablestock use accounts for nearly 50 pounds and processed potatoes the balance.

Foreign trade in U.S. potatoes is small. The U.S. is a net exporter. Japan is the largest importer of U.S. processed potatoes, primarily taking french fries. Canada exports fresh potatoes to the U.S. which are used mostly for seed.

Retail fresh potato prices have averaged over $0.30 a pound since 1990, versus an average in the mid $0.20's in the 1980s. Frozen potato prices have also trended higher, averaging close to $0.90 per pound since 1992.

Futures Markets

Potato futures are traded on the Marche a Terme International de France (MATIF) and the London Commodity Exchange (LCE). Options trade on the LCE.

Salient Statistics of Potatoes in the United States

Crop Year	Acreage Planted (1,000 Acres)	Acreage Harvested (1,000 Acres)	Yield Per Harvested Acre Cwt.	Total Production (In Thousands of Cwt.)	Farm Disposition: Used Where Grown: Seed & Feed (In Thousands of Cwt.)	Farm Disposition: Used Where Grown: Shrinkage & Loss (In Thousands of Cwt.)	Farm Disposition: Sold[2] (In Thousands of Cwt.)	Farm Price $ Cwt.	Value of Production[3] (Million $)	Value of Sales (Million $)	Stocks on Jan. 1 1,000 Cwt	Foreign Trade[5] (Fresh): Domestic Exports (Millions of Lbs.)	Foreign Trade[5] (Fresh): Imports (Millions of Lbs.)	Consumption[5] Per Capita (in Pounds): Fresh	Consumption[5] Per Capita (in Pounds): Total
1988	1,285	1,259	283	356,438	5,810	25,067	325,561	6.02	2,144	1,958	196,760	421,985	388,394	49.6	122.4
1989	1,305	1,282	289	370,444	5,722	24,974	339,748	7.36	2,717	2,501	177,750	467,836	509,347	50.0	127.1
1990	1,400	1,371	293	402,110	5,949	28,329	367,832	6.08	2,409	2,240	173,550	327,333	482,903	45.8	127.7
1991	1,408	1,375	304	417,622	5,995	32,429	379,198	4.96	2,043	1,880	194,460	341,682	437,349	46.4	130.4
1992	1,339	1,315	323	425,367	5,925	33,807	385,637	5.52	2,336	2,129	211,005	537,939	273,515	48.9	132.4
1993	1,385	1,317	326	428,763	5,931	30,152	392,610	6.17	2,637	2,424	215,990	539,345	541,382	49.9	137.0
1994[1]	1,414	1,383	338	467,924	5,954	37,246	424,724	5.58	2,596	2,371	217,800	655,026	405,899	50.1	140.7
1995[1]	1,388	1,375	323	442,309							237,560			49.2	139.3

[1] Preliminary. [2] For all purposes, including food, seed processing & livestock feed. [3] Farm weight basis, excluding canned and frozen potatoes.
Source: Economic Research Service, U.S. Department of Agriculture

U.S. Cold Storage Stocks of All Frozen Potatoes (First of Month) In Millions of Pounds

Year	Jan.	Feb.	Mar.	Apr.	May	June	July	Aug.	Sept.	Oct.	Nov.	Dec.
1988	882.6	899.0	977.7	965.1	950.7	963.9	1,000.8	882.5	835.0	917.9	1,047.5	1,044.4
1989	988.7	927.4	944.3	947.3	968.7	986.7	961.5	739.9	611.3	734.2	878.7	938.0
1990	917.3	932.7	995.6	1,041.2	1,059.0	1,061.3	977.6	769.3	688.1	852.5	995.6	999.5
1991	975.8	993.3	988.9	1,041.5	1,052.3	1,167.2	1,216.5	935.5	880.1	985.5	1,148.0	1,037.2
1992	980.8	996.5	1,036.3	1,082.7	1,077.6	1,137.3	1,131.4	966.4	948.7	949.1	1,067.1	1,038.7
1993	963.2	971.2	1,028.2	1,046.6	912.7	979.5	989.8	932.8	902.8	1,019.5	1,184.7	1,130.7
1994	1,006.4	1,019.9	1,057.1	1,054.4	1,050.5	1,118.9	1,099.9	979.8	1,028.2	1,108.7	1,189.0	1,163.5
1995[1]	1,096.6	1,156.0	1,170.3	1,170.6	1,138.0	1,125.4	1,132.3	992.4	992.6	1,145.3	1,225.6	1,179.2

[1] Preliminary. *Source: Agricultural Statistics Board, U.S. Department of Agriculture*

Potato Crop Production Estimates, Stocks & Disappearance in the U.S. In Millions of Cwt.

	Crop Production Estimates					Total Storage Stocks[2]						Fall Crop				
	Total Crop			Fall Crop			Following Year					1,000 Cwt.				
Year	Oct. 1	Nov. 1	Dec. 1	Oct. 1	Nov. 1	Dec. 1	Jan. 1	Feb. 1	Mar. 1	Apr. 1	May 1	Production	Disappearance (Sold)	Dec. 1 Stocks	Average Price $/Cwt.	Value of Sales $1,000
1982	350.0	350.0	349.3	306.9	308.9	206.5	179.0	150.2	122.5	90.1	57.3	309,134	272,611	206,525	3.92	1,067,863
1983	329.8	329.8	325.7	292.7	292.7	192.5	165.3	138.9	112.7	81.7	50.4	294,679	265,598	192,150	5.46	1,449,394
1984	358.8	358.8	361.6	310.0	346.1	201.4	173.4	144.8	118.4	86.4	52.5	312,662	279,270	201,410	5.03	1,402,425
1985	—	400.4	404.1	—	307.5	235.5	202.8	171.5	138.7	104.5	65.4	343,984	295,032	235,475	3.42	1,007,953
1986	—	352.3	352.3	—	342.7	209.4	180.9	154.5	128.7	95.1	59.8	307,928	284,721	209,435	4.68	1,335,419
1987	—	361.5	—	—	309.9	225.9	196.8	167.3	138.8	105.9	70.0	335,607	309,279	225,890	3.69	1,142,731
1988	—	352.1	—	—	322.7	206.4	177.8	151.1	124.5	92.6	59.4	305,623	284,205	206,420	5.82	1,652,864
1989	—	367.3	—	—	342.5	202.1	173.6	144.3	116.6	84.3	50.7	316,097	295,605	202,050	6.76	1,999,104
1990	—	393.2	—	—	371.7	225.5	194.5	162.9	134.5	101.2	63.0	344,200	320,033	225,500	5.42	1,734,476
1991	—	417.6	—	—	379.5	242.1	211.0	178.5	145.8	108.9	69.1	363,541	334,893	242,070	4.16	1,393,749
1992	—	425.4	—	—	372.4	246.8	216.0	184.6	152.8	115.8	75.0	368,516	341,209	246,820	5.17	1,762,984
1993	—	414.8	—	—	372.4	249.7	217.8	186.1	154.1	116.0	73.9	391,565	351,161	249,710	5.65	1,981,017
1994	—	458.5	—	—	412.4	271.9	237.6	201.9	168.8	128.8	87.5	425,525	379,047	271,890	5.06	1,919,023
1995[1]	—	444.8	—	—	402.4	252.1	219.0	184.8				401,879		252,080		

[1] Preliminary. [2] Held by growers and local dealers in the fall producing areas. *Source: Agricultural Statistics Board, U.S. Department of Agriculture*

United States Potato Production by Seasonal Groups In Thousands of Cwt.

		Spring			Summer			Fall									
Year	Winter	California	Florida	Total	New Mexico	Virgina	Total	Colorado	Idaho	Maine	Minnesota	North Dakota	Oregan	Washington	Wisconsin	Total
1982	2,263	9,563	5,657	20,964	1,274	2,475	22,770	12,825	91,785	27,030	11,520	17,250	21,105	52,800	22,575	309,134
1983	2,193	8,330	5,121	18,338	1,625	1,001	18,701	13,950	85,990	22,560	10,313	20,480	20,710	54,080	18,910	294,679
1984	2,640	11,115	6,740	23,798	2,639	1,540	23,086	17,225	86,500	21,360	13,775	20,615	23,515	56,925	21,350	313,088
1985	2,691	10,588	6,643	22,986	2,860	3,300	27,794	17,920	102,515	28,215	14,145	23,630	26,888	63,630	24,130	353,638
1986	2,991	7,605	7,031	19,865	2,790	1,112	20,689	18,810	90,220	21,930	13,650	21,600	23,172	61,950	20,125	318,198
1987	2,501	7,881	5,567	18,988	3,500	1,974	22,833	19,500	99,710	23,240	16,330	24,050	25,924	66,960	22,100	344,438
1988	2,616	7,546	6,753	20,110	3,060	2,048	20,154	19,040	102,610	22,000	13,860	15,525	20,735	63,250	20,000	313,558
1989	2,764	7,875	6,860	20,852	4,025	1,440	22,155	20,603	102,475	22,000	13,860	15,070	23,308	64,310	23,120	324,673
1990	2,343	8,438	8,714	24,163	3,400	1,980	23,097	22,750	119,070	20,520	14,280	16,675	23,450	67,980	23,075	352,507
1991	2,609	8,284	6,600	20,636	3,450	1,485	22,647	23,800	122,175	18,170	17,160	30,030	22,170	75,435	23,275	371,730
1992	2,998	7,238	7,750	21,535	952	1,980	21,309	22,110	127,050	24,300	16,080	27,690	21,075	69,300	25,160	379,525
1993	2,552	7,508	6,068	19,654	1,290	1,760	14,922	25,270	126,192	19,890	14,780	21,090	23,103	88,500	22,588	391,565
1994	2,372	7,790	8,588	22,646	1,088	1,425	17,381	25,795	138,801	18,375	20,035	28,200	27,514	88,920	25,740	425,525
1995[1]	2,473	6,230	7,830	20,193	1,365	2,040	17,764	23,808	131,274	17,160	20,790	25,410	23,760	80,850	27,135	401,879

[1] Preliminary. *Source: Agricultural Statistics Board, U.S. Department of Agriculture*

Utilization of Potatoes in the United States In Thousands of Cwt.

	Sales											Non-sales			
		For Processing							Other Sales						
Crop Year	Table Stock	Chips, Shoestrings	For Dehydration	Frozen French Fries	Other Frozen Products	Canned Potatoes	Other Canned Products[2]	Starch & Flour	Livestock Feed	Seed	Total Sale	Used on Farms Where Grown	Shrinkage & Loss	Total Non-sales	Total
1982	120,232	40,650	27,720	76,013	17,290	2,743	1,839	4,636	6,308	19,413	316,844	4,707	31,045	38,287	355,131
1983	107,295	43,311	26,754	74,350	19,655	2,137	1,991	3,028	3,734	20,870	303,125	4,605	24,664	30,601	333,726
1984	113,187	42,339	27,845	87,350	20,322	2,589	1,834	3,401	4,662	22,752	326,281	4,407	30,057	35,758	362,039
1985	125,006	42,217	29,958	94,741	17,856	2,971	1,610	3,489	8,098	19,895	345,841	5,060	52,707	60,768	406,609
1986	109,331	45,814	28,445	96,244	15,708	2,790	1,308	2,808	3,992	20,700	327,140	5,070	28,355	34,603	361,743
1987	129,097	40,593	30,823	101,377	18,305	2,958	1,597	2,184	3,808	21,023	351,765	4,521	31,901	37,555	389,320
1988	108,348	44,539	28,786	95,466	17,558	2,941	2,031	1,416	3,330	21,146	325,561	4,827	25,067	30,877	356,438
1989	113,932	43,071	32,187	100,459	19,115	3,138	1,858	898	2,800	22,290	339,748	4,735	24,974	30,696	370,444
1990	119,545	44,489	38,838	108,455	23,915	2,526	2,075	1,699	3,264	23,026	367,832	5,035	28,329	34,278	402,110
1991	126,953	45,850	40,395	111,128	23,097	2,465	1,886	1,739	3,652	22,033	379,198	4,988	32,429	38,424	417,622
1992	127,215	48,455	38,078	112,496	23,016	2,710	2,557	1,610	3,928	23,529	385,637	4,746	33,807	39,730	425,367
1993	123,802	48,987	40,795	121,087	25,190	1,879	2,458	1,691	2,498	24,223	392,610	4,808	30,152	36,083	428,693
1994[1]	134,654	49,549	41,381	136,531	26,362	2,503	2,891	2,176	4,147	24,530	424,724	4,744	37,246	43,200	467,924

[1] Preliminary. [2] Hash, stews and soups. *Source: Agricultural Statistics Board, U.S. Department of Agriculture*

POTATOES

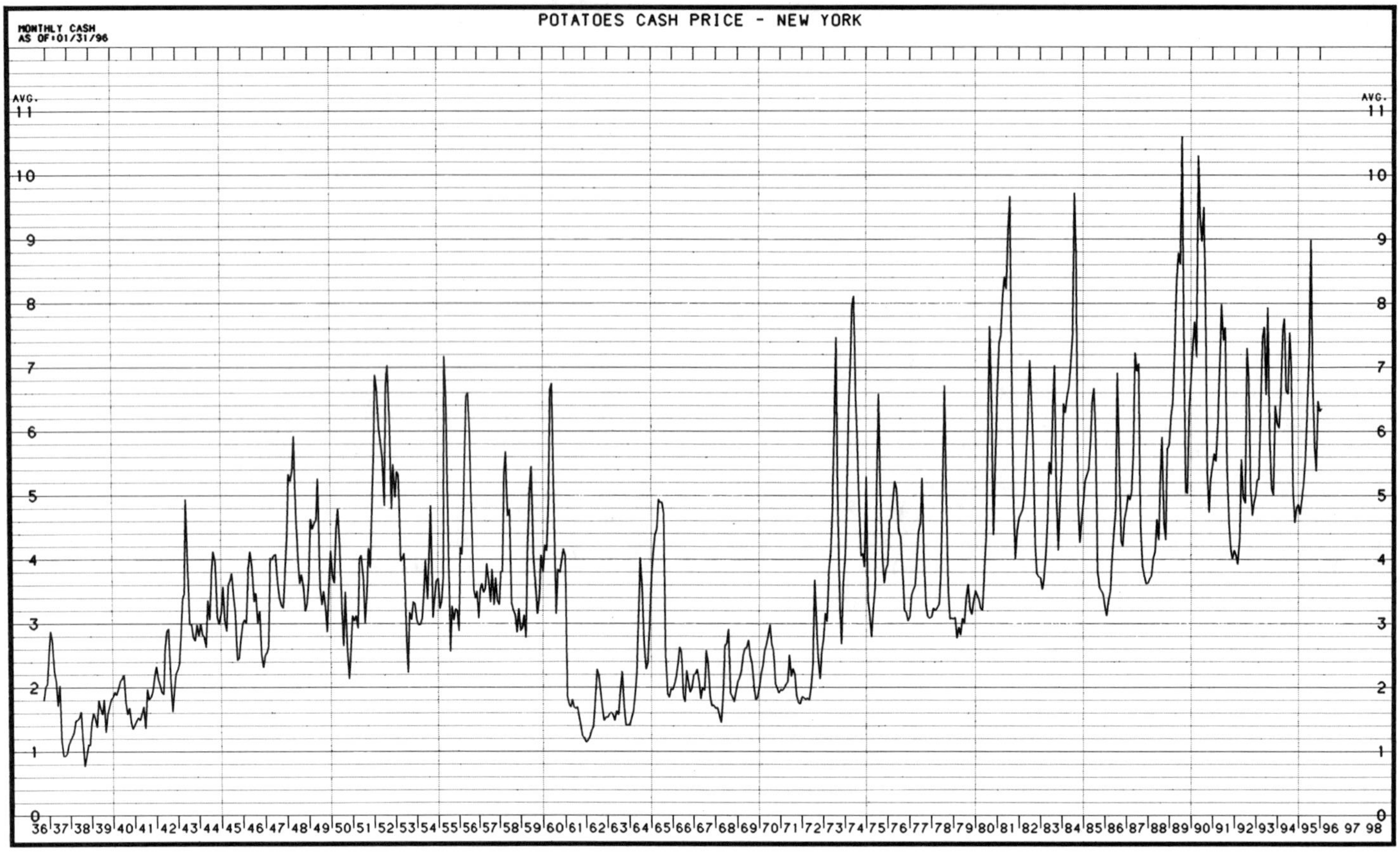

Potatoes U.S. Total Per Capita Utilization in Pounds (Farm Weight)

			Processing				
Year	Total	Fresh	Freezing	Chips & Shoe-string	Dehy-drating	Canning	Total
1986	126.0	48.8	46.3	18.2	10.9	1.8	77.2
1987	126.0	47.9	47.9	17.6	10.8	1.8	78.1
1988	122.4	49.6	43.3	17.2	10.4	1.9	72.8
1989	127.1	50.0	46.8	17.5	10.8	2.0	77.1
1990	127.7	45.8	50.2	17.0	12.8	1.9	81.9
1991	130.4	46.4	51.3	17.3	13.7	1.7	84.0
1992	132.4	48.9	51.0	17.5	13.2	1.8	83.5
1993	136.9	49.7	54.5	17.6	13.4	1.7	87.2
1994	140.8	49.1	59.4	17.1	13.5	1.7	91.7
1995[1]	140.2	49.8	58.4	17.0	13.3	1.7	90.4
1996[2]	140.6	49.8	58.8	16.9	13.4	1.7	90.8

[1] Preliminary. [2] Forecast. *Source: Agricultural Statistics Board, U.S. Department of Agriculture*

U.S. Average Price Received by Farmers for Potatoes In Dollars Per Cwt.

Year	Jan.	Feb.	Mar.	Apr.	May	June	July	Aug.	Sept.	Oct.	Nov.	Dec.	Season Average
1985	5.22	5.31	5.40	5.80	6.44	6.67	5.84	3.83	3.56	3.51	3.46	3.26	3.92
1986	3.12	3.35	3.50	3.99	4.39	4.79	6.91	5.68	4.28	4.20	4.63	4.78	5.03
1987	5.01	4.93	5.05	5.66	7.23	6.94	7.06	4.52	3.89	3.74	3.62	3.63	4.38
1988	3.70	3.74	4.02	4.11	4.62	4.30	5.28	5.91	4.55	4.30	5.72	5.79	6.02
1989	6.24	6.43	7.34	8.33	8.78	8.61	10.60	7.58	5.06	5.03	6.32	6.81	7.36
1990	7.36	7.71	9.17	10.30	9.32	8.96	9.50	8.09	5.36	4.73	5.24	5.46	6.08
1991	5.66	5.53	6.15	7.03	7.98	7.51	7.95	5.39	4.51	4.06	3.99	4.29	4.96
1992	4.07	4.08	4.64	5.16	4.43	4.71	7.00	6.64	4.89	4.55	4.90	5.06	5.52
1993	5.15	5.29	6.06	7.19	7.18	6.45	7.61	6.05	5.12	4.96	6.40	6.12	6.22
1994	6.02	6.43	7.67	6.69	6.59	6.67	7.49	6.99	5.03	4.57	4.80	4.86	5.36
1995[1]	4.88	4.92	5.16	5.55	6.28	7.19	8.98	7.00	5.75	5.38	6.26	6.31	

[1] Preliminary. *Source: Agricultural Statistics Board, U.S. Department of Agriculture*

United States Potatoes Processed[1], Eight States In Thousands of Cwt.

States	Storage Season	to Dec. 1	to Jan. 1	to Feb. 1	to Mar. 1	to Apr. 1	to May 1	Entire Season
Idaho and Oregon-Malheur Co	1986-7	13,200	17,980	21,910	27,070	33,360	38,970	55,470
	1987-8	18,260	23,320	28,680	34,340	40,380	46,440	64,495
	1988-9	18,740	24,270	29,420	34,720	41,360	48,080	64,425
	1989-90	22,200	28,140	34,240	40,270	46,330	51,810	66,010
	1990-1	24,780	31,100	37,550	44,220	51,030	58,660	78,500
	1991-2	22,980	28,910	35,700	42,840	50,260	57,290	78,690
	1992-3	22,180	29,080	35,710	42,800	50,090	57,090	80,570
	1993-4	24,090	30,540	37,150	44,720	53,070	61,440	85,780
	1994-5	26,620	34,230	42,330	49,890	57,990	66,680	90,300
	1995-6	27,310	35,040	43,260				
Maine[2]	1986-7	2,100	2,835	3,345	3,865	4,500	5,195	6,995
	1987-8	1,770	2,440	3,145	3,745	4,410	4,865	6,745
	1988-9	1,685	2,190	2,830	3,455	4,230	4,915	6,915
	1989-90	2,055	2,660	3,510	4,000	4,620	5,210	6,900
	1990-1	2,105	2,690	3,420	3,900	4,460	5,120	6,750
	1991-2	2,015	2,450	3,050	3,350	3,900	4,445	5,210
	1992-3	1,195	1,630	2,205	2,720	3,390	4,020	5,055
	1993-4	1,350	1,720	2,210	2,505	2,890	3,275	4,555
	1994-5	1,505	1,840	2,265	2,540	2,985	3,330	4,770
	1995-6	1,335	1,685	2,200				
Washington and Oregon-Other	1986-7	21,530	25,510	28,530	33,595	39,610	44,865	56,910
	1987-8	22,265	25,950	30,790	35,800	40,900	44,925	58,085
	1988-9	19,200	23,455	27,280	31,960	37,575	41,795	51,555
	1989-90	23,635	28,015	33,170	38,610	44,510	49,595	57,695
	1990-1	24,780	29,830	35,170	39,950	45,600	50,780	61,450
	1991-2	26,345	30,570	35,320	41,320	47,120	52,605	65,210
	1992-3	26,840	31,550	35,950	41,670	46,530	51,630	63,510
	1993-4	28,260	33,350	39,010	45,020	51,290	57,180	70,690
	1994-5	28,670	33,480	39,120	46,070	52,940	59,540	76,780
	1995-6	30,000	35,170	39,460				
Other States[3]	1986-7	6,240	8,405	10,330	12,320	14,690	16,750	20,975
	1987-8	5,750	7,370	9,200	11,250	13,305	15,270	20,155
	1988-9	5,805	7,450	9,040	10,645	12,340	14,075	18,385
	1989-90	6,340	8,010	9,860	11,535	13,240	15,100	20,610
	1990-1	6,585	8,605	10,405	12,425	14,635	17,010	24,005
	1991-2	7,515	9,350	11,580	13,585	15,685	17,935	24,990
	1992-3	7,140	9,220	11,265	13,305	15,550	17,555	25,070
	1993-4	7,605	9,515	11,605	13,720	16,080	18,705	25,690
	1994-5	9,725	13,110	15,630	18,260	21,115	24,060	32,260
	1995-6	12,360	15,330	18,415				
Total	1986-7	43,070	54,730	64,115	76,850	92,160	105,780	140,350
	1987-8	48,045	59,080	71,815	85,135	98,995	111,500	149,480
	1988-9	45,430	57,365	68,570	80,780	95,505	108,865	144,280
	1989-90	54,230	66,825	80,780	94,415	108,700	121,715	151,215
	1990-1	58,250	72,225	86,545	100,495	115,725	131,570	170,705
	1991-2	58,855	71,280	85,650	101,095	116,965	132,275	174,100
	1992-3	57,355	71,480	85,130	100,495	115,560	130,295	174,205
	1993-4	61,305	75,125	89,975	105,965	123,330	140,600	186,715
	1994-5	66,520	82,660	99,345	116,760	135,030	153,610	204,110
	1995-6	71,005	87,225	10,335				

[1] Total quantity received and used for processing regardless of the state in which the potatoes were produced. Excluding quantities used for potato chips in Maine, Michigan, Minnesota, North Dakota or Wisconsin. [2] Includes Maine grown potatoes only. [3] Michigan, Minnesota, North Dakota and Wisconsin.
Source: National Agricultural Statistics Service, U.S. Department of Agriculture

Rapeseed (Canola)

Rapeseed (or Canola) is the world's third largest oilseed crop behind soybeans and cottonseed. World production in 1995/96 of a record high 32.9 million tons was slightly more than 13 percent of total world oilseed production of about 251 million tons. In the mid 1980s the crop averaged about 17 million tons, in the first half of the 1990s production averaged over 25 million tons. In 1995/96, rapeseed production of nearly 33 million tons was less than 2 million tons under cottonseed. In the early 1990s, the difference exceeded 8 million tons. If the trend persists rapeseed will soon be the world's second largest oilseed crop, but still well under soybeans. Total 1995/96 world supplies of 36.8 million tons includes a carryover of 3.4 million tons; the world 1995/96 (July/June) crush of a record high 28.6 million tons compares with the previous year's record 26.2 million.

World rapeseed production is widespread. China produces almost one fourth of total production—a record high 8.7 million tons in 1995/96, up from 6.9 million in 1994/95. Canada is a not too distant second with 6.6 million tons in 1995/96 versus a record high 7.1 million in 1994/95; in the early 1990s, Canada produced on average of 4 million tons annually. Rapeseed is also produced in Europe; collectively it is the largest producing area with a record large 8.1 million tons in 1995/96 versus 7 million in 1994/95, with Germany the largest single producer. Rape/canola oil is viewed as a growth miracle with production and use increasing about 73 percent from the mid-1980s. In foreign trade rapeseed is second only to soybeans, but world trade in 1995/96 was expected to slip and contribute to a buildup in carryover to 4.5 million tons, a record high.

U.S. production of Canola seed is small but growing, as producers see a strong demand for canola oil. A record 459,000 acres were planted for the 1995/96 crop, up 30 percent from 1994/95. Contributing to the acreage increase was the flexibility provisions of the 1990 farm legislation. The Environmental Protection Agency's permission to evaluate pesticides for use on canola also encourages wider U.S. cultivation. The Northern Plains have been plagued in recent years by wheat scab, and adding canola to the rotation helps break the disease cycle. Still, production is well under demand, necessitating continued reliance on canola seed imports, mostly from Canada and estimated at 573 million pounds in 1995/96. The U.S. crush in 1995/96 was expected to near one billion pounds while total demand for canola seed (including exports of 209 million pounds) was estimated at 1.15 billion pounds, up 10 million from 1994/95. In the mid 1980's, the canola seed crush, imports, and carryover stocks were insignificant. Production of canola oil in 1995/96 of 343 million pounds compares with 299 million the previous year. Canola oil imports of 969 million pounds in 1995/96. mostly from Canada, compares with 904 million in 1994/95. Aside from the Government enticements to increase canola acreage, the primary reasons for the gains include: (1) the development of low-erucic canola varieties that can be grown in the U.S., (2) the wider acceptance of canola oil in cooking due to its lower content of saturated fats, and (3) it's priced competitively against sunflowerseed oil. Canola oil is now readily accepted as a salad and cooking oil; it is reported to be 94 percent saturated fat free, the lowest of any leading oil. Moreover, the U.S. remains dependent on imported canola oil to satisfy domestic usage. Demand for canola meal has also grown impressively as a livestock feed due to very aggressive pricing by producers; domestic usage of meal in 1995/96 of a record high 1.1 million short tons compares with only 389,000 in 1990.

Rapeseed prices are highly sensitive to changes in either supply or demand. Futures values tend to be volatile. Futures rose sharply in the spring of 1995 from under $390 per ton to $435 (basis January 1996) by mid-summer, then lost almost the entire gain by late summer before staging another rally into the Fall.

Futures Market

Canola futures and options are traded on the Winnipeg Commodity Exchange (WPG) and quoted in Canadian dollars per ton. The market generally has the largest open interest among the futures traded on the WPG. Rapeseed futures are traded on the Marche a Terme International de France (MATIF).

World Production of Rapeseed In Thousands of Metric Tons

Year	Australia	Bangladesh	Canada	China	Czechoslovakia	Denmark	France	Germany	India	Pakistan	Poland	Sweden	United Kingdom	Former U.S.S.R.	World Total
1982-3	7	120	2,225	5,656	178	334	1,147	878	2,207	246	533	320	580	47	14,804
1983-4	17	131	2,609	4,287	314	309	906	859	2,608	217	554	318	565	69	14,259
1984-5	32	140	3,412	4,205	300	474	1,305	1,017	3,073	234	911	327	925	55	16,935
1985-6	87	261	3,498	5,607	285	544	1,340	1,184	2,681	250	1,073	320	895	74	18,699
1986-7	77	229	3,787	5,881	306	618	1,071	1,472	2,605	217	1,298	321	940	144	19,550
1987-8	66	222	3,847	6,605	337	556	2,645	1,723	3,455	204	1,192	250	1,353	296	23,435
1988-9	58	207	4,218	5,044	380	504	2,303	1,642	4,377	249	1,199	250	1,040	420	22,646
1989-90	78	217	3,209	5,436	387	655	1,748	1,908	4,125	233	1,586	370	976	424	22,096
1990-1	99	228	3,266	6,958	380	793	1,926	2,155	5,152	228	1,206	367	1,258	506	25,301
1991-2	170	248	4,224	7,436	490	734	2,270	3,030	5,863	219	1,043	252	1,308	410	28,534
1992-3	179	244	3,872	7,653	430	406	1,810	2,617	4,872	207	758	247	1,159	388	25,601
1993-4[1]	294	252	5,480	6,939	466	417	1,550	2,848	5,390	215	594	313	1,256	325	27,039
1994-5[2]	309	250	7,100	7,436	551	366	1,800	2,896	5,200	220	756	214	1,298	355	29,696
1995-6[3]	620		6,586	8,800	765	340	2,700	3,130	5,400		1,300	228	1,306	375	33,164

[1] Preliminary. [2] Estimate. [3] Forecast. *Source: The Oil World*

World Supply and Distribution of Rapeseed & Products In Thousands of Metric Tons

Crop Year	Rapeseed Production	Rapeseed Exports	Rapeseed Imports	Rapeseed Crush	Rapeseed Ending Stocks	Rapeseed Meal Production	Rapeseed Meal Exports	Rapeseed Meal Imports	Rapeseed Meal Consumption	Rapeseed Meal Ending Stocks	Rapeseed Oil Production	Rapeseed Oil Exports	Rapeseed Oil Imports	Rapeseed Oil Consumption	Rapeseed Oil Ending Stocks
1979-80	10,081	2,102	2,403	8,714	1,708	5,206	520	640	5,316	149	3,365	643	571	3,295	159
1980-1	11,104	2,305	2,366	10,477	1,489	6,297	808	636	6,075	199	3,933	814	756	3,914	210
1981-2	12,345	2,142	2,216	11,959	911	7,331	845	683	7,182	186	4,383	824	775	4,404	140
1982-3	14,804	2,469	2,540	13,826	740	8,449	768	871	8,500	238	4,991	841	790	4,925	155
1983-4	14,263	2,537	2,704	13,312	647	8,130	1,198	1,303	8,206	267	4,856	984	980	4,827	180
1984-5	16,935	3,153	3,291	15,369	1,033	9,419	1,463	1,451	9,454	220	5,602	1,298	1,199	5,497	186
1985-6	18,699	3,632	3,648	16,986	1,267	10,260	1,823	1,734	10,109	282	6,233	1,313	1,203	5,978	331
1986-7	19,550	4,577	4,923	18,439	1,037	11,112	1,692	2,225	11,568	359	6,849	1,662	1,409	6,540	387
1987-8	23,383	4,456	4,296	20,370	1,250	12,264	2,113	2,088	12,139	169	7,701	1,852	1,806	7,461	922
1988-9	22,646	4,417	4,610	20,252	3,760	12,160	2,709	2,675	12,213	81	7,671	1,939	1,807	7,775	687
1989-90	22,096	2,831	2,891	21,075	3,240	12,709	1,681	1,773	12,721	160	7,944	1,624	1,730	8,000	743
1990-1	25,301	2,526	2,563	23,231	3,130	14,035	1,960	1,888	14,010	114	8,760	1,599	1,595	8,719	781
1991-2	28,534	2,719	2,664	25,332	3,700	15,286	2,538	2,528	15,261	128	9,515	1,538	1,663	9,585	836
1992-3	25,601	3,125	3,000	23,865	780	14,451	2,726	2,656	14,362	147	9,071	1,182	1,199	9,182	742
1993-4[1]	27,039	4,097	4,058	25,259	790	15,150	2,610	2,732	15,303	114	9,723	1,595	1,522	9,525	836
1994-5[2]	29,696	4,482	4,540	26,743	1,040	16,080	2,503	2,500	16,076	115	10,347	2,159	2,135	10,019	1,139
1995-6[3]	33,164	4,145	4,110	28,800	1,120	17,275	2,635	2,635	17,260	130	11,098	1,977	2,005	11,144	1,122

[1] Preliminary. [2] Estimate. [3] Forecast. *Source: The Oil World*

Salient Statistics of Rapeseed and Canola Oil in the United States In Millions of Pounds

Crop Year Beginning June 1	Rapeseed (Canola Seed): Supply: Stocks June 1	Production	Imports	Total	Disappearance: Crush	Exports	Total[3]	Canola Oil: Supply: Stocks June 1	Production	Imports	Total	Disappearance: Domestic	Exports	Total
1987	3	27	2	32	30	0	30	4	14	273	291	263	0	263
1988	2	39	37	78	71	4	75	29	54	430	513	486	8	494
1989	3	95	231	329	298	10	308	20	130	391	541	510	6	516
1990	21	97	141	259	195	32	227	24	18	583	625	577	7	584
1991	32	191	2	225	109	97	212	41	32	815	888	801	15	816
1992	13	144	27	184	59	104	174	71	49	861	981	898	16	914
1993	10	252	773	1,036	850	78	941	67	406	902	1,375	1,228	76	1,304
1994[1]	95	447	630	1,173	899	227	1,139	137	299	938	1,374	1,165	153	1,318
1995[2]	34	547	573	1,155	889	209	1,114	54	334	1,001	1,389	1,213	110	1,323

[1] Preliminary. [2] Estimate. [3] Forecast. *Source: Economic Research Service, U.S. Department of Agriculture*

Wholesale Price of Rapeseed Oil, Refined (Denatured), in Tanks at New York In Cents Per Pound

Year	Jan.	Feb.	Mar.	Apr.	May	June	July	Aug.	Sept.	Oct.	Nov.	Dec.	Average
1985	55.20	55.20	55.20	NA	NA	68.30	67.90	64.00	62.50	62.50	62.50	60.50	61.40
1986	60.00	60.00	60.00	60.00	60.00	60.00	60.00	60.00	60.50	60.50	60.50	60.50	60.10
1987	60.50	62.00	62.50	62.50	64.25	69.50	69.50	65.00	63.50	63.50	63.50	63.50	64.15
1988	63.56	63.50	63.50	63.50	63.50	63.50	63.50	63.50	63.50	64.63	66.25	70.00	64.37
1989	70.00	70.00	80.25	80.25	80.25	80.75	80.25	80.25	80.25	80.25	80.25	80.25	78.58
1990	81.75	82.25	82.23	82.25	82.25	82.25	82.25	82.25	79.25	77.25	77.25	81.00	81.02
1991	82.25	82.25	82.25	82.25	82.25	82.25	82.25	82.25	82.25	82.25	82.25	82.25	82.25
1992	82.25	82.25	82.25	82.25	82.25	82.25	82.25	82.25	67.25	62.25	62.25	62.25	76.00
1993	62.25	62.25	62.25	62.25	55.88	53.75	53.25	53.00	53.00	52.00	52.50	50.00	56.03
1994[1]	43.75	43.75	43.75	43.75	43.75	43.75							43.75

[1] Preliminary. NA = Not available. *Source: Economic Research Service, U.S. Department of Agriculture*

Average Open Interest of Rapeseed Futures in Winnipeg In 20 Metric Ton Units

Year	Jan.	Feb.	Mar.	Apr.	May	June	July	Aug.	Sept.	Oct.	Nov.	Dec.
1985	19,122	22,206	21,260	22,202	19,611	17,591	17,675	19,058	16,757	14,511	14,717	17,232
1986	15,553	18,146	19,741	20,435	22,262	19,193	17,192	20,594	22,570	26,838	28,391	28,972
1987	25,143	32,141	34,152	31,564	30,761	28,903	26,599	24,083	25,075	25,893	23,049	26,576
1988	28,875	33,387	31,798	34,056	34,587	31,318	30,224	29,509	26,289	29,510	28,974	29,221
1989	22,435	20,889	18,591	22,690	24,587	21,025	22,280	22,027	16,153	21,556	20,981	21,749
1990	18,431	20,340	17,599	19,825	24,718	22,546	23,073	24,353	24,872	25,688	18,706	22,057
1991	22,000	22,829	24,815	26,637	30,072	28,240	28,288	27,547	27,558	29,079	23,880	20,117
1992	15,943	17,556	20,559	21,410	23,727	28,885	26,013	25,674	28,049	32,724	35,693	37,375
1993	34,098	37,658	36,715	38,210	38,231	29,743	39,763	43,844	50,616	55,107	54,998	54,475
1994	50,335	55,280	54,899	58,012	60,567	55,434	54,733	57,044	57,049	54,375	55,045	49,475
1995	47,579	43,662	36,530	32,580	38,361	42,961	43,607	42,828	51,067	57,638	46,640	45,444

Source: Winnipeg Commodity Exchange

Average Price of Cash Canola at Vancouver In Canadian Dollars Per Tonne

Year	Jan.	Feb.	Mar.	Apr.	May	June	July	Aug.	Sept.	Oct.	Nov.	Dec.
1985	381.52	387.69	385.37	398.63	393.49	375.08	354.84	330.12	334.24	313.57	314.21	321.75
1986	321.49	304.19	294.97	283.29	282.19	267.79	252.73	234.95	239.20	246.00	252.73	244.59
1987	242.61	227.73	219.03	221.67	243.97	256.27	247.85	235.66	243.24	257.22	267.19	281.15
1988	302.56	303.16	294.22	305.27	336.31	413.98	395.28	381.19	379.83	349.68	333.96	344.35
1989	329.54	321.64	333.29	331.44	335.18	306.10	300.49	289.44	297.10	293.79	303.10	302.54
1990	300.01	301.45	311.00	318.78	322.24	303.89	300.83	299.43	292.74	295.23	290.08	290.01
1991	285.01	280.36	291.50	298.57	293.83	277.25	258.12	269.40	275.00	270.30	262.90	261.60
1992	264.15	273.35	282.70	276.85	288.08	292.35	272.20	282.26	320.62	302.10	327.22	331.57
1993	344.22	329.26	328.67	325.06	318.85	319.23	331.29	322.85	311.29	311.66	331.44	366.37
1994	408.60	413.10	422.23	454.90	481.44	484.95	388.63	382.54	381.70	379.99	401.38	432.35
1995	431.85	440.41	456.13	425.40	404.27	414.31	426.49	405.94	405.89	413.29	416.03	423.77

Source: Winnipeg Commodity Exchange

Rayon and Other Synthetic Fibers

Worldwide Cellulosic Fiber Production In Thousands of Metric Tons

Year	Austria	Brazil	China	Czech Republic	Finland	Germany	India	Japan	Poland	Romania	Taiwan	United Kingdom	United States	Former U.S.S.R.	Yugo-slavia	Total
1986	123.9	50.4	183.0	55.2	55.0	276.7	140.0	320.0	72.0	64.0	119.9	58.0	280.7	589.0	71.1	2,860
1987	120.0	48.9	187.0	55.2	54.0	274.6	167.5	300.5	73.3	66.0	119.6	55.0	274.6	591.5	63.3	2,826
1988	132.0	51.5	184.4	58.3	60.4	277.1	174.1	290.6	74.2	75.6	125.8	64.0	278.3	601.0	68.0	2,896
1989	136.0	55.0	204.0	56.9	64.8	278.4	198.7	272.9	65.6	95.9	147.6	55.0	263.3	584.0	71.1	2,943
1990	135.0	54.5	214.3	55.0	63.8	199.1	216.7	275.8	36.2	59.9	147.9	71.0	229.2	544.0	72.7	2,757
1991	120.0	53.0	242.0	33.5	47.4	118.0	215.4	266.4	25.6	38.0	149.1	63.0	220.7	401.7	49.3	2,433
1992	128.3	54.2	249.0	39.3	56.0	139.9	219.9	254.4	22.1	28.5	139.3	65.0	224.5	292.3	18.2	2,327
1993[1]	131.2	56.7	273.0	41.0	56.5	127.1	238.9	244.4	23.6	13.3	130.8	67.2	228.9	258.3	15.0	2,283
1994[1]	134.3	62.8	338.0	41.7	58.5	136.2	239.7	218.9	18.0	11.5	149.3	67.4	226.0	176.0	6.0	2,325
1995[2]	142.0	71.3	365.0	51.2	62.0	147.0	302.0	290.7	49.0	44.0	153.0	69.5	279.4	588.4	51.0	3,252

[1] Preliminary. [2] Producing capacity. *Source: Fiber Economics Bureau, Inc.*

Worldwide Noncellulosic Fiber Production (Except Olefin) In Thousands of Metric Tons

Year	Brazil	China	France	Germany	India	Italy/ Malta	Japan	Rep. of Korea	Mexico	Romania	Spain	Taiwan	United Kingdom	United States	Former U.S.S.R.	Total
1986	237.0	747.4	167.2	745.0	220.7	576.9	1,355.6	862.4	296.3	199.7	276.2	1,232.1	208.2	2,918.8	589.0	12,927
1987	248.1	846.0	161.0	759.3	266.0	564.6	1,340.6	970.1	333.2	201.9	268.5	1,391.3	203.0	3,094.3	591.5	13,741
1988	239.7	1,074.5	159.1	926.3	321.6	568.2	1,351.9	1,115.0	340.3	192.3	302.3	1,430.2	193.0	3,146.9	601.0	14,418
1989	245.8	1,223.2	152.1	952.3	366.7	547.7	1,380.9	1,189.9	352.8	159.3	252.3	1,523.1	178.5	3,119.4	874.0	14,747
1990	207.8	1,342.8	137.2	777.0	436.6	578.3	1,425.0	1,269.7	366.8	139.9	255.0	1,621.5	179.8	2,886.0	893.5	14,894
1991	219.1	1,488.9	107.0	797.0	439.6	564.6	1,429.8	1,365.2	395.3	138.8	241.1	1,841.4	179.3	2,902.9	804.8	15,273
1992	218.2	1,586.7	105.2	817.3	538.0	589.9	1,448.8	1,451.4	426.6	110.1	257.0	2,042.6	187.4	2,980.6	656.8	15,911
1993[1]	234.4	1,652.9	103.7	758.8	604.4	551.6	1,365.1	1,581.3	406.5	103.5	240.3	2,122.8	174.3	3,016.1	549.8	16,084
1994[1]	236.3	2,034.0	124.7	807.6	679.4	599.9	1,398.1	1,673.5	484.9	118.5	273.6	2,295.9	161.3	3,193.3	658.9	17,718
1995[2]	352.6	2,736.0	183.9	932.4	934.3	664.0	1,837.2	1,895.2	613.3	217.6	316.6	2,494.5	195.1	3,684.1	1,247.0	23,010

[1] Preliminary. [2] Producing capacity. *Source: Fiber Economics Bureau, Inc.*

World Production of Synthetic Fibers In Thousands of Metric Tons

	Noncellulosic Fiber Production (Except Olefin) — By Fibers				— World Total			Glass Fiber Production							
Year	Acrylic & Mod-acrylic	Nylon & Aramid	Polyester	Other Fibers[3]	Yarn & Monofil-aments	Staple & Tow & Fiberfill	Total	Europe	Japan	Other Americas	United States	Total	China	Former U.S.S.R.	Cigarette Tow Pro-duction
1986	2,445	3,500	6,842	140	5,683	7,244	12,927	364	240	35	630	1,299	50	100	362
1987	2,521	3,638	7,438	144	6,040	7,701	13,741	407	300	50	725	1,517	55	110	400
1988	2,452	3,725	8,102	138	6,572	7,845	14,417	465	340	65	730	1,655	65	125	412
1989	2,341	3,795	8,459	152	6,847	7,900	14,747	470	345	65	735	1,680	70	133	443
1990	2,320	3,738	8,678	158	7,035	7,859	14,894	445	371	60	675	1,631	75	120	464
1991	2,385	3,605	9,116	167	7,241	8,032	15,273	441	293	75	650	1,561	65	133	480
1992	2,363	3,662	9,729	157	7,673	8,238	15,911	442	307	83	700	1,652	75	130	475
1993	2,288	3,586	10,068	142	7,899	8,185	16,084	508	312	86	794	1,865	77	133	482
1994[1]	2,474	3,921	11,157	166	8,993	8,725	17,718	545	313	87	959	2,076	78	133	536
1995[2]	3,000	5,457	14,258	295	11,832	11,178	23,010	653	346	105	1,019	2,323	130	190	

[1] Preliminary. [2] Producing capacity. [3] Alginate, azion, spandex, saran, etc. *Source: Fiber Economics Bureau, Inc.*

U.S. Artificial (Cellulosic) Distribution In Millions of Pounds

	Yarn & Monofilament — Producers' Shipments					Staple & Tow — Producers' Shipments					
Year	Domestic	Exports	Total	Imports	Domestic Con-sumption	Domestic	Exports	Total	Imports	Domestic Con-sumption	Glass Fiber Ship-ments
1986	192.1	20.2	212.3	17.0	209.1	373.5	30.8	404.3	17.4	390.9	1,339.3
1987	166.8	24.9	191.7	12.8	179.6	383.6	32.4	416.0	13.8	397.4	1,513.1
1988	182.6	34.1	216.7	17.6	200.2	386.0	20.5	406.5	20.4	406.4	1,587.6
1989	187.3	31.7	219.0	26.3	213.6	338.2	16.2	354.4	54.0	392.2	1,530.1
1990	172.7	34.0	206.7	24.2	196.9	291.7	12.5	304.2	111.6	403.3	1,519.1
1991	179.9	32.3	212.2	30.8	210.7	255.5	8.1	263.6	92.0	347.5	1,488.5
1992	182.9	35.1	218.0	32.1	215.0	260.7	6.9	267.6	85.6	346.3	1,629.7
1993	196.5	31.5	228.0	40.4	236.9	273.6	10.3	283.9	89.5	363.1	1,780.6
1994[1]	190.3	32.9	223.2	32.9	223.2	252.3	30.7	283.0	65.7	318.0	2,115.0

[1] Preliminary. *Source: Fiber Economics Bureau, Inc.*

RAYON AND OTHER SYNTHETIC FIBERS

Man-Made Fiber Production in the United States In Millions of Pounds

	Artificial (Cellulosic) Fibers: Rayon & Acetate			Synthetic (Noncellulosic) Fibers: Yarn & Monofilament				Synthetic (Noncellulosic) Fibers: Staple & Tow							
Year	Filament Yarn & Monofilament	Staple & Tow	Total Cellulostic	Nylon	Polyester	Olefin	Total Yarn	Nylon	Polyester	Acrylic & Modacrylic	Olefin	Total Staple	Total Noncellulosic	Total Manufactured Fibers	Total Glass Fiber
1986	215	404	619	1,606	1,173	1,058	3,837	908	2,132	616	335	3,991	7,826	8,447	1,389
1987	191	414	605	1,697	1,179	1,134	4,010	992	2,362	592	360	4,306	8,316	8,921	1,598
1988	214	400	614	1,728	1,228	1,224	4,180	942	2,452	588	364	4,346	8,526	9,140	1,609
1989	217	363	580	1,759	1,209	1,257	4,225	981	2,385	543	382	4,291	8,516	9,096	1,620
1990	206	299	505	1,671	1,107	1,417	4,194	990	2,090	505	406	3,991	8,185	8,690	1,488
1991	213	273	486	1,667	1,208	1,408	4,282	869	2,202	454	459	3,984	8,266	8,752	1,433
1992	220	275	495	1,651	1,270	1,528	4,449	904	2,308	439	474	4,125	8,573	9,068	1,543
1993	227	278	505	1,700	1,284	1,659	4,643	959	2,274	433	483	4,149	8,791	9,296	1,750
1994[1]	225	273	498	1,805	1,492	1,870	5,167	935	2,366	442	549	4,292	9,459	9,957	2,114
1995[2]	208	290	498	1,829	1,597	1,907	5,333	874	2,290	432	521	4,117	9,450	9,948	2,246

[1] Preliminary. [2] Estimate. *Source: Fiber Economics Bureau, Inc.*

U.S. Domestic Distribution of Synthetic (Noncellulosic) Fibers In Millions of Pounds

	Yarn & Monofilament: Producers' Shipments: Domestic								Staple & Tow: Producers' Shipments: Domestic								
Year	Nylon	Polyester	Olefin	Total	Exports	Total	Imports	Domestic Consumption	Nylon	Polyester	Acrylic & Modacrylic	Olefin	Total	Exports	Total	Imports	Domestic Consumption
1986	1,479.6	1,092.4	1,049.2	3,621.2	200.6	3,821.8	126.1	3,747.3	894.9	1,998.6	531.2	312.7	3,737.4	239.8	3,977.2	182.8	3,920.2
1987	1,554.3	1,113.4	1,135.5	3,803.2	214.7	4,017.9	123.9	3,927.1	966.0	2,201.0	479.3	341.1	3,987.4	325.6	4,313.0	189.0	4,176.4
1988	1,572.4	1,157.4	1,199.8	3,929.6	260.5	4,190.1	116.3	4,045.9	944.9	2,311.8	421.1	344.2	4,022.0	344.8	4,366.8	196.2	4,218.2
1989	1,575.3	1,110.7	1,226.0	3,912.0	237.9	4,149.9	182.2	4,094.2	955.3	2,261.3	414.8	363.4	3,994.8	253.3	4,248.1	192.4	4,187.2
1990	1,537.5	1,046.2	1,404.9	3,988.6	265.1	4,253.7	154.7	4,143.3	950.2	2,015.4	352.2	387.9	3,705.7	278.9	3,984.6	209.8	3,915.5
1991	1,493.9	1,114.0	1,380.6	3,988.5	246.9	4,235.4	174.8	4,163.3	835.0	2,127.9	319.2	437.5	3,719.6	277.8	3,997.4	263.1	3,982.7
1992	1,570.1	1,229.6	1,496.1	4,295.8	194.8	4,490.6	209.3	4,505.1	891.7	2,202.1	322.3	441.0	3,857.1	267.2	4,124.3	397.7	4,255.0
1993	1,612.7	1,228.4	1,631.5	4,472.6	174.6	4,647.2	295.8	4,768.4	907.9	2,157.8	333.0	468.2	3,866.9	297.1	4,164.0	509.0	4,375.9
1994[1]	1,700.0	1,402.8	1,838.2	4,941.0	204.9	5,145.9	377.7	5,318.7	911.7	2,221.3	319.6	489.0	3,941.6	390.9	4,332.5	622.9	4,564.5

[1] Preliminary. *Source: Fiber Economics Bureau, Inc.*

U.S. Mill Consumption of Fiber & Products & Per Capita Consumption In Millions of Pounds

	Cellulosic Fibers				Noncellulosic Fibers								Per Capita[4] Mill Consumption (Pounds)				
Year	Yarn & Monofilament	Staple & Tow	Net Waste	Total Cellulostic	Noncellulostic	Net Waste	Total Noncellulostic	Total Manufactured Fibers[2]	Cotton	Wool	Other Fibers[3]	Grand Total	Man-made Fibers[2]	Cotton	Wool	Other Fibers[3]	Total All Fibers
1986	209.1	390.9	8.3	608.3	7,667.5	178.1	7,845.6	8,453.9	3,301.7	164.5	103.3	12,023.4	39.9	20.4	1.7	2.4	64.4
1987	179.6	397.4	8.6	585.6	8,103.5	172.6	8,276.1	8,861.7	3,736.5	167.6	104.8	12,870.6	41.3	23.7	1.7	2.5	69.2
1988	200.2	406.4	5.8	612.4	8,264.1	140.9	8,405.0	9,017.4	3,470.1	156.1	83.8	12,727.4	40.9	21.4	1.5	2.1	65.9
1989	213.6	392.2	-5.0	600.8	8,281.4	127.4	8,408.8	9,009.6	3,985.9	139.6	77.9	13,213.0	40.6	23.4	1.1	2.0	67.1
1990	196.9	403.3	-1.3	598.9	8,058.8	179.3	8,238.1	8,837.0	4,036.5	135.4	75.7	13,084.6	39.3	23.2	1.1	2.2	65.8
1991	210.7	347.5	-1.7	556.5	8,135.9	168.8	8,304.7	8,861.2	4,347.5	159.0	78.6	13,446.3	39.1	24.6	1.2	2.0	66.9
1992	215.0	346.3	-3.6	557.7	8,748.3	192.9	8,941.2	9,498.9	4,714.7	159.1	76.3	14,449.0	41.5	27.6	1.2	1.9	72.2
1993	236.9	363.1	-5.6	594.4	9,135.5	198.6	9,334.1	9,928.5	4,921.9	166.6	73.8	15,090.8	43.2	29.2	1.3	1.8	75.5
1994[1]	223.2	318.0	-21.4	519.8	9,883.2	97.2	9,980.4	10,505.4	5,191.6	163.3	73.4	15,933.7	45.4	30.2	1.4	2.2	79.2

[1] Preliminary. [2] Excludes Glass Fiber. [3] Includes silk, linen, jute and sisel & others. [4] Mill consumption plus imports less exports of semimanufactured and unmanufactured products. *Source: Fiber Economics Bureau, Inc.*

Producer Price Index of Grey Synthetic Broadwovens 1982 = 100

Year	Jan.	Feb.	Mar.	Apr.	May	June	July	Aug.	Sept.	Oct.	Nov.	Dec.	Average
1986	102.4	102.5	102.5	103.0	102.4	102.6	102.7	101.5	100.3	101.0	100.9	101.0	101.9
1987	101.9	101.9	102.2	103.4	103.9	105.3	106.4	106.9	107.9	108.6	109.0	109.2	105.6
1988	110.0	111.1	111.6	111.8	112.2	113.0	113.4	113.8	113.0	113.5	113.9	114.6	112.7
1989	114.3	112.0	112.2	112.2	112.1	113.1	114.7	115.0	115.0	115.8	115.9	115.3	114.0
1990	115.6	115.7	115.6	115.7	115.5	115.6	115.7	115.2	115.3	115.6	115.8	116.1	115.7
1991	115.7	114.7	114.4	114.1	114.3	113.9	114.8	116.4	116.5	116.5	116.8	118.2	115.5
1992	119.0	119.9	120.3	120.9	121.8	122.0	122.6	122.0	121.7	120.8	119.4	119.9	120.9
1993	119.6	119.1	119.1	119.2	117.1	118.4	118.0	118.0	116.9	117.3	115.2	114.5	117.7
1994	113.5	112.8	112.9	113.2	113.2	113.3	113.1	113.3	114.1	111.8	112.9	113.8	113.2
1995[1]	114.8	116.8	116.7	116.3	116.6	117.1	115.4	114.8	118.8	116.4	114.7		

[1] Preliminary. *Source: Bureau of Labor Statistics, U.S. Department of Commerce*

Rice

Rice is the world's second most popular foodstock after wheat. However, international trading in rice is relatively small (about 5 percent) compared to world production as much of the crop is consumed where it is produced. Still, a record large world import demand of 19.4 million tons (milled basis) was realized in 1995, up 21 percent from 1994. Generally, its rare to find a country with annual rice imports in excess of 1 million tons, but in 1995 Indonesia imported about 2.6 million tons and China 2 million. World import demand is expected to fall in 1996 to 16.4 million tons, but world trade would still be at its second highest level, while world stocks are projected at their tightest since 1976/77. With relatively little of world production trading freely, prices can be very sensitive to changes in supply and demand such as 1995 reports of flood damage in Thailand. Strong world prices were expected to hold into 1996.

World rice production in 1995/96 of 351.7 million metric tons (milled) was down 3.4 million from the 1994/95 record. World demand was estimated at a record large 363 million tons, which if realized, would place ending world stocks at 42.8 million tons, the lowest in more than twenty years.

The world's largest producer and consumer is China with about a third of each; production in 1995 of 124 million tons compares with 123.2 million in 1994. India is the second largest producer with 79 million tons in 1995, 2.6 million under the 1994 record but still enough to add to stocks and permit larger exports. Thailand, whose 1995 rice production was about 10 percent of China's, is the largest exporter; the U.S., with even less production, is second. Importing nations are far more numerous. The Western hemisphere is the primary destination, paced by Mexico and Brazil.

U.S. rough rice production in 1995/96 of 174.2 million cwt. (rough) was down 11 percent from the record large 197.8 million produced in 1994/95. The smaller crop reflected smaller acreage and lower yields. U.S. rice acreage peaked in 1981 at 3.8 million acres and has never returned to that level; 3.2 million were planted in 1995/96. The long grain yield for the 1995/96 crop of 5,387 pounds/acre compares with 5,609 pounds in 1994/95, while the medium and short grain yields were 6,667 and 6,866 pounds, respectively. U.S. rice exports in 1995/96 of 88 million cwt. compare with 100 million in 1994/95. Still, U.S. ending 1995/96 stocks were expected to fall 20 percent from a year earlier to 25.1 million cwt. (rough), representing only 13.1 percent of total use, the lowest since 1980/81.

U.S. rice prices, farm level, in 1995/96 were forecast to range between \$7.00 and \$8.00 per cwt., well above the \$6.74 per cwt. in 1994/95, the increase reflecting the smaller U.S. crop and strong foreign demand.

Futures Market

Rough rice futures and options are traded on the Chicago Board of Trade (CBOT).

World Rice Supply and Distribution[4] In Thousands of Metric Tons

		Exports			Imports					Utilization			Ending Stocks		
Year	Production	U.S.	Non-U.S.	Total	Brazil	Iran	Saudi Arabia	Unaccounted	Total	China	India	Total	China	India	Total
1991-2	516,760	2,107	11,975	14,082	456	926	760	1,276	14,082	128,537	74,975	351,698	27,510	13,500	56,660
1992-3	521,391	2,644	12,231	14,875	715	1,037	869	1,945	14,875	127,000	75,368	354,853	29,602	10,600	54,281
1993-4[1]	522,649	2,794	13,251	16,045	975	475	750	1,470	16,045	128,000	76,045	357,018	25,173	12,900	50,024
1994-5[2]	533,923	3,000	16,527	19,527	700	1,400	750	928	19,527	129,000	77,307	362,115	21,074	13,450	48,529
1995-6[3]	532,535	2,900	13,265	16,165	1,000	800	800	1,225	16,165	130,000	80,000	365,215	17,874	10,850	42,772

[1] Preliminary. [2] Estimate. [3] Forecast. [4] Production is on a rough basis; all other data are reported on a milled basis. *Source: Foreign Agricultural Service, U.S. Department of Agriculture*

World Exports of Rice (Milled Basis), by Country of Origin In Thousands of Metric Tons

Year	Bangladesh	Brazil	Burma	China	Egypt	India	Indonesia	Japan	Kazakhstan	Rep. of Korea	Pakistan	Philippines	Russia	Thailand	Vietnam
1991-2	27,378	10,100	12,800	183,810	3,447	112,031	44,680	12,005	522	7,428	4,865	9,132	772	20,400	22,179
1992-3	27,513	9,901	13,400	186,220	3,908	109,313	48,231	13,216	468	7,257	4,674	9,523	755	19,917	21,703
1993-4[1]	27,064	10,515	15,086	177,700	4,198	118,467	48,185	9,793	403	6,511	5,993	9,923	769	19,200	23,182
1994-5[2]	25,252	10,885	16,034	175,930	4,565	121,898	46,638	14,973	277	6,882	5,171	10,475	538	21,364	23,712
1995-6[3]	27,753	10,000	16,897	180,000	3,387	118,512	46,000	13,503	262	6,469	5,401	10,500	538	20,985	24,242

[1] Preliminary. [2] Estimate. [3] Forecast. *Source: Foreign Agricultural Service, U.S. Department of Agriculture*

World Exports of Rice (Milled Basis), by Country of Origin In Thousands of Metric Tons

Year	Agrentina	Australia	Burma	China	Egypt	European Union	Guyana	India	Indonesia	Pakistan	Taiwan	Thailand	Uruguay	Vietnam	United States
1991	75	450	176	689	159	391	54	711	0	1,297	229	3,988	260	1,048	2,197
1992	204	500	185	933	209	376	114	563	60	1,358	188	4,776	327	1,914	2,107
1993	276	500	223	1,374	133	153	122	625	469	937	101	4,798	451	1,765	2,644
1994[1]	175	600	619	1,519	262	175	150	600	225	1,375	117	4,738	400	2,000	2,794
1995[2]	350	550	800	50	150	250	160	3,500	0	1,400	200	5,600	485	2,000	3,000
1996[3]	425	575	1,000	200	50	175	175	1,500	0	1,100	150	5,250	450	2,000	2,900

[1] Preliminary. [2] Estimate. [3] Forecast. *Source: Foreign Agricultural Service, U.S. Department of Agriculture*

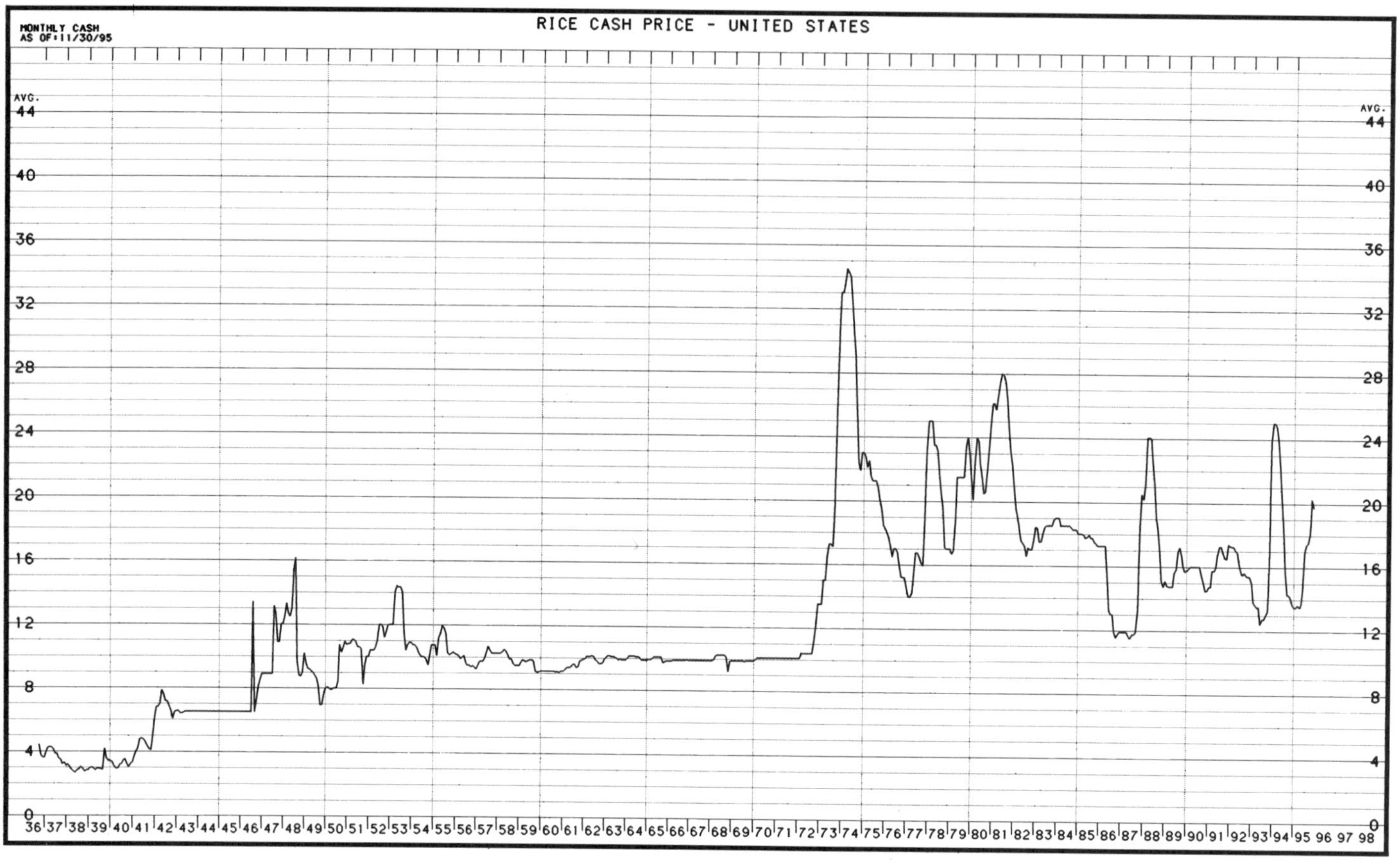

Average Wholesale Price of Rice No. 2 (Medium)[1] Southwest Louisiana   In Dollars Per Cwt. Bagged

Year	Aug.	Sept.	Oct.	Nov.	Dec.	Jan.	Feb.	Mar.	Apr.	May	June	July	Average
1981-2	26.40	24.20	22.90	21.20	20.00	18.80	17.80	16.10	16.00	16.40	16.20	16.00	19.30
1982-3	16.50	16.50	16.50	16.70	17.80	17.30	16.50	16.50	16.50	17.10	17.50	17.50	16.90
1983-4	17.50	17.50	17.50	17.50	17.50	17.50	17.50	17.50	17.50	17.50	17.50	17.50	17.50
1984-5	16.00	16.00	15.50	15.50	15.50	15.50	15.50	16.00	16.20	16.30	18.00	16.20	16.00
1985-6	16.00	16.00	16.00	16.00	16.00	16.00	15.67	15.50	14.60	11.90	12.00	11.35	14.75
1986-7	10.00	10.00	10.00	10.00	10.00	10.00	10.00	10.50	11.25	11.15	11.20	11.20	10.45
1987-8	11.10	11.95	16.60	17.25	16.75	18.50	19.80	20.15	20.00	18.00	17.40	16.70	17.00
1988-9	16.40	16.20	14.50	14.50	14.00	13.90	13.75	13.50	13.50	14.60	14.65	15.75	14.60
1989-90	15.55	15.30	14.80	14.30	14.04	14.80	15.13	15.13	15.50	15.75	15.65	15.30	15.10
1990-1	14.75	13.90	13.50	13.50	13.50	14.90	14.90	15.05	16.05	16.15	16.50	16.35	14.90
1991-2	15.85	16.00	16.00	16.00	16.00	16.00	15.90	15.50	15.50	15.15	14.50	14.50	15.60
1992-3	14.50	14.00	14.50	14.15	13.40	13.40	13.00	12.80	12.40	11.94	12.00	12.00	13.15
1993-4	12.25	12.45	15.65	21.95	24.00	24.00	23.88	23.80	24.00	23.70	22.00	20.00	20.65
1994-5	18.30	15.88	15.00	15.00	14.00	13.80	14.16	14.38	14.38	14.70	14.75	14.55	14.91
1995-6[2]	15.44	17.50	20.25	20.13	14.00								

[1] U.S. No. 2--broken not to exceed 4%. [2] Preliminary. *Source: Economic Research Service, U.S. Department of Agriculture*

U.S. Rice (Rough) Production by Type and Variety   In Thousands of Hundred of Pounds (Cwt.)

Year	Long Grain	Medium Grain	Short Grain	Total	Year	Long Grain	Medium Grain	Short Grain	Total
1988	119,364	36,891	3,642	159,897	1992	128,015	50,633	1,010	179,658
1989	109,161	41,441	3,885	154,487	1993	103,064	51,873	1,173	156,110
1990	107,806	47,328	954	156,088	1994	133,445	63,390	944	197,779
1991	109,137	47,567	753	157,457	1995[1]	122,168	51,152	903	174,223

[1] Preliminary. *Source: National Agricultural Statistics Service, U.S. Department of Agriculture*

Salient Statistics of Rice, Rough & Milled (Rough Equivalent) in the United States   In Millions of Cwt.

Crop Year Beginning August	Supply: Stocks August 1	Supply: Production	Supply: Imports	Supply: Total Supply	Disappearance: Domestic: Food	Domestic: Brewers	Domestic: Seed	Domestic: Total	Residual	Exports	Total Disappearance	CCC Stocks July 31	Government Support Program: Put Price Support	Loan Rate ($ Per Cwt.): Rough[3]: Long	Rough[3]: Medium	Rough[3]: All Classes	Milled Long
1990-1	26.3	156.1	4.8	187.2	63.7	15.3	3.6	82.6	9.0	71.0	162.6	.1	143.7	6.68	6.21	6.50	10.84
1991-2	24.6	159.4	5.3	189.2	67.1	15.4	3.9	86.4	9.0	66.4	161.8	.4	108.3	6.65	6.11	6.50	10.74
1992-3	27.4	179.7	6.1	213.2	69.0	15.1	3.6	87.7	9.0	77.0	173.7	.1	125.8	6.66	6.13	6.50	10.74
1993-4	39.4	156.1	6.9	202.5	71.2	15.1	4.2	90.5	11.0	75.2	176.7	0	30.9	6.66	6.13	6.50	10.75
1994-5[1]	25.8	197.8	7.3	230.9	74.0	15.1	4.1	93.2	5.4	92.0	199.5	.1	131.2	6.65	6.12	6.50	10.72
1995-6[2]	31.4	174.2	8.3	213.9	77.0	15.1	4.1	96.2	8.0	86.0	190.2	0	64.2	6.65	6.11	6.50	10.69

[1] Preliminary. [2] Estimate. [3] Loan rate for each class of rice is the sum of the whole kernels' loan rate weighted by its milling yield (average 56%) and the broken kernels' loan rate weighted by its milling yield (average 12%). *Source: Economic Research Service, U.S. Department of Agriculture*

Acreage, Yield, Production and Prices of Rice in the United States

Crop Year	Acreage Harvested (1,000 Acres): Southern States	California	United States	Yield Per Harvested Acre (In Lbs.): California	United States	Production 1,000 Cwt.: Southern States	California	United States	Value of Production $1,000	Wholesale Prices ($ Per Cwt.): Arkansas[2]	Houston[3]	Milled Rice, Average C.I.F. at Rotterdam ($ Per Metric Ton): U.S. No. 2[4]	Thai "A"[5]	Thai "B"[5]
1990-1	2,428	395	2,823	7,700	5,529	125,659	30,429	156,088	1,047,242	15.55	15.55	340	405	339
1991-2	2,425	350	2,775	8,100	5,674	129,107	28,350	157,457	1,200,629	16.20	17.15	359	396	328
1992-3	2,738	394	3,132	8,500	5,736	146,168	33,490	179,658	1,057,272	14.30	15.15	287	385	290
1993-4	2,396	437	2,833	8,300	5,510	119,839	36,271	156,110	1,246,875	21.20	20.75	413	413	335
1994-5	2,831	485	3,316	8,500	5,964	156,555	41,224	197,779		14.47	14.69	325	412	331
1995-6[1]	2,663	448	3,111	7,800	5,635	137,953	36,270	174,223		18.07	19.16	401	NA	417

[1] Preliminary. [2] F.O.B. mills, Arkansas, medium. [3] Houston, Texas (long grain). [4] Milled, 4%, container, FAS. 5 SWR, 100%, bulk. NA = Not available. *Source: Economic Research Service, U.S. Department of Agriculture*

U.S. Exports of Milled Rice, by Country of Destination   In Thousands of Metric Tons

Year Beginning October	Canada	Germany	Haiti	Iran	Ivory Coast	Jamaica	Mexico	Netherlands	Peru	Russia[2]	Saudi Arabia	Senegal	South Africa	Switzerland	United Kingdom	Total
1990-1	127.4	49.9	124.8	0	69.4	75.5	96.5	91.6	61.5	0	189.1	63.2	115.9	108.6	38.8	2,395.1
1991-2	143.7	44.9	116.9	11.6	73.4	46.3	157.0	67.7	43.6	55.6	179.6	61.7	136.6	94.2	59.8	2,279.0
1992-3	146.0	67.6	152.9	184.3	107.3	39.4	241.5	120.9	61.6	74.8	223.5	91.5	122.1	71.2	72.2	2,709.9
1993-4	141.3	41.7	57.2	60.4	34.2	53.8	234.0	92.8	47.0	6.4	180.5	90.1	110.9	64.8	82.4	2,432.5
1994-5[1]	160.0	43.1	210.2	240.6	92.0	88.5	309.6	170.3	81.8	0	176.1	28.1	106.9	91.2	58.7	3,763.1

[1] Preliminary. [2] Formerly part of the U.S.S.R.; data not reported separately until 1992. *Source: Economic Research Service, U.S. Department of Agriculture*

U.S. Rice Exports by Export Program   In Thousands of Metric Tons

Fiscal Year	PL 480	Section 416	CCC Credit Programs[2]	CCC African Relief Exports	EEP[3]	Export Programs[4]	Exports Outside Specified Export Programs	Total U.S. Rice Exports	% Export Programs as a Share of Total Exports
1990	351	0	663	0	0	1,038	1,398	2,437	43
1991	411	0	183	0	76	669	1,611	2,280	29
1992	382	0	220	0	358	982	1,177	2,159	45
1993	497	0	235	0	278	1,108	1,486	2,594	43
1994	111	0	155	0	46	319	2,010	2,329	14
1995[1]	87	0	263	0	113	468	2,563	3,031	15

[1] Preliminary. [2] May not completely reflect exports made under these programs. [3] Sales not shipments. [4] Adjusted for estimated overlap between CCC export credit and EEP shipments. *Source: Economic Research Service, U.S. Department of Agriculture*

Average Price Received by Farmers for Rice (Rough) in the U.S.   In Dollars Per Hundred Pounds (Cwt.)

Year	Aug.	Sept.	Oct.	Nov.	Dec.	Jan.	Feb.	Mar.	Apr.	May	June	July	Average[2]
1990-1	6.66	6.21	6.02	6.29	6.13	6.39	6.75	7.07	7.43	7.44	7.43	7.21	6.68
1991-2	7.16	7.67	7.65	7.84	7.98	7.84	7.97	7.78	7.46	7.18	6.97	6.99	7.58
1992-3	6.60	6.41	6.40	6.42	6.39	6.36	6.06	5.64	5.52	5.24	5.02	4.92	5.89
1993-4	5.19	5.21	6.10	8.06	8.91	8.98	10.10	10.20	9.93	10.00	8.88	7.80	7.98
1994-5	6.87	6.89	6.47	6.53	6.56	6.78	6.71	6.64	6.70	6.75	7.03	7.17	6.78
1995-6[1]	7.64	7.92	8.77	9.13	9.25								

[1] Preliminary. [2] Weighted average by sales. *Source: Economic Research Service, U.S. Department of Agriculture*

Rubber

According to the International Rubber Study Group (IRSG), the recovery in the world rubber industry got under way in 1994, sparked by sharply higher prices. In 1993, there were sharp declines in both consumption and production, but by 1994 consumption in most countries was on the increase. Natural rubber increased more quickly than synthetic rubber resulting in a decline in synthetic rubber's share of total rubber consumption.

In 1994, natural rubber consumption increased for the third year in a row. Natural rubber production, which fell sharply in 1993, increased in 1994. Asian countries posted strong increases in consumption. The smaller producing countries in Africa and Asia had sharp increases in production. Rubber output by the major producers also increased.

The IRSG estimates that world production of synthetic rubber in 1994 was 8.81 million tonnes, up three percent from 1993. The U.S. is the world's largest producer of synthetic rubber. In 1994, U.S. production was 2.39 million tonnes, up nearly ten percent from 1993. The next largest producer of synthetic rubber was Japan with 1994 output of 1.35 million tonnes, up three percent from 1993. German production was put at 642,000 tonnes, up 13 percent from 1993. Russian production fell sharply to 590,000 tonnes, down 43 percent from 1993. Canadian synthetic rubber production was 232,000 tonnes in 1994, up close to 18 percent.

World production of natural rubber in 1994 was 5.72 million tonnes, seven percent more than in 1993. The major producer is Thailand. 1994 production was estimated at 1.72 million tonnes, up 11 percent from 1993. Thailand has seen substantial increases in natural rubber production for several years. As recently as 1984, Thailand's production was 629,000 tonnes. The next largest producer is Indonesia with output in 1994 of 1.36 million tonnes or nearly five percent more than in 1993. Malaysian production was estimated at 1.1 million tonnes , up close to three percent. China's output in 1994 rose almost five percent to 341,000 tonnes. India's production increased over eight percent to 464,000 tonnes. Other producers of natural rubber are Nigeria, Sri Lanka, the Philippines and Vietnam.

World consumption of synthetic rubber in 1994 was 8.87 million tonnes, up one percent from 1993. U.S. consumption was up almost six percent to 2.12 million tonnes. Japan's consumption was virtually unchanged at 1.03 million tonnes. German synthetic rubber consumption was 535,000 tonnes, up close to ten percent from 1993. French consumption of 325,000 tonnes was up over three percent.

World consumption of natural rubber in 1994 was 5.64 million tonnes, up almost five percent. The U.S. is the largest consumer of natural rubber with 1994 use at just over a million tonnes, up nearly four percent. Japan consumed 640,000 tonnes, up over one percent.

World stocks of synthetic rubber on January 1, 1995, were 854,000 tonnes, down four percent from 1993. World natural rubber stocks on January 1, 1995, were 390,000 tonnes, down 17 percent from 1993. U.S. rubber stocks on January 1, 1995, were 45,200 tonnes, down 37 percent.

World net exports of natural rubber in 1994 were 3.79 million tonnes, down three percent. The major exporter was Thailand at 1.61 million tonnes, up 15 percent.

The IRSG outlook for 1995 was positive based on expected improvements in the world economy. The U.S. car industry was expected to have very good sales though current economic indicators point to some slowing in growth. European growth rates were expected to remain good.

The rubber industry in Central and Eastern Europe was expected to continue recovering. The pace of recovery should be helped by improvement in Western Europe. The Czech Republic, Poland, and Slovakia should see improved economies. Privatization of smaller businesses have largely been completed. One problem area is the former Soviet Union where financial instability has hampered growth.

Economic growth in Asia is expected to increase. Japanese tire manufacturers have forecast a 2.9 percent increase in demand in 1995. South Korea was planning a ten percent increase in tire production in 1995. Natural rubber producers have seen increasing local consumption.

Chinese rubber demand is an important factor in the market. China has a large population and its economy is growing rapidly. Chinese natural rubber output is expected to show little change in 1995 which could lead to a shortage and increased imports. China has seen a large increase in synthetic rubber consumption. China appears to be putting more emphasis on synthetic rubber consumption.

Futures Markets

Rubber futures are traded on the Kobe Rubber Exchange (KRE), the Tokyo Commodity Exchange, (TOCOM), the Kuala Lumpur Commodity Exchange (KLCE), and the Singapore Commodity Exchange Ltd.

U.S. Imports of Natural Rubber (Includes Latex & Guayule) In Thousands of Metric Tons

Year	Jan.	Feb.	Mar.	Apr.	May	June	July	Aug.	Sept.	Oct.	Nov.	Dec.	Total
1985[2]	72.8	72.8	89.5	65.0	86.0	48.9	60.9	46.0	41.4	70.6	73.0	65.5	792.3
1986	66.7	71.5	77.9	84.5	48.4	54.9	70.1	45.2	63.9	73.5	54.0	56.7	721.0
1987	55.9	91.3	82.0	33.3	64.6	58.9	64.2	47.6	59.4	57.7	63.9	78.9	769.1
1988	83.2	69.6	87.0	68.6	67.2	64.9	49.5	83.3	59.1	69.3	77.4	74.7	791.8
1989	99.3	52.2	99.1	74.6	87.5	63.8	77.9	65.6	69.1	69.5	78.9	69.1	880.9
1990	72.3	58.6	81.9	63.1	89.5	77.7	60.4	61.0	83.0	55.7	81.7	75.7	820.1
1991	59.9	54.1	69.5	90.9	59.6	56.7	53.4	52.4	65.5	74.4	71.3	68.9	776.2
1992	77.5	75.2	84.7	64.7	79.0	73.8	80.5	77.2	73.9	81.3	68.1	77.5	913.4
1993	95.3	79.9	93.9	86.3	74.1	81.2	83.6	77.8	69.2	73.4	86.0	86.9	987.6
1994[1]	87.5	74.7	102.6	78.9	88.3	77.8	66.7	85.0	78.8	89.3	70.0	76.0	975.6
1995[1]	81.7	86.9	102.3	90.2	94.1	93.4	78.0	81.0	81.5				

[1] Preliminary. [2] Data prior to 1985 are in thousands of long tons. *Source: International Rubber Study Group*

World Rubber Production[1] In Thousands of Metric Tons

	Natural										Synthetic						
Year	China	India	Indo-nesia	Malaysia	Nigeria	Philip-pines	Sri Lanka	Thailand	Vietnam	World Total	Canada	Ger-many	Japan	United Kingdom	United States	Russia[3]	World Total
1985	187.9	198.3	1,130.2	1,469.5	51.6	150.1	137.5	723.8	52.5	4,400	209.2	447.6	1,158.0	232.6	2,026.0	2,125.0	8,960
1986	209.7	219.0	1,049.2	1,538.6	36.8	146.0	137.8	786.0	54.0	4,490	187.1	452.5	1,150.1	249.2	2,119.1	2,320.0	9,260
1987	237.6	227.4	1,203.3	1,578.7	55.3	147.2	121.8	925.6	55.0	4,840	179.8	468.4	1,191.9	257.0	2,182.1	2,366.0	9,450
1988	239.8	254.8	1,235.0	1,661.6	80.5	51.6	122.4	978.9	60.0	5,020	197.0	499.6	1,298.8	312.8	2,334.7	2,435.0	10,160
1989	242.8	288.6	1,256.0	1,415.6	118.4	56.7	110.7	1,178.9	85.0	5,150	188.0	507.6	1,352.7	311.4	2,261.4	2,358.0	10,150
1990	264.2	323.5	1,262.0	1,291.0	152.0	61.2	113.1	1,271.1	103.0	5,120	195.0	524.5	1,425.8	274.3	2,114.5	2,277.0	9,910
1991	296.4	360.2	1,284.0	1,255.7	155.7	59.6	103.9	1,340.8	87.0	5,240	180.0	504.4	1,377.3	251.3	2,050.0	2,105.0	9,270
1992	309.0	383.0	1,387.0	1,173.2	126.0	56.9	106.1	1,531.0	114.0	5,460	206.0	544.7	1,388.0	280.1	2,300.0	1,495.0	9,240
1993[2]	326.0	428.1	1,301.3	1,074.3	105.0	56.0	104.2	1,551.4	90.0	5,340	197.0	569.7	1,309.8	289.8	2,180.0	1,030.0	8,580
1994[2]	341.0	464.0	1,360.8	1,100.6	95.0	58.0	105.3	1,722.4	88.0	5,720	232.0	642.0	1,349.0	290.7	2,390.0	590.0	8,810

[1] Including rubber in the form of latex. [2] Preliminary. *Source: International Rubber Study Group*

World Consumption of Natural and Synthetic Rubber In Thousands of Metric Tons

	Natural									Synthetic						
Year	Australia	Brazil	Canada	France	Ger-many	Japan	United Kingdom	United States	World Total	Canada	France	Ger-many	Japan	United Kingdom	United States	World Total
1985	35.8	97.6	95.0	156.0	202.2	539.9	126.0	764.0	4,350	173.0	311.8	411.3	947.5	201.0	1,962.0	9,000
1986	30.6	105.6	86.0	158.7	198.7	535.0	130.0	743.0	4,460	190.2	315.0	426.0	910.0	195.0	2,019.6	9,280
1987	35.5	115.4	98.0	170.0	198.5	568.0	134.0	789.0	4,800	210.0	316.4	453.4	946.0	216.0	2,017.3	9,650
1988	40.5	125.3	82.5	181.0	203.6	623.0	140.0	858.3	5,100	202.0	315.0	471.0	1,042.0	226.5	2,016.8	9,940
1989	43.5	124.3	84.9	184.0	221.1	657.0	132.5	866.9	5,190	191.1	358.0	476.0	1,103.0	240.0	2,051.0	10,070
1990	34.0	121.3	84.0	179.0	208.7	677.0	136.0	807.5	5,200	185.4	351.0	511.0	1,133.0	223.0	1,820.8	9,710
1991	34.0	125.0	76.3	183.0	210.7	689.5	119.0	755.8	5,100	183.9	342.0	502.0	1,118.5	201.0	1,768.1	9,290
1992	36.5	119.4	86.5	179.0	212.8	685.4	124.5	910.2	5,390	198.0	365.4	506.0	1,080.6	231.0	1,959.6	9,300
1993[1]	45.0	125.0	91.5	168.5	174.9	631.0	119.0	966.7	5,390	210.0	314.7	488.0	1,022.0	212.0	2,001.0	8,690
1994[1]	48.5	132.0	106.0	179.8	178.0	639.8	135.0	1,001.7	5,640	240.0	325.2	535.0	1,026.2	217.0	2,117.6	8,780

[1] Preliminary. *Source: International Rubber Study Group*

World Stocks of Natural & Synthetic Rubber (by Countries) on January 1 In Thousands of Metric Tons

		In Producing Countries									In Consuming Countries (Reported Stocks)				
Year	Total Synthetic	Africa	Cam-bodia	Indo-nesia	Malaysia	Singa-pore	Sri Lanka	Thailand	Vietnam	Other Asia	Total Natural	Brazil	India	Japan	United States	Total
1985	1,790	------	1.0	95.0	228.8	36.8	10.2	41.3	5.0	30.0	545	15.9	58.0	70.7	96.4	925
1986[2]	1,750	17.8	1.0	90.0	191.8	22.0	12.2	47.1	6.0	16.0	520	13.5	58.2	70.7	95.2	238
1987	1,710	16.2	1.0	90.0	207.3	21.6	23.6	32.5	6.0	15.1	530	13.3	85.5	61.9	73.0	234
1988	1,520	19.1	1.0	100.0	208.5	21.6	20.0	37.8	6.0	13.8	510	13.5	58.2	70.7	95.2	224
1989	1,800	23.2	1.0	100.0	286.5	32.2	23.2	53.0	6.0	6.7	540	20.5	80.9	97.2	61.7	260
1990	988	26.9	1.0	110.0	248.3	24.0	27.0	53.7	8.0	7.3	510	16.0	78.4	105.6	92.0	292
1991	1,011	21.7	1.0	114.0	190.3	20.2	29.8	74.9	11.0	7.1	490	12.0	92.9	91.6	94.3	291
1992	973	24.4	1.0	68.0	196.1	25.9	17.3	80.1	9.0	6.9	450	9.0	106.0	92.7	109.4	317
1993	965	22.6	1.0	70.0	187.2	15.3	16.0	79.8	12.0	7.1	500	2.0	90.9	82.9	108.0	284
1994[1]	892	22.2	1.0	40.0	159.2	10.6	17.2	104.2	9.0	7.2	470	5.0	96.4	85.4	71.3	258
1995[1]	854	20.8	1.0	40.0	187.0	10.5	16.5	89.4	8.0	8.5	390	4.0	94.1	72.9	45.2	216

[1] Preliminary. [2] Prior to 1986, data shown for all consuming countries. *Source: International Rubber Study Group*

Net Exports of Natural Rubber from Producing Areas In Thousands of Metric Tons

Year	Cambodia	Guat-emala	Indonesia	Liberia	Malaysia	Nigeria	Sri Lanka	Thailand	Vietnam	Other Africa[2]	Other Asia[3]	World Total
1985	14.0	10.6	1,000.9	87.2	1,465.8	29.1	120.4	685.3	35.5	69.0	29.8	3,640
1986	20.0	6.2	958.7	90.4	1,485.2	26.0	110.0	755.2	35.0	78.0	35.2	3,630
1987[4]	20.0	10.4	1,092.8	91.1	1,578.5	43.7	106.0	873.2	35.0	94.0	28.1	3,950
1988	21.0	9.8	1,132.0	105.6	1,563.6	65.8	99.3	906.4	37.9	107.0	36.8	4,070
1989	32.0	11.0	1,151.8	106.0	1,364.8	101.3	86.0	1,100.6	57.7	115.0	38.2	4,170
1990	28.0	13.4	1,077.3	40.0	1,185.6	121.0	86.7	1,150.8	75.9	120.0	37.6	3,990
1991	21.0	14.3	1,220.0	19.0	1,041.2	139.0	76.4	1,231.9	62.9	122.0	44.0	4,020
1992	20.0	15.7	1,268.1	28.0	939.1	107.0	78.6	1,412.9	80.9	134.0	44.6	4,060
1993[1]	21.0	16.9	1,214.3	3.0	769.8	87.0	69.6	1,393.6	63.0	134.0	52.8	3,920
1994[1]	32.0	22.3	1,244.8	31.0	782.1	76.0	69.1	1,605.0	59.0	142.2	65.0	3,790

[1] Preliminary. [2] Includes Cameroon, Cote d'Ivoire, Gabon, Ghana and Zaire. [3] Includes Myanmar, Papua New Guinea and the Philippines. [4] Prior to 1987, data shown for Central American Common Market (C.A.C.M.) *Source: International Rubber Study Group*

RUBBER

Average Spot Crude Rubber Prices (Smoked Sheets[1]) in New York   In Cents Per Pound

Year	Jan.	Feb.	Mar.	Apr.	May	June	July	Aug.	Sept.	Oct.	Nov.	Dec.	Average
1983	44.0	48.5	57.8	57.8	56.8	54.5	58.3	59.3	60.5	60.5	58.3	-----	56.0
1984	57.3	58.3	58.0	56.8	51.8	47.0	46.0	46.0	46.0	43.0	42.8	42.0	49.6
1985	42.3	42.3	41.8	42.3	40.8	42.0	40.3	41.8	41.8	43.8	42.5	39.8	41.8
1986	40.7	42.8	42.0	39.2	40.1	41.0	43.5	43.5	45.3	46.9	44.7	44.7	42.9
1987	45.9	46.5	43.8	47.4	49.1	50.6	53.5	53.7	54.2	53.8	53.1	54.0	50.5
1988	54.6	53.8	54.9	55.7	58.6	67.6	66.1	63.8	60.1	55.2	53.0	54.1	58.1
1989	56.0	59.3	54.1	55.2	52.1	49.5	49.2	47.2	46.1	46.1	45.6	44.8	50.4
1990	44.7	45.8	45.9	45.6	45.8	46.0	45.8	47.5	48.4	46.5	46.3	47.1	46.3
1991	47.5	48.8	49.1	46.0	45.2	45.3	44.6	44.4	44.3	44.5	44.8	44.2	45.7
1992	43.1	44.0	44.5	45.9	46.4	46.6	46.8	47.1	46.9	47.8	48.0	48.0	46.3
1993	48.5	48.3	46.4	44.2	43.8	43.8	43.3	43.9	44.5	44.2	44.9	44.7	45.0
1994	44.9	46.1	49.6	50.8	51.4	55.1	62.5	66.4	67.2	73.5	71.8	77.4	59.7
1995	85.7	92.6	94.2	93.4	89.5	80.6	72.1	68.5	70.7	73.6	83.2	83.4	82.3

[1] No. 1 ribbed, plantation rubber.   *Source: Wall Street Journal*

Natural Rubber Prices in London   In British Pounds Per Metric Ton

Year	Jan.	Feb.	Mar.	Apr.	May	June	July	Aug.	Sept.	Oct.	Nov.	Dec.	Average
Buyers' Price RSS 1 (CIF)													
1993	644.4	683.5	635.7	584.2	576.1	585.0	588.0	597.3	593.9	599.4	605.1	610.9	608.6
1994	612.6	639.5	686.0	698.9	712.6	771.7	878.5	886.8	884.7	911.8	875.8	1,004.5	797.0
1995	1,141.9	1,170.8	1,209.6	1,189.2	1,174.9	1,004.9	894.9	886.0	921.4	946.7	1,082.6	1,099.7	1,060.2
Buyers' Prices RSS 3 (CIF)													
1993	614.4	667.5	625.3	578.0	566.3	573.2	575.6	581.5	565.3	570.5	574.8	578.1	589.2
1994	586.2	629.2	671.0	688.2	706.0	766.0	872.6	880.8	875.0	901.8	866.8	975.2	784.9
1995	1,122.9	1,157.0	1,188.2	1,174.2	1,161.0	988.2	882.7	859.2	911.3	941.4	1,074.2	1,093.6	1,046.2
Sellers' Prices SMR 20 (CIF)													
1993	602.5	640.6	607.1	585.6	571.8	571.5	568.1	568.8	550.0	546.9	571.2	598.0	581.8
1994	619.4	658.8	718.5	757.5	713.8	719.8	780.6	821.0	823.1	877.5	897.5	1,088.1	789.6
1995	1,227.5	1,228.8	1,151.5	1,116.9	1,053.0	926.3	796.9	839.1	871.2	887.5	1,066.5	1,065.0	1,019.2

Source: International Rubber Study Group

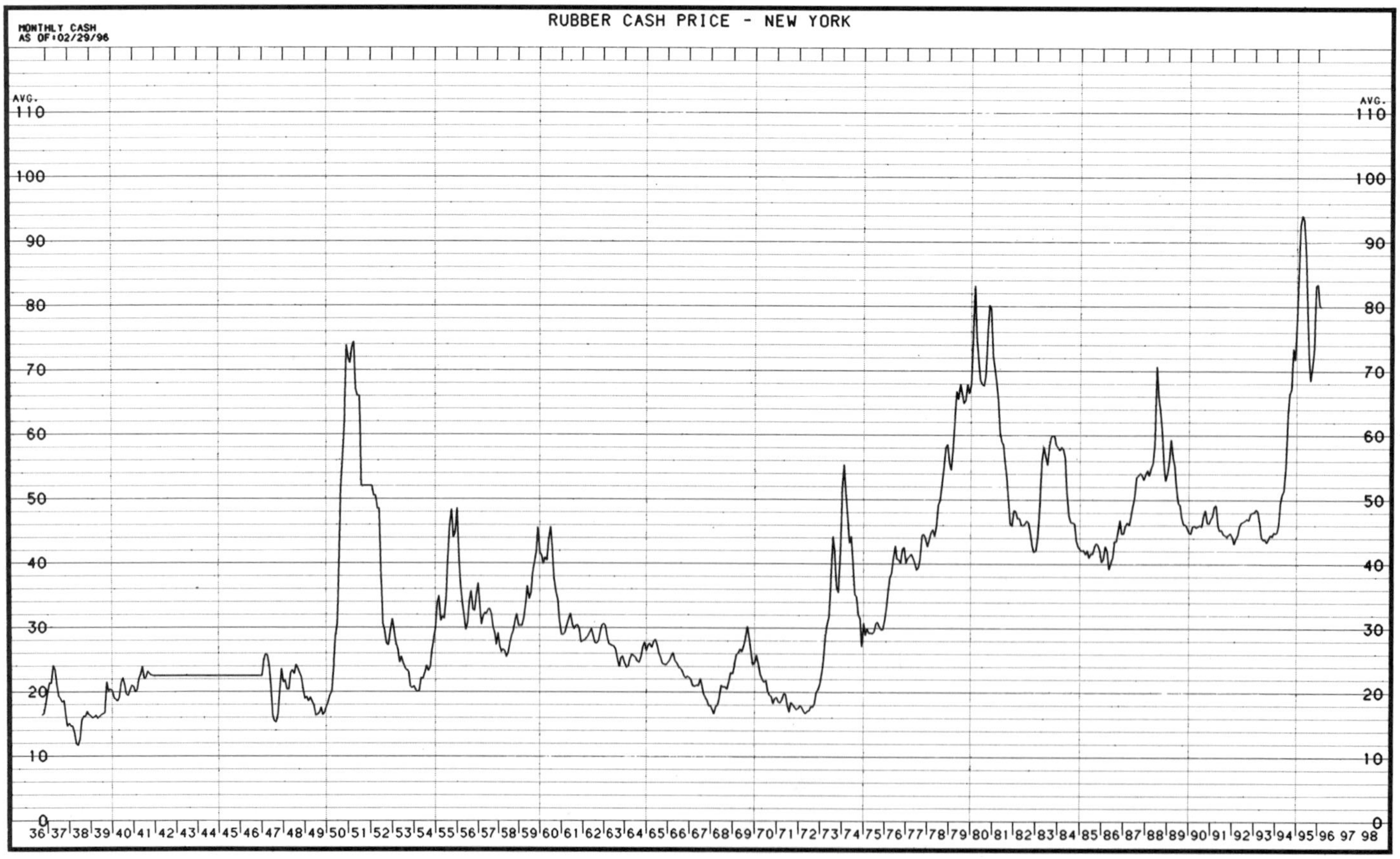

Consumption of Natural Rubber in the United States In Thousands of Metric Tons

Year	Jan.	Feb.	Mar.	Apr.	May	June	July	Aug.	Sept.	Oct.	Nov.	Dec.	Total
1984	73.8	56.8	83.1	68.2	65.1	42.4	73.9	56.1	63.7	58.3	55.4	54.1	750.7
1985	71.8	65.7	91.5	51.7	89.0	45.2	55.4	47.3	68.1	47.2	65.7	52.4	774.7
1986	59.4	71.8	71.3	81.9	45.5	54.6	69.9	49.9	57.0	80.3	50.8	51.2	743.0
1987	49.9	85.4	81.3	62.3	62.6	56.3	67.4	61.4	61.9	57.4	60.6	69.4	789.0
1988	80.9	66.3	91.6	60.8	68.7	66.2	53.5	80.6	64.6	74.5	75.4	75.2	858.3
1989	89.9	51.1	96.6	68.4	87.9	65.1	82.7	70.8	72.0	62.1	84.6	50.9	866.9
1990	62.6	57.3	79.0	65.2	87.4	73.9	57.4	74.1	78.8	59.8	75.6	69.8	807.5
1991	60.0	60.0	65.0	65.0	65.0	60.0	55.0	55.0	65.0	70.0	65.0	66.0	755.8
1992	83.4	63.3	85.9	66.9	80.6	78.6	82.6	79.5	70.2	84.6	64.4	70.2	910.2
1993	96.3	76.0	93.4	93.4	67.9	76.8	77.3	84.9	72.0	73.6	82.9	72.2	966.7
1994[1]	92.8	84.9	93.1	82.7	89.6	84.6	76.2	87.8	74.8	90.1	66.4	78.7	1,001.7
1995[1]	70.5	75.8	98.4	90.3	92.2	93.3	85.0	82.7	83.1				

[1] Preliminary. *Source: International Rubber Study Group*

Stocks of Natural Rubber in the United States, Beginning of the Month In Thousands of Metric Tons

Year	Jan.	Feb.	Mar.	Apr.	May	June	July	Aug.	Sept.	Oct.	Nov.	Dec.
1984	80.8	95.2	95.7	87.7	87.8	91.4	88.5	87.0	84.8	86.2	87.3	91.3
1985	96.4	94.3	97.3	91.4	101.9	95.9	95.6	97.9	93.9	84.9	81.1	85.1
1986	95.2	97.0	96.9	100.4	98.6	98.6	96.7	93.8	86.4	91.6	75.3	78.2
1987	38.5	76.7	78.8	70.2	80.2	79.5	79.0	82.5	77.0	70.6	65.9	65.5
1988	72.5	74.9	75.3	70.7	74.6	72.9	71.6	68.7	71.2	63.9	57.9	58.4
1989	61.7	71.1	67.5	77.4	82.2	86.7	86.2	86.2	88.1	83.3	87.7	83.9
1990	92.0	100.2	100.2	101.6	97.1	97.3	99.8	101.6	87.2	90.3	84.7	89.6
1991	94.3	94.0	88.0	93.0	119.0	113.0	110.0	108.0	106.0	106.0	110.0	117.0
1992	109.4	103.6	112.7	110.4	107.5	105.9	101.1	99.0	96.7	100.3	97.0	100.7
1993	108.0	49.4	53.3	53.7	46.7	52.9	57.3	63.6	56.5	53.7	53.4	56.5
1994[1]	71.3	65.9	55.7	65.2	61.4	60.0	53.2	43.8	41.0	45.0	44.2	47.8
1995[1]	45.2	56.4	67.5	71.4	71.2	72.6	73.0	66.0	64.4	62.8		

[1] Preliminary. *Source: International Rubber Study Group*

Stocks of Synthetic Rubber in the United States, Beginning of the Month In Thousands of Metric Tons

Year	Jan.	Feb.	Mar.	Apr.	May	June	July	Aug.	Sept.	Oct.	Nov.	Dec.
1984	277.9	284.1	277.2	277.0	294.6	305.0	302.3	309.3	300.6	312.0	301.4	285.9
1985	272.1	281.2	271.8	288.6	294.0	398.0	247.8	295.8	413.5	397.3	374.9	367.0
1986	213.9	352.8	217.5	397.7	403.0	238.6	247.5	239.9	233.4	236.5	231.1	224.6
1987	235.6	247.0	249.5	242.6	239.9	242.2	241.8	251.9	240.6	222.8	213.6	213.8
1988	229.0	237.8	235.1	229.6	237.5	246.2	249.6	261.0	259.9	258.6	259.0	258.2
1989	276.3	288.9	287.7	294.4	289.6	300.4	303.7	308.7	314.1	323.4	329.6	414.8
1990	404.0	393.5	392.5	385.8	406.8	397.5	395.0	414.9	420.8	419.6	405.0	393.9
1991	403.7	406.0	403.0	404.0	402.0	388.0	394.0	385.0	356.0	334.0	330.0	325.0
1992	403.7	386.0	381.2	383.9	393.2	389.2	372.8	382.7	382.1	375.1	378.6	401.1
1993	406.9	345.9	345.7	346.0	340.5	351.8	342.1	341.6	333.6	326.4	319.9	321.4
1994[1]	331.1	313.3	313.3	307.9	306.0	314.2	302.5	323.2	318.5	304.6	299.4	299.5
1995[1]	305.4	307.4	302.8	293.5	319.4	315.6	325.9	349.2	355.7	354.6		

[1] Preliminary. *Source: International Rubber Study Group*

Production of Synthetic Rubber in the United States In Thousands of Metric Tons

Year	Jan.	Feb.	Mar.	Apr.	May	June	July	Aug.	Sept.	Oct.	Nov.	Dec.	Total
1984	155.6	162.3	187.9	171.7	171.1	156.8	139.7	145.5	147.9	154.4	122.4	116.5	1,829
1985	155.2	153.9	170.1	160.5	171.1	164.6	154.4	146.7	159.6	174.5	189.4	160.2	1,936
1986	183.3	173.0	190.3	193.2	191.4	183.7	166.7	178.4	173.0	179.7	158.3	147.5	2,156
1987	169.9	161.6	182.1	166.0	154.2	139.5	150.4	154.2	160.3	153.6	149.2	131.8	1,838
1988	166.5	156.7	189.1	178.6	167.8	164.9	155.3	170.5	178.6	186.7	145.6	174.7	2,335
1989	206.3	177.5	193.6	174.1	179.7	175.0	186.2	164.2	176.0	191.0	182.9	194.8	2,261
1990	173.5	180.1	182.5	187.8	174.6	172.0	171.9	180.9	180.4	190.3	167.4	153.1	2,115
1991	168.0	163.0	184.0	174.0	173.0	159.0	154.0	133.0	159.0	159.0	173.0	164.0	2,050
1992	180.0	190.0	200.0	210.0	200.0	190.0	190.0	200.0	210.0	200.0	195.0	175.0	2,300
1993	120.0	160.0	220.0	190.0	200.0	180.0	190.0	180.0	180.0	180.0	190.0	180.0	2,180
1994[1]	180.0	180.0	210.0	200.0	210.0	200.0	200.0	210.0	190.0	210.0	200.0	200.0	2,390
1995[1]	210.0	200.0	210.0	210.0	230.0	220.0	210.0	220.0	200.0				

[1] Preliminary. *Source: International Rubber Study Group*

RUBBER

Consumption of Synthetic Rubber in the United States   In Thousands of Metric Tons

Year	Jan.	Feb.	Mar.	Apr.	May	June	July	Aug.	Sept.	Oct.	Nov.	Dec.	Total
1984	131.7	140.2	158.2	146.3	146.2	156.7	135.6	170.3	170.5	180.4	158.2	147.2	1,828
1985	177.5	175.4	180.5	166.7	167.1	171.0	147.1	173.9	151.5	184.1	166.3	147.2	2,062
1986	155.8	169.5	159.6	154.8	163.6	137.9	139.8	150.6	171.6	174.3	154.0	140.3	1,802
1987	160.7	145.0	175.7	157.6	163.9	148.0	151.5	168.5	160.6	177.5	145.8	155.7	2,020
1988	162.8	166.1	182.8	160.6	163.1	157.8	161.9	163.6	172.2	185.1	167.6	174.1	2,017
1989	158.5	166.8	186.8	163.1	172.1	166.3	160.9	171.1	162.5	170.6	180.5	150.5	2,051
1990	159.6	158.7	161.6	144.1	161.5	151.6	137.1	149.5	155.6	175.3	147.1	119.1	1,821
1991	145.0	140.0	160.0	150.0	160.0	135.0	140.0	140.0	160.0	140.0	150.0	149.0	1,768
1992	167.8	159.5	174.7	158.9	162.6	184.2	154.5	177.7	180.2	171.5	155.1	148.2	1,960
1993	161.3	154.4	189.4	172.8	164.5	173.6	166.0	173.9	162.0	169.4	162.3	151.4	2,001
1994[1]	177.7	160.8	191.8	173.0	173.5	187.5	164.9	187.1	176.0	178.8	175.7	170.8	2,118
1995[1]	186.8	180.3	193.8	176.7	210.6	186.5	158.5	188.4	180.9				

[1] Preliminary. *Source: International Rubber Study Group*

Exports of Synthetic Rubber in the United States   In Thousands of Metric Tons

Year	Jan.	Feb.	Mar.	Apr.	May	June	July	Aug.	Sept.	Oct.	Nov.	Dec.	Total
1986	23.9	28.1	24.4	36.0	26.1	25.4	26.8	32.3	34.8	30.9	28.2	27.5	366.0
1987	32.4	33.2	36.1	37.1	39.4	36.9	34.1	33.3	38.8	33.5	37.5	37.1	470.5
1988	39.7	37.4	41.8	41.7	40.4	41.1	29.8	44.0	38.6	37.2	36.3	32.1	514.0
1989	42.4	45.7	55.0	41.3	54.4	51.3	43.7	48.2	54.5	54.6	43.6	44.4	450.6
1990	45.6	39.0	50.2	42.6	42.7	41.0	37.4	43.1	42.0	50.8	50.3	39.0	523.7
1991	43.8	46.1	44.0	45.2	47.9	40.4	42.8	43.2	43.1	46.3	47.3	42.2	532.3
1992	52.3	55.1	51.3	59.1	58.2	51.6	46.5	52.8	58.0	51.4	48.1	39.7	624.1
1993	47.1	34.1	57.7	47.4	52.4	46.9	46.9	43.8	48.8	46.6	49.0	41.9	562.6
1994[1]	48.8	46.4	55.4	57.0	52.4	49.6	50.2	62.8	60.7	59.9	56.9	55.0	655.1
1995[1]	54.9	51.6	62.7	55.6	58.6	58.6	50.0	54.9	53.0				

[1] Preliminary. *Source: International Rubber Study Group*

Production of Tyres (Car and Truck) in the United States   In Thousands of Units

Year	Jan.	Feb.	Mar.	Apr.	May	June	July	Aug.	Sept.	Oct.	Nov.	Dec.	Total
1984	16,749	17,498	19,122	16,988	18,043	18,557	15,546	18,078	17,333	19,136	16,645	15,682	209,375
1985	18,381	17,375	18,704	17,388	16,781	15,216	12,989	16,635	16,844	17,626	15,198	13,786	196,923
1986	16,306	15,966	16,968	16,037	15,003	14,647	14,203	16,112	16,540	18,180	15,144	15,183	190,289
1987	16,879	16,593	17,733	16,680	16,982	16,548	15,796	16,723	17,204	18,956	16,455	16,428	202,978
1988	17,345	18,027	19,305	17,642	17,403	17,941	15,022	18,058	18,115	19,138	17,253	16,102	211,351
1989	18,944	18,102	19,670	19,224	19,090	18,312	14,835	18,288	16,963	18,400	16,323	14,721	212,870
1990	19,017	17,376	19,522	17,680	17,990	18,186	14,996	18,555	17,612	19,965	16,077	13,687	210,663
1991	17,713	17,375	16,208	17,017	19,360	16,419	14,354	17,784	17,045	19,588	16,354	15,173	202,391
1992	18,772	18,762	20,356	19,065	18,874	19,380	17,273	20,306	19,975	21,602	18,384	17,501	230,250
1993	---------	61,809	---------	---------	60,752	---------	---------	57,702	---------	---------	57,184	---------	237,447
1994[1]	---------	63,586	---------	---------	63,331	---------	---------	57,018	---------	---------	59,665	---------	243,600

[1] Preliminary. [2] Estimate. *Source: International Rubber Study Group*

Foreign Trade of Tyres (Car and Truck) in the United States   In Thousands of Units

	Imports					Exports				
Year	First Quarter	Second Quarter	Third Quarter	Fourth Quarter	Total	First Quarter	Second Quarter	Third Quarter	Fourth Quarter	Total
1986	9,346	10,148	11,458	10,215	41,167	1,268	1,146	1,267	1,474	5,223
1987	11,584	12,820	11,722	11,341	47,467	2,095	2,327	2,389	3,371	10,182
1988	11,383	12,059	12,383	12,783	48,608	4,203	4,120	3,712	4,034	16,069
1989	12,802	14,518	12,609	12,749	52,678	4,104	4,254	5,267	4,704	18,329
1990	13,713	13,564	11,951	11,633	50,861	5,453	5,532	6,031	6,730	23,746
1991	12,011	13,008	11,320	10,158	46,497	6,407	6,388	6,623	6,342	25,760
1992	10,760	12,496	11,850	12,285	47,391	6,243	6,475	7,125	6,646	26,489
1993[1]	12,311	12,303	12,457	12,697	49,768	6,989	6,987	7,081	6,960	28,017
1994[2]	14,600	14,600	14,600	14,900	58,700	7,900	7,900	7,900	7,900	31,600

[1] Preliminary. [2] Estimate. *Source: International Rubber Study Group*

Rye

U.S. rye production in the 1990s averaged about 10.5 million bushels versus an annual average during the 1980's of more than 20 million bushels. The downward trend is likely to continue, further solidifying rye as a minor U.S. crop. Imports, although small in quantity, have averaged about 4.5 million bushels during the past few years, nearly half of U.S. production. The major producing states are Georgia and South Dakota, accounting for nearly a third of total production. In 1995/96, (June/May) production totaled 9.9 million bushels versus 11.3 million in 1994/95; the decrease reflecting a seven percent decline in harvested acreage to a near record low 378,000 acres. The average yield was 26.3 bushels/acre, down 1.6 bushels from 1994/95.

Rye is used as an animal feed and as an ingredient in bread and some whiskeys. In the U.S., about a third of the total supply is used as a feedstuff, a third as a foodstuff, and the balance as seed and for whisky. So far virtually no U.S. rye has been exported during the 1990s. Carryover stocks have recently averaged about 1.5 million bushels. A USDA price support program exists for rye, but due to the crop's declining importance little of the crop has been acquired by the CCC since the late 1980s.

On a world basis production has also fallen, but the slide may abate if import demand from the Far East continues to grow. World production in the mid-1980s averaged more than 30 million tons annually, so far in the 1990s production has averaged around 25 million tons with higher output earlier in the decade. The reason for the slide was not adverse yield, but a steady decline in acreage. Eastern Europe is the major producing area: Russia, the Ukraine, and Poland generally account for more than half of total world output, and Germany about 15 percent. Much of the world's crop is consumed domestically, except for Canada, who exports most of its crop to the U.S. World trade in 1995/96, was estimated at 2.4 million metric tons, the highest since 1991/92, when 2.5 million tons shipped. The Republic of Korea is now the world's largest importer, with nearly one million tons in 1995/96, nearly twice that of 1994/95; Korea imported no rye from 1992 through 1994. China has also increased its import demand from virtually nothing earlier in the 1990s, to 500,000 tons in 1995/96. Japan's imports average about 400,000 tons. Eastern Europe supplies most of the world's rye exports.

World Production of Rye In Thousands of Metric Tons

Crop Year	Agrentina	Austria	Canada	Czech Republic[5]	Denmark	France	Germany	Hungary	Netherlands	Poland	Russia[4]	Spain	Turkey	Ukraine[4]	United States	World Total
1983-4	130	348	827	751	315	278	3,738	138	26	8,781	-----	253	380	14,000	689	31,407
1984-5	140	380	664	710	608	321	4,493	192	25	9,540	-----	325	360	13,400	827	33,398
1985-6	100	339	569	620	565	283	4,382	163	19	7,600	-----	295	360	15,700	524	32,217
1986-7	60	284	609	547	546	200	4,224	172	19	7,074	-----	220	350	15,248	496	30,782
1987-8	88	309	493	496	513	275	3,928	186	25	6,816	-----	320	350	18,055	503	33,034
1988-9	42	356	267	530	366	260	3,419	245	28	7,232	-----	357	360	18,517	373	32,989
1989-90	70	381	873	708	487	270	3,867	200	33	6,216	-----	336	320	18,288	347	33,412
1990-1	96	396	599	736	545	240	3,988	226	36	6,044	-----	267	240	21,193	258	36,861
1991-2	45	350	339	484	395	210	3,324	221	34	5,899	-----	242	240	14,061	248	27,359
1992-3	34	278	265	255	308	205	2,422	140	34	3,981	13,890	230	240	1,160	304	28,656
1993-4[1]	62	290	320	300	323	190	2,984	110	35	5,000	9,150	300	230	1,180	263	26,090
1994-5[2]		320	390	280	380	180	3,450	200		5,300	6,000	220	250	940	290	21,890
1995-6[3]		340	300	330	500	180	4,480	170		6,300	4,100	200	260	1,000	250	21,640

[1] Preliminary. [2] Estimate. [3] Forecast. [4] Formerly part of the U.S.S.R.; data not reported separately until 1992. [5] Formerly part of Czechoslovakia; data not reported separately until 1992. *Source: Foreign Agricultural Service, U.S. Department of Agriculture*

Production of Rye in the United States In Thousands of Bushels

Year	Georgia	Illinois	Indiana	Kansas	Michigan	Minnesota	Nebraska	North Dakota	Ohio	Oklahoma	Pennylvania	South Carolina	South Dakota	Texas	Virginia	Wisconsin
1983	1,470	336	270	220	600	4,960	1,265	4,320	210	780	578	320	8,740	450	312	300
1984	1,760	308	336	312	588	6,650	1,392	5,400	175	704	578	546	10,800	240	378	216
1985	2,070	256	308	300	651	3,300	1,242	2,640	172	828	470	532	4,440	400	312	234
1986	1,785	210	280	210	713	1,600	1,035	4,250	175	840	630	391	4,440	190	364	168
1987	1,540	144	162	270	640	1,200	1,150	5,115	180	360	525	528	5,040	150	435	100
1988	1,890	140	210	130	650	920	1,375	1,350	185	720	684	720	2,250	150	560	120
1989	1,610	312	204	80	825	1,088	600	1,064	155	532	576	644	3,240	126	264	360
1990	1,320	165	124	130	580	868	750	780	175	420	496	594	1,870	140	256	465
1991	1,300	162	100	115	360	648	1,000	992	155	665	297	630	1,152	228	264	435
1992	1,560	280	156	130	496	720	1,040	1,496	175	798	720	675	1,666	280	288	330
1993	1,380	224	150	693	420	667	500	1,050	150	660	340	380	1,600	363	165	260
1994	1,890	144	120	325	442	810	546	700	170	945	320	600	1,485	435	252	875
1995[1]	1,155	240	116	400	544	609	480	680	180	720	330	440	1,650	380	175	480

[1] Preliminary. *Source: Agricultural Statistics Board, U.S. Department of Agriculture*

RYE

Salient Statistics of Rye in the United States In Thousands of Bushels

Crop Year Beginning June 1	Supply: Stocks June 1	Supply: Production	Supply: Imports	Supply: Total Supply	Disappearance: Domestic Use: Food	Disappearance: Domestic Use: Industry	Disappearance: Domestic Use: Seed	Disappearance: Domestic Use: Feed & Residual	Disappearance: Domestic Use: Total	Disappearance: Exports	Disappearance: Total Disappearance	Acreage: Planted (1,000 Acres)	Acreage: Harvested for Grain (1,000 Acres)	Yield Per Harvested Acre Bushels
1986-7	21,869	19,067	1,000	41,936	3,500	2,000	3,700	13,653	22,853	500	23,353	2,334	661	28.8
1987-8	18,583	19,526	1,204	39,313	3,500	2,000	3,800	10,601	19,901	500	20,401	2,428	671	29.1
1988-9	18,912	14,689	200	33,801	3,500	2,000	3,200	11,401	20,101	3,400	23,501	2,374	595	24.7
1989-90	10,300	13,647	30	23,977	3,500	2,000	3,000	9,035	17,535	800	18,335	2,014	484	28.2
1990-1	5,642	10,176	3,895	19,713	3,500	2,000	3,000	7,673	16,173	213	16,386	1,625	375	27.1
1991-2	3,327	9,761	4,542	17,630	3,500	2,000	3,000	7,563	16,063	53	16,116	1,671	396	24.6
1992-3	1,523	11,952	3,099	16,100	3,500	2,000	3,000	6,000	14,500	0	14,500	1,582	406	29.4
1993-4[1]	1,555	10,340	4,600	16,495	3,600	2,000	3,000	6,900	15,500	0	15,500	1,493	381	27.1
1994-5[2]	971	11,341	4,400	16,700	3,600	2,000	3,000	6,600	15,200	0	15,200	1,613	407	27.9
1995-6[3]	1,500	9,928	4,500	15,900	3,600	2,000	3,000	5,700	14,300	100	14,400	1,612	378	26.3

[1] Preliminary. [2] Estimate. [3] Forecast. *Source: Economic Research Service, U.S. Department of Agriculture*

U.S. Rye Crop Production Reports and CCC Operations In Thousands of Bushels

Crop Year Beginning June 1	Official Crop Reports: July 1	Official Crop Reports: Aug. 1	Official Crop Reports: Dec. 1	Official Crop Reports: Final	National Average Support Rate: $ Per Bushel	National Average Support Rate: % of Parity	Placed Under Loan Total	Percentage of Production	Acquired by CCC
1986-7	------	17,892	19,498	19,067	1.63	38	5,900	30.9	2,600
1987-8	------	19,098	19,718	19,526	1.55	38	8,600	44.1	1,600
1988-9	------	15,062	------	14,689	1.50	37	300	2.0	800
1989-90	------	13,610	------	13,647	1.40	32	600	4.4	0
1990-1	------	10,098	------	10,176	1.33	31	200	2.0	0
1991-2	------	9,761	------	9,761	1.38	32	100	1.0	0
1992-3	------	11,952	------	11,952	1.46	34	200	1.7	0
1993-4[1]	------	10,340	------	10,340	1.46	34	100	1.0	0
1994-5[2]	------	11,138	------	11,341	1.61	37	.1	1.0	0
1995-6[3]	------	9,928	------	9,928	1.61		.1	0	0

[1] Preliminary. [2] Estimate. [3] Forecast. *Source: National Agricultural Statistics Service, U.S. Department of Agriculture*

Average Price of Cash Rye No. 2 at Minneapolis In Cents Per Bushel

Year	July	Aug.	Sept.	Oct.	Nov.	Dec.	Jan.	Feb.	Mar.	Apr.	May	June	Average
1984-5	227	209	207	206	221	227	231	230	235	236	235	248	226
1985-6	210	215	223	233	248	259	246	228	226	226	219	178	226
1986-7	156	151	160	168	173	202	195	185	185	173	196	163	176
1987-8	165	165	175	198	199	189	185	189	175	167	181	278	189
1988-9	266	264	264	247	269	280	268	268	264	270	257	201	260
1989-90	206	203	214	235	229	225	245	220	222	241	242	232	226
1990-1	215	222	220	220	190	245	252	243	242	242	245	245	232
1991-2	216	238	195	288	288	279	251	263	235	235	235	245	247
1992-3	245	241	267	295	303	298	288	290	300	289	285	282	282
1993-4	280	270	280	354	387	427	430	430	452	460	400	383	372
1994-5	360	336	305	305	305	305	285	267	270	270	270	270	296
1995-6	287	298	299	300	300	350							

Source: Agricultural Marketing Service, U.S. Department of Agriculture

Average Open Interest[1] of Rye Futures in Winnipeg In 20 Metric Ton Units

Year	Jan.	Feb.	Mar.	Apr.	May	June	July	Aug.	Sept.	Oct.	Nov.	Dec.
1984	2,224	4,566	3,980	3,883	3,731	3,023	2,888	5,430	7,098	6,320	5,894	4,158
1985	4,267	4,826	4,175	4,227	3,893	3,919	4,031	5,022	4,872	5,478	4,289	3,786
1986	4,287	4,335	3,302	4,211	3,039	2,553	2,900	3,317	3,479	2,767	2,827	2,031
1987	2,128	2,406	1,892	2,813	3,778	4,427	2,866	3,167	4,209	3,228	3,211	2,494
1988	2,690	2,645	2,760	2,809	2,176	3,635	3,562	3,628	3,537	3,139	2,827	2,160
1989	2,382	2,556	1,768	1,586	1,666	1,963	1,990	3,027	3,004	2,954	3,434	2,537
1990	2,828	2,840	1,943	2,335	2,500	2,408	2,673	3,062	2,669	2,379	2,116	1,625
1991	1,713	1,834	1,765	1,685	1,165	1,078	1,017	1,447	1,724	1,842	1,630	1,168
1992	1,153	1,954	2,330	2,336	1,996	1,902	1,385	1,642	1,416	1,218	965	1,058
1993	935	1,053	785	860	792	760	644	623	558	461	476	476
1994	472	474	275	113	51	40	34	37	20	23	17	22
1995[2]	20	20	34	42	31	31	17	15	15			

[1] Data prior to 1986 are for end of month. [2] Trading of contract ceased on September 20, 1995. *Source: Winnipeg Commodity Exchange*

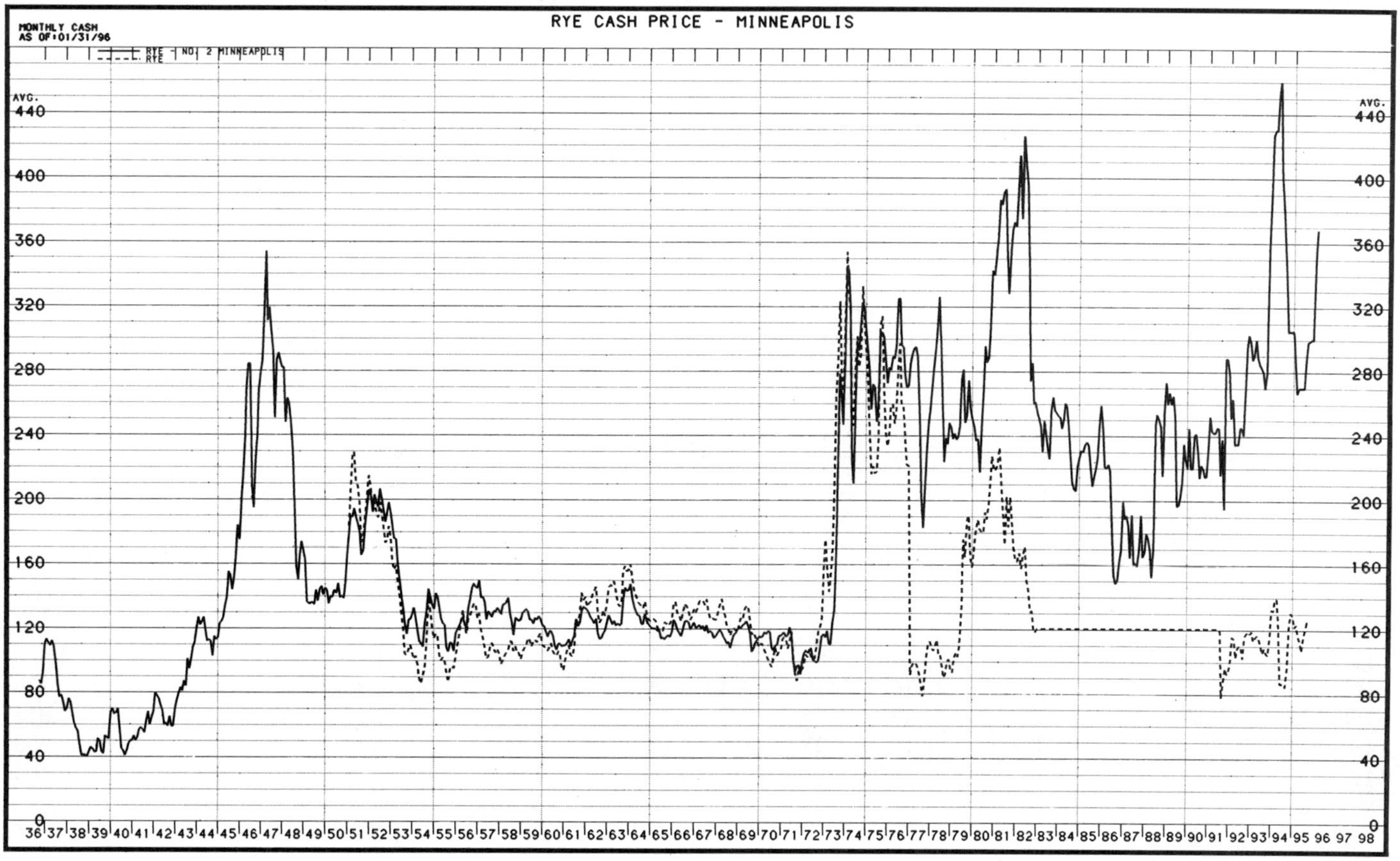

Salt

Salt is the most important mineral feedstock in the chemical industry. Sodium chloride, commonly known as salt, is a universal commodity used by virtually every person in the world. Salt is an important compound with approximately 14,000 different uses. World salt resources are virtually unlimited. Almost every country has salt deposits or solar evaporation operations. Salt substitutes are calcium chloride, calcium magnesium acetate, hydrochloric acid and potassium chloride.

Total U.S. salt production rose two percent in 1994 compared to 1993. Rock salt production rose six percent due to strong demand for de-icing salt. The 1994 Bureau of Mines survey indicated 27 companies currently operate 67 salt-producing plants in 14 states. The leading States in terms of total salt sold or used were Louisiana, 34 percent; Texas 20 percent; New York 15 percent; and Kansas seven percent. Louisiana, New York, and Ohio were major rock salt-producing states.

U.S. salt production accounted for 22 percent of total world production. Production and trade in salt increased from 1993. Total world production of all types of salt decreased slightly. The market for chlorine was depressed and there have been environmental problems associated with emissions of chlorinated compounds which could effect the near term outlook for the chloralkali industry, the largest consumer of salt.

In March 1994, the U.S.'s largest underground salt mine had a major roof collapse. It occurred at the Akzo Salt's Retsof mine near Rochester, N.Y. The annual rock salt production capacity was 3.63 million tonnes. Parts of the mine flooded and efforts to fix it were unsuccessful.

A record 47.2 million tonnes of domestic and imported salt was consumed in the U.S. in 1994. Salt producers reported that the major end users were chemicals, 39 percent; ice control, 35 percent; distributors, 10 percent; food and agricultural, 6 percent; industrial, 6 percent; primary water treatment, 1 percent; and other including exports, 3 percent.

World Production of All Salt   In Thousands of Metric Tons

Year	Australia	Canada	China	France	Germany	India	Italy	Japan	Mexico	Netherlands	Poland	Spain	Ukraine[3]	United Kingdom	United States	World Total
1987	7,150	11,165	19,800	8,642	18,299	10,915	4,702	1,540	7,047	4,386	6,807	3,522	16,976	7,806	36,943	197,010
1988	7,165	10,687	22,000	7,575	17,861	9,204	4,289	1,363	6,788	3,693	6,179	3,880	14,800	6,130	34,325	185,542
1989	7,069	11,021	28,000	8,267	17,129	9,603	4,186	1,367	6,703	3,756	4,670	3,090	15,000	6,720	35,251	191,660
1990	7,227	11,261	20,000	6,605	15,719	9,503	4,432	1,377	7,135	3,653	4,055	3,377	14,700	6,434	36,918	183,000
1991	7,791	11,993	24,100	6,500	14,900	9,503	3,954	1,380	7,533	3,417	3,840	3,400	14,000	6,828	35,902	185,000
1992	7,690	11,171	28,100	6,116	12,700	9,503	3,820	1,405	7,395	3,628	3,887	3,770	4,400	6,101	34,784	178,000
1993[1]	7,740	10,900	29,530	5,260	12,700	9,502	3,070	1,380	7,490	3,500	3,820	3,410	4,000	6,200	39,800	181,000
1994[2]	7,800	11,500	29,700	5,440	12,700	9,500	3,100	1,390	7,460	3,500	3,800	3,400	3,500	5,700	39,800	180,000

[1] Preliminary. [2] Estimate. [3] Formerly part of the U.S.S.R.; data not reported separately until 1992. *Source: U.S. Bureau of Mines*

Salient Statistics of the Salt Industry in the United States   In Thousands of Metric Tons

Year	Net Import Reliance as a % of Apparent Consumption	Average Value FOB Mine Vacuum & Open Pan $ Ton	Production: Total	Production: Open & Vacuum Pan	Production: Solar	Production: Rock	Production: Brine	Sold or Used by Producers: Open & Vacuum Pan	Sold or Used by Producers: Rock Salt	Sold or Used by Producers: Brine	Sold or Used by Producers: Total Salt	Sold or Used by Producers: Value[3] Million $	Imports for Consumption	Exports: Total	Exports: To Canada	Apparent Consumption
1987	11	94.21	33,515	3,426	2,830	11,095	16,164	3,426	10,855	16,442	33,106	684.2	5,186	491	433	37,801
1988	11	97.71	35,534	3,469	3,065	11,567	17,434	3,467	11,703	17,782	35,326	699.3	4,966	802	650	39,490
1989	10	102.22	35,632	3,606	2,849	12,682	16,496	3,599	15,364	16,509	35,250	776.8	5,519	1,422	1,240	39,347
1990	9	110.58	36,794	3,662	2,985	12,772	17,374	3,655	13,056	17,724	36,916	826.7	5,969	2,266	2,087	40,619
1991	11	114.75	36,316	3,654	2,813	11,188	18,660	3,623	11,064	18,640	35,902	801.5	6,188	1,777	1,288	40,313
1992	11	113.20	36,016	3,811	3,221	11,411	17,574	3,763	10,910	34,784	34,784	802.6	5,394	992	718	39,186
1993[1]	12	111.99	39,200	3,864	2,960	14,253	18,100	3,850	13,401	18,100	38,200	904.0	5,868	688	499	43,400
1994[2]	19	112.00	39,800	3,700	3,020	15,100	18,000	3,670	14,900	18,000	39,500	956.0	9,630	742	573	48,400

[1] Preliminary. [2] Estimate. [3] Values are fob mine or refinery and do not include cost of cooperage or containers. *Source: U.S. Bureau of Mines*

Salt Sold or Used by Producers in the U.S. by Classes & Consumers or Uses   In Thousands of Metric Tons

Year	Chemical[2]	Tanning Leather	Textile & Dyeing	Meat Packers	Canning	Baking	Agricultural Distribution	Feed Dealers	Feed Manufacturers	Rubber	Oil	Paper & Pulp	Metal Processing	Water Treatment	Grocery Stores	Water Conditioning Distrib.	Ice Control and/or Stabilization
1987	18,715	124	237	452	296	158	302	995	416	145	597	387	311	392	1,007	1,063	9,878
1988[3]	18,810	112	208	417	252	138	320	905	396	24	743	341	339	420	866	953	10,093
1989	18,105	105	211	394	263	152	530	810	363	31	653	338	363	469	880	880	10,397
1990	19,258	99	206	543	288	155	562	999	495	41	719	257	314	449	811	1,019	10,253
1991	20,014	76	232	370	255	142	546	1,097	335	138	554	237	293	432	897	889	9,360
1992	18,538	67	271	389	252	161	553	1,020	392	34	1,208	230	217	435	849	899	7,814
1993	19,273	67	313	418	322	152	808	1,120	476	37	1,220	110	216	419	823	527	13,600
1994[1]	18,400	82	304	410	342	157	842	1,070	478	33	1,290	150	239	440	934	505	16,400

[1] Preliminary. [2] Chlralkali producers and other chemical. [3] Reported in thousands of short tons prior to 1988. *Source: U.S. Bureau of Mines*

Sheep & Lambs

The U.S. inventory of sheep and lambs declined steadily during the first half of the 1990s, but in mid-1995 the pace of the contraction moderated. The breeding flock on July 1, 1995 of around 70,000 head was up slightly from January. U.S. slaughter in 1995 was expected to exceed the January l, inventory by five percent, but a sharp cut in exports was expected to hold the year's herd reduction to 13 percent of the beginning inventory versus an 18 percent decline in 1994.

1995 commercial lamb production of 284 million pounds compares with 304 million in 1994. The U.S. is a net importer of lamb, mostly from New Zealand and Australia. Per capita disappearance of lamb in the U.S. is small, totaling only 1.2 pounds in 1994 and 1995.

Wholesale carcass lamb prices traded at record highs toward mid-1995, holding in the mid to upper $70/cwt. range, $15 above the like 1994 period and apparently reflecting strong hotel-restaurant demand. From a pricing aspect, the industry had been notorious for sharp swings in wholesale prices, but increased forward contracting of supplies and quarterly price contracts by hotels and restaurants apparently took root in 1995. If the trend continues, it's expected to add some sorely needed stability to the industry.

World Sheep and Goat Numbers in Specified Countries, January 1 In Thousands of Head

Year	Agrentina	Australia	China	France	Greece	India	Italy	Kazakhstan[4]	New Zealand	Romania	Russia[4]	South Africa	Spain	Turkey	United Kingdom	United States
1986	29,243	155,561	-----	11,241	10,122	54,460	11,300	35,485	67,854	18,609	63,400	29,481	17,300	47,000	24,540	9,983
1987	28,998	158,800	166,220	10,580	10,000	55,482	11,451	36,408	69,204	18,762	64,100	29,753	17,600	43,500	25,976	10,334
1988	29,202	162,500	180,340	10,360	10,512	51,684	11,450	36,388	64,244	18,900	63,000	29,640	20,310	40,000	27,820	10,784
1989	29,345	171,292	201,527	11,495	10,694	155,204	11,623	36,498	64,600	16,210	62,700	30,935	23,797	45,700	29,045	10,858
1990	28,571	177,841	211,642	11,208	10,150	157,706	11,695	36,223	60,569	15,442	61,300	38,349	22,730	45,300	29,521	11,363
1991	27,552	173,982	210,021	11,071	9,759	160,207	10,848	35,700	57,852	14,062	58,200	37,585	24,037	45,000	30,147	11,200
1992	25,706	161,073	206,210	11,761	9,694	161,084	11,749	34,556	55,162	13,879	55,300	36,076	24,625	44,700	28,932	11,507
1993	24,500	140,542	207,329	11,451	9,659	162,155	11,724	34,420	52,568	12,079	51,400	35,770	24,615	44,600	29,493	10,906
1994[1]	23,500	132,609	217,314	11,505	9,604	163,156	11,835	34,208	50,298	12,276	43,700	33,800	23,872	44,000	29,333	9,742
1995[2]	21,626	121,000	240,530	11,389	9,559	164,242	12,070	24,955	50,135	12,119	35,900	33,385	23,900	43,000	29,484	8,895
1996[3]	21,839	124,000	260,000	11,300	9,386	165,660	12,100	20,000	49,300	12,000	31,900	34,230	23,900	42,300	29,524	8,350

[1] Preliminary. [2] Estimate. [3] Forecast. [4] Formerly part of the U.S.S.R.; data not reported separately until 1986. *Source: Foreign Agricultural Service, U.S. Department of Agriculture*

Salient Statistics of Sheep & Lamb in the United States In Thousands of Head

	--Inventory, Jan. 1--				--- Marketings[3]---		---------- Slaughter ----------					Production	------ Farm Value, Jan. 1 ------	
Year	Without New Crop Lambs	With New Crop Lambs	Lamb Crop	Total Supply	Sheep	Lambs	Farm	Commercial	Total[4]	Net Exports	Total Disappearance	(Live Weight) Mil. Lbs.	All Million $	$ Per Hear
1986	10,145	11,029	7,356	19,385	1,280	6,067	127	5,638	5,762	100	7,160	725.9	684.0	67.4
1987	10,572	11,417	7,190	18,607	1,195	6,194	111	5,200	5,312	15	6,693	733.1	799.3	75.7
1988	10,945	11,799	7,205	19,004	1,566	5,939	99	5,294	5,393	134	6,988	707.1	985.0	90.0
1989	10,858	11,674	7,721	19,395	1,058	6,492	98	5,466	5,563	188	7,086	775.6	894.9	82.4
1990	11,358	12,132	7,685	19,817	1,616	6,322	96	5,654	5,750	448	7,552	758.4	901.5	79.3
1991	11,174	11,930	7,651	19,581	1,777	6,566	92	5,722	5,813	787	7,792	762.8	734.9	65.6
1992	10,797	11,507	7,225	18,732	1,999	6,371	89	5,497	5,585	770	7,624	709.9	658.3	61.2
1993	10,201	10,906	6,379	17,285	1,809	6,089	72	5,184	5,256	750	7,185	651.2	702.8	70.2
1994[1]	9,079	9,714	5,897	15,644			76	4,938	5,014	760	6,744		638.6	70.3
1995[2]	8,008	8,886	5,604	14,490			80	4,562	4,642	420	5,882			

[1] Preliminary. [2] Estimate. [3] Excludes interfarm sales. [4] Includes all commercial and farm. *Source: Economic Research Service, U.S. Department of Agriculture*

Sheep and Lambs on Farms in the United States, January 1 In Thousands of Head

Year	California	Colorado	Idaho	Iowa	Minnesota	Missouri	Montana	New Mexico	Ohio	South Dakota	Texas	Utah	Wyoming	Total[3]
1986	1,065	600	320	350	213	101	423	525	275	540	1,810	484	819	9,983
1987	980	690	314	375	237	110	523	480	300	605	1,930	464	775	10,334
1988	990	755	324	405	258	103	530	489	270	610	1,960	478	865	10,945
1989	940	825	287	420	290	125	600	516	246	590	1,870	503	837	10,858
1990	1,000	840	286	490	285	138	663	495	270	590	2,090	509	805	11,363
1991	1,015	710	272	465	300	134	683	462	305	640	2,000	508	830	11,200
1992	995	710	273	345	293	111	658	445	215	602	2,140	488	870	10,749
1993	995	685	250	320	245	97	554	405	190	591	2,000	490	885	10,500
1994	1,120	647	266	267	231	91	534	340	198	550	1,895	442	813	9,742
1995[1]	1,060	545	270	294	190	83	490	315	162	530	1,700	445	790	8,886
1996[2]	1,000	535	273	345	185	73	465	265	153	500	1,650	395	680	8,457

[1] Preliminary. [2] Estimate. [3] Includes sheep & lambs on feed for market and stock sheep & lambs. *Source: Economic Research Service, U.S. Department of Agriculture*

SHEEP AND LAMBS

Average Wholesale Price of Slaughter Lambs (Choice) at San Angelo, Texas   In Dollars Per 100 Pounds

Year	Jan.	Feb.	Mar.	Apr.	May	June	July	Aug.	Sept.	Oct.	Nov.	Dec.	Average
1987	78.56	75.75	86.50	93.12	94.50	84.83	76.84	71.83	70.05	66.25	65.00	73.83	78.09
1988	83.53	77.25	83.75	76.50	72.67	59.38	59.00	56.19	59.50	63.94	65.55	68.83	68.84
1989	68.13	68.83	70.90	78.17	73.56	72.63	67.79	67.28	63.81	59.63	56.06	60.83	67.30
1990	54.80	60.38	63.69	63.13	62.25	53.56	53.25	51.20	51.75	52.50	50.42	48.08	55.42
1991	47.63	45.81	54.88	55.50	57.70	55.75	55.50	54.31	53.25	51.20	52.08	54.92	53.21
1992	58.56	57.69	66.55	74.63	68.88	64.50	58.17	52.38	53.61	52.81	56.93	67.25	61.00
1993	69.88	73.38	75.50	71.25	62.50	57.75	57.00	58.97	66.08	63.75	65.69	68.44	65.85
1994	56.67	62.31	61.19	51.25	60.94	66.92	75.33	79.50	76.08	69.96	73.60	67.50	66.77
1995[1]	65.38	75.08	73.75	68.58	77.20	81.63	83.70	87.00	80.00	75.90	72.00	70.50	75.89

[1] Preliminary. *Source: Economic Research Service, U.S. Department of Agriculture*

Federally Inspected Slaughter of Sheep & Lambs in the United States   In Thousands of Head

Year	Jan.	Feb.	Mar.	Apr.	May.	June	July	Aug.	Sept.	Oct.	Nov.	Dec.	Total
1987	418	390	432	477	363	407	411	400	459	446	399	439	5,042
1988	380	408	535	388	414	413	387	442	452	437	418	447	5,122
1989	418	415	505	393	435	423	398	476	440	468	467	457	5,295
1990	479	431	481	466	465	426	430	463	422	490	465	449	5,469
1991	495	449	546	436	442	388	431	438	456	501	449	471	5,504
1992	468	422	481	503	374	419	427	400	470	452	413	460	5,290
1993	380	384	476	461	396	462	394	413	410	391	403	430	5,002
1994	383	409	515	402	418	377	302	382	384	381	393	411	4,756
1995[1]	373	363	456	420	355	347	296	355	344	356	364	358	4,388

[1] Preliminary. *Source: Economic Research Service, U.S. Department of Agriculture*

Cold Storage Holdings of Lamb and Mutton, on First of Month   In Thousands of Pounds

Year	Jan.	Feb.	Mar.	Apr.	May	June	July	Aug.	Sept.	Oct.	Nov.	Dec.
1987	12,603	11,550	13,565	13,595	13,248	13,997	12,007	9,311	8,468	6,978	7,036	8,637
1988	7,949	8,069	6,190	7,056	7,639	8,018	8,738	8,537	7,253	6,827	6,396	6,001
1989	6,115	7,267	6,487	6,947	6,135	6,827	8,003	7,841	7,731	7,057	7,707	7,990
1990	7,625	7,844	8,468	7,905	8,390	8,052	9,685	10,107	9,144	8,929	8,458	8,099
1991	8,414	9,438	9,829	8,070	7,277	8,436	8,002	6,917	6,130	5,287	5,739	6,659
1992	6,296	7,255	6,670	8,455	8,580	9,870	10,968	11,711	9,314	8,751	8,520	8,406
1993	7,864	6,343	6,620	6,661	11,064	11,181	13,152	13,495	12,241	12,615	11,843	10,161
1994	8,372	9,198	9,507	11,194	11,505	11,368	12,124	12,026	11,016	9,261	8,946	8,796
1995[1]	10,913	11,620	10,826	12,691	14,934	13,992	12,306	10,679	10,240	7,412	7,503	7,846

[1] Preliminary. *Source: Economic Research Service, U.S. Department of Agriculture*

Average Price Received by Farmers for Sheep in the U.S.   In Dollars Per Hundred Pounds (Cwt.)

Year	Jan.	Feb.	Mar.	Apr.	May	June	July	Aug.	Sept.	Oct.	Nov.	Dec.	Average
1987	31.60	32.20	30.70	28.60	28.30	25.70	28.50	32.00	32.50	31.50	30.90	32.30	30.40
1988	34.70	30.10	29.70	26.00	23.90	23.20	25.00	25.30	25.00	25.30	27.80	29.10	27.09
1989	34.20	35,70	30.30	25.40	21.60	22.20	24.60	23.40	23.10	22.70	29.50	31.10	26.98
1990	32.20	30.90	30.00	23.50	19.70	19.60	24.70	24.30	18.90	19.20	20.40	22.40	23.82
1991	23.50	19.90	21.50	21.30	18.30	21.00	20.30	19.20	18.90	18.20	19.80	22.60	20.38
1992	28.10	29.80	31.60	28.30	23.10	22.60	24.00	25.80	25.00	25.30	25.50	33.20	26.86
1993	33.10	35.20	36.10	27.30	29.10	28.90	29.00	28.50	25.80	24.60	25.70	30.30	29.47
1994	35.10	37.00	34.30	29.60	29.30	33.60	30.10	29.40	27.90	27.30	30.50	34.70	31.57
1995[1]	32.80	37.50	31.90	29.40	27.70	29.20	28.90	27.00	26.00	23.50	23.90	25.20	28.58

[1] Preliminary. *Source: Economic Research Service, U.S. Department of Agriculture*

Average Price Received by Farmers for Lambs in the U.S.   In Dollars Per Hundred Pounds (Cwt.)

Year	Jan.	Feb.	Mar.	Apr.	May	June	July	Aug.	Sept.	Oct.	Nov.	Dec.	Average
1987	76.60	76.00	80.80	86.10	90.10	83.50	78.70	76.10	76.80	71.90	65.70	72.80	77.93
1988	80.70	80.40	80.20	74.80	72.60	60.20	60.00	59.80	64.20	66.20	66.30	68.60	69.50
1989	67.40	68.40	72.50	75.20	73.10	70.60	68.60	66.60	65.90	62.00	58.70	59.00	67.33
1990	56.40	59.80	66.00	62.90	59.80	55.40	54.40	54.00	52.80	51.90	50.10	48.60	56.01
1991	48.00	45.80	51.10	54.80	57.60	55.30	57.70	53.40	51.80	51.70	50.70	52.00	52.49
1992	53.50	55.20	63.40	69.30	68.80	65.60	62.20	55.90	56.70	55.40	58.20	65.20	60.78
1993	67.30	72.70	76.00	68.10	61.50	55.70	53.90	59.20	64.50	64.50	65.80	66.00	64.60
1994	60.60	59.40	58.60	54.50	54.50	63.00	72.80	75.50	71.20	68.00	70.60	69.10	64.82
1995[1]	67.50	70.40	74.80	74.40	80.40	85.70	85.70	85.70	82.70	77.90	77.00	77.70	78.33

[1] Preliminary. *Source: Economic Research Service, U.S. Department of Agriculture*

Silk

The Food and Agricultural Organization of the United Nations (FAO) reported that world production of silk in 1994 was 114,509 tonnes, up three percent from 1993. The world's major producer of silk is China, where production in 1994 was estimated by the FAO at 84,001 tonnes, an increase of nine percent from 1993. For several years, Chinese silk production has been on the rise. As recently as 1985, China produced 38,956 tonnes of silk. The next largest producer was India with 1994 estimated production of 17,000 tonnes, an increase of just over six percent from the previous year. The next largest producer is North Korea, where 1994 output was estimated at 4,800 tonnes, up four percent. Brazilian production was put at 2,450 tonnes, unchanged from 1993. Japan's silk output fell 40 percent to 2,400 tonnes. Other producers include Thailand, Uzbekistan, South Korea and Iran.

World exports of silk in 1993 were estimated at 34,799 tonnes, up 32 percent from 1992. The major exporters included China, Brazil, and North Korea. World imports in 1993 were put at 35,391 tonnes, up 25 percent. The major importers included Japan, Italy, South Korea and India.

Futures Markets

Raw silk is traded in Japan on the Kobe Raw Silk Exchange (KSE). Dry Cocoons are traded on the Manila International Futures Exchange Inc., (MIFE).

World Production of Silk In Metric Tons

Year	Brazil	China	India	Iran	Japan	North Korea	South Korea	Kyrgyzstan[3]	Tajikistan[3]	Thailand	Turkey	Turkmenistan[3]	Uzbekistan[3]	Viet Nam	World Total
1985	1,200	38,956	7,029	280	9,591	3,500	1,436	-----	-----	1,300	80	-----	3,908	330	68,090
1986	1,200	39,098	9,300	280	8,336	3,600	1,342	-----	-----	1,400	85	-----	3,710	350	69,178
1987	1,800	40,940	9,498	900	7,864	3,700	1,413	-----	-----	1,200	216	-----	4,200	360	72,597
1988	1,900	42,041	10,255	900	6,862	3,800	1,355	-----	-----	1,250	251	-----	4,300	420	73,866
1989	1,697	50,244	10,500	537	6,078	4,000	1,400	-----	-----	1,250	250	-----	3,900	400	80,745
1990	1,693	55,003	11,000	537	6,000	4,200	971	-----	-----	1,250	290	-----	4,094	500	85,987
1991	2,077	60,002	14,000	537	5,527	4,400	837	-----	-----	1,300	180	-----	4,100	500	93,880
1992	2,296	70,302	15,000	537	5,085	4,500	870	1,200	300	1,300	105	600	2,200	500	105,220
1993[1]	2,450	76,801	16,000	537	4,000	4,600	683	1,000	300	1,500	135	500	2,000	550	111,473
1994[2]	2,450	84,001	17,000	550	2,400	4,800	683	NA	NA	1,500	135	NA	NA	588	114,509

[1] Preliminary. [2] Estimate. [3] Formerly part of the U.S.S.R.; data not reported separately until 1992. NA = Not available.
Source: Food and Agricultural Organization of the United Nations

World Trade of Silk by Selected Countries In Metric Tons

	Imports								Exports						
Year	France	Hong Kong	India	Italy	Japan	South Korea	United States	World Total	Brazil	China	Hong Kong	Japan	North Korea	Russia[2]	World Total
1985	919	3,233	2,000	6,463	7,928	2,567	736	27,929	581	15,939	3,911	897	850	2,845	27,855
1986	572	3,179	2,100	7,133	8,943	3,747	475	29,835	692	16,349	4,115	586	1,060	2,816	27,931
1987	770	6,652	2,100	7,339	8,342	5,582	661	35,864	648	18,368	7,778	794	1,200	3,367	34,886
1988	771	7,489	1,411	8,094	10,259	4,851	435	39,216	670	20,168	8,553	442	1,200	4,432	37,276
1989	1,012	6,362	1,400	7,740	8,512	3,763	535	35,968	534	19,314	6,748	417	1,100	5,754	39,064
1990	796	3,928	1,647	4,775	7,111	3,204	326	27,322	1,064	13,066	4,102	380	1,200	1,703	27,977
1991	579	4,347	2,100	5,297	6,933	3,519	439	29,623	2,052	15,178	4,186	405	900	2,000	29,188
1992	693	4,400	2,843	4,337	5,137	3,627	288	28,233	1,552	13,474	4,358	701	800	410	26,435
1993[1]	960	5,475	4,700	5,634	5,982	4,494	375	35,391	1,495	15,652	7,204	904	350	166	34,799

[1] Preliminary. [2] Formerly part of the U.S.S.R.; data not reported separately until 1992. *Source: Food and Agricultural Organization of the United*

U.S. Raw Silk Deliveries In Bales of 132-Pounds

Year	Jan.	Feb.	Mar.	Apr.	May	June	July	Aug.	Sept.	Oct.	Nov.	Dec.	Total
1984	715	537	455	315	636	655	229	672	532	562	391	538	6,237
1985	462	689	344	480	415	NA	NA	NA	NA	NA	NA	NA	4,813
1986	410	504	197	244	225	227	555	NA	NA	NA	NA	NA	4,272
1987	411	680	572	526	245	447	253	327	330	470	239	448	4,948
1988	292	430	559	317	302	189	203	613	310	126	367	108	3,816
1989	358	234	471	329	405	564	353	401	288	317	475	442	4,637
1990	455	352	387	158	342	150	248	53	49	103	152	139	2,588
1991	124	126	206	187	100	250	445	305	220	345	325	351	2,984
1992	145	192	425	209	122	459	173	166	146	223	249	132	2,641
1993	457	173	281	215	315	197	NA	NA	NA	NA	NA	NA	3,066
1994[1]	363	71	224	233	227	479	315	227	195	193	315	201	3,043

[1] Preliminary. NA = Not available. *Source: Fiber Economics Bureau, Inc.*

Silver

Silver prices spiked to their highest level of the 1990s during the second quarter and then lapsed into a lethargic trading affair during the second half of the year. By year end, nearby futures prices were trading at $5.16 per ounce versus a low for the year of $4.34 and a high of $6.16. Many variables impact on silver's price with some rooted in tangible supply/demand data, but intangibles such as inflation fears often have greater impact. Also, a belief persists suggesting a direct tandem price correlation between gold and silver. Silver, often called the poor man's gold, tends to have greater price volatility than gold. Overriding these variables at times are computer/chart based signals that can quickly trigger price swings in either direction.

In the spring of 1995, the buoyancy in the equity markets suggested that the economy's strength was not dissipating, which in turn was seen as buoying industrial demand for silver and triggering a cost push inflation. Moreover, the flip side of the outlook suggested that any economic slippage would force an easing of credit and rekindled inflation fears. Speculative buying of silver quickened with a 25 percent price appreciation from late March to mid-May. Fueling the price advance were declining silver inventories at COMEX approved vaults, but that did not necessarily mean increased silver consumption, but more likely a reallocation of inventory placement. COMEX silver stocks in mid-1995 of 181 million ounces compared with 240 million ounces a year earlier. Total U.S. silver stocks at yearend 1994 were not definitively known, but at least 10,400 metric tons were held in futures exchange approved vaults, about the same as a year earlier.

World mine production of silver in 1994 of 13,900 metric tons was the lowest since 1986 and compares with a high of 16,600 tons in 1990. Forecasts for the next few years put mine production around 15,000 tons, with metal's ore recovery more a function of the price of the host metals associated with silver, such as copper. Mexico is the world's largest producer with about 2,330 tons in 1994. U.S. production in 1994 of 1,480 tons compares with 1,645 in 1993 and a high of 2,121 tons in 1990. Nevada is the largest producing state. Forecasts of U.S. mine production in the second half of the 1990s range between 1,400 to 2,000 tons. The worldwide recovery of silver from secondary supplies such as scrap and old coinage is expected to remain large; in the U.S. secondary production totaled 1,700 metric tons in 1994 versus 2,020 in 1993.

World silver consumption in recent years has lagged production resulting in a buildup in inventories, but not necessarily reportable stocks. Silver is hoarded, either in the form of coinage or bullion, as a speculative hedge against economic uncertainties. World industrial use of silver averaged about 565 million ounces from 1990 to 1993 while coinage use averaged near 600 million. The U.S. is the largest user for industrial use and coinage with 130 million ounces in 1993 versus 127 million in 1992. More than half of U.S. usage has generally been for photographic needs. U.S. coinage needs have jumped since the early 1980s when two million ounces were used, escalating a record high 12.2 million in 1987, and then falling to an annual average of nine million in the 1990s. The U.S. imported 66 million ounces of silver in 1994, the lowest since 1987, the bulk of which came from Canada and Mexico. U.S. exports of refined silver of 28 million ounces in 1994 compares with 22.6 million in 1993.

Silver's 1995 price range of $4.34-$6.16 compared to $4.53-$5.79 in 1994.

Futures Markets

Silver futures are traded on the Tokyo Commodity Exchange (TOCOM), the Chicago Board of Trade (CBOT), the Mid America Commodity Exchange (MidAm), and the New York Mercantile Exchange, COMEX division (COMEX). Options are traded on the European Options Exchange (EOE-Optiebeurs), the CBOT, and the COMEX.

World Mine Production of Silver, by Selected Countries In Thousands of Kilograms (Metric Tons)

Year	Australia	Bolivia	Brazil	Canada[3]	Chile	China	Japan	Kazakhstan[4]	Rep. of Korea	Mexico	Peru	Poland	South Africa	Spain	Sweden	United States	World Total[2]
1980	767	190	24	1,037	298	78	268	1,431	71	1,557	1,381	766	222	141	166	1,005	10,661
1981	743	199	24	1,129	361	78	280	1,446	95	1,646	1,460	640	235	166	161	1,265	11,246
1982	907	170	24	1,314	382	78	306	1,459	101	1,840	1,305	657	216	118	168	1,252	11,543
1983	1,033	187	15	1,106	468	78	307	1,468	105	1,978	1,570	678	203	47	207	1,351	12,058
1984	972	142	26	1,327	490	78	324	1,474	117	2,343	1,651	744	218	290	239	1,387	13,064
1985	1,086	111	32	1,197	517	80	339	1,490	124	2,153	1,811	831	208	367	231	1,227	13,051
1986	1,023	95	58	1,088	500	90	351	1,500	157	2,303	1,926	829	222	327	263	1,074	13,034
1987	1,119	142	110	1,375	500	100	281	1,510	209	2,415	2,054	831	208	350	254	1,241	14,019
1988	1,118	232	124	1,443	507	110	252	2,500	227	2,359	1,552	1,063	200	353	208	1,661	15,484
1989	1,075	267	114	1,371	545	125	156	2,500	239	2,400	1,840	1,003	180	668	228	2,008	16,425
1990	1,173	311	171	1,501	655	130	150	2,500	238	2,425	1,930	832	161	500	243	2,121	16,600
1991	1,180	376	154	1,339	678	150	171	2,200	265	2,295	1,930	899	171	208	239	1,855	15,600
1992	1,248	282	162	1,220	1,029	170	178	900	333	2,098	1,610	798	183	160	210	1,804	14,600
1993[1]	1,090	333	165	896	970	200	137	900	330	2,420	1,630	767	192	159	255	1,645	14,300
1994[2]	1,060	350	170	758	980	210	133	800	340	2,330	1,700	770	196	160	276	1,480	13,900

[1] Preliminary. [2] Estimate. [3] Shipments. [4] Formerly part of the U.S.S.R.; data not reported separately until 1992. *Source: U.S. Bureau of Mines*

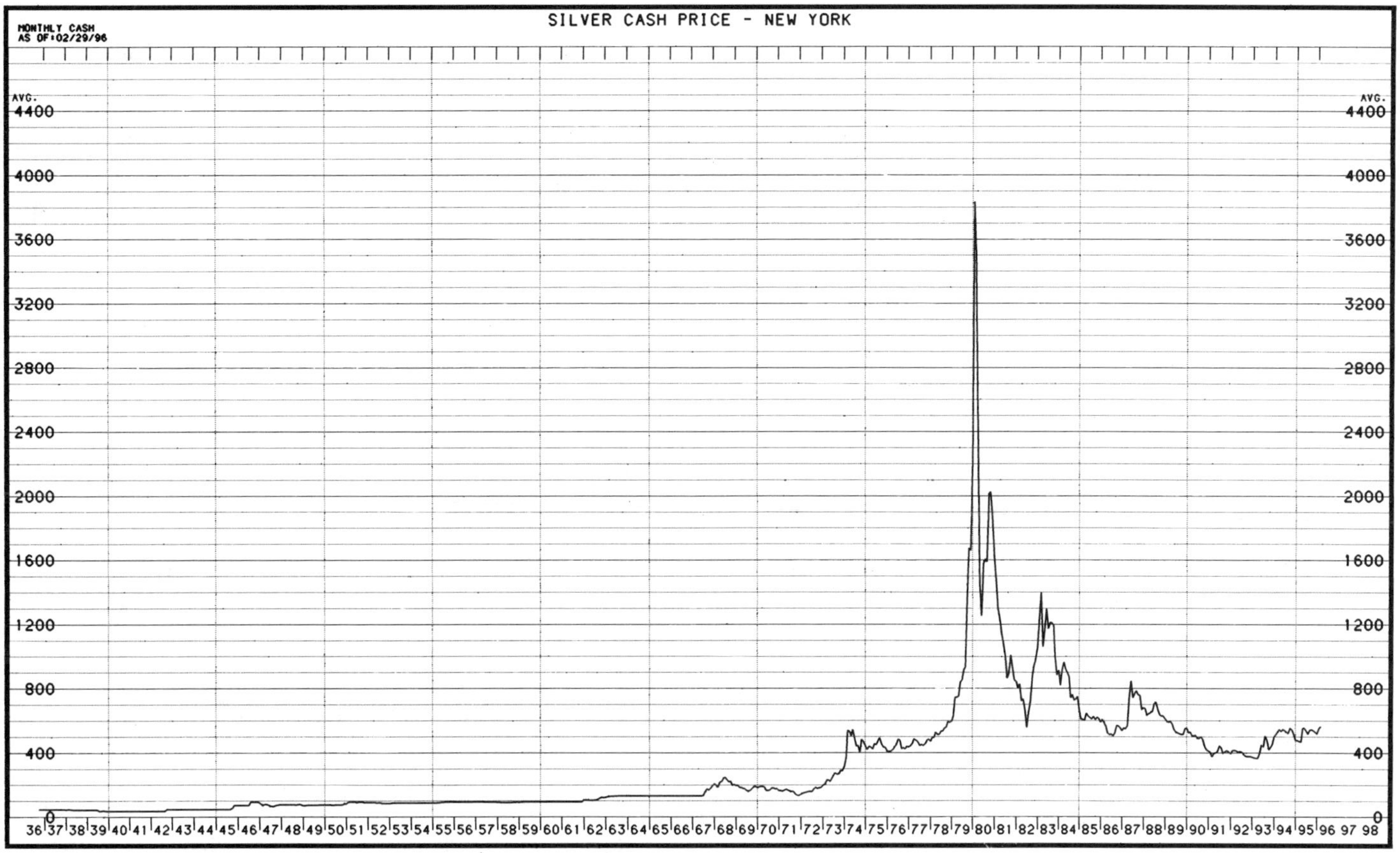

Average Price of Silver in New York (Handy & Harman) In Cents Per Troy Ounce (.999 Fine)

Year	Jan.	Feb.	Mar.	Apr.	May	June	July	Aug.	Sept.	Oct.	Nov.	Dec.	Average
1972	147.31	150.36	153.64	157.20	158.30	156.90	173.58	184.61	177.67	181.06	183.25	197.60	168.45
1973	201.66	223.62	230.92	220.72	240.12	262.09	270.56	263.65	267.51	288.56	285.99	313.67	255.96
1974	363.70	535.90	532.55	503.60	543.18	489.61	441.55	443.14	404.88	482.98	469.39	439.13	470.80
1975	419.27	437.00	434.53	420.92	453.81	448.91	470.45	492.50	451.60	432.86	433.24	408.50	441.97
1976	406.27	408.64	418.91	435.05	448.85	481.17	477.95	423.70	429.52	422.51	437.27	434.68	435.38
1977	440.90	452.74	484.16	477.71	469.20	444.30	449.81	444.43	453.86	476.32	482.84	470.60	462.30
1978	493.40	493.57	526.80	511.59	511.95	531.59	533.07	549.50	557.48	591.79	586.49	592.95	540.02
1979	625.45	741.69	745.35	749.25	836.57	853.83	913.50	933.43	1,395.92	1,678.07	1,655.27	2,179.28	1,108.97
1980	3,827.21	3,508.50	2,413.33	1,384.09	1,253.29	1,574.76	1,605.97	1,589.71	2,014.38	2,018.14	1,864.82	1,639.33	2,063.29
1981	1,475.15	1,306.50	1,236.91	1,091.73	1,084.75	1,000.07	863.11	892.29	1,003.55	925.12	854.68	843.16	1,048.09
1982	803.05	826.79	721.30	731.07	667.35	557.79	649.67	713.61	872.52	946.75	991.83	1,058.63	795.03
1983	1,239.57	1,396.37	1,061.87	1,169.43	1,295.26	1,174.93	1,208.75	1,209.56	1,191.50	984.13	883.73	912.07	1,143.93
1984	818.24	912.65	965.11	922.05	897.20	874.38	741.57	761.30	726.34	731.68	748.89	669.42	814.07
1985	609.82	606.95	601.36	645.83	628.05	617.18	610.43	624.68	605.37	618.80	613.39	588.78	614.22
1986	605.30	587.37	563.93	522.91	511.48	515.26	504.93	521.83	568.29	566.69	559.56	536.40	547.00
1987	552.88	548.76	568.16	742.79	843.90	741.09	767.84	784.74	759.05	755.80	666.18	679.02	700.85
1988	673.25	632.48	641.28	647.83	654.26	703.68	714.65	670.80	636.48	628.45	627.53	610.83	653.46
1989	597.17	589.08	592.98	579.08	544.70	528.02	523.65	517.93	513.30	513.30	546.53	554.28	550.00
1990	524.30	527.84	505.82	504.58	507.39	490.60	485.90	498.15	479.03	436.59	416.90	406.84	482.00
1991	402.82	372.34	396.90	397.07	404.07	438.85	430.38	393.80	403.60	410.22	406.05	390.90	403.92
1992	412.08	413.71	410.36	403.00	406.83	405.64	394.89	379.67	376.33	373.66	376.32	370.98	393.62
1993	367.93	364.39	364.80	396.36	445.02	437.50	503.74	480.61	417.19	433.45	450.25	496.83	429.84
1994	513.14	527.24	545.11	530.87	543.64	539.34	528.65	519.54	552.88	544.10	519.60	476.88	528.42
1995	476.36		464.83		555.25	535.27	517.58	539.59	540.78	534.48	529.30	514.75	520.82

Source: American Metal Market

SILVER

World Silver Consumption[1] In Millions of Troy Ounces

	Industrial Uses										Coinage							
Year	Canada	France	Germany	India	Italy	Japan	Mexico	United Kingdom	United States	World Total	Austria	Canada	France	Germany	Mexico	United States	World Total	World Total
1973	10.4	22.5	60.0	13.0	41.5	69.0	16.5	31.0	196.4	522.5	6.3	6.6	.1	7.0	NA	.9	28.5	551.0
1974	10.3	21.0	55.0	15.0	38.6	46.5	10.2	25.0	176.0	470.0	5.7	9.0	3.6	7.6	NA	1.0	31.6	501.6
1975	10.3	21.0	38.9	13.0	28.9	46.4	8.8	28.0	157.7	407.7	9.1	10.4	1.8	5.4	NA	2.7	33.4	441.1
1976	9.3	31.8	52.9	18.0	32.1	60.7	10.2	28.0	170.6	484.7	6.9	8.4	6.2	1.8	NA	1.3	30.0	514.7
1977	9.1	32.6	48.1	17.6	33.8	63.2	8.6	32.2	153.6	459.9	8.9	.5	7.1	4.6	4.2	.1	34.5	494.4
1978	9.6	24.6	42.0	20.0	41.8	64.9	9.1	29.0	160.2	452.4	9.6	1.0	9.0	3.6	6.6	0	39.5	491.9
1979	7.3	24.1	39.8	19.0	33.3	68.8	8.6	27.6	157.3	448.2	4.0	.8	10.6	3.7	5.0	.2	31.0	479.2
1980	8.7	19.8	31.9	19.0	21.8	61.5	4.9	19.5	124.7	364.3	2.3	.2	.1	0	6.1	.1	15.0	379.3
1981	8.5	18.9	29.3	19.0	21.5	59.6	5.0	18.4	116.7	355.4	3.1	.3	.1	.5	0	.2	9.5	364.9
1982	9.0	17.1	32.7	16.1	20.8	63.2	5.7	18.1	118.8	361.4	4.5	.3	1.4	.3	0	1.8	12.0	373.4
1983	8.9	16.5	30.3	12.9	15.0	72.1	3.5	17.7	116.3	356.5	1.8	.4	2.2	0	0	2.1	10.2	366.7
1984	9.3	17.1	32.2	16.1	19.4	78.8	5.5	19.2	114.8	376.2	2.4	.3	3.9	0	2.5	2.0	13.7	389.9
1985	9.1	17.0	34.1	20.9	23.9	72.6	8.0	19.1	118.7	500.0	4.9	.3	2.2	0	3.5	.4	13.4	513.4
1986	9.6	17.1	36.3	22.5	33.7	78.5	7.7	19.0	118.9	542.3	1.2	1.3	2.2	0	2.0	10.3	26.8	569.1
1987	10.4	17.6	39.1	20.1	38.6	90.9	6.9	21.1	115.1	538.7	.6	1.2	2.2	3.2	2.3	12.2	30.4	569.1
1988	11.0	21.3	44.0	22.4	37.9	100.4	7.1	22.8	112.0	568.6	.6	1.1	2.2	3.2	2.0	7.9	25.3	593.9
1989	12.0	22.1	46.7	25.6	43.1	100.8	7.2	24.6	120.0	599.2	.4	3.3	2.2	3.2	1.7	6.8	26.3	625.5
1990	4.0	22.4	51.7	42.3	45.7	106.9	14.1	24.7	118.9	651.8	.5	1.9	2.2	2.4	1.2	9.1	31.6	683.4
1991	3.1	21.9	52.2	42.8	50.8	108.8	14.8	25.0	113.0	653.1	.6	.9	2.0	5.5	1.6	10.5	28.1	681.2
1992	1.0	27.5	49.3	58.0	58.9	104.9	16.1	25.7	115.2	679.2	.5	.8	2.1	5.4	8.7	8.1	33.3	712.5
1993	.9	26.9	45.6	110.0	54.6	104.7	16.9	27.7	118.1	721.6	.5	1.2	1.0	2.6	17.1	7.9	39.5	761.1
1994[2]	.8	27.1	45.0	91.1	48.1	107.8	16.6	31.6	126.5	706.4	.5	1.5	1.0	7.0	13.0	8.2	42.9	749.3

[1] Non-communist areas only. [2] Preliminary. NA = Not available. *Source: The Silver Institute*

U.S. Mine Production of Recoverable Silver In Metric Tons

Year	Arizona	Idaho	Montana	Nevada	Total	Year	Arizona	Idaho	Montana	Nevada	Total
1985	152	586	125	154	1,227	1990	173	442	220	646	2,125
1986	140	349	148	199	1,074	1991	148	337	222	578	1,848
1987	114	NA	185	379	1,241	1992	153	255	195	586	1,740
1988	152	340	192	608	1,661	1993[1]	157	190	125	713	1,604
1989	171	439	194	625	2,007	1994[2]	177	158	71	602	1,380

[1] Preliminary. [2] Estimate. NA = Not available. *Source: U.S. Bureau of Mines*

U.S. Consumption of Silver, by End Use In Millions of Troy Ounces

Year	Batteries	Brazing Alloys & Solders	Catalysts	Electrical Contacts - Conductors	Mirrors	Photo-graphic Materials	Jewerly	Sterling Ware	Silver-plate	Total Net Industrial Con-sumption	Coinage	Total Con-sumption
1979	4.6	10.9	5.6	33.5	1.9	66.0	5.4	13.1	8.1	157.3	.2	157.4
1980	6.0	8.5	3.0	27.8	.7	49.8	5.9	9.1	4.4	124.7	.1	124.8
1981	3.8	7.7	3.8	26.4	.6	51.0	5.4	4.4	3.9	116.7	.2	116.8
1982	4.2	7.4	2.4	27.7	1.0	51.8	6.3	6.6	3.3	118.8	1.8	120.7
1983	2.6	5.8	2.4	26.3	1.0	51.8	6.9	7.0	3.2	116.3	2.1	118.4
1984	2.7	5.9	2.4	25.6	1.0	55.3	5.8	3.6	3.5	114.8	2.7	117.5
1985	2.5	5.6	2.4	27.5	1.0	57.9	5.8	3.5	3.7	118.6	.4	118.9
1986	3.7	6.4	2.3	27.4	1.0	55.4	4.6	3.9	3.7	118.9	10.3	129.2
1987	2.4	5.6	2.4	22.7	1.0	60.2	4.2	3.8	2.5	115.3	12.2	127.5
1988	2.5	NA	2.6	23.0	1.1	62.5	2.9	3.5	2.6	112.0	7.9	119.9
1989	2.8	NA	2.8	23.5	1.1	65.2	2.4	3.4	2.7	120.0	6.8	126.8
1990	3.0	NA	3.0	22.8	1.2	67.0	2.0	3.5	2.8	118.9	9.1	128.0
1991	3.1	NA	3.3	18.3	1.1	65.0	2.0	3.5	2.8	113.0	10.5	123.5
1992	3.1	NA	3.8	18.3	1.2	63.5	3.0	3.9	2.9	115.2	8.1	123.3
1993	3.3	NA	4.0	18.8	1.3	64.0	3.3	4.0	3.0	118.1	7.9	126.0
1994[1]	----------	----------	46.7	----------	----------	----- 67.8 -----		----- 12.0 -----		126.5	8.2	134.7

[1] Preliminary. NA = Not available. *Source: The Silver Institute*

Commodity Exchange, Inc. (COMEX) Warehouse of Stocks of Silver In Millions of Troy Ounces

Year	Jan. 1	Feb. 1	Mar. 1	Apr. 1	May 1	June 1	July 1	Aug. 1	Sept. 1	Oct. 1	Nov. 1	Dec. 1
1984	127.4	123.7	116.8	117.2	115.3	114.3	121.8	120.3	116.2	115.0	113.4	115.4
1985	118.9	121.5	122.3	106.6	106.0	104.2	133.7	140.8	141	143.6	149.2	153.7
1986	155.2	142.3	145.9	151.3	154.9	144.6	151.9	150.7	158.6	156.8	138.1	145.1
1987	144.9	150.2	160.0	157.9	157.7	156.1	152.5	151.9	158.6	155.7	154.8	155.8
1988	156.3	156.3	156.9	155.8	161.3	164.3	167.1	169.7	175.6	178.8	175.3	178.5
1989	174.4	179.2	190.6	194.3	200.4	204.1	206.0	207.3	210.4	212.3	226.6	237.9
1990	238.8	240.8	243.4	252.1	253.8	255.4	251.6	251.5	255.8	260.2	258.6	257.7
1991	265.3	266.2	263.8	260.7	263.4	263.5	266.1	275.8	270.7	270.2	265.9	260.6
1992	270.7	270.0	279.6	269.6	262.3	268.0	268.4	271.8	274.7	278.6	278.6	280.7
1993	275.3	271.7	273.6	268.4	266.0	271.4	273.9	278.4	278.7	275.7	275.4	277.1
1994	263.5	252.9	250.8	239.4	241.4	233.8	237.4	246.9	250.0	254.0	259.2	265.1
1995	260.7	264.0	235.1	211.0	189.7	184.6	181.3	175.8	156.5	156.5	156.1	156.9

Source: Commodity Exchange, Inc. of New York (COMEX)

United States Production[1] of Refined Silver from all Sources In Metric Tons

Year	Jan.	Feb.	Mar.	Apr.	May	June	July	Aug.	Sept.	Oct.	Nov.	Dec.	Total
1983	9,121	8,533	9,063	9,653	7,663	10,210	8,579	8,342	7,886	8,738	9,880	12,058	112,200
1984	7,094	8,414	8,446	9,827	10,423	8,921	8,879	11,226	8,971	8,386	10,200	13,920	116,400
1985	8,414	7,930	8,645	9,238	9,344	9,850	8,578	9,885	8,191	8,429	8,987	11,467	109,000
1986	7,897	7,835	7,340	8,727	7,547	7,129	3,988	6,404	6,932	7,869	8,216	10,197	90,081
1987	8,170	6,098	7,047	7,946	8,473	7,839	8,777	7,731	7,703	6,692	6,955	9,024	92,455
1988	7,852	7,264	9,453	7,956	7,891	9,453	10,562	9,903	7,374	8,074	9,545	9,726	105,053
1989	10,025	9,488	9,883	9,650	12,006	8,956	7,722	9,337	7,978	7,901	10,099	8,999	112,044
1990	8,938	7,839	7,106	8,725	8,571	8,819	8,230	7,747	7,619	8,019	9,732	8,106	99,451
1991	8,767	6,715	7,378	7,334	9,162	7,579	7,070	8,165	8,444	8,335	8,023	8,614	95,586
1992[2]	----------	1,064	----------	----------	1,031	----------	----------	933	----------	----------	557	----------	3,921
1993	----------	1,032	----------	----------	1,080	----------	----------	795	----------	----------	712	----------	4,059
1994[3]	----------	802	----------	----------	908	----------	----------	808	----------	----------	803	----------	3,321

[1] Output of commercial bars .999 fine, including U.S. Mint purchases of crude. Production is from both foreign and domestic silver. [2] Prior to 1992, shown in thousands of troy ounces. [3] Preliminary. *Source: U.S. Bureau of Mines*

SILVER

U.S. Exports of Refined Silver to Selected Countries In Thousands of Troy Ounces

Year	Australia	Canada	France	Germany	Hong Kong	Japan	Singapore	South Korea	Switzer-land	United Arab Emirates	United Kingdom	Uruguay	Other Countries	Total
1987	NA	2,086	134	261	NA	5,426	NA	NA	NA	NA	2,568	NA	157	11,241
1988	NA	1,073	157	480	NA	6,030	NA	166	70	NA	4,894	NA	82	14,270
1989	NA	2,597	61	519	NA	5,997	NA	588	88	NA	3,722	NA	55	13,828
1990	NA	2,586	64	749	NA	16,568	1,005	298	74	NA	2,060	152	93	23,664
1991	NA	736	22	350	755	6,519	1,593	2,823	8	3,462	8,628	259	73	25,318
1992	593	2,177	44	140	497	4,554	2,126	NA	70	6,922	10,856	671	47	29,274
1993	520	4,910	--	34	1,002	3,414	2,500	1,492	38	4,403	3,673	530	44	22,673
1994[1]	NA	4,289	NA	8	456	9,275	16	3,084	NA	3,627	4,896	1,353	193	27,902

[1] Preliminary. NA = Not available, included in "Other Countries," if any. *Source: American Bureau of Metal Statistics*

U.S. Imports of Silver from Selected Countries In Thousands of Troy Ounces

	Ores and Concentrates				Refined Bullion						
Year	Canada	Mexico	Other Countries	Total	Canada	Chile	Mexico	Peru	Uruguay	Other Countries	Total
1987	650	1,561	59	2,681	16,665	113	40,779	243	NA	71	67,959
1988	288	1,511	31	6,151	31,361	211	37,471	11	NA	139	72,663
1989	56	129	28	225	37,203	724	53,262	2,761	1,958	0	98,429
1990	12	189	2	203	33,518	1,671	40,204	8,141	2,265	165	86,741
1991	42	277	29	348	25,389	6,640	34,448	13,748	NA	17	81,198
1992	646	126	11	814	24,937	2,002	40,230	16,841	400	2	85,572
1993	299	836	11	1,147	28,622	1,058	27,241	12,709	NA	28	70,189
1994[1]	369	3,805	5	4,271	28,678	1,923	22,135	12,663	NA	32	66,141

[1] Preliminary. NA = Not available, included in "Other Countries," if any. *Source: American Bureau of Metal Statistics*

Average Open Interest of Silver Futures at New York (COMEX) In Contracts

Year	Jan.	Feb.	Mar.	Apr.	May	June	July	Aug.	Sept.	Oct.	Nov.	Dec.
1983	39,122	49,642	45,929	49,603	51,481	50,738	42,589	48,332	49,920	51,782	54,999	59,067
1984	62,135	64,640	68,763	72,204	65,424	62,890	61,644	63,700	63,655	66,339	78,744	78,492
1985	82,285	83,773	74,987	75,583	74,587	76,985	71,610	73,325	71,100	81,987	87,775	86,249
1986	82,915	81,670	75,891	79,653	74,781	72,411	67,063	74,916	79,376	81,192	93,567	88,962
1987	93,442	94,823	94,366	114,498	98,917	91,469	82,200	87,131	79,747	84,420	78,669	71,204
1988	76,788	79,031	68,994	66,187	69,137	83,428	84,517	82,793	82,369	85,261	92,026	90,081
1989	93,582	95,876	93,953	99,598	90,996	86,804	83,466	88,886	85,248	88,406	91,459	93,606
1990	94,397	93,713	96,182	96,701	95,784	103,575	99,098	99,668	92,436	91,093	84,181	80,364
1991	91,685	101,352	99,564	99,791	94,921	105,646	97,554	95,536	87,079	90,791	89,765	91,390
1992	97,179	93,352	88,445	96,427	87,355	84,002	80,879	81,695	74,265	72,090	77,633	72,296
1993	80,155	86,241	87,127	100,985	105,931	102,539	107,537	109,427	93,891	93,316	101,576	110,029
1994	112,584	116,652	112,745	119,314	121,296	126,255	122,138	118,081	113,261	117,224	126,666	134,099
1995	132,158	139,806	132,317	129,063	112,723	108,941	101,842	111,251	95,433	101,763	105,453	95,551

Source: New York Mercantile Exchange, COMEX Division

Volume of Trading of Silver Futures at New York (COMEX) In Thousands of Contracts

Year	Jan.	Feb.	Mar.	Apr.	May	June	July	Aug.	Sept.	Oct.	Nov.	Dec.	Total
1983	502.7	601.4	446.6	452.9	516.1	623.7	454.3	656.5	492.0	569.0	596.9	512.7	6,433
1984	570.8	698.8	695.7	629.9	626.7	587.4	554.7	601.5	431.3	449.2	534.2	362.3	6,698
1985	531.8	488.0	518.4	449.8	424.8	377.9	377.7	388.5	267.7	314.0	332.8	349.9	4,821
1986	394.0	368.9	277.6	438.8	280.1	336.1	187.9	317.8	454.6	286.7	338.9	168.2	3,850
1987	247.3	248.0	343.2	932.7	438.6	486.4	378.7	502.7	390.3	468.1	355.9	263.7	5,056
1988	274.1	301.1	348.9	313.9	341.1	726.9	638.9	411.7	299.9	268.4	475.4	264.4	4,665
1989	317.2	408.5	447.3	354.2	278.5	484.7	272.3	360.4	224.9	261.1	622.1	345.4	4,377
1990	343.2	413.3	210.2	364.1	328.5	433.8	242.3	524.8	201.3	308.4	323.7	219.8	3,914
1991	309.8	420.1	446.5	396.0	255.5	547.5	344.7	320.6	268.7	253.0	349.7	242.6	3,801
1992	408.2	320.2	229.0	332.4	184.8	295.4	197.9	266.3	173.2	125.5	355.7	127.7	3,016
1993	167.2	332.5	243.0	453.9	433.5	523.9	503.9	531.8	428.4	338.2	520.6	373.0	4,856
1994	489.1	555.1	484.1	585.1	516.4	729.4	339.3	535.7	377.5	445.0	589.2	348.3	5,994
1995	390.5	501.5	541.8	592.6	500.5	476.5	280.7	655.8	344.2	272.4	447.1	179.8	5,183

Source: New York Mercantile Exchange, COMEX Division

Soybean Meal

Soybean meal, of which the U.S. produces about one-third of the world's total production, is a high protein feed used in formulating livestock and poultry rations, and is obtained from the processing (crush) of soybeans. Brazil is the second largest producer with about half the U.S. total. Soybean meal ranks as the world's top protein meal with about 60 percent of total production. Cottonseed and rapeseed meal account for a combined total of about 20 percent.

World soybean meal production has increased nearly 50 percent since the mid-1980s when about 60 million metric tons were produced to over 85 million tons in the mid-1990s. Percentagewise, China's production gain has been the most dynamic, nearly tripling during the decade, although it still lags well under U.S. production. Brazil's production during the period increased about 50 percent. However, part of the growth in production was indirectly derived from the strong worldwide demand for vegetable oils. Perhaps even more striking has been the growth in world soybean meal trade which reached a record high 31.5 million tons in 1994/95 and was expected to increase further in 1995/96. Significantly, much of the gains in foreign trade during 1995/96 will come from Latin America and Asia, perhaps as much as eight percent over 1994/95, which will more than offset possible meal import slippage from the former USSR. Also, more stable economic growth in Eastern European nations will marginally lift meal imports; and in the European Union meal imports are forecast to reach a record 16.8 million tons, the sixth consecutive year of increasing demand and continuing a trend that has run counter to expectations. Contributing to the gain in EU imports is the larger than expected growth in poultry production, the primary user of soybean meal, and legislative factors that dampened EU oilseed production, notably rapeseed and sunflower that in turn abetted the demand for soybean meal.

U.S. soymeal production in 1995/96 reached a near record large 33 million short tons, putting total supplies for the season (beginning October 1) at 33.4 million tons including a .2 million ton carryover. Total supplies in the early 1990s averaged near 30 million tons. Domestic usage has climbed steadily since 1990 and expected to total a record high 27 million tons in 1995/96, up nearly .3 million tons from 1994/95. The gain in meal use largely reflects increases in poultry production. Cattle accounts for little soybean meal use, hogs a little more.

U.S. soybean meal exports peaked in 1979 at 7.9 million tons, slipping to 4.9 million by 1984. Exports in 1995/96 were forecast at 6.3 million tons, a shade under 1994/95, but about .3 million tons more than initially expected. The decline in the U.S. share of global meal trade is attributed largely to increased competition from South America, notably Brazil. Future demand for meal exports is now strongly linked to economic developments in the former Soviet bloc, as demand for U.S. meal has slipped from traditional buyers in Western Europe. If the 1995/96 supply/demand forecasts are realized, ending carryover on September 30, 1996 should total about 250,000 tons, unchanged from a year earlier.

Soybean meal prices were expected to average between \$195-\$220 per ton in 1995/96 versus \$162.55 in 1994/95, the lowest since 1984/85, basis 48 percent protein, Decatur, Illinois. Futures, however, at yearend 1995 surged to almost \$240 a ton, basis March 1996. During the past decade, the highest season average was in 1988/89 at \$252.40.

Futures Markets

Soybean meal futures and options are traded on the Chicago Board of Trade. A smaller futures contract is traded on the Mid-America Commodity Exchange.

World Soybean Meal Supply & Demand In Thousands of Metric Tons

Year Beginning Oct. 1	Production					Exports			Imports		Consumption			Ending Stocks		
	Brazil	China	EC-12	United States	Total	Brazil	United States	Total	France	Total	EC-12	United States	Total	Brazil	United States	Total
1985-6	9,690	2,190	10,220	22,635	61,060	7,380	5,476	23,140	3,670	23,950	18,730	17,318	61,790	610	192	2,860
1986-7	11,280	3,000	10,740	25,182	67,210	8,370	6,617	25,940	3,660	26,630	19,240	18,539	67,680	520	218	3,070
1987-8	10,130	3,980	10,400	25,460	67,555	7,350	6,191	24,560	3,110	25,310	18,930	19,344	67,660	970	140	3,720
1988-9	11,360	3,570	9,100	22,630	64,230	8,680	4,940	24,980	2,910	26,310	17,810	17,680	66,050	790	160	3,220
1989-90	12,350	3,020	10,580	25,150	70,089	9,430	4,830	26,010	3,480	25,730	19,900	20,220	68,950	1,114	290	4,070
1990-1	11,160	3,280	9,950	25,700	69,500	8,200	4,960	26,890	3,430	27,200	20,190	20,810	70,130	860	260	3,660
1991-2	11,740	2,750	10,530	27,060	73,200	8,780	6,300	28,620	3,550	28,250	21,170	20,870	73,360	520	210	3,140
1992-3	12,170	3,480	10,980	27,550	76,100	8,170	5,650	27,600	3,500	27,610	22,240	22,000	75,510	600	190	3,740
1993-4	14,480	5,830	9,850	27,680	80,720	10,380	4,860	30,110	3,800	29,890	22,650	22,940	80,750	510	140	3,500
1994-5[1]	16,070	6,550	11,430	30,180	87,130	10,650	6,090	31,620	4,030	31,460	24,280	24,080	86,470	990	200	4,000
1995-6[2]	15,700	5,870	11,290	29,960	87,030	11,000	5,530	31,620	3,860	31,610	23,860	24,490	87,220	690	200	3,750

[1] Preliminary. [2] Forecast. *Source: Foreign Agricultural Service, U.S. Department of Agriculture*

SOYBEAN MEAL

Stocks (at Oil Mills)[2] of Soybean Cake & Meal in the United States — In Thousands of Short Tons

Year	Oct. 1	Nov. 1	Dec. 1	Jan. 1	Feb. 1	Mar. 1	Apr. 1	May 1	June 1	July 1	Aug. 1	Sept. 1
1976-7	354.9	423.5	427.7	353.9	384.7	429.9	412.6	449.0	408.3	390.7	399.0	270.4
1977-8	228.3	270.0	239.8	245.1	251.7	239.7	227.3	308.2	263.3	191.1	262.6	234.1
1978-9	242.9	210.4	178.2	260.5	215.1	198.7	210.4	231.6	207.4	205.3	232.2	140.3
1979-80	224.3	204.1	164.2	207.7	158.7	160.6	219.1	193.9	265.0	262.0	232.4	225.1
1980-1	189.7	211.1	350.0	221.8	209.7	214.4	232.2	184.4	254.0	209.7	156.1	199.7
1981-2	233.8	309.2	314.8	279.4	315.7	324.9	190.3	172.1	309.3	224.9	209.1	189.7
1982-3	175.2	342.8	349.6	332.3	400.2	422.8	341.0	356.1	341.5	272.3	365.2	378.5
1983-4	474.1	419.3	466.8	391.1	475.8	446.7	460.7	418.6	427.2	391.2	355.5	242.7
1984-5	255.4	236.1	285.7	336.8	319.6	334.1	444.6	429.8	495.8	569.6	562.5	458.0
1985-6	386.9	318.4	369.2	358.4	372.4	281.3	386.6	300.8	282.4	278.7	250.6	298.3
1986-7	211.7	218.0	387.3	240.3	311.2	277.5	235.8	244.0	321.7	261.3	292.9	301.3
1987-8	240.2	267.6	311.8	296.2	390.4	304.9	243.7	299.5	255.6	294.4	437.4	264.6
1988-9	153.5	267.8	295.6	353.6	442.3	395.7	237.9	296.8	260.4	218.0	264.9	152.0
1989-90	172.9	220.5	194.3	328.2	254.0	262.0	311.8	307.9	252.6	262.5	267.7	232.0
1990-1	318.3	290.9	313.6		455.8			527.8			425.0	
1991-2		285.0		281.0	258.3	291.3	315.6	310.4	310.2	274.7	260.5	209.9
1992-3	230.0	307.9	411.3	360.8	440.0	420.5	336.9	268.5	328.4	257.3	386.1	353.8
1993-4	204.4	375.1	282.3	290.1	230.0	283.1	277.3	333.0	325.2	254.3	267.5	144.9
1994-5[1]	149.6	240.9	231.6	241.1	197.7	227.1	173.1	382.7	337.6	222.6	252.0	203.8
1995-6[1]	223.4	196.9	241.3	347.2	261.9							

[1] Preliminary. [2] Including millfeed and lecithin. *Source: Economic Research Service, U.S. Department of Agriculture*

Supply and Distribution of Soybean Meal in the United States In Thousands of Short Tons

Year Beginning Oct. 1	Supply: For Stocks Oct. 1	Supply: Production	Supply: Total Supply	Distribution: Domestic	Distribution: Exports	Distribution: Total	$ Ton Decatur 48% Protein Solvent	$ Tonne Decatur 44% Solvent	$ Tonne Brazil FOB 45-46% Protein	$ Tonne Rotterdam CIF
1988-9	153	24,943	25,113	19,496	5,444	24,940	252.40	257	241	259
1989-90	173	27,719	27,928	22,291	5,319	27,610	186.48	192	181	204
1990-1	318	28,325	28,688	22,934	5,469	28,403	181.40	187	178	198
1991-2	285	29,831	30,183	23,008	6,945	29,953	189.20	194	184	203
1992-3	230	30,364	30,687	24,251	6,232	30,483	193.75	201	185	207
1993-4[1]	204	30,514	30,788	25,283	5,356	30,638	192.86	199	182	202
1994-5[2]	150	33,265	33,479	26,538	6,717	33,256	162.55	167	172	184
1995-6[3]	223	33,067	33,350	27,150	6,000	33,150	210-235	209	215	220

[1] Preliminary. [2] Estimate. [3] Forecast. *Source: Economic Research Service, U.S. Department of Agriculture*

U.S. Exports of Soybean Cake & Meal by Country of Destination In Thousands of Metric Tons

Year	Algeria	Australia	Canada	Dominican Republic	Egypt	Ireland	Italy	Japan	Mexico	Netherlands	Philippines	Russia[2]	Spain	United Kingdom	Venezuela	Total
1988	411.4	35.5	718.1	92.7	195.8	29.6	543.6	33.0	332.3	553.9	110.6	1,122.0	71.2	29.6	851.3	6,348
1989	389.1	7.7	569.2	66.2	165.9	5.7	188.6	10.8	269.5	269.0	59.1	1,417.9	44.2	29.6	283.8	4,712
1990	373.5	28.2	555.5	130.5	174.8	7.5	146.4	20.8	253.0	229.7	200.7	1,568.4	19.6	32.0	332.2	4,826
1991	323.5	99.4	651.2	142.6	118.6	7.5	33.5	24.1	303.6	339.8	150.4	2,271.0	5.5	29.6	405.9	5,536
1992	237.8	75.9	582.5	146.7	56.5	57.2	93.4	167.2	454.4	420.0	434.8	765.1	92.3	70.6	473.8	6,236
1993	266.1	90.6	646.7	200.8	120.6	84.1	91.5	208.7	187.8	580.8	295.7	697.1	203.8	32.1	425.0	5,536
1994[1]	248.3	247.0	706.3	209.2	142.0	36.8	27.1	76.9	367.5	465.6	257.9	159.5	92.6	80.9	258.9	4,825

[1] Preliminary. [2] Formerly part of the U.S.S.R.; data not reported separately until 1992. *Source: The Oil World*

Production of Soybean Cake & Meal[2] in the U.S. In Thousands of Short Tons

Crop Year	Oct.	Nov.	Dec.	Jan.	Feb.	Mar.	Apr.	May	June	July	Aug.	Sept.	Total	Yield of Meal from Soybeans in lbs.
1988-9	2,235.5	2,399.4	2,390.0	2,359.8	2,036.3	2,218.8	2,126.6	2,061.2	1,802.9	1,749.2	1,804.4	1,758.6	24,943	47.43
1989-90	2,246.2	2,492.5	2,519.6	2,548.6	2,187.2	2,432.3	2,263.7	2,224.2	2,183.4	2,196.6	2,237.1	2,187.3	27,718	47.63
1990-1	2,508.8	2,513.2	2,431.5	----------	7,082.0	----------	----------	6,640.8	----------	----------	7,148.9	----------	28,325	47.47
1991-2	---------	7,920.4	----------	2,665.5	2,393.8	2,544.4	2,411.3	2,262.5	2,372.4	2,434.2	2,429.0	2,397.3	29,831	47.51
1992-3	2,698.1	2,697.3	2,763.4	2,781.2	2,430.4	2,691.3	2,519.1	2,536.3	2,373.0	2,324.1	2,188.3	2,361.8	30,364	47.54
1993-4	2,707.1	2,714.8	2,696.7	2,632.3	2,458.1	2,696.3	2,510.0	2,446.4	2,330.7	2,398.0	2,406.6	2,517.1	30,514	47.62
1994-5[1]	2,812.5	2,903.5	3,027.8	3,007.5	2,755.0	3,048.5	2,829.8	2,697.9	2,492.1	2,565.4	2,589.8	2,535.8	33,265	47.32
1995-6[1]	2,891.2	2,946.9	2,761.9	2,730.1										47.29

[1] Preliminary. [2] At oil mills; including millfeed and lecithin. *Source: Economic Research Service, U.S. Department of Agriculture*

Average Open Interest of Soybean Futures at the Chicago Board of Trade In Contracts

Year	Jan.	Feb.	Mar.	Apr.	May	June	July	Aug.	Sept.	Oct.	Nov.	Dec.
1988	65,643	63,960	61,100	66,950	73,264	80,444	71,643	76,295	80,753	75,439	77,466	71,443
1989	71,792	71,599	67,542	58,923	58,794	64,212	59,547	60,925	59,271	60,038	63,552	57,219
1990	60,010	71,773	74,762	76,897	77,307	69,658	63,824	62,033	58,915	68,888	76,899	70,901
1991	62,172	60,017	56,179	59,107	49,973	57,068	55,629	54,342	67,765	68,627	68,263	71,900
1992	67,575	56,453	55,370	59,528	57,204	60,519	66,315	66,861	66,648	72,403	73,255	72,881
1993	63,178	70,384	64,550	66,121	78,386	74,191	91,435	73,770	75,267	77,065	83,802	85,039
1994	87,612	91,142	82,193	89,453	85,553	81,721	84,461	82,691	85,508	94,483	101,030	98,717
1995	97,661	101,253	101,846	99,898	90,237	86,090	83,712	74,233	79,450	85,290	103,824	110,193

Source: Chicago Board of Trade

Volume of Trading of Soybean Meal Futures at the Chicago Board of Trade In Thousands of Contracts

Year	Jan.	Feb.	Mar.	Apr.	May	June	July	Aug.	Sept.	Oct.	Nov.	Dec.	Total
1988	393.7	371.5	350.4	396.3	497.3	584.3	482.0	427.7	449.6	446.3	533.1	424.0	5,313
1989	408.1	320.7	382.4	388.8	406.7	403.8	410.7	393.1	382.8	364.8	330.1	294.8	4,487
1990	308.6	276.4	400.2	428.4	421.0	398.3	460.2	435.3	401.6	476.3	448.7	448.5	4,904
1991	323.4	281.8	310.3	429.3	296.8	412.5	484.3	463.6	394.7	410.8	351.6	339.6	4,498
1992	368.7	290.5	312.6	312.2	388.1	381.0	426.0	333.6	327.6	320.2	327.9	357.1	4,146
1993	295.5	288.1	346.6	307.9	356.7	518.2	575.5	460.5	402.4	315.6	469.3	380.6	4,718
1994	405.6	339.8	330.7	380.7	467.2	456.3	384.5	354.4	366.3	317.4	370.4	420.5	4,594
1995	283.6	307.5	404.4	410.9	532.7	479.6	610.8	491.8	481.9	449.0	523.4	625.6	5,601

Source: Chicago Board of Trade

SOYBEAN MEAL

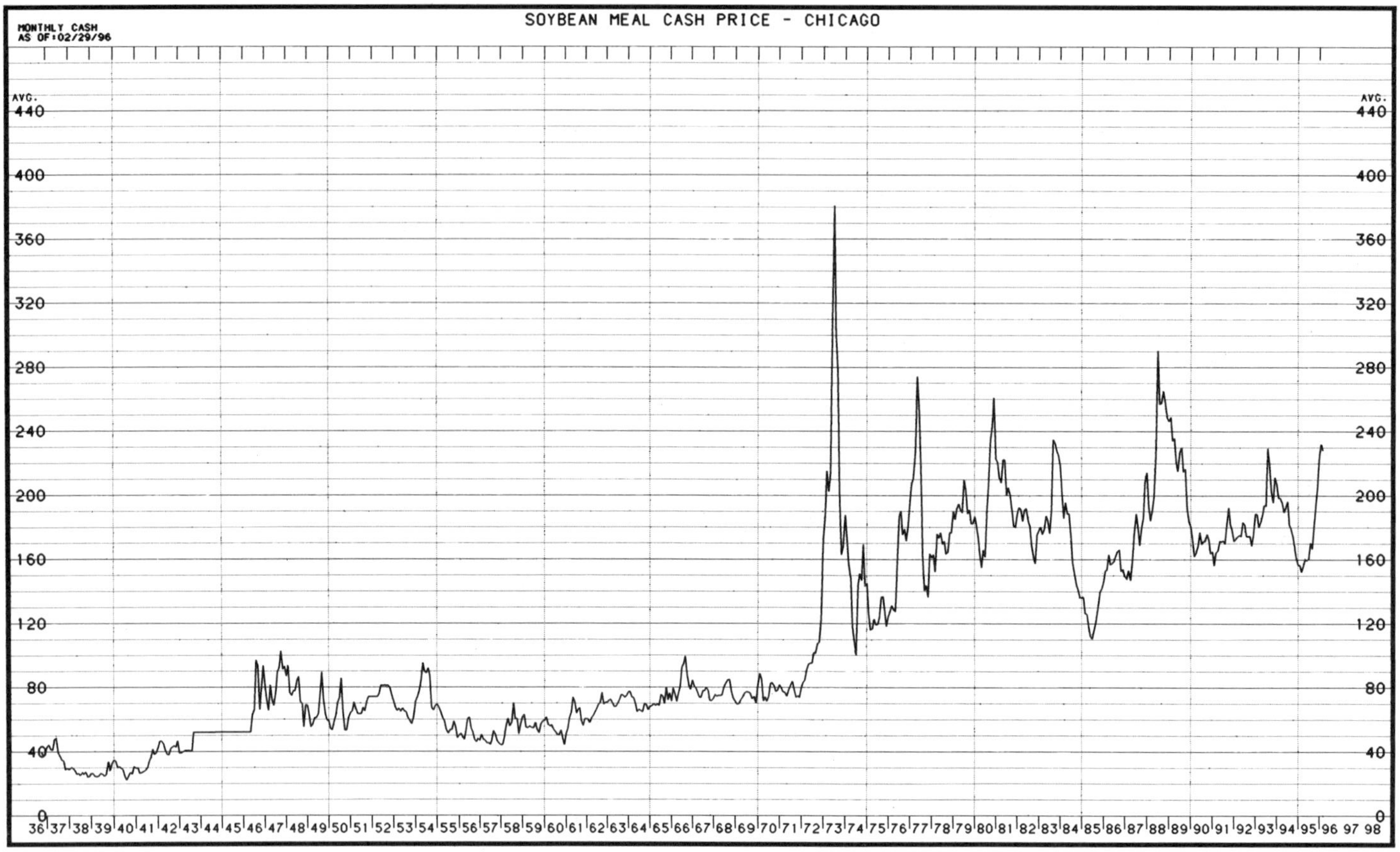

Average Price of Soybean Meal (48% Solvent) at Decatur In Dollars Per Short Ton--Bulk

Year	Oct.	Nov.	Dec.	Jan.	Feb.	Mar.	Apr.	May	June	July	Aug.	Sept.	Average
1984-5	156.50	150.00	150.50	146.80	137.40	137.50	128.60	120.75	119.40	122.75	128.75	137.90	136.40
1985-6	146.40	152.25	153.60	162.00	162.50	174.90	167.90	168.90	170.40	174.40	178.75	182.40	166.20
1986-7	165.40	167.40	164.30	158.00	169.25	161.20	173.40	190.00	200.70	196.50	186.40	195.20	177.31
1987-8	201.60	224.75	231.70	211.75	199.60	207.60	218.25	238.60	305.40	275.10	273.80	284.00	239.35
1988-9	280.10	268.90	266.90	270.10	252.10	254.00	238.00	232.30	246.25	251.00	234.30	234.90	252.40
1989-90	208.10	194.90	191.60	183.80	172.90	176.40	178.00	189.40	182.00	183.92	186.75	190.00	186.48
1990-1	185.40	174.25	175.90	167.00	174.50	177.60	182.50	182.10	183.25	181.00	188.75	204.25	181.38
1991-2	196.30	190.25	183.10	184.00	185.40	185.90	187.20	195.25	203.90	186.25	186.00	187.00	189.21
1992-3	180.60	181.90	187.60	188.75	179.90	183.60	187.40	193.25	193.10	229.90	219.10	199.90	193.75
1993-4	194.50	209.40	206.00	198.30	198.40	195.40	188.90	193.75	195.50	181.10	178.60	174.50	192.86
1994-5	168.50	161.30	156.90	156.40	151.30	156.90	161.90	159.10	160.40	170.45	166.70	180.80	162.55
1995-6	193.92	204.07	223.60	232.00									159.02

Source: Economic Research Service, U.S. Department of Agriculture

Soybean Oil

World soybean oil production in 1995/96 neared a record large 20 million metric tons versus the previous high of 19.5 million in 1994/95. U.S. production is nearly twice that of Brazil, the world's second largest bean oil producer. Of the important vegetable oils, soyoil is the world's largest with palm oil second and rapeseed oil a distant third. World usage of soyoil in 1995/96 will lag production but still set a new record high. World carryover stocks at the end of 1995/96 were expected to increase to 1.9 million tons from the 1.5 million tons on hand a year earlier.

Global soybean oil exports in 1995/96 were forecast at or near a record high. Foreign trade in soyoil is quite diversified. Exports are concentrated among producing areas while imports are scattered. Argentina is generally the largest exporter and Brazil second. U.S. exports during the past few years have averaged about 10-15 percent of production. U.S. soybean oil imports are insignificant.

A near record crush and positive extraction rate put 1995/96 U.S. soybean oil production at a record high 15.7 billion pounds, the fourth consecutive season of record production. The oil content of U.S. soybeans correlates directly with temperatures and sunshine during the pod-filling stages, which proved favorable during August, 1995. Carryin stocks on October 1, 1995 totaled about 1 billion pounds; the U.S. supply in 1995/96 may total a record high 16.7 billion pounds. Total disappearance during 1995/96 was expected to lag the record high 15.8 billion pounds in 1994/95, triggering a buildup in carryover supplies to an estimated 1.6 billion pounds, still well under the record 2.2 billion carryover at the end of 1991/92.

The slippage in 1995/96 demand was due mostly to a drop in exports, to 2.0 billion pounds from 2.7 billion in 1994/95. China was a major vegetable oil buyer in 1994/95, their objective to build up stocks and dampen inflation pressures; apparently the import policy worked. China's oil import needs in 1995/96 were expected to drop. Moreover, hefty supplies of competing oil was expected to dampen foreign demand for U.S. soybean oil. Domestic use, meanwhile, has stagnated in recent years at about 13 billion pounds, but compares very favorably with the 10 billion pound average during the first half of the 1980s.

Crude soybean oil prices (basis Decatur) in 1995/96 were expected to range from 24.00¢ to 28.50¢ per pound versus a 27.71¢ per pound average in 1994/95. It should be noted that soybean oil prices do not necessarily move in tandem with soybean meal, as these two products have been known to move in opposite directions for short periods of time. The fourth quarter of 1995 is a good example.

Futures Markets

Soybean oil futures and options are traded on the Chicago Board of Trade.

World Supply & Demand of Soybean Oil In Thousands of Metric Tons

Year Beginning Oct. 1	Production				Exports			Imports		Consumption					Stocks[3]	
	Brazil	EC-12	United States	Total	Brazil	United States	Total	India	Total	Brazil	EC-12	India	United States	Total	United States	Total
1986-7	2,730	2,360	5,798	15,200	950	538	3,900	360	3,790	1,930	1,460	450	4,915	14,760	782	1,990
1987-8	2,440	2,280	5,890	15,240	610	850	3,800	420	3,770	1,930	1,560	620	4,960	15,110	950	2,090
1988-9	2,740	2,010	5,320	14,630	700	750	3,710	30	3,490	2,140	1,590	410	4,800	14,870	780	1,660
1989-90	2,980	2,350	5,900	16,000	870	610	3,940	30	3,970	2,000	1,610	340	5,480	15,950	590	1,740
1990-1	2,679	2,243	6,082	15,909	686	356	3,635	20	3,587	2,136	1,661	370	5,515	15,886	810	1,988
1991-2	2,815	2,337	6,507	16,851	658	748	3,558	100	3,487	2,167	1,703	442	5,554	16,366	1,016	2,470
1992-3	2,910	2,540	6,250	17,170	690	640	4,200	40	4,070	2,280	1,980	560	5,920	17,360	710	2,000
1993-4	3,470	2,240	6,330	18,180	1,350	690	4,830	40	4,740	2,320	1,850	710	5,870	18,320	500	1,770
1994-5[1]	3,850	2,620	7,060	19,850	1,570	1,220	5,990	150	5,860	2,470	1,970	650	5,860	19,700	520	1,780
1995-6[2]	3,760	2,570	7,120	19,840	1,300	890	5,380	130	5,410	2,560	1,930	790	5,920	19,560	840	2,090

[1] Preliminary. [2] Forecast. [3] End of season. *Source: Foreign Agricultural Service, U.S. Department of Agriculture*

Supply & Distribution of Soybean Oil in the U.S. In Millions of Pounds

					Domestic Disappearance									
						Food					Non-Food			
Year Beginning Oct. 1	Production	Imports	Stocks Oct. 1	Exports	Total Domestic	Shortening	Margarine	Cooking & Salad Oils	Other Edible	Total Food	Paint & Varnish	Resins & Plastics	Total Non-Food	Total Disappearance
1986-7	12,783	15	947	1,187	10,833	3,359	1,161	5,054	138	10,213	63	109	300	12,020
1987-8	12,974	194	1,725	1,873	10,930	3,627	1,629	5,043	130	10,429	54	106	285	12,803
1988-9	11,737	137	2,092	1,661	10,591	3,419	1,537	4,497	137	9,636	35	124	282	12,252
1989-90	13,004	22	1,715	1,353	12,083	3,934	1,754	4,726	124	10,537	38	112	272	13,436
1990-1	13,408	17	1,305	780	12,164	4,090	1,811	4,693	130	10,722	49	106	295	12,944
1991-2	14,345	1	1,786	1,648	12,245	4,091	1,911	4,961	148	11,112	46	98	301	13,893
1992-3	13,778	10	2,239	1,419	13,054	4,465	1,970	4,717	254	11,505	38	95	296	14,473
1993-4	13,951	68	1,555	1,529	12,941	4,772	1,841	5,004	221	11,838	46	115	304	14,471
1994-5[1]	15,613	17	1,103	2,680	12,916	4,714	1,693	5,546	222	12,175	49	124	287	15,597
1995-6[2]	15,640		1,137	1,825	13,050									14,875

[1] Preliminary. [2] Forecast. *Source: Economic Research Service, U.S. Department of Agriculture*

SOYBEAN OIL

Crude and Refined Stocks of Soybean Oil in the U.S., at End of Month In Millions of Pounds

Crop Year Beginning Oct.		Oct.	Nov.	Dec.	Jan.	Feb.	Mar.	Apr.	May	June	July	Aug.	Sept.
1991-2	Crude	------------	------------	1,955.9	1,915.8	2,156.8	2,175.8	2,211.3	2,213.9	2,216.8	2,205.0	2,126.8	2,026.2
	Refined	------------	------------	259.8	243.7	245.7	224.3	211.2	219.6	209.7	215.9	236.0	213.2
1992-3	Crude	1,856.1	1,885.0	2,041.5	2,177.8	2,110.4	2,029.0	2,068.9	2,006.4	1,967.0	1,848.8	1,518.6	1,352.9
	Refined	220.2	220.2	238.6	232.3	226.4	217.1	229.0	234.3	207.0	211.8	201.2	201.9
1993-4	Crude	1,239.6	1,209.9	1,189.3	1,184.2	1,184.0	1,192.3	1,329.8	1,346.2	1,330.0	1,352.6	1,124.0	904.7
	Refined	213.1	189.7	217.5	230.4	216.9	209.8	223.5	220.6	223.8	218.2	215.4	198.4
1994-5[1]	Crude	850.8	811.4	826.6	880.6	876.7	838.3	860.5	893.9	885.9	906.3	895.3	905.7
	Refined	204.7	215.5	231.7	236.2	252.1	221.3	229.1	236.5	225.8	235.7	204.7	231.0
1995-6[1]	Crude	990.4	908.9	1,154.4									
	Refined	205.5	223.1	254.6									

[1] Preliminary. *Source: Bureau of Census, U.S. Department of Commerce*

U.S. Exports of Soybean Oil[1], by Country of Destination In Metric Tons

Year Beginning Oct. 1	Bolivia	Canada	Ecuador	Ethiopia	Haiti	India	Israel	Mexico	Morocco	Pakistan	Panama	Peru	Philip-pines	Turkey	Vene-zuela	Grand Total
1984-5	2,691	12,915	44,721	23,966	16,110	62,805	874	45,422	3,758	168,437	8,034	11,399	2,822	0	51,882	752,918
1985-6	1,560	6,105	16,689	17,300	9,474	37,562	560	49,109	3,236	274,935	2,780	1,602	3,000	0	17,108	570,297
1986-7	2,293	6,940	18,814	561	6,940	47,098	560	21,883	59,547	146,663	2,975	1,292	5,926	0	18,652	538,466
1987-8	2,123	7,344	19,050	17,605	3,411	151,600	416	11,537	35,821	396,737	3,736	1,144	6,734	17,098	4,866	850,015
1988-9	998	5,364	30,930	8,960	2,846	28,127	454	17,730	80,023	453,067	6,695	5,778	3,657	0	29,055	753,576
1989-90	1,037	5,443	26,314	22,858	1,688	16,391	442	4,435	77,985	309,502	3,174	5,206	1,868	0	8,198	613,902
1990-1	1,549	3,790	20,832	14,948	4,946	13,544	321	11,087	73,255	66,209	8,123	6,566	3,006	16,460	0	353,959
1991-2	1,829	11,153	528	19,619	4,737	67,577	356	23,383	127,602	250	11,143	32,696	1,996	81,976	13	747,465
1992-3	280	28,585	17	8,272	6,753	49,452	480	44,194	57,995	0	641	36,340	634	58,436	0	643,796
1993-4[2]	0	3,714	0	19,709	1,603	46,846	200	10,795	31,563	72,204	248	22,751	100	34,920	26	578,470
1994-5[2]		23,435	12,698	7,374	38,272	28,949		50,682	29,053	25,500		8,332		5,750		1,179,768

[1] Crude & refined oil combined as such. [2] Preliminary. *Source: Economic Research Service, U.S. Department of Agriculture*

U.S. Production of Crude Soybean Oil[2] In Millions of Pounds

Year	Oct.	Nov.	Dec.	Jan.	Feb.	Mar.	Apr.	May	June	July	Aug.	Sept.	Total
1984-5	996	1,072	1,096	1,027	879	946	918	983	919	913	869	853	11,468
1985-6	1,040	1,053	1,096	1,086	895	1,005	935	953	882	910	875	887	11,617
1986-7	1,163	1,172	1,152	1,186	1,110	1,149	1,047	1,038	981	1,014	891	881	12,783
1987-8	1,120	1,207	1,208	1,170	1,092	1,187	1,133	1,087	996	994	879	901	12,974
1988-9	1,047	1,109	1,110	1,106	952	1,041	1,010	977	856	836	855	843	11,737
1989-90	1,057	1,146	1,161	1,187	1,022	1,142	1,067	1,050	1,036	1,038	1,059	1,038	13,004
1990-1	1,188	1,168	1,138	------	3,331	------	------	3,171	------	------	3,412	------	13,408
1991-2	------	3,772	------	1,270	1,147	1,228	1,167	1,096	1,152	1,177	1,179	1,158	14,345
1992-3	1,238	1,200	1,239	1,247	1,102	1,216	1,148	1,152	1,083	1,070	1,006	1,078	13,778
1993-4	1,241	1,228	1,218	1,192	1,122	1,231	1,155	1,123	1,070	1,099	1,104	1,168	13,951
1994-5[1]	1,328	1,342	1,403	1,400	1,289	1,419	1,333	1,275	1,183	1,205	1,228	1,208	15,613
1995-6[1]	1,353	1,359	1,381										

[1] Preliminary. [2] Not seasonally adjusted. *Source: Economic Research Service, U.S. Department of Agriculture*

U.S. Production of Refined Soybean Oil In Millions of Pounds

Year	Oct.	Nov.	Dec.	Jan.	Feb.	Mar.	Apr.	May	June	July	Aug.	Sept.	Total
1984-5	907.6	835.5	821.2	838.7	796.1	835.5	865.0	899.5	773.1	763.9	806.2	794.4	9,937
1985-6	865.7	834.8	790.0	804.2	751.1	819.5	783.0	808.5	816.8	780.2	830.1	834.8	9,719
1986-7	911.3	848.1	850.0	790.2	763.6	900.7	871.2	826.9	871.3	921.8	898.6	946.5	10,400
1987-8	975.5	925.8	902.5	880.3	843.4	925.6	843.5	894.1	890.1	947.4	903.6	838.7	10,771
1988-9	867.1	826.9	800.8	776.7	709.6	830.1	800.6	867.4	801.4	791.4	866.6	866.6	9,805
1989-90	936.8	912.0	873.9	887.8	800.6	800.6	812.7	952.8	915.1	903.7	931.1	935.7	10,745
1990-1	1,028.0	980.6	934.7	------	2,717.1	------	------	2,865.5	------	------	2,952.8	------	11,479
1991-2	------	2,918.1	------	933.8	876.7	1,041.3	973.1	993.3	977.9	979.2	997.6	1,040.7	11,732
1992-3	1,095.6	999.4	951.0	960.1	935.4	1,054.9	1,039.7	950.6	1,042.8	978.2	1,066.7	1,109.7	12,184
1993-4	1,094.3	1,053.5	1,030.8	960.1	945.5	1,056.6	1,018.5	1,012.0	1,017.3	968.0	1,107.2	1,044.6	12,308
1994-5[1]	1,123.0	1,079.2	1,060.6	1,002.5	968.2	1,063.6	1,010.4	1,077.0	993.5	940.9	1,076.8	1,039.8	12,435
1995-6[1]	1,119.2	1,088.8	1,018.5										

[1] Preliminary. *Source: Bureau of Census, U.S. Department of Commerce*

Soybean Oil Consumption in End Products in the U.S. In Millions of Pounds

Year	Jan.	Feb.	Mar.	Apr.	May	June	July	Aug.	Sept.	Oct.	Nov.	Dec.	Total
1984	827.6	821.7	837.8	781.1	857.4	824.4	744.7	772.2	780.6	932.0	883.4	856.1	9,919
1985	989.0	804.0	867.1	885.9	940.8	810.5	825.9	856.1	863.7	922.4	864.2	851.6	10,481
1986	836.7	794.0	889.7	849.1	850.3	856.8	835.1	843.1	890.3	927.6	840.6	891.2	10,305
1987	800.9	799.4	862.0	869.6	824.4	918.9	932.7	902.9	949.6	961.4	876.0	891.5	10,589
1988	913.9	820.5	930.0	839.9	870.5	937.9	936.5	907.3	829.1	862.2	829.1	846.6	10,524
1989	780.8	729.5	834.7	800.8	851.9	854.2	774.7	876.9	876.2	923.2	889.7	887.0	10,080
1990	901.3	815.7	952.0	893.6	950.9	927.8	866.0	905.4	895.7	984.1	912.9	878.0	10,883
1991		2,690.3			2,831.8			2,837.7			2,907.8		11,268
1992	880.4	867.0	1,010.1	947.9	956.7	962.1	935.5	932.4	1,019.8	1,061.7	951.8	946.1	11,472
1993	934.5	942.2	1,092.6	1,044.6	981.2	1,036.0	1,019.3	1,097.3	1,103.3	1,123.6	1,092.1	1,029.2	12,496
1994	924.5	939.1	1,084.7	1,040.6	1,001.4	1,023.8	974.9	1,119.2	1,075.4	1,123.3	1,103.4	1,063.8	12,474
1995[1]	991.1	950.0	1,093.8	1,006.2	1,077.3	1,020.8	948.7	1,046.1	1,042.3	1,092.0	1,067.7	994.8	12,331

[1] Preliminary. *Source: Bureau of Censue, U.S. Department of Commerce*

U.S. Exports of Soybean Oil (Crude & Refined) In Millions of Pounds

Year	Jan.	Feb.	Mar.	Apr.	May	June	July	Aug.	Sept.	Oct.	Nov.	Dec.	Total
1984	161.3	289.9	258.9	163.3	208.3	157.3	140.0	73.0	156.3	200.3	214.6	189.6	2,068
1985	66.7	198.3	184.9	66.9	52.4	138.8	174.4	70.1	102.8	125.4	38.1	74.3	1,293
1986	80.6	100.7	92.8	124.0	50.7	115.1	44.6	187.7	223.4	118.2	27.4	22.8	1,188
1987	67.9	74.0	52.1	28.2	47.4	85.0	175.6	261.0	224.8	100.1	139.0	134.0	1,389
1988	25.7	281.0	279.4	87.7	138.6	269.0	157.2	78.1	183.2	200.1	110.6	119.9	1,931
1989	104.5	65.8	112.4	105.5	161.4	72.1	159.3	181.1	265.6	116.2	82.5	113.4	1,540
1990	95.4	136.2	164.4	33.0	112.0	161.9	122.6	82.8	132.9	85.4	43.9	12.1	1,183
1991		71.8			132.3			434.8			336.1		975
1992	140.0	171.9	134.6	155.4	69.1	129.1	163.7	205.2	142.5	169.5	113.2	91.6	1,686
1993	146.8	188.0	143.3	61.1	154.8	75.4	59.9	116.0	99.7	190.4	88.6	200.2	1,524
1994	120.4	144.6	94.4	46.1	111.6	36.1	57.7	184.6	254.0	154.8	303.2	305.9	1,813
1995[1]	217.4	367.6	564.2	236.2	90.8	160.4	91.0	109.4	79.4	69.3	205.4		2,191

[1] Preliminary. *Source: Economic Research Service, U.S. Department of Agriculture*

SOYBEAN OIL

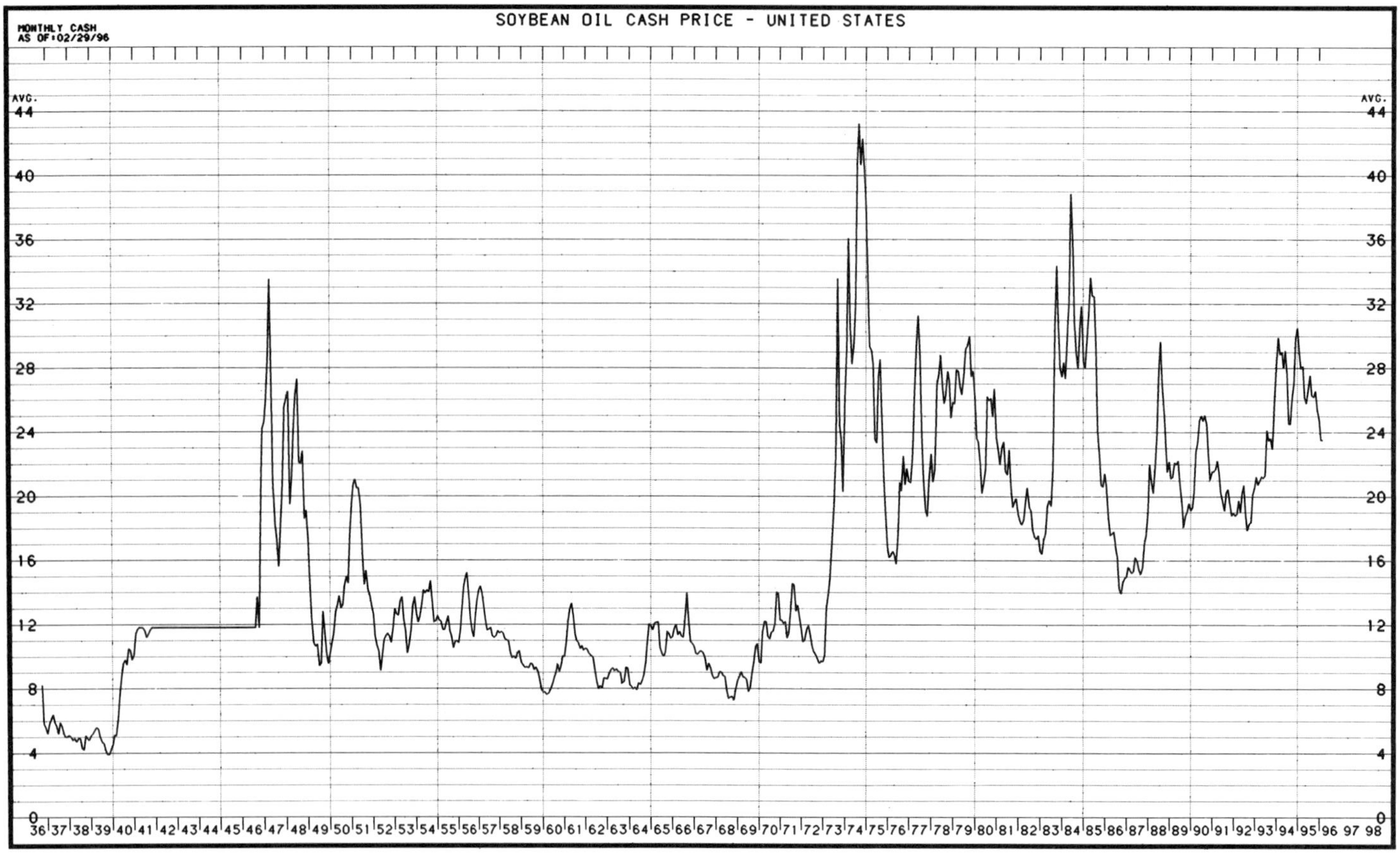

U.S. Stocks of Soybean Oil (Crude & Refined) at Factory & Warehouse   In Millions of Pounds

Year	Oct. 1	Nov. 1	Dec. 1	Jan. 1	Feb. 1	Mar. 1	Apr. 1	May 1	June 1	July 1	Aug. 1	Sept. 1
1984-5	721	597	580	777	884	724	716	666	707	732	724	716
1985-6	632	636	810	969	1,167	1,181	1,247	1,219	1,360	1,225	1,321	1,152
1986-7	947	964	1,269	1,507	1,837	2,017	2,352	2,344	2,416	2,339	2,184	1,979
1987-8	1,725	1,661	1,834	2,050	2,391	2,239	2,343	2,385	2,570	2,361	2,203	2,212
1988-9	2,092	2,046	2,303	2,540	2,703	2,902	2,893	2,759	2,743	2,683	2,427	2,070
1989-90	1,715	1,515	1,532	1,605	1,718	1,703	1,695	1,716	1,551	1,422	1,433	1,380
1990-1	1,305	1,216	1,320	------------	1,464	------------	------------	1,875	------------	------------	1,853	------------
1991-2	------------	1,786	------------	2,217	2,159	2,402	2,400	2,423	2,433	2,427	2,421	2,363
1992-3	2,239	2,076	2,111	2,280	2,410	2,337	2,246	2,298	2,241	2,174	2,061	1,720
1993-4	1,555	1,453	1,400	1,407	1,415	1,401	1,402	1,553	1,567	1,554	1,571	1,339
1994-5[1]	1,103	1,056	1,027	1,055	1,117	1,129	1,060	1,090	1,130	1,112	1,142	1,100
1995-6[1]	1,137	1,196	1,132	1,411								

[1] Preliminary. *Source: Economic Research Service, U.S. Department of Agriculture*

Average Prices of Crude Domestic Soybean Oil (in Tank Cars) F.O.B. Decatur   In Cents Per Pound

Year	Oct.	Nov.	Dec.	Jan.	Feb.	Mar.	Apr.	May	June	July	Aug.	Sept.	Average
1984-5	30.56	31.86	28.44	28.01	29.64	31.40	33.63	32.49	32.46	29.07	24.08	22.54	29.52
1985-6	20.71	20.62	21.39	20.63	18.64	17.56	17.65	17.79	16.80	16.22	14.28	13.94	18.02
1986-7	14.63	14.88	14.94	15.60	15.40	15.21	15.31	16.22	15.96	15.41	15.16	15.58	15.36
1987-8	17.03	17.55	19.00	21.98	20.94	20.22	21.67	23.56	27.68	29.65	27.16	25.55	22.67
1988-9	23.42	21.55	22.16	21.13	21.21	22.11	21.97	22.23	20.75	19.66	18.08	18.77	21.09
1989-90	19.02	19.57	19.11	19.28	20.27	22.80	23.35	24.72	25.03	24.69	25.05	24.45	22.28
1990-1	22.59	21.05	21.55	21.56	21.66	22.21	21.50	20.23	19.65	19.05	20.23	20.46	21.00
1991-2	19.57	18.78	18.99	18.77	18.88	19.74	19.00	20.15	20.71	18.82	17.87	18.28	19.10
1992-3	18.36	20.10	20.52	21.23	20.72	21.00	21.24	21.15	21.30	24.13	23.47	23.61	21.40
1993-4	22.98	25.37	28.09	29.91	28.84	29.03	27.94	29.10	27.60	24.53	24.51	26.11	27.00
1994-5[1]	27.06	29.84	30.61	29.01	28.15	28.33	27.16	26.00	26.78	27.60	26.56	26.26	27.71
1995-6[1]	26.56	25.41	24.76	23.69									

[1] Preliminary. *Source: Economic Research Service, U.S. Department of Agriculture*

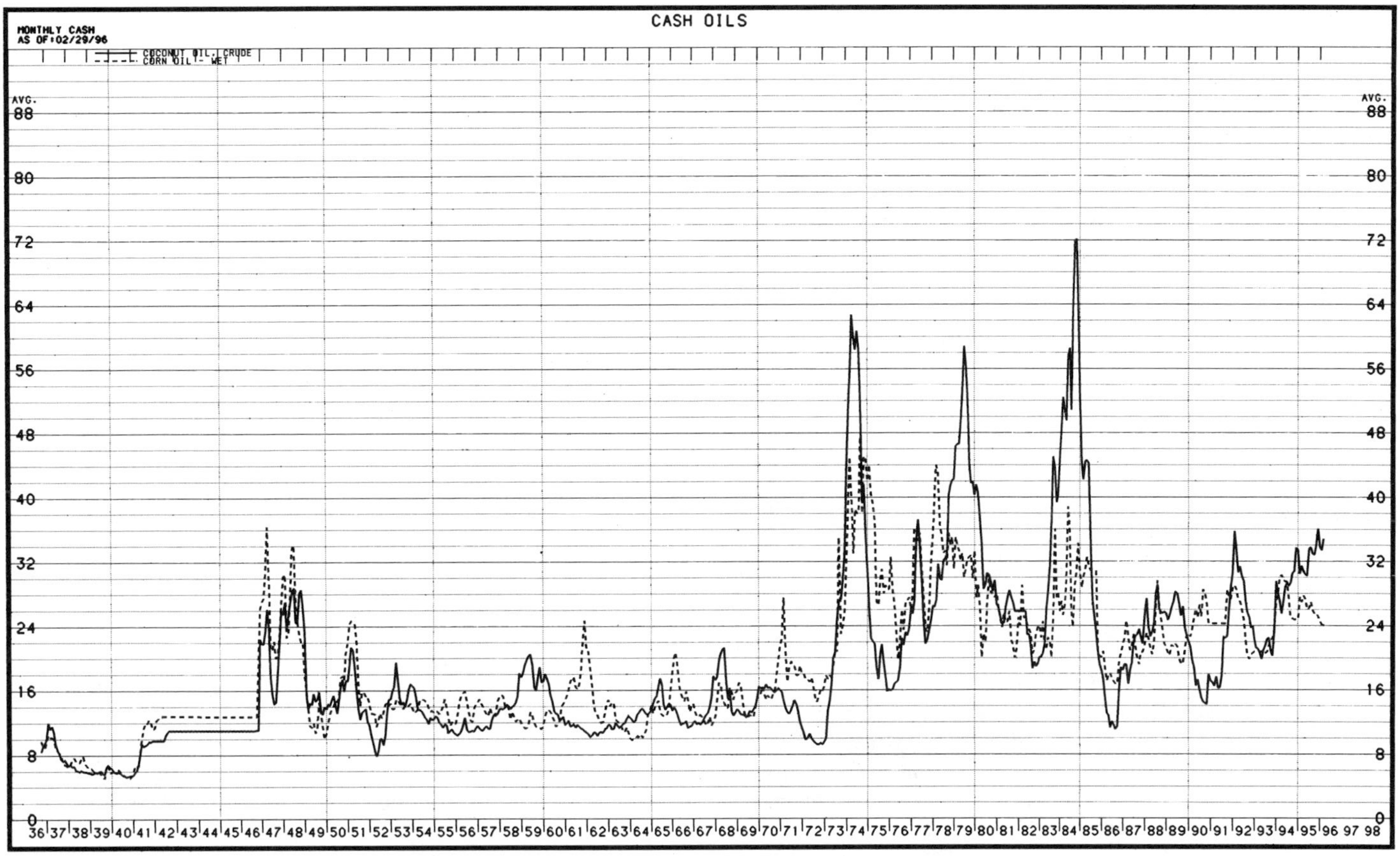

Average Open Interest of Soybean Oil Futures at the Chicago Board of Trade In Contracts

Year	Jan.	Feb.	Mar.	Apr.	May	June	July	Aug.	Sept.	Oct.	Nov.	Dec.
1984	61,271	59,187	53,640	57,139	65,025	61,391	54,517	47,204	45,349	40,365	43,138	42,943
1985	37,482	42,458	47,038	56,246	58,675	60,357	55,448	53,111	53,351	47,026	42,732	46,469
1986	48,384	52,875	55,877	56,114	53,063	60,035	63,034	60,095	54,905	57,256	69,227	67,871
1987	71,509	81,610	73,916	75,154	82,843	86,672	83,041	68,373	65,973	68,860	73,194	79,985
1988	85,953	88,260	86,472	85,712	87,253	94,791	95,931	87,566	86,994	82,541	82,477	75,688
1989	77,741	81,676	78,235	77,249	73,623	76,572	70,644	68,652	63,751	63,911	69,248	68,166
1990	73,368	80,842	87,615	92,845	103,116	103,747	88,763	81,310	73,841	78,548	86,786	75,995
1991	72,987	71,607	76,800	70,361	70,954	73,870	73,864	70,058	66,128	61,227	69,657	63,901
1992	68,619	73,919	75,508	68,749	65,084	71,507	64,450	72,569	70,228	65,243	76,168	76,908
1993	73,683	68,887	66,803	68,598	65,814	73,892	83,730	72,746	64,927	62,348	80,136	94,990
1994	97,198	99,640	100,334	98,659	97,595	83,165	93,994	88,196	81,735	86,901	108,327	114,928
1995	101,171	103,856	97,715	87,300	76,175	75,171	81,650	77,064	70,410	71,652	85,241	84,138

Source: Chicago Board of Trade

Volume of Trading of Soybean Oil Futures at the Chicago Board of Trade In Thousands of Contracts

Year	Jan.	Feb.	Mar.	Apr.	May	June	July	Aug.	Sept.	Oct.	Nov.	Dec.	Total
1984	358.3	346.5	337.7	360.0	513.7	436.7	353.6	280.8	244.2	269.5	288.0	220.5	4,010
1985	264.2	256.0	311.6	405.0	416.4	308.7	341.1	281.5	233.0	270.0	281.5	278.4	3,647
1986	263.1	235.9	254.0	311.7	273.8	262.0	296.0	237.9	202.7	324.8	261.4	259.6	3,183
1987	347.3	304.8	267.7	303.4	374.2	363.9	356.3	267.6	301.1	349.8	315.1	361.2	3,912
1988	437.0	390.7	346.8	442.7	399.2	580.2	461.4	403.6	390.0	303.1	377.3	364.2	4,896
1989	317.8	347.7	368.1	384.7	426.4	386.3	414.5	348.8	320.8	341.0	344.2	298.6	4,301
1990	294.1	397.1	413.9	447.7	488.8	441.5	462.3	405.6	319.2	344.1	370.2	266.3	4,651
1991	330.2	259.4	355.0	342.1	364.6	322.9	433.8	399.8	303.2	340.6	297.9	369.3	4,119
1992	344.2	293.1	400.0	255.8	381.8	352.3	413.1	298.0	425.9	346.8	365.8	405.5	4,283
1993	341.4	281.1	378.4	291.5	261.6	434.7	513.3	444.6	449.3	302.1	465.2	448.6	4,612
1994	442.0	401.6	366.0	391.2	442.4	378.2	397.5	357.9	415.4	476.9	516.7	477.4	5,063
1995	424.4	363.7	464.4	355.9	457.7	418.2	377.4	330.5	303.9	317.2	431.7	366.4	4,611

Source: Chicago Board of Trade

Soybeans

U.S. 1995 soybean production slipped to 2.2 billion bushels (61 million tons) from the record large 1994 crop of 2.5 billion bushels (63 million tons); the total representing about 47 percent of world production of 127.6 million metric tons versus 137.8 million in 1994/95. World output in the late-1980s averaged under 100 million tons.

The U.S. is in no danger of losing its ranking as the world's largest soybean producer although percentagewise Brazil, Argentina, and China's output has grown faster during the past decade. China, the world's third largest producer after Brazil, is in danger of losing its position to Argentina, although the growth of China's economy should maintain a strong domestic demand for soybean meal and provide farmers with enough incentive to maintain a large bean crop; estimated at 15 million tons in 1995/96 versus a record large 16.3 million in 1994/95. However, as China's economy becomes more market sensitive, growers are apt to switch to higher price crops as apparently happened in 1995 with the area planted to soybeans down six percent as farmers moved heavily into corn and cotton production. Brazil's 1995/96 soybean crop, which is sown about the time the U.S. crop has been harvested, was initially forecast at 24.3 million tons versus 25.5 million in 1994/95; later estimates were pared to about 23.3 million partially due to an extended drought in Southern Brazil during planting time. This helped lift Chicago soybean futures in late 1995 to a two-year high. Argentina's 1995/96 production was forecast at a record high 12.5 million tons, up slightly from 1994/95. Unlike Brazil, Argentine soybean farmers have significantly lower production costs and a better transportation structure. Brazil's soybean acreage is generally about twice that of Argentina, but yield per acre is lower. Brazil's crop year encompasses February to January; Argentina's is April to March. India, the fifth largest producer, was expected to match their record high production of four million tons in 1992/93 with their 1995/96 crop.

World soybean trade in 1995/96 was forecast at 31.6 million tons, down two percent from 1994/95 during which trade was buoyed by larger U.S. supplies, healthy crush margins in the European Union, and unusually high Brazilian imports; conditions that do not exist for 1995/96. However, the 1995/96 early trade picture, especially for U.S. exports, was clouded due to the dollar's slippage against the key European currencies. The U.S. generally accounts for about two-thirds of world exports; 69 percent in 1994/95, a sharp rebound from the historic low of 57 percent in 1993/94. Importing nations are numerous, the biggest are generally Japan, Germany, and the Netherlands. In either case, the world's lower 1995/96 new supply will lag demand and shrink world carryover by September 1996 to about 24 percent under a year earlier, the lowest total since 1984.

U.S. farmers planted 63.1 million acres to soybeans in 1995, up 1.2 million from 1994. Record acreage was planted in most midwestern states. A wet spring in the upper midwest delayed grain plantings, making soybeans the best alternative. The harvested acreage was put at 61.7 million acres with an average yield of 35.4 bushels per acre, versus the record high 41.9 bushels in 1994/95. During the past seven years, total U.S. acreage for corn and soybeans, including set side programs, averaged about 143.5 million acres, with corn using about 80 to 81 million. However, there is an estimated 8 million acres in the Conservation Reserve Program, (CRP) a portion of which could be released in 1996 if prices escalate too far during 1995/96, which the run to $7.50 in late 1995 could do.

U.S. soybean carryover stocks on August 31, 1995, of 335 million bushels brought total 1995/96 supplies to more than 2.5 billion bushels versus 2.7 billion in 1994/95. Total disappearance in 1995/96 will drop due to the season's higher price, but still exceed the new supply and require a draw on carryover of at least 120 million bushels. The USDA forecast ending 1995/96 stocks at 215 million bushels, which could prove optimistic if Brazil's crop comes in short and fosters a stronger foreign demand for U.S. beans, especially from China. The lowest carryover in recent years was 182 million bushels as of September 1, 1989, which in the mid 1990s might be viewed as close to the bare minimum level, and not yet an unrealistic total for 1995/96 ending carryover. The season's estimated crush of a record high 1.4 billion bushels is marginally higher than 1994/95; exports were initially estimated at 800 million bushels versus 838 million in 1994/95, while seed and residual use was placed near 110 million bushels, down sharply from 153 million a year earlier.

The USDA's initial average price received by farmers in 1995/96 of $5.50 to 6.50 per bushel is likely to prove well under the final average considering the $1.25/bushel rise during the first half of the season. The average 1994/95 price was $5.45/bushel and compares with a high during the past decade of $7.42 in 1988/89.

U.S. Farm Program

The effective marketing loan rate for the 1995 crop was $4.92 ($5.02 less 2 percent origination fee) as it has been since 1991.

Futures Markets

Soybean futures are traded on the Bolsa de Mercadorias & Futuros (BM&F), the Kansai Agricultural Commodities Exchange (KANEX), the Tokyo Grain Exchange (TGE), the Manila International Futures Exchange Inc. (MIFE), the Chicago Board of Trade (CBOT), and the Mid America Commodity Exchange (MidAm). Options are traded on the TGE, the CBOT, and the MidAm.

World Production of Soybeans   In Thousands of Metric Tons

Crop Year[4]	Argentina	Bolivia	Brazil	Canada	China	India	Indonesia	Japan	Rep. of Korea	Meixco	Romania	Paraguay	Thailand	United States	former USSR	World Total
1986-7	7,000	81	17,300	960	11,610	891	900	245	199	660	472	950	356	52,868	703	98,100
1987-8	9,700	158	18,020	1,267	12,470	980	950	287	203	750	350	1,100	338	52,746	712	103,810
1988-9	6,500	294	23,600	1,100	11,650	1,400	1,285	277	239	300	340	1,620	517	42,153	880	95,650
1989-90	10,750	173	20,340	1,219	10,227	1,806	1,315	272	252	984	304	1,575	672	52,354	956	107,367
1990-1	11,500	352	15,750	1,262	11,000	2,602	1,400	220	233	575	141	1,300	530	52,416	880	104,155
1991-2	11,315	384	19,456	1,460	9,713	2,492	1,555	197	183	725	179	1,315	436	54,065	830	108,050
1992-3	11,240	278	22,710	1,455	10,304	3,106	1,870	188	176	573	126	1,794	435	59,546	620	117,508
1993-4[1]	12,300	491	24,963	1,851	15,310	4,000	1,655	101	170	483	95	1,796	480	50,920	650	116,916
1994-5[2]	12,200	550	25,500	2,251	16,000	3,300	1,600	99	170	430	91	2,200	480	68,490	560	136,490
1995-6[3]	12,500	620	23,300	2,100	15,000	4,000	1,700	110	180	370		1,950	460	59,620	540	125,260

[1] Preliminary. [2] Estimate. [3] Forecast. [4] Split year includes Northern Hemisphere crops harvested in the late months of the first year shown combined with Southern Hemisphere crops harvested in the early months of the following year. *Source: Foreign Agricultural Service, U.S. Department of Agriculture*

Supply and Distribution of Soybeans in the United States   In Millions of Bushels

Crop Year Beginning Sept. 1	Supply: Stocks, Sept. 1: Farms	Supply: Stocks, Sept. 1: Mills, Elevators[2]	Supply: Stocks, Sept. 1: Total	Supply: Production	Supply: Total Supply	Distribution: Crushings	Distribution: Exports	Distribution: Seed, Feed & Residual	Distribution: Total Distribution
1986-7	167.1	369.3	536	1,943	2,479	1,179	757	106	2,042
1987-8	108.0	328.5	436	1,938	2,375	1,174	804	95	2,073
1988-9	105.1	197.4	302	1,549	1,855	1,058	527	87	1,673
1989-90	87.3	94.7	182	1,924	2,109	1,146	622	101	1,870
1990-1	86.0	153.1	239	1,926	2,169	1,187	557	95	1,840
1991-2	118.4	210.6	329	1,987	2,319	1,254	684	103	2,041
1992-3	105.0	173.4	278	2,190	2,471	1,279	770	130	2,179
1993-4	125.0	167.3	292	1,871	2,170	1,276	589	96	1,961
1994-5[1]	59.1	150.0	209	2,517	2,731	1,405	838	153	2,396
1995-6[3]	105.1	229.7	335	2,152	2,492	1,390	800	111	2,301

[1] Preliminary. [2] Also warehouses. [3] Estimates. *Source: Economic Research Service, U.S. Department of Agriculture*

U.S. Soybean Price Support Program & Official Crop Production Reports   In Millions of Bushels

Crop Year Beginning Sept.	Quantity Put Under Support	% of Production	Stocks Sept. 1	National Average Support: % of Parity	National Average Support: $ Per Bu.	Crop Production Reports In Thousands of Bushels: Aug. 1	Sept. 1	Oct. 1	Nov. 1	Dec. 1	Final
1986	327.6	16.9	536.4	39	4.77	1,979,773	1,979,773	1,991,763	2,009,333	2,007,033	1,942,558
1987	274.7	14.2	436.4	39	4.77	2,000,349	1,956,859	1,968,069	1,959,949	1,904,712	1,938,087
1988	120.1	7.8	302.5	40	4.77	1,473,986	1,472,376	1,501,381	1,511,876	----------	1,548,841
1989	208.9	10.9	182.0	37	4.53	1,905,300	1,889,265	1,926,385	1,936,545	----------	1,926,806
1990	241.4	12.5	239.1	36	4.50	1,836,017	1,834,602	1,823,462	1,903,832	----------	1,925,947
1991	158.8	8.0	329.0	40	5.02	1,868,825	1,816,825	1,933,570	1,961,840	----------	1,986,539
1992	182.1	8.3	278.4	41	5.02	2,079,487	NA	NA	NA	----------	2,190,354
1993	87.1	4.8	292.3	40	5.02	1,902,023	1,909,188	1,890,808	1,833,788	----------	1,870,958
1994	375.0	14.6	209.1		4.92	2,282,367	2,316,077	2,458,087	2,522,527	----------	2,516,694
1995[1]	62.3	2.9	335.0		4.92	2,245,901	2,284,551	2,190,661	2,182,991	----------	2,151,834

[1] Preliminary. NA = Not available. *Source: National Agricultural Statistics Service, U.S. Department of Agriculture*

Soybean Stocks in the United States   In Thousands of Bushels

Year	On Farms: Mar. 1	On Farms: Jun. 1	On Farms: Sept. 1	On Farms: Dec. 1	Off Farms[1]: Mar. 1	Off Farms[1]: Jun. 1	Off Farms[1]: Sept. 1	Off Farms[1]: Dec. 1	Total Stocks: Mar. 1	Total Stocks: Jun. 1	Total Stocks: Sept. 1	Total Stocks: Dec. 1
1986	NA	411,740	167,090	1,061,000	NA	437,186	369,275	895,637	NA	848,926	536,365	1,956,637
1987	589,000	282,100	107,950	865,300	749,958	554,654	328,497	889,981	1,338,958	836,754	436,447	1,755,281
1988	553,100	304,900	105,050	650,000	594,620	351,382	197,426	716,812	1,147,720	656,282	302,476	1,366,812
1989	415,000	229,200	87,320	793,400	475,246	235,311	94,709	816,583	890,246	464,511	182,029	1,609,983
1990	535,800	255,300	86,000	754,000	519,705	340,614	153,139	929,963	1,055,505	595,914	239,139	1,683,963
1991	555,500	336,500	118,400	810,000	634,619	387,022	210,642	968,957	1,190,119	723,522	329,042	1,778,957
1992	505,000	279,000	105,000	876,100	672,343	416,671	173,437	959,885	1,177,343	695,671	278,437	1,835,985
1993	576,900	319,800	124,970	697,400	638,667	363,613	167,314	876,220	1,215,567	683,413	292,284	1,573,620
1994	425,700	195,000	59,080	985,800	595,917	360,260	150,037	1,116,156	1,021,617	555,260	209,117	2,101,956
1995	635,300	348,800	105,130	861,500	734,898	443,072	229,684	971,914	1,370,198	791,872	334,814	1,833,414

[1] Includes stocks at mills, elevators, warehouses, terminals and processors. NA = Not available. *Source: National Agricultural Statistics Service, U.S. Department of Agriculture*

SOYBEANS

U.S. Commercial Stocks of Soybeans on the First of the Month In Millions of Bushels

Year	Jan.	Feb.	Mar.	Apr.	May	June	July	Aug.	Sept.	Oct.	Nov.	Dec.
1983	53.6	58.2	57.5	55.7	55.9	44.7	34.9	35.8	42.5	47.0	78.8	83.0
1984	77.2	74.4	65.2	58.6	49.2	41.1	35.4	20.8	7.9	6.7	23.3	41.7
1985	41.1	44.0	38.2	33.3	22.8	14.7	12.7	11.3	6.9	9.6	47.6	60.9
1986	61.7	63.9	57.3	53.6	40.2	30.5	24.9	24.5	24.8	30.1	52.5	61.5
1987	62.0	61.4	56.9	52.5	49.4	46.3	38.4	26.0	16.6	21.3	56.5	57.1
1988	63.0	66.9	63.6	61.2	54.6	51.7	53.2	54.5	46.0	41.6	74.7	80.9
1989	81.3	75.6	63.8	53.4	35.8	31.2	21.1	18.6	14.1	11.4	62.1	71.3
1990	65.8	62.1	57.8	53.2	56.2	54.4	48.1	41.4	26.1	24.1	89.7	90.7
1991	90.2	78.1	70.5	56.2	43.5	35.5	33.3	25.5	25.3	29.7	80.6	84.0
1992	76.0	75.9	67.1	67.8	58.5	57.2	51.7	32.1	18.6	59.0	75.1	79.9
1993	71.5	63.5	54.5	48.5	44.0	32.1	26.6	24.4	15.8	9.6	52.3	60.2
1994	62.6	65.3	54.4	46.3	40.7	34.7	29.9	24.3	19.8	11.5	68.1	83.4
1995	80.7	72.5	67.8	63.5	51.8	50.8	44.3	35.7	33.6	23.0	60.8	59.7

Source: Livestock Division, U.S. Department of Agriculture

Salient Statistics of Soybeans in the United States

Crop Year	Planted (1,000 Acres)	Acreage Harvested (1,000 Acres)	Yield Per Acre (Bu.)	Farm Price ($ Bu.)	Farm Value (Million Dollars)	Pounds Per Bushel Crushed: Yield of Oil	Pounds Per Bushel Crushed: Yield of Meal	U.S. Exports of Soybeans Crop Year (Oct.-Sept.) in Thousands of Metric Tons: Grand Total	Bel.-Luxem.	Canada	Germany	Japan	Netherlands	Spain	Taiwan	former USSR
1978-9	64,708	63,663	29.4	6.66	12,450	11.07	47.63	20,117	420	352	1,486	3,865	4,012	1,475	1,271	1,178
1979-80	71,411	70,343	32.1	6.28	14,204	10.74	48.01	23,818	584	392	1,318	3,868	6,035	2,203	780	813
1980-1	60,930	67,813	26.5	7.57	13,601	11.09	47.93	19,712	670	345	1,791	3,816	3,839	1,383	1,063	NA
1981-2	67,543	66,163	30.1	6.07	12,005	10.72	47.86	25,285	1,404	310	2,135	4,196	5,349	3,855	1,059	683
1982-3	70,884	69,442	31.5	5.71	12,463	10.76	47.88	24,634	1,259	324	1,813	4,580	4,648	2,313	1,300	199
1983-4	63,779	62,525	26.2	7.83	12,775	11.26	47.36	20,215	882	248	967	4,394	2,988	1,800	1,382	408
1984-5	67,755	66,113	28.1	5.84	10,748	11.05	47.15	16,279	658	140	718	3,828	2,857	1,084	1,389	0
1985-6	63,145	61,599	34.1	5.05	10,571	11.01	47.27	20,158	784	114	934	4,293	3,056	1,519	1,506	1,519
1986-7	60,405	58,312	33.3	4.78	9,263	10.86	47.08	20,600	888	206	1,393	4,024	3,540	1,775	1,968	71
1987-8	58,180	57,172	33.9	5.88	11,391	11.04	47.76	21,870	825	154	1,416	3,914	4,267	1,593	1,857	831
1988-9	58,840	57,373	27.0	7.42	11,488	11.16	47.43	14,356	474	113	601	3,251	2,531	1,152	1,439	240
1989-90	60,820	59,538	32.3	5.69	10,916	11.17	47.63	16,933	666	276	818	3,480	2,721	1,565	2,016	342
1990-1	57,795	56,512	34.1	5.74	11,042	11.23	47.47	15,161	413	156	760	3,584	2,085	1,027	1,087	354
1991-2	59,180	58,011	34.2	5.58	11,092	11.42	47.51	19,277	797	76	814	3,891	3,167	1,459	2,034	543
1992-3	59,180	58,233	37.6	5.60	12,154	10.84	47.54	20,400	814	249	893	3,984	3,362	1,424	2,369	46
1993-4[1]	60,135	57,347	32.6	6.40	11,575	10.87	47.62	16,364	602	26	807	3,527	2,661	921	1,700	NA
1994-5[2]	61,670	60,859	41.4	5.48	12,068	11.08	47.32	23,584	778	0	1,228	4,061	4,130	1,714	2,586	NA
1995-6[2]	62,575	61,624	34.9	6.55-7.55		11.24	47.59									

[1] Preliminary. [2] Forecast. NA = Not available. *Source: Economic Research Service, U.S. Department of Agriculture*

Production of Soybeans for Beans in the U.S., by Selected States In Millions of Bushels

Year	Arkansas	Illinois	Indiana	Iowa	Kentucky	Louisiana	Michigan	Minnesota	Mississippi	Missouri	Nebraska	North Carolina	Ohio	South Carolina	Tennessee
1978	115.2	309.5	144.2	283.1	40.8	76.0	21.6	146.2	81.7	155.0	42.5	40.3	127.7	32.3	56.9
1979	144.2	379.1	159.1	306.4	54.0	93.8	30.3	162.6	118.9	183.6	54.7	45.8	144.8	39.8	70.7
1980	65.3	309.9	157.7	318.4	36.0	67.0	30.4	149.9	61.6	135.5	53.1	34.7	135.4	20.8	45.9
1981	99.0	351.5	151.8	326.0	47.9	64.2	29.1	139.2	75.6	155.6	78.7	46.3	99.8	31.0	61.1
1982	105.6	354.2	173.3	306.6	51.3	75.4	35.3	169.1	92.3	171.0	78.8	52.5	133.2	39.6	61.0
1983	70.3	267.0	122.5	278.6	24.5	68.1	33.8	151.8	58.9	103.0	59.0	33.0	105.0	23.6	31.5
1984	101.4	284.1	150.1	264.6	42.3	66.8	32.1	172.9	76.8	108.7	66.3	46.5	137.6	29.8	48.1
1985	98.1	382.5	185.1	309.7	41.8	44.1	34.6	160.0	70.7	180.4	85.0	39.1	160.6	24.6	45.3
1986	66.0	360.0	157.3	350.7	35.8	35.0	28.8	162.8	41.7	170.6	93.1	36.7	146.6	13.7	35.5
1987	71.5	330.6	174.0	343.7	24.0	38.8	38.2	181.4	47.8	154.6	83.4	32.8	147.3	15.7	28.8
1988	83.2	234.9	115.5	251.1	24.1	56.6	35.1	124.8	49.5	112.1	70.8	35.4	99.9	18.6	32.0
1989	75.2	354.0	166.1	322.9	36.9	38.5	38.9	185.0	40.0	121.8	81.9	41.9	125.4	20.2	29.8
1990	90.5	354.9	171.4	327.9	39.0	42.0	43.3	179.4	39.9	124.5	81.4	32.4	135.7	13.9	33.8
1991	89.6	341.3	171.6	349.5	36.7	30.7	52.8	195.3	46.8	135.1	82.4	38.6	135.7	13.7	31.5
1992	104.3	405.5	194.4	359.5	42.2	35.1	47.5	172.8	59.5	161.5	103.3	36.5	147.2	14.7	33.3
1993	92.3	387.0	223.1	257.3	38.0	31.2	54.7	115.0	42.9	118.8	90.0	30.0	156.2	7.8	32.2
1994	115.6	429.1	215.3	442.9	42.4	31.9	57.0	224.0	57.0	173.3	134.4	41.9	173.6	15.7	38.3
1995[1]	86.7	373.5	194.2	398.2	41.4	26.0	59.8	232.0	37.8	130.5	99.5	26.8	153.1	12.7	34.6

[1] Preliminary. *Source: Agricultural Statistics Board, U.S. Department of Agriculture*

Soybean Stocks at U.S. Mills on First of Month In Millions of Bushels

Crop Year	Sept.	Oct.	Nov.	Dec.	Jan.	Feb.	Mar.	Apr.	May	June	July	Aug.
1978-9	37.9	31.9	138.4	149.4	127.3	112.4	124.0	120.9	96.7	71.1	73.0	55.6
1979-80	37.5	39.2	166.5	184.5	163.3	145.4	130.7	118.6	95.8	79.7	75.7	73.9
1980-1	56.9	80.4	166.0	172.0	138.7	125.9	105.4	97.2	84.4	67.8	49.2	43.9
1981-2	33.4	31.5	105.8	135.2	114.5	99.8	84.6	79.2	72.2	60.8	51.2	43.6
1982-3	30.0	29.0	114.2	145.5	125.1	116.2	98.5	96.2	84.6	69.8	62.0	55.4
1983-4	58.6	63.9	124.5	142.3	124.0	125.3	114.8	105.3	94.2	101.7	83.4	57.7
1984-5	35.3	19.7	53.9	116.4	98.4	85.9	65.8	69.7	65.2	53.4	47.6	36.0
1985-6	26.7	25.7	92.8	113.4	119.9	124.6	97.5	84.9	67.6	53.2	40.7	40.2
1986-7	28.5	38.3	108.1	127.4	117.2	113.1	105.4	90.2	85.2	72.9	63.6	49.8
1987-8	31.2	65.7	158.5	155.5	145.0	141.8	139.3	133.8	113.9	95.4	90.1	66.2
1988-9	59.7	61.4	136.6	147.4	138.6	131.9	112.0	99.2	72.8	52.5	46.1	31.0
1989-90	23.8	24.5	96.3	108.5	89.7	93.6	91.4	83.5	73.0	67.5	58.8	46.9
1990-1	45.2	34.5	130.1	130.7		106.5			78.5			61.2
1991-2	------		67.0		126.9	121.4	109.6	94.7	79.8	73.5	65.7	56.2
1992-3	43.8	46.3	132.3	137.4	119.1	111.2	97.2	90.1	83.6	67.7	67.1	55.3
1993-4	42.0	28.0	108.6	114.9	120.9	126.1	118.5	119.7	98.7	97.8	90.0	63.5
1994-5[1]	47.9	46.8	114.1	124.3	108.0	114.7	114.3	112.6	94.1	81.2	69.1	55.1
1995-6[1]	52.8	54.2	125.3	128.8								

[1] Preliminary. *Source: Economic Research Service, U.S. Department of Agriculture*

Soybean Exports from the United States In Millions of Bushels

Year	Sept.	Oct.	Nov.	Dec.	Jan.	Feb.	Mar.	Apr.	May	June	July	Aug.	Total
1980-1	41.4	60.3	75.0	74.5	71.7	55.5	103.2	60.0	69.6	41.8	29.6	41.8	724.3
1981-2	50.9	100.8	103.7	73.6	84.3	89.4	79.0	85.7	90.6	59.8	53.8	57.5	929.1
1982-3	58.0	94.4	93.6	90.1	86.3	87.2	84.4	73.3	58.5	67.7	51.6	60.2	905.2
1983-4	53.9	67.6	69.2	74.5	80.4	79.7	78.8	68.5	56.8	41.1	39.2	30.7	686.6
1984-5	19.0	40.9	93.5	84.8	70.3	72.6	59.8	60.4	33.1	18.2	19.2	26.3	598.2
1985-6	31.5	55.3	79.6	94.1	84.7	92.1	89.9	80.4	57.2	28.7	26.6	20.4	740.7
1986-7	30.2	89.7	96.6	89.0	71.7	73.8	67.8	53.9	37.6	37.9	54.3	54.5	756.9
1987-8	59.4	101.1	100.4	81.1	80.8	97.0	78.5	66.7	39.7	29.3	30.4	37.2	801.7
1988-9	26.7	50.2	61.3	69.3	66.3	56.1	66.8	40.8	23.2	31.2	16.4	18.3	526.5
1989-90	17.9	74.0	76.6	65.7	76.3	74.9	87.3	43.6	22.8	35.2	20.8	28.3	623.4
1990-1	27.9	29.8	62.8	55.8		190.1			117.7		73.9		557.9
1991-2	26.8		235.6		73.8	90.6	63.3	56.6	28.3	27.3	42.6	39.2	683.9
1992-3	50.1	98.0	84.2	73.6	89.1	104.7	79.7	48.7	34.6	39.4	42.7	24.6	769.5
1993-4	30.1	73.6	72.4	73.9	71.0	67.8	53.6	34.8	27.5	26.7	17.1	40.7	589.1
1994-5[1]	42.3	99.9	78.5	104.2	89.3	91.4	83.1	80.7	45.2	35.5	41.2	46.7	838.1
1995-6[1]	70.7	77.4	65.5										

[1] Preliminary. *Source: Economic Research Service, U.S. Department of Agriculture*

Volume of Trading in Soybean Futures at the Chicago Board of Trade In Millions of Bushels

Year	Jan.	Feb.	Mar.	Apr.	May	June	July	Aug.	Sept.	Oct.	Nov.	Dec.	Total
1982	3,120	3,497	4,478	4,484	3,517	4,245	4,017	3,822	3,197	4,014	4,282	3,198	45,828
1983	3,942	3,820	4,247	4,375	4,259	4,409	6,224	8,799	7,852	8,071	6,793	5,609	68,402
1984	5,550	5,247	6,008	4,945	7,300	6,323	5,314	4,045	2,505	3,687	3,427	2,463	56,813
1985	3,315	2,749	2,657	2,821	2,766	3,309	3,779	2,581	2,525	3,364	3,881	3,213	36,961
1986	3,692	2,484	2,435	2,976	2,546	2,199	2,925	2,049	1,812	3,266	2,473	1,811	30,668
1987	2,174	1,816	1,794	3,118	3,969	4,356	3,785	1,935	2,305	4,109	3,674	3,859	36,894
1988	4,436	4,252	4,284	4,822	6,339	7,975	5,574	5,214	4,516	5,235	5,001	4,777	62,485
1989	5,222	4,265	4,760	4,720	4,587	4,466	3,977	3,172	2,854	4,011	3,247	2,893	48,174
1990	3,278	2,673	4,133	4,422	5,630	5,209	5,188	4,528	3,214	5,660	4,299	3,275	67,887
1991	3,725	3,104	3,577	4,040	3,422	3,881	4,962	4,716	3,312	4,381	2,856	3,095	44,871
1992	4,022	3,692	3,440	2,794	4,369	5,273	4,666	3,154	2,861	4,337	3,066	3,327	45,001
1993	3,417	3,123	3,379	3,806	3,890	6,435	8,216	5,900	4,625	4,811	5,940	4,707	58,247
1994	5,673	4,493	4,610	4,597	5,792	5,985	4,462	3,442	3,113	4,285	4,129	3,166	53,745
1995	3,070	2,860	3,998	3,491	4,747	5,254	5,984	4,085	4,001	5,639	4,202	5,727	53,058

Source: Chicago Board of Trade

SOYBEANS

Average Open Interest of Soybean Futures at Chicago Board of Trade In Millions of Bushels

Year	Jan.	Feb.	Mar.	Apr.	May	June	July	Aug.	Sept.	Oct.	Nov.	Dec.
1980	542,923	555,696	506,850	512,455	501,404	544,760	669,411	716,959	836,481	994,450	1,069,985	1,083,919
1981	760,433	618,363	556,355	586,500	516,510	517,640	497,162	452,323	440,217	472,908	485,995	482,498
1982	404,223	406,528	393,035	460,729	418,686	391,052	374,053	380,213	355,169	397,810	425,089	438,322
1983	442,828	456,830	416,479	505,813	462,581	420,022	455,472	670,320	714,951	748,973	655,300	631,981
1984	558,727	544,108	564,202	535,411	546,508	495,022	360,313	286,738	270,991	326,171	353,568	356,011
1985	348,140	364,738	327,450	317,610	306,381	329,845	314,415	324,314	315,912	353,915	375,558	367,207
1986	377,175	375,378	374,277	382,321	342,736	333,767	303,102	290,679	298,112	366,628	410,962	405,791
1987	373,975	374,970	384,749	448,282	472,715	460,889	396,495	364,262	373,807	524,582	537,224	589,553
1988	592,560	617,929	609,312	692,576	763,473	849,772	644,812	574,151	598,951	607,404	558,608	603,549
1989	598,499	572,342	579,959	513,682	484,011	472,263	417,035	379,628	404,830	503,966	482,161	493,360
1990	478,591	496,834	556,976	615,027	655,864	590,047	483,946	458,531	489,646	599,204	625,678	617,759
1991	546,555	552,104	551,590	534,973	511,847	516,809	457,245	430,659	490,248	571,031	562,037	563,908
1992	574,356	591,586	663,193	605,856	606,990	689,478	581,040	534,148	520,573	628,670	594,385	571,307
1993	608,628	633,411	633,405	690,776	689,104	713,606	998,406	917,111	818,236	798,207	805,850	843,468
1994	888,241	836,087	780,293	737,844	728,991	751,017	660,050	605,630	634,736	735,989	685,934	681,753
1995	691,726	693,969	689,213	693,120	667,663	715,597	718,354	677,921	722,043	836,000	873,873	970,104

Source: Chicago Board of Trade

Spread Between Value of Products and Soybean Price in the U.S. In Cents Per Bushel

Year	Sept.	Oct.	Nov.	Dec.	Jan.	Feb.	Mar.	Apr.	May	June	July	Aug.	Average
1980-1	36	36	29	19	30	20	29	22	9	11	11	21	23
1981-2	35	15	4	22	19	26	25	22	24	16	21	24	21
1982-3	33	47	30	31	21	22	15	18	30	27	25	39	28
1983-4	42	40	23	40	28	7	8	14	26	24	41	31	27
1984-5	46	49	37	23	19	18	36	35	25	33	28	29	37
1985-6	40	49	43	43	40	27	32	29	25	18	28	48	35
1986-7	90	60	44	50	44	77	51	63	72	83	85	77	66
1987-8	108	134	166	167	131	83	89	89	133	125	135	107	122
1988-9	111	131	109	95	90	73	70	72	61	93	107	155	97
1989-90	171	141	113	87	78	58	70	85	109	103	97	99	101
1990-1	99	77	58	64	63	73	79	75	72	74	91	99	77
1991-2	118	120	94	82	74	74	75	78	87	104	80	83	89
1992-3	98	93	87	93	94	77	77	79	82	84	120	97	90
1993-4	95	108	105	92	93	99	88	85	89	88	94	118	96
1994-5	146	167	143	137	130	109	114	109	86	102	87	90	118
1995-6	90	107											538

Source: Economic Research Service, U.S. Department of Agriculture

Soybean Crushed (Factory Consumption) in the U.S. In Millions of Bushels--One Bushel=60 Pounds

Year	Sept.	Oct.	Nov.	Dec.	Jan.	Feb.	Mar.	Apr.	May	June	July	Aug.	Total
1980-1	81.0	97.8	98.5	94.1	92.2	79.6	88.7	85.4	82.3	73.4	72.3	74.6	1,020
1981-2	75.4	104.5	97.6	102.5	94.9	86.7	85.1	81.0	86.6	77.1	70.6	67.8	1,030
1982-3	76.0	100.2	108.1	111.9	110.0	93.0	94.6	81.8	83.7	81.5	81.6	85.7	1,108
1983-4	86.6	96.4	86.6	89.4	93.8	79.2	86.0	74.6	79.4	70.6	69.0	71.1	983
1984-5	65.5	89.2	98.9	101.1	94.5	80.8	85.6	83.2	89.3	82.7	82.0	77.5	1,030
1985-6	76.5	94.3	96.7	100.8	99.6	81.4	91.6	84.4	86.3	79.6	83.1	78.4	1,053
1986-7	79.4	107.0	109.4	107.6	110.3	102.3	106.0	95.9	95.3	90.6	92.6	82.4	1,179
1987-8	79.7	102.5	111.2	110.8	106.7	99.8	107.6	102.6	98.0	89.2	88.0	78.3	1,174
1988-9	79.9	94.4	101.0	100.7	99.8	85.8	93.5	89.6	87.0	76.0	74.0	75.9	1,058
1989-90	74.1	94.8	104.1	105.4	107.2	91.8	102.1	95.1	93.4	92.0	92.2	94.2	1,146
1990-1	92.1	106.1	106.0	102.7	------------	297.9	-----------	------------	280.1	-----------	202.5	-----------	1,187
1991-2	98.9	------------	333.3	-----------	112.0	100.8	107.2	101.6	95.2	100.0	102.3	102.3	1,254
1992-3	101.2	113.9	113.1	116.2	116.8	102.2	113.0	105.9	106.5	99.9	98.0	92.2	1,279
1993-4	98.4	113.7	114.4	114.1	110.7	103.3	113.3	105.6	103.0	97.2	101.0	101.0	1,276
1994-5[1]	105.9	119.3	122.5	128.5	127.3	116.5	128.1	119.4	114.2	105.6	108.4	109.5	1,405
1995-6[1]	107.4	120.5	123.3	125.0									

[1] Preliminary. *Source: Economic Research Service, U.S. Department of Agriculture*

Average Price Received by Farmers for Soybeans in the U.S. In Cents Per Bushel

Year	Sept.	Oct.	Nov.	Dec.	Jan.	Feb.	Mar.	Apr.	May	June	July	Aug.	Average
1980-1	759	768	818	780	780	750	759	760	740	705	713	671	757
1981-2	621	606	603	600	613	604	604	617	627	612	599	559	604
1982-3	522	506	534	546	556	566	582	609	606	590	627	757	565
1983-4	828	796	780	774	785	728	768	783	812	799	695	650	783
1984-5	609	607	601	582	591	577	588	588	570	562	542	510	584
1985-6	499	485	492	501	516	518	523	523	525	519	511	499	505
1986-7	485	455	464	467	470	469	473	490	520	536	525	502	478
1987-8	502	504	536	563	573	596	605	639	698	818	850	833	588
1988-9	793	753	743	753	769	741	751	729	720	705	683	607	742
1989-90	570	554	566	564	565	556	565	582	597	588	597	600	570
1990-1	599	587	578	572	572	565	577	577	559	555	536	566	575
1991-2	564	549	548	545	554	559	567	566	587	594	559	540	560
1992-3	535	526	536	546	558	556	565	573	581	564	657	655	571
1993-4	621	601	632	664	672	671	673	657	677	672	592	558	640
1994-5[1]	547	530	536	541	547	540	551	555	556	568	590	583	548
1995-6[1]	599	615	639	676	695								

[1] Preliminary. *Source: Economic Research Service, U.S. Department of Agriculture*

SOYBEANS

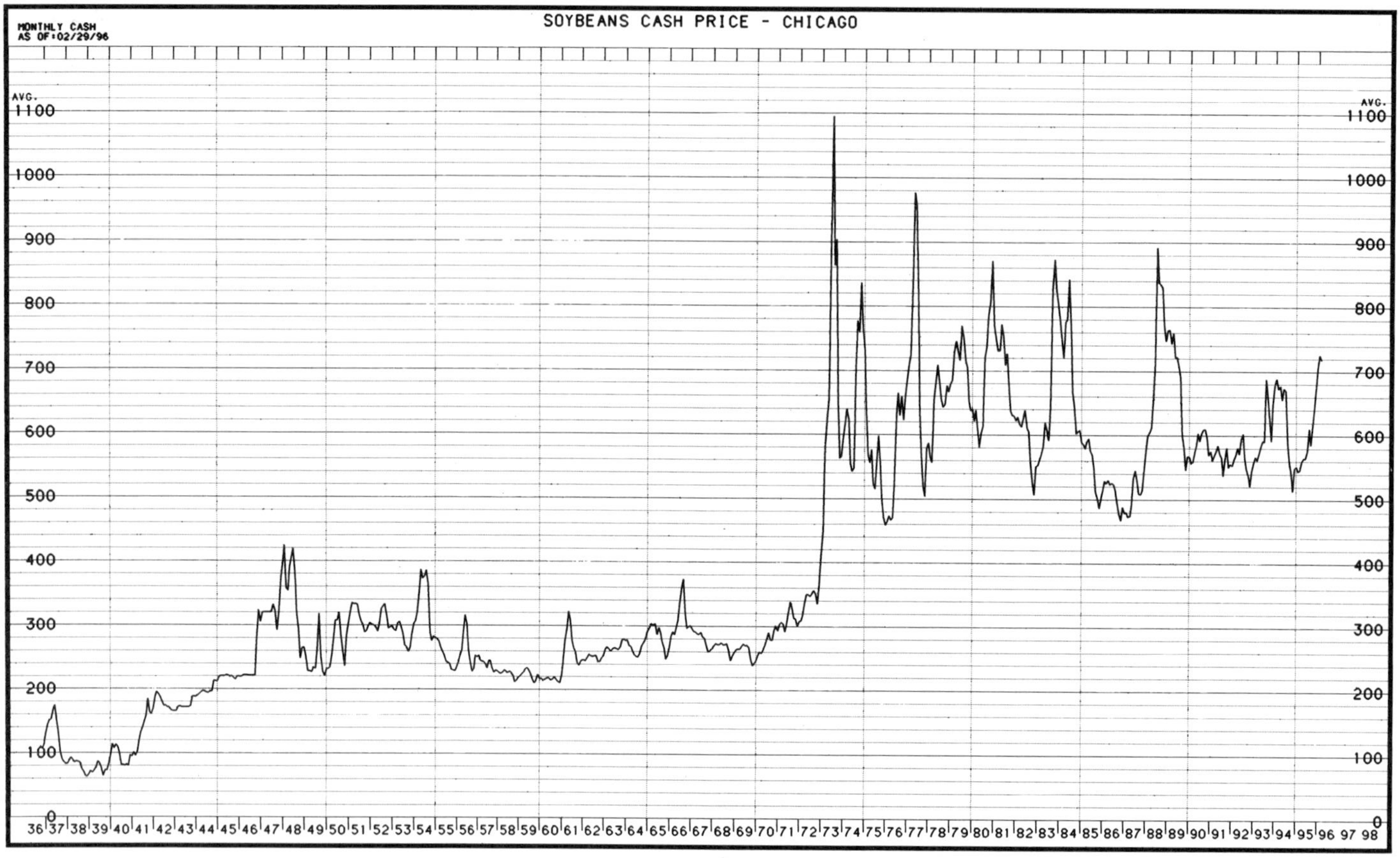

Average Cash Price of No. 1 Yellow Soybeans at Illinois Processor In Cents Per Bushel

Year	Sept.	Oct.	Nov.	Dec.	Jan.	Feb.	Mar.	Apr.	May	June	July	Aug.	Average
1976-7	516	622	655	686	706	726	825	960	942	825	640	549	721
1977-8	642	507	584	594	573	565	658	681	701	676	662	647	624
1978-9	704	672	668	681	689	728	745	727	721	768	764	728	716
1979-80	813	656	652	653	636	642	607	580	604	610	722	745	660
1980-1	644	827	891	773	757	734	737	772	758	713	736	694	753
1981-2	540	630	628	623	630	624	616	642	656	631	620	573	618
1982-3	540	526	570	573	581	586	598	635	627	606	659	846	612
1983-4	893	846	820	777	767	737	797	798	861	791	685	663	786
1984-5	621	627	625	607	604	597	608	613	595	588	565	528	598
1985-6	519	505	519	532	545	538	547	540	544	543	533	500	530
1986-7	496	489	508	469	498	489	492	512	552	563	547	528	512
1987-8	527	532	564	594	617	621	630	671	731	913	859	852	676
1988-9	852	792	767	783	783	760	778	739	740	725	708	606	753
1989-90	600	564	570	582	572	585	600	600	620	609	619	626	596
1990-1	628	614	587	591	576	585	592	601	589	583	554	578	590
1991-2	598	568	571	568	577	581	593	585	609	619	580	564	584
1992-3	554	535	560	572	582	575	587	597	607	606	689	679	595
1993-4	643	606	664	694	701	686	692	670	689	685	603	576	659
1994-5[1]	557	531	566	567	558	560	574	578	580	577	623	602	573
1995-6[1]	632	656											

[1] Preliminary. *Source: Economic Research Service, U.S. Department of Agriculture*

Stock Index Futures, U.S.

1995 was phenomenal for the U.S. equity markets as the major indices soared to new highs on near fever pitched, record trading volume. The occasional corrections proved short lived and only fueled the rush into equities by so-called bargain hunters. Indeed, the bullish momentum seem to feed upon itself as the year progressed.

Ironically, a rational for the strength was a slowing domestic economy, seemingly headed for a "soft landing." The equity markets quickly interpreted bad economic news as good, and vice versa; the assumption being that the Federal Reserve would check the economy's slippage with an easier monetary policy—and if they didn't act immediately, it was just a matter of time before they did. Interest rates did edge lower during the year, heightening the flow of capital into equities and out of low yielding bank deposits. Money poured into stock mutual funds; in November alone $16.7 billion (net) was received, up from $11 billion in October. At the end of the year mutual fund assets exceeded a record high $2 trillion.

At yearend, the Treasury's 30-year bond yield of 5.94 percent was at a two-year low versus a 7.87 percent yield a year earlier. As if emphasizing the markets' deep rooted positive psychology, which abetted the very strong technical profile, or perhaps it was the other way around, was the near partial shutdown of the federal government, not once, but twice in late 1995, as the smoldering political impasse over the Government's deficit boiled over. The uncertainty triggered a 101 point drop in the Dow-Jones on December 18, the biggest decline in four years, but the loss had no follow through in the closing days of 1995.

The bellwether Dow-Jones 30 Industrial Average closed 1995 at a near record high 5,117.12, up 1,283 points or 33.5 percent from 1994, versus a 2.1 percent gain in 1994. On 69 trading days, the D-J scored new highs, the most ever in a single year. Among the broader indices, the S & P 500 Stock Index rose 34 percent, and the corporate high tech dominated NASDAQ jumped 40 percent. Trading volume on the New York Stock Exchange totaled nearly 87 billion shares versus 72.5 billion in 1994; on the NASDAQ, volume swelled to 102 billion versus 74 billion.

The economic news in 1995 was mixed: real growth slowed and the number of new jobs created was about half that of 1994. The monthly unemployment totals, however, held steady at about 5.7 percent as corporate America continued to pursue a "lean and mean" approach for cutting costs. Consumer credit debt, not including mortgages and home equity loans, surpassed $1 trillion in October, a record high and placing the share of monthly disposable income to repay debt at 17 percent. Consumer confidence at yearend was 98.7 percent, as determined by the Conference Board using a 1985 base of 100.

Since 1996 is a major election year the pressure on the Fed to ease is apt to intensify, notwithstanding the Fed's theoretical independence from political pressure. The variables that might put monetary policy on hold are (1) greater inflationary pressures than seen in 1995; (2) a gridlock setting for reconciling the federal government's budgetary problems; (3) any serious FOREX weakness in the U.S. dollar. On balance, 1996 could be another good year for the market, but a repeat of 1995 will be a tough act to follow.

Futures Markets

S & P 500 futures and options and the S & P Midcap Index of 400 stocks are traded on the Chicago Mercantile Exchange (CME). Options on the S & P Midcap Index are traded on the American Stock Exchange (AMEX). A New York Stock Exchange Composite index is traded on the New York Futures Exchange (NYFE). Other U.S. stock indices listed for futures and/or options trading include: the Value Line Arithmetic Index and mini Value line Index, and the Major Market Index and Russell 2000 Index.

Dow Jones Industrial Average (30 Stocks)

Year	Jan.	Feb.	Mar.	Apr.	May	June	July	Aug.	Sept.	Oct.	Nov.	Dec.	Average
1988	1,947.4	1,980.7	2,044.3	2,036.1	1,988.9	2,104.9	2,104.2	2,051.3	2,080.1	2,144.3	2,099.0	2,148.6	2,061.0
1989	2,234.7	2,304.3	2,283.1	2,348.9	2,439.6	2,494.9	2,554.0	2,691.1	2,693.4	2,692.0	2,642.5	2,728.5	2,508.9
1990	2,679.2	2,614.2	2,700.1	2,708.3	2,793.8	2,894.8	2,934.2	2,681.9	2,550.7	2,460.5	2,518.6	2,610.9	2,678.9
1991	2,587.6	2,863.0	2,920.1	2,925.5	2,928.4	2,968.1	2,978.2	3,006.1	3,010.4	3,019.7	2,986.1	2,958.6	2,929.3
1992	3,227.1	3,257.3	3,247.4	3,294.1	3,376.8	3,337.8	3,329.4	3,307.4	3,293.9	3,198.7	3,238.5	3,303.2	3,284.3
1993	3,277.7	3,367.3	3,440.7	3,423.6	3,478.2	3,513.8	3,529.4	3,597.0	3,592.3	3,625.8	3,674.7	3,744.1	3,522.1
1994	3,868.4	3,905.6	3,817.0	3,661.5	3,708.0	3,737.6	3,718.3	3,797.5	3,880.6	3,868.1	3,792.5	3,770.3	3,793.8
1995	3,872.5	3,953.7	4,062.8	4,230.7	4,391.6	4,510.8	4,684.8	4,639.3	4,746.8	4,760.5	4,935.8	5,136.1	4,493.8

Source: The Wall Street Journal

Dow Jones Transportation (20 Stocks)

Year	Jan.	Feb.	Mar.	Apr.	May	June	July	Aug.	Sept.	Oct.	Nov.	Dec.	Average
1988	756.0	790.1	861.3	853.7	820.2	873.1	881.2	856.1	879.5	923.1	916.2	955.4	863.8
1989	1,009.3	1,073.2	1,046.3	1,098.0	1,139.8	1,158.9	1,223.1	1,407.1	1,462.7	1,342.0	1,188.1	1,183.0	1,194.3
1990	1,139.8	1,083.4	1,160.3	1,164.8	1,163.1	1,181.9	1,150.0	951.1	881.3	850.8	848.1	908.4	1,040.3
1991	962.4	1,110.3	1,113.2	1,139.1	1,167.6	1,205.1	1,204.6	1,204.7	1,182.4	1,283.1	1,237.1	1,233.3	1,170.2
1992	1,378.7	1,412.2	969.9	1,356.9	1,380.4	1,333.3	1,303.1	1,254.6	1,275.2	1,286.2	1,375.9	1,430.1	1,349.6
1993	1,488.1	1,533.2	1,541.6	1,619.7	1,583.4	1,533.9	1,553.7	1,631.6	1,623.9	1,660.5	1,732.6	1,763.2	1,605.5
1994	1,812.1	1,810.4	1,719.9	1,614.7	1,602.2	1,619.2	1,596.2	1,602.8	1,553.7	1,485.8	1,473.7	1,415.3	1,608.8
1995	1,515.8	1,547.2	1,584.6	1,648.9	1,646.2	1,699.3	1,852.1	1,883.9	1,961.4	1,922.9	2,008.3	2,029.5	1,775.0

Source: The Wall Street Journal

STOCK INDEX FUTURES

Dow Jones Public Utilities (15 Stocks)

Year	Jan.	Feb.	Mar.	Apr.	May	June	July	Aug.	Sept.	Oct.	Nov.	Dec.	Average
1987	221.6	222.4	217.8	204.6	200.5	203.0	203.4	208.0	198.2	188.7	182.5	176.0	202.2
1988	182.2	185.0	177.7	171.4	169.3	180.0	178.7	178.6	179.9	185.0	184.1	185.2	179.8
1989	188.9	186.6	182.8	188.0	196.3	206.7	215.5	218.1	216.0	216.6	221.0	232.1	205.7
1990	223.2	221.2	217.0	210.7	212.4	211.2	205.0	210.1	199.8	207.2	210.3	210.6	210.8
1991	205.3	213.7	213.2	214.5	211.2	204.6	199.6	204.4	208.0	213.5	216.7	219.3	210.3
1992	215.7	206.8	204.4	206.1	213.2	212.5	219.1	220.2	220.0	217.2	217.7	220.2	214.4
1993	222.0	234.2	240.0	242.1	237.8	241.5	246.5	252.0	253.0	243.1	227.1	227.1	238.9
1994	222.3	215.6	207.0	196.5	185.5	182.9	181.8	188.9	179.6	179.9	177.7	181.0	191.6
1995	186.9	194.0	187.9	192.7	197.6	204.5	202.5	202.8	207.2	216.4	215.3	221.4	202.4

Source: The Wall Street Journal

Standard & Poor's 500 Composite Price Index

Year	Jan.	Feb.	Mar.	Apr.	May	June	July	Aug.	Sept.	Oct.	Nov.	Dec.	Average
1987	264.5	280.9	292.5	289.3	289.1	301.4	310.1	329.4	318.7	280.2	245.0	241.0	286.8
1988	250.5	258.1	265.7	262.6	256.1	270.7	269.1	263.7	268.0	277.4	271.0	276.5	265.8
1989	285.4	294.0	292.7	302.3	313.9	323.7	331.9	246.6	247.3	247.4	340.2	348.6	322.8
1990	340.0	330.5	338.5	338.2	350.3	360.4	360.0	330.8	315.4	307.1	315.3	328.8	334.6
1991	325.5	362.3	372.3	379.7	378.0	378.3	380.2	389.4	387.2	386.9	385.9	388.5	376.2
1992	416.1	412.6	407.4	407.4	414.8	408.3	415.1	417.9	418.5	412.5	422.8	435.6	415.8
1993	435.2	441.7	450.2	443.1	445.3	448.1	447.3	454.1	459.2	463.9	462.9	466.0	451.4
1994	473.0	471.6	463.8	447.2	451.0	454.8	451.4	464.2	467.0	463.8	461.0	455.2	460.3
1995	465.3	481.9	493.2	507.9	523.8	539.4	557.4	559.1	578.8	582.9	595.5	614.6	541.6

Source: The Wall Street Journal

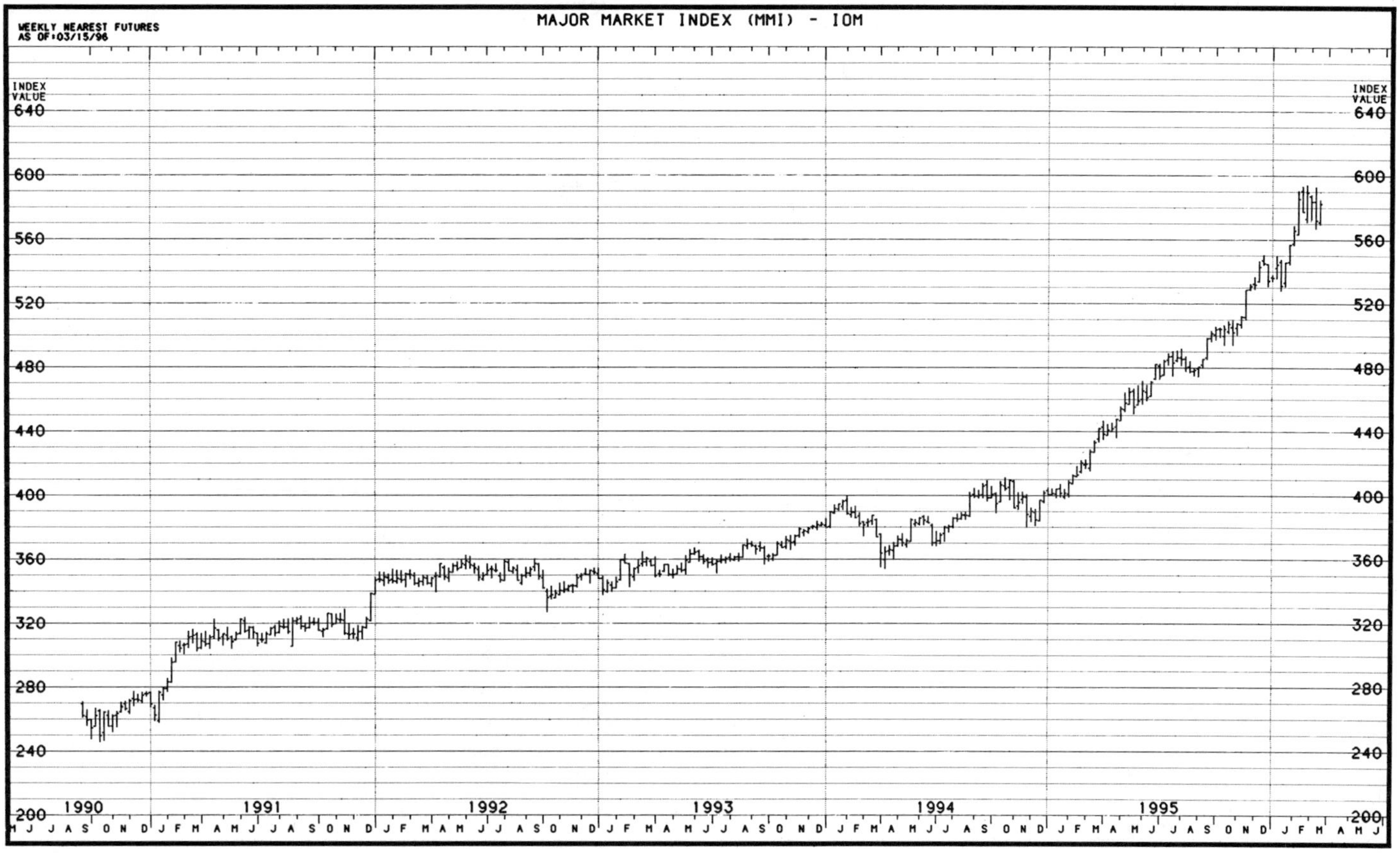
WEEKLY NEAREST FUTURES
AS OF:03/15/96
MAJOR MARKET INDEX (MMI) - IOM
INDEX VALUE
640
600
560
520
480
440
400
360
320
280
240
200
1990
1991
1992
1993
1994
1995
M J J A S O N D J F M A M J J A S O N D J F M A M J J A S O N D J F M A M J J A S O N D J F M A M J J A S O N D J F M A M J J A S O N D J F M A M J

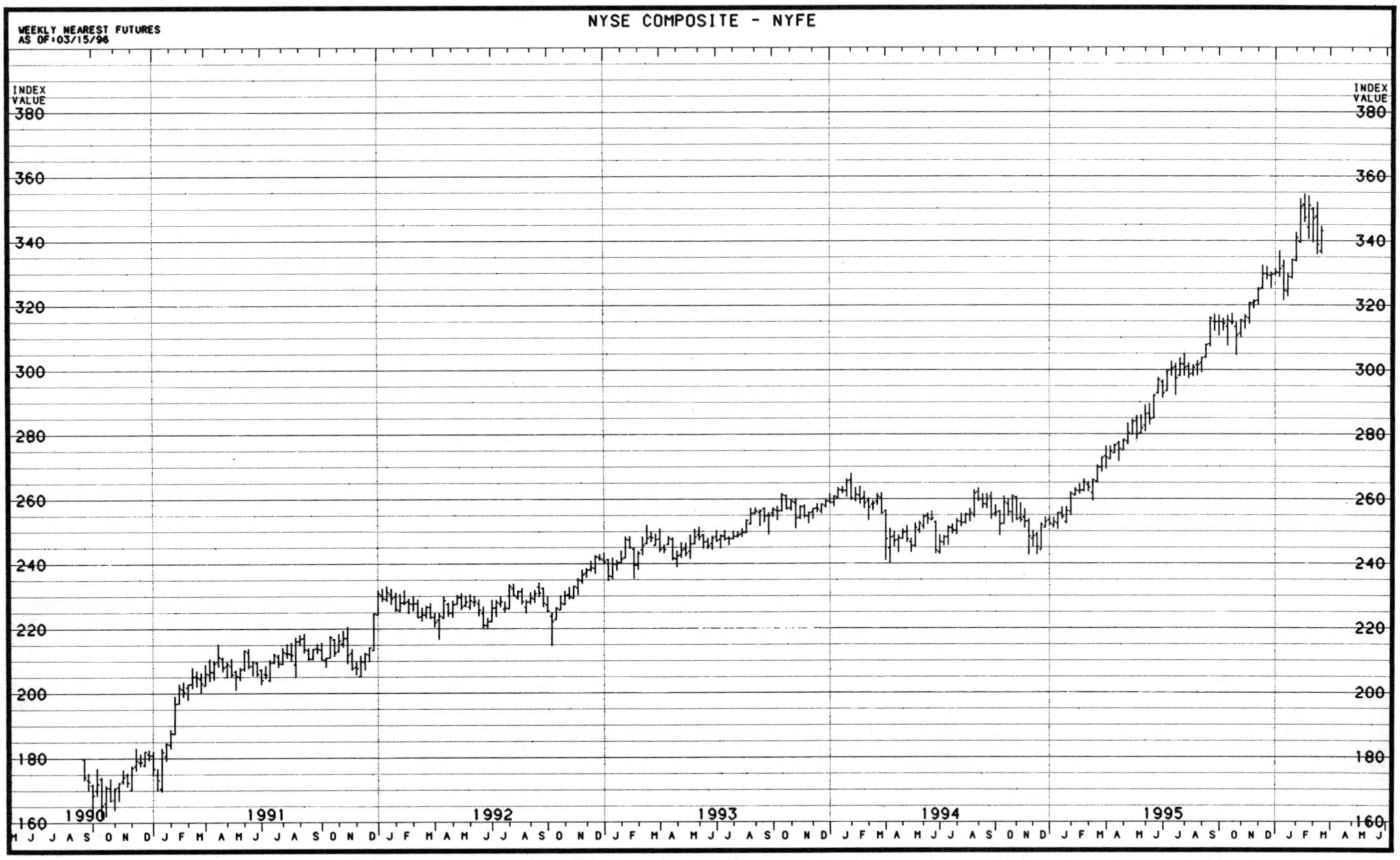
WEEKLY NEAREST FUTURES
AS OF:03/15/96
NYSE COMPOSITE - NYFE
INDEX VALUE
380
360
340
320
300
280
260
240
220
200
180
160
1990
1991
1992
1993
1994
1995
M J J A S O N D J F M A M J J A S O N D J F M A M J J A S O N D J F M A M J J A S O N D J F M A M J J A S O N D J F M A M J J A S O N D J F M A M J

WEEKLY NEAREST FUTURES
AS OF:03/15/96
S&P 500 INDEX - IOM
INDEX VALUE
800
750
700
650
600
550
500
450
400
350
300
250
1990
1991
1992
1993
1994
1995

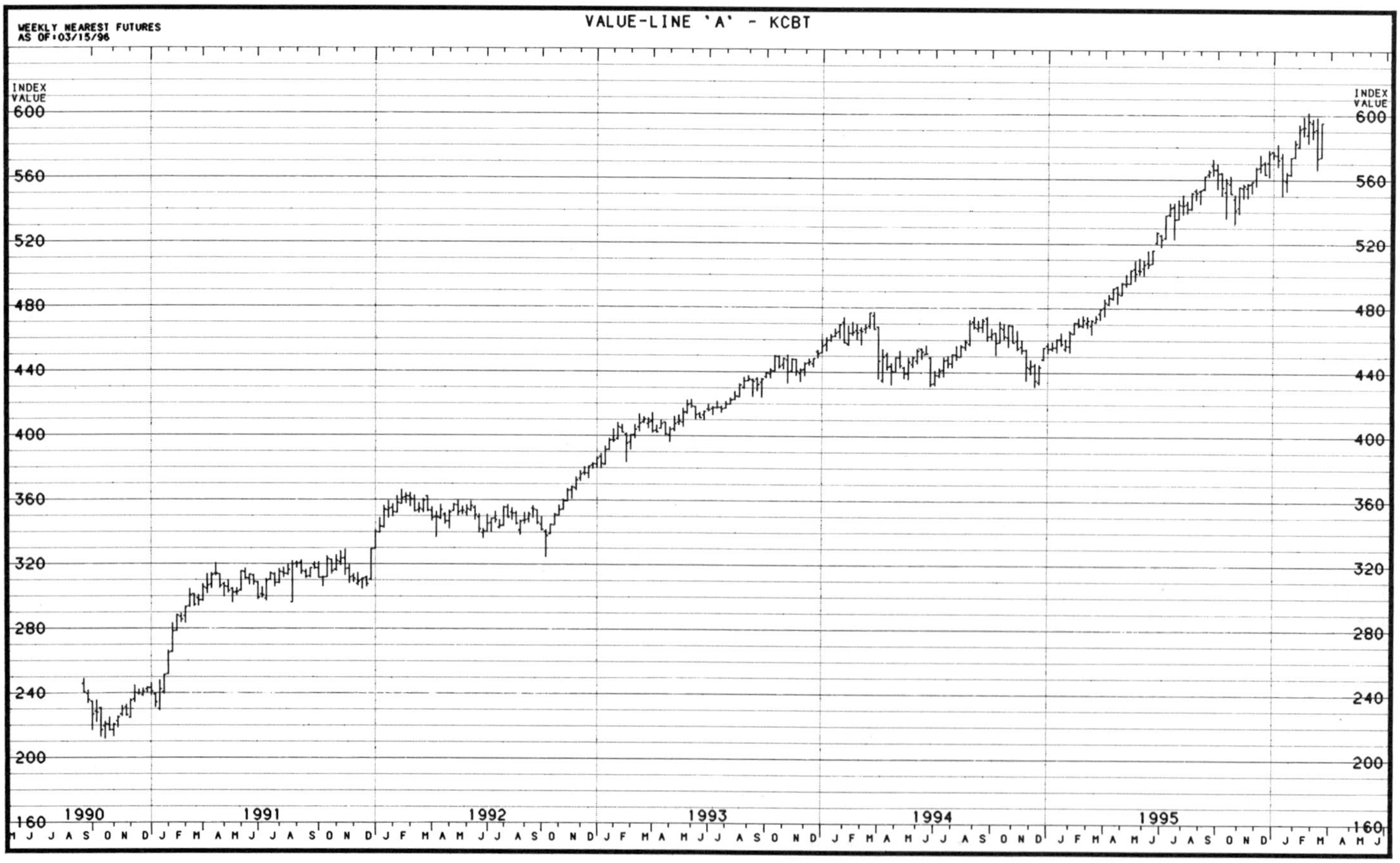
WEEKLY NEAREST FUTURES
AS OF:03/15/96
VALUE-LINE 'A' - KCBT
INDEX VALUE
600
560
520
480
440
400
360
320
280
240
200
160
1990
1991
1992
1993
1994
1995

Composite of Leading Indicators 1987 = 100

Year	Jan.	Feb.	Mar.	Apr.	May	June	July	Aug.	Sept.	Oct.	Nov.	Dec.	Average
1987	99.0	99.3	99.4	99.5	99.7	100.2	100.9	101.0	101.0	100.6	99.8	99.6	100.0
1988	99.4	100.0	100.0	100.0	99.9	100.6	100.0	100.2	100.1	100.1	100.0	100.5	100.1
1989	100.9	100.7	100.1	100.4	99.6	99.4	99.2	99.1	99.2	98.9	99.0	99.4	99.7
1990	99.4	98.9	99.4	99.2	99.4	99.3	99.1	98.4	97.8	97.2	96.5	96.5	98.4
1991	96.0	96.4	96.8	96.8	97.0	97.0	97.9	97.7	97.7	97.6	97.4	97.2	97.1
1992	97.5	97.8	98.1	98.1	98.3	98.2	98.1	97.9	97.8	98.0	98.2	99.2	98.1
1993	98.9	99.1	98.4	98.4	98.1	98.1	97.9	98.3	98.7	99.2	99.6	100.3	98.8
1994[1]	100.5	110.7	101.3	101.4	101.5	101.7	101.7	102.3	102.5	102.3	102.4	102.6	101.8
1995[1]	102.6	102.4	101.9	101.3	101.1	101.3	101.1	101.3	101.2	100.7			

[1] Preliminary. *Source: Bureau of Economic Analysis, U.S. Department of Commerce*

Civilian Unemployment Rate 1982 = 100

Year	Jan.	Feb.	Mar.	Apr.	May	June	July	Aug.	Sept.	Oct.	Nov.	Dec.	Average
1987	6.6	6.6	6.5	6.5	6.3	6.2	6.1	6.0	5.9	6.0	5.9	5.8	6.2
1988	5.7	5.7	5.7	5.5	5.6	5.4	5.5	5.6	5.4	5.3	5.3	5.3	5.5
1989	5.4	5.2	5.0	5.3	5.2	5.3	5.3	5.3	5.3	5.3	5.3	5.3	5.3
1990	5.3	5.3	5.3	5.4	5.3	5.3	5.5	5.6	5.7	5.7	5.9	6.1	5.5
1991	6.2	6.5	6.7	6.6	6.8	6.9	6.8	6.8	6.8	6.9	6.9	7.1	6.7
1992	7.1	7.3	7.3	7.2	7.5	7.7	7.6	7.6	7.5	7.4	7.3	7.3	7.4
1993	7.1	7.0	7.0	7.0	6.9	7.0	6.8	6.7	6.7	6.7	6.5	6.4	6.8
1994[1]	6.7	6.6	6.5	6.4	6.1	6.1	6.1	6.0	5.8	5.7	5.6	5.4	6.1
1995[1]	5.7	5.4	5.5	5.8	5.7	5.6	5.7	5.6	5.6	5.5			

[1] Preliminary. *Source: Bureau of Economic Analysis, U.S. Department of Commerce*

Capacity Utilization Rates (Total Industry) Percent

Year	Jan.	Feb.	Mar.	Apr.	May	June	July	Aug.	Sept.	Oct.	Nov.	Dec.	Average
1987	79.6	80.0	80.3	80.2	80.4	80.8	81.5	81.5	81.3	82.0	82.2	82.6	81.0
1988	82.7	82.6	82.7	82.9	83.3	83.3	84.0	84.0	84.0	84.3	84.4	84.6	83.6
1989	84.8	84.0	83.7	84.2	83.8	83.6	83.7	83.9	83.6	83.5	83.3	82.3	83.7
1990	82.7	83.2	83.4	83.1	83.4	83.7	83.8	83.6	83.5	82.7	81.0	80.4	82.9
1991	80.0	79.1	78.4	78.6	79.1	79.6	80.0	79.8	79.9	79.8	79.3	78.8	79.4
1992	78.0	78.3	78.4	78.7	79.1	79.5	80.0	79.7	79.3	80.2	80.8	81.0	79.8
1993	81.2	81.5	81.6	81.4	81.0	81.1	81.3	81.4	81.4	81.7	82.3	82.9	81.5
1994[1]	82.7	83.2	83.7	83.6	83.8	84.1	84.1	84.5	84.0	84.4	84.6	85.1	83.9
1995[1]	85.1	84.7	84.6	84.0	83.7	83.5	83.3	83.9	83.7	83.2			

[1] Preliminary. *Source: Bureau of Economic Analysis, U.S. Department of Commerce*

Manufacturers New Orders, Durable Goods In Billions of 1987 Dollars

Year	Jan.	Feb.	Mar.	Apr.	May	June	July	Aug.	Sept.	Oct.	Nov.	Dec.	Total
1987	79.68	84.09	84.78	83.76	83.48	85.66	84.02	83.84	85.98	86.81	85.89	86.86	1,014.85
1988	83.26	85.42	85.34	85.73	87.82	87.78	85.15	87.58	87.98	87.93	89.88	92.62	1,046.49
1989	90.82	89.12	86.34	89.73	87.85	86.77	82.76	90.45	87.84	87.60	109.02	110.41	1,098.71
1990	98.75	101.07	107.48	102.92	107.01	103.48	106.04	104.85	102.77	106.37	95.59	99.80	1,236.13
1991	96.39	96.04	91.52	94.81	96.68	95.46	106.62	102.27	94.89	97.83	87.76	92.39	1,145.58
1992[2]	95.63	95.19	96.92	98.62	96.46	99.55	96.42	96.39	96.80	100.85	98.63	107.31	1,182.69
1993	114.64	116.99	112.96	112.61	109.77	114.50	111.08	113.68	115.01	117.87	120.10	122.20	1,381.61
1994[1]	126.86	124.58	125.24	125.61	126.94	128.04	122.78	130.42	130.73	129.43	133.21	135.37	1,539.32
1995[1]	136.29	134.99	134.63	128.34	131.39	131.00	128.29	134.71	138.67	137.34			

[1] Preliminary. [2] Prior to 1993, shown in 1982 dollars. *Source: Bureau of Economic Analysis, U.S. Department of Commerce*

Change in Manufacturing and Trade Inventories In Billions of Dollars

Year	Jan.	Feb.	Mar.	Apr.	May	June	July	Aug.	Sept.	Oct.	Nov.	Dec.	Average
1987	61.2	24.9	45.4	30.0	69.1	41.5	19.6	3.5	27.1	104.4	61.6	76.8	47.1
1988	31.6	64.3	49.5	48.3	47.4	90.3	42.2	84.7	60.1	.1	44.0	107.0	55.8
1989	78.4	69.7	50.6	76.8	82.0	71.2	53.7	18.5	-14.7	34.8	47.2	-14.9	46.1
1990	15.8	6.0	22.1	39.3	67.8	-19.7	61.6	55.1	36.8	21.3	26.9	-51.3	23.5
1991	65.0	-24.7	-96.3	-23.1	-39.3	-37.4	-6.7	-.1	36.3	15.5	13.7	45.8	-4.3
1992	-56.1	1.4	8.5	31.4	-4.0	50.5	34.1	17.6	-11.5	3.9	17.7	14.2	9.0
1993	35.4	26.1	49.8	31.8	18.8	12.0	16.6	17.0	24.8	18.0	42.8	-7.9	23.8
1994[1]	24.8	51.0	-10.5	54.2	117.4	52.5	62.8	79.5	60.9	78.6	63.2	32.6	55.6
1995[1]	145.5	89.0	79.8	113.9	51.4	43.7	56.8	45.2	33.9				

[1] Preliminary. *Source: Bureau of Economic Analysis, U.S. Department of Commerce*

STOCK INDEX FUTURES

Comparison of International Stock Price Indexes 1967 = 100

Year	Jan.	Feb.	Mar.	Apr.	May	June	July	Aug.	Sept.	Oct.	Nov.	Dec.	Average
United States													
1990	369.8	359.5	368.2	367.9	381.0	392.0	391.6	359.8	343.1	334.1	343.0	357.6	364.0
1991	354.1	394.1	405.0	413.0	411.2	411.5	413.6	423.6	421.2	420.8	419.8	422.6	409.2
1992	452.6	448.8	443.1	443.2	451.2	444.1	451.5	454.6	455.2	448.7	460.0	473.9	452.2
1993	473.4	480.5	489.7	482.0	484.3	487.4	486.6	494.0	499.6	504.6	503.5	506.9	491.0
1994[1]	514.5	513.0	504.5	486.5	490.5	494.8	491.0	505.0	508.0	504.5	501.5	495.2	500.8
1995[1]	506.1	524.2	536.4	552.5	569.8	586.7	606.3	608.2	629.6	634.1			
Canada													
1990	418.6	416.6	411.2	377.5	404.7	400.4	402.4	378.1	357.0	348.2	356.0	368.0	386.6
1991	369.8	391.2	395.0	392.0	400.7	391.6	400.0	397.5	382.8	397.3	390.3	396.9	392.1
1992	406.3	404.7	385.6	379.2	382.8	382.8	389.1	384.5	372.6	377.0	370.8	378.6	384.5
1993	373.5	390.0	407.1	428.2	437.4	448.2	448.3	467.5	450.9	480.9	472.3	488.3	441.1
1994[1]	514.7	499.9	489.2	482.2	488.9	454.8	472.2	491.5	492.0	484.9	462.5	474.9	484.0
1995[1]	454.0	466.1	487.4	483.6	502.7	511.5	521.5	510.4	511.9	503.9			
France													
1990	900.4	856.2	872.4	938.4	949.5	932.2	899.7	796.5	714.6	726.8	713.9	719.4	835.0
1991	694.7	740.0	822.6	820.1	840.7	810.1	810.1	832.6	871.7	861.7	856.9	809.7	814.2
1992	891.2	907.8	920.4	951.3	969.4	938.8	895.3	858.0	900.4	845.5	861.7	866.9	900.6
1993	868.7	908.6	945.8	944.5	901.9	907.7	954.5	1,021.3	1,007.1	1,047.2	1,023.8	1,111.5	970.2
1994[1]	1,145.8	1,141.4	1,095.8	1,072.1	1,075.8	987.1	998.2	1,030.6	975.9	943.0	970.1	977.3	1,034.4
1995[1]	925.2	921.2	902.1	954.6	988.9	961.1	969.1	976.4	931.3	893.5			
Germany[2]													
1990	370.8	384.6	396.3	399.5	389.5	385.3	393.7	348.9	308.8	297.8	292.4	299.9	355.6
1991	280.5	300.8	314.8	324.2	327.9	339.3	329.1	326.3	330.2	315.8	313.2	301.3	317.0
1992	315.1	326.7	331.6	334.9	337.7	335.8	316.2	292.2	285.2	266.3	269.8	269.1	306.7
1993	277.9	291.9	296.8	293.4	286.3	293.4	311.6	325.4	322.9	337.9	345.7	363.1	312.2
1994[1]	374.2	372.7	380.2	396.9	399.8	373.1	372.0	389.4	379.8	361.7	362.4	359.2	376.8
1995[1]	361.7	366.0	343.6	338.9	349.6	354.6	364.1	373.8	376.4	360.9			
Italy													
1990	418.6	440.1	439.9	455.3	468.9	485.6	457.4	387.9	354.4	338.4	302.2	312.9	409.1
1991	289.1	318.0	336.5	342.0	331.6	355.9	335.2	325.8	315.2	304.7	306.4	299.4	321.7
1992	321.3	326.2	312.1	311.0	302.2	298.0	267.0	260.1	240.1	260.5	475.2	453.4	288.6
1993	497.5	528.2	534.4	544.2	575.2	560.0	580.0	634.4	633.1	617.2	575.2	622.7	575.2
1994[1]	646.8	703.3	699.9	815.6	823.9	757.1	738.5	721.2	710.2	668.9	668.9	651.7	717.2
1995[1]	691.6	697.8	643.4	644.1	682.7	656.5	667.5	690.2	675.3	623.4			
Japan													
1990	2,498.2	2,427.8	2,175.1	1,959.4	2,142.6	2,155.2	2,119.1	1,833.0	1,644.4	1,592.1	1,572.2	1,579.4	1,974.9
1991	1,542.4	1,696.8	1,785.2	1,803.2	1,776.2	1,712.1	1,639.9	1,593.0	1,612.8	1,694.0	1,631.8	1,533.4	1,668.4
1992	1,474.7	1,426.0	1,333.0	1,176.0	1,242.8	1,176.0	1,132.7	1,093.9	1,242.8	1,177.8	1,151.6	1,197.7	1,235.4
1993	1,157.0	1,171.5	1,233.8	1,411.5	1,468.9	1,462.9	1,468.9	1,510.4	1,506.4	1,490.6	1,381.9	1,308.7	1,381.4
1994[1]	1,376.0	1,445.1	1,466.9	1,457.0	1,488.6	1,526.2	1,498.5	1,494.6	1,441.2	1,433.3	1,383.9	1,383.9	1,449.6
1995[1]	1,344.3	1,277.1	1,190.1	1,182.2	1,180.2	1,109.1	1,176.3	1,257.3	1,306.9	1,296.4			
United Kingdom													
1990	1,123.4	1,086.7	1,060.8	1,031.9	1,048.2	1,118.0	1,109.6	1,030.1	971.1	974.1	969.3	993.4	1,043.0
1991	969.9	1,048.2	1,138.5	1,168.0	1,158.3	1,157.1	1,168.0	1,200.5	1,221.6	1,207.1	1,177.6	1,130.6	1,145.5
1992	1,177.6	1,195.7	1,178.2	1,207.1	1,284.2	1,178.8	1,147.5	1,094.5	1,131.8	1,187.2	1,240.2	1,281.8	1,192.1
1993	1,302.2	1,324.5	1,351.0	1,325.3	1,326.4	1,341.0	1,325.3	1,405.7	1,414.1	1,440.2	1,430.8	1,509.1	1,375.0
1994[1]	1,584.3	1,584.3	1,520.6	1,488.3	1,472.6	1,409.9	1,430.8	1,503.9	1,463.2	1,427.7	1,441.3	1,413.1	1,478.3
1995[1]	1,420.4	1,420.4	1,421.4	1,472.6	1,514.4	1,539.4	1,567.2	1,599.4	1,608.4	1,587.5			

[1] Preliminary. [2] Federal Republic of Germany. Not seasonally adjusted. *Source: Economic and Statistics Administration, U.S. Department of Census*

Corporate Profits After Tax--Quarterly In Billions of Dollars

Year	I	II	III	IV	Average	Year	I	II	III	IV	Average
1988	159.9	166.9	173.2	175.6	168.9	1992	229.7	272.3	274.3	295.9	275.4
1989	173.6	161.1	152.4	166.3	163.4	1993	258.9	284.8	288.9	310.2	289.2
1990	167.1	166.1	179.4	NA	128.2	1994[1]	299.4	321.4	329.5	337.9	322.0
1991	189.7	182.7	189.6	207.4	210.7	1995[1]	350.7	353.6			

[1] Preliminary. *Source: Bureau of Economic Analysis, U.S. Department of Commerce*

Productivity: Index of Output Per Hour, All Persons, Nonfarm Business--Quarterly 1982 = 100

Year	I	II	III	IV	Average	Year	I	II	III	IV	Average
1988	111.0	110.5	111.5	112.0	111.3	1992	110.6	111.1	114.3	115.3	113.7
1989	111.6	111.9	112.6	111.0	111.8	1993	114.8	114.2	115.8	117.0	115.4
1990	110.7	110.7	110.8	NA	83.1	1994[1]	117.9	116.6	117.3	118.6	117.4
1991	107.9	108.4	108.6	109.6	108.7	1995[1]	119.3	120.7	121.3		

[1] Preliminary. *Source: Bureau of Economic Analysis, U.S. Department of Commerce*

Consumer Confidence, The Conference Board 1985 = 100

Year	Jan.	Feb.	Mar.	Apr.	May	June	July	Aug.	Sept.	Oct.	Nov.	Dec.	Average
1987	90.4	90.2	90.8	92.8	91.1	91.5	93.7	94.4	93.6	89.3	83.1	86.8	90.6
1988	90.8	91.6	94.6	91.2	94.8	94.7	93.4	97.4	97.3	94.1	93.0	91.9	93.7
1989	97.9	95.4	94.3	91.5	90.7	90.6	92.0	89.6	95.8	93.9	115.1	113.0	96.7
1990	106.5	106.7	110.6	107.3	107.3	102.4	101.7	84.7	85.6	62.6	61.7	61.3	61.2
1991	55.1	59.4	81.1	79.4	76.4	78.0	77.7	76.1	72.9	60.1	52.7	52.5	68.5
1992	50.2	47.3	56.5	65.1	71.9	72.6	61.2	59.0	57.3	54.6	65.6	78.1	61.6
1993	76.7	68.5	63.2	67.6	61.9	58.6	59.2	59.3	63.8	60.5	71.9	79.8	65.9
1994[1]	82.6	79.9	86.7	92.1	88.9	92.5	91.3	90.4	89.5	89.1	100.4	103.4	90.6
1995[1]	101.4	99.4	100.2	104.6	102.0	94.6	101.4	102.4	97.3	96.3			

[1] Preliminary. *Source: Bureau of Economic Analysis, U.S. Department of Commerce*

Average Open Interest of NYSE Composite Stock Index Futures at New York In Contracts

Year	Jan.	Feb.	Mar.	Apr.	May	June	July	Aug.	Sept.	Oct.	Nov.	Dec.
1987	11,851	12,725	13,420	13,469	12,534	10,808	11,476	16,863	15,994	11,721	9,688	6,837
1988	5,530	5,760	6,013	6,785	8,372	7,400	7,003	7,668	6,689	6,816	7,600	6,419
1989	6,460	7,211	7,860	7,605	8,001	6,771	6,386	6,247	6,449	7,045	6,491	6,084
1990	6,350	6,098	5,443	4,925	5,129	5,160	4,732	6,079	6,003	5,272	4,983	4,554
1991	4,736	5,720	5,264	5,488	6,190	6,010	5,056	5,997	5,869	5,512	6,438	6,195
1992	5,216	5,290	5,469	4,575	4,867	5,858	6,491	7,049	6,647	6,034	6,430	5,890
1993	5,033	5,083	4,113	3,613	4,222	4,340	3,714	4,178	3,997	4,315	4,721	4,539
1994	4,653	4,471	4,823	3,720	3,839	3,969	3,903	3,982	4,142	4,494	4,244	4,617
1995	3,695	4,159	4,113	3,476	3,396	3,254	3,205	3,029	2,966	2,683	3,125	3,403

Source: New York Futures Exchange

Average Open Interest of KC Value Line Stock Index Futures at Kansas City In Contracts

Year	Jan.	Feb.	Mar.	Apr.	May	June	July	Aug.	Sept.	Oct.	Nov.	Dec.
1987	10,600	11,155	10,358	6,952	7,306	6,059	4,734	5,748	4,377	4,029	2,918	2,170
1988	1,538	1,655	2,814	3,059	3,266	2,269	1,570	1,389	1,332	1,229	1,564	1,580
1989	1,394	1,189	1,288	1,262	1,421	1,513	1,615	1,710	1,522	1,250	1,200	1,182
1990	1,245	1,355	1,463	1,514	1,544	1,404	1,311	1,297	1,250	1,210	1,325	1,381
1991	1,534	2,211	2,107	2,326	2,384	2,138	1,860	1,884	1,764	1,509	1,857	2,100
1992	2,127	2,208	1,657	1,169	1,117	1,049	833	867	1,029	962	1,101	1,632
1993	1,999	1,822	1,356	934	1,188	1,118	1,100	1,181	1,039	1,057	1,302	1,461
1994	1,921	1,649	1,289	768	839	823	812	850	898	915	1,011	1,478
1995	1,600	1,365	1,077	802	759	648	580	565	568	489	627	1,025

Source: Kansas City Board of Trade

Average Open Interest of Maxi Major Market Stock Index Futures at Chicago In Contracts

Year	Jan.	Feb.	Mar.	Apr.	May	June	July	Aug.	Sept.	Oct.	Nov.	Dec.
1987	8,078	8,843	7,627	9,860	8,072	5,860	7,793	10,109	10,794	7,726	4,268	3,464
1988	2,442	2,849	3,901	6,309	8,000	4,890	3,072	2,957	3,591	5,878	4,956	7,206
1989	7,060	6,421	5,554	6,335	6,280	4,130	6,213	5,235	4,043	7,169	4,835	5,552
1990	5,274	4,273	5,261	5,847	7,686	8,773	8,398	6,480	7,837	8,106	7,873	9,891
1991	9,705	9,856	7,894	7,739	7,715	7,130	5,519	5,501	5,042	4,296	3,877	5,118
1992	5,326	5,568	4,627	4,776	5,495	5,518	4,505	4,336	4,681	4,409	4,236	5,771
1993	5,880	5,122	3,730	3,137	3,116	2,913	2,033	1,903	1,849	2,040	2,867	3,699
1994	3,467	3,722	4,048	4,280	4,516	5,015	4,517	3,690	2,937	3,842	3,511	1,899
1995	2,009	3,457	2,397	1,263	1,297	1,048	1,015	746	705	334	313	344

Source: Chicago Board of Trade

STOCK INDEX FUTURES

Average Open Interest of S & P 500 Index Futures at Chicago In Contracts

Year	Jan.	Feb.	Mar.	Apr.	May	June	July	Aug.	Sept.	Oct.	Nov.	Dec.
1986	61,697	73,610	90,736	75,590	93,638	95,400	101,017	109,169	121,724	136,823	144,103	128,305
1987	107,367	116,765	119,444	110,154	127,090	131,406	115,722	127,385	128,930	139,741	141,059	130,387
1988	115,006	120,909	114,792	114,269	129,134	116,524	104,644	118,008	120,657	121,970	137,715	131,134
1989	129,453	136,285	137,068	136,664	140,627	128,578	116,935	129,989	129,949	126,039	126,444	117,875
1990	112,196	124,279	124,460	118,350	127,718	118,865	113,050	132,568	159,607	151,990	157,440	160,260
1991	148,112	168,803	158,994	148,106	157,103	154,848	142,665	152,067	151,609	144,279	153,898	145,324
1992	147,434	143,013	141,942	136,991	141,757	149,962	153,035	163,613	168,263	170,065	178,342	179,942
1993	164,614	173,691	178,939	174,277	182,896	190,053	182,189	191,311	208,390	195,109	201,374	196,175
1994	188,225	195,824	210,065	200,818	219,109	299,567	217,028	227,871	237,934	230,594	243,581	251,370
1995	213,502	221,314	222,792	210,052	221,648	226,682	210,012	211,304	208,906	201,397	220,890	223,764

Source: International Monetary Market; Chicago Mercantile Exchange

Stock Index Futures, Worldwide

Most of the world's equity markets moved higher during 1995, no doubt influenced by the performance of the U.S. market which outpaced them all. The bellwether Dow-Jones 30 Industrial stock average jumped 33 percent, the S & P 500 was up 34 percent, and the NASDAQ index, which is heavily weighted with high-tech corporations surged 40 percent; all on record trading volume. The only other equity market indices that showed worthwhile gains for the year of 15 percent to 20 percent were Hong Kong's Hang Seng, the United Kingdom's FT-100, and the Swiss SBC General. There were also some losses: Italy's BCI index and Thailand's Bangkok Set each lost more than 10 percent; Taiwan's weighted index fell about 30 percent; and Japan's Nikkei index fell about 5 percent.

Mexico's IPC index showed the greatest turnaround relative to 1994, a year that the index collapsed following the peso's surprise devaluation. The 1995 gain of 15 percent contrasted the 45 percent slide in 1994. The Hong Kong market also reversed from a loss in 1994 of about 30 percent to the aforementioned gain. On balance, most European markets posted lackluster results due to slack economic growth across the continent despite efforts to prime the economies with easier monetary policies. However, when viewed in a longer term perspective, the world's equity markets in the first half of the 1990s have generally performed well. The major exception among the industrialized nations has been Japan, where the Nikkei 225 index has yet to recover from the 1990-92 break that halved its value.

In the U.S., stocks reacted very positively to a slowing domestic economy and the perception that monetary policy would be eased to create what was called a virtual non-inflationary "soft landing," and it appeared to work. Moreover, as interest rates eased, the equity markets were seen as the best alternative for capital and it flowed into equities in record volume, abetted by hefty pension monies from mutual funds, corporations, and individuals with 401K and IRA funds. While a repeat of the 1995 action is apt to be difficult in 1996, the bullish roots were well entrenched as the new year began.

Germany's DAX index traded in a relatively narrow range during 1995, ending the year with about a 6 percent gain. The action was disappointing considering the Bundesbank's easier policy and generally excellent corporate profits; the chemical industry did especially well. However, the good earnings may have already been discounted as evidenced by the relatively high P/E ratios in 1995. Also, the dividend yield of about 2.03 percent was below the annual average of 2.27 percent between 1987-1994.

In France, the CAC 40 index fell slightly in 1995. Although monetary policy was eased, labor strife nearly paralyzed the country in late 1995 and raised questions as to whether the Government can boost employment, restrain the budget deficit, and keep the French franc steady against the D-mark. It's a tall order that injects caution towards French equities.

In the U.K., equities were buoyed by several factors, including: corporate mergers and acquisitions; the bull move in the U.S. which the U.K. market tends to follow; a strong bond market; and expectations of an easier monetary policy in 1996. A warning flag, however, is the relatively low U.K. average dividend yield of under four percent in 1995 versus a five percent yield during the past twenty years. Despite Europe's mixed results in 1995, forecasts for the equity markets were generally positive for 1996.

Canada's TSE index gained about ten percent during 1995. The price/earnings ratio was deemed favorable as was the monetary climate, but consumer spending was sluggish during the year and a sense of consumer pessimism pervaded over the state of the economy. Also, the Quebec secession issue is not apt to fade, injecting some risk into the Canadian dollar's value and caution into equities.

Japan's Nikkei 225 index and Topix index strengthened in late 1995, but the move failed to rally equities enough to bring the year to a positive gain. Japan's economy stalled in 1995, inventories were accumulating, and exports showed signs of declining. Inflationary pressures, however, remained the lowest among the industrialized nations despite the easier monetary policy executed by Japan's Central Bank in 1995. Low-cost money was expected to buoy the economy in 1996, which if realized may give Japan's equity markets a long awaited shot in the arm.

For the Asian equity markets, Hong Kong had the best return in 1995. Ironically, it's the area which probably has the greatest uncertainty as 1997 nears and the question of China's intentions towards the island remain the proverbial enigma within a puzzle.

Futures Markets

A number of stock index futures and options markets are traded in the world's major financial centers. The Chicago Mercantile Exchange (CME) offers the S & P 500, the S & P Midcap 400, the Major Market Index and the Russell 2000 index. A Nikkei 225 stock average is traded in Chicago, Tokyo, Osaka and Singapore. In New York, the NYSE Composite index is offered. The Kansas City Board of Trade (KC) lists the Value Line index. The Canadian 25 stock index is traded on the Toronto Futures Exchange (TFE). The Sydney Futures Exchange (SFE) trades the Australian All-Ordinaries Share Price index. In Europe, the FT-SE 100 index is traded on the London International Financial Futures Exchange (LIFFE); in Paris, the CAC-40 stock index is traded on the MATIF.

STOCK INDEX FUTURES, WORLDWIDE

WEEKLY CASH
AS OF:03/15/96
CAC 40 INDEX / CASH
CASH
INDEX VALUE
2600
2500
2400
2300
2200
2100
2000
1900
1800
1700
1600
1500
1993
1994
1995
1996
M A M J J A S O N D J F M A M J J A S O N D J F M A M J J A S O N D J F M A M J J

WEEKLY CASH
AS OF:03/15/96
DTB GERMAN STOCK INDEX (DAX)
CASH
INDEX VALUE
2600
2500
2400
2300
2200
2100
2000
1900
1800
1700
1600
1500
1993
1994
1995
1996
M A M J J A S O N D J F M A M J J A S O N D J F M A M J J A S O N D J F M A M J J

WEEKLY CASH
AS OF:03/15/96
TOPIX INDEX / CASH
CASH
2000
1900
1800
1700
1600
1500
1400
1300
1200
1100
1000
900
1993
1994
1995
1996
M A M J J A S O N D J F M A M J J A S O N D J F M A M J J A S O N D J F M A M J J

WEEKLY CASH
AS OF:03/15/96
TORONTO 300 INDEX
CASH
5400
5200
5000
4800
4600
4400
4200
4000
3800
3600
3400
3200
1993
1994
1995
1996
M A M J J A S O N D J F M A M J J A S O N D J F M A M J J A S O N D J F M A M J J

STOCK INDEX FUTURES, WORLDWIDE

Sugar

World sugar production and consumption in 1995/96 (September/August) was estimated at a record high 118.3 and 117.1 million metric tons, respectively (raw value). The surplus of 1.2 million tons for 1995/96, together with a similar increase in 1994/95, will bring the global carryover to about 21.2 million tons on August 31, 1996. The 1993/94 ending stock total of 18.5 million tons was the lowest of the 1990s, and the primary reason world prices pushed to a five year high of nearly 16 cents per pound early in 1995. The price strength proved short lived, however, as the market took more note of sugar's changing statistical setting with prices falling by mid-1995 to under 10 cents, before finding a footing that supported a recovery back to 11 1/2 cents during the fourth quarter.

World production in 1995/96 was up at least 500,000 tons from initial estimates as crops proved larger in Asia and Latin America. Production totaled 115.8 million tons in 1994/95. Through the first half of the 1990s, world production trended irregularly higher; the 1995/96 crop comparing with 113.5 million in 1990/91. Global sugar use increased somewhat faster, paced almost entirely by expanding usage in the developing countries; the 1995/96 consumption topping 1994/95 by at least 2.75 million tons. Sugar's annual consumption growth is weak in the world's industrialized economies, the U.S., EC, and Japan, where sugar markets are mature, and alternative caloric and high-intensity sweeteners are popular.

The world produces more cane sugar than beet sugar; on the consumer level the two are identical with the term sucrose applied to either. Generally, it takes 1.07 tons of raw sugar to produce 1.0 ton of refined sugar.

European production is entirely beet sugar. Western Europe's 1995/96 crop of 17.1 million tons was up 600,000 from 1994/95; collectively it is the world's largest producing region. France and Germany are the largest producers, accounting for nearly half of the region's total production.

In Eastern Europe, sugar production increased 900,000 in 1995/96 due to improved yields, but overall output still lagged most prior years. Poland's 1995/96 crop of 1.7 million tons compares with 2.2 million in 1990/91; the Russian Federation totals were 1.9 million and 2.6 million, respectively. In the Ukraine—Eastern Europe's largest producer—the 1995/96 crop of 4 million tons compares with 5.4 million in 1990/91; the decline reflects less acreage sown to beetsugar and inefficient farm management policies.

In Asia, India is both the world's largest cane producer and single sugar producing nation; production in 1995/96 of 16 million tons compares with the record large 16.4 million in 1994/95. Thailand's 1995/96 crop of 5.5 million tons nearly equaled 1994/95, three-quarters of which is exported. China's 1995/96 crop of 6.4 million compares with 6 million in 1994/95 and crops in excess of 8 million tons a few years earlier.

In Latin America, Brazil produced a record large 12.6 million tons in 1995/96 versus 12.4 million in 1994/95; production earlier in the 1990s averaged close to 9 million tons. Cuba, once the world's leading cane producer, shows little chance for regaining the title; the 1995/96 crop of 4 million tons, while up from 3.3 million in 1994/95, is nearly half the 7.6 million produced in 1990/91. In late 1995, Russia and Cuba signed a three year extension of an oil-for-sugar swap arrangement in which Russia will receive 4 million tons of sugar in 1996, 1997, and 1998, while Cuba receives an equivalent monetary value in oil. The swap appeared to have little effect on world sugar prices.

U.S. sugar production in 1995/96 of 7.65 million short tons was 4.2 percent less than 1994/95. The beet crop was estimated at 4.4 million versus the year earlier record large 4.55 million. Sugar cane production, however, fell 187,000 tons to 3.25 million tons. Beet sugar accounts for almost 60 percent of U.S. sugar production. U.S. sugar consumption in 1995/96 was up only one percent, or 90,000 short tons from 1994/95's 9.42 million tons. Between 1986 and 1994, usage grew about two percent a year. The slippage in use reflects continued encroachment of HFCS (high fructose corn syrup) and weak demand from major industrial users for bakery and candy products. HFCS production and usage was forecast at 8.15 million tons in 1995/96, up 4.5 percent; HFCS consistently sells at a discount of four to eight cents (depending on the grade) to refined sugar, encouraging the substitution of corn sweeteners for sugar where technically feasible. On a per capita basis, U.S. refined sugar use has been stagnant at about 30 kilograms versus an EC average close to 40 kg.

One-fourth of world production enters the export/import market, about 30.7 million metric tons in 1995/96 half of which is refined sugar. Six nations account for the bulk of exports: Cuba, the EC, Ukraine, Australia, Thailand, and Brazil. Global importers are less concentrated; the top six importers are Russia, the EC, U.S., Japan, China, and Korea. U.S. imports of foreign grown sugar are subject to a quota. The fiscal 1995/96 tariff rate import quota (TRQ) for raw sugar was 1,117,195 metric tons versus 1.59 million tons in 1994/95. The U.S. also imports products containing sugar that may not be subject to a quota.

Futures Markets

Sugar futures are traded on the Bolsa de Mercadorias & Futuros (BM&F), the Marche a Terme International de France (MATIF), Kansai Agricultural Commodities Exchange (KANEX), the Tokyo Grain Exchange (TGE), the Manila International Futures Exchange Inc. (MIFE), the London Commodity Exchange (LCE), and the New York Coffee, Sugar, and Cocoa Exchange Inc. (CSCE). Options are traded on the KANEX, the TGE, the LCE, and the CSCE.

SUGAR

World Sugar Production, Supply & Stocks/Consumption Ratio   In Thousands of Metric Tons (Raw Value)

Marketing Year	Beginning Stocks	Production	Imports	Total Supply	Exports	Domestic Consumption	Ending Stocks	Stocks/ Consumption Percentage
1986-7	25,636	103,951	27,458	157,045	27,458	106,470	23,117	21.7
1987-8	23,117	103,786	27,076	153,979	27,076	106,554	20,349	19.1
1988-9	20,349	105,562	28,671	154,582	28,671	106,516	19,395	18.2
1989-90	19,395	108,772	33,179	161,346	33,179	108,709	19,458	17.9
1990-1	19,458	113,484	32,558	165,500	32,558	111,926	21,016	18.8
1991-2	21,016	116,512	30,822	168,350	30,822	113,926	23,602	20.7
1992-3	23,602	112,088	29,605	165,295	29,605	114,627	21,063	18.4
1993-4	21,063	109,838	29,997	160,898	29,997	112,512	18,389	16.4
1994-5[1]	18,389	115,562	30,459	164,410	30,459	114,524	19,426	17.0
1995-6[2]	19,426	118,016	31,336	168,778	31,336	116,612	20,830	17.8

[1] Preliminary. [2] Forecast. *Source: Foreign Agricultural Service, U.S. Department of Agriculture*

World Production of Sugar (Centrifugal Sugar-Raw Value)   In Thousands of Metric Tons

Year	Australia	Brazil	China	Cuba	France	Germany	India	Indonesia	Mexico	Philippines	Poland	South Africa	Thailand	United States	Ukraine[3]	World Total
1984-5	3,548	9,300	4,627	8,100	4,301	3,146	7,071	1,709	3,436	1,767	1,878	2,514	2,533	5,289	8,587	100,267
1985-6	3,404	8,100	5,535	7,200	4,297	3,430	7,983	1,728	3,928	1,561	1,811	2,287	2,586	5,473	8,260	98,798
1986-7	3,457	8,650	5,774	7,220	3,707	3,469	9,474	2,024	3,970	1,350	1,891	2,289	2,639	6,246	8,700	103,951
1987-8	3,528	8,457	4,706	7,400	3,966	2,968	10,000	2,127	3,806	1,400	1,823	2,165	2,704	6,483	9,560	103,786
1988-9	3,680	8,582	5,312	8,100	4,372	3,003	10,150	1,889	3,678	1,600	1,825	2,240	4,055	6,089	8,900	105,562
1989-90	3,797	7,793	5,618	8,000	4,204	4,087	12,575	2,080	3,100	1,750	1,865	2,289	3,502	6,070	5,627	108,772
1990-1	3,637	7,900	6,765	7,620	4,736	4,675	13,707	2,120	3,900	1,718	2,214	2,152	3,954	6,330	5,369	113,484
1991-2	3,192	9,200	8,492	7,030	4,413	4,250	15,249	2,250	3,500	2,010	1,640	2,429	5,062	6,627	4,178	116,512
1992-3	4,367	9,800	8,300	4,280	4,723	4,401	12,456	2,300	4,330	2,060	1,567	1,600	3,750	7,111	3,965	112,088
1993-4	4,412	9,930	6,505	4,000	4,725	4,736	11,660	2,480	3,780	1,809	2,170	1,243	3,975	6,945	4,188	109,838
1994-5[1]	5,082	12,400	6,000	3,300	4,369	3,985	16,345	2,450	4,556	1,650	1,492	1,766	5,448	7,191	3,600	115,562
1995-6[2]	4,950	13,000	6,500	4,000	4,600	4,200	15,150	2,200	4,250	1,800	1,790	1,790	5,700	6,895	4,000	118,016

[1] Preliminary. [2] Forecast. [3] Formerly part of the U.S.S.R.; data not reported separately until 1989. *Source: Foreign Agricultural Service, U.S. Department of Agriculture*

World Stocks of Centrifugal Sugar at Beginning of Marketing Year   In Thousands of Metric Tons (Raw Value)

Year	Australia	Brazil	China	Cuba	France	Germany	India	Iran	Italy	Japan	Mexico	Netherlands	Philippines	Switzerland	United Kingdom	United States	World Total
1986-7	348	981	2,057	550	1,042	692	2,166	296	256	227	1,620	270	283	246	420	1,499	25,636
1987-8	310	845	1,679	360	1,034	707	2,960	296	439	192	1,485	233	209	237	398	1,358	23,117
1988-9	236	771	2,575	460	710	432	2,700	246	479	180	577	223	160	205	338	1,194	20,349
1989-90	256	1,382	2,674	340	642	409	1,315	246	332	242	605	114	275	200	343	1,128	19,395
1990-1	256	1,164	1,350	475	434	330	2,376	220	425	192	750	58	308	197	300	1,111	19,458
1991-2	220	757	1,350	500	689	428	3,563	275	475	85	1,505	125	242	172	228	1,371	21,016
1992-3	194	950	2,002	500	589	340	5,245	300	333	110	910	137	515	149	281	1,340	23,602
1993-4	156	880	905	130	701	358	3,501	400	375	144	1,040	147	679	144	416	1,546	21,063
1994-5[1]	156	455	570	50	765	511	2,731	400	170	140	575	75	412	139	450	1,213	18,389
1995-6[2]	190	732	1,030	50	302	226	5,176	270	105	144	666	39	83	124	374	1,068	19,429

[1] Preliminary. [2] Forecast. *Source: Foreign Agricultural Service, U.S. Department of Agriculture*

Average Refined Beet Sugar[1] (Wholesale)--Midwest Market   In Cents Per Pound

Year	Jan.	Feb.	Mar.	Apr.	May	June	July	Aug.	Sept.	Oct.	Nov.	Dec.	Average
1984	26.85	26.50	26.50	26.50	26.50	26.25	25.75	25.31	25.00	24.60	24.12	24.00	25.66
1985	23.50	23.42	23.00	23.12	23.55	23.12	23.25	23.50	23.44	23.13	22.50	22.62	23.18
1986	23.45	23.31	23.25	23.50	23.30	23.00	23.38	24.20	24.19	23.50	23.00	23.00	23.38
1987	23.30	23.50	23.50	23.50	24.15	24.44	24.50	24.50	24.00	22.85	22.50	22.50	23.60
1988	23.25	22.75	22.75	23.45	24.19	25.25	27.10	27.75	27.50	27.25	26.75	27.80	25.44
1989	28.75	29.00	29.50	29.50	29.50	29.50	29.38	29.25	29.06	28.20	29.50	31.38	29.06
1990	30.50	30.50	30.50	30.50	30.50	30.50	30.50	30.50	30.50	29.13	28.60	27.38	29.97
1991	26.88	26.50	26.50	26.13	26.00	25.75	25.50	25.50	25.00	24.94	24.60	24.50	25.65
1992	25.40	26.50	26.50	26.50	26.40	26.00	25.00	25.00	25.00	24.90	24.13	23.90	25.44
1993	23.25	23.00	23.00	23.50	23.50	23.50	25.50	27.75	27.50	27.50	27.25	26.50	25.15
1994	25.75	25.50	25.50	24.50	24.75	25.25	25.00	25.00	24.70	25.00	25.38	26.50	25.15
1995[2]	25.50	25.50	25.50	25.50	25.13	25.10	24.75	24.75	25.50	25.75	28.13		

[1] These are f.o.b. basis prices in bulk, not delivered prices. [2] Preliminary. *Source: Economic Research Service, U.S. Department of Agriculture*

World Raw Sugar Price[1] In Cents Per Pound

Year	Jan.	Feb.	Mar.	Apr.	May	June	July	Aug.	Sept.	Oct.	Nov.	Dec.	Average
1984	6.95	6.58	6.42	5.96	5.58	5.48	4.51	4.01	4.11	4.66	4.41	3.51	5.18
1985	3.59	3.66	3.78	3.37	2.77	2.74	3.15	4.35	5.14	5.01	5.53	5.37	4.04
1986	4.87	5.55	7.07	8.36	7.64	6.36	5.58	5.50	4.67	5.42	5.93	5.66	6.05
1987	6.47	7.32	7.51	6.64	6.71	6.40	6.03	5.57	5.79	6.60	7.28	8.25	6.71
1988	9.64	8.40	8.48	8.49	8.85	10.52	14.04	11.09	10.18	10.29	10.82	11.28	10.17
1989	6.69	10.49	11.54	12.14	11.93	12.63	14.01	13.96	14.13	14.42	15.02	13.52	12.79
1990	14.38	14.63	15.39	15.24	14.62	12.99	11.92	10.92	11.00	9.77	10.00	9.72	12.55
1991	8.88	8.57	9.22	8.55	7.88	9.37	10.26	9.45	9.39	9.10	8.79	9.03	9.04
1992	8.43	8.06	8.22	9.53	9.62	10.52	10.30	9.78	9.28	8.66	8.54	8.15	9.09
1993	8.27	8.61	10.75	11.30	11.87	10.35	9.60	9.30	9.52	10.27	10.10	10.47	10.03
1994	10.29	10.80	11.71	11.10	11.79	12.04	11.73	12.05	12.62	12.75	13.88	14.76	12.13
1995[2]	14.87	14.43	14.58	13.63	13.49	13.99	13.46	13.75	12.72	11.94	11.96		

[1] Contract No. 11 fob stowed Caribbean port, including Brazil, bulk spot price. [2] Preliminary. *Source: Economic Research Service, U.S. Department of Agriculture*

Raw Sugar N.Y. Spot Price (C.I.F., Duty/Free Paid, Contract #12 & #14) In Cents Per Pound

Year	Jan.	Feb.	Mar.	Apr.	May	June	July	Aug.	Sept.	Oct.	Nov.	Dec.	Average
1984	21.51	21.90	22.00	22.03	22.01	22.06	21.89	21.72	21.70	21.56	21.40	21.10	21.74
1985	20.72	20.38	20.91	20.97	21.09	21.27	21.23	20.59	19.51	18.68	18.89	19.89	20.34
1986	20.67	21.01	20.95	20.85	20.88	20.99	20.97	20.87	20.87	21.08	21.17	21.12	20.95
1987	21.50	21.76	21.76	21.81	22.01	22.06	22.07	21.88	21.88	21.69	21.75	21.76	21.83
1988	21.83	22.11	22.16	22.16	22.13	22.54	23.43	21.90	21.77	21.74	21.70	21.99	22.12
1989	21.88	22.07	22.12	22.30	22.45	22.99	23.56	23.57	23.50	23.14	23.24	22.84	22.81
1990	23.11	22.93	23.58	23.81	23.58	23.33	23.42	23.27	23.23	23.29	23.15	22.47	23.26
1991	21.86	21.42	21.46	21.23	21.29	21.42	21.25	21.83	22.06	21.76	21.75	21.50	21.57
1992	21.38	21.56	21.36	21.38	21.04	20.92	21.10	21.34	21.55	21.61	21.39	21.11	21.31
1993	20.76	21.16	21.56	21.76	21.36	21.42	21.89	21.85	21.97	21.80	21.87	22.00	21.62
1994	22.00	21.95	21.95	22.08	22.18	22.44	22.72	21.84	21.78	21.58	21.57	22.35	22.04
1995[1]	22.65	22.69	22.46	22.76	23.10	23.09	24.47	23.18	23.21	22.67	22.60		

[1] Preliminary. *Source: Economic Research Service, U.S. Department of Agriculture*

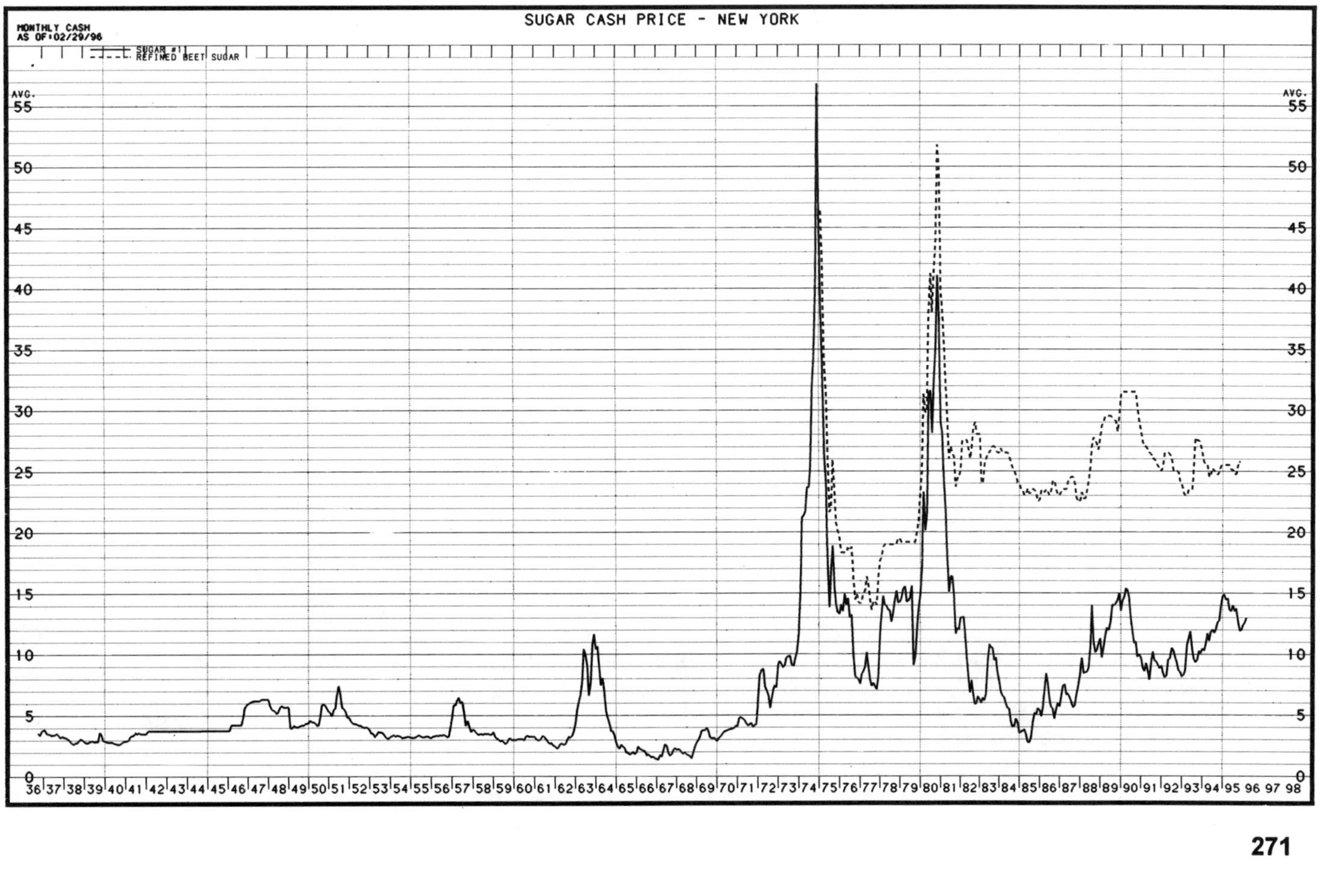

SUGAR

Centrifugal Sugar (Raw Value) Imported into Selected Countries In Thousands of Metric Tons

Year	Algeria	Canada	China	France	Germany	Iran	Israel	Rep. of Korea	Malaysia	Morocco	Nigeria	Russia[4]	Peru	United Kingdom	United States	World Total
1987-8	700	928	3,199	361	194	800	257	1,000	741	295	505	4,515	222	1,323	1,140	27,076
1988-9	650	711	2,462	382	630	650	-----	1,109	797	283	400	5,300	126	1,429	1,753	28,671
1989-90	840	824	1,132	357	482	774	260	1,110	841	276	396	4,550	130	1,350	2,351	33,179
1990-1	990	1,109	1,055	343	209	875	280	1,233	900	350	480	3,580	237	1,143	2,619	32,558
1991-2	980	961	1,230	398	173	825	290	1,258	921	380	560	3,850	267	1,442	2,071	30,822
1992-3	980	1,095	506	487	154	780	300	1,233	900	408	430	3,500	305	1,352	1,827	29,605
1993-4[1]	990	1,219	874	395	142	950	300	1,258	958	417	510	3,150	342	1,363	1,604	29,997
1994-5[2]	1,000	1,110	3,000	372	170	820	300	1,345	1,000	433	400	2,700	280	1,405	1,630	30,459
1995-6[3]	1,000	1,070	2,500	375	150	830	300	1,340	1,050	490	400	3,100	320	1,405	2,082	31,336

[1] Preliminary. [2] Estimate. [3] Forecast. [4] Formerly part of the U.S.S.R.; data not reported separately until 1989-90. *Source: Foreign Agricultural Service, U.S. Department of Agriculture*

Centrifugal Sugar (Raw Value) Exported from Selected Countries In Thousands of Metric Tons

Year	Australia	Brazil	Czech Republic[4]	Cuba	Dominican Republic	France	Germany	Mauritius	Mexico	Netherlands	Philippines	South Africa	Swaziland	Thailand	United Kingdom	World Total
1987-8	2,797	2,131	200	6,500	531	2,535	1,572	687	967	366	129	925	394	1,891	340	27,076
1988-9	2,860	1,371	140	7,420	550	2,804	1,264	690	410	446	210	900	428	3,004	366	28,671
1989-90	2,927	1,500	91	7,065	393	2,748	1,539	589	17	548	271	927	449	2,611	385	33,179
1990-1	2,819	1,300	133	6,800	328	2,751	1,857	621	285	538	286	757	469	2,741	255	32,558
1991-2	2,345	1,607	100	6,100	344	2,682	1,557	590	50	379	178	969	474	3,657	368	30,822
1992-3	3,476	2,425	95	3,800	327	2,822	1,607	621	0	523	253	123	409	2,332	300	29,605
1993-4[1]	3,663	2,861	144	3,300	346	2,894	1,785	590	0	626	261	27	395	2,718	410	29,997
1994-5[2]	4,100	4,178	50	2,600	295	3,050	1,450	508	170	288	170	347	296	3,800	404	30,459
1995-6[3]	4,000	4,800	40	3,250	275	2,550	1,100	540	100	300	180	500	300	4,000	400	31,336

[1] Preliminary. [2] Estimate. [3] Forecast. [4] Formerly part of Czechoslovakia.; data not reported separately until 1989-90. *Source: Foreign Agricultural Service, U.S. Department of Agriculture*

United States Sugar (Cane & Beet) Supply and Utilization In Thousands of Short Tons (Raw Value)

	Supply								Utilization						
	Production			Offshore Receipts									Domestic Disappearance		
Year	Cane	Beet	Total	Foreign	Territories	Total	Beginning Stocks	Total Supply	Total Use	Exports	Net Changes in Invisible Stocks	Refining Loss Adjustment	In Polyhydric Alcohol[4]	Total	Per Capita
1987-8	3,324	3,822	7,146	1,272	19	1,291	1,508	10,027	8,701	383	-27	8	9	7,608	62.5
1988-9	3,316	3,396	6,712	2,025	12	2,037	1,326	10,155	8,911	460	7	53	6	7,689	62.4
1989-90	3,157	3,466	6,623	2,568	0	2,568	1,244	10,503	9,279	561	53	7	10	7,933	63.7
1990-1	3,124	3,854	6,978	2,825	0	2,825	1,224	11,027	9,503	627	-86	61	8	9,503	64.6
1991-2	3,641	3,845	7,486	2,194	0	2,194	1,524	11,024	9,547	554	-13	0	11	9,547	64.4
1992-3	3,446	4,392	7,838	2,039	0	2,039	1,477	11,354	9,650	405	48	0	15	8,916	64.6
1993-4[1]	3,565	4,090	7,655	1,772	0	1,772	1,704	11,131	9,794	454	7	0	15	9,195	64.9
1994-5[2]	3,434	4,493	7,927	1,875	0	1,875	1,338	11,117	9,884	502	45	0	10	9,218	64.6
1995-6[3]	3,390	4,100	7,490	2,288	0	2,288	1,450	11,011	9,820	400	0	0	14	9,420	64.8

[1] Preliminary. [2] Estimate. [3] Forecast. [4] Includes feed use. *Source: Economic Research Service, U.S. Department of Agriculture*

Sugar Cane for Sugar & Seed and Production of Cane Sugar and Molasses in the United States

			Production					Farm Value		Sugar Production			Molasses Made	
										Raw Value				
Year	Acreage Harvested 1,000 Acres	Yield of Cane Per Havested Acre Net Tons	for Sugar (1,000 Tons)	for Seed (1,000 Tons)	Total (1,000 Tons)	Sugar Yield Per Acre Short Tons	Farm Price $ Per Ton	of Cane Used for Sugar (1,000 Dollars)	of Cane Used for Sugar & Seed (1,000 Dollars)	Total 1,000 Tons	Per Ton of Cane Lbs.	Refined Basis 1,000 Tons	Edible (1,000 Gallons)	Total[3] (1,000 Gallons)
1987	824	35.5	28,026	1,192	29,218	4.11	29.1	916,801	851,664	3,434	238	3,115	1,630	191,360
1988	845	35.4	28,479	1,425	29,904	4.14	29.4	836,810	877,817	3,489	239	3,176	1,925	197,608
1989	852	34.5	28,069	1,357	29,426	3.83	29.2	819,057	857,678	3,244	226	2,967	1,990	197,732
1990	794	35.4	26,475	1,661	28,136	4.20	30.8	815,630	863,497	3,226	238	2,945	1,405	186,487
1991	897	33.7	28,960	1,292	30,252	3.95	29.0	840,194	876,479	3,497	237	3,206	1,825	193,117
1992	925	32.8	28,873	1,490	30,363	3.79	28.1	811,350	852,235	3,437	234	3,193	1,460	184,974
1993[1]	948	32.8	29,652	1,449	31,101	3.82	28.5	846,132	886,285	3,533	235	3,351	1,480	189,954
1994[1]	937	33.0	29,405	1,524	30,929	3.96				3,596		3,308		190,541
1995[2]	932	32.9	29,041	1,620	30,661	3.76				3,390				

[1] Preliminary. [2] Estimate. [3] Excludes edible molasses. *Source: Economic Research Service, U.S. Department of Agriculture*

U.S. Sugar Beets, Beet Sugar, Pulp & Molasses Produced from Sugar Beets & Raw Sugar Spot Prices

Year of Harvest	Acreage Planted (1,000 Acres)	Acreage Harvested (1,000 Acres)	Yield Per Harvested Acre Tons	Production 1,000 Tons	Sugar Yield Per Acre Sh. Tons	Price[3] Dollars	Farm Value $1,000	Sugar Production: Equivalent Raw Value[4] (1,000 Short Tons)	Sugar Production: Refined Basis (1,000 Short Tons)	Raw Sugar Prices: World[5] Refined #5 (Cents Per Pound)	Raw Sugar Prices: Cof., Sugar Exch. #11 World (Cents Per Pound)	Raw Sugar Prices: Cof., Sugar Exch. N.Y. Duty Paid (Cents Per Pound)	Wholesale List Price HFCS (42%) Midwest
1986	1,232	1,191	21.1	25,162	2.87	35.90	901,771	3,281	3,066	8.47	6.05	20.95	18.07
1987	1,267	1,252	22.4	28,072	3.19	38.20	1,073,584	3,998	3,736	8.75	6.71	21.83	16.50
1988	1,327	1,301	19.1	24,810	2.70	41.20	1,022,284	3,507	3,278	12.01	10.17	22.12	16.47
1989	1,324	1,295	19.4	25,131	2.66	42.10	1,058,298	3,442	3,217	17.15	12.79	22.81	19.24
1990	1,400	1,377	20.0	27,513	2.79	43.00	1,182,221	3,842	3,591	17.32	12.55	23.26	19.69
1991	1,427	1,412	20.3	28,203	2.68	38.50	1,085,728	3,729	3,485	13.41	9.04	21.57	20.93
1992	1,437	1,412	20.6	29,143	3.10	41.40	1,206,480	4,386	4,099	12.39	9.09	21.31	20.70
1993[1]	1,438	1,409	18.6	26,249	2.87	38.50	1,085,728	4,047	3,792	12.79	10.03	21.62	18.83
1994[1]	1,476	1,443	22.2	31,994	3.11	39.00	1,023,687	4,579	4,090	15.66	12.13	22.04	20.17
1995[2]	1,442	1,425	20.3	28,892	2.88			4,100					

[1] Preliminary. [2] Estimate. [3] Includes support payments, but excludes Government sugar beet payments. [4] Refined sugar multiplies by the factor of 1.07. [5] F.O.B. Europe. *Source: Economic Research Service, U.S. Department of Agriculture*

Sugar Deliveries and Stocks in the United States In Thousands of Short Tons (Raw Value)

Year	Quota Allocation	Actual Imports	Deliveries by Primary Distributors: Cane Sugar Refineries	Beet Sugar Factories	Importers of Direct Consumption Sugar	Mainland Cane Sugar Mills[3]	Total Deliveries	Total Domestic Consumption	Stocks (January 1): Cane Sugar Refineries[4]	Beet Sugar Factories	Commodity Credit Corp.	Refiners' Raw	Mainland Cane Mills	Total
1986	1,849.9	1,845.7	4,594	3,077	28	3	7,702	8,422	197	1,189	220	523	834	2,964
1987	1,003.4	997.1	4,454	3,656	18	4	8,131	8,897	211	1,304	177	516	830	3,038
1988	1,056.7	1,024.8	4,290	3,832	20	5	8,147	8,557	184	1,546	0	401	996	3,128
1989	3,093.1	2,995.8	4,764	3,449	76	6	8,295	8,952	187	1,372	0	487	1,008	3,053
1990	2,314.9	2,242.8	4,998	3,570	39	8	8,615	9,309	155	1,412	0	381	899	2,947
1991	1,526.7	1,477.0	4,786	3,713	30	11	8,540	9,470	168	1,327	0	371	812	2,729
1992	2,500.0	2,275.4	4,808	3,966	52	7	8,936	8,772	194	1,336	0	619	890	3,039
1993[1]	[5]	[5]	4,781	4,087	52	10	9,064	8,922	183	1,640	0	507	895	3,225
1994[1]	1,458.3	230.6	4,928	4,170	78		9,322	9,080	218	1,696	0	438	1,160	3,512
1995[2]	1,564.0	168.6							181	1,594	6	448	916	3,145

[1] Preliminary. [2] Estimate. [3] Sugar for direct consumption only. [4] Refined. [5] Combined with 1992. *Source: Economic Research Service, U.S. Department of Agriculture*

Sugar, Refined--Delivered to End User in the U.S. In Thousands of Short Tons

Year	Bakery & Cereal Products	Beverages	Confectionery[2]	Hotels, Restaurant & Institutions	Ice Cream & Dairy Products	Canned, Bottled & Frozen Foods	All Other Food Uses	Retail Grocers[3]	Wholesale Grocers[4]	Non-food Uses	Non-Industrial Uses	Industrial Uses	Total Deliveries
1986	1,432	266	1,051	84	447	387	443	1,066	1,867	138	3,075	4,164	7,238
1987	1,513	212	1,146	91	449	398	534	996	2,040	149	3,199	4,400	7,599
1988	1,541	237	1,107	89	394	354	529	940	2,200	121	3,316	4,283	7,614
1989	1,532	215	1,187	106	426	342	637	1,026	2,051	126	3,259	4,465	7,730
1990	1,608	228	1,279	108	462	332	642	1,077	2,130	109	3,391	4,660	8,051
1991	1,632	204	1,277	100	439	331	623	1,182	2,079	88	3,469	4,594	8,063
1992	1,719	164	1,246	101	429	315	649	1,230	2,104	69	3,668	4,591	8,259
1993	1,785	158	1,292	108	424	336	725	1,235	2,075	85	3,589	4,805	8,394
1994[1]	1,952	156	1,313	93	453	322	704	1,269	2,039	77	3,598	4,977	8,575

[1] Preliminary. [2] And related products. [3] Chain stores, supermarkets. [4] Jobbers, sugar dealers. *Source: Economic Research Service, U.S. Department of Agriculture*

U.S. Deliveries[1] of All Sugar by Primary Distributors by Quarters In Thousands of Short Tons (Raw Value)

Year	First Quarter	Second Quarter	Third Quarter	Fourth Quarter	Total	Year	First Quarter	Second Quarter	Third Quarter	Fourth Quarter	Total
1984	2,029	2,121	2,238	2,066	8,454	1990	1,837	1,911	2,154	2,149	8,051
1985	1,909	1,972	2,150	2,044	8,035	1991	1,878	1,955	2,173	2,057	8,063
1986	1,819	1,907	2,069	1,991	7,786	1992	1,985	2,178	2,390	2,273	8,826
1987	1,908	2,001	2,146	2,112	8,167	1993	2,039	2,172	2,432	2,277	8,920
1988	1,951	1,983	2,147	2,107	8,188	1994	2,121	2,265	2,532	2,260	9,178
1989	1,923	2,051	2,181	2,185	8,340	1995[2]	2,105	2,311	2,537		6,953

[1] Includes for domestic consumption and for export. [2] Preliminary. *Source: Economic Research Service, U.S. Department of Agriculture*

SUGAR

Average Open Interest of World Sugar (#11) Futures at New York In Contracts

Year	Jan.	Feb.	Mar.	Apr.	May	June	July	Aug.	Sept.	Oct.	Nov.	Dec.
1984	80,937	79,379	84,043	90,879	88,648	91,792	85,155	95,839	89,421	84,488	85,805	83,433
1985	88,595	88,208	81,731	84,538	86,437	90,837	84,727	91,241	92,998	79,755	92,348	98,473
1986	92,744	92,403	106,334	113,717	100,925	93,288	85,582	87,092	90,033	82,403	86,598	90,652
1987	98,697	103,115	95,910	93,886	96,153	98,463	97,889	98,401	100,395	99,286	103,205	126,916
1988	147,508	147,629	132,539	133,524	137,472	167,829	159,071	137,351	135,121	115,138	119,873	144,931
1989	123,554	126,504	146,798	157,254	146,878	162,097	186,211	179,077	168,840	152,276	171,354	164,757
1990	164,235	160,509	163,155	168,962	170,351	161,320	133,208	121,665	112,065	109,986	110,047	108,939
1991	124,637	129,361	114,432	115,704	110,142	105,607	106,406	107,852	102,546	91,649	90,976	93,827
1992	96,255	105,166	93,774	109,137	95,101	106,310	96,038	87,089	77,740	69,023	74,292	93,039
1993	91,426	105,147	123,023	115,400	112,085	101,843	94,296	94,932	91,312	92,832	96,246	99,592
1994	108,936	123,148	137,582	115,060	117,030	126,843	106,749	118,057	141,361	140,011	171,843	191,801
1995	186,893	167,451	149,027	152,600	127,978	121,877	114,027	119,787	114,069	119,561	140,008	157,779

Source: Coffee, Sugar & Cocoa Exchange, Inc. of New York

Volume of Trading of World Sugar (#11) Futures at New York In Contracts

Year	Jan.	Feb.	Mar.	Apr.	May	June	July	Aug.	Sept.	Oct.	Nov.	Dec.	Total
1984	192,451	205,499	252,489	227,150	175,268	213,491	163,955	228,279	263,419	234,008	154,735	124,579	2,449,549
1985	273,316	265,967	215,540	210,046	193,527	237,904	263,842	338,816	323,387	224,856	216,340	249,398	3,012,929
1986	308,044	268,053	382,053	519,027	343,746	289,900	281,124	235,555	328,830	258,744	173,612	195,126	3,583,814
1987	387,630	381,393	323,047	381,972	278,857	313,001	248,133	235,263	367,074	331,052	268,226	337,851	3,853,499
1988	603,565	605,773	348,510	391,971	474,693	705,498	807,381	422,101	450,116	276,010	332,463	381,040	5,819,121
1989	499,199	520,018	575,486	600,852	557,386	660,521	624,969	517,295	526,834	328,469	456,485	375,927	6,243,361
1990	519,886	523,591	588,021	505,492	598,320	532,937	384,116	441,608	448,195	372,925	303,065	206,645	5,424,801
1991	313,915	510,163	388,672	477,954	286,120	534,639	309,836	352,351	366,007	240,812	253,201	234,876	4,268,546
1992	376,704	395,793	255,501	583,535	246,360	454,854	264,528	275,677	334,962	163,263	168,470	147,844	3,667,481
1993	330,474	481,506	507,370	518,292	415,283	390,261	255,581	307,181	368,194	222,082	272,579	217,142	4,285,945
1994	289,593	486,222	360,787	472,388	407,343	443,002	252,012	349,079	471,899	316,330	484,943	387,620	4,719,218
1995	591,861	489,274	472,519	478,757	352,000	485,131	298,756	402,358	360,086	246,584	278,906	254,850	4,711,082

Source: Coffee, Sugar & Cocoa Exchange, Inc. of New York

Sulfur

Elemental sulfur is used in the synthesis of sulfur compounds. It finds use in construction where it is added to concrete to aide in corrosion resistance. It is also added to asphalt for highway construction.

U.S. production of frasch sulfur in the first quarter of 1995 was 759,000 tonnes. Data for the April-July period was withheld to avoid disclosing company proprietary data. The data is included under natural gas production of sulfur. For the first seven months of 1994, frasch sulfur production was 1.67 million tonnes. Petroleum sulfur production for the January-July 1995 period was 2.88 million tonnes, compared to 2.89 million tonnes in the same period of 1994. Natural gas production of sulfur in the January-July 1995 period was 2.32 million tonnes. The data for April-July included production of frasch sulfur. In January-July 1994, natural gas sulfur production was 1.32 million tonnes. For the first seven months of 1995, all sulfur production was 5.96 million tonnes compared to 5.87 million tonnes in the same period of 1994.

U.S. consumption of sulfur by domestic sources for the January-June 1995 period was 4.69 million tonnes, down one percent from the same period of 1994. U.S. imports of sulfur for consumption in the first half of 1995 were 1.05 million tonnes, up from 644,000 tonnes in the same period of 1994. For the first half of 1995, U.S. imports of sulfur from Canada were 813,000 tonnes, up sharply from 403,000 tonnes in the first half of 1994. Imports of sulfur from Mexico in the first half of 1995 were 240,000 tonnes compared to 241,000 tonnes in the first half of 1994.

U.S. imports of sulfuric acid in the January-June 1995 period were 992,000 tonnes with sulfur content of 324,000 tonnes. In the same period of 1994, imports were 1.1 million tonnes with sulfur content of 353,000 tonnes. Imports from Canada were 851,000 tonnes while imports from Europe were 61,000 tonnes. For January-June 1995, U.S. exports of sulfur were 567,000 tonnes compared to 368,000 a year before, while exports of sulfuric acid were 96,000 tonnes versus 72,000 tonnes in the first half of 1994.

World Production of Sulfur (All Forms) In Thousands of Metric Tons

Year	Canada	China	Finland	France	Germany	Iraq	Italy	Japan	Mexico	Poland	Romania	Russia[3]	Saudi Arabia	Spain	Ukraine[3]	United States	World Total
1987	6,687	4,500	599	1,263	2,139	957	564	2,349	2,461	5,187	690	9,750	1,432	1,195	------	10,539	56,968
1988	6,908	4,750	600	1,181	2,153	1,185	618	2,432	2,378	5,200	750	10,765	1,378	1,177	------	10,746	59,160
1989	6,600	5,170	527	1,036	1,701	1,330	640	2,559	2,372	5,137	725	9,900	1,423	1,211	------	11,592	58,924
1990	6,790	5,370	636	1,049	1,550	1,180	587	2,630	2,413	4,902	660	9,025	1,435	1,147	------	11,560	57,800
1991	7,130	5,910	636	1,199	1,282	300	480	2,630	2,094	4,173	600	8,100	2,000	905	------	10,820	54,500
1992	7,487	5,470	607	1,150	1,164	600	470	2,750	2,302	3,152	585	2,150	1,630	860	1,200	10,663	48,500
1993[1]	8,450	6,030	607	1,260	1,170	800	475	2,920	1,670	2,130	580	2,000	1,600	687	1,000	10,959	48,900
1994[2]	9,140	6,030	-----	1,100	1,240	800	500	2,900	2,920	2,380	-----	1,830	1,600	702	1,000	11,500	51,000

[1] Preliminary. [2] Estimate. [3] Formerly part of the U.S.S.R.; data not reported separately until 1992. *Source: U.S. Bureau of Mines*

Salient Statistics of Sulfur in the United States In Thousands of Metric Tons (Sulfur Content)

	Production of											Sales Value of Shipments F.O.B. Mine/Plant		
	Elemental Sulfur													
	Native	Recovered												
Year	Sulfur[3] - Frasch	Petroleum & Coke	Natural Gas	Total	By-product Sulfuric Acid[4]	Other Sulf. Acid Compounds	Production (All Forms)	Imports Sulfuric Acid[4]	Exports Sulfuric Acid[4]	Producer Stocks, Dec. 31[5]	Apparent Consumption (All Forms)	Frasch ($ Per Tonne)	Recovered ($ Per Tonne)	Average ($ Per Tonne)
1987	3,202	3,622	2,539	6,161	1,003	173	10,539	1,599	98	2,316	11,323	107.15	79.63	89.78
1988	3,174	3,941	2,503	6,444	1,125	3	10,746	1,996	147	1,112	12,712	99.24	77.03	85.95
1989	3,888	3,971	2,539	6,510	1,190	4	11,592	2,260	146	1,301	12,685	100.18	78.70	86.62
1990	3,726	4,199	2,337	6,536	1,294	4	11,560	2,571	162	1,423	13,056	91.17	73.89	80.14
1991	2,869	4,243	2,402	6,645	1,302	4	10,820	3,020	149	1,194	12,932	87.05	64.17	71.45
1992	2,320	4,524	2,524	7,048	1,292	3	10,663	2,725	139	809	12,747	58.15	44.47	48.14
1993[1]	1,904	4,820	2,905	7,720	1,430	3	11,100	2,440	145	1,382	11,800	51.60	25.06	31.86
1994[2]	2,960	4,924	2,242	7,160	1,380		11,500	2,130	140	1,160	12,400	W	W	28.60

[1] Preliminary. [2] Estimate. [3] Or sulfur ore. [4] Basis 100% H_2SO_4, sulfur equivalent. [5] Frasch & recovered. W = Withheld. *Source: U.S. Bureau of Mines*

Sulfur Consumption & Foreign Trade of the United States In Thousands of Metric Tons (Sulfur Content)

	Consumption			Sulfuric Acid Sold or Used, by End Use[2]						Foreign Trade					
										Exports			Imports		
Year	Native Sulfur (Frasch)	Recovered Sulfur	Total Elemental Form	Total Sulfuric Acid	Pulpmills & Paper Products	Inorganic Chemicals[3]	Synthetic Rubber & Plastic	Phosphatic Fertilizers	Petroleum Refining[4]	Frasch	Recovered	Value Thous. $	Frasch	Recovered	Value Thous. $
1987	3,938	6,209	10,147	11,092	262	412	253	7,556	793	465	777	139,431	793	806	152,096
1988	4,956	6,628	11,584	12,334	280	435	339	8,404	786	464	759	131,863	1,079	917	185,864
1989	4,536	6,955	11,491	12,563	320	423	383	8,642	683	330	694	107,126	1,086	1,174	209,465
1990	4,457	7,301	11,758	12,600	290	653	273	8,664	400	348	624	109,327	1,129	1,442	206,450
1991	3,931	7,694	11,625	12,842	279	901	272	8,311	383	448	748	119,713	1,259	1,760	241,749
1992	3,083	8,368	11,451	12,340	296	617	278	8,300	385	362	604	69,662	845	1,877	129,894
1993	1,331	9,046	10,377	11,886	304	549	259	7,906	388	246	410	39,726	100	1,935	49,800
1994[1]	W	11,100	NA	12,000	295	448	256	8,700	236	----	899	48,400	----	1,650	62,000

[1] Preliminary. [2] Sulfur equivalent. [3] Including inorganic pigments, paints & allied products, and other inorganic chemicals & products. [4] Including other pertroleum and coal products. NA = Not available. W = Withheld. *Source: U.S. Bureau of Mines*

Sunflowerseed and Oil

Sunflowerseed is the world's fourth ranking oilseed crop, but production is only a fifth of soybean's total. The U.S. produces less than ten percent of world production, but plays a larger role in the world export market. World production in 1995/96 of 23.8 million metric tons was a record high as large increases in the former Soviet Union (FSU) and Eastern Europe more than offset declines in the European Union, notably Spain, Germany, and France. Policy changes in the FSU and Eastern Europe, that allow producers to sell their product to Western Europe, has encouraged FSU farmers to increase sunflowerseed acreage and cultivation methods which they did for the 1995/96 crop. World production in 1994/95 totaled 23.7 million tons versus a 1990s average of 22 million. However, unlike soybeans, for which most of the crop is crushed for meal, sunflowerseed has nearly equal amounts of meal and oil produced, although on balance more meal is realized than oil.

The acreage planted to sunflowerseed production in the U.S. since the late 1970s shows an irregular pattern, but currently appears to be on the upswing. A record 5.6 million acres were planted in 1979, falling to an average of only 2 million between 1986-1990, and about 3.6 million for the 1994 and 1995 crops. The Dakotas are the largest producing states. In the same period production ranged from a record high 73 million cwt. in 1979, down to a yield ravaged 17.6 million cwt. in 1989, and 45.7 million cwt. in 1995.

U.S. sunflower meal production in 1995/96 of 635,000 metric tons compares with 653,000 in 1994/95. Carryin supplies are generally small, 5000 tons for 1995/96 and a like amount forecast as of August 31,1996. Usage in 1995/96 of 636,000 tons compares with 658,000 in 1994/95, of which nearly 10 percent will be exported. Sunflower oil production in 1995/96 of 513,000 tons compares with 528,000 the previous year. However, unlike meal, the bulk of U.S. sunflower oil production is exported; 365,000 tons in 1995/96 versus a record 405,000 in 1994/95. Carryover oil as of August 31, 1996, is forecast at 36,000 tons, up 6000 from a year earlier.

U.S. sunfloweroil exports are dependent on a number of variables. Generally, sunflower oil trades at a premium to soybean oil, but the pattern reversed in 1994/95 which helped boost exports. Also, some countries, like Mexico, have a preference for sunflower oil, although in 1994/95 the peso's devaluation dampened oil imports from the U.S. The U.S. also exports sunflower seed, much of it going to the European Union. Seed exports of 245,000 tons in 1995/96 compare with 260,000 in 1994/95.

The 1995/96 sunflower oil price was forecast at $568 to $612 per metric tons versus $619 in 1994/95, basis average crude Minneapolis. The sunflower meal price was forecast to range from $111 to $131 per metric ton versus $72 in 1994/95, basis 28 percent protein.

The average price received by farmers for sunflowerseed was forecast to range between $253-247 per ton versus $237 in 1994/95.

World Production of Sunflowerseed In Thousands of Metric Tons

Crop Year	Argentina	Australia	Bulgaria	Myanmar (Burma)	China	France	Hungary	India	Romania	South Africa	Spain	Turkey	United States	Former U.S.S.R.	Yugoslavia	World Total
1991-2	3,880	123	434	124	1,422	2,570	813	1,194	612	589	1,026	650	1,639	5,643	463	22,733
1992-3	3,100	70	595	87	1,473	2,110	765	1,185	774	250	1,343	950	1,181	5,734	440	21,642
1993-4	4,010	127	442	96	1,340	1,643	702	1,400	696	362	1,309	815	1,167	5,230	460	21,390
1994-5[1]	5,500	128	596	102	1,430	2,091	664	1,410	764	438	984	740	2,194	4,470	380	23,977
1995-6[2]	5,600	165	690		1,490	2,000	700	1,500	960	437	500	800	2,075	5,750	435	24,890

[1] Preliminary. [2] Forecast. *Source: The Oil World*

Sunflowerseed Statistics in the United States In Thousands of Metric Tons

Crop Year Beginning September	Harvested Acres 1,000	Harvested Yield Per Cwt.	Farm Price $ Per Metric Ton	Value of Production Mil. $	Supply: Stocks, Sept. 1	Supply: Production	Supply: Imports	Supply: Total	Disappearance: Crush	Disappearance: Exports	Disappearance: Non-Oil Use & Seed	Disappearance: Total
1991-2	2,673	13.52	192	316.8	85	1,639	75	1,799	952	163	422	1,537
1992-3	2,043	12.55	215	254.3	262	1,163	47	1,472	923	118	363	1,404
1993-4	2,486	10.35	284	332.0	69	1,167	25	1,261	661	99	429	1,189
1994-5[1]	3,430	14.10	237	511.0	71	2,194	42	2,306	1,313	287	604	2,203
1995-6[2]	3,484	13.13	230-244		103	1,817	34	1,954	1,195	161	523	1,879

[1] Preliminary. [2] Forecast. *Source: Economic Research Service, U.S. Department of Agriculture*

Sunflowerseed Product Statistics in the United States In Thousands of Metric Tons

Crop Year Beginning October	Sunflower Oil: Supply: Stocks, Oct. 1	Supply: Production	Supply: Total[3]	Disappearance: Exports	Disappearance: Domestic	Disappearance: Total	Price $ Per Metric Ton[4]	Sunflower Meal: Supply: Stocks, Oct. 1	Supply: Production	Supply: Total[3]	Disappearance: Exports	Disappearance: Domestic	Disappearance: Total	Price $ Per Metric Ton 28% Protein
1991-2	21	413	438	214	179	393	476	5	498	510	53	451	503	85
1992-3	45	331	376	266	85	351	558	6	440	451	48	401	449	98
1993-4	25	263	292	204	59	262	683	2	327	331	37	291	328	104
1994-5[1]	29	528	558	444	78	521	619	5	653	660	89	566	655	72
1995-6[2]	37	478	516	375	102	477	532-592	5	590	596	64	526	591	123-148

[1] Preliminary. [2] Forecast. [3] Includes imports. [4] Crude at Minneapolis. *Source: Economic Research Service, U.S. Department of Agriculture*

Tall Oil

Tall oil is the major by-product of the kraft or sulfate processing of pinewood. After pulping, the resulting liquor concentrate is skimmed. These skimmings are then acidified to produce crude tall oil.

Crude tall oil contains 40-50 percent resin acids; 40-55 percent fatty acids; and 5-10 percent sterols, alcohols, and other neutral components. When distilled, these resins and fatty acids are consumed in alkyd and synthetic resins, lubricants, adhesives, soaps and detergents, linoleum, flotation agents, and water proofing agents.

The U.S. Department of Commerce, Bureau of Census, reported that U.S. tall oil production in the October-December 1994 quarter was 320.3 million pounds. For the same quarter of 1993, production was 352.8 million pounds. For the crop year of 1993-94 (October-September), U.S. tall oil production was 1.27 billion pounds. Tall oil consumption for calendar year 1994 was 1.044 billion pounds, 17 percent more than in 1993. The inedible products tall oil is used in are resin and plastics, soap, paint, varnish, lubricants, and fatty acids. In December 1994, inedible product use of tall oil was 88.5 million pounds. Fatty acids production used 75.9 million pounds, while lubricants used 413,000 pounds, and plastics and resins 499,000 pounds.

Stocks of tall oil have been declining. On January 1, 1995, stocks of crude tall oil were 103.5 million pounds. On January 1, 1994, stocks were 103.7 million pounds. On January 1, 1992, they were 188.9 million. Stocks of refined tall oil at the beginning of 1995 were 13.5 million pounds. At the start of 1994 they were 10.7 million pounds, while at the beginning of 1992 they were 35 million pounds.

U.S. Tall Oil Consumption in Inedible Products In Millions of Pounds

Year	Jan.	Feb.	Mar.	Apr.	May	June	July	Aug.	Sept.	Oct.	Nov.	Dec.	Total
1988	109.2	111.0	108.0	112.3	112.3	104.0	105.9	110.6	111.4	103.1	100.0	91.5	1,270
1989	111.5	107.7	107.3	102.9	102.9	105.0	101.6	111.9	88.8	88.8	84.3	82.8	1,196
1990	100.4	105.9	91.2	86.5	86.5	84.6	78.5	82.4	69.1	69.7	78.4	78.2	1,017
1991	-------	249.1	-------	-------	237.3	-------	-------	223.1	-------	-------	230.5	-------	940
1992	77.8	7.5	73.2	67.6	77.8	74.8	71.5	78.4	77.1	78.9	63.8	69.2	884
1993	68.6	64.8	73.1	68.1	76.3	68.8	79.0	78.1	78.0	75.4	78.4	83.2	892
1994	117.4	98.8	124.0	118.4	115.0	118.8	106.8	114.9	119.8	113.7	101.9	113.0	1,363
1995[1]	99.8	93.6	96.9	95.8	87.3	96.5	93.1	102.3	89.4	91.6	100.5	89.0	1,136

[1] Preliminary. *Source: Bureau of Census, U.S. Department of Commerce*

Tall Oil Production in the United States In Millions of Pounds

Crop Year		Oct.	Nov.	Dec.	Jan.	Feb.	Mar.	Apr.	May	June	July	Aug.	Sept.	Total
1989-90	Crude	123.2	121.2	107.0	92.1	120.0	137.1	134.6	126.7	122.1	118.0	120.6	102.4	1,437.0
	Refined	9.3	8.1	6.6	6.0	5.2	4.8	5.5	4.7	4.8	5.3	3.3	5.7	69.3
1990-1	Crude	120.8	119.1	126.5	-------	389.5	-------	-------	362.4	-------	-------	375.0	-------	1,469.6
	Refined	5.6	6.2	4.2	-------	15.7	-------	-------	15.3	-------	-------	17.6	-------	64.6
1991-2	Crude	-------	342.7	-------	131.4	121.5	131.2	133.2	121.9	129.8	130.6	129.9	119.7	1,372.2
	Refined	-------	15.7	-------	5.4	5.6	6.2	W	W	W	W	W	W	W
1992-3	Crude	120.2	114.7	122.7	119.4	128.4	142.1	131.8	120.0	126.6	117.0	104.3	117.3	1,347.2
1993-4	Crude	107.5	120.7	124.6	127.0	115.4	148.1	131.0	119.1	109.1	108.7	110.8	117.4	1,322.0
1994-5[1]	Crude	111.1	114.5	115.1	108.3	108.1	123.0	111.1	116.5	118.2	116.4	119.2	102.9	1,261.6
1995-6[1]	Crude	109.8	105.2	102.6										

[1] Preliminary. W = Withheld proprietary data. *Source: Bureau of Census, U.S. Department of Commerce*

Tall Oil Stocks in the United States In Millions of Pounds

Crop Year		Oct. 1	Nov. 1	Dec. 1	Jan. 1	Feb. 1	Mar. 1	Apr. 1	May 1	June 1	July 1	Aug. 1	Sept. 1
1989-90	Crude	112.7	130.4	145.2	133.9	114.0	112.6	106.6	114.1	106.9	103.5	108.3	104.8
	Refined	23.4	25.8	28.5	23.3	22.2	21.4	20.3	16.6	17.2	17.2	18.0	15.7
1990-1	Crude	101.5	83.1	76.6	-------	144.5	-------	-------	119.8	-------	-------	140.4	-------
	Refined	15.3	34.0	35.8	-------	29.7	-------	-------	30.2	-------	-------	33.9	-------
1991-2	Crude	-------	139.1	-------	188.9	153.9	163.1	163.2	156.9	158.4	161.0	190.7	186.1
	Refined	-------	36.0	-------	35.0	35.0	35.7	36.2	13.5	16.1	15.2	15.9	28.4
1992-3	Crude	173.3	167.5	143.7	137.8	162.5	170.8	184.7	187.3	165.3	179.2	173.1	149.9
	Refined	17.4	18.1	13.8	14.1	14.0	12.6	13.7	9.4	7.7	7.3	7.5	7.2
1993-4	Crude	132.8	124.0	113.0	103.7	109.5	109.7	118.2	124.4	112.6	105.3	101.1	97.5
	Refined	7.0	7.5	8.5	10.7	13.7	13.5	13.5	12.0	10.2	9.7	11.6	10.9
1994-5[1]	Crude	86.3	82.7	94.1	104.1	107.6	117.2	123.4	132.1	118.1	132.3	134.7	135.0
	Refined	12.0	14.4	16.3	15.9	15.4	14.1	11.7	10.8	10.2	10.0	9.9	8.9
1995-6[1]	Crude	117.5	112.9	100.3									
	Refined	11.6	7.9	6.0									

[1] Preliminary. *Source: Bureau of Census, U.S. Department of Commerce*

Tallow and Greases

U.S. edible tallow stocks on January 1, 1994, were 33 million pounds (rendered basis). The stocks were unchanged from the prior year. Production of edible tallow was 1.51 billion pounds, up six percent from 1993, making total supplies 1.56 billion pounds. Domestic use of tallow was estimated by USDA at 1.23 billion pounds, up nine percent from the year before. Exports were put at 295 million pounds, down from 310 million in 1993. Total use was 1.52 billion pounds. Per capita domestic disappearance of edible tallow in 1994 was 4.7 pounds, up from 4.4 pounds in 1993. The average wholesale price of loose edible tallow, Chicago, in 1994 was 18.42 cents per pound, up from 16.20 cents per pound in 1993. The USDA estimates that U.S. usage of tallow in food products in 1994 was 731 million pounds, with per capita usage of 2.8 pounds. In 1993, this use of tallow was 565 million pounds.

According to the USDA, world tallow and grease production is expected to remain relatively stable in 1995 at 7.8 million tonnes, about one half percent more than 1994. Most areas of the world will see minor increases in 1995, although there could be declines in Eastern Europe, Russia and Oceania. Trade in tallow and grease was expected to decline. While less exports were expected from Oceania, less imports were expected by Mexico, South America, and the European Union. U.S. exports of tallow were expected to increase in 1995. Edible tallow exports were expected to flatten out while inedible tallow exports were expected to continue to trend higher, particularly to countries in the Mediterranean area. Economic problems in Mexico have affected U.S. tallow exports to that country. The devaluation of the peso and slower economic growth will reduce U.S. exports. For 1995, inedible tallow exports were forecast to decline to 120,000 tonnes from 146,785 tonnes in 1994. Exports of edible tallow in 1995 were put at 65,000 tonnes, down from 81,965 tonnes in 1994.

The Mexican tallow industry is unable to produce enough tallow to meet domestic needs. Imports, while still high, were expected to decline nine percent in 1995. Canadian tallow and grease production in 1994 increased with a rise in cattle slaughter. Another increase was expected in 1995 based on continued growth in cattle slaughter. Canada exports tallow to the Netherlands, Japan, and Algeria.

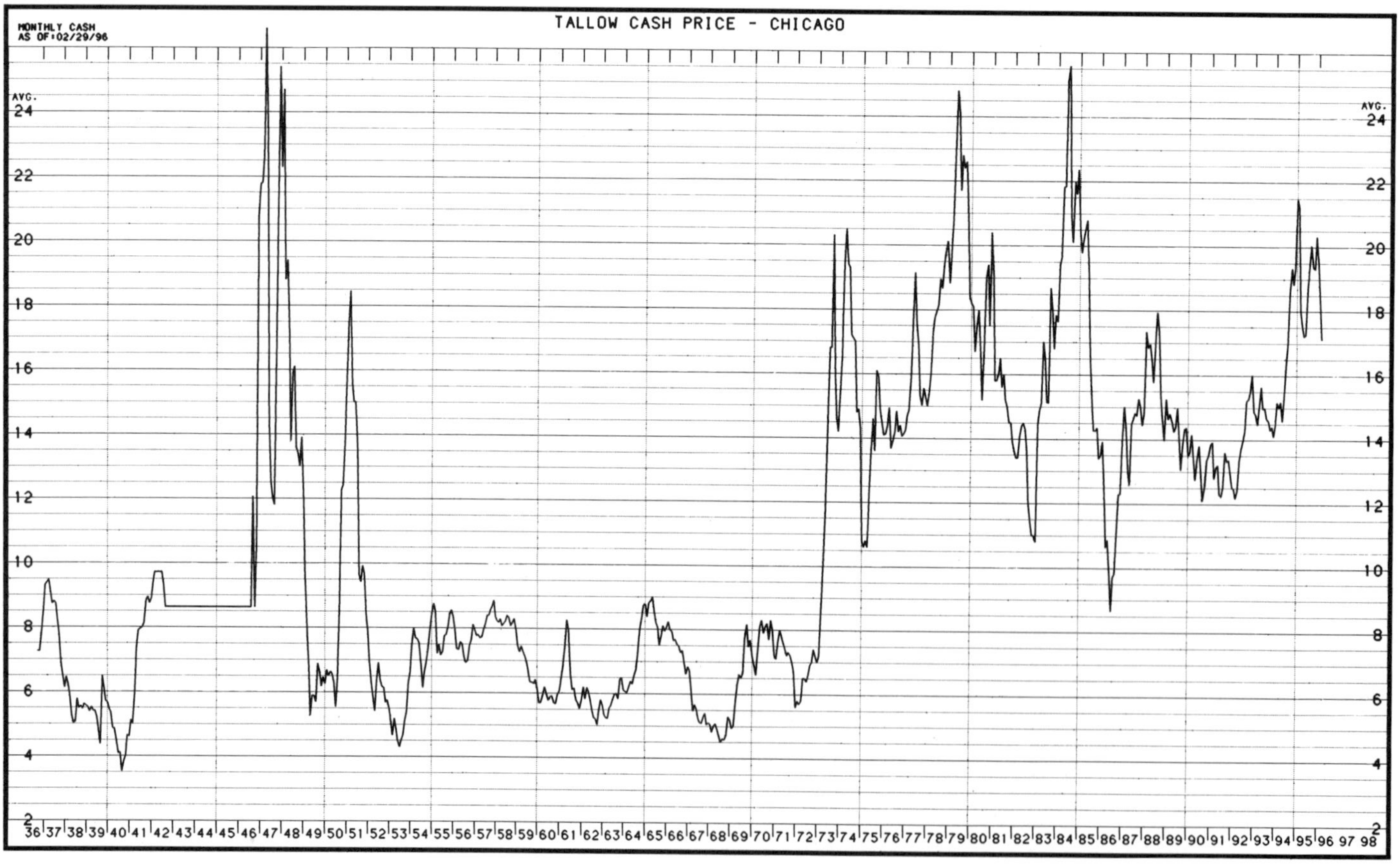

World Production of Tallow and Greases (Edible and Inedible) In Thousands of Metric Tons

Year	Agren-tina	Aust-ralia	Brazil	Canada	Den-mark	France	Ger-many	Italy	Japan	Rep. of Korea	Mexico	Nether-lands	New Zealand	Russia[4]	United Kingdom	United States	World Total
1985	293	305	220	216	60	180	250	115	212	0	69	103	156	370	230	3,373	6,527
1986	305	328	200	217	69	175	256	115	215	25	58	119	126	375	220	3,375	6,580
1987	289	350	170	205	70	182	282	110	219	46	43	127	132	380	233	3,190	6,420
1988	279	456	190	200	65	186	278	100	218	53	54	125	146	370	200	3,382	6,726
1989	278	489	272	203	83	179	280	90	168	60	65	125	133	400	207	3,212	6,614
1990	285	530	340	193	122	185	270	96	164	85	55	150	132	108	230	3,180	6,538
1991	268	472	336	212	129	275	197	99	153	121	58	150	134	106	225	3,309	6,677
1992	260	526	345	209	118	240	178	98	165	115	59	163	145	115	212	3,487	7,511
1993[1]	250	446	340	213	104	206	167	96	150	120	62	159	135	110	215	3,700	7,572
1994[2]	250	418	350	224	100	220	165	94	144	130	65	156	137	110	225	3,720	7,723
1995[3]	255	467	360	245	100	220	164	93	139	130	62	152	135	110	229	3,888	7,995

[1] Preliminary. [2] Estimate. [3] Forecast. [4] Formerly part of the U.S.S.R.; data not reported separately until 1990.
Source: Foreign Agricultural Service, U.S. Department of Agriculture

Salient Statistics of Tallow and Greases (Inedible) in the United States In Millions of Pounds

	Supply				Consumption			Wholesale Prices, ¢ Per Lb.	
Year	Production	Stocks Jan. 1	Total	Exports	Soap	Feed	Total	Edible, (Loose) Chicago	Inedible, Chicago No. 1
1985	5,827	368	6,195	2,737	535	1,363	2,782	20.1	14.3
1986	5,543	362	5,905	2,562	482	1,604	2,917	13.5	9.0
1987	5,602	316	5,918	2,491	571	1,727	3,082	15.6	14.9
1988	6,158	407	6,565	2,807	461	1,864	3,147	17.9	16.6
1989	5,848	399	6,247	2,679	368	1,919	3,194	15.8	14.4
1990	5,217	374	6,097	2,267	402	2,000	3,061	14.6	13.7
1991	5,759	357	6,116	1,936	392	1,748	2,949	14.3	13.3
1992	5,768	349	6,117	2,276	334	1,954	3,050	15.5	14.4
1993[1]	6,621	309	6,930	2,117	300	1,995	3,018	16.2	14.9
1994[1]	6,364	320	6,665	2,866	301	2,183	3,246	18.4	17.4

[1] Preliminary. [2] Estimate. *Sources: Economic Research Service, U.S. Department of Agriculture; Bureau of Census, U.S. Department of Commerce*

Edible Tallow: Supply and Disappearance in the U.S. In Millions of Pounds, Rendered Basis

	Supply			Disappearance					
Year	Stocks Jan. 1	Production	Total	Domestic	Exports	Total	Direct Use	Baking or Frying Fats	Per Capita (Lbs.)
1985	36	1,611	1,647	1,526	80	1,606	457	1,015	6.4
1986	41	1,523	1,564	1,469	62	1,531	428	973	6.1
1987	33	1,258	1,291	1,186	65	1,251	220	890	4.9
1988	40	1,296	1,336	1,149	139	1,288	197	840	4.7
1989	48	1,167	1,215	975	202	1,177	223	752	3.9
1990	34	1,202	1,247	955	251	1,206	342	637	3.8
1991	41	1,515	1,944	1,197	333	1,530	604	460	3.9
1992	33	1,414	1,456	1,109	306	1,415	537	427	4.7
1993	41	1,499	1,556	1,204	316	1,519	700	404	4.4
1994[1]	36	1,542	1,596	1,268	277	1,544	722	405	4.7
1995[2]	52	1,548	1,610	1,305	265	1,570		374	

[1] Preliminary. [2] Forecast. *Sources: Economic Research Service, U.S. Department of Agriculture; Bureau of Census, U.S. Department of Commerce*

Average Wholesale Price of Tallow, Inedible, No. 1 Packers (Prime), Delivered, Chicago In Cents Per Lb.

Year	Jan.	Feb.	Mar.	Apr.	May	June	July	Aug.	Sept.	Oct.	Nov.	Dec.	Average
1985	17.50	17.50	17.50	17.70	16.10	14.30	13.60	12.10	11.40	11.50	11.30	11.50	14.33
1986	12.00	11.80	9.40	8.90	8.70	7.60	7.80	7.80	8.10	8.40	8.50	9.50	9.04
1987	15.84	15.15	13.03	12.98	15.42	14.73	15.17	14.50	15.53	15.23	15.17	15.56	14.86
1988	18.00	17.08	17.25	16.17	15.93	17.18	18.81	17.44	16.00	15.02	14.18	16.33	16.62
1989	14.90	16.00	14.86	14.60	14.70	15.10	14.48	13.52	14.13	15.25	15.50	15.50	14.88
1990	14.87	14.50	14.47	13.77	13.66	NA	13.50	10.12	12.00	13.42	14.09	14.75	13.56
1991	13.88	14.28	14.43	14.80	13.02	12.36	12.96	14.00	13.50	13.68	13.08	12.50	13.54
1992	12.25	12.63	12.68	13.25	13.75	13.98	14.75	15.42	15.25	15.94	16.75	16.13	14.40
1993	15.36	14.70	15.24	16.15	15.41	14.51	14.36	14.53	14.66	14.62	14.69	14.63	14.91
1994	15.00	15.00	15.22	15.19	15.25	15.63	16.67	18.64	19.50	19.78	20.38	22.48	17.40
1995[1]	21.75	18.86	18.00	17.75	17.50	17.77							18.61

[1] Preliminary. *Source: Economic Research Service, U.S. Department of Agriculture*

Tea

The U.S. Department of Agriculture, in a survey of the six major tea producing countries (approximately 75 percent of world production) forecasts 1995 output at 1.96 million tonnes. This would be marginally below the 1994 output of 1.97 million tonnes. The lower output is due to smaller crops in India, Sri Lanka, and Argentina, while larger crops were reported in China and Kenya. Indonesian tea production was expected to remain unchanged.

In India, dry weather and uneven rainfall in the major growing regions adversely affected the 1995 harvest. India's production was estimated at 715,000 tonnes, down four percent from the 1994 crop of 743,800 tonnes. The industry's targeted output was 735,000 tonnes. Most of the decline was in orthodox (whole leaf) tea, which is more expensive to grow than cut, tear, and curl tea. For 1995, tea acreage harvested was 428,000 hectares, up marginally from 1994. While there have been efforts to increase planted acreage and the industry's processing capacity, production has been in decline forcing the Indian Government to reduce its year 2000 production target from 1,000,000 tons to 860,000 tons.

The Indian tea industry has decided to concentrate on producing quality tea because consumer trends are toward lighter, quality teas. Due to concerns over pesticide residues, there have been efforts to restrict chemical use and shift to more organic methods of weed and pest control.

For China, 1995 tea output is forecast by the USDA to reach 590,000 tonnes, up marginally from the 1994 output of 588,000 tonnes. Harvested acreage was put at 860,000 hectares, up from 851,000 tonnes in 1994. The Government and the Internal Trade Ministry have developed a plan for the tea industry. It focuses on encouraging tea farmers to produce high-quality teas, develop new varieties, boost yields, and further process low-grade teas and tea by-products. The primary tea grown in China is green tea for local consumption. While retail prices have increased, green tea consumption has been rising. Black (manufactured) tea is produced primarily for the export market.

In Sri Lanka, 1995 production was put by USDA at 240,000 tonnes, down from 245,000 tonnes in 1994. Harvested acreage was put at 220,000 hectares, down slightly from 1994. Poor weather resulted in reduced production in the first half of 1995. Traditionally, Sri Lanka produces orthodox tea.

For Kenya, the 1995 crop is estimated at 230,000 tonnes, up from 206,800 tonnes in 1994. Harvested acreage was 102,000 hectares, up from 94,000 hectares in 1994. The major reason for the better crop was improved weather. While Kenya is growing more tea, the industry is hampered by inadequate financing, insufficient processing capacity, poor roads, and a shortage of vehicles.

Indonesian production was forecast to be unchanged at 140,000 tonnes. Harvested acreage was 96,000 hectares, unchanged from 1994. Weather was not favorable due to drought. Indonesia produces high-quality tea but future expansion will be limited by a lack of land.

Argentinian production was estimated at 40,000 tonnes, down from 48,700 tonnes in 1994. Dry weather adversely affected the crop.

World Tea Production, in Major Producing Countries In Thousands of Metric Tons

Year	Argentina	Bangladesh	China	India	Indonesia	Iran	Japan	Kenya	Malawi	Mozambique	Sri Lanka	Taiwan	Tanzania	Turkey	Former USSR[2]	Grand Total
1984	46.0	38.2	414.0	639.9	126.2	46.8	92.5	116.2	37.5	11.0	209.2	24.4	16.5	113.7	151.1	2,194
1985	35.0	43.3	432.0	656.2	132.3	41.5	95.5	147.1	40.0	7.0	215.3	23.2	16.5	137.1	152.1	2,292
1986	40.0	37.6	461.0	620.8	129.5	48.5	93.6	143.3	39.0	5.0	212.7	23.9	15.1	148.3	146.6	2,285
1987	43.0	40.6	508.0	665.3	126.1	45.6	96.3	155.8	31.9	3.0	214.6	25.6	14.5	140.7	120.0	2,356
1988	44.0	43.6	545.0	700.0	133.8	55.6	89.8	164.0	40.2	1.5	228.2	23.6	14.6	166.4	118.0	2,490
1989	48.0	39.1	535.0	688.1	141.4	46.0	90.5	180.6	39.5	1.8	208.0	22.1	17.0	141.6	119.2	2,444
1990	50.0	45.9	540.0	720.3	145.2	44.0	89.9	197.0	39.1	2.0	234.1	22.3	18.4	126.7	123.2	2,528
1991	40.0	45.2	542.0	741.7	133.4	45.0	87.9	203.6	40.5	2.0	241.6	21.4	19.3	135.3	110.0	2,541
1992	59.0	46.0	580.0	703.9	163.0	55.0	92.1	188.1	28.1	1.5	178.9	20.7	18.4	144.0	55.0	2,439
1993	50.0	49.0	600.0	758.1	168.0	57.0	92.0	211.4	39.5	1.5	237.0	21.0	21.0	117.0	75.0	2,645
1994	48.7	51.0	588.0	743.8	140.0	75.0	86.0	206.8	42.0	1.0	245.0		22.0	125.0		2,623

[1] Preliminary. [2] Mostly Georgia and Azerbaijan. *Sources: Foreign Agricultural Service, U.S.D.A..; Food and Agriculture Organization of the United Nations*

World Tea Exports from Producing Countries In Metric Tons

Year	Argentina	Bangladesh	Brazil	China	India	Indonesia	Japan	Kenya	Malawi	Mozambique	P. New Guinea	Sri Lanka	Taiwan	Vietnam	Zimbabwe	Grand Total
1983	44,733	29,989	8,135	125,072	208,476	63,603	2,124	100,645	35,833	13,440	7,234	157,786	11,572	10,000	8,267	867,718
1984	42,102	23,100	9,301	145,346	217,400	85,664	2,787	91,198	37,208	7,550	7,530	204,226	11,862	11,000	9,835	942,733
1985	30,657	30,306	8,807	136,864	214,021	90,121	1,805	126,086	37,777	3,190	7,025	197,580	9,127	12,000	10,036	957,083
1986	36,279	27,675	10,851	172,028	203,149	78,957	1,261	116,456	40,189	1,820	5,213	207,567	9,011	12,500	11,819	997,534
1987	33,647	21,606	8,073	174,274	201,891	90,422	1,107	134,779	33,404	2,100	5,491	200,774	7,375	13,000	10,105	978,368
1988	34,258	26,187	9,686	198,289	200,956	92,687	1,260	138,201	36,961	830	5,834	219,710	7,631	14,800	14,190	1,039,313
1989	43,335	23,426	9,400	204,584	211,622	114,709	671	163,188	39,891	800	5,439	203,763	6,745	15,016	12,768	1,121,251
1990	45,966	26,970	7,976	195,471	209,085	110,964	322	169,586	43,039	700	5,375	215,251	5,853	24,698	11,507	1,141,026
1991	36,029	26,860	7,347	190,188	215,144	110,207	289	175,625	41,185	1,339	3,747	212,017	5,317	7,953	11,304	1,206,282
1992[1]	36,530	23,643	8,211	180,834	166,359	121,243	290	166,518	37,100	400	5,638	181,259	5,296	12,967	6,088	1,121,849
1993[2]	44,258	33,054	8,335	206,659	170,000	123,925	328	188,390	35,265	100	3,400	134,742	-----	16,200	6,700	1,187,617

[1] Preliminary. [2] Estimate. *Source: Food and Agriculture Organization of the United Nations*

TEA

United States Imports of Tea   In Metric Tons

Year	Agren-tina	Brazil	China	Ger-many	India	Indo-nesia	Kenya	Malawi	Nether-lands	Papua New Guinea	Sri Lanka	Total	Passed for U.S. Entry by Type: Black Teas	Green Teas	Oolong Teas	Mixed Teas	Total
1980	7,009	3,534	6,461	104	5,886	11,205	9,438	2,476	4,729	282	14,655	79,239	78,753	3,841	429	591	83,614
1981	10,345	2,806	7,962	205	4,159	13,913	6,762	2,147	5,936	200	12,216	83,819	80,857	3,754	541	755	85,907
1982	10,011	3,537	7,143	289	4,724	14,676	5,498	2,356	7,668	56	12,991	86,299	78,273	3,290	541	768	82,872
1983	15,114	3,926	6,399	646	2,894	14,352	4,536	1,288	4,657	25	8,106	77,318	71,709	2,371	517	551	75,148
1984	18,142	3,611	9,622	1,161	3,758	15,501	3,932	915	4,792	76	9,383	88,256	82,486	5,385	646	634	89,151
1985	15,234	4,281	10,877	3,046	2,943	12,844	4,152	935	4,213	62	9,796	79,206	69,210	6,570	811	618	77,209
1986	16,367	5,554	16,925	2,535	3,884	16,270	4,330	1,205	4,053	14	7,756	90,549	81,036	5,543	722	471	87,772
1987	15,897	5,418	16,728	3,422	3,042	10,395	4,145	1,991	3,258	75	4,799	77,391	70,881	6,590	770	496	78,737
1988	13,815	4,147	22,950	5,198	3,625	14,380	6,198	1,645	3,843	321	5,919	90,144	79,430	4,547	689	572	85,238
1989	17,219	4,735	19,641	5,731	2,914	12,293	6,005	1,871	2,508	571	5,693	89,582	78,898	5,870	804	634	86,206
1990	17,100	3,882	19,579	4,931	2,565	10,650	3,996	1,585	2,633	822	3,762	76,997	70,885	5,183	845	534	77,447
1991	19,457	3,453	21,859	4,834	2,648	13,477	4,056	1,958	1,839	1,153	3,702	84,330	76,762	5,056	704	412	82,934
1992	22,879	3,679	24,026	4,408	2,893	16,350	4,357	2,650	811	831	3,907	91,365	83,510	5,551	788	526	90,375
1993	21,268	2,684	24,035	3,961	2,912	13,247	3,938	3,146	937	1,126	3,750	84,893	77,796	4,470	768	538	83,572
1994[1]	25,120	3,843	24,549	4,481	3,705	15,011	3,406	3,865	640	1,087	4,842	96,184	90,873	4,517	689	397	96,476

[1] Preliminary. *Source: Foreign Agricultural Service, U.S. Department of Agriculture*

U.S. Per Capita Consumption of Specific Beverages and Tea Sales by U.S. Retail Stores

Year	Per Capita Consumption (In Gallons): Soft Drinks	Coffee[2]	Beer	Milk	Tea[2]	Bottled Water	Juices	Powder Drinks	Wine[3]	Distilled Spirits	Sales by Retail Stores[4] (In Metric Tons): Tea Bags	Loose Tea	Instant Tea	Instant Mixes	Herbal	Total
1980	34.2	27.2	24.3	20.6	7.3	2.7	7.7	6.0	2.1	2.0	37,857	3,680	17,124	12,100	645	71,406
1981	NA	NA	NA	NA	NA	NA	NA	NA	NA	NA	39,697	3,255	15,850	11,959	1,010	71,771
1982	35.6	26.6	24.4	19.7	7.5	3.3	6.8	6.0	2.2	1.9	40,638	3,023	14,905	11,742	1,875	72,183
1983	NA	NA	NA	NA	NA	NA	NA	NA	NA	NA	41,876	2,685	14,878	13,136	2,096	74,671
1984	38.8	26.4	23.9	19.7	7.2	4.0	6.6	6.4	2.3	1.9	40,685	2,329	13,287	12,192	2,109	70,602
1985	40.8	26.8	23.8	19.8	7.3	5.2	7.9	6.3	2.4	1.8	40,951	2,081	12,688	11,412	2,151	69,283
1986	42.1	25.8	24.1	19.9	7.3	5.7	7.3	6.0	2.4	1.7	40,410	1,816	12,065	10,573	2,350	67,214
1987	NA	NA	NA	NA	NA	NA	NA	NA	NA	NA	32,596	1,124	7,226	10,437	2,141	53,524
1988	46.0	25.4	23.7	19.3	7.4	7.2	7.1	5.2	2.2	1.6	31,924	939	6,521	10,589	2,191	52,164
1989	46.7	26.4	23.6	19.6	7.2	8.1	8.0	5.4	2.1	1.5	35,359	1,045	7,606	11,322	2,380	58,060
1990	47.7	26.4	24.1	19.4	7.0	8.0	7.1	5.7	2.0	1.5	34,806	972	6,858	11,659	2,458	57,153
1991	47.8	26.5	23.3	19.4	6.7	8.0	7.6	5.9	1.9	1.4	35,068	871	6,561	12,599	2,380	58,060
1992	48.0	26.1	23.0	19.1	6.8	8.2	7.1	5.8	2.0	1.3	35,025	749	5,761	12,846	2,477	57,607
1993	49.0	25.4	22.9	18.9	6.9	8.8	7.0	5.5	1.7	1.3	34,534	730	5,239	13,283	2,581	57,697
1994[1]	50.6	23.4	22.6	18.9	7.1	9.2	7.0	5.4	1.7	1.3						

[1] Preliminary. [2] Based on 3-year moving average. [3] Includes wine coolers beginning 1985. [4] Excludes sales by hotels, restaurants and institutional users. NA = Not available. *Source: Foreign Agricultural Service, U.S. Department of Agriculture*

London Auction Tea Prices   In U.S. Cents Per Pound

Year	Jan.	Feb.	Mar.	Apr.	May	June	July	Aug.	Sept.	Oct.	Nov.	Dec.	Average
1980	102.4	105.7	102.4	100.4	104.2	106.8	100.9	102.5	95.1	92.4	101.3	98.1	101.0
1981	98.6	101.2	100.5	97.9	94.7	90.4	84.6	80.0	81.7	87.4	91.3	91.6	91.7
1982	92.0	94.2	88.5	84.7	84.8	83.3	79.9	80.8	86.7	91.4	89.8	96.1	87.7
1983	98.5	93.1	89.8	92.1	91.0	85.2	86.6	90.6	99.0	117.4	158.8	163.8	105.5
1984	194.2	169.0	166.7	160.4	161.3	144.8	130.3	133.2	154.1	164.2	155.2	147.9	156.8
1985	143.1	127.3	110.4	98.6	75.2	74.6	71.5	72.2	73.3	78.7	80.2	75.3	90.0
1986	82.1	85.7	91.5	91.3	85.9	79.7	79.8	86.5	91.6	94.1	93.6	88.6	87.5
1987	89.7	83.6	83.2	67.9	65.4	60.8	69.5	72.3	72.7	84.1	87.4	94.0	77.6
1988	96.1	88.0	87.2	83.6	77.3	75.3	66.4	67.2	74.7	82.5	87.4	89.4	81.3
1989	87.5	82.4	80.6	77.3	76.7	80.4	88.1	83.2	97.7	118.4	106.7	115.5	91.2
1990	114.7	95.9	87.3	88.5	84.8	82.6	86.3	79.2	84.1	100.0	103.8	99.6	92.2
1991	107.2	90.2	83.6	84.3	78.7	73.8	70.4	73.5	79.6	84.4	89.4	89.7	83.7
1992	78.7	73.8	76.1	89.6	98.2	95.7	93.7	100.6	99.2	91.4	93.7	105.4	91.3
1993	108.6	92.5	86.9	80.6	78.3	75.9	74.7	75.8	82.4	90.9	84.3	84.4	84.6
1994	74.7	78.9	84.7	84.3	83.4	90.2	82.4	83.3	91.2	86.5	81.4	78.1	83.3
1995[1]	74.0	76.8	77.9	76.3	74.6	66.0	65.7	68.3	74.2	80.2			

[1] Preliminary. *Source: Foreign Agricultural Service, U.S. Department of Agriculture*

Tin

Tin is manufactured into a coating for steel containers used to preserve foods and beverages. In addition, it is utilized in solder alloys, electroplating, ceramics and plastic.

1994 world tin mine output was about the same as in the previous two years, mostly as a result of efforts by producers to restrict production. Stocks of tin still were excessive, reaching about 35,000 tonnes at the end of the year. Despite the large stocks, tin prices reached three year highs in the second half of 1995. Most of the move higher was attributed to speculative buying pressures. Stocks of tin at the London Metal Exchange were low and held in relatively tight hands. Because of the high prices and tightening stocks market analysts were looking for China, who many felt was the only producing country which could, to substantially increase exports. Under the Association of Tin Producing Countries export quota scheme, China was committed to limiting exports to 20,000 tonnes in 1995. There were some questions about Chinese abilities to hold exports to those levels. For the first six months of 1995, Chinese exports of tin were reported to be near 18,000 tonnes.

At the Association of Tin Producing Countries meeting in late 1995, it was reported that Vietnam, Portugal, Peru, and Myanmar might join the Association. Brazil was expected to join in 1996.

According to the Bureau of Mines, tin was mined in 28 countries in 1994, with the top five accounting for three-fourths of the world total of 183,000 tonnes. China was the largest producer with 27 percent of the world total, followed by Indonesia with 19 percent, Brazil with 15 percent, Bolivia nine percent, and Peru eight percent. World tin reserves were estimated at seven million tonnes and were considered adequate to meet the world's tin requirements in the near future. The bulk of the world's reserves are in Asia and South America.

For the first time in many years there was no tin mine production in the U.S. In recent years, the only tin mine in the U.S. was located in Alaska. There has also been no primary tin smelter in the U.S. for several years. Any domestic tin mine output has been shipped to foreign smelters.

The U.S. is believed to be the world's largest producer of secondary tin. Tin metal recovered from new tinplate scrap and from used tin cans was the only type of secondary tin available in the marketplace as free tin. Other secondary tin was available in scrap materials as an alloying ingredient. Secondary tin from recycled fabricated parts was a major source of material, particularly for the solder, brass, and bronze industries.

In terms of primary tin, the Bureau of Mines reported that 25 firms consumed about 86 percent of the primary tin used in the U.S. in 1994. The major uses were: can and containers, 32 percent; electrical, 22 percent; transportation, 11 percent; construction, 10 percent; and other, 25 percent.

In the U.S., over the January-July 1995 period, scrap production of tin from brass and bronze was 6,300 tonnes. For all of 1994, production was 4,800 tonnes. Consumption of primary tin in the first seven months of 1995 was 19,000 tonnes compared to 33,300 tonnes for all of 1994. Consumption of secondary tin was 5,900 tonnes compared to 9,400 tonnes in 1994.

Tin stocks in the U.S. at the end of July 1995 were 3,840 tonnes, compared to 3,210 tonnes at the end of June 1995, and 2,820 tonnes at the end of 1994.

Tinplate production in July 1995 was 110,000 tonnes with tin content of 675 tonnes. For all of 1994, tinplate production was 1.53 million tonnes with tin content of 9,400 tonnes.

U.S. imports of tin metal (unwrought tin) in the January-June 1995 period were 16,200 tonnes. For all of 1994 they were 32,400 tonnes. The major suppliers were Brazil, Indonesia, Bolivia, China, and Malaysia. U.S. imports of other tin products in the first six months of 1995 were 14,700 tonnes, compared to 12,300 tonnes in all of 1994. Most of the imports were waste, scrap , and tin alloys.

U.S. exports of tin metal in the first half of 1995 were 1,450 tonnes compared to total 1994 exports of 2,560 tonnes.

Futures Markets

Tin futures are traded on the London Metals Exchange (LME) and on the Kuala Lumpur Commodity Exchange (KLCE). Options are traded on the LME.

World Mine Production of Tin In Metric Tons (Contained Tin)

Year	Australia	Bolivia	Brazil	China	Indonesia	Malaysia	Nigeria	Peru	Portugal	Russia[3]	South Africa	Thailand	United Kingdom	Zaire	Zimbabwe	World Total
1989	7,709	15,849	50,232	40,000	31,263	32,034	217	5,082	63	16,000	1,306	14,922	3,846	2,346	1,130	232,857
1990	7,377	17,249	39,149	42,000	30,200	28,468	192	5,134	4,780	15,000	1,140	14,635	3,400	2,221	1,120	221,000
1991	5,700	16,830	29,253	42,100	30,061	20,710	217	6,559	8,330	13,500	1,042	14,937	2,330	1,522	1,060	201,000
1992	6,610	16,516	27,500	43,800	29,400	14,339	186	9,680	6,560	6,000	582	11,484	2,040	1,020	950	182,000
1993[1]	8,060	18,634	26,500	49,100	29,000	10,384	186	13,900	10,100	5,000	450	6,380	2,230	700	800	187,000
1994[2]	6,400	16,200	27,000	50,000	34,000	6,460	180	14,000	12,000	4,100	500	4,000	1,900	700	800	183,000

[1] Preliminary. [2] Estimate. [3] Formerly part of the U.S.S.R.; data not reported separately until 1992. *Source: U.S. Bureau of Mines*

World Smelter Primary Production of Tin In Metric Tons

Year	Australia	Bolivia	Brazil	China	Indonesia	Japan	Malaysia	Mexico	Russia[2]	South Africa	Spain	Thailand	United Kingdom	Zimbabwe	World Total
1989	424	9,448	44,240	29,500	29,916	808	50,874	4,752	18,000	1,306	1,767	14,571	3,584	848	221,569
1990	312	12,567	37,580	35,000	30,389	816	49,067	5,004	16,000	1,140	600	15,512	6,100	838	246,000
1991	268	14,663	25,776	36,400	30,415	716	42,722	2,262	13,000	1,042	600	11,255	1,661	796	205,000
1992	240	14,393	27,000	39,600	31,915	821	45,598	2,590	6,000	592	600	10,679		716	195,000
1993[1]	222	14,500	26,900	52,000	30,400	804	40,100	1,640	5,000	452	500	8,100		657	194,000
1994[1]	240	15,300	30,000	53,000	31,100	706	42,000	1,700	4,100		700	8,100		82	199,000

[8] Preliminary. [2] Formerly part of the U.S.S.R.; data not reported separately until 1992. *Source: U.S. Bureau of Mines*

Tin Foreign Trade of the United States In Metric Tons

		Imports (For Consumption)														
		Concentrates[3] (Ore)			Unwrought Tin Metal											
Year	Exports (Metal[2])	Total All Ore	Bolivia	Peru	Total All Metal	Australia	Belgium	Bolivia	Brazil	China	Indonesia	Malaysia	Nigeria	Singapore	Thailand	United Kingdom
1980	595	840	528	-----	45,982	145	190	5,597	2,031	858	6,477	15,548	770	864	12,414	416
1981	2,361	232	-----	232	45,874	552	-----	8,277	1,129	2,032	7,096	13,163	520	656	11,967	46
1982	5,769	1,961	192	1,416	27,939	334	10	4,340	2,409	2,632	5,744	2,364	124	600	9,116	55
1983	1,340	969	257	341	34,048	390	45	5,739	5,604	1,938	6,004	4,704	265	1,029	7,436	18
1984	1,429	3,272	271	2,502	41,224	288	137	5,438	10,220	1,640	4,985	6,622	60	781	9,531	583
1985	1,478	1,616	22	1,506	33,830	266	-----	1,815	11,021	4,513	4,586	379	-----	1,886	6,373	48
1986	1,547	3,936	259	3,676	35,768	94	-----	4,893	9,456	2,955	4,149	6,230	-----	691	1,901	730
1987	1,318	2,953	732	2,165	41,150	1,406	302	3,476	13,089	8,044	4,001	4,959	79	743	1,460	467
1988	1,209	2,837	923	1,914	43,493	1,342	-----	3,926	16,213	6,223	5,334	5,317	41	1,342	670	1,354
1989	904	216	-----	149	33,988	1,420	-----	4,795	10,572	4,793	5,162	2,392	-----	456	180	391
1990	658	-----	-----	-----	33,810	1,660	-----	8,472	6,535	4,339	4,695	3,873	-----	40	60	227
1991	970	1	1	-----	29,102	1,105	221	8,912	4,489	5,281	4,425	1,751	-----	100	-----	344
1992	1,888	-----	-----	-----	27,314	300	1	4,623	8,167	5,389	3,854	2,799	-----	320	427	-----
1993	2,598	-----	-----	-----	33,682	-----	1	8,027	11,366	4,202	5,678	846	-----	220	-----	6
1994[1]	2,560	-----	-----	-----	32,400	-----	3	7,260	9,990	3,230	6,620	1,389	-----	140	-----	666

[1] Preliminary. [2] Excludes re-exports from 1979. [3] Tin content. *Source: U.S. Bureau of Mines*

United States Tin (Pig) Consumption (Total) In Metric Tons

Year	Jan.	Feb.	Mar.	Apr.	May	June	July	Aug.	Sept.	Oct.	Nov.	Dec.	Total
1980	5,500	5,300	5,750	5,300	4,600	4,100	3,700	3,900	4,150	4,300	4,050	3,750	56,362
1981	4,300	4,400	4,100	4,600	4,400	4,350	3,900	4,200	3,950	3,900	3,400	2,950	54,373
1982	3,400	3,300	3,750	5,100	5,000	5,100	4,900	4,700	4,700	4,600	4,500	4,400	53,450
1983	4,400	4,700	4,900	4,700	4,700	4,800	4,300	4,600	4,700	4,800	4,400	4,800	55,800
1984	4,600	4,300	5,300	3,900	4,500	4,400	4,100	4,400	4,100	4,000	3,300	3,500	50,400
1985	4,000	3,900	4,600	4,500	4,600	4,400	4,200	4,400	4,300	4,500	4,200	4,000	51,600
1986	4,300	4,000	4,200	4,500	4,400	4,400	4,100	4,100	4,000	4,300	3,900	3,900	50,100
1987	4,100	3,900	4,200	4,700	4,300	4,200	4,400	4,400	4,400	4,300	4,600	4,400	44,219
1988	4,600	4,700	4,800	4,700	5,300	5,600	5,300	5,300	5,500	5,600	4,900	4,900	45,073
1989	4,800	4,700	4,300	4,500	4,500	4,100	4,000	4,200	4,100	4,300	4,000	3,300	46,371
1990	4,000	4,000	4,200	4,100	4,200	4,100	4,100	4,300	4,100	4,100	4,200	3,900	44,363
1991	4,100	3,900	4,100	4,300	4,100	4,200	3,900	4,100	4,000	4,300	4,100	4,000	49,000
1992	3,800	3,800	3,800	3,800	3,700	3,800	3,800	3,500	3,600	3,600	3,400	3,300	45,090
1993	3,400	3,500	3,600	3,600	3,500	3,600	3,500	3,600	3,500	3,500	3,500	3,400	47,107
1994[1]	3,500	3,700	3,700	3,600	3,600	3,700	3,500	3,400	2,500	3,600	3,600	3,400	42,700
1995[1]	3,500	3,600	3,680	3,726	3,877	3,833	3,544	3,895	3,811				

[1] Preliminary. *Source: U.S Bureau of Mines*

United States Tin Stocks (Pig -- Industrial) In Metric Tons

Year	Jan. 1	Feb. 1	Mar. 1	Apr. 1	May 1	June 1	July 1	Aug. 1	Sept. 1	Oct. 1	Nov. 1	Dec. 1
1980	4,238	7,720	6,882	7,527	5,443	7,263	6,592	6,544	6,051	5,180	5,208	5,086
1981	5,504	5,968	5,745	5,229	5,725	5,978	6,227	6,465	5,663	5,710	5,325	5,563
1982	5,988	3,872	3,490	3,829	5,222	4,953	4,653	3,888	2,910	2,940	2,970	3,437
1983	3,152	4,609	3,513	3,815	4,026	3,527	3,634	3,931	4,091	3,604	3,074	3,180
1984	3,020	2,968	2,268	2,840	2,646	3,119	2,795	2,688	2,837	2,495	2,512	2,326
1985	2,592	2,766	2,283	2,407	2,228	2,853	3,042	2,762	2,663	2,985	4,121	4,913
1986	5,665	5,310	4,692	3,097	4,127	3,987	4,032	4,166	4,246	3,497	3,554	4,681
1987	4,802	5,232	6,394	6,321	7,263	8,087	6,663	4,288	5,373	5,533	6,402	5,460
1988	4,428	4,490	5,989	5,631	5,868	6,128	6,456	5,665	4,350	4,171	4,371	4,781
1989	4,943	4,242	3,894	4,320	3,717	4,945	4,912	5,597	5,872	6,241	5,313	5,530
1990	6,072	5,975	5,824	6,401	4,959	3,298	3,792	3,592	3,836	4,762	4,819	4,829
1991	6,337	6,677	6,688	6,177	5,993	5,991	6,348	6,739	6,544	8,544	6,616	6,347
1992	3,024	3,022	3,369	2,844	2,877	2,901	2,651	3,111	3,321	3,454	3,654	3,178
1993	3,221	3,572	4,450	4,483	3,898	3,609	4,648	4,652	4,561	3,709	3,262	3,535
1994[1]	3,651	4,635	3,775	3,967	3,471	3,470	3,825	3,027	2,891	2,980	2,844	2,908
1995[1]	2,741	3,931	3,850	2,780	3,000	3,080	3,210	3,910	3,800	3,880		

[1] Preliminary. *Source: U.S. Bureau of Mines*

TIN

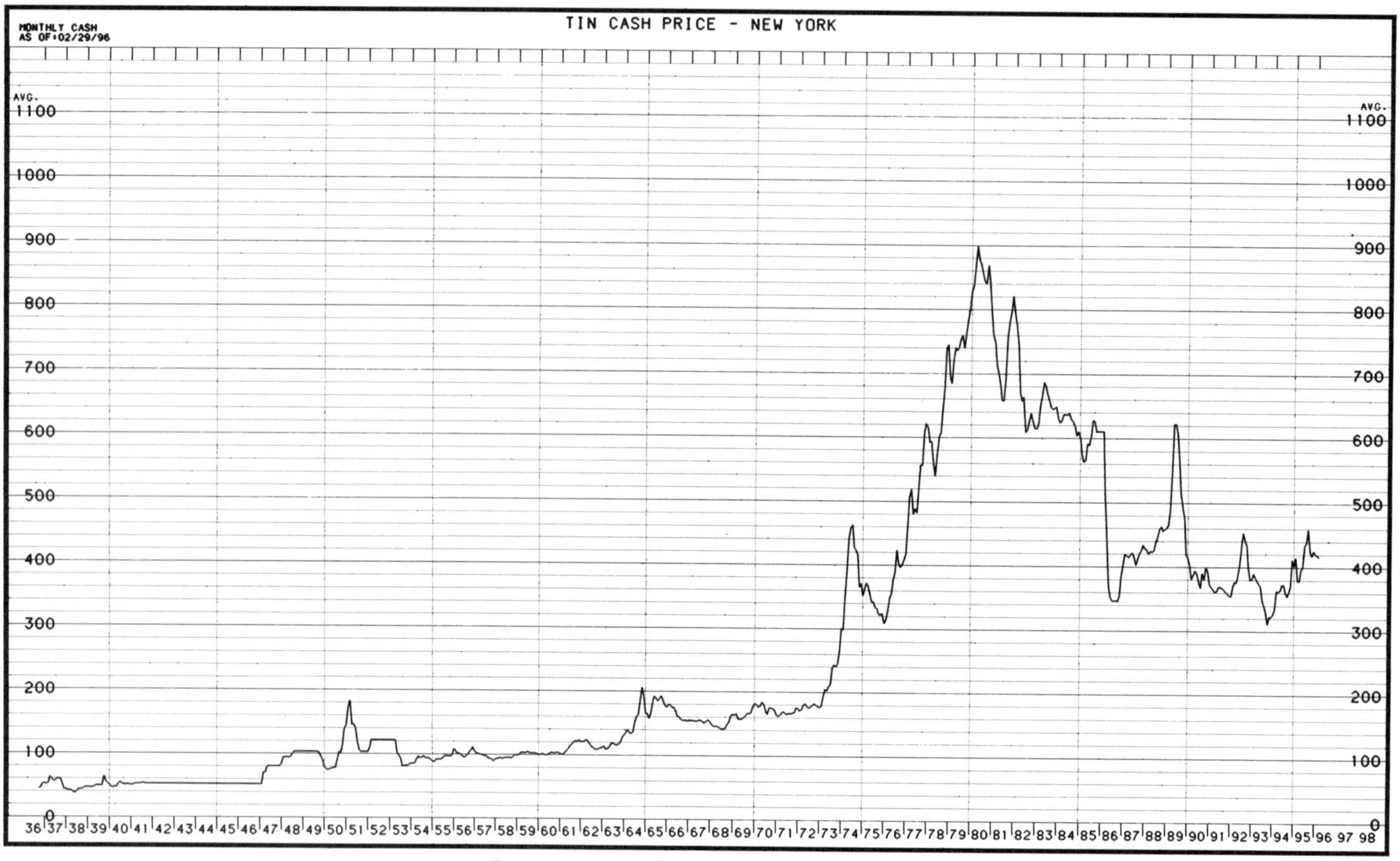

Average Price of Ex-Dock Tin in New York[1] In Cents Per Pound

Year	Jan.	Feb.	Mar.	Apr.	May	June	July	Aug.	Sept.	Oct.	Nov.	Dec.	Average
1978	591.19	595.93	557.48	537.85	570.58	600.95	606.21	641.80	679.66	739.69	758.84	695.86	631.34
1979	684.56	724.57	746.14	740.06	745.18	760.14	712.31	739.93	762.03	785.54	801.23	830.88	756.87
1980	836.46	866.39	900.23	872.21	861.84	845.19	836.95	834.61	861.92	832.92	788.67	751.36	840.73
1981	739.94	705.76	691.70	677.38	652.07	652.77	680.22	746.06	777.36	798.70	813.00	801.59	728.05
1982	787.41	749.93	669.51	649.58	662.35	643.00	638.00	636.33	644.33	627.94	627.93	630.18	663.88
1983	648.90	653.89	669.18	692.29	683.36	670.54	663.13	653.10	649.31	650.65	653.02	636.71	660.34
1984	590.60	592.10	603.40	605.10	601.70	602.20	593.50	594.70	590.20	578.60	574.40	566.10	591.05
1985	542.10	532.00	533.80	559.10	557.70	576.30	594.90	593.80	578.60	580.50	NQ	NQ	564.88
1986	NQ	NQ	350.64	274.98	265.04	260.28	261.51	261.26	260.69	267.48	292.84	308.26	280.30
1987	321.56	320.39	317.66	320.98	323.60	316.96	307.59	314.63	321.86	324.81	332.21	327.65	320.83
1988	326.68	321.12	324.79	323.85	325.28	337.37	342.18	351.14	355.20	347.84	351.10	352.42	338.25
1989	355.80	377.77	419.64	486.72	484.42	474.15	458.64	415.80	395.99	379.67	329.10	324.79	408.54
1990	317.89	296.28	302.41	308.97	307.02	295.86	288.09	287.48	279.20	296.11	292.27	261.82	295.41
1991	269.97	268.00	264.51	265.78	271.78	272.30	270.55	269.02	265.86	264.50	262.26	262.05	267.21
1992	261.30	267.79	267.52	277.20	290.05	313.07	331.10	322.19	315.66	291.60	268.54	271.76	289.81
1993	280.40	280.91	277.43	275.67	269.62	255.35	252.31	230.17	213.22	220.02	224.88	236.90	251.41
1994	249.55	267.55	261.20	258.49	277.79	282.43	276.11	265.35	279.39	292.17	325.83	346.21	281.84
1995	374.77		266.45		283.62	314.33	316.06	331.64	304.12	297.77	304.47	300.28	35

[1] Data prior to 1984 are for Straits (Alloyer Price). NQ = No quote. *Source: American Metal Market*

Tin Plate Production & Tin Recovered in the United States In Metric Tons

	Tin Content of Tinplate Produced				Tin Recovered from Scrap by Form of Recovery								
		Tinplate (All Forms)											
Year	Tinplate Waste	Gross Weight	Tin Content (Tonne)	Tin per Tonne of Plate (Kilograms)	Tin Metal	Bronze & Brass	Solder	Type Metal	Babbitt	Anti-monial Lead	Chemical Com-pounds	Misc.[2]	Grand Total
1980	311,770	3,699,920	16,346	4.4	1,703	10,402	4,423	525	378	856	321	30	18,638
1981	284,505	3,288,662	13,306	4.0	1,587	8,894	3,035	576	261	791	265	29	15,438
1982	208,074	2,712,678	10,936	4.0	1,067	6,971	2,723	222	237	1,015	447	101	12,783
1983	166,186	2,586,810	9,328	3.6	1,180	8,517	3,072	172	185	803	182	94	14,205
1984	151,540	2,409,399	8,659	3.6	1,107	9,146	3,653	142	123	894	301	51	15,417
1985	146,041	2,215,042	9,321	4.2	1,302	8,045	3,565	122	88	791	186	10	14,109
1986	120,186	2,068,246	8,660	4.2	1,134	7,996	3,676	197	66	891	W	17	13,977
1987	141,842	2,302,173	10,357	4.5	1,353	10,245	3,765	66	77	623	W	30	16,159
1988	149,054	2,375,809	11,582	4.9	578	9,939	3,619	70	112	902	W	29	15,249
1989	153,542	2,263,769	11,764	5.2	569	10,305	3,225	46	116	952	W	W	15,213
1990	156,419	2,467,205	11,750	4.8	186	13,312	2,876	46	28	739	W	4	17,187
1991	166,647	2,468,769	11,482	4.7	234	11,719	W	44	24	928	W	2,705	12,949
1992	195,760	1,620,007	9,821	6.1	137	12,761	W	47	78	704	W	181	13,727
1993[1]	196,874	1,625,132	9,945	6.0	112	10,670	W	43	51	796	W	W	11,672
1994[1]	189,000	1,530,000	9,400	6.1									

[1] Preliminary. [2] Includes foil, terne metal, cable lead, and items indicated by symbol "W". W = Withheld proprietary data. *Source: U.S. Bureau of Mines*

U.S. Consumption of Primary and Secondary Tin In Metric Tons

			Net Receipts							
Year	Net Import Reliance as a % of Apparent Consumption	Industry Stocks Jan. 1[2]	Primary	Secondary	Scrap	Total	Available Supply	Stocks Dec. 31 (Total Available Less Total Processed)	Total Processed	Consumed in Manu-facturing Products
1981	77	8,835	41,162	5,692	8,050	54,904	63,739	8,640	55,099	54,373
1982	68	8,717	35,843	6,507	7,830	50,180	58,897	12,328	46,569	46,295
1983	73	7,549	36,494	5,412	7,435	49,341	56,890	11,098	45,792	45,547
1984	74	8,063	38,813	6,110	6,791	51,714	59,777	11,145	48,632	48,315
1985	72	8,430	38,006	8,904	7,471	54,381	62,811	13,928	48,883	48,669
1986	74	9,336	35,475	11,636	6,346	53,457	62,793	18,915	43,878	43,524
1987	74	9,876	38,401	11,707	6,635	56,743	66,619	21,887	44,731	44,219
1988	78	10,217	39,421	12,472	6,707	58,600	68,817	23,586	46,232	45,602
1989	77	9,242	37,760	10,901	8,168	56,829	66,071	19,184	46,887	46,463
1990	71	13,551	38,473	9,501	6,534	54,508	68,059	22,578	45,481	45,165
1991	74	12,502	36,126	1,622	8,370	46,118	58,620	13,540	45,080	44,805
1992	80	12,038	34,327	2,279	8,412	45,018	57,056	11,669	45,387	45,120
1993	84	8,556	37,700	3,280	8,768	49,700	58,300	11,566	46,700	46,600
1994[1]	84	9,530	33,000	4,160	4,930	42,000	51,600	9,940	41,600	41,400

[1] Preliminary. [2] Includes tin in transit to the U.S. *Source: U.S. Bureau of Mines*

Consumption of Tin in the United States by Finished Products In Metric Tons (Contained Tin)

												Total	
Year	Tinplate[2]	Solder	Babbitt	Bronze & Brass	Tinning	Chemicals[3]	Tin Powder	Bar Tin & Anodes	White Metal	Other	Total	Primary	Secondary
1981	13,306	15,799	3,844	7,041	2,491	4,417	983	455	1,201	1,788	54,373	40,229	14,144
1982	11,134	13,142	1,915	4,400	1,887	W	906	509	1,177	11,225	46,295	33,019	13,276
1983	9,462	14,120	2,881	4,583	1,759	W	793	654	937	10,358	45,547	34,301	11,246
1984	8,825	17,249	2,684	4,998	1,748	W	1,057	526	958	11,396	48,315	37,201	11,114
1985	9,321	18,621	1,488	4,330	1,511	W	976	466	937	12,100	48,669	36,524	12,145
1986	8,660	15,810	1,324	3,502	1,437	W	1,002	449	1,134	10,204	43,522	33,324	10,198
1987	10,357	15,240	1,060	3,559	1,398	W	W	703	1,175	10,704	44,219	35,620	8,599
1988	11,582	15,288	926	3,934	1,406	W	W	557	1,131	10,777	45,601	37,529	8,072
1989	11,764	16,370	794	3,693	1,505	W	711	619	1,074	9,926	46,456	36,603	9,853
1990	11,750	16,443	763	3,166	1,707	6,275	563	603	1,045	2,850	45,165	36,770	8,395
1991	11,482	16,296	941	2,896	1,465	6,564	539	436	868	3,318	44,805	35,138	9,667
1992	9,821	18,461	916	2,916	1,275	6,301	573	919	974	2,964	45,090	34,983	10,137
1993	9,650	19,000	823	3,093	1,249	6,446	608	946	789	3,927	46,600	34,600	11,900
1994[1]	9,480	15,000	627	3,080	1,230	5,740	625	855	756	3,990	41,400	32,900	8,490

[1] Preliminary. [2] Includes small quantity of secondary pig tin and tin acquired in chemicals. [3] Including tin oxide. W = Withheld proprietary data.
Source: U.S. Bureau of Mines

Titanium

Titanium's unique properties of having one-half the density of steel, excellent strength, and immunity to corrosion make it an ideal construction material for engines and airframes. Pure titanium metal is called "sponge" because of its porous cellular form. The sponge is processed to form an ingot, and the ingot is processed by mills to make plate sheet tubing. There are titanium sponge plants in the U.S., Japan, Great Britain, China, and the former Soviet Union. Other uses of titanium mill products are in pollution control devices, desalination plants, chemical processing, and in tubing for power plants and oil refineries. Titanium dioxide finds use as a white pigment for exterior paints, paper production, and pigment for ink and porcelain enamels.

U.S. production of titanium ingot in the second quarter of 1995 was 9,780 tonnes, up from the first quarter production of 9,580 tonnes. For all of 1994, titanium ingot production was 29,500 tonnes. Production of titanium sponge was withheld to avoid disclosing company proprietary data. Production of titanium mill products in second qtr. 1995 was 5,910 tonnes, up from 5,909 tonnes in the first quarter.

Consumption of titanium sponge over the first six months of 1995 totaled 10,600 tonnes. For all of 1994, titanium sponge consumption was 17,200 tonnes. Consumption of titanium scrap in the first half of 1995 was 9,840 tonnes while for all of 1994 it was 15,700 tonnes. Consumption of titanium ingot was 15,300 tonnes in the first half 1995 while for 1994 it was 24,300 tonnes. Net shipments of titanium mill products over the January-June 1995 period was 9,270 tonnes with 43 percent of the total forging and extrusion billet, 13 percent titanium rod and bar and 43 percent other mill products. For all of 1994, net shipments of titanium mil products was 15,600 tonnes.

U.S. imports of titanium sponge in the first half of 1995 were 4,380 tonnes compared to 6,470 tonnes for all of 1994. Titanium waste and scrap imports in the first half of 1995 were 3,630 tonnes compared to 5,870 tonnes for all of 1994. Total imports of all titanium products were 10,200 tonnes compared to 15,600 tonnes for all of 1994.

U.S. exports of all titanium products including scrap, sponge and ingot in the first half 1995 were 4,310 tonnes while for all of 1994 they were 9,660 tonnes.

Government stocks of titanium sponge at the end of June 1995 were 33,400 tonnes, the same as at the end of 1994.

Average Titanium Prices in the United States

Year	Ilmenite F.O.B. Australian Ports[2] \$ Tonne[4]	Slag, 85% TiO_2 F.O.B. Richards Bay, South Africa \$ Tonne[4]	Rutile Large Lots Bulk, F.O.B. U.S. East Coast[3] \$ Tonne[5]	Rutile Bagged F.O.B. Australian Ports \$ Tonne[5]	Avg. Price of Grade A Titanium Sponge, F.O.B. Shipping Point (Dollars Per Pound)	Titanium Metal Sponge (Dollars Per Pound)	Titanium Dioxide Pigments, F.O.B. U.S. Plants: Anatase (Dollars Per Pound)	Titanium Dioxide Pigments, F.O.B. U.S. Plants: Rutile (Dollars Per Pound)
1984	36-38	200	320-340	339-359	5.70	5.55	.69	.75
1985	38-42	212	350-360	371-386	5.70	3.50-4.00	.72-.73	.78
1986	47-53	225-230	355-375	398-422	4.32	3.90-4.30	.75-.77	.80-.82
1987	46-52	235-245	355-375	398-418	4.06	4.00-4.20	.75-.77	.80-.82
1988	64-77	250-275	NA	547-572	4.21	4.25-4.75	.92-.95	.95-.97
1989	67-75	275-300	540-550	553-632	5.11	4.80-5.30	1.01-1.02	1.04-1.05
1990	69-77	285-310	550-580	693-770	5.31	4.75	.99	1.01
1991	68-76	295-325	606-650	515-545	5.25	4.75	.99	.99
1992	58-62	310	510-520	380-414	3.96	3.50-4.00	.99	.92-.95
1993	61-64	330	NA	370-400	3.75	3.50-4.00	.99	.92-.95
1994[1]	74-80	334	351-372	450-480	3.96	3.75-4.25	.94-.96	.92-.94
1995[6]	72-78	343	NA	427-444		3.75-4.25	.94-.96	.92-.94

[1] Preliminary. [2] Prior to 1984 prices are for TiO_2 F.O.B. Atlanta Seaboard. [3] Prior to 1984 prices are for F.O.B. Eastern Ports. [4] Prices prior to 1984 are per long ton. [5] Prices prior to 1988 are per short ton. [6] Estimate. NA = Not available. *Source: U.S. Bureau of Mines*

Salient Statistics of Titanium in the United States In Metric Tons

Year	Titanium Dioxide Pigment: Production	Titanium Dioxide Pigment: Imports[3]	Titanium Dioxide Pigment: Apparent Consumption	Ilmenite: Imports[3]	Ilmenite: Consumption	Titanium Slag: Imports[3]	Titanium Slag: Consumption	Rutile[4]: Imports[3]	Rutile[4]: Consumption	Exports of Titanium Products: Ores & Concentrates	Exports of Titanium Products: Scrap	Exports of Titanium Products: Dioxide & Pigments	Exports of Titanium Products: Ingots, Billets, Etc.
1983	659,710	138,922	741,065	348,366	583,250	247,845	225,541	163,325	238,937	4,391	5,379	91,702	1,371
1984	834,889	193,501	916,198	409,605	783,391	209,839	200,858	180,508	317,902	8,651	4,109	106,124	2,071
1985[5]	783,393	178,001	893,195	459,765	685,896	264,742	228,635	162,988	276,944	25,183	6,133	93,624	2,039
1986	844,274	183,862	908,055	422,401	731,436	328,285	250,677	158,595	298,601	4,821	5,809	104,734	1,922
1987	878,558	174,219	966,169	307,515	744,266	408,785	251,423	197,937	320,505	4,023	5,083	108,889	2,467
1988	926,746	185,468	991,536	394,170	679,008	434,641	300,013	231,124	352,356	9,368	5,939	118,422	2,083
1989	1,006,581	166,346	947,259	411,751	659,584	386,146	414,830	264,895	366,143	19,832	5,474	212,197	2,702
1990	978,659	147,592	925,447	345,907	688,948	373,623	390,537	274,605	369,454	18,765	5,487	202,288	2,371
1991	991,976	166,094	935,829	213,886	738,089	408,302	341,379	240,120	368,643	26,912	4,568	211,854	1,700
1992	1,137,038	169,260	999,930	294,585	684,882	537,118	539,323	317,399	460,969	34,665	2,770	270,422	1,455
1993[1]	1,161,469	171,939	1,028,311	301,000	693,940	476,000	545,809	371,481	464,825	15,202	3,893	261,000	1,511
1994[2]	1,250,000	176,000	1,100,000	336,000	W	472,000	583,000	332,000	510,000	19,000	4,120	313,000	1,559

[1] Preliminary. [2] Estimate. [3] For consumption. [4] Natural and synthetic. [5] Data shown in short tons prior to 1985. W = Withheld proprietary data.
Source: U.S. Bureau of Mines

World Production of Titanium Ilmenite Concentrates In Thousands of Metric Tons

Year	Australia[2]	Brazil	China	India	Malaysia	Norway	Sierra Leone	Sri Lanka	Thailand	Ukraine[3]	World Total	Titaniferous Slag[4] Canada	Titaniferous Slag[4] South Africa
1980	1,553	18.6	NA	185.1	208.3	912.5	NA	37.4	NA	460	5,420	934	379
1981	1,478	17.5	150.0	179.1	190.4	727.1	NA	88.2	NA	470	5,266	837	408
1982	1,289	12.5	150.0	168.6	111.6	608.2	NA	75.3	NA	475	4,496	737	420
1983	1,003	33.6	154.0	148.2	245.5	612.8	NA	90.1	NA	480	4,108	700	460
1984[5]	1,681	45.1	154.0	154.3	296.0	718.5	NA	112.5	NA	485	5,091	800	460
1985	1,433	76.4	140.0	143.0	314.7	735.8	NA	114.9	1.0	445	4,737	845	435
1986	1,252	75.5	140.0	140.0	414.9	803.6	NA	129.9	13.5	450	4,705	850	435
1987	1,509	169.3	140.0	140.0	509.2	852.3	5.6	128.5	27.1	455	3,937	925	650
1988	1,622	142.2	150.0	229.7	486.3	898.0	42.1	74.3	18.3	460	4,033	1,025	400
1989	1,714	144.2	150.0	240.7	533.7	929.8	62.3	101.4	17.0	460	4,353	1,040	725
1990	1,621	114.1	150.0	280.0	530.2	814.5	54.6	66.4	10.7	430	4,072	1,046	840
1991	1,381	69.1	150.0	312.0	336.3	625.0	60.4	60.9	17.1	400	3,360	701	808
1992	1,810	76.6	150.0	300.0	337.7	708.0	60.3	33.3	3.0	250	3,720	753	884
1993	1,821	90.6	155.0	320.0	289.0	713.0	62.9	76.9	20.8	200	3,750	653	892
1994[1]	1,805	91.0	155.0	300.0	116.0	700.0	47.0	60.4	16.0	150	3,440	764	744

[1] Preliminary. [2] Includes leucoxene. [3] Formerly part of the U.S.S.R.; data not reported separately until 1992. [4] Approximately 10% of total production is ilmenite. Beginning in 1988, 25% of Norway's ilmenite production was used to produce slag containing 75% TiO_2. [5] Data prior to 1985 are shown in thousands of short tons. NA = Not available. *Source: U.S. Bureau of Mines*

World Production of Titanium Rutile Concentrates In Metric Tons

Year	Australia	Brazil	India	Sierre Leone	South Africa	Sri Lanka	Thailand	Ukraine[2]	World Total
1980	343,639	472	5,908	52,356	53,000	14,097	NA	11,000	480,472
1981	254,432	190	7,397	55,992	55,000	14,662	NA	11,000	398,673
1982	243,277	258	6,374	52,590	52,000	7,950	NA	11,000	373,449
1983	180,089	510	6,100	79,146	62,000	8,921	NA	11,000	347,766
1984[3]	187,860	454	6,600	100,641	62,000	7,129	NA	11,000	375,684
1985	211,615	713	6,800	80,611	55,000	8,558	110	10,000	373,407
1986	215,774	495	7,000	97,100	55,000	8,443	48	10,000	393,860
1987	246,263	324	7,000	113,300	55,000	7,200	92	10,000	439,179
1988	230,637	1,514	5,000	126,358	55,000	5,255	128	10,000	433,892
1989	243,000	2,613	9,931	128,198	60,000	5,589	150	10,000	459,331
1990	245,000	1,814	11,000	144,284	64,056	5,460	NA	9,500	481,114
1991	201,000	1,094	13,635	154,800	77,000	3,085	76	9,000	460,000
1992	183,000	1,800	10,000	148,990	84,000	2,741	281	5,000	436,000
1993	186,000	1,740	13,900	152,000	85,000	2,643	87	4,000	445,000
1994[1]	223,000	1,800	14,000	137,000	78,000	2,410	100	3,000	459,000

[1] Preliminary. [2] Formerly part of the U.S.S.R.; data not reported separately until 1992. [3] Data prior to 1985 are shown in short tons. NA = Not available. *Source: U.S. Bureau of Mines*

World Production of Titanium Sponge Metal & U.S. Consumption of Titanium Concentrates

Year	Production of Titanium (In Metric Tons) — Sponge Metal[2]: China	Japan	Russia[3]	United Kingdom	United States	Total	U.S. Consumption of Titanium Concentrates, by Products (In Metric Tons) — Ilmenite (TiO_2 Content): Pigments	Misc.	Total	Rutile (TiO_2 Content): Welding Rod Coatings	Pigments	Misc.	Total
1980	NA	21,257	45,000	2,600	NA	NA	502,108	11,207	513,315	6,876	211,599	59,407	277,882
1981	2,000	27,500	42,000	2,600	26,419	100,519	501,301	9,721	511,022	6,944	192,779	66,873	266,596
1982	1,500	18,600	44,000	2,600	15,600	82,300	345,618	6,775	35,293	5,275	184,403	35,435	225,113
1983	2,000	11,600	45,000	2,000	13,966	74,000	468,279	6,006	474,285	3,649	210,949	35,820	250,418
1984	2,000	16,938	46,000	2,500	24,326	92,000	492,658	6,319	498,977	3,911	231,808	62,920	298,639
1985	2,000	16,938	47,000	1,500	23,257	91,000	474,561	6,450	481,011	4,881	239,893	41,714	286,488
1986	2,000	18,000	48,000	1,500	17,500	87,000	511,070	1,655	512,725	7,667	244,178	57,539	309,384
1987[4]	2,000	11,105	49,000	1,500	19,675	83,000	463,072	1,817	510,449	4,168	271,658	56,558	332,384
1988	2,000	16,500	46,000	1,500	24,000	88,000	429,736	590	429,737	3,737	262,998	64,641	331,376
1989	2,000	21,000	46,000	1,500	25,225	95,725	419,329	414	419,743	3,603	271,208	71,178	345,989
1990	2,000	25,630	47,000	1,500	24,679	101,000	445,502	726	446,228	4,047	271,637	71,373	347,057
1991	2,000	18,945	20,000	2,000	13,366	56,000	476,145	495	476,640	6,931	286,741	42,200	335,872
1992	2,000	14,554	20,000	2,000	W	38,554	425,876	647	426,523	W	405,875	32,553	438,428
1993	2,000	14,400	20,000	1,000	W	37,000	434,097	451	434,548	W	405,784	30,223	436,007
1994[1]	2,000	14,000	15,000	----	W	31,000	W	637	W	W	460,000	18,500	478,000

[1] Preliminary. [2] Unconsolidated metal in various forms. [3] Formerly part of the U.S.S.R.; data not reported separately until 1993. [4] Data prior to 1988 are shown in short tons. NA = Not available. W = Withheld proprietary data. *Source: U.S. Bureau of Mines*

Tobacco

The U.S. Department of Agriculture forecasts U.S. tobacco production to decline 15 percent to 1.35 billion pounds from 1.58 billion in 1994. While harvested acreage increased marginally to 675,000 acres, yields per acre fell 15 percent to 1,996 pounds per acre. This was the lowest tobacco yield since the late sixties.

The U.S.-grown tobacco supply for 1995-96 is forecast to fall because carryin stocks (July 1 for flue-cured and cigar wrapper types; October 1 for all other types) are likely to decline five percent from a year earlier to 2.33 billion pounds. Stocks of imported leaf rose two percent to 1.05 billion pounds.

U.S. cigarette consumption continued to trend lower in 1995. This marks the eleventh consecutive year of decline in cigarette use. The decline is attributed to higher cigarette retail prices, an increasing number of prohibitions and restrictions on where people can smoke, continuing publicity about the relationship between smoking and health, and declining social acceptance of cigarette smoking.

In August 1995, President Clinton authorized the Food and Drug Administration (FDA) to regulate cigarettes and smokeless tobacco products as drugs because of their nicotine content. This initiative was an attempt to curb the use of tobacco products by youths. The Clinton Administration rejected voluntary control proposals by some cigarette manufacturers but indicated specific measures to eliminate smoking by minors could be legislated. The FDA has published proposed regulations governing tobacco product sales and advertising. Among the proposals would be the prohibition of vending machine sales of cigarettes and prohibiting tobacco brand-name sponsorship of sporting events.

Americans smoked an estimated 484 billion cigarettes in 1994-95 (July-June), down slightly from the previous year. Per capita cigarette consumption for 18 year olds and over was 2,470 with an estimated weight of 4.15 pounds of tobacco. This was down two percent from the previous year. The share of discount-brand cigarettes fell to 30 percent of the market in 1994-95 compared to 33 percent a year before. Low-tar, low-nicotine cigarettes accounted for a slightly higher proportion than a year earlier, but below the record high of 1981. Per capita consumption is forecast at about 123.5 packs of 20 cigarettes, the lowest level since 1941.

Total U.S. cigarette production in 1994-95 was estimated by USDA at 737 billion units. Exports of U.S. cigarettes jumped sharply to 239.3 billion, up almost 21 percent from the previous year. For the 1994-95 (July-June) period, Belgium-Luxembourg (entry point for Europe) imported 83.4 billion cigarettes while Japan imported 61.3 billion.

U.S. consumption of large cigars and cigarillos in 1994-95 was estimated at 2.29 billion pounds, up four percent from the previous year. This was the second consecutive year that consumption has risen. The trend in cigar consumption had been lower for many years. Consumption of small cigars was also expected to increase to 1.45 billion pounds, up close to six percent from the prior year.

U.S. consumption of smoking tobacco, which is used in pipes and roll-your-own cigarettes was estimated at 14.1 million pounds, down 7.7 percent from the year before. Chewing tobacco production was estimated at 64.8 million pounds, down one percent from a year earlier. Snuff consumption continues to trend higher. Dry snuff output in 1994-95 was estimated at 5.9 million pounds, up over seven percent from the previous year while moist snuff output was estimated at 54.4 million pounds, up two percent.

Retail prices of tobacco products were about two percent higher in July 1995 compared to a year earlier. Manufacturers had lowered the prices of premium-brand cigarettes more than 25 percent in August 1993 to slow the gains made by discount cigarettes. Prices were increased slightly in November 1993 and went unchanged until they were increased three percent in May 1995.

Five states imposed tax hikes in 1995 averaging 14 cents a pack. The average State tax on cigarettes was 31.4 cents per pack of 20 in Virginia to 81.5 cents in Washington. Many cities and local governments also tax cigarettes and 43 states impose sales taxes on cigarettes. The Federal excise tax has been 24 cents per pack since January 1, 1993.

U.S. exports of unmanufactured tobacco during 1994-95 were 432 million pounds. Exports declined because of sufficient supplies of lower-priced tobacco in other countries. The value of unmanufactured tobacco exports for 1994-95 was $1.3 billion.

World cigarette trade increased 20 percent in 1994. Shipments from the U.S., Germany, Hong Kong, the Netherlands, and Great Britain were higher. World cigarette production increased four percent in 1994 due to increases in the U.S., Germany, and China. China accounts for about a third of world production. China's rate of production increase has been declining. Chinese cigarette production rose one percent while the rest of the world increased four percent. During most of the last decade, world production outside China was relatively stagnant.

World Production of Leaf Tobacco In Metric Tons

Year	Brazil	Canada	China	France	Greece	India	Indonesia	Italy	Japan	Kyrgyzstan[3]	Pakistan	Philippines	Turkey	United States	Zimbabwe	World Total
1986	385.0	70.1	1,707.0	38.6	148.8	439.4	154.1	145.5	118.2	321.0	78.3	72.8	161.5	528.0	117.0	6,005
1987	410.0	61.4	1,943.0	33.9	144.0	460.2	154.0	162.1	104.4	296.0	69.0	79.4	184.7	539.3	131.5	6,160
1988	419.0	69.8	2,731.3	29.4	184.4	367.4	137.8	184.4	85.8	242.0	69.5	68.8	218.8	621.2	123.7	6,835
1989	462.0	75.6	2,830.4	29.2	197.3	492.8	146.9	197.3	74.4	233.2	71.1	73.3	269.5	620.2	135.2	7,111
1990	435.0	63.1	2,627.5	28.3	134.4	564.4	158.9	214.8	80.5	292.7	68.0	70.1	295.6	737.7	139.8	7,106
1991	422.0	78.7	3,030.7	29.5	165.7	555.9	164.9	193.3	69.9	250.5	80.8	82.3	239.4	754.9	178.1	7,564
1992	577.0	71.8	3,499.0	23.1	196.5	584.4	145.4	150.8	79.4	18.2	108.0	114.9	331.8	780.9	211.4	8,293
1993	608.0	86.1	3,451.0	25.8	148.0	580.6	152.8	135.7	67.4	55.6	106.0	102.5	338.1	731.9	235.3	8,300
1994[1]	442.0	71.5	2,238.0	27.4	135.4	528.0	160.0	130.7	79.5	45.0	106.8	56.0	187.7	718.0	177.8	6,388
1995[2]	398.0	79.3	2,350.0	25.0	131.9	524.5	169.8	132.5	75.0	21.0	106.5	63.7	210.3	604.0	210.0	6,376

[1] Preliminary. [2] Estimate. [3] Formerly part of the U.S.S.R.; data not reported separately until 1992. *Source: Foreign Agricultural Service, U.S. Department of Agriculture*

Production and Consumption of Tobacco Products in the United States

Year	Cigarettes -Billions-	Cigars[3] -Millions-	Chewing Tobacco: Plug	Twist	Looseleaf	Total	Smoking Tobacco	Snuff[4]	Consumption[5] of Per Capita[6]: Cigarettes	Cigars[3]	Cigarettes	Cigars[3]	Smoking Tobacco	Chewing Tobacco	Total Products
			Million Pounds						Number		Pounds				
1986	658.0	2,932	10.4	1.4	69.6	81.4	19.4	47.5	3,274.0	35.8	5.7	.59	.29	.93	6.56
1987	689.4	2,133	9.9	1.4	67.3	78.7	18.0	46.2	3,197.0	31.7	5.5	.52	.27	.89	6.30
1988	694.5	1,980	8.9	1.4	65.6	75.9	17.8	48.6	3,096.0	29.1	5.4	.47	.25	.86	6.11
1989	677.2	2,010	8.3	1.3	64.9	74.5	17.0	49.7	2,926.0	27.9	4.9	.46	.22	.82	5.67
1990	709.7	1,896	7.4	1.3	64.3	72.9	16.4	53.1	2,817.0	26.2	4.8	.43	.20	.79	5.48
1991	694.5	1,740	6.7	1.2	64.3	72.2	15.7	54.3	2,713.0	24.9	4.7	.41	.19	.79	5.41
1992	718.5	1,741	5.9	1.2	61.6	69.7	14.9	57.5	2,640.0	24.1	4.7	.40	.17	.74	5.38
1993	661.0	1,795	5.3	1.1	58.0	64.4	13.7	59.1	2,539.0	23.9	4.5	.39	.17	.70	5.12
1994[1]	725.6	1,916	4.6	1.1	26.8	62.5	13.4	59.5	2,493.0	24.3	4.6	.40	.16	.71	5.30
1995[2]	745.0	2,040	4.2	1.1	58.0	63.3	12.7	60.7							

[1] Preliminary. [2] Estimate. [3] Large cigars and cigarillos. [4] Includes loose-leaf. [5] Consumption of tax-paid tobacco products. Unstemmed processing weight. [6] 18 years and older. *Source: Economic Research Service, U.S. Department of Agriculture*

Production of Tobacco in the United States In Thousands of Pounds

Year	Connecticut	Florida	Georgia	Indiana	Kentucky	Maryland	Massachusetts	Missouri	North Carolina	Ohio	Pennsylvania	South Carolina	Tennessee	Virginia	West Virginia	Wisconsin
1986	3,062	13,303	67,890	12,095	314,940	21,120	622	4,389	444,790	13,574	21,830	75,480	82,821	73,524	2,640	11,860
1987	2,716	13,804	72,160	11,070	304,845	13,338	653	3,519	466,592	12,044	20,700	94,080	87,291	76,900	2,592	8,370
1988	2,971	17,152	85,880	10,945	355,024	11,970	767	4,422	552,627	14,497	18,175	100,125	93,142	92,177	2,720	6,906
1989	2,793	17,755	87,200	13,237	366,551	8,103	746	5,450	541,056	15,925	17,925	103,680	79,820	93,814	1,885	11,248
1990	3,007	19,044	103,845	15,050	442,253	9,656	805	5,928	639,639	18,915	19,780	109,905	112,218	110,269	2,720	13,346
1991	2,831	15,312	80,600	18,920	479,794	12,900	830	6,825	634,655	22,776	20,765	111,180	121,524	116,849	3,420	15,191
1992	2,258	19,575	100,980	18,900	524,378	11,931	740	3,298	609,873	21,840	20,840	112,320	146,556	111,459	3,623	13,100
1993	2,533	18,673	96,320	17,415	455,080	12,255	738	4,760	608,415	18,900	18,260	110,760	139,423	99,544	3,600	6,643
1994	2,682	16,575	80,660	15,265	453,687	12,750	792	8,015	599,833	18,360	18,360	108,100	132,289	106,092	3,550	5,910
1995[1]	3,347	17,352	84,000	13,650	375,150	11,475	851	5,670	483,720	17,347	15,685	105,000	104,344	81,807	3,400	6,200

[1] Preliminary. *Source: Agricultural Statistics Board, U.S. Department of Agriculture*

Salient Statistics of Tobacco in the United States

Year	Acres Harvested 1,000 Acres	Yield Per Acre Pounds	Production Million Pounds	Farm Price ¢ Lb.	Farm Value Million $	Tobacco (July-June) Exports[2]	Imports[3]	U.S. Exports of: Cigarettes	Cigars & Cheroots	All Tobacco	Smoking Tobacco[4]	Stocks of Tobacco[5] Various Types: All Tobacco	Fire Cured[6]	Cigar Filler[7]	Maryland
						Million Pounds		Millions				Million Pounds			
1986	581.6	1,998	1,163	152.2	1,771	533.6	487.1	63,945	62	591	41.8	3,815	94.4	54.8	45.6
1987	586.3	2,028	1,191	157.1	1,871	500.0	480.3	100,246	145	573	43.3	3,406	93.0	43.3	42.0
1988	634.0	2,160	1,370	164.6	2,254	476.7	394.6	118,499	87	555	43.9	2,909	79.2	35.1	37.6
1989	678.4	2,016	1,367	170.8	2,335	485.9	365.0	141,782	78	582	46.6	2,714	75.9	31.8	27.0
1990	732.3	2,218	1,625	173.8	2,827	487.4	415.0	164,301	72	631	58.0	2,401	70.2	26.9	19.3
1991	763.4	2,179	1,664	177.3	2,951	511.0	502.2	179,200	70	499	63.2	2,232	66.7	25.6	12.1
1992	784.4	2,195	1,722	177.7	3,059	528.8	881.0	205,600	76	574	59.1	2,280	61.6	26.7	9.4
1993	746.4	2,161	1,613	175.3	2,830	529.7	707.8	195,476	67	458	62.5	2,412	64.0	26.7	7.5
1994[1]	671.1	2,359	1,583	177.4	2,808	442.1	537.5	220,200	74	529	77.0	2,588	69.7	24.1	8.4
1995[1]	675.3	1,968	1,329					240,000	77			2,541	80.5	20.5	11.5

[1] Preliminary. [2] Domestic. [3] For consumption. [4] In bulk. [5] Flue-cured and cigar wrapper, year beginning July1; for all other types, October 1. [6] Kentucky-Tennessee types 22-23. [7] Types 41-46. *Source: Economic Research Service, U.S. Department of Agriculture*

Tobacco Production in the U.S., by Types In Thousands of Pounds (Farm-Sale Weight)

Types	11-14	21	22	23	31	32	35-36	37	41	41-61	51	54	55	61
1986	644,563	3,538	26,554	11,179	407,922	27,750	11,050	162	15,200	29,254	1,750	5,502	6,358	1,684
1987	690,914	2,600	17,524	7,451	419,360	20,738	6,849	130	13,300	23,296	1,864	5,670	2,700	1,590
1988	813,212	2,920	19,804	8,020	477,208	18,445	7,415	127	11,700	22,372	1,630	5,016	1,890	2,108
1989	808,350	2,480	18,463	7,980	482,568	17,825	6,430	104	10,725	25,512	1,256	7,648	3,600	2,283
1990	939,234	2,762	22,931	9,285	597,927	16,316	7,491	102	13,120	30,278	1,160	9,328	4,018	2,652
1991	911,887	3,563	20,620	8,704	658,181	19,920	8,776	156	13,735	32,587	1,433	9,799	5,392	2,228
1992	906,025	2,567	23,736	10,486	719,552	18,771	10,332	124	14,000	30,098	1,484	8,460	4,640	1,514
1993	886,908	1,872	26,985	12,060	633,838	18,335	11,123	104	12,180	22,094	1,694	4,690	1,953	1,577
1994	869,920	2,403	31,723	14,205	612,398	19,770	11,797	124	11,340	20,680	1,808	4,180	1,686	1,666
1995[1]	743,712	1,540	27,110	11,184	498,917	17,935	8,977	77	9,225	19,623	2,353	4,300	1,900	1,845

[1] Preliminary. *Source: Agricultural Statistics Board, U.S. Department of Agriculture*

TOBACCO

U.S. Exports of Unmanufactured Tobacco In Millions of Pounds (Declared Weight)

Year	Australia	Belgium-Luxem.	Denmark	Egypt	France	Germany	Ireland	Italy	Japan	Nether-lands	Norway	Sweden	Switzer-land	Thailand	United Kingdom	Total U.S. Exports
1984	8.2	9.4	19.8	37.4	5.1	66.0	8.0	31.3	92.1	22.3	4.7	11.5	25.3	14.6	31.8	542.7
1985	7.3	11.5	16.2	41.2	9.9	76.7	7.3	28.7	102.0	20.9	3.3	15.8	23.9	17.8	18.4	548.9
1986	11.7	10.1	14.5	46.5	8.4	82.7	3.4	22.5	83.2	31.2	4.3	10.2	11.5	13.0	21.8	477.5
1987	8.5	8.2	15.6	11.0	6.7	69.3	1.2	22.4	105.4	32.1	3.3	8.0	12.6	7.5	16.7	430.0
1988	9.0	9.7	16.4	15.7	5.7	87.2	2.0	32.4	70.4	41.0	3.7	12.0	15.5	13.5	19.6	481.8
1989	6.2	12.3	13.8	.4	4.8	75.4	1.3	17.1	105.3	43.2	3.6	8.3	10.4	15.7	18.4	485.9
1990	8.3	12.4	15.1	.5	5.7	75.9	1.6	19.3	106.5	45.3	3.4	9.5	13.3	22.2	20.5	492.5
1991	7.7	11.0	14.8	4.6	6.5	82.8	4.3	19.9	83.1	42.8	3.5	8.3	14.8	19.5	18.9	499.3
1992	6.9	21.4	15.6	.2	4.2	93.3	2.5	19.0	131.0	49.9	3.4	8.8	7.5	16.9	24.3	574.4
1993	5.7	12.8	15.5	7.8	4.3	52.1	2.4	7.3	124.7	38.1	3.8	8.1	6.1	17.8	20.8	458.0
1994[1]	6.4	12.3	14.9	.3	3.1	54.1	1.3	11.3	126.2	30.9	1.6	7.3	6.0	19.0	14.7	433.9

[1] Preliminary. *Source: Economic Research Service, U.S. Department of Agriculture*

U.S. Salient Statistics for Flue-Cured Tobacco (Types 11-14) In Millions of Pounds

Crop Year	Acres Harvested 1,000	Yield Per Acre Pounds	Mar-ketings	Stocks July 1	Total Supply	Exports	Domestic Disap-pearance	Total Disap-pearance	Farm Price ¢ Lb.	Placed Under Gov't Loan Mil. Lb.	Price Support Level ¢ Lb.	Loan Stocks Nov. 30	Loan Stocks Uncom-mitted
1985-6	357.1	2,241	789	2,080	2,870	435	477	912	171.9	132.2	169.9	922.4	767.7
1986-7	308.3	2,099	667	1,958	2,625	393	480	873	152.7	55.5	143.8	752.9	475.9
1987-8	324.6	2,129	683	1,752	2,435	385	537	922	158.7	24.8	143.5	630.4	397.7
1988-9	366.4	2,219	796	1,513	2,309	363	522	885	161.3	15.2	144.2	421.9	328.4
1989-90	390.7	2,069	838	1,424	2,262	387	567	954	167.4	28.4	146.8	314.5	218.2
1990-1	416.9	2,253	920	1,308	2,228	403	609	1,012	167.3	74.4	148.8	226.4	223.8
1991-2	402.6	2,265	882	1,216	2,098	403	472	875	172.3	49.9	152.8	153.7	174.5
1992-3	401.5	2,257	901	1,223	2,124	420	509	929	172.6	81.8	156.0	223.6	129.0
1993-4	400.1	2,217	892	1,195	2,087	359	433	792	168.1	204.9	157.7	330.5	317.5
1994-5[1]	359.5	2,420	807	1,295	2,102	346	569	915	169.8	97.7	158.3	298.5	396.5
1995-6[2]	386.2	1,926	854	1,187	2,041	330	520	850	179.4		159.7	348.0	60.0

[1] Preliminary. [2] Estimate. *Source: Economic Research Service, U.S. Department of Agriculture*

U.S. Salient Statistics for Burley Tobacco (Type 31) In Millions of Pounds

Crop Year	Acres Harvested 1,000	Yield Per Acre Pounds	Mar-ketings	Stocks Oct. 1	Total Supply	Exports	Domestic Disap-pearance	Total Disap-pearance	Farm Price ¢ Lb.	Gross Sales[3]	Price Support Level ¢ Lb.	Loan Stocks Nov. 30	Loan Stocks Uncom-mitted
1985-6	255.1	2,247	542	1,462	2,004	151	425	576	159.7	494.0	148.8	570.3	566.0
1986-7	210.7	1,936	420	1,426	1,846	165	402	567	156.5	409.9	148.8	544.0	479.6
1987-8	215.9	1,943	428	1,279	1,706	157	478	635	156.3	374.2	148.8	332.9	231.0
1988-9	226.4	2,109	468	1,073	1,541	164	414	578	161.0	351.5	150.0	243.4	117.7
1989-90	244.4	1,975	498	963	1,461	169	446	614	167.2	398.1	153.2	314.5	91.6
1990-1	270.6	2,204	592	847	1,439	199	475	674	175.3	467.8	155.8	226.4	52.0
1991-2	312.0	2,110	657	765	1,422	209	407	616	178.8	501.5	158.4	62.3	32.8
1992-3	332.7	2,163	700	807	1,507	183	385	568	181.5	502.4	164.9	131.2	71.7
1993-4	299.7	2,115	627	939	1,566	152	400	552	181.6	492.4	168.3	178.8	141.9
1994-5[1]	266.3	2,300	568	1,014	1,582	159	464	623	184.1	455.7	171.4	345.2	380.8
1995-6[2]	246.6	2,023	520	959	1,479	155	455	610	184.5	341.6	172.5	343.5	38.5

[1] Preliminary. [2] Estimate. [3] Before Christmas holidays. *Source: Economic Research Service, U.S. Department of Agriculture*

Exports of Tobacco from the United States (Quantity and Value) In Metric Tons

Year	Unmanufactured: Flue-Cured	Unmanufactured: Value $1,000	Unmanufactured: Burley	Unmanufactured: Value $1,000	Unmanufactured: Total	Unmanufactured: Value $1,000	Manufactured	Value $1,000
1991	115,481	776,654	61,852	441,223	226,463	1,427,630	NA	4,574,086
1992	146,100	983,478	64,481	483,743	260,526	1,650,559	58,115	4,509,395
1993	111,636	752,646	51,892	389,964	207,747	1,306,067	49,669	4,253,286
1994[1]	107,411	749,305	49,859	367,856	196,792	1,302,745	63,837	5,367,220
1995[2] [3]	79,937	568,393	38,423	295,264	144,245	965,751	58,291	3,846,661

[1] Preliminary. [2] Forecast. [3] For the period January-September. NA = Not available. *Source: Foreign Agricultural Service, U.S. Department of Agriculture*

Tung Oil

Tung oil is derived for the seeds of the tung tree and is used as an industrial lubricant and drying agent. The tung tree is found mainly in China, the leading producer and exporter of tung oil.

World production of tung oil in 1993 was estimated at 83,000 tonnes. China is by far the largest producer of tung oil with about three-quarters of world production. There are a number of other smaller producers, the most important being Argentina and Paraguay.

The publication *Oil World* noted that world trade in tung oil increased in the 1994-95 (October-September) crop year. World exports of tung oil were put at 46,500 tonnes, a six year high. China, which has increased its exports considerably in the last two years, Argentina, and Paraguay are the leading exporters. The major importers of tung oil are the U.S., Japan, and Taiwan. In the 1994-95 season, import requirements for Japan, Taiwan, and Western Europe increased.

With increased production of tung oil, prices have fallen considerably. The USDA reports that the price of tung oil, f.o.b., New York, in the January-April 1993 period were $1.30 per pound. By the first quarter of 1994, the average price was $0.83 per pound. For the January-June 1995 period, the average price of tung oil was $0.60 per pound.

World Tung Oil Trade In Metric Tons

	Imports										Exports					
Year	Germany	Hong Kong	Italy	Japan	Netherlands	South Korea	Taiwan	United Kingdom	United States	World Total	Argentina	China	EC-12	Hong Kong	Paraguay	World Total
1988	341	7,118	699	10,688	585	2,234	-----	848	6,407	43,639	5,061	26,933	1,097	7,343	5,213	46,201
1989	1,193	4,119	344	13,137	631	2,533	1,538	1,037	6,474	44,496	9,506	24,248	518	4,085	8,296	47,254
1990	1,078	4,176	149	12,424	1,095	3,249	3,152	924	4,046	36,590	8,557	16,069	402	4,454	8,347	38,500
1991	1,138	6,476	109	11,890	543	3,035	4,957	862	5,646	39,766	8,522	14,485	476	7,182	9,039	40,600
1992	1,036	8,509	178	13,326	782	3,722	6,676	893	4,996	44,146	5,808	20,867	231	8,174	4,221	40,269
1993[1]	720	5,222	164	6,549	1,351	3,490	3,595	608	4,270	29,793	2,497	16,990	369	6,004	2,295	29,200
1994[2]	900	7,843	273	8,628	1,680	3,300	7,200	495	5,401	39,805	2,550	25,000	440	6,476	3,800	39,218

[1] Preliminary. [2] Estimate. *Source: The Oil World*

U.S. Consumption of Tung Oil in Inedible Products In Thousands of Pounds

Year	Jan.	Feb.	Mar.	Apr.	May	June	July	Aug.	Sept.	Oct.	Nov.	Dec.	Total
1988	2,169	1,143	988	1,117	1,072	878	713	1,148	1,276	2,751	2,509	4,317	20,081
1989	4,106	3,360	3,074	2,717	2,313	2,508	2,511	2,512	2,541	2,845	2,668	2,510	33,665
1990	2,573	646	680	823	795	923	712	738	607	626	472	611	10,206
1991	----------	1,953	----------	----------	1,555	----------	----------	1,334	----------	----------	1,100	----------	5,942
1992	435	459	574	498	502	694	572	705	674	873	530	790	7,306
1993	958	966	693	1,041	833	1,022	867	1,427	1,354	860	585	593	11,199
1994	608	592	635	1,408	1,558	840	861	910	480	392	660	382	9,326
1995[1]	427	503	976	1,389	1,437	1,387	1,886	2,830	2,549	2,645	2,455	2,126	20,610

[1] Preliminary. *Source: Bureau of Census, U.S. Department of Commerce*

U.S. Stocks of Tung Oil at Factories & Warehouses In Thousands of Pounds

Year	Jan. 1	Feb. 1	Mar. 1	Apr. 1	May 1	June 1	July 1	Aug. 1	Sept. 1	Oct. 1	Nov. 1	Dec. 1
1988	3,224	4,501	5,296	4,374	4,304	3,500	3,913	3,797	3,422	4,999	3,821	3,498
1989	3,739	3,012	3,867	3,526	3,225	3,216	4,836	3,860	3,640	5,450	4,649	5,037
1990	5,448	4,648	2,744	2,529	3,164	2,859	2,003	1,553	1,880	1,018	1,913	2,374
1991	1,829	----------	----------	2,997	----------	----------	1,379	----------	----------	963	----------	----------
1992	1,608	2,421	2,439	1,605	1,323	1,540	847	1,348	2,162	1,724	2,560	3,545
1993	3,122	2,038	2,390	2,120	2,966	1,773	866	815	1,596	1,217	1,635	1,752
1994	1,551	2,053	1,507	2,049	2,091	2,591	2,148	1,562	820	2,455	1,712	1,909
1995[1]	1,764	1,490	1,055	3,193	2,554	2,551	2,369	2,116	2,038	2,361	2,210	2,048

[1] Preliminary. *Source: Bureau of Census, U.S. Department of Commerce*

Average Price of Tung Oil (Imported, Drums) F.O.B. New York In Cents Per Pound

Year	Jan.	Feb.	Mar.	Apr.	May	June	July	Aug.	Sept.	Oct.	Nov.	Dec.	Average
1988	57.63	58.00	58.00	56.88	53.50	52.00	51.00	49.80	49.00	48.25	44.75	44.00	51.90
1989	41.00	41.00	41.00	41.00	41.00	41.00	41.00	41.00	41.00	41.00	41.00	41.00	41.00
1990	41.00	41.00	41.00	59.00	59.00	58.25	58.00	58.00	58.00	55.50	62.00	70.00	55.06
1991	70.00	63.00	61.50	63.00	63.00	61.50	61.00	61.00	61.00	61.00	61.00	70.00	63.08
1992	70.00	70.00	70.00	76.00	82.00	130.00	130.00	130.00	132.00	131.50	132.00	130.00	106.96
1993	130.00	130.00	130.00	130.00	117.00	130.00	130.00	130.00	107.50	100.00	94.75	93.00	118.52
1994	93.00	79.25	78.00	78.00	78.00	78.00	78.00	78.00	78.00	74.40	60.00	60.00	76.05
1995[1]	60.00	60.00	60.00	60.00	60.00	60.00							60.00

[1] Preliminary. *Source: Economic Research Service, U.S. Department of Agriculture*

Tungsten

Tungsten has unique high-temperature properties that can be used in the production of numerous end-use items. It has a high melting point, high density, good corrosion resistance, and good thermal and electrical conductivity properties. It has excellent wear-resistance and cutting properties. Nearly 60 percent of tungsten is used to produce tungsten carbide. Tungsten carbide is used for cutting tools, mining and drilling tools, dies, bearings and armor-piercing projectiles. Nearly 25 percent of tungsten use is in unalloyed tungsten, which is formed into wire and employed in filaments for incandescent and fluorescent lamps. Tungsten is also used in fireproofing material.

Total reported domestic consumption of tungsten in primary end-use categories increased by about seven percent in 1994 compared to 1993. According to the U.S. Bureau of Mines, demand increased in the cemented carbide end-use sectors that included the combined cutting tool, mining tool, oil drilling equipment, and wear-resistant component industries. Demand for tungsten chemicals and directly usable tungsten scrap also increased in 1994.There was a decrease in demand for mill products made from metal powder and directly reusable tungsten scrap.

Reported U.S. consumption of tungsten concentrate for the January-May 1995 period was 2,950 tonnes. For 1994 the total was 3,630 tonnes. Reported tungsten scrap consumption in the first five months of 1995 was 843 tonnes compared to 2,070 tonnes in 1994. Reported consumption of intermediate products was 4,790 tonnes compared to 7,940 tonnes in 1994.

U.S. imports of tungsten in the first four months of 1995 were 4,450 tonnes. The major suppliers were China and Russia. U.S. exports of tungsten in the January-April 1995 period were 835 tonnes. For all of 1994, exports were 2,490 tonnes. The major markets were Canada, Germany and Japan.

World Concentrate Production of Tungsten In Metric Tons (Contained Tungsten[3])

Year	Australia	Austria	Bolivia	Brazil	Burma	China	Kazakhstan[4]	Mongolia	Peru	Portugal	Rep. of Korea	Russia[4]	World Total
1986	1,600	1,387	1,095	875	715	15,000	------	1,500	742	1,637	2,455	9,200	43,480
1987	1,150	1,250	638	800	493	21,000	------	1,500	205	1,207	2,375	9,200	42,474
1988	1,261	1,235	900	738	307	30,000	------	1,000	432	1,382	2,029	9,200	50,869
1989	1,371	1,517	1,118	679	233	30,200	------	600	970	1,376	1,701	9,300	51,038
1990	1,086	1,378	1,014	316	443	32,000	------	500	1,536	1,410	1,361	8,800	51,900
1991	237	1,314	1,065	223	356	31,800	------	300	1,232	971	780	8,000	48,200
1992	159	1,490	851	205	531	25,000	200	260	802	1,870	247	6,500	40,400
1993[1]	23	104	262	245	524	21,600	150	250	398	1,280	200	5,000	32,000
1994[2]	11		450	250	580	16,500	100	250	800	1,000		4,000	25,500

[1] Preliminary. [2] Estimate. [3] Conversion factors: WO_3 to W, multiply by 0.7931; 60% WO_3 to W, multiply by 0.4758. [4] Formerly part of the U.S.S.R.; data not reported separately until 1992. *Source: U.S. Bureau of Mines*

Salient Statistics of Tungsten in the U.S. In Metric Tons (Contained Tungsten)

Year	Net Import Reliance as a % Apparent Consumption	Total Consumption	Consumption of Tungsten Products by End Uses: Steel: Tool	Steel: Stainless & Heat Assisting	Steel: Alloy Steel[3]	Superalloys	Cutting & Wear Resistant Materials	Products Made from Metal Powder	Miscellaneous	Chemical and Ceramic	Exports	Imports for Consumption	Stocks at End of Year — Concentrates: Consumers	Stocks at End of Year — Concentrates: Producers
1987	79	5,506	306	68	28	212	3,911	W	2,662	41	2	4,414	329	21
1988	86	7,832	317	73	77	279	4,651	2,066	748	84	172	8,045	499	21
1989	84	7,725	258	62	W	258	5,018	1,828	476	52	203	7,896	1,261	10
1990	81	5,878	342	64	74	325	4,985	2,181	464	50	139	6,420	1,077	16
1991	91	5,309	243	44	W	287	4,801	1,941	614	44	21	7,837	1,778	26
1992	86	4,313	407	52	66	25	4,211	1,309	828	W	38	2,477	702	44
1993[1]	82	2,866	388	43	40	282	5,064	1,434	2	37	63	1,721	592	44
1994[2]	94	3,630	529	20	19	300	5,920	1,200	W	108	44	2,960	756	44

[1] Preliminary. [2] Estimate. [3] Other than tool. W = Withheld proprietary data. *Source: U.S. Bureau of Mines*

Tungsten Prices (Monthly Average) In U.S. Dollars

Year	Jan.	Feb.	Mar.	Apr.	May	June	July	Aug.	Sept.	Oct.	Nov.	Dec.	Average
European Market (London), 65% WO_3 Basis, C.I.F.[1] -- $ Per Metric Ton													
1991	44.16	47.75	48.54	53.69	56.38	57.00	57.89	61.25	63.00	63.00	63.00	63.00	56.56
1992	61.50	61.00	61.00	61.00	60.57	59.21	57.50	57.50	55.75	51.67	50.00	45.00	56.81
1993	45.00	42.63	37.50	36.38	33.94	33.00	32.44	27.75	27.89	32.13	33.00	33.00	34.56
1994	29.94	29.94	37.71	35.38	35.38	37.09	38.10	38.10	42.03	45.36	47.63	49.56	38.85
U.S. Spot Quotations, 65% WO_3, Basis C.I.F., U.S. Ports (Including Duty) -- $ Per Short Ton													
1991	39.80	46.00	47.63	57.00	58.00	59.38	61.00	61.70	62.50	62.13	57.00	57.00	55.76
1992	57.00	57.00	56.25	54.40	52.50	50.88	49.50	49.00	49.00	48.10	43.75	43.50	50.91
1993	43.50	43.50	42.00	40.50	40.50	40.50	40.50	35.63	34.00	34.00	34.00	34.00	38.55
1994	37.48	40.79	44.10	44.10	44.10	44.53	47.95	48.50	48.50	48.50	48.50	48.50	45.46

[1] Combined wolframite and scheelite quoations. *Source: U.S. Bureau of Mines*

Turkeys

U.S. turkey production has risen from 4.5 billion pounds in 1990 to an estimated 5.2 billion in 1995. During this period the industry has shifted a larger proportion of retail sales to prepackaged turkey parts and away from whole birds. The additional processing required to cut up and package turkey cuts, such as breast and legs, has increased the supply of edible trimmings, which processors sell in several forms, including mechanically deboned turkey (MDT). Two promising markets for MDT are the export market, and as a relatively low-cost meat protein which can be easily incorporated into sausage and other meat products.

U.S. per capita ready to cook weight turkey consumption reached a record high 18.3 pounds in 1995 versus 18 pounds in 1994. An increase to 19.2 pounds is forecast for 1996. In the mid 1980s per capita use averaged about 12 pounds. There's a time tested seasonality to consumption: the October-December quarter accounts for more than a third of total use, followed by a sharp tapering off in the January-March period. Prices follow a similar pattern, peaking generally in the fourth quarter and trending lower during the first quarter, basis 8-16 pound hens in New York. However, changes in consumer food tastes that favor poultry could have the effect of ironing out, but not changing, turkey's traditional seasonality.

Federally inspected turkey production in 1995 was estimated at a record high 5.2 billion pounds versus 5.0 billion in 1994. An estimated 5.4 billion pounds is forecast for 1996. Attractive net returns to producers during 1995, averaging about five cents per pound, have encouraged production. Good returns are also expected in 1996 despite higher feed costs in late 1995. The Thanksgiving period is a time tested seasonality of strong consumer demand for turkeys prior to which the monthly slaughter averages more than 25 million birds.

Turkey exports soared to an estimated 328 million pounds in 1995, up 17 percent from 280 million in 1994. The turkey export statistics now include the aforementioned MDT which added 34.6 million pounds to the 1994 total. Total exports are forecast at 345 million pounds in 1996, up five percent. The sharp gain in 1995 exports reflected increased shipments to Russia that more than offset lower exports to Mexico, traditionally the largest export market. The bulk of the shipments to Russia were defined as "other prepared or preserved meat, meat offal, or blood of turkey." The average export value of these products going to Russia in 1995 was less than $0.40 a pound.

Wholesale turkey prices during 1995 averaged near $0.65/lb., about unchanged from 1994. Due to the expected large production in 1996, prices are forecast to range between $0.60-0.65/lb.

Turkey Meat Production and Consumption by Selected Countries   In Thous. of Metric Tons (Ready-to-Cook)

	Production								Consumption							
Year	Canada	France	Germany	Israel	Italy	Russia	United Kingdom	United States	Canada	France	Germany	Israel	Italy	Russia	United Kingdom	United States
1990	129	432	145	52	279	54	223	2,048	125	315	208	44	272	92	211	1,992
1991	131	487	149	60	273	45	242	2,088	126	342	240	46	265	75	236	2,060
1992	132	558	159	68	269	37	246	2,167	129	357	272	61	268	72	228	2,086
1993	128	532	169	77	266	35	252	2,176	126	321	280	60	256	39	249	2,090
1994[1]	133	568	183	85	269	30	253	2,239	128	322	294	73	245	44	258	2,126
1995[2]	142	600	188	98	287	28	263	2,321	132	330	300	85	254	53	268	2,208
1996[3]	142	630	193	100	280	25	263	2,423	134	338	305	87	245	50	269	2,306

[1] Preliminary. [2] Estimate. [3] Forecast. *Source: Foreign Agricultural Service, U.S. Department of Agriculture*

Salient Statistics of Turkeys in the U.S.

						Ready-to-Cook-Basis							Wholesale Ready-to-Cook	
			Liveweight						Consumption		Production Costs			
Year	Poults Placed[3] (In Thousands)	Number Raised[4] (In Thousands)	Produced Mil. Lbs.	Price ¢ Per Lb.	Value of Production Million $	Production (Million Pounds)	Beginning Stocks (Million Pounds)	Exports (Million Pounds)	Total (Million Pounds)	Per Capita Lbs.	Feed (Liveweight Basis)	Total (Liveweight Basis)	Production Costs	3-Region Weighted Average Price[5]
1982	184,241	165,464	3,175.1	39.5	1,254.7	2,481	238	51	2,456	10.6	24.50	36.30	60.10	60.87
1983	182,122	170,723	3,335.5	38.0	1,269.1	2,594	204	47	2,585	11.0	26.60	39.80	65.40	60.33
1984	184,238	171,296	3,384.4	48.9	1,654.9	2,606	162	27	2,611	11.0	27.50	41.20	67.60	74.38
1985	198,683	185,427	3,704.0	49.1	1,819.5	2,826	125	27	2,765	11.6	21.40	35.10	60.10	75.56
1986	225,380	207,232	4,147.2	47.0	1,948.4	3,171	150	27	3,101	12.9	21.10	34.80	59.80	73.00
1987	264,228	240,438	4,894.9	34.8	1,703.1	3,745	178	33	3,580	14.7	19.40	33.10	57.60	57.21
1988	261,406	242,421	5,059.1	38.6	1,957.3	3,930	266	51	3,844	15.7	24.60	38.30	64.20	60.69
1989	290,678	261,280	5,465.5	40.9	2,234.4	4,181	250	41	4,109	16.6	26.70	40.40	66.80	65.75
1990	304,863	282,450	6,029.6	39.4	2,378.6	4,567	236	54	4,390	17.6	23.40	37.10	62.60	62.35
1991	308,083	285,110	6,110.7	38.4	2,344.7	4,658	306	103	4,541	18.0	22.72	36.42	61.83	60.79
1992	307,823	288,980	6,333.8	37.7	2,387.7	4,835	264	171	4,599	18.0	23.06	36.76	62.25	60.48
1993	308,871	287,650	6,432.6	39.0	2,509.1	4,798	272	212	4,608	17.9	22.20	35.86	61.12	63.20
1994[1]	317,468	286,605	6,609.8	40.4	2,671.7	4,937	249	246	4,686	18.0	23.80	37.50	63.20	65.90
1995[2]	321,600	292,626				5,241	254	250	4,896	18.6	20.40	34.10	59.00	59.40

[1] Preliminary. [2] Estimate. [3] Poults placed for slaughter by hatcheries. [4] Turkeys placed August1-July 31. [5] Regions include central, eastern and western. Central region receives twice the weight of the other regions in calculating the average. *Source: Economic Research Service, U.S. Department of Agriculture*

TURKEYS

U.S. Basis of Turkey-Feed Price Ratio In Pounds[1]

Year	Jan.	Feb.	Mar.	Apr.	May	June	July	Aug.	Sept.	Oct.	Nov.	Dec.	Average
1984	6.0	5.5	5.3	5.4	5.2	5.3	5.9	6.4	7.0	8.0	8.9	9.6	6.5
1985	7.9	6.5	6.2	6.1	6.2	6.6	7.4	8.5	9.5	10.8	10.7	10.6	8.1
1986	6.3	6.4	6.5	6.7	7.2	8.5	9.9	10.8	11.7	12.6	11.8	9.7	9.0
1987	7.9	8.2	8.0	7.9	7.3	7.0	7.1	7.1	6.8	6.5	6.9	7.5	7.3
1988	6.2	5.5	5.2	5.0	4.9	4.5	5.3	5.6	6.2	6.7	6.7	5.3	5.6
1989	4.8	5.3	5.5	5.9	6.1	6.3	6.1	6.6	6.0	6.4	6.8	6.5	6.0
1990	5.9	5.7	6.1	5.9	6.0	6.2	6.4	6.7	7.0	7.6	7.7	6.7	6.5
1991	6.0	6.3	6.4	6.5	6.7	6.9	7.2	7.1	7.0	6.5	6.4	6.5	6.6
1992	6.0	5.8	6.0	6.0	6.0	6.1	6.5	6.8	6.7	7.1	7.2	7.1	6.4
1993	6.3	6.4	6.6	6.5	6.6	6.7	6.4	6.4	6.9	7.2	6.7	6.1	6.5
1994	5.4	5.4	5.5	5.8	5.9	6.0	7.0	7.4	7.4	7.9	8.0	7.3	6.6
1995[2]	6.7	6.4	6.5	6.4	6.3	6.2	6.0	6.3	6.4	6.3	6.5	5.7	6.3

[1] Pounds of feed equal in value to one pound of turkey, liveweight. [2] Preliminary. *Source: Economic Research Service, U.S. Department of Agriculture*

Average Price Received by Farmers for Turkeys in the United States (Liveweight) In Cents Per Pounds

Year	Jan.	Feb.	Mar.	Apr.	May	June	July	Aug.	Sept.	Oct.	Nov.	Dec.	Average
1984	46.50	40.80	41.20	42.90	42.30	42.00	43.70	45.40	46.70	51.30	56.30	60.00	46.59
1985	50.30	40.50	39.50	39.20	38.50	40.60	44.00	47.50	51.80	56.90	58.40	59.10	47.19
1986	35.60	36.30	36.90	38.10	40.90	45.90	49.30	50.90	51.40	53.00	51.50	43.00	44.40
1987	35.10	35.80	35.70	36.30	35.50	34.10	33.50	32.10	31.30	30.20	34.00	38.40	34.33
1988	32.30	29.70	28.40	28.40	29.80	32.10	40.40	42.00	45.40	48.40	47.90	38.30	36.93
1989	35.50	38.40	40.30	42.00	43.60	43.80	41.20	40.80	36.40	38.20	40.70	39.30	40.02
1990	35.40	33.70	36.40	36.60	38.30	38.70	39.10	40.20	40.30	42.50	42.30	36.90	38.37
1991	33.60	35.10	37.00	37.60	38.30	38.70	39.10	40.10	40.20	37.00	37.00	38.10	37.65
1992	36.30	35.50	37.00	37.00	37.70	37.70	37.90	37.80	37.50	38.50	39.40	39.30	37.63
1993	35.60	35.70	37.60	37.60	37.70	37.60	38.70	39.60	41.10	43.20	42.70	40.80	38.99
1994	37.00	37.30	38.40	39.20	39.90	40.30	40.60	42.10	43.10	44.50	44.30	42.20	40.74
1995[1]	39.30	37.20	38.30	38.30	38.20	39.30	39.80	41.80	43.70	45.30	47.70	44.00	41.08

[1] Preliminary. *Source: Economic Research Service, U.S. Department of Agriculture*

Wholesale Price of Turkeys[1] (Hens, 8-16 Lbs.) N.Y. In Cents Per Pound

Year	Jan.	Feb.	Mar.	Apr.	May	June	July	Aug.	Sept.	Oct.	Nov.	Dec.	Average
1984	72.19	64.72	66.08	66.95	66.85	67.00	68.57	72.42	76.24	82.61	91.49	97.31	74.37
1985	74.05	65.62	67.04	64.62	62.64	68.13	72.84	78.37	82.37	90.20	93.11	86.88	75.49
1986	60.25	61.67	63.94	64.61	67.08	73.83	77.85	80.46	81.21	83.17	80.68	71.11	72.16
1987	55.25	58.47	60.34	58.33	55.26	55.72	56.30	56.14	56.14	54.73	60.73	66.45	57.82
1988	52.79	47.09	47.01	46.90	49.29	57.14	70.82	70.46	76.02	79.64	75.97	61.59	61.23
1989	59.03	62.17	65.71	68.33	72.08	72.98	66.40	62.61	57.88	67.61	72.45	72.70	66.66
1990	55.55	55.16	58.86	59.62	61.27	62.88	63.37	66.57	68.99	76.15	73.70	56.05	63.18
1991	53.49	55.76	59.10	60.32	62.32	62.68	63.41	64.66	64.38	60.52	63.07	65.18	61.24
1992	58.74	55.00	58.77	60.00	60.03	59.46	57.02	57.80	61.02	63.92	65.57	65.14	60.21
1993	58.05	56.83	58.41	58.98	58.81	58.35	59.76	63.43	66.73	71.28	71.76	68.20	62.55
1994	60.09	59.32	60.98	61.58	63.14	64.61	65.26	66.39	68.98	73.13	74.01	70.35	65.65
1995[2]	60.71	58.54	60.04	60.05	60.57	62.76	64.78	68.54	72.92	76.73	80.31	70.35	66.36

[1] Ready-to-cook. [2] Preliminary. *Source: Economic Research Service, U.S. Department of Agriculture*

Certified Federally Inspected Turkey Slaughter in the U.S. (Ready-to-Cook Weights) In Millions of Pounds

Year	Jan.	Feb.	Mar.	Apr.	May	June	July	Aug.	Sept.	Oct.	Nov.	Dec.	Total
1984	138.1	139.0	155.1	163.1	202.6	223.6	242.3	279.6	255.4	320.8	271.7	182.8	2,574
1985	157.7	148.0	176.4	177.3	212.5	238.5	271.1	295.2	288.3	341.5	282.5	210.7	2,800
1986	187.5	175.0	193.6	205.2	236.4	275.8	307.6	299.4	331.4	365.8	307.1	248.2	3,133
1987	215.4	212.8	241.9	255.0	274.1	335.8	358.8	357.4	383.9	411.4	373.5	297.0	3,717
1988	255.7	266.9	314.0	276.6	331.3	373.2	322.4	377.3	365.8	395.7	371.7	272.8	3,923
1989	254.1	248.1	301.3	268.8	356.9	388.6	360.4	430.3	385.7	422.6	423.1	334.9	4,175
1990	334.0	298.3	351.1	328.4	384.1	389.2	395.7	444.0	382.9	478.4	446.2	328.6	4,561
1991	365.6	322.0	329.7	375.8	398.2	380.7	402.2	421.8	404.8	482.0	419.2	349.9	4,652
1992	362.9	331.7	361.3	385.2	374.2	435.0	451.8	411.9	431.3	467.6	423.0	393.1	4,829
1993	354.1	322.7	382.9	391.9	378.7	446.7	419.3	426.9	436.0	451.4	461.8	375.3	4,848
1994	347.8	342.0	400.9	380.6	415.6	457.9	405.6	483.6	447.7	453.6	453.9	397.5	4,992
1995[1]	389.1	371.2	435.0	371.9	443.4	482.1	413.1	451.1	424.0	483.0	466.7	390.6	5,123

[1] Preliminary. *Source: Economic Research Service, U.S. Department of Agriculture*

Turkey Per Capita Consumption in the U.S. In Pounds

Year	Jan.	Feb.	Mar.	Apr.	May	June	July	Aug.	Sept.	Oct.	Nov.	Dec.	Total
1985	.7	.6	.7	.6	.8	.8	.9	.9	1.0	1.3	2.3	1.1	11.6
1986	.7	.7	.9	.7	.8	.9	.9	1.0	1.1	1.4	2.5	1.3	12.9
1987	.8	.8	.9	.9	.9	1.0	1.1	1.1	1.3	1.7	2.8	1.3	14.7
1988	1.0	.9	1.2	.9	1.2	1.3	1.1	1.3	1.4	1.5	2.6	1.3	15.7
1989	1.0	1.0	1.2	.9	1.2	1.1	1.3	1.4	1.5	1.7	2.9	1.4	16.6
1990	1.2	1.1	1.2	1.1	1.3	1.2	1.3	1.5	1.4	1.9	2.9	1.4	17.6
1991	1.4	1.1	1.2	1.3	1.4	1.3	1.3	1.4	1.4	1.9	3.0	1.5	18.0
1992	1.1	1.1	1.2	1.3	1.2	1.3	1.4	1.4	1.4	1.8	3.1	1.6	18.0
1993	1.2	1.0	1.4	1.2	1.2	1.3	1.2	1.3	1.4	1.8	3.2	1.5	17.8
1994	--------	3.5	--------	--------	3.8	--------	--------	4.4	--------	--------	6.1	--------	17.8
1995[1]	--------	3.6	--------	--------	3.9	--------	--------	4.2	--------	--------	6.1	--------	17.8
1996[2]	--------	3.9	--------	--------	3.9	--------	--------	4.3	--------	--------	6.4	--------	18.5

[1] Preliminary. [2] Estimate. *Source: Economic Research Service, U.S. Department of Agriculture*

Storage Stocks of Turkeys (Frozen) in the United States In Millions of Pounds

Year	Jan. 1	Feb. 1	Mar. 1	Apr. 1	May 1	June 1	July 1	Aug. 1	Sept. 1	Oct. 1	Nov. 1	Dec. 1
1984	161.8	161.5	145.8	144.4	142.2	180.9	226.3	278.2	331.3	390.6	415.4	195.7
1985	125.3	124.1	129.5	131.1	157.0	183.7	243.3	304.7	387.8	444.5	484.1	208.2
1986	150.2	159.2	163.6	150.5	188.9	229.5	297.8	388.1	449.3	511.6	543.2	249.0
1987	178.2	198.1	211.4	226.0	250.8	298.1	381.6	472.7	560.0	640.8	629.9	321.5
1988	282.4	281.8	321.5	339.0	370.7	410.1	456.8	496.2	551.9	572.8	583.3	303.5
1989	249.7	262.5	263.1	269.2	298.7	355.6	454.6	496.9	574.3	569.3	571.8	258.6
1990	235.9	268.4	276.3	317.9	354.9	405.6	481.3	541.7	593.1	623.6	625.1	338.4
1991	306.4	302.5	342.2	370.0	408.5	453.4	503.1	571.3	625.8	667.2	653.0	305.5
1992	264.1	325.5	354.1	392.3	430.2	486.8	580.1	662.1	684.2	734.4	714.7	320.5
1993	271.7	314.7	359.8	359.2	424.4	474.0	556.1	624.2	678.6	713.8	683.6	290.6
1994	249.1	279.8	304.8	346.5	399.1	461.4	539.2	288.1	623.4	648.6	636.2	280.7
1995[1]	254.4	317.6	367.5	444.4	480.4	553.4	618.6	673.0	678.2	686.0	644.4	269.1

[1] Preliminary. *Source: Economic Research Service, U.S. Department of Agriculture*

Turkey (Whole) Costs to Selected Retailers in the U.S. In Cents Per Pound

Year	Jan.	Feb.	Mar.	Apr.	May	June	July	Aug.	Sept.	Oct.	Nov.	Dec.	Average
1984	78.40	73.70	74.80	75.20	75.60	75.90	77.00	79.80	83.50	89.30	97.70	104.50	82.12
1985	84.00	75.30	75.90	73.30	71.80	75.90	80.40	84.30	89.50	97.00	99.80	95.90	83.59
1986	72.60	71.10	72.30	72.90	76.30	83.30	86.30	90.00	90.20	92.70	91.90	80.30	81.66
1987	63.80	65.80	67.60	67.00	65.50	65.00	64.70	63.30	64.30	64.30	68.00	75.70	66.25
1988	63.30	58.00	57.60	56.40	57.80	68.30	72.30	78.50	83.30	87.50	84.50	70.40	69.83
1989	67.60	66.90	71.90	75.10	79.40	80.60	74.40	71.80	67.80	73.28	79.80	79.60	74.02
1990	65.20	64.60	67.30	69.40	70.10	70.10	68.70	73.60	76.60	81.90	82.30	66.40	71.35
1991	62.30	63.06	66.61	66.78	69.70	70.00	70.30	72.20	72.80	69.10	70.80	73.90	68.96
1992	67.90	65.80	68.10	68.70	69.24	69.04	65.70	68.10	69.60	72.30	74.00	74.90	69.45
1993	67.85	67.22	67.94	68.80	68.40	68.19	67.08	72.07	74.91	78.37	80.08	75.03	71.33
1994	70.30	69.40	70.60	70.90	72.00	72.58	72.77	74.75	77.32	79.89	83.33	77.34	74.27
1995[1]	69.54	67.08	68.47	68.62	70.05	72.49	74.18	77.77	81.60	84.89	86.50	77.50	74.89

[1] Preliminary. *Source: Economic Research Service, U.S. Department of Agriculture*

Turkey (Whole) Retail-to-Consumer Price Spread in the U.S. In Cents Per Pound

Year	Jan.	Feb.	Mar.	Apr.	May	June	July	Aug.	Sept.	Oct.	Nov.	Dec.	Average
1984	14.3	20.6	20.8	19.1	21.7	23.2	24.3	20.9	18.8	14.5	-0.4	1.5	16.6
1985	25.1	32.0	29.4	31.1	31.2	27.0	23.6	20.1	17.8	10.5	4.4	7.2	21.6
1986	33.7	36.7	32.5	31.3	27.1	19.0	19.3	19.5	21.7	20.2	16.2	21.8	24.9
1987	39.8	37.4	35.4	33.4	37.3	40.1	41.1	41.8	39.0	38.3	22.0	13.6	34.9
1988	29.8	34.9	33.4	33.0	35.1	24.6	23.7	21.0	17.3	16.5	14.7	26.7	25.9
1989	29.8	29.9	25.7	23.2	20.7	20.7	30.2	32.3	34.2	28.9	13.4	15.4	25.4
1990	33.7	33.7	32.1	27.7	29.8	29.7	32.1	27.8	26.7	23.7	8.8	29.6	27.9
1991	37.1	38.1	31.2	33.7	30.9	32.0	32.6	31.2	30.3	34.9	20.8	17.5	30.9
1992	28.2	29.2	27.0	29.4	29.6	29.5	33.3	32.5	31.4	27.2	15.4	18.1	27.5
1993	30.0	31.7	32.6	31.9	32.3	34.5	35.8	29.7	27.7	25.0	13.6	20.4	28.8
1994	27.5	29.7	28.1	25.1	27.1	28.8	28.7	27.6	27.1	25.5	13.9	20.3	25.8
1995[1]	28.5	32.0	33.7	32.1	32.7	32.8	30.8	28.2	27.0	20.1	10.6	21.2	27.5

[1] Preliminary. *Source: Economic Research Service, U.S. Department of Agriculture*

Uranium

The future of uranium dioxide use in the U.S. continues to be clouded by public resistance to the development and use of nuclear power facilities. The major uses for uranium are for power generation as well as in military weapons. Both of these areas are likely to show steady or reduced usage. Both the U.S. and the former Soviet Union are in the process of dismantling their nuclear arsenals. Other former states of the Soviet Union, such as the Ukraine, are expected to join the process. This has proven to be a technically difficult and very expensive undertaking. Part of the plan is for Russia to take highly enriched uranium removed from nuclear weapons and dilute it to produce low-enriched uranium for use by American nuclear power plants.

For the U.S., the Energy Information Administration reports that in 1994 mine production of U3O8 was 2.5 million pounds, up from two million pounds in 1993. In 1992 mine production fell to a low of one million pounds. As recently as 1989, production was 9.7 million pounds. Uranium concentrate production in 1994 was 3.4 million pounds, some 300,000 pounds more than in 1993. U3O8 concentrate production is far below the levels seen between 1986 and 1989 when annual production averaged 13.4 million pounds, peaking in 1989 when it reached 13.8 million.

Uranium concentrate shipments in 1994 were 6.3 million pounds, up close to 90 percent from the 1993 shipment total of 3.4 million pounds. The recent peak in uranium concentrate shipments was in 1989 at 14.8 million pounds.

Deliveries of uranium from suppliers to U.S. utilities under domestic purchases in 1994 was 22.7 million pounds, up 46 percent from the 1993 total of 15.5 million pounds. Foreign purchase contracts or imports in 1994 were 36.6 million pounds, up 74 percent from the 1993 level of 21 million pounds.

Uranium prices have been declining for many years. In January 1980, the price of uranium averaged about $42 per pound. In 1994, the average price of delivered uranium was $10.30 per pound, down sharply from $13.14 in 1993. In 1985, the average price was $31.43 per pound. The average price for delivered uranium under foreign purchases was $8.95 per pound, down from $10.53 the year before. Export sales of delivered uranium in 1994 totaled 18 million pounds, up sharply from the 1993 total of three million pounds.

Commercial inventories of U3O8 at the end of 1994 were 86.3 million pounds, down 18 percent from the 1993 stocks of 105.7 million pounds. At year-end 1985, commercial inventories were 176.9 million pounds, while at the end of 1990 they were 129.1 million pounds.

Utility stocks of natural uranium at the end of 1994 were 42.5 million pounds, down 27 percent from the 1993 year-end stocks of 57.9 million pounds. Utility stocks of enriched uranium at the end of 1994 were 24.2 million pounds, up from 23.3 million in 1993.

Domestic supplier stocks of natural uranium at end of year 1994 were 15.5 million pounds, down from 19.1 million at the end of 1993. Enriched uranium stocks were four million pounds.

Canada's Rio Algom Ltd. reported in the summer of 1995 that it would close the Stanleigh uranium mine in Elliot Lake, Ontario on June 30 1996. This date will mark the conclusion of deliveries of uranium under a contract with Ontario Hydro. The mine still has ample reserves to continue operations but the ore is of low grade and cannot compete with the more cost-effective Saskatchewan uranium mines.

World Production of Uranium Oxide (U_3O_8) Concentrate In Short Tons (Uranium Content)

Year	Australia	Canada	China	Czech Rep. & Slovakia	France	Gabon	Germany	India	Namibia	Niger	South Africa	Spain	United States	Former U.S.S.R.	World Total
1985	4,200	14,150	NA	NA	4,150	1,200	NA	NA	4,400	4,150	6,350	NA	5,550	NA	45,150
1986	5,400	15,250	NA	NA	4,250	1,100	NA	NA	4,500	4,100	6,000	NA	6,550	NA	48,200
1987	4,902	16,127	NA	NA	4,377	1,030	26	164	4,590	3,848	5,219	322	6,500	NA	47,745
1988	4,580	15,646	NA	NA	4,377	1,194	58	194	4,551	3,845	5,039	348	6,500	NA	46,846
1989	4,752	14,855	1,039	2,989	4,183	1,157	4,961	273	4,000	3,874	3,810	229	6,919	18,849	75,264
1990	4,589	11,400	1,039	2,600	3,661	922	3,864	273	4,030	3,682	3,169	213	4,443	18,199	64,642
1991	4,909	10,609	1,039	2,340	3,204	882	1,569	260	3,185	3,853	2,248	254	3,975	13,650	53,458
1992[1]	3,032	12,087	1,039	2,040	2,755	702	325	299	2,199	3,855	2,449	241	2,822	11,205	46,124
1993[2]	2,949	11,990	1,300	911	2,220	769	195	260	2,168	3,786	2,261	238	2,587	10,491	43,027

[1] Preliminary. [2] Estimate. NA = Not available. *Source: American Bureau of Metal Statistics, Inc.*

Month-End Uranium (U_3O_8) Transaction Values[1] In Dollars Per Pound

Year	Jan.	Feb.	Mar.	Apr.	May	June	July	Aug.	Sept.	Oct.	Nov.	Dec.	Average
1985	16.20	15.70	15.05	14.90	14.45	14.60	14.75	15.10	15.10	15.75	15.80	16.55	15.33
1986	16.55	16.70	16.70	17.10	17.15	17.20	17.50	17.45	17.35	17.25	17.30	17.35	17.13
1987	17.35	16.90	16.95	17.00	17.20	17.10	17.30	17.55	18.20	18.05	17.80	17.20	17.38
1988	16.85	16.65	16.55	16.45	16.10	15.80	15.45	15.00	14.50	14.40	13.30	12.50	15.30
1989	12.25	12.00	11.25	11.00	10.75	10.45	9.95	9.80	9.80	9.65	9.55	9.40	10.49
1990	9.25	9.05	8.75	8.65	8.55	8.80	9.75	10.80	11.40	10.10	9.30	9.15	9.46
1991	9.40	9.45	9.35	9.30	9.30	9.20	9.15	8.95	8.70	8.35	7.45	7.50	8.84
1992	7.55	7.80	7.95	7.90	7.85	7.80	7.75	7.85	7.95	8.40	8.55	8.75	8.01
1993	8.80	8.60	8.80	9.20	8.70	8.90	8.20	8.80	9.05	8.45	8.60	-----	8.74

[1] Transaction value is a weighted average price of recent natural uranium sales transactions, based on prices paid on transactions closed within the previous 3-month period for which delivery is scheduled within one year of the transaction date; at least 10 transactions involving a sum total of at least 2 million pounds of U_3O_8 equivalent. *Source: American Metal Market*

Reported Average Price Settlements for Purchases by U.S. Utilities and Domestic Suppliers In $ Per Lb.[2]

Year of Delivery	Contract Price	Market Price[1]	Price & Cost Floor	Total	Contract & Market	Year of Delivery	Contract Price	Market Price[1]	Price & Cost Floor	Total	Contract & Market
	Averages of Reported Prices						Averages of Reported Prices				
1983	39.90	24.05	50.67	36.18	38.21	1989	20.87	11.48	22.50	15.42	19.56
1984	33.60	16.87	44.71	31.88	32.65	1990	17.94	9.18	19.40	11.65	15.70
1985	34.74	15.46	35.62	27.15	31.43	1991	13.94	9.04	21.84	12.62	13.66
1986	32.58	16.93	41.06	27.39	30.01	1992	13.16	8.65	18.35	13.89	13.45
1987	29.16	17.53	34.34	22.85	27.37	1993	14.96	9.57	14.87	11.03	13.14
1988	28.20	16.12	33.52	21.59	26.15	1994	10.68	9.76	20.03	10.57	10.63

[1] No floor. [2] U_3O_8 equivalent. Note: Price excludes uranium delivered under litigation settlements. Price is given in year-of-delivery dollars.
Source: Energy Information Adminstration, U.S. Department of Energy

U.S. Uranium Industry Statistics In Millions of Pounds U_3O_8

Year	Production: Mine	Production: Concentrate	Concentrate Shipments	Employment – Person Years: Exploration	Mining	Milling	Processing	Total[1]	Deliveries to U.S. Utilities[2]	Avg. Price Delivered Uranium $/lb. U_3O_8	Imports	Avg. Price Delivered Uranium Imports $/lb. U_3O_8	Exports
1985	8.6	11.314	11.760	163	1,212	514	557	2,446	21.7	31.43	11.7	20.08	5.3
1986	8.3	13.500	10.641	162	954	513	490	2,120	18.9	30.01	14.4	20.07	1.6
1987	6.0	12.991	11.558	183	819	432	568	2,002	20.8	27.37	15.9	19.14	1.0
1988	9.5	13.130	12.791	144	849	572	576	2,141	17.6	26.15	17.0	19.03	4.3
1989	9.7	13.837	14.808	86	659	367	471	1,583	18.4	19.56	13.7	16.75	2.5
1990	5.9	8.885	12.957	73	664	304	293	1,335	20.5	15.70	26.6	12.55	2.4
1991	5.2	7.952	8.437	52	411	191	361	1,016	26.8	13.66	23.1	15.55	3.5
1992	1.0	5.645	6.853	51	219	129	283	682	23.4	13.45	45.4	11.34	20.9
1993	2.0	3.063	3.374	36	133	65	145	380	15.5	13.14	41.9	10.53	21.3
1994	2.5	3.352	6.319	41	157	105	149	452	22.7	10.30	57.6	8.95	46.9

[1] Does not include 491 person years in 1993 and 528 person years in 1994 for employment in reclamation work. [2] From suppliers under domestic purchases.
Source: Energy Information Administration, U.S. Department of Energy

Commercial and U.S. Government Stocks of Uranium, End of Year In Millions of Pounds U_3O_8 Equivalent

Year	Utility: Natural Uranium	Utility: Enriched Uranium[1]	Domestic Supplier: Natural Uranium	Domestic Supplier: Enriched Uranium[1]	Total Commercial Stocks	DOE-Owned & USEC-Held: Natural Uranium	DOE-Owned & USEC-Held: Enriched Uranium
1990	61.5	41.2	22.0	4.4	129.1	59.8	32.8
1991	70.9	27.1	18.7	2.0	118.7	46.8	36.7
1992	66.5	25.5	19.1	6.1	117.3	45.8	23.1
1993	57.9	23.3	19.1	5.4	105.7	52.4	26.9
1994	42.5	24.2	15.5	4.0	86.3	53.8	20.5

[1] Includes amount reported as UF_6 at enrichment suppliers. DOE = Department of Energy USEC = U.S. Energy Commission.
Source: Energy Information Administration, U.S. Department of Energy

Vanadium

Vanadium is used in the production of carbon and alloy steels and plates, structural bar, and pipe steels. It is commercially important as an oxidation catalyst. Vanadium finds uses in ceramics as a coloring agent, enhances strength and toughness, and can be used in tools. Ferrovanadium is an iron alloy used in steel. Vanadium pentoxide finds use in dyeing and printing applications. Vanadium is critical in the production of aerospace titanium alloys and as a catalyst in the production of maleic anhydride and sulfuric acid.

According to the U.S. Bureau of Mines, total reported consumption of vanadium in June 1995 rose 18 percent from consumption in May to 386,000 kilograms. This was also about 27 percent more than the consumption in June 1994. Small to moderate decreases in the full alloy, tool, and superalloy end use categories were more than offset by small to large increases in the carbon, stainless and heat-resisting, and high strength, low-alloy, end use categories. In June 1995, vanadium consumption for ferrovanadium was 358,000 kilograms, up from 300,000 kilograms in May. Consumption of vanadium oxide was 1,120 kilograms. Stocks of ferrovanadium in June 1995 were 334,000 kilograms. Total vanadium stocks were 363,000 kilograms.

In terms of vanadium consumption by end use category in June 1995 steel consumed 354,000 kilograms, while over the January-June 1995 period steel used 1.94 million kilograms of vanadium. Carbon steel production used 40 percent, stainless and heat-resisting steel less than 1 percent, full alloy steel 22 percent, high-strength low alloy steel 28 percent, tool steel 10 percent, and unspecified steel the remainder.

Vanadium also finds use in other areas. These include cast irons, superalloys, as well as chemical and ceramic uses. Total use of vanadium in the January-June 1994 period was 2.13 million kilograms. For all of 1994, use was 3.94 million kilograms.

In the January-May 1995 period, U.S. exports of aluminum-vanadium master alloy were 423,000 kilograms with the major export markets being Mexico and Canada. Ferrovanadium exports were 143,000 kilograms with 108,000 kilograms shipped to Canada. Vanadium pentoxide exports were 38,800 kilograms with Germany taking 24,300 kilograms. Other vanadium oxides and hydroxides were 419,000 kilograms, most of which was exported to Canada. Vanadium metal exports, including waste and scrap, were 73,700 kilograms as the United Kingdom took 52,000 kilograms and Ireland 16,800.

Over the January-May 1995 period, U.S. imports of ferrovanadium were 972,000 kilograms, vanadium pentoxide imports were 328,000 kilograms, and vanadium metal imports were 466,000 kilograms.

World Production of Vanadium by Country In Metric Tons (Contained Vanadium)

	From Ores, Concentrates and Slag						From Petroleum Residues, Ash, Spent Catalysts			
			Republic of South Africa							
Year	China[3]	Russia[4]	Content of Pentoxide & Vanadate Products	Content of Vanadiferous Slag Product	Total	Total[5]	Japan[6]	United States[7]	Total	World Grand Total
1986	4,500	9,600	5,761	9,600	15,361	29,461	843	2,114	2,957	32,418
1987	4,500	9,600	5,842	10,100	15,942	30,042	728	2,275	3,003	33,045
1988	4,500	9,600	6,330	11,300	17,631	31,731	728	2,950	3,678	35,409
1989	4,500	9,600	7,270	11,300	18,567	32,967	868	2,389	3,257	36,224
1990	4,500	9,000	7,100	10,000	17,106	33,900	700	2,308	3,008	36,900
1991	4,500	8,500	6,500	8,460	14,962	31,700	404	2,250	2,650	34,300
1992	4,700	11,000	6,300	7,730	14,033	29,900	245	1,347	1,590	31,500
1993[1]	5,000	10,000	8,400	6,650	15,100	30,300	252	2,867	3,120	33,400
1994[2]	5,000	10,000	8,600	7,100	15,700	30,900	300	2,740	3,040	33,900

[1] Preliminary. [2] Estimate. [3] In vanadiferous slag product. [4] Formerly part of the U.S.S.R.; data not reported separately until 1992. [5] Excludes U.S. production. [6] In vanadium pentoxide products. [7] In vandium pentoxide and ferrovandium products. *Source: U.S. Bureau of Mines*

Salient Statistics of Vanadium In Metric Tons (Contained Vanadium)

		Vanadium Consumption by Uses in U.S.								Exports			Imports			
Year	Consumer & Producer Stocks, Dec. 31	Tool Steel	Cast Irons	Hign Strength, Low Alloy	Stainless & Heat Resisting	Superalloys	Carbon	Full Alloy	Total	Average $ Per Lb. V_2O_5	Vanadium Pentoxide, Anhydride	Oxides & Hydroxides	Ferrovanadium	Ores, Slag, Residues	Vanadium Pentoxide, Anhydride	Oxides & Hydroxides	Ferrovanadium
1987	2,057	422	23	1,212	59	9	1,086	740	4,221	3.50	742	-----	311	2,054	207	-----	310
1988	1,266	481	20	1,339	41	9	1,259	887	4,834	3.40	620	-----	462	2,025	219	-----	108
1989	1,736	420	18	1,225	96	38	1,103	898	4,646	6.17	1,171	1,080	399	4,210	133	106	527
1990	1,082	421	18	1,122	38	42	994	814	4,081	4.21	819	976	271	3,826	83	217	244
1991	935	242	15	919	37	14	919	739	3,293	2.85	700	1,110	94	882	133	110	420
1992	1,084	453	17	989	28	13	1,262	828	4,079	2.28	26	1,113	213	838	206	103	592
1993[1]	900	373	21	981	33	13	1,413	789	3,973	1.45	126	895	219	1,454	70	19	1,630
1994[2]	1,000	424	31	979	26	16	1,680	777	4,290	1.55	335	1,050	374	1,900	294	3	1,910

[1] Preliminary. [2] Estimate. W = Withheld proprietary data. *Source: U.S. Bureau of Mines*

Vegetables

According to the USDA, 1994 U.S. vegetable production (including potatoes, sweet potatoes and dry beans) increased ten percent from 1993. Production of fresh-market vegetables and melons increased just one percent, while output of vegetables for processing was up 22 percent, potatoes were up seven percent, dry edible beans were up 33 percent, and sweet potatoes were up 21 percent.

USDA noted that there was a record-large processing vegetable crop of over 18 million tons which was a result of increased acreage and yields. For the 13 processing vegetable crops, ten increased while production declines were seen in asparagus, carrots and cauliflower. There were record yields and production for processing sweet corn and tomatoes. Sweet corn production was the result of a 26 percent increase in yields to a record 7.2 tons per acre. Tomato acreage rose 14 percent and yields were up six percent. The USDA estimates that about 85 percent of processing vegetable production is canned.

For 1995, U.S. fresh tomato production was estimated at 3.4 billion pounds, down six percent from 1994. Fresh head lettuce production in 1995 was estimated at 5.97 billion pounds, down five percent. Fresh onion production was put at 2.05 billion pounds, down three percent. Per capita use was estimated at 7.5 pounds. Fresh carrot production in 1995 was 1.98 billion pounds, down five percent. Per capita consumption was estimated at 7.4 pounds. Fresh celery production was forecast at 1.9 billion pounds, down five percent. Per capita use was estimated at 6.5 pounds. Fresh cabbage production was estimated at 2.58 billion pounds, about the same as last season. Per capita consumption of cabbage was 9.7 pounds.

Commercial and Fresh Vegetables: Index of Prices Received by U.S. Growers

Year	Jan.	Feb.	Mar.	Apr.	May	June	July	Aug.	Sept.	Oct.	Nov.	Dec.	Annual
					Commercial[1]		1990-92 = 100						
1989	122	107	103	112	101	100	111	99	95	100	90	99	103
1990	135	122	92	81	89	89	94	98	102	111	114	100	102
1991	95	84	114	107	131	109	91	88	90	88	109	88	100
1992	97	118	144	106	93	94	102	113	115	125	109	121	111
1993	119	125	108	164	126	100	105	109	112	95	102	124	116
1994	111	108	91	86	96	103	97	94	103	116	121	161	107
1995[2]	125	114	156	176	148	117	93	98	115	103			
						Fresh[3]	1982 = 100						
1989	93	120	111	107	140	117	111	96	82	101	84	88	104
1990	164	203	137	75	78	84	93	79	79	96	118	87	108
1991	89	87	88	113	157	138	102	83	82	74	113	76	100
1992	118	155	148	100	90	81	86	115	115	149	108	133	117
1993	129	126	117	179	164	81	98	111	117	90	141	167	127
1994	146	99	96	91	91	95	105	96	107	114	128	245	118
1995[2]	164	149	159	199	167	127	107	95	153	114	116	126	140

Indexes are not seasonally adjusted. [1] Includes fresh and processing vegetable. [2] Preliminary. [3] Producer Price Index (0113-02).
Source: National Agricultural Statistics Service, U.S. Department of Agriculture

U.S. Processed Vegetables: Monthly Producer Price Index 1982 = 100

Year	Jan.	Feb.	Mar.	Apr.	May	June	July	Aug.	Sept.	Oct.	Nov.	Dec.	Annual
						Canned[1] (0244)							
1989	118.7	119.7	119.8	119.4	119.1	118.6	118.9	118.8	118.9	118.0	117.8	118.0	118.8
1990	117.9	117.8	118.0	118.8	118.2	118.5	116.5	115.2	115.4	114.4	114.9	114.0	116.6
1991	114.8	114.8	115.1	113.8	114.0	113.3	114.0	112.2	110.9	111.2	110.1	109.8	112.8
1992	110.3	109.7	109.3	108.9	109.8	109.4	109.5	109.6	109.2	109.1	109.5	109.8	109.5
1993	110.1	109.8	109.7	109.1	108.8	109.9	111.1	109.6	110.4	111.5	112.3	112.6	110.4
1994	113.1	116.1	116.8	116.5	117.9	118.0	118.9	118.1	116.0	116.0	114.2	113.1	116.2
1995[2]	112.6	114.3	114.9	113.1	117.6	117.4	118.6	117.5	117.6	117.7	118.7	119.5	116.6
						Frozen (0245)							
1989	113.1	114.3	114.8	115.3	115.3	115.7	115.5	116.2	116.2	115.3	116.4	117.0	115.4
1990	117.6	117.9	118.4	118.9	120.1	117.6	118.1	118.3	118.5	118.6	118.6	119.0	118.5
1991	118.4	118.5	118.3	117.9	118.1	117.5	117.8	117.2	117.4	116.6	116.5	116.8	117.6
1992	116.6	116.1	116.2	116.4	116.3	115.5	115.4	115.4	116.7	116.3	117.5	118.0	116.4
1993	118.0	118.0	117.9	118.7	119.9	121.1	121.3	122.1	122.6	123.2	123.7	125.4	121.0
1994	125.5	126.1	126.1	126.4	126.9	127.0	126.4	126.4	125.2	124.9	124.7	125.0	125.9
1995[2]	125.1	124.8	124.9	124.9	124.2	123.6	123.1	123.6	124.4	124.9	123.7	124.1	124.3

[1] Includes canned vegetables and juices, including hominy and mushrooms. [2] Preliminary. *Source: Bureau of Labor Statistics, U.S. Department of Labor*

VEGETABLES

U.S. Per Capita Use of Selected Commercially Produced Fresh and Processing Vegetables

Pounds, Farm Weight Basis

Crop	1985	1986	1987	1988	1989	1990	1991	1992	1993	1994[9]	1995[10]
Asparagus, all	.9	1.0	1.0	1.0	1.0	1.0	1.0	1.0	1.0	.9	1.0
Fresh	.3	.3	.6	.6	.6	.6	.6	.6	.6	.6	.6
Canning	.3	.3	.3	.3	.3	.3	.3	.3	.3	.2	.3
Freezing	.1	.1	.1	.1	.1	.1	.1	.1	.1	.1	.1
Snap Beans, all	7.0	6.7	6.7	6.7	7.1	6.7	7.0	7.2	7.3	7.4	7.4
Fresh	1.3	1.3	1.2	1.2	1.2	1.1	1.1	1.5	1.5	1.5	1.5
Canning	3.8	3.9	3.8	3.8	3.9	3.7	4.1	4.0	4.0	3.9	3.9
Freezing	1.9	1.5	1.7	1.7	2.0	1.9	1.8	1.7	1.8	2.0	2.0
Broccoli, all[1]	4.5	4.7	5.3	6.2	6.0	5.6	5.4	5.8	5.2	5.1	5.0
Fresh	2.6	3.0	3.1	3.8	3.8	3.4	3.1	3.4	2.9	2.8	2.7
Freezing	1.9	1.7	2.2	2.4	2.2	2.2	2.3	2.4	2.3	2.3	2.3
Carrots, all[2]	9.7	9.5	11.4	10.5	11.5	11.6	11.4	11.9	12.6	11.7	11.1
Fresh	6.5	6.5	8.3	7.1	8.1	8.3	7.7	8.3	8.2	7.9	7.4
Canning	.9	.8	.8	.9	.9	.9	1.0	1.0	1.2	1.0	1.0
Freezing	2.3	2.2	2.3	2.5	2.5	2.4	2.7	2.6	3.2	2.8	2.7
Cauliflower, all[1]	2.7	3.1	3.0	3.1	3.1	3.0	2.6	2.5	2.4	2.0	1.8
Fresh	1.8	2.2	2.1	2.2	2.3	2.2	2.0	1.8	1.7	1.4	1.2
Freezing	.9	.9	.9	.9	.8	.8	.6	.7	.7	.6	.6
Celery, fresh	7.0	6.6	6.6	7.2	7.5	7.2	6.8	7.4	7.1	6.8	6.5
Sweet Corn, all[3]	26.2	25.8	24.7	24.9	24.4	26.3	26.4	27.8	28.0	27.0	28.0
Fresh	6.4	6.1	6.3	5.8	6.5	6.7	5.9	6.9	7.0	7.8	7.5
Canning	11.9	12.1	10.6	10.4	9.5	11.0	11.1	11.9	11.2	10.0	10.7
Freezing	7.9	7.6	7.8	8.7	8.4	8.6	9.4	9.0	9.8	9.2	9.8
Cucumbers, all	10.2	9.9	10.6	10.1	10.0	9.7	9.7	9.6	9.7	9.9	10.0
Fresh	4.4	4.6	5.1	4.8	4.8	4.7	4.6	5.0	5.3	5.3	5.3
Pickles	5.8	5.3	5.5	5.3	5.2	5.0	5.1	4.6	4.4	4.6	4.7
Melons	24.1	24.6	24.3	23.8	26.5	24.6	23.4	24.5	25.0	26.0	25.4
Watermelon	13.5	12.8	13.0	13.5	13.6	13.3	12.8	14.8	14.6	15.4	14.7
Cantaloupe	8.5	9.4	9.1	7.9	10.4	9.2	8.7	8.5	8.7	8.8	8.8
Honeydew	2.1	2.4	2.2	2.4	2.5	2.1	1.9	2.1	1.7	1.8	1.9
Lettuce, Head	23.7	21.9	25.7	27.0	28.8	27.8	26.1	25.9	24.6	22.5	21.2
Onions, all	15.2	15.6	14.9	16.2	16.4	17.1	17.3	17.6	18.1	17.5	18.2
Fresh	13.6	13.7	13.4	14.5	14.8	15.1	15.7	16.2	16.0	16.5	16.7
Green peas, all[4]	4.2	4.1	3.7	3.7	3.7	4.2	4.2	4.1	3.5	3.6	3.7
Canning	2.1	2.2	2.0	1.8	1.7	2.0	1.9	2.1	1.6	1.5	1.6
Freezing	2.1	1.9	1.7	1.9	2.0	2.2	2.3	2.0	1.9	2.1	2.1
Tomatoes, all	78.2	79.5	81.0	78.1	86.2	90.9	92.8	89.2	92.4	90.9	94.1
Fresh	15.0	15.9	15.8	16.8	16.8	15.5	15.4	15.5	16.0	15.7	15.1
Canning	63.2	63.6	65.2	61.3	69.4	75.4	77.4	73.7	76.4	75.2	79.0
Subtotal, all[8]	242.9	241.3	247.5	248.4	262.9	266.9	266.3	271.3	274.5	268.0	270.5
Fresh	126.4	125.2	131.3	134.4	141.8	137.5	133.3	141.5	141.2	140.0	136.0
Canning	95.3	95.6	95.5	91.2	98.7	107.0	109.6	107.3	108.3	105.4	110.5
Freezing	19.6	18.6	19.3	21.1	20.8	20.4	21.8	21.1	22.9	21.6	22.5
Potatoes, all	122.4	126.0	126.0	122.4	127.1	127.7	130.4	132.4	137.0	140.7	139.3
Fresh	46.3	48.8	47.9	49.6	50.0	45.8	46.4	48.9	49.9	50.1	49.2
Processing	76.1	77.2	78.1	72.8	77.1	81.9	84.0	83.5	87.1	90.6	90.1
Sweetpotatoes, all	5.4	4.4	4.4	4.1	4.1	4.6	4.0	4.3	3.9	4.7	4.4
Total, all items	381.9	382.8	387.1	385.9	403.9	410.0	412.1	419.7	427.1	425.2	426.4

[1] All production for processing broccoli and cauliflower is for freezing. [2] Industry allocation suggests that 27% of processing carrot production is for canning and 73% is for freezing. [3] On-cob basis. [4] In-shell basis. [5] Includes artichokes, brussel sprouts, eggplant, endive/excarole, garlic, radishes and spinach. [6] Includes beets, chile peppers and spinach. [7] Includes green lima beans, spinach and miscellaneous freezing vegetables. [8] Fresch, canning and freezing data do not add to the total because onions are for dehydrating are included in total. [9] Preliminary. [10] Forecast. *Source: Economic Research Service, U.S. Department of Agriculture*

Fresh Vegetables: Average Prices Received by U.S. Growers Dollars Per Cwt.

Year	Jan.	Feb.	Mar.	Apr.	May	June	July	Aug.	Sept.	Oct.	Nov.	Dec.	Season Average
Broccoli													
1993	32.60	28.10	28.60	23.70	22.30	26.80	24.50	20.00	36.60	22.40	24.20	30.00	26.60
1994	23.50	21.40	19.50	21.80	27.10	21.10	21.60	18.50	38.60	37.00	57.70	46.00	31.60
1995[1]	26.60	35.00	54.10	33.90	26.50	27.30	19.50	34.10	27.70	25.70			31.04
Carrots													
1993	18.00	13.20	11.20	12.70	11.20	10.20	9.04	10.10	9.98	10.30	11.00	10.90	11.90
1994	10.70	10.50	11.50	10.30	12.10	12.10	13.60	16.40	15.30	15.50	15.10	15.60	13.20
1995[1]	19.50	16.80	19.20	20.10	19.70	15.20	14.60	15.90	15.10	14.90			17.10
Cauliflower													
1993	34.30	29.10	24.70	44.90	26.90	37.00	28.30	29.30	38.70	27.40	21.60	30.90	31.20
1994	24.80	24.90	23.10	20.80	32.30	29.10	32.00	24.20	34.20	31.30	42.50	30.10	29.60
1995[1]	32.00	33.30	53.80	68.10	47.70	37.60	26.90	34.20	25.40	21.90			38.09
Celery													
1993	24.00	35.60	27.40	16.50	14.40	9.45	9.41	11.80	14.20	13.30	11.50	11.10	14.80
1994	11.40	8.85	7.78	8.34	13.50	8.92	12.40	14.90	12.60	12.00	13.90	25.50	11.80
1995[1]	24.30	25.80	20.20	30.70	23.80	15.40	11.30	11.00	15.90	12.80			19.12
Corn, Sweet													
1993	23.30	39.20	25.20	23.50	20.60	17.70	18.50	16.80	14.70	22.10	16.60	24.30	17.80
1994	26.80	17.60	26.40	17.90	22.00	22.40	19.00	14.40	15.60	21.30	21.50	35.10	17.70
1995[1]	32.20	43.60	28.30	15.70	15.00	15.40	17.40	15.20	19.00	19.00			22.08
Lettuce, Head													
1993	10.80	18.70	14.30	37.80	12.60	11.50	18.80	14.90	16.80	12.20	10.50	8.28	16.00
1994	8.05	11.60	9.69	11.60	11.40	13.90	10.40	11.00	17.00	22.30	22.10	37.50	13.00
1995[1]	13.50	9.44	29.30	49.20	48.50	15.60	12.50	16.50	25.90	17.00			23.74
Tomatoes													
1993	38.30	21.90	21.20	45.20	58.10	22.90	23.30	32.70	29.80	19.40	31.60	57.60	31.70
1994	41.50	19.30	24.50	16.50	20.70	30.70	28.20	29.20	23.20	28.30	30.90	37.20	27.20
1995[1]	41.60	27.00	43.80	20.50	14.40	33.30	20.50	14.90	18.40	23.40			25.78

[1] Preliminary. *Source: National Agricultural Statistics Service, U.S. Department of Agriculture*

Frozen Vegetables: January 1 & July 1 Cold Storage Holdings In Thousands of Pounds

	1991	1992		1993		1994		1995		1996[1]
Crop	July 1	Jan. 1	July 1	Jan. 1	July 1	Jan. 1	July 1	Jan. 1	July 1	Jan. 1
Asparagus	19,990	9,673	17,597	7,791	22,307	14,782	19,175	9,808	15,493	9,689
Lima Beans	60,760	100,392	49,264	65,047	26,164	49,594	24,093	59,440	29,783	60,208
Snap Beans	113,486	248,737	116,360	190,465	73,907	184,418	71,457	244,681	87,436	224,297
Broccoli	137,670	88,286	150,460	143,486	194,061	134,774	152,312	109,076	110,075	136,850
Brussels sprouts	20,856	22,216	13,000	26,467	12,029	34,338	20,166	30,191	18,181	18,883
Carrots	109,649	203,637	99,743	254,040	176,830	260,993	165,748	271,244	176,054	307,645
Cauliflower	56,277	88,234	40,636	71,135	32,461	60,683	40,077	77,243	49,561	65,008
Corn, Sweet[2]	233,433	470,816	285,023	489,019	239,379	493,411	119,206	645,985	199,148	648,994
Mixed vegetables	59,383	57,422	53,945	47,721	42,013	44,916	51,737	58,272	59,414	60,492
Okra	21,087	51,643	33,548	44,679	18,387	16,341	31,799	62,491	43,367	39,954
Onions	31,049	32,137	27,829	34,230	24,787	36,101	31,296	51,244	42,810	48,761
Black-eyed peas	13,449	19,416	7,323	12,559	4,636	9,605	3,159	13,157	3,145	9,994
Green peas	220,022	272,691	229,461	305,164	177,245	261,338	218,032	260,487	219,669	281,349
Peas and carrots	6,730	6,583	8,228	6,921	7,506	15,363	14,063	9,329	9,034	10,401
Spinach	107,268	53,293	83,863	56,182	79,337	47,159	120,542	70,010	100,274	68,940
Squash	48,804	50,618	43,597	54,708	40,941	61,679	53,763	64,533	39,494	57,785
Southern greens	31,462	27,496	21,458	27,173	22,251	31,786	29,194	29,993	30,079	21,659
Other vegetables	192,357	274,768	216,709	295,028	211,523	258,611	238,554	241,252	189,124	319,519
Total	1,483,732	2,243,853	1,498,044	2,300,040	1,405,764	2,015,892	1,404,373	2,288,336	1,422,141	2,390,428
Potatoes	1,213,532	970,012	1,131,381	963,167	989,818	1,006,416	1,099,850	1,083,747	1,116,454	1,123,744
Grand total	2,697,264	3,213,865	2,629,425	3,263,207	2,395,582	3,022,308	2,504,223	3,372,083	2,538,595	3,514,172

[1] Preliminary. [2] Cut-basis with cob corn converted to cut-basis using a factor of 0.4706. *Source: National Agricultural Statistics Service, U.S. Department of Agriculture*

Wheat

World wheat production in 1995/96 of 535 million metric tons was eight million tons lower than initially expected, but were it not for a large increase in India's crop the world total may have dipped under 530 million tons. Production in 1994/95 totaled 523 million tons. World consumption was forecast at 550 million tons, marginally higher than in 1994/95. Assuming the 1995/96 supply/demand totals are realized, world stocks at the end of the season would fall to 98.5 million tons versus 114 million a year earlier. The projected stocks-to-usage ratio of 17.9 percent was the lowest on record, but a shade higher than initially forecast. World wheat production trended irregularly higher since the mid-1980s, totaling a shade under 500 million tons in 1985/86 and a record high 588 million in 1990/91, but carryover stocks trended lower. The major unsettling factor in wheat's statistical setting during the past ten years have been developments in the former Soviet Union.

China is the world's largest wheat producer with nearly 20 percent of total production—100 million tons in 1995/96, versus 99 million in 1994/95, and a record high 106 million in 1993/94. China's 1995/96 wheat consumption is placed at a record large 112 million tons, which if realized is thought to require imports of about 11 million tons. However, just how much China will import is uncertain as China's stock of wheat is unknown, as is the government's willingness to utilize their carryover supplies. Despite China's steadily rising wheat usage and production that consistently trails use, import totals have little consistency; imports in 1993/94 totaled only 4.3 million tons. Apparently China's import needs are very price sensitive; world prices quickly strengthen on talk, real or otherwise, of Chinese purchases, which in turn quickly blunt their interest.

The Russian Federation, once the world's largest importer, now trails a number of countries. Russia's 1995/96 imports of only 3.5 million tons compare with 14 million tons early in the 1990s. Russia's lack of foreign exchange and/or credit accounts for the drop in imports. Russia's wheat production, meanwhile, continues to slide, forecast at 30.5 million tons in 1995/96 versus 32.1 million in 1994/95, and an average of more than 40 million tons earlier in the 1990s. However, domestic use has also dropped, estimated at 38.6 million tons in 1995/96, versus 42.6 million in 1994/95, and more than 50 million on average early in the 1990s.

The U.S. is the world's largest wheat exporter, shipping on average about one-third of the world total. In 1995/96 this was 32.5 million tons compared to expected world exports of 95.3 million tons. In 1994/95, the totals were 32 million tons and 97 million, respectively. The EC-12 and Canadian 1995/96 exports were forecast at 18 million tons each, versus 16.8 million and 21.3 million, respectively in 1994/95. Australia's exports of 12 million tons in 1995/96 compare with 7.9 million in 1994/95. Generally, only four regions account for the bulk of world wheat exports, while importing nations are scattered.

The U.S. 1995 wheat crop of 2.18 billion bushels compares with 2.32 million in 1994/95. The decline reflected a lower average yield—35.9 bushels per acre versus 38.2—and planted acreage of 69.1 million acres versus 72.2 million, respectively. The hard red varieties of wheat account for more than half of U.S. production, 1.3 billion bushels in 1995/96 versus 1.5 billion in 1994/95. Kansas is the largest producing state followed by Oklahoma. North Dakota is the largest spring wheat producing state. Durum wheat production totaled 102 million bushels in 1995/96 versus 97 million in 1994/95, most of which is produced in North Dakota and Minnesota.

The U.S. imports some wheat, about 100 million bushels in 1995/96, versus 92 million in 1994/95. Canada is the largest source of U.S. imports. Carryin stocks as of June 1, 1995, of 507 million bushels compare with 568 million a year earlier, and the lowest since 1992/93's carryin of 475 million. The U.S. wheat supply for 1995/96, of 2.8 billion bushels, compares with 3.0 billion in 1994/95. Total usage in 1995/96, of about 2.4 billion bushels, compares with nearly 2.5 billion in the previous two seasons. Exports, at 1.2 billion bushels, account for one half the total disappearance and are marginally higher than in 1994/95. Food use takes about two-thirds of domestic usage, feed about 20 percent, and seed the balance. If the 1995/96 supply/demand estimates are realized, ending stocks on May 31, 1995, would total only 395 million bushels, dropping the stock to use ratio to 17 percent, versus 20 percent a year earlier. This ratio is often used to forecast prices; the smaller it is the greater the likelihood for higher prices as the crop year progresses.

The tightening global supply firmed prices in the first half of the 1995/96 crop year with little sign of any viable slippage towards the end of calendar year 1995. The 1995/96 average price received by farmers was forecast to range from a record high $4.20 to $4.50 a bushel.

U.S. Farm Program

The 1995 target price for wheat was $4.00 per bushel, unchanged from 1993 and the price support was $2.58, also unchanged.

Futures Markets

Wheat futures and options are traded on the London Commodity Exchange (LCE), the Chicago Board of Trade (CBOT), the Kansas City Board of Trade (KCBT), the Minneapolis Grain Exchange (MGE) and the Mid America Commodity Exchange (MidAm). Feed wheat futures and options are traded on the Winnipeg Commodity Exchange (WCE).

World Production of Wheat — In Thousands of Metric Tons

Crop Year	Argentina	Australia	Canada	China	France	Germany	India	Italy	Pakistan	Russia[4]	Spain	Turkey	United Kingdom	United States	World Total
1984-5	13,200	18,666	21,199	87,820	33,241	10,223	45,476	10,057	10,882	68,600	5,800	13,300	14,957	70,618	511,463
1985-6	8,500	16,127	24,252	85,810	29,262	9,866	44,069	8,516	11,703	78,100	5,326	12,700	12,045	66,001	498,810
1986-7	9,000	16,700	31,850	90,295	26,500	10,406	46,885	9,070	13,922	92,306	4,292	14,000	13,900	56,793	529,419
1987-8	8,800	12,442	25,950	85,840	27,234	9,932	44,323	9,381	12,020	83,312	5,768	13,000	11,940	57,362	502,300
1988-9	8,400	14,060	15,995	85,432	29,660	11,922	46,169	7,952	12,675	84,445	6,173	16,000	11,750	49,320	500,300
1989-90	10,150	14,214	24,796	90,807	32,100	14,482	54,110	7,413	14,419	87,151	5,200	12,500	14,030	55,428	533,001
1990-1	10,900	15,066	32,098	98,229	33,600	15,242	49,850	8,108	14,429	49,596	4,759	16,000	14,000	74,292	587,995
1991-2	9,880	10,557	31,946	96,000	34,594	16,610	55,134	9,416	14,565	38,900	5,000	16,500	14,400	53,891	542,132
1992-3	9,800	16,184	29,871	101,590	32,777	15,542	55,690	8,938	15,684	46,170	4,356	15,500	14,000	67,135	561,793
1993-4[1]	9,700	16,479	27,232	106,390	29,630	15,767	57,210	7,900	16,157	43,500	5,000	16,500	12,900	65,220	559,342
1994-5[2]	11,000	8,903	23,122	99,300	30,900	16,480	59,130		15,114	32,100		14,700	13,310	63,167	521,879
1995-6[3]	8,500	17,000	25,430	100,000	31,000	17,800	65,200		16,948	28,000		15,500	14,150	59,481	533,590

[1] Preliminary. [2] Estimate. [3] Forecast. [4] Formerly part of the U.S.S.R.; data not reported separately until 1990-91. *Source: Foreign Agricultural Service, U.S. Department of Agriculture*

World Wheat Supply & Demand — In Millions of Metric Tons/Hectares

Crop Year	Area Harvested	Yield	Production	World Trade	Utilization Total	Ending Stocks	Stocks as % of Utilization
1988-9	219.7	2.26	496.0	115.6	527.4	147.7	28.0
1988-9	217.4	2.28	495.0	104.3	524.3	118.4	22.6
1989-90	225.8	2.36	533.2	103.9	532.7	118.9	22.3
1990-1	231.4	2.54	588.0	101.0	561.5	145.4	25.9
1991-2	222.5	2.44	542.1	110.8	554.7	132.8	23.9
1992-3	223.1	2.52	561.8	112.7	549.6	145.0	26.4
1993-4[1]	221.1	2.53	559.1	99.7	563.4	140.6	25.0
1994-5[2]	214.3	2.44	521.9	97.2	548.7	113.9	20.8
1995-6[3]	217.2	2.46	533.6	97.5	550.0	97.5	17.7

[1] Preliminary. [2] Estimate. [3] Forecast. *Source: Foreign Agricultural Service, U.S. Department of Agriculture*

Salient Statistics of Wheat in the United States

Crop Year	Planting Intentions	Acreage Harvested: Winter	Acreage Harvested: Spring	Acreage Harvested: All	Average - All Yield Per Acre in Bushels	Value of Production $1,000	Foreign Trade[5]: Domestic Exports[2]	Foreign Trade[5]: Imports[3]	Per Capita[4] Consumption: Flour	Per Capita[4] Consumption: Cereal
	1,000 Acres						Millions of Bushels		In Pounds	
1987-8	65,829	39,332	16,613	55,945	37.7	5,497,712	1,587.9	16.1	130.0	3.7
1988-9	65,529	39,800	13,389	53,189	34.1	6,683,999	1,414.9	22.7	130.0	3.8
1989-90	76,615	41,509	20,680	62,189	32.7	7,542,464	1,232.0	22.5	129.6	4.0
1990-1	77,041	49,721	19,382	69,103	39.5	7,184,427	1,069.5	36.4	135.8	4.3
1991-2	69,881	39,506	18,297	57,803	34.3	5,956,642	1,282.3	40.7	136.5	4.5
1992-3	72,219	42,123	20,638	62,761	39.3	7,978,911	1,353.6	70.0	138.3	4.7
1993-4	72,168	43,811	18,901	62,712	38.2	7,812,000	1,227.8	108.8	139.0	5.0
1994-5[1]	70,349	41,335	20,415	61,770	37.6	8,006,000	1,188.3	91.9		
1995-6[1]	69,177	40,993	19,978	60,971	35.8		1,275.0	70.0		

[1] Preliminary. [2] Includes flour milled from imported wheat. [3] Total wheat, flour & other products. [4] Civilian only. [5] Year beginning June.
Source: Economic Research Service, U.S. Department of Agriculture

Supply and Distribution of Wheat in the United States — In Millions of Bushels

Crop Year Beginning June	Supply: Stocks, June 1: On Farms	Supply: Stocks, June 1: Mills, Elevators[3]	Supply: Stocks, June 1: Total Stocks	Supply: Production	Supply: Imports[4]	Supply: Total Supply	Domestic Disappearance: Food	Domestic Disappearance: Seed	Domestic Disappearance: Feed & Residual[5]	Domestic Disappearance: Total	Exports[4]	Total Disappearance
1987-8	560.0	1,260.9	1,820.9	2,107.7	16.1	3,945	720.7	85.0	290.2	1,096.0	1,587.9	2,684
1988-9	525.0	735.8	1,260.8	1,812.2	22.7	3,096	725.8	103.0	150.5	979.2	1,414.9	2,394
1989-90	289.0	412.6	701.6	2,036.6	22.5	2,761	748.9	104.3	139.1	992.3	1,232.0	2,224
1990-1	212.5	324.0	536.5	2,729.8	36.4	3,303	789.8	92.9	482.1	1,365.1	1,069.5	2,435
1991-2	341.2	524.7	868.1	1,980.1	40.7	2,889	789.5	97.7	244.5	1,131.6	1,282.3	2,414
1992-3	144.6	327.2	475.0	2,466.8	70.0	3,012	834.8	99.1	193.6	1,127.5	1,353.6	2,481
1993-4	183.8	345.3	530.7	2,396.4	108.8	3,036	871.7	96.3	271.7	1,239.7	1,227.8	2,467
1994-5[1]	175.3	393.2	568.5	2,321.0	91.9	2,981	852.5	89.2	344.8	1,286.5	1,188.3	2,475
1995-6[2]	168.4	343.2	506.6	2,185.5	85.0	2,777	860.0	106.0	200.0	1,166.0	1,225.0	2,391

[1] Preliminary. [2] Estimate. [3] Also warehouses and all off-farm storage not otherwise disignated, including flour mills. [4] Imports & exports are for wheat, including flour & other products in terms of wheat. [5] Mostly feed use. *Source: Economic Research Service, U.S. Department of Agriculture*

WHEAT

Stocks, Production and Exports of Wheat by Class In Millions of Bushels

Year Beginning June	Hard Spring June 1 Stocks	Hard Spring Production	Hard Spring Exports[3]	Durum[2] June 1 Stocks	Durum[2] Production	Durum[2] Exports[3]	Hard Winter June 1 Stocks	Hard Winter Production	Hard Winter Exports[3]	Soft Red Winter June 1 Stocks	Soft Red Winter Production	Soft Red Winter Exports[3]	White June 1 Stocks	White Production	White Exports[3]
1988-9	402	181	194	83	45	20	567	882	639	75	473	315	135	232	247
1989-90	219	433	280	60	92	55	302	711	359	39	549	345	81	251	193
1990-1	155	555	201	50	122	53	215	1,196	369	32	344	230	85	313	216
1991-2	279	431	380	62	104	45	360	901	559	80	325	105	87	219	193
1992-3	131	707	438	55	100	47	194	967	464	41	427	210	54	266	195
1993-4	171	512	266	49	70	54	204	1,066	486	43	401	173	64	347	249
1994-5[1]	201	515	292	28	97	40	227	971	422	45	434	212	67	304	222
1995-6[1]	193	475	325	26	102	40	194	824	385	37	450	255	57	334	220

[1] Preliminary. [2] Includes "Red Durum." [3] Includes flour made from U.S. wheat & shipments to territories. [4] Estimate.
Source: Economic Research Service, U.S. Department of Agriculture

Seeded Acerage, Yield and Production of Wheat in the United States

Year	Seeded Acreage--1,000 Acres Winter	Other Spring	Durum	All	Yield Per Harvested Acre (Bushels) Winter	Other Spring	Durum	All	Production (1,000,000 Bushels) Winter	Other Spring	Durum	All
1988	48,800	13,393	3,336	65,529	39.2	19.5	15.7	34.1	1,561.9	205.5	44.8	1,812.2
1989	55,091	17,733	3,791	76,615	35.0	28.8	25.1	32.7	1,454.6	489.7	92.2	2,036.6
1990	56,748	16,723	3,570	77,041	40.7	36.7	34.9	39.5	2,024.2	583.1	122.4	2,729.8
1991	51,024	15,604	3,253	69,881	34.7	33.4	32.5	34.3	1,371.6	504.6	104.0	1,980.1
1992	50,922	18,750	2,547	72,219	38.2	41.8	39.7	39.3	1,609.3	757.6	99.9	2,466.8
1993	51,587	18,340	2,241	72,168	40.2	33.7	33.6	38.2	1,760.1	565.8	70.5	2,396.4
1994	49,197	18,329	2,823	70,349	40.2	31.8	35.6	37.6	1,661.9	562.3	96.7	2,321.0
1995[1]	48,726	17,016	3,436	69,177	37.7	32.2	30.5	35.8	1,547.3	535.9	102.3	2,185.5

[1] Preliminary. *Source: Economic Research Service, U.S. Department of Agriculture*

Production of Winter Wheat in the United States In Thousands of Bushels

Year	Colorado	Idaho	Illinois	Indiana	Kansas	Michigan	Missouri	Montana	Nebraska	Ohio	Oklahoma	Oregon	South Dakota	Tennessee	Texas	Washington
1984	110,400	56,700	70,400	48,300	431,200	45,600	84,050	66,960	81,000	48,400	190,800	66,150	61,200	21,400	150,000	148,800
1985	134,550	46,110	36,750	37,100	433,200	45,000	49,920	22,400	89,700	58,900	165,000	51,840	44,080	8,000	187,200	115,200
1986	92,800	51,850	36,080	30,100	336,600	30,600	18,810	64,000	76,000	48,300	150,800	53,940	57,600	10,725	120,000	102,900
1987	93,750	60,000	56,050	34,800	366,300	19,200	35,420	79,200	85,800	46,400	129,600	49,500	55,080	14,350	100,800	104,025
1988	75,900	50,820	67,500	35,000	323,000	26,040	75,950	39,900	72,000	46,000	172,800	46,860	21,590	21,500	89,600	108,500
1989	57,200	56,700	105,020	51,920	213,600	33,920	86,950	54,000	55,350	62,730	153,900	48,900	35,100	18,900	60,000	68,900
1990	84,150	69,000	91,200	50,440	472,000	41,250	76,000	87,500	85,500	79,650	201,600	54,600	57,600	17,640	130,200	138,600
1991	71,300	49,000	44,800	28,800	363,000	24,080	48,000	76,000	67,200	52,920	135,000	41,600	45,500	7,680	84,000	40,600
1992	70,500	55,250	62,100	25,000	363,800	35,280	64,800	65,250	55,500	59,095	168,150	42,900	33,600	13,440	129,200	102,000
1993	94,350	67,150	68,200	34,840	388,500	22,140	53,200	102,900	73,500	52,520	156,600	61,060	56,550	13,940	118,400	162,500
1994	76,500	56,880	50,400	38,430	433,200	30,740	50,400	64,750	71,400	68,440	143,100	55,680	43,200	15,000	75,400	124,200
1995[1]	102,600	58,520	68,110	39,600	286,000	37,200	47,970	54,800	86,100	73,810	109,200	57,750	56,240	15,980	75,600	133,300

[1] Preliminary. *Source: Crop Reporting Board, U.S. Department of Agriculture*

United States Official Winter Wheat Crop Production Reports In Thousands of Bushels

Crop Year	May 1	June 1	July 1	August 1	September 1	Current December	Final
1984-5	1,979,366	1,972,776	2,021,918	2,045,088	2,036,028	2,060,646	2,060,266
1985-6	1,974,228	1,892,438	1,854,254	1,842,884	1,839,284	1,827,195	1,826,625
1986-7	1,603,127	1,578,277	1,553,026	1,532,526	1,532,526	1,519,143	1,520,433
1987-8	1,549,344	1,577,489	1,574,439	2,125,097	2,114,492	1,565,176	1,565,381
1988-9	1,620,257	1,570,417	1,568,052	1,554,812	1,560,970	1,561,145	1,561,910
1989-90	1,430,148	1,407,898	1,461,924	1,466,049	1,451,746	1,453,842	1,454,642
1990-1	2,091,614	2,089,234	2,035,087	2,054,287	2,036,059	----------	2,030,874
1991-2	1,495,943	1,449,418	1,361,316	1,371,946	1,372,182	----------	1,372,617
1992-3	1,618,017	1,618,017	1,573,901	1,600,931	NA	----------	1,609,284
1993-4	1,807,657	1,824,062	1,821,345	1,788,005	1,788,005	----------	1,760,143
1994-5	1,657,938	1,674,563	1,658,426	1,670,436	1,670,436	----------	1,661,043
1995-6[1]	1,638,211	1,608,396	1,529,950	1,552,230	1,552,230	----------	1,547,311

[1] Preliminary. NA = Not available. *Source: Crop Reporting Board, U.S. Department of Agriculture*

Wheat

Production of All Spring Wheat in the United States In Thousands of Bushels

	Durum Wheat							Other Spring Wheat									
Year	Arizona	Cali-fornia	Minne-sota	Mon-tana	North Dakota	South Dakota	Total Durum	Colo-rado	Idaho	Minne-sota	Mon-tana	North Dakota	Oregon	South Dakota	Utah	Wash-ington	Total Other
1986	4,176	6,525	1,326	4,320	80,000	1,560	97,907	3,630	29,900	98,050	70,200	198,400	4,465	49,500	1,650	13,950	472,230
1987	3,825	5,130	1,218	5,320	74,100	3,024	92,617	3,630	25,500	98,400	66,700	189,100	3,420	48,600	1,653	10,260	449,687
1988	4,300	5,605	840	2,070	31,200	816	44,831	3,640	24,700	49,450	18,000	70,500	4,940	15,600	1,188	16,120	205,460
1989	7,560	8,715	1,044	6,030	66,000	2,880	92,229	4,900	34,720	96,900	85,000	174,000	4,935	45,100	990	41,710	489,747
1990	4,136	5,346	1,320	4,465	103,700	3,204	122,171	2,800	30,600	134,750	53,900	277,200	3,016	67,200	1,170	11,480	583,124
1991	3,705	3,360	960	5,907	88,350	1,675	103,957	2,700	32,660	64,170	81,600	212,350	2,300	49,000	1,127	58,000	504,565
1992	3,740	5,115	470	4,851	81,700	990	99,906	3,619	44,840	137,500	79,050	382,200	4,900	85,000	1,056	17,640	757,608
1993	4,500	3,800	240	3,534	57,970	432	70,476	2,640	43,200	69,750	99,900	274,350	3,900	54,540	1,225	15,080	565,821
1994	8,554	5,605	275	5,340	76,375	598	96,747	3,234	43,400	70,000	100,500	278,775	2,900	51,480	1,012	9,800	562,291
1995[1]	8,514	6,800	360	7,950	77,760	896	102,280	2,660	44,800	70,400	133,000	221,400	5,928	33,600	1,950	20,470	535,948

[1] Preliminary. *Source: Crop Reporting Board, U.S. Department of Agriculture*

Average Wheat Farm Prices for Leading Classes in the U.S. In Dollars Per Bushel

Year	June	July	Aug.	Sept.	Oct.	Nov.	Dec.	Jan.	Feb.	Mar.	Apr.	May	Average
						Winter Wheat							
1993-4	2.72	2.76	2.83	2.88	3.00	3.21	3.43	3.41	3.36	3.26	3.24	3.17	3.11
1994-5	3.09	2.99	3.23	3.57	3.79	3.76	3.75	3.67	3.61	3.47	3.45	3.65	3.50
1995-6[1]	3.77	4.07	4.22	4.47	4.72	4.79	4.88	4.80	5.08				4.53
						Durum Wheat							
1993-4	3.18	3.26	3.43	3.92	4.23	4.91	4.92	4.97	5.36	5.71	5.70	4.93	4.54
1994-5	4.59	4.32	4.30	4.51	4.89	4.88	4.67	4.61	4.68	4.61	4.48	4.82	4.61
1995-6[1]	5.20	5.29	5.33	5.87	5.83	5.63	5.80	5.66	5.68				5.59
						Other Spring Wheat							
1993-4	3.21	3.50	3.51	3.37	3.50	3.67	3.75	3.69	3.68	3.64	3.68	3.63	3.57
1994-5	3.51	3.28	3.19	3.38	3.52	3.51	3.56	3.50	3.40	3.38	3.34	3.53	3.43
1995-6[1]	3.78	4.26	4.19	4.27	4.47	4.61	4.72	4.66	4.83				4.42

[1] Preliminary. *Source: Agricultural Statistics Board, U.S. Department of Agriculture*

United States Grindings of Wheat by Mills In Millions of Bushels (60 Pounds Each)

Year	July	Aug.	Sept.	Oct.	Nov.	Dec.	Jan.	Feb.	Mar.	Apr.	May	June	Total
1986-7	60.0	65.4	65.9	69.2	65.8	64.1	59.3	60.2	62.7	62.8	66.1	64.2	765.7
1987-8	62.3	66.3	65.8	69.5	66.7	62.5	59.6	58.4	61.2	58.0	65.7	63.8	759.8
1988-9	63.6	70.0	66.0	70.0	69.7	63.8	65.0	60.8	60.4	60.7	64.7	59.6	773.3
1989-90	58.5	70.6	63.6	67.4	65.1	58.7	63.4	64.0	66.7	61.6	63.6	60.6	763.8
1990-1	62.3	73.2	65.7	74.9	73.9	64.3	66.7	65.2	63.2	67.6	69.9	60.9	807.8
1991-2	65.3	71.2	67.7	72.2	73.5	65.6	65.7	66.0	65.6	67.3	67.0	67.2	814.3
1992-3	70.0	77.3	71.9	77.9	71.9	65.5	68.1	70.0	76.2	72.0	69.6	67.9	858.2
1993-4	69.2	75.2	74.1	75.8	77.0	76.3	70.0	68.3	81.1	73.0	73.0	70.6	883.8
1994-5	68.9	78.7	76.3	77.9	75.9	71.1	69.0	65.1	76.8	66.5	74.6	71.8	872.5
1995-6[1]	69.8	77.7	74.0	78.3	74.7	69.8							

[1] Preliminary. *Source: Bureau of Census, U.S. Department of Commerce*

Comparative Average Cash Wheat Prices In Dollars Per Bushel

					Minneapolis					Export Prices[2] (U.S. $ per Metric Ton)				
Crop Year Beginning June	Received by U.S. Farmers	No. 2 Soft Red Winter Chicago	No. 1 Hard Red Ordinary Protein Kansas City	No. 2 Soft Red Winter St. Louis	No. 1 Dark Northern Spring 14%	No. 1 Hard Amber Durum	No. 1 Soft White Portland Oregon	No. 2 Western White Pacific N.W.	No. 2 Soft White Toledo	Aust-ralian Standard Wheat	Canada Vancouver No. 1 CWRS 13 1/2 %	Argentina F.O.B. B.A.	U.S. Gulf No. 2 H.W.	Rotter-dam C.I.F. U.S. No. 2 Hard Winter
1986-7	2.42	2.76	2.72	2.87	3.07	3.57	2.90	2.59	2.66	120	161	88	117	148
1987-8	2.57	2.89	2.96	2.95	3.15	4.13	3.06	2.74	2.94	115	134	89	114	141
1988-9	3.72	4.00	4.17	4.08	4.36	5.53	4.53	4.13	3.90	150	177	125	146	176
1989-90	3.72	3.92	4.22	3.94	4.16	4.25	4.28	3.88	3.80	176	202	151	171	190
1990-1	2.61	2.74	2.94	2.81	3.06	3.48	3.16	2.75	2.59	144	158	107	137	164
1991-2	3.00	3.49	3.77	3.32	3.82	3.61	4.11	3.66	3.41	137	141	99	129	154
1992-3	3.24	3.49	3.67	3.54	3.91	3.88	4.11	3.73	3.18	165	177	122	152	173
1993-4[1]	3.26	3.20	3.60	3.23	5.02	5.76	3.53	NA	3.16	154	192	131	141	200
1994-5[1]	3.42	3.62	3.97	3.62	4.26	5.98	4.16	NA	3.37	162	199	NA	150	210

[1] Preliminary. [2] Calendar year. NA = Not available. *Source: Economic Research Service, U.S. Department of Agriculture*

Wheat

Wheat Government Loan Program Data in the United States   Loan Rates (Cents Per Bushel)

Crop Year Beginning June	National Average[3]	Target Rate	Farm Loan Prices: Corn Belt (Soft Red Winter)	Central & Southern Plains (Hard Winter)	Northern Plains (Spring & Durum)	Pacific Northwest (White)	Placed Under Loan	% of Production	Acquired by CCC Under Program	Stocks Ending May 31: Total Stocks	Total CCC Stocks	Outstanding: CCC Loans	Farmer-Owned Reserve	"Free"
							Millions of Bushels							
1987-8	228	438	235	226	228	239	472	22.4	147	1,821	830	236	632	123
1988-9	221	423	233	221	221	232	106	5.8	45	1,261	283	178	467	334
1989-90	206	410	214	204	206	217	113	5.6	62	702	191	19	287	205
1990-1	195	400	200	194	195	206	405	14.8	90	536	117	30	144	246
1991-2	204	400	209	200	204	214	143	7.2	1	868	163	217	14	475
1992-3	221	400	232	220	221	237	240	9.8	.1	475	152	20	50	253
1993-4[1]	245	400	251	243	245	269	258	14.7	.3	531	150	47	28	305
1994-5[2]	258	400	253	257	258	271	231	10.0	0	569	150	67	6	345
1995-6[2]	258	400					103	4.7	0	507	142	64	0	301

[1] Preliminary. [2] Estimate. [3] The national average loan rate at the farm as a percentage of the parity-priced wheat at the beginning of the marketing year.
Source: Agricultural Marketing Service, U.S. Department of Agriculture

Exports of Wheat (Only)[2] from the United States   In Thousands of Bushels

Year	June	July	Aug.	Sept.	Oct.	Nov.	Dec.	Jan.	Feb.	Mar.	Apr.	May	Total
1987-8	119,769	157,706	112,758	119,945	101,680	71,166	113,609	140,228	143,959	149,146	152,830	147,667	1,530,462
1988-9	121,842	111,498	107,562	127,564	93,153	93,309	100,149	115,846	127,060	141,780	115,916	90,658	1,346,336
1989-90	90,490	137,933	131,176	150,697	89,336	68,664	81,813	78,343	87,647	104,903	84,576	71,572	1,177,152
1990-1	88,235	80,831	93,617	107,786	84,488	76,800	56,444	66,473	91,313	112,809	88,526	81,760	1,029,072
1991-2	59,167	79,319	97,794	94,991	124,155	136,385	112,771	132,413	115,126	103,024	116,850	59,764	1,231,759
1992-3	75,045	96,382	99,290	92,723	132,232	108,235	111,389	111,584	118,607	118,782	126,845	104,540	1,295,653
1993-4	85,874	103,836	100,516	104,732	100,618	112,667	121,900	109,389	87,250	96,873	71,575	82,838	1,178,068
1994-5	73,364	66,314	103,941	117,555	101,450	107,549	104,139	93,735	97,478	98,876	85,251	75,006	1,124,658
1995-6[1]	78,355	88,649	119,797	131,424	117,679	105,535	99,175						

[1] Preliminary.. [2] Grains. *Source: Economic Research Service, U.S. Department of Agriculture*

United States Wheat and Flour Imports and Exports   In Thousands of Bushels

Crop Year Beginning June	Imports: Wheat: Suitable for Milling	Unfit for Human Consumption	Grain	Flour & Products[2]	Total	Exports: P.L. 480	Foreign Donations Sec. 416	Aid[3]	Total concessional	CCC Export Credit	Export Enhancement Program	Total U.S. Wheat Exports
			-- Wheat Equivalent --			In Thousands of Metric Tons						
1986-7	14,837	984	15,821	5,430	21,250	3,927	406	1	4,334	8,125	12,214	28,204
1987-8	9,020	969	9,989	6,097	16,086	3,321	1,186	292	4,800	9,273	26,679	40,523
1988-9	15,870	NA	15,870	6,798	22,668	3,020	138	806	3,964	8,897	17,906	37,774
1989-90	13,548	NA	12,583	9,884	22,467	2,985	0	28	3,065	7,759	12,806	27,999
1990-1	25,540	NA	25,574	10,832	36,407	2,975	0	0	3,067	8,339	15,150	26,792
1991-2	30,924	NA	31,019	9,675	40,598	2,286	0	0	2,416	13,334	21,111	34,322
1992-3[1]	56,859	NA	56,859	13,142	69,415	2,332	0	0	3,195	8,538	21,832	36,081
1993-4[1]	91,287	NA	91,288	17,529	108,860	1,804	0	0	2,178	5,874	18,157	31,132

[1] Preliminary. [2] Includes macaroni, semolina & similar products. [3] Shipments mostly under the Commodity Import Program, financed with foreign aid funds. NA = Not available. *Source: Economic Research Service, U.S. Department of Agriculture*

Wheat Stocks in the United States   In Millions of Bushels

Year	On Farms: Mar. 1	June 1	Sept. 1	Dec. 1	Off Farms: Mar. 1	June 1	Sept. 1	Dec. 1	Total Stocks: Mar. 1	June 1	Sept. 1	Dec. 1
1987	794.0	560.0	1,168.0	971.0	1,456.4	1,260.9	1,820.5	1,534.3	2,250.4	1,820.9	2,988.5	2,505.3
1988	748.0	525.0	798.0	620.0	1,175.5	735.8	1,455.6	1,095.9	1,923.5	1,260.8	2,253.6	1,715.9
1989	463.0	289.0	832.0	592.0	764.7	412.6	1,086.0	830.5	1,227.7	701.6	1,918.0	1,422.5
1990	376.0	212.5	1,000.0	763.2	567.1	324.0	1,409.5	1,144.8	943.1	536.5	2,409.5	1,909.5
1991	532.9	341.2	828.0	564.8	863.3	524.7	1,212.7	877.3	1,396.3	865.9	2,040.7	1,442.1
1992	275.6	144.6	979.4	672.0	611.7	327.2	1,128.2	918.5	887.2	471.9	2,107.6	1,590.5
1993	378.0	183.8	987.0	653.1	670.3	346.8	1,145.6	932.6	1,048.3	530.7	2,132.6	1,585.7
1994	363.2	175.3	859.8	575.6	664.8	393.2	1,209.7	920.6	1,028.0	568.5	2,069.5	1,491.1
1995[1]	335.3	163.4	743.6	477.0	633.8	343.2	1,137.5	860.9	969.1	506.6	1,881.1	1,337.9

[1] Preliminary. NA = Not available. *Source: Crop Reporting Board, U.S. Department of Agriculture*

Wheat Supply and Distribution in Canada, Australia and Agrentina In Millions of Metric Tons

Crop Year	Canada (Year Beginning Aug. 1): Supply: Stocks Aug. 1	New Crop	Total Supply	Disappearance: Domestic	Exports[3]	Australia (Year Beginning Oct. 1): Supply: Stocks Oct. 1	New Crop	Total Supply	Disappearance: Domestic	Exports[3]	Argentina (Year Beginning Dec. 1): Supply: Stocks Dec. 1	New Crop	Total Supply	Disappearance: Domestic	Exports[3]
1984-5	9.2	21.2	30.2	5.2	17.5	7.5	18.7	26.2	2.9	15.8	1.3	13.2	14.5	4.6	9.4
1985-6	7.6	24.3	31.9	5.6	17.7	8.6	16.2	24.8	2.9	16.0	.5	8.5	9.0	4.4	4.3
1986-7	8.6	31.4	40.0	6.4	20.8	5.9	16.1	22.0	2.7	15.6	.3	8.9	9.2	4.5	4.4
1987-8	12.7	25.9	38.7	7.9	23.5	3.8	12.4	16.1	3.5	9.9	.2	8.8	9.0	4.5	3.7
1988-9	7.3	15.9	23.2	5.8	12.4	2.8	14.1	16.8	2.9	11.3	.8	8.4	9.2	4.7	4.0
1989-90	5.0	24.8	29.8	6.5	16.9	2.6	14.2	16.8	3.0	10.8	.5	10.2	10.7	4.5	6.1
1990-1	6.4	32.1	38.5	6.5	20.5	3.0	15.1	18.1	3.5	11.7	0	10.9	10.9	4.5	4.8
1991-2	10.3	31.9	42.3	7.8	24.5	2.8	10.6	13.4	3.4	7.1	.8	9.9	10.7	4.6	5.8
1992-3	10.1	29.9	40.1	8.1	19.7	2.9	16.2	19.1	4.2	9.9	.3	9.8	10.1	4.3	5.9
1993-4[1]	12.2	27.2	39.5	9.3	19.1	5.0	16.5	21.5	4.1	13.7	0	9.7	9.7	4.3	5.0
1994-5[1]	11.1	23.1	34.3	6.9	21.5	3.7	8.9	12.7	4.4	5.9	.4	11.0	11.4	4.3	6.9
1995-6[2]	5.9	25.4	31.4	7.2	18.9	2.4	17.0	19.4	4.4	13.0	.2	8.5	8.7	4.2	4.3

[1] Preliminary. [2] Forecast. [3] Including flour. *Source: Foreign Agricultural Service, U.S. Department of Agriculture*

United States Wheat Quarterly Supply and Disappearance In Millions of Bushels

Crop Year Beginning June 1	Supply: Beginning Stocks	Production	Imports[3]	Total Supply	Disappearance: Domestic Use: Food	Seed	Feed & Residual[7]	Total	Exports[3]	Total Disap-pearance	Ending Stocks: Gov't Owned[4]	Privately Owned[5]	Total Stocks
1988-9	1,261.0	1,812.2	22.6	3,096	725.8	103.0	150.5	979.2	1,414.9	2,394.1	190.5	511.1	701.6
June-Aug.	1,261.0	1,812.2	8.6	3,082	183.3	1.0	282.2	466.4	361.6	828.1	250.0	2,003.6	2,253.6
Sept.-Nov.	2,254.0	---------	6.3	2,260	197.3	67.0	-49.4	214.9	329.0	543.9	213.0	1,502.9	1,715.9
Dec.-Feb.	1,716.0	---------	3.7	1,720	173.4	3.0	-44.5	131.9	360.0	491.9	203.2	1,024.5	1,227.7
Mar.-May	1,228.0	---------	4.1	1,232	171.8	32.0	-37.8	166.0	364.2	530.2	190.5	511.1	701.6
1989-90	701.6	2,036.6	23.4	2,761	748.9	104.3	139.1	992.3	1,232.0	2,224.3	116.6	419.9	536.5
June-Aug.	701.6	2,036.6	5.9	2,744	190.7	1.7	264.9	457.4	368.7	826.1	167.9	1,750.1	1,918.0
Sept.-Nov.	1,918.0	---------	7.1	1,925	191.7	70.3	-87.8	174.1	328.6	502.7	154.5	1,268.0	1,422.5
Dec.-Feb.	1,423.0	---------	4.7	1,427	184.3	2.7	37.4	224.4	259.6	484.0	136.5	806.6	943.1
Mar.-May	943.1	---------	5.8	948	182.2	29.6	-75.4	136.4	275.1	411.5	116.6	419.9	536.5
1990-1	536.5	2,729.8	36.4	3,303	789.8	92.9	482.4	1,365.1	1,069.5	2,434.5	162.7	705.4	868.1
June-Aug.	536.5	2,729.8	8.0	3,274	194.1	1.7	399.7	595.5	267.7	863.1	104.6	2,306.5	2,411.1
Sept.-Nov.	2,409.5	---------	13.4	2,425	210.6	62.9	-38.3	235.2	279.4	514.5	129.9	1,780.0	1,909.9
Dec.-Feb.	1,908.0	---------	7.8	1,918	191.0	2.1	101.5	294.6	225.5	520.0	152.5	1,245.2	1,397.7
Mar.-May	1,396.0	---------	7.2	1,405	194.1	26.3	19.5	239.9	296.9	536.8	162.7	705.4	868.1
1991-2	868.1	1,980.1	40.7	2,889	789.5	97.2	244.5	1,131.6	1,282.3	2,413.9	152.0	323.0	475.0
June-Aug.	868.1	1,980.1	7.8	2,856	189.4	1.2	359.1	549.6	251.7	801.3	162.8	1,891.9	2,054.7
Sept.-Nov.	2,054.7	---------	7.3	2,062	213.0	62.2	-26.9	248.3	365.9	614.2	160.7	1,287.1	1,447.8
Dec.-Feb.	1,447.8	---------	10.7	1,459	192.9	2.4	-0.5	194.8	371.7	566.5	156.9	735.1	892.0
Mar.-May	892.0	---------	14.9	907	194.2	31.9	-87.3	138.9	293.0	431.9	152.0	323.0	475.0
1992-3	475.0	2,466.8	70.0	3,012	834.3	99.1	194.2	1,127.6	1,353.6	2,481.2	150.0	380.7	530.7
June-Aug.	475.0	2,466.8	20.1	2,962	212.1	1.4	345.3	558.8	282.6	841.4	151.6	1,969.0	2,120.6
Sept.-Nov.	2,120.6	---------	16.4	2,137	218.8	63.4	-81.9	200.3	345.0	545.3	151.1	1,440.6	1,591.7
Dec.-Feb.	1,591.7	---------	17.4	1,609	196.7	2.6	5.2	204.5	356.3	560.8	150.4	897.9	1,048.3
Mar.-May	1,048.3	---------	16.1	1,064	206.7	31.7	-74.4	164.0	369.7	533.7	150.0	380.7	530.7
1993-4	530.7	2,396.4	108.8	3,036	869.3	96.3	274.1	1,239.7	1,227.8	2,467.4	150.3	418.2	568.5
June-Aug.	530.7	2,396.4	14.6	2,942	211.3	1.3	295.8	508.4	300.7	809.1	149.9	1,982.7	2,132.6
Sept.-Nov.	2,132.6	---------	30.1	2,163	225.3	60.9	-38.5	247.7	329.2	577.0	150.3	1,435.4	1,585.7
Dec.-Feb.	1,585.7	---------	26.9	1,613	210.1	2.3	39.9	252.3	332.3	584.6	150.4	877.6	1,028.0
Mar.-May	1,028.0	---------	37.2	1,065	222.6	31.8	-23.2	231.2	265.5	496.7	150.3	418.2	568.5
1994-5[1]	568.5	2,320.6	90.0	2,981	852.0	89.0	345.0	1,223.0	1,188.0	2,523.0	142.1	364.5	506.6
June-Aug.	568.5	2,320.6	30.7	2,920	212.3	1.6	376.0	590.7	259.6	850.3	146.4	1,923.1	2,069.5
Sept.-Nov.	2,069.5	---------	21.4	2,091	229.0	61.9	-29.0	257.5	338.2	595.7	142.8	1,348.3	1,491.1
Dec.-Feb.	1,491.0	---------	18.0	1,509	202.0	2.0	26.0	230.0	310.0	540.0	142.3	826.8	969.1
Mar.-May	969.0	---------	22.0	991	209.0	24.0	-28.0	205.0	280.0	485.0	142.1	364.5	506.6
1995-6[2]	507.0	2,186.0	85.0	2,777	860.0	106.0	200.0	1,166.0	1,225.0	2,391.0	120.0	226.1	346.1
June-Aug.	1,881.0	2,186.0	23.0	2,715	215.0	8.0	308.0	531.0	303.0	834.0	141.5	1,739.6	1,881.1
Sept.-Nov.	1,338.0	---------	17.0	1,898	226.0	65.0	-91.0	200.0	360.0	560.0	141.2	1,196.7	1,337.9

[1] Preliminary. [2] Forecast. [3] Imports & exports include flour and other products expressed in wheat equivalent. [4] Uncommitted, Government only. [5] Includes total loans. [6] Includes alcoholic beverages. *Source: Economic Research Service, U.S. Department of Agriculture*

WHEAT

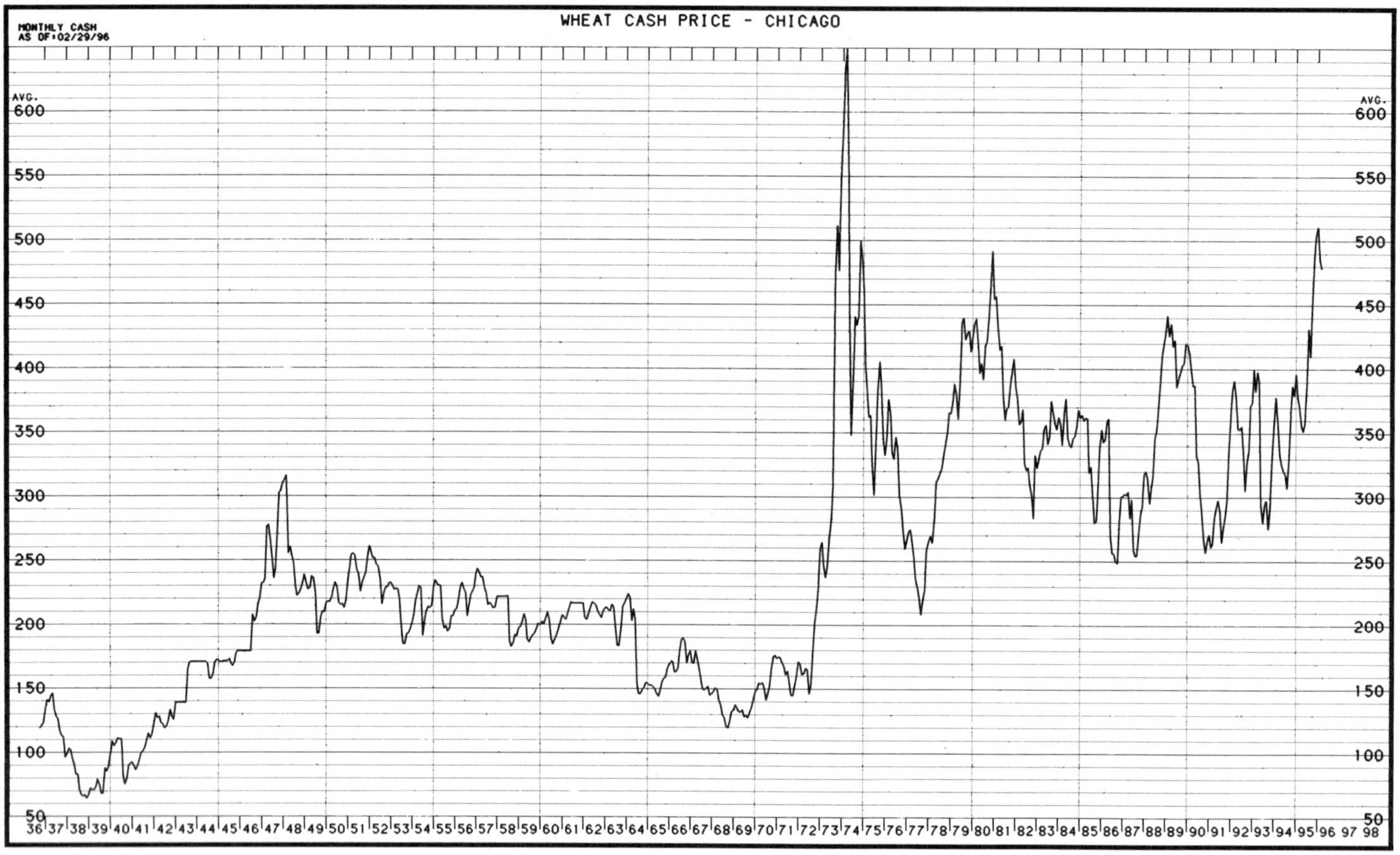

Average Price of No. 2 Soft Red Winter (30 Days) Wheat at Chicago In Dollars Per Bushel

Year	June	July	Aug.	Sept.	Oct.	Nov.	Dec.	Jan.	Feb.	Mar.	Apr.	May	Average
1982-3	3.31	3.36	3.35	3.18	2.98	3.33	3.23	3.32	3.40	3.36	3.51	3.55	3.32
1983-4	3.53	3.59	3.71	3.62	3.56	3.42	3.55	3.47	3.34	3.57	3.65	3.65	3.56
1984-5	3.51	3.44	3.49	3.47	3.51	3.62	3.49	3.51	3.55	3.58	3.63	3.34	3.51
1985-6	3.27	3.09	2.87	2.83	3.04	3.33	3.46	3.34	3.37	3.40	3.39	3.25	3.22
1986-7	2.52	2.58	2.44	2.36	2.57	2.73	2.76	2.87	2.91	3.11	3.16	3.08	2.76
1987-8	2.63	2.54	2.61	2.77	2.82	2.80	3.00	3.23	3.23	2.94	3.02	3.13	2.89
1988-9	3.56	3.52	3.61	3.84	4.07	4.09	4.25	4.39	4.30	4.31	4.04	4.07	4.00
1989-90	3.87	3.92	3.94	3.93	4.07	4.07	4.13	4.03	3.92	3.61	3.83	3.71	3.92
1990-1	3.26	3.04	2.83	2.62	2.62	2.41	2.52	2.50	2.53	2.76	2.80	2.83	2.73
1991-2	2.86	2.79	2.97	3.24	3.50	3.57	3.79	4.12	4.15	3.71	3.53	3.68	3.49
1992-3	3.60	3.39	3.09	3.24	3.39	3.60	3.59	3.77	3.67	3.58	3.72	3.19	3.49
1993-4	2.82	3.03	3.12	2.99	3.02	3.29	3.53	3.67	3.48	3.20	3.15	3.15	3.20
1994-5	3.21	3.14	3.34	3.63	3.97	3.85	3.99	3.88	3.74	3.49	3.51	3.64	3.62
1995-6	3.94	NQ	4.26	4.55	NQ	4.97	5.13	5.02					

NQ = No quote. *Source: Agricultural Marketing Service, U.S. Department of Agriculture*

Stocks of Wheat Flour Held by Mills in the United States In Thousands of Sacks (100 Pounds Each)

Year	Jan. 1	April 1	July 1	Oct. 1	Year	Jan. 1	April 1	July 1	Oct. 1
1984	3,805	3,780	3,763	3,833	1990	5,207	5,072	5,818	7,980
1985	4,230	4,363	5,040	5,052	1991	8,051	5,474	8,115	6,336
1986	4,847	4,740	5,141	5,101	1992	5,660	5,210	5,841	5,864
1987	5,228	4,900	5,581	5,258	1993	5,487	4,863	6,197	5,882
1988	5,858	4,508	4,822	5,303	1994[1]	5,611	5,904	5,834	6,020
1989	4,800	4,423	5,116	5,489	1995[1]	7,060	6,761	6,421	6,844

[1] Preliminary. *Source: U.S. Department of Commerce*

Commercial Stocks of Domestic Wheat[1] in the United States, at First of Month — In Millions of Bushels

Year	July	Aug.	Sept.	Oct.	Nov.	Dec.	Jan.	Feb.	Mar.	Apr.	May	June
1985-6	312.5	434.8	474.8	510.9	504.2	473.9	446.3	435.7	413.0	400.3	399.0	407.2
1986-7	437.5	483.7	494.7	475.9	472.7	445.0	435.0	420.0	410.1	393.3	381.1	366.8
1987-8	417.8	436.5	443.7	451.9	439.9	421.4	387.1	361.1	302.6	261.2	235.6	203.7
1988-9	291.6	334.2	342.4	340.8	331.1	297.2	293.7	266.5	213.3	181.1	150.1	114.4
1989-90	130.5	171.6	211.7	211.8	196.0	180.2	164.2	150.4	127.9	109.7	87.2	77.8
1990-1	121.8	212.7	289.7	290.2	284.6	264.8	243.7	237.7	------	------	174.5	174.5
1991-2	244.8	275.5	296.9	308.2	271.0	264.8	249.8	227.0	205.2	180.7	170.9	209.1
1992-3	269.6	290.5	202.5	228.2	231.9	202.7	185.5	169.5	153.3	132.6	112.9	87.0
1993-4	102.9	145.1	171.8	194.9	199.3	174.9	169.5	168.3	162.2	143.8	127.3	111.3
1994-5	145.7	203.9	243.0	269.7	268.6	238.2	199.5	181.0	162.5	150.2	108.7	91.8
1995-6	92.3	161.7	201.1	234.3	228.3	200.2	178.7	175.2				

[1] Domestic wheat in storage in public and private elevators in 39 markets and wheat afloat in vessels or barges at lake and seaboard ports, the first Saturday of the month. *Source: Livestock Division, U.S. Department of Agriculture*

Average Open Interest of All Wheat Futures Contracts at Chicago & Kansas City — In Thousands of Bushels

	Chicago[1]												Kansas City[2]
Year	Jan.	Feb.	Mar.	Apr.	May	June	July	Aug.	Sept.	Oct.	Nov.	Dec.	Jan.
1986	165,634	160,985	162,241	176,466	178,596	187,200	177,405	173,918	173,247	183,853	152,193	125,838	71,056
1987	128,805	137,113	147,187	154,030	160,892	175,160	176,293	200,085	199,244	194,362	163,349	152,801	66,850
1988	192,824	209,322	206,533	217,011	209,546	283,122	283,710	280,121	342,077	372,677	348,955	313,480	112,972
1989	334,519	315,770	323,343	308,643	301,955	349,492	335,590	327,315	307,555	261,229	260,113	270,586	156,530
1990	271,124	281,973	284,920	257,741	283,120	319,096	322,882	298,960	286,186	291,155	279,248	235,303	142,888
1991	242,983	257,602	279,608	268,339	265,149	294,983	274,730	261,417	276,101	306,286	288,394	259,224	128,872
1992	307,419	350,761	294,787	268,528	254,891	251,702	300,579	310,357	250,467	272,821	288,463	246,317	177,990
1993	251,644	239,291	224,427	241,772	256,763	279,143	293,523	321,674	293,017	307,481	314,383	252,615	148,971
1994	269,558	240,064	225,548	237,148	222,762	273,110	285,754	326,938	365,999	392,094	354,076	335,752	196,237
1995	333,575	338,842	279,865	278,059	339,373	451,038	506,753	454,001	457,527	519,934	512,376	497,108	197,235

[1] Chicago Board of Trade. [2] Kansas City Board of Trade. *Source: Commodity Futures Trading Commission*

WHEAT

Average Price of No. 1 Hard Red Winter (Ordinary Protein) Wheat, at Kansas City   In Cents Per Bushel

Year	June	July	Aug.	Sept.	Oct.	Nov.	Dec.	Jan.	Feb.	Mar.	Apr.	May	Average
1988-9	379	377	378	403	413	418	425	440	437	432	446	455	417
1989-90	444	428	424	418	428	436	439	430	413	404	413	391	422
1990-1	360	311	289	282	281	278	278	271	277	294	298	304	294
1991-2	299	291	310	331	364	376	406	466	451	433	402	390	377
1992-3	391	352	327	356	360	378	381	397	375	374	359	351	367
1993-4	333	338	334	337	352	339	415	400	380	364	363	365	360
1994-5	360	348	370	405	431	424	427	406	398	387	386	422	397
1995-6	472	498	476	500	528	534	551	540					

Source: Economic Research Service, U.S. Department of Agriculture

Average Price of No. 1 Dark Northern Spring Wheat at Minneapolis (14% Protein)   In Cents Per Bushel

Year	June	July	Aug.	Sept.	Oct.	Nov.	Dec.	Jan.	Feb.	Mar.	Apr.	May	Average
1988-9	432	423	424	432	433	422	426	444	440	456	447	455	436
1989-90	441	436	418	408	411	412	423	421	406	396	408	409	416
1990-1	396	356	305	284	285	280	282	283	285	300	307	310	306
1991-2	304	294	310	321	368	378	411	436	456	436	428	444	382
1992-3	442	404	365	379	385	394	388	405	387	387	380	371	391
1993-4	396	480	488	490	517	550	545	532	529	494	499	505	502
1994-5	420	414	400	427	440	441	437	421	409	411	430	461	426
1995-6	489	552	506	527	552	563	580	562					

Source: Economic Research Service, U.S. Department of Agriculture

Average Price[1] Received by Farmers for Wheat in the U.S.   In Cents Per Bushel

Year	June	July	Aug.	Sept.	Oct.	Nov.	Dec.	Jan.	Feb.	Mar.	Apr.	May	Average[2]
1988-9	337	350	361	374	384	388	394	402	403	407	403	401	372
1989-90	385	378	374	372	375	372	379	371	356	348	349	340	372
1990-1	308	279	258	246	243	239	240	242	243	253	260	264	255
1991-2	255	250	263	280	307	325	344	354	378	372	365	364	300
1992-3	343	315	301	320	321	329	331	337	333	330	326	311	324
1993-4	284	285	296	310	325	347	363	358	360	370	356	343	326
1994-5	321	304	325	357	376	375	374	369	361	352	349	366	352
1995-6	384	411	426	453	473	482	488	483	503				

[1] Weighted average by sales. [2] Includes an allownace for unredeemed loans at average loan value. *Source: Economic Research Service, U.S. Department of Agriculture*

Average Producer Price Index of Wheat Flour (Spring[1])   June 1983 = 100

Year	July	Aug.	Sept.	Oct.	Nov.	Dec.	Jan.	Feb.	Mar.	Apr.	May	June	Average
1988-9	107.0	107.7	110.0	110.5	109.0	109.1	110.7	110.0	112.4	109.5	112.0	112.7	110.5
1989-90	112.1	110.7	109.5	108.5	108.7	109.6	109.4	109.0	106.9	108.8	107.9	106.0	100.2
1990-1	99.7	93.4	92.0	91.2	89.4	89.8	88.7	90.2	92.0	93.0	94.0	93.0	94.5
1991-2	91.3	94.1	96.3	100.1	97.5	102.7	109.7	116.4	111.5	110.3	109.2	111.0	107.3
1992-3	104.9	99.6	104.1	104.4	104.7	103.5	107.5	108.1	107.2	108.4	105.2	104.7	105.2
1993-4	103.7	107.2	102.1	107.3	108.4	112.5	111.8	110.5	109.9	107.9	109.0	106.4	108.1
1994-5	100.8	101.2	109.2	112.0	111.2	111.4	110.7	108.7	107.4	109.8	113.5	118.6	109.5
1995-6	125.2	126.7	129.6	131.5	132.7	133.5							

[1] Standard patent. *Source: Bureau of Labor Statistics, U.S. Department of Commerce (0212-0301)*

World Wheat Flour Production (Monthly Average)   In Thousands of Metric Tons

Year	Australia[3]	France	Germany	Hungary	India	Japan	Kazakhstan	Rep. of Korea	Mexico	Poland	Russia	Sweden	Turkey	United Kingdom	Yugoslavia
1988	105.5	433.6	282.0	98.0	363.3	372.1	159.1	141.0	198.6	236.3	NA	38.4	111.2	333.0	183.8
1989	109.0	435.6	280.0	102.2	391.3	378.4	164.0	134.5	207.0	241.1	NA	40.1	136.4	333.0	193.4
1990	114.9	442.7	218.1	102.4	394.3	374.3	163.5	134.7	209.4	150.6	NA	41.0	112.9	328.0	175.5
1991	112.7	464.8	341.1	97.7	398.0	390.3	167.8	130.4	207.3	128.6	NA	47.7	111.1	326.0	160.4
1992	113.9	465.2	327.0	106.9	400.0	NA	161.0	129.4	223.3	167.1	NA	44.6	112.2	NA	NA
1993	116.3	480.6	336.4	75.0	399.4	367.6	155.3	129.5	214.0	113.4	449.5	44.8	122.1	327.3	82.0
1994[1]	126.1	470.8	378.8	62.9	400.0	387.2	157.0	132.6	219.8	150.5	348.0	45.2	104.9	333.9	65.0
1995[2]		484.0	369.1	74.5	400.0	382.7	103.7	137.6	214.3	101.9	281.3		107.1	343.5	71.5

[1] Preliminary. [2] Estimate. [3] Average of twelve months ending June 30. NA = Not available. *Source: United Nations*

United States Wheat Flour Production In Millions of Sacks (100 Pounds Each)

Year	July	Aug.	Sept.	Oct.	Nov.	Dec.	Jan.	Feb.	Mar.	Apr.	May	June	Total
1987-8	27.6	30.1	29.3	31.3	29.8	28.0	26.5	26.5	27.1	26.0	29.2	28.6	340.0
1988-9	28.5	31.4	29.4	31.3	31.1	28.5	29.1	27.1	27.0	27.2	28.6	26.6	345.8
1989-90	26.6	32.3	29.8	31.8	30.0	27.8	27.9	28.0	29.2	27.0	27.6	26.7	354.3
1990-1	27.7	33.7	29.9	32.2	32.7	29.1	29.4	29.5	29.5	29.4	29.2	29.1	362.3
1991-2	29.2	31.8	30.1	32.2	32.7	29.2	29.3	29.3	29.4	30.0	29.8	29.8	363.0
1992-3	31.1	34.2	31.9	34.6	32.2	29.2	30.6	31.3	34.1	32.0	31.0	30.3	382.4
1993-4	30.7	33.3	32.9	33.5	34.0	33.8	30.9	30.2	35.9	32.3	32.2	31.1	390.8
1994-5	30.5	34.9	34.2	35.0	33.7	31.7	30.8	29.2	34.4	29.8	33.3	32.1	389.5
1995-6[1]	30.9	34.3	32.8	34.9	33.2	31.0							

[1] Preliminary. *Source: Bureau of Census, U.S. Department of Commerce*

United States Wheat Flour Exports (Grain Equivalent[2]) In Thousands of Bushels

Year	June	July	Aug.	Sept.	Oct.	Nov.	Dec.	Jan.	Feb.	Mar.	Apr.	May	Total
1987-8	5,450	6,816	4,749	3,999	3,418	6,746	4,316	6,934	2,556	823	2,463	2,520	50,790
1988-9	7,036	6,400	6,002	2,402	7,908	3,368	6,086	4,108	6,040	3,974	6,469	5,205	64,998
1989-90	907	1,897	5,775	8,917	3,579	6,817	3,606	4,943	3,124	4,466	6,132	3,287	53,450
1990-1	1,035	2,207	2,785	1,464	3,303	3,407	4,480	2,698	3,809	6,301	3,719	3,525	38,733
1991-2	5,582	5,362	4,207	3,743	1,179	2,222	3,140	2,549	5,549	4,630	3,771	4,579	46,514
1992-3	3,257	5,284	2,856	2,325	3,840	4,641	3,903	2,325	7,744	5,832	7,499	5,285	54,789
1992-3	3,257	5,284	2,856	2,325	3,840	4,641	3,903	2,325	7,744	5,832	7,499	5,285	54,789
1993-4	4,408	3,793	1,811	3,642	3,840	3,416	3,170	5,838	4,390	6,099	4,198	3,368	47,972
1994-5[1]	2,922	6,824	5,636	3,407	3,105	4,721	4,734	2,805	7,085	7,617	6,945	6,005	61,806

[1] Preliminary. [2] Includes meal, groats and durum. *Source: Economic Research Service, U.S. Department of Agriculture*

Supply and Distribution of Wheat Flour in the United States

Year	Wheat Ground 1,000 Bu.	Milfeed Production 1,000 Tons	Flour Production[3]	Flour & Product Imports[2]	Total Supply	Exports: Flour	Exports: Products[2]	Domestic Disappearance	Total Population July 1 Millions	Per Capita Disappearance Pounds
			1,000 Cwt.							
1987	767,507	6,260	341,565	2,663	344,228	28,880	144	315,204	242.8	130
1988	769,699	6,163	344,154	2,727	346,881	24,097	185	322,599	245.0	132
1989	761,021	6,072	342,762	3,337	346,099	25,265	180	320,654	247.3	130
1990	788,186	6,109	354,348	3,623	357,971	18,872	273	338,826	249.9	136
1991	808,966	6,436	362,311	4,070	366,381	20,044	440	345,897	252.6	137
1992	833,339	6,707	370,829	5,037	375,866	20,711	619	354,536	255.4	139
1993	871,408	6,963	387,419	6,233	393,652	23,241	548	369,863	258.1	143
1994	884,707	7,186	392,519	9,048	401,567	24,234	733	376,599	260.7	144
1995[1]	868,265	7,115	386,820	9,305	396,125	24,343	716	371,066	263.0	141

[1] Preliminary. [2] Import and exports of macaroni and noodle products (flour equivalent), reporting methods changed in 1990. [3] Commercial production of wheat flour, whole wheat, industrial and durum flour and farina reported by Bureau of Census. *Source: Economic Research Service, U.S. Department of Agriculture*

Wheat and Flour -- Price Relationship at Milling Centers In Dollars

Crop Year (June-May)	At Kansas City: Cost of Wheat to Produce 100 lb. Flour[1]	Wholesale Price of: Bakery Flour 100 lb. Flour[2]	Wholesale Price of: By-Products Obtained 100 lb. Flour[3]	Total Products: Actual	Total Products: Over Cost of Wheat	At Minneapolis: Cost of Wheat to Produce 100 lb. Flour[1]	Wholesale Price of: Bakery Flour 100 lb. Flour[2]	Wholesale Price of: By-Products Obtained 100 lb. Flour[3]	Total Products: Actual	Total Products: Over Cost of Wheat
1987-8	7.15	7.96	1.14	9.10	1.95	7.18	9.39	.89	10.28	3.10
1988-9	9.62	10.21	1.68	11.89	2.27	9.94	10.39	1.62	12.01	2.07
1989-90	9.58	10.41	1.45	11.86	2.28	9.48	10.00	1.36	11.36	1.89
1990-1	6.86	7.78	1.29	9.07	2.21	6.98	7.73	1.21	8.94	1.96
1991-2	8.58	9.53	1.26	10.79	2.21	8.71	9.39	1.16	10.55	1.84
1992-3	8.53	9.65	1.28	10.93	2.40	8.91	10.12	1.15	11.27	2.37
1993-4	10.03	10.34	1.46	11.79	1.77	11.45	12.50	1.28	13.77	2.33
1994-5	9.25	10.50	1.21	11.71	2.46	9.71	11.01	1.04	12.05	2.34
1995-6 I	11.51	12.45	1.21	13.66	2.15	11.76	12.70	1.06	13.76	2.00
II	12.50	12.88	1.79	14.68	2.18	12.48	13.07	1.57	14.63	2.15
Dec.[4]	13.02	13.10	2.33	15.43	2.41	13.22	13.35	2.10	15.45	2.22
Jan.[4]	12.81	12.60	2.41	15.01	2.20	12.81	12.75	2.03	14.78	1.97

[1] Based on 73% extraction rate, cost of 2.28 bushels: at Kansas City, No. 1 hard winter, 13 % protein; and at Minneapolis, No. 1 dark northern spring, 14% protein. [2] Quoted as mid-month bakers' standard patent at Kansas City and spring standard patent at Minneapolis, bulk basis. [3] Assumed 50-50 millfeed distribution between bran and shorts or middlings, bulk basis. *Source: Agricultural Marketing Service, U.S. Department of Agriculture*

Wool

World wool production (greasy) was estimated at 5.6 billion pounds (3.3 billion, clean) in 1995/96 versus 5.9 billion in 1994/95 and an average of seven billion pounds in the early 1990s. Usage in 1994/95 of 3.5 billion pounds (clean) equaled 1993/94 and compares with 3.9 billion in the late 1980s. The slippage can be partially attributed to declining world sheep numbers, to one billion head in 1994/95 from an average of 1.1 billion head in the late 1980s. In Australia, the world largest wool producer, sheep numbers declined from 163 million head in 1990/91 to 123 million in 1995/96, and wool production (clean) dropped from 1,541 million pounds to 1,050 million pounds over the same period.

1996/96 production in New Zealand, the world's second largest wool producer, was 434 million pounds. New Zealand's sheep herd in early 1995 was placed at 49 million, the lowest in 34 years. China, whose sheep inventory is the world's largest, 127 million head in 1994/95, produced 287 million pounds of wool. Russia, with sheep numbers down to only 75 million head in 1994/95 from 135 million in 1990/91 produced 337 million pounds of wool versus 472 million pounds. U.S. wool production is insignificant.

Despite the slippage in world wool production and use during the first half of the 1990s, global foreign trade increased. Exports (greasy) in 1994/95 of nearly 3 billion pounds compared with 2.7 billion in 1993/94. Australia exported 1.3 billion pounds, New Zealand 500 million pounds and Argentina 102 million pounds. Importing nations are numerous; but the leaders include China whose imports have increased from 70 million pounds in 1990/91 to 553 million in 1994/95. Japan, The U.K., Italy, and France import generally no less than 200 million pounds each.

Imports to the former USSR have dropped from 283 million pounds in 1989/90 to only 9 million pounds in 1994/95. U.S. imports have averaged 115 million pounds during the past few years, equal to 90 million pounds clean. Australian wool accounts for almost 80 percent of U.S. imports. Global wool prices are a function of origin and grade; South African wool is generally more than twice Australian prices, while the latter are somewhat higher than New Zealand's prices.

The total 1995 U.S. supply of raw wool is 189 million pounds, clean, 9 percent below 1994 and so far the lowest supply of the 1990s. Stocks have also declined sharply, to 37 million pounds at yearend 1995 from 52 million a year earlier. Mill use, however, has held steady since 1991 at about 150 million pounds, necessitating a drawdown of stocks. Wool prices in the U.S. rose from $2.43 a pound in July, 1994 to a four year high of $3.08 in mid-1995, and then fell to $2.42 by October, basis Australian grade 64's.

Futures Markets

Wool futures are traded on the Sydney Futures Exchange (SFE), the Nagoya Textile Exchange, the Osaka Textile Exchange, the Tokyo Commodity Exchange (TOCOM), and the New Zealand Futures & Options Exchange Ltd. (NZFOE).

World Production of Wool In Metric Tons-Degreased

Year	Argentina	Australia	China	Kazakhstan[3]	New Zealand	Pakistan	Romania	Russia[3]	South Africa	United Kingdom	United States	Uruguay	World Total
1987	73,311	573,200	124,800	------	308,400	31,400	25,640	273,000	45,000	44,466	20,560	55,000	1,932,887
1988	81,200	546,585	112,000	------	310,100	32,450	28,000	286,800	46,200	47,000	21,660	54,000	1,931,251
1989	87,600	622,000	120,111	------	302,800	34,800	20,900	284,400	46,500	52,765	21,665	60,000	2,011,693
1990	85,800	724,000	122,400	64,750	233,000	28,200	26,500	136,050	49,500	53,358	21,140	58,100	2,029,209
1991	75,400	699,000	123,000	62,640	227,000	28,900	19,196	122,700	51,000	51,055	20,830	56,500	1,953,339
1992	74,200	574,000	121,500	63,000	221,000	29,600	16,800	107,400	48,500	50,876	19,980	50,700	1,780,613
1993[1]	58,000	557,000	122,000	60,000	193,000	30,400	15,600	95,000	45,000	48,693	20,220	49,410	1,679,305
1994[2]	51,000	581,800	132,600	60,100	204,600	31,000	16,900	87,000	45,000	50,300	16,500	49,800	1,713,471

[1] Preliminary. [2] Estimate. [3] Formerly part of the U.S.S.R.; data not reported separately until 1990. *Source: Food and Agriculture Organization of the United Nations*

Wool Goods[1] Production in the United States In Millions of Yards

Year	First Quarter	Second Quarter	Third Quarter	Fourth Quarter	Total Year	Year	First Quarter	Second Quarter	Third Quarter	Fourth Quarter	Total Year
1986	37.7	38.8	27.3	30.2	134.1	1991	38.0	48.7	41.4	41.5	169.6
1987	48.0	45.9	36.0	40.9	168.9	1992	45.7	47.2	43.9	39.5	176.3
1988	50.6	53.0	43.0	43.9	190.5	1993	48.4	48.9	43.9	42.8	184.0
1989	48.3	50.9	40.1	37.0	176.3	1994[2]	49.1	51.1	39.4	39.0	178.6
1990	38.0	38.7	32.6	31.4	140.7	1995[2]	45.9	45.9	35.2	34.2	161.2

[1] Woolen and worsted woven goods, except woven felts. [2] Preliminary. *Source: Bureau of Census, U.S. Department of Commerce*

Consumption of Apparel Wool in the United States In Millions of Pounds--Clean Basis

Year	Jan.	Feb.	Mar.	Apr.	May	June	July	Aug.	Sept.	Oct.	Nov.	Dec.	Total
1990	---------	31.5	---------	---------	31.7	---------	---------	26.9	---------	---------	30.5	---------	120.6
1991	---------	31.6	---------	---------	37.1	---------	---------	34.6	---------	---------	33.9	---------	137.2
1992	---------	36.4	---------	---------	35.1	---------	---------	33.6	---------	---------	31.1	---------	136.1
1993	---------	35.5	---------	---------	35.9	---------	---------	35.5	---------	---------	34.4	---------	141.4
1994	---------	36.3	---------	---------	35.6	---------	---------	32.7	---------	---------	34.0	---------	138.6
1995[1]	---------	37.1	---------	---------	36.2	---------	---------	29.9	---------	---------	28.6	---------	131.8

[1] Preliminary. *Source: Bureau of Census, U.S. Department of Commerce*

Salient Statistics of Wool in the United States

Year	Sheep & Lambs Shorn[4] 1,000	Weight per Fleece Lbs.	Shorn Wool Production 1,000 Lbs	Price per Lb.	Value of Production 1,000 $	Shorn Wool Support (¢ Per Lb.)	Shorn Wool Payment Rate (¢ Per Lb.)	Total Wool Production	Raw Wool (Clean Content): Domestic Production	Exports Domestic Wool	Dutiable Imports for Consump.[3] 48s&Finer	Total New Supply[2]	Duty Free Imports (Not Finer than 46's)	Mill Consumption: Apparel	Mill Consumption: Carpet
								Thousands of Pounds							
1986	10,827	7.82	84,372	66.8	56,331	178	111.2	84,372	44,548	788	66,090	140,751	30,901	126,768	9,960
1987	10,922	7.75	84,450	91.7	77,009	181	89.3	84,450	44,590	1,037	74,054	148,673	31,066	129,677	13,092
1988	11,531	7.76	89,482	138.0	124,993	178	40.0	89,482	47,246	1,247	72,324	142,740	24,417	117,069	15,633
1989	11,314	7.89	89,220	124.0	110,537	177	53.0	89,220	47,108	1,188	77,003	152,860	29,889	120,534	14,122
1990	11,222	7.84	88,033	80.0	69,534	182	102.0	88,033	46,481	2,736	50,328	115,461	21,355	120,622	12,124
1991	11,009	7.97	87,740	55.0	47,178	188	133.0	87,740	46,327	3,867	68,242	128,916	18,166	137,187	14,352
1992	10,521	7.88	82,943	74.0	60,162	197	123.0	82,819	43,728	3,413	65,457	129,599	23,802	136,143	14,695
1993	9,976	7.77	77,535	51.0	39,077	204	153.0	77,319	40,824	2,529	76,001	138,606	21,876	141,380	15,431
1994[1]	8,882	7.73	68,643	78.0	52,419				36,500	2,900	64,889		24,645	138,563	14,739

[1] Preliminary. [2] Production minus exports plus imports; stocks not taken into consideration. [3] Appearal wool includes all dutiable wool; carpet wool includes all duty-free wool. [4] Includes sheep shorn at commercial feeding yards. *Source: Economic Research Service, U.S. Department of Agriculture*

Shorn Wool Prices

Year	U.S. Farm Price Shorn Wool Greasy Basis[1] ¢ per Lb.	Australian Offering Price, Clean[2]: Grade 70's Type 61	Grade 64's Type 63	Grade 62's Type 64	Grade 60/62's Type 64A	Grade 58's-56's 433-34	Market Indicator[3] Cents/Kg.	Graded Territory Shorn Wool, Clean Basis[4]: 62's Staple 3" & up	60's Staple 3" & up	58's Staple 3 1/4" & up	56's Staple 3 1/4" & up	54's Staple 3 1/2" & up
		Dollars per Pound						Dollars per Pound				
1986	66.80	2.60	2.26	2.13	1.91	1.64	533	1.71	1.54	1.42	1.36	1.31
1987	91.70	4.35	3.14	2.76	2.37	2.11	626	2.28	1.97	1.75	1.60	1.47
1988	138.00	7.43	4.77	4.16	3.62	3.08	1,003	3.47	2.78	2.39	2.08	1.90
1989	124.00	5.82	4.21	3.86	3.44	2.81	990	3.14	2.61	2.06	2.04	1.91
1990	80.00	4.76	3.60	3.26	2.87	2.46	870	2.06	1.66	1.45	1.30	1.18
1991	55.00	3.56	2.32	2.02	1.87	1.68	627	1.58	1.31	1.14	1.03	.93
1992	74.00	2.58	2.32	2.17	2.10	1.94	557	1.81	1.61	1.47	1.35	1.23
1993	51.00	2.08	1.70	1.55	1.49	1.44	488	1.23	1.13	1.05	.99	.94
1994	78.00	3.72	2.43	2.02	1.96	1.84	547	1.75	1.50	1.26	1.27	1.21

[1] Annual weighted average. [2] F.O.B. Australian Wool Corporation South Carolina warehouse in bond. [3] Index of prices of all wool sold in Australia for the crop year July-June. [4] Wool principally produced in Texas and Rocky Mountain States. *Source: Economic Research Service, U.S. Department of Agriculture*

Average Wool Prices[1]--Australian--64's, Type 62, Duty Paid--U.S. Mills In Cents Per Pound

Year	Jan.	Feb.	Mar.	Apr.	May	June	July	Aug.	Sept.	Oct.	Nov.	Dec.	Average
1986	231	229	231	238	252	242	NA	229	224	230	240	250	236
1987	252	259	288	325	327	335	332	373	341	348	347	356	324
1988	391	468	496	564	564	513	489	467	461	488	472	475	487
1989	511	484	454	429	414	403	405	410	414	417	417	420	431
1990	417	404	403	414	406	342	338	352	355	343	332	332	370
1991	334	335	209	221	271	286	NA	248	229	215	274	270	242
1992	259	270	277	264	268	246	NA	224	210	192	195	193	236
1993	186	176	170	158	179	169	167	154	153	171	175	176	170
1994	204	216	205	223	249	258	243	248	259	256	273	297	244
1995	291	297	302	302	307	308	292	284	266	236	240	237	280

[1] Raw, clean basis. NA = Not available. *Source: Economic Research Service, U.S. Department of Agriculture*

Average Wool Prices--Domestic[1]--Graded Territory, 64's, Staple 2 3/4 & Up--U.S. Mills In Cents Per Pound

Year	Jan.	Feb.	Mar.	Apr.	May	June	July	Aug.	Sept.	Oct.	Nov.	Dec.	Average
1986	193	189	180	188	198	198	193	190	190	190	190	190	191
1987	193	202	216	260	270	270	270	300	295	300	300	300	265
1988	315	397	435	453	463	460	450	450	450	463	475	450	438
1989	450	438	410	375	375	365	350	350	350	350	333	300	370
1990	294	287	287	284	275	257	242	235	235	235	225	220	256
1991	217	210	163	167	203	230	230	167	156	148	148	155	158
1992	163	203	195	196	199	218	210	188	210	193	168	168	193
1993	158	148	132	127	135	140	138	140	130	129	133	133	124
1994	140	150	170	201	226	230	230	235	250	238	238	252	213
1995	245	252	265	288	295	285	261	250	235	185	188	192	245

[1] Raw, shorn, clean basis. *Source: Economic Research Service, U.S. Department of Agriculture*

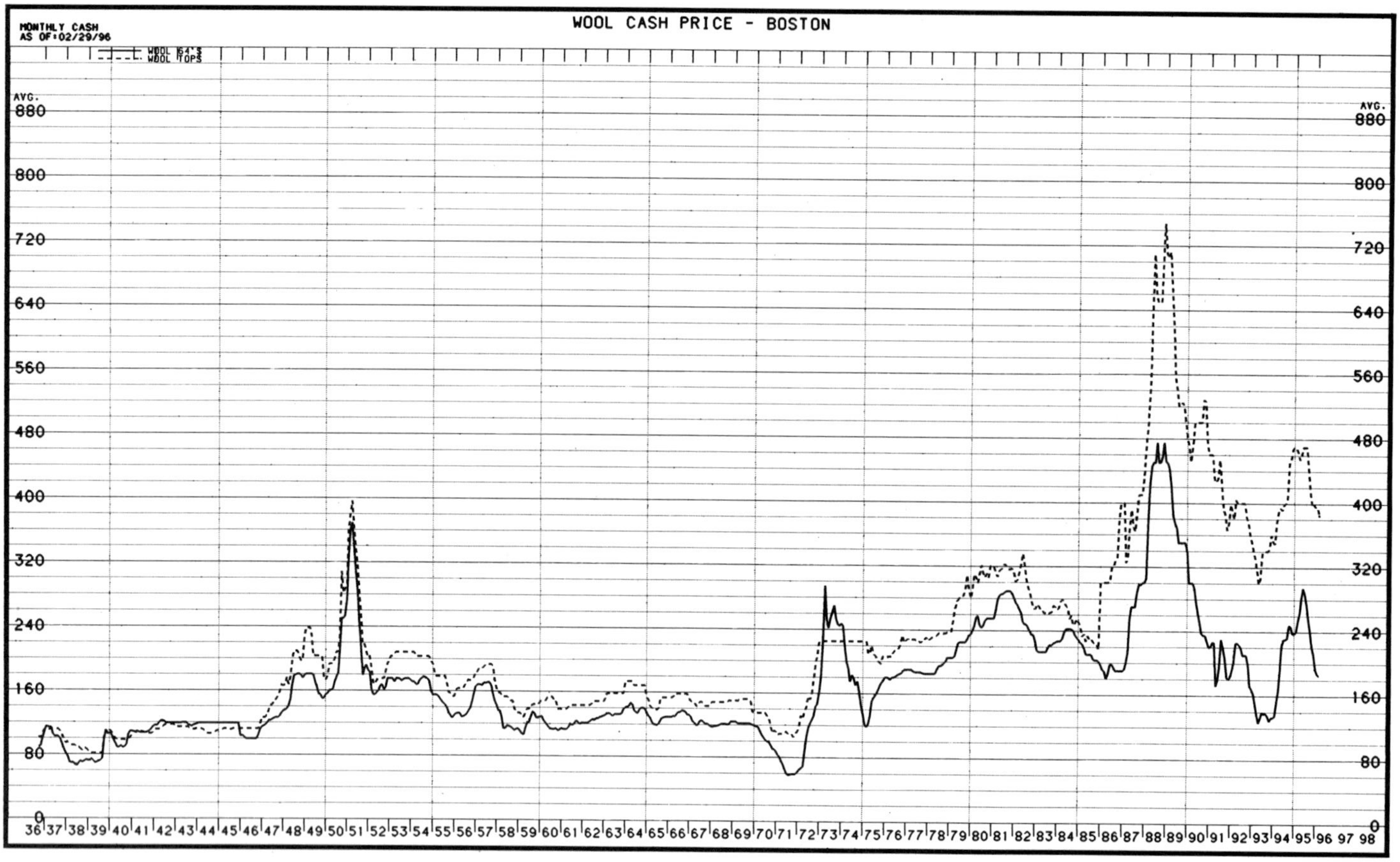

Wool: Mill Consumption, by Grades in the U.S., Scoured Basis In Thousands of Pounds

	Apparel Wool[1]							
	Woolen System			Worsted System				
Year	60's & Finer	Coarser Than 60's	Total	60's & Finer	Coarser Than 60's	Total	All Total	Carpet Wool[2]
1984	32,913	32,247	65,160	39,686	24,136	63,822	128,982	13,088
1985	28,046	27,694	55,740	33,646	16,665	50,311	106,051	10,562
1986	34,122	32,167	66,289	41,719	18,760	60,479	126,768	9,960
1987	32,401	28,613	61,014	53,814	14,849	68,663	129,677	13,092
1988	23,769	20,876	44,645	54,553	17,871	72,424	117,069	15,633
1989	24,123	21,803	45,935	56,065	18,534	74,599	120,534	14,122
1990	26,173	24,941	51,114	50,630	18,878	69,508	120,622	12,124
1991	31,961	26,599	58,560	56,521	22,106	78,627	137,187	14,352
1992[3]	33,878	25,600	59,478	58,495	18,170	76,665	136,143	14,695
1993[4]	40,895	26,624	67,519	58,834	15,027	73,861	141,380	15,431
1994[4]	35,960	26,038	61,998	59,599	16,966	76,565	138,563	14,739

[1] Domestic & duty-paid foreign. [2] Duty-free foreign. [3] Preliminary. [4] Estimate. *Source: Economic Research Service, U.S. Department of Agriculture*

United States Imports[1] of Unmanufactured Wool (Clean Yield) In Millions of Pounds

Year	Jan.	Feb.	Mar.	Apr.	May	June	July	Aug.	Sept.	Oct.	Nov.	Dec.	Total
1984	11.2	9.0	7.8	7.8	10.4	6.7	9.6	6.4	6.0	6.9	5.6	6.8	94.2
1985	10.7	5.8	6.0	5.7	7.1	4.9	7.3	4.5	6.9	7.1	5.5	8.0	79.5
1986	10.2	8.8	7.6	7.5	8.0	8.6	7.8	6.3	7.0	5.0	9.2	10.8	97.0
1987	8.6	8.2	9.5	8.7	13.4	8.9	8.6	8.4	6.7	7.0	8.2	9.0	105.1
1988	12.0	12.7	8.8	9.1	8.6	7.4	7.7	5.0	3.3	6.7	8.6	6.7	96.7
1989	8.7	11.3	9.0	13.1	10.3	8.3	10.0	6.9	3.9	10.4	5.1	9.8	106.9
1990	7.3	9.2	4.7	8.2	5.0	4.8	3.4	5.5	5.0	6.9	7.5	4.2	71.7
1991	10.7	6.9	5.4	5.5	7.3	8.1	9.2	7.0	4.4	7.8	5.1	9.0	86.5
1992	10.2	8.1	7.3	10.6	8.8	6.2	6.9	5.0	3.9	5.5	9.1	7.8	89.3
1993	7.8	8.7	8.5	9.3	11.0	9.6	9.7	8.7	5.7	7.7	7.2	8.4	100.3
1994	10.0	7.7	7.7	12.7	7.5	7.7	6.9	6.5	4.1	5.7	8.2	7.3	92.0
1995[2]	10.4	7.7	10.8	6.0	11.5	5.2	7.3						

[1] Data are imports for consumption. [2] Preliminary. *Source: Economic Research Service, U.S. Department of Agriculture*

Zinc

Zinc is utilized as a protective coating on other metals, such as iron or steel, in a process known as galvanizing. Zinc also has use as an alloy with copper to make brass, and as an alloying compound with aluminum and magnesium.

The International Lead and Zinc Study Group (ILZSG) reported that world zinc metal consumption in the first seven months of 1995 totaled 4.24 million tonnes, up 5.8 percent from 4.008 million tonnes in the same period of 1994. Western world consumption is estimated to have increased by 217,000 tonnes or 6.4 percent to 3.594 million tonnes year-on-year.

Mined production of zinc totaled 3.94 million tonnes in the January-July 1995 period, up from 3.848 million in the same period of 1994. Refined zinc production in the first seven months of 1995 is estimated to have been 4.198 million tonnes, up less than one percent from production of 4.126 million tonnes in the 1994 period.

Stocks of refined zinc held by western world producers were 312,000 tonnes at the end of July 1995, down 5,000 tonnes from the previous month. Stocks in London Metal Exchange warehouses trended lower and at the end of August were 761,400 tonnes, down 423,800 tonnes over the first eight months of the year.

The ILZSG forecast that growth in western world zinc consumption should continue in 1996, but at a slower rate than in 1995. For 1995, zinc consumption is forecast to grow by 5.7 percent to 6.18 million tonnes, reflecting strong growth in Southeast Asia. In the western world the rate of growth is expected to be 1.7 percent to 6.29 million tonnes.

Demand in the U.S. and Europe is expected to increase by about 1.5 percent, but a decline of 6.2 percent is expected in Japan.

Mined zinc output in the western world is expected to increase by 4.9 percent to 5.39 million tonnes in 1995, with metal production rising one percent to 5.43 million tonnes. For 1996, the ILZSG forecast a 7.5 percent increase in mined output to 5.79 million tonnes, though metal production was expected to rise two percent to 5.54 million tonnes.

In Eastern countries, zinc demand is expected to increase to 1.12 million tonnes in 1995 and 1.15 million tonnes in 1996. Metal production was forecast to increase by 1.4 percent to 1.78 million tonnes in 1995, and a further 4.2 percent to 1.86 million tonnes in 1996 due to increased use by China.

For the world as a whole, the ILZSG put mine output at 6.98 million tonnes in 1995 and 7.42 million tonnes in 1996. Metal output in 1995 is out at 7.21 million tonnes, while in 1996 it is forecast at 7.39 million tonnes. Zinc consumption in 1995 is estimated at 7.30 million tonnes, while in 1996 it is forecast at 7.43 million tonnes.

The U.S., during the January-May 1995 period, mined 251,000 tonnes of recoverable zinc, up from 224,000 tonnes in the same period of 1994, and 557,000 tonnes for all of 1994. Smelter production of slab zinc in the 1995 period was 156,000 tonnes, up from 151,000 tonnes in the 1994 period, and 355,000 tonnes for all of 1994. Zinc oxide production over the first five months of 1995 was 51,700 tonnes gross weight, compared to 53,800 tonnes in January-May 1994, and 131,000 tonnes for all of 1994.

U.S. consumption of slab zinc for the first five months of 1995 was 232,000 tonnes, down from 278,000 tonnes in the 1994 period, and 623,000 tonnes for all of 1994. Zinc metal consumption in the 1995 period was 584,000 tonnes, down from 437,000 tonnes in January-May 1994, and 1.19 million tonnes in all of 1994.

Imports of slab zinc in the January-April 1995 period were 340,000 tonnes, up from 304,000 tonnes in the same period of 1994, and 793,000 tonnes for all of 1994. Total stocks of slab zinc at the end of May 1995 were 60,300 tonnes, compared to 54,400 tonnes at the end of May 1994.

Futures Markets

Zinc futures and options are traded on the London Metal Exchange (LME).

U.S. Historical Salient Zinc Statistics In Metric Tons

Year	Slab Zinc Production: Primary	Slab Zinc Production: Secondary	Mine Production (Recovered)	Imports for Consumption: Slab Zinc	Imports for Consumption: Ore (Zinc Content)	Exports: Slab Zinc	Exports: Ore (Zinc Content)	Consumption: Slab Zinc[3]	Consumption: Consumed as Ore	Consumption: All Classes[4]	Net Import as a % of Consumption	High-Grade, Price ¢ Per Lb.
1980	340,456	29,396	317,103	410,163	182,370	302	54,457	811,146	58,986	1,142,409	60	37.43
1981	346,563	50,192	312,418	612,007	245,710	323	54,232	840,875	60,643	1,189,369	65	44.56
1982	228,176	74,288	303,160	456,233	66,809	341	77,289	795,000	35,515	1,038,600	58	38.47
1983	235,694	69,390	275,294	617,679	63,156	427	60,168	933,000	36,912	1,246,300	65	41.39
1984	253,432	78,113	252,768	639,228	86,172	760	30,579	980,000	45,487	1,344,000	68	48.60
1985	261,209	72,563	226,545	610,900	90,186	1,011	23,264	961,000	39,886	1,257,000	70	40.37
1986	253,369	62,912	202,983	665,126	75,786	1,938	3,269	999,000	19,236	1,274,000	73	38.00
1987	261,345	82,589	216,327	705,985	46,464	1,082	16,921	1,052,000	2,536	1,324,000	69	41.92
1988	241,294	88,492	244,314	748,130	62,966	482	33,590	1,089,000	2,412	1,340,000	70	60.20
1989	260,305	97,904	275,883	711,554	40,974	5,532	78,877	1,060,000	2,107	1,311,000	61	82.02
1990	262,704	95,708	515,355	631,742	46,684	1,238	220,446	992,000	2,178	1,240,000	41	74.59
1991	253,276	124,078	517,804	549,137	45,419	1,253	381,416	933,000	2,098	1,165,000	24	52.77
1992[1]	272,000	128,000	523,430	644,482	44,523	565	307,114	1,035,000	2,400	1,276,000	30	58.38
1993[2]	240,000	141,000	488,374	723,563	33,093	1,410	311,278	1,140,000	2,200	1,350,000	45	46.15
1994[2]	217,000	139,000	570,000	793,000	27,374	6,310	389,000	1,190,000	2,400	1,420,000	41	49.26

[1] Preliminary. [2] Estimate. [3] Data through 1981 are reported consumption of slab zinc; 1982 forward, data are apparent consumption of slab zinc.
[4] Based on apparent consumption of slab zinc plus zinc content of ores and concentrates and secondary materials used to make zinc dust and chemicals.
Source: U.S. Bureau of Mines

ZINC

World Smelter Production of Zinc[3] In Thousands of Metric Tons

Year	Australia	Belgium	Canada	France	Germany	Italy	Japan	Kazak-hstan[4]	Mexico	Norway	Peru	Poland	Spain	United Kingdom	United State	World Total
1989	296.5	306.0	669.7	265.8	372.0	259.5	714.7	977.0	193.3	120.4	126.7	163.7	246.4	79.8	358.2	7,245
1990	308.5	356.5	591.8	263.1	350.3	264.4	731.6	890.0	199.3	125.1	120.6	132.2	252.7	93.3	358.4	7,178
1991	326.5	385.1	660.6	299.6	345.7	263.8	778.7	800.0	189.1	124.9	154.6	126.0	262.2	100.7	375.8	7,310
1992	338.0	310.6	671.7	319.0	383.1	253.0	780.6	250.0	151.6	127.6	138.0	134.6	365.9	96.8	399.5	7,230
1993[1]	321.0	300.8	662.0	310.0	381.0	254.0	745.0	250.0	209.9	129.0	165.0	150.0	328.0	102.0	381.8	7,400
1994[2]	331.0	310.0	693.0	310.0	360.0	260.0	713.0	175.0	220.0	132.0	165.0	156.0	325.0	96.8	356.0	7,360

[1] Preliminary. [2] Estimate. [3] Secondary metal included. [4] Formerly part of the U.S.S.R.; data not reported separately until 1992. *Source: U.S. Bureau of Mines*

Consumption (Reported) of Slab Zinc in the United States by Industries and Grades In Metric Tons

		By Industries					By Grades			
Year	Total	Gal-vanizers	Brass Products	Zinc-Base Alloy[3]	Zinc Oxide	Other	Special High Grade	High Grade	Remelt and Other	Prime Western
1989	884,655	444,603	95,798	189,690	70,417	84,147	458,020	120,433	94,340	214,410
1990	801,969	388,421	104,276	171,771	67,532	69,969	445,427	92,424	78,265	210,373
1991	764,038	364,629	97,952	169,883	64,035	67,539	421,316	91,468	57,786	189,930
1992[1]	814,228	396,480	112,990	165,598	71,224	67,936	414,661	119,660	56,185	223,723
1993[2]	1,035,000	532,400	139,500	222,000	63,448	141,100	403,696	116,500	71,202	182,309
1994[2]	859,000	395,000	107,000	196,000	68,300	92,400	486,000	112,000	68,400	192,000

[1] Preliminary. [2] Estimate. [3] Die casters. *Source: U.S. Bureau of Mines*

Zinc Foreign Trade of the United States In Metric Tons

	Imported for Consumption							Zinc Ore & Manufactures Exported						
								Blocks, Pigs, Anodes, etc.		Wrought & Alloys				
Year	Ores[1]	Blocks, Pigs, Slabs	Sheets, Plates, Other	Waste & Scrap	Dross, Ashes, Fume	Dust, Powder & Flakes	Total Value $1,000	Un-wrought	Un-wrought Alloys	Sheets, Plates & Strips	Angles, Bars, Rods, etc.	Waste & Scrap	Dust (Blue Powder)	Zinc Ore & Con-centrates
1988	62,699	749,133	4,100	5,727	6,346	7,652	884,524	482	5,748	3,814	2,016	103,732	2,221	33,590
1989	40,974	711,554	3,066	9,367	9,031	7,253	1,241,659	5,532	2,423	16,515	2,653	108,086	8,137	78,877
1990	46,684	631,742	929	31,720	6,411	8,834	1,049,940	1,238	4,566	11,881	3,731	109,316	8,701	220,446
1991	45,419	549,137	539	31,596	6,483	15,424	687,879	1,253	4,224	10,385	6,151	96,314	5,737	381,416
1992	44,523	644,482	171	31,176	11,813	17,051	910,289	----- 5,886 ----		NA	NA	82,088	5,889	307,114
1993[2]	33,093	723,563	136	38,079	11,862	16,218	799,999	----- 8,765 ----		NA	NA	46,385	6,727	311,278
1994[3]	27,374	793,000	475	51,700	12,200	12,000	878,100	---- 13,220 ----		NA	NA	58,300	6,603	389,000

[1] Zinc content. [2] Preliminary. [3] Estimate. NA = Not available. *Source: U.S. Bureau of Mines*

U.S. Mine Production of Recoverable Zinc In Thousands of Metric Tons

Year	Jan.	Feb.	Mar.	Apr.	May	June	July	Aug.	Sept.	Oct.	Nov.	Dec.	Total
1988	16.8	18.2	22.3	21.9	22.0	22.4	18.8	21.5	19.9	19.9	19.9	19.3	244.3
1989	22.2	20.8	22.9	22.4	23.4	24.3	20.8	25.3	23.1	25.1	22.8	20.9	275.9
1990	26.9	24.8	26.4	26.2	27.9	45.6	50.7	57.1	44.7	42.7	40.4	43.6	515.4
1991	45.5	41.9	43.8	45.5	49.4	36.9	43.0	47.4	49.5	39.0	33.4	38.0	517.8
1992	41.5	48.8	47.7	40.3	40.7	40.4	46.2	49.1	47.6	36.2	40.4	42.2	520.1
1993	48.0	42.5	46.4	39.5	43.0	40.7	33.5	32.1	35.9	41.8	41.4	43.4	488.3
1994[1]	43.2	40.2	48.4	44.0	47.9	47.1	52.5	47.1	50.1	41.6	46.0	48.0	557.0
1995[1]	49.8	48.1	52.8	45.6	54.5	50.0	50.2	55.0					

[1] Preliminary. *Source: U.S. Bureau of Mines*

U.S. Consumption of Slab Zinc by Fabricators In Thousands of Metric Tons

Year	Jan.	Feb.	Mar.	Apr.	May	June	July	Aug.	Sept.	Oct.	Nov.	Dec.	Total
1988	79.5	76.4	110.3	97.9	110.7	84.6	73.9	111.8	100.0	97.5	87.2	88.1	1,089.0
1989	90.0	81.4	96.0	81.6	97.0	82.1	76.1	101.2	81.2	92.0	92.7	78.0	1,060.0
1990	82.4	79.2	88.0	74.0	79.4	91.0	102.8	100.0	73.0	86.0	73.0	67.1	826.5
1991	80.0	69.0	65.9	67.8	68.3	68.8	73.6	78.0	79.3	85.9	84.2	82.0	764.0
1992	93.8	77.2	85.0	89.9	76.0	76.9	47.2	53.8	52.2	53.5	50.3	47.6	814.2
1993	50.9	49.2	55.8	59.2	60.8	55.7	44.6	49.1	47.0	52.7	50.9	51.0	774.0
1994[1]	50.8	53.7	55.7	58.5	58.7	52.7	48.0	53.2	53.6	53.9	52.5	45.0	623.0
1995[1]	51.3	57.0	58.1	57.7	53.1	56.9	44.2	51.5					

[1] Preliminary. *Source: U.S. Bureau of Mines*

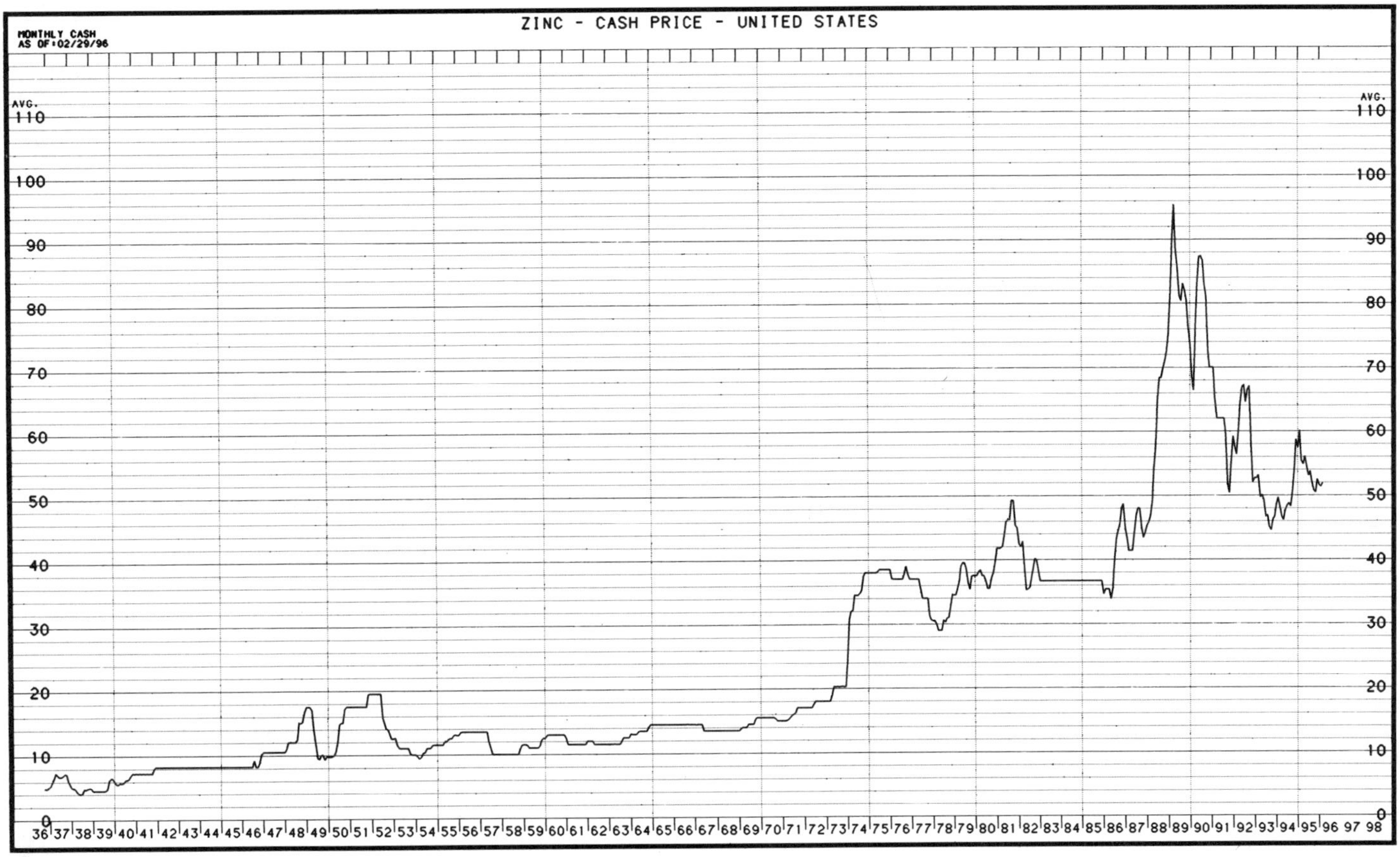

Average Price of Zinc, Prime Western Slab (Delivered U.S. Basis) In Cents Per Pound

Year	Jan.	Feb.	Mar.	Apr.	May	June	July	Aug.	Sept.	Oct.	Nov.	Dec.	Average
1987	43.33	41.38	41.38	41.38	44.15	46.92	48.00	48.00	44.87	43.38	44.10	45.38	44.36
1988	45.90	46.93	49.36	54.14	57.74	65.08	68.38	68.38	69.88	71.07	72.54	75.37	62.07
1989	81.58	89.01	95.38	87.76	85.38	81.06	80.38	83.26	81.88	80.31	76.57	73.38	83.00
1990	71.33	66.47	77.37	83.12	87.38	87.38	86.54	82.45	81.00	72.30	70.00	70.00	77.95
1991	70.00	64.53	62.00	62.00	62.00	62.00	62.00	N.Q.	N.Q.	50.44	54.85	59.22	60.90
1992	57.62	56.40	60.19	64.12	66.83	67.29	64.57	66.47	67.12	57.84	52.16	52.71	61.11
1993	52.70	53.18	49.72	50.07	49.27	46.75	46.90	45.08	44.54	46.21	46.54	48.69	48.30
1994	49.64	48.29	46.70	46.16	47.66	48.42	48.81	48.26	50.55	53.81	58.64	57.41	50.36
1995	60.11		54.84		54.61	53.08	53.75	52.00	50.77	50.42	52.52	51.60	53.37

NQ = No quote. *Source: American Metal Market*